COC = ch 3, 8, 12

Business Analysis & Valuation

Using Financial Statements

Text & Cases

Krishna G. Palepu, PhD

Thomas D. Casserly Jr. Professor of Business Administration
Harvard University

Victor L. Bernard, PhD, CPA

Price Waterhouse Professor of Accounting
University of Michigan

Paul M. Healy, PhD, ACA

Nanyang Technological University Chair in Management
Massachusetts Institute of Technology

SOUTH-WESTERN College Publishing

An International Thomson Publishing Company

Acquisitions Editor: Mark R. Hubble
Sponsoring Editor: David L. Shaut
Senior Development Editor: Ken Martin
Production Editor: Marci Dechter
Production Supplier: Julia Chitwood
Cover Design: Bruce Design
Cover Photograph: Reza Estakhrian/Tony Stone Images
Internal Design: Michael Stratton
Marketing Manager: Sharon Oblinger

AM66AA
Copyright © 1996
by South-Western Publishing Co.
Cincinnati, Ohio

I(T)P
International Thomson Publishing
South-Western Publishing Co. is an ITP Company. The ITP trademark is used under license.

ISBN: 0-538-84332-2

2 3 4 5 6 7 8 9 0 D 2 1 0 9 8 7 6 5

Printed in the United States of America

Library of Congress Cataloging-in-Publication Data

Palepu, Krishna G.
    Business analysis and valuation : using financial statements : text and cases / Krishna G. Palepu, Victor L. Bernard, Paul M. Healy.
      p. cm.
   ISBN 0-538-84332-2
    1. Business enterprises—Valuation.   2. Financial statements.
  3. Business enterprises—Valuation—Case studies.   I. Bernard, Victor L.
(Victor Lewis).   II. Healy, Paul M.   III. Title.
HF5681.V3P3 1995
658.15—dc20   95-24971
                                        CIP

This book is dedicated to the memory and spirit of

Vic Bernard

Scholar, colleague, friend

Krishna Palepu joined the Harvard Business School faculty in 1983 after receiving Bachelors and Masters degrees in physics from Andhra University, an MBA from the Indian Institute of Management, and a PhD from MIT. He has taught courses in finance and control, financial statement analysis, and competitive strategy in the Harvard MBA and Executive Educations programs, and he is currently co-leading a Harvard senior executive program on India and China, "Managing Global Opportunities in the Emerging Markets of Asia." Professor Palepu's research focuses on analyzing corporate finance and investment strategies and the process through which firms communicate these strategies to the capital markets. He has published numerous research papers and teaching cases on corporate disclosure, financing and dividend policies, and mergers and restructurings. He is also Associate Editor of several leading research journals, including the *Journal of Accounting and Economics, Accounting Review*, the *Journal of Financial Economics,* and the *Journal of Corporate Finance.* In addition to extensive consulting work, Professor Palepu serves on the International Board of the Academy of Management Excellence in India and of the EuroMBA Program of the Helsinki University of Technology in Finland.

Vic Bernard, who passed away November 14, 1995, was a CPA and held a PhD from the University of Illinois. He was Director of the Paton Accounting Center at the University of Michigan and Director of Research for the American Accounting Association. His research examined issues in financial reporting, financial statement analysis, and financial economics. He was one of ten persons in the last 30 years to have received the AAA/AICPA Notable Contributions to Accounting Literature Award more than once (in 1991 and 1993).

Paul Healy joined the MIT Sloan School of Management faculty in 1983, where he teaches financial accounting and financial statement analysis. He received his BCA Honors (1st class) in Accounting and Finance from Victoria University, New Zealand, and his MS in Economics and PhD in Business from the University of Rochester. Prior to coming to the U.S., he worked for Arthur Young and ICI Ltd. in New Zealand. Professor Healy received Sloan School awards for Teaching Excellence in 1991 and 1992. In 1993–94, he served as Deputy Dean at the Sloan School, and in 1994–95, he visited London Business School and Harvard Business School. Professor Healy's research, which has been published in *Accounting Review,* the *Journal of Accounting and Economics,* the *Journal of Accounting Research,* and the *Journal of Financial Economics,* includes studies of how firms' disclosure strategies affect their costs of capital, how investors interpret firms' dividend policy and capital structure decisions, the performance of merging firms after mergers, and the effect of managerial compensation and lending contracts on financial reporting. In 1990, he was awarded the AAA/AICPA Notable Contributions to Accounting Literature Award for his article, "The Effect of Bonus Schemes on Accounting Decisions."

Financial statements are the basis for a wide range of business analysis. Managers use them to monitor and judge their firm's performance relative to its competitors, to communicate with external investors, to help judge what financial policies they should pursue, and to evaluate potential new businesses to acquire as part of their investment strategy. Securities analysts use financial statements to rate and value companies they recommend to clients. Bankers use them in deciding whether to extend a loan to a client and to determine the loan's terms. Investment bankers use them as a basis for valuing and analyzing prospective buyouts, mergers, and acquisitions. And consultants use them as a basis for competitive analysis for their clients. Not surprisingly, therefore, we find that there is a strong demand among business students for a course that provides a framework for using financial statement data in a variety of business analysis and valuation contexts. The purpose of this book is to provide such a framework for business students and practitioners.

KEY FEATURES

This book differs from other texts in business and financial analysis in a number of important ways. In the first two parts of the book, we introduce and develop a framework for business analysis and valuation using financial statement data. In Part 3, we show how this framework can be applied to a variety of decision contexts. We use Compaq Computer Corporation, whose annual report data are provided in Part 5, to illustrate both the framework and the applications. Part 4 provides a variety of cases that can be used to develop the concepts discussed in the text.

Framework for Analysis

In the framework section, we identify four key analysis components:

- Business Strategy Analysis
- Accounting Analysis
- Financial Analysis
- Prospective Analysis

The first of the components, business strategy analysis, involves developing an understanding of the business and competitive strategy of the firm being analyzed.

Accounting analysis implies examining how accounting rules and conventions represent the firm's business economics and strategy in its financial statements and, if necessary, developing adjusted accounting measures of performance. Financial analysis utilizes financial ratio and cash flow measures of operating, financing, and investing performance of a company, relative either to key competitors or historical performance. Finally, under prospective analysis we show how to develop forecasted financial statements and how to use these to make estimates of firm value. Our discussion of valuation includes traditional cash flow methods as well as methods linked more directly to accounting numbers.

While we cover all four components of business analysis and valuation in the book, we recognize that the extent of their use depends on the user's decision context. For example, bankers are likely to use business strategy analysis, accounting analysis, financial analysis, and the forecasting portion of prospective analysis; they are less likely to be interested in formally valuing a prospective client.

Application of Framework to Decision Contexts

The decision contexts that we include in the third part of the book are:

- Securities Analysis
- Credit Analysis
- Merger and Acquisition Analysis
- Corporate Financing Policies Analysis
- Management Communications Analysis

For each of these topics we present an overview chapter to provide a foundation for class discussions. Where possible we discuss relevant institutional details and results of academic research that are useful in applying the analysis concepts developed in the first section of the book. For example, the chapter on credit analysis shows how banks and rating agencies analyze financial statement data to develop lending decisions and to rate public debt issues. This chapter also discusses academic research on how to analyze whether a company is financially distressed.

Case Approach

We have found that a course in business analysis and valuation is significantly enhanced, both for teachers and students, by using cases as a pedagogical tool. Students want to develop "hands-on" experience in applying the concepts of business analysis and valuation in decision contexts similar to those they will encounter in the business world. Cases achieve this objective in a natural way by presenting practical issues that might otherwise be ignored in a traditional classroom exercise. Our cases all present business analysis and valuation issues in a specific decision context, and we find that this makes the material more interesting and exciting.

USING THE TEXT

The text is most effectively used in a second-year MBA elective course or in a capstone course for an undergraduate business program.

Prerequisites

To get the most out of the text, students should have completed basic courses in financial accounting, finance, and either business strategy or business economics. The text provides a concise overview of some of these topics, primarily as background for preparing the cases. But it would probably be difficult for students with no prior knowledge in these fields to use the chapters as stand-alone coverage of them. We have integrated only a small amount of business strategy material into each case.

The extent of accounting knowledge required for the cases varies considerably. Some cases require only a basic understanding of accounting issues, whereas others require a more detailed knowledge at the level of a typical intermediate financial accounting course. However, we have found it possible to teach even these more complex cases to students without a strong accounting background by providing additional reading on the topic. For some cases, the Teaching Manual includes a primer on the relevant accounting issue, which instructors can hand out to help students prepare the case.

How to Use the Text and Case Materials

The materials can be used in a variety of ways. We teach the course using almost a pure case approach, adding relevant lecture sections as needed. However, a lecture class could be presented first, followed by an appropriate case. It is also possible to use the text material primarily for a lecture course and include some of the cases as in-class illustrations of the concepts discussed in the text. Alternatively, lectures could be used as a follow-up to the cases to more clearly lay out the conceptual issues raised in the discussion of the cases.

We have designed the cases so that they can be taught at a variety of levels. For students who need more structure to work through a case, the Teaching Manual includes a set of detailed questions which the instructor can hand out before class. For students who need less structure, there are recommended questions at the end of each case.

ACKNOWLEDGMENTS

We gratefully acknowledge the help of Jeff Abarbanell (University of Michigan) and G. Peter Wilson (MIT) for valuable discussions on pedagogical issues. We are also grateful for the contributions of colleagues who co-authored four cases: Mary Barth (Harvard University), Roosevelt Financial Group, Inc.; Ken Merchant (University of Southern

California), Kansas City Zephyrs Baseball Club; and G. Peter Wilson, Hawkeye Bank Corporation and Morlan International. We also thank the Harvard Business School for permission to include a number of their cases.

We appreciate the help of Paul Asquith (MIT), Edouard De Vitry D'Avaucourt, Raguvir Gurumurthy, Charles Lee (University of Michigan), Renu Nallicheri, PNC Bank Corp., Dr. Charles Schalhorn (Eastman Kodak), Cholthicha Srivisal, Anant Sundaram, and Eleanor Westney (MIT) in developing the case materials. Research assistant help was provided by Marlene Plumlee and Rory Stace. We also wish to thank our colleagues who gave us feedback on our materials, particularly Tom Frecka (Notre Dame), Jeff Abarbanell, and Amy Sweeney (Harvard University). We also thank Brian Belt (University of Missouri-Kansas City), Marlin R. H. Jensen (Auburn University), Ron King (Washington University), James M. Wahlen (University of North Carolina), and David A. Ziebart (University of Illinois) for reviewing the initial outline of this project.

We are also very grateful to Mark Hubble for encouraging us to undertake this project, and to Ken Martin, Marci Dechter, and Julia Chitwood for their patient editorial and production help. We thank Bianca Baggio for providing excellent help in putting the manuscript together.

contents

Part 4   CASES IN FINANCIAL STATEMENT ANALYSIS

Part 5   COMPAQ COMPUTER CORPORATION

p a r t 1

Introduction

chapter 1

A Framework for Doing Business Analysis Using Financial Statements

The purpose of this chapter is to outline a comprehensive framework for financial statement analysis. Because financial statements provide the most widely available data on public corporations' economic activities, investors and other stakeholders rely on financial reports to assess the plans and performance of firms and corporate managers.

A variety of questions can be addressed by doing business analysis using financial statements, as shown in the following examples:

- A security analyst may be interested in asking: "How well is the firm I am following performing? Did the firm meet my performance expectations? If not, why not? What is the value of the firm's stock given my assessment of the firm's current and future performance?"
- A loan officer may need to ask: "What is the credit risk involved in lending a certain amount of money to this firm? How well is the firm managing its liquidity and solvency? What is the firm's business risk? What is the additional risk created by the firm's financing and dividend policies?"
- A management consultant might ask: "What is the structure of the industry in which the firm is operating? What are the strategies pursued by various players in the industry? What is the relative performance of different firms in the industry?"
- A corporate manager may ask: "Is my firm properly valued by investors? Is our investor communication program adequate to facilitate this process?"
- A corporate manager could ask: "Is this firm a potential takeover target? How much value can be added if we acquire this firm? How can we finance the acquisition?"
- An independent auditor would want to ask: "Are these financial statements consistent with my understanding of this business and its recent performance? Do these

financial reports communicate the current status and significant risks of the business?"

Financial statement analysis is a valuable activity when managers have complete information on a firm's strategies and a variety of institutional factors make it unlikely that they fully disclose this information. In this setting, outside analysts attempt to create "inside information" from analyzing financial statement data, thereby gaining valuable insights about the firm's current performance and future prospects.

To understand the contribution that financial statements analysis can make, it is important to understand the institutional forces that shape financial statements. Therefore, we present first a brief description of these forces; then we discuss the steps that an analyst must perform to extract information from financial statements and to provide valuable forecasts.

FROM BUSINESS ACTIVITIES TO FINANCIAL STATEMENTS

Corporate managers are responsible for acquiring physical and financial resources from the firm's environment and using them to create value for the firm's investors. Value is created when the firm earns a return on its investment in excess of the cost of capital. Managers formulate business strategies to achieve this goal, and they implement them through business activities. A firm's business activities are influenced by its economic environment and its own business strategy. The economic environment includes the firm's industry, its input and output markets, and the regulations under which the firm operates. The firm's business strategy determines how the firm positions itself in its environment to achieve a competitive advantage.

As shown in Figure 1-1, a firm's financial statements summarize the economic consequences of its business activities. The firm's business activities in any time period are too numerous to be reported individually to outsiders. Further, some of the activities undertaken by the firm are proprietary in nature, and disclosing these activities in detail could be a detriment to the firm's competitive position. The firm's accounting system provides a mechanism through which business activities are selected, measured, and aggregated into financial statement data.

An analyst using financial statement data to do business analysis has to be aware that financial reports are influenced both by the firm's business activities and by its accounting system. A key aspect of financial statement analysis, therefore, involves understanding the influence of the accounting system on the quality of the financial statement data being used in the analysis. The institutional features of accounting systems discussed below determine the extent of that influence.

Accounting System Feature 1: Accrual Accounting

One of the fundamental features of corporate financial reports is that they are prepared using accrual rather than cash accounting. Unlike cash accounting, accrual accounting

Figure 1-1 From Business Activities to Financial Statements

Business Environment

Labor Markets
Capital Markets
Product Markets:
    Suppliers
    Customers
    Competitors
Business Regulations

Business Activities

Operating Activities
Investment Activities
Financing Activities

Business Strategy

Scope of Business:
    Degree of Diversifi-
      cation
    Type of Diversification
Competitive Positioning:
    Cost Leadership
    Differentiation
Key Success Factors and
    Risks

Accounting Environment

Capital Market Structure
Contracting and
    Governance
Accounting Conventions
    and Regulations
Tax and Financial
    Accounting Linkages
Third-Party Auditing
Legal System for
    Accounting Disputes

Accounting System

Measure and
    report economic
    consequences
    of business
    activities.

Accounting Strategy

Choice of Accounting
    Policies
Choice of Accounting
    Estimates
Choice of Reporting
    Format
Choice of Supplementary
    Disclosures

Financial Statements

Managers' Superior
    Information on
    Business Activities
Estimation Errors
Distortions from
    Managers' Account-
    ing Choices

distinguishes between the recording of costs and benefits associated with economic activities and the actual payment and receipt of cash. Net income is the primary periodic performance index under accrual accounting. To compute net income, the effects of economic transactions are recorded on the basis of *expected,* not necessarily *actual,* cash receipts and payments. Expected cash receipts from the delivery of products or services are recognized as revenues, and expected cash outflows associated with these revenues are recognized as expenses.

The need for accrual accounting arises from investors' demand for financial reports on a periodic basis. Because firms undertake economic transactions on a continual basis, the arbitrary closing of accounting books at the end of a reporting period leads to a fundamental measurement problem. Since cash accounting does not report the full economic consequence of the transactions undertaken in a given period, accrual accounting is designed to provide more complete information on a firm's periodic performance.

Accounting System Feature 2: Accounting Standards and Auditing

The use of accrual accounting lies at the center of many important complexities in corporate financial reporting. Because accrual accounting deals with *expectations* of future cash consequences of current events, it is subjective and relies on a variety of assumptions. Who should be charged with the primary responsibility of making these assumptions? A firm's managers are entrusted with the task of making the appropriate estimates and assumptions to prepare the financial statements because they have intimate knowledge of their firm's business.

The accounting discretion granted to managers is potentially valuable because it allows them to reflect inside information in reported financial statements. However, since investors view profits as a measure of managers' performance, managers have incentives to use their accounting discretion to distort reported profits by making biased assumptions. Further, the use of accounting numbers in contracts between the firm and outsiders provides another motivation for management manipulation of accounting numbers. Income management distorts financial accounting data, making them less valuable to external users of financial statements. Therefore, the delegation of financial reporting decisions to corporate managers has both costs and benefits.

A number of accounting conventions have evolved to ensure that managers use their accounting flexibility to summarize their knowledge of the firm's business activities, and not to disguise reality for self-serving purposes. For example, the measurability and conservatism conventions are accounting responses to concerns about distortions from managers' potentially optimistic bias. Both these conventions attempt to limit managers' optimistic bias by imposing their own pessimistic bias.

Accounting standards known as Generally Accepted Accounting Principles (GAAP), promulgated by the Financial Accounting Standards Board (FASB) and similar standard-setting bodies in other countries, also limit potential distortions that managers can introduce into reported numbers. Uniform accounting standards attempt to reduce managers' ability to record similar economic transactions in dissimilar ways, either over time or across firms.

Increased uniformity from accounting standards, however, comes at the expense of reduced flexibility for managers to reflect genuine business differences in their firm's financial statements. Rigid accounting standards work best for economic transactions whose accounting treatment is not predicated on managers' proprietary information. However, when there is significant business judgment involved in assessing a transaction's economic consequences, rigid standards which prevent managers from using their superior business knowledge would be dysfunctional. Further, if accounting standards are too rigid, they may induce managers to expend economic resources to restructure business transactions to achieve a desired accounting result.

Auditing, broadly defined as a verification of the integrity of the reported financial statements by someone other than the preparer, ensures that managers use accounting rules and conventions consistently over time, and that their accounting estimates are reasonable. Therefore, auditing improves the quality of accounting data.

Third-party auditing may also reduce the quality of financial reporting because it constrains the kind of accounting rules and conventions that evolve over time. For example, the FASB considers the views of auditors in the standard-setting process. Auditors are likely to argue against accounting standards producing numbers that are difficult to audit, even if the proposed rules produce relevant information for investors.

The legal environment in which accounting disputes between managers, auditors, and investors are adjudicated can also have a significant effect on the quality of reported numbers. The threat of lawsuits and resulting penalties have the beneficial effect of improving the accuracy of disclosure. However, the potential for a significant legal liability might also discourage managers and auditors from supporting accounting proposals requiring risky forecasts, such as forward-looking disclosures.

Accounting System Feature 3: Managers' Reporting Strategy

Because the mechanisms that limit managers' ability to distort accounting data add noise, it is not optimal to use accounting regulation to eliminate managerial flexibility completely. Therefore, real-world accounting systems leave considerable room for managers to influence financial statement data. A firm's reporting strategy, that is, the manner in which managers use their accounting discretion, has an important influence on the firm's financial statements.

Corporate managers can choose accounting and disclosure policies that make it more or less difficult for external users of financial reports to understand the true economic picture of their businesses. Accounting rules often provide a broad set of alternatives from which managers can choose. Further, managers are entrusted with making a range of estimates in implementing these accounting policies. Accounting regulations usually prescribe *minimum* disclosure requirements, but they do not restrict managers from *voluntarily* providing additional disclosures.

A superior disclosure strategy will enable managers to communicate the underlying business reality to outside investors. One important constraint on a firm's disclosure strategy is the competitive dynamics in product markets. Disclosure of proprietary information about business strategies and their expected economic consequences may hurt the firm's competitive position. Subject to this constraint, managers can use financial statements to provide information useful to investors in assessing their firm's true economic performance.

Managers can also use financial reporting strategies to manipulate investors' perceptions. Using the discretion granted to them, managers can make it difficult for investors to identify poor performance on a timely basis. For example, managers can choose accounting policies and estimates to provide an optimistic assessment of the firm's true performance. They can also make it costly for investors to understand the true performance by controlling the extent of information that is disclosed voluntarily.

The extent to which financial statements are informative about the underlying business reality varies across firms—and across time for a given firm. This variation in accounting quality provides both an important opportunity and a challenge in doing business analysis. The process through which analysts can separate noise from information in financial statements, and gain valuable business insights from financial statement analysis, is discussed next.

FROM FINANCIAL STATEMENTS TO BUSINESS ANALYSIS

Because managers' insider knowledge is a source both of value and distortion in accounting data, it is difficult for outside users of financial statements to separate true information from distortion and noise. Not being able to undo accounting distortions completely, investors "discount" a firm's reported accounting performance. In doing so, they make a probabilistic assessment of the extent to which a firm's reported numbers reflect economic reality. As a result, investors can have only an imprecise assessment of an individual firm's performance. Financial analysts can add value by improving investors' understanding of a firm's current performance and its future prospects.

Effective financial statement analysis is valuable because it attempts to get at managers' inside information from public financial statement data. Because analysts do not have direct access to this information, they rely on their knowledge of the firm's industry and its competitive strategies to interpret financial statements. Successful analysts have at least as good an understanding of the industry economics as do the firm's managers, and a reasonably good understanding of the firm's competitive strategy. Although outside analysts have an information disadvantage relative to the firm's managers, they are more objective in evaluating the economic consequences of the firm's investment and operating decisions. Figure 1-2 provides a schematic overview of how business analysts use financial statements to accomplish four key steps: (1) business strategy analysis, (2) accounting analysis, (3) financial analysis, and (4) prospective analysis.

Analysis Step 1: Business Strategy Analysis

The purpose of business strategy analysis is to identify key profit drivers and business risks, and to assess the company's profit potential at a qualitative level. Business strategy analysis involves analyzing a firm's industry and its strategy to create a sustainable competitive advantage. This qualitative analysis is an essential first step because it enables the analyst to frame the subsequent accounting and financial analysis better. For example, identifying the key success factors and key business risks allows the identification

Figure 1-2 Doing Business Analysis Using Financial Statements

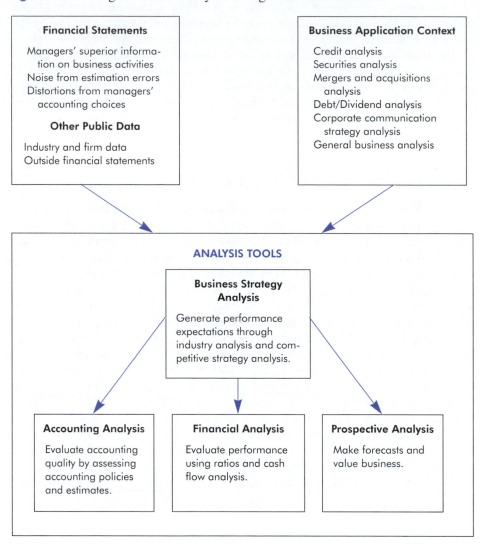

of key accounting policies. Assessment of a firm's competitive strategy facilitates evaluating whether current profitability is sustainable. Finally, business analysis enables the analyst to make sound assumptions in forecasting a firm's future performance.

Analysis Step 2: Accounting Analysis

The purpose of accounting analysis is to evaluate the degree to which a firm's accounting captures the underlying business reality. By identifying places where there is accounting flexibility, and by evaluating the appropriateness of the firm's accounting policies and estimates, analysts can assess the degree of distortion in a firm's accounting numbers. Another important step in accounting analysis is to "undo" any accounting distortions by recasting a firm's accounting numbers. Sound accounting analysis improves the reliability of conclusions from financial analysis, the next step in financial statement analysis.

Analysis Step 3: Financial Analysis

The goal of financial analysis is to use financial data to evaluate the current and past performance of a firm and to assess its sustainability. There are two important skills related to financial analysis. First, the analysis should be systematic and efficient. Second, the analysis should allow the analyst to use financial data to explore business issues. Ratio analysis and cash flow analysis are the two most commonly used financial tools. Ratio analysis focuses on evaluating a firm's product market performance and financial policies; cash flow analysis focuses on a firm's liquidity and financial flexibility.

Analysis Step 4: Prospective Analysis

Prospective analysis, which focuses on forecasting a firm's future, is the final step in business analysis. Two commonly used techniques in prospective analysis are financial statement forecasting and valuation. Both these tools allow the synthesis of the insights from business analysis, accounting analysis, and financial analysis in order to make predictions about a firm's future.

The predictions from a sound business analysis are useful to a variety of parties and can be applied in various contexts. The exact nature of the analysis will depend on the context. The contexts that we will examine include securities analysis, credit evaluation, mergers and acquisitions, evaluation of debt and dividend policies, and assessing corporate communication strategies. The four analytical steps described above are useful in each of these contexts. Appropriate use of these tools, however, requires a familiarity with the economic theories and institutional factors relevant to the context.

SUMMARY AND CONCLUSIONS

Financial statements provide the most widely available data on public corporations' economic activities; investors and other stakeholders rely on them to assess the plans and performance of firms and corporate managers. Accrual accounting data in financial statements are noisy, and unsophisticated investors can assess firms' performance only imprecisely. Financial analysts who understand managers' disclosure strategies have an opportunity to create inside information from public data, and they play a valuable role in enabling outside parties to evaluate a firm's current and prospective performance.

This chapter has outlined the framework for doing business analysis with financial statements, using the four key steps: business strategy analysis, accounting analysis, financial analysis, and prospective analysis. The remainder of the chapters in this book describe these steps in greater detail and discuss how they can be used in a variety of business contexts.

p a r t 2

Business Analysis Tools

chapter 2

Business Strategy Analysis

Business strategy analysis is an important starting point for the analysis of financial statements. Strategy analysis allows the analyst to probe the economics of the firm at a qualitative level so that the subsequent accounting and financial analysis is grounded in business reality. Business strategy analysis also allows the identification of the firm's profit drivers and key risks. This, in turn, enables the analyst to assess the sustainability of the firm's performance and make realistic forecasts of future performance.

A firm's value is determined by its ability to earn a return on its capital in excess of the cost of capital. What determines whether or not a firm is able to accomplish this goal? While a firm's cost of capital is determined by the capital markets, its profit potential is determined by its own strategic choices: (1) the choice of an industry or a set of industries in which the firm operates (industry choice), and (2) the manner in which the firm intends to compete with other firms in its chosen industry or industries (competitive positioning). Business strategy analysis, therefore, involves industry analysis and competitive strategy analysis.[1] In this chapter, we will briefly discuss both these steps, and use information from Compaq Computer Corporation to illustrate the application of the concepts discussed.[2]

INDUSTRY ANALYSIS

In analyzing a firm's profit potential, an analyst has to first assess the profit potential of each of the industries in which the firm is competing, because the profitability of various industries differs systematically and predictably over time. For example, the annual after-tax returns on equity (ROE) for all U.S. manufacturing companies between 1971 and 1990 was 12.6 percent. However, the average returns varied widely across specific industries: the average annual ROE during the period 1971–1990 was 15.2 percent for the food and kindred products industry, 12.5 percent for the paper and allied products industry, and 3.9 percent for the iron and steel industry.[3] What causes these profitability differences?

There is a vast body of research in industrial organization on the influence of industry structure on profitability.[4] Relying on this research, strategy literature suggests that the average profitability of an industry is influenced by the "five forces" shown in Figure 2-1.[5] According to this framework, the intensity of competition determines the potential for creating abnormal profits by the firms in an industry. Whether or not the potential profits are kept by the industry is determined by the relative bargaining power of the

Figure 2-1 Industry Structure and Profitability

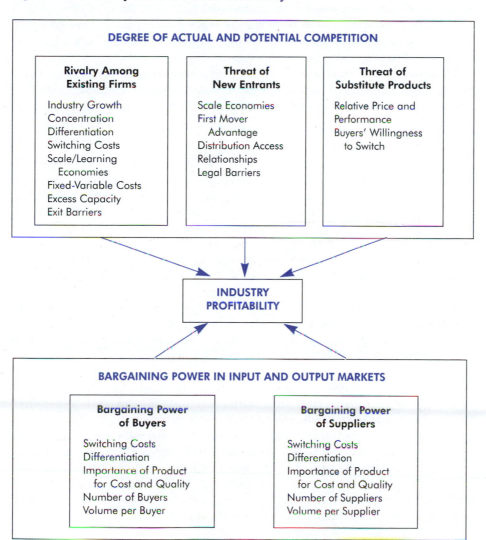

firms in the industry and their customers and suppliers. We will discuss each of these industry profit drivers in more detail below.

DEGREE OF ACTUAL AND POTENTIAL COMPETITION

At the most basic level, the profits in an industry are a function of the maximum price that customers are willing to pay for the industry's product or service. One of the key determinants of the price is the degree to which there is competition among suppliers of the same or similar products. At one extreme, if there is a state of perfect competition in the industry, micro-economic theory predicts that prices will be equal to marginal cost, and there will be few opportunities to earn super-normal profits. At the other extreme, if the industry is dominated by a single firm, there will be potential to earn monopoly profits. In reality, the degree of competition in most industries is somewhere in between perfect competition and monopoly.

There are three potential sources of competition in an industry: (1) rivalry between existing firms, (2) threat of entry of new firms, and (3) threat of substitute products or services. We will discuss each of these competitive forces in the following paragraphs.

Competitive Force 1: Rivalry among Existing Firms

In most industries, the average level of profitability is primarily influenced by the nature of rivalry among existing firms in the industry. In some industries, firms compete aggressively, pushing prices close to (and sometimes below) the marginal cost. In other industries, firms do not compete aggressively on price. Instead, they find ways to coordinate their pricing, or compete on non-price dimensions, such as innovation or brand image. Several factors determine the intensity of competition between existing players in an industry:

INDUSTRY GROWTH RATE.   If an industry is growing very rapidly, existing firms need not grab market share from each other to grow. In contrast, in stagnant industries, the only way existing firms can grow is by taking share away from the other players. In this situation, one can expect price wars among firms in the industry.

CONCENTRATION AND BALANCE OF COMPETITORS.   The number of firms in an industry and their relative sizes determine the degree of concentration in an industry.[6] The degree of concentration influences the extent to which firms in an industry can coordinate their pricing and other competitive moves. For example, if there is one dominant firm in an industry (such as IBM in the mainframe computer industry in the 1970s), it can set and enforce the rules of competition. Similarly, if there are only two or three equal-sized players (such as Coke and Pepsi in the U.S. soft-drink industry), they can implicitly cooperate with each other to avoid destructive price competition. If an industry is fragmented, price competition is likely to be severe.

DEGREE OF DIFFERENTIATION AND SWITCHING COSTS.   The extent to which firms in an industry can avoid head-on competition depends on the extent to which they can differentiate their products and services. If the products in an industry are very similar, customers are ready to switch from one competitor to another purely on the basis of price. Switching costs also determine customers' propensity to move from one product to another. When switching costs are low, there is a greater incentive for firms in an industry to engage in price competition.

SCALE/LEARNING ECONOMIES AND THE RATIO OF FIXED TO VARIABLE COSTS.   If there is a steep learning curve or there are other types of scale economies in an industry, size becomes an important factor for firms in the industry. In such situations, there are incentives to engage in aggressive competition for market share. Similarly, if the ratio of fixed to variable costs is high, firms have an incentive to reduce prices to utilize installed capacity. The airline industry, where price wars are quite common, is an example of this type of situation.

EXCESS CAPACITY AND EXIT BARRIERS.   If capacity in an industry is larger than customer demand, there is a strong incentive for firms to cut prices to fill capacity. The problem of excess capacity is likely to be exacerbated if there are significant barriers for firms to exit the industry. Exit barriers are high when the assets are specialized, or if there are regulations which make exit costly.

Competitive Force 2: Threat of New Entrants

The potential for earning abnormal profits will attract new entrants to an industry. The very threat of new firms entering an industry potentially constrains the pricing of existing firms within it. Therefore, the ease with which new firms can enter an industry is a key determinant of its profitability. Several factors determine the height of barriers to entry in an industry:

ECONOMIES OF SCALE.   When there are large economies of scale, new entrants face the choice of having either to invest in a large capacity which might not be utilized right away, or to enter with less than the optimum capacity. Either way, new entrants will at least initially suffer from a cost disadvantage in competing with existing firms. Economies of scale might arise from large investments in research and development (the pharmaceutical or jet engine industries), in brand advertising (soft-drink industry), or in physical plant and equipment (telecommunications industry).

FIRST MOVER ADVANTAGE.   Early entrants in an industry may deter future entrants if there are first mover advantages. For example, first movers might be able to set industry standards, or enter into exclusive arrangements with suppliers of cheap raw materials. They may also acquire scarce government licenses to operate in regulated industries. Finally, if there are learning economies, early firms will have an absolute cost advantage over new entrants. First mover advantages are also likely to be large when there are significant switching costs for customers once they start using existing products. For example, switching costs faced by the users of Microsoft's DOS operating system make it difficult for software companies to market a new operating system.

ACCESS TO CHANNELS OF DISTRIBUTION AND RELATIONSHIPS.   Limited capacity in the existing distribution channels and high costs of developing new channels can act as a powerful barriers to entry. For example, a new entrant into the domestic auto industry in the U.S. is likely to face formidable barriers because of the difficulty of developing a dealer network. Similarly, new consumer goods manufacturers find it difficult to obtain supermarket shelf space for their products. Existing relationships between firms and customers in an industry also make it difficult for new firms to enter an industry. Industry examples of this include auditing, investment banking, and advertising.

LEGAL BARRIERS.   There are many industries in which legal barriers, such as patents and copyrights in research-intensive industries, limit entry. Similarly, licensing regulations limit entry into taxi services, medical services, broadcasting, and telecommunications industries.

Competitive Force 3: Threat of Substitute Products

The third dimension of competition in an industry is the threat of substitute products or services. Relevant substitutes are not necessarily those that have the same form as the existing products, but those that perform the same function. For example, airlines and car rental services might be substitutes for each other when it comes to travel over short distances. Similarly, plastic bottles and metal cans substitute for each other as packaging in the beverage industry. In some cases, threat of substitution comes not from customers' switching to another product but from utilizing technologies that allow them to do without, or use less of, the existing products. For example, energy conserving technologies allow customers to reduce their consumption of electricity and fossil fuels.

The threat of substitutes depends on the relative price and performance of the competing products or services, and on customers' willingness to substitute. Customers' perception of whether two products are substitutes depends to some extent on whether they perform the same function for a similar price. If two products perform an identical function, then it would be difficult for them to differ from each other in price. However, customers' willingness to switch is often the critical factor in making this competitive dynamic work. For example, even when tap water and bottled water serve the same function, many customers may be unwilling to substitute the former for the latter, enabling bottlers to charge a price premium. Similarly, designer label clothing commands a price premium even if it is not superior in terms of basic functionality, because customers place a value on the image offered by designer labels.

RELATIVE BARGAINING POWER IN INPUT AND OUTPUT MARKETS

While the degree of competition in an industry determines whether or not there is *potential* to earn abnormal profits, the *actual profits* are influenced by the industry's bargaining power with its suppliers and customers. On the input side, firms enter into transactions with suppliers of labor, raw materials and components, and finances. On the output side, firms either sell directly to the final customers, or enter into contracts with intermediaries in the distribution chain. In all these transactions, the relative economic power of the two sides is important to the overall profitability of the industry firms.

Competitive Force 4: Bargaining Power of Buyers

Two factors determine the power of buyers: price sensitivity and relative bargaining power. Price sensitivity determines the extent to which buyers care to bargain on price; relative bargaining power determines the extent to which they will succeed in forcing the price down.[7]

PRICE SENSITIVITY.   Buyers are more price sensitive when the product is undifferentiated and there are few switching costs. The sensitivity of buyers to price also depends on the importance of the product to their own cost structure. When the product represents a large fraction of the buyers' cost (for example, the packaging material for soft-drink producers), the buyer is likely to expend the resources necessary to shop for a lower cost alternative. In contrast, if the product is a small fraction of the buyers' cost (for example, windshield wipers for automobile manufacturers), it may not pay to expend resources to search for lower-cost alternatives. Further, the importance of the product to the buyers' product quality also determines whether or not price becomes the most important determinant of the buying decision.

RELATIVE BARGAINING POWER.   Even if buyers are price sensitive, they may not be able to achieve low prices unless they have a strong bargaining position. Relative bargaining power in a transaction depends, ultimately, on the cost to each party of not doing business with the other party. The buyers' bargaining power is determined by the number of buyers relative to the number of suppliers, volume of purchases by a single buyer, number of alternative products available to the buyer, buyers' costs of switching from one product to another, and the threat of backward integration by the buyers. For example, in the automobile industry, car manufacturers have considerable power over component manufacturers because auto companies are large buyers, with several alternative suppliers to choose from, and switching costs are relatively low. In contrast, in the personal computer industry, computer makers have low bargaining power relative to the operating system software producers because of high switching costs.

Competitive Force 5: Bargaining Power of Suppliers

The analysis of the relative power of suppliers is a mirror image of the analysis of the buyer's power in an industry. Suppliers are powerful when there are only a few companies and there are few substitutes available to their customers. For example, in the soft-drink industry, Coke and Pepsi are very powerful relative to the bottlers. In contrast, metal can suppliers to the soft drink industry are not very powerful because of intense competition among can producers and the threat of substitution of cans by plastic bottles. Suppliers also have a lot of power over buyers when the suppliers' product or service is critical to buyers' business. For example, airline pilots have a strong bargaining power in the airline industry. Suppliers also tend to be powerful when they pose a credible threat of forward integration. For example, IBM is powerful relative to mainframe computer leasing companies because of IBM's unique position as a mainframe supplier, and its own presence in the computer leasing business.

APPLYING INDUSTRY ANALYSIS: THE PERSONAL COMPUTER INDUSTRY

Let us consider the above concepts of industry analysis in the context of Compaq's industry—the IBM and compatible personal computer (PC) industry—in 1993.[8] The industry began in 1981 when IBM announced its PC with Intel's microprocessor and Microsoft's DOS operating system, and grew by 1992 to become a $62 billion dollar industry. Despite this spectacular growth, however, the industry in 1993 was characterized by low profitability. Even the largest companies in the industry, such as IBM, Compaq, and Dell, reported poor performance in the early 1990s, and were forced to undergo internal restructuring. What accounted for this low profitability? What was the industry's future profit potential?

COMPETITION IN THE PERSONAL COMPUTER INDUSTRY.   The competition was very intense for a number of reasons:

- The industry was highly fragmented, with many firms producing virtually identical products. Even the largest firm in the industry, IBM, had only about a 15 percent market share, and the ten largest firms in the industry accounted for only 53 percent of the industry.
- Component costs accounted for 80–90 percent of total costs of a personal computer, and volume purchases of components reduced these costs. Therefore, there was intense competition for market share among competing manufacturers.
- Products produced by different firms in the industry were virtually identical, and there were few opportunities to differentiate the products. While brand name and service were dimensions that customers valued in the early years of the industry, they became less important as PC buyers became more informed about the technology.

- Switching costs across different brands of personal computers were relatively low because the clones were essentially identical to IBM computers.
- Access to distribution was not a significant barrier, as demonstrated by Dell Computers, which distributed its computers through direct mail. The advent of computer superstores like CompUSA also mitigated this constraint, since these stores were willing to carry several brands.
- Since virtually all the components needed to produce a personal computer were available for purchase, there were very few barriers to entering the industry. In fact, Michael Dell started Dell Computer Company in the early 1980s by assembling PCs in his University of Texas dormitory room.
- Apple's Macintosh computers offered significant competition as a substitute product. Work stations produced by Sun, DEC, and other vendors were also potential substitutes at the higher end of the personal computer market.

THE POWER OF SUPPLIERS AND BUYERS.   Suppliers and buyers had significant power over firms in the industry for these reasons:

- Key hardware and software components for personal computers were controlled by firms with virtual monopoly. Intel dominated the microprocessor production for the personal computer industry, and Microsoft controlled the operating system market with its DOS and Windows operating systems.
- Buyers gained more power during the ten years from 1983 to 1993. Corporate buyers, who represented a significant portion of the customer base, were highly price sensitive since the expenditure on PCs represented a significant cost to their operations. Further, as they became knowledgeable about personal computer technology, customers were less influenced by brand name in their purchase decision. Buyers increasingly viewed PCs as commodities, and used price as the most important consideration in their buying decision.

As a result of the intense rivalry and low barriers to entry in the personal computer industry, there was severe price competition among different manufacturers. Further, there was tremendous pressure on firms to spend large sums of money to introduce new products rapidly, maintain high quality, and provide excellent customer support. Both these factors led to a low profit potential in the industry. The power of suppliers and buyers reduced the profit potential further. Thus, while the personal computer industry represented a technologically dynamic industry, its profit potential was poor.

Because there were few indications of change in the basic structure of the personal computer industry, there was little likelihood of viable competition emerging to challenge the domination of Microsoft and Intel in the input markets. Attempts by industry leaders like IBM to create alternative proprietary technologies have not succeeded, and barriers to entry are likely to continue. Threats from Apple are only likely to increase with the development of the PowerPC chip, as well as Apple's willingness to license its own operating system to clone manufacturers. As a result, the profitability of the PC industry may not improve significantly any time in the near future.

Limitations of Industry Analysis

A potential limitation of the industry analysis framework discussed in this chapter is the assumption that industries have clear boundaries. In reality, it is often not easy to clearly demarcate industry boundaries. For example, in analyzing Compaq's industry, should one focus on the IBM-compatible personal computer industry or the personal computer industry as a whole? Should one include workstations in the industry definition? Should one consider only the domestic manufacturers of personal computers, or also manufacturers abroad? Inappropriate industry definition will result in incomplete analysis and inaccurate forecasts.

COMPETITIVE STRATEGY ANALYSIS

The profitability of a firm is influenced not only by its industry structure but also by the strategic choices it makes in positioning itself in the industry. While there are many ways to characterize a firm's business strategy, as Figure 2-2 shows, there are two generic

Figure 2-2 Strategies for Creating Competitive Advantage

Cost Leadership

Supply same product or service at a lower cost.

Economies of scale and scope
Efficient production
Simpler product designs
Lower input costs
Low-cost distribution
Little research and development or
    brand advertising
Tight cost control system

Differentiation

Supply a unique product or service at a cost lower than the price premium customers will pay.

Superior product quality
Superior product variety
Superior customer service
More flexible delivery
Investment in brand image
Investment in research and
    development
Control system focus on creativity
    and innovation

Competitive Advantage

- Match between firm's core competencies and key success factors to execute strategy

- Match between firm's value chain and activities required to execute strategy

- Sustainability of competitive advantage

competitive strategies: (1) cost leadership and (2) differentiation.[9] Both these strategies can potentially allow a firm to build a sustainable competitive advantage.

Strategy researchers have traditionally viewed cost leadership and differentiation as mutually exclusive strategies. Firms that straddle the two strategies are considered to be "stuck in the middle" and are expected to earn low profitability.[10] These firms run the risk of not being able to attract price conscious customers because their costs are too high; they are also unable to provide adequate differentiation to attract premium price customers.[11]

SOURCES OF COMPETITIVE ADVANTAGE

Cost leadership enables a firm to supply the same product or service offered by its competitors at a lower cost. Differentiation strategy involves providing a product or service that is distinct in some important respect valued by the customer. For example, in retailing, Nordstrom has succeeded on the basis of differentiation by emphasizing exceptionally high customer service. In contrast, Filene's Basement Stores is a discount retailer competing purely on a low cost basis.

Competitive Strategy 1: Cost Leadership

Cost leadership is often the clearest way to achieve competitive advantage. In industries where the basic product or service is a commodity, cost leadership might be the only way to achieve superior performance. There are many ways to achieve cost leadership, including economies of scale and scope, economies of learning, efficient production, simpler product design, lower input costs, and efficient organizational processes. If a firm can achieve cost leadership, then it will be able to earn above-average profitability by merely charging the same price as its rivals. Conversely, a cost leader can force its competitors to cut prices and accept lower returns, or to exit the industry.

Firms that achieve cost leadership focus on tight cost controls. They make investments in efficient scale plants, focus on product designs that reduce manufacturing costs, minimize overhead costs, make little investment in risky research and development, and avoid serving marginal customers. They have organizational structures and control systems that focus on cost control.

Competitive Strategy 2: Differentiation

A firm following the differentiation strategy seeks to be unique in its industry along some dimension that is highly valued by customers. For differentiation to be successful, the firm has to accomplish three things. First, it needs to identify one or more attributes of a product or service that customers value. Second, it has to position itself to meet the chosen customer need in a unique manner. Finally, the firm has to achieve differentiation at a cost that is lower than the price the customer is willing to pay for the differentiated product or service.

Drivers of differentiation include providing superior intrinsic value via product quality, product variety, bundled services, or delivery timing. Differentiation can also be achieved by investing in signals of value, such as brand image, product appearance, or reputation. Differentiated strategies require investments in research and development, engineering skills, and marketing capabilities. The organizational structures and control systems in firms with differentiation strategies need to foster creativity and innovation.

While successful firms choose between cost leadership and differentiation, they cannot completely ignore the dimension on which they are not primarily competing. Firms which target differentiation still need to focus on costs, so that the differentiation can be achieved at an acceptable cost. Similarly, cost leaders cannot compete unless they achieve at least a minimum level on key dimensions on which competitors might differentiate, such as quality and service.

ACHIEVING AND SUSTAINING COMPETITIVE ADVANTAGE

The choice of competitive strategy does not automatically lead to the achievement of competitive advantage. To achieve competitive advantage, the firm has to have the capabilities needed to implement and sustain the chosen strategy. Both cost leadership and differentiation strategy require that the firm make the necessary commitments to acquire the core competencies needed, and structure its value chain in an appropriate way. Core competencies are the economic assets that the firm possesses, whereas the value chain is the set of activities that the firm performs to convert inputs into outputs. The uniqueness of a firm's core competencies and its value chain and the extent to which it is difficult for competitors to imitate them determines the sustainability of a firm's competitive advantage.[12]

To evaluate whether or not a firm is likely to achieve its intended competitive advantage, the analyst should ask the following questions:

- What are the key success factors and risks associated with the firm's chosen competitive strategy?
- Does the firm currently have the resources and capabilities to deal with the key success factors and risks?
- Has the firm made irreversible commitments to bridge the gap between its current capabilities and the requirements to achieve its competitive advantage?
- Has the firm structured its activities (such as research and development, design, manufacturing, marketing and distribution, and support activities) in a way that is consistent with its competitive strategy?
- Is the company's competitive advantage sustainable? Are there any barriers that make imitation of the firm's strategy difficult?
- Are there any potential changes in the firm's industry structure (such as new technologies, foreign competition, changes in regulation, changes in customer requirements) that might dissipate the firm's competitive advantage? Is the company flexible enough to address these changes?

APPLYING BUSINESS STRATEGY ANALYSIS

Once again, let us consider the concepts of business strategy analysis in the context of Compaq Computers. Compaq was the leading IBM compatible computer maker, with a market share of approximately 10 percent by 1993. After several years of strong performance, the company reported a decline in profits in 1992. However, with new management and a fine-tuning of its strategy, Compaq reported a strong profit performance once again in 1993.

Bill Gurley of CS First Boston summarized Compaq's business strategy that led to this superior performance in a difficult industry as follows:

Compaq Computer Corporation has emerged as the leading independent vendor of IBM/PC compatible computers, second only to the IBM PC Company itself in shipments and revenues. The company has achieved this position by establishing itself as a low cost producer without sacrificing its commitment to quality. As part of its strategy, Compaq has focused on revenue growth and market share gains rather than margin increases. Compaq has converted these market share gains into further volume-driven cost advantages. The company has then passed these cost advantages on to the customer in terms of lower pricing, thus generating further growth. The strategy is working, and we expect Compaq will continue to outperform its competitors and Wall Street's earnings forecasts in the process.[13]

As Gurley's analysis suggests, Compaq distinguished itself from IBM by being a low cost producer, and it differentiated itself from other PC clone makers by investing in a brand name with an image of high quality, industry leading service, and continual introduction of new products. Compaq's competitive strategy produced these results:

- As a result of its brand image, Compaq commanded a slight price premium of about 5–6 percent over other IBM clones.
- Compaq had a significant cost advantage because of its ability to purchase components in large volumes. These components account for 80–90 percent of PC manufacturing costs. For example, Gurley suggests that Compaq followed a low-cost manufacturing strategy by creating vertically integrated manufacturing lines which significantly reduce direct labor costs and overhead costs. As a result of both lower input costs and manufacturing efficiencies, Compaq's cost of goods sold was approximately 70 percent, several percentage points lower than the ratio for Dell and other IBM compatible manufacturers.
- Compaq also lowered its operating expenses in 1992 and 1993 by focusing on tight cost controls.

In an industry with very small gross margins, the price premium and lower costs enabled Compaq to earn one of the highest net profit margins.

Although Compaq's strategy gave it a competitive advantage over both IBM and other PC clone makers, the long-term sustainability of Compaq's position was questionable. For example, if IBM's PC operations were better managed under its new management, Compaq could be dominated by IBM in terms of technical innovation, customer service, and brand image. Similarly, it ran the risk of being dominated by low-cost clone makers like Packard-Bell and Gateway 2000, which avoided some of the costs incurred by Compaq without significantly sacrificing product quality and features. In either case, Compaq is likely to lose its current price premium, leading to significantly lower profits. How soon this happens will be determined to some extent by the strategies and actions taken by Compaq's competitors, something not in the control of Compaq's management.

SUMMARY AND CONCLUSIONS

Business strategy analysis is an important starting point for the analysis of financial statements because it allows the analyst to probe the economics of the firm at a qualitative level. Strategy analysis also allows the identification of the firm's profit drivers and key risks, enabling the analyst to assess the sustainability of the firm's performance and make realistic forecasts of future performance.

Whether or not a firm is able to earn a return on its capital in excess of its cost of capital is determined by its own strategic choices: (1) the choice of an industry or a set of industries in which the firm operates (industry choice) and (2) the manner in which the firm intends to compete with other firms in its chosen industry or industries (competitive positioning). Business strategy analysis involves both of these choices.

Industry analysis consists of identifying the economic factors which drive the industry profitability. In general, an industry's average profit potential is influenced by the degree of rivalry among existing competitors, the ease with which new firms can enter the industry, the availability of substitute products, the power of buyers, and the power of suppliers. To perform industry analysis, the analyst has to assess the current strength of each of these forces in an industry and make forecasts of any likely future changes.

Competitive strategy analysis involves identifying the basis on which the firm intends to compete in its industry. In general, there are two potential strategies that could provide a firm with a competitive advantage: cost leadership and differentiation. Cost leadership involves offering the same product or service that other firms offer at a lower cost. Differentiation involves satisfying a chosen dimension of customer need better than the competition, at an incremental cost that is less than the price premium that customers are willing to pay. To perform strategy analysis, the analyst has to identify the firm's intended strategy, assess whether or not the firm possesses the competencies required to execute the strategy, and recognize the key risks that the firm has to guard against. The analyst also has to evaluate the sustainability of the firm's strategy.

The insights gained from industry analysis can be useful in performing the remainder of the financial statement analysis. In accounting analysis, the analyst can examine whether a firm's accounting policies and estimates are consistent with its stated business strategy. For example, a firm's choice of functional currency in accounting for its international operations should be consistent with the level of integration between domestic and international operations that the business strategy calls for. Similarly, a firm that mainly sells housing to low income customers should have higher bad debts expenses.

Strategy analysis is also useful in guiding financial analysis. For example, in a cross-sectional analysis the analyst should expect firms with cost leadership strategy to have lower gross margins and higher asset turnover than firms that follow differentiated strategies. In a time series analysis, the analyst should closely monitor any increases in expense ratios and asset turnover ratios for low cost firms, and any decreases in investments critical to differentiation for firms that follow differentiation strategy.

Business strategy analysis also helps in prospective analysis. First, it allows the analyst to assess whether, and for how long, differences between the firm's performance and its industry performance are likely to persist. Second, strategy analysis facilitates forecasting investment outlays the firm has to make to maintain its competitive advantage.

NOTES

1. The discussion presented here is intended to provide a basic background in business strategy analysis. For a more complete discussion of the strategy concepts, see, for example, *Contemporary Strategy Analysis* by Robert M. Grant (Cambridge, MA: Blackwell Publishers, 1991).

2. Most of the 1992 annual report for Compaq Computer Corporation is in Part 5 at the end of the text.

3. These data are taken from *Selected Profitability Data on U.S. Industries and Companies* by Anita M. McGahan (Boston: Harvard Business School Publishing Division, 9-792-066).

4. For a summary of this research, see *Industrial Market Structure and Economic Performance,* second edition, by F. M. Scherer (Chicago: Rand McNally College Publishing Co., 1980).

5. See *Competitive Strategy* by Michael E. Porter (New York: The Free Press, 1980).

6. The four-firm concentration ratio is a commonly used measure of industry concentration; it refers to the market share of the four largest firms in an industry.

7. While the discussion here uses the buyer to connote industrial buyers, the same concepts also apply to buyers of consumer products. Throughout this chapter, we use the terms buyers and customers interchangeably.

8. The data on the personal computer (PC) industry discussed here and elsewhere in this chapter is drawn from a survey by Bill Gurley, "PC Profile 1993," CS First Boston, November 1993.

9. For a more detailed discussion of these two sources of competitive advantage, see Michael E. Porter, *Competitive Advantage: Creating and Sustaining Superior Performance* (New York: The Free Press, 1985).

10. Ibid.

11. In recent years, one of the strategic challenges faced by corporations is having to deal with competitors who achieve differentiation with low cost. For example, Japanese auto manufacturers have successfully demonstrated that there is no necessary trade-off between quality and cost. Similarly, in recent years several highly successful retailers like Wal-Mart and Home Depot have been able to combine high quality, high service, and low prices. These examples suggest that combining low cost and differentiation strategies is possible when a firm introduces a significant technical or business innovation. However, such cost advantage and differentiation will be sustainable only if there are significant barriers to imitation by competitors.

12. See *Competing for the Future* by Gary Hammel and C. K. Prahalad (Boston: Harvard Business School Press, 1994) for a more detailed discussion of the concept of core competencies and their critical role in corporate strategy.

13. "Compaq Computer Corporation" by J. Gurley, CS First Boston, November 29, 1993, p. 4.

chapter 3

Accounting Analysis

The purpose of accounting analysis is to evaluate the degree to which a firm's accounting captures its underlying business reality.[1] By identifying places where there is accounting flexibility, and by evaluating the appropriateness of the firm's accounting policies and estimates, analysts can assess the degree of distortion in a firm's accounting numbers. Another important skill is recasting a firm's accounting numbers using cash flow and footnote information to "undo" any accounting distortions. Sound accounting analysis improves the reliability of conclusions from financial analysis, the next step in financial statement analysis.

OVERVIEW OF THE INSTITUTIONAL FRAMEWORK FOR FINANCIAL REPORTING

There is typically a separation between ownership and management in public corporations. Financial statements serve as the vehicle through which owners keep track of their firms' financial situation. On a periodic basis, firms typically produce three financial reports : (1) an income statement that describes the operating performance during a time period, (2) a balance sheet that states the firm's assets and how they are financed, and (3) a cash flow statement (or in some countries, a funds flow statement) that summarizes the cash flows of the firm. These statements are accompanied by several footnotes and a message and narrative discussion written by the management.

To evaluate effectively the quality of a firm's financial statement data, the analyst needs to first understand the basic features of financial reporting and the institutional framework that governs them, as discussed in the following sections.

Building Blocks of Accrual Accounting

One of the fundamental features of corporate financial reports is that they are prepared using accrual rather than cash accounting. Unlike cash accounting, accrual accounting distinguishes between the recording of costs and benefits associated with economic activities and the actual payment and receipt of cash. Net income is the primary periodic performance index under accrual accounting. To compute net income, the effects of economic transactions are recorded on the basis of *expected*, not necessarily *actual*, cash receipts and payments. Expected cash receipts from the delivery of products or services are recognized as revenues, and expected cash outflows associated with these revenues are recognized as expenses.

While there are many rules and conventions that govern a firm's preparation of financial statements, there are only a few conceptual building blocks that form the foundation of accrual accounting. The principles that define a firm's assets, liabilities, equities, revenues, and expenses are as follows[2]:

- **Assets** are economic resources owned by a firm that (a) are likely to produce future economic benefits and (b) are measurable with a reasonable degree of certainty.
- **Liabilities** are economic obligations of a firm arising from benefits received in the past that are (a) required to be met with a reasonable degree of certainty and (b) at a reasonably well-defined time in the future.
- **Equity** is the difference between a firm's net assets and its liabilities.

These definitions lead to the fundamental relationship that governs a firm's balance sheet:

Assets = Liabilities + Equity

While the balance sheet is a summary at one point in time, the income statement summarizes a firm's revenues and expenses and its gains and losses arising from changes in assets and liabilities in accord with the following definitions:

- **Revenues** are economic resources earned during a time period. Revenue recognition is governed by the realization principle, which proposes that revenues should be recognized when (a) the firm has provided all, or substantially all, the goods or services to be delivered to the customer and (b) the customer has paid cash or is expected to pay cash with a reasonable degree of certainty.
- **Expenses** are economic resources used up in a time period. Expense recognition is governed by the matching and the conservatism principles. Under these principles, expenses are (a) costs directly associated with revenues recognized in the same period, or (b) costs associated with benefits that are consumed in this time period, or (c) resources whose future benefits are not reasonably certain.
- **Profit** is the difference between a firm's revenues and expenses in a time period.[3]

Delegation of Reporting to Management

While the basic definitions of the elements of a firm's financial statements are simple, their application in practice often involves complex judgments. For example, how should revenues be recognized when a firm sells land to customers and also provides customer financing? If revenue is recognized before cash is collected, how should potential defaults be estimated? Are the outlays associated with research and development activities, whose payoffs are uncertain, assets or expenses when incurred? Do frequent flyer reward programs create accounting liabilities for airline companies? If so, when and at what value?

Because corporate managers have intimate knowledge of their firms' businesses, they are entrusted with the primary task of making the appropriate judgments in portraying myriad business transactions using the basic accrual accounting framework. The accounting discretion granted to managers is potentially valuable because it allows them to reflect inside information in reported financial statements. However, since investors view profits as a measure of managers' performance, managers have an incentive to use their accounting discretion to distort reported profits by making biased assumptions. Further, the use of accounting numbers in contracts between the firm and outsiders provides a motivation for management manipulation of accounting numbers.

Income management distorts financial accounting data, making them less valuable to external users of financial statements. Therefore, the delegation of financial reporting decisions to managers has both costs and benefits. Accounting rules and auditing are mechanisms designed to reduce the cost and preserve the benefit of delegating financial reporting to corporate managers.

Generally Accepted Accounting Principles

Given that it is difficult for outside investors to determine whether managers have used their accounting flexibility to signal their proprietary information or merely to disguise reality, a number of accounting conventions have evolved to mitigate the problem. Accounting conventions and standards promulgated by the standard-setting bodies limit potential distortions that managers can introduce into reported accounting numbers. In the United States, the Securities and Exchange Commission (SEC) has the legal authority to set accounting standards. The SEC typically relies on private sector accounting bodies to undertake this task. Since 1973, accounting standards in the United States have been set by the Financial Accounting Standards Board (FASB). There are similar private sector or public sector accounting standard-setting bodies in many other countries. In addition, the International Accounting Standards Committee (IASC) has been attempting to set worldwide accounting standards, though IASC's pronouncements are not legally binding as of now.

Uniform accounting standards attempt to reduce managers' ability to record similar economic transactions in dissimilar ways either over time or across firms. Thus they create a uniform accounting language and increase the credibility of financial statements by limiting a firm's ability to distort them. Increased uniformity from accounting standards, however, comes at the expense of reduced flexibility for managers to reflect genuine business differences in a firm's accounting decisions. Rigid accounting standards work best for economic transactions whose accounting treatment is not predicated on managers' proprietary information. However, when there is a significant business judgment involved in assessing a transaction's economic consequences, rigid standards are likely to be dysfunctional, because they prevent managers from using their superior business knowledge. Further, if accounting standards are too rigid, they may induce managers to expend economic resources to restructure business transactions to achieve a desired accounting result.

External Auditing

Broadly defined as a verification of the integrity of the reported financial statements by someone other than the preparer, external auditing ensures that managers use accounting rules and conventions consistently over time, and that their accounting estimates are reasonable. In the United States, all listed companies are required to have their financial statements audited by an independent public accountant. The standards and procedures to be followed by independent auditors are set by the American Institute of Certified Public Accountants (AICPA). These standards are known as Generally Accepted Auditing Standards (GAAS). While auditors issue an opinion on published financial statements, it is important to remember that the primary responsibility of the statements still rests with corporate managers.

Auditing improves the quality and credibility of accounting data by limiting a firm's ability to distort financial statements to suit its own purposes. However, third-party auditing may also reduce the quality of financial reporting because it constrains the kind of accounting rules and conventions that evolve over time. For example, the FASB considers the views of auditors in the standard-setting process. Auditors are likely to argue against accounting standards that produce numbers which are difficult to audit, even if the proposed rules produce relevant information for investors.

Legal Liability

The legal environment in which accounting disputes between managers, auditors, and investors are adjudicated can also have a significant effect on the quality of reported numbers. The threat of lawsuits and resulting penalties have the beneficial effect of improving the accuracy of disclosure. However, the potential for a significant legal liability might also discourage managers and auditors from supporting accounting proposals requiring risky forecasts, such as forward-looking disclosures This type of concern is often expressed by the auditing community in the U.S.

Limitations of Accounting Analysis

Because the mechanisms that limit managers' ability to distort accounting data themselves add noise, it is not optimal to use accounting regulation to eliminate managerial flexibility completely. Therefore, real-world accounting systems leave considerable room for managers to influence financial statement data. The net result is that information in corporate financial reports is noisy and biased, even in the presence of accounting regulation and external auditing.[4] The objective of accounting analysis is to evaluate the degree to which a firm's accounting captures its underlying business reality and to "undo" any accounting distortions. When potential distortions are large, accounting analysis can add considerable value.[5]

Factors Influencing Accounting Quality

There are three potential sources of noise and bias in accounting data: (1) the noise and bias introduced by rigidity in accounting rules, (2) random forecast errors, and (3) systematic reporting choices made by corporate managers to achieve specific objectives. Each of these factors is discussed below.

ACCOUNTING RULES.   Accounting rules introduce noise and bias because it is often difficult to restrict management discretion without reducing the information content of accounting data. For example, the Statement of Financial Accounting Standards No. 2 issued by the FASB requires firms to expense research outlays when they are incurred. Clearly, some research expenditures have future value while others do not. However, because SFAS No. 2 does not allow firms to distinguish between the two types of expenditures, it leads to a systematic distortion of reported accounting numbers. Broadly speaking, the degree of distortion introduced by accounting standards depends on how well uniform accounting standards capture the nature of a firm's transactions.

FORECAST ERRORS.   Another source of noise in accounting data arises from pure forecast error, because managers cannot predict future consequences of current transactions perfectly. For example, when a firm sells products on credit, accrual accounting requires managers to make a judgment on the probability of collecting payments from customers. If payments are deemed "reasonably certain," the firm treats the transactions as sales, creating accounts receivable on its balance sheet. Managers then make an estimate of the proportion of receivables that will not be collected. Because managers do not have perfect foresight, actual defaults are likely to be different from estimated customer defaults, leading to a forecast error. The extent of errors in managers' accounting forecasts depends on a variety of factors, including the complexity of the business transactions, the predictability of the firm's environment, and unforeseen economy-wide changes.

MANAGERS' ACCOUNTING CHOICES.   Corporate managers also introduce noise and bias into accounting data through their own accounting decisions. Managers have a variety of incentives to exercise their accounting discretion to achieve certain objectives, leading to systematic influences on their firms' reporting[6]:

- *Accounting-based debt covenants.* Managers may make accounting decisions to meet certain contractual obligations in their debt covenants. For example, firms' lending agreements with banks and other debt holders require them to meet covenants related to interest coverage, working capital ratios, and net worth, all defined in terms of accounting numbers. Violation of these constraints may be costly because it allows lenders to demand immediate payment of their loans. Managers of firms close to violating debt covenants have an incentive to select accounting policies and estimates to reduce the probability of covenant violation. The debt covenant motivation for managers' accounting decisions has been analyzed by a number of accounting researchers.[7]
- *Management compensation.* Another motivation for managers' accounting choice comes from the fact that their compensation and job security are often tied to reported profits. For example, many top managers receive bonus compensation if they exceed certain prespecified profit targets. This provides motivation for managers to choose accounting policies and estimates to maximize their expected compensation.[8]
- *Corporate control contests.* In corporate control contests, including hostile takeovers and proxy fights, competing management groups attempt to win over the firm's shareholders. Accounting numbers are used extensively in debating managers' performance in these contests. Therefore, managers may make accounting decisions to influence investor perceptions in corporate control contests.[9]
- *Tax considerations.* Managers may also make reporting choices to trade off between financial reporting and tax considerations. For example, U.S. firms are required to use LIFO inventory accounting for shareholder reporting in order to use it for tax reporting. Under LIFO, when prices are rising, firms report lower profits, thereby reducing tax payments. Some firms may forgo the tax reduction in order to report higher profits in their financial statements.[10]
- *Regulatory considerations.* Since accounting numbers are used by regulators in a variety of contexts, managers of some firms may make accounting decisions to influence regulatory outcomes. Examples of regulatory situations where accounting numbers are used include antitrust actions, import tariffs to protect domestic industries, and tax policies.[11]
- *Capital market considerations.* Managers may make accounting decisions to influence the perceptions of capital markets. When there are information asymmetries between managers and outsiders, this strategy may succeed in influencing investor perceptions, at least temporarily.[12]
- *Stakeholder considerations.* Managers may also make accounting decisions to influence the perception of important stakeholders in the firm. For example, since labor unions can use healthy profits as a basis for demanding wage increases, managers may make accounting decisions to decrease income when they are facing union contract negotiations. In countries like Germany, where labor unions are

strong, these considerations appear to play an important role in firms' accounting policy. Other important stakeholders that firms may wish to influence through their financial reports include suppliers and customers.

- *Competitive considerations.* The dynamics of competition in an industry might also influence a firm's reporting choices. For example, a firm's segment disclosure decisions may be influenced by its concern that disaggregated disclosure may help competitors in their business decisions. Similarly, firms may not disclose data on their margins by product line for fear of giving away proprietary information. Finally, firms may discourage new entrants by making income-decreasing accounting choices.

In addition to accounting policy choices and estimates, the level of disclosure is also an important determinant of a firm's accounting quality. Corporate managers can choose disclosure policies that make it more or less costly for external users of financial reports to understand the true economic picture of their businesses. Accounting regulations usually prescribe minimum disclosure requirements, but they do not restrict managers from voluntarily providing additional disclosures. Managers can use various parts of the financial reports, including the Letter to the Shareholders, Management Discussion and Analysis, and footnotes, to describe the company's strategy, its accounting policies, and the firm's current performance. There is wide variation across firms in how managers use their disclosure flexibility.[13]

DOING ACCOUNTING ANALYSIS

In this section we will discuss a series of steps that an analyst can follow to evaluate a firm's accounting quality. Later in the chapter, an analysis of Compaq's accounting quality in 1992 is presented to illustrate the application of the concepts discussed.

Step 1: Identify Key Accounting Policies

As discussed in the chapter on business strategy analysis, a firm's industry characteristics and its own competitive strategy determine its key success factors and risks. One of the goals of financial statement analysis is to evaluate how well these success factors and risks are being managed by the firm. In accounting analysis, therefore, the analyst should identify and evaluate the policies and the estimates the firm uses to measure its critical factors and risks.

For example, one of the key success factors in the leasing business is to make accurate forecasts of residual values of the leased equipment at the end of the lease terms. For a firm in the equipment leasing industry, therefore, one of the most important accounting policies is the way residual values are recorded. Residual values influence the company's reported profits and its asset base. If residual values are over-estimated, the firm runs the risk of having to take large write-offs in the future.

Key success factors in the banking industry include interest and credit risk management; in the retail industry, inventory management is a key success factor; and for a manufacturer competing on product quality and innovation, research and development and product defects after the sale are key areas of concern. In each of these cases, the analyst has to identify the accounting measures the firm uses to capture these business constructs, the policies that determine how the measures are implemented, and the key estimates embedded in these policies. For example, the accounting measure a bank uses to capture credit risk is its loan loss reserves, and the accounting measure that captures product quality for a manufacturer is its warranty expenses and reserves.

Step 2: Assess Accounting Flexibility

Not all firms have equal flexibility in choosing their key accounting policies and estimates. Some firms' accounting choice is severely constrained by accounting standards and conventions. For example, even though research and development is a key success factor for biotechnology companies, managers have no accounting discretion in reporting on this activity. Similarly, even though marketing and brand building are key to the success of consumer goods firms, they are required to expense all their marketing outlays. In contrast, managing credit risk is one of the critical success factors for banks, and bank managers have the freedom to estimate expected defaults on their loans. Similarly, software developers have the flexibility to decide at what points in their development cycles the outlays can be capitalized.

If managers have little flexibility in choosing accounting policies and estimates related to their key success factors (as in the case of biotechnology firms), accounting data are likely to be not as informative for understanding the firm's economics. In contrast, if managers have considerable flexibility in choosing the policies and estimates (as in the case of software developers), accounting numbers have the potential to be informative, depending upon how managers exercise this flexibility.

Regardless of the degree of accounting flexibility a firm's managers have in measuring their key success factors and risks, they will have some flexibility with respect to several other accounting policies. For example, all firms have to make choices with respect to depreciation policy (straight-line or accelerated methods), inventory accounting policy (LIFO, FIFO, or Average Cost), policy for amortizing goodwill (write-off over forty years or less), and policies regarding the estimation of pension and other post-employment benefits (expected return on plan assets, discount rate for liabilities, and rate of increase in wages and health care costs). Since all these policy choices can have a significant impact on the reported performance of a firm, they offer an opportunity for the firm to manage its reported numbers.

Step 3: Evaluate Accounting Strategy

When managers have accounting flexibility, they can use it either to communicate their firm's economic situation or to hide true performance. Some of the strategy questions one could ask in examining how managers exercise their accounting flexibility include the following:

- How do the firm's accounting policies compare to the norms in the industry? If they are dissimilar, is it because the firm's competitive strategy is unique? For example, consider a firm that reports a lower warranty allowance than the industry average. One explanation is that the firm competes on the basis of high quality and has invested considerable resources to reduce the rate of product failure. An alternative explanation is that the firm is merely understating its warranty liabilities.

- Does management face strong incentives to use accounting discretion for earnings management? For example, is the firm close to violating bond covenants? Or, are the managers having difficulty meeting accounting-based bonus targets? Does management own significant stock? Is the firm in the middle of a proxy fight or union negotiations? Managers may also make accounting decisions to reduce tax payments, or to influence the perceptions of the firm's competitors.

- Has the firm changed any of its policies or estimates? What is the justification? What is the impact of these changes? For example, if warranty expenses decreased, is it because the firm made significant investments to improve quality?

- Have the company's policies and estimates been realistic in the past? For example, firms may overstate their revenues and understate their expenses during the year by manipulating quarterly reports, which are not subject to a full-blown external audit. However, the auditing process at the end of the fiscal year forces such companies to make large fourth-quarter adjustments, providing an opportunity for the analyst to assess the quality of the firm's interim reporting. Similarly, firms that expense acquisition goodwill too slowly will be forced to take a large write-off later. A history of write-offs may be, therefore, a sign of prior earnings management.

- Does the firm structure any significant business transactions so that it can achieve certain accounting objectives? For example, leasing firms can alter lease terms (the length of the lease or the bargain purchase option at the end of the lease term) so that the transactions qualify as sales-type leases for the lessors. Firms may structure a takeover transaction (equity financing rather than debt financing) so that they can use the pooling of interests method rather than the purchase method of accounting. Finally, a firm can alter the way it finances (coupon rate and the terms of conversion for a convertible bond issue) so that its reported earnings per share is not diluted. Such behavior may suggest that the firm's managers are willing to expend economic resources merely to achieve an accounting objective.

Step 4: Evaluate the Quality of Disclosure – read foot notes

Managers can make it more or less easy for an analyst to assess the firm's accounting quality and to use its financial statements to understand business reality. While accounting rules require a certain amount of minimum disclosure, managers have considerable choice in the matter. Disclosure quality, therefore, is an important dimension of a firm's accounting quality.

In assessing a firm's disclosure quality, an analyst could ask the following questions:

- Does the company provide adequate disclosures to assess the firm's business strategy and its economic consequences? For example, some firms use the Letter to the Shareholders in their annual report to clearly lay out the firm's industry conditions, its competitive position, and management's plans for the future. Others use the Letter to puff up the firm's financial performance and gloss over any competitive difficulties the firm might be facing.
- Do the footnotes adequately explain the key accounting policies and assumptions and their logic? For example, if a firm's revenue and expense recognition policies differ from industry norms, the firm can explain its choices in a footnote. Similarly, when there are significant changes in a firm's policies, footnotes can be used to disclose the reasons.
- Does the firm adequately explain its current performance? The Management Discussion and Analysis section of the firm's annual report provides an opportunity to help analysts understand the reasons behind the firm's performance changes. Some firms use this section to link financial performance to business conditions. For example, if profit margins went down in a period, was it because of price competition or because of increases in manufacturing costs? If the selling and general administrative expenses went up, was it because the firm is investing in a differentiation strategy, or because unproductive overhead expenses were creeping up?
- If accounting rules and conventions restrict the firm from measuring its key success factors appropriately, does the firm provide adequate additional disclosure to help outsiders understand how these factors are being managed? For example, if a firm invests in product quality and customer service, accounting rules do not allow the management to capitalize these outlays, even when the future benefits are certain. The firm's Management Discussion and Analysis can be used to highlight how these outlays are being managed and their performance consequences. For example, the firm can disclose physical indexes of defect rates and customer satisfaction so that outsiders can assess the progress being made in these areas and the future cash flow consequences of these actions.
- If a firm is in multiple business segments, what is the quality of segment disclosure? Some firms provide excellent discussion of their performance by product segments and geographic segments. Others lump many different businesses into one broad segment. The level of competition in an industry and management's willingness to share desegregated performance data influence a firm's quality of segment disclosure.
- How forthcoming is the management with respect to bad news? A firm's disclosure quality is most clearly revealed by the way management deals with bad news. Does it adequately explain the reasons for poor performance? Does the company clearly articulate its strategy, if any, to address the company's performance problems?

- How good is the firm's investor relations program? Does the firm provide fact books with detailed data on the firm's business and performance? Is the management accessible to analysts?

Step 5: Identify Potential Red Flags — *read foot notes*

In addition to the above analysis, a common approach to accounting quality analysis is to look for "red flags" pointing to questionable accounting quality. These indicators suggest that the analyst should examine certain items more closely or gather more information on them. Some common red flags are:

- *Unexplained changes in accounting, especially when performance is poor.* This may suggest that managers are using their accounting discretion to "dress up" their financial statements.[14]
- *Unexplained transactions that boost profits.* For example, firms might undertake balance sheet transactions, such as asset sales or debt for equity swaps, to realize gains in periods when operating performance is poor.[15]
- *Unusual increases in accounts receivable in relation to sales increases.* This may suggest that the company might be relaxing its credit policies or artificially loading up its distribution channels to record revenues during the current period. If credit policies are relaxed unduly, the firm may face receivable write-offs in the subsequent periods as a result of customer defaults. If the firm accelerates shipments to the distribution channels, it may either face product returns or reduced shipments in the subsequent periods.
- *Unusual increases in inventories in relation to sales increases.* If the inventory build-up is due to an increase in finished goods inventory, it could be a sign that the demand for the firm's products is slowing down, suggesting that the firm may be forced to cut prices (and hence earn lower margins) or write down its inventory. A build-up in work-in-progress inventory tends to be good news on average, probably signaling that managers expect an increase in sales. If the build-up is in raw materials, it could suggest manufacturing or procurement inefficiencies, leading to an increase in cost of goods sold (and hence lower margins).[16]
- *An increasing gap between a firm's reported income and its cash flow from operating activities.* While it is legitimate for accrual accounting numbers to differ from cash flows, there is usually a steady relationship between the two if the company's accounting policies remain the same. Therefore, any *change* in the relationship between reported profits and operating cash flows might indicate subtle changes in the firm's accrual estimates. For example, a firm undertaking large construction contracts might use the percentage-of-completion method to record revenues. While earnings and operating cash flows are likely to differ for such a firm, they should bear a steady relationship to each other. Now suppose the firm increases revenues in a period through an aggressive application of the percentage-of-comple-

tion method. Then its earnings will go up, but its cash flow remains unaffected. This change in the firm's accounting quality will be manifested by a *change* in the relationship between the firm's earnings and cash flows.

- *An increasing gap between a firm's reported income and its tax income.* Once again, it is quite legitimate for a firm to follow different accounting policies for financial reporting and tax accounting, as long as the tax law allows it.[17] However, the relationship between a firm's book and tax accounting is likely to remain constant over time, unless there are significant changes in tax rules or accounting standards. Thus, an *increasing* gap between a firm's reported income and its tax income may indicate that the firm's financial reporting to shareholders has become more aggressive. As an example, consider that warranty expenses are estimated on an accrual basis for financial reporting, but are recorded on a cash basis for tax reporting. Unless there is a big change in the firm's product quality, these two numbers bear a consistent relationship to each other. Therefore, a change in this relationship can be an indication either that the product quality is changing significantly or that financial reporting estimates are changing.

- *A tendency to use financing mechanisms like research and development partnerships and the sale of receivables with recourse.* While these arrangements may have a sound business logic, they can also provide management with an opportunity to understate the firm's liabilities and/or overstate its assets.[18]

- *Unexpected large asset write-offs.* This may suggest that management is slow to incorporate changing business circumstances into its accounting estimates. Asset write-offs may also be a result of unexpected changes in business circumstances.[19]

- *Large fourth-quarter adjustments.* A firm's annual reports are audited by the external auditors, but its interim financial statements are usually only reviewed. If a firm's management is reluctant to make appropriate accounting estimates (such as provisions for uncollectable receivables) in its interim statements, it could be forced to make adjustments at the end of the year as a result of pressure from its external auditors. A consistent pattern of fourth-quarter adjustments, therefore, may indicate an aggressive management orientation towards interim reporting.[20]

- *Qualified audit opinions or changes in independent auditors that are not well justified.* These may indicate a firm's aggressive attitude or a tendency to "opinion shop."

- *Related-party transactions or transactions between related entities.* These transactions may lack the objectivity of the marketplace, and managers' accounting estimates related to these transactions are likely to be more subjective and potentially self-serving.

While the preceding list provides a number of red flags for potentially poor accounting quality, it is important to do further analysis before reaching final conclusions. Each of the red flags has multiple interpretations; some interpretations are based on sound business reasons, and others indicate questionable accounting. It is, therefore, best to use the red flag analysis as a starting point for further probing, not as an end point in itself.[21]

Step 6: Undo Accounting Distortions

If the accounting analysis suggests that the firm's reported numbers are misleading, analysts should attempt to restate the reported numbers to reduce the distortion to the extent possible. It is, of course, virtually impossible to undo all the distortion using outside information alone. However, some progress can be made in this direction by using the cash flow statement and the financial statement footnotes.

A firm's cash flow statement provides a reconciliation of its performance based on accrual accounting and cash accounting. If the analyst is unsure of the quality of the firm's accrual accounting, the cash flow statement provides an alternative benchmark of its performance. The cash flow statement also provides information on how individual line items in the income statement diverge from the underlying cash flows. For example, if an analyst is concerned that the firm is aggressively capitalizing certain costs that should be expensed, the information in the cash flow statement provides a basis to make the necessary adjustment.

Financial statement footnotes also provide a lot of information that is potentially useful in restating reported accounting numbers. For example, when a firm changes its accounting policies, it provides a footnote indicating the effect of that change if it is material. Similarly, some firms provide information on the details of accrual estimates such as the allowance for bad debts. The tax footnote usually provides information on the differences between a firm's accounting policies for shareholder reporting and tax reporting. Since tax reporting is often more conservative than shareholder reporting, the information in the tax footnote can be used to estimate what the earnings reported to shareholders would be under more conservative policies.

ACCOUNTING ANALYSIS PITFALLS

There are several potential pitfalls in accounting analysis that an analyst should avoid. First, it is important to remember that from an analyst's perspective, conservative accounting is not the same as "good" accounting. Financial analysts are interested in evaluating how well a firm's accounting captures business reality in an unbiased manner, and conservative accounting can be as misleading as aggressive accounting in this respect. Further, conservative accounting often provides managers with opportunities for "income smoothing." Income smoothing may prevent analysts from recognizing poor performance in a timely fashion.

A second potential mistake is to confuse unusual accounting with questionable accounting. While unusual accounting choices might make a firm's performance difficult to compare with other firms' performance, such an accounting choice might be justified if the company's business is unusual. For example, firms that follow differentiated strategies, or firms that structure their business in an innovative manner to take advantage of particular market situations may make unusual accounting choices to properly reflect their business. Therefore, it is important to evaluate a company's accounting choices in the context of its business strategy.

Another potential pitfall in accounting analysis arises when an analyst attributes all changes in a firm's accounting policies and accruals to earnings management motives.[22] Accounting changes might be merely reflecting changed business circumstances. For example, as already discussed, a firm that shows unusual increases in its inventory might be preparing for a new product introduction. Similarly, unusual increases in receivables might merely be due to changes in a firm's sales strategy. Unusual decreases in the allowance for uncollectable receivables might be reflecting a firm's changed customer focus. It is therefore important for an analyst to consider all possible explanations for accounting changes and investigate them using the qualitative information available in a firm's financial statements.

APPLICATION OF ACCOUNTING ANALYSIS CONCEPTS TO COMPAQ COMPUTER CORPORATION

As discussed in the prior chapter on Business Strategy Analysis, Compaq's strategy in the personal computer industry in 1992 was to compete as a low-cost producer with a high quality and service image. Compaq sold its computers through large computer retailers. The key success factors for Compaq, therefore, were: (1) keeping manufacturing costs and administrative overhead low, (2) investing in product quality and service, and (3) keeping good relations with its retailers. In this section, we will analyze Compaq's accounting quality in its 1992 financial statements as a way to apply the concepts discussed above.[23]

Since Compaq's business was essentially assembling components into a personal computer and marketing it, its operating cycle (the time from purchasing materials to collecting cash from its customers) was relatively short. As a result, the firm faced few complex choices in its accrual accounting. Some of Compaq's key accounting policies and estimates were:

- *Accounting for inventory.* Compaq used FIFO accounting, which is normally a less conservative policy than LIFO. However, since prices of inputs and outputs in the personal computer industry have been decreasing, FIFO is a more conservative accounting choice for Compaq.
- *Revenue recognition.* Compaq sold computers to retailers, and recognized revenue upon shipping the computers. While this is standard practice, Compaq faced some risks with this policy. First, Compaq allowed for returns of computers sold, and it had to estimate them properly. In the personal computer industry, where technology changes rapidly, there was a risk of inventory obsolescence being borne by Compaq. Second, Compaq guaranteed financing of the inventory by some of its distributors. (See the footnote on Commitments and Contingencies in Compaq's annual report.) As a result, the company was essentially financing its distributors and hence was bearing the risk of customer defaults to an extent greater than indicated by its accounts receivable on the balance sheet.

- *Outlays on new product development, quality, and customer service.* While these are some of the critical success factors for Compaq, accounting rules provided little flexibility to Compaq's management in dealing with these outlays, so Compaq expensed all such outlays when incurred. As a result, an analyst has to rely on information outside the financial statements in assessing how effective these activities were.
- *Warranty expenses.* The company had a policy of producing high quality products. To assure customers of its confidence in its product quality, Compaq offered warranties on its products. The warranty liability associated with current period sales, therefore, was an important accounting estimate for Compaq. The warranty reserve, as indicated in the Note 7, Other Current Liabilities, increased by 87 percent from $39 million in 1991 to $73 million in 1992, even though sales increased by only 25 percent. Some of the increase in warranty reserve in 1992 was attributable to a new three-year warranty Compaq began offering that year. It is also possible that the reserve in 1991 was unusually low. It would be useful to probe this issue further to fully understand the nature of this estimate.
- *Allowance for doubtful accounts.* As mentioned earlier, since the company recognized revenues when it shipped products to computer retailers, there was some default risk associated with its receivables. The allowance for doubtful accounts was 2.9 percent of the receivables in 1991, but it dropped to 2.5 percent in 1992. What was the reason for this change? Did the company take steps to improve its credit screening, or was the company not providing for adequate reserves? Or, was the company merely responding to the improved credit situation of its customers because of the overall improvement in the economy?

In addition to the above items, the following red flags could be investigated further:

- Compaq's accounts receivable to sales ratio increased from 19 percent in 1991 to 24 percent in 1992. Similarly, the inventory to sales ratio increased from 13 to 20 percent in 1992. While both these increases may be attributable to the many new products that Compaq introduced in 1992, it would be useful to probe this issue further.
- Compaq sold its equity interest in Connor Peripherals in 1992, recording a gain of about $85.7 million dollars. This gain accounts for a large part of the $141 million increase in Compaq's pre-tax income between 1991 and 1992. The company did not provide a sound explanation for the timing of this asset sale.
- The company's tax footnote shows that the difference between warranty expense recognized for financial reporting and tax reporting changed dramatically between 1990, 1991, and 1992. Deferred taxes arising out of this item were negative $2.95 million in 1990, $.098 million in 1991, and negative $6.68 million in 1992, consistent with our prior analysis that the provision in financial reports was unusually low in 1991. Once again, this issue needs to be investigated further.

Compaq's disclosure was generally adequate, but not excellent. The company provided a good description of its strategy, why its gross margins declined in 1992, how it managed its operating expenses during that year, and the factors that were likely to influence the company's future performance. However, Compaq did not provide a good explanation for a number of issues raised above. For example, why did Compaq's accounts receivable and inventory increase significantly in 1992? Why did it reduce its allowance for doubtful accounts as a proportion of accounts receivable? Why did it sell its stake in Connor Peripherals in 1992? Also, the company provided neither an adequate discussion of the potential threats to the sustainability of its competitive advantage in its industry, nor the steps the company was taking to protect its position.

In reaching a final conclusion on Compaq's accounting quality, it is important to assess management's motivations in 1992. The company reported a dramatic drop in earnings in 1991, and a new management team was subsequently put in place. The new management was implementing a turnaround strategy during 1992. It is likely that Compaq's managers were keen on showing that their restructuring strategy was paying off so that they could rally the company's suppliers, customers, employees, and investors behind the new management team. Compaq's top managers were also compensated based on the company's accounting profits. All these factors could have motivated Compaq's managers to use their accounting discretion to increase reported income in 1992. Therefore, while there may have been a real improvement in the company's fundamentals, reported results in 1992 may have also been helped by its accounting.

SUMMARY AND CONCLUSIONS

In summary, accounting analysis is an important step in the process of analyzing corporate financial reports. The purpose of accounting analysis is to evaluate the degree to which a firm's accounting captures the underlying business reality. Sound accounting analysis improves the reliability of conclusions from financial analysis, the next step in financial statement analysis.

There are six key steps in accounting analysis. The analyst begins by identifying the key accounting policies and estimates, given the firm's industry and its business strategy. The second step is to evaluate the degree of flexibility available to managers, given the accounting rules and conventions. Next, the analyst has to evaluate how managers exercise their accounting flexibility and the likely motivations behind managers' accounting strategy. The fourth step involves assessing the depth and quality of a firm's disclosures. The analyst should next identify any red flags needing further investigation. The final accounting analysis step is to restate accounting numbers to remove any noise and bias introduced by the accounting rules and management decisions.

NOTES

1. Accounting analysis is sometimes also called quality of earnings analysis. We prefer to use the term accounting analysis, since we are discussing a broader concept than merely a firm's earnings quality.

2. These definitions paraphrase the definitions by the Financial Accounting Standards Board, Statement of Financial Accounting Concepts No. 6, "Elements of Financial Statements" (1985). Our intent is to present the definitions at a conceptual, not technical, level. For more complete discussion of these and related concepts, see the FASB's *Statements of Financial Accounting Concepts*.

3. Strictly speaking, the comprehensive net income of a firm also includes gains and losses from increases and decreases in equity from non-operating activities or extraordinary items.

4.. Thus, although accrual accounting is theoretically superior to cash accounting in measuring a firm's periodic performance, the distortions it introduces can make accounting data less valuable to users. If these distortions are large enough, current cash flows may measure a firm's periodic performance better than accounting profits. The relative usefulness of cash flows and accounting profits in measuring performance, therefore, varies from firm to firm. For empirical evidence on this issue, see "Accounting earnings and cash flows as measures of firm performance: The role of accounting accruals" by Patricia M. Dechow, *Journal of Accounting and Economics* 18, 1994.

5. For example, Abraham Brilloff published a series of accounting analyses of public companies in *Barron's* magazine over several years. On average, the stock prices of the analyzed companies changed by about 8 percent on the day these articles were published, indicating the potential value of performing such analysis. For a more complete discussion of this evidence, see "Brilloff and the Capital Market: Further Evidence" by George Foster, Stanford University working paper, 1985.

6. For a complete discussion of these motivations, see *Positive Accounting Theory* by Ross L. Watts and Jerold L. Zimmerman (Englewood Cliffs, NJ: Prentice-Hall, 1986).

7. The most convincing evidence supporting the covenant hypothesis is reported in a study of the accounting decisions by firms in financial distress: "Debt-covenenat violations and managers' accounting responses," Amy Patricia Sweeney, *Journal of Accounting and Economics* 17, 1994.

8. A number of studies examine the bonus hypothesis and report evidence consistent with the view that managers' accounting decisions are influenced by compensation considerations. See, for example, "The effect of bonus schemes on accounting decisions," Paul M. Healy, *Journal of Accounting and Economics* 12, 1985.

9. "Managerial competition, information costs, and corporate governance: The use of accounting performance measures in proxy contests," Linda DeAngelo, *Journal of Accounting and Economics* 10, 1988.

10. The trade-off between taxes and financial reporting in the context of managers' accounting decisions is discussed in detail in *Taxes and Business Strategy* by Myron Scholes and Mark Wolfson (Englewood Cliffs, NJ: Prentice-Hall, 1992). Many empirical studies have examined firms' LIFO/FIFO choice.

11. Several researchers have documented that firms affected by such situations have a motivation to influence regulators' perceptions through their accounting decisions. For example, Jones documents that firms seeking import protections make income-decreasing accounting decisions in "Earnings management during import relief investigations," J. Jones, *Journal of Accounting Research* 29, 1991.

12. "The effect of firms' financial disclosure strategies on stock prices," Paul Healy and Krishna Palepu, *Accounting Horizons* 7, 1993. See also "Causes and consequences of aggressive financial reporting," P. Dechow, R. Sloan, and A. Sweeney, *Contemporary Accounting Research,* forthcoming.

13. Financial analysts pay considerable attention to managers' disclosure strategies; the Financial Analysts' Federation publishes annually a report evaluating U.S. firms' disclosure strategies.

For a discussion of these ratings, see "Cross-sectional Determinants of Analysts' Ratings of Corporate Disclosures" by Mark Lang and Russ Lundholm, *Journal of Accounting Research* 31, Autumn 1993: 246–271.

14. For a detailed analysis of a company that made such changes, see "Anatomy of an Accounting Change" by Krishna Palepu in *Accounting & Management: Field Study Perspectives,* edited by William J. Bruns, Jr., and Robert S. Kaplan (Boston: Harvard Business School Press, 1987).

15. An example of this type of behavior is documented by John Hand in his study, "Did Firms Undertake Debt-Equity Swaps for an Accounting Paper Profit or True Financial Gain?," *The Accounting Review* 64, October 1989.

16. For an empirical analysis of inventory build-ups, see "Do Inventory Disclosures Predict Sales and Earnings?" by Victor Bernard and James Noel, *Journal of Accounting, Auditing, and Finance,* Fall 1991.

17. This is true by and large in the United States and in several other countries. However, in some countries, such as Germany and Japan, tax accounting and financial reporting are closely tied together, and this particular red flag is not very meaningful.

18. For research on accounting and economic incentives motivating the formation of R&D partnerships, see "Motives for Forming Research and Development Financing Organizations," by Anne Beatty, Philip G. Berger, and Joseph Magliolo, *Journal of Accounting & Economics* 19, 1995.

19. For an empirical examination of asset-write-offs, see "Write-offs as Accounting Procedures to Manage Perceptions" by John A. Elliott and Wayne H. Shaw, *Journal of Accounting Research,* Supplement, 1988.

20. Richard R. Mendenhall and William D. Nichols report evidence consistent with the hypothesis that managers take advantage of their discretion to postpone reporting bad news until the fourth quarter. See "Bad News and Differential Market Reactions to Announcements of Earlier-Quarter versus Fourth-Quarter Earnings," *Journal of Accounting Research,* Supplement, 1988.

21. This type of analysis is presented in the context of provisions for bad debts by Maureen McNichols and G. Peter Wilson in their study, "Evidence of Earnings Management from the Provisions for Bad Debts," *Journal of Accounting Research,* Supplement, 1988.

22. This point has been made by several accounting researchers. For a summary of research on earnings management, see "Earnings Management" by Katherine Schipper, *Accounting Horizons,* December 1989: 91–102.

23. Most of the 1992 Annual Report for Compaq Computer Corporation is given in Part 5 at the end of the text.

CASES

Anacomp, Inc.

Comdisco, Inc. (A)

Comdisco, Inc. (B)

CUC International, Inc.

Harnischfeger Corporation

Hawkeye Bancorporation

IBM and Fujitsu

Kansas City Zephryrs Baseball Club, Inc.

Morlan International, Inc.

Oracle Systems Corporation

Patten Corporation

Siemens

Southwestern Fuel Systems, Inc.

Thousand Trails, Inc.

E. Wedel, S.A.

chapter 4

Financial Analysis

The goal of financial analysis is to assess the performance of a firm in the context of its stated goals and strategy. There are two principal tools of financial analysis: ratio analysis and cash flow analysis. Ratio analysis involves assessing how various line items in a firm's financial statements relate to one another. Cash flow analysis allows the analyst to examine the firm's liquidity and how the firm is managing its operating, investing, and financing cash flows.

Financial analysis is used in a variety of contexts. As we will discuss in later chapters, financial analysis is useful in credit evaluation, financial distress prediction, security analysis, mergers and acquisitions analysis, and corporate financial policy analysis. In all these contexts, financial analysis is a key input for making sound predictions about a company's future prospects.

RATIO ANALYSIS

The value of a firm is determined by its profitability and growth. As Figure 4-1 shows, a firm's profitability and growth are influenced by its product market and financial market strategies. The product market strategy is implemented through the firm's operating policies and investment strategies. Financial market strategies are implemented through financing and dividend policies.

The four levers managers can use to achieve their growth and profit targets are (1) operating management, (2) investment management, (3) financing strategy, and (4) dividend policies. The objective of ratio analysis is to evaluate the effectiveness of the firm's policies in each of these areas. Effective ratio analysis involves relating the financial numbers to the underlying business factors in as much detail as possible. While ratio analysis may not give an analyst all the answers regarding a firm's performance, it will help the analyst frame questions for further probing.

Figure 4-1 Drivers of a Firm's Profitability and Growth

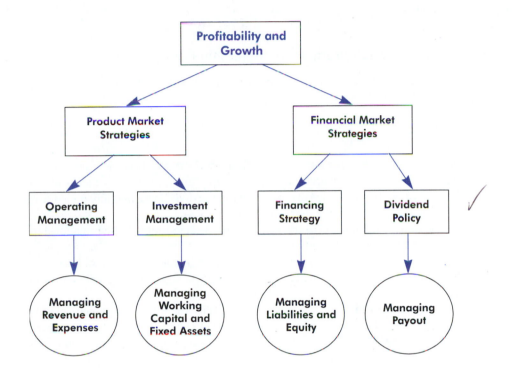

In ratio analysis, the analyst can (1) compare ratios for a firm over several years (a time-series comparison), (2) compare ratios for the firm and other firms in the industry (cross-sectional comparison), and/or (3) compare ratios to some absolute benchmark. In a time-series comparison, the analyst can hold firm-specific factors constant and examine the effectiveness of a firm's strategy over time. Cross-sectional comparison facilitates examining the relative performance of a firm within its industry, holding industry-level factors constant. For most ratios, there are no absolute benchmarks. The exceptions are measures of rates of return, which can be compared to the cost of the capital associated with the investment. For example, subject to distortions caused by accounting, the rate of return on equity (ROE) can be compared to the cost of equity capital.

In our discussion below, we will use Compaq Computer Corporation to illustrate these approaches. We will compare Compaq's ratios in 1992 with its own ratios in 1991 and with the 1992 ratios for Apple and Dell, two other prominent personal computer companies.[1] Recall from Chapter 2 that Compaq was the leading seller of IBM-compatible personal computers, and followed a volume-driven low-cost strategy. Compaq tried to differentiate itself from other personal computer makers through quality, innovation, and service. Dell was the second largest producer of IBM clones. Unlike Compaq, Dell competed purely on a cost basis. Apple, in contrast, competed on the basis of differentiation. Apple's computers were not IBM compatible, and they used a distinct microprocessor and software.

Measuring Overall Profitability: Return on Equity

The starting point for a systematic analysis of a firm's performance is its return on equity (ROE), defined as:

$$ROE = \frac{\text{Net income}}{\text{Shareholders equity}}$$

ROE is a comprehensive indicator of a firm's performance because it provides an indication of how well managers are employing the funds invested by the firm's shareholders to generate returns. On average over long periods, large publicly traded firms in the U.S. generate ROEs in the range of 11 to 13 percent.

In the long run, the value of the firm's equity is determined by the relationship between its ROE and its cost of equity capital.[2] That is, those firms that are expected over the long run to generate ROEs in excess of the cost of equity capital should have market values in excess of book value, and vice versa. (We will return to this point in more detail in Chapter 6.)

A comparison of ROE with the cost of capital is useful not only for contemplating the value of the firm, but also in considering the path of future profitability. The generation of consistent supernormal profitability will, absent significant barriers to entry, attract competition. For that reason, ROEs tend over time to be driven by competitive forces toward a "normal" level—the cost of equity capital. Thus, one can think of the cost of equity capital as establishing a benchmark for the ROE that would be observed in a long-run competitive equilibrium. Deviations from this level arise for two general reasons. One is the industry conditions and competitive strategy that cause a firm to generate supernormal (or subnormal) economic profits, at least over the short run. The second is distortions due to accounting.

Table 4-1 shows the ROE for Compaq, Apple Computer, and Dell. The first row in the table displays ROE based on reported earnings. In the second row, we recalculate ROE, excluding some gains and losses that are unlikely to reoccur and that do not reflect the product of ongoing operations. For Compaq, we exclude its gain on the sale of Conner Peripherals, Inc. in 1992, and its restructuring charges in 1991 and 1992.[3] These adjustments are only intended to be illustrative, and are not the only ones an analyst might make. The approach presented in Chapter 3 raises several issues that, depending on investigation, might cause an analyst to make further adjustments. There are no adjustments for Apple or Dell, because they disclosed no unusual, nonoperating gains or losses for 1992.

Regardless of whether we look at adjusted or unadjusted amounts in either 1991 or 1992, Compaq's ROE was lower than reasonable estimates of the cost of equity capital

Table 4-1 Return on Equity for Compaq and Selected Competitors

Ratio	Compaq 1991	Compaq 1992	Apple 1992	Dell 1992
Return on equity	6.8%	10.6%	24.2%	27.5%
Return on equity, adjusted for unusual gains/losses	11.0%	10.2%	24.2%	27.5%

for a firm in an industry as risky as the PC industry. (In Chapter 6, we will estimate that Compaq's cost of equity capital lies in the range of 12 to 15 percent.) Moreover, even though the *reported* earnings suggest a major improvement at Compaq, there is none evident in the adjusted amounts. The reason is that the reported improvement was largely due to a reduction in restructuring charges and a gain on the sale of Conner, as opposed to an improvement in operations.

Understanding Profit Drivers: Decomposing ROE

Compaq's ROE in 1992 was not only less than the cost of capital, it was also less than that of Apple (24.2%) and Dell (27.5%). In the following paragraphs we will attempt to gain a deeper understanding of why Compaq's ROE in 1992 differs from its own ROE in 1991, and from the ROEs of Apple and Dell.

A company's ROE is affected by two factors: how profitably it employs its assets and how big the firm's asset base is relative to shareholders' investment. To understand the effect of these two factors, ROE can be decomposed into return on assets (ROA) and a measure of financial leverage, as follows:

$$
\begin{aligned}
\text{ROE} &= \text{ROA} \times \text{Financial leverage} \\
&= \frac{\text{Net income}}{\text{Assets}} \times \frac{\text{Assets}}{\text{Shareholders' equity}}
\end{aligned}
$$

ROA tells us how much profit a company is able to generate for each dollar of assets invested. Financial leverage indicates how many dollars of assets the firm is able to deploy for each dollar invested by its shareholders.

The measure of ROA shown above is commonly used, but it involves an internal inconsistency. Specifically, the denominator includes the assets claimed by all providers of capital to the firm, but the numerator includes only the earnings available to equity holders. An alternative measure of ROA begins to deal with this problem by expressing profits on a pre-interest basis. The numerator then can be labeled EBILAT, or earnings before interest, less adjusted taxes. The term "adjusted taxes" reflects the fact that we add back to net income the tax benefit of the interest expense deduction[4]:

$$\text{Pre-interest ROA} \quad = \quad \frac{\text{EBILAT}}{\text{Assets}} \quad = \quad \frac{\text{Net income} + \text{Interest expense} \times (1 - \text{tax rate})}{\text{Assets}}$$

Even the pre-interest ROA suffers from a shortcoming, in that the numerator reflects the returns available only to equity holders and holders of interest-bearing debt, and yet the denominator includes *all* assets—even those financed with non-interest-bearing debt. Another alternative measure is return on net assets (RONA), or return on capital (ROC), which uses EBILAT in the numerator and places equity and interesting-bearing debt in the denominator[5]:

$$\text{RONA (or ROC)} \quad = \quad \frac{\text{Net income} + \text{Interest expense} \times (1 - \text{Tax rate})}{\text{Equity} + \text{Debt}}$$

The appropriate benchmark for evaluating RONA (or ROC) is the weighted average cost of debt and equity capital, or WACC. In the long run, the value of the firm is determined by where RONA (or ROC) stands relative to this norm. Moreover, over the long run, and absent some barrier to competitive forces, RONA will tend to be pushed towards the weighted average cost of capital. Since the WACC is lower than the cost of equity capital, RONA (or ROC) tends to be pushed to a level lower than that to which ROE tends. The average RONA (or ROC) for large firms in the U.S., over long periods of time, is in the range of 9 to 11 percent.

A fourth measure of asset returns, called operating ROA, focuses on operating returns only and excludes any income earned by the firm from its cash and short-term investments. The appropriate denominator for this return is debt plus equity minus cash and short-term investments.[6]

Operating ROA   =

$$\frac{\text{Net income} + (\text{Interest expense} - \text{Interest income}) \times (1 - \text{Tax rate})}{\text{Equity} + \text{Debt} - \text{Cash and short-term investments}}$$

The four alternative return on asset measures are presented in Table 4-2 for Compaq, Apple, and Dell. The pre-interest ROA does not differ significantly from the ROA because none of the firms have much interest-bearing debt. However, RONA and Operating ROA differ significantly from ROA for all the firms.

We can see that Compaq's RONA and its operating ROA were less than any reasonable estimate of its weighted average cost of capital in 1991.[7] While there was an increase in this ratio between 1991 and 1992, this increase was attributable to unusual and non-operating items. When these items are excluded, Compaq showed little improvement in any return on asset measure in Table 4-2. Moreover, all the return on asset measures were significantly lower than those for Apple and Dell. For Apple and Dell, there was a large difference between ROA (or pre-interest ROA) and RONA (or operating ROA) because both these firms had large cash and short-term investments. This shows that, at least for some firms, it is important to make adjustments to the simple ROA measure to take into account the interest expense, interest income, and financial assets.

Table 4-2 Return on Assets for Compaq, Apple, and Dell

Ratio	Compaq 1991	Compaq 1992	Apple 1992	Dell 1992
Return on assets (ROA)	4.6%	6.8%	12.6%	11.0%
Pre-interest ROA	5.4	7.6	12.0	11.5
RONA or ROC	7.6	11.9	22.6	25.5
Operating ROA	8.6	13.3	54.0	30.6
Amounts adjusted for unusual, non-operating gains:				
Return on assets (ROA)	7.5%	6.5%	12.6%	11.0%
Pre-interest ROA	8.3	7.3	12.7	11.5
RONA or ROC	11.7	11.5	22.6	25.5
Operating ROA	10.7	10.5	54.0	30.6

To begin our investigation of *why* the return on assets was so low for Compaq, we decompose ROA, showing it as a product of two factors:

$$\text{ROA} = \frac{\text{Net income}}{\text{Sales}} \times \frac{\text{Sales}}{\text{Assets}}$$

The ratio of net income to sales is called net profit margin or return on sales (ROS). The ratio of sales to assets is known as asset turnover. The profit margin ratio indicates how much the company is able to keep as profits for each dollar of sales it makes. Asset turnover indicates how many sales dollars the firm is able to generate for each dollar of its assets. In the above decomposition, we use the traditional measure of ROA, but analogous decompositions are possible for pre-interest ROA, RONA, and operating ROA.

Table 4-3 displays the three drivers of ROE for our computer firms: profit margin, asset turnover, and financial leverage. Compaq's ROE increased between 1991 and 1992 in part because its net profit margin increased from 4 percent to 5.2 percent. However, this increase in ROS based on *reported* earnings was entirely due to unusual gains and losses. The profit margin excluding the effects of unusual gains and losses actually eroded in 1992, from 6.5 to 5.3 percent. Compaq's ROE improved in 1992 also because its asset turnover and financial leverage increased marginally. However, as discussed below, relative to Apple and Dell, Compaq's asset turnover was not impressive; nor did it take advantage of as much leverage.

Both Apple and Dell had an ROA that was almost twice as large as Compaq's ROA, though for different reasons. Apple's ROA was larger than Compaq's primarily because of its higher net profit margins. In contrast, Dell's superior ROA was entirely due to its larger asset turnover. Apple's higher net profit margins were a result of its successful differentiation strategy, and Dell's higher asset turnover suggests that its low-cost strategy was working well.

Table 4-3 Key Drivers of Return on Equity

Ratio	Compaq 1991	Compaq 1992	Apple 1992	Dell 1992
Net profit margin (or ROS)	4.0%	5.2%	7.48%	5.05%
× Asset turnover	1.16	1.30	1.68	2.17
= Return on assets	4 .64%	6.76%	12.57%	10.96%
× Financial leverage	1.46	1.57	1.93	2.51
= Return on equity	6.8%	10.6%	24.2%	27.5%

In addition, both Apple and Dell had higher financial leverage relative to Compaq. Thus, Dell had a higher ROE than Compaq because it used its assets more productively and relied less on equity financing. Apple had a higher ROE than Compaq because its sales were more profitable, and it also leveraged its shareholders' investment more effectively. Below, we explore further the factors that are behind the ratios in Table 4-3.

Assessing Operating Management: Decomposing Net Profit Margins

A firm's net profit margin or return on sales (ROS) shows the profitability of the company's operating activities. Further decomposition of a firm's ROS allows an analyst to assess the efficiency of the firm's operating management. A popular tool used in this analysis is the common-sized income statement in which all the line items are expressed as a ratio of sales revenues.

Common-sized income statements make it possible to compare trends in income statement relationships over time for a firm, and trends across different firms in an industry. Income statement analysis allows the analyst to ask the following types of questions: (1) Are the company's margins consistent with its stated competitive strategy? (For example, a differentiation strategy should usually lead to higher gross profit margins than a low-cost strategy.) (2) Are the company's margins changing? Why? What are the underlying business causes—changes in competition, changes in input costs, or poor overhead cost management? (3) Is the company managing its overhead and administrative costs well? What are the business activities driving these costs? Are these activities necessary?

To illustrate how the income statement analysis can be used, we show common-sized income statements for Compaq, Apple, and Dell in Table 4-4.

GROSS PROFIT MARGINS.   The difference between a firm's sales and cost of sales is gross profit. Gross profit margin indicates the extent to which revenues exceed direct costs associated with sales. It is computed as:

$$\text{Gross profit margin} \quad = \quad \frac{\text{Sales} - \text{Cost of sales}}{\text{Sales}}$$

Gross profit margin is influenced by two factors: (1) the price premium that a firm's products or services command in the marketplace and (2) the efficiency of the firm's procurement and production process. The price premium a firm's products or services can command is influenced by the degree of competition and the extent to which its products are unique. A firm's cost of sales can be low when it can purchase its inputs at a lower cost than competitors and/or run its production processes efficiently. This is generally the case when a firm has a low-cost strategy.

Table 4-4 indicates that Compaq's gross profit margins in 1992 decreased to 29.1 percent from 37.2 percent in 1991. The company explained in its annual report that this decline was prompted by price competition in the PC industry. Dell's gross profit margins in 1992 were even lower at 22.3 percent. This suggests that Compaq was able to either charge a premium relative to Dell's prices, or to reduce its input and manufacturing costs. Both are consistent with Compaq's stated strategy of volume-driven cost leadership and premium pricing based on differentiation on service and quality.

Table 4-4 Common-Sized Income Statements

Line Item	Compaq 1991	Compaq 1992	Apple 1992	Dell 1992
Sales revenue	100.0%	100.0%	100.0%	100.0%
Cost of goods sold	62.8	70.9	56.3	77.7
Gross profit	**37.2**	**29.1**	**43.7**	**22.3**
Research and development	6.0	4.2	8.5	2.1
Selling, general, and administrative costs	22.1	17.0	23.8	13.3
Earnings before other income and expense	**9.1**	**7.9**	**12.8**	**7.3**
Other expense (income)	4.4	0.7	0.7	(0.2)
Earnings before taxes	**4.7**	**7.2**	**12.1**	**7.1**
Provision for taxes	1.3	2.4	4.6	2.1
Earnings from consolidated companies	3.4	4.8	7.5	5.0
Equity in net income of affiliated companies and other items	0.6	0.4	–	–
Net income	**4.0**	**5.2**	**7.5**	**5.0**
Net income excluding restructuring costs and gain on sale of investments	**6.5**	**5.0**	**7.5**	**5.0**

In contrast to Dell, Apple had a significantly larger gross profit margin than Compaq's. This is probably attributable to the fact that Apple followed a differentiation strategy in the PC industry. Its computers used software and hardware that was distinctly different from the IBM and compatible computers; they competed on the basis of ease in using and networking capabilities. Apple's differentiation strategy apparently allowed it to earn superior gross profit margins relative to both Compaq and Dell, primarily because of the price premium Apple's products commanded in the marketplace.

OPERATING EXPENSES.   A company's operating expenses are influenced by the activities it needs to undertake to implement its competitive strategy. As discussed in Chapter 2, firms with differentiation strategies have to undertake specific activities to achieve differentiation. A company competing on the basis of quality and rapid introduction of new products is likely to have higher research and development (R&D) costs relative to a company competing purely on a cost basis. Similarly, a company that attempts to build a brand image, distributes its products through full-service retailers, and provides after-sales service is likely to have higher selling and administrative costs than a company that sells through warehouse retailers or direct mail and does not provide much customer support.

A company's operating expenses are also influenced by the way it manages its overhead activities. The efficiency with which operating expenses are controlled is likely to be especially important for firms competing on the basis of low cost. However, even for differentiators, it is important to assess whether the cost of differentiation is commensurate with the price premium earned in the marketplace.

Focusing once again on Table 4-4, one can see that Compaq's operating expenses, including R&D and selling, general, and administrative (SG&A) costs, decreased significantly between 1991 and 1992. In its annual report, Compaq's management attributed this decline to the success of its new cost control efforts. Compaq also had significantly higher "other expenses" in 1991, primarily because of a large restructuring charge. While Compaq also had a restructuring charge in 1992, this charge was offset by a gain from the sale of its stock in Connor Peripherals, as discussed in Chapter 3. Thus, even though Compaq achieved significant cost reductions in R&D, and SG&A, its profits before other income and expenses went down from 9.1 percent to 7.9 percent of sales. This suggests that Compaq's operating cost reduction efforts in 1992 were not adequate to cover the decline in the company's gross profit margin. Only because Compaq had a one-time gain from the sale of its stake in Connor, the company's profit before taxes as a percent of sales went up from 4.7 percent to 7.2 percent.

Relative to Compaq, Dell had significantly lower operating expenses as a percent of sales, because Dell invested less both in R&D and in selling expenses. This is consistent with Dell's strategy of competing purely on a cost basis and selling its computers through direct mail. In fact, Compaq's higher operating expenses appear to fully offset the higher gross profit margin it was able to earn by emphasizing quality and service. As a result, earnings before taxes as a percent of sales for Dell and Compaq were similar, even though they achieved this through different business strategies.

Apple's operating expenses were significantly higher than Compaq's. Once again, this is consistent with Apple's differentiation strategy, which required additional expenses for R&D and marketing. Even with these additional expenses, Apple was able to achieve higher pre-tax earnings because its price premium more than offset its cost of differentiation.

TAX EXPENSE.   Taxes are an important element of a firm's total expenses. A wide variety of tax planning techniques allows a firm to attempt to reduce its tax expenses. There are two measures one can use to evaluate a firm's tax expense. One is the ratio of tax expense to sales. The second measure is the ratio of tax expense to earnings before taxes (also known as the average tax rate). The firm's tax footnote provides a detailed account of why its average tax rate differs from the statutory tax rate.

When evaluating a firm's tax planning, the analyst should ask two questions: (1) Are the company's tax policies sustainable? Or is the current tax rate influenced by one-time tax credits? (2) Do the firm's tax planning strategies lead to other business costs? For example, if the operations are located in tax havens, how does this affect the company's profit margins and asset utilization? Are the benefits of tax planning strategies (reduced taxes) greater than the increased business costs, such as lower labor productivity and higher transportation costs?

Table 4-4 shows that Compaq's tax rate did not change significantly between 1991 and 1992. Compaq's taxes as a percent of sales was also comparable to Dell's ratio. Apple's tax expense as a percent of sales was significantly higher than for Compaq, but it was because Apple's pre-tax earnings were also higher. The average tax rate for Compaq (33%) and Apple (29%) were indeed comparable.

Evaluating Investment Management: Decomposing Asset Turnover

Asset turnover is the second driver of a company's return on equity. Since firms invest considerable resources in their assets, using them productively is critical to a firm's overall profitability. A detailed analysis of asset turnover allows the analyst to evaluate the effectiveness of a firm's investment management.

There are two primary areas of asset management: (1) working capital management and (2) management of long-term assets. Working capital is the difference between a firm's current assets and current liabilities. The components of working capital that analysts focus on primarily are accounts receivable, inventory, and accounts payable. A certain amount of investment in working capital is necessary for a firm to run its normal operations. For example, a firm's credit policies and distribution policies determine its optimal level of accounts receivable. The nature of the production process and the need for buffer stocks determine the optimal level of inventory. Finally, accounts payable is a routine source of financing for a firm's working capital, and payment practices in an industry determine the normal level of accounts payable.

The following ratios are useful in analyzing a firm's working capital management:

$$\text{Current asset turnover} \quad = \quad \frac{\text{Sales}}{\text{Current assets}}$$

$$\text{Working capital turnover} \quad = \quad \frac{\text{Sales}}{\text{Current assets} \, - \, \text{Current liabilities}}$$

$$\text{Accounts receivable turnover} \quad = \quad \frac{\text{Sales}}{\text{Accounts receivable}}$$

$$\text{Inventory turnover} \quad = \quad \frac{\text{Cost of goods sold}}{\text{Inventory}}$$

$$\text{Accounts payable turnover} \quad = \quad \frac{\text{Purchases}}{\text{Accounts payable}} \quad or \quad \frac{\text{Cost of goods sold}}{\text{Accounts payable}}$$

$$\text{Days' receivables} \quad = \quad \frac{\text{Accounts receivable}}{\text{Average sales per day}}$$

$$\text{Days' inventory} \quad = \quad \frac{\text{Inventory}}{\text{Average cost of goods sold per day}}$$

$$\text{Days' payables} \quad = \quad \frac{\text{Accounts payable}}{\text{Average purchases (or cost of goods sold) per day}}$$

Current asset turnover and working capital turnover indicate how many dollars of sales a firm is able to generate for each dollar invested in current assets or working capital. Accounts receivable turnover, inventory turnover, and accounts payable turnover allow the analyst to examine how productively the three principal components of working capital are being used. Days' receivables, days' inventory, and days' payables are another way to evaluate the efficiency of a firm's working capital management. These reflect the number of days of operating activity (sales, production, and purchases, respectively) that are supported by the level of investment in the firm's receivables, inventory, and payables.[8]

Property, plant, and equipment (PP&E) is the most important long-term asset in a firm's balance sheet. The amount of sales generated by a dollar invested in PP&E is measured by the ratio:

$$\text{PP\&E turnover} \quad = \quad \frac{\text{Sales}}{\text{Property, plant, and equipment}}$$

The ratios listed above allow the analyst to explore a number of business questions: (1) How well does the company manage its inventory? Does the company use modern manufacturing techniques? Does it have good vendor and logistics management systems? If inventory ratios are changing, what is the underlying business reason? Are new products being planned? Is there a mismatch between demand forecasts and actual sales? (2) How well does the company manage its credit policies? Are these policies consistent with its marketing strategy? Is the company artificially increasing sales by loading distribution channels? (3) Is the company taking advantage of trade credit? Is it relying too much on trade credit? If so, what are the implicit costs? (4) Is the company's investment in plant and equipment consistent with its competitive strategy? Does the company have a sound policy of acquisitions and divestitures?

We present in Table 4-5 the asset turnover ratios for Compaq, Apple, and Dell. Recall that Compaq's asset turnover remained relatively stagnant between 1991 and 1992. Table 4-5 shows that Compaq's current asset turnover worsened in 1992 relative to 1991. The principal reason is that the company's receivables and inventory turned more slowly in 1992. Days' receivables increased from 70 to 88, and days' inventory increased from 78 to 105. The slow turnover of receivables and inventory are important to Compaq's overall asset productivity because these two items accounted for 79 percent of the company's current assets and 58 percent of its total assets in 1992.

Despite the worsening of current asset turnover, Compaq's working capital turnover improved marginally in 1992 because of an increase in days' payables from 35 to 65. Thus, while Compaq increased its investments in receivables and inventory significantly in 1992, its net investment in working capital did not increase correspondingly because the company also stretched its payables. These patterns in the company's working capital ratios were not well explained in the company's 1992 annual report, making it difficult for an outside analyst to understand the business reasons behind them without further probing.

Compaq's 1992 asset turnover ratios were also significantly different from Apple's and Dell's ratios, principally because both Dell and Apple had significantly higher turnovers of current assets and working capital. Apple turned its inventories and receivables faster and paid its suppliers sooner than did Compaq. Dell also had better receivables and inventory turnovers, though its payables turnover was comparable to Compaq's.

Table 4-5 Asset Management Ratios

Ratio	Compaq 1991	Compaq 1992	Apple 1992	Dell 1992
Current asset turnover	1.84	1.77	1.99	2.36
Working capital turnover	2.85	3.02	3.32	5.61
Accounts receivable turnover	5.24	4.15	6.52	5.38
Inventory turnover	4.70	3.48	6.88	5.16
Accounts payable turnover	10.50	5.63	9.35	5.30
Days' receivables	70	88	56	68
Days' inventory	78	105	53	71
Days' payables	35	65	39	69
PP&E turnover	3.71	5.08	15.33	28.6

In terms of PP&E utilization, Compaq showed a significant improvement between 1991 and 1992. However, relative to Apple and Dell, Compaq's PP&E productivity was significantly lower. In 1992, while Compaq realized five dollars in sales for each dollar invested in PP&E, Apple realized fifteen dollars and Dell realized more than twenty-eight dollars. The impact of these differences on the overall profitability of the three companies, however, was not very large because PP&E represented only a small fraction of the total assets for all three companies.

Evaluating Financial Management: Examining Financial Leverage

Financial leverage enables a firm to have an asset base larger than its equity. The firm can augment its equity through borrowing and the creation of other liabilities, such as accounts payable, accrued liabilities, and deferred taxes. Financial leverage increases a firm's ROE as long as the cost of the liabilities is less than the return from investing these funds. Financial leverage, however, also increases the firm's risk. Unlike equity, liabilities have predefined payment terms, and the firm faces risk of financial distress if it fails to meet these commitments.

There are a number of ratios to evaluate the degree of risk arising from a firm's financial leverage. These ratios are described in the following sections.

CURRENT LIABILITIES AND SHORT-TERM LIQUIDITY.   The following ratios are useful in evaluating the risk related to a firm's current liabilities:

$$\text{Current ratio} \; = \; \frac{\text{Current assets}}{\text{Current liabilities}}$$

$$\text{Quick ratio} \; = \; \frac{\text{Cash} \; + \; \text{Short-term investments} \; + \; \text{Accounts receivable}}{\text{Current liabilities}}$$

$$\text{Cash ratio} \; = \; \frac{\text{Cash} \; + \; \text{Short-term investments}}{\text{Current liabilities}}$$

$$\text{Operating cash flow ratio} \; = \; \frac{\text{Cash flow from operations}}{\text{Current liabilities}}$$

All the above ratios attempt to measure the firm's ability to repay its current liabilities. The first three compare a firm's current liabilities with its short-term assets, which can be used to repay the current liabilities. The fourth ratio focuses on the ability of the firm's operations to generate the resources needed to repay its current liabilities.

Since both current assets and current liabilities have comparable duration, the current ratio is a key index of a firm's short-term liquidity. Analysts view a current ratio of more than 1 to be an indication that the firm can cover its current liabilities with the cash realized from its current assets. However, the firm can face a short-term liquidity problem even with a current ratio exceeding 1 when some of its current assets are not easy to liquidate. The quick ratio and the cash ratio capture the firm's ability to cover its current liabilities from liquid assets. The quick ratio assumes that the firm's accounts receivable are liquid. This is true in industries where the credit-worthiness of the customers is beyond dispute, or when receivables are collected in a very short period. However, when these conditions do not prevail, the cash ratio, which considers only cash and marketable securities, is a better indication of a firm's ability to cover its current liabilities in an emergency. Operating cash flow is another measure of the firm's ability to cover its current liabilities with cash generated from operations of the firm.

We report the liquidity ratios for Compaq, Apple, and Dell in Table 4-6. Compaq's liquidity situation in 1992 was very comfortable, as indicated by a current ratio of 2.4 and a quick ratio of 1.40. However, both these ratios and the cash ratio deteriorated in 1992 relative to 1991. Further, because Compaq had a negative cash flow from operations in 1992, its operating cash flow ratio worsened significantly. Apple's liquidity in 1992 was certainly stronger than Compaq's. Apple had a cash ratio of 1, suggesting that it could meet all its current liabilities by merely liquidating its cash and marketable securities. Dell was in the weakest liquidity position among the three computer makers, in part due to the company's attempt to minimize its investment in working capital as part of its low-cost strategy.

DEBT AND LONG-TERM SOLVENCY.   A company's financial leverage is also influenced by its debt financing policy. There are several potential benefits from debt financing. First, debt is typically cheaper than equity because the firm promises predefined payment terms to debt holders. Second, in most countries, interest on debt financing is tax deductible, whereas dividends to shareholders are not tax deductible. Third, debt financing can impose discipline on the firm's management and motivate it to reduce wasteful expenditures. Fourth, it is often easier for management to communicate its proprietary information on the firm's strategies and prospects to private lenders than to public capital markets. Such communication can potentially reduce a firm's cost of capital.

Table 4-6 Liquidity Ratios

Ratio	Compaq		Apple	Dell
	1991	1992	1992	1992
Current ratio	2.79	2.41	2.50	1.72
Quick ratio	1.68	1.40	1.77	0.95
Cash ratio	0.71	0.37	1.00	0.19
Operating cash flow ratio	0.62	*	0.62	*

* Not meaningful because cash flow from operations was negative.

For all these reasons, it is optimal for firms to use at least some debt in their capital structure.

Too much reliance on debt financing is, however, potentially costly to the firm's shareholders. The firm will face financial distress if it defaults on the interest and principal payments. Debt holders also impose covenants on the firm, restricting the firm's operating, investing, and financing decisions.

The optimal capital structure for a firm is determined primarily by its business risk. A firm's cash flows are easier to predict when there is little competition or little threat of technological changes. Such firms have low business risk, and hence they can rely heavily on debt financing. In contrast, if a firm's operating cash flows are highly volatile and its capital expenditure needs are unpredictable, it may have to rely primarily on equity financing. Managers' attitudes toward risk and financial flexibility also often determine a firm's debt policies.

There are a number of ratios which help the analyst in this area. To evaluate the mix of debt and equity in a firm's capital structure, the following ratios are useful:

$$\text{Liabilities-to-equity ratio} = \frac{\text{Total liabilities}}{\text{Shareholders' equity}}$$

$$\text{Debt-to-equity ratio} = \frac{\text{Short-term debt} + \text{Long-term debt}}{\text{Shareholders' equity}}$$

$$\text{Debt-to-capital ratio} = \frac{\text{Short-term debt} + \text{Long-term debt}}{\text{Short-term debt} + \text{Long-term debt} + \text{Shareholders' equity}}$$

The first ratio restates the assets-to-equity ratio (one of the three primary ratios underlying ROE) by subtracting 1 from it. The second ratio provides an indication of how many dollars of debt financing the firm is using for each dollar invested by its shareholders. The third ratio gives the proportion of debt in the total capital of the firm.

The ease with which a firm can meet its interest payments is an indication of the degree of risk associated with its debt policy. The interest coverage ratio provides a measure of this construct:

$$\text{Interest coverage (earnings basis)} = \frac{\text{Net income} + \text{Interest expense} + \text{Tax expense}}{\text{Interest expense}}$$

$$\text{Interest coverage (cash basis)} = \frac{\text{Cash flow from operations} + \text{Interest paid} + \text{Taxes paid}}{\text{Interest paid}}$$

The earnings-based coverage ratio indicates the dollars of earnings available for each dollar of required interest payment. The cash flow-based coverage ratio indicates the dollars of cash generated by operations for each dollar of required interest payment. In both these ratios, the denominator is the interest expense. In the numerator, we add taxes back because taxes are computed only after interest expense is deducted. A coverage ratio of 1 implies that the firm is barely covering its interest expense through its operating activities, which is a very risky situation. The larger the coverage ratio, the greater the cushion the firm has to meets its interest obligations.[9]

Some of the business questions to ask when the analyst is examining a firm's debt policies are: (1) Does the company have enough debt? Is it exploiting the potential benefits of debt—interest tax shields, management discipline, easier communication? (2) Given its business risk, does the company have too much debt? What type of debt covenant restrictions does the firm face? Is it bearing the costs of too much debt and risking potential financial distress and reduced business flexibility? (3) What is the company doing with the borrowed funds? Investing in working capital? Investing in fixed assets? Are these investments profitable? (4) Is the company borrowing money to pay dividends? If so, what is the justification?

We report the debt and coverage ratios for Compaq, Apple, and Dell in Table 4-7. The financial leverage for all three companies primarily comes from current liabilities. For example, in 1992, while Compaq had 57 cents in liabilities for each dollar of equity, it had no interest-bearing debt.[10] In fact, while Compaq increased its reliance on non-interest-bearing liabilities in 1992, the company paid off all its interest-bearing debt. Relative to Compaq, Apple and Dell had higher liabilities as a proportion of their equity. However, once again, most of these liabilities were non-interest-bearing. Both the firms had only a modest amount of interest-bearing debt. The low debt ratios for all three companies are a result of the high business risk associated with the PC industry.

Compaq had a comfortable interest coverage ratio in 1991, and it improved further in 1992 if one takes into account earnings-based coverage. However, if reported earnings are adjusted for unusual items, Compaq's coverage remained flat at approximately 8 in both 1991 and 1992. Further, the company's cash flow-based coverage deteriorated dramatically in 1992. Apple and Dell had a significantly better interest coverage position relative to Compaq.

Table 4-7 Debt and Interest Coverage Ratios

Ratio	Compaq 1991	Compaq 1992	Apple 1992	Dell 1992
Liabilities-to-equity	0.46	0.57	0.93	1.51
Debt-to-equity	0.04	0	0.08	0.13
Debt-to-capital	0.04	0	0.08	0.12
Interest coverage (earnings based)	5.7	8.4	98.1	19.1
Interest coverage (cash flow based)	14.5	−0.34	112.9	−7.8

Dupont

Putting It All Together: Assessing Sustainable Growth Rate

Analysts often use the concept of sustainable growth as a way to evaluate a firm's ratios in a comprehensive manner. A firm's sustainable growth rate is defined as:

Sustainable growth rate   =   ROE × (1 − Dividend payout ratio)

We discussed the analysis of ROE in the previous four sections. The dividend payout ratio is defined as:

$$\text{Dividend payout ratio} \quad = \quad \frac{\text{Cash dividends paid}}{\text{Net income}}$$

A firm's dividend payout ratio is a measure of its dividend policy. As we will discuss in detail in a later chapter, firms pay dividends for several reasons. Dividends are a way for the firm to return to its shareholders any cash generated in excess of its operating and investment needs. When there are information asymmetries between a firm's managers and its shareholders, dividend payments can serve as a signal to shareholders about managers' expectations of the firm's future prospects. Firms may also pay dividends to attract a certain type of shareholder base.

The sustainable growth rate is the rate at which a firm can grow, keeping its profitability and financial policies unchanged. A firm's return on equity and its dividend payout policy determine the pool of funds available for growth. Of course, the firm can grow at a rate different from its sustainable growth rate if either its profitability, or payout policy, or financial leverage changes. Therefore, the sustainable growth rate is a benchmark against which a firm's growth plans can be evaluated. Figure 4-2 shows how a firm's sustainable growth rate can be linked to all the ratios discussed in this chapter. These linkages allow an analyst to examine the drivers of a firm's current sustainable growth rate. If the firm intends to grow at a rate higher than its sustainable growth rate, one could assess which of the ratios are likely to change in the process. Such an analysis can lead to asking these kinds of business questions: Where is the change going to take place? Is management expecting profitability to increase? Or is it expecting asset productivity to improve? Are these expectations realistic? Is management planning adequately for these changes? If the profitability is not likely to go up, will the firm increase its financial leverage or cut dividends? What is the likely impact of these financial policy changes?

Table 4-8 shows the sustainable growth rate and its components for Compaq, Apple, and Dell. Compaq's sustainable growth rate was equal to its return on equity because the firm did not pay cash dividends in either 1991 or in 1992. The sustainable growth rate for Compaq went up in 1992 relative to 1991 because its ROE increased. The analysis presented in the previous sections shows how Compaq has been able improve its ROE. For example, an important reason for the ROE increase was the difference in unusual gains and losses Compaq reported in the two years. If these gains and losses were excluded, Compaq's sustainable growth rate declined from 11 percent to 10.2 percent.

Figure 4-2 Sustainable Growth Rate Framework for Financial Ratio *Dupont*
Analysis

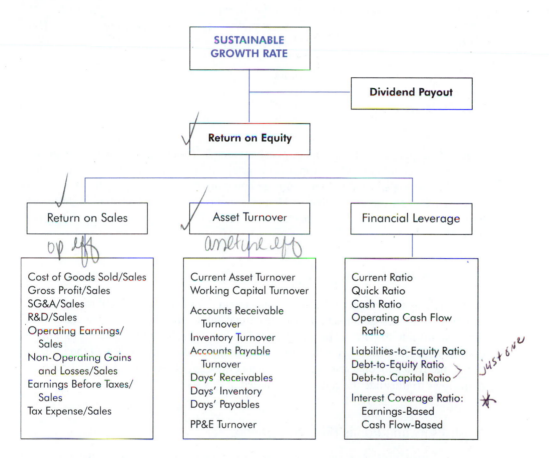

The analysis also shows that Compaq's sustainable growth rate in 1992 was positively influenced by its cost cutting and its increase in accounts payable. It was adversely influenced by the decrease in gross profit margins and the increase in receivables and inventory. Thus, if Compaq was to grow faster in 1993 than its 1992 sustainable growth rate, it had to improve its gross profit margins or reduce its inventory and receivables or further reduce its operating costs. Compaq could also grow by further increasing its days' payables, but this could strain the company's relations with its suppliers. The final option for Compaq to grow faster than its sustainable growth rate was to increase its debt. Since Compaq had no debt in 1992, this was feasible. However, Compaq's cash flow coverage of its interest in 1992 was only 1. A significant improvement in operating cash flow would have been needed to service the additional borrowing.

Table 4-8 Sustainable Growth Rate

Ratio	Compaq 1991	Compaq 1992	Apple 1992	Dell 1992
ROE	6.8%	10.6%	24.2%	27.5%
Dividend payout ratio	0	0	0.11	0
Sustainable growth rate	6.8%	10.6%	21.5%	27.5%

Like Compaq, Dell also did not pay cash dividends. Hence, Dell's sustainable growth rate was also equal to its ROE. Apple, however, paid modest dividends, equal to 11 percent of its earnings in 1992. As a result, the company's sustainable growth rate was less than its ROE. However, relative to Compaq, both Apple and Dell had significantly higher room for growth without having to alter any of their financial and operating policies.

CASH FLOW ANALYSIS

Ratio analysis focuses on analyzing a firm's income statement (net profit margin analysis) or its balance sheet (asset turnover and financial leverage). The analyst can get further insights into the firm's operating, investing, and financing policies by examining its cash flows. Cash flow analysis also provides an indication of the quality of the information in the firm's income statement and balance sheet. As before, we will use Compaq's cash flows to illustrate the concepts discussed in this section.

Cash Flow and Funds Flow Statements

All U.S. companies are required to include a statement of cash flows in their financial statements under Statement of Financial Accounting Standard No. 95 (SFAS 95). In the reported cash flow statement, firms classify their cash flows into three categories: cash flow from operations, cash flow related to investments, and cash flow related to financing activities. Cash flow from operations is the cash generated by the firm from the sale of goods and services after paying for the cost of inputs and operations. Cash flow related to investment activities shows the cash paid for capital expenditures, intercorporate investments and acquisitions, and cash received from the sales of long-term assets. Cash flow related to financing activities shows the cash raised from (or paid to) the firm's stockholders and debt holders.

Firms use two cash flow statement formats: the direct format and the indirect format. The key difference between the two formats is the way they report cash flow from operating activities. In the direct cash flow format, which is used by only a small number of firms in practice, operating cash receipts and disbursements are reported directly. In the indirect format, firms derive their operating cash flows by making adjustments to net income. Because the indirect format links the cash flow statement with the firm's income statement and balance sheet, many analysts and managers find this format more useful. As a result, current U.S. accounting rules require firms using the direct format to report operating cash flows in the indirect format as well.

Recall from Chapter 3 that net income differs from operating cash flows because revenues and expenses are measured on an accrual basis. There are two types of accruals embedded in net income. First, there are current accruals, such as credit sales and unpaid expenses. Current accruals result in changes in a firm's current assets (such as accounts receivable, inventory, and prepaid expenses), and current liabilities (such as accounts payable and accrued liabilities). The second type of accruals included in the income statement is non-current accruals, such as depreciation, deferred taxes, and equity income from unconsolidated subsidiaries. To derive cash flow from operations from net income, adjustments have to be made for both these types of accruals. In addition, adjustments have to be made for non-operating gains and losses included in net income, such as profits from asset sales.

Most firms outside the U.S. report a funds flow statement rather than a cash flow statement. Prior to SFAS No. 95, U.S. firms also reported a similar statement. It is useful for analysts to know how to convert a funds flow statement into a cash flow statement.

Funds flow statements typically provide information on a firm's working capital from operations, defined as net income adjusted for non-current accruals and gains from the sale of long-term assets. As discussed above, cash flow from operations essentially involves a third adjustment, the adjustment for current accruals. Thus, it is relatively straightforward to convert working capital from operations to cash flow from operations by making the relevant adjustments for current accruals related to operations.

Information on current accruals can be obtained by examining changes in the firm's current assets and current liabilities Typically, operating accruals represent changes in all the current asset accounts other than cash and cash equivalents, and changes in all the current liabilities other than notes payable and the current portion of long-term debt.[11] Cash from operations can be calculated as:

Working capital from operations
- − Increase (or + decrease) in accounts receivable
- − Increase (or + decrease) in inventory
- − Increase (or + decrease) in other current assets, excluding cash and cash equivalents
- + Increase (or − decrease) in accounts payable
- + Increase (or − decrease) in other current liabilities excluding notes payable and debt

Funds flow statements also often do not classify investing and financing flows. In this case, the analyst has to classify the line items in the funds flow statement into these two categories by evaluating the nature of the business transactions that give rise to the flow represented by the line items.

Analyzing Cash Flow Information

Cash flow analysis can be used to address a variety of questions regarding the firm's cash flow dynamics:

- How strong is the firm's internal cash flow generation? Is the cash flow from operations positive or negative? If it is negative, why? Is it because the company is growing? Is it because its operations are unprofitable? Or is it having difficulty managing its working capital properly?
- Does the company have the ability to meet its short-term financial obligations, such as interest payments, from its operating cash flow? Can it continue to meet these obligations without reducing its operating flexibility?
- How much cash did the company invest in growth? Are these investments consistent with its business strategy? Did the company use internal cash flow to finance growth, or did it rely on external financing?
- Does the company have excess cash flow after investing in capital investments? Is it a long-term trend? What plans does management have to deploy the free cash flow?
- Did the company pay dividends from internal free cash flow, or did it have to rely on external financing? If the company had to fund its dividends from external sources, is the company's dividend policy sustainable?
- What type of external financing does the company rely on—equity, short-term debt, or long-term debt? Is the financing consistent with the company's overall business risk?

While the information in reported cash flow statements can be used to answer these questions directly for some firms, it may not always be easy to do so for several reasons. First, even though SFAS No. 95 provides broad guidelines on the format of a cash flow statement, there is still significant variation across firms in how cash flow data are disclosed. Therefore, to facilitate a systematic analysis and comparison across firms, analysts often recast the information in the cash flow statement, using their own cash flow model. Second, firms include interest expense and interest income in computing their cash flow from operating activities. However, these two items are not strictly related to a firm's operations. Interest expense is a function of financial leverage, and interest income is derived from financial assets rather than operating assets. Therefore, it is useful to restate the cash flow statement to take this into account.

Analysts use a number of different approaches to restate the cash flow data. One popular model, called the Total Cash Flow Analysis, is given in Table 4-9. This model shows clearly what one would expect from a firm that is healthy and has a sound financial management.

Table 4-9 Total Cash Flow Analysis of Compaq Computer Corporation

Cash Flow Effects of Various Activities	1991	1992
Net income	**130.9**	**213.2**
Adjustments for non-current operating accruals and non-operating items:		
Depreciation	165.8	159.5
Deferred taxes	(9.6)	34.1
Equity (income)/loss in affiliated companies	(19.8)	(15.2)
(Gain)/Loss on sale of assets and investments	4.2	(71.3)
Interest expense less interest and dividend income (net of related taxes)	2.7	5.9
Other*	204.8	(69.8)
Total	**348.1**	**43.2**
Cash flow from operations before working capital investments and interest payments	**479.0**	**256.4**
Cash flow effects of investment in working capital:		
(Increase)/Decrease in accounts receivable	2.2	(362.3)
(Increase)/Decrease in inventories	106.8	(397.6)
Increase/(Decrease) in accounts payable	(96.8)	320.7
(Increase)/Decrease in other current assets, excluding cash and cash equivalents	(186.1)	128.1
Increase/(Decrease) in other current liabilities, excluding debt	91.8	1.2
Total	**(82.1)**	**(309.9)**
Cash flow from operations after investment in working capital, before interest payments	**396.9**	**(53.5)**
Interest expense (net of taxes)	(22.1)	(25.3)
Interest income (net of taxes)	19.4	19.4
Cash flow from operations after investment in working capital and interest payments	**394.2**	**(59.4)**
Cash flow effects of investment in long-term assets:		
(Purchase)/Sale of property, plant, and equipment	(188.8)	(159.2)
(Purchase)/Sale of investments	(135.0)	376.4
Other	(16.6)	13.0
Total	**(340.4)**	**230.2**
Free cash flow before dividend payments and external financing activities	**53.8**	**170.8**
Dividend payments	0	0
Free cash flow after dividend payments	**53.8**	**170.8**
Cash flow effects of external financing activities:		
Stock repurchase	(82.2)	(215.5)
Sale of equity	22.6	56.8
Repayment of debt	(0.5)	(73.5)
Exchange rate gains (losses) on cash and cash equivalents	23.8	(34.1)
Total	**(36.3)**	**(266.3)**
Net cash flow after external financing	**17.5**	**(95.5)**

*Derived as a plug number because Compaq's cash flow statement does not disclose all details necessary to calculate this figure. It includes provision for restructuring costs.

The Total Cash Flow Analysis presents cash flow from operations in two stages. The first step computes cash flow from operations before working capital investments. In computing this cash flow, the model excludes interest expense and interest income. A firm should generate a positive cash flow from operations in steady state, provided it collects more cash from its customers than it spends on its operating expenses. Most firms, however, use some of this cash flow for working capital items, such as accounts receivable, inventories, and accounts payable. A firm's net investment in working capital is a function of its credit policies (accounts receivable), payment policies (payables, prepaid expenses, and accrued liabilities), and expected growth in sales (inventories). Thus, in interpreting a firm's cash flow from operations after working capital, it is important to keep in mind the firm's growth strategy, its industry characteristics, and its credit policies.

The next step in the Total Cash Flow Analysis is to compare the cash flow from operations after working capital investments with the firm's interest payments. If cash flow from operations is less than a firm's interest payments, it has to liquidate its assets or raise external capital to meet its interest obligations. Clearly, such a situation is unhealthy from a financial management perspective.

The Total Cash Flow Analysis focuses next on cash flows related to long-term investments. These investments take the form of capital expenditures, intercorporate investments, and mergers and acquisitions. Any positive operating cash flow after making interest payments allows the firm to pursue long-term growth opportunities. If the firm's operating cash flows after interest are not sufficient to finance its long-term investments, it has to rely on external financing to fund its growth. Such firms have less flexibility to pursue long-term investments than firms that can fund their growth internally. There are both costs and benefits from being able to fund growth internally. The cost is that managers can use the internally generated free cash flow to fund unprofitable investments. Such wasteful capital expenditures are less likely if managers are forced to rely on external capital suppliers. However, reliance on external capital markets may make it difficult for managers to undertake long-term risky investments if it is not easy to communicate to the capital markets the benefits from such investments.

Any excess cash flow after these long-term investments is free cash flow available for dividend payments. It is not prudent for a firm to pay dividends unless it has a positive free cash flow on a sustained basis. Thus, the Total Cash Flow Analysis compares cash flow after long-term investments with the firm's dividend payments. A negative cash flow after dividend payments is a signal that the firm's dividend policy may be subject to change. If the firm has a positive free cash flow after dividend payments, it can be used for repayment of debt or for repurchase of shares.

The Total Cash Flow Analysis suggests that the analyst should focus on a number of cash flow measures: (1) cash flow from operations before investment in working capital and interest payments, to examine whether or not the firm is able to generate a cash surplus from its operations; (2) cash flow from operations after investment in working capital to assess how the firm's working capital is being managed; (3) cash flow from operations after interest payments to assess the firm's ability to meet its interest obligations; (4) free cash flow before dividend payments to assess the firm's financial flexibility to finance long-term investments internally; (5) free cash flow after dividend payments to examine whether or not the firm's dividend policy is sustainable; and (6) net cash flow after external financing to examine the firm's financing policies. These measures have to be evaluated in the context of the company's business, its growth strategy, and its financial policies. Further, changes in these measures from year to year provide valuable information on the stability of the cash flow dynamics of the firm.

The Total Cash Flow Analysis can also be used to assess a firm's earnings quality, as discussed in Chapter 3. The reconciliation of a firm's net income with its cash flow from operations facilitates this exercise. Some of the questions an analyst can probe in this respect are:

- Are there significant differences between a firm's net income and its operating cash flow? Is it possible to clearly identify the sources of this difference? Which accounting policies contribute to it? Are there any one-time events contributing to the difference?
- Is the relationship between cash flow and net income changing over time? Why? Is it because of changes in business conditions or because of changes in the firm's accounting policies and estimates?
- What is the time lag between the recognition of revenues and expenses and the receipt and disbursement of cash flows? What type of uncertainties need to be resolved in between?
- Are the changes in receivables, inventories, and payables normal? If not, is there adequate explanation for the changes?

Analyzing Compaq's Cash Flow

In its 1992 annual report, Compaq used the direct format to report its cash flows. This statement shows that Compaq's 1992 operations led to a cash deficit of $59.4 million. At the bottom of the statement, the firm showed why there was a negative cash flow from operations, even though the firm reported a net income of over $213 million during 1992. Compaq's cash flow statement shows that the difference in its operating cash flow and net income arose from the three types of adjustments discussed above. For example, the company adjusted the net income for depreciation expense, deferred taxes, and equity in income of an affiliated company, all non-current accruals. It also adjusted for changes in a number of current assets and current liabilities. Finally, the company adjusted for non-operating gains from the sale of an investment in an affiliated company and losses on disposal of assets.

Compaq also reported that its investment activities resulted in a positive cash flow of $230 million in 1992. While the company invested $159.2 million in new plant and equipment, it was able to offset this investment with cash flows realized from the sale of stock in Connor Peripherals, Inc. and in Silicon Graphics, Inc. Compaq's financing activities in 1992 consumed $232.1 million, primarily as a result of stock repurchases and debt repayments.

Compaq's reported cash flow statement does not provide adequate information to address the types of questions raised at the beginning of the previous section. For example, Compaq reported that its cash flow from operations was negative, largely because of a $456 million increase in its net current assets. However, it provided few details on the nature of these increases. To facilitate further analysis, we show in Table 4-9 the cash flow data for Compaq in 1991 and 1992, using the Total Cash Flow Analysis model.

Compaq generated $256.4 million in cash from operations in 1992 before its investments in working capital and the net interest payments are considered. However, because of significant investments in accounts receivable and inventories, Compaq's cash flow from operations after working capital investments became negative, even after a very large increase in its accounts payable. As a result, Compaq had a negative cash flow from operations before its interest payments. The firm paid its interest payments in part out of its interest income, and in part by drawing down its cash balance.

Compaq's cash flow pattern in 1992 differed significantly from the pattern in 1991. In that year, the firm generated a positive cash flow from operations, even after considering its investments in working capital and interest payments. This suggests that something changed in the firm's cash flow dynamics. Did the firm lose control of its inventory and receivables? Or were these increases merely a result of a surge in the firm's production and sales activities in the fourth quarter of 1992? Unfortunately, the firm provided few explanations. While it is not uncommon for growth firms like Compaq to have a negative cash flow from operations, the difference between 1991 and 1992 suggests that further investigation is warranted.

Another interesting aspect of Compaq's operating cash flow in 1992 was the large gap between its cash flow and net income. This gap was caused to some extent by one-time events, such as the gain on the sale of investments. It was also caused by a significant increase in accounts receivable. As discussed in Chapter 3, both these aspects, which were not present in 1991, raise questions about the sustainability of Compaq's 1992 earnings.

The negative cash flow from operations was not a major concern for Compaq's liquidity in 1992 because Compaq generated $376.4 million in cash by shrinking its long-term investments in affiliated companies. Thus, even after spending $159.2 million on plant and equipment, the firm had a positive cash flow from investment activities. It is unlikely, however, that Compaq could repeat this performance in subsequent years, since it did not have other investments it could liquidate, and its growth plans called for additional investments in plant and equipment.

As a result of its investment sales in 1992, Compaq had a free cash flow of $170.8 million before dividend payments and external financing activities. Compaq was not paying a regular cash dividend. However, the firm used its free cash flow to pay down its debt and repurchase its stock.

Overall, Compaq's liquidity was strong, and given the firm's low financial leverage, there was little cause for concern regarding the firm's financial risk. The one area that merits further analysis is the firm's working capital management. This conclusion is consistent with the ratio analysis of Compaq presented earlier.

SUMMARY AND CONCLUSIONS

There are two key tools of financial analysis: ratio analysis and cash flow analysis. Both these tools allow the analyst to examine the firm's performance and its financial condition, given its strategy and goals. Ratio analysis involves assessing the firm's income statement and balance sheet data. Cash flow analysis relies on the firm's cash flow statement.

The starting point for ratio analysis is the company's ROE. The next step is to evaluate the three drivers of ROE—net profit margin, asset turnover, and financial leverage. Net profit margin reflects a firm's operating management, asset turnover reflects its investment management, and financial leverage reflects its liability management. Each of these areas can be further probed by examining a number of ratios. For example, common-sized income statement analysis allows a detailed examination of a firm's net margins. Similarly, turnover of key working capital accounts, such as accounts receivable, inventory, and accounts payable, and turnover of the firm's fixed assets allows further examination of a firm's asset turnover. Finally, short-term liquidity ratios, debt policy ratios, and coverage ratios provide a means of examining a firm's financial leverage.

A firm's sustainable growth rate, the rate at which it can grow without altering its operating, investing, and financing policies, is determined by its ROE and its dividend policy. Therefore, the concept of sustainable growth provides a way to integrate the ratio analysis and to evaluate whether or not a firm's growth strategy is sustainable. If a firm's plans call for growing at a rate above its current sustainable rate, then the analyst can examine which of the firm's ratios is likely to change in the future.

Cash flow analysis supplements ratio analysis in examining a firm's operating activities, investment management, and financial risks. Firms in the U.S. are currently required to report a cash flow statement summarizing their operating, investing, and financing cash flows. Firms in other countries typically report working capital flows, but it is possible to use this information to create a cash flow statement.

Since there are wide variations across firms in the way cash flow data are reported, analysts often use a standard format to recast cash flow data. We discussed in this chapter a popularly used cash flow model called the Total Cash Flow Analysis. This model allows the analyst to assess whether a firm's operations generate cash flow before investments in working capital, and how much cash is being invested in the firm's working capital. It also enables the analyst to calculate the firm's free cash flow after investments in long-term investments, an indication of the firm's ability to sustain its dividend payments. Finally, the Total Cash Flow Analysis shows how the firm is financing itself and whether or not its financing patterns are too risky.

The insights gained from analyzing a firm's financial ratios and its cash flows are valuable in making forecasts about a firm's future prospects. We turn to this topic in the next three chapters.

NOTES

1. We use the financial statements for the years ending December 31, 1991 and 1992 for Compaq, the year ending September 25, 1992 for Apple, and the year ending January 31, 1993 for Dell. The differences in the fiscal years for the three companies introduce some noise in the comparison of their ratios.

2. In computing ROE, one can either use the beginning equity, ending equity, or an average of the two. Conceptually, the average equity is appropriate, particularly for rapidly growing companies. However, for most companies, this computational choice makes little difference as long as the analyst is consistent. Therefore, analysts most often use ending balances for simplicity. This comment applies to all ratios discussed in this chapter, where one of the items in the ratio is a flow variable (items in the income statement or cash flow statement) and the other item is a stock variable (items in the balance sheet). Throughout this chapter, we use the ending balances of the stock variables for computational simplicity.

3. These adjustments to earnings are made assuming a 40 percent tax effect. Throughout this chapter we use a 40 percent tax rate based on a 34 percent federal tax rate for corporations and a 6 percent state and local tax rate.

4. When ROA is defined in this way, it can be reconciled with ROE as follows:

$$\text{ROE} \; = \; \text{Pre-interest ROA} \; \times \; \frac{\text{Earnings}}{\text{EBILAT}} \; \times \; \text{Financial leverage}$$

5. ROE can be expressed as a function of RONA, as follows:

$$\text{ROE} \; = \; \text{RONA} \; \times \; \frac{\text{Earnings}}{\text{EBILAT}} \; \times \; \frac{\text{Equity} \, + \, \text{Debt}}{\text{Assets}} \; \times \; \text{Financial leverage}$$

6. Strictly speaking, part of a cash balance is needed to run the firm's operations, so only the excess cash balance should be subtracted in the denominator of this ratio. However, firms do not provide this information, so we subtract all cash balances in our definition and computations. An alternative possibility is to subtract only short-term investments and ignore the cash balance completely.

7. Compaq has no debt, so its WACC is equal to its cost of equity capital. Thus, it is estimated to be in the range of 12 to 15 percent. See Chapter 6 for further discussion.

8. There are a number of practical issues related to the calculation of the above ratios. First, in calculating all the turnover ratios, the assets used in the calculations can be either year-end values or an average of the beginning and ending balances in a year. We use the year-end values here for simplicity. Second, strictly speaking, one should use credit sales to calculate accounts receivable turnover and days' receivables. However, since it is usually difficult to obtain data on credit sales, total sales are used instead. Similarly, in calculating accounts payable turnover or days' payables, cost of goods sold is substituted for purchases because of data availability.

9. One could also construct coverage ratios to take into account not only interest expense but also other fixed charges, such as lease payment obligations and required debt repayments.

10. As mentioned in Chapter 3, Compaq had some off-balance-sheet liabilities that are not included in the calculation of these debt ratios. In fact, some of Compaq's interest expense was related to these off-balance-sheet liabilities, including dealer-financing arrangements.

11. Changes in cash and marketable securities are excluded because this is the amount being explained by the cash flow statement. Changes in short-term debt and the current portion of long-term debt are excluded because these accounts represent financing flows, not operating flows.

CASES

Anacomp, Inc.
Comdisco, Inc. (A)
Eastman Kodak Company and Fuji Photo Film Company, Ltd.
The Gap, Inc.
The Home Depot, Inc.

chapter 5

Prospective Analysis: Forecasting

Most financial statement analysis tasks are undertaken with a forward-looking decision in mind. And much of the time, it is useful to summarize the view developed in the analysis with an explicit forecast. Managers need forecasts for planning and to provide performance targets. Analysts need forecasts to help communicate their view of the firm's prospects to investors. Bankers and debt market participants need forecasts to assess the likelihood of loan repayment. Moreover, there are a variety of contexts (including but not limited to security analysis) where the forecast is usefully summarized in the form of an estimate of the firm's value—an estimate that can be viewed as the best attempt to reflect in a single summary statistic the manager's or analyst's view of the firm's prospects.

Prospective analysis includes two tasks—forecasting and valuation—that together represent approaches to explicitly summarizing the analyst's forward-looking views. In this chapter, we focus on forecasting. Valuation is the topic of the following two chapters.

RELATION OF FORECASTING TO OTHER ANALYSES

Forecasting is not so much a separate analysis as it is a way of summarizing what has been learned through business strategy analysis, accounting analysis, and financial analysis. For example, a projection of the future profitability of Compaq as of early 1993 must be grounded ultimately in an understanding of questions such as:

- *From business strategy analysis:* What will Compaq's shift in business strategy in 1992 mean for future margins and sales volume? Can Compaq continue to command price premiums even as it emphasizes cost leadership and market share? What will Compaq's drive for market share imply about the need for working capital and capital expenditures?

- *From accounting analysis:* Are there any aspects of Compaq's accounting that suggest past earnings are either stronger or weaker than they appear on the surface? If so, what are the implications for future earnings?
- *From financial analysis:* What are the sources of the improvement in Compaq's net margin in 1992? Do they suggest that the improvement is sustainable? Has Compaq's shift in business strategy translated into improvements in asset utilization in 1992? Can any such improvements in efficiency be sustained or enhanced? Why is Compaq so conservative in its design of capital structure? Would a more aggressive stance enhance profitability enough to offset the increased risk of distress?

THE TECHNIQUES OF FORECASTING

A forecast can be no better than the business strategy analysis, the accounting analysis, and the financial analysis underlying it. However, there are certain techniques and knowledge that can help a manager or analyst to structure the best possible forecast, conditional on what has been learned in the previous steps. Below, we summarize an approach to structuring the forecast, some information useful in getting started, and some detailed steps used to forecast earnings, balance sheet data, and cash flows.

The Overall Structure of the Forecast

The best way to forecast future performance is to do it comprehensively, by producing not only an earnings forecast, but a forecast of cash flows and the balance sheet as well. A comprehensive approach is useful, even in cases where one might be interested primarily in a single facet of performance, because it guards against unrealistic implicit assumptions. For example, if an analyst forecasts growth in sales and earnings for several years without explicit consideration of the required increases in working capital and plant assets and the associated financing, the forecast might possibly imbed unreasonable assumptions about asset turnover, leverage, or equity capital infusions.

A comprehensive approach involves many forecasts, but in most cases they are all linked to the behavior of a few key "drivers." The drivers vary according to the type of business involved, but for businesses outside the financial services sector, the sales forecast is nearly always one of the key drivers, profit margin is another. When asset turnover is expected to remain stable—an often realistic assumption—working capital accounts and investment in plant should track the growth in sales closely. Most major expenses also track sales, subject to expected shifts in profit margins. By linking forecasts of such amounts to the sales forecast, one can avoid internal inconsistencies and unrealistic implicit assumptions.

In many contexts, the manager or analyst is interested ultimately in a forecast of cash flows, not earnings per se. Nevertheless, even forecasts of cash flows tend to be grounded in practice on forecasts of accounting numbers, including sales and earnings. Of course, it would be possible in principle to move *directly* to forecasts of cash flows—

inflows from customers, outflows to suppliers and laborers, and so forth—and in some businesses, this is a convenient way to proceed. In most cases, however, the growth prospects and profitability of the firm are more readily framed in terms of accrual-based sales and operating earnings. These amounts can then be converted to cash flow measures by adjusting for the effects of non-cash expenses and expenditures for working capital and plant.

Getting Started: Points of Departure

Every forecast has, at least implicitly, an initial "benchmark" or point of departure— some notion of how a particular amount, such as sales or earnings, would be expected to behave in the absence of detailed information. For example, in beginning to contemplate 1993 profitability for Compaq, one must start somewhere. A possibility is to begin with the 1992 performance; another starting point might be the 1992 performance, adjusted for recent trends. A third possibility that might seem reasonable—but one that generally turns out not to be very useful—is the average performance over several prior years.

By the time one has completed a business strategy analysis, an accounting analysis, and a detailed financial analysis, the resulting forecast might differ significantly from the original point of departure. Nevertheless, simply for purposes of having a starting point that can help anchor the detailed analysis, it is useful to know how certain key financial statistics behave "on average."

In the case of some key statistics, such as earnings, a point of departure or benchmark based only on prior behavior of the number is more powerful than one might expect. Research demonstrates that some such benchmarks for earnings are not much less accurate than the forecasts of professional security analysts, who have access to a rich information set. (We return to this point in more detail below.) Thus, the benchmark is often not only a good starting point, but also close to the amount forecast after detailed analysis. Large departures from the benchmark could be justified only in cases where the firm's situation is demonstrably unusual.

Reasonable points of departure for forecasts of key accounting numbers can be based on the evidence summarized below. Such evidence may also be useful for checking the reasonableness of a completed forecast.

THE BEHAVIOR OF SALES.   For typical firms, annual sales follow approximately a process labeled a "random walk with drift."[1] For such a process, the forecast for year $t+1$ is simply the amount observed for year t, plus a "drift" that reflects the average change in the series over prior years. Thus, the evidence indicates that for typical firms, sales behavior is very much a reflection of "what you have done for me lately." Sales information more than one year old is useful only to the extent that it contributes to the average annual trend.

The implication of the evidence is that, in beginning to contemplate future sales possibilities, a useful number to start with is last year's sales. Long-term trends in sales tend to be sustained on average, and so they are also worthy of consideration. The average level of sales over several prior years is not. If quarterly data are also considered, then some consideration should usually be given to any departures from the long-run trend that occurred in the most recent quarter. For most firms, these most recent changes tend to be partially repeated in subsequent quarters.[2]

THE BEHAVIOR OF EARNINGS.   Earnings have also been shown, on average, to follow a process that can be approximated by a "random walk" or "random walk with drift." Thus, the prior year's earnings is a good starting point in considering future earnings potential. As will be explained in more detail later in the chapter, it is reasonable to adjust this simple benchmark for the earnings changes of the most recent quarter (that is, changes versus the comparable quarter of the prior year, and after controlling for the long-run trend in the series). However, even a simple random walk forecast—one that predicts next year's earnings will be equal to last year's earnings—is surprisingly useful. One study documents that professional analysts' year-ahead forecasts are only 22 percent more accurate (on average) than a simple random walk forecast.[3] Thus, early in a year, an earnings forecast will *usually* not differ dramatically from a random walk benchmark.

THE BEHAVIOR OF RETURNS ON INVESTMENT.   Given that prior earnings serves as a useful benchmark for future earnings, one might expect the same to be true of rates of return on investment, such as return on equity (ROE). That, however, is not the case, for two reasons. First, even though the *average* firm tends to sustain the current earnings level, that is not true of firms with unusual levels of ROE. Firms with abnormally high (or low) ROE tend to experience earnings declines (or increases).[4]

Second, firms with higher ROEs tend to expand their investment bases more quickly than others, which causes the denominator of the ROE to increase. Of course, if firms could earn returns on the new investments that match the returns on the old ones, then the level of ROE would be maintained. However, firms have difficulty pulling that off. Firms with higher ROEs tend to find that, as time goes by, their earnings growth does not keep pace with growth in their investment base, and ROE ultimately falls.

The resulting behavior of ROE and other measures of return on investment is characterized as "mean reverting": firms with above-average or below-average rates of return tend to revert over time to a "normal" level within three to ten years (for ROE, historically in the range of 10 to 14 percent for U.S. firms).[5] Figure 5-1 documents this effect for U.S. firms for 1972–1991. In each year, firms are divided into ten groups based on their ROEs. The ROEs of each group are then traced through subsequent years. The most profitable group of firms initially, with ROEs of 34 percent, experience a decline to 15 percent within three years and are never above 13 percent after 5 years. Those with the lowest initial ROEs (–21 percent) experience an increase to breakeven within four years.

Figure 5-1 Path of ROE Over Time

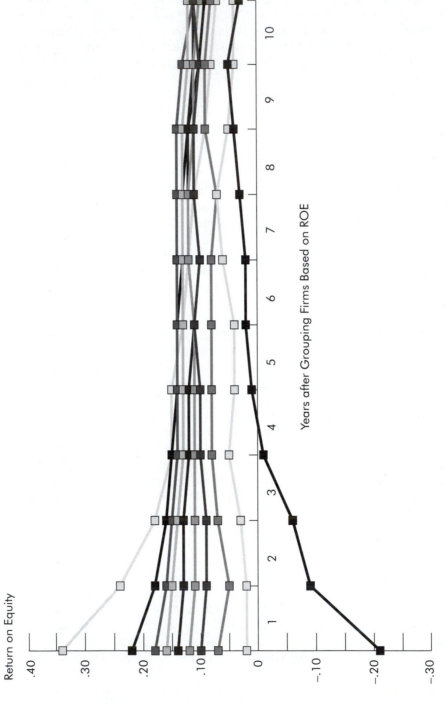

Explanation: Firms are grouped in deciles in year 0, based on ROE. The graph then plots ROE for each of the ten groups for the subsequent ten years. Based on data for U.S. industrial firms, 1972–1991; the number of firms per year varies from 1640 to 2306.

All but the three initially most unprofitable groups revert to "normal" levels of ROE—within the range of 10 to 14 percent—by the fifth year.

The pattern in Figure 5-1 is not a coincidence. It is exactly what the economics of competition would predict. The tendency of high ROEs to fall is a reflection of high profitability attracting competition. The tendency of low ROEs to rise reflects the mobility of capital away from unproductive ventures and toward more profitable ones.

Despite the general tendencies documented in Figure 5-1, there are some firms whose ROEs may remain at above- or below-normal levels for long periods of time. In some cases, the phenomenon reflects the strength of a strong brand name (e.g., Coca-Cola), but often it is purely an artifact of accounting methods. Good examples in the U.S. are pharmaceutical firms, whose major economic asset (the intangible value of research and development) is not recorded on the balance sheet and is therefore excluded from the denominator of ROE. For those firms, one could reasonably expect high ROEs—in excess of 20 percent—over the long run, even in the face of strong competitive forces.

THE BEHAVIOR OF PROFIT MARGINS.   The behavior of rates of return on investment offers a lesson for the behavior of profit margins as well. Recall from Chapter 4 that ROEs and profit margins are linked as follows:

ROE   =   Profit margin × Asset turnover × Adjusted leverage

Asset turnover tends to be rather stable, in part because it is so much a function of the technology of an industry. Leverage also tends to be stable, simply because management policies on capital structure aren't often changed. Profit margins stand out as the most variable component of ROE. If the forces of competition drive abnormal ROEs toward more normal levels, the change is most likely to arrive in the form of changes in profit margins.

The implication is that profit margins, like ROEs, tend to be driven by competition to "normal" levels over time. However, what constitutes "normal" varies widely according to the technology employed within an industry and the corporate strategy pursued by a firm—both of which influence turnover and leverage.[6] For example, assume that asset turnover hovers around 1.5 and that there is no leverage (i.e., financial leverage = assets/equity = 1.0). Then if competition drives ROE toward a "normal" level of, say, 13 percent, the profit margin must be driven to about 8.7 percent:

$$ROE = \text{Profit margin} \times \text{Asset turnover} \times \text{Financial leverage}$$

$$13\% = \text{Profit margin} \times 1.5 \times 1.0$$

Profit margin = 8.7%

However, if the technology in the industry were such that asset turnover could be sustained at 2.5, then competition would tend to drive the profit margin lower, to 5.2 percent ($13\% = 5.2\% \times 2.5 \times 1.0$). In a fully competitive equilibrium, profit margins should remain high for firms that must operate with a low turnover, and vice versa.

The implication of the above discussion of rates of return and profit margins is that a reasonable point of departure for a forecast of such a statistic should consider more than just the most recent observation. One should also consider whether that rate or margin is above or below a normal level. If so, and absent detailed information to the contrary, one would expect some movement over time toward the norm. Of course, this centralizing tendency might be overcome in some cases where, for example, the firm has erected barriers to competition that can protect margins, even for extended periods. The lesson from the evidence, however, is that such cases are the exceptional ones.

As we proceed with the steps involved in producing a detailed forecast, the reader will note that we draw to some extent on the above evidence of the behavior of accounting numbers. However, it is important to keep in mind that a knowledge of *average* behavior will not apply to all firms well. The art of financial statement analysis requires not only knowing what the "normal" patterns are but also knowing how to identify those firms that will *not* follow the norm.

Elements of the Detailed Forecast

The steps that could be followed in producing a comprehensive forecast are summarized in the following paragraphs. We assume that the firm being analyzed is among the vast majority for which the forecast would reasonably be anchored by a sales forecast.

THE SALES FORECAST.   The first step in most forecasting exercises is the sales prediction. There is no generally accepted approach to forecasting sales. The approach should be tailored to the context and should reflect the factors considered in the prior steps of the analysis. For example, for a large retail firm, a sales forecast would normally consider the prior year's sales, increases due purely to expansion of the number of retail outlets, and "comparable store growth," which captures growth in sales in already existing stores. The forecast of growth might consider such factors as customer acceptance of new product lines, marketing plans, changes in pricing strategies, competitors' behavior, and the expected state of the economy. Another approach—and possibly the only feasible one when little history exists—is to estimate the size of the target market, project the degree of market penetration, and then consider how quickly that degree of penetration can be achieved.

Table 5-1 presents a forecast of sales and earnings for Compaq Computer Corporation, produced by an analyst at Duff & Phelps in February 1993. The 1993 sales forecast, a 30 percent increase over the prior year, is approximately consistent with a continuation of sales levels achieved by Compaq in the latter half of 1992, after the introduction of a major set of new products. Thus, the forecast is roughly a random walk forecast, but based only on the last two quarters' sales. In commenting on the forecast, the analyst recognized at least three factors that might support a more optimistic view on sales: (1) Compaq's large sales backlog at the end of 1992; (2) the firm's shift in its corporate strategy towards higher unit volume through more aggressive pricing; and (3) the existence

Table 5-1 Analyst's Forecast of Compaq 1993 Earnings

	1992 Actual Results		1993 Forecast	
	$ millions	% of sales	$ millions	% of sales
Sales	$4,100	100%	$5,330	100%
Cost of sales	2,905	71%	3,944	74%
Gross margin	1,195	29%	1,386	26%
Research and development costs	173	4%	160	3%
Selling, general, and administrative expense	699	17%	746	14%
Other income and expense	28	1%	0	0%
Earnings before taxes	295	7.2%	479	9.0%
Provision for taxes	97	2.4%	158	3.0%
Earnings from consolidated companies	198	4.8%	321	6.0%
Equity in net income of affiliated company	15	0.4%	0	0.0%
Net income	$213	5.2%	$321	6.0%
ROE	.11		.15	
EPS: primary	$2.58		NA	
EPS: fully diluted	$2.52		$3.80	

Source: *Common Stock Summary: Compaq Computer Corporation*, Duff & Phelps Investment Research Company (Chicago, Illinois), February 1993.

of enough excess manufacturing capacity to accommodate a sales increase of nearly 40 percent without adding facilities. Nevertheless, the forecast was for no further improvement in earnings over the last two quarters, with higher unit sales being offset by lower prices, because (1) competitors were selling what the analyst considered similar products at comparable or lower prices; (2) overall industry growth was expected to slow; and (3) price pressure was expected to intensify even further as firms in the industry engaged in their ongoing "struggle for low-cost producer status."

The Duff & Phelps forecast appears to be based largely on analysis that views the firm as a whole. An alternative approach—not feasible for all firms—is to build a sales forecast on a product-by-product basis. Table 5-2 presents such a forecast, produced by First Boston analyst Bill Gurley in late 1993, about nine months after the Duff & Phelps forecast was released. By this time, it was clear that Compaq was performing much better than expected early in the year—1993 sales were now expected to be up 73 percent over the prior year.

Table 5-2 Analyst's Detailed Sales Forecast for Compaq, November 1993

Revenue Calculation for 1993

	First Quarter, A			Second Quarter, A			Third Quarter, A			Fourth Quarter, A			Year 1993, E		
	Units	Price	Revenue	Units	Price	Revenue	Units	Price	Revenue	Units	Price	Revenue	Units	Price	Revenue
Servers:															
ProLiant	0		$0	0		$0	2	$14,600	$26	7	$15,400	$108	9	$15,236	$134
Systempro	5	$14,500	65	5	$14,500	73	5	$13,475	67	2	$12,200	24	17	$13,911	230
Prosignia	12	6,400	74	15	6,425	96	16	6,800	109	19	6,900	131	62	6,665	410
	16	8,678	139	20	8,444	169	23	8,880	202	28	9,404	263	87	8,911	773
Desktop:															
Deskpro/M	155	2,776	430	151	2,695	407	150	2,710	407	160	2,800	448	616	2,746	1,692
Deskpro/I-/XE	135	1,751	236	137	1,700	233	135	1,685	227	145	1,750	254	552	1,722	951
Prolinea	208	1,421	296	210	1,380	290	225	1,350	304	245	1,300	319	888	1,360	1,208
Presario	0		0	0		0	30	1,210	38	100	1,195	120	130	1,198	156
	498	1,932	962	498	1,867	930	540	1,804	974	650	1,753	1,140	2186	1,832	4,006
Portable:															
Portable 486	5	4,700	24	5	4,900	25	4	4,950	20	4	4,950	20	18	4,867	88
Concerto	0	0	0	0	0	0	8	2,300	18	32	2,250	72	40	2,260	90
LTE Lite	105	2,635	277	103	2,750	283	105	2,750	289	115	2,750	316	428	2,722	1,165
Contura	106	1,736	184	110	1,810	199	115	1,900	219	130	1,950	254	461	1,855	855
Sub-Notebook	0		0	0		0	0		0	0		0	0		0
PDA	0		0	0		0	0		0	0		0	0		0
	216	2,242	484	218	2,325	507	232	2,351	545	281	2,354	662	947	2,321	2,198
Peripherals:															
Pagemarq Printers	9	2,895	26	10	2,700	27	11	2,200	24	12	2,000	24	42	2,411	101
Total	739	$2,180	$1,611	746	$2,188	$1,632	806	$2,167	$1,746	971	$2,151	$2,089	3262	$2,170	$7,078

Revenue Calculation for 1994

	First Quarter, A			Second Quarter, A			Third Quarter, A			Fourth Quarter, A			Year 1994, E		
	Units	Price	Revenue	Units	Price	Revenue	Units	Price	Revenue	Units	Price	Revenue	Units	Price	Revenue
Servers:															
ProLiant	8	$16,000	$128	9	$16,600	$141	9	$16,500	$149	11	$16,300	$179	37	$16,353	$597
Systempro	1	0	0	0	0	0	0	0	0	0	0	0	1	0	0
Prosignia	20	7,040	141	21	7,040	144	22	6,900	152	28	6,850	192	91	6,947	629
	29	9,432	269	29	9,842	285	31	9,687	300	39	9,515	371	128	9,613	1,226
Desktop:															
Deskpro/M	155	2,850	442	155	2,850	442	155	2,800	434	165	2,750	454	630	2,812	1,771
Deskpro/I-/XE	145	1,800	261	150	1,750	263	150	1,700	255	155	1,650	256	600	1,724	1,034
Prolinea	235	1,300	306	210	1,350	284	205	1,350	277	235	1,300	306	885	1,323	1,171
Presario	115	1,250	144	130	1,190	155	145	1,134	164	210	1,080	227	600	1,149	690
	650	1,772	1,152	645	1,771	1,143	655	1,724	1,130	765	1,623	1,242	2715	1,719	4,666
Portable:															
Portable 486	4	5,050	20	5	4,810	24	4	4,581	18	5	4,362	22	18	4,688	84
Concerto	50	2,400	120	65	2,350	153	70	2,238	157	80	2,132	171	265	2,264	600
LTE Lite	105	2,750	289	100	2,750	275	100	2,750	275	115	2,750	316	420	2,750	1,155
Contura	115	1,800	207	105	1,850	194	105	1,850	194	110	1,800	198	435	1,824	794
Sub-Notebook	5	1,100	6	15	1,100	17	20	1,050	21	30	1,000	30	70	1,043	73
PDA	0	0	0	0	0	0	10	1,300	13	30	1,250	38	40	1,263	51
	279	2,299	641	290	2,285	663	309	2,195	678	370	2,092	774	1248	2,209	2,756
Peripherals:															
Pagemarq Printers	15	1,900	29	20	1,800	36	22	2,400	53	29	2,286	68	86	2,135	184
Total	973	$2,150	$2,091	984	$2,161	$2,126	1017	$2,125	$2,161	1203	$2,039	$2,453	4177	$2,115	$8,832

Source: B. Gurley, "Compaq Computer Corporation: Initiation of Coverage," C S First Boston (November 29, 1993).

In Table 5-2, Gurley presents estimates of *actual* units sold and prices for each of 14 major Compaq product lines for the first three quarters of 1993, and associated *forecasts* for the fourth quarter of 1993 and for each quarter of 1994. Compaq management releases some breakdown of sales activity, but not at this level of detail. Gurley's estimates are based on information from a variety of sources in addition to management, including suppliers, competitors, retail outlets, and other firms that research the industry (such as Dataquest). The forecasts incorporate a detailed understanding of the various products and their features, distribution networks, and the prices that can be commanded in light of competition and the Compaq brand name. Overall, while Gurley recognizes that a repeat of 1993's expected 73 percent sales increase is not likely, he still projects a 25 percent jump in 1994. Following the normal increase during the holiday season in 1993, sales are projected to be maintained at that level during 1994 and to jump again in the fourth quarter of 1994.

Although built product by product, Gurley's projections are supported by thinking at both the product and overall firm level. Gurley explains that his projection of 1994 sales growth in excess of the industry average is based on three factors: (1) the benefits of consolidation as "natural selection plays out," (2) strong positioning, thanks to new products in the hot markets for servers and portables, and (3) opportunities for increased penetration in the fast-growing home PC market, resulting from favorable pricing and a popular product (Presario) introduced in the latter half of 1993. The explanation is offered in the context of a view that Compaq's new emphasis on a low-cost, high-volume approach is "the single most sustainable corporate strategy for a PC vendor that wishes to compete on a global basis,"[7] and that Compaq's brand image will help make this strategy succeed.

THE FORECAST OF EXPENSES AND EARNINGS. Expenses should be forecast item by item, since different expenses may be driven by different factors. However, most major expenses are clearly related to sales and are therefore naturally framed as fractions of sales. These include cost of sales and selling, general, and administrative expenses. Research and deveolpment need not track current sales closely; however, research and development generally tracks sales at least roughly over the long run. Other expenses are more closely related to drivers other than sales. Interest expense is driven by debt levels and interest rates. Depreciation expense should be forecast in a way consistent with the firm's depreciation policy. Under straight-line depreciation, the expense would tend to be a fairly stable fraction of beginning depreciable plant. Tax provisions are driven by pretax income and factors that have a permanent impact on tax payments (such as tax rates applicable to certain foreign subsidiaries). Equity in the income of affiliates is determined by whatever drives the affiliate's earnings.

In the case of Compaq, the three largest expenses—cost of sales, research and development, and selling, general and administrative expense—were all forecast by Duff & Phelps as fractions of sales (see Table 5-1). Cost of sales was expected to increase as a fraction of sales, causing the gross margin percentage to decline to 26 percent from 29 percent. This projected decline reflects a continuation of a trend in gross margin that existed for five consecutive quarters, based on Compaq's shift in corporate strategy and increasing competition based on price. By the last quarter of 1992, the gross margin percentage had already fallen to 26.9 percent, down from 37 percent a year earlier. Thus, the forecast of 26 percent for 1993 is only slightly lower than the margin already experienced recently. In Table 5-1, research and development and selling, general, and administrative are both expected to decline in 1993 as fractions of sales, because some economies are expected from Compaq's increased emphasis on sales volume and market share.

In long-range forecasts (to be presented in detail in Chapter 6), Duff & Phelps projected a continuing decline in gross margins, to 20 percent: "what the IBM PC company is living with now and appears to expect to live with in the future."[8] This view is consistent with our statements in Chapter 2 that, over the long run, it is not clear that Compaq can sustain a competitive advantage over IBM and some other PC assemblers. The decline in gross margin is projected to be accompanied by reductions in selling, general, and administrative costs as a fraction of sales, so as to leave Compaq with a competitive net margin. Thus, the forecasts are consistent with the behavior of margins described previously; that is, they are expected over several years to revert to a more normal level.

Remaining expenses are not driven directly by sales. The "other" category includes interest income, interest expense, and a number of transitory gains and losses that are nearly offsetting in 1992. The analyst projected zero for 1993, or grouped the items within another expense category. Tax expense is forecast as a fraction of pretax income, assuming that fraction will continue to hold at 33 percent. Equity in the income of an affiliate will fall to zero because the associated investment was liquidated in 1992.

The forecasts of sales and expenses produce an expected net margin of 6 percent and a return on equity of approximately 15 percent. Both are improvements over 1992's rather ordinary overall performance, but are slightly weaker than the performance of late 1992, when ROEs hit 19 percent after new product lines were introduced. The producer of the forecast notes that "though Compaq has a large backlog going into the first quarter, which we do not like to bet against, we do not believe that a 19%+ ROE is sustainable in an industry where elasticity [of demand is high]—[we expect] flat revenues on more units for 1993." The expected reversion to a more normal level of ROE is consistent with the average behavior of ROE described previously. It is also consistent with Chapter 2's statements about the difficulty of maintaining a competitive advantage in this industry.

THE FORECAST OF BALANCE SHEET ACCOUNTS.   Since various balance sheet accounts may be driven by different factors, they are usually best forecast individually. However, several accounts, including operating working capital accounts and plant assets, are driven over the long run by sales activity. Thus, these accounts can be forecast as fractions of sales, allowing for any expected changes in the efficiency of asset utilization. If management plans for capital expenditures are known, they would clearly be useful in forecasting plant assets. Other accounts may depend on a variety of factors, including policies on capital structure and dividends.

Table 5-3 presents Duff & Phelps' December 1993 forecast of 1994 income statement and balance sheet accounts for Compaq.[9] This forecast was produced around the same time as the First Boston sales forecast given in Table 5-2, and it reflects the stronger-than-anticipated experience of the first three quarters of 1993. The actual results for

Table 5-3 Analyst's Forecast of Compaq 1994 Earnings and Balance Sheet

	1993 Actual Results		1994 Forecast	
	$ millions	% of sales	$ millions	% of sales
Statement of earnings				
Sales	$7,191	100.0%	$8,712	100.0%
Cost of sales	5,493	76.4%	6,774	77.8%
Gross margin	1,698	23.6%	1,938	22.2%
Research and development	169	2.4%	218	2.5%
Selling, general, and administrative expense	837	11.6%	994	11.4%
Other expense (income)	76	1.1%	36	0.4%
Earnings before taxes	616	8.6%	690	7.9%
Provision for taxes	154	2.1%	173	2.0%
Net income	$462	6.4%	$517	5.9%
Balance sheet				
Cash and equivalents	$ 627	9%	$1,151	13%
Receivables	1,377	19%	1,500	17%
Inventories	1,123	16%	1,238	14%
Prepaid expenses and other	164	2%	157	2%
Total current assets	3,291	46%	4,046	46%
Property, plant, & equipment	779	11%	801	9%
Other assets	14	0%	25	0%
Total assets	4,084	57%	4,872	56%
Accounts payable	637	9%	813	9%
Income tax payable	69	1%	94	1%
Other current liabilities	538	7%	624	7%
Total current liabilities	1,244	17%	1,531	18%
Deferred income taxes	186	3%	220	3%
Shareholders equity	2,654	37%	3,121	36%
Total liabilities and equity	$4,084	57%	$4,872	56%

Sources: Actual results from Compaq Computer 1993 Annual Report; forecasts from *Company Analysis: Compaq Computer Corporation*, Duff & Phelps Investment Research Company (Chicago, Illinois), December 1993.

1993 are presented in Table 5-3 for purposes of comparison. Those results were not yet known at the forecast date, but analysts were able to project them with a high level of accuracy.

Most balance sheet account forecasts maintain relations to sales that are consistent from 1993 to 1994. In particular, total asset utilization is nearly constant. Receivables, inventory, and plant are forecast to decline slightly, relative to sales, reflecting increased efficiency as Compaq's shift to a high-volume strategy is more fully realized. However, this efficiency is largely offset by a dramatic projected increase in cash balances. The net effect is that total assets as a fraction of sales decline only slightly.

An alternative approach to balance sheet projection would be to assume the *change* in each balance sheet account is linked to the *change* in sales. For example, one might forecast that inventory balances will increase by 15 to 20 percent of sales increases. The weakness of this approach is that it takes the beginning balances as given and adjusts from those points. The approach is problematic because working capital accounts at a given point in time often reflect some unusual deviation from the norm. (For example, beginning-of-year accruals might have ballooned, depending on where payday falls on the calendar.) More importantly, the firm's strategy may suggest a shift from the beginning-of-year position. In Compaq's case, the shift to a high-volume strategy is expected by Duff & Phelps to reduce the amounts of inventory and receivables needed per dollar of sales.

Liability and equity accounts are maintained at nearly identical fractions of sales, reflecting a presumed maintenance of the current capital structure policy. Both Duff & Phelps and First Boston assume that Compaq will continue to shun debt. But First Boston analyst Gurley notes that ROE could improve substantially if Compaq began to take on more leverage. We will return to the question of what capital structure would be best for Compaq in Chapter 11.

THE FORECAST OF CASH FLOWS.   The forecast of earnings and balance sheet accounts implies a forecast of cash flows, which can be constructed as described in Chapter 4. Table 5-4 illustrates the projection of cash flows for Compaq for 1994. Most of the amounts can be calculated from the earnings and balance sheet data already presented in Table 5-3. The exceptions are the projections of capital expenditures, interest expense, depreciation expense, and deferred taxes, all of which are provided in (or can be calculated from) the Duff & Phelps report.

Duff & Phelps forecasts capital expenditures for 1994 at $218 million, up from 1993's $145 million. Capital expenditures are difficult to forecast without some guidance from management, and Compaq announced only after the release of the Duff & Phelps forecast that 1994 capital expenditures would probably be closer to $250 million. In the absence of such information, a good rule of thumb is to assume that the ratio of plant to sales will remain relatively stable, and that capital expenditures will be whatever amount is needed to maintain that ratio. If sales are growing, then capital expenditures will exceed depreciation.

Table 5-4 Forecast of Compaq 1994 Free Cash Flows

	Dollars in Millions
Net income	**$517**
Adjustments for non-current operating accruals:	
✓ Deferred taxes	34
Depreciation	211
	762
Adjustment for interest expense less interest income (net of related tax effect)	22
Cash flow from operations before working capital investments and interest payments	**784**
Investment in working capital:	
✓ Receivables	(123)
✓ Inventories	(115)
✓ Prepaid expenses and other	7
✓ Accounts payable	176
✓ Income tax payable	25
✓ Other current liabilities	87
Other adjustments	(76)
	(19)
Cash from operations after investment in working capital, before interest payments	**765**
Interest expense less interest income (net of tax)	22
Cash from operations after investment in working capital, after interest payments	**743**
Capital expenditures	(218)
Free cash flow	**$525**

Based on earnings and balance sheet data in Table 5-3 and detailed income statement and capital expenditure projections from Duff & Phelps December 1993 report. Cash flow projection does not match that published by Duff & Phelps due to differences between expected and actual 1993 balance sheet amount (not yet published at time of Duff & Phelps report).

For purposes of producing a cash flow forecast from earnings, the two noncash expenses, depreciation and deferred taxes, are required. Of course, both of these are already embedded in our earnings forecast, but they were not made explicit in Table 5-3. Compaq has $1,310 million in gross depreciable plant at the beginning of 1994, and depreciation expense has been running at about 13 percent of gross plant—suggesting an average depreciable life of about 8 years. Thus, one might expect depreciation in 1994 to be about .13 × $1,310, or $170 million, plus some modest increase for the increment added to plant in 1994. The Duff & Phelps forecast of depreciation ($211 million) seems high relative to this amount.[10] The Duff & Phelps forecast of the increase in deferred taxes maintains a constant ratio of the balance of deferred taxes to sales. This represents a reasonable approximation, although with knowledge of the details of Compaq's tax situation, one might be able to produce a more accurate forecast. For example, a key determinant of the change in deferred taxes is warranty expenses that are not deductible until paid. Such amounts can change dramatically when the pace of sales changes.

The forecast suggests Compaq's earnings will translate into a nearly equivalent amount of free cash flow. At first blush, this is surprising, because Compaq is expected to grow so fast, and growth requires additional investment. The key to the projection is that receivables and inventory will increase more slowly than sales, and that the increases can be financed largely through increases in payables and other current liabilities. First Boston analyst Gurley was not as optimistic as Duff & Phelps about Compaq's ability to contain working capital increases in the face of higher sales. However, if the projection in Table 5-4 materializes, Compaq will generate a substantial amount of free cash flow—$525 million—even while supporting increased sales volume. Duff & Phelps forecasts for 1995 and beyond suggest continued high levels of cash generation, in the range of $295 to $450 million per year. Unless accumulation of billions of dollars of cash is efficient for Compaq (which seems doubtful), some reconsideration of Compaq's no-dividend policy or consideration of share buybacks may be in order. We will return to the question of what dividend policy might be best for Compaq in Chapter 11.

Sensitivity Analysis

The projections discussed thus far represent nothing more than a "best guess." Managers and analysts are typically interested in a broader range of possibilities. For example, in considering the likelihood that short-term financing will be necessary, it would be wise to produce projections based on a more pessimistic view of profit margins and asset turnover. Alternatively, an analyst estimating the value of Compaq should consider the sensitivity of the estimate to the key assumptions about sales growth, profit margins, and asset utilization. What if competitor reaction to Compaq's high-volume strategy requires more dramatic price cuts than anticipated? What if the anticipated improvements in inventory turnover do not materialize? What if Compaq begins to include some debt in its capital structure?

There is no limit to the number of possible scenarios that can be considered. However, to provide some feel for the range of possible profit and cash flow outcomes that could arise for Compaq in 1994, Table 5-5 considers sales growth rates from 10 to 30 percent, and profit margins from 4 to 8 percent. These assumptions bracket the expected values used above—21 percent sales growth and 5.9 percent profit margin. All the projections hold asset turnover constant, and they assume no use of debt.

Judgments about what alternative scenarios are reasonably possible are difficult to make, but history can provide some guidance. The lowest profit margin considered in Table 5-5, 4 percent, is equal to the lowest level experienced in Compaq's recent history (in 1991). While weaker performance may be unlikely, margins below that level have

Table 5-5 Forecast of Compaq 1994 Earnings and Cash Flows: Sensitivity Analysis

Alternative Scenarios Considered

Sales growth	10%	10%	10%	21%	21%	21%	30%	30%	30%
Profit margin	4%	5.9%	8%	4%	5.9%	8%	4%	5.9%	8%

Implied Sales, Earnings, and Free Cash Flows (millions of dollars)

Sales	$7,910	$7,910	$7,910	$8,712	$8,712	$8,712	$9,348	$9,348	$9,348
Earnings	316	469	633	348	517	697	374	555	748
Free cash flow	506	659	822	356	525	705	238	419	612

Notes: The base case (with 21% sales growth and 5.9% profit margin) is that presented in detail in Tables 5-3 and 5-4.
Alternative scenarios assume that asset turnover and leverage remain constant.

clearly been experienced by others in the industry, even as recently as 1993. Note that if Compaq's gross margin fell to the 20 percent that IBM generates in its PC division, with no decline in selling, general, and administrative expense, Compaq's net profit margin would vanish entirely. The lowest sales increase considered in Table 5-5 is 10 percent. Coming off a year where sales increased by 75 percent and new product lines were very successful late in the fourth quarter, and in light of Compaq's corporate strategy and overall industry growth rates, sales growth of 10 percent appears to be quite pessimistic.

Turning to the more optimistic projections, we could note that an 8 percent net profit margin may appear at first glance to be well within the range of achievable performance. It is lower than the double-digit performance turned in by Compaq in every year from 1987 through 1990. However, in light of Compaq's shift in corporate strategy and the increased price pressure in the industry, a return to those high margin days seems extremely unlikely. An 8 percent margin would require holding the line on gross margin while continuing to achieve efficiencies in selling, general, and administrative expense—not very likely in light of industry competition and Compaq's new strategy. Looking at sales growth, a 30 percent increase for the year is only 6 percent higher than what one would project if fourth-quarter 1993 sales volumes were maintained throughout 1994. Even much higher sales growth rates are not out of the question.

Sensitivity analysis can be useful in helping to identify the key drivers of profits and cash flows. An interesting (and not unusual) feature of the analysis in Table 5-5 is that the stronger the sales growth, the *weaker* the free cash flows. The reason is that greater sales growth requires larger investments in working capital. Overall, free cash flow estimates range from a low of $238 million with the combination of high growth and low margins, to a high of $822 million with low growth and high margins. Although one should also contemplate the possibility of slower inventory and receivables turns than considered thus far, the analysis suggests that Compaq is not likely to face a "cash squeeze" during 1994—and that the firm may well have to confront the question of what to do with excess cash.

SEASONALITY AND INTERIM FORECASTS

Thus far, we have concerned ourselves with annual forecasts. However, especially for security analysts in the U.S., forecasting is very much a quarterly game. Forecasting quarter-by-quarter raises a new set of questions. How important is seasonality? What is a useful point of departure: the most recent quarter's performance? the comparable quarter of the prior year? some combination of the two? How should quarterly data be used in producing an annual forecast? Does the item-by-item approach to forecasting used for annual data apply equally well to quarterly data? Full consideration of these questions lies outside the scope of this chapter, but we can begin to answer some of them.

Seasonality is a more important phenomenon in sales and earnings behavior than one might guess. It is present for more than just the retail sector firms that benefit from holiday sales. Seasonality also results from weather-related phenomena (e.g., for electric and gas utilities, construction firms, and motorcycle manufacturers), new product introduction patterns (e.g., for the automobile industry), and other factors. Analysis of the time series behavior of earnings for U.S. firms suggests that at least some seasonality is present in nearly every major industry.

The implication for forecasting is that one cannot focus only on performance of the most recent quarter as a point of departure. In fact, the evidence suggests that, in forecasting earnings, if one had to choose only one quarter's performance as a point of departure, it would be the comparable quarter of the prior year, not the most recent quarter. Note how consistent this finding is with the reports of analysts or the financial press. When they discuss a quarterly earnings announcement, it is nearly always evaluated relative to the performance of the comparable quarter of the prior year, not the most recent quarter.

Research has produced models that forecast sales, earnings, and earnings per share, based solely on prior quarters' observations. Such models are not used by many analysts, since analysts have access to much more information than such simple models contain. However, the models are useful for helping those unfamiliar with the behavior of earnings data to understand how it tends to evolve through time. Such an understanding can provide useful general background, a point of departure in forecasting that can be adjusted to reflect details not revealed in the history of earnings, or a "reasonableness" check on a detailed forecast.

Using Q_t to denote earnings (or EPS) for quarter t, and $E[Q_t]$ as its expected value, one model of the earnings process that fits well across a variety of industries is the so-called Foster model[11]:

$$E[Q_t] = Q_{t-4} + \delta + \phi[Q_{t-1} - Q_{t-5}]$$

Foster shows that a model of the same form also works well with sales data. The form of the Foster model confirms the importance of seasonality, because it shows that the starting point for a forecast for quarter t is the earnings four quarters ago (Q_{t-4}). It states that, when constrained to using only prior earnings data, a reasonable forecast of earnings for quarter t includes the following elements:

the earnings of the comparable quarter of the prior year (Q_{t-4});

a long-run trend in year-to-year quarterly earnings increases (δ); and

a fraction (ϕ) of the year-to-year increase in quarterly earnings experienced most recently $(Q_{t-1} - Q_{t-5})$.

The parameters δ and ϕ can easily be estimated for a given firm with a simple linear regression model available in most spreadsheet software.[12] For most firms, the parameter ϕ tends to be in the range of .25 to .50, indicating that 25 to 50 percent of an increase in quarterly earnings tends to persist in the form of another increase in the subsequent quarter. The parameter δ reflects, in part, the average year-to-year change in quarterly earnings over past years, and it varies considerably from firm to firm.

Research indicates that the Foster model produces one-quarter-ahead forecasts that are off, on average, by $.30 to $.35 per share.[13] Such a degree of accuracy stacks up surprisingly well with that of security analysts, who obviously have access to much information ignored in the model. As one would expect, most of the evidence supports analysts' being more accurate, but the models are good enough to be "in the ball park" in most circumstances. Thus, while it would certainly be unwise to rely completely on such a naive model, an understanding of the typical earnings behavior reflected by it is useful.

Compaq's quarterly EPS for years prior to 1994 behaved as shown in Table 5-6. Note the strong presence of seasonality. The fourth quarter of the year has been the strongest in every year except 1989 and 1991. On average, the fourth quarter accounts for 36 percent of annual earnings.

If we used the Foster model to forecast EPS for the first quarter of 1994, we would start with EPS of the comparable quarter of 1993, or $1.23. We would then expect some additional upward trend in EPS, and a partial repetition of the most recent quarter's increase ($1.74 − $1.11). More specifically, when the parameters δ and ϕ are estimated with the data in Table 5-6,[14] the Foster model predicts EPS of $1.62.

Table 5-6 Compaq Quarterly Earnings per Share, 1987–1993

Quarter ended:	1993	1992	1991	1990	1989	1988	1987
March	$1.23	$0.50	$1.26	$1.08	$0.99	$0.60	$0.27
June	1.21	0.35	0.23	1.17	0.99	0.72	0.39
September	1.26	0.59	−0.82	1.38	1.02	0.69	0.48
December	1.74	1.11	0.77	1.50	0.93	1.08	0.63
Annual EPS	$5.45	$2.58	$1.49	$5.14	$3.89	$3.15	$1.80

$$E\,[Q_t] \;=\; Q_{t-4} \;+\; .08 \;+\; .49\,[Q_{t-1} - Q_{t-5}]$$

$$= \;1.23 \;+\; .08 \;+\; .49\,[1.74 - 1.11] \;=\; 1.62$$

The model can be extended to forecast earnings two quarters ahead, and even to produce a forecast for all quarters of the next year. The issue that arises here is that, in forecasting earnings two quarters ahead, one needs earnings one quarter ahead, and yet next quarter's earnings are still unknown. The proper resolution of the issue is to substitute the *forecast* of next quarter's earnings. Our forecast of earnings for Compaq for the second quarter of 1994, based on data through the fourth quarter of 1993, is $1.48:

$$E\,[Q_{t+1}] \;=\; Q_{t-3} \;+\; .08 \;+\; .49\,[E\,(Q_t) - Q_{t-4}]$$

$$= \;1.21 \;+\; .08 \;+\; .49\,[1.62 - 1.23] \;=\; 1.48$$

The $1.62 forecast for the first quarter of 1994, naive as it is, is not far from the $1.69 average analyst forecast for Compaq in the March/April 1994 time frame (just after the 1993 earnings were announced). It is not surprising that the naive model produces a lower forecast, in light of the detailed information that we considered earlier. The model assumes that only 49 percent of the EPS increase of the most recent quarter will carry forward into 1994, but there are sound reasons to expect more at this point in Compaq's history. The most recent quarter's EPS reflects a long-term shift in the firm's corporate strategy and the profitability of hot new products that are still very early in their product life cycle.

The Foster model is not intended as a potential substitute for the hard work of producing a detailed forecast. Forecasting quarterly earnings should be done using the same approach used earlier for annual earnings, a line-item by line-item projection. However, the model does remind us of some important issues. First, it underscores that, due to seasonality, a reasonable starting point in quarterly forecasting is usually the comparable quarter of the prior year, not the most recent quarter. Second, it indicates that recent increases in profitability should *usually* not be extrapolated fully into the future—for Compaq's EPS, on average, only 49 percent of such changes tend to persist.

SUMMARY AND CONCLUSIONS

Forecasting represents the first step of prospective analysis, and serves to summarize the forward-looking view that emanates from business strategy analysis, accounting analysis, and financial analysis. Although not every financial statement analysis is accompanied by such an explicit summarization of a view of the future, forecasting is still a key tool for managers, consultants, security analysts, commercial bankers and other credit analysts, investment bankers, and others.

The best approach to forecasting future performance is to do it comprehensively: produce not only an earnings forecast but a forecast of cash flows and the balance sheet as well. Such a comprehensive approach provides a safeguard against internal inconsistencies and unrealistic implicit assumptions. The approach described here involves line-by-line analysis, so as to recognize that different items on the income statement and balance sheet are influenced by different drivers. Nevertheless, it remains true that a few key projections, such as sales growth and profit margin, usually drive most of the projected numbers.

The forecasting process should be embedded in an understanding of how various financial statistics tend to behave on average, and what might cause a firm to deviate from that average. Absent detailed information to the contrary, one would expect sales and earnings numbers to persist at their current levels, adjusted for overall trends of recent years. However, rates of return on investment (ROEs) tend, over several years, to move from abnormal to normal levels—close to the cost of equity capital—as the forces of competition come into play. Profit margins also tend to shift to normal levels, but for this statistic "normal" varies widely across firms and industries, depending on the levels of asset turnover and leverage. Some firms are capable of creating barriers to entry that enable them to fight these tendencies toward normal returns, even for many years, but these firms are the unusual cases.

For some purposes, including short-term planning and security analysis, forecasts for quarterly periods are desirable. One important feature of quarterly data is seasonality. At least some seasonality exists in the sales and earnings data of nearly every industry. An understanding of a firm's peaks and valleys throughout the year is a necessary ingredient of a good forecast of performance on a quarterly basis.

There are a variety of contexts (including but not limited to security analysis) where the forecast is usefully summarized in the form of an estimate of the firm's value—an estimate that, after all, can be viewed as the best attempt to reflect in a single summary statistic the manager's or analyst's view of the firm's prospects. That process of converting a forecast into a value estimate is labeled valuation. It is to that topic that we turn in the following two chapters.

NOTES

1. Among the few to have studied the statistical behavior of sales are Foster (1977) and Hopwood and McKeown (1985). They examine quarterly data, but their evidence is roughly consistent with annual sales behaving as indicated here.

2. See George Foster, "Quarterly Accounting Data: Time Series Properties and Predictive Ability Results," *The Accounting Review* (January 1977): 1–21; and William Hopwood and James McKeown, "The Incremental Information Content of Expenses over Sales," *Journal of Accounting Research* (Spring 1985): 161–174.

3. See Patricia O'Brien, "Analysts' Forecasts as Earnings Expectations," *Journal of Accounting and Economics* (January 1988): 53–83.

4. See Robert Freeman, James Ohlson, and Stephen Penman, "Book Rate-of-Return and Prediction of Earnings Changes: An Empirical Investigation," *Journal of Accounting Research* (Autumn 1982): 639–653.

5. See Stephen H. Penman, "An Evaluation of Accounting Rate-of-Return," *Journal of Accounting, Auditing, and Finance* (Spring 1991): 233–256; Eugene Fama and Kenneth French, "Size and Book-to-Market Factors in Earnings and Returns," *Journal of Finance* (March 1995): 131–156; and Victor Bernard, "Accounting-Based Valuation Methods: Evidence on the Market-to-Book Anomaly and Implications for Financial Statements Analysis," working paper, University of Michigan (1994). Ignoring the effects of accounting artifacts, ROEs should be driven in a competitive equilibrium to a level approximating the cost of equity capital.

6. A "normal" profit margin is that which, when multiplied by the turnover achievable within an industry through a viable corporate strategy, yields a return on investment that just covers the cost of capital. However, as mentioned above, accounting artifacts can cause returns on investment to deviate from the cost of capital for long periods, even in a competitive equilibrium.

7. B. Gurley, "Compaq Computer Corporation: Initiation of Coverage," C S First Boston (November 29, 1993).

8. M. G. Brandon, "Compaq Computer Corporation: Company Analysis," Duff & Phelps Investment Research Company (December 1993).

9. We present forecasts of balance sheet accounts and cash flows as of December 1993, because such details were not made available in the February 1993 forecast discussed above.

10. Duff & Phelps does not discuss its forecast of depreciation or the underlying rationale. Indeed, they do not publish a forecast of depreciation expense per se, but it can be inferred from capital expenditures and the forecast change in net plant.

11. See Foster, op. cit. A somewhat more accurate model is furnished by Brown and Rozeff, but it requires iterative statistical techniques for estimation. See Lawrence D. Brown and Michael Rozeff, "Univariate Time Series Models of Quarterly Accounting Earnings per Share," *Journal of Accounting Research* (Spring 1979): 179–89.

12. To estimate the model, we write it in terms of realized earnings (as opposed to expected earnings), and move Q_{t-4} to the left-hand side:

$$Q_t - Q_{t-4} \;=\; \delta + \phi \, [Q_{t-1} - Q_{t-5}] \; + \; e_t$$

We now have a regression where $(Q_t - Q_{t-4})$ is the dependent variable, and its lagged value—$(Q_{t-1} - Q_{t-5})$—is the independent variable. Thus, to estimate the equation, prior earnings data must first be expressed in terms of year-to-year changes. The change for one quarter is then regressed against the change for the most recent quarter. The intercept provides an estimate of δ, and the slope is an estimate of ϕ. The equation is typically estimated using 24 to 40 quarters of prior earnings data.

13. See O'Brien, op. cit.

14. See note 12 for a description of the estimation process. The series for the dependent variable would be $(1.74 - 1.11)$, $(1.26 - 0.59)$, $(1.21 - 0.35)$, and so on. The series for the independent variable would be the corresponding lagged values: $(1.26 - 0.59)$, $(1.21 - 0.35)$, $(1.23 - 0.50)$, and so on.

CASES

Boston Celtics, Inc.
The Gap, Inc.
Revco D.S., Inc.
The Timberland Company

chapter 6

Prospective Analysis: Valuation Based on Discounted Cash Flows

The previous chapter introduced forecasting, the first stage of prospective analysis. In this and the following chapter we will describe the second and final stage of prospective analysis—valuation.

Valuation is the process of converting a forecast into an estimate of the value of a firm or some component of the firm. At some level, nearly every business decision involves valuation (at least implicitly). Within the firm, capital budgeting involves consideration of how a particular project would affect firm value. Strategic planning focuses on how value would be influenced by larger sets of actions. Outside the firm, security analysts conduct valuation to support their buy/sell decisions, and potential acquirers (often with the assistance of their investment bankers) estimate the value of target firms and the synergies they might offer. Valuation is necessary to price an initial public offering and to inform parties to sales, estate settlements, and divisions of property involving ongoing business concerns. Even credit analysts, who typically do not explicitly estimate firm value, must at least implicitly consider the value of the firm's equity "cushion" if they are to maintain a complete view of the risk associated with lending activity.

In practice, a wide variety of valuation approaches are employed. For example, in evaluating the fairness of a takeover bid, investment bankers commonly use five to ten different methods of valuation. Among the available methods are the following:

- *Discounted cash flow (DCF) analysis.* This approach involves the production of detailed, multiple-year forecasts of cash flows. The forecasts are discounted at an estimated cost of capital to arrive at an estimated present value.
- *Discounted abnormal earnings.* In principle, this approach is equivalent to DCF analysis, but it is more directly linked to accounting numbers. The approach expresses the value of the firm's equity as the sum of the book value and the discounted forecasts of abnormal earnings.

• *Valuation based on price multiples.* This family of approaches does not involve a detailed, multi-year forecast. Instead, a current measure of performance or single forecast of performance is converted into a price through application of some price multiple for other presumably comparable firms. For example, firm value can be estimated by applying a price-to-earnings ratio to a forecast of the firm's earnings for the coming year. Other commonly used multiples include price-to-book ratios and price-to-sales ratios.

Here we discuss valuation based on discounted cash flow analysis. The next chapter deals with accounting-based valuation techniques, including both discounted abnormal earnings valuation and valuation based on price multiples.

OVERVIEW OF DISCOUNTED CASH FLOW (DCF) ANALYSIS

It is well accepted among financial theorists that the value of the firm should be equal to the present value of future dividends. Thus, all valuation approaches should ultimately be consistent with this principle. DCF analysis is the most popular way of operationalizing this principle.[1] It focuses on discounting cash flows from operations after investment in working capital, less capital expenditures.

Valuation based on DCF analysis can be structured in either of two ways:

• Forecast cash flows available to *equity holders,* and then discount the expected cash flows at the cost of equity capital. The result is an estimated value of equity.
• Forecast cash flows available to *all providers of capital* (debt and equity), and then discount the expected cash flows at the weighted average cost of (debt and equity) capital. Under this approach, one arrives at an estimated value of the firm, which must be reduced by the value of debt to arrive at an equity value.

The second approach is more widely used in practice because it does not require explicit forecasts of changes in debt balances. (A good forecast, however, would be grounded in an understanding of these changes as well as all other key elements of the firm's financial picture.) Based on its widespread use in practice, we will describe the second approach to DCF analysis. It involves the following steps:

Step 1: Forecast free cash flows available to debt and equity holders over a finite forecast horizon (usually 5 to 10 years). The final year of the horizon is called the "terminal year."

Step 2: Forecast free cash flows beyond the terminal year, based on some simplifying assumption.

Step 3: Discount free cash flows at the weighted average cost of capital (WACC)—that is, the required return on the combination of debt and equity capital. The discounted amount represents the estimated value of free cash flows available to debt and equity holders as a group.

Step 4: To arrive at the estimated value of equity, subtract from the discounted free cash flows the estimated current market value of debt. If there are non-operating assets held by the firm that have been ignored in the previous cash flow forecasts (e.g., marketable securities or real estate held for sale), then add their value.

Below, we illustrate the four steps as we convert an analyst's long-range forecasts for Compaq into an estimate of the firm's value at the end of 1993. The long-range forecasts are those of the same Duff & Phelps analyst whose year-ahead forecast was examined in Chapter 5. Thus, the valuation serves as an illustration of how the analyst could determine whether his specific forecasts imply a price for Compaq that is higher or lower than the existing market price at the time.

For purposes of applying DCF valuation techniques, Compaq represents a special case in that it has no debt at the end of 1993. Thus, our calculations will be the same, whether we compute the value of debt and equity (based on cash flows *before* debt service, discounted at the weighted average cost of capital) or compute the value of equity directly (based on discounted cash flows *after* debt service, discounted at the cost of equity capital). However, our discussion will include guidance on how to value firms with debt.

STEP 1 OF DCF: FORECAST FREE CASH FLOWS

Under DCF analysis, free cash flows are defined as cash flows from operations after investment in working capital, less capital expenditures. Since the DCF approach described here calls for cash flows available to *all* providers of capital—holders of short-term debt,[2] long-term debt, and equity—cash from operations should be expressed on a *pre-interest* but *post-tax* basis. That is, interest expense on debt should not be deducted in arriving at free cash flow, and amounts deducted for taxes should reflect what tax payments would be due if the firm had no interest deduction.[3]

Table 6-1 presents forecasts, as of December 1993, of free cash flows for Compaq Computer for 1994 through 2000. The forecasts are based largely on those of Duff & Phelps but include some augmentations and adjustments.[4] In Table 5-4 we calculated free cash flows for 1994; but Table 6-1 presents data for several additional years as well.

There are a number of factors an analyst would have to consider carefully in producing long-range forecasts like those in Table 6-1. They are included in many of the questions raised in our discussion of business strategy analysis and financial analysis. For example, the analyst must ask:

- To what extent is Compaq's currently above-normal profit margin dependent on its brand name, and how long can the associated price premium be sustained? Can a brand name established when Compaq focused on a product differentiation strategy command a substantial price premium now that the company is shifting toward producing computers more like the industry standard? How well insulated is the competitive advantage of all vendors of personal computers from the power of two key suppliers, Microsoft (producer of software) and Intel (producer of processors)?

Table 6-1 Analyst Forecast of Compaq Earnings, Cash Flows, and Balance Sheets: 1994–2000

(all amounts other than ratios in millions of dollars)

	1993	1994F	1995F	1996F	1997F	1998F	1999F	2000F
Sales	$7,191	$8,712	$10,454	$12,023	$13,225	$14,547	$16,002	$17,601
Net earnings	$462	$517	$565	$609	$628	$639	$702	$773
Earnings before noncash expenses	$580	$762	$848	$922	$970	$949	$1044	$1148
Investment in working capital and other adjustments	(340)	(19)	(293)	(264)	(206)	(215)	(237)	(260)
Cash from operations	$240	$743	$555	$658	$764	$734	$807	$888
Capital expenditures	(145)	(218)	(261)	(301)	(331)	(364)	(400)	(441)
Free cash flows	$95	$525	$294	$357	$433	$370	$407	$448
Key forecast drivers and other statistics:								
Sales growth rate	75.3%	21.2%	20.0%	15.0%	10.0%	10.0%	10.0%	10.0%
Gross margin percentage	23.6%	22.2%	21.5%	21.0%	20.5%	20.0%	20.0%	20.0%
R&D expense/Sales	2.4%	2.5%	2.5%	2.5%	2.5%	2.5%	2.5%	2.5%
SG&A expense/Sales	11.6%	11.4%	11.3%	11.2%	11.1%	11.1%	11.1%	11.1%
Net profit margin	6.4%	5.9%	5.4%	5.1%	4.7%	4.4%	4.4%	4.4%
Cash/Sales	8.7%	7.8%	6.5%	5.6%	5.1%	4.7%	4.2%	3.8%
Receivables/Sales	19.1%	17.2%	17.2%	17.2%	17.2%	17.2%	17.2%	17.2%
Inventory/Sales	15.6%	14.2%	14.4%	14.4%	14.5%	14.5%	14.5%	14.5%
Current assets/Sales	45.8%	41.0%	39.9%	39.1%	38.7%	38.2%	37.8%	37.4%
Net plant/Sales	10.8%	9.2%	7.9%	7.1%	6.6%	6.6%	6.6%	6.6%
Current liabilities/Sales	17.3%	17.6%	17.6%	17.6%	17.6%	17.6%	17.6%	17.6%
Sales turnover	1.990	2.054	2.220	2.267	2.279	2.313	2.336	2.357
Leverage	1.551	1.600	1.693	1.743	1.777	1.798	1.812	1.825
Return on average equity	0.198	0.195	0.203	0.200	0.192	0.183	0.186	0.189
Return on beginning equity	0.230	0.195	0.214	0.209	0.198	0.190	0.193	0.197
Total assets	$4,084	$4,398	$5,019	$5,586	$6,022	$6,556	$7,144	$7,791
Shareholders' equity	$2,654	$2,646	$2,917	$3,169	$3,364	$3,633	$3,928	$4,253

Forecasts of earnings and balance sheet details for 1994–1997 are based on Company Analysis: Compaq Computer Corporation, Duff & Phelps Investment Research Company (Chicago, Illinois). December 1993. Forecasts for 1998–1999 are based on Duff & Phelps forecasts of 20% gross margin beyond 1997, an assumed constant ratio of sales to expenses other than cost of sales, and maintenance of 1997 sales growth rate. Balances of cash and shareholders' equity as forecast by Duff & Phelps have been reduced to reflect distribution of all free cash flow beginning in 1994, and a $50 adjustment for the difference between actual 1993 earnings and amounts expected by Duff & Phelps at the time forecasts were prepared. However, cash balances of at least 3.8% of sales are assumed necessary to support operations.

- To what extent is Compaq's above-normal profit margin a function of cost advantages? Can these advantages be sustained? If Compaq's vertically integrated manufacturing is an advantage, how quickly could it be mimicked? Compaq also enjoys an agreement with IBM that exempts them from royalty patents, giving them a 2 to 3 percent cost advantage over most competitors—but that advantage lasts only until the late 1990s and, of course, gives Compaq no advantage over IBM itself.
- How much longer can Compaq's sales grow at above-industry rates? How much more market share can be garnered through Compaq's shift to cost leadership and more competitively priced products? Where does Compaq stand in the life cycle of its major products? What are the opportunities for expansion into markets beyond those where Compaq is already a leader (U.S., Canada, and Europe)?

Taking these and other considerations into account, Duff & Phelps forecasts that sales growth will decline from 25 percent in 1994 to 20 percent in 1995, and that Compaq will ultimately grow at a pace more in keeping with the industry. Compaq's strategy and the forces of competition are expected to drive gross margin down to 20 percent by 1998, similar to IBM's current gross margin on PCs. The declining gross margin leaves a forecast of net margin that falls to 4.4 percent by 1998.

Most balance sheet accounts are forecast to grow proportionately with sales. One exception is net plant; Compaq is forecast to utilize plant more efficiently, perhaps because of the ongoing improvements in their production operations and the excess capacity they had in 1993.[5] We also assume cash balances will decline as a fraction of sales, relative to the cash-rich position held at the end of 1993. (This implies initiation of dividends in 1994.[6]) The combination of the above effects—declining margins and increased asset utilization—produces an ROE that remains high (about 19 percent) by current industry norms, and probably higher than the cost of equity capital. Thus, one would expect Compaq might have difficulty extrapolating that rate of return over an even larger investment base, moving beyond 2000.

Table 6-1 includes not only sales and earnings forecasts, but also cash flow forecasts. Recall that the free cash flows needed for our DCF valuation are those available to equity *and* debt holders; normally it would be necessary to adjust cash flows so that they are forecast on a before-interest basis (net of associated tax benefit). In Compaq's case, there is no debt, so adding back interest expense is not required. Compaq does report an expense it labels as interest, but its unusual nature makes it more practical to treat it here like an operating expense and forecast cash flows after this expense.[7]

STEP 2 OF DCF: FORECAST CASH FLOWS BEYOND THE "TERMINAL YEAR"

The forecasts in Table 6-1 extend only through the year 2000, and thus 2000 is the "terminal year." (Selection of an appropriate terminal year is discussed later.) Since the value of the firm depends on cash flows over the remainder of Compaq's life, the analyst must adopt some assumption that simplifies the process of forecasting cash flows beyond the year 2000.

The Competitive Equilibrium Assumption

Duff & Phelps projects that by the year 2000, Compaq's sales, earnings, and cash flows from operations will all be growing at an annual rate of 10 percent. What should we assume beyond 2000? Can we assume a continuation of the 10 percent growth rate or is some other pattern more reasonable?

Clearly a continuation of a 10 percent sales growth rate is unrealistic over a very long horizon. That rate would likely outstrip inflation in the dollar and the real growth rate of the world economy. Over many years, it would imply that Compaq would grow to a size greater than that of all other firms in the world combined. But what would be a suitable alternative assumption? Should we expect the firm's sales growth rate to ultimately settle down to the rate of inflation? To a higher rate, the nominal growth rate in GNP? Or to some other rate?

Ultimately, the answers to such questions depend on the kinds of long-range considerations raised earlier. One must consider how much longer the rate of growth in industry sales can outstrip the general growth in the world economy, and how long Compaq's competitive advantages can enable it to grow faster than the overall industry. Clearly, looking seven or more years into the future, any forecasts of sales growth rates are likely to be subject to considerable error.

Fortunately, in many if not most situations, how we deal with the seemingly imponderable questions about long-range growth in sales simply *does not matter very much!* In fact, under plausible economic assumptions, there is no practical need to consider sales growth beyond the terminal year. Such growth may be *irrelevant* so far as the firm's current value is concerned.

How can long-range growth in sales *not* matter? The reasoning revolves around the forces of competition. Competition tends to constrain firms' ability to identify, on a consistent basis, growth opportunities that generate super-normal profits. (Recall the evidence in Chapter 5 concerning the reversion of ROEs to normal levels over horizons of five to ten years.) Certainly, a firm may at a point in time maintain a competitive advantage that permits it to achieve returns in excess of the cost of capital. When that advantage is protected with patents or a strong brand name, the firm may even be able to maintain it for many years—perhaps indefinitely. With hindsight, we know that some such firms—like Coca Cola and Wal-Mart—were able not only to maintain their competitive edge, but to expand it across dramatically increasing investment bases. But in the face of competition, one would typically not expect a firm to continue to extend its supernormal profitability to new, *additional* projects *year after year.* Ultimately, we would expect high profits to attract enough competition to drive the firm's return down to a normal level. Each new project would generate cash flows with a present value no greater than the cost of the investment—the investment would be a "zero net present value" project. Since the benefits of the project are offset by its costs, it does nothing to enhance the current value of the firm, and the associated growth can be ignored.

The appendix to this chapter presents a simple illustration to clarify the point. In the appendix, we consider a wide range of growth in sales for the year 2001: from no growth at all to $3 billion of additional sales. The amount of investment needed to support an additional $1.00 of sales is assumed to be $0.242, which holds the ratio of operating assets to sales constant at the year 2000 levels. We also assume that the impact of *incremental* sales on earnings is 3.15 percent of sales. Under these assumptions, and using a cost of capital of 13 percent (discussed later), the appendix shows that the additional sales—whether zero, $1 billion, or $3 billion—do *nothing* to enhance the current value of the firm.

The key assumption is that the incremental profit margin is 3.15 percent of the sales increase. Under that assumption, $1.00 of additional sales yields $.0315 of additional annual cash flow—just enough to cover the required 13 percent return on the investment of $0.242 in net working capital, plant, and other assets needed to support the higher sales level. The benefit of the added cash inflow is thus equal to its cost, and the incremental value of the added sales is zero.

The assumption about incremental profits is not arbitrary but based on the notion that over the long run, competitive forces drive incremental margins to the point of incremental costs. Margins any higher than this attract competition that forces the margins down. Margins below this level drive investment away until the margins recover.

Note that if we ignore sales increases beyond 2000, we are *not* assuming that Compaq's abnormal profitability will be driven away completely. In fact, if we treat sales and earnings as if they will remain constant after 2000, we are treating Compaq as if it will preserve its higher-than-normal margin on its year-2000 sales base *forever.* Another way to say this is that we assume the abnormally high year-2000 ROE (19 percent) is maintained on the equity base that exists in 2000, but that the incremental return on any added equity will be equal to the cost of capital, so that the aggregate ROE will fall slowly from 19 percent toward the cost of capital.

DCF valuation does not *require* this "competitive equilibrium assumption." If the analyst expects that supernormal margins can be extended to new markets for many years, it can be accommodated within the context of a DCF analysis. At a minimum, as we will discuss later, the analyst may expect that supernormal margins can be maintained on markets that grow at the rate of inflation. However, the important lesson here is that the rate of growth in sales beyond the forecast horizon is not a relevant consideration *unless* the analyst believes that the growth can be achieved while generating supernormal incremental margins—competition may make that a difficult trick to pull off.

Terminal Value As If There Is No Sales Growth Beyond Terminal Year

If we invoke the competitive equilibrium assumption as of the year 2001, then it does not matter what sales growth rate we use beyond that year, and we may as well simplify our arithmetic by treating sales as if they will be constant at the year 2000 level. Earnings will remain at \$773 million; free cash flow will also be \$773 million per year[8]:

Earnings (for firms with debt, add back interest, net of tax)	\$773
Deferred taxes (balance sheet account remains constant)	0
Depreciation (\$369), less capital expenditures (\$369)	0
Investment in incremental working capital (balances constant)	0
Free cash flow	\$773

Since the cash flows are constant beginning in 2001, it is simple to discount those flows. Again assuming a discount rate of 13 percent, the present value of the cash flows for the years beyond 2000 is thus equal to the 2001 flow of \$773 million, divided by .13:

$$\text{Present value of cash flows beyond 2000} \quad = \quad \frac{\$773}{.13} \quad = \quad \$5{,}943$$

This represents the value of the cash flows as of the end of the year 2000. The value as of the end of 1993 would be obtained by discounting \$5,943 million for seven years:

$$\text{Present value of cash flows beyond 2000, as of 1993} \quad = \quad \frac{\$5{,}943}{(1.13)^7} \quad = \quad \$2{,}526$$

The amount \$2,526 million is the so-called "terminal value" of the firm. It represents a large fraction of the total value of the firm, as we will see shortly.

Terminal Value Based on a Price Multiple

An alternative approach to terminal value calculation is to apply a multiple to cash flows or earnings in the terminal period. In its most simple form, the analyst simply capitalizes earnings (before interest, less adjusted taxes) by a "normal" PE ratio.

The approach is not so ad hoc as it might at first appear. Note that under the assumption of no sales growth, cash flows beyond 2000 remain constant and equal to earnings. Capitalizing this cash flow in perpetuity by dividing by the cost of capital (.13) is equivalent to multiplying earnings by a PE of 7.7. Thus, applying a multiple in this range is similar to discounting all free cash flows beyond 2000, while invoking the competitive equilibrium assumption.

The mistake to avoid here is to capitalize the future earnings or cash flows using a multiple that is too high. The PE multiple might be high currently because the market anticipates much abnormally profitable growth. However, once that growth is realized, the PE multiple should fall to a normal level. It is that normal PE, applicable to a stable firm or one that can grow only through zero net present value projects, that should be used in the terminal value calculation. Thus, multiples in the range of 7 to 10—close to the reciprocal of the WACC—should be used here.[9] Higher multiples are justifiable only when the terminal year is closer and there are still abnormally profitable growth opportunities beyond that point.

Allowing for Growth Beyond the Terminal Year, and Dealing with Long-Run Inflation

The approaches described above each appeal in some way to the "competitive equilibrium assumption." However, there are circumstances where the analyst is willing to assume that the firm may defy competitive forces and earn abnormal rates of return on new projects for many years. In the case of Compaq, we could ask whether its current competitive advantage is protected by barriers that will allow it to extend its supernormal profitability well beyond its current market, and even into the 21st century. Note that some of the advantages mentioned earlier—for example, the unique exemptions from royalty payments to IBM—will definitely dissipate within a decade, on not only incremental sales but also the existing sales base. Compaq's vertically integrated approach to manufacturing, if it does involve advantages, could be mimicked by others, given enough time. What about Compaq's other advantages, including its brand name? Does it offer any competitive edge as Compaq extends its sales well beyond the current base and into new markets?

If the analyst believes supernormal profitability can be extended to larger markets for many years, one possibility is to project earnings and cash flows over a longer horizon, until the competitive equilibrium assumption can reasonably be invoked.

Another possibility is to project growth in cash flows at some constant rate. Consider the following. By treating Compaq as if its competitive advantage can be maintained only on the *nominal* sales level achieved in the year 2000, we were assuming that in *real* terms its competitive advantage would shrink. Let's say that the analyst expects Compaq can maintain its advantage (through supplies of new and more advanced products to a similar customer base) on a sales base that remains constant in real terms—that grows beyond the year 2000 at the expected long-run inflation rate of 3.5 percent. The computations implied by these assumptions are described below. The approach is more aggressive than the one described earlier, but it may be more realistic. After all, there is no obvious reason why the *real* size of the investment base on which Compaq earns abnormal returns during the twenty-first century should depend on inflation rates.

The approach just described still relies to some extent on the competitive equilibrium assumption. The assumption is now invoked to suggest that supernormal profitability can be extended only to an investment base that remains constant in real terms. However, there is nothing about the DCF method that requires any reliance on the competitive equilibrium assumption. The calculations described below could be used with *any* rate of growth in sales. The question is not whether the arithmetic is available to handle such an approach, but rather how realistic it is.

Let's stay with the approach that assumes Compaq will extend its supernormal margins to sales that grow beyond 2000 at the rate of inflation. How would free cash flows beyond 2000 behave? There are two incorrect approaches that are easy to fall into at this point. One might think that since free cash flows in the year 2001 were $773 million under our no-growth assumption, they would simply grow from that point at a 3.5 percent rate under our new assumptions. Alternatively, one might note that free cash flows in the year 2000 were $448 million (see Table 6-1), and then apply a 3.5 percent growth factor to that amount. Both approaches are wrong: the first one overstates value and the second one understates it. They ignore the fact that 3.5 percent growth in *sales* does not necessarily imply 3.5 percent growth in *cash flows*. The latter is heavily influenced by changes in amounts invested in net working capital and plant, and those shift dramatically when sales growth rates change.

Table 6-2 correctly projects free cash flows for the years 2000 through 2003, assuming that sales increase by 3.5 percent in 2001 and beyond, and that profit margins, asset turnover, and leverage remain constant. Note that in 2001, earnings increase at the same rate as sales: by 3.5 percent. In contrast, free cash flows jump 45 percent! Why? Because free cash flows reflect not just the firm's earnings experience, but also the amount invested to support growth. As the firm's growth slows from 10 percent in 2000 to 3.5 percent in 2001, the cash required to support working capital growth is slashed (by more

Table 6-2 Forecast of Free Cash Flows Beyond 2000, with 3.5 Percent Sales Growth and Constant Profit Margins

	Forecast for terminal year	Forecast beyond terminal year *as if sales growth only keeps pace with inflation*		
	2000	2001	2002	2003
Sales growth	10.0%	3.5%	3.5%	3.5%
Profit margin	4.4%	4.4%	4.4%	4.4%
Earnings (for firm with debt, add back interest, net of tax:	$773	$800	$828	$857
Earnings growth	10.0%	3.5%	3.5%	3.5%
Earnings before depreciation and deferred taxes	$1,148	$1,184	$1,225	$1,268
Investment in net working capital[a]	(260)	(122)	(126)	(131)
Capital expenditures[b]	(441)	(409)	(424)	(438)
Free cash flow	$448	$651	$674	$697
Free cash flow growth	10.0%	45.0%	3.5%	3.5%

Present value of free cash flows in 2001 and beyond:

$$\text{Present value in 2000} = \frac{\text{2001 free cash flow}}{(\text{cost of capital} - \text{growth rate})} = \frac{\$651}{(.13 - .035)} = \$6,850$$

$$\text{Present value in 1993} = \frac{\$6,850}{(1.13)^7} = \$2,912$$

a. Net working capital accounts (including cash balances needed to support operations) are maintained at the same ratio to sales as in 1988 (19.8 percent) through 2000 (see Table 6-1).
b. Capital expenditures are amounts necessary to maintain net plant at 6.6 percent of sales. Depreciation is projected at 31.9 percent of beginning net plant.

than half), and capital expenditures fall as well (by about 7 percent). The upshot is a free cash flow growth rate that is much higher than the earnings growth rate in that year. However, beyond 2001, as the sales growth rate remains constant, the growth in earnings and working capital remains constant, and therefore the growth in free cash flows also remains constant, at 3.5 percent.

Since the rate of cash flow growth is constant beginning in 2001, it is simple to discount those flows. For a given discount rate r, any cash flow stream growing at the constant rate g can be discounted by dividing the cash flows in the first year by the amount $(r - g)$. Once again assuming a discount rate of 13 percent and our cash flow growth rate of 3.5 percent, the present value of the cash flows for the years beyond 2000 is as follows:

$$\text{Present value of cash flows beyond 2000} = \frac{\$651}{(.13 - .035)} = \$6,850$$

This is the present value as of the end of the year 2000; when we discount that amount to the end of 1993, we obtain $2,912 (see Table 6-2). This represents our terminal value estimate under the new set of assumptions. It is about $400 million higher than our terminal value estimate based on no growth in abnormal profitability.

Selecting the Terminal Year

A question begged by the above discussion is how long the forecast horizon should be. When the competitive equilibrium assumption is used, the answer is whatever time is required for the firm's returns on incremental investment projects to reach that equilibrium—an issue that turns on the sustainability of the firm's competitive advantage. As indicated in Chapter 5, the historical evidence indicates that most firms in the U.S. should expect ROEs to revert to normal levels within five to ten years. But for the typical firm, we can justify ending the forecast horizon even earlier—note that the return on *incremental* investment can be normal even while the return on *total* investment (and therefore ROE) remains abnormal. Thus, a five- to ten-year forecast horizon should be more than sufficient for most firms. Exceptions would include firms so well insulated from competition (perhaps due to the power of a brand name) that they can extend their investment base across new markets for many years and still expect to generate supernormal returns. In 1995 the Wrigley Company, producer of chewing gum that is still extending its brand name to untapped markets in other nations, appears to be such a firm.

In the case of Compaq, the terminal year used is seven years beyond the current one. Table 6-1 shows that the return on capital (in this case, ROE) is forecast to decline only gradually over these seven years, from the unusually high 20 percent in 1993 to a level that holds steady at 18 to 19 percent by the late 1990s. If profit margins could be maintained at the projected 4.4 percent on ever-increasing sales, this high ROE could be achieved even on new investment in 2001 and beyond. However, even a slight decline in the margin—in the initial year, to about 4.3 percent—would, in the face of continued 10 percent sales growth, be enough to render the return on the *incremental* investment no higher than the cost of capital. Thus, the performance we have already projected for the terminal year 2000 is not far removed from a competitive equilibrium, and extending the forecast horizon by a few more years would have little impact on the calculated value. Even if we project continuation of the 4.4 percent margin through 2003 with 10 percent annual sales increases (and with the competitive equilibrium assumption invoked thereafter), the final estimated firm value would increase by only about 5 percent. Large changes in our value estimate would arise only if the analyst is willing to assume abnormal rates of return on investments well into the twenty-first century—and in light of our analysis of industry conditions, such an assumption would be tenuous indeed. The upshot is that an analyst could argue that the terminal year used here for Compaq should be extended from the seventh year to, say, the tenth year or even a few years beyond that point, depending on the perceived sustainability of its competitive advantage. However, because we are already assuming Compaq is close to a competitive equilibrium in the year 2000, the final value estimate would not be particularly sensitive to this change.

STEP 3 OF DCF: DISCOUNT EXPECTED FREE CASH FLOWS

Table 6-3 illustrates how the projected cash flows from the previous tables should be discounted to the present, using a range of weighted average costs of capital from 11 to 15 percent. The terminal value used in Table 6-3 is the one that assumes Compaq can maintain its abnormal rate of return forever on the sales volume achieved in the terminal

Table 6-3 Valuation of Compaq Based on Discounted Free Cash Flows, December 1993

		1994	1995	1996	1997	1998	1999	2000	beyond 2000
		(dollar amounts in millions)							
Free cash flow		$525	$294	$357	$433	$370	$407	$448	$773*
Discount factor, at 13%		1.13	1.28	1.44	1.63	1.84	2.08	2.35	
Discounted free cash flow		$465	$230	$247	$266	$201	$195	$190	$2,526*
Sum of discounted free cash flows, at 13%	$4,320								
Discounted value at 11%	$5,293								
Discounted value at 12%	$4,763								
Discounted value at 14%	$3,946								
Discounted value at 15%	$3,625								

> The present value calculations treat all cash flows as if they occur at the end of the year. To assume that, on average, cash flows occur half way through the year, multiply the discounted value by $(1 + r/2)$, where r is the discount rate. When $r = 13\%$, the discounted value would be adjusted from $4,320 to $4,600.

*Terminal value calculation: When sales are treated as if they will not grow beyond 2000 while margins stay constant, cash flows rise to $773 in 2001 and remain at that level (see text). The present value of the $773 in perpetuity is $5,943 ($773/.13) at the end of 2000, and $2,526 ($5,943 / (1.13)^7) at the end of 1993.

If we allow for growth in sales beyond 2000 at the rate of expected inflation (3.5 percent), the terminal value based on a 13 percent discount rate rises to $2,912 (see Table 6-2). Estimated firm value rises to $4,706 and, when adjusted to reflect the arrival of cash flows halfway through the year, becomes $5,012.

year 2000, but not on any sales growth beyond that point. We will also discuss value estimates that allow for long-range growth in sales at the rate of inflation.

Computing a Discount Rate

Thus far, the discount rates used have been offered without explanation. How would they be estimated by the analyst?

Since Compaq is debt-free, there is no distinction between the cost of equity capital and the weighted average cost of capital (WACC). However, in general, the proper discount rate to use here is the WACC, because we are discounting cash flows available to both debt and equity holders. The WACC is calculated by weighting the costs of debt and equity capital according to their respective market values:.

$$\text{WACC} = \frac{V_D}{V_D + V_E} \times r_D(1 - T) + \frac{V_E}{V_D + V_E} \times r_E$$

where V_D = the market value of debt; V_E = the market value of equity

r_D = the cost of debt capital; r_E = the cost of equity capital

T = the tax rate reflecting the marginal tax benefit of interest

WEIGHTING THE COSTS OF DEBT AND EQUITY.   The weights assigned to debt and equity represent their respective fractions of total capital provided, measured in terms of market values. Computing a market value for debt should not be difficult. It is reasonable to use book values if interest rates have not changed significantly since the time the debt was issued. Otherwise, the value of the debt can be estimated by discounting the future payouts at current market rates of interest applicable to the firm.

What is included in debt? Should short-term as well as long-term debt be included? Should payables and accruals be included? The answer is revealed by considering how we calculated free cash flows. Those free cash flows are the returns to the providers of the capital to which the WACC applies. The cash flows are those available *before* servicing short-term and long-term debt, which indicates that both short-term and long-term debt should be considered a part of capital when computing the WACC. Servicing of other liabilities, such as accounts payable or accruals, should already have been considered when computing free cash flows. Thus, internal consistency requires that operating liabilities not be considered a part of capital when computing the WACC.

The tricky problem we face is assigning a market value to equity. That is the very amount we are trying to estimate in the first place! How can the analyst possibly assign a market value to equity at this intermediate stage, given that the estimate will not be known until all steps in the DCF analysis are completed?

One common approach to the problem is to insert "target" ratios of debt to capital $[V_D/(V_D + V_E)]$ and equity to capital $[V_E/(V_D + V_E)]$ at this point. For example, one might expect that a firm will, over the long run, maintain a capital structure that is 40 percent debt and 60 percent equity. The long-run focus is reasonable, because we are discounting cash flows over a long horizon.

Another way around the problem is to use some reasonable guess for the value of equity at this stage—perhaps based on some multiple of next year's earnings forecast. The guess can be used as a weight for purposes of calculating an initial estimate of the WACC, which in turn can be used in the discounting process to generate an initial estimate of the value of equity. That initial estimate can then be used in place of the guess to arrive at a new WACC, and a second estimate of the value of equity can be produced. This process can be repeated until the value used to calculate the WACC and the final estimated value converge.

ESTIMATING THE COST OF DEBT.   The cost of debt (r_D) should be based on current market rates of interest. For privately-held debt, such rates are not quoted, but stated interest rates may provide a suitable substitute if interest rates have not changed much since the debt was issued. The cost of debt should be expressed on a net-of-tax basis, because it is after-tax cash flows that are being discounted. In most settings, the market rate of interest can be converted to a net-of-tax basis by multiplying by one minus the marginal corporate tax rate.

ESTIMATING THE COST OF EQUITY.   Estimating the cost of equity (r_E) can be difficult, and a full discussion of the topic lies beyond the scope of this chapter. At any rate, even an extended discussion would not supply answers to all the questions that might be raised in this area, because the field of finance is in a state of flux over what constitutes an appropriate measure of the cost of equity.

One possibility is to use the capital asset pricing model (CAPM), which expresses the cost of equity as the sum of a required return on riskless assets, plus a premium for systematic risk:

$$r_E \;=\; r_F \;+\; \beta \,[\,E\,(r_M) \;-\; r_F\,]$$

where r_F is the riskless rate;

[$E[r_M] - r_F$] is the risk premium expected for the market as a whole, expressed as the excess of the expected return on the market index over the riskless rate;

and β is the systematic risk of the equity.

To compute r_E, one must estimate three parameters: the riskless rate r_F; the market risk premium [$E(r_M) - r_F$], and systematic risk, β. For r_F, analysts often use the rate on intermediate-term Treasury bonds, based on the observation that it is cash flows beyond the short term that are being discounted.[10] When r_F is measured in that way, then average common stock returns (based on the returns to Standard and Poor's 500 index) have exceeded that rate by 7.6 percent over the 1926–1993 period.[11] This excess return constitutes an estimate of the market risk premium [$E(r_M) - r_F$]. Finally, systematic risk (β) reflects the sensitivity of the firm's value to economy-wide market movements. Historically, Compaq's stock price has changed 1.2 percent for each 1 percent change in the market index, indicating that Compaq's β is approximately 1.2.[12] Putting these estimates together and noting that in late 1993 rates on ten-year U.S. government bonds were 5.8 percent, we estimate that Compaq's cost of equity capital is about 15 percent:

$$r_E = r_F + \beta [E(r_M) - r_F] = .058 + 1.20[.076] = .149$$

Although the above CAPM is often used to estimate the cost of capital, the evidence indicates that the model is incomplete. Assuming stocks are priced competitively, stock returns should be expected just to compensate investors for the cost of their capital. Thus, long-run average returns should be close to the cost of capital and should (according to the CAPM) vary across stocks according to their systematic risk. However, factors beyond only systematic risk seem to play some role in explaining variation in long-run average returns. The most important such factor is labeled the "size effect": smaller firms (as measured by market capitalization) tend to generate higher returns in subsequent periods. Why this is so is unclear. It could either indicate that smaller firms are riskier than indicated by the CAPM, or that they are underpriced at the point their market capitalization is measured, or some combination of both. Average stock returns for U.S. firms (including NYSE, AMEX, and NASDAQ firms) varied across size deciles from 1926–1993, as shown in Table 6-4.

In the case of Compaq, we have a firm that is large. Based on any reasonable multiple of earnings, Compaq's market value would lie in either the largest or next-largest decile

Table 6-4 Stock Returns and Firm Size

Size decile	Market value of largest company in decile, in 1993 (millions of dollars)	Average annual stock return, 1926–1993	Fraction of total NYSE value represented by decile (in 1993)
1–smallest	$ 60.3	22.3%	0.1%
2	146.3	18.2	0.4
3	253.5	17.1	0.9
4	406.0	16.2	1.4
5	612.3	15.7	2.1
6	1,017.6	15.7	3.4
7	1,537.5	14.7	5.0
8	2,812.7	14.1	8.5
9	5,311.2	13.3	16.1
10–largest	81,891.3	11.2	62.0

Source: Ibbotson Associates (1994).

of the distribution above. On that basis alone, one might expect that equity holders would be satisfied with a return on equity that is relatively low. The table indicates that historically, investors in firms in the top two deciles of the size distribution have realized returns of only 11.2 to 13.3 percent. If we place Compaq close to the breakpoint between the top two deciles, based on reasonable estimates of its size, then the value-weighted average of the two deciles' returns, 11.6 percent, would be the best indicator of Compaq's cost of capital. Note, however, that if we use firm size as an indicator of the cost of capital, we are implicitly assuming that large size is indicative of lower risk. Yet finance theorists have not developed a well-accepted explanation for why that should be the case.

One method for combining the cost of capital estimates is based on the CAPM and the "size effect."[13] The approach calls for adjustment of the CAPM-based cost of capital, based on the difference between the average return on the market index used in the CAPM (Standard and Poor's 500) and the average return on firms of the size comparable to the firm being evaluated. Thus, since firms of Compaq's size have, on average, earned returns of 11.6 percent, or 0.7 percent less than the 12.3 percent return on the market index, we would adjust the cost of capital downward by the difference. Our resulting cost of capital estimate is about 14 percent:

$$r_E = r_F + \beta[E(r_M) - r_F] + r_{size} = (.058 + 1.2[.076] - .007) = .142$$

In light of the continuing debate on how to measure the cost of capital, it is not surprising that managers and analysts often consider a range of estimates. We will present estimates based on costs of capital from 11 to 15 percent, which bracket the estimates based on size alone and those based on either CAPM or the combined CAPM and size model. The 13 percent amount used thus far in our discussion lies between these estimates. However, we will also refer in our discussion to computations based on 14 percent, which comes closest to the estimate based on the CAPM adjusted for the size effect.

The Discounted Amount

In Table 6-3, we discounted Compaq's projected cash flows using the previously discussed range of cost of capital estimates. Since there is no debt, the weighted average cost of capital is equal to the cost of equity capital.

Table 6-3 indicates that, based on a cost of capital of 13 percent, we estimate Compaq's value at about $4.3 billion. If we allow for abnormally profitable growth in sales beyond the year 2000 at the rate of inflation, the estimate rises to $4.7 billion. Using a cost of capital of 14 percent would of course produce lower estimates ($3.9 billion and $4.2 billion, respectively). Note that Compaq's terminal value always represents a large fraction of the total discounted cash flows. It is not unusual for the terminal value to be so important. Since the terminal value estimate is hinged on the long-run earnings forecast, the latter thus becomes key to a good valuation.

That the terminal value is so large can leave an analyst feeling quite uncomfortable about a DCF-based estimate. After all, most of the value of Compaq is being attributed to cash flows that won't be realized until at least seven years go by—and few analysts would feel confident about forecasts that far into the future. Unfortunately for our nerves, that's just the way the world is. Growing companies chew up cash in the near term, and most of their value is derived from cash flows well out in the horizon. We can use simpler valuation techniques (such as the application of multiples to current earnings) that may not make this issue explicit, but those techniques don't make the underlying reality go away. Equity valuation is very much a game of projecting what earnings and cash flows will be years from now, and such projections are inherently uncertain. DCF valuation techniques can't eliminate that uncertainty, but they can produce estimates of value that are at least consistent with the best long-run projections the analyst can generate.

The primary calculations in Table 6-3 treat all cash flows as if they arrive at the end of the year. Of course, they are likely to arrive throughout the year. If we assume for the sake of simplicity that cash flows will arrive mid-year, then we should adjust our value estimates upward by the amount $1+r/2$, where r is the discount rate. For the case of a 13 percent discount rate, the value estimate rises from \$4,320 million to \$4,600 million. Using a 14 percent cost of capital would yield an adjusted estimate of approximately \$4,220 million. Comparable amounts that allow for growth in sales beyond 2000 at the rate of inflation are \$5,012 million (based on a 13 percent discount rate) and \$4,512 (using 14 percent).

STEP 4 OF DCF: CALCULATE THE VALUE OF EQUITY

In general, the present value calculated above is the value of both debt and equity. The final step in the calculation is to convert this amount to the value of equity by subtracting the market value of debt (short-term and long-term). Note that we do not subtract the value of other liabilities, such as accounts payable. Their influence on firm value has already been considered in the process of forecasting free cash flows.

If the firm maintains any nonoperating assets that will generate cash flows not considered in our forecasts, the value of those assets must be added at this stage. Common examples are marketable securities, land held for sale, and excess pension fund assets (to the extent the benefit of the latter has not already been reflected in earnings projections). Adjustments should also be made for the expected cost of any obligations not recorded on the balance sheet and not already considered in earnings projections. For example, if the firm faced a possible cost to repair environmental damage and that amount was not accrued in the accounts, such a cost should be considered here. On the other hand, unrecorded obligations on operating leases need not be considered here, assuming that the earnings projections already reflect expected rent payments on such leases.

In Compaq's case there is no debt, and no major unrecorded liabilities exist for which adjustments are needed. Also, Compaq has no major nonoperating assets, with the possible exception of its cash balance. Should the value of cash be added as an adjustment to our existing present value estimate? The answer depends on whether we have already considered the earnings generated by cash in our projections of future cash flows. Although we did not present the detailed breakdown of earnings in the Table 6-1 forecasts from Duff & Phelps, the forecast does include interest income from cash equivalents. (The amount in 1994 is $45 million.) In addition, since some cash balances are required simply to keep operations running, cash contributes to the generation of cash from operations. The value of cash is thus already embedded in our present value estimate, and to make a further adjustment now would constitute double-counting. An alternative approach would be to treat at least some portion of cash and cash equivalents as a nonoperating asset, exclude the interest income on that asset from the cash flow projections, and add its current value to the present value of the projected cash flows. However, since some cash is necessary just to maintain operations, only the "excess" cash should be a candidate for such treatment.

A final set of adjustments would be required in cases where the firm has potentially dilutive securities outstanding. The market value of options and warrants, as well as the market value of the conversion feature of convertible securities, should be deducted from firm value. Estimation of such amounts can be quite complex and lies outside the scope of this chapter. However, for many if not most firms, the amounts involved are relatively small. Compaq, like most firms, has employee stock options outstanding, but they represent claims to shares constituting only $2/10$ of one percent of the firm's outstanding stock. Their value would be an even smaller fraction of the *value* of outstanding shares, because there is a cost (the exercise price) associated with exercising the options.

To summarize, the value of equity (based on a 13 percent cost of capital and treating cash flows as if they arrive mid-year) is calculated as follows:

Value of free cash flows to debt and equity holders	$4,600
− Value of debt	0
+ Value of nonoperating assets	0
− Expected cost of unrecorded obligations	0
− Value of options, warrants, and conversion features	0
Value of currently outstanding equity	$4,600

The value of currently outstanding equity is divided by the number of outstanding shares to arrive at an estimated per-share value of the stock. Given our previous estimated equity value of $4.6 billion for Compaq and their 84.3 million shares outstanding, our estimate of the per-share value is $54. The indicated per-share value falls to $50 on the basis of a cost of capital of 14 percent.

Had we used the more aggressive terminal value assumptions presented in Table 6-2 —which allowed for abnormally profitable long-run growth in sales at the rate of inflation and are probably more realistic—our per-share estimate based on a 13 percent cost of capital would have been $59. The price estimate would be $53, based on a 14 percent cost of capital.

Taking a Look at the Estimate

The estimates are lower than the $74 market price at the time of the release of the forecasts on which we relied. There can be only two explanations. One is that the market is using a lower cost of capital. An 11 percent cost of capital with the more aggressive terminal value assumptions of Table 6-2 implies a per-share value of $76. However, this explanation is difficult to justify because it ignores any premium for systematic risk.

The other possibility is simply that the market was more optimistic than the Duff & Phelps analyst on whose forecasts we have built.[14] The Duff & Phelps forecasts for 1994 are close to those of the median of the 33 analysts who issued forecasts for Compaq during the last two months of 1993. However, there was divergence about that median, and during this period of quickly rising expectations (the price had been below $60 just two months earlier), the median could be outdated relative to the expectations of market agents "driving" the stock price. Some analysts were forecasting 1994 EPS at levels nearly 20 percent higher than Duff & Phelps' forecast. One of Compaq's lead analysts (at C.S. First Boston) issued an EPS forecast that was only 6 percent higher than Duff & Phelps for 1994 but at least 15–20 percent higher over the longer term.

In order to "justify" the price at which Compaq traded in late 1993, the most plausible scenarios would involve a combination of forecasts more optimistic than Duff & Phelps' and a cost of capital below 15 percent. (We return to this point in more detail in Chapter 8.)

With hindsight, we know that the optimists proved correct in this case, as Compaq's stock rose to over $100 during the months after our forecast. During this period it became clear that Compaq would likely overtake IBM as the market share leader in personal computers, while still maintaining strong profit margins. By March of 1994, consensus EPS forecasts for 1994 were 35 percent higher than reflected in our valuation.

SUMMARY AND CONCLUSIONS

Valuation is the process by which forecasts of performance are converted into estimates of price. A variety of valuation techniques are employed in practice, and there is no single method that clearly dominates others. In fact, since each technique involves different advantages and disadvantages, there are gains to considering several approaches simultaneously.

In this chapter, we discussed one of the most widely used valuation techniques—discounted cash flow analysis. The method involves forecasting future free cash flows over a finite horizon, discounting them at an estimated cost of capital, and adding an appropriate terminal value estimate to reflect the value of cash flows beyond the forecast horizon.

Discounted cash flow analysis is, in practice, typically grounded in forecasts of earnings and other accounting numbers. In the following chapter, we discuss methods of valuation that are based more directly on accounting forecasts.

APPENDIX

The Competitive Equilibrium Assumption: How can sales growth NOT affect current firm value?

A key step in DCF valuation is the invoking of the competitive equilibrium assumption. When we invoke that assumption beyond the final year of the forecast (the year 2000 in our Compaq example), any additional growth in sales is assumed to have no impact on the current value of the firm. How can this be?

In Table 6-A, we take the forecasts of Table 6-1 as a given. Those forecasts carry us through the year 2000. Then we consider four different sales projections for the year 2001, ranging from no increase to a $3 billion increase (17 percent growth). We assume that the ratio of net working capital, net plant, and other assets, minus deferred taxes, remains as it stood in 2000, at .242.[15] Thus, the incremental investment to support, say, a $3 billion sales increase is $3 billion × .242, or $726 million.

If sales rise, projected earnings should also rise. The key assumption in Table 6-A—and one we explain momentarily—is that the *increment* to earnings is equal to 3.15 percent of sales. When added to the existing profits, this produces an overall margin that is slightly lower at higher sales levels. For example, the margin is 4.4 percent if sales remain constant, but only 4.2 percent if sales rise by $3 billion to $20.6 billion.

Now we consider the impact of the various sales projections on the cash flows and estimated value of the firm. To focus attention for the time being on the impact of *only* the change in sales experienced in 2001, let's assume that sales beyond 2001 stay constant at the levels projected for that year. Then annual free cash flows beyond 2001 will also stay constant and equal to the earnings for 2001. Why? Consider the adjustments necessary to move from earnings to free cash flows. The adding back of depreciation is offset exactly by capital expenditures, as the firm's net plant balance will be held constant (because sales beyond 2001 are held constant). With no further change in the scale of the firm, the change in deferred taxes will be zero, as will be the investment in additional working capital. The upshot is a perpetuity of free cash flow equal to earnings. The implied annual cash flows for the various sales levels are shown in Table 6-A, and are compared with the cash flows ($773 million) in the base case of no growth in sales. For example, if sales grow by $3 billion, free cash flows are $94 million higher than the

Table 6-A Impact on Value of Different Sales Projections for 2001

Projected sales level in 2001:	$17,601	$18,601	$19,601	$20,601
Projected sales increase	0	1,000	2,000	3,000
Projected earnings, assuming incremental margin is 3.15 % of incremental sales	$773	$804	$836	$867
Project net profit margin	4.4%	4.3%	4.3%	4.2%
Implied annual free cash flow, holding sales constant at new level*	$773	$804	$836	$867
Incremental annual free cash flow due to sales increase (ignoring impact of initial investment)	0	31	63	94
Present value of perpetuity of incremental free cash flow at 13%	0	242	484	726
Cash flow impact of investment required to support higher sales	0	−242	−484	−726
Enhancement of current firm value caused by increase in sales (present value of cash flow, less investment)	$ 0	$ 0	$ 0	$ 0

*Beyond 2001, with sales and earnings held constant at the level achieved in 2001, earnings and free cash flows will be equal to each other (and equal to earnings of 2001), as explained in the text. In the year 2001, free cash flows for the four different sales levels will be as follows:

Earnings	$773	$ 804	$ 836	$ 867
+ Depreciation (.319 of beginning net plant)	369	369	369	369
+ Deferred tax change (.025 of sales change)	0	25	50	75
− Investment in net working capital and other assets (.201 of change in sales)	0	−201	−402	−605
− Capital expenditures (sufficient to bring net plant to 6.6 % of sales)	−369	−435	−501	−567
Free cash flow	$773	$ 562	$ 352	$ 141
Incremental free cash flow versus base case	$ 0	$−211	$−421	$−632

Note that the incremental free cash flows in 2001 reflect two impacts:

Incremental free cash flow due to additional profits caused by sales increase in 2001	$ 0	$ 31	$ 63	$ 94
Reduction in free cash flow due to added investment required in 2001	0	−242	−484	−726
	$ 0	$−211	$−421	$−632

In Table 6-A, the present value of the perpetuity of incremental free cash flow includes the effect in 2001 of the second-to-last row above. The next-to-last row is treated separately, as the impact of investment.

base case in all years beyond 2001. The same increment to cash flows is present in 2001 as well, although bottom-line free cash flows in that year will also reflect the cost of investment needed to generate the higher sales levels. (See notes to Table 6-A). The upshot in the case of the $3 billion sales increase is that $726 million of cash investment generates a perpetuity of $94 million of additional annual cash flow.

So what is the value of the incremental cash flow generated by the various levels of sales growth in 2001? Given that the increment is constant over all future years, we can calculate its present value simply by dividing by the discount rate. Using a discount rate of 13 percent, the value of the $94 million increment to free cash flows caused by a $3 billion growth in sales is $726 million. How does that growth influence the current value of the firm's equity? *Not at all!* The value of the additional cash flows—$726 million—is offset precisely by the cost of the investment needed to support the higher sales level. The increment to sales—whether $1 billion or $2 billion or $3 billion—is zero net present value project. We can ignore it altogether and still arrive at the same estimate of the value of the firm. We could extend the same logic to additional sales growth in 2002, 2003, and so on, but the final conclusion would be the same: the rate of sales growth would have no impact on the current value of the firm.

NOTES

1. The present value of future dividends and the present value of future cash flows generate identical firm valuations, provided free cash flows are equivalent in value to those ultimately distributed by the firm to its owners. This requirement holds as long as any cash flows not used for reinvestment in operations are held in what are *expected* to be zero net present value projects, such as fairly priced marketable securities.

2. Short-term debt excludes operating liabilities, such as accounts payable and most accruals.

3. Compaq's situation on this dimension is unusual, in that they report interest expense even though they have no debt. For reasons discussed below, it is more practical to treat Compaq's interest expense as an operating expense, and to forecast cash flows net of this expense.

4. The forecasts of earnings and cash flow through 1997 are based on those of Duff and Phelps, reformatted to conform to the approach described here. To produce forecasts for 1998 through 2000, it is assumed that sales continue to grow at the same pace maintained in 1997, while gross margins fall to the 20 percent level forecast by Duff & Phelps for "the out years." Balance sheet forecasts are also based on those of Duff & Phelps (with extrapolations beyond 1997), except for cash balances. As explained, we assume distribution of cash (as dividends) and lower cash balances beginning in 1994.

5. Even though Duff & Phelps forecasts a decline in the ratio of net plant to sales, it forecasts capital expenditures to remain relatively constant as a fraction of sales. This seems unusual, in that it implies a decline in the average useful life of plant, and a corresponding increase in the rate of depreciation. In our forecasts beyond 1997, net plant is held constant as a fraction of sales at the 1997 level (6.6 percent). Depreciation is forecast at 31.9 percent of beginning net plant, roughly consistent with the average experience projected over 1994–1996. Capital expenditures are projected at amounts sufficient to maintain net plant at 6.6 percent of sales.

6. Perhaps in the interest of simplicity and because cash balances were not relied on explicitly by Duff & Phelps, their forecast of cash assumed that all free cash flows would be retained. As a result, the cash balance rises as a fraction of total assets from 11 percent in 1992 to a forecasted 29 percent in 1997. In Table 6-1, we assume that cash balances beyond 1994 remain at their 1994 level, which implies that all free cash flows are distributed to owners. Holding the cash balance constant causes the ratio of cash to total assets to fall from 15 percent in 1994 to 9 percent in 2000. For valuation purposes, the key is to maintain internally consistent treatment of cash balances and interest income. We could assume higher cash balances *and* higher interest income if we reduced distributions to owners, but in principle a similar valuation should be obtained.

7. Most of Compaq's interest expense represents reimbursements of dealers' cost of financing their payments to Compaq for inventory still on the dealer floor. Compaq's expense is thus a marketing cost that comes in a form similar to interest on factored receivables. Duff and Phelps forecasts the expense in amounts roughly proportional to sales. In valuing Compaq, one could either discount cash flows *before* this expense and arrive at the value of the commitment to dealers plus the value of equity, or discount cash flows *after* this expense and arrive at the value of equity directly. Because this interest expense is so closely tied to sales volume, we include it with other operating expenses, discount cash flows *net* of this expense, and arrive at a value of equity directly. In most other situations, interest expense is associated with debt, in which case we would discount cash flows *before* interest expense to arrive at the value of debt plus equity.

8. In the forecasts for 2001 and beyond, we continue to maintain the same ratio between balance sheet accounts and sales that was assumed for 2000 (see Table 6-1). Thus, with no change in sales, there is no required investment in net working capital. Depreciation ($369 million) is forecast at 31.9 percent of beginning net plant, consistent with the year 2000, and capital expenditures ($369 million) are forecast in the amount necessary to maintain net plant at 6.6 percent of sales.

9. If the analyst expects the firm to maintain abnormally profitable rates of return on sales that grow at the rate of inflation, a higher capitalization rate (based on the reciprocal of the weighted average cost of capital measured in *real* terms) could be justified. However, the amount capitalized must reflect the cash investment necessary to support the sales growth.

10. See Copeland, T. T. Koller, and J. Murrin, *Valuation: Measuring and Managing the Value of Companies,* 2nd edition (New York: John Wiley and Sons, 1994). Theory calls for the use of a short-term rate, but if that rate is used here, a difficult practical question rises: How does one reflect the premium required for expected inflation over long horizons? While the premium could, in principle, be treated as a portion of the term $[E(r_M) - r_F]$, it is probably easier to use an intermediate- or long-term riskless rate that presumably reflects expected inflation.

11. The average return reported here is the arithmetic mean, as opposed to the geometric mean. Ibbotson and Associates explain why this estimate is appropriate in this context. See Ibbotson and Associates, *Stocks, Bonds, Bills, and Inflation 1993 Yearbook,* (Chicago, 1994).

12. One way to estimate systematic risk is to regress the firm's stock returns over some recent time period against the returns on the market index. The slope coefficient represents an estimate of β. More fundamentally, systematic risk depends on the firm's degree of leverage and how sensitive the firm's operating profits are to shifts in economy-wide activity. Financial analysis that assesses these financial and operating risks should be useful in arriving at reasonable estimates of β.

13. Ibbotson and Associates, op. cit.

14. The Duff & Phelps report was issued in conjunction with a downgrade in their recommendation to investors from "buy" to "accumulate." Since the preponderance of analysts' recommendations are "buys," this could be viewed as a relatively negative signal.

15. As indicated in Table 6-1, the ratio of current assets to sales for 2000 is forecast at .374; the ratio of current liabilities to sales is .176. Net working capital is thus .198 times sales. The ratio of net plant to sales is .066, and the ratio of other long-lived assets to sales is .003. The deferred tax liability is .025 times sales. Total net investment required to support $1 of additional sales is thus .198 + .066 + .003 − .025, or .242.

CASES

Boston Celtics, Inc.
The Gap, Inc.
Thousand Trails, Inc.
The Timberland Company

7

Prospective Analysis: Accounting-Based Valuation Techniques

$\mathbf{W}$e conclude our discussion of prospective analysis with a description of accounting-based valuation techniques. In the previous chapter on discounted cash flow analysis, we noted that as the method is typically applied, its cash flow projections are grounded in forecasts of sales, profit margins, and other accounting numbers. Here, we describe an alternative valuation technique that is consistent with DCF, but which is linked more directly to accounting measures. This approach expresses the value of the firm's equity as the sum of the book value of equity and discounted expectations of future abnormal earnings.

Another set of valuation techniques based directly on accounting numbers involves the use of price multiples: price-earnings multiples, price-to-book multiples, and others. Intelligent application of these techniques requires an understanding of the determinants of the various multiples. Valuation based on discounted abnormal earnings provides a framework for describing those determinants.

VALUATION BASED ON DISCOUNTED ABNORMAL EARNINGS

The recognition that DCF valuation is often grounded in forecasts of accounting measures raises a question: Is there a way to estimate value by discounting some accounting measure directly? For years, the finance literature suggested that there is no acceptable way to map accounting numbers into an estimate of firm value, without first converting the accounting numbers into cash flows. It was pointed out that accounting numbers fail to reflect the timing of cash inflows and the investments necessary to generate them, and that accounting numbers are subject to manipulation and influenced by method choices that should not affect firm value. More recently, some in both the practicing and academic communities have rediscovered a notion that has long existed in the literature: It is possible to estimate equity value by discounting accounting numbers directly, so long as the proper technique is used.[1]

In principle, the accounting-based valuation described below should deliver the same estimate as DCF. In fact, we will structure our illustration based on Compaq so as to assure that such is the case. However, the technique frames the valuation task differently and can thus potentially cause the analyst to focus attention on different issues. We will return to this point after having laid out the calculations.

Estimating Value Based on Discounted Abnormal Earnings

We begin with a simple and intuitively appealing notion. Specifically, if a firm can earn only a normal rate of return on its book value, then investors should be willing to pay no more than book value to acquire an interest. Investors should pay more or less than book value if earnings are above or below this normal level. Thus, the deviation of the firm's market value from its book value depends on the firm's power to generate "abnormal earnings."

We define normal earnings as a normal rate of return multiplied by the beginning book value of equity. The normal rate of return is equal to the cost of equity capital—the same cost of equity that we use (along with the cost of debt) in the context of DCF valuation. Thus, abnormal earnings are as follows:

$$\text{Abnormal earnings} \ = \ \text{Earnings} \ - \ [\,\text{Cost of equity capital} \ \times \ \text{Beginning book value}\,]$$

The value of the firm's equity is now viewed as the sum of the current book value plus the discounted expected future abnormal earnings. Using the operation $E_t[\,\cdot\,]$ to represent the expected value as of time t, the value can be expressed as:

Value of equity at time $t \ =$

$$\text{Book value of equity at time } t \ + \ \sum_{\tau \ = \ t+1}^{\infty} \frac{E_t \, [\,\text{Abnormal earnings for year } \tau\,]}{(\,1 \ + \ \text{Cost of equity}\,)^{\tau}}$$

Table 7-1 illustrates the calculations for Compaq. Using the projected earnings and book values from Table 6-1 and assuming that the cost of equity capital is 13 percent, we calculate the abnormal earnings for each future year. Those abnormal earnings are then discounted at 13 percent and added to the current book value to arrive at an estimated value of equity.

The calculations for the terminal value, which represents the present value of the stream of abnormal earnings beyond 2000, are also presented in Table 7-1. The result is an estimated value equal to that obtained with DCF valuation: $4.3 billion, when we treat sales as constant beyond 2000. Nearly two-thirds of that value is already represented in the beginning book value reported by Compaq. Another fraction is reflected in the

Table 7-1 Valuation of Compaq Based on Book Value and Abnormal Earnings, December 1993

	1994	1995	1996	1997	1998	1999	2000	beyond 2000
				(dollar amounts in millions)				
Book value, 1993	$2,654							
Earnings forecast	$517	$565	$609	$628	$639	$702	$773	$773*
Book value, beginning	$2,654	$2,646	$2,917	$3,169	$3,364	$3,633	$3,928	$4,253*
Residual earnings:								
Earnings – r (book value)	$172	$221	$230	$216	$202	$230	$262	$220*
Discount factor, at 13%	1.13	1.28	1.44	1.63	1.84	2.08	2.35	
Discounted abnormal earnings	$152	$173	$159	$132	$109	$110	$112	$718*
Book value plus sum of discounted abnormal earnings	$4,320							

*Terminal value calculation: When sales are treated as if they will not grow beyond 2000 while margins stay constant, earnings remain at $773 in 2001 and beyond. Book value, which rises to $4,253 at the end of 2000 to accommodate the growth occurring during that year, remains at this level thereafter. Abnormal earnings are thus $773 – (.13 × $4253), or $220 per year. The present value of the $220 in perpetuity is $1,690 at the end of 2000 ($220/.13) and $718 at the end of 1993 [$1,690 / (1.13)⁷].

 If sales were treated as if they grew at a 3.5 percent rate beyond 2000 while holding margins constant, earnings would rise 3.5 percent each year, to $800 in 2001, $828 in 2002, and so on. Book value would be $4,253 at the beginning of 2001 and would also rise by 3.5 percent each year. Abnormal earnings would be $247 in 2001 [$800 – (.13 × $4,253)], and would rise 3.5 percent each year. The present value of the growing abnormal earnings stream would be $2,597 in 2000 [$247/(.13–.035)] and $1,104 as of the end of 1993. The sum of book value and discounted abnormal earnings would be $4,706—or $5,012 after multiplication by [1 + (.13/2)] to account for cash flows arriving halfway through the year, rather than at year's end. Indicated per share value would be $59.

When adjusted to assume that cash flows occur halfway through year, the amount is $4,320 × (1 + .13/2) = $4,600, or $54 per share.

discounted abnormal earnings for 1994 through 2000. Only about 17 percent of the value is attributed to abnormal earnings of the years beyond 2000. Contrast this with the terminal value calculated under DCF, which represented 58 percent of total value. We will return to this point later, and explain how the technique built on abnormal earnings reduces the role of the terminal value.

Estimating Terminal Value Based on Discounted Abnormal Earnings

When valuation is based on abnormal earnings, the terminal value is the present value of the abnormal earnings beyond the terminal year. As indicated in Table 7-1, abnormal earnings beyond 2000 are projected to be $220 per year.[2] The present value of those abnormal earnings in perpetuity (at 13 percent) is $1,690. Discounting that amount to 1993 yields a terminal value of $718 million. When we add this to the initial book value and the discounted abnormal earnings from years 1994 through 2000, we ultimately arrive at an indicated value per share of $54. (See Table 7-1 for details.)

If we had treated sales as if they would grow by 3.5 percent, with margins holding constant at 4.4 percent, the terminal value would have been $2,597 million as of 2000, and $1,104 million as of the end of 1993. (See the notes to Table 7-1.) Price per share would be $59, as opposed to our base case of $54.

The terminal value as of 2000—$1,690 million or $2,597 million, according to the calculations above—is an estimate of the difference between the market value and the book value of equity in that year. Thus, projecting the terminal value is equivalent to projecting the future market-to-book premium. With that in mind, other approaches to terminal value estimation come to mind. For example, one could consider what the future price-to-book multiple might be and apply that to the projected book value to arrive at an estimated premium. An appropriate multiple would be one that is "normal": one that allows for the possibility of supernormal profits on assets in place, but not for further growth with abnormal profitability. Average price-to-book ratios in the U.S. have been about 1.6 over the years. Interestingly, applying this amount to Compaq's projected book value for 2000 would have produced a terminal value estimate of $2,552 million [$4,253 million $\times (1.6 - 1.0)$]—nearly identical to our more optimistic estimate above.

The Role of Accounting Methods in Valuation Based on Discounted Abnormal Earnings

It may seem odd that firm value is expressed here as a function of accounting numbers. We know that accounting methods per se should have no influence on firm value (except as those choices influence the analyst's view of future real performance). Yet the valuation approach used here is based on numbers—earnings and book value—that vary with accounting method choices. How, then, can the valuation approach deliver correct estimates?

It turns out that, because accounting choices must affect both earnings *and* book value, and because of the self-correcting nature of double-entry bookkeeping (all "distortions" of accounting must ultimately reverse), estimated values based on the above method will not be affected by accounting choices.[3] As an example, let's assume that managers are conservative, choosing to expense some unusual costs that could have been capitalized as inventory, and thus causing earnings and ending book value to be lower by $100 times the required rate of return. For the time being, let's say the accounting choice has no influence on the analyst's view of the firm's real performance.

Our accounting-based valuation approach starts with book value, which is $100 lower as the result of the accounting choice. However, the choice also causes future abnormal earnings to be higher, for two reasons. First, future earnings will be higher (by $100) when the inventory is sold in a later period at a lower cost of sales. Second, in the meantime, the benchmark for normal earnings (based on book value of equity) will be lower by $100 times the required rate of return. Let's say the inventory isn't sold until two years after the accounting adjustment. Then assuming a discount rate of 13 percent, the impact of the writedown on our calculation of value is as follows:

		Dollar impact			Present value
Reduction in current book value:		−$100			−$100.00
Increase in abnormal earnings of year 1					
-due to lower book value ($.13 \times \$100$) =		13	÷	1.13 =	11.50
Increase in abnormal earnings of year 2					
-due to lower book value ($.13 \times \$100$) =	13				
-due to lower cost of sales =	$\underline{100}$				
		113	÷	1.13^2 =	$\underline{88.50}$
Impact of accounting choice on present value:					$0.00

The impact of the lower current book value of equity and the higher future abnormal earnings offset exactly, leaving no impact of the writedown on firm value.

The above discussion makes it appear as if the analyst would be indifferent to the accounting methods used. There are several reasons why this is not necessarily true. First, as discussed in Chapter 3, a firm's accounting choices can, in general, influence analysts' perceptions of the real performance of the firm. In the above example, the managers' choice to expense some inventoriable costs could reveal new information about the salability of the inventory. If so, the choice per se would affect expectations of future earnings and cash flows in ways beyond those considered above. The estimated value of the firm would presumably be lower—but it would still be the same regardless of whether the valuation is based on DCF or on discounted abnormal earnings.

Second, as explained below, the accounting methods used can have an important impact on what fraction of the firm's value is captured within the forecast horizon, and what remains in the terminal value. "High quality accounting" permits a more complete reflection of the value over short horizons. In fact, the analyst may choose to adjust the accounting so as to move toward that end.

Cash-Flow-Based Valuation Versus Accounting-Based Valuation

In principle, valuation based on discounted abnormal earnings delivers exactly the same estimate as DCF-based methods. Our Compaq illustration has been carefully constructed so as to preserve this equivalence.[4] However, the analyst could still consider the differences between the two approaches important. First, the alternatives frame the valuation task differently and can in practice focus the analyst's attention on different issues. The accounting-based approach can be framed in a way that immediately focuses attention on the same key measure of performance, ROE, that is decomposed in a standard financial analysis. Second, if it is more natural to think about future performance in terms of accounting returns, and if the analyst faces a context where a "back-of-the-envelope" estimate of value would be of use, the accounting-based technique can be simplified to deliver such an estimate (as shown below). Such an estimate could also be easily generated through, say, an application of some PE multiple, but that approach would involve restrictive assumptions not required here.

LINKAGE TO "VALUE DRIVERS."   Previously, we expressed the value of equity as the sum of book value and discounted abnormal earnings. We can reframe the task by scaling all of these amounts by book value, in which case our job is to estimate the price-to-book ratio, as opposed to the price itself. Under this approach, the valuation task would be described by the equation shown below. As before, we use the operator $E_t[\cdot]$ to indicate the expected value as of time t.

$$\frac{V_t}{b_t} = 1 + \frac{E_t[(ROE_{t+1} - r_E)]}{(1 + r_E)} + \frac{E_t[(ROE_{t+2} - r_E)(1 + g_{t+1})]}{(1 + r_E)^2}$$

$$+ \frac{E_t[(ROE_{t+3} - r_E)(1 + g_{t+1})(1 + g_{t+2})]}{(1 + r_E)^3} + \ldots$$

where V_t = estimated value of equity at time t

b_t = book value at time t

r_E = cost of equity capital

g_{t+n} = growth in book value in year $t+n$ $= \dfrac{(b_{t+n} - b_{t+n-1})}{b_{t+n-1}}$

The ratio of market value to book value is expressed directly in terms of future abnormal ROE, which is simply future ROE less the cost of equity capital $(ROE_{t+n} - r_E)$. Firms with expected positive abnormal ROE are assigned price-to-book ratios greater than one, and those with below-normal ROEs take on ratios below one. The deviation about one depends not only on the amount of abnormal ROE, but also the amount of growth in book value. The valuation task is framed in terms of two key questions about the firm's "value drivers":

- How much greater (or smaller) than normal will the firm's ROE be?
- How quickly will the firm's investment base (book value) grow?

If desired, the equation can be rewritten so that future ROEs are expressed as the product of their components: profit margins, sales turnover, and leverage. Thus, the approach permits us to build directly on projections of the same accounting numbers utilized in financial analysis (see Chapter 4), without the need to convert projections of those numbers into cash flows. Yet in the end, the estimate of value should be the same as that from DCF.[5]

A "SHORTCUT" TECHNIQUE.   The recognition that valuation based on discounted abnormal earnings can be framed entirely in terms of future ROEs and growth in book value suggests that it might permit a "shortcut" to estimating value. Indeed, the approach is amenable to producing quick and simple estimates of value without relying on assumptions as restrictive as, say, those implicit in the simple application of a PE multiple. "Back of the envelope" estimates are useful in a variety of contexts where the cost and time involved in a detailed DCF analysis is not justifiable. More than that, such estimates can provide a good "sanity check" on the detailed analysis. It is easy in the detailed analysis to become so "preoccupied by the trees that one loses sight of the forest"— inadvertently introducing internally inconsistent or unreasonable assumptions.

To illustrate the accounting-based valuation "shortcut," assume that the analyst believes that Compaq will continue to generate an ROE in the range of 19 percent for the foreseeable future, and that sales and book value will grow at a rate of 20 percent. However, beyond three years, any growth is ignored, assuming it comes only in the form of zero net present value projects. Applying the formula shown earlier in this section, while imposing these assumptions, the indicated ratio of market value to book value is 1.72, as shown below.[6]

$$\frac{V_t}{b_t} = 1 + \frac{(.19 - .13)}{(1.13)} + \frac{(.19 - .13)(1.20)}{(1.13)^2} + \frac{(.19 - .13)(1.20)^2}{(1.13)^3}$$

$$+ \frac{(.19 - .13)(1.20)^3 / (.13)}{(1.13)^3} = 1.72$$

A price-to-book ratio of 1.72 suggests a current price per share of $54, which happens to be equal to our earlier projection. We could easily have allowed for growth in abnormal earnings of 3.5 percent for all years beyond the third, raising our implied price to $60, again close to the amount from our detailed analysis.[7] The estimates are close because our projections for the next three years are similar to those used earlier, and because growth beyond the third year has relatively little impact on our estimate. Of course, if the long-run sales growth had been projected to enhance value more substantially, our rough estimate would have been too low.

The shortcut is not much more difficult than applying a PE multiple, and yet it provides the flexibility to entertain any desired combination of abnormal profitability, growth, and discount rates. For example, if desired, we could have allowed for a longer period of abnormally profitable growth and/or for ROEs that revert to more normal levels through time. The technique can be used to gain a quick feel for what a reasonable value might be, or for considering how value would be impacted by various "what if" scenarios. In fact, armed with information about current ROE, an understanding of how ROE is likely to change in the future, and a sense for likely sales growth rates, one can produce a "back-of-the-envelope" estimate of firm value very quickly. Such an approach should not, however, be viewed as a perfect substitute for the more detailed analyses described earlier.

IMPACT OF ACCOUNTING METHODS ON TERMINAL VALUE ESTIMATES. As indicated earlier, terminal value estimates tend to represent a much smaller fraction of total value when the accounting-based valuation technique is used. On the surface, this would appear to mitigate concerns about the aspect of valuation that leaves the analyst most uncomfortable. Is this apparent advantage real? As explained below, the answer turns on how well value is already reflected in the accountant's book value.

Earnings-based valuation does not make DCF's terminal value problem go away, but it does reframe it. DCF terminal values include the present value of *all* expected cash flows beyond the forecast horizon. Under accounting-based valuation, that value is broken into two parts: the present values of *normal* and *abnormal* earnings beyond the terminal year. The terminal value in the accounting-based technique includes only the abnormal earnings; the present value of normal earnings is already reflected in the original book value or growth in book value over the forecast horizon.

The accounting-based approach, then, recognizes that current book value and earnings over the forecast horizon already reflect many of the cash flows expected to arrive after the forecast horizon. The accounting-based approach builds on these products of accrual accounting directly. The DCF approach, on the other hand, "unravels" all of the accruals, spreads the resulting cash flows over longer horizons, and then reconstructs its own "accruals" in the form of discounted expectations of future cash flows. The essential difference between the two approaches is that accounting-based valuation recognizes that the accrual process may already have performed a portion of the valuation task, whereas the DCF approach ultimately moves back to the primitive cash flows underlying the accruals.

The usefulness of the accounting-based perspective thus hinges on how well the accrual process reflects future cash flows. The approach is most convenient when the accounting is "unbiased," so that ROEs can be abnormal only as the result of economic rents and not as a product of the accounting itself.[8] In that case, as the forecast horizon extends to the point where the firm is expected to approach a competitive equilibrium and earn only a normal return on its projects, expected ROE would approach the cost of capital. Subsequent abnormal earnings would be zero, and the terminal value at that point would be nil. In this extreme case, *all* of the firm's value is reflected in the book value and earnings projected over the forecast horizon.

Of course, accounting rarely works so well. For example, in most countries research and development costs are expensed, and book values fail to reflect any research and development assets. This reduces the denominator of the ROE. As a result, firms that spend heavily on research and development, such as pharmaceuticals, tend on average to generate abnormally high ROEs, even in the face of stiff competition. Purely as an artifact of research and development accounting, abnormal earnings would be expected to remain positive indefinitely for such firms, and the terminal value could represent a substantial fraction of total value.

If desired, the analyst can alter the accounting approach used by the firm in her or his own projections. "Better" accounting would be viewed as that which reflects a larger fraction of the firm's value in book values and earnings over the forecast horizon.[9] This same view underlies analysts' attempts to "normalize" earnings. The adjusted numbers are intended to provide better indications of value, even though they reflect performance only over a short horizon.

TECHNIQUES OF VALUATION BASED ON PRICE MULTIPLES

Both the DCF valuation method and valuation based on discounted abnormal earnings require detailed, multi-year forecasts. In that sense, the methods place heavy demands on the analyst. Moreover, given that the valuation depends so heavily on forecasts of performance several years into the future, the analyst may feel less than confident about the final range of estimates. An alternative approach is to value the firm based on price multiples of "comparable" firms. Under this approach, one relies on the market to undertake the difficult task of considering the short- and long-term prospects for growth and profitability and their implications for the values of the seemingly comparable firms. Then the analyst *assumes* that the pricing of those other firms is applicable to the firm at hand.

Application of price multiples for comparable firms seems straightforward on the surface. One simply identifies firms in the same industry, calculates the desired multiple—e.g., price-earnings or price-to-book—and then applies the multiple to the firm being valued.

Unfortunately, application of price multiples is not so simple as it would appear. Identification of firms that are really comparable is often quite difficult. There are also some choices to be made concerning how the multiples will be calculated. Finally, explaining why multiples vary across firms, and how applicable another firm's multiple is to the one at hand, requires a sound understanding of the determinants of each multiple.

Below, we address some of these issues with the aid of Table 7-2, which compares various multiples for Compaq with those of three other industry players. One could view Table 7-2 as a foundation for assessing how favorably priced Compaq is relative to others. Alternatively, if one imagined that Compaq were a private firm with no observable market price, one could consider the multiples for other firms as indicators of how one might price Compaq.

Table 7-2 Selected Price Multiples for Compaq and "Comparable" Firms

Price multiple	Compaq Computer	Comparable Firms		
		AST Research	Apple Computer	Dell Computer
Trailing PE based on four most recently reported quarters' EPS	14.3	17.4	12.7	NM
Leading PE based on forecast 1994 EPS	11.5	12.6	18.1	12.6
Unlevered[a] **price/sales ratio** based on four most recently reported quarters' sales	.89	.50	.44	.36
Unlevered[a] **price/sales ratio** based on forecast 1994 sales	.75	.34	.39	.27
Price-to-book ratio, based on book value as reported in most recent quarter	2.48	2.22	1.72	2.61
Unlevered[b] **price-to-"cash flow" ratio**, based on 1993 EBITDA	6.7	9.5	4.6	NM

a. Unlevered price/sales ratio $= \dfrac{(Market\ value\ of\ equity\ +\ Debt)}{Sales}$

b. Unlevered price/"cash flow" ratio $= \dfrac{(Market\ value\ of\ equity\ +\ Debt)}{Earnings\ before\ interest,\ depreciation,\ and\ amortization}$

Selecting Comparable Firms

Ideally, price multiples used in a comparable firm analysis would be those for firms with the most similar operating and financial characteristics. Firms within the same industry are the most obvious candidates. However, even within narrowly defined industries, it is often difficult to find multiples for similar firms. Compaq's closest competitor in the personal computer (PC) market is IBM, but IBM is involved in much more than the production and sale of PCs. Moreover, IBM does not reveal financial data for its PC division; even if it did, there is no observable market price for only that part of the business.

Similar issues arise with DEC and Hewlett-Packard. Another close competitor, NCR, cannot be used in the comparison because it exists as a division within ATT. Yet another player, NEC, produces more than just PCs and presents another difficulty as well: Even though its financials are converted to U.S. GAAP, it is unlikely that, as a Japanese firm, its accounting policies are truly similar to those that would be used by a U.S. firm. Gateway and Packard Bell are also close competitors but, as private firms in 1993, they had no price data. Commodore International produces desktop computers, but it was facing so much financial difficulty in late 1993 that its price multiples are difficult to interpret and probably not applicable to a healthy company like Compaq.

Compaq competitors that are publicly held and that focus almost primarily on production of desktop computers include Apple, AST Research, and Dell—the firms whose multiples appear in Table 7-2. Even among this small set, there are some problems in drawing comparisons. Dell is coming off losses in 1993, and so its trailing price/earnings ratio is not meaningful. AST Research does not have the strength of brand that Compaq has developed, and so its profit margins are lower. As explained below, this affects the comparability of some ratios but not others. Apple has maintained a strong brand image and high margins in the past, but is adjusting later than Compaq to new market realities. Thus, while Compaq's earnings are already on the rebound in 1993, Apple may still face another year or two of mediocre earnings growth.

Differences such as those found here inevitably arise in valuation based on price multiples. One way of dealing with the problem is to average across *all* firms in the industry. However, the analyst using that approach can only hope that various sources of noncomparability cancel each other out, so that the firm being valued is a "typical" industry member. Another approach is to focus on those firms within the industry that are most similar, as we do in Table 7-2. As explained below, this should be done with the recognition that what constitutes comparability varies according to which multiple is being applied. We will return to this topic after discussing some technical issues.

Use of Forecasts Versus Past Performance

Price multiples can include, in the denominator, measures of either past or future performance. Which is best? Note that prices should be based on expected future performance. Thus, using historical data in the denominator of a price multiple is justified only in the sense that the denominator is viewed as an indicator of the future. If a reliable forecast is directly available, it would generally be preferred as the basis for a multiple. However, such forecasts are typically available only for larger firms.

Table 7-2 presents PE ratios based on both past earnings (a *trailing* PE multiple) and on forecasts of fiscal 1994 earnings (a *leading* PE multiple). In the interests of using the latest data in the trailing PE multiple, the denominator includes the EPS of the most recent four quarters, even though those quarters may span different fiscal years.

Trailing PE multiples can be distorted substantially by the transitory gains and losses or other unusual performance of the most recent year. With that in mind, we have excluded from the denominator of Apple's PE multiple a large nonrecurring loss. Absent such an adjustment, Apple's PE would have been nearly 50! Even after eliminating such nonrecurring items, PEs can still be distorted, however. For example, Dell suffered an operating loss in 1993 that analysts do not expect to see repeated, rendering their trailing PE nonmeaningful.

Leading multiples can also be distorted, but are less likely to include one-time gains and losses in the denominator, simply because such items are difficult to anticipate in forecasts. All of the leading PE multiples in Table 7-2 are within a "normal" range, 11.5 to 18.1.

Adjusting Multiples for Leverage

Price multiples should be calculated in a way that preserves consistency between the numerator and denominator. Consistency is an issue for those ratios where the denominator reflects performance *before* servicing debt. Examples include the price-to-sales multiple and any multiple of operating earnings or operating cash flows. When calculating these multiples, the numerator should include not just the market value of equity, but the value of debt as well. This is not an issue for Compaq or Apple, neither of which carry any debt. However, both AST Research and Dell do have debt in their capital structure. In the case of AST Research, the trailing price-to-sales multiple was adjusted for debt as follows:

$$\frac{(\text{Market value of equity} + \text{Debt})}{\text{Sales}} = \frac{(\text{Stock price} \times \text{Shares}) + \text{Debt}}{\text{Sales}}$$

$$= \frac{(\$23 \times 31.6 \text{ million}) + \$92 \text{ million}}{\$1645 \text{ million}} = .50$$

Interpreting and Comparing Multiples

Even across these relatively closely related firms, some of the price multiples vary considerably. For example, Compaq's unlevered price-to-sales ratio is much higher than that of any of the "comparable" firms. Does this suggest that Compaq is relatively overpriced? Or is there some other explanation? If Compaq had no observable market price, how appropriate would it be to apply the price-to-book multiples of the other firms to estimate the value of Compaq?

Careful analysis of such questions requires consideration of the determinants of each multiple: the factors that might explain why some firms' multiples should be higher than others.

- *Price-earnings ratios* should vary positively with differences in expected future growth in (abnormal) earnings, and negatively with risk.[10] In the special case where no growth is expected in the current level of earnings, or where such growth will come only as the product of additional investment in zero-net-present-value projects, the PE ratio should be approximately equal to the reciprocal of the cost of equity capital, thus placing it in the range of 6 to 10.[11] In early 1995, the market priced U.S. auto manufacturers at multiples in the range of 5 to 7, reflecting an expectation of essentially no growth in abnormal earnings.

  The leading PE ratios for Compaq, AST Research, and Dell all indicate that market agents expect moderate growth in (abnormal) earnings beyond the coming year. The ratios are all within the range of 11.5 to 12.6. Apple holds a higher multiple of forecast 1994 earnings, at 18.1. The higher multiple reflects the market's expectation that much of Apple's rebound will not occur until *after* 1994. In fact, Apple stands as the only firm in the set for which analysts are projecting a decline in earnings in 1994. The upshot is that Apple's higher multiple should *not* be taken as an indication that it is overpriced, or that Compaq is underpriced. The difference is expected, based on the likely path of earnings growth for the two firms.

- *Price-to-book ratios.* The theoretical determinants of a price-to-book ratio are provided in the previous discussion of valuation based on discounted abnormal earnings. Price-to-book ratios should vary across firms according to differences in their future ROEs, growth in book value, and risk (the driver of differences in discount rates).

    Compaq and Dell have relatively high price-to-book ratios. That should be expected, because analysts are expecting high ROEs (in the upper teens) for both firms in the future, along with strong growth in book value. Apple's price-to-book ratio is relatively low, but that again is to be expected. *Value Line* forecasts ROE for Apple to be only about 10 percent in 1994, rising to about 13.5 percent over a four-year horizon. AST Research sits in the middle of the price-to-book distribution, as does its forecast long-range ROE (15 percent).

- *Price-to-sales ratios* can be viewed as the product of price-earnings ratios and earnings-to-sales ratios. Thus, in addition to the factors that explain variation in PE ratios, price-to-sales ratios should vary with expected profit margins. Firms with higher expected margins should be worth more in dollar sales. This is why one would expect, for example, a pharmaceutical company to have a higher price-to-sales ratio than a grocery store chain; or why one would expect the price-to-sales ratio to be higher when a firm carries a strong brand name.

    The price-to-sales ratio is the one multiple for which Compaq appears on the surface to be most out of line with its competitors. Its ratio is more than twice as large as the average of the others. Given that differences in the PE ratios were much smaller, the differences in price-to-sales ratios are explainable only if Compaq can maintain a higher profit margin. Indeed, that is expected. Projected operating margins are (according to *Value Line*) substantially larger than those of the other firms. This is consistent with the view of Compaq's strength of brand name and cost efficiencies, expressed earlier.

- *Price-to-cash flow ratios,* as used in practice, rarely employ a pure cash flow measure in the denominator. Cash flow from operations is often affected by temporary fluctuations in working capital accounts, and thus provides a noisy indicator of value as it stands alone. Instead, the price-cash flow multiples used in practice usually refer to a multiple of earnings before depreciation, or some similar measure. A commonly used denominator is EBITDA, or operating earnings before interest, taxes, depreciation, and amortization. Note that such a ratio should be unlevered (including the value of debt in the numerator) because the denominator reflects earnings before interest.

    Table 7-2 presents the unlevered multiple of trailing EBITDA for the most recent year. Leading multiples are not presented because forecasts of EBITDA are not widely available. Compaq's "cash flow" multiple lies between that of AST and Apple; Dell's multiple is not meaningful. The pattern is consistent with the trailing PE multiples; it reflects the market's expectation of a large rebound from 1993 for AST and continuing difficulties at Apple.

The above discussion helps highlight that a firm can be high on one multiple and low on another, because they are determined by different factors. Consider the two most commonly used multiples, price-earnings (PE) and price-to-book (PB).[12] Both multiples vary positively with future earnings prospects. However, PB is determined by the future level of earnings *relative to book value*, and the growth in book value. PE is determined by growth in future earnings, *relative to the earnings* in the denominator of PE. Apple has a relatively high leading PE, because earnings are expected to grow substantially from the depressed level forecast for the coming year. However, even after the rebound occurs, earnings are not expected to be high *relative to book value* (i.e., ROE is not expected to be high), and thus the PB ratio is lower than that for the other firms in Table 7-2.

In general, as illustrated in Table 7-2, the PB and PE ratios are *both* high only when a firm is expected to grow quickly, and to enjoy abnormally high ROEs during the growth period and/or after the growth occurs. These are the "rising stars." Other firms, which might be called "falling stars," may still be enjoying high ROEs on existing investments but are no longer growing fast. Such firms would have high PBs, but relatively low PEs. Many recovering firms, like Apple, are expected to rebound from temporarily low earnings levels but will be prevented by competition from returning to a point of abnormally high ROEs. They should have high PEs and relatively low PBs. Finally, firms whose earnings have little prospect for either growth or high ROEs—the "dogs"—will carry low PBs and low PEs.

What Can Be Learned from Analysis of Price Multiples

Overall, the variation in multiples across the firms in Table 7-2 appears explainable and therefore not necessarily indicative that Compaq's pricing is either more or less favorable than that of other firms. If Compaq had no market price and we were turning to the multiples of the other firms to suggest how it should be priced, the differences in the determinants of multiples discussed above should be taken into account. For example, given Compaq's relatively high expected margins, it would be unreasonable to apply the other firms' sales multiples directly to Compaq. Some upward adjustment would be in order. In terms of future earnings growth, the firms are more similar, and thus an application to Compaq of other firms' PE multiples—with the possible exception of Apple's—would be more reasonable.

Note that the multiples in Table 7-2 do not provide us with a great deal of confidence in statements about Compaq's pricing. Even if Compaq were, for example, underpriced by 10 percent, the sort of analysis in Table 7-2 would probably not make that evident.

Alternatively, if Compaq had no market price and we were attempting to estimate it, the multiples in Table 7-2 would only be suggestive of a reasonable *range* of values rather than a pinpoint estimate.

The differences that exist across firms—even firms as closely related as those in Table 7-2—render pricing based on multiples an inherently crude technique. The analyst can reduce the impact of such differences by focusing on *average* multiples across the comparable firms, but there is still no guarantee that the average applies perfectly to the firm being valued. Valuations based on detailed forecasts may take on the appearance of delivering more precision, but there is nearly always a high degree of uncertainty surrounding the long-run forecasts.

The bottom line is that valuation of firms is a difficult and uncertain business, and no technique can alter that underlying reality. The analyst can only apply the techniques as intelligently as possible, so that estimation error results only from underlying economic uncertainties and not from avoidable misjudgments in applying the valuation method.

Multiples Based on Formulae

Our discussion thus far has focused on price multiples based on comparable firms, but it is also possible to construct multiples based on various formulae. Perhaps the most widely known example is the "Gordon-Shapiro growth formula," which expresses the price (P) as a function of the current dividend (d), based on estimates of the cost of equity capital (r) and future dividend growth (g):

$$P = \frac{d}{(r - g)}$$

If the firm retains the fraction k of the firm's earnings (E), and thus $d = E(1 - k)$, then the implied price-earnings multiple should be:

$$\frac{P}{E} = \frac{(1 - k)}{(r - g)}$$

This formula assumes dividends can grow at the same rate in perpetuity. Almost inevitably, that assumption is so unrealistic as to call into question the practical value of the formula. It is obviously of no use in pricing Compaq, which currently pays no dividends and for which expectations of dividends in the near term are quite uncertain.

Miller and Modigliani provide a somewhat less restrictive approach.[13] They consider a setting where growth may continue for a period of any length, but is relevant to the firm's current value for only T years, because beyond that point the expected return on investment (r^*) will be driven by competition to the cost of capital (r). That is, we expect the firm to find abnormally profitable projects for only T years. Beyond that point, only zero net present value projects are expected. If over the T-year horizon the firm reinvests the fraction k of its earnings, then the price-earnings ratio should be:

$$\frac{P}{E} = \frac{1 + Tk\,(r^* - r)}{r}$$

This formula also has shortcomings. For example, it implicitly assumes that the rate of return on investment r^* expected in the future is equal to that which generated the earnings E.[14] As explained in Chapter 5, it is generally unrealistic to assume that rates of return on investment will remain constant.

Price-earnings multiples based on restrictive formulae like those above are probably best viewed as useful devices for thinking about valuation. They should not be used as methods of estimating value in practical situations. The previously discussed "shortcut" technique based on discounted abnormal earnings provides an alternative that is less restrictive.

DETAILED VALUATION VERSUS USE OF MULTIPLES

Valuation based on either DCF or discounted abnormal earnings requires detailed, multiple-year forecasts about a variety of parameters, including growth, profitability, and cost of capital. These techniques supply the proper conceptual template for thinking about what creates value, and they offer the advantage of forcing the analyst to make his or her forecasts explicit. Doing so can help avoid unrealistic or internally inconsistent assumptions, but it places high demands on the analyst. Moreover, the detailed approaches are vulnerable to the analyst's idiosyncratic estimation errors. Recall how great an impact on estimated value can arise from a 2 percent shift in the cost of capital—and errors of that magnitude are understandable given the current uncertainty about how the cost of capital should be measured.

Valuation based on multiples for comparable firms is less demanding. It can also avoid some vulnerability to the analyst's idiosyncratic estimation error by "letting the market decide" some of the valuation parameters. For example, application of a price-earnings multiple does not require explicit specification of a firm's cost of capital or growth rate. It simply assumes that whatever such parameters' values may be, they are similar to those for firms deemed "comparable." Of course, how much is gained (or lost!) by relying on the market's pricing of other firms depends critically on how closely comparable those firms are. Such reliance also involves a certain circularity. If all equity valuation were based solely on comparables, then mispricing of one firm would translate into mispricing in another firm, and so on. To avoid this never-ending spiral, someone must ultimately conduct an analysis based on something other than mere comparables.

Each of the alternatives offers its own set of advantages. There is no "best" valuation method, which explains why analysts tend to "triangulate" by applying several methods in the same context.

SUMMARY AND CONCLUSIONS

In this chapter we described several accounting-based valuation techniques. One approach expresses the value of the firm's equity as book value plus discounted expectations of future abnormal earnings. The approach is conceptually sound, consistent with DCF analysis, and it offers the advantage of being framed directly in terms of the drivers of firm value (ROE, profit margins, growth, and so forth).

Valuation techniques based on price multiples are commonly used in practice. They place fewer demands on the analyst; they also take direct advantage of information known in the marketplace and embedded in other firms' prices, even when that information may not be known to the analyst using the multiple. The primary difficulty with using price multiples lies in identifying firms that are truly comparable. An understanding of the determinants of various multiples can help the analyst assess the degree of comparability and explain why differences in multiples should be expected across firms.

The various alternatives to valuation each offer their own strengths and weaknesses. In a given setting, some are more useful than others. However, there are typically gains to be had by considering several approaches simultaneously.

NOTES

1. See G. A. D. Preinreich, "Annual Survey of Economic Theory: The Theory of Depreciation," *Econometrica* (July 1938): 219–241; Edgar O. Edwards and Philip W. Bell, *The Theory and Measurement of Business Income,* (Berkeley: University of California Press, 1961); Victor L. Bernard, "Accounting-Based Valuation Techniques, Market-to-Book Ratios, and Implications for Financial Statements Analysis," working paper, University of Michigan (1994); James Ohlson, "Earnings, Book Value, and Dividends in Security Valuation," *Contemporary Accounting Research* (Spring 1995); G. Bennett Stewart, *The Quest for Value,* second edition (New York: HarperCollins, 1994).

One version of the approach, based on Stewart's economic value added (EVA) model, has quickly gained acceptance in practice since 1990. Stewart's approach could be viewed as an application or extension of a valuation technique first described by Preinreich and then reintroduced to the literature by Edwards and Bell, Bernard, and especially Ohlson, among others.

2. The abnormal earnings drop in 2001 despite earnings remaining constant. The reason is that book value during 2000 was still growing at a 10 percent rate, so that the benchmark for normal earnings—based on beginning book value—is higher in 2001 than in 2000.

3. Valuation based on discounted abnormal earnings does require one property of the forecasts: that they be consistent with "clean surplus accounting." Such accounting requires the following relation:

End-of-period book value =

   Beginning book value + Earnings − Dividends ± Capital contributions/Withdrawals

Clean surplus accounting rules out situations where some gain or loss is excluded from earnings but is still used to adjust the book value of equity. For example, under U.S. GAAP, gains and losses on foreign currency translations are handled this way. In applying the valuation technique described here, the analyst would need to deviate from GAAP in producing forecasts and treat such gains/losses as a part of earnings. However, the technique does *not* require clean surplus accounting to have been applied *in the past*. So the existing book value, based on U.S. GAAP or any other set of principles, can still serve as the starting point. All the analyst needs to do is apply clean surplus accounting in his or her forecasts. That much is not only easy, but is usually the natural thing to do anyway. Our Duff & Phelps forecasts, for example, were consistent with clean surplus accounting.

4. Some special aspects of Compaq's case make it easier to preserve this equivalence. First, there is no debt, so there is no question about maintaining internally consistent estimates of the WACC (used in DCF to discount cash flows) and the cost of equity capital (used here for discounting abnormal earnings). Second, beginning in 1994, we treat all free cash flows as if they are distributed as dividends, not reinvested. The DCF method *assumes* that free cash flows are reinvested in zero net present value projects. As implemented here, the accounting-based valuation method permits but does not assume this. Third, our approach to long-range forecasting assures that once sales growth reaches a steady state beyond the terminal year, both abnormal earnings growth and free cash flow growth do so as well.

5. It may seem surprising that one can estimate value with no explicit attention to two of the cash flow streams considered in DCF analysis: investments in working capital and capital expenditures. The accounting-based technique recognizes that these investments cannot possibly contribute to value without impacting abnormal earnings, and that therefore only their earnings impacts need be considered. For example, the benefit of an increase in inventory turnover surfaces in terms of its impact on ROE (and thus, abnormal earnings), without the need to consider explicitly the cash flow impacts involved.

6. The first three terms to the right of the 1 include abnormal ROE, scaled up by the amount of prior growth in book value and discounted to the present. The final term recognizes that the scaled abnormal ROE of the third year—$(.19 - .13)(1.20)^2$—is now assumed to remain constant in perpetuity, and so it can be capitalized by dividing by $(.13)$ and then discounted to the present with the factor $(1.13)^3$. Given that book value is assumed to grow at a rate that exceeds the ROE, the calculation implicitly assumes some (small) capital infusions.

7. To do this, simply capitalize the fourth term by $(.13 - .035)$ rather than $(.13)$. The indicated market-to-book ratio would then be 1.93, and the implied price per share would be $60.

8. Unbiased accounting is that which, in a competitive equilibrium, produces an expected ROE equal to the cost of capital. The actual ROE thus reveals the presence of economic rents. Market-value accounting is a special case of unbiased accounting that produces an expected ROE equal to the cost of capital, even when the firm is *not* in a competitive equilibrium. That is, market-value accounting reflects the present value of future economic rents in book value, driving the expected ROEs to a normal level. For a discussion of unbiased and biased accounting, see Gerald Feltham and James Ohlson, "Valuation and Clean Surplus Accounting for Operating and Financial Activities," *Contemporary Accounting Research* (forthcoming, Spring 1995).

9. In his book on EVA valuation, Bennett Stewart (op. cit.) recommends a number of accounting adjustments, including the capitalization of research and development.

10. An underappreciated point is that PE ratios vary according to expected changes in *abnormal* earnings, not earnings per se. If earnings will grow *only* as the result of additional investment that will produce normal rates of return, that should have no impact on the current *price* of the firm and therefore no impact on the PE ratio as a whole. See Patricia Fairfield, "P/E, P/B, and the Present Value of Future Dividends," *Financial Analysts Journal* (July/August 1994): 23–31; and

Stephen Penman, "The Articulation of Price-Earnings Ratios and Market-to-Book Ratios and the Evaluation of Growth," working paper, University of California at Berkeley (1994).

11. More precisely, a trailing PE ratio for a no-growth firm should be equal to $\left(\dfrac{1+r}{r} - \dfrac{div}{E} \right)$ where r = cost of equity capital and $\dfrac{div}{E}$ = dividend payout ratio during the period over which earnings were measured. Thus, with a 50 percent dividend payout and a 13 percent cost of capital, the PE ratio in the no-growth case would be (1.13/.13) − .50, or 8.2. See Fairfield (op. cit.) and Penman (op. cit.).

12. For a more detailed explication of the points drawn here, see Penman (op. cit.).

13. See Merton Miller and Franco Modigliani, "Dividend Policy, Growth, and the Valuation of Shares," *Journal of Business* 34 (1961): 411–433.

14. See Penman (op. cit.) for further discussion.

CASES

Boston Celtics
The Computer Industry in 1992
The Gap, Inc.
IBM and Fujitsu
Siemens
The Timberland Company

p a r t 3

Business Analysis Applications

chapter 8

Equity Security Analysis

Equity security analysis is the evaluation of a firm and its prospects from the perspective of a current or potential investor in the firm's stock. Security analysis is one step in a larger investment process that involves (1) establishing the objectives of the investor or fund, (2) forming expectations about the future returns and risks of individual securities, and then (3) combining individual securities into portfolios to maximize progress toward the investment objectives.

Security analysis is the foundation for the second step, projecting future returns and assessing risk. Security analysis is typically conducted with an eye towards identification of mispriced securities, in hopes of generating returns that more than compensate the investor for risk. However, that need not be the case. For analysts who do not have a comparative advantage in identifying mispriced securities, the focus should be on gaining an appreciation for how a security would affect the risk of a given portfolio, and whether it fits the profile that the portfolio is designed to maintain.

Security analysis is undertaken by individual investors, by analysts at brokerage houses (sell-side analysts), by analysts that work at the direction of funds managers for various institutions (buy-side analysts), and others. The institutions employing buy-side analysts include mutual funds, pension funds, insurance companies, universities, and others.

A variety of questions are dealt with in security analysis:

- A sell-side analyst asks: How do my forecasts compare to those of the analysts' consensus? Is the observed market price consistent with that consensus? Given my expectations for the firm, does this stock appear to be mispriced? Should I recommend this stock as a buy, a sell, or a hold?
- A buy-side analyst for a "value stock fund" offered to mutual fund investors asks: Does this stock possess the characteristics we seek in our fund? That is, does it have a relatively low ratio of price to earnings, book value, and other fundamental indicators? Do its prospects for earnings improvement suggest good potential for high future returns on the stock?

- An individual investor asks: Does this stock offer the risk profile that suits my investment objectives? Does it enhance my ability to diversify the risk of my portfolio? Is the firm's dividend payout rate low enough to help shield me from taxes while I continue to hold the stock?

As the above questions underscore, there is more to security analysis than estimating the value of stocks. Nevertheless, for most sell-side and buy-side analysts, the key goal remains the identification of mispriced stocks.

MARKET EFFICIENCY AND THE PRICING OF EQUITY SECURITIES

How a security analyst should invest his or her time depends on how quickly and efficiently information flows through markets and becomes reflected in security prices. In the extreme, information would be reflected in security prices fully and immediately upon its release. This is essentially the condition posited by the *efficient markets hypothesis*. This hypothesis states that security prices reflect all available information, as if such information could be costlessly digested and translated immmediately into demands for buys or sells without regard to frictions imposed by transactions costs. Under such conditions, it would be impossible to identify mispriced securities on the basis of public information.

In a world of efficient markets, the expected return on any equity security is just enough to compensate investors for the unavoidable risk the security involves. Unavoidable risk is that which cannot be "diversified away" simply by holding a portfolio of many securities. Given efficient markets, the investor's strategy shifts away from the search for mispriced securities and focuses instead on maintaining a well diversified portfolio. Aside from this, the investor must arrive at the desired balance between risky securities and short-term government bonds. The desired balance depends on how much risk the investor is willing to bear for a given increase in expected returns.

The above discussion implies that investors who accept that stock prices already reflect available information have no need for analysis involving a search for mispriced securities. Of course, if all investors adopted this attitude, no such analysis would be conducted, mispricing would go uncorrected, and markets would no longer be efficient! This is why the efficient markets hypothesis cannot represent an equilibrium in a strict sense. In equilibrium, there must be just enough mispricing to provide incentives for the investment of resources in security analysis.

The existence of some mispricing, even in equilibrium, does not imply that it is sensible for just anyone to engage in security analysis. Instead, it suggests that securities analysis is subject to the same laws of supply and demand faced in all other competitive industries: it will be rewarding only for those with the strongest comparative advantage. How many analysts are in that category is a question that cannot be settled at a theoretical level, but it need not be many. In the case of Compaq, which is among the larger companies in the United States, there are only about 30 professional analysts who formally track and report on the firm. Only a subset of these analysts are considered the "key movers" of the stock. There are many others, however, including most buy-side analysts, who track the firm on their own account without issuing any formal reports to outsiders. For the smallest publicly traded firms in the U.S., there is typically no formal following by analysts, and would-be investors and their advisors are left to themselves to conduct securities analysis.

Market Efficiency and the Role of Financial Statement Analysis

The degree of market efficiency that arises from competition among analysts and other market agents is an empirical issue addressed by a large body of research spanning the last three decades. Such research has important implications for the role of financial statements in security analysis. Consider, for example, the implications of an extremely efficient market, where information is fully impounded in prices within minutes of its revelation. In such a market, agents could profit from digesting financial statement information in two ways. First, the information would be useful to the select few who receive newly-announced financial data, interpret it quickly, and trade on it within minutes. Second, and probably more important, the information would be useful for gaining an understanding of the firm, so as to place the analyst in a better position to interpret other news (from financial statements as well as other sources) as it arrives.

On the other hand, if securities prices fail to reflect financial statement data fully, even days or months after its public revelation, there is a third way in which market agents could profit from such data. That is to create trading strategies designed to exploit any systematic ways in which the publicly available data are ignored or discounted in the price-setting process.

Market Efficiency and Managers' Financial Reporting Strategies

The degree to which markets are efficient also has implications for managers' approaches to communicating with their investment communities. The issue becomes most important when the firm pursues an unusual strategy, or when the usual interpretation of financial statements would be misleading in the firm's context. In such a case, the communication avenues managers can successfully pursue depend not only on management's credibility, but also on the degree of understanding present in the investment community. We will return to the issue of management communications in more detail in Chapter 12.

Evidence on Market Efficiency

There is an abundance of evidence consistent with a high degree of efficiency in the primary U.S. securities markets.[1] In fact, during the 1960s and 1970s, the evidence was so one-sided that the efficient markets hypothesis gained widespread acceptance within the academic community and had a major impact on the practicing community as well.

Evidence pointing to very efficient securities markets comes in several forms:

- When information is announced publicly, the markets react *very* quickly.
- It is difficult to identify specific funds or analysts who have consistently generated abnormally high returns.
- A number of studies suggest that stock prices reflect a rather sophisticated level of fundamental analysis.

While a large body of evidence consistent with efficiency exists, recent years have witnessed a re-examination of the once widely accepted thinking. A sampling of the research includes the following:

- On the issue of the speed of stock price response to news, a number of studies suggest that even though prices react quickly, the initial reaction tends to be incomplete.[2]
- A number of studies point to trading strategies that could have been used to outperform market averages.[3]
- Some related evidence—still subject to ongoing debate about its proper interpretation—suggests that, even though market prices reflect some relatively sophisticated analyses, prices still do not fully reflect all the information that could be garnered from publicly available financial statements.[4]

The controversy over the efficiency of securities markets is unlikely to end soon. However, there are some lessons that are accepted by most researchers. First, securities markets not only reflect publicly available information, they also anticipate much of it before it is released. The open question is what fraction of the response remains to be impounded in price once the day of the public release comes to a close. Second, even in most studies that suggest inefficiency, the degree of mispricing is relatively small for large stocks.

Finally, even if some of the evidence is currently difficult to align with the efficient markets hypothesis, it remains a useful benchmark (at a minimum) for thinking about the behavior of security prices. The hypothesis will continue to play that role unless it can be replaced by a more complete theory. Some researchers are developing theories that encompass the existence of market agents who trade for inexplicable reasons, and prices that differ from so-called "fundamental values," even in equilibrium.

APPROACHES TO FUND MANAGEMENT AND SECURITIES ANALYSIS

Approaches used in practice to manage funds and analyze securities are quite varied. One dimension of variation is the extent to which the investments are actively or passively managed. Another variation is whether a quantitative or a traditional fundamental approach is used. Security analysts also vary considerably in terms of whether they produce formal or informal valuations of the firm.

Active Versus Passive Management

Active portfolio management relies heavily on security analysis to identify mispriced securities. The passive portfolio manager serves as a price taker, avoiding the costs of security analysis and turnover while typically seeking to hold a portfolio designed to match some overall market index or sector performance. Combined approaches are also possible. For example, one may actively manage 20 percent of a fund balance while passively managing the remainder. The widespread growth of passively managed funds in the U.S. over the past twenty years serves as testimony to many fund managers' belief that earning superior returns is a difficult thing to do.

Quantitative Versus Traditional Fundamental Analysis

Actively managed funds must depend on some form of security analysis. Some funds employ "technical analysis," which attempts to predict stock price movements on the basis of market indicators (prior stock price movements, volume, etc.). In contrast, "fundamental analysis," the primary approach to security analysis, attempts to evaluate the current market price relative to projections of the firm's future earnings and cash-flow generating potential. Fundamental analysis involves all the steps described in the previous chapters of this book: business strategy analysis, accounting analysis, financial analysis, and prospective analysis (forecasting and valuation).

In recent years, some analysts have supplemented traditional fundamental analysis, which involves a substantial amount of subjective judgment, with more quantitative approaches. The quantitative approaches themselves are quite varied. Some involve simply "screening" stocks on the basis of some set of factors, such as trends in analysts' earnings revisions, price-earnings ratios, price-book ratios, and so on. Whether such approaches are useful depends on the degree of market efficiency relative to the screens.

Quantitative approaches can also involve implementation of some formal model to predict future stock returns. Longstanding statistical techniques such as regression analysis and probit analysis can be used, as can more recently developed, computer-intensive techniques such as neural network analysis. Again, the success of these approaches depends on the degree of market efficiency and whether the analysis can exploit information in ways not otherwise available to market agents as a group.

Quantitative approaches play a more important role in security analysis today than they did a decade or two ago. However, by and large, analysts still rely primarily on the kind of fundamental analysis involving complex human judgments, as outlined in our earlier chapters.

Formal Versus Informal Valuation

Full-scale, formal valuations based on the kind of discounted cash flow methods described in Chapter 6 have become more common, especially in recent years. However, less formal approaches are also possible. For example, an analyst can compare his or her long-term earnings projection with the consensus forecast to generate a buy or sell recommendation. Alternatively, an analyst might recommend a stock because his or her earnings forecast appears relatively high in comparison to the current price. Another possible approach might be labeled "marginalist." This approach involves no attempt to value the firm. The analyst simply assumes that if he or she has unearthed favorable (unfavorable) information believed not to be recognized by others, the stock should be bought (sold).

Unlike many security analysts, investment bankers produce formal valuations as a matter of course. Investment bankers, who estimate values for purposes of bringing a private firm to the public market, for evaluating a merger or buyout proposal, or for purposes of periodic managerial review, must document their valuation in a way that can readily be communicated to management and (if necessary) to the courts.

THE PROCESS OF A COMPREHENSIVE SECURITY ANALYSIS

Given the variety of approaches practiced in security analysis, it is impossible to summarize all of them here. Instead, we briefly outline steps to be included in a comprehensive security analysis. The amount of attention focused on any given step varies among analysts.

Selection of Candidates for Analysis

No analyst can effectively investigate more than a small fraction of the securities on a major exchange, and thus some approach to narrowing the focus must be employed. Sell-side analysts are often organized within an investment house by industry or sector. Thus, they tend to be constrained in their choices of firms to follow. However, from the perspective of a fund manager or an investment firm as a whole, there is usually the freedom to focus on any firm or sector.

Some fund managers direct the energies of their analysts toward identification of stocks that fit some desired risk profile. Individual investors who seek to maintain a well diversified portfolio without holding many stocks also need information about the nature of a firm's risks. Thus, the analyst could first ask:

- What is the risk profile of this firm? How volatile are its earnings stream and its stock price? What are the key possible bad outcomes? What is the upside potential? How closely linked are the firm's risks to the health of the overall economy? Are the risks largely diversifiable, or are they systematic?

For the manager of funds with certain desired characteristics (e.g., growth stocks, "value" stocks, technology stocks, cyclical stocks), the following questions might also be raised:

- Does this firm possess the characteristics of a growth stock? What is the expected pattern of sales and earnings growth for the coming years? Is the firm reinvesting most or all of its earnings?
- Does the firm match the characteristics desired in our "income funds"? Is it a mature or maturing company, prepared to "harvest" profits and distribute them in the form of high dividends?
- Is the firm a candidate for a "value fund"? Does it offer measures of earnings, cash flow, and book value that are high relative to the price?

An alternative approach is to screen firms on the basis of some hypothesis about mispricing—perhaps with follow-up detailed analysis of stocks that meet the specified criteria. For example, one fund managed by a large U.S. insurance company screens stocks on the basis of recent "earnings momentum," as reflected in revisions in the earnings projections of sell-side and buy-side analysts. Upward revisions trigger investigations for possible purchase. The fund operates on the belief that earnings momentum is a positive signal of future price movements. Another fund complements the earnings momentum screen with one based on recent short-term stock price movements, in the hopes of identifying earnings revisions not yet reflected in stock prices.

Inferring Market Expectations

If the security analysis is conducted with an eye toward the identification of mispricing, it must ultimately involve a comparison of the analyst's expectations with those of "the market." One possibility is to view the observed stock price as the reflection of market expectations and to compare the analyst's own estimate of value with that price. However, a stock price is only a "summary statistic." It is useful to have a more detailed idea of the market's expectations about a firm's future performance, expressed in terms of sales, earnings, and other measures. For example, assume an analyst has developed potentially unrecognized information about near-term sales. Whether in fact the information is unrecognized and whether a buy recommendation is appropriate can be easily determined if the analyst knows the market consensus sales forecast.

Around the world, a number of agencies summarize analysts' forecasts of sales and earnings. Forecasts for the next year or two are commonly available, and for many firms a long-run earnings growth projection is also available—typically for three-to-five years. In the U.S., some agencies provide continuous on-line updates to such data, so that if an analyst revises a forecast, that can be made known to fund managers and other analysts within seconds.

As useful as analysts' forecasts of sales and earnings are, they do not represent a complete description of expectations about future performance, and there is no guarantee that consensus analyst forecasts are the same as those reflected in market prices. However, armed with the model in Chapters 6 and 7 that expresses price as a function of future cash flows or earnings, an analyst can draw some educated inferences about the expectations embedded in stock prices.

In Chapter 6, our primary estimate of the value of Compaq stock in December 1993 was $59, based on analyst forecasts from Duff & Phelps—forecasts that were very close to the consensus analyst forecast at the time.[5] However, the observed stock price was substantially higher, at $74. The discrepancy raises questions about what the market is really expecting, and whether a particular projection of future earnings has already been impounded in the market price. What if an analyst had information suggesting expected long-run earnings should be 10 percent higher than the median published analyst forecast? Does that suggest the analyst should label the stock a "buy"? Or have market agents already embedded such information in the price, even though the published consensus does not yet reflect it?

By altering the amounts assumed for key value drivers and arriving at combinations that generate an estimated value equal to the observed market price, the analyst can infer what the market may have been expecting for Compaq in late 1993. Table 8-1 below summarizes the "base case" combinations from Chapter 6 as well as other combinations that generate higher values. The lightly shaded cells represent combinations of assumptions that are consistent with market prices close to the observed price (in the range of $70 to $80). The more darkly shaded cells indicate combinations that produce an estimated price much higher than the market price (above $80).

Table 8-1 indicates that in order to explain an observed market price of $74 while holding the cost of capital at 13 percent, one must project a *combination* of higher sales growth *and* higher margins than we projected in Chapter 6. However, the strong competition in the industry would probably make margins any higher than 5 percent difficult to achieve over such a long period. Five percent is sufficient to produce ROEs in the range of about 22 percent, in excess of long-run industry norms and the cost of capital. More optimistic sales forecasts would be easier to justify. Although the industry is expected to grow at a rate of only 10 to 15 percent in the short run, and at a slower pace in the long run, Compaq is currently expanding market share to remain above that rate. First Boston analyst Gurley expects that the future will be harsh on the less efficient clone assemblers that produce 40 percent of PCs, and projects that low-cost producers with a recognized brand name may continue to take market share from those firms for several years. In the most optimistic scenario above, Compaq achieves *average* 17 percent growth over 1993–2000, implying nearly 16 percent in the late 1990s—substantially higher than the expected long-run industry growth rate. Progress toward such growth appears to be already reflected in the price.

Another lesson from the table is that none of the cases considered produce an estimated value as high as the observed price when the cost of capital is as high as 14 percent—which, in turn, is still slightly lower than our estimate in Chapter 6, based on the capital asset pricing model (CAPM) and the size effect. Thus, either market agents perceive Compaq as less risky than our model in Chapter 6 assumed, or market agents are even more optimistic than the most optimistic scenario considered above.

Table 8-1 Alternative Assumptions about Value Drivers for Compaq, Including Combinations Consistent with Observed Market Price of $74

| | Average annual sales growth, 1993 to 2000 | | | | | |
| | Base case: Sales growth = 13.6% | | Projected sales growth = 15%* | | Projected sales growth = 17%* | |
	Base case	Other case	Base case	Other case	Base case	Other case
Profit margin declines by year 2000 to:	4.4%	5.0%	4.4%	5.0%	4.4%	5.0%
Implied earnings level in year 2000:	$773	$880	$840	$960	$950	$1,080
Implied price, based on cost of capital of:						
14 percent	$ 54	$ 60	$ 56	$ 66	$ 60	$ 68
13 percent	$ 59	$ 67	$ 63	$ 73	$ 67	$ 76
12 percent	$ 67	$ 75	$ 71	$ 83	$ 76	$ 87

*The base case was altered to produce average sales growth of 15 percent (17 percent) from 1993 to 2000, by altering projected growth rates in 1997 through 2000 from 10 percent to 12.31 percent (15.75 percent). Sales in the year 2000 are projected at $19,128 ($21,581).

Security analysis need not involve such a detailed attempt to infer market expectations. However, whether the analysis is made explicit or not, a good analyst understands what economic scenarios could plausibly be reflected in the observed price. It is useful to know, for example, that the price is *already* reflecting expectations of supernormal margins for Compaq, and that any further price appreciation is more likely to be hinged on spreading those high margins over an even larger market share. The market appears to be quite optimistic about Compaq's future, despite how difficult it is to sustain a competitive advantage in the PC industry.

Developing the Analyst's Expectations

Ultimately, a security analyst must compare his or her own view of a stock with the view embedded in the market price. The analyst's own view is generated using the same tools discussed in Chapters 2 through 7: business strategy analysis, accounting analysis, financial analysis, and prospective analysis. Thus, key questions in the analysis will be:

- How profitable is the firm? In light of industry conditions, the firm's corporate strategy, and its barriers to competition, how sustainable is that rate of profitability?
- What are the opportunities for growth for this firm?
- How risky is this firm? How vulnerable are operations to general economic down-

turns? How highly levered is the firm? What does the riskiness of the firm imply about its cost of capital?

- How do answers to the above questions compare to the expectations embedded in the observed stock price?

The final product of the work described in Chapters 2 through 7 is, of course, a forecast of the firm's future earnings and cash flows and an estimate of the firm's value. However, that final product is less important than the understanding of the business and its industry that the analysis provides. It is such understanding that positions the analyst to interpret new information as it arrives and to infer its implications. A good illustration is provided by our Compaq analyst, Bill Gurley.

By early April of 1994, it was apparent that sales volume at Compaq was running well in excess of the expectations analysts held at the end of 1993. Not only were sales expanding more quickly than projected, but profit margins were *increasing* at the same time! Accordingly, Compaq's stock price had shot up to $100. The consensus earnings forecasts for 1994 and 1995 were running at $7.03 per share and $8.19 per share, respectively, up from 1993's actual EPS of $5.44.[6]

As optimistic as the market was about Compaq at the time, analyst Gurley saw reason for even further optimism. The basis for Gurley's view lay in signals about future sales volume. One signal came directly from management: its announced intention to increase worldwide market share to 14 percent in 1994. However, a second confirming signal was inferred. It was based on Gurley's understanding of Compaq's cash position, its recent decision to issue $300 million of debt, and its statement that the proceeds would be used in part to finance working capital. Given its cash balance at the end of 1993 and the relation between its sales and working capital, Gurley estimated that Compaq could not possibly require more cash to finance inventory and receivables unless it were planning for sales volume in excess of $11.4 billion—a nearly 60 percent increase over 1993. On that basis, Gurley forecast 1994 sales "conservatively" at $10.5 billion, 1994 EPS at $7.95, and 1995 EPS at $10.00. Assuming that Compaq's growth prospects beyond 1995 would justify a higher-than-industry-average PE multiple of 15 in 1995, Gurley projected the price would reach $150 per share in that year. He rated the stock a "buy," even at $100. In fact, the stock did rise to over $110 within the month and to over $125 (on a split-adjusted basis) later in 1994.[7]

Gurley's work illustrates how the understanding developed from a thorough fundamental analysis can enhance one's ability to recognize the import of newly arriving information. Viewed in isolation, a debt issue would not necessarily have any implications for sales volume. However, in the context of an understanding of Compaq's current cash position, its relation of working capital to sales, and other factors, Gurley saw in the debt issue an action that confirmed management's optimistic disclosures about future sales.

The Final Product of Security Analysis

For sell-side analysts like Bill Gurley, or buy-side analysts who must communicate with fund managers, the final product of security analysis is a recommendation to buy, sell, or hold the stock (or some more refined ranking). The recommendation is supported by a set of forecasts and a report summarizing the foundation for the recommendation. Analysts' reports often delve into significant detail. For example, Gurley's April 1994 buy recommendation was supported by a 10-page report, complete with line-by-line income statement forecasts for each quarter of 1994 and for the year 1995.

FINANCIAL STATEMENT DATA AND SECURITY PRICES

While security analysis clearly involves much information beyond the financial statements, those statements play an important role. Much research over the past three decades has helped describe the role of financial statement data in the setting of security prices. An understanding of that role provides an appreciation for the importance of that data in security analysis, as well as market agents' ability to digest such data.

A thorough review of research on financial statement data and security prices lies well outside the scope of this chapter. However, we can summarize a few of the key findings from the literature.

Earnings and book value are good indicators of stock prices.

Accounting earnings and book values ignore important aspects of the firm's economic landscape, are subject to distortion by managers, and are not adjusted for inflation in the U.S. and most other countries. One could (and the financial press frequently does) reasonably question whether accounting numbers are good indicators of the expected cash flows that should drive stock prices.

It turns out that, in spite of the widely discussed shortcomings of accounting systems, earnings and book value offer a good reflection of much of the information in security prices. In the U.S., the combination of book value (per-share) and earnings explains, in a typical year, nearly two-thirds of the cross-sectional variation in stock prices.[8] Such a finding indicates that book value and earnings provide good starting points for predicting the cash flows that should drive prices.

That book value and earnings do not summarize the information in prices more completely should not be surprising. There are a number of factors that influence prices that accounting systems are not designed to capture well, including, for example, the value of brand assets, growth opportunities, and research and development.

Explaining variation in the *level* of a firm's stock prices is one thing; explaining stock returns, which depend on *changes* in those levels, is quite another. The latter is clearly the more challenging task. It is necessary to not only identify factors that explain value, but also to determine to what extent information about the factors became known to market agents within the interval over which the price changes are measured. Researchers have in fact had difficulty explaining more than a small fraction of the variance in stock returns over years or shorter intervals. Earnings data are the most powerful of the factors that have been studied, but even so, the explanatory power is relatively low. A combination of earnings and earnings changes (both expressed relative to price at the beginning of the year) explains only about 5–15 percent of the variation in annual stock returns.[9]

To summarize, the picture that emerges is that earnings data provide somewhat noisy indicators of value—good enough to approximate whether the stock price should be closer to, say, $10 than $5, but not sufficiently precise to provide clear indications of whether that price level might have changed by, for example, 10 percent rather than 5 percent over the past year. Thus, while the earnings number is a good starting point for analysis, more information is certainly required to track stock prices.

Market agents can anticipate much of the information in earnings.

To say that financial statement data *reflect* much of the information in prices does not necessarily mean that when those data are reported, they convey *new* information. Indeed, market agents have access to a variety of information sources more timely than financial statements, and they use these sources to anticipate the data ultimately revealed in financial statements.

Figure 8-1 describes the extent to which the key financial statement datum—earnings—is anticipated by market agents.[10] In the figure, firms are divided into 10 groups, based on the extent to which quarterly earnings have changed from prior quarters. (The earnings change is labeled SUE, for standardized unexpected earnings.) The importance of the earnings information is evident in how much the stock price performance differs across the groups. The top performers experience a three-month stock price increase 4.2 percent greater than a control group, while those at the bottom underperform by 6.1 percent. However, note that most (about 60 percent) of this movement occurs *before* the week of the earnings announcement. This underscores that there are sources more timely than earnings that reflect the same information that will ultimately be reflected in earnings.

How does the market anticipate the earnings announcement? In some cases, management itself reveals information. For example, on several occasions in 1993 and 1994, Compaq's management made statements to the press and in financial analysts' meetings about their progress in gaining market share. That information should improve market agents' ability to forecast earnings. Sometimes management will make explicit statements about the range in which earnings are likely to be. Even in the absence of such direct information channels, however, it should be possible to anticipate to some extent how well a firm is performing. In the case of Compaq, one could learn through discussions with retail outlets, suppliers, competitors, and industry news sources. Even general information about the state of the economy, the retail sector, and the computer industry should permit more educated guesses about how well the firm is performing.

The findings summarized in Figure 8-1 offer an important lesson for security analysts. Specifically, it's not good enough to be aware of earnings as soon as they are announced. A good analyst also tracks more timely information sources.

A final comment on Figure 8-1 pertains to stock price movements *after* the earnings are announced. Note that for those firms with earnings increases, the stock prices continue to rise, and for those with earnings decreases, the prices continue to fall (relative to the control group). This is the phenomenon that was mentioned briefly in the section

Figure 8-1 Stock Price Movements Before and After Quarterly Earnings Announcements

Stock return relative to control group (%)

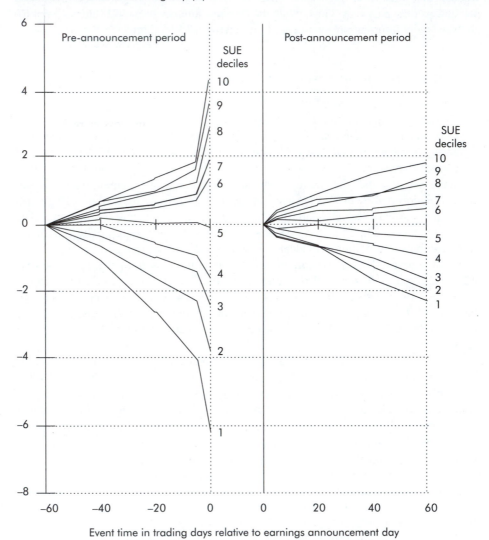

Event time in trading days relative to earnings announcement day

Explanation: Firms are grouped into ten portfolios based on "standardized unexpected earnings," or SUE: actual earnings less a statistical forecast, and scaled by the standard deviation of past unexpected earnings. Stock returns (less those for a size control group) are then cumulated over the 60 days before and after the earnings announcement for each of the ten groups.

on market efficiency. The figure suggests that even though most of the response to earnings occurs on a timely basis, some portion of the response appears to be delayed.

Financial statement details matter.

Throughout our discussion of business strategy analysis, accounting analysis, financial analysis, and prospective analysis, we drew on financial statement information beyond simply earnings. Moreover, in the chapter on accounting analysis, we pointed to a number of items in the financials that could temper one's view of the quality of earnings. Assuming market agents are capable of conducting similar analyses, we would expect stock prices to reflect financial statement details beyond just earnings.

A large number of studies have examined the relation between stock prices and financial statement data beyond earnings. For example, one study focused on roughly a dozen financial statement variables that could be useful in assessing the quality of earnings: disproportionate inventory and receivables buildups, increases in gross margin percentage, and other factors.[11] The results confirm that stock prices reflect such variables. In other words, one can explain variation in stock prices better when armed not just with earnings but also with the factors that help analysts interpret the quality of earnings.

Many studies have also examined the extent to which footnote disclosures are related to stock price behavior. For example, one study examined the extent to which unrealized gains in banks' investment portfolios are reflected in stock prices.[12] The conclusion of most studies in this area is that prices at least approximately reflect the details in footnotes. Thus, the evidence is consistent with the footnotes presenting important data and with analysts "doing their homework." Whether market agents do a *complete* job of digesting footnote data is less clear.

Research on the relation of stock prices to financial statement details continues, and many of the questions in the area remain unsettled.[13] A few general comments on the current state of understanding can be offered. First, many financial statement details are important, in the sense that they reflect factors that drive stock prices. Second, whether market agents learn about such details from the financial statements themselves or from more timely sources is difficult to know. (Most studies are not sharp enough to answer this question.) Third, whether stock prices reflect financial statement details completely and immediately remains a subject of debate, with some studies on both sides of the issue. One implication of the research for security analysts is that to stay abreast of the market one must be able to gather and interpret the kind of information reflected in the financial statement details—either by going directly to the statements or (preferably) to more timely sources.

SUMMARY AND CONCLUSIONS

Equity security analysis is the evaluation of a firm and its prospects from the perspective of a current or potential investor in the firm's stock. Security analysis is one component of a larger investment process that involves (1) establishing the objectives of the investor or fund, (2) forming expectations about the future returns and risks of individual securities, and then (3) combining individual securities into portfolios to maximize progress toward the investment objectives.

Some security analysis is devoted primarily to assuring that a stock possesses the proper risk profile and other desired characteristics prior to inclusion in an investor's portfolio. However, especially for many professional buy-side and sell-side security analysts, the analysis is also directed toward the identification of mispriced securities. In equilibrium, such activity will be rewarding for those with the strongest comparative advantage. They will be the ones able to identify any mispricing at the lowest cost and exert pressure on the price so as to correct the mispricing. What kinds of efforts are productive in this domain depends on the degree of market efficiency. A large body of evidence exists that is supportive of a high degree of efficiency in the U.S. market, but recent evidence has reopened the debate on this issue.

In practice, a wide variety of approaches to fund management and security analysis are employed. However, at the core of the analyses are the same steps outlined in Chapters 2 through 7 of this book: business strategy analysis, accounting analysis, financial analysis, and prospective analysis (forecasting and valuation). For the professional analyst, the final product of the work is, of course, a forecast of the firm's future earnings and cash flows, and an estimate of the firm's value. However, that final product is less important than the understanding of the business and its industry, which the analysis provides. It is such understanding that positions the analyst to interpret new information as it arrives and infer its implications.

While security analysis clearly involves much information beyond the financial statements, those statements play an important role. Much research over the past three decades has helped describe the role of financial statement data in the setting of security prices. The research shows conclusively that financial statements reflect much of the information that drives prices. However, whether market agents acquire the information directly from the financial statements themselves or from more timely sources is less clear. Much of the information in financial statements appears to be anticipated before its release. Finally, whether stock prices reflect financial statement details completely and immediately remains a subject of debate. One implication of the research for security analysts is that to stay abreast of the market, one must be able to gather and interpret the kind of information reflected in the financial statement details—either by going directly to the statements or (preferably) to more timely sources.

NOTES

1. For a recent review of evidence on market efficiency, see Eugene Fama, "Efficient Capital Markets: II," *Journal of Finance* (December 1991): 1575–1618.

2. For example, see V. Bernard and J. Thomas, "Evidence that Stock Prices Do Not Fully Reflect the Implications of Current Earnings for Future Earnings," *Journal of Accounting and Economics* (December 1990): 305–341.

3. A good example, in which a "value stock" strategy is examined, is in Josef Lakonishok, Andre Shleifer, and Robert Vishny, "Contrarian Investment, Extrapolation, and Risk," *Journal of Finance* (December 1994): 1541–1578.

4. For example, see J. Ou and S. Penman, "Financial Statement Analysis and the Prediction of Stock Returns," *Journal of Accounting and Economics* (November 1989a): 295–330; R. Holth-

ausen and D. Larcker, "The Prediction of Stock Returns Using Financial Statement Information," *Journal of Accounting and Economics* (June/September 1992): 373–412; and Richard Sloan, "Do Stock Prices Fully Impound Information in Accruals about Future Earnings?" working paper, University of Pennsylvania (1995).

5. The $59 estimate is based on a 13 percent discount rate, and it allows for growth in sales and abnormal earnings beyond 2000 at the rate of inflation.

6. Consensus forecasts are from the March/April 1994 edition of I/B/E/S Quarterly Company Data.

7. Compaq's sales volume for 1994 ultimately reached $10.9 billion. EPS was $9.63 on a split-adjusted basis. The stock price peaked at $133 during early 1995 (on a split-adjusted basis), and fell back to $90 in the spring of 1995.

8. On average across time, 66 percent of the variance in price per share is explained by book value per share and the rank of earnings per share. See Victor Bernard, "Accounting-Based Valuation, the Determinants of Market-to-Book Ratios, and Implications for Financial Statements Analysis," working paper, University of Michigan (January 1994).

9. For two of several discussions of research in this area, see Baruch Lev, "On the Usefulness of Earnings and Earning Research: Lessons and Directions from Two Decades of Empirical Research," *Journal of Accounting Research*, supplement 1989: 153–197; and Peter Easton, Trevor Harris, and James Ohlson, "Aggregate Accounting Earnings Can Explain Most of Security Returns," *Journal of Accounting and Economics* (June/September 1992): 119–142.

10. V. Bernard and J. Thomas, "Post-Earnings-Announcement Drift: Delayed Price Response or Risk Premium?" *Journal of Accounting Research* (Supplement 1989): 1–36. For seminal work on the timeliness of earnings information, see R. Ball and P. Brown, "An Empirical Evaluation of Accounting Income Numbers," *Journal of Accounting Research* (Autumn 1968): 159–178; and William H. Beaver, "The Information Content of Annual Earnings Announcements," *Journal of Accounting Research* (Supplement, 1968), 67–92.

11. Baruch Lev and Ramu Thiagarajan, "Fundamental Information Analysis," *Journal of Accounting Research* (Autumn 1993): 190–215.

12. M. Barth, "Fair value accounting: Evidence from investment securities and the market valuation of banks," *The Accounting Review* (January 1994), 1–25.

13. For some incomplete reviews of work in this area, see Victor Bernard, "Capital Markets Research in Accounting During the 1980's: A Critical Review," in *The State of Accounting Research As We Enter the 1990's,* Thomas J. Frecka, editor. (Urbana: University of Illinois Press, 1989): 72–120; and Victor Bernard and Katherine Schipper, "Recognition and Disclosure in Financial Reporting," working paper, University of Michigan (November 1994).

CASES

Anacomp, Inc.	The Murray Ohio Manufacturing Co.
CUC International (A)	Southwestern Fuel Systems, Inc.
The Gap, Inc.	Thousand Trails, Inc.
Hawkeye Bancorporation	The Timberland Company
Morlan International, Inc.	E. Wedel, S.A.

chapter 9

Credit Analysis and Distress Prediction

C redit analysis is the evaluation of a firm from the perspective of a holder or potential holder of its debt, including trade payables, loans, and public debt securities. A key element of credit analysis is the prediction of the likelihood a firm will face financial distress.

Credit analysis is involved in a wide variety of decision contexts:

- A potential supplier asks: Should I sell products or services to this firm? The associated credit will be extended only for a short period, but the amount is large and I should have some assurance that collection risks are manageable.
- A commercial banker asks: Should we extend a loan to this firm? If so, how should it be structured? How should it be priced?
- If the loan is granted, the banker must later ask: Are we still providing the services, including credit, that this firm needs? Is the firm still in compliance with the loan terms? If not, is there a need to restructure the loan, and if so, how? Is the situation serious enough to call for accelerating the repayment of the loan?
- A pension fund manager, insurance company, or other investor asks: Are these debt securities a sound investment? What is the probability that the firm will face distress and default on the debt? Does the yield provide adequate compensation for the default risk involved?
- An investor contemplating purchase of debt securities in default asks: How likely is it that this firm can be turned around? In light of the high yield on this debt, relative to its current price, can I accept the risk that the debt will not be repaid in full?

Although credit analysis is typically viewed from the perspective of the financier, it is obviously important to the borrower as well:

- A manager of a small firm asks: What are our options for credit financing? Would the firm qualify for bank financing? If so, what type of financing would be possible? How costly would it be? Would the terms of the financing constrain our flexibility?

- A manager of a large firm asks: "What are our options for credit financing? Is the firm strong enough to raise funds in the public market? If so, what is our debt rating likely to be? What required yield would that rating imply?

Finally, there are third parties—those other than borrowers and lenders—who are interested in the general issue of how likely it is that a firm will avoid financial distress:

- An auditor asks: How likely is it that this firm will survive beyond the short run? In evaluating the firm's financials, should I consider it a going concern?
- An actual or potential employee asks: How confident can I be that this firm will be able to offer employment over the long term?
- A potential customer asks: What assurance is there that this firm will survive to provide warranty services, replacement parts, product updates, and other services?
- A competitor asks: Will this firm survive the current industry shakeout? What are the implications of potential financial distress at this firm for my pricing and market share?

THE MARKET FOR CREDIT

An understanding of credit analysis requires an appreciation for the various players in the market for credit. We describe those players briefly here, and discuss the suppliers of credit to Compaq and its competitors.

Suppliers of Credit

The major suppliers in the market for credit are described below.

COMMERCIAL BANKS.   Commercial banks are very important players in the market for credit. Since banks tend to provide a range of services to a client, and have intimate knowledge of the client and its operations, they have a comparative advantage in extending credit in settings where (1) knowledge gained through close contact with management reduces the perceived riskiness of the credit and (2) credit risk can be contained through careful monitoring of the firm.

A constraint on bank lending operations is that the credit risk be relatively low, so that the bank's loan portfolio will be of acceptably high quality to bank regulators. Because of the importance of maintaining public confidence in the banking sector and the desire to shield government deposit insurance from risk, governments have incentives to constrain banks' exposure to credit risk. Banks also tend to shield themselves from the risk of shifts in interest rates by avoiding fixed-rate loans with long maturities. Since most of banks' capital comes from short-term deposits, such long-term loans leave them exposed to increases in interest rates, unless the risk can be hedged with derivatives. Thus, banks are less likely to play a role when a firm requires a very long-term commitment to financing. However, in some such cases they assist in providing a placement of the debt with, say, an insurance company, a pension fund, or a group of private investors.

OTHER FINANCIAL INSTITUTIONS.   Banks face competition in the commercial lending market from a variety of sources. In the U.S., there is competition from savings and loans, even though the latter are relatively more involved in financing mortgages. Finance companies compete with banks in the market for asset-based lending (i.e., the secured financing of specific assets, such as receivables, inventory, or equipment). Insurance companies are involved in a variety of lending activities. Since life insurance companies face obligations of a long-term nature, they often seek investments of long duration (e.g., long-term bonds or loans to support large, long-term commercial real estate and development projects). Investment bankers are prepared to place debt securities with private investors or in the public markets (discussed below). Various government agencies are another source of credit.

PUBLIC DEBT MARKETS.   Some firms have the size, strength, and credibility necessary to bypass the banking sector and seek financing directly from investors, either through sales of commercial paper or through the issuance of bonds. Such debt issues are facilitated by the assignment of a debt rating. In the U.S., Moody's and Standard and Poor's are the two largest rating agencies. A firm's debt rating influences the yield that must be offered to sell the debt instruments. After the debt issue, the rating agencies continue to monitor the firm's financial condition. Changes in the rating are associated with fluctuation in the price of the securities.

Banks often provide financing in tandem with a public debt issue or other source of financing. In highly-levered transactions, such as leveraged buyouts, banks commonly provide financing along with a public debt issue that would have a lower priority in case of bankruptcy. The bank's "senior financing" would typically be scheduled for earlier retirement than the public debt, and it would carry a lower yield. For smaller or startup firms, banks often provide credit in conjunction with equity financing from venture capitalists. Note that in the case of both the leveraged buyout and the startup company, the bank helps provide the cash needed to make the deal happen, but does so in a way that shields it from risks that would be unacceptably high in the banking sector.

SELLERS WHO PROVIDE FINANCING.   Another sector of the market for credit are manufacturers and other suppliers of goods and services. As a matter of course, such firms tend to finance their customers' purchases on an unsecured basis for periods of 30 to 60 days. Suppliers will, on occasion, also agree to provide more extended financing, usually with the support of a secured note. A supplier may be willing to grant such a loan in the expectation that the creditor will survive a cash shortage and remain an important customer in the future. However, the customer would typically seek such an arrangement only if bank financing is unavailable, because it could constrain flexibility in selecting among and/or negotiating with suppliers.

Sources of Credit for Compaq and Its Competitors

In our prior discussion of Compaq Computer, we indicated that the firm had no debt, but that it had the capacity to assume leverage if desired. In March of 1994, Compaq did assume $300 million of debt. At that time, Compaq had a $300 million line of credit on which it could have drawn. However, not surprisingly, Compaq bypassed its financial institutions and went directly to the public debt markets to raise the funds. Despite the volatility in the computer industry, Compaq's strong balance sheet and earnings potential allowed it to issue debt with an investment grade rating. The issue included $150 million of 5-year notes with a yield of 6.5 percent and $150 million of 10-year notes at 7.25 percent—rates that were quite favorable, even relative to most other investment-grade bonds trading at the time.

Compaq's direct competitors discussed in Chapter 7 include two with debt: AST Research and Dell Computer. Neither firm matches Compaq's size or financial strength and, accordingly, their arrangements for financing are quite different. AST Research relies on a revolving credit facility from a consortium of eight major international banks. Dell appealed to the public debt markets for financing in 1993, but was forced to offer a yield of 11 percent to facilitate the issue (at a time when investment grade bonds were selling for yields in the range of 7 to 8 percent).

THE CREDIT ANALYSIS PROCESS

At first blush, credit analysis might appear less difficult than the valuation task discussed in Chapters 6 and 7. After all, a potential creditor ultimately cares only about whether the firm is strong enough to pay its debts at the scheduled times. The firm's exact value, its upside potential, or its distance from the threshold of credit-worthiness may not appear so important. Viewed in that way, credit analysis may seem more like a "zero-one" decision: either the credit is extended, or it is not.

It turns out, however, that credit analysis involves more than "just" establishing credit-worthiness. First, there are ranges of credit-worthiness, and it is important to understand where a firm lies within that range for purposes of pricing and structuring a loan. Moreover, if the creditor is a bank or other financial institution with an expected continuing relationship with the borrower, the borrower's upside potential is important, even though downside risk must be the primary consideration in credit analysis. A firm that offers growth potential also offers opportunities for income-generating financial services.

Given this broader view of credit analysis, it should not be surprising that it involves most of the same issues already discussed in the prior chapters on business strategy analysis, accounting analysis, financial analysis, and prospective analysis. Perhaps the greatest difference is that credit analysis rarely involves any explicit attempt to estimate the value of the firm's equity. However, the determinants of that value are relevant in credit analysis, because a larger equity cushion translates into lower risk for the creditor.

Below we describe one series of steps that is used by commercial lenders in credit analysis. Of course, not all commercial lenders follow the same process, but the steps are representative of typical approaches. The approach used by commercial lenders is of interest in its own right and illustrates a comprehensive credit analysis. However, analysis by others who grant credit often differs. For example, even when a manufacturer conducts some credit analysis prior to granting credit to a customer, it is typically much less extensive than the analysis conducted by a banker because the credit is very short-term and the manufacturer is willing to bear some credit risk in the interest of generating a profit on the sale.

We present the steps in a particular order, but they are in fact all interdependent. Thus, analysis at one step may need to be rethought, depending on the analysis at some later step.

Step 1: Consider the Nature and Purpose of the Loan

Understanding the purpose of a loan is important not just for deciding whether it should be granted, but also for structuring the loan. Loans might be required for only a few months, for several years, or even as a permanent part of a firm's capital structure. Loans might be used for replacement of other financing, to support working capital needs, or to finance the acquisition of long-term assets or another firm.

The required amount of the loan must also be established. In the case of small and medium-sized companies, a banker would typically prefer to be the sole financier of the business, in which case the loan would have to be large enough to retire existing debt. The preference for serving as the sole financier is not just to gain an advantage in providing a menu of financial services to the firm. It also reflects the desirability of not permitting another creditor to maintain a superior interest that would give it a higher priority in case of bankruptcy. If other creditors are willing to subordinate their positions to the bank, that would of course be acceptable so far as the bank is concerned.

In many cases, the commercial lender deals with firms that may have parent-subsidiary relations. The question of to whom one should lend then arises. The answer is usually the entity that owns the assets that will serve as collateral (or that could serve as such if needed in the future). If this entity is the subsidiary and the parent presents some financial strength independent of the subsidiary, a guarantee of the parent could be considered.

Step 2: Consider the Type of Loan and Available Security

The type of loan considered is a function of not only its purpose, but also the financial strength of the borrower. Thus, to some extent, the loan type will be dictated by the financial analysis described in the following step in the process. Some of the possibilities are as follows:

- *Open line of credit.* An open line of credit permits the borrower to receive cash up to some specified maximum on an as-needed basis for a specified term, such as one year. To maintain this option, the borrower pays a fee (e.g., 3/8 of 1 percent) on the unused balance, in addition to the interest on any used amount. An open line of credit is useful in cases where the borrower's cash needs are difficult to anticipate.

- *Revolving line of credit.* When it is clear that a firm will need credit beyond the short run, financing may be provided in the form of a "revolver." Sometimes used to support working capital needs, the borrower is scheduled to make payments as the operating cycle proceeds and inventory and receivables are converted to cash. However, it is also expected that cash will continue to be advanced so long as the borrower remains in good standing. In addition to interest on amounts outstanding, a fee is charged on the unused line.
- *Working capital loan.* Such a loan is used to finance inventory and receivables, and is usually secured. The maximum loan balance may be tied to the balance of the working capital accounts. For example, the loan may be allowed to rise to no more than 80 percent of receivables less than 60 days old.
- *Term loan.* Term loans are used for long-term needs and are often secured with long-term assets, such as plant or equipment. Typically, the loan will be amortized, requiring periodic payments to reduce the loan balance.
- *Mortgage loan.* Mortgages support the financing of real estate, have long terms, and require periodic amortization of the loan balance.
- *Lease financing.* Lease financing can be used to facilitate the acquisition of any asset, but is most commonly used for equipment, including vehicles. Leases may be structured over periods of 1 to 15 years, depending on the life of the underlying asset.

Much bank lending is done on a secured basis, especially with smaller and more highly levered companies. Security will be required unless the loan is short-term and the borrower exposes the bank to minimal default risk. When security is required, one consideration is whether the amount of available security is sufficient to support the loan. The amount that a bank will lend on given security involves business judgment, and it depends on a variety of factors that affect the liquidity of the security in the context of a situation where the firm is distressed. The following are some rules of thumb often applied in commercial lending to various categories of security:

- *Receivables.* Accounts receivable are usually considered the most desirable form of security because they are the most liquid. One large regional bank allows loans of 50 to 80 percent of the balance of nondelinquent accounts. The percentage applied is lower when (1) there are many small accounts that would be costly to collect in the case the firm is distressed; (2) there are a few very large accounts, such that problems with a single customer could be serious; and/or (3) the customer's financial health is closely related to that of the borrower, so that collectibility is endangered just when the borrower is in default. On the latter score, banks often refuse to accept receivables from affiliates as effective security.
- *Inventory.* The desirability of inventory as security varies widely. The best case scenario is inventory consisting of a common commodity that can easily be sold to other parties if the borrower defaults. More specialized inventory, with appeal to only a limited set of buyers, or inventory that is costly to store or transport, is less desirable. The large regional bank mentioned above lends up to 60 percent on raw materials, 50 percent on finished goods, and 20 percent on work in process.

- *Machinery and equipment.* Machinery and equipment is less desirable as collateral. It is likely to be used, and it must be stored, insured, and marketed. Keeping the costs of these activities in mind, banks typically will loan only up to 50 percent of the estimated value of such assets in a forced sale, such as an auction.
- *Real estate.* The value of real estate as collateral varies considerably. Banks will often lend up to 80 percent of the appraised value of readily salable real estate. However, a factory designed for a unique purpose would be much less desirable.

When security is required to make a loan viable, a commercial lender will estimate the amounts that could be loaned on each of the assets available as security. Unless the amount exceeds the required loan balance, the loan would not be extended.

Even when a loan is not secured initially, a bank can require a "negative pledge" on the firm's assets—a pledge that the firm will not use the assets as security for any other creditor. In that case, if the borrower begins to experience difficulty and defaults on the loan, and if there are no other creditors in the picture, the bank can demand the loan become secured if it is to remain outstanding.

Step 3: Analyze the Potential Borrower's Financial Status

This portion of the analysis involves all the steps discussed in our chapters on business strategy analysis, accounting analysis, and financial analysis. The emphasis, however, is on the firm's ability to service the debt at the scheduled rate. The focus of the analysis depends on the type of financing under consideration. For example, if a short-term loan is considered to support seasonal fluctuations in inventory, the emphasis would be on the ability of the firm to convert the inventory into cash on a timely basis. In contrast, a term loan to support plant and equipment must be made with confidence in the long-run earnings prospects of the firm.

Some of the questions to be addressed in this analysis are:

- *Business strategy analysis*:
  How does this business work? Why is it valuable? What is its strategy for sustaining or enhancing that value? How well qualified is the management to carry out that strategy effectively? Is the viability of the business highly dependent on the talents of the existing management team?
- *Accounting analysis*:
  How well do the firm's financial statements reflect its underlying economic reality? Are there reasons to believe that the firm's performance is stronger or weaker than reported profitability would suggest? Are there sizable off-balance-sheet liabilities (e.g., operating leases) that would affect the potential borrower's ability to repay the loan?
- *Financial analysis*:
  Is the firm's level of profitability unusually high or low? What are the sources of any unusual degree of profitability? How sustainable are they? What risks are associated with the operating profit stream?

How highly levered is the firm?

What is the firm's funds flow picture? What are its major sources and uses of funds? Are funds required to finance expected growth? How great are fund flows expected to be, relative to the debt service required? Given the possible volatility in those fund flows, how likely is it that they could fall to a level insufficient to service debt and meet other commitments?

Ultimately, the key question in the financial analysis is how likely it is that cash flows will be sufficient to repay the loan. With that question in mind, lenders focus much attention on solvency ratios: the magnitude of various measures of profits and cash flows relative to debt service and other requirements. To the extent such a ratio exceeds one, it indicates the "margin of safety" the lender faces. When such a ratio is combined with an assessment of the variance in its numerator, it provides an indication of the probability of nonpayment.

Ratio analysis from the perspective of a creditor differs somewhat from that of an owner. For example, there is greater emphasis on cash flows and earnings available to *all* claimants (not just owners) *before* taxes (since interest is tax-deductible and paid out of pre-tax dollars). To illustrate, the creditor's perspective is apparent in the following solvency ratio, called the "funds flow coverage ratio":

$$\text{Funds flow coverage} = \frac{\text{EBIT} + \text{Depreciation}}{\text{Interest} + \dfrac{\text{Debt repayment}}{(1 - \text{tax rate})} + \dfrac{\text{Preferred dividends}}{(1 - \text{tax rate})}}$$

We see earnings before both interest and taxes in the numerator. This measures the numerator in a way that can be compared directly to the interest expense in the denominator, because interest expense is paid out of pre-tax dollars. In contrast, any payment of principal scheduled for a given year is nondeductible and must be made out of after-tax profits. In essence, with a 50 percent tax rate, one dollar of principal payment is "twice as expensive" as a one-dollar interest payment. Scaling the payment of principal by (1 - tax rate) accounts for this. The same idea applies to preferred dividends, which are not tax deductible.

The funds flow coverage ratio provides an indication of how comfortably the funds flow can cover unavoidable expenditures. The ratio excludes payments such as common dividends and capital expenditures on the premise that they could be reduced to zero to make debt payments if necessary.[1] Clearly, however, if the firm is to survive in the long run, funds flow must be sufficient to not only service debt but also maintain plant assets. Thus, long-run survival requires a funds flow coverage ratio well in excess of 1.[2]

It would be overly simplistic to establish any particular threshold above which a ratio indicates a loan is justified. However, a creditor clearly wants to be in a position to be repaid on schedule, even when the borrower faces a reasonably foreseeable difficulty. That argues for lending only when the funds flow coverage is expected to exceed 1, even in a recession scenario—and higher if some allowance for capital expenditures is prudent.

The financial analysis should produce more than an assessment of the risk of nonpayment. It should also identify the nature of the significant risks. At many commercial banks, it is standard operating procedure to summarize the analysis of the firm by listing the key risks that could lead to default and factors that could be used to control those risks if the loan were made. That information can be used in structuring the detailed terms of the loan so as to trigger default when problems arise, at a stage early enough to permit corrective action.

Step 4: Utilize Forecasts to Assess Payment Prospects

Already implicit in some of the above discussion is a forward-looking view of the firm's ability to service the loan. Good credit analysis should also be supported by explicit forecasts. The basis for such forecasts is usually management, but, not surprisingly, lenders do not accept such forecasts without question.

In forecasting, a variety of scenarios should be considered—including not just a "best guess" but also a "pessimistic" scenario. Ideally, the firm should be strong enough to repay the loan even in this scenario. Ironically, it is not necessarily a decline in sales that presents the greatest risk to the lender. If managers can respond quickly to the dropoff in sales, it should be accompanied by a liquidation of receivables and inventory, which enhances cash flow for a given level of earnings. The nightmare scenario is one that involves large negative profit margins, perhaps because managers are caught by surprise by a downturn in demand and are forced to liquidate inventory at substantially reduced prices.

At times, it is possible to reconsider the structure of a loan so as to permit it to "cash flow." That is, the term of the loan might be extended, or the amortization pattern changed. Often, a bank will grant a loan with the expectation that it will be continually renewed, thus becoming a permanent part of the firm's financial structure. (Such a loan is labeled an "evergreen.") In that case, the loan will still be written as if it is due within the short term, and the bank must assure itself of a viable "exit strategy." However, the firm would be expected to service the loan by simply covering interest payments.

Step 5: Assemble the Detailed Loan Structure, Including Loan Covenants

If the analysis thus far indicates that a loan is in order, it is then time to pull together the detailed structure: type of loan, repayment schedule, loan covenants, and pricing. The first two items were discussed above. Here we discuss loan covenants and pricing.

WRITING LOAN COVENANTS.   Loan covenants specify mutual expectations of the borrower and lender by specifying actions the borrower will and will not take. Some covenants require certain actions (such as regular provision of financial statements); others preclude certain actions (such as undertaking an acquisition without the permission of the lender); still others require maintenance of certain financial ratios. Violation of a covenant represents an event of default that could cause immediate acceleration of the debt payment, but in most cases the lender uses the default as an opportunity to reexamine the situation and either waive the violation or renegotiate the loan.

Loan covenants must strike a balance between protecting the interests of the lender and providing the flexibility management needs to run the business. The covenants represent a mechanism for insuring that the business will remain as strong as the two parties anticipated at the time the loan was granted. Thus, required financial ratios are typically based on the levels that existed at that time, perhaps with some allowance for deterioration but often with some expected improvement over time.

The particular covenants included in the agreement should contain the significant risks identified in the financial analysis, or to at least provide early warning that such risks are surfacing. Some commonly used financial covenants include:

- *Maintenance of minimum net worth.* This covenant assures that the firm will maintain an "equity cushion" to protect the lender. Covenants typically require a level of net worth rather than a particular level of income. In the final analysis, the lender may not care whether that net worth is maintained by generating income, cutting dividends, or issuing new equity. Tying the covenant to net worth offers the firm the flexibility to use any of these avenues to avoid default.
- *Minimum coverage ratio.* Especially in the case of a long-term loan, such as a term loan, the lender may want to supplement a net worth covenant with one based on coverage of interest or total debt service. The funds flow coverage ratio presented above would be an example. Maintenance of some minimum coverage helps assure that the ability of the firm to generate funds internally is strong enough to justify the long-term nature of the loan.
- *Maximum ratio of total liabilities to net worth.* This ratio constrains the risk of high leverage and prevents growth without either retaining earnings or infusing equity.
- *Minimum net working capital balance or current ratio.* Constraints on this ratio force a firm to maintain its liquidity by using cash generated from operations to retire current liabilities (as opposed to acquiring long-lived assets).
- *Maximum ratio of capital expenditures to earnings before depreciation.* Constraints on this ratio help prevent the firm from investing in growth (including the illiquid assets necessary to support growth) unless such growth can be financed internally, with some margin remaining for debt service.

In addition to such financial covenants, loans sometimes place restrictions on other borrowing activity, pledging of assets to other lenders, selling of substantial parts of assets, engaging in mergers or acquisitions, and payment of dividends.

Covenants are included in not only private lending agreements with banks, insurance companies, and others, but also in public debt agreements. However, public debt agreements tend to have less restrictive covenants, for two reasons. First, negotiations resulting from a violation of public debt covenants are costly (possibly involving not just the trustee, but also bondholders), and so they are written to be triggered only in serious circumstances. Second, public debt is usually issued by stronger, more creditworthy firms. (The primary exception would be high-yield debt issued in conjunction with leveraged buyouts.) For the most financially healthy firms, with strong debt ratings, very few covenants will be used—only those necessary to limit dramatic changes in the firm's operations, such as a major merger or acquisition.

Earlier, we indicated that Dell Computer's debt financing came in the form of publicly issued notes. The major covenants on the notes impose limitations on future borrowing and restrictions on dividends. However, if Dell's debt achieves an investment-grade rating in the future, those covenants are to be relaxed.

LOAN PRICING.   A detailed discussion of loan pricing falls outside the scope of this text. The essence of pricing is to assure that the yield on the loan is sufficient to cover (1) the lender's cost of borrowed funds; (2) the lender's costs of administering and servicing the loan; (3) a premium for exposure to default risk; and (4) at least a normal return on the equity capital necessary to support the lending operation. The price is often stated in terms of a deviation from a bank's prime rate—the rate charged to stronger borrowers. For example, a loan might be granted at prime plus 1½ percent. An alternative base is LIBOR, or the London Interbank Offer Rate, the rate at which large banks from various nations lend large blocks of funds to each other.

Banks compete actively for commercial lending business, and it is rare that a yield includes more than 2 percentage points to cover the cost of default risk. If the spread to cover default risk is, say, 1 percent, and the bank recovers only 50 percent of amounts due on loans that turn out bad, then the bank can afford only 2 percent of their loans to fall into that category. This underscores how important it is for banks to conduct a thorough analysis and to contain the riskiness of their loan portfolio.

FINANCIAL STATEMENT ANALYSIS AND PUBLIC DEBT

Fundamentally, the issues involved in analysis of public debt are no different from those of bank loans and other private debt issues. Institutionally, however, the contexts are different. Bankers can maintain very close relations with clients so as to form an initial assessment of their credit risk and monitor their activities during the loan period. In the case of public debt, the investors are distanced from the issuer. To a large extent, they must depend on professional debt analysts, including debt raters, to assess the riskiness of the debt and monitor the firm's ongoing activities. Such analysts and debt raters thus serve an important function in closing the information gap between issuers and investors.

The Meaning of Debt Ratings

As indicated above, the two major debt rating agencies in the U.S. are Moody's and Standard and Poor's. Using the Standard and Poor's labeling system, the highest possible rating is AAA. Firms with this rating are large and have strong and steady earnings and little leverage. Only about 1 to 2 percent of the public industrial companies rated by Standard & Poor's have the financial strength to merit this rating. Among the few in 1995 are Exxon, Merck, General Electric, and Nippon Telegraph and Telephone—all among the largest, most profitable firms in the world. Proceeding downward from AAA, the ratings are AA, A, BBB, BB, B, CCC, CC, C, and D, where "D" indicates debt in default. To be considered investment grade, a firm must achieve a rating of BBB or higher. Many funds are precluded by their charters from investing in any bonds below that grade. Table 9-1 presents examples of firms in rating categories AAA through CCC, as well as average values for selected financial ratios across all firms in each category.

Note that even to achieve a grade of BBB is difficult. General Motors, the second most profitable corporation in the U.S. in 1994, and with rising earnings in early 1995, was still rated as "only" BBB—barely investment grade—in 1995. In this case, the bond raters recalled the string of losses that GM suffered in the early 1990s, recognizing the riskiness of the GM profit stream. Sears Roebuck is another large, profitable firm ranked "only" as BBB—and, like GM, it has suffered losses in the recent past. Overall, firms in the BBB class are only moderately leveraged, with about 40 percent of long-term capitalization coming in the form of debt. Earnings tend to be relatively strong, as indicated by a pre-tax interest coverage (EBIT/interest) of 2.5 and a funds flow debt coverage (working capital from operations/total debt) of nearly 30 percent.

The difficulty of achieving an investment-grade rating is also revealed by Compaq's experience in the debt markets in 1994. Consider this: Compaq's debt represents only 7.4 percent of long-term capital, and even if Compaq's $300 million debt issue had been outstanding for the entire year, pre-tax earnings would have been *56 times* interest expense. In fact, Compaq's cash balances were more than sufficient to retire the entire debt issue immediately! On the basis of such information, one might expect Compaq would easily qualify as AAA. However, Standard and Poor's classified the debt as BBB, and Moody's gave it a comparable rating. The reason is that the bond raters do not focus on a single year's performance. They consider the volatility of earnings in the past and the risk of downturns in the future. In commenting on the rating, Standard and Poor's stated, "Compaq Computer Corp.'s rating reflects the volatile nature of the personal computer hardware industry, offset by Compaq's competitive cost position in an environment of aggressive price competition; technological leadership in an industry characterized by short product cycles; improved customer focus; and strong balance sheet."[3]

Interestingly, the debt markets were apparently more confident in Compaq than the debt raters. The debt was issued at par at rates of 6.5 percent and 7.25 percent (depending on maturity) at a time when other BBB issues were yielding about 8 percent. The rates faced by Compaq were similar to those carried by AAA debt.

Firms with below investment-grade ratings tend to face some significant risk, even though many are quite profitable. Table 9-1 places United Airlines in the BB category. In 1995 it is the leading U.S. airline in terms of revenues, but one that was profitable in 1994 and 1995 only after having suffered severe losses in the early 1990s. The B category includes Stone Container Corporation, a highly leveraged producer of corrugated containers that experienced losses from 1991 through early 1995. The CCC category includes firms whose long-term capital is three-fourths debt, on average. An illustrative CCC firm is Spectravision, a provider of in-room movies to the lodging industry. Spectravision emerged from bankruptcy in 1992 and has since operated at a loss, with negative book value.

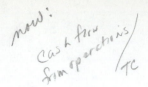

Table 9-1 Debt Ratings: Example Firms and Median Financial Ratios by Category

S&P debt rating	Example firms in 1995	Percentage of public industrials given same rating by S&P*	Median ratios for overall category over three years prior to rating—1991–1993 (industrials only)			
			Pre-tax return on long-term capital	Pre-tax interest coverage	Working capital from operations to total debt	Long-term debt to total capital
AAA	General Electric Merck and Co. Nippon T & T	1.2%	24.5%	19.9	136.8%	11.0%
AA	McDonald's Corp. Wal-Mart Stores, Inc. J. P. Morgan	5.4	18.4	8.9	75.1	19.3
A	Ford Motor Company Citicorp	16.2	13.7	4.7	44.3	30.9
BBB	General Motors Sears Roebuck and Co.	19.5	9.7	2.5	29.3	39.5
BB	Revco United Airlines	26.1	9.6	1.6	17.9	50.5
B	Stone Container Corp. Northwest Airlines	28.6	6.4	0.7	8.5	58.9
CCC	Spectravision, Inc. Presidio Oil Co.	1.1	5.5	0.5	1.5	75.4

*Ratings are as of September 1994; firms included in set for analysis only if data were publicly available 1989–1993.
Source: Standard and Poor's *Global Sector Review* (October 1994).

Factors That Drive Debt Ratings

The Compaq illustration seems to suggest that it would be difficult to predict debt ratings purely on the basis of financial statement data. In turns out that the Compaq example is unusual, however. Research demonstrates that a majority of the variation in debt ratings can be explained as a function of selected financial statement ratios, even as used within a quantitative model that incorporates no subjective human judgment. Some debt rating agencies rely heavily on quantitative models, and such models are commonly used by insurance companies, banks, and others to assist in the evaluation of the riskiness of debt issues for which a public rating is not available.

Table 9-2 lists the factors used by three different firms in their quantitative debt-rating models. The firms include one insurance company and one bank, which use the models in their private placement activities, and an investment research firm, which employs the

Table 9-2 Factors Used in Quantitative Models of Debt Ratings

	Firm 1	Firm 2	Firm 3
Profitability measures	Return on long-term capital	Return on long-term capital	Return on long-term capital
Leverage measures	Long-term debt to capitalization	Long-term debt to capitalization Total debt to total capital	Long-term debt to capitalization
Profitability and leverage	Interest coverage Cash flow to long-term debt	Interest coverage Cash flow to long-term debt	Fixed charge coverage Coverage of short-term debt and fixed charges
Firm size	Sales	Total assets	
Other		Standard deviation of return Subordination status	

model in evaluating its own debt purchases and holdings. In each case, profitability and leverage play an important role in the rating. One firm also uses firm size as an indicator, with larger size associated with higher ratings.

Several researchers have estimated quantitative models used for debt ratings. Two of these models, developed by Kaplan and Urwitz and shown in Table 9-3, highlight the relative importance of the factors.[4] Model 1 has the greater ability to explain variation in bond ratings. However, it includes some factors based on stock market data, which are not available for all firms. Model 2 is based solely on financial statement data.

The factors in Table 9-3 are listed in the order of their statistical significance in Model 1. An interesting feature is that the most important factor explaining debt ratings is not a financial ratio at all—it is simply firm size! Large firms tend to get better ratings than small firms. Whether the debt is subordinated or unsubordinated is next most important, followed by a leverage indicator. Profitability appears less important, but in part that reflects the presence in the model of multiple factors (ROA and interest coverage) that capture profitability. It is only the explanatory power that is *unique* to a given variable that is indicated by the ranking in Table 9-3. Explanatory power common to the two variables is not considered.

When applied to a sample of bonds that were not used in the estimation process, the Kaplan-Urwitz model (1) predicted the rating category correctly in 44 of 64 cases, or 63 percent of the time. Where it erred, the model was never off by more than one category, and in about half of those cases its prediction was more consistent with the market yield on the debt than was the actual debt rating. Interestingly, application of the model to Compaq (using 1993 data and assuming that $300 million of debt had been incorporated in Compaq's capital structure during the year) produces a predicted AAA rating—incon-

Table 9-3 Kaplan-Urwitz Models of Debt Ratings

| | | Coefficients | |
Firm or debt characteristic	Variable reflecting characteristic	Model 1	Model 2
	Model intercept	5.67	4.41
Firm size	Total assets[a]	.0010	.0012
Subordination status of debt	1 = subordinated; 0 = unsubordinated	–2.36	–2.56
Leverage	Long-term debt to total assets	–2.85	–2.72
Systematic risk	Market model beta, indicating sensitivity of stock price to market-wide movements (1 = average)[b]	–.87	NA
Profitability	Net income to total assets	5.13	6.40
Unsystematic risk	Standard deviation of residual from market model (average = .10)[b]	–2.90	NA
Riskiness of profit stream	Coefficient of variation in net income over 5 years (standard deviation / mean)	NA	–.53
Interest coverage	Pre-tax funds flow before interest to interest expense	.007	.006

The score from the model is converted to a bond rating as follows:
If score > 6.76, predict AAA
   score > 5.19, predict AA
   score > 3.28, predict A
   score > 1.57, predict BBB
   score < 0.00, predict BB

a. *The coefficient in the Kaplan-Urwitz model was estimated at .005 (Model 1) and .006 (Model 2). Its scale has been adjusted to reflect that the estimates were based on assets measured in dollars from the 1960s and 1970s. Given that $1 from 1970 is approximately equivalent to $5 in 1995, the original coefficient estimate has been divided by 5.*
b. *Market model is estimated by regressing stock returns against the return on the market index, using monthly data for prior five years.*

sistent with the actual rating, but consistent with the market yield on the debt issued in early 1994.[5]

    Given that debt ratings can be explained so well in terms of a handful of financial ratios, one might question whether ratings convey any *news* to investors—anything that could not already have been garnered from publicly available financial data. The answer to the question is yes, at least in the case of debt rating downgrades. That is, downgrades are greeted with drops in both bond and stock prices.[6] To be sure, the capital markets anticipate much of the information reflected in rating changes. However, that is not surprising, given that the changes often represent reactions to recent known events, and that the rating agencies typically indicate in advance that a change is being considered.

PREDICTION OF DISTRESS AND TURNAROUND

The key task in credit analysis is assessing the probability that a firm will face financial distress and fail to repay a loan. A related analysis, relevant once a firm begins to face distress, involves considering whether it can be turned around. In this section, we consider evidence on the predictability of these states.

The prediction of either distress or turnaround is a complex, difficult, and subjective task that involves all of the steps of analysis discussed throughout this book: business strategy analysis, accounting analysis, financial analysis, and prospective analysis. Purely quantitative models of the process can rarely serve as substitutes for the hard work the analysis involves. However, research on such models does offer some insight into which financial indicators are most useful in the task. Moreover, there are some settings where extensive credit checks are too costly to justify, and where quantitative distress prediction models are useful. For example, the commercially available "Zeta" model is used by some manufacturers and other firms to assess the credit-worthiness of their customers.[7]

Several distress prediction models have been developed over the years.[8] They are similar to the debt rating models, but instead of predicting ratings, they predict whether a firm will face some state of distress within one year, typically defined as bankruptcy. One study suggests that the factors most useful (on a stand-alone basis) in predicting bankruptcy one year in advance are[9]:

$$1. \text{ Profitability} \;=\; \left[\frac{\text{Net income}}{\text{Net worth}}\right]$$

$$2. \text{ Volatility} \;=\; \left[\text{Standard deviation of}\left(\frac{\text{Net income}}{\text{Net worth}}\right)\right]$$

$$3. \text{ Financial leverage} \;=\; \left[\frac{\text{Market value of equity}}{(\text{Market value of equity} + \text{Book value of debt})}\right]$$

The evidence indicates that the key to whether a firm will face distress is its level of profitability, the volatility of that profitability, and how much leverage it faces. Interestingly, liquidity measures turn out to be much less important. Current liquidity won't save an unhealthy firm if it is losing money at a fast pace.

Of course, if one were interested in predicting distress, there would be no need to restrict attention to one variable at a time. A number of multi-factor models have been designed to predict financial distress. One such model is the Altman Z-score model[10]:

$$Z \;=\; .717(X_1) + .847(X_2) + 3.11(X_3) + .420(X_4) + .998(X_5)$$

where X_1 = net working capital/total assets

X_2 = retained earnings/total assets

X_3 = EBIT/total assets

X_4 = shareholders' equity/total liabilities

X_5 = sales/total assets

The model predicts bankruptcy when Z < 1.20. The range between 1.20 and 2.90 is labeled the "gray area." As an example, and not surprisingly, Compaq stands well above the threshold for survival, based on its 1993 data:

$$Z = .717(.50) + .847(.51) + 3.11(.15) + .420(2.13) + .998(1.76) = 3.91$$

Such models have some ability to predict failing and surviving firms. Altman reports that when the model was applied to a holdout sample containing 33 failed and 33 non-failed firms (the same proportion used to estimate the model), it correctly predicted the outcome in 63 of 66 cases. However, the performance of the model would degrade substantially if applied to a holdout sample where the proportion of failed and nonfailed firms was not forced to be the same as that used to estimate the model.

Simple distress prediction models like the Altman model cannot serve effectively as a replacement for in-depth analysis of the kind discussed throughout this book. But they provide a useful reminder of the power of financial statement data to summarize important dimensions of the firm's performance. Even in the absence of direct information about management expertise, corporate strategy, engineering know-how, and market position, financial ratios can reveal much about who will make it and who will not.

SUMMARY AND CONCLUSIONS

Credit analysis is the evaluation of a firm from the perspective of a holder or potential holder of its debt. Credit analysis is important to a wide variety of economic agents—not just bankers and other financial intermediaries, but also public debt analysts, industrial companies, service companies, and others.

At the heart of credit analysis lie the same techniques described in Chapters 2 through 5: business strategy analysis, accounting analysis, financial analysis, and portions of prospective analysis. The purpose of the analysis is not just to assess the likelihood that a potential borrower will fail to repay the loan. It is also important to identify the nature of the key risks involved, and how the loan might be structured to mitigate or control those risks. A well-structured loan provides the lender with a viable "exit strategy," even in the case of default. A key to this structure is properly designed accounting-based covenants.

Fundamentally, the issues involved in analysis of public debt are no different from those involved in evaluating bank loans or other private debt. Institutionally, however, the contexts are different. Investors in public debt are usually not close to the borrower and must rely on other agents, including debt raters and other analysts, to assess creditworthiness initially, and on a continuing basis. Debt ratings, which depend heavily on firm size and financial measures of performance, have an important influence on the market yields that must be offered to issue debt.

The key task in credit analysis is the assessment of the probability of default. The task is complex, difficult, and to some extent, subjective. Nevertheless, a small number of key financial ratios are sufficient to predict financial distress with impressive accuracy. The most important financial indicators for this purpose are profitability, volatility of profits, and leverage.

NOTES

1. The same is true of preferred dividends. However, when preferred stock is cumulative, any dividends missed must be paid later, when and if the firm returns to profitability.

2. Other relevant coverage ratios are discussed in Chapter 4.

3. *Standard and Poor's Credit Week* (March 14, 1994), p. 73.

4. Robert Kaplan and G. Urwitz, "Statistical Models of Bond Ratings: A Methodological Inquiry," *Journal of Business* (April 1979): 231–261.

5. Using Model 2 and assuming that the debt issue increases leverage without changing total assets, we obtain:

$$4.41 + .0012(4084) - 2.56(0) - 2.72(.07) + 6.4(.11) - .53(.46) + .006(29.9) = 9.77$$

6. See Robert Holthausen and Richard Leftwich, "The Effect of Bond Rating Changes on Common Stock Prices," *Journal of Financial Economics* (September 1986): 57–90; and John Hand, Robert Holthausen, and Richard Leftwich, "The Effect of Bond Rating Announcements on Bond and Stock Prices," *Journal of Finance* (June 1992): 733–752.

7. See Edward Altman, *Corporate Financial Distress* (New York: John Wiley, 1983).

8. See Edward Altman, "Financial Ratios, Discriminant Analysis, and the Prediction of Corporate Bankruptcy," *Journal of Finance* (September 1968): 589–609; Altman, 1983, op. cit.; William Beaver, "Financial Ratios as Predictors of Distress," *Journal of Accounting Research,* supplement, 1966: 71–111; James Ohlson, "Financial Ratios and the Probabilistic Prediction of Bankruptcy," *Journal of Accounting Research* (Spring 1980): 109–131; and Mark Zmijewski, "Predicting Corporate Bankruptcy: An Empirical Comparison of the Extant Financial Distress Models," working paper, SUNY at Buffalo, 1983.

9. Zmijewski, op. cit.

10. Altman, 1983, op. cit.

CASES

Debt Ratings in the Chemical Industry
Pageturner Bookstores, Inc.
Power Line, Inc.
Vitronics Corporation

chapter 10

Mergers and Acquisitions

Mergers and acquisitions have long been a popular form of corporate investment, particularly in countries with Anglo-American forms of capital markets. There is no question that these transactions provide a healthy return to target stockholders. However, their value to acquiring shareholders is less understood. Many skeptics point out that given the hefty premiums paid to target stockholders, acquisitions tend to be negative-valued investments for acquiring stockholders.

A number of questions can be examined using financial analysis for mergers and acquisitions:

- Securities analysts can ask: Does a proposed acquisition create value for the acquiring firm's stockholders?
- Risk arbitrageurs can ask: What is the likelihood that a hostile takeover offer will ultimately succeed, and are there other potential acquirers likely to enter the bidding?
- Acquiring management can ask: Does this target fit our business strategy? If so, what is it worth to us, and how can we make an offer that can be successful?
- Target management can ask: Is the acquirer's offer a reasonable one for our stockholders? Are there other potential acquirers that would value our company more than the current bidder?
- Investment bankers can ask: How can we identify potential targets that are likely to be a good match for our clients? And how should we value target firms when we are asked to issue fairness opinions?

In this chapter we focus primarily on the use of financial statement data and analysis by financial analysts interested in evaluating whether a merger creates value for the acquiring firm's stockholders. However, our discussion can also be applied to these other merger contexts.

Our discussion of whether acquisitions create value for acquirers focuses on evaluating motivations for acquisitions, the pricing of offers, and the methods of financing, as well as assessing the likelihood that an offer will be successful. Throughout the chapter we use AT&T's $7.5 billion acquisition of NCR in 1991 to illustrate how financial analysis can be used in a merger context.[1]

MOTIVATION FOR MERGER OR ACQUISITION

There are a variety of reasons that firms merge or acquire other firms. Some acquiring managers may want to increase their own power and prestige. Others, however, realize that business combinations provide an opportunity to create new economic value for their stockholders. New value can be created in the following ways:

1. *Taking Advantage of Economies of Scale.* Mergers are often justified as a means of providing the two participating firms with increased economies of scale. Economies of scale arise when one firm can perform a function more efficiently than two. For example, AT&T and NCR both design and manufacture UNIX-based personal computers. Following a merger, they will probably be able to take advantage of economies of scale in research and development by reducing the number of researchers working on similar new products. The combined firm may also be able to economize on management costs, including accounting and corporate finance functions and corporate management.

2. *Improving Target Management.* Another common motivation for acquisition is to improve target management. A firm is likely to be a target if it has systematically under-performed its industry. Historical poor performance could be due to bad luck, but it could also be due to the firm's managers making poor investment and operating decisions, or deliberately pursuing goals which increase their personal power but cost stockholders.

3. *Combining Complementary Resources.* Firms may decide that a merger will create value by combining complementary resources of the two partners. For example, a merger between a firm with a strong research and development unit, such as AT&T, and a firm in the same industry with a strong distribution unit, such as NCR, may benefit both firms. Of course, they could both separately invest to strengthen their respective distribution and R&D units. However, it may well be cheaper to combine resources through a merger.

4. *Capturing Tax Benefits.* In the U.S. the 1986 Tax Reform Act eliminated many of the tax benefits from mergers and acquisitions. However, several merger tax benefits remain. The major benefit is the acquisition of operating tax losses. If a firm does not expect to earn sufficient profits to fully utilize operating loss carryforward benefits, it may decide to buy another firm which is earning profits. The operating losses and loss carryforwards of the acquirer can then be offset against the target's taxable income.[2] A second tax benefit often attributed to mergers is the

tax shield that comes from increasing leverage for the target firm. This was particularly relevant for leveraged buyouts in the 1980s.

5. *Providing Low-Cost Financing to a Financially Constrained Target.* If capital markets are imperfect, perhaps because of information asymmetries between management and outside investors, firms can face capital constraints. Information problems are likely to be especially severe for newly formed, high-growth firms. These firms can be difficult for outside investors to value since they have short track records, and their financial statements provide little insight into the value of their growth opportunities. Further, since they typically have to rely on external funds to finance their growth, capital market constraints for high-growth firms are likely to affect their ability to undertake profitable new projects. Public capital markets are therefore likely to be costly sources of funds for these types of firms. An acquirer that understands the business and is willing to provide a steady source of finance may therefore be an attractive option.

6. *Increasing Product-Market Rents.* Firms also can have incentives to merge to increase product-market rents. By merging and becoming a dominant firm in the industry, two smaller firms can collude to restrict their output and raise prices, thereby increasing their profits. This circumvents problems that arise in cartels of independent firms, where firms have incentives to cheat on the cartel and increase their output.

While product-market rents make sense for firms as a motive for merging, the two partners are unlikely to announce their intentions when they explain the merger to their investors, since most countries have anti-trust laws which regulate mergers between two firms in the same industry. For example, in the U.S. there are three major anti-trust statutes—The Sherman Act of 1890, The Clayton Act of 1914, and The Hart Scott Rodino Act of 1976.

While many of the motivations for acquisitions are likely to create new economic value for shareholders, some are not. Firms that are flush with cash but have few new profitable investment opportunities are particularly prone to using their surplus cash to make acquisitions. Stockholders of these firms would probably prefer that managers pay out any surplus or "free" cash flows as dividends, or use the funds to repurchase their firm's stock. However, these options reduce the size of the firm and the assets under management's control. Management may therefore prefer to invest the free cash flows to buy new companies, even if they are not valued by stockholders. Of course, managers will never announce that they are buying a firm because they are reluctant to pay out funds to stockholders. They may explain the merger using one of the motivations discussed above, or they may argue that they are buying the target at a bargain price.

Another motivation for mergers that is valued by managers but not stockholders is diversification. Diversification was a popular motivation for acquisitions in the 1960s and early 1970s. Acquirers sought to dampen their earnings volatility by buying firms in unrelated businesses. Diversification as a motive for acquisitions has since been widely discredited. Modern finance theorists point out that in a well functioning capital market, investors can diversify for themselves and do not need managers to do so for them. In addition, diversification has been criticized for leading firms to lose sight of their major competitive strengths and to expand into businesses where they do not have expertise.

Financial Analysis of Merger Motivations

In evaluating a proposed merger, financial analysts are interested in determining whether the merger creates new wealth for acquiring and target stockholders, or whether it is motivated by managers' desires to increase their own power and prestige. Financial analysis is likely to include:

- *Learning about the motivation(s) for an acquisition and any anticipated benefits through public disclosures by acquirers or targets.*
- *Comparing the industries of the target and acquirer.* Are the firms related horizontally or vertically? How close are the business relations between them? If the businesses are unrelated, is the acquirer cash-rich and reluctant to return free cash flows to stockholders?
- *Evaluating the key operational strengths of the target and the acquirer.* Are these strengths complementary? For example, does one firm have a renowned research group and the other a strong distribution network?
- *Assessing whether the acquisition is a friendly one, supported by target management, or hostile.* A hostile takeover is more likely to occur for targets with poorperforming management who oppose the acquisition to preserve their jobs.
- *Comparing the pre-merger performance of the two firms.* Performance metrics are likely to include ROE, gross margins, general and administrative expenses to sales, and working capital management ratios. On the basis of these measures, is the target a poor performer in its industry, implying that there are opportunities for improved management? Is the acquirer in a declining industry and searching for new directions?
- *Assessing the tax position of both firms.* What are the average and marginal current tax rates for the target and the acquirer? Does the acquirer have operating loss carryforwards and the target taxable profits?

This analysis should help the analyst understand what specific benefits, if any, the merger is likely to generate.

Motivation for AT&T's Acquisition

Prior to 1984, AT&T was a regulated utility providing telephone services and manufacturing-related equipment. However, in 1982 the company signed a Consent Agreement with the Department of Justice (DOJ) to divest its Bell operating companies, which provided short-distance telephone services. This agreement followed eight years of negotiations with the DOJ over allegations that AT&T monopolized the telephone services and telephone equipment industries. In return for agreeing to this divestiture, AT&T was granted permission to enter the computer industry, which had previously been off-limits to the company.

Management argued that the Consent Agreement permitted the firm to concentrate on linking its telecommunications with computer and information services. The company could finally begin to take advantage of advances in computer science, particularly the development of UNIX operating systems that had been made at its renowned research park, Bell Labs. However, prior to 1990, the company had not been particularly successful in implementing this strategy. The financial press estimated that the firm's computer operations lost at least $2 billion between 1984 and 1990. Losses for 1990 alone were estimated at between $10 million and $300 million on sales of $1.5 billion.

AT&T's management decided that the best approach to its computer problems involved increasing its presence in computer operations and began searching for a suitable acquisition candidate. NCR, which had a corporate culture similar to AT&T's, emerged as the ideal target from this search. It also had compatible product lines and a similar policy of using UNIX operating systems. However, NCR was stronger than AT&T in networking and had an international computer marketing presence and customer base. Consistent with its desire to use NCR to develop its expertise in computer operations, AT&T announced that it would combine both companies' computer operations under NCR's management.

In summary, given AT&T's strategy of combining telecommunications and computer technologies and services, the acquisition of NCR appeared to make some economic sense. However, some analysts who were critical of AT&T's overall strategy argued that the acquisition would probably not create value for AT&T's stockholders, and that AT&T should concede that its entry into the computer business was a costly mistake.

ACQUISITION PRICING

A well thought-out economic motivation for a merger or acquisition is a necessary but not sufficient condition for it to create value for acquiring stockholders. The acquirer must be careful to avoid overpaying for the target. Overpayment makes the transaction highly desirable and profitable for target stockholders, but it diminishes the value of the deal to acquiring stockholders. A financial analyst can use the following methods to assess whether the acquiring firm is overpaying for the target.

Analyzing Premium Offered to Target Stockholders

One popular way to assess whether the acquirer is overpaying for a target is to compare the premium offered to target stockholders to premiums offered in similar transactions. If the acquirer offers a relatively high premium, the analyst is typically led to conclude that the transaction is less likely to create value for acquiring stockholders.

Premiums differ significantly for friendly and hostile acquisitions. Premiums tend to be about 30 percent higher for hostile deals than for friendly offers, implying that hostile acquirers are more likely to overpay for a target.[3] There are several reasons for this. First, a friendly acquirer has access to the internal records of the target, making it much less likely that it will be surprised by hidden liabilities or problems once it has completed the deal. In contrast, a hostile acquirer does not have this advantage in valuing the target and is forced to make assumptions, which may later turn out to be false. Second, the delays that typically accompany a hostile acquisition often provide opportunities for competing bidders to make an offer for the target, leading to a bidding war.

Comparing a target's premium to values for similar types of transactions is straightforward to compute, but it has several practical problems. First, it is not obvious how to define a comparable transaction. Figure 10-1 shows the average premiums paid for U.S. targets between 1989 and 1993 relative to stock prices one month and one week prior to the first acquisition announcement. Average one-month premiums have varied dramatically during this period, ranging from 53 percent in 1989 to 72 percent in 1993.

Figure 10-1 Average Premium Paid for Mergers and Acquisitions in the Period 1989 to 1993

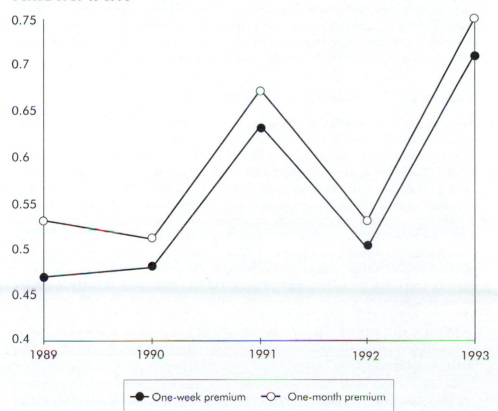

A second problem in using premiums offered to target stockholders to assess whether an acquirer overpaid is that measured premiums can be misleading if an offer is anticipated by investors. The stock price run-up for the target will then tend to make estimates of the premium appear relatively low. This limitation can be partially offset by using target stock prices one month prior to the acquisition offer as the basis for calculating premiums. However, in some cases offers may have been anticipated for even longer than one month.

Finally, using target premiums to assess whether an acquirer overpaid ignores the value of the target to the acquirer after the acquisition. This value can be viewed as:

Value of target after acquisition = Value as independent firm + Value of merger benefits

The value of the target before acquisition is the present value of the free cash flows for the target if it were to remain an independent entity. This is likely to be somewhat different from the firm's stock price prior to any merger announcement, since the pre-takeover price is a weighted average of the value of the firm as an independent unit and its value in the event of a takeover. The benefits of the merger include such effects as improvements in target operating performance from economies of scale, improved management, or tax benefits, as well as any spillover benefits to the acquirer from the acquisition. Clearly, acquirers will be willing to pay higher premiums for targets which are expected to generate higher merger benefits. Thus, examining the premium alone cannot determine whether the acquisition creates value for acquiring stockholders.

Analyzing Value of the Target to the Acquirer

A second and more reliable way of assessing whether the acquirer has overpaid for the target is to compare the offer price to the estimated value of the target to the acquirer. This latter value can be computed using the valuation techniques discussed in Chapters 6 and 7. The most popular methods of valuation used for mergers and acquisitions are earnings multiples and discounted cash flows. Since a comprehensive discussion of these techniques is provided earlier in the book, we focus here on implementation issues that arise for valuing targets in mergers and acquisitions. We recommend first computing the value of the target as an independent firm. This provides a way of checking whether the valuation assumptions are reasonable, since for publicly listed targets we can compare our estimate with pre-merger market prices. It also provides a useful benchmark for thinking about how the target's performance, and hence its value, is likely to change once it is acquired.

EARNINGS MULTIPLES.   To estimate the value of a target to an acquirer using earnings multiples, we have to forecast earnings for the target and decide on an appropriate earnings multiple.

Step One: Forecasting Earnings. Earnings forecasts are usually made by first forecasting next year's net income for the target, assuming no acquisition. Historical sales growth rates, gross margins, and average tax rates are useful in building a pro forma income model. Once we have forecasted the income for the target prior to an acquisition, we can incorporate into the pro forma model any improvements in earnings performance that we expect to result from the acquisition. Performance improvements can be modeled as:

- Higher operating margins through economies of scale in purchasing, or increased market power;
- Reductions in expenses as a result of consolidating research and development staffs, sales forces, and/or administration; or
- Lower average tax rates from taking advantage of operating tax loss carryforwards.

Forecasting earnings after acquisition requires some caution since, as we discuss later, an acquisition accounted for using purchase accounting will typically lead to increased goodwill amortization and depreciation expenses for revalued assets after the acquisition. These effects should be ignored in estimating future earnings for price-earnings valuation.

Step Two: Determining Price-Earnings Multiple. How do we determine the earnings multiple to be applied to our earnings forecasts? If the target firm is listed, it may be tempting to use the pre-acquisition price-earnings multiple to value post-merger earnings. However, there are several limitations to this approach. First, for many targets, earnings growth expectations are likely to change after a merger, implying that there will be a difference between the pre- and post-merger price-earnings multiples. Post-merger earnings should then be valued using a multiple for firms with comparable growth and risk characteristics. (See discussion in Chapter 7.) A second problem is that pre-merger price-earnings multiples are unavailable for unlisted targets. Once again, it becomes necessary to decide which types of listed firms are likely to be good comparables. Finally, if a pre-merger price-earnings multiple is appropriate for valuing post-merger earnings, care is required to ensure that the multiple is calculated prior to any acquisition announcement, since the price will increase in anticipation of the premium to be paid to target stockholders.

The following table summarizes how price-earnings multiples are used to value a target firm before an acquisition (assuming it will remain an independent entity), and to estimate the value of a target to a potential acquirer:

Summary of Price-Earnings Valuation for Targets

Value of target as an independent firm	Target earnings forecast for the next year, assuming no change in ownership, multiplied by its *pre-merger* PE multiple.
Value of target to potential acquirer	Target *revised* earnings forecast for the next year, incorporating the effect of any operational changes made by the acquirer, multiplied by its *post-merger* PE multiple.

LIMITATIONS OF PRICE-EARNINGS VALUATION.   As explained in Chapter 6, there are serious limitations to using earnings multiples for valuation. In addition to these limitations, the method has several more that are specific to merger valuations:

1. PE multiples assume that merger performance improvements come either from an immediate increase in earnings or from an increase in earnings growth (and hence an increase in the post-merger PE ratio). In reality, improvements and savings can come in many forms—gradual increases in earnings from implementing new operating policies, elimination of over-investment, better management of working capital, or paying out excess cash to stockholders. These types of improvements are not naturally reflected in PE multiples.
2. PE models do not easily incorporate any spillover benefits from an acquisition for the acquirer, since they focus on valuing the earnings of the target.

DISCOUNTED CASH FLOWS OR ABNORMAL EARNINGS.   As discussed in Chapters 6 and 7, we can also value a company using the discounted free cash flow and discounted abnormal earnings methods. These require us to first forecast the free cash flows or abnormal earnings for the firm and then discount them at the cost of capital.

Step One: Forecast Free Cash Flows/Abnormal Earnings. A pro forma model of expected future income and cash flows for the firm provides the basis for forecasting free cash flows/abnormal earnings. As a starting point, the model should be constructed under the assumption that the target remains an independent firm. The model should reflect our best estimates of future sales growth, cost structures, working capital needs, investment and research and development needs, and cash requirements for known debt retirements, developed from financial analysis of the target. Under the free cash flow approach, the pro forma model will forecast free cash flows to either the firm or to equity, typically for a period of five to ten years. The abnormal earnings method requires that we forecast abnormal earnings for as long as the firm expects new investment projects to earn more than their cost of capital. Once we have a model of the free cash flows or abnormal earnings, we can incorporate any improvements in free cash flows/earnings that we expect to result from the acquisition. These will include the cost savings, cash received from asset sales, benefits from eliminating over-investment, improved working capital management, and paying out excess cash to stockholders.

Step Two: Compute the Discount Rate. If we are valuing the target's post-acquisition cash flows to the firm, the appropriate discount rate is the weighted average cost of capital for the target, using its expected *post-acquisition* capital structure. Alternatively, if the target equity cash flows are being valued directly or if we are valuing abnormal earnings, the appropriate discount rate is the target's *post-acquisition cost of equity* rather than its weighted average cost of capital (WACC). Two common mistakes are to use the acquirer's cost of capital or the target's *pre-acquisition* cost of capital to value the post-merger cash flows/abnormal earnings from the target.

The computation of the target's post-acquisition cost of capital can be complicated if the acquirer plans to make a change to the target's capital structure after the acquisition, since the target's costs of debt and equity will change. However, the net effect of these changes on the weighted average cost of capital is likely to be quite small unless the revision in leverage has a significant effect on the target's interest tax shields or its likelihood of financial distress.

The following table summarizes how the discounted cash flow/abnormal earnings methods can be used to value a target before an acquisition (assuming it will remain an independent entity), and to estimate the value of a target firm to a potential acquirer.

Summary of Discounted Cash Flow/Abnormal Earnings Valuation for Targets

Value of target without an acquisition	(a) Present value of free cash flows to target equity assuming no acquisition, discounted at *pre-merger* cost of equity; or
	(b) Present value of free cash flows to target debt and equity assuming no acquisition, discounted at *pre-merger* WACC, less value of debt; or
	(c) Present value of abnormal earnings to target stockholders assuming no acquisition, discounted at *pre-merger* cost of equity.
Value of target to potential acquirer	(a) Present value of free cash flows to target equity, *including benefits from merger,* discounted at *post-merger* cost of equity; or
	(b) Present value of free cash flows to target, *including benefits from merger,* discounted at *post-merger* WACC, less value of debt; or
	(c) Present value of abnormal earnings to target stockholders, *including benefits from merger,* discounted at *post-merger* cost of equity.

Step Three: Analyze Sensitivity. Once we have estimated the expected value of a target, we will want to examine the sensitivity of our estimate to changes in the model assumptions. For example, answering the following questions can help the analyst assess the risks associated with an acquisition.

- What happens to the value of the target if it takes longer than expected for the benefits of the acquisition to materialize?
- What happens to the value of the target if the acquisition prompts its primary competitors to respond by also making an acquisition? Will such a response affect our plans and estimates?

AT&T's Pricing of NCR

AT&T's $7.5 billion price for NCR represents a 120 percent premium to target stockholders (adjusted for market-wide changes during the merger negotiation period). This is certainly substantially higher than typical premiums during this period and in part reflects opposition to the acquisition from NCR's management. AT&T's initial offer for the firm was $85 per share. The final price, which was accepted by target management, was $110.

AT&T's pricing of NCR also appears to be aggressive in terms of traditional forms of valuation. At the time of the announcement of AT&T's offer, the typical PE value for firms in the computer industry was 12.9 and NCR's PE was 11.5, yet AT&T's final offer valued NCR at 18 times current earnings. If these benefits are realized immediately, the total annual performance improvements from the acquisition for the new firm is equivalent to 50 percent of NCR's pre-merger earnings, a challenging target. Of course AT&T's management believed some of these benefits would come from increased earnings from its own operations.

The market reaction to acquisition announcements suggests that analysts believed that AT&T overpaid for NCR—AT&T's stock price dropped by 13 percent (again adjusted for market-wide changes), or $4.9 billion, during the negotiation period. Given the $3.7 billion premium that AT&T paid for NCR, this decline in AT&T equity implies that analysts believed that AT&T would actually destroy value in NCR! Subsequent short-term financial results for AT&T's computer operations (which includes NCR) support the market's skepticism. NCR's 1991 earnings were $100 million (26 percent) below projections made to AT&T. AT&T's loss from computer operations in 1993 was $99 million (including a $190 million restructuring charge). For the first quarter of 1994 the firm reported an operating loss of $61 million (including another restructuring charge of $120 million).

In summary, it appears from preliminary results and market assessments of the acquisition that AT&T overpaid for NCR. Indeed, the market believed that AT&T would actually destroy NCR's value as an independent firm, raising questions about the merits of AT&T's overall technology strategy.

ACQUISITION FINANCING

Even if an acquisition is undertaken to create new economic value and is priced judiciously, it may still destroy shareholder value if it is inappropriately financed. Several financing options are available to acquirers, including issuing stock or warrants to target stockholders, or acquiring target stock using surplus cash or proceeds from new debt. The trade-offs between these options from the standpoint of target stockholders usually hinge on their tax and transaction cost implications. For acquirers, they can affect the firm's capital structure and the financial reporting of the transaction and provide new information to investors.

As we discuss below, the financing preferences of target and acquiring stockholders can diverge. Financing arrangements can therefore increase or reduce the attractiveness of an acquisition from the standpoint of acquiring stockholders. As a result, a complete analysis of an acquisition will include an examination of the implications of the financing arrangements for the acquirer.

Effect of Form of Financing on Target Stockholders

As noted above, the key financing considerations for target stockholders are the tax and transaction cost implications of the acquirer's offer.

TAX EFFECTS OF DIFFERENT FORMS OF CONSIDERATION.   Target stockholders care about the after-tax value of any offer they receive for their shares. In the U.S., whenever target stockholders receive cash for their shares, they are required to pay capital gains tax on the difference between the takeover offer price and their original purchase price. Alternatively, if they receive shares in the acquirer as consideration and the acquisition is undertaken as a tax-free reorganization, they can defer any taxes on the capital gain until they sell the new shares.

U.S. tax laws appear to cause target stockholders to prefer a stock offer to a cash one. This is certainly likely to be the case for a target founder who still has a significant stake in the company. If the company's stock price has appreciated over its life, the founder will face a substantial capital gains tax on a cash offer and will therefore probably prefer to receive stock in the acquiring firm. However, cash and stock offers can be tax-neutral for some groups of stockholders. For example, consider the tax implications for risk arbitrageurs, who take a short-term position in a company that is a takeover candidate in the hope that other bidders will emerge and increase the takeover price. They have no intention of holding stock in the acquirer once the takeover is completed, and will pay ordinary income tax on any short-term trading gain. Cash and stock offers therefore have identical after-tax values for risk arbitrageurs. Similarly, tax-exempt institutions are likely to be indifferent to whether an offer is in cash or stock.

TRANSACTION COSTS AND THE FORM OF FINANCING.   Transaction costs are another factor related to the form of financing that can be relevant to target stockholders. Transaction costs are incurred when target stockholders sell any stock received as consideration for their shares in the target. These costs will not be faced by target stockholders if the bidder offers them cash. Transaction costs are unlikely to be significant for investors who intend to hold the acquirer's stock following a stock acquisition. However, they may be relevant for investors who intend to sell, such as risk arbitrageurs.

Effect of Form of Financing on Acquiring Stockholders

For acquiring stockholders, the costs and benefits of different financing options usually depend on how the offer affects their firm's capital structure, any information effects associated with different forms of financing, and the accounting methods of recording the acquisition.

CAPITAL STRUCTURE EFFECTS OF FORM OF FINANCING.   In acquisitions where debt financing or surplus cash are the primary form of consideration for target shares, the acquisition increases the financial leverage of the acquirer. This increase in leverage may be part of the acquisition strategy, since one way an acquirer can add value to an inefficient firm is to lower its taxes by increasing interest tax shields. However, in many acquisitions an increase in post-acquisition leverage is a side effect of the method of financing and not part of a deliberate tax-minimizing strategy. The increase in leverage can then potentially reduce shareholder value for the acquirer by increasing the risk of financial distress.

To assess whether an acquisition leads an acquirer to have too much leverage, financial analysts can assess the acquirer's financial risk following the proposed acquisition by these methods:

- Assessing the pro forma financial risks for the acquirer under the proposed financing plan. Popular measures of financial risk include debt-to-equity and interest-coverage ratios, as well as projections of cash flows available to meet debt repayments. The ratios can be compared to similar performance metrics for the acquiring and target firms' industries. Do post-merger ratios indicate that the firm's probability of financial distress has increased significantly?
- Examining whether there are important off-balance sheet liabilities for the target and/or acquirer which are not included in the pro forma ratio and cash flow analysis of post-acquisition financial risk.
- Determining whether the pro forma assets for the acquirer are largely intangible, and therefore sensitive to financial distress. Measures of intangible assets include such ratios as market to book equity and tangible assets to the market value of equity.

INFORMATION PROBLEMS AND THE FORM OF FINANCING.   As we discuss in Chapter 11, information asymmetries between managers and external investors can make managers reluctant to raise equity to finance new projects. Managers' reluctance arises from their fear that investors will interpret the decision as an indication that the firm's stock is overvalued. In the short term, this effect can lead managers to deviate from the firm's long-term optimal mix of debt and equity. As a result, acquirers are likely to prefer to use internal funds or debt to finance an acquisition, since these forms of consideration are less likely to be interpreted negatively by investors.

The information effects imply that firms forced to use stock financing are likely to face a stock price decline when investors learn of the method of financing. From the viewpoint of financial analysts, the financing announcement may therefore provide valuable news about the pre-acquisition value of the acquirer. However, it should have no implications for analysis of whether the acquisition creates value for acquiring shareholders, since the news reflected in the financing announcement is about the *pre-acqui-sition* value of the acquirer and not about the *post-acquisition* value of the target to the acquirer.

A second information problem arises if the acquiring management does not have good information about the target. Stock financing then provides a way for acquiring stockholders to share the information risks with target shareholders. If the acquirer finds out after the acquisition that the value of the target is less than previously anticipated, the accompanying decline in the acquirer's equity price will be partially borne by target stockholders who continue to hold the acquirer's stock. In contrast, if the target's shares were acquired in a cash offer, any post-acquisition loss would be fully borne by the acquirer's original stockholders. The risk-sharing benefits from using stock financing appears to be widely recognized for acquisitions of private companies, where public information on the target is largely unavailable. In practice, it appears to be considered less important for acquisitions of large public corporations.

FORM OF FINANCING AND POST-ACQUISITION ACCOUNTING.   Finally, the form of financing has an effect on the acquirer's financial statements following the acquisition. Two methods of reporting for the acquisition are permitted under U.S. accounting—purchase and pooling of interests.

Under the *purchase method,* the acquirer writes up the assets of the target to their market value, and records the difference between the purchase price and the market value of the target's tangible net assets as goodwill. In the U.S. and most other countries, goodwill is subsequently amortized to earnings over a period of from 5 to 40 years. In contrast, U.K. companies typically write off any goodwill against shareholders' equity.

The *pooling-of-interests method* of accounting for mergers, which is rarely used outside the U.S., requires acquirers to show the target's assets, liabilities, and equity at their original book values. Thus, no goodwill is recorded, and subsequent earnings need not be reduced by the amortization of goodwill.

An acquirer's decision on a method of financing an acquisition largely determines its method of accounting for the transaction. A number of conditions must be satisfied for an acquirer to use the pooling-of-interests method to account for an acquisition. If these conditions are not satisfied, the acquirer is required to use purchase accounting. The most significant of these conditions are that: (1) the acquirer issues voting common shares (not cash) in exchange for substantially all of the voting common shares (at least 90 percent) of the acquired company; and (2) the acquisition occurs in a single transaction.

Some managers seem to believe that there is a benefit to shareholders from using the pooling-of-interests method for recording an acquisition. They argue that investors use earnings to value a firm's stock. Since the pooling-of-interests method leads to higher earnings than the purchase method by avoiding amortization of goodwill (at least until the asset is fully depleted), pooling must therefore lead to higher stock prices. However, while the two methods do have different earnings implications for the firm, they do not lead to different cash flows. They therefore do not alter the economic value of the firm. Thus, for the financial analyst, the choice of financing largely determines the accounting methods used to prepare an acquirer's pro forma balance sheets and income statements. But these accounting effects are not relevant to the question of whether the acquisition creates value for acquiring stockholders.

In summary, the form of financing has important tax and transaction cost implications for target stockholders. It can also have important capital structure, information, and merger accounting implications for acquirers. From the perspective of the financial analyst, the effect of any corporate tax benefits from debt financing should already be reflected in the valuation of the target. Information and accounting effects are not relevant to the value of the acquisition. However, the analyst does need to consider whether demands by target stockholders for consideration in cash lead the acquirer to have a post-acquisition capital structure which increases the risk of financial distress to a point that is detrimental for stockholders. Thus, part of the financial analyst's task in analyzing the value of an acquisition is to determine how it affects the acquirer's capital structure and its risks of financial distress.

AT&T's Financing of NCR

AT&T offered NCR's shareholders the right to exchange 100 percent of their shares for AT&T stock, valued at $110 per NCR share, unless AT&T was not satisfied that an all-stock merger could be accounted for as a pooling of interests. In that case, target stockholders would exchange 40 percent of their shares for AT&T stock and 60 percent for cash, where both stock and cash were valued at $110 per share. High and low collars were added to the stock deal to ensure that NCR's stockholders were protected in the event of a decline in AT&T's stock price. In either event the acquisition was to be treated as a tax-free purchase of stock.

AT&T's offer is unusual because it indicates that the firm had a strong preference for having the acquisition accounted for under the pooling-of-interests method. AT&T's managers argued that it was important for the firm to use pooling-of-interests accounting to avoid any goodwill amortization, which would hurt the firm's earnings and stock price. And certainly, goodwill amortization would have hurt earnings: pro forma estimates indicate that 1990 earnings per share for AT&T (including the earnings of NCR) would have been $2.42 under the pooling-of-interests method and only $1.97 under the purchase method. However, it is not so obvious that this earnings decline would have affected the stock price.

In summary, AT&T chose to finance NCR with a 100 percent stock offer, primarily to ensure that it could use pooling-of-interests accounting. Because this is a very conservative approach, the financing of the acquisition does not impose additional financial risks on AT&T's stockholders. However, AT&T's explanation of the offer should raise questions for analysts about whether the form of the offer really maximized value for AT&T's existing shareholders.

ACQUISITION OUTCOME

The final question of interest to the analyst evaluating a potential acquisition is whether it will indeed be completed. If an acquisition has a clear value-based motive, the target is priced appropriately, and its proposed financing does not create unnecessary financial risks for the acquirer, it may still fail because the target receives a higher competing bid or because of opposition from entrenched target management. Therefore, to evaluate the likelihood that an offer will be accepted, the financial analyst has to understand whether there are potential competing bidders who could pay an even higher premium to target stockholders than is currently offered. They also have to consider whether target management is entrenched and, to protect their jobs, likely to oppose an offer.

Other Potential Acquirers

If there are other potential bidders for a target, especially ones who place a higher value on the target, there is a strong possibility that the bidder in question will be unsuccessful. Target management and stockholders have an incentive to delay accepting the initial offer to give potential competitors time to also submit a bid. From the perspective of the initial bidder, this means that the offer could potentially reduce stockholder value by the cost of making the offer (including substantial investment banking and legal fees). In practice, a losing bidder can usually recoup these losses, and sometimes even make healthy profits from selling to the successful acquirer any shares it has accumulated in the target.

How can the financial analyst determine whether there are other potential acquirers for a target and how they value the target? There are several ways:

- Identify other firms that could also implement the initial bidder's acquisition strategy. For example, if this strategy relies on developing benefits from complementary assets, look for potential bidders who also have assets complementary to the target. If the goal of the acquisition is to replace inefficient management, what other firms in the target's industry could provide management expertise?
- Examine competitors of the acquirer. Could any of these firms provide an even better fit for the target?

Target Management Entrenchment

If target managers are entrenched and fearful for their jobs, it is likely that they will oppose a bidder's offer. Some firms have implemented "golden parachutes" for top managers to counteract their concerns about job security at the time of an offer. Golden parachutes provide top managers of a target firm with attractive compensation rewards should the firm get taken over. However, many firms do not have such schemes, and opposition to an offer from entrenched management is a very real possibility.

What indicators of entrenched management can financial analysts use in assessing the likely success of an acquisition? One indicator is the existence of a golden parachute plan for target management. A second indicator is the existence of takeover defenses for the target. Many such defenses were used during the turbulent 1980s, when mergers and acquisitions were at their peak. Some of the most widely adopted include poison pills, staggered boards, super-majority rules, dual-class recapitalizations, fair-price provisions, ESOP plans, and changes in firms' states of incorporation (to states with more restrictive anti-takeover laws)

While the existence of takeover defenses for a target indicates that its management is likely to fight a bidding firm's offer, defenses have typically not prevented an acquisition from taking place. Instead, they tend to cause delays, which increase the likelihood that there will be competing offers made for the target, including offers by friendly parties solicited by target management, called "white knights." Takeover defenses therefore increase the likelihood that the bidder in question will be outbid for the target, or that it will have to increase its offer significantly to win a bidding contest. Given these risks, some have argued that acquirers are now less likely to embark on a potentially hostile acquisition.

Analysis of Outcome of AT&T's Offer for NCR

AT&T had good reason to be concerned about the outcome of an offer for NCR. NCR had rejected AT&T's preliminary friendly offers made to the company before any public announcement, indicating that target management intended to oppose the offer and use whatever anti-takeover measures were at their disposal. NCR followed up this opposition by creating a qualified ESOP and announcing a special dividend of $1 and a $.02 per share regular dividend increase, all intended to prohibit AT&T from using pooling of interests to account for the acquisition. NCR's opposition certainly increased the likelihood that either AT&T would overpay for NCR, or that it would be forced to drop its offer. No competing offers for NCR emerged, probably because the high price offered by AT&T scared off any competitors. The acquisition was finally completed on September 19, 1991, ten months after AT&T's initial offer.

SUMMARY AND CONCLUSIONS

This chapter summarizes how financial statement data and analysis can be used by financial analysts interested in evaluating whether an acquisition creates value for an acquiring firm's stockholders. Obviously, much of this discussion is also likely to be relevant to other merger participants, including target and acquiring management and their investment banks.

For the external analyst, the first task is to identify the acquirer's acquisition strategy. We discuss a number of strategies. Some of these are consistent with maximizing acquirer value, including acquisitions to: take advantage of economies of scale; improve target management; combine complementary resources; capture tax benefits; provide low-cost financing to financially constrained targets; and increase product-market rents.

However, other strategies appear to benefit managers more than stockholders. For example, some unprofitable acquisitions are made because managers are reluctant to return free cash flows to shareholders, or because managers want to lower the firm's earnings volatility by diversifying into unrelated businesses.

The financial analyst's second task is to assess whether the acquirer is offering a reasonable price for the target. Even if the acquirer's strategy is based on increasing shareholder value, it can overpay for the target. Target stockholders will then be well rewarded but at the expense of acquiring stockholders. We show how the ratio, pro forma, and valuation techniques discussed earlier in the book can all be used to assess the worth of the target to the acquirer.

The method of financing an offer is also relevant to a financial analyst's review of an acquisition proposal. If a proposed acquisition is financed with surplus cash or new debt, it increases the acquirer's financial risk. Financial analysts can use ratio analysis of the acquirer's post-acquisition balance sheet and pro forma estimates of cash flow volatility and interest coverage to assess whether demands by target stockholders for consideration in cash lead the acquirer to increase its risk of financial distress.

Finally, the financial analyst is interested in assessing whether a merger is likely to be completed once the initial offer is made, and at what price. This requires the analyst to determine whether there are other potential bidders, and whether target management is entrenched and likely to oppose a bidder's offer.

NOTES

1. Much of our discussion is based on analysis of the acquisition presented by Thomas Lys and Linda Vincent in "An Analysis of the Value Destruction in AT&T's Acquisition of NCR," *Journal of Financial Economics,* forthcoming.

2. Of course, another possibility is for the profitable firm to acquire the unprofitable one. However, in the U.S., the IRS will disallow the use of tax loss carryforwards by an acquirer if it appears that an acquisition was tax-motivated.

3. See Paul Healy, Krishna Palepu, and Richard Ruback, "Which Mergers Are Profitable—Strategic or Financial?," unpublished working paper, 1992, MIT Sloan School of Management and Harvard Business School.

CASES

Darty-Kingfisher
Schneider and Square D
Thousand Trails, Inc.

chapter 11

Corporate Financing Policies

In this chapter, we discuss how firms set their capital structure and dividend policies to maximize shareholder value. There is a strong relation between these two decisions. For example, a firm's decision to retain internally-generated funds rather than paying them out as a dividend can also be thought of as a financing decision. It is not surprising, therefore, to find that many of the factors that are important in setting capital structure (such as taxes, costs of financial distress, agency costs, and information costs) are also relevant for dividend policy decisions. In the following sections we discuss these factors, how they affect capital structure and dividend policy, as well as how the financial analysis tools, discussed in Part 2 of this book, can be used to evaluate capital structure and dividend policy decisions.

A variety of questions are dealt with in analysis of corporate financing policies:

- Securities analysts can ask: Given its capital structure and dividend policy, how should we position a firm in our fund—as a growth or income stock?
- Takeover specialists can ask: Can we improve stockholder value for a firm by changing its financial leverage or by increasing dividend payouts to owners?"
- Management can ask: Have we selected a capital structure and dividend policy which supports our business objectives?
- Credit analysts can ask: What risks do we face in lending to this company, given its business and current financial leverage?

Throughout our discussion, we take the perspective of an external analyst who is evaluating whether a firm has selected a capital structure and dividend policy that maximize shareholder value. However, our discussion obviously also applies to management's decisions about what debt and dividend policies it should implement.

FACTORS THAT DETERMINE FIRMS' DEBT POLICIES

When financial analysts evaluate a firm's capital structure, two related questions typically emerge. First, in the long term, what is the best mix of debt and equity for creating stockholder value? And second, if managers are considering new investment initiatives in the short-term, what type of financing should they use? Two popular models of capital structure provide help in thinking about these questions. The static model of capital structure examines how trade-offs between the benefits and costs of debt determine a firm's long-term optimal mix of debt and equity. And the dynamic model examines how information effects can lead a firm to deviate from its long-term optimal capital structure as it seeks financing for new investments. We discuss both models, since they have somewhat different implications for thinking about capital structure.

To show how financial analysis can be used to help managers make capital structure decisions, we examine financial leverage for Compaq Computer, the company we have discussed throughout these chapters. Throughout the section we discuss factors that are relevant to Compaq's optimal long-term mix of debt and equity and its financing of new capital projects. As you can see from the table below, Compaq has a very conservative capital structure. Its cash and marketable securities actually outweigh interest-bearing debt, so that reported financial leverage is negative. This low leverage is somewhat offset by modest off-balance-sheet liabilities for noncancelable operating leases, factored receivables, and guarantees on finance company loans to the company's resellers. It is difficult to quantify the effects of these liabilities on Compaq's leverage.

THE OPTIMAL LONG-TERM MIX OF DEBT AND EQUITY

To determine the best long-term mix of debt and equity capital for a firm, we need to consider the benefits and costs of financial leverage. By trading off these benefits and costs, we can decide whether a firm should be financed mostly with equity or mostly with debt.

TABLE 11-1 Net Interest-Bearing Debt and Equity for Compaq Computer for the Years Ended December 31, 1991 and 1992

	1992	1991
Interest-bearing debt	0	73,456
Less: cash and short-term investments	356,747	452,174
Net debt	(356,747)	(378,718)
Book stockholders' equity	2,006,691	1,930,704
Net interest-bearing debt to book equity	(18%)	(20%)

Benefits of Leverage

The major benefits of financial leverage typically include corporate tax shields on interest and improved incentives for management.

CORPORATE INTEREST TAX SHIELD.   In the U.S., and in many other countries for that matter, tax laws provide a form of government subsidy for debt financing which does not exist for equity financing. This arises from the corporate tax deductibility of interest against income. No such corporate tax shield is available for dividend payments or for retained earnings. Debt financing therefore has an advantage over equity, since the interest tax shield from debt provides additional income to debt- and equity-holders. This higher income translates directly into higher firm values for leveraged firms in relation to unleveraged firms.

Some practitioners and theorists have pointed out that the corporate tax benefit from debt financing is potentially offset by a personal tax disadvantage of debt. That is, since the holders of debt must pay relatively high tax rates on interest income, they require that corporations offer high pre-tax yields on debt. This disadvantage is particularly severe when interest income is taxed at a higher rate than capital gains on equity. However, under current U.S. tax laws, personal tax rates on interest income and capital gains are identical, implying that personal tax effects are unlikely to eliminate the corporate tax benefits of debt.

Therefore, the corporate tax benefits from debt financing should encourage firms with high effective tax rates and few forms of tax shield other than interest to have highly-leveraged capital structures. In contrast, firms that have tax shield substitutes for interest, such as depreciation, or that have operating loss carryforwards and hence do not expect to pay taxes, should have capital structures that are largely equity.

What tax benefits is Compaq forgoing? In evaluating Compaq's financial leverage, analysts would probably want to know how much the firm could save in taxes if management modified its current policy of zero debt. To evaluate the tax effects of additional debt, analysts can use accounting, financial ratio, and prospective analysis to answer the following types of questions:

- What is Compaq's average income tax rate? How does this rate compare with the average tax rate and financial leverage for the firm's major competitors?
- What portion of Compaq's tax expense is deferred taxes versus current taxes?
- What is Compaq's marginal corporate tax rate likely to be?
- Does Compaq have tax loss carryforwards or other tax benefits? How long are they expected to continue?
- What non-interest tax shields are currently available to the firm? For example, are there sizable tax shields from accelerated depreciation?
- Based on pro forma income and cash flow statements, what are our estimates for Compaq's taxable income for the next five to ten years? What non-interest tax

shields are available to the firm? Finally, what would be the tax savings from using some debt financing?

Analysis of Compaq's tax footnote indicates that the firm's average current tax rate in 1992 is 21.4 percent. This rate is lower than the statutory rate of 34 percent because the firm's Singapore operations receive a tax holiday, expected to continue through at least 1997. The firm has only a modest depreciation tax shield, since depreciable assets are a relatively small percentage of total assets. And as we discussed in Chapter 5, Compaq is likely to continue generating impressive taxable income in the foreseeable future. Thus, it certainly appears that the firm could reduce its tax burden and create additional value for stockholders by adding some debt to its capital structure.

MANAGEMENT INCENTIVES FOR VALUE CREATION.   A second benefit of debt financing is that it focuses management on value creation, thus reducing conflicts of interests between managers and shareholders. Conflicts of interest can arise when managers make investments that are of little value to stockholders and/or spend the firm's funds on perks, such as overly spacious office buildings and lavish corporate jets. Firms are particularly prone to these temptations when they are flush with cash but have few promising new investment opportunities, often referred to as a "free cash flow" situation. These firms' stockholders would generally prefer that their managers pay out any free cash flows as dividends or use the funds to repurchase stock. However, these options reduce the size of the firm and the assets under management's control. Management may therefore invest the free cash flows in new projects, even if they are not valued by stockholders, or spend the cash flows on management perks.

How can debt help reduce management's incentives to over-invest and to overspend on perks? The primary way is by reducing resources available to fund these types of outlays, since firms with relatively high leverage face pressures to generate cash flows to meet payments of interest and principal.

Could Compaq benefit from using debt to improve management focus? Compaq's lack of debt may increase opportunities for managers to spend free cash flows on perks or to invest in projects that are not valued by stockholders. Financial ratio and prospective analysis can help analysts assess whether there are currently free cash flow inefficiencies at Compaq as well as risks of future inefficiencies. Symptoms of excessive management perks and investment in unprofitable projects include the following:

- *Does Compaq have high ratios of general and administrative expenses and overhead to sales?* If its ratios are higher than those for its major competitors, one possibility is that management is wasting money on perks.
- *Is Compaq making significant new investments in unrelated areas?* If it is difficult to rationalize these new investments, Compaq might have a free cash flow problem.
- *Does Compaq have high levels of expected operating cash flows (net of essential capital expenditures and debt retirements) from pro forma income and cash flow statements?*

- *Does Compaq have poor management incentives to create additional shareholder value,* evidenced by a weak linkage between management compensation and firm performance?

Currently Compaq does not appear to have any problems with inefficient investment of free cash flows. It operates in a highly competitive industry which has gone through a difficult few years, it has remained very focused and invested only in related businesses, and its selling, general and administrative expenses are only 17 percent of sales in 1992, down from 22 percent in 1991. Further, management indicates that it plans to keep a tight rein on administrative expenses as part of the firm's new strategy. Thus, there currently appears to be little value in using debt to improve management focus.

However, as shown in Chapter 5's prospective analysis of Compaq, if the firm's new strategy pays off, its cash flows will mushroom. Analysts have some concerns that, if this occurs, the firm might waste these resources on acquisitions instead of paying them out to stockholders. One way for management to ensure that it does not end up making unprofitable future investments with free cash flows is to increase leverage in 1993.

Costs of Leverage: Financial Distress

As a firm increases its leverage, it increases the likelihood of financial distress, where it is unable to meet interest or principal repayment obligations to creditors. This may force the firm to declare bankruptcy or to agree to restructure its financial claims.

Financial distress can be expensive, since restructurings of a firm's ownership claims typically involve costly legal negotiations. It can also be difficult for distressed firms to raise capital to undertake profitable new investment opportunities. Finally, financial distress can intensify conflicts of interest between stockholders and the firm's debtholders, increasing the cost of debt financing.

LEGAL COSTS OF FINANCIAL DISTRESS.   When a firm is in serious financial distress, its owners' claims are likely to be restructured. This can take place under formal bankruptcy proceedings or out of bankruptcy. Restructurings are likely to be costly, since the parties involved have to hire lawyers, bankers, and accountants to represent their interests, and they have to pay court costs if there are formal legal proceedings. These are often called the *direct* costs of financial distress.

COSTS OF FORGONE INVESTMENT OPPORTUNITIES.   When a firm is in financial distress and particularly when it is in bankruptcy, it may be very difficult for it to raise additional capital for new investments, even though they may be profitable for all the firm's owners. In some cases, bankrupt firms are run by court-appointed trustees, who are unlikely to take on risky new investments—profitable or not. Even for a firm whose management supports new investment, the firm is likely to be capital constrained. Creditors are unlikely to approve the sale of nonessential assets unless the proceeds are used to first repay their claims. Potential new investors and creditors will be wary of the firm because they do not want to become embroiled in the legal disputes themselves. Thus, in all likelihood the firm will be unable to make significant new investments, potentially diminishing its value.

COSTS OF CONFLICTS BETWEEN CREDITORS AND STOCKHOLDERS.   When a firm is performing well, both creditors' and stockholders' interests are likely to coincide. Both want the firm's managers to take all investments which increase the value of the firm. However, when the firm is in financial difficulty, conflicts can arise between different classes of owners. Creditors become concerned about whether the firm will be able to meet its interest and principal commitments. Shareholders become concerned that their equity will revert to the creditors if the firm is unable to meet its outstanding obligations. Thus, managers are likely to face increased pressure to make decisions which serve the interests of only one form of owner, typically stockholders, rather than making decisions in the best interests of all owners. For example, managers have incentives to issue additional debt with equal or higher priority, to invest in riskier assets, or to pay liquidating dividends, since these actions reduce the value of outstanding creditors' claims and benefit stockholders. When it is costly to completely eliminate this type of game playing, creditors will simply reduce the amount they are willing to pay the firm for the debt when it is issued, increasing the costs of borrowing for the firm's stockholders.

OVERALL EFFECTS OF FINANCIAL DISTRESS.   The costs of financial distress discussed above offset the tax and monitoring benefits of debt. As a result, firms that are more likely to fall into financial distress or for which the costs of financial distress are especially high should have relatively low financial leverage. Firms are more likely to fall into financial distress if they have high business risks, that is, if their revenues and earnings before interest are highly sensitive to fluctuations in the economy. Financial distress costs are also likely to be relatively high for firms whose assets are easily destroyed in financial distress. For example, firms with human capital and brand intangibles are particularly sensitive to financial distress since dissatisfied employees and customers can leave or seek alternative suppliers. In contrast, firms with tangible assets can sell their assets if they get into financial distress, providing additional security for lenders and lowering the costs of financial distress. Firms with intangible assets are therefore less likely to be highly leveraged than firms whose assets are mostly tangible.

FINANCIAL DISTRESS COSTS FOR COMPAQ.   As the above discussion implies, Compaq's optimal financial leverage will depend on its underlying business risks and asset types. If the firm's business risks are relatively high or its assets can be easily destroyed by financial distress, changing the mix of debt and equity towards more debt may actually destroy shareholder value. Analysts can use ratio, cash flow, and pro forma analysis to assess Compaq's business risks and whether its assets are easily destroyed by financial distress. Their analysis should focus on:

- *Comparing indicators of business risk for Compaq and other firms in the computer industry with the economy.* Popular indicators of business risk include the ratio of fixed operating expenses (such as depreciation on plant and equipment) to sales, the volatility of return on assets, as well as the relation between indicators of Compaq's performance and indicators of performance for the economy as a whole.
- *Examining the competitive nature of the industry.* Since Compaq is in a highly competitive industry, its performance is very sensitive to changes in strategy by its competitors.
- *Determining whether Compaq's assets are largely intangible and therefore sensitive to financial distress,* using such ratios as market to book equity.

Although Compaq is not highly capital intensive, it does face significant business risk because of the high degree of competition in the industry. There is intense pressure in the personal computer industry to develop more powerful machines and to lower prices. Thus, Compaq's business risks arise from shocks to the industry from introductions of new technology and price wars. To compound these risks, many of Compaq's research and development assets are human ones that can leave if the firm gets into financial difficulty. Therefore, for Compaq the risks of financial distress are relatively high.

Determining the Long-Term Optimal Mix of Debt and Equity

The above discussion implies that the optimal mix of debt and equity for a firm can be estimated by trading off the corporate interest tax shield and monitoring benefits of debt against the costs of financial distress. As the firm becomes more highly leveraged, the costs of leverage presumably begin to outweigh the tax and monitoring benefits of debt.

However, there are several practical difficulties in trying to estimate a firm's optimal financial leverage. One difficulty is quantifying some of the costs and benefits of leverage. For example, it is not easy to value the expected costs of financial distress or any management incentive benefits from debt. There are no easy answers to this problem. The best that we can do is to qualitatively assess whether the firm faces free cash flow problems, and whether it faces high business risks and has assets that are easily destroyed by financial distress. These qualitative assessments can then be used to adjust the more easily quantified tax benefits from debt to determine whether the firm's financial leverage should be relatively high, low, or somewhere in between.

A second practical difficulty in deciding whether a firm should have high, low, or medium financial leverage is quantifying what we mean by high, low, and medium. One way to resolve this question is to use indicators of financial leverage, such as debt-to-equity ratios, for the market as a whole as a guide on leverage ranges. To provide a rough sense of what companies usually consider to be high, medium, and low financial leverage, Figures 11-1 and 11-2 show ranges of debt-to-market-equity and debt-to-book-equity ratios for public firms in the period 1984 to 1993 for a variety of countries.

FIGURE 11-1 Ratio of Net Interest-Bearing Debt to Market Equity from 1984 to 1993 for the 25th, 50th, and 75th Percentiles of Public Firms by Country

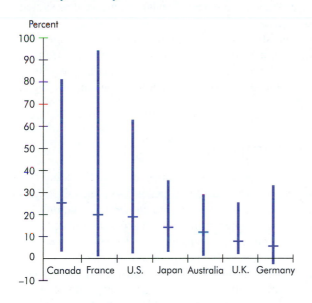

FIGURE 11-2 Ratio of Net Interest-Bearing Debt to Book Equity from 1984 to 1993 for the 25th, 50th, and 75th Percentiles of Public Firms by Country

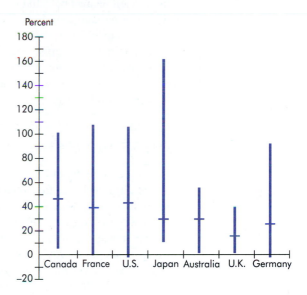

For U.S. firms, the median net interest-bearing debt-to-market-equity ratio from 1984 to 1993 is 19 percent. In contrast, the firm at the 25th percentile has zero net debt and the firm at the 75th percentile has a 63 percent ratio. Debt-to-book-equity ratios for U.S. firms are –6 percent for the firm at the 25th percentile, 44 percent for the median firm, and 106 percent for the firm at the 75th percentile.[1] It is interesting to note that for all the countries reported, more than 25 percent of the public firms have almost no net debt. In addition, firms in the U.S., Canada, and France appear to have systematically higher debt-to-equity ratios than firms in the U.K., Germany, and Australia.[2] However, some of these comparisons should not be taken too literally, since accounting practices vary considerably by country. For example, until relatively recently, reports for Japanese, German, and French companies were frequently unconsolidated, potentially understating their reported leverage.

THE OPTIMAL MIX OF DEBT AND EQUITY FOR COMPAQ.   Like other firms in its industry, Compaq's capital structure is currently quite conservative.[3] As we discussed above, Compaq could generate significant tax benefits from changing this policy and increasing financial leverage. However, given the current competitive situation in the industry, this would come at a cost—it would increase the likelihood of financial distress.

The personal computer industry is one of the most competitive in the U.S. By using equity financing, Compaq has ensured that it has "breathing room" to respond to any new technological or pricing challenges. This flexibility helped the firm to weather the financial problems faced in 1991. It also provides an important way for the firm to buttress itself against potential future problems as it embarks on its aggressive new strategy to cut prices and squeeze operating costs.

If Compaq's new strategy is successful, its cash position is likely to be impressive. Analysts raise concerns about whether the firm will use these free cash flows to make unprofitable acquisitions. One way for management to answer these concerns is to increase leverage, thereby reducing incentives to waste free cash flows on unprofitable acquisitions and investments.

THE FINANCING OF NEW PROJECTS

The second model of capital structure focuses on how firms make new financing decisions. Proponents of this dynamic model argue that there can be short-term frictions in capital markets which cause deviations from long-run optimal capital structure. One source of friction arises when managers have better information about their firm's future performance than outside investors. This could lead managers to deviate from their long-term optimal capital structure as they seek financing for new investments.

To see how information asymmetries between outside investors and management can create market imperfections and potentially affect short-term capital structure decisions, consider management's options for financing a proprietary new project that it expects to be profitable. One financing option is to use retained earnings to cover the investment outlay. However, what if the firm has no retained earnings available today? If it pays dividends, it could perhaps cut dividends to help pay for the project. But as we discuss later, investors usually interpret a dividend cut as an indication that the firm's management anticipates poor future performance. A dividend cut is therefore likely to lead to a stock price decline, albeit temporary, which management would probably prefer to avoid. Also, many firms do not pay dividends.

A second financing option is to borrow additional funds to finance the project. However, if the firm is already highly leveraged, the tax shield benefits from debt are likely to be relatively modest and the potential costs of financial distress relatively high, making additional borrowing unattractive.

The final financing option available to the firm is to issue new equity. However, if investors know that management has superior information on the firm's value, they are likely to interpret an equity offer as an indication that management believes that the firm's stock price is higher than the intrinsic value of the firm. The announcement of an equity offer is therefore likely to lead to a drop in the price of the firm's stock, raising the firm's cost of capital, and potentially leading management to abandon a perfectly good project.

The above discussion implies that if the firm has internal cash flows available or is not already highly-leveraged, it is relatively straightforward for it to arrange financing for the new project. Otherwise, management has to decide whether it is worthwhile undertaking the new project, given the costs of cutting dividends, issuing additional debt, or issuing equity to finance the project. The information costs of raising funds through these means lead managers to have a "pecking order" for new financing. Managers first use internal cash to fund investments, and only if this is unavailable do they resort to external financing. Further, if they have to use external financing, managers first use debt financing. New equity issues are used only as a last resort because of the difficulties that investors have in interpreting these issues.[4]

One way for management to mitigate the information problems of using external financing is to ensure that the firm has financial slack. Management can create financial slack by reinvesting free cash flows in marketable securities, so that it doesn't have to go to the capital market to finance a new project. It could also choose to have relatively low levels of debt, so that the firm can borrow easily in the future.

In summary, information asymmetries between managers and external investors can make managers reluctant to raise new equity to finance new projects. Managers' reluctance arises from their fear that investors will interpret the decision as an indication that the firm's stock is overvalued. In the short-term, this effect can lead managers to deviate from the firm's long-term optimal mix of debt and equity.

Compaq's Options for Raising Financing for New Investments

The above discussion implies that in the short-term Compaq should attempt to finance new projects primarily with retained earnings. Further, it suggests that the firm would be well advised to maintain financial slack to ensure that it is not forced to use costly external financing. To assess Compaq's financing options, we would ask the following types of questions:

- What is the value of current cash reserves (not required for day-to-day working capital needs) that could be used for new capital outlays? What operating cash resources are expected to become available in the coming few years? Do these internal resources cover Compaq's expected cash needs for new investment and working capital associated with its new operating strategy?
- How do Compaq's future cash needs for investment change as its operating performance deteriorates or improves? Are its investment opportunities relatively fixed, or are they related to current operating cash flow performance? Investment opportunities for many firms decline during a recession and increase during booms, enabling them to consistently use internal funds for financing. However, firms with stable investment needs should build financial slack during booms so that they can support investment during busts.
- If internal funds are not readily available, what opportunities does Compaq have to raise low-cost debt financing? Normally, a firm which has virtually zero debt could do this without difficulty. However, if it is in a volatile industry or has mostly intangible assets, debt financing may be costly.

- If Compaq has to raise costly equity capital, are there ways to focus investors on the value of the firm's assets and investment opportunities to lower any information asymmetries between managers and investors? For example, management might be able to disclose additional information about the uses and expected returns from the new funds.

Compaq's long-term optimal mix of debt and equity should continue to be mostly equity. Given its expected continued growth in operating cash flows, the need for external financing is likely to be minimal in the foreseeable future. Further, if the firm does face a future short-term cash shortfall—perhaps because of difficulties in implementing its new business strategy or the financing of new growth—it could easily raise additional low-cost debt. In 1993, Compaq actually registered $300 million of debt and negotiated a $300 million line of credit to provide for additional working capital needs associated with its growth.

Summary of Debt Policy

There are no easy ways to quantify the best mix of debt and equity for a firm and its best financing options. However, some general principles are likely to be useful in thinking about these questions. We have seen that the benefits from debt financing are likely to be highest for firms with:

high marginal tax rates and few non-interest tax shields, making interest tax shields from debt valuable;

high, stable income/cash flows and few new investment opportunities, increasing the monitoring value of debt and reducing the likelihood that the firm will fall into financial distress or require costly external financing for new projects; and

high tangible assets that are not easily destroyed by financial distress.

As we illustrated with Compaq, the financial analysis tools developed in Part 2 of the book are useful in rating a firm's interest tax shield benefits, its business risk and investment opportunities, and its major asset types. This information can then be used to judge whether there are benefits from debt or whether the firm would be better off using equity financing to support its business strategies.

FACTORS THAT DETERMINE FIRMS' DIVIDEND POLICIES

What factors should a firm consider when setting its dividend policy? Do investors prefer firms to pay out profits as dividends or to retain them for reinvestment? As we noted above, many of the factors that affect dividends are similar to those examined in the section on capital structure decisions. This should not be too surprising, since a firm's dividend policies also affect its financing decisions. Thus, dividends provide a means of reducing free cash flow inefficiencies. They also have tax implications for investors and can reduce a firm's financial slack. Finally, lending contracts can affect a firm's dividend payouts to protect lenders' interests.

Below we discuss the factors that are relevant to managers' dividend decisions and how financial analysis tools can be used in this decision process. To provide a context for our discussion, we again consider the case of Compaq Computer, using our financial analysis tools to discuss factors that are relevant to Compaq's dividend policy.

Dividends as a Way of Reducing Free Cash Flow Inefficiencies

As we discussed earlier, conflicts of interest between managers and shareholders can affect a firm's optimal capital structure; they also have implications for dividend policy decisions. Stockholders of a firm with free cash flows and few profitable investment opportunities want managers to adopt a dividend policy with high payouts. This will deter managers from growing the firm by reinvesting the free cash flows in new projects that are not valued by stockholders or from spending the free cash flows on management perks. In addition, if managers of a firm with free cash flows wish to fund a new project, most stockholders would prefer that they do so by raising new external capital rather than cutting dividends. Stockholders can then assess whether the project is genuinely profitable or simply one of management's pet projects.

Compaq's Use of Dividends for Improving Management Focus

Earlier we discussed how ratio and cash flow analysis can help Compaq's management assess whether the firm faces free cash flow inefficiencies, and how pro forma analysis can help indicate the likelihood of future free cash flow problems. The same analysis can help management to decide whether Compaq should initiate dividends. As of December 31, 1992, Compaq had never paid a dividend. By committing to pay dividends, management can reduce opportunities to overspend on perks or invest in projects that do not create value for stockholders.

Compaq does not currently appear to have a serious free cash flow problem, so that there is little benefit from using dividends as a way to improve management focus. However, if its new strategy pays off, management may want to consider initiating a dividend to maintain pressure to lower administrative and operating costs, and to reduce the risk of investing free cash flows in unrelated businesses.

Tax Costs of Dividends

What are the implications for dividend policy if dividends and capital gains are taxed, particularly at different rates? Classical models of the tax effects of dividends predict that if the capital gains tax rate is less than the rate on dividend income, investors will prefer that the firm either pay no dividends, so that they subsequently take gains as capital accumulation, or that the firm undertakes a stock repurchase, which qualifies as a capital distribution. Even if capital gains are slightly higher than dividend tax rates, investors are still likely to prefer capital gains to dividends, since they do not actually have to realize their capital gains. They can delay selling their shares and thereby defer paying the taxes on any capital appreciation. The longer investors wait before selling their stock, the lower the value of the capital gains tax. Only if capital gains tax rates are substantially higher than the rates on ordinary income are investors likely to favor dividend distributions over capital gains.

Today many practitioners and theorists believe that taxes play only a minor role in determining a firm's dividend policy, since a firm can attract investors with different tax preferences. Thus, a firm that wishes to pay high dividend rates will attract stockholders that are tax-exempt institutions, which do not pay taxes on dividend income. In contrast, a firm that prefers to pay low dividend rates will attract stockholders who have high marginal tax rates and prefer capital gains to dividend income.

Dividends and Financial Slack

We discussed earlier how managers' information advantage over dispersed investors can increase a firm's cost of external funds. One way to avoid having to raise costly external funds is to have a conservative dividend policy which creates financial slack in the organization. By paying only a small percentage of income as dividends and reinvesting the free cash flows in marketable securities, management reduces the likelihood that the firm will have to go to the capital market to finance a new project.

Managers of firms with high intangible assets and growth opportunities are particularly likely to have an information advantage over dispersed investors, since accounting information for these types of firms is frequently a poor indicator of future performance. Accountants, for example, do not attempt to value R&D, intangibles, or growth opportunities. These types of firms are therefore more likely to face information problems and capital market constraints. To compound this problem, high-growth firms are typically heavily dependent on external financing, since they are not usually able to fund all new investments internally. Any capital market constraints are therefore likely to affect their ability to undertake profitable new projects.

Because paying dividends reduces financial slack and is thus costly, a firm's dividend policy can help management communicate effectively with external investors. Investors recognize that managers will only increase their firm's dividend rate if they anticipate that the payout does not have a serious effect on the firm's future financing options. Thus, the decision to increase dividends can help investors appreciate management's optimism about the firm's future performance and its ability to finance growth.

Compaq's Financial Slack Costs and Dividend Initiation

As we discussed earlier, financial analysis tools can help assess how much financial slack Compaq should maintain. If the firm's projected cash needs for new investments are stable in relation to operating cash flows, management might decide that it is important to build significant financial slack during boom periods to help fund investments during busts. Similarly, if the firm's opportunities to raise low-cost debt are limited because it is in a volatile industry or has mostly intangible assets, financial slack may be valuable. Management may then decide that the initiation of dividend payments will not benefit stockholders, since it increases the risk that the firm will have to raise high-cost external capital in the future, lower dividends, or even forgo a profitable new project.

In Compaq's case, the cash flow needs for working capital are significant, because of its current high sales growth. Management might then decide that it is in the shareholders' best interests to delay initiating dividend payments until the growth has stabilized. This strategy protects against the risk of competitors' introductions of new technology and price wars. However, once growth stabilizes in the longer term, Compaq is more likely to have sufficient financial slack, so that management will almost surely have to initiate dividends to avoid holding huge cash balances.

Lending Constraints and Dividend Policy

One of the concerns of a firm's creditors is that when the firm is in financial distress, managers will pay a large dividend to stockholders. This problem is likely to be particularly severe for a firm with highly liquid assets, since its managers can pay a large dividend without selling assets. To limit these types of games, managers agree to restrict dividend payments to stockholders. Such dividend covenants usually require the firm to maintain certain minimum levels of retained earnings and current asset balances, which effectively limit dividend payments when it is facing financial difficulties. However, these constraints on dividend policy are unlikely to be severe for a profitable firm. Since Compaq does not have any significant debt, this constraint is not relevant.

Determining Optimal Dividend Payouts

One question that arises in using the above factors to determine dividend policy is defining what we mean by high, low, and medium dividend payouts. To provide a rough sense of what companies usually consider to be high, medium, and low dividend payouts and yields, Figures 11-3 and 11-4 show ranges of these ratios for public firms in the period 1984 to 1993 for a variety of countries.

In the U.S., more than 25 percent of publicly-listed firms do not pay dividends. The median payout is 16 percent and the rate for the firm at the 75th percentile is 49 percent. Payout rates in Germany, Australia, U.K., Japan, Canada, and France are somewhat

FIGURE 11-3 Dividend Payout Ratio from 1984 to 1993 for the 25th, 50th, and 75th Percentiles of Public Firms by Country

FIGURE 11-4 Dividend Yield from 1984 to 1993 for the 25th, 50th, and 75th Percentiles of Public Firms by Country

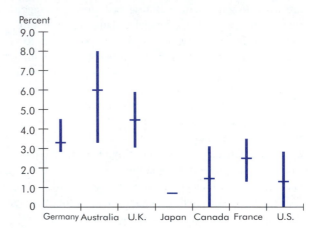

higher than in the U.S., with median firms paying out between 28 percent and 51 percent of profits. Dividend yields in the U.S. also tend to be somewhat lower than many other countries. The median dividend yield in the U.S. is about 1 percent, substantially lower than yields in Germany, Australia, the U.K., and France. It is interesting to see that dividend yields in Japan are less than 1 percent, with almost no variation between firms at the 75th and 25th percentiles.

Should Compaq initiate dividends?

Given its expected continued growth in operating cash flows for 1993 and 1994, Compaq should be able to afford to cover both moderate dividend payouts and new capital needs from internal funds. Further, the firm's conservative capital structure provides considerable financial slack in the event of a future short-term cash shortfall. Paying dividends also reduces the firm's free cash flows and thus maintains pressure on management to continue lowering operating and administrative costs.

If management is confident that the new business strategy will pay off, it might want to consider initiating a modest dividend as early as 1992. This could provide a strong optimistic signal to investors about the outcome of the strategy change. Otherwise, management might prefer to wait until the results of the strategy change become clearer.

In general, analysts predict that Compaq will not initiate dividends in the next few years. However, based on their forecasts of future growth, analysts presume that the firm will begin paying dividends within the coming five years. Otherwise, Compaq is likely either to have huge cash balances or to invest in unprofitable projects.

A Summary of Dividend Policy

Just as it is difficult to provide a simple formula to help management compute its optimal capital structure, it is difficult to formalize a firm's optimal dividend policy. However, we are able to identify several factors that appear to be important:

- High-growth firms should have low dividend payout ratios, and they should use their internally generated funds for reinvestment. This minimizes any costs from capital market constraints on financing growth options.
- Firms with high and stable operating cash flows and few investment opportunities should have high dividend payouts to reduce managers' incentives to reinvest free cash flows in unprofitable ventures.
- Firms should probably not worry too much about tax factors in setting dividend policy. Whatever their policy, they will be able to attract a clientele of investors. Firms that select high dividend payouts will attract tax-exempt institutions or corporations, and firms that pay low or no dividends will attract individuals in high tax brackets.
- Firms' financial covenants can have an impact on their dividend policy decisions. Firms will try to avoid being too close to their constraints in order to minimize the possibility of cutting their dividend.

SUMMARY AND CONCLUSIONS

This chapter examined how firms make optimal capital structure and dividend decisions. We show that a firm's optimal long-term capital structure is largely determined by its expected tax status, business risks, and types of assets. The benefits from debt financing are expected to be highest for firms with: high marginal tax rates and few non-interest tax shields, making interest tax shields valuable; high, stable income/cash flows and few new investment opportunities, increasing the monitoring value of debt and reducing the likelihood that the firm will fall into financial distress; and high tangible assets that are not easily destroyed by financial distress.

We also show that, in the short-term, managers can deviate from their long-term optimal capital structure when they seek financing for new investments. In particular, managers are reluctant to raise external financing, especially new equity, for fear that outside investors will interpret their action as meaning that the firm is overvalued. This information problem has implications for how much financial slack a firm is likely to need to avoid facing these types of information problems.

Optimal dividend policy is determined by many of the same factors—firms' business risks and their types of assets. Thus, dividend rates should be highest for firms with high and stable cash flows and few investment opportunities. By paying out relatively high dividends, these firms reduce the risk of managers investing free cash flows in unprofitable projects. Conversely, firms with low, volatile cash flows and attractive investment opportunities, such as start-up firms, should have relatively low dividend payouts. By reinvesting operating cash flows and reducing the amount of external financing required for new projects, these firms reduce their costs of financing.

Financial statement analysis can be used to better understand a firm's business risks, its expected tax status, and whether its assets are primarily assets in place or growth opportunities. Useful tools for assessing whether a firm's current capital structure and dividend policies maximize shareholder value include accounting analysis to determine off-balance-sheet liabilities, ratio analysis to help understand a firm's business risks, and cash flow and pro forma analysis to explore current and likely future investment needs.

NOTES

1. Firms can have a negative ratio, since the denominator is net debt, that is, interest-bearing debt less cash and marketable securities. A negative ratio for a firm indicates that its cash holdings exceed debt.

2. Japanese firms appear to be relatively highly leveraged when leverage is measured using debt to book equity, but only modestly leveraged using debt to market equity.

3. Apple also has no debt, and both Dell and AST have debt-to-long-term-capital ratios of about 25%.

4. These issues are discussed by Stewart Myers and Nicholas Majluf in "Corporate Financing and Investment Decisions When Firms Have Information That Investors Do Not Have," *Journal of Financial Economics* (June 1984): 187–221.

CASE

The Murray Ohio Manufacturing Co.

12

Management Communications

Management communication is increasingly important as firms invest in complex product and production technologies and in intangible assets such as research and development. These outlays can be quite difficult for outsiders to value, since they do not have access to the same data as management. As we discuss in this chapter, financial reports provide a low-cost way for management to communicate with investors. However, financial reports are not always effective as a communication vehicle. We therefore examine how alternative forms of communication can be used by management to mitigate information problems with external investors.

Several questions can be addressed by analyzing management's communication strategy:

- Management can ask: Is our current communication strategy effective in helping investors understand the firm's business strategy and expected future performance, thereby ensuring that our stock price is not seriously over- or undervalued?
- Securities analysts can ask: Do management's communications provide us with credible information that is useful for forecasting a firm's future performance? What types of information can we reasonably expect management to provide us? And how should we interpret information provided by management?

Throughout this book we have focussed primarily on showing how financial statement data can be helpful for *analysts* and *outside investors* in making a variety of decisions. In this chapter we change our emphasis and focus primarily on *management's* use of financial analysis to help communicate effectively with external users. However, as we note above, analysis of management's communication strategy is also likely to be useful to securities analysts.

To illustrate how managers can use financial analysis to help set their communication strategy, we examine the communication issues facing Compaq Computer, the company we have discussed throughout this book. In 1992, Compaq's performance deteriorated significantly, and in response management changed the firm's operating strategy. As discussed below, this change raises several questions for Compaq's management as it communicates with outside investors.

COMMUNICATING WITH INVESTORS

Some managers argue that communication problems are not worth worrying about. They maintain that as long as managers make investment and operating decisions that enhance shareholder value, investors will value their performance and the firm's stock accordingly. While this is true in the long run, since all information is eventually public, it may not hold in the short- or even medium-term. If investors do not have access to the same information as management, they will probably find it difficult to value new and innovative investments. In an efficient capital market, they will not consistently over- or undervalue these new investments, but their valuations will tend to be noisy. This can make stock prices relatively noisy, leading management at various times to consider their firms to be either seriously over- or undervalued.

Does it matter if a firm's stock is over- or undervalued for a period? Most managers would prefer to not have their stock undervalued, since it makes it more costly to raise new financing. They may also worry that undervaluation is likely to increase the chance of a takeover by a hostile acquirer, with an accompanying reduction in their job security. Managers of firms that are overvalued may be concerned about the market's assessment, since they are legally liable for failing to disclose information relevant to investors. They may therefore not wish to see their stock seriously overvalued, even though overvaluation provides opportunities to issue new equity at favorable rates.

A Word of Caution

It is natural that many managers believe their firms are undervalued by the capital market. This frequently occurs because it is difficult for managers to be realistic about their company's future performance. After all, it is part of their job to sell the company to new employees, customers, suppliers, and investors. In addition, forecasting the firm's future performance objectively requires them to judge their own capabilities as managers. Thus, many managers may argue that investors are uninformed and that their firm is undervalued. Only some can back that up with solid evidence.

We recommend that before jumping to the conclusion that their firm is undervalued, managers should analyze their firm's performance and compare their own forecasts of future performance with those of analysts, using the following approach:

- *Is there a significant difference between internal management forecasts of future earnings and cash flows and those of outside analysts?*

- *Do any differences between managers' and analysts' forecasts arise because of different expectations about economy-wide performance?* Managers may understand their own businesses better than analysts, but they may not be any better at forecasting macroeconomic conditions.
- *Can managers identify any factors with the firm that might explain a difference between analysts' and managers' forecasts of future performance?* For example, are analysts unaware of positive new R&D results, do they have different information about customer responses to new products and marketing campaigns, etc.? These types of differences could indicate that the firm faces an information problem.

If management decides that the firm does face a genuine information problem, it can begin to consider whether and how this could be redressed. Is the problem potentially serious enough that it is worth doing something to alter investors' perceptions? Or is the problem likely to resolve itself within a short period? Does the firm have plans to raise new equity or to use equity to acquire another company? Is management's job security threatened? As we discuss below, there is a wide range of options for management in this situation.

Communication Issues for Compaq's Managers

As we discussed earlier, Compaq experienced deteriorating performance in 1991. In that year, the firm's sales declined by 9 percent, return on equity dropped to 7 percent (from 30 percent in 1990), and the stock price dropped from a high of $74.25 to a low of $22.13. As a result of this deterioration, the firm replaced its founding CEO and changed its business strategy to focus on increasing market share. This was to be accomplished by introducing new programs in pricing, product development, distribution and marketing, and service support.

Having decided to make management and strategy changes, Compaq's management faced several communication questions. One approach was to make no major effort to communicate the new plans to external investors, letting subsequent earnings and cash flow improvements speak for themselves. A second approach was to publicize the change in strategy, discuss the logic that underlay the decision—perhaps projecting how it would affect the firm's future earnings performance—and even implement financial policy changes to indicate that management was optimistic about the firm's future performance. Both approaches have pluses and minuses. By publicizing a strategy change, Compaq's management would be alerting the firm's competitors to the change, potentially increasing the likelihood of retaliation. However, this approach also reduces the risk that investors will misvalue Compaq, since they will have access to some of the same information as management about the firm's future prospects.

In making their decision about how to communicate the strategy change, management would want to consider the following questions:

- *What competitive retaliation is likely if Compaq provides a clear signal that management is optimistic about the firm's strategy change? How does this affect the value of the strategy?*
- *Do investors seriously undervalue the firm, given its new strategy?* This requires management to estimate pro forma earnings or cash flows for Compaq under the new strategy and then to use these projections to model the value of the firm's stock.
- *Is Compaq's strategy dependent on new financing? If so, can the firm raise new capital from low-cost debt, or will it be forced to raise new equity just when the market undervalues its stock?*

If Compaq's managers decide to follow a proactive communication strategy to explain the firm's new operating strategy to investors and analysts, they have several options. They can use the firm's financial reports to attempt to show that the long-term future is strong. Alternatively, they can use non-accounting forms of communication, such as increased disclosure of non-accounting data or the selection of financial policies that signal optimism to investors.

COMMUNICATION THROUGH FINANCIAL REPORTING

Financial reports are the least costly and the most popular format for management communication. Below we discuss the role of financial reporting as a means of investor communication, the institutions that make accounting information credible, and when it is likely to be ineffective.

Accounting as a Means of Management Communication

As we discussed in Chapter 3, financial reports are an important medium for management communication with external investors. Reports provide investors with an explanation of how their money has been invested, a summary of the performance of those investments, and a discussion of how current performance fits within the firm's overall philosophy and strategy.

Accounting reports not only provide a record of past transactions, they also reflect management estimates and forecasts of the future. For example, they include estimates of bad debts, forecasts of the lives of tangible assets, and implicit forecasts that outlays will generate future cash flow benefits that exceed their cost. Since management is likely to be in a position to make forecasts of these future events that are more accurate than those of external investors, financial reports are a potentially useful form of communicating with investors. However, investors are also likely to be skeptical of reports prepared by management, since managers have conflicts of interest in providing information that will be used to assess their own performance.

Investors' Concerns About the Credibility of Accounting Communication

It is difficult for managers to be truly impartial in providing external investors with information about their firm's performance. Management has a natural incentive to want to "sell" the company, in part because that is its job and in part because it is reluctant to provide information that jeopardizes its own job security. Reporting consistently poor earnings increases the likelihood that top management will be replaced, either by the board of directors or by an acquirer who takes over the firm to improve its management. Consequently, investors sometimes believe that accounting communications lack credibility.

Factors That Increase the Credibility of Accounting Communication

A number of mechanisms mitigate conflicts of interest in financial reporting and increase the credibility of accounting information that is communicated to stockholders. These include accounting standards, auditing, monitoring of management by financial analysts, and management reputation.

ACCOUNTING STANDARDS AND AUDITING.   Accounting standards promulgated by the Financial Accounting Standards Board (FASB) and the Securities Exchange Commission (SEC) provide guidelines for managers on how to make accounting decisions and provide outside investors with a way of interpreting these decisions. Uniform accounting standards attempt to reduce managers' ability to record similar economic transactions in different ways, either over time or across firms. Compliance with these standards is enforced by external auditors who attempt to ensure that managers' estimates are reasonable. Auditors therefore reduce the likelihood of earnings management.

MONITORING BY FINANCIAL ANALYSTS.   Financial intermediaries, such as analysts, also limit management's ability to manage earnings. Financial analysts specialize in developing firm- and industry-specific knowledge, enabling them to assess the quality of a firm's reported numbers and to make any necessary adjustments. Analysts evaluate the appropriateness of management's forecasts implicit in accounting method choices and reported accruals. This requires a thorough understanding of the firm's business and the relevant accounting rules used in the preparation of its financial reports. Superior analysts adjust reported accrual numbers, if necessary, to reflect economic reality, perhaps by using the cash flow statement and the footnote disclosures.

Analysts' business and technical expertise as well as their legal liability and incentives differ from those of auditors. Consequently, analyst reports can provide information to investors on whether the firm's accounting decisions are appropriate, or whether managers are overstating the firm's economic performance to protect their jobs.

MANAGEMENT REPUTATION.   A third factor that can counteract external investors' natural skepticism about financial reporting is management reputation. Managers that expect to have an ongoing relation with external investors and financial intermediaries may be able to build a track record for unbiased financial reporting. By making accounting estimates and judgments that are supported by subsequent performance, managers can demonstrate their competence and reliability to investors and analysts. As a result, managers' future judgments and accounting estimates are more likely to be viewed as credible sources of information.

Limitations of Financial Reporting for Investor Communication

While accounting standards, auditing, monitoring of management by financial analysts, and management concerns about its reputation increase the credibility and informativeness of financial reports, these mechanisms are far from perfect. Consequently, there are times when financial reporting breaks down as a means for management to communicate with external investors. These breakdowns can arise when: (1) there are no accounting rules to guide practice or the existing rules do not distinguish between poor and successful performers, (2) auditors and analysts do not have the expertise to judge new products or business opportunities, or (3) management faces credibility problems.

ACCOUNTING RULES.   Despite the rapid increase in new accounting standards, accounting rules frequently do not distinguish between good and poor performers. For example, current accounting rules do not permit managers to show on their balance sheets in a timely fashion the benefits of investments in quality improvements, human resource development programs, research and development, and customer service.

Some of the problems with accounting standards arise because it takes time for standard setters to develop appropriate standards for many new types of economic transactions. Other difficulties arise because standards are the result of compromises between different interest groups (e.g., auditors, investors, corporate managers, and regulators).

AUDITOR AND ANALYST EXPERTISE.   While auditors and analysts have access to proprietary information, they do not have the same understanding of the firm's business as managers. The divergence between managers' and auditors'/analysts' business assessments is likely to be most severe for firms with distinctive business strategies, or firms that operate in emerging industries. In addition, auditors' decisions in these circumstances are likely to be dominated by concerns about legal liability, hampering management's ability to use financial reports to communicate effectively with investors.

MANAGEMENT CREDIBILITY.   When is management likely to face credibility problems with investors? There is very little evidence on this question. However, we expect that managers of new firms, firms with volatile earnings, firms in financial distress, and firms with poor track records in communicating with investors will find it difficult to be seen as credible reporters.

If management faces a credibility problem, financial reports are likely to be viewed with considerable skepticism. Investors will then view financial reporting estimates that increase income as evidence that management is padding earnings. This makes it very difficult for management to use financial reports to communicate positive news about future performance.

Compaq's Accounting Communication

For Compaq, the change in operating strategy is likely to have certain effects on future measures of accounting performance:

1. The cost-cutting measures aimed at increasing manufacturing and administrative efficiency are likely to lead to layoffs and restructuring costs.
2. Given the elasticity of demand for PC products and Compaq's brand name, the more aggressive pricing policy should lead to a surge in demand for the company's products and hence superior revenue growth.
3. Plans to extend its current one-year product warranty to three years will increase warranty costs and customer satisfaction.
4. Plans to pursue an aggressive research and development strategy to ensure that it maintains its technological edge will lead R&D costs to continue to grow in the coming years.

Compaq's management is likely to be in the best position to understand how long it will take the company to successfully implement its strategy, and how long it will take for this success to be reflected in earnings performance. Financial reporting can provide management with a number of ways to convey its intentions to investors:

- Write-offs of major restructuring outlays indicate the costs of implementing the new strategy and the seriousness of management efforts to reorganize the firm. Write-offs are likely to be viewed positively by investors if they are one-time events which show management's commitment to increasing productivity and efficiency. They are likely to be less effective if management consistently understates write-offs, so that there are further write-offs in subsequent years.
- Outlays associated with implementing the strategy change and that have future benefits could be capitalized, signaling to investors that management and the firm's auditors are confident that the changes will be successful.
- Inventory build-ups can provide investors with information on how much of an increase in volume that management is anticipating as a result of its more aggressive pricing policy.
- Estimates of future costs associated with the new strategy, such as increased warranty expenses, are required to be reported as liabilities on the firm's balance sheet, helping investors to understand the financial implications of additional services provided.

Compaq faced restructuring costs associated with reducing its costs of manufacturing and administration. These included costs of $135 million in 1991 and $73 million in

1992, for layoffs of personnel and costs of reorganizing its operations to increase efficiency. These charges are likely to help investors appreciate management's commitment to making significant operational changes and the magnitude of the reorganization required. However, they do not provide much new information about the expected financial benefits of the changes. Given the limitations on capitalizing R&D and brand capital in the U.S., there are no opportunities for management to capitalize any outlays associated with increased customer service or R&D, despite their likely future benefits. However, estimated additional warranty costs could provide new information for investors on the financial implications of increased customer service. Compaq anticipated it had a strategic edge over generic PC manufacturers in providing two years of additional warranty, since its returns tended to be lower than those of the generics. Warranty liabilities therefore provide investors with management estimates of future returns and product quality, both good indicators of customer satisfaction. Finally, Compaq doubled its inventory in 1992, largely to prepare for expected sales growth from the introduction of new models and pricing reductions.

OTHER FORMS OF COMMUNICATING WITH INVESTORS

Given the limitations of accounting standards, auditing, and monitoring by financial analysts, as well as the reporting credibility problems faced by management, firms that wish to communicate effectively with external investors are often forced to use alternative media. Below we discuss three alternative ways that managers can communicate with external investors and analysts: meetings with analysts to publicize the firm, expanded voluntary disclosure, and using financing policies to signal management expectations. These forms of communication are typically not mutually exclusive. For example, at meetings with analysts, management usually discloses additional information that is helpful in valuing the firm.

Analyst Meetings

One popular way for managers to help mitigate communication problems is to meet regularly with financial analysts that follow the firm. At these meetings, management will field questions about the firm's current financial performance as well as discuss its future business plans. As noted above, management typically provides additional disclosures to analysts at these meetings. In addition to holding analyst meetings, many firms appoint a director of public relations, who provides further regular contact with analysts seeking more information on the firm.

Voluntary Disclosure

One way for managers to improve the credibility of their financial reporting is through voluntary disclosure. Accounting rules usually prescribe minimum disclosure requirements, but they do not restrict managers from voluntarily providing additional information. These could include an articulation of the company's long-term strategy, specification of non-financial leading indicators which are useful in judging the effectiveness of the strategy implementation, explanation of the relation between the leading indicators and future profits, and forecasts of future performance. Voluntary disclosures can be reported in the firm's annual report, in brochures created to describe the firm to investors, in management meetings with analysts, or in investor relations responses to information requests.

One constraint on expanded disclosure is the competitive dynamics in product markets. Disclosure of proprietary information on strategies and their expected economic consequences may hurt the firm's competitive position. Managers then face a trade-off between providing information that is useful to investors in assessing the firm's economic performance, and withholding information to maximize the firm's product market advantage.

A second constraint in providing voluntary disclosure is management's legal liability. Forecasts and voluntary disclosures can potentially be used by dissatisfied shareholders to bring civil action against management for providing misleading information. This seems ironic, since voluntary disclosures should provide investors with additional information. Unfortunately, it can be difficult for courts to decide whether managers' disclosures were good-faith estimates of uncertain future events which later do not materialize, or whether management manipulated the market. Consequently, many corporate legal departments recommend against management providing much voluntary disclosure.

Finally, management credibility can limit a firm's incentives to provide voluntary disclosures. If management faces a credibility problem in financial reporting, any voluntary disclosures it provides are also likely to be viewed skeptically. In particular, investors may be concerned about what management is not telling them, particularly since such disclosures are not audited.

Selected Financial Policies

Managers can also use financing policies to communicate effectively with external investors. Financial policies that are useful in this respect include dividend payouts, stock repurchases, financing choices, and hedging strategies.

DIVIDEND PAYOUT POLICIES.   As we discussed in Chapter 11, a firm's cash payout decision can provide information to investors on managers' assessments of the firm's future prospects. This arises because dividend payouts tend to be sticky, in the sense that managers are reluctant to cut dividends. Thus, managers will only increase dividends when they are confident that they are able to sustain the increased rate in future years. Consequently, investors interpret dividend increases as signals of managers' confidence in the quality of current and future earnings.

STOCK REPURCHASES.   In some countries, such as the U.S. and the U.K., managers can use stock repurchases to communicate with external investors. Under a stock repurchase, the firm buys back its own stock, either through a purchase on the open market, through a tender offer, or through a negotiated purchase with a large stockholder. Of course a stock repurchase, particularly a tender offer repurchase, is an expensive way for management to communicate with outside investors. Firms typically pay a hefty premium to acquire their shares in tender offer repurchases, potentially diluting the value of the shares that are not tendered or not accepted for tender. In addition, the fees to investment banks, lawyers, and share solicitation fees are not trivial.

FINANCING CHOICES.   Firms that have problems communicating with external investors may be able to use financing choices to reduce them. For example, a firm that is unwilling to provide proprietary information to help dispersed public investors value it may be willing to provide such information to a knowledgeable private investor—which can become a large stockholder/creditor—or a bank that agrees to provide the company with a significant new loan. A firm with credibility problems in financial reporting can sell stock or issue debt to an informed private investor such as a large customer who has superior information about the quality of product or service.

Such changes in financing and ownership can mitigate communication problems in two ways. First, the terms of the new financing arrangement and the credibility of the new lender or stockholder can provide investors with information to reassess the value of the firm. Second, the accompanying increased concentration of ownership and the role of large block holders in corporate governance can have a positive effect on valuation. If investors are concerned about management's incentives to increase shareholder value, the presence of a new block shareholder or significant creditor on the board can be reassuring. This type of monitoring arises in leveraged buyouts, start-ups backed by venture capital, and in firms with equity partnership investments. In Japanese and German corporations, it may also arise because large banks own both debt and equity and have close working relationships with firms' managers.

Of course, in the extreme, management can decide that the best option for the firm is to no longer continue operating as a public company. This can be accomplished by a management buyout, where a buyout group (including management) leverages its own investment (using bank or public debt finance), buys the firm, and takes it private. The buyout firm hopes to run the company for several years and then take it public again, hopefully with a track record of improved performance that enables investors to value the firm more effectively.

HEDGING.   An important source of mispricing arises if investors are unable to distinguish between unexpected changes in reported earnings due to management performance and transitory shocks that are beyond managers' control (e.g., foreign currency translation gains and losses). Managers can counteract these effects by hedging such "accounting" risks. Even though hedging is costly, it may be valuable if it reduces information problems that potentially lead to misvaluation.

Compaq's Use of Other Communications

Many of the non-accounting forms of communication discussed above are available to Compaq's management. The firm can meet with analysts to explain the new strategy, present the logic that underlies it, provide analysts with information on leading indicators that will foretell the strategy's success, and even forecast future earnings.

Compaq's management can also change financial policies to indicate its optimism to investors. By repurchasing the firm's own stock, initiating a dividend, or raising new debt or equity financing from a respected and knowledgeable investor, Compaq's management may be able to persuade investors that the firm's future is bright. One important difference between this type of communication and additional disclosure is that the firm does not provide potentially proprietary information to competitors. The signal therefore indicates to competitors that Compaq's management is bullish on the new strategy, but it does not provide details of key dimensions of the strategy or implementation issues.

Compaq opted to use a relatively passive voluntary disclosure strategy in communicating with investors. The Financial Analysts Federation's ratings of the firm's voluntary disclosure actually declined between 1990 and 1991. Although analysts that rated the firm commended it for continuing to provide overall good coverage, despite the declining performance, the company's ratings dropped from above average for the industry in 1990 to average or slightly below average in 1991.

However, Compaq has been willing to use financial policies to communicate more effectively with investors. For example, on May 16, 1991, the Board of Directors voted to repurchase on the open market up to ten million shares of common stock, representing approximately 12 percent of the shares outstanding at the beginning of 1991.[1] This decision was made in response to the 30 percent stock price drop that occurred on May 15–16, following the announcement that second-quarter earnings had fallen by 15 percent. The announcement of the repurchase decision, made on May 17, was accompanied by a statement from top management and the Board that they were confident that the company's earnings problems were temporary. In contrast to typical repurchase announcements, the market reaction to this event was subdued—the stock held at $35.25. In 1992, Compaq announced that it had begun hedging its net income from foreign currency risks. This could potentially assist in communicating with investors if management was concerned that foreign currency risks might obscure earnings information about the outcome of the change in operating strategy.

It is interesting that the above communications by Compaq's management were largely ineffective in changing investors' perceptions of the firm's future performance. Indeed, it wasn't until late 1992, when there were actual earnings improvements, that the firm's stock price began to recover.

SUMMARY AND CONCLUSIONS

This chapter discussed firms' strategies for communicating with investors. Communication with investors can be useful because managers typically have better information on their firm's current and expected future performance than outside analysts and investors. By communicating effectively with investors, management can potentially reduce this information gap, lowering the likelihood that the stock will be mispriced or volatile. This can be important for firms that wish to raise new capital, avoid takeovers, or whose management is concerned that its true job performance is not reflected in the firm's stock.

The typical way for firms to communicate with investors is through financial reporting. Accounting standards and auditing make the reporting process a way for managers to not only provide information about the firm's current performance, but to indicate, through accounting estimates, where they believe the firm is headed in the future. However, financial reports are not always able to convey the types of forward-looking information that investors need. Accounting standards often do not permit firms to capitalize outlays that provide significant future benefits to the firm, such as R&D outlays.

A second way that management can communicate with investors is through non-accounting means. We discussed several such mechanisms, including: meeting with financial analysts to explain the firm's strategy, current performance and outlook; disclosing additional information, both quantitative and qualitative, to provide investors with similar information as management's; and using financial policies (such as stock repurchases, dividend increases, and hedging) to help signal management's optimism about the firm's future performance.

In this chapter we have stressed the importance of communicating effectively with investors. However, firms also have to communicate with other stakeholders, including employees, customers, suppliers, and regulatory bodies. Many of the same principles discussed here can also be applied to management communication with these other stakeholders.

NOTE

1. The company carried through on its repurchase commitment. Three million shares were acquired in 1991, at a cost of $95.5 million, and an additional seven million were acquired at a cost of $202.2 million in 1992.

CASES

Comdisco, Inc. (A)
Comdisco, Inc. (B)
CUC International, Inc. (A)
Harnischfeger Corporation
Oracle Systems Corporation
Patten Corporation
Roosevelt Financial Group, Inc. (A)

p a r t 4

Cases in Financial Statement Analysis

Anacomp, Inc.

O n September 10, 1982, Anacomp, a computer software company, released its first annual report after being listed on the New York Stock Exchange. Prior
to 1982, the company's stock was traded on the over-the-counter market. In the annual
report Anacomp's management outlined the company's strategy for new software systems development:

> Anacomp is committed to being the world's leading supplier of software and
> services to the banking industry. Anacomp and its subsidiaries have licensed soft-
> ware products, sold data processing services, or entered into software consulting
> agreements with more than 200 billion-dollar financial institutions around the
> world. But the bank marketplace is changing rapidly. Regulatory and technologi-
> cal changes are blurring the distinctions between banks and other financial insti-
> tutions. Bank customers—both retail and wholesale—are becoming more
> sophisticated and more demanding. Bankers require computer systems which en-
> courage total customer relationships, adapt quickly to product changes, and meet
> requirements of round-the-clock banking.
>
> Since 1979, Anacomp has been developing a totally new generation of banking
> computer software systems to serve those evolving needs. Anacomp's software de-
> velopment effort is one the most substantial ever undertaken by an independent
> computer services vendor. It is based on an Anacomp innovation—the software
> R&D partnership—and on the philosophy of getting prospective customers in-
> volved in developing the software products they will eventually use.
>
> In 1979, when its net worth was $10 million, Anacomp recognized the oppor-
> tunity to develop at a cost of $12 million a major new IBM-based real-time retail
> banking system. The development was expected to take several years to complete.
> Anacomp selected the limited partnership alternative to buffer the company's
> stockholders from the financial risks involved. To help assure the development of
> a superior product, Anacomp also sought the participation of a cross-section of
> major financial institutions—the ultimate users of the bank product. To induce
> these banks to become co-developers, it was necessary to show that the required
> funding was in place and that Anacomp's commitment was firmly established. A

This case was prepared by Professor Krishna Palepu as the basis for class discussion rather than to illustrate either
effective or ineffective handling of an administrative situation. Copyright © 1987 by the President and Fellows of
Harvard College. Harvard Business School case 9-187-153.

limited partnership was the best way to induce four "primary development banks" to contribute collectively $6 million and 24 software development people for two years to the project.

The same considerations were present in each of the four subsequent partnerships—BANKSERV 10000, CEFT, CDA, and CIBS. Each partnership assumed development risks; except for BANKSERV 10000, each project involved several major banks acting as co-developers with Anacomp. Any product developed becomes the property of the partnership. Anacomp has the option to purchase the products but is under no obligation to exercise this option; Anacomp did purchase the CIS and BANKSERV 10000 systems in 1982. In total, more than $60 million has been raised since 1979 for investment in the development of new wholesale and retail banking software products.

COMPANY BACKGROUND

Anacomp, Inc., based in Indianapolis, Indiana, began as a computer and data services company in 1969. The company was founded by Ronald Palamara, a Ph.D. in computer sciences. Among the computer services offered by the company were the design and implementation of computer software systems and the management of customers' computer facilities. The company also operated customers' data centers, offered data processing and microfilming services, and sold micrographic equipment. The company viewed that its future growth would primarily come from the design and development of software for the banking industry.

Prior to 1980, the company's principal proprietary software system for commercial banks and thrift institutions was the Customer Integrated/Reference File (CI/RF) system. CI/RF integrated a customer's banking relationships—such as checking, savings, loans, etc.—and incorporated them into a single record. The system was utilized by banks in 20 states throughout the United States, including Manufacturers Hanover Trust and Sumitomo Bank of California. The system and software primarily used a computer language designed for computers manufactured by NCR Corporation.

Beginning in 1980 Anacomp announced plans to develop a number of new software systems for the banking and financial services industry. For the retail banking industry the company was developing two new products: the Continuous Integrated System (CIS) and the BANKSERVE 10000 system. CIS was claimed to be the first on-line real-time retail banking transactions processing system designed for IBM computers. The BANK-SERVE 10000 system would allow banks to share networks of point-of-sale terminals or automated teller machines on a national or regional basis.

Anacomp had also announced plans to develop a full line of software systems to help banks deal more efficiently with their wholesale customers—companies, institutions, and other banks. The Corporate Electronic Funds Transfer (CEFT) system was expected to combine three banking functions: an electronic funds transfer mechanism that would take payments from external sources, a money transfer component which would automate the bank's internal paying and receiving functions, and a corporate funds control

a

component which would allow the bank to monitor its own cash position and the cash position of each customer. The Corporate Deposit and Analysis (CDA) system, another wholesale banking product that Anacomp targeted for development, was expected to automate the bank's depository relationships with large corporations and other banks.

In August 1982 the company announced that it was initiating the development of yet another new software system, Corporate International Banking System (CIBS). CIBS was the most complex system the company planned to date, and was intended to help a large international bank automate certain internal treasury operations, generate complete information on the bank's foreign currency positions, and automate the processing of letters of credit and documentary credit collections.

Anacomp's management believed that the above software systems, if successfully developed and implemented, would enable the company to become a leading supplier of software and services to the banking industry.

INDUSTRY AND COMPETITION[1]

The computer services industry was marked by very rapid growth. In 1981, computer service revenues totaled $18.9 billion, up 23 percent from $15.4 billion a year, according to INPUT, a leading international consulting firm. INPUT had estimated that the industry growth rate between 1981 and 1986 would be approximately 23 percent per annum.

There were three major segments of the computer services industry: processing services, professional services, and software products. The companies in the processing area offered customers access to a large computer facility in which batch processing, remote computing services, and facilities management services were performed. This segment accounted for 57 percent of total computer services revenues in 1981 and was expected to grow at a compound annual rate of 17 percent between 1981 and 1986. The companies in the professional services segment provided customers alternatives to in-house data processing. These services included custom-made computer systems and programming to perform specialized tasks, as well as the management of data processing facilities. The professional services segment, which accounted for 23 percent of total computer services industry revenues in 1981, was expected to grow 29 percent annually from 1981 to 1986. Software products, the third segment of the software services industry, was the fastest-growing sector. Software products consist of instructions that guide computer equipment through tasks. This segment was expected to grow at an annual compound growth rate of 33 percent between 1981 and 1986.

The high growth rates of the computer services industry were being fueled by the large number of computers installed and customers' realization of the value computer services can have in lifting their productivity. Hardware, the premiere growth area of the 1960s and 1970s, had since taken on a commodity-like status as a result of progressively lower manufacturing costs. Computer services, on the other hand, increased in value and in price.

a

3

1. Material in this section is drawn from Standard and Poor's Industry surveys on office equipment systems and services, October 21, 1982.

The computer services industry in 1982 consisted of some 5,000 companies ranging from small software operations to giants such as IBM and Control Data Corporation. Smaller companies in the industry generally concentrated on serving particular market niches; their performance depended on factors influencing these small sectors.

There was active competition in each of the areas of services provided by Anacomp. In the computer service area, Anacomp competed with other computer service companies, manufacturers of mainframe computers, and companies developing in-house computer service capabilities. In the data center service business, Anacomp competed with other data processing and micrographic service companies. Anacomp believed that the services performed by it represented only a small portion of the market in each of the fields it operated.

The computer services industry was subject to rapid technological change requiring constant adaptation to provide competitive service. Competition in the computer services industry was based primarily on technical capability and expertise, pricing, quality of work, and ability to meet system development deadlines. In the other areas of Anacomp's business, competition was based upon the reliability and timeliness of the services and products provided.

TOP MANAGEMENT

The names, ages, and current and former positions of Anacomp's executive officers in September 1982 were as follows:

Ronald D. Palamara, Ph.D., age 42, has served as Chairman and President for more than the past five years.

Stanley E. Hirschfeld, age 47, became Senior Vice President of Corporate Development during 1981. For more than the prior five years, he served as Vice President-Finance and Secretary of Anacomp.

Ralph C. McAuley, age 47, became President of Anacomp's Computer Services group during 1981. For more than the five prior years, he served as Vice President of Data Processing Services.

John J. Flanigan, age 42, became Group Vice President of Data Services during 1981. During the prior five-year period, he served as Vice President of Data Processing Services.

Christopher Duffy, age 44, became Vice President and Chief Administrative Officer during 1981. For more than the five prior years, he served as Vice President and General Manager of an Indianapolis television station.

Myles Hannan, age 44, became Vice President-Finance, General Counsel and Secretary during 1981. During 1979 and 1980, he served as Vice President-Law and Administration for Delaware North Companies, Incorporated. For more than the prior two years he served as Vice President-Legal and Staff Divisions of the Stop & Shop Companies, Inc.

William C. Ater, age 40, became Vice President of Administration during 1981. During 1979 and 1980, he served as Anacomp's Vice President of Bank Data Processing. For more than the prior two years, he served in various computer management positions with NCR Corporation.

As of the end of fiscal 1981, all officers and directors as a group owned 15.1 percent of Anacomp's common stock and were paid $2.9 million in cash and cash equivalent forms of remuneration during the year.

NEW SOFTWARE SYSTEMS DEVELOPMENT

Anacomp organized and financed its new software development in a unique manner. During the fiscal year ended June 30, 1980, Anacomp initiated the development of a major new computer software system called Continuous Integrated System (CIS) to be marketed to major financial institutions. According to Anacomp's management, CIS would represent a major advance over the company's current CI/RF system.

Anacomp stated that, in view of the anticipated significant development expenditure for the CIS system, the company had entered into an agreement in November 1979 with a limited partnership, RTS Associates. Under this agreement, Anacomp agreed to develop the CIS system on behalf of the partnership. In return, RTS agreed to pay a development fee of $6 million, of which $2.2 million was paid in 1980. Upon completion of the development of the CIS system, Anacomp agreed to market CIS for five years on a commission basis. Anacomp also had the option to acquire all rights to the CIS system at the greater of its appraised fair market value or RTS's investment plus a fixed profit. RTS had the right to extend Anacomp's five-year marketing agreement an additional five years or to cancel it if Anacomp did not use its best efforts to market CIS.

RTS Associates' payments for the CIS development expenses were financed by (1) an investment of $1.444 million by the partners, (2) a $3.25 million bank loan to RTS, secured by bank letters of credit and personal guarantees of the limited partners, and (3) a $2.2 million loan to RTS, personally guaranteed by the limited partners, from Anacomp, with interest at 11 percent per annum payable quarterly through December 31, 1981, and with principal and interest payable thereafter in 84 equal monthly installments. In addition, if the CIS development expenses exceeded $6 million and therefore RTS was required to pay further development fees, Anacomp agreed to loan RTS, without recourse to the limited partners, up to $1.5 million to complete the CIS system.

Several officers and directors of Anacomp were affiliated with the corporate general partner of RTS, and were also investors in the limited partnership arrangement. Ronald Palamara, Chairman of the Board and President of Anacomp, and three other directors of Anacomp, were also directors and officers of the corporate general partner of RTS. The ownership interest of Anacomp's officers and directors in the limited partnership amounted to 38.5% of the total.

During the fiscal year 1981, thirteen major banks, including the National Bank of North America in New York, the Shawmut National Bank in Boston, Provident National Bank in Philadelphia, and the First National Bank in Kansas City, contracted with Anacomp to participate as advisory banks in the CIS project for a nonrefundable fee of $150,000 each. The arrangement permitted each bank to review the project during development and provide input regarding changes to enhance the ultimate marketability of CIS.

a

5

In June 1982, Anacomp announced that the CIS system development was completed. The company also announced that it purchased the system from RTS Associates for $16 million.

FINANCIAL PERFORMANCE

After reporting a strong increase in revenues and profits from 1978 to 1981, Anacomp reported a slower revenue growth and a decline in profits in fiscal 1982. Dr. Palamara commented that the 1982 performance was a short-term aberration, and that the company's long-term strategy and prospects were sound:

> Fiscal 1982 marked the beginning of one era and the end of another for Anacomp. A new era began with five events having tremendous long-term significance for Anacomp: the purchase of two major software products, the completion of our most significant acquisition, an offering of $50 million in convertible debentures, the formation of history's largest software research and development partnership, and Anacomp's listing on the New York Stock Exchange. Thus, despite a difficult fourth quarter which was affected by several non-recurring items and resulted in lower earnings for the year, fiscal 1982 was perhaps the most significant year of achievements in Anacomp's history.
>
> Judged solely by the numbers, of course, 1982 does not seem especially memorable. . . . In terms of positioning the company for future growth, however, 1982 may well be remembered as the most significant year in Anacomp's history. . . .
>
> We believe that Anacomp's performance in future years will demonstrate that the company is well along in its evolution from a small, explosive-growth firm to a nationally recognized market leader.

Dr. Palamara projected record financial results in fiscal 1983. He also assured investors that Anacomp would place renewed emphasis on improving the company's profitability and reducing its financial leverage.

Exhibit 1 shows Anacomp's stock price data around the time of its 1982 results. An abridged version of the company's annual report is presented in Exhibit 2.

QUESTIONS

1. Evaluate Anacomp's new product development strategy. What are the risks and benefits of this strategy for Anacomp's shareholders? *and get financial analysis*
2. How is Anacomp's accounting influenced by the way the company organizes and finances its new product development?
3. Compare Anacomp's cash flow performance with its accounting performance. What is your evaluation of the company's financial condition?
4. What is your assessment of Anacomp's future? *Conclusions*

take for statement and import into spreadsheet

Exhibit 1   Anacomp—Stock Price and Trading Volume Data

EXHIBIT 1
Anacomp—Stock Price and Trading Volume Data

Trading	Anacomp Trading Volume (thousands)	Anacomp Closing Price (dollars)	S&P 500 Composite Closing
9/1/82	109	10.875	118.25
9/2/82	92	10.875	120.38
9/3/82	437	11.125	122.68
9/7/82	120	10.875	121.37
9/8/82	231	11.000	122.20
9/9/82	230	10.750	121.97
9/10/82	417	10.625	120.97
9/13/82	284	10.375	122.24

Anacomp's common stock beta = 1.3 (Value Line estimate)

STOCK TRADING INFORMATION

	Stock Price		
	High	Low	Cash Dividends
Fiscal Year 1981			
First quarter	$15.63	$10.63	$.026
Second quarter	19.88	13.75	.026
Third quarter	16.50	12.75	.026
Fourth quarter	18.38	15.13	.030
Fiscal Year 1982			
First quarter	16.63	11.25	.030
Second quarter	14.00	11.88	.030
Third quarter	12.25	10.00	.030
Fourth quarter	13.38	10.88	.030

OTHER INFORMATION

Interest rate on 3-month Treasury bills:	8.2%
Interest rate on 20-year government bonds:	12.2%
P/E ratio for Standard & Poor's 400 Industrials:	23.2

a

7

Exhibit 2   Anacomp, Inc.—Abridged 1982 Annual Report

EXHIBIT 2

Anacomp, Inc.—Abridged 1982 Annual Report

To our Shareholders

Fiscal 1982 marked the beginning of one era and the end of another for Anacomp.

A new era began with five events having tremendous long-term significance for Anacomp: the purchase of two major software products, the completion of our most significant acquisition, an offering of $50 million in convertible debentures, the formation of history's largest software research and development partnership and Anacomp's listing on the New York Stock Exchange. Thus, despite a difficult fourth quarter which was affected by several non-recurring items and resulted in lower earnings for the year, fiscal 1982 was perhaps the most significant year of achievements in Anacomp's history.

Judged solely by the numbers, of course, 1982 does not seem especially memorable. Although revenues rose slightly over 1981, earnings per share declined due to the impact of fourth quarter results, which reflected several one-time changes and short-term factors. These factors are described in detail in our fourth quarter report.

In terms of positioning the company for future growth, however, 1982 may well be remembered as the most significant year in Anacomp's history.

- In January, Anacomp completed a $50 million offering of 13⅞ percent convertible subordinated debentures which, after an original issue discount, increased the company's working capital position by $41 million.

- Listing on the New York Stock Exchange in April recognized Anacomp's stature in the computer services industry and provided the opportunity for greater visibility as the computer reaches out to new, worldwide markets.

- During June of the year, Anacomp purchased two major retail banking software systems which we had been developing for investment partnerships. CIS, a totally integrated system that we believe will revolutionize retail banking in the 1980s, was purchased for nearly $16 million. CIS has already attracted a financial commitment from nearly 35 banks, seven of which had signed substantial license agreements by the end of the year. BANKSERV® 10000, a system to provide banks with a new level of electronic transaction switching and processing capabilities, was purchased for $2.3 million.

- Also during June, Anacomp signed an agreement with IBM Corporation which gives us the capability to be a primary source of supply for a bank's branch automation requirements.

- The acquisition of 24 micrographic data imaging centers from DSI Corporation and Kalvar Corporation in May provided the ability to deliver Anacomp services to an even broader base of regular, repetitive customers, and the opportunity to offer new services through an expanded delivery system.

- After the close of the fiscal year, funding for the CIBS research and development partnership was completed with the closing of the final portion of $26.25 million in partnership interests. The partnership will contract with Anacomp to develop CIBS, Corporate International Banking System, a complex software system for use by large banks and other financial institutions engaged in international business.

a

8

Exhibit 2   Anacomp, Inc.—Abridged 1982 Annual Report

We believe Anacomp's performance in future years will demonstrate that the company is well along in its evolution from a small, explosive-growth firm to a nationally recognized market leader.

To ensure that Anacomp's evolution will result in a stable company, with performance attractive to investors, Anacomp will be placing renewed emphasis in several areas. These areas will include our rate of return, where we anticipate achieving a superior return on investment from the maturation of software projects, existing operations, plus the addition of quality investments.

We also expect to reduce our leverage ratio over the next few years by calling our convertible debt, when this becomes practical, and by taking other appropriate measures. We will continue to employ strategic planning approaches in all our business units. Lastly, we will seek out those acquisitions which blend with our long-term goals.

We have projected record financial results in fiscal 1983 as the company asserts its leadership in bank software and micrographic data imaging. We appreciate the continued support of our stockholders and employees which makes that goal achievable.

Sincerely,

Ronald D. Palamara, Ph.D.
President and Chairman of the Board

September 10, 1982

MANAGEMENT'S DISCUSSION AND ANALYSIS OF FINANCIAL CONDITION AND RESULTS OF OPERATIONS

Anacomp, Inc. and Subsidiaries

General

In September 1980, Anacomp completed a public offering of $30,000,000 of 9½% Convertible Subordinated Debentures due 2000. In January 1981, Anacomp completed an offering outside the United States of $12,500,000 of 9% Convertible Subordinated Debentures due 1996, with warrants to purchase a like amount of debentures. In January 1982, Anacomp completed the public offering of $50,000,000 of 13⅞% Convertible Subordinated Debentures due 2002. The Debentures were offered at an original issue discount of 15%, with net proceeds of $41,125,000, and carry an effective cost of 16.6%. The cash from these offerings has been used to finance the expansion of receivables and unbilled revenues, to retire long-term debt, to provide funds for acquisitions, and to increase working capital. During the past three years, Anacomp has completed the acquisition of eleven business entities. The acquisitions and the debenture offerings accounted for the major changes in Anacomp's financial condition and results of operations.

Financial Condition and Liquidity

During 1982, working capital increased $1,949,000. The major source of working capital, other than operations, was the increase in long-term debt, primarily the result of the

Exhibit 2   Anacomp, Inc.—Abridged 1982 Annual Report

January offering of $50,000,000 of debentures and to a lesser extent the exercise of warrants to purchase $1,289,000 of additional 9% debentures. The major use of working capital was the purchase of computer software systems from limited partnerships. Other major uses of working capital were the purchase of marketable securities held as long-term investments, the retirement of long-term debt, and additions of fixed assets. During the year, cash was used to finance the increase in unbilled revenues, to purchase 92% of the shares of DSI Corporation, and to pay certain software development costs. As a result, the current ratio at June 30, 1982, is 2.40, compared to 3.84 at June 30, 1981. At June 30, 1982, Anacomp had $35,000,000 of available but unused lines of credit that could be used if needed to provide short-term financing. Negotiations are currently being held with a group of banks to establish a revolving credit arrangement which will replace the existing lines of credit.

At the present time, Anacomp has no major commitments to acquire assets or facilities which will require a substantial outlay of working capital. It is anticipated that the current acquisition program will continue in the future as opportunities present themselves.

Anacomp currently expects to incur approximately $6,000,000 during 1983 on enhancements to a computer software system, of which approximately $3,000,000 is expected to be funded by others. The project is being undertaken because the results will yield a product with improved marketability, which at the same time will meet commitments to certain customers.

Operations—Fiscal 1982 Compared to 1981

Revenues for 1982 increased only 3% over fiscal 1981, with the increase being generated primarily by internal growth and the addition of internally generated projects. Software development projects, especially two new projects contracted for by major banks and limited partnerships, and higher levels of sales of minicomputers and microcomputers and related software, contributed the largest portion of the increase. Revenues were also increased by certain data centers. These increases, along with smaller increases in other areas, were largely offset by reduced revenue being generated by other data centers as a result of a consolidation of certain operations.

Total operating costs and expenses increased 10.4% during fiscal 1982. Personnel costs and outside services costs associated with the increased software development activity were the major factors in the increase. Other contributors to the increase were higher supply costs, equipment-related costs, and the cost of computer hardware sales, each caused by higher levels of activity. Also, amortization of purchased software added to the overall increase, along with generally higher prices for all purchased goods and services. These increases were partially offset by cost reductions from the synergism obtained from prior acquisitions, a reduction in costs as a result of consolidating certain administrative functions and, in the third quarter, from the recovery of previously recorded expenses.

Margins for the current periods were substantially lower than the prior year due to the emphasis on completing large systems development projects as opposed to generating new license fees for other products. Margins earned on development work have typically been less than those earned from software licensing and related activities. The reduction in revenue in certain data centers has also tended to reduce margins, as the revenue losses have preceded to some extent the current cost reduction and consolidation efforts.

Interest expense increased in the convertible year as a result of the interest on the 9½% Convertible Subordinated Debentures offered during fiscal 1981 and the 13⅞%

Exhibit 2   Anacomp, Inc.—Abridged 1982 Annual Report

Convertible Subordinated Debentures offered in January 1982. Interest income was derived from investing the proceeds from these offerings not otherwise utilized. Due to the uses of cash mentioned previously and a lowering of interest rates on investments, interest income decreased throughout the current period.

The extraordinary credit arose from the sale of a branch office which had been acquired in 1981 in a transaction accounted for as a pooling of interests. The amount of the credit is the gain realized, net of related income taxes.

The provision for income taxes reflects the normal tax relating to the income reported for financial statement purposes after recognizing the impact of investment tax credits, non-deductible expenses, and the effect of interest due from the under-depositing of tax payments as a result of the denial of a request for a change in certain reporting policies for tax purposes.

Fiscal 1981 Compared to 1980

Of the $34,725,000 increase in revenue, the major portion was attributable to acquisitions included for the first time in 1981, or for the full period in 1981, plus internal growth generated by those acquisitions. Other changes in revenue for the year resulted primarily from new software development sales and non-recurring licensing agreements (especially from new software systems for banks, financed in part by limited partnerships), offset in part by reduced revenues due to declining activity in certain data centers and the completion of certain non-repetitive software projects.

Direct costs of service and equipment increased 54%, primarily from the costs associated with the recent acquisitions plus increased expenses required to support increased software development, and rising costs for personnel and other services. Selling, general and administrative expenses increased 17% from the costs associated with the recent acquisitions plus the expenses necessary to manage the rapidly growing company and from rising personnel costs. The increases in other direct operating and selling, general and administrative costs were offset in part by a savings of approximately $1,255,000 being realized during 1981 due to a change in the funding of Anacomp's contribution to the Thrift Plan for Employees.

Interest income increased from interest earned by cash investment programs and from the interest earned on notes receivable.

Interest expense increased primarily from the interest on the recently issued 9% and 9½% Convertible Subordinated Debentures, with other increases from debt incurred to finance acquisitions and interest on short-term borrowings, offset somewhat by lower interest on the 10% Convertible Subordinated Debentures due to conversions to equity.

Other income included the gain from a transaction with Kalvar which resulted from an agreement whereby Anacomp sold to Kalvar its Kalvar preferred stock for Kalvar common stock and sold its option to acquire additional Kalvar common stock in exchange for a promissory note from Kalvar.

The provision for income taxes reflects the normal tax relating to the income reported for financial statement purposes after giving effect to the benefits obtained from investment tax credits and from the exclusion of dividend income. The expected tax rate for fiscal 1981 was revised downward during the fourth quarter as a result of a large capital gain arising primarily from the transaction with Kalvar.

a

11

Exhibit 2   Anacomp, Inc.—Abridged 1982 Annual Report

SELECTED FINANCIAL DATA

Anacomp, Inc., and Subsidiaries

(dollars in thousands, except per share amounts)	1982	1981	1980	1979	1978
For the year ended June 30					
Revenues	$109,599	$106,368	$71,643	$41,662	$23,433
Income before provision for income taxes and extraordinary credit	3,622	13,997	7,787	5,045	3,154
Income before extraordinary credit	2,779	7,938	4,627	2,704	1,542
Net income	4,609	7,938	4,627	2,704	1,542
Earnings per common and common equivalent share:					
Income before extraordinary credit	$.30	$.87	$.70	$.57	$.39
Net income	.50	.87	.70	.57	.39
Earnings per common share assuming full dilution:					
Income before extraordinary credit	$.29	$.83	$.66	$.51	$.32
Net income	.48	.83	.66	.51	.32
Cash dividends declared per common share	.12	.11	.10	.09	.06
As of June 30					
Current assets	$ 99,044	$ 75,453	$33,453	$16,200	$ 9,869
Current liabilities	41,276	19,634	22,079	11,452	3,561
Working capital	7,768	55,819	11,374	4,748	6,308
Total assets	211,660	130,798	76,950	30,069	14,182
Long-term debt	105,208	50,591	10,608	8,162	3,993
Stockholders' equity	61,035	55,891	44,077	10,211	6,639
Book value per common share	$6.59	$6.18	$5.56	$2.14	$1.55
Number of employees	2,300	2,000	1,800	895	430
Number of holders of common stock	7,930	5,575	3,810	1,955	1,225

a

12

Exhibit 2   Anacomp, Inc.—Abridged 1982 Annual Report

CONSOLIDATED BALANCE SHEET

Anacomp, Inc. and Subsidiaries

	June 30	
(dollars in thousands, except per share amounts)	1982	1981
Assets		
Current assets:		
Cash (including temporary investments)	$ 34,519	$29,392
Accounts and notes receivable, less allowances for doubtful accounts of $1,915 and $1,210, respectively	25,284	23,216
Unbilled revenues	18,534	15,863
Inventories	4,469	3,014
Deferred CIBS development costs (Note 3)	5,647	—
Prepaid expenses (including income taxes of $3,018 and $1,242, respectively)	10,591	3,968
Total current assets	99,044	75,453
Property and equipment, at cost less accumulated depreciation and amortization of $10,189 and $8,660, respectively	25,112	14,930
Cost of computer software systems purchased, less accumulated depreciation of $1,584 and $186, respectively	20,363	1,747
Excess of purchase price over net assets of businesses acquired, less accumulated amortization of $2,319 and $1,285, respectively	42,646	24,291
Other assets	24,495	14,377
	$211,660	$130,798

(continued)

a

13

Exhibit 2   Anacomp, Inc.—Abridged 1982 Annual Report

CONSOLIDATED BALANCE SHEET (continued)

	June 30	
(dollars in thousands, except per share amounts)	1982	1981
Liabilities and Stockholders' Equity		
Current liabilities:		
Notes payable, banks	$ 14,000	$ —
Current portion of long-term debt	2,907	2,359
Accounts payable	8,151	8,787
Accrued salaries, wages and bonuses	4,604	3,863
Accrued interest payable	5,129	1,747
Income taxes	—	419
Other accrued liabilities	6,485	2,459
Total current liabilities	41,276	19,634
Long-term debt, net of current portion:		
Convertible subordinated debentures	86,274	43,340
Other long-term debt	18,934	7,251
Total long-term debt	105,208	50,591
Deferred income taxes	3,177	4,015
Minority interest	964	667
Stockholder's equity:		
Preferred stock—$1 par value, authorized 1,000,000 shares, none issued	—	—
Common stock—$1 par value, authorized 25,000,000 shares, 9,256,544 and 9,042,722 issued, respectively	9,257	9,043
Capital in excess of par value of common stock	37,305	35,207
Unrealized losses on marketable securities	(899)	(233)
Retained earnings	15,372	11,874
Total stockholders' equity	61,035	55,891
	$211,660	$130,798

a

14

Exhibit 2   Anacomp, Inc.—Abridged 1982 Annual Report

CONSOLIDATED STATEMENT OF INCOME

Anacomp, Inc., and Subsidiaries

	Year Ended June 30		
(dollars in thousands, except per share amounts)	1982	1981	1980
Revenues			
Services provided	$88,045	$87,304	$58,781
Equipment sold	21,554	19,064	12,862
	109,599	106,368	71,643
Operating costs and expenses			
Costs of services provided	67,302	62,464	40,342
Costs of equipment sold	16,764	13,900	9,172
Selling, general and administrative expenses	19,888	17,821	15,284
	103,954	94,185	64,798
	5,645	12,183	6,845
Interest income	5,525	3,204	485
Interest expense	(8,158)	(4,090)	(1,381)
Other, net	610	2,700	1,838
	(2,023)	1,814	942
Income before provision for income taxes and extra-ordinary credit	3,622	13,997	7,787
Provision for income taxes	843	6,059	3,160
Income before extraordinary credit	2,779	7,938	4,627
Extraordinary credit, net of related tax	1,830	—	—
Net income	$ 4,609	$ 7,938	$ 4,627
Earnings per common and common equivalent share			
Income before extraordinary credit	$.30	$.87	$.70
Extraordinary credit	.20	—	—
Net income	$.50	$.87	$.70
Earnings per common share assuming full dilution			
Income before extraordinary credit	$.29	$.83	$.66
Extraordinary credit	.19	—	—
Net income	$.48	$.83	$.66
Cash dividends declared per share	$.12	$.11	$.10

Exhibit 2   Anacomp, Inc.—Abridged 1982 Annual Report

CONSOLIDATED STATEMENT OF CHANGES IN FINANCIAL POSITION

Anacomp, Inc., and Subsidiaries

(dollars in thousands)	Year Ended June 30		
	1982	1981	1980
Working capital was provided by:			
Income before extraordinary credit	$2,779	$7,938	$4,627
Charges to income not requiring an outlay of working capital:			
Depreciation and amortization	6,708	4,368	3,026
Deferred income taxes	(1,314)	3,951	2
Other	143	416	331
Working capital provided by operations	8,316	16,673	7,986
Working capital provided by extraordinary credit	742	—	—
Dispositions of property and equipment	702	218	2,001
Decrease in investment in Computer Micrographics, Inc.	—	—	1,733
Long-term debt incurred	55,680	43,636	7,158
Issuances of common stock	2,236	4,813	28,371
Other	3,224	1,024	(84)
	70,900	66,364	47,165
Working capital was applied to:			
Additions to property and equipment	11,172	3,533	5,171
Excess of purchase price over net assets of businesses acquired	19,791	4,172	18,900
Noncurrent assets of companies acquired in purchase transactions	5,315	1,088	4,593
Noncurrent liabilities of businesses acquired in purchase transactions	(2,892)	(1,040)	(2,199)
Purchase of computer software systems	20,014	1,734	—
Increase in investments	6,099	4,806	2,027
Increase in other assets	4,441	1,977	4,443
Reduction of long-term debt	3,900	4,693	6,911
Cash dividends declared	1,111	956	693
	68,951	21,919	40,539
	$ 1,949	$44,445	$ 6,626

Exhibit 2   Anacomp, Inc.—Abridged 1982 Annual Report

(dollars in thousands)	Year Ended June 30		
	1982	1981	1980
Increase in working capital represented by:			
Increase (decrease) in current assets:			
Cash (including temporary investments)	$5,127	$24,649	$1,484
Accounts and notes receivable	2,068	6,841	8,333
Unbilled revenues	2,671	7,283	5,605
Inventories	1,455	513	1,383
Deferred CIBS development costs	5,647	—	—
Prepaid expenses	6,623	2,714	448
Decrease (increase) in current liabilities:			
Notes payable	(14,000)	4,000	(3,250)
Current portion of long-term debt	(548)	791	(315)
Accounts payable	636	(1,022)	(4,716)
Accrued salaries, wages and bonuses	(741)	(1,185)	(683)
Accrued interest payable	(3,382)	(1,639)	(48)
Income taxes	419	1,162	286
Other accrued liabilities	(4,026)	338	(1,901)
Increase in working capital	$ 1,949	$44,445	$6,626

The accompanying notes are an integral part of the consolidated financial statements.

a

17

Exhibit 2   Anacomp, Inc.—Abridged 1982 Annual Report

NOTES TO CONSOLIDATED FINANCIAL STATEMENTS

Anacomp, Inc. and Subsidiaries
(dollars in thousands, except per share amounts)

Note 1. Summary of Significant Accounting Policies

Consolidation

The consolidated financial statements include the accounts of Anacomp, Inc. ("Anacomp") and its majority-owned subsidiaries except Anacomp Leasing Company, Inc., an immaterial wholly-owned subsidiary, which is reflected in the equity method in the accompanying financial statements. Intercompany transactions have been eliminated. Certain amounts in the 1981 and 1980 financial statements have been reclassified to conform to the 1982 presentation.

Revenue Recognition

Revenues are generally recognized as follows:

(1) Data preparation, data processing, facility management and computer output microfilm ("COM") services and sales are recognized as the services are performed or products are shipped.

(2) Revenues from granting perpetual licenses of existing software systems which do not require substantial modification are recognized at the time the license agreement is executed, if collectibility is reasonably assured and the software system is delivered to the customer.

(3) Revenues from contracts for development and/or modifications to existing software systems are recognized under methods which approximate the percentage-of-completion method, except for revenues from development contracts with certain limited partnerships which are reported on the completed contract method, other than immaterial amounts reported for 1980 (see Note 3). Losses on such contracts are recognized when identified.

Revenue recognized under items (2) and (3) may precede the date at which the customer may be billed pursuant to the contract terms. Substantially all unbilled revenue is collected in the year subsequent to the year revenue is recognized.

The subject of revenue recognition for development contracts with limited partnerships including certain arrangements described in (3) above is presently under review by the Financial Accounting Standards Board (FASB). Anacomp will comply with any Statement of Financial Standards issued by the FASB. In April, 1982, the FASB issued an exposure draft entitled "Research and Development Arrangements." Anacomp believes that it is in substantial compliance with the exposure draft, and that approval of the draft by the FASB would not result in an adjustment to the amounts presented in the financial statements.

Exhibit 2 Anacomp, Inc.—Abridged 1982 Annual Report

Inventories

Inventories are stated at the lower of cost or market, cost being determined primarily on the specific identification basis. The cost of the inventories is distributed as follows:

	June 30		
	1982	1981	1980
Equipment held for resale	$3,084	$1,899	$1,315
Operating supplies	1,385	1,115	1,186
	$4,469	$3,014	$2,501

Purchased Computer Software Systems

Purchased computer software systems held for licensing to others are earned at cost less accumulated depreciation. Depreciation is recorded over the estimated marketing lives of the software, and is computed based on the greater of the amount calculated using either a percent-of-revenue or the straight-line method. The percent-of-revenue method is based on the total estimated future revenues expected to be derived from sales of the software, while straight-line depreciation is provided using estimated marketing lives of five to ten years.

Amortization of Excess Purchase Price over Net Assets

Excess of purchase price over net assets of business acquired is amortized on the straight-line method over the estimated useful life, currently ranging from five to twenty years, if determined, and over 40 years if life is indeterminate.

Earnings per Share

The computation of earnings per common and common equivalent share is based upon the weighted average number of common shares outstanding during the year plus (in years in which they have a dilutive effect) the effect of common shares contingently issuable, primarily from stock options, conversion of subordinated debentures issued during fiscal 1981 and, for 1980, common shares purchased in July 1980, in connection with an employment agreement (see Note 13). Interest expense, net of taxes, on the subordinated debentures is added to net income in the computation of earnings per common and common equivalent share.

The fully diluted per share computation reflects the effect of common shares contingently issuable upon conversion of each convertible subordinated debenture outstanding in years in which such conversions would cause dilution. Interest expense, net of income taxes, on the debentures assumed to be converted is added to net income in the computation of fully diluted earnings per share. Fully diluted earnings per share also reflects additional dilution related to stock options due to the use of the year-end market price, when higher than the average price for the year.

a

19

Exhibit 2   Anacomp, Inc.—Abridged 1982 Annual Report

The weighted average number of common and common equivalent shares used to compute earnings per share is 9,281,640, 9,425,788 and 6,624,955 for 1982, 1981 and 1980, respectively. The average number of shares used to compute earnings per common share assuming full dilution is 9,667,794, 11,457,335 and 7,149,132 for the respective years. The numbers of shares for all years are adjusted for all stock splits and stock dividends declared.

Vacation Pay

In November 1980, the Financial Accounting Standards Board issued Statement of Financial Accounting Standards No. 43 (SFAS No. 43), "Accounting for Compensated Absences," which requires the accrual of vacation pay earned but not taken. The provisions of SFAS No. 43 require the restatement of prior periods and therefore the cumulative effect as of July 1, 1979, is shown as an adjustment to retained earnings at that date. The effect of this change was to reduce net income by $97 ($.01 per share) in 1982, $72 ($.01 per share) in 1981 and $273 ($.03 per share) in 1980.

Note 3. Major Software Products and Related Party Transactions

CIS

In June 1982, Anacomp purchased for $16,000 a major new computer software system called CIS (Continuous Integrated System) developed by Anacomp for RTS Associates ("RTS"), a limited partnership formed in 1979. Several officers and directors of Anacomp who are affiliated with RTS's general partner are also investors in RTS, aggregating approximately 39% of the combined general and limited partnership units. The remaining partnership interests are owned by persons not affiliated with Anacomp. Anacomp contracted to develop the system on a best-efforts basis, and RTS agreed to pay a development fee of $6,000, of which $4,750 was paid through 1981, and an additional $1,250 during 1982. RTS paid Anacomp an additional $1,500 after actual costs to Anacomp exceeded $6,000. Anacomp had previously loaned $2,200 to RTS, personally guaranteed by the limited partners, and loaned the additional $1,500 as provided for in the development agreement. RTS paid all such loans in full out of the proceeds of the sale of the CIS system.

Concurrent with the development of CIS for the RTS partnership, a complimentary project was being developed for four CIS Primary Development Banks. Each bank committed $1,500 to fund modifications of the CIS project to conform to their specific requirements and thereby obtained a nonexclusive license to CIS as so modified. Under the terms of the Primary Development Bank agreements, 10% of any revenue from licensing CIS to others will accrue to each of the banks until such time as their entire $1,500 development fee has been recovered. At June 30, 1982, seven other banks had entered into, or committed to enter into, license agreements for CIS.

During 1981 and 1982, twenty major banks contracted with Anacomp to participate as Advisory Development Banks on the CIS project for a nonrefundable fee of $150. The fee permits each bank to review the project during development and provide input, which is not binding to Anacomp, regarding changes which would enhance the marketability of CIS. Anacomp defers a portion of this fee which will be recognized as services are provided to the participating banks throughout the terms of their contracts.

Exhibit 2   Anacomp, Inc.—Abridged 1982 Annual Report

EFT

During fiscal 1981, Anacomp initiated and completed development of a new computer software switching system called H-10000 to be marketed to major financial institutions. Anacomp entered into an agreement with EFT Partners, Ltd. ("EFT"), a limited partnership formed in the fall of 1980. Several officers and directors of Anacomp purchased limited partnership units in EFT, aggregating approximately 31% of the partnership units, and Kranzley & Co., a wholly-owned subsidiary of Anacomp, was the general partner. The remaining limited partnership interests were owned by persons not affiliated with Anacomp. Anacomp agreed to develop and market the system, and EFT agreed to pay a development fee of $1,000, of which $910 was paid during 1981 and an additional $90 during 1982. The contract was reported on the completed contract basis; revenue and profits were recognized upon completion during the fourth quarter of 1981. In June 1982, Kranzley & Co. exercised its right under the purchase option to buy the interests of the limited partners at the appraised fair market value for the H-10000 system of $2,300.

CEFT

During fiscal 1981, Anacomp entered into an agreement with CEFT Partners, Ltd. ("CEFT"), a limited partnership formed in December 1980, and primary development banks to jointly develop a new computer funds transfer software system to be marketed to major financial institutions. Certain officers, directors and employees of Anacomp purchased limited partnership units in CEFT aggregating approximately 9% of the limited partnership units. The remaining partnership interest and the general partnership interest are owned by persons not affiliated with Anacomp.

Under the development agreement, Anacomp agreed to develop the new system on a best-effort basis. The agreement permits Anacomp to contract with primary development banks to provide development fees up to $1,000 in addition to the $2,100 development fee to be paid by the partnership. In June 1981, the general partner agreed to permit Anacomp to increase the bank fees allowable to $2,000 on this project. Contracts with five banks aggregating $2,000 have been completed.

Anacomp has acquired rights to a system owned by a major bank at a cost of $500 to assist and expedite the completion of the system. A portion of this cost has been charged to expense as a system development cost and the remainder is being amortized over the expected marketing life of the purchased system in its unmodified form.

The system was certified as being complete in July 1982, and Anacomp has agreed to market it for seven years on an exclusive commission basis. Anacomp has the option to acquire all rights to the system at the greater of (a) fair market value or (b) $3,000 to $5,000, depending on the date the option is exercised. Revenues earned on this software development project were $3,150 and $942 during fiscal 1981 and 1982.

CBS

During fiscal 1981, Anacomp entered into an agreement with CBS Partners, Ltd. ("CBS"), a limited partnership formed in April 1981, and primary development banks to jointly develop a wholesale banking computer software system to be marketed to major financial institutions. Certain officers, directors and employees of Anacomp purchased

Exhibit 2   Anacomp, Inc.—Abridged 1982 Annual Report

limited partnership units in the partnership aggregating approximately 20% of the limited partnership units. The remaining limited partnership interest and the general partnership interest are owned by persons not affiliated with Anacomp. Under the development agreement, Anacomp agreed to develop the new system on a best-efforts basis. The agreement permits Anacomp to contract with primary development banks to provide development fees up to $3,750 in addition to the $4,500 development fee to be paid by the partnership. Contracts with three banks aggregating $3,750 have been completed.

Anacomp has acquired rights to a wholesale banking system owned by a major bank at a cost of $1,350 to assist and expedite the completion of the system. A portion of this cost is being charged to expense as a system development cost and the remainder is being amortized over the expected marketing life of the purchased system in its unmodified form.

Upon completion of the system, Anacomp has agreed to market it for seven years on an exclusive commission basis. Anacomp has the option to acquire all rights to CBS at the greater of (a) fair market value or (b) $7,000 to $9,000, depending on the date the option is exercised. Revenues earned on this software development project were $2,620 and $4,319 during 1981 and 1982.

CIBS

Subsequent to June 30, 1982, Anacomp entered into an agreement with CIBS Partners, Limited ("CIBS"), a limited partnership formed in April 1981, to develop new software systems for large banks engaged in international business. Certain officers, directors and employees of Anacomp purchased limited partnership units in CIBS aggregating approximately 6.5% of the limited partnership units. The remaining limited partnership interests are owned by persons not affiliated with Anacomp. Anacomp is the sole holder of $400 of the non-voting preferred stock of the corporate general partner. The partnership payments under the development agreements are to be funded with $26,250 of partners' capital investment.

Under the development agreement, Anacomp has agreed to develop the new systems on a best-efforts basis. The agreement permits Anacomp to contract with primary development banks to provide development fees up to $12,000 in addition to the $23,000 development fee to be paid by the partnership. A contract with one bank for $500 has been completed.

Upon completion of the systems, Anacomp has agreed to lease the systems for five years on an exclusive basis at rental based on a percentage of license fees generated. Anacomp has the option to acquire all rights to the systems during the three-year period commencing one year after completion of the systems at total prices ranging from $46,400 to $59,700, plus a share of licensing fees generated thereafter, depending on the year in which the option is exercised.

At June 30, 1982, the Company considered the funding for this project to be imminent. Accordingly, costs of $5,647, including $2,750 to acquire rights to certain software incurred in commencing the development of CIBS, were deferred until such time as project funding became available in August 1982. Such costs will be charged to operations in fiscal 1983.

Exhibit 2   Anacomp, Inc.—Abridged 1982 Annual Report

Other

During fiscal 1980, a group of officers and directors of Anacomp formed a limited partnership which purchased a computer system and leased it to Anacomp at a competitive rental rate. In May 1982, the Company purchased the computer equipment from the partnership for $1,167, which was its appraised value.

Note 5. Cash, Cash Investments and Short-Term Borrowings

Cash balances at June 30, 1982 and 1981, include temporary investments of $34,380 and $26,550, respectively, at costs which approximate market value. Of the amounts invested at June 20, 1982, $10,000 is pledged as collateral for the short-term borrowings from banks of $10,000 and is restricted as to withdrawal.

At June 20, 1982, Anacomp has short-term lines of credit from banks in the amount of $39,000, of which $35,000 is unused. Anacomp has agreed to maintain compensating balances, not restricted as to withdrawal, on certain of these lines. The average of compensating balances on these lines was approximately 5% of the available lines during fiscal 1982.

Note 7. Other Assets

The following comprise other assets:

	June 30	
	1982	1981
Investment in Kalvar Corporation, including $1,028 note receivable in both years and income bond and preferred stock in 1982	$ 6,428	$ 3,398
Marketable securities valued at the lower of cost or market	6,068	3,665
Notes receivable, RTS Associates	—	2,095
Notes receivable, other	4,132	400
Employment and non-compete agreements, less accumulated amortization of $1,297 and $848, respectively	491	737
Deferred debenture costs, less accumulated amortization of $313 and $152, respectively	3,470	2,026
Deferred charges, other	3,906	2,056
	$24,495	$14,377

a

23

Exhibit 2   Anacomp, Inc.—Abridged 1982 Annual Report

Note 8. Long-Term Debt

Long-term debt is comprised of the following:

	June 30	
	1982	1981
10% Convertible Subordinated Debentures due November 1, 1988	$ 758	$ 915
9½% Convertible Subordinated Debentures due September 1, 2000	29,925	29,925
9% Convertible Subordinated Debentures due January 15, 1996	13,789	12,500
13⅞% Convertible Subordinated Debentures due January 15, 2002 (net of unamortized original issue discount of $7,440	42,560	—
Notes payable to banks at an average rate of 15.5% at June 30, 1982, due in installments to 1985	12,880	1,436
Other	8,203	8,174
	108,115	52,950
Less current portion	2,907	2,359
	$105,208	$50,591

Other debt includes equipment purchase notes, debtor to finance acquisitions, mortgages and obligations under capitalized financial leases. These items have effective costs of 9¾% to 15% and are payable in installments over varying periods extending to 2006. Shares representing substantially all of the operations of DSI are pledged as collateral for a note with a discounted balance of $2,793 at June 30, 1982. At June 30, 1982, processing equipment with an aggregate book value of approximately $3,600 is pledged as collateral under certain of the debt agreements.

Anacomp is guarantor of a bank loan to Anacomp's wholly-owned leasing subsidiary. At June 30, 1982, the balance of the debt being guaranteed is $480.

At June 30, 1982, the aggregate maturities of long-term debt through fiscal year 1987 are: 1983, $2,907; 1984, $12,972; 1985, $3,482; 1986, $347; and 1987, $219.

Note 9. Capital Stock

Stock Dividends and Stock Splits

The Board of Directors declared the following stock dividends and stock splits during the three years ended June 30, 1982:

January, 1980—five-for-four stock split
March, 1981—five-for-four stock split

Exhibit 2   Anacomp, Inc.—Abridged 1982 Annual Report

All applicable share and per share amounts have been restated to reflect the stock dividends and stock splits. All conversion prices and stock option data have also been adjusted to give effect to the stock dividends and stock split.

Note 10. Segment Information

Anacomp operates in two business segments—data center services and computer services. Data center services consist of providing computer output microfilm ("COM") and computer processing for banks and credit unions through a network of branch offices, where Anacomp's equipment and personnel process data for numerous customers at each branch site. Computer services consist of providing computer software, primarily to large financial institutions, and managing computer facilities for large customers, primarily state and local governments.

	Year Ended June 30, 1982			Year Ended June 30, 1981		
	Consolidated	Data Center Services	Computer Services	Consolidated	Data Center Services	Computer Services
Revenues	$109,599	$67,418	$42,181	$106,368	$67,899	$38,469
Operating profit	12,451	8,504	3,947	18,191	7,294	10,897
Income before taxes	3,622			13,997		
Depreciation and amortization	6,054	3,636	2,418	3,859	2,527	1,332
Corporate depreciation and amortization	654			509		

	June 30, 1982			June 30, 1981		
Identifiable assets	$155,039	$84,785	$70,254	$93,737	$57,332	$36,405
Corporate assets	56,621			37,061		
	$211,660			$130,798		

Approximately 19% of Anacomp's fiscal 1982 consolidated revenues were provided by major computer services contracts which extend beyond one year, including those contracts in process discussed in Note 3. Contracts of this type provided 18% of the 1981 and 20% of the 1980 revenue. This included system licensing and modification contracts, which accounted for 13% of revenues in 1982, 11% in 1981 and 1980, and facility management arrangements, which accounted for 6% of revenue in 1982, 7% in 1981 and 9% in 1980.

Revenues from various federal, state and local government agencies amounted to approximately 11% of revenue in 1982 and 1981, and 14% in 1980.

Exhibit 2   Anacomp, Inc.—Abridged 1982 Annual Report

Note 11. Income Taxes

Deferred taxes are provided where differences exist between the period in which transactions affect taxable income and the period in which they enter into the determination of income for financial reporting purposes. Investment tax credits are reflected in income in the year realized by reducing the current provision for federal taxes on income.

The following table sets forth the components of the provision for income taxes:

Year ended June 30,	1982	1981	1980
Charge equivalent to realized tax benefits of pre-acquisition losses of acquired companies	$ 67	$ 164	$ 250
Charge equivalent to realized tax benefits from early disposition of shares issued under qualified stock option and stock purchase plans	76	252	81
Charge equivalent to realized tax benefits from certain acquisition expenditures	276	—	—
Taxes currently payable:			
Federal	2,536	1,034	2,263
State	889	602	377
Deferred	(3,001)	4,007	189
	$ 843	$6,059	$3,160

The deferred income tax effects of timing differences are as follows:

Year ended June 30,	1982	1981	1980
Excess of tax over book depreciation	$1,906	$265	$189
Use of cash basis accounting for tax purposes	(3,830)	3,830	—
Accrued interest on convertible debentures	(1,282)	(436)	—
Election of installment sale for tax purposes	506	(8)	—
Deferred income of foreign subsidiary	109	187	—
Deferred income of DISC	(156)	140	—
Transfer from deferred to currently payable	(264)	—	—
Other	10	29	—
	$(3,001)	$4,007	$189

The following is a reconciliation of income taxes calculated at the United States federal statutory rate to the provision for income taxes:

Exhibit 2   Anacomp, Inc.—Abridged 1982 Annual Report

Year Ended June 30,	1982	1981	1980
Provision for taxes on income at statutory rate	$1,666	$6,439	$3,582
Investment tax credit	(1,950)	(333)	(377)
State income taxes, net of federal income tax benefit	569	325	204
Nondeductible amortization of intangible assets	474	332	169
Difference between capital gain and statutory tax rates	—	(316)	(269)
Dividend deduction of 85% of dividend income	(119)	(179)	—
Interest on tax deposits, net of federal income tax benefit	302	—	—
Other	(99)	(209)	(149)
	$ 843	$6,059	$3,160

At June 30, 1982, certain subsidiaries of Anacomp have net operating loss carryforwards of approximately $1,997. The carryforwards pertain to preacquisition losses of the subsidiaries and therefore can be utilized only to the extent that the subsidiaries produce taxable income in the future. Any tax benefit resulting from the utilization of these carryforwards will reduce the intangible assets recorded at the time of purchase of the subsidiaries. The carryforwards expire in the following fiscal years: 1992, $357; 1993, $774; 1994, $514; and 1995, $352.

Note 12. Other Income and Extraordinary Credit

Year Ended June 30,	1982	1981	1980
Gain (loss) on transaction with Kalvar	$(725)	$ 898	$1,567
Gain on sale of certain assets	630	855	25
Other	705	947	246
	$610	$2,700	$1,838

The extraordinary credit in 1982 arose from the sale of a branch office which had been acquired in 1981 as part of an acquisition accounted for as a pooling of interests. The gain was $2,541 before income taxes, determined at the capital gains rate of $711.

Note 13. Lease and Other Commitments

Anacomp has commitments under long-term operating leases, principally for building space, covering periods generally up to five years. The following summarizes by year the future minimum lease payments due within the next five years and under all noncancellable operating lease obligations which extend beyond one year.

Exhibit 2   Anacomp, Inc.—Abridged 1982 Annual Report

Fiscal	As of June 30
1983	$3,933
1984	3,159
1985	2,362
1986	1,605
1987	565
1988 and thereafter	626
Total minimum payments required	$12,250

Anacomp and Dr. Ronald D. Palamara, president and chairman of Anacomp, are parties to a March 27, 1980, employment and noncompetition agreement pursuant to which Anacomp agreed (a) to pay Dr. Palamara commencing July 1, 1980, a base annual salary of $125 plus an amount equal to 3.54% of Anacomp's annual income before income taxes in excess of $1,000, (b) to make a one-time payment of $430 in July, 1980, to Dr. Palamara for his agreement not to compete with Anacomp for three years following any termination of service with Anacomp and (c) to sell Dr. Palamara, in July, 1980, 428,688 shares of Anacomp common stock for a consideration of $6.08 per share, that being the per share market price on the date of the agreement. Of the $6.08 per share consideration, Dr. Palamara agreed to pay $1.22 per share and granted Anacomp a right of first refusal to purchase such shares upon any resale by Dr. Palamara or subsequent holders at $4.86 below the sale price, $4.86 being the balance of the $6.08 per share consideration.

Note 15. Supplementary Income Statement Information

Supplementary income statement information follows.

Year ended June 30,	1982	1981	1980
Maintenance and repairs	$4,475	$3,738	$2,271
Depreciation and amortization of property, equipment and purchased computer software systems	$4,789	$2,938	$2,246
Amortization of intangible assets	$1,919	$1,430	$780
Taxes other than payroll and income taxes	$1,000	$507	$410
Rents	$7,503	$8,084	$4,819

Exhibit 2   Anacomp, Inc.—Abridged 1982 Annual Report

REPORT OF INDEPENDENT ACCOUNTANTS

To the Board of Directors and Stockholders of Anacomp, Inc.

We have examined the consolidated balance sheet of Anacomp, Inc. and Subsidiaries as of June 30, 1982 and 1981, and the related consolidated statements of income, stockholders' equity, and changes in financial position for each of the three years in the period ended June 30, 1982. Our examinations were made in accordance with generally accepted auditing standards and, accordingly, included such tests of the accounting records and such other auditing procedures as we considered necessary in the circumstances.

In our opinion, the financial statements referred to above present fairly the consolidated financial position of Anacomp, Inc. and Subsidiaries as of June 30, 1982 and 1981, and the consolidated results of their operations and changes in financial position for each of the three years in the period ended June 30, 1982, in conformity with generally accepted accounting principles applied on a consistent basis, after restatement for the change, with which we concur, in the method of accounting for vacation pay as described in Note 1 to the financial statements.

Coopers & Lybrand

Indianapolis, Indiana
September 1982

a

29

On November 2, 1986, John Taggart, a partner of Smith Barney, Harris Upham & Co., received a call from legal counsel for the owners of the Boston Celtics, Don Gaston, Alan Cohen, and Paul Dupee. The trio wished to explore the possibility of a partial sale of the team. A meeting was arranged for the following Wednesday.

At the meeting the owners explained that they wished to sell only a minority interest in the team, since they wanted to retain control over the franchise. They had acquired the team on August 9, 1981, for $18,984,961. Since then NBA franchise prices had soared. Public interest in the sport was at an all-time high, and the NBA had recently renegotiated a lucrative television contract with CBS through the 1989–90 season. Further, the Celtics had just completed a highly successful season, winning the NBA Championship. The owners needed advice on how to implement a partial sale. In particular, they wanted to know how the sale should be structured, what the team was worth, and what a noncontrolling interest in the team would be worth.

THE NATIONAL BASKETBALL ASSOCIATION

The National Basketball Association (NBA) is the only major professional basketball league in the U.S. It was organized in 1949 and currently has 23 member teams, each of which operates a professional basketball team in a major U.S. city. The teams are organized into two Conferences, with two Divisions within each Conference. A list of the teams operating in each Division and Conference during the 1986–87 season is reported in Exhibit 1.

During the NBA regular season, which extends from late October to mid-April, each team plays a total of 82 games against members of both Conferences. Half of the games are played at home, and half are played away, in the opposing team cities. At the end of the regular season, 16 of the 23 teams qualify for the NBA Playoffs to determine the NBA champion for the season. These 16 teams consist of the champions of each of the four Divisions, together with the six teams in each Conference with the next best winning percentages during the regular season. The playoffs consist of three rounds in each Conference, with the fourth and final round matching the winners of the Eastern and Western

This case was prepared for class discussion by Paul M. Healy of the MIT Sloan School of Management.

Conferences to determine the NBA champion. The first round is a best-of-five game series, while all subsequent rounds are best-of-seven game series.

Under NBA regulations, at the end of each season, teams are allotted rights to draft new players entering the league. The rules are designed to help strengthen the weakest teams in the league and to increase competition between teams. Thus, the teams with the worst record from the previous year usually have the rights to draft and sign the top-rated new players.

The league also has strict rules on the salaries paid to players, and on players' rights to change teams. Under the 1983 collective bargaining agreement between the NBA owners and the Players' Association, a cap is set for team salaries for each year. Teams are permitted exceptions under this salary cap to replace or re-sign their own veteran players. The salary cap is designed so that total player salaries and benefits for a given season are at least 53 percent of the adjusted gross revenues of all NBA teams for the prior season. The league rules also set minimum individual player salaries ($75,000 per year for the 1986–87 season). This collective bargaining agreement expires at the end of the 1986–87 season.

THE BOSTON CELTICS

The Boston Celtics were formed in 1949 as one of the original NBA franchises. Since its inception, the team has been the most successful sports team in any major sports league, winning 16 NBA championships between 1959 and 1986.

The team generates revenues from two main sources—the sale of tickets to home games, and the licensing of television and radio rights. Other revenues include licensing fees from the sale of items using the team's insignia. Its major expenses are for team costs.

Ticket Revenues

Under NBA rules, the Celtics receive all revenues from the sale of tickets to regular season home games and no revenue from regular season away games. The team also retains revenues from the sale of tickets to home exhibition games, net of appearance fees paid to the visiting team, and appearance fees for exhibition games played elsewhere. The Celtics play most of their games in the Boston Garden, which has a seating capacity of 14,890 and is located in downtown Boston. The team has sold out the Boston Garden for 270 consecutive home games. Thus, variability in revenues arises primarily from changes in ticket prices and from success in the playoffs, which determines the number of home games the team plays during the season.

Ticket prices for regular season home games during the 1985–86 season at the Boston Garden ranged from $8.00 to $23.00 per game. For the 1986–87 season, ticket prices will range from $9.00 to $26.00 per game. The average ticket price for regular season home games was $12.83 during the 1983–84 season, $14.74 during the 1984–85 season,

$16.72 during the 1985–86 season, and is anticipated to be $18.49 during the 1986–1987 season. As noted above, the team has an impressive record in the playoffs, winning the championship sixteen times since 1959. The team record in the regular season and the playoffs is reported in Exhibit 2.

Television and Radio Rights

The Celtics receive revenues from NBA agreements with CBS Sports and Turner Broadcasting System Inc., from local television and cable television contracts, and from a local radio station agreement. In the year ended June 30, 1986, local television, cable, and radio contracts amounted to $5,314,000, or 24 percent of total revenues.

The NBA agreement with CBS Sports grants CBS exclusive U.S. television rights to broadcast between 34 and 44 NBA games per season, including regular season games, playoff games, and the NBA All-Star game. The current agreement extends through the 1989–90 season and requires CBS to pay a fee to the NBA each season. The fee for the 1986–87 season is $39,000,000, and rises to $47,500,000 for the 1989–90 season. These payments are shared equally by each NBA member team. The Celtics' share of the CBS payment during the 1985–86 season was approximately $956,000, and will increase to $1,696,000 for the 1986–87 season. The NBA will enter into a new television contract after the 1989–90 season.

Under the NBA agreement with Turner Broadcasting System Inc. (TBS), TBS has exclusive U.S. television rights to broadcast up to 55 exhibition and regular season games and up to 20 playoff games. The games are telecast on WTBS-TV in Atlanta for distribution nationally through cable television. Under the agreement, which expires at the end of the 1987–88 basketball season, TBS pays the NBA an annual fee of $12,000,000 for the 1986–87 season and $13,000,000 for the 1987–88 season. These payments are distributed equally among the NBA member teams. The Boston Celtics received approximately $478,000 during the 1985–86 season and will receive approximately $522,000 during the 1986–87 season.

In addition, the Celtics have contracts with local television stations. An agreement with WLVI-TV, which expires at the end of the 1989–90 season, permits the Boston TV station to telecast up to six exhibition games, between 25 and 40 regular season games, and all home and away playoff games not preempted by the national NBA network contracts. A similar agreement with Sportschannel New England Limited Partnership grants the firm cable television rights to between 32 and 41 regular season home games and all playoff home games not preempted by the NBA's national television contracts. This agreement expires at the end of the 1986–87 season.

Finally, the Celtics also sell rights to broadcast their games to a local radio station. In 1983, RKO General, Inc., the owner of WRKO Radio, acquired the rights to broadcast all of the team's games through the end of the 1986–87 season. In October 1986, a new agreement was signed with WEEI, another local radio station, to cover games from the 1987–88 season through the 1993–94 season.

b

33

Other Revenues

The Celtics share equally with other members of the NBA in the earnings of NBA Properties, Inc. This company was organized in 1967 to license the manufacture and sale of items such as sneakers, basketballs, warm-up jackets, and sweatshirts, as well as certain nonsports items, which use official NBA team names and insignias. The Celtics retain the right to use their insignia and symbols to promote the team in their home territory and for retail sales in their home arena.

Team Costs

The major costs for the team are salaries for players and coaches. NBA rules permit each team to maintain a roster of 12 players during each regular season and up to 20 players in the off season. Exhibit 3 reports information on the players under contract with the Celtics on November 25, 1986, and aggregate contract payments to be made in future years to current players and 19 past players. These payments are each mostly guaranteed, implying that they must be paid during the remainder of each player's contract even if the player is released or, in some cases, injured.

In the 1986 draft, the Celtics selected five draft choices. The first round draft choice, Len Bias, a forward from the University of Maryland, died shortly after the 1986 draft. The Boston Celtics have not added any of the other draft choices to their roster.

Under its contracts with its head coach, K. C. Jones, and assistant coaches Jimmy Rodgers and Chris Ford, the Celtics made total compensation payments of $437,000 during the 1985–86 season, and are required to make salary payments of $540,000 during the 1986–87 season and $475,000 during the 1987–88 season.

SALE OF THE BOSTON CELTICS

Two crucial decisions faced the Celtics' owners in their deliberations over a partial sale of the team. First, should the team be sold privately or publicly? And, second, should the firm be organized as a limited liability company or as some form of partnership? Normally, Taggart would consider a private sale to be the only option available to the owners of a sports franchise. However, in the case of the Celtics, a public sale might also be viable. Under a private sale, Smith Barney, Harris Upham & Co. would find a single buyer or group of buyers for up to 49 percent of the outstanding shares of the Boston Celtics, Inc. The sale by the current owners would then be taxed at capital gains rates. Under the Tax Reform Act of 1986, capital gains tax rates in 1987 were due to increase to the same level as ordinary income rates, from 20 percent to 34 percent.

A public sale of a share of the Celtics would entail listing the firm's stock on a public exchange, and an initial public offering of up to 49 percent of the firm's stock. Although no professional sports team had gone public before, Taggart believed that the name recognition of the Celtics made this a unique opportunity. A public sale satisfied the existing owners' wish to retain control of the franchise, and any gain on the sale was taxable at capital gains rates.

Taggart was also intrigued by the possibility of organizing the team as a Master Limited Partnership. The first Master Limited Partnership (MLP) was formed and sold to the public in 1981. The number and dollar amount of new MLPs grew steadily through mid-1986. In a limited partnership two classes of partners are created, general partners and limited partners. The general partner manages the organization and has unlimited liability for partnership debts. The limited partner has no right to participate in the management of the organization, but has limited liability. Limited partnerships have been used to finance research and development, and oil and gas exploration, but have never before been used for a sports franchise.

There are several differences in tax treatment of limited partnerships and corporations. Partners of limited partnerships are taxed at personal rates on their share of the firm's profits each year. Under the Tax Reform Act of 1986 corporate tax rates are expected to be 34 percent, whereas personal tax rates are 28 or 33 percent. In addition, limited partnerships eliminate the double taxation faced under corporate ownership. Partnership profits are taxed only once, at the personal level, whereas corporate profits are first taxed at corporate rates, and then taxed again at personal ordinary income or capital gains rates for dividends and capital gains.

After discussing these forms of ownership with the team owners and his partners, Taggart recommended organizing the firm as a Master Limited Partnership. Under the agreement, the existing owners will become General Partners and own 60 percent of the 6.5 million units to be issued by the partnership. The General Partners will retain control of the management of the organization and will receive a minimum of $750,000 per year for these services. The new investors will be Limited Partners and will own 40 percent of the partnership units.

To help him establish a price for the team, the owners provided Taggart with financial statements for the team, presented in Exhibit 4. They noted that the short-term bank debt of $1,100,000 outstanding in June 1986 had already been paid off. In addition, record-keeping costs were expected to increase under a partnership, requiring the purchase of a new accounting system for $220,000. This outlay would be amortized on a straight-line basis over five years. Finally, annual costs of operating the new accounting system and complying with NYSE and SEC requirements would be $31,000. Despite this information, Taggart was unsure how to value the firm. No other sports franchises were publicly listed. Private sales of other sports franchises were not truly comparable to this sale since they also involved changes in control. Finally, Taggart was concerned about how the market would value the offer since the company appeared to be extremely risky, its success depending largely on the success of the team.[1]

b

35

----

1. In early November 1986, 30-year government securities yielded 7.6%, 3-month treasuries yielded 6.2%, and AA industrial bonds yielded 9.3%.

Boston Celtics, Inc.

QUESTIONS

1. Why are the owners interested in selling part of the Celtics at this time? What are the benefits of using the Master Limited Partnership form of ownership?
2. Analyze the financial performance of the Celtics. *get the in analysis*
3. Using information provided in the prospectus and your analysis in question 2, forecast cash flows for the Celtics for the period 1987 to 1991.
4. What is the value of the Celtics? At what price do you recommend that the owners offer units to prospective owners under the initial public offering?

EXHIBIT 1
List of Teams in National Basketball Divisions and Conferences During the 1986–87 Season

Eastern Conference		Western Conference	
Atlantic Division	**Central Division**	**Midwest Division**	**Pacific Division**
Boston Celtics	Atlanta Hawks	Dallas Mavericks	Golden State Warriors
New Jersey Nets	Chicago Bulls	Denver Nuggets	Los Angeles Clippers
New York Knicks	Cleveland Cavaliers	Houston Rockets	Los Angeles Lakers
Philadelphia 76ers	Detroit Pistons	Sacramento Kings	Phoenix Suns
Washington Bullets	Indiana Pacers	San Antonio Spurs	Portland Trailblazers
		Utah Jazz	Seattle SuperSonics

EXHIBIT 2
Boston Celtics Playoff Record

Season	Regular Season Record	Regular Season, Place of Finish in Division	Playoff Results
1985–86	67-15	First	NBA Champions
1984–85	63-19	First	Lost in championship finals
1983–84	62-20	First	NBA Champions
1982–83	56-26	Second	Lost in Conference semifinals
1981–82	63-19	First	Lost in Conference finals
1980–81	62-20	First	NBA Champions
1979–80	61-21	First	Lost in Conference finals
1978–79	29-53	Fifth	
1977–78	32-50	Third	
1976–77	44-38	Second	Lost in Conference semifinals
1975–76	54-28	First	NBA Champions
1974–75	60-22	First	Lost in Conference finals
1973–74	56-26	First	NBA Champions
1972–73	68-14	First	Lost in Conference finals
1971–72	56-26	First	Lost in Conference finals

b

Exhibit 3   Boston Celtics Players under Contract on November 25, 1986

EXHIBIT 3

Boston Celtics Players under Contract on November 25, 1986

Name	Position	Height	Age	Years in NBA	Last Season under Contract
Danny Ainge	Guard	6'5"	27	5	1991–92
Larry Bird	Forward	6'9"	29	7	1990–91
Rick Carlisle	Guard	6'5"	26	2	1988–89
Dennis Johnson	Guard	6'4"	32	10	1988–89
Greg Kite	Center	6'11"	25	3	1988–89
Kevin McHale	Forward	6'10"	28	6	1991–92
Robert Parish	Center	7'1½"	33	10	1989–90
Fred Roberts	Forward	6'10"	26	3	1987–88
Jerry Sichting	Guard	6'1"	29	6	1989–90
David Thirdkill	Forward	6'7"	26	4	1987–88
Sam Vincent	Guard	6'2"	23	1	1987–88
Bill Walton	Center	6'11"	33	12	1987–88
Scott Wedman	Forward	6'7"	34	12	1987–88

EXHIBIT 4

Boston Celtics Aggregate Contract Payments Owing to
Current and Past Players

Fiscal Year	Current Compensation Payments	Deferred Compensation Payments
1987	$6,350,000	$2,192,200
1988	7,127,000	2,089,200
1989	5,855,000	2,596,200
1990	5,110,000	2,199,600
1991 and thereafter	5,590,000	4,085,600

Exhibit 5   Financial Statements for Boston Celtics, Incorporated

EXHIBIT 5
Financial Statements for Boston Celtics, Incorporated

BALANCE SHEETS

	June 30,	
	1985	1986
ASSETS		
CURRENT ASSETS		
Cash and cash equivalents	$ 55,626	$ 1,292,971
Accounts receivable	1,297,376	1,040,623
Deferred game costs		
Prepaid income taxes		182,433
Prepaid expenses and other assets	59,512	135,333
TOTAL CURRENT ASSETS	1,412,514	2,651,360
NOTES RECEIVABLE	820,000	925,000
FRANCHISE AND OTHER RELATED ASSETS		
Deferred player acquisition costs, less amortization of $4,548,642 at June 30, 1985 and $7,222,963 at June 30, 1986 and September 30, 1986	6,785,361	5,514,740
National Basketball Association Franchise, less amortization of $308,480 at June 30, 1985 and $462,720 at June 30, 1986 and September 30, 1986	5,861,102	5,706,862
Media and other contracts, less amortization of $445,207 at June 30, 1985, $684,250 at June 30, 1986 and $717,130 at September 30, 1986	271,923	32,880
	12,918,386	11,254,482
EQUIPMENT AND IMPROVEMENTS—at cost, less allowances for depreciation and amortization of $74,203 at June 30, 1985, $141,809 at June 30, 1986 and $128,310 at September 30, 1986	97,312	107,082
	$15,248,212	$14,937,924

(continued)

b

39

Exhibit 5 Financial Statements for Boston Celtics, Incorporated

BALANCE SHEETS (continued)

	June 30,	
	1985	1986
LIABILITIES AND STOCKHOLDERS' EQUITY		
CURRENT LIABILITIES		
Accounts payable and accrued expenses	$228,122	$498,269
Accrued players' compensation	715,597	893,311
Liability for refundable tickets	734,331	1,087,538
Note payable to bank		1,100,000
Deferred game revenues		
Current portion of deferred compensation	647,770	879,256
Dividend payable on Preferred Stock	101,300	
Income taxes payable	340,931	
TOTAL CURRENT LIABILITIES	2,768,051	4,458,374
LONG-TERM DEBT	7,200,000	
DEFERRED REVENUE	1,000,000	800,000
DEFERRED COMPENSATION, less current portion	2,888,283	3,868,679
DEFERRED INCOME TAXES	963,000	
STOCKHOLDERS' EQUITY		
Common Stock, no par value—authorized 1,000 shares, issued and outstanding 100 shares	50,000	50,000
Retained earnings	378,878	5,760,871
	428,878	5,810,871
COMMITMENTS AND CONTINGENCIES		
	$15,248,212	$14,937,924

Exhibit 5   Financial Statements for Boston Celtics, Incorporated

STATEMENTS OF OPERATIONS

	Period from September 27, 1983 to June 30, 1984	Year ended June 30,	
		1985	1986
Regular Season Revenues			
Ticket sales	$ 8,168,029	$ 9,605,380	$11,092,727
Television and radio	3,778,536	4,609,010	6,747,532
Other, principally advertising	593,133	655,543	713,748
	12,539,698	14,869,933	18,554,007
Costs of Regular Season Revenues			
Team	6,322,059	7,473,078	8,112,787
Game	1,666,637	1,900,401	2,030,744
General and administrative	1,409,160	1,336,459	1,381,625
Selling and promotional	295,313	402,671	407,888
	9,693,169	11,112,609	11,933,044
	2,846,529	3,757,324	6,620,963
Revenues from playoffs, net of costs of $2,028,069, $1,813,596 and $1,910,565 in the periods ended June 30, 1984, 1985 and 1986	1,713,778	1,841,490	1,822,941
Amortization of NBA franchise and other related assets	(3,010,344)	(3,038,302)	(3,086,404)
Income (loss) from operations	1,549,963	2,560,512	5,357,500
Interest expense	(1,043,469)	(848,193)	(598,224)
Interest income	81,648	17,417	71,717
Income (loss) before income taxes	588,142	1,729,736	4,830,993
Provision (credit) for income taxes	370,000	940,000	(551,000)
Net income (loss)	$218,142	$789,736	$5,381,993

b

41

Exhibit 5   Financial Statements for Boston Celtics, Incorporated

STATEMENTS OF CASH FLOWS

	Period from September 27, 1983 to June 30, 1984	Year ended June 30,	
		1985	1986
Cash Flows from Operating Activities			
Regular season receipts:			
Ticket sales	$ 8,013,323	$ 9,809,861	$11,642,848
Television and radio	4,056,636	4,109,910	6,780,434
Other, principally advertising	563,720	667,457	660,318
	12,633,679	14,587,228	19,083,600
Regular season expenditures:			
Team expenses	5,316,186	7,044,393	8,259,542
Game expenses	1,666,377	1,900,631	2,030,774
General and administrative expenses	1,099,860	1,264,585	1,157,642
Selling and promotional expenses	274,843	555,573	404,846
	8,357,266	10,765,182	11,852,804
	4,276,413	3,822,046	7,230,796
Playoff receipts	3,589,681	3,874,618	3,599,817
Playoff expenditures	1,907,530	1,742,018	1,755,764
	1,682,151	2,132,600	1,844,053
	5,958,564	5,954,646	9,074,849
Interest and taxes paid	(459,201)	(719,238)	(979,501)
Payment of deferred compensation	(937,918)	(534,174)	(613,514)
Net Cash Flows from Operating Activities	4,561,445	4,701,234	7,481,834
Cash Flows from Investing Activities			
Purchase of NBA franchise and related assets	15,000,000		
Notes receivable from players	500,000	320,000	105,000
Purchases of equipment and improvements	121,232	32,355	63,877
Other (receipts) expenditures	(2,289)	(41,945)	(125,688)
Net Cash Used by (Provided from) Investing Activities	15,618,943	310,410	43,189
Cash Flows from Financing Activities			
Proceeds from long-term debt	9,000,000		
Proceeds from sale of Preferred Stock	3,000,000		
Proceeds from sale of Common Stock	50,000		
Redemption of Preferred Stock		(3,000,000)	
Repayment of long-term debt	(600,000)	(1,200,000)	(6,100,000)
Dividends on Preferred Stock	(167,700)	(360,000)	(101,300)
Dividend on Common Stock			
Net Cash Provided (Used) by Financing Activities	11,282,300	(4,560,000)	(6,201,300)
Net increase (decrease) in cash	$ 224,802	$ (169,176)	$ 1,237,345
Cash at beginning of period		224,802	55,626
Cash at End of Period	$ 224,802	$ 55,626	$ 1,292,971

b

42

Exhibit 5   Financial Statements for Boston Celtics, Incorporated

STATEMENTS OF CASH FLOWS (continued)

	Period from September 27, 1983 to June 30, 1984	Year ended June 30, 1985	Year ended June 30, 1986
Schedule reconciling net income (loss) to net cash flows from operating activities:			
Net income (loss)	$ 218,142	$ 789,736	$ 4,418,993
Items not affecting cash flows:			
Amortization	3,010,344	3,038,302	3,086,404
Depreciation	31,709	42,494	54,107
Provision for income taxes	370,000	593,000	
Deferred compensation earned	380,167	331,729	346,567
Accrued interest on deferred compensation liability	255,878	360,308	478,829
Deferred revenue	1,000,000		(200,000)
Deferred expenses assumed in acquisition	209,203		
	5,257,301	4,365,833	3,765,907
Net effect of change in certain working capital items:			
Accounts receivable	(1,058,491)	(238,885)	256,753
Deferred game costs			
Accounts payable, accrued expenses and accrued compensation	1,260,304	(362,141)	447,861
Liability for refundable tickets	(184,544)	376,475	353,207
Deferred game revenues			
Accrued income taxes		340,931	(340,931)
Other	6,651	(36,541)	(383,942)
	23,920	79,839	332,948
Other payments not affecting net income (loss):			
Deferred compensation payments	(937,918)	(534,474)	(813,514)
Signing bonus payments			(222,500)
Net Cash Flows from Operating Activities	$ 4,561,445	$ 4,701,234	$ 7,481,834

b

43

Exhibit 5   Financial Statements for Boston Celtics, Incorporated

NOTES TO FINANCIAL STATEMENTS

Note A – Organization

On August 9, 1983, Boston Celtics Incorporated (the "Company"), entered into an Agreement for Purchase and Sale of Assets with Boston Celtics Corporation whereby the Company acquired the National Basketball Association ("NBA") franchise to operate a professional basketball team in the City of Boston, Massachusetts, certain contractual rights and related operating assets in exchange for cash and assumption of certain obligations. The Company commenced operations on September 27, 1983. The cost ($18,984,961) of the acquisition (the "Acquisition") was allocated principally to the NBA franchise, player contracts and other contract rights based on the estimated fair market value of these assets. The cost comprised cash of $15,000,000; the assumption of liabilities of $3,680,064 for deferred compensation and assumption of other net liabilities of $304,897.

Note B – Significant Accounting Policies

Revenue and Cost Recognition: Revenues and costs are recognized in the accompanying financial statements when revenues and related costs are earned and incurred, respectively. Tickets sales and television and radio broadcasting fees generally are recorded as revenue at the time the game to which the proceeds relate has been played. Team costs, principally player and coaches' salaries, related fringe benefits and insurance, and game costs, principally NBA attendance assessments, arena rentals and travel, are recorded as expense on the same basis. Consequently, advance ticket sales and advance payments on television and radio broadcasting contracts and payments for team and game costs not earned or incurred are recorded as deferred game revenues and deferred game costs, respectively. General and administrative and promotional costs are expensed as incurred. Amortization (see below) is provided ratably as games are played based upon the estimated useful life of the related asset.

Player Acquisition Costs: The allocation of the purchase price to player contracts acquired in the Acquisition was based upon estimated fair market value. These costs are being amortized on the straight-line method over an average contract life of five years. The costs of player contracts acquired from other teams are amortized over the life of the respective players' contracts. At termination of a player's services, the unamortized balance of contract costs, net of sale proceeds, if any, is charged to expense.

National Basketball Association Franchise: The cost ascribed to the NBA franchise was recorded at fair market value and is being amortized on the straight-line method over a period of 40 years.

Media and Other Contracts: The costs ascribed to these contracts, principally broadcasting, lease and employment contract rights, were recorded at fair market value and are being amortized on the straight-line method over the terms of the specific agreements, which range from two to four years.

Equipment and Improvements: These assets are stated at cost. Depreciation and amortization is provided over the estimated useful lives of the assets using an accelerated method.

Pension Costs: Pension expense includes amortization of players' prior service costs over a 30-year period. The Company's policy is to fund pension costs as accrued.

Income Taxes: The Company, until July 1, 1985, provided for federal and state income taxes based upon income recorded for financial statement purposes. Deferred taxes, consequently, result from differences between financial statement and income tax reporting as a result of the Company's use of cash basis accounting and a different method of amortizing player costs for tax purposes. On July 1, 1985, the stockholders of the Company elected to be taxed under the provisions of the Internal Revenue Code applicable to S Corporations (see Note J).

Financial Statements: The statement of operations for the period from September 27, 1983 to June 30, 1984 is equivalent to a full year's operations because it includes all revenues for such year and because deferred game and operating expenses ($209,203) of the prior owner for the period from

b

Exhibit 5   Financial Statements for Boston Celtics, Incorporated

July 1, 1983 to September 26, 1983 were reimbursed to such owner and have been charged to operations of the Company for the fiscal year ended June 30, 1984. The accompanying financial statements do not present earnings or dividend per share information because it is not meaningful with respect to the contemplated liquidation of the Company and formation of a limited partnership to purchase the Company's assets and liabilities from its stockholders.

b

C

Comdisco Inc., the world's leading independent lessor of IBM computers, would seem like a company Wall Street ought to love. Annual revenues are up fourfold since 1978, to an estimated $600 million in the fiscal year that ended September 30. Earnings per share have grown at an even more torrid tempo, and return on shareholders' equity is running at an estimated 35%. Yet at a recent price of $37, the stock was selling at 15 times projected earnings in fiscal 1984—a tepid multiple for a company whose earnings could grow at a 30% clip over the next five years.

⋮

Just about the only thing wrong with Comdisco is the tainted reputation that computer-leasing companies acquired as a result of the well-known bankruptcies of OPM Leasing and Itel. Securities analysts, though, see no similarities between Comdisco and those fiascos. OPM Leasing turned out to be a spectacularly fraudulent operation, and Itel's downfall resulted in large part from overly optimistic accounting assumptions, coupled with a large inventory of obsolete equipment. Comdisco's accounting couldn't be more conservative, analysts say. They add that the company has managed, through the use of ingenious leasing arrangements, to eliminate almost all exposure to equipment obsolescence. Comdisco, asserts John Keefe of Drexel Burnham Lambert, has practically nothing to fear from any future IBM decision.[1]

The quotes above appeared in the Personal Investing Section of *Fortune* magazine in October 1983.

BUSINESS HISTORY AND OPERATIONS

Comdisco, Inc. is a Chicago-based company founded in 1969 by its current chairman of the board and president, Kenneth Pontikes. The company originally began as an IBM computer dealer. As demand for computer leasing started to grow during the late 1970s, the company started emphasizing leasing operations. By 1982, leasing old and new IBM computer equipment constituted the primary business activity of the company, and Comdisco had become the largest computer leasing company. Comdisco's customers

This case was prepared by Professor Krishna G. Palepu as the basis for class discussion rather than to illustrate either effective or ineffective handling of an administrative situation. Copyright © 1986 by the President and Fellows of Harvard College. Harvard Business School case 9-186-299.

1. *Reprinted with permission from* Fortune, *October 31, 1983.*

were primarily large corporations. In 1982, the company had business relationships with 70 percent of the Fortune 500 companies, including 49 of the 50 largest U.S. companies.

The computer remarketing industry had many participants: small independent operators, larger private organizations, and leasing subsidiaries of conglomerates. Comdisco was one of the few independent public corporations in the industry. The firms in the industry were primarily of two types: broker/dealers or third-party lessors. The broker/dealers obtained for customers computer equipment from either a vendor or current user; third-party lessors provided lease financing. Comdisco engaged in both these activities.

Comdisco achieved its dominance in the computer leasing industry through a strategy of full-service leasing. Under this strategy, the company offered its customers a number of services which were not offered by competitors. Comdisco's subsidiaries, Comdisco Technical Services, Inc. and Comdisco Transport, Inc., specialized in equipment refurbishment, delivery, installation, de-installation, and technical planning and site preparation. Comdisco Maintenance Services, another subsidiary, offered a low-cost alternative to IBM's maintenance service. Comdisco Disaster Recovery Services, Inc. was established to provide another valuable service to the company's customers: contingent data processing capacity to be used when a customer's own data center had unavoidable failures. Through this service, Comdisco's customers had access to four fully operational data centers as a backup to their own data centers, to be used in the event of a natural disaster or accident.

Comdisco's broad customer base provided the company with a number of competitive advantages. First, taking advantage of its access to 10,000 important users of IBM equipment in the U.S., the company created a proprietary data base of their computing needs. This data base provided Comdisco's sales force with current and timely information on potential customers and their requirements. Second, being the leading IBM dealer, Comdisco maintained large inventories of a broad range of IBM equipment. Comdisco's personnel closely monitored IBM's new products and pricing policies. This product knowledge combined with large inventories enabled the company to assist customers with their computer acquisition plans and to offer quick deliveries. Finally, using its data base, the company could help its customers sell their old hardware when they acquired new equipment from Comdisco.

While the above strategy enabled Comdisco to establish its dominance over others in the computer leasing industry, the company was still potentially vulnerable to competition from IBM itself since IBM equipment accounted for most of Comdisco's revenues. In 1981, IBM formed a financing subsidiary, IBM Credit Corporation, to provide customer financing. Shortly after that, IBM announced its intention to enter into computer leasing and established a joint venture for this purpose with Merrill Lynch and Metropolitan Life Insurance. A number of industry analysts felt that this might result in increased competition for companies like Comdisco.

Comdisco's management, however, felt that IBM's recent moves did not pose a threat to the company's competitive position because IBM's entry into leasing would enhance the tarnished image of the computer leasing business, a net benefit to the industry. They also believed that, as IBM began to emphasize outright sale of its equipment over short-term rentals, many of IBM's customers might be forced to look for other lessors like Comdisco who offered short-term leases. This was likely to provide additional business opportunities which would offset any loss of long-term lease business to IBM.

While equipment leasing to computer users was Comdisco's primary activity, the company also offered tax-oriented leases to investors who were primarily interested in the tax benefits associated with leasing. In recent years, the financial services income from the tax advantaged transactions accounted for a growing portion of the company's revenues.

ACCOUNTING POLICIES FOR LEASING

Comdisco offered computer equipment to its customers through a variety of lease arrangements. Using the terminology of Financial Accounting Standards Board's Statement No. 13, Comdisco's leases can be classified into one of three types: sales-type leases, direct financing leases, or operating leases.

Classification

Both sales-type and direct financing leases transferred substantially all the benefits and risks inherent in the ownership of the leased property to the lessee. A sales-type lease usually gave rise to a dealer's profit or loss for Comdisco. Therefore, in a sales-type lease, the fair value of the leased equipment (normal selling price) at the inception of the lease differed from the cost or carrying amount. In contrast, in a direct financing lease, the primary service that Comdisco offered was the financing of the equipment's acquisition by a lessee. In such a lease, the fair value of the equipment was equal to the cost or carrying amount. Comdisco earned only a financing income (interest) and no dealer's profit. An operating lease was a simple rental of the equipment, and Comdisco retained ownership of the equipment throughout the lease term.

Under FASB's guidelines, the accounting classification of a lease was based on whether or not it satisfied certain conditions:

1. The lease transfers ownership of the equipment to the lessee by the end of the lease term.
2. The lease contains an option allowing the lessee to purchase the property at a bargain price.
3. The lease term is equal to 75 percent or more of the estimated economic life of the property.
4. The present value of the rental is equal to 90 percent or more of the fair market value of the leased property.
5. Collectibility of the payments from the lessee is reasonably predictable.
6. No important uncertainties surround the amount of cost yet to be incurred by the lessor.

C

49

A lease meeting *at least one* of the first four conditions and *both* of the last two conditions was classified as a sales-type lease or direct financing lease. Such a lease was treated as a sales-type lease if the fair value of the leased equipment was different from its carrying amount; otherwise it was classified as a direct financing lease. A lease that did not meet the combination of conditions just described was classified as an operating lease.

Accounting Treatment: Comdisco as Lessor

The accounting treatment in Comdisco's financial statements for the above three types of leases was as follows:

OPERATING LEASE.   Lease revenue consisted of monthly rentals; the cost of equipment was recorded as leased equipment. The difference between the cost and the estimated residual value at the end of the lease term was depreciated on a straight-line basis over the lease term. Salesmen's commissions and other initial direct costs were capitalized as deferred charges and were amortized on a straight-line basis.

SALES-TYPE LEASE.   At the inception of the lease, the present value of rentals was treated as sales revenue. Equipment cost less the present value of the residual was recorded as cost of sales. The present value of rentals and of the residual was recorded on the balance sheet as net investment in sales-type lease. As each lease payment was received, the net investment was reduced and interest income was recognized.

DIRECT FINANCING LEASE.   At the inception of the lease, the cost of the leased equipment was recorded as net investment in the direct financing lease. As each lease payment was received, the net investment was reduced by the corresponding amount. The difference between the sum of the lease payments and the cost of the leased equipment was unearned profit from the direct financing lease, and it was recognized monthly so as to produce a constant rate of return on the net investment.

Accounting Treatment: Comdisco as Lessee

In addition to the above leases where Comdisco was a lessor, it was also often a lessee: the company acquired equipment from computer vendors and others through leasing arrangements. If such a lease met at least one of the first four conditions listed earlier, it was classified by Comdisco as a capital lease; otherwise, it was classified as an operating lease. The accounting treatment of the leases where Comdisco was a lessee was as follows:

OPERATING LEASE.   Monthly rentals were treated as rental expense.

CAPITAL LEASE.   At the inception of the lease, the present value of lease rentals was recorded as a capital lease asset. An equal amount was also recognized as a liability—

C

an obligation under the capital lease. The capital lease asset was depreciated over the lease term. When a lease payment was made, the obligation under capital lease was reduced and interest expense on the lease obligation was recognized.

NONRECOURSE DISCOUNTING OF LEASE PAYMENTS

In order to finance its investment in leased assets, Comdisco often assigned the stream of lease payments to a financial institution at a fixed interest rate on a nonrecourse basis. In return, Comdisco received from the financial institution a loan equal to the present value of the lease payment stream. The financial institution received the lease payments from the lessee as repayments of the loan. In the event of default by a lessee, the financial institution had a first lien on the underlying leased equipment, with no further recourse against the company.

For operating leases, proceeds from discounting were recorded on the balance sheet as discounted lease rentals liability. As lessees made payments to the financial institutions, discounted lease rentals were reduced by the interest rate method. For sales-type leases and direct financing leases, proceeds from discounting were not included in discounted lease rentals. Instead, future rentals were eliminated from the net investment in sales-type or direct financing leases, and any gain or loss on the financing was immediately recognized in the income statement.

TAX ADVANTAGED TRANSACTIONS

In addition to leasing equipment to computer users, Comdisco undertook leasing transactions with investors who were interested in tax shelters. While the specific terms and conditions of these tax advantaged transactions varied, a typical transaction was as follows:

1. After the inception of the initial user lease and independent of it, Comdisco sold all the leased equipment to a third-party investor. This sale usually occurred three to nine months after the commencement of the initial user lease. The sales price equaled the then current fair market value of the equipment. The payment from the investor to Comdisco consisted of: (a) cash and a negotiable interest-bearing promissory note due within two years for 10–22 percent of the sales price (the "equity payment") and (b) an installment note for the balance payable over an 84-month period.
2. Simultaneously with the sale, Comdisco leased the equipment back from the investors for 84 months. The lease payments under the leaseback obligation were equal to the installment payments receivable by Comdisco from the investor (1.b).
3. As part of the leaseback arrangement, during the 61st through 84th months of the leaseback period, the investor shared in the re-lease proceeds that the company received from subleasing the equipment to a user. Upon the expiration of the leaseback period, the investor had the exclusive right to the equipment.

The net result of the above transaction was that Comdisco gave up the depreciation tax benefit, a portion of the rental revenues for months 61–84, and 100 percent of the equipment value after the 84th month. In return, the company received the nonrefundable equity payment (1.a).

If the equipment sold to the investor was originally under an operating lease, the equity payment was recorded by Comdisco as financial services revenue in the period in which the tax advantaged transaction occurred. From the fourth quarter of 1983, the company began to allocate as cost of financial services a portion of the net book value of the equipment at lease termination. For sales-type and direct financing leases, the equity payment was first applied to reduce a portion of the residual value of the equipment shown in the balance sheet (as investment in sales-type and direct financing leases). This is because the company's ability to recover the residual value was decreased due to the rental sharing under the tax advantaged transaction. The excess of the equity payment over the residual value reduction was recorded as financial services revenue in the period in which the tax advantaged transaction occurred.

RECENT PERFORMANCE

During the ten years ending in 1982, Comdisco's sales and profits grew rapidly. During fiscal 1982 the company reported $29.4 million profits on revenues of $471.6 million, representing an 88 percent increase in profits and 56 percent increase in sales during the year. (See Exhibit 3 for an abridged version of the 1982 annual report.) The company continued its strong growth performance in fiscal 1983. The company's profits and revenues in the first nine months of the fiscal year were $36.1 million and $401.4 million, respectively. (See Exhibit 2 for the company's interim report for this period.)

In Comdisco's second quarterly report for 1983, Kenneth Pontikes commented on the company's future:

> These new activities, along with the continued growth of the company's lease and customer base, enhance the company's long term growth prospects. The company's history of outstanding performance and the recent issuance of $250,000,000 of convertible subordinated debentures, which further strengthened the company's capital base, provide it with the flexibility required for continued growth in today's marketplace.

The company's shares, listed on The New York Stock Exchange, reflected this optimistic outlook: their price appreciated from about $9 in January 1982 to $37 by the end of September 1983. Exhibit 1 shows the movement of Comdisco's stock price and Standard and Poor's 500 index from January 1982 to September 1983. Comdisco's stock price increased by more than 300 percent during this period compared to a roughly 40 percent increase in Standard and Poor's 500 index. However, as the *Fortune* magazine comments indicate, many analysts considered Comdisco's stock to be still undervalued and expected it to continue to outperform the market.

QUESTIONS

1. Evaluate Comdisco's business activities and the company's strategy.
2. Using the information in Comdisco's financial statements and footnotes, fill in the following to the extent possible (use plug figures if necessary):

Account	Balance as of 9/30/81	Increases during fiscal '82	Decreases during fiscal '82	Balance as of 9/30/82
Obligations under capital leases	_____ +	_____ –	_____ =	_____
Discounted lease rentals	_____ +	_____ –	_____ =	_____
Net investment in sales-type and direct financing leases	_____ +	_____ –	_____ =	_____

Identify the business transactions that would have given rise to the changes identified in the above accounts.

3. Analyze the relative contribution of rentals, sales of computer equipment, and financial services to Comdisco's reported profits during fiscal years 1981 and 1982 and the first nine months of fiscal year 1983. What are the reasons for the differences in the profit margins of these three activities? Which activity is contributing most to Comdisco's profits?
4. Evaluate the quality of Comdisco's disclosure in its annual report regarding the company's lease accounting policies. Do you think the disclosure is adequate to evaluate the company's performance?

C

EXHIBIT 1
Movement of Comdisco's Stock and S&P 500 Index, January 1982–September 1983

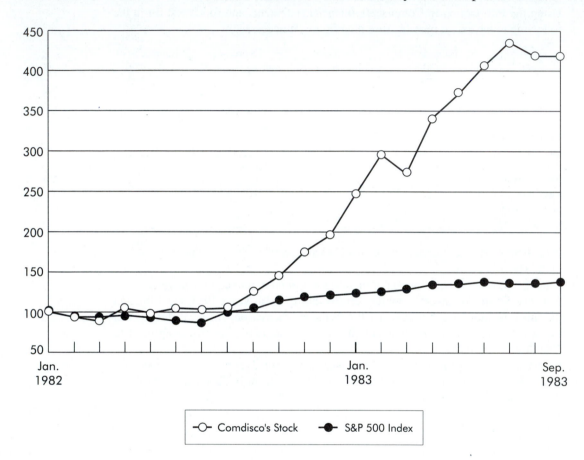

C

54

EXHIBIT 2
Comdisco, Inc. Quarterly Report, Third Quarter Ended June 30, 1983

To Our Stockholders

I am pleased to report net earnings of $13,199,000 or $.45 per share for the third quarter of fiscal 1983. These results represent increases of 127% and 96%, respectively, over the three months ended June 30, 1982 when net earnings were $5,824,000 or $.23 per share. Earnings improved as a result of increased profitability of financial services activities, increased leasing of computer equipment and a lower effective tax rate. Total revenue for the quarter ended June 30, 1983 was $127,455,000 compared to $94,691,000 for the prior year period. The increase in total revenue was primarily due to the continued growth of the Company's lease base. In the third quarter of fiscal 1983, the Company entered into 850 new leases with total revenue of $266.1 million during the initial lease terms. These figures compare to 605 new leases and $180.4 million of revenue for the year earlier period.

Net earnings for the nine months ended June 30, 1983 were $36,064,000, or $1.25 per share, representing increases of 69% and 51%, respectively, over the prior year period. Total revenue for the first nine months of fiscal 1983 amounted to $401,367,000 compared to $334,189,000 for the nine months ended June 30, 1982. The Company's impressive results for the first nine months of fiscal 1983 were primarily due to its active participation in the peripheral equipment and 3081 and 3083 processor markets, which have resulted in increased computer equipment sales, leasing and financial services activities. In addition, deliveries by IBM of the 3081 and 3083 processors have stimulated both sale and leasing of displaced IBM 3033 processors.

On July 21, 1983, the Board of Directors declared a cash dividend of $.04 per share to be paid on September 9, 1983 to stockholders of record as of August 19, 1983. This is the twenty-seventh consecutive quarterly cash dividend declared since the Company commenced paying cash dividends in 1977.

In April 1983, the Company announced its Corporate Lease Line Program, an expanded leasing program designed to meet the growing demand for lease financing of office and industrial equipment. The Corporate Lease Line Program expands the Company's array of complementary services and capitalizes on its expertise in providing customers with innovative and cost effective financing options.

During the third quarter of fiscal 1983, the Company began operations of a newly established, wholly owned subsidiary, Comdisco Resources, Inc. ("CRI"). Initially CRI will be primarily engaged, through joint ventures with established partners, in the acquisition of mineral and royalty rights in producing domestic oil and gas properties and the acquisition of onshore leasehold interests, primarily for resale to others for oil and gas exploration and development. For fiscal 1983 and 1984, investments of approximately $32.0 million and $13.0 million, respectively, have been budgeted by CRI.

These new activities, along with the continued growth of the Company's lease and customer base, enhance the Company's long term growth prospects. The Company's history of outstanding financial performance and the recent issuance of $250,000,000 of convertible subordinated debentures, which further strengthened the Company's capital base, provide it with the flexibility required for continued growth in today's marketplace.

Kenneth N. Pontikes
Chairman of the Board and President
August 10, 1983

55

CONSOLIDATED STATEMENTS OF EARNINGS AND RETAINED EARNINGS
For the Three and Nine Months Ended June 30, 1983 and 1982 (unaudited)

(in thousands except per share data)	Three Months Ended June 30		Nine Months Ended June 30	
	1983	1982	**1983**	1982
Revenue				
Rental	$ 70,056	$53,462	$193,520	$148,434
Sale of computer equipment	29,159	24,113	129,626	110,108
Financial services	15,493	12,890	50,073	62,040
Other	12,747	4,226	28,148	13,607
Total Revenue	127,455	94,691	401,367	334,189
Cost and Expenses				
Equipment depreciation, amortization and rental	56,647	40,378	152,586	115,325
Cost of computer equipment	26,112	21,318	114,631	99,659
Financial services	1,524	1,065	3,614	6,641
Selling, general and administrative	13,938	10,722	43,060	38,074
Interest	14,035	12,016	38,112	34,560
Total Costs and Expenses	112,256	85,499	352,003	294,259
Earnings before income taxes	15,199	9,192	49,364	39,930
Income taxes	2,000	3,368	13,300	18,568
Net earnings	$ 13,199	5,824	36,064	21,362
Retained earnings at beginning of period	$ 92,445	$58,223	$71,268	$43,359
Net earnings	13,199	5,824	36,064	21,362
Dividends paid	(1,150)	(394)	(2,838)	(1,068)
Retained earnings at end of period	$104,494	$63,653	$104,494	$ 63,653
Net earnings per common and common equivalent share	.45	.23	1.25	.83
Cash dividends per common share	.04	.03	.11	.09
Common and common equivalent shares outstanding	29,611	29,118	29,234	28,918

CONSOLIDATED BALANCE SHEET
June 30, 1983 and 1982 (unaudited) and September 30, 1982 (unaudited)

	June 30		September 30
(in thousands except number of shares)	**1983**	1982	1982
Assets			
Cash and marketable securities (at cost which approximates market)	**$175,215**	$ 4,586	$ 39,762
Receivables	**66,430**	38,854	45,055
Inventory of computer equipment	**48,914**	38,716	35,382
Investment in sales-type and direct financing leases	**63,735**	28,541	23,682
Leased and other equipment	**703,759**	532,969	534,611
Less: accumulated depreciation and amortization	**263,401**	174,408	192,714
Net equipment	**440,358**	358,561	341,897
Other assets and deferred charges	**55,925**	43,446	50,901
	$850,577	$512,704	$536,679
Liabilities and Stockholders' Equity			
Note payable	**$ —**	$ 2,650	$ 2,385
Subordinated debentures	**262,250**	62,250	62,250
Accounts payable	**29,001**	26,982	19,110
Obligations under capital leases	**14,669**	20,122	18,636
Income taxes	**42,817**	31,585	36,197
Other liabilities	**45,139**	39,219	45,265
Discounted lease rentals	**280,976**	247,899	261,780
	674,852	430,707	445,623
Stockholders' equity:			
Common stock $.10 par value			
Authorized 50,000,000 shares; issued 28,768,366 and 11,757,418 shares at June 30, 1983 and 1982, respectively (11,769,043 at September 30, 1982)	**2,877**	1,176	1,177
Additional paid-in capital	**68,718**	17,657	18,965
Deferred translation adjustment	**(364)**	(489)	(354)
Retained earnings	**104,494**	63,653	71,268
Total stockholders' equity	**175,725**	81,997	91,056
	$850,577	$512,704	$536,679

C

57

CONSOLIDATED STATEMENTS OF CHANGES IN FINANCIAL POSITION
For the Nine Months Ended June 30, 1983 and 1982 (unaudited)

(in thousands)	1983	1982
Source of Funds		
Total provided by operations	$123,798	$133,285
Issuance of common stock upon conversion of 13% convertible debentures, net	52,465	—
Proceeds from issuance of subordinated debentures	245,250	—
Discounted lease rentals	141,002	92,535
Other	305	2,624
	562,820	228,444
Application of Funds		
Increase in leased equipment and inventory	238,304	175,193
Decrease in note payable	2,385	795
Redemption of convertible debentures	50,000	—
Reduction of discounted lease rentals and obligations under capital leases	126,332	45,611
Other assets and deferred charges	7,508	11,039
Other	2,838	1,068
	427,367	233,706
Increase (decrease) in cash and marketable securities	135,453	(5,262)
Cash and marketable securities at beginning of period	39,762	9,848
Cash and marketable securities at end of period	$175,215	$4,586

Notes to Consolidated Financial Statements

June 30, 1983 and 1982 (unaudited)

1. Principles of Reporting

The accompanying consolidated financial statements include the accounts of the Company and its wholly-owned subsidiaries after elimination of intercompany accounts and transactions. In the opinion of management, the accompanying consolidated financial statements contain all adjustments necessary for a fair presentation. The Company has a fiscal year that ends September 30.

The balance sheet at September 30, 1982 has been derived from the audited financial statements at that date.

2. Subordinated Debentures

On November 4, 1982, the Board of Directors announced the redemption of all of the Company's 13% Convertible Subordinated Debentures Due 2001 (the "Convertible Debentures") at a redemption price of $1,117 for each $1,000 principal amount of Convertible Debenture, plus accrued and unpaid interest to December 6, 1982. The Convertible Debentures were convertible into shares of common stock of the Company, at the option of the Convertible Debenture holder, at a conversion price of $9.75 per share. Common stock issued upon conversion of $49,839,000 principal amount of the convertible Debentures totaled 5,111,360 shares.

On May 4, 1983, the Company completed the sale of $250,000,000 principal amount of its 8% Convertible Subordinated Debentures Due May 1, 2003 (the "Debentures"). The Debentures are convertible into common stock of the Company at the rate of $36.50 per share. An aggregate of 6,849,315 shares has been reserved for issuance upon conversion of the Debentures. Temporarily, the net proceeds from the Debentures, which amounted to approximately $245,250,000, have been invested in short-term instruments and used to finance an increase in the Company's lease portfolio pending receipt of cash upon discounting of the related lease receivables.

3. Income Taxes

The rates used in computing the provision for federal income taxes at June 30, 1983 and 1982 vary from the statutory tax rate primarily due to investment tax credits generated in the respective years and Domestic International Sales Corporation (DISC) tax benefits. During the third quarter of fiscal 1983, the Company generated substantial investment tax credits resulting from the increase in leasing activity. Accordingly, the Company estimates that the annual effective tax rate will be approximately 27% for fiscal 1983 compared to the estimated rates of 33% and 40% used in the first six months of fiscal 1983 and the first nine months of fiscal 1982, respectively. The reduction in the estimated income tax rate resulted in an increase of approximately $2,100,000 in net earnings or $.07 per share in the third quarter of fiscal 1983. The effective tax rate for the quarter and nine months ended June 30, 1982 varies from the estimated annual rate due to a reinstatement of deferred income taxes resulting from the sale of investment tax credits which had been used to reduce deferred income taxes at September 30, 1981.

4. Common Stock

All references in the financial statements and notes to the number of common shares and per share data have been adjusted for the two-for-one stock split distributed in March 1983.

C

59

Exhibit 3   Comdisco, Inc. Annual Report for Fiscal Year 1982 (abridged)

EXHIBIT 3

Comdisco, Inc. Annual Report for Fiscal Year 1982 (abridged)

To Our Stockholders

In fiscal 1982 Comdisco continued its outstanding performance with record earnings and revenues. Net earnings of $29.4 million, or $2.27 per share, represented increases of 88% and 68%, respectively, over fiscal 1981, while total revenue increased 56% to $471.6 million. These results were achieved despite the recessionary economic environment. The compound annual growth rate in net earnings over the last five years is an exceptional 43%. The primary factors contributing to the record earnings in fiscal 1982 were the increased volume and profitability of financial services activity, the growth of the Company's lease and customer bases, and the ability of the Company to capitalize on the active market for IBM 3033 processors and disk storage devices.

The higher level of financial services activity was the result of tax-advantaged leasing transactions associated with the Company's lease portfolio of used equipment and also the arrangement of "tax benefit transfers" that were structured under the Economic Recovery Tax Act of 1981. Late in fiscal 1982, Congress passed the Tax Equity and Fiscal Responsibility Act of 1982, which included legislation that will eventually eliminate "tax benefit transfers." This will cause the arrangement of traditional leveraged leases to re-emerge as a primary financial services activity of the Company.

The growth of Comdisco's lease base continued on a strong trend in fiscal 1982 as more users committed themselves to the leasing of equipment. The Company significantly increased its activity in the leasing of peripheral equipment. During fiscal 1982 the Company entered into 2,259 new leases with total revenue of $701.6 million during the initial term of these leases. This compares to 1,620 leases and $338.8 million in revenue during fiscal 1981.

The initial deliveries by IBM of its 3081 processor stimulated activity in all Comdisco's businesses. The Company participated in the lease placement of 3081 processors, and in the remarketing of the displaced 3033 processors. The Company's increased marketing efforts led to a 31% increase in its customers, which include most of the largest corporations in the United States. In fiscal 1981 Comdisco set up a "mid-range" marketing force that has successfully expanded the Company's customer base among medium-sized corporations. Comdisco's foreign subsidiaries continued to increase their marketing presence and also produced record results in the twelve months ended September 30, 1982. Fiscal 1982 also saw the continued refinement of Comdisco's computerized marketing data base that tracks user information for virtually all large IBM systems installed in the United States.

Two of Comdisco's newer subsidiaries, Comdisco Disaster Recovery Services and Comdisco Technical Services, made significant progress in fiscal 1982. The addition of the Texas Disaster Recovery Center by December 31, 1982 will bring the number of centers to four, providing further evidence that Comdisco Disaster Recovery Services can provide its customers with the most comprehensive disaster backup services available. Comdisco Technical Services expanded its equipment installation and facilities planning operations and showed increased profitability.

Probably as significant as the record earnings results achieved in fiscal 1982, was the strengthening of Comdisco's financial position. Total assets increased 33% to $536.7 million, while stockholders' equity increased 55% to $9.1 million. The announcement in early November 1982 of the redemption of the Company's $50 million convertible debentures is anticipated to increase stockholders' equity to approximately $140 million and will reduce the Company's interest expense by $6.5 million per year. In addition, the Company had nearly $40 million in cash and marketable securities at September 30, 1982 while borrowing under various revolving credit agreements was zero. Because of its improved financial position, Comdisco is ideally situated to capitalize on opportunities in its traditional marketplace as well as those that arise in other areas.

Exhibit 3   Comdisco, Inc. Annual Report for Fiscal Year 1982 (abridged)

In September 1982 Raymond F. Sebastian, formerly President of Comdisco Financial Services (CFS), was appointed to the position of Senior Vice President/ Corporate Development of Comdisco and will devote full time to the analysis of various investment opportunities available to the Company. He was replaced as President of CFS by Basil R. Twist, Jr. who, with Mr. Sebastian, has formulated the strategies that have made CFS so successful since its formation in 1976. Michael J. O'Connell has resigned as Executive Vice President of Comdisco effective January 1, 1983 to pursue other endeavors, but will continue as a Director. Mr. O'Connell has been with Comdisco since 1971 and has made valuable contributions to the Company's success.

In March 1982 Comdisco split its common stock 3-for-2 and paid dividends in fiscal 1982 totaling $.23 per share, an increase of 28% over the prior year, as adjusted. More importantly, return on average stockholders' equity has averaged 34.0% over the last five years. This has occurred over a period of time in which most of the Company's borrowings, other than discounted lease rentals, have been eliminated.

Comdisco begins fiscal 1983 in a strong capital position with high liquidity, a strong, competitive market position and a comprehensive array of complementary services for its customers. The Company provides leasing and other cost-effective services which continue to be attractive despite the current economic outlook. The delivery of more IBM 3081 processors will also increase opportunities for Comdisco in its marketplace.

Perhaps more so than many companies, Comdisco relies on the determination, skill and creative energies of its employees for its past and future success. This is another factor that gives me much optimism for Comdisco's continued success. With the ongoing dedication of Comdisco's employees and the support of the Company's customers and stockholders, I am confident that Comdisco's superior growth rates in earnings and revenue can be maintained.

Kenneth N. Pontikes
Chairman of the Board and
President

November 11, 1982

Management's Discussion and Analysis of Financial Condition and Result of Operations

Summary

The Company continued to achieve outstanding growth during fiscal 1982 as total revenue and net earnings increased 56% and 88%, respectively, compared to fiscal 1981. Increases in revenue and net earnings were accomplished despite the recessionary economic climate. Total revenue for fiscal 1982 and 1981 was $471.6 million and $301.5 million respectively. Net earnings increased from $15.6 million, or $1.35 a share, in fiscal 1981 to a record of $29.4 million, or $2.27 a share in fiscal 1982. The primary factors contributing to the record earnings were the increased volume and profitability of financial services activity, the growth of the Company's lease and customer base, and the ability of the Company to capitalize on the active market for 3033 processors and disk storage devices.

Revenue

Total revenue for fiscal 1982 reflected increases in all activities. In fiscal 1981, total revenue increased 19% over fiscal 1980 total revenue, as a result of higher revenue from all activities other than sale of computer equipment. For the five year period ended September 30, 1982, the Company has achieved an annual compound growth rate of 25% for total revenue.

The growth of the Company's lease base continued on a strong trend during fiscal 1982. This growth has been achieved as a result of the increased demand for leasing, broader penetration of the market, and the increase of activity levels created by initial product deliveries by IBM. Leasing offers computer users flexibility through short term commitments and conserves capital in a weak economy. As a result of this growth, rental revenue of $206.6 million in fiscal 1982 and $131.6 million in fiscal 1981 represented increases of 57% and 62%, respectively, over the preceding year.

Revenue from the sale of computer equipment increased during fiscal 1982 as a result of the active market for the IBM 3033 processor. The market for 3033 processors was stimulated by initial deliveries

C

61

Exhibit 3   Comdisco, Inc. Annual Report for Fiscal Year 1982 (abridged)

of IBM's 3081 processor and by the impact of IBM purchase price reductions on the 3033, which improved its price/performance ratio. Revenue from the sale of computer equipment declined 16% in fiscal 1981 compared to fiscal 1980, primarily due to computer users' increased preference for leasing.

Financial services revenue totaled $73.9 million in fiscal 1982 in comparison to $30.8 million in fiscal 1981. The increase in financial services revenue was primarily the result of tax-advantaged computer leasing transactions associated with a portion of the Company's lease portfolio of used equipment and also tax benefit transfers that were structured under the Economic Recovery Tax Act of 1981. Fiscal 1981 financial services revenue increased 119% over fiscal 1980 due to higher revenue from tax leveraged leases with third-party investors.

Cost and Expenses

Total costs and expenses of $417.8 million for fiscal 1982 increased 49% over total costs and expenses of $280.2 million in fiscal 1981. Fiscal 1981 total costs and expenses were 15% higher than fiscal 1980. The increases were the result of the growth in the Company's lease portfolio and customer base and the continuing expansion in marketing of the Company's services.

Selling, general and administrative expenses were $51.8 million in fiscal 1982, $28.5 million in fiscal 1981 and $19.3 million in fiscal 1980. The increases were primarily due to costs associated with the Company's expanding marketing activities, including higher commissions and administrative expenses.

The increases in interest expense in fiscal 1982 and fiscal 1981 were due to increased discounted lease rentals as a result of the growth in the Company's leasing activity. Interest expense on discounted leases, which is a non-cash expense, is the largest component of total interest expense (69% and 46% of total interest expense in fiscal 1982 and 1981, respectively). The Company finances leases by assigning the noncancellable rentals to financial institutions on a nonrecourse basis at a fixed interest rate and receives from the lender the present value of the rental payments (the discounted amount). As rental payments are made directly to the lender, the Company recognizes interest expense.

Income Taxes

Income taxes as a percentage of earnings before income taxes were 45.4% in fiscal 1982 compared to 26.8% in fiscal 1981 and 20.8% in fiscal 1980. Note 7 of Notes to Consolidated Financial Statements provides details about the Company's income tax provisions and effective tax rates. The higher effective tax rate in fiscal 1982 was attributable to lower investment tax credits due to the sale of such benefits by the Company as permitted under the Economic Recovery Tax Act of 1981 (the "Act"). The Act liberalized the leasing provisions of the tax law and made it possible for corporations which cannot use all their current year tax deductions and credits to transfer them to other corporations. The tax benefit transfers completed by the Company in fiscal 1982 provided cash flow benefits which otherwise would not have been available until future years.

International Operations

The Company operated principally in three geographic areas during fiscal 1982 and 1981; United States, Europe and Canada. The Company has subsidiaries in Belgium, Germany, Switzerland, the Netherlands, France, the United Kingdom and Canada. These subsidiaries offer services similar to those offered in the United States.

A more favorable environment in fiscal 1982 resulted in an increase in revenue from international operations of 42% from $55.9 million in fiscal 1981 to $79.6 million in fiscal 1982. The prior year's results had been depressed as a result of computer users deferring action pending shipment of new products. International revenues represented 17% of the Company's total revenue in fiscal 1982, and 18% in fiscal 1981.

Market and Dividend Information

The Company's common stock is traded on the New York Stock Exchange under the symbol CDO. The following table shows the quarterly price range and dividends paid for fiscal years 1982 and 1981, adjusted to reflect the three-for-two and five-for-four common stock splits effected in March 1982 and 1981, respectively.

Exhibit 3 Comdisco, Inc. Annual Report for Fiscal Year 1982 (abridged)

	1982			1981		
Qtr.	High	Low	Div.	High	Low	Div.
1st	$18.00	$11.75	$.05	$13.27	$ 7.87	$.04
2nd	18.00	13.50	.06	15.50	11.50	.05
3rd	19.25	15.50	.06	16.09	13.17	.05
4th	23.00	15.00	.06	15.33	10.67	.05

At September 30, 1982, there were approximately 2,900 record holders of common stock.

Financial Position

During fiscal 1982, the Company's financial position and liquidity improved significantly, with cash and marketable securities amounting to $39.8 million at September 30, 1982 compared to $9.8 million at September 30, 1981. These improvements were due to an increased earnings level and continued emphasis on effective asset management. Major sources and uses of funds are set forth in the Consolidated Statements of Changes in Financial Position.

At September 30, 1982, the Company had $45 million of available borrowing capacity under various lines of credit from commercial banks. During fiscal 1982, the Company entered into agreements for the purpose of issuing commercial paper which may be used from time to time to meet some of the Company's short term debt requirements. These facilities ensure the availability of significant funds to finance additional growth.

The trend of computer users toward leasing rather than purchasing computer equipment is expected to continue due to economic conditions, IBM pricing policies, and new product announcements. The major portion of funds required by the Company to finance the purchase of equipment acquired for leasing is generated by assigning the noncancelable rentals to various financial institutions at fixed interest rates on a nonrecourse basis.

In June 1981, the Company sold $50 million of 13% convertible subordinated debentures. The proceeds of the lower cost, fixed-rate long term debt were used to replace bank borrowings. The Company had no short term debt at September 30, 1982.

Total notes and debentures as a percentage of total capital (the sum of notes and debentures payable, discounted lease rentals and stockholders' equity)

has declined in each of the last three fiscal years, to 16% at September 30, 1982, compared to 29% at September 30, 1980. Improved earnings have contributed to the high returns on average stockholders' equity. This key financial measure of performance reached 39.2% in fiscal 1982, compared with 30.6% in fiscal 1981. The Company's strong financial position and history of earnings growth provide a solid base for obtaining the necessary financial resources to finance additional growth and for investment opportunities.

Ratios

The following table presents ratios which illustrate the changes and trends for the last three fiscal years:

	1982	1981	1980
Return on average stockholders' equity	39.2%	30.6%	18.0%
Return on average assets	6.2%	4.9%	3.5%
Earnings before income taxes (as a percentage of revenue)	11.4%	7.1%	3.5%
Net earnings (as a percentage of revenue)	6.2%	5.2%	2.8%

C

63

Exhibit 3 Comdisco, Inc. Annual Report for Fiscal Year 1982 (abridged)

CONSOLIDATED FINANCIAL STATEMENTS

FIVE YEAR SELECTED FINANCIAL DATA

Years Ended September 30,	1982	1981	1980	1979	1978
Consolidated Summary of Earnings (in thousands):					
Revenue					
Rental	$206,592	$131,571	$ 80,979	$ 60,947	$ 42,524
Sale of computer equipment	166,705	125,384	149,708	149,983	103,995
Financial services	73,879	30,837	14,079	9,991	4,046
Other	24,454	13,746	8,348	4,355	2,717
Total Revenue	471,630	301,538	253,114	225,276	153,282
Cost and expenses					
Equipment depreciation, amortization and rental	160,523	99,413	68,328	47,698	32,260
Cost of computer equipment	149,654	111,784	134,595	128,470	93,176
Financial services	8,617	6,784	4,878	5,108	1,768
Selling, general and administrative	51,785	28,529	19,341	16,176	9,246
Interest	47,242	33,657	16,988	13,319	10,360
Total cost and expenses	417,821	280,167	244,130	210,771	146,810
Earnings before income taxes	53,809	21,371	8,984	14,505	6,472
Income taxes	24,432	5,730	1,870	3,900	1,550
Net earnings	$ 29,377	$ 15,641	$ 7,114	$ 10,605	$ 4,922
Common and Common Equivalent Share Data:					
Net earnings	$ 2.27	$ 1.35	$ .65	$ 1.07	$ .53
Stockholders' equity	$ 7.74	$ 5.17	$ 3.95	$ 3.50	$ 1.77
Average shares outstanding (in thousands)	14,487	12,270	11,051	9,929	9,222
Cash dividends paid	$ .23	$ .18	$ .15	$ .12	$ .06
Financial Position (in thousands):					
Total assets	$536,679	$404,507	$229,170	$173,950	$144,223
Total long-term debt	83,271	84,945	29,055	25,573	25,447
Discounted lease rentals	261,780	197,672	85,612	74,569	61,703
Stockholders' equity	91,056	58,746	43,565	35,508	14,994

Common and common equivalent share data have been adjusted to reflect a three-for-two stock split effected in February 1978, a two-for-one common stock split effected July 1978, a three-for-two common stock split effected in February 1979, a five-for-four common stock split effected in March 1981, and a three-for-two common stock split effected in March 1982.

Exhibit 3   Comdisco, Inc. Annual Report for Fiscal Year 1982 (abridged)

CONSOLIDATED BALANCE SHEETS
(in thousands except number of shares)

September 30,	1982	1981
ASSETS		
Cash and marketable securities (at cost of $3,909 in 1982 and $1,883 in 1981 which approximates market)	$ 39,762	$ 9,848
Receivables:		
Accounts and notes (Net of allowance for doubtful accounts of $628 in 1982 and $528 in 1981)	41,368	28,379
Other	3,687	3,827
Inventory of computer equipment	35,382	25,036
Net investment in sales-type and direct financing leases	23,682	17,890
Leased and other equipment:		
Leased computer equipment	502,494	374,044
Capitalized leases—computer equipment	24,158	23,225
Buildings, furniture and other	7,959	4,184
Total equipment	534,611	401,453
Less: accumulated depreciation and amortization	192,714	115,073
Net equipment	341,897	286,380
Other assets and deferred charges	50,901	33,147
	$536,679	$404,507
LIABILITIES AND STOCKHOLDERS' EQUITY		
Note payable to bank	$ 2,385	$ 3,445
Convertible subordinated debentures	50,000	50,000
Subordinated debentures	12,250	12,250
Accounts payable	19,110	27,492
Obligations under capital leases	18,636	19,250
Income taxes:		
Current	6,076	—
Deferred	30,121	13,017
Other liabilities	45,265	22,635
Discounted lease rentals	261,780	197,672
	445,623	345,761
Stockholders' equity:		
Common stock $.10 par value. Authorized 50,000,000 shares in 1982 and 15,000,000 shares in 1981; issued 11,769,043 shares (7,571,151 in 1981)	1,177	757
Additional paid-in capital	18,965	14,630
Deferred translation adjustment	(354)	—
Retained earnings	71,268	43,359
Total stockholders' equity	91,056	58,746
	$536,679	$404,507

See accompanying notes to consolidated financial statements.

C

65

Exhibit 3   Comdisco, Inc. Annual Report for Fiscal Year 1982 (abridged)

CONSOLIDATED STATEMENTS OF EARNINGS
(in thousands except per share data)

Years Ended September 30,	1982	1981	1980
Revenue			
Rental	$206,592	$131,571	$ 80,979
Sale of computer equipment	166,705	125,384	149,708
Financial services	73,879	30,837	14,079
Other	24,454	13,746	8,348
Total revenue	471,630	301,538	253,114
Cost and Expenses			
Equipment depreciation, amortization and rental	160,523	99,413	68,328
Cost of computer equipment	149,654	111,784	134,595
Financial services	8,617	6,784	4,878
Selling, general and administrative	51,785	28,529	19,341
Interest	47,242	33,657	16,988
Total costs and expenses	417,821	280,167	244,130
Earnings before income taxes	53,809	21,371	8,984
Income taxes	24,432	5,730	1,870
Net Earnings	$ 29,377	$ 15,641	$ 7,114
Net Earnings Per Common and Common Equivalent Share	$ 2.27	$ 1.35	$ .65

See accompanying notes to consolidated financial statements.

Exhibit 3   Comdisco, Inc. Annual Report for Fiscal Year 1982 (abridged)

CONSOLIDATED STATEMENTS OF STOCKHOLDERS' EQUITY
(in thousands)

Years Ended September 30, 1982, 1981 and 1980

	Common Stock $.10 Par Palue	Additional Paid-in Capital	Retained Earnings	Deferred Translation Adjustment
Balance at September 30, 1979	$ 541	$12,405	$22,56	$ —
Net earnings	—	—	7,114	—
Dividends paid	—	—	(865)	—
Stock options exercised	46	639	—	—
Income tax benefits resulting from exercise of non-qualified stock options	—	1,123	—	—
Balance at September 30, 1980	587	14,167	28,811	—
Net earnings	—	—	15,641	—
Dividends paid	—	—	(1,093)	—
Stock split	148	(148)	—	—
Stock options exercised	22	611	—	—
Balance at September 30, 1981	757	14,630	43,359	—
Cumulative amount as of September 30, 1981	—	—	—	(232)
Net earnings	—	—	29,377	—
Dividends paid	—	—	(1,468)	—
Stock split	391	(400)	—	—
Stock options exercised	14	835	—	—
Common stock issued	15	2,648	—	—
Translation adjustment	—	—	—	(122)
Income tax benefits resulting from exercise of non-qualified stock options	—	1,252	—	—
Balance at September 30, 1982	$1,177	$18,965	$71,26	$(354)

See accompanying notes to consolidated financial statements.

Exhibit 3   Comdisco, Inc. Annual Report for Fiscal Year 1982 (abridged)

CONSOLIDATED STATEMENTS OF CHANGES IN FINANCIAL POSITION
(in thousands)

Years Ended September 30,	1982	1981	1980
Source of Funds:			
From operations			
Net earnings	$ 29,377	$ 15,641	$ 7,114
Noncash charges (credits) to operations:			
Depreciation and amortization	133,902	77,528	46,212
Increase in receivables	(12,849)	(5,531)	(12,278)
Investment in sales-type and direct financing leases	(5,792)	(11,732)	323
Income taxes	23,180	5,730	747
Increase in accounts payable and accrued liabilities	14,248	18,611	11,322
Other, net	474	(1,233)	2,490
Total provided from operations	182,540	99,014	55,930
Proceeds from issuance of subordinated debentures	—	48,560	—
Increase (decrease) in notes payable	(1,060)	(33,460)	25,339
Obligations under capital leases	5,663	14,249	2,885
Discounted lease rentals	145,626	183,557	62,786
Other	4,201	924	766
	336,970	312,844	147,706
Application of Funds:			
Increase in leased equipment and inventory	190,180	202,002	75,361
Reduction of discounted lease rentals and obligations under capital leases	87,795	75,781	55,916
Purchase of subordinated debentures	—	2,162	—
Capitalized leases—computer equipment	5,663	14,249	2,885
Other assets and deferred charges	21,950	12,343	13,555
Cash dividends	1,468	1,093	865
	307,056	307,630	148,582
Increase (decrease) in cash and marketable securities	29,914	5,214	(876)
Cash and marketable securities at beginning of year	9,848	4,634	5,510
Cash and marketable securities at end of year	$ 39,762	$ 9,848	$ 4,634

See accompanying notes to consolidated financial statements.

Exhibit 3   Comdisco, Inc. Annual Report for Fiscal Year 1982 (abridged)

NOTES TO CONSOLIDATED FINANCIAL STATEMENTS

1. Summary of Significant Accounting Policies

Principles of Consolidation: The accompanying consolidated financial statements include the accounts of the Company and its wholly-owned subsidiaries after elimination of intercompany accounts and transactions.

Revenue Recognition: Leases are accounted for either as sales-type, direct financing or operating leases. Lease terms generally range from four months to five years. Revenue from sales-type leases is recorded upon acceptance of the equipment by the customer and is reflected as sale of computer equipment. Revenue from direct financing leases is recorded over the term of the lease as interest income calculated using the interest method. Rental revenue from operating leases is recognized in equal monthly amounts over the term of the lease.

Revenue from the sale of computer equipment and the related cost of equipment is reflected in earnings at the time of acceptance of the equipment by the customer.

Revenue from the sale of equipment subject to operating leases is recognized at the closing of the transactions and is included as sale of computer equipment in fiscal 1981 and 1980. In addition to this revenue, the Company is also entitled to the use of such equipment subsequent to the lease expiration date for periods ranging generally from six months to four years. Revenue, if any, from the re-leasing of such equipment during this period is recognized upon acceptance of the equipment by the customer and is reflected as other revenue.

Under the provisions of the Economic Recovery Tax Act of 1981, the Company sold the tax benefits (investment tax credits and cost recovery allowances) on new equipment purchased for the Company's lease portfolio. The proceeds from the sale of tax benefits are recorded as financial services revenue. Also included as financial services revenue are fees for arranging tax benefit transfer agreements with third parties.

Fees from the sale of equipment included in the Company's lease portfolio of used equipment are recognized at the closing of the transactions and included as financial services revenue. Such transac-

tions, which are structured as tax advantaged leases, entitle the Company to the use of such equipment for periods ranging generally from one to six years subsequent to the initial lease expiration date.

The Company, through its CFS subsidiary, has entered into certain computer equipment transactions in which it has leased equipment (the "Lease") and in turn has subleased such equipment (the "Sublease"). In substantially all of these transactions, the Lease term exceeds the Sublease term. Monthly Sublease rentals are greater than the monthly Lease rentals; however, the present value of the total Sublease rentals ("Sublease Proceeds") may be less than the present value of the total Lease rentals ("Lease Obligations") due to the difference in lease terms. Rentals from the sublease are discounted by the Company with a financial institution on a nonrecourse basis. An escrow account is established to fund the Company's obligations under the lease for the period after the expiration of the Sublease. In the event the Sublease Proceeds exceed the Lease Obligations, the Company recognizes profit. When Lease Obligations exceed the Sublease Proceeds, no profit is recognized and the next excess Lease Obligation is deferred to be recovered from the Company's right to future rentals during the remaining term of the Lease. At September 30, 1982 and 1981, $21,258,000 and $10,148,000, respectively, of costs were deferred in connection with such transactions and are included in the balance sheet caption "Other assets and deferred charges." The Company recognized $3,113,000, $4,286,000, and $1,890,000 of interest income on investments held in escrow during the years ended September 30, 1982, 1981 and 1980, respectively.

Inventory of Computer Equipment: Inventory of computer equipment is stated at the lower of cost or market.

Equipment, Depreciation and Amortization: Leased equipment owned by the Company is generally recorded at cost. Depreciation and amortization of leased equipment are computed on the straight-line method for financial reporting purposes to estimated fair market value at lease termination (See Note 2).

C

69

Exhibit 3   Comdisco, Inc. Annual Report for Fiscal Year 1982 (abridged)

Deferred Lease Costs: Salesmen's commissions and other direct expenses related to operating leases are deferred and amortized over the lease term.

Income Taxes and Investment Tax Credits: Deferred income taxes have been provided for income and expenses which are recognized in different periods for income tax purpose than for financial reporting purposes. Investment tax credits are accounted for on a flow-through basis.

Profit Sharing Plan: The Company has a profit sharing plan covering all employees. Company contributions to the plan are based on a percentage of employees' compensation, as defined. Profit sharing payments are based on amounts accumulated on an individual employees basis. Profit sharing expense for the years ended September 30, 1982, 1981 and 1980 amounted to $590,000, $489,000 and $178,000, respectively.

Earnings Per Share: Earnings per common and common equivalent share are computed based on the weighted average number of common and common equivalent shares outstanding during each period including the assumed conversion of the 13% convertible subordinated debentures, after elimination of the related interest expense (net of tax) and after giving retroactive effect to the three-for-two split effected in March 1982 (See Note 9). Dilutive stock options included in the number of common and common equivalent shares are based on the treasury stock method. The number of common and common equivalent shares used in the computation of earnings per share for the years ended September 30, 1982, 1981 and 1980 were 14,486,738, 12,269,703 and 11,050,277, respectively.

Foreign Currency Translation: Fiscal 1982 consolidated financial statements have been prepared in accordance with Financial Accounting Standards Board Statement No. 52, "Foreign Currency Translation," the provisions of which were adopted by the Company on a prospective basis as of October 1, 1981. Previous consolidated financial statements have been prepared in accordance with Statement No. 8, "Accounting for the Translation of Foreign Currency Transactions and Foreign Currency Financial Statements." The effect of the change was not material.

2. Depreciable Lives

Effective October 1, 1980 the Company extended its estimates of depreciable lives of certain IBM peripheral equipment. Effective January 1, 1981 the Company extended its estimates of depreciable lives and salvage values of certain IBM peripheral equipment. Previously, this equipment was depreciated to zero by September 30, 1983. The changes in estimates were made based on revised market conditions and reflect current estimates of the equipment's useful lives and salvage values. The effect of the changes on recorded leased equipment at the effective dates of the changes was an increase in net earnings of $4,488,000 (net of income taxes of $4,142,000), or $.37 per share, for the year ended September 30, 1981.

3. Investment in Sales-Type and Direct Financing Leases

The following table lists the components of the net investment in sales-type and direct financing leases as of September 30:

	1982	1981
	(in thousands)	
Minimum lease payments receivable	$24,142	$18,504
Estimated residual values of leased property	12,324	9,160
Less unearned income	12,784	9,774
Net investment in sales-type and direct financing leases	$23,682	$17,890

Future minimum lease payments to be received under the above lease agreements are as follows:

Years ending September 30	Sales-type and direct financing leases
	(in thousands)
1983	$ 7,306
1984	7,416
1985	5,534
1986	2,637
1987	1,249
	$24,142

The Company finances most sales-type and direct financing leases by assigning the non-cancellable

Exhibit 3   Comdisco, Inc. Annual Report for Fiscal Year 1982 (abridged)

rentals on a non-recourse basis. The proceeds from the assignment reduce the investment in sales-type and direct financing leases. Any gain or loss on the assignment is recognized at the time of such assignment.

4. Capitalized Leases

Capitalized leases – computer equipment at September 30 is comprised of the following:

	1982	1981
	(in thousands)	
Capitalized leases – computer equipment	$24,158	$23,225
Less accumulated amortization	15,354	12,099
Net capitalized leases – computer equipment	$ 8,804	$11,126

At September 30, 1982, the Company, as lessee, was obligated to pay rentals under capitalized leases. The related equipment has been subleased and accounted for either as operating leases or as direct financing leases. The following table summarizes minimum rentals payable by the Company as lessee under capitalized leases:

Years ending September 30	Capitalized leases
	(in thousands)
1983	$ 8,196
1984	6,987
1985	4,801
1986	2,618
1987	1,810
Later years	521
Total minimum lease payments	24,933
Less imputed interest (9% to 17%)	6,297
Present value of net mimum lease payments	$18,636

Total minimum lease payments for capitalized leases have not been reduced by minimum non-cancelable sublease rentals of $16,094,000 due the Company in the future.

5. Bank Borrowings and Compensating Balances

The Company has a revolving credit agreement which entitles the Company to borrow up to $25,000,000 on an unsecured basis. The agreement, which expires March 31, 1983, carries an interest cost of prime rate (13.5% at September 30, 1982) and includes a fee of 3/8% per annum of the average daily unused amount. If the Company or the bank elects not to renew the agreement, the loan becomes a two-year term loan payable in equal quarterly installments with an interest cost of prime rate plus 1%. Under the agreement, the Company is required to maintain a defined debt to net worth ratio and dividend payments cannot exceed 20% of consolidated net earnings subsequent to September 30, 1980. At September 30, 1982, approximately $4,280,000 of retained earnings were available for payment of dividends.

In accordance with the terms of the agreement, the Company is required to maintain average cash balances with the bank equal to 5% of the $25,000,000 loan commitment. The amount of unused available borrowings under the agreement was $25,000,000 at September 30, 1982.

At September 30, 1982, the Company had additional unused lines of credit totaling $20,000,000 under which borrowings would bear interest at the prime rate. Under the agreements, the Company is required to maintain compensating balances equal to 5% of the outstanding borrowings.

6. Note Payable to Bank and Subordinated Debentures

Note Payable to Bank: The note payable to bank at September 30, 1982 and 1981 was an 11¾% term note payable in quarterly installments through December, 1984.

13% Convertible Subordinated Debentures: In June 1981, the Company issued $50,000,000 of 13% convertible subordinated debentures ("Convertible Debentures") due in 2001. Issue costs of $1,440,000 relating to the Convertible Debenture may be converted into shares of common stock of the Company, prior to maturity, at the option of the convertible Debenture holder at a conversion price of $19.50 per share.

The Convertible Debentures are redeemable in full or in part at the option of the company beginning in 1981 at an amount equal to 113.0% of the principal amount of the Convertible Debentures, the premium on redemption declining 1.3% per annum

C

71

Exhibit 3   Comdisco, Inc. Annual Report for Fiscal Year 1982 (abridged)

commencing in 1982 through 1991, and redeemable thereafter at par.

11½% Subordinated Debentures: At September 30, 1982, $12,250,000 of 11½% subordinated debentures (the "Debentures") due December 1, 1992, were outstanding. Annual sinking fund payments of $1,350,000 (9% of the aggregate original principal amount) commence December 1, 1982, and are calculated to retire 90% of the issue prior to maturity. During fiscal 1981, the Company, in connection with future sinking fund requirements, acquired $2,750,000 principal amount of the outstanding debentures which resulted in a gain of $318,000 (net of income taxes of $270,000).

Both the Debentures and the Convertible Debentures are subordinated to all senior indebtedness as defined in the indenture agreements. At September 30, 1982, the Company's senior indebtedness was approximately $2,473,000.

The annual maturities and sinking fund requirements of the note payable and subordinated debentures for the next five years are as follows:

Years ending September 30	Aggregate Maturities
	(in thousands)
1983	$1,060
1984	1,060
1985	1,565
1986	1,350
1987	1,350

7. Income Taxes

The following data relate to the provision for income taxes for the years ended September 30:

	1982	1981	1980
Provision in lieu of income taxes	$1,252	—	$1,123
Current:			
Federal	5,000	—	—
State	1,076	—	—
	6,076	—	—
Deferred:			
Federal	16,281	4,216	147
State	273	553	220
Foreign	550	961	380
	17,104	5,730	747
Total tax provision	$24,432	$5,730	$1,870

	1982	1981	1980
Earnings before income taxes:			
Domestic	$51,166	$18,992	$8,203
Foreign	2,643	2,379	781
Total	$53,809	$21,371	$8,984

Income tax benefits of $1,252,000 and $1,123,000 resulting from the exercise of non-qualified stock options were utilized to reduce the current Federal tax provision in fiscal 1982 and 1980, respectively.

The reasons for the difference between the U.S. Federal income tax rate of 46% and the effective income tax rate were as follows:

	Percentage of Pretax Earnings		
Years ended September 30,	1982	1981	1980
U.S. Federal income tax	46.0%	46.0%	46.0%
Increase (reduction) resulting from:			
Domestic International Sales Corporation tax benefit	(.1)	(1.2)	(6.8)
Reduction of deferred income taxes applicable to investment tax credit carryforward	—	(20.4)	(20.1)
Investment tax credit	(2.0)	—	—
State income taxes, net of U.S. tax benefit	1.4	1.2	1.1
Other – net	.1	1.2	.6
	45.4%	26.8%	20.8%

The Company has not provided for income taxes on the unremitted earnings of the Domestic International Sales Corporation (DISC) subsidiary aggregating $4,253,000 through September 30, 1982, since the Company intends to postpone indefinitely the remittance of such earnings.

Deferred income taxes provided for timing differences were as follows:

Years ended September 30,	1982	1981	1980
	(in thousands)		
Sale of tax benefits	$38,661	—	—
Difference between depreciation for tax purposes and financial statement purposes	(18,125)	6,311	570
Deferred compensation expense	754	(754)	—
Deferred leasing income	2,934	(2,093)	—
Deferred leasing costs	1,518	1,164	793
Portion of undistributed earnings in DISC	(178)	(454)	231

Exhibit 3   Comdisco, Inc. Annual Report for Fiscal Year 1982 (abridged)

Years ended September 30,	1982	1981	1980
Difference between leases accounted for as sales-type leases for financial statement purposes and operating leases for tax purposes	(23,601)	194	2,915
Reinstatement (reduction) of deferred income taxes applicable to:			
Investment tax credit carryforward	12,021	(4,356)	(1,803)
Tax net operating loss realization (carryforward)	—	2,323	(650)
Income tax benefit resulting from exercise of non-qualified stock options	—	1,903	(1,123)
Other – net	3,120	1,492	(186)
	$17,104	$5,730	$747

8. Discounted Lease Rentals

Leased equipment owned by the Company is financed by assigning the noncancellable rentals to various lenders at fixed interest rates on a nonrecourse basis. The proceeds from the assignment of the lease rentals (discounted lease rentals) represent payments due under the lease discounted to their present value at the interest rate charged by the lender, generally ranging from 10% to 19%. The difference between monthly rentals due under discounted leases and the amortization of related discounted lease rentals represents interest expense. This expense amounted to $32,527,000, $15,468,000 and $8,380,000 in 1982, 1981 and 1980, respectively. In the event of default by the lessee, the lender has a first lien against the underlying leased equipment, with no further recourse against the Company.

9. Common Stock and Additional Paid-in Capital

On January 27, 1982, the Board of Directors declared a three-for-two split of the Company's common stock. This distribution was subject to the stockholders approval, which was obtained, amending the Certificate of Incorporation increasing the number of authorized shares from 15,000,000 to 50,000,000 with the par value remaining at $.10

per share. On January 28, 1981, the Board of Directors of the Company declared a five-for-four split of the Company's common stock. All references in the financial statements and notes to the number of shares of common stock and per share amounts have been adjusted for the aforementioned stock splits.

On November 18, 1981, the Board of Directors approved the Settlement Agreement (the "Agreement") between the Company and participants in the Residual Incentive Compensation Plan (the "Plan") related to vested residual computer interests. The Plan provided in part for the allocation of a percentage interest in the residual value of computer equipment to the participants. The Agreement was approved by the stockholders on March 15, 1982, and pursuant to the terms of the Agreement, the Company distributed to participants in accordance with the terms of the Plan, the aggregate sum of $3,000,000 plus 150,000 shares of the Company's common stock.

Dividends on Common Stock: Common stock dividends paid were $.23 per share in 1982 compared with $.18 in 1981 and $.15 in 1980. Certain officers and directors of the Company and their affiliates, owning an aggregate of 5,028,645 shares (43%) of the outstanding common stock at September 30, 1982, have waived their rights to any cash dividends through February 1, 1983 and did not receive any of the previously mentioned cash dividends.

At September 30, 1982, the Company had reserved the following number of common shares for future issuance:

1979 Stock Option Plan	334,438
1981 Stock Option Plan	750,000
Employee Stock Purchase Plan	147,358
Conversion of Convertible Subordinated Debentures	2,564,103
	3,795,899

10. Stock Options and Stock Purchase Plan

On November 18, 1981, the Board of Directors amended the Company's 1979 Stock Option Plan (the "1979 Plan") to qualify the plan as an incentive stock option plan in accordance with the provisions

C

73

Exhibit 3 Comdisco, Inc. Annual Report for Fiscal Year 1982 (abridged)

of the Economic Recovery Tax Act of 1981. All outstanding stock options, which retained their original option price, are eligible for treatment as incentive stock options subject to certain limitations as defined in the amended 1979 Plan.

On January 27, 1982, the stockholders approved the 1981 Stock Option Plan (the "1981 Plan"). An aggregate of 750,000 shares were reserved for issuance pursuant to the exercise of options under the 1981 plan.

The Comdisco, Inc. Employee Stock Purchase Plan (the "Stock Plan") was adopted by the Board of Directors on November 17, 1981. An aggregate of 150,000 shares was reserved for issuance under the Stock Plan.

The changes in the number of shares under the option plans during 1982, 1981 and 1980 were as follows:

	1982	1981	1980
	(in thousands except option price range)		
Number of shares:			
Shares under option beginning of the year	512	861	1,119
Options granted	169	—	612
Options exercised	(188)	(349)	(870)
Shares under option end of year	493	512	861
Aggregate option price:			
Shares under option beginning of year	$2,533	$3,257	$480
Options granted	3,284	—	3,187
Options exercised	(850)	(724)	(410)
Shares under option end of the year	$4,967	$2,533	$3,257
Options exercisable at end of year	58	164	12
Aggregate option price of exercisable options outstanding at end of year	$295	$722	$19
Options available for future grant at end of year	591	11	11
Option price range	$4.90–$19.38	$1.35–$7.00	$.12–$7.00

11. Operating Leases

The following table summarizes the Company's future rentals receivable and payable under non-cancellable operating leases existing at September 30, 1982 for computer equipment and rentals payable for non-computer equipment and office space:

Years ending Sept. 30	Computer equipment		Rents payable on subleased equipment	Other rents payable
	Rents Receivable on Equipment			
	Owned	Subleased		
1983	$180,581	$21,704	$25,497	$2,033
1984	107,125	13,269	12,197	1,735
1985	43,115	5,799	5,002	1,600
1986	7,237	1,742	792	1,033
1987	352	544	—	233
Later years	11	—	—	77

Total rental income and related expense for the years ended September 30, 1982, 1981 and 1980 applicable to computer sublease activities are as follows:

Years ending September 30	Rental income	Rental expense
	(in thousands)	
1982	$23,633	$27,455
1981	24,152	22,415
1980	22,614	22,455

12. Commitments and Contingent Liabilities

At September 30, 1982, the Company was obligated under the following commitments: (1) to purchase computer equipment in the approximate aggregate amount of $31,768,000, (2) to sell computer equipment in the approximate aggregate amount of $20,926,000, and (3) to lease computer equipment to others with an aggregate initial term rental of approximately $55,107,000.

The Company has arranged for approximately $74,000,000 of letters of credit, primarily as guarantees for certain of the Company's sublease obligations and for future purchases of IBM equipment. The cost of such letters of credit range between ½% and ¾% per annum of the amount outstanding.

Exhibit 3   Comdisco, Inc. Annual Report for Fiscal Year 1982 (abridged)

Accountants' Report

The Stockholders and Board of Directors Comdisco, Inc.:

We have examined the consolidated balance sheets of Comdisco, Inc. and subsidiaries as of September 30, 1982 and 1981 and the related consolidated statements of earnings, stockholders' equity and changes in financial position for each of the years in the three year period ended September 30, 1982. Our examinations were made in accordance with generally accepted auditing standards and, accordingly, included such tests of the accounting records and such other auditing procedures as we considered necessary in the circumstance.

In our opinion, the aforementioned consolidated financial statements present fairly the financial position of Comdisco, Inc. and subsidiaries at September 30, 1982 and 1981 and the results of their operations and the changes in their financial position for each of the years in the three-year period ended September 30, 1982, in conformity with generally accepted accounting principles applied on a consistent basis.

Peat, Marwick, Mitchell & Co.
Chicago, Illinois
November 9, 1982

Quarterly Financial Data

Summarized Quarterly Financial data for the fiscal years ended September 30, 1982 and 1981, is as follows:

(in thousands of dollars except per share amounts)

Quarter ended:	December 31		March 31		June 30		September 30	
	1981	1980	1982	1981	1982	1981	1982	1981
Total revenue	$121,189	$78,833	$118,309	$64,450	$94,691	$75,722	$137,441	$82,533
Net earnings	9,604	3,285	5,934	3,146	5,824	4,075	8,015	5,135
Net earnings per common and common equivalent share	$.73	$.29	$.47	$.27	$.46	$.35	$.61	$.42

Comdisco, Inc. (B)

A published report implying that the accounting practices of computer leasing giant Comdisco, Inc. could result in overstated earnings has provoked strong rebuttals from the leasing industry while rattling the skeleton of the OPM Leasing Services, Inc. scandal.

The report appeared last week in Barron's financial weekly and suggested that internal and external forces are mixing to create a potential disaster scenario for Comdisco as well as other third-party lessors. Meanwhile, the report stated, company officers, including founder and chairman Kenneth Pontikes, have gone on a Comdisco stock-selling spree in the past two years, getting rich in the process.

After publication of the report, Comdisco's stock lost nearly 37% of its paper value in one frenzied day of trading last Monday, falling from $38 to $24 per share.[1]

The October 17, 1983 issue of *Computerworld* magazine carried the above report on Comdisco, Inc.

BUSINESS HISTORY AND OPERATIONS[2]

Comdisco, Inc. is a Chicago-based company founded in 1969 by its current chairman of the board and president, Kenneth Pontikes. The company originally began as an IBM computer dealer. As demand for computer leasing started to grow during the late 1970s, the company started emphasizing leasing operations. By 1982, leasing old and new IBM computer equipment constituted the primary business activity of the company, and Comdisco had become the largest computer leasing company. Comdisco's customers were primarily large corporations. In 1982, the company had business relationships with 70 percent of the Fortune 500 companies, including 49 of the 50 largest U.S. companies.

This case was prepared by Professor Krishna G. Palepu as the basis for class discussion rather than to illustrate either effective or ineffective handling of an administrative situation. Copyright © 1987 by the President and Fellows of Harvard College. Harvard Business School case 9-186-299.

1. *Reprinted with permission from Computerworld, October 17, 1983*
2. *This section and the next, Tax Advantaged Transactions, can be skipped by those who read Comdisco, Inc. (A) (case 9-186-299).*

The computer remarketing industry had many participants: small independent operators, larger private organizations, and leasing subsidiaries of conglomerates. Comdisco was one of the few independent public corporations in the industry. The firms in the industry were primarily of two types: broker/dealers or third-party lessors. The broker/dealers obtained for customers computer equipment from either a vendor or current user; third-party lessors provided lease financing. Comdisco engaged in both these activities.

Comdisco achieved its dominance in the computer leasing industry through a strategy of full-service leasing. Under this strategy, the company offered its customers a number of services which were not offered by competitors. Comdisco's subsidiaries, Comdisco Technical Services, Inc. and Comdisco Transport, Inc., specialized in equipment refurbishment, delivery, installation, de-installation, and technical planning and site preparation. Comdisco Maintenance Services, another subsidiary, offered a low-cost alternative to IBM's maintenance service. Comdisco Disaster Recovery Services, Inc. was established to provide another valuable service to the company's customers: contingent data processing capacity to be used when a customer's own data center had unavoidable failures. Through this service, Comdisco's customers had access to four fully operational data centers located as a backup to their own data centers, to be used in the event of a natural disaster or accident.

Comdisco's broad customer base provided the company with a number of competitive advantages. First, taking advantage of its access to 10,000 important users of IBM equipment in the U.S., the company created a proprietary data base of their computing needs. This data base provided Comdisco's sales force with current and timely information on potential customers and their requirements. Second, being the leading IBM dealer, Comdisco maintained large inventories of a broad range of IBM equipment. Comdisco's personnel closely monitored IBM's new products and pricing policies. This product knowledge combined with large inventories enabled the company to assist customers with their computer acquisition plans and to offer quick deliveries. Finally, using its data base, the company could help its customers sell their old hardware when they acquired new equipment from Comdisco.

While the above strategy enabled Comdisco to establish its dominance over others in the computer leasing industry, the company was still potentially vulnerable to competition from IBM itself since IBM equipment accounted for most of Comdisco's revenues. In 1981, IBM formed a financing subsidiary, IBM Credit Corporation, to provide customer financing. Shortly after than, IBM announced its intention to enter into computer leasing and established a joint venture for this purpose with Merrill Lynch and Metropolitan Life Insurance. A number of industry analysts felt that this might result in increased competition for companies like Comdisco.

Comdisco's management, however, felt that IBM's recent moves did not pose a threat to the company's competitive position because IBM's entry into leasing would enhance the tarnished image of the computer leasing business, a net benefit to the industry. They also believed that, as IBM began to emphasize outright sale of its equipment over short-term rentals, many of IBM's customers might be forced to look for other lessors like

Comdisco who offered short-term leases. This was likely to provide additional business opportunities which would offset any loss of long-term lease business to IBM.

While equipment leasing to computer users was Comdisco's primary activity, the company also offered tax-oriented leases to investors who were primarily interested in the tax benefits associated with leasing. In recent years, the financial services income from the tax advantaged transactions accounted for a growing portion of the company's revenues.

TAX ADVANTAGED TRANSACTIONS

In addition to leasing equipment to computer users, Comdisco undertook leasing transactions with investors who were interested in tax shelters. While the specific terms and conditions of these tax advantaged transactions varied, a typical transaction was as follows:

1. After the inception of the initial user lease and independent of it, Comdisco sold all the leased equipment to a third party investor. This sale usually occurred three to nine months after the commencement of the initial user lease. The sales price equaled the then current fair market value of the equipment. The payment from the investor to Comdisco consisted of: (a) cash and a negotiable interest-bearing promissory note due within two years for 10–22 percent of the sales price (the "equity payment") and (b) an installment note for the balance payable over an 84-month period.
2. Simultaneously with the sale, Comdisco leased the equipment back from the investors for 84 months. The lease payments under the leaseback obligation were equal to the installment payments receivable by Comdisco from the investor (1.b).
3. As part of the leaseback arrangement, during the 61st through 84th months of the leaseback period, the investor shared in the re-lease proceeds that the company received from subleasing the equipment to a user. Upon the expiration of the leaseback period, the investor had the exclusive right to the equipment.

The net result of the above transaction was that Comdisco gave up the depreciation tax benefit, a portion of the rental revenues for months 61–84, and 100 percent of the equipment value after the 84th month. In return, the company received the nonrefundable equity payment (1.a).

If the equipment sold to the investor was originally under an operating lease, the equity payment was recorded by Comdisco as financial services revenue in the period in which the tax advantaged transaction occurred. From the fourth quarter of 1983, the company began to allocate as cost of financial services a portion of the net book value of the equipment at lease termination. For sales-type and direct financing leases, the equity payment was first applied to reduce a portion of the residual value of the equipment shown in the balance sheet (as investment in sales-type and direct financing leases). This is because the company's ability to recover the residual value was decreased due to the rental sharing under the tax advantaged transaction. The excess of the equity payment over the residual value reduction was recorded as financial services revenue in the period in which the tax advantaged transaction occurred.

THE BARRON'S ARTICLE

The October 10, 1983 issue of *Barron's,* a widely circulated financial weekly, carried an article on Comdisco, "Something Doesn't Compute: A Hard Look at Comdisco's Accounting." The article, excerpts from which are given in Exhibit 2, focused on four areas: the company's accounting, competition from IBM Credit Corporation, the company's tax advantaged leasing program, and the sale of company stock by insiders.

The article attracted considerable attention on Wall Street, leading to hectic trading of the company's stock. The company's stock price dropped from $38.250 to $22.875 by the end of the week, representing a loss of about $453.5 million in the market value of the company (see Exhibit 1 for data on Comdisco's stock price).

In response to these events, Kenneth Pontikes, president of Comdisco, issued a letter to shareholders on October 12, 1983. The letter addressed the issues raised in the *Barron's* article and attempted to rebut the charges (see Exhibit 3). Pontikes concluded:

> *[Finally,] it is important for you, our stockholders, to understand completely that Comdisco is stronger financially than it has ever been; that we have greater opportunities before us than at any time in our history; and that management is dedicated to retaining stockholder confidence and enhancing stockholder wealth.*

Shortly after the above developments, Comdisco released its annual report for fiscal 1983 (Exhibit 4).

QUESTIONS

1. Evaluate *Barron's* criticism of Comdisco's accounting and the company's response. Do you agree with the company or *Barron's*?
2. Compare the level of disclosure in Comdisco's annual reports in the (A) and (B) cases. Do you think the company's poor disclosure prior to 1983 made it vulnerable to the attack by *Barron's*? Would the market reaction to the *Barron's* article have been different if the company had a better disclosure policy?
3. Do you think Comdisco's stock in November 1983 was a "buy"?

EXHIBIT 1

Movement of Comdisco's Stock Price and S&P 500 Index, January 1982–November 1983

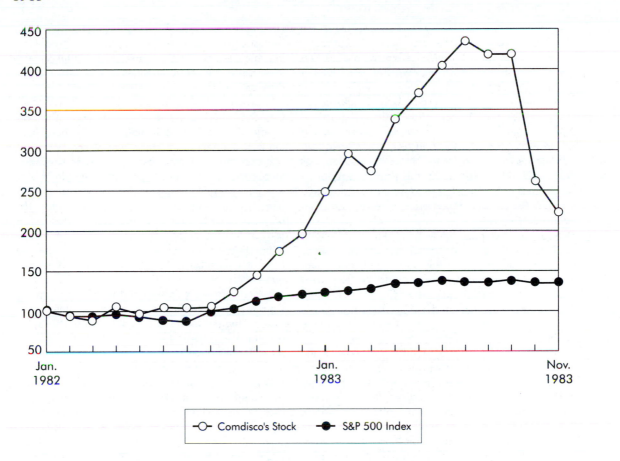

C

81

EXHIBIT 2

"Something Doesn't Compute—A Hard Look at Comdisco Accounting Practices"[3]

Rhonda Brammer, *Barron's*, October 10, 1983:

Twenty years ago, Ken Pontikes sold computer tapes and tab cards for IBM. He was paid $5,000 a year. When he lit out on his own five years later—starting up a one-man brokerage business in computers—his whole idea, he says "was to make a nice living." That start-up operation today is Chicago-based Comdisco, the biggest computer leasing company in the country. And yes, the 43-year-old Pontikes is making a living. His compensation was $2.4 million last year. So far this year, he's reported stock sales of $2.6 million. And his stake in the company, at the current market price, is worth $200 million plus.

His company could now be ranked an old-timer in the volatile computer leasing business, but its meteoric stock market rise is a recent phenomenon. In 1977, for example, shares could be had for a fraction of a dollar. As late as 1982, investors could have bought the stock under 7. Those same shares now sell at 38, just four points shy of their all-time high.

The spectacular rise in the stock reflects the transformation of the company itself, from a computer brokerage business—one that basically matched up computer buyers and sellers for a fee—into a complex financial service operation. Today, Comdisco not only buys and leases computers, but also re-sells the leased equipment in intricately structured tax shelters. The marketing men of a decade ago have been joined by a cadre of lawyers and accountants—tough, shrewd professionals, paid handsomely to keep one step ahead of the IRS. It's a new emphasis that has done wonders for the bottom line. Since 1980, sales have almost doubled, hitting $472 million in the 1982 fiscal year ended September. More important—thanks to the tax shelters—over the like stretch earnings expanded more than fourfold, to $29 million.

But past is not necessarily prologue. And Comdisco may be running into trouble on several fronts.

First, sources close to the IRS say that computer-leasing tax shelters are the object of wrathful scrutiny these days. The very guidelines around which Comdisco structures deals are being rewritten.

Second, IBM is moving into territory where Comdisco had been undisputed king. The IBM Credit Corp. is pushing its way into third-party leasing with partners none other than Merrill Lynch and Metropolitan Life Insurance. By next year, say industry observers, the Armonk giant will rank No. 1. And with its enormous supplies of cheap capital, IBM already is offering surprisingly aggressive rates. This ominous trend threatens to put an increasing squeeze on the profit margins of computer leasing outfits like Comdisco. To compete they may well have no choice but to take calculated—and dangerous—financial risks.

Finally, there's some controversial accounting. Comdisco's method of accounting for "fees" from tax-advantaged leases is a matter unresolved by the accounting profession—and a potentially explosive issue. Right now, Comdisco has significant latitude in the level of profits it reports and the amount of residual values it carries on the balance sheet. The details are complex, but essentially Comdisco often records what it calls "fees" from tax-advantaged transactions as straight profit—without offsetting such "fees" against the company's investment in the equipment. It thereby keeps on its books a significant investment, recorded in "leased computer equipment" or "net investment in sales and direct financing leases"—an investment it hopes to recoup from the residual value when the equipment is re-leased.

And if there are no residual values when the equipment comes off lease? Well, based on information supplied by the company's financial department, if *all* equipment was considered to have zero residual value, Comdisco's entire net worth, as of the end of fiscal 1982, would vanish.

Obviously, the way residual values are treated affects earnings, too. When Comdisco reasons that it will recoup its net investment after the equipment is released, it books the "fee" from the sale of the tax shelter as pure profit. If, instead, it subtracted its investment in equipment from this fee—recovered the investment and took it off the balance sheet—earnings would be a mere fraction of the substantial sums currently reported.

This method of accounting is thus disturbing on several scores. First, it's possible the residual values simply aren't there. Comdisco insists its assumptions are conservative—and they may well be—but all leasing companies have made such assertions, even the defunct ones. If there's a miscalculation, and the equipment should come off lease and suddenly be worthless, that means Comdisco would face a write-off.

Not to be overlooked, either, is the matter of when profits are recognized by Comdisco. Why should a company be allowed to report earnings today when it won't see the cash for four or five years, if ever? And finally, at the very least, financial statements might reasonably be expected to disclose net investment and assumed residual values, as well as detailed descriptions of how "fees" are booked.

None of this, however, is to say that Comdisco's accounting breaks the rules. Quite the contrary. "The accounting profession hasn't addressed the issue on this type of transaction," John Vosicky, Comdisco's vice president of accounting and financial controls, correctly points out. "One could argue that you could take the entire fee into income right away—on everything. Another could argue you reduce your investment completely, and you don't recognize anything until that investment is covered."

: :

To better understand the accounting, consider a typical transaction, which in itself is no simple matter. The "tax-advantaged" leases, in order to get by the IRS, often involve layers of companies. And the shuffling of papers in sale-leaseback transactions can, in short order, obscure the economic realities of the deals.

But here are the basics.

Comdisco finds a user who wants to lease a computer for say, five years, and buys a machine for $100. Comdisco then takes the lease to the bank, and borrows the discounted value of the payments. A typical present value for the lease payments might be $85.

This borrowing from the bank appears on Comdisco's balance sheet as "discounted lease rentals," but the contract is so structured that the risk is essentially transferred to the bank. "These are hell-or-high water agreements," insists one Comdisco executive. If anything goes wrong—if the user fails to make his payments—all the bank can do is confiscate the equipment. It has no recourse to Comdisco. So at this point, Comdisco's investment has effectively been reduced from $100 to $15.

Then comes the "tax advantaged" part of the deal. Comdisco sells the computer to an investor who is looking for a tax shelter. And here things start to get tricky.

Comdisco collects, say, $17 in cash, from the investor and then agrees to take a seven-year note for the remaining $83 of the purchase price of the equipment. At the same time, it signs a seven-year leaseback with the investor, so the rental payments the investor gets are spread over seven years. It's neatly arranged so the rental payments of this leaseback are precisely enough to cover the payments on the seven-year note. Put another way, Comdisco pays the investor rent, and the investor turns right around and pays this rent back to Comdisco as interest and principal on the note. It's a wash—a paper transaction. It's a nifty tax deal that has no effect on the actual user of the equipment, who continues to make his payments to the bank, which, in turn, reduces Comdisco's discounted lease receivables.

So has Comdisco made money? Well, it has paid $100 for a computer and borrowed $85 from the bank, to be paid off in five years by the user's rental payments. That leaves a $15 net investment. But it's also received $17 cash from the investor, and then shuffled papers so that an $83 note from the investor is exactly offset by lease payables of $83. Comdisco also retains the right to share the proceeds of re-leasing the computer in years six and

C

83

seven with the investor. The bottom line is this: the $17 in cash offsets the $15 net investment. Comdisco is $2 richer.

So the income statement shows $2?

Not likely. All those high-paid lawyers and accountants on staff argue the $17 cash payment is a "fee"—for, among other things, putting the deal together. Clearly the $17 is theirs; they don't have to give it back. So in many cases Comdisco takes the entire fee as profit. It shows earnings of $17, even though it has only $2 in the cash register.

Where's the other $15? The difference between the reported profits and the actual cash sits quietly on the balance sheet—in "leased computer equipment" or sometimes in "net investment in sales-type and direct finance leases." That's the amount Comdisco hopes to recover from re-leasing the computer in years six and seven. But by booking the entire $17, it has effectively taken this assumed residual value into earnings on day one.

Now if in years six and seven, Comdisco re-leases the computer for, say $20, it can report a $5 profit. If the re-leasing brings in only $15, Comdisco has broken even. It has simply replaced the $15 paper asset on the balance sheet with a more spendable $15 in cash. But what if re-leasing brings in only $5? That presents a nasty problem—indeed, that means that Comdisco is looking at a $10 write-off.

⋮

Nor is the way "fees" are treated an idle, theoretical matter. It is vitally important to Comdisco's bottom line. For such fees comprise the bulk of the company's "financial services" revenues. And although revenues from computer sales and rentals are two to three times greater, the company's big profit center is clearly financial services. Peter Labe, an analyst at Smith Barney, a firm that has done investment banking for Comdisco, claims in a recent report that financial services "account for the bulk of corporate profits."

Comdisco doesn't dispute it. "No question," says Comdisco's Vosicky, "a large percentage of the profits are attributed to tax-advantaged transactions."

About 80%–90%?

"I wouldn't say 90%," says Vosicky. "It depends on how you want to slice the pie." Profitability, he points out, depends on the allocation of general and administrative expenses. And Comdisco financials do not break out this information.

"I think it would be correct to say," continues Vosicky, "that the primary reason for the earnings increase is because of tax-advantaged transactions or financial services."

The bulk of the increase rather than the bulk of earnings?

"Yes."

In other words, the big leap in pretax earnings from $21 million in 1981 to $53 million in 1982 is primarily because of the tax-advantaged deals?

"Yes. I think that would be fair to say."

And if all fees had been reduced by the amount of investment in the equipment, how much less would financial services revenues have been in 1982?

"A lot of that revenue came from safe harbor leasing transactions where we don t have any investment . . . ."

But if the investment in equipment on all the *other* leases in 1982 was netted out, how much would financial services be reduced?

"It would probably be cut in half," replies Vosicky. "I would think at least cut in half."

And so this year, with no safe harbor leases, netting out all the investment in equipment would cause an even greater drop in financial services?

"Yet, it would."

Insofar as Comdisco reports profits now from the equipment leased—and leaves residual value on the books to be recovered later—it increases its exposure to obsolescence. And as of September 1982, the date of the most recent balance sheet with full footnotes, that exposure was considerable, at least in comparison with the company's net worth.

⋮

Exhibit 3   Letter to Comdisco, Inc. Shareholders

EXHIBIT 3
Letter to Comdisco, Inc. Shareholders

October 12, 1983

Dear Stockholders:

As I'm sure most of you know by now, the October 10, 1983 issue of *Barron's* includes an article about our Company. I believe the article and its subsequent impact on the price of the Company's stock entitle our stockholders to a clarification of the facts underlying the key issues raised. The article emphasizes four main areas: (1) The Company's accounting; (2) competition from IBM Credit Corporation; (3) our tax advantaged investment program; and (4) sales by insiders.

Accounting

The article raises questions concerning the Company's accounting policy with respect to the investment risk taken on leased equipment and implies that our policy with respect to payments from tax advantaged leases could result in an overstatement of income. Under the Company's depreciation policy, our leased equipment portfolio as of June 30, 1983 will be depreciated to a net book value at lease termination of $112,000,000. The estimated fair market value of this equipment at lease termination (as provided by independent forecasts from International Data Corporation, a highly regarded equipment valuation expert) was in excess of $279,000,000, a coverage ratio of nearly 2.5 to 1. The facts demonstrate that the Company's policies are conservative, and have created a potential significant source of future earnings. The specific financial implications of our policies are as follows:

(1) Equipment Values

While generally accepted accounting principles require varied accounting treatments for different types of leases, the central issue is the same for all of the Company's leases: Is the Company's depreciation policy reasonable, thus eliminating the likelihood of a future write-off? The answer is that our depreciation policy is reasonable, and, in fact, produced book values of leased equipment which are substantially less than the values estimated by independent industry experts, as shown by the table below:

Total Lease Portfolio at June 30, 1983 (000's omitted)

Lease Type	Net Book Value at Lease Termination	Estimated Fair Market Value at Lease Termination*	IBM List Price
Operating leases	$92,000	$208,000	$876,000
Sales type and direct financing leases	20,000	63,000	847,000
Other	—	8,000	60,000
	$112,000	$279,000	$1,783,000

*Source: International Data Corporation

As shown above, fair market value estimates prepared by International Data Corporation provide a substantial margin over the Company's net book value at lease termina-

C

85

Exhibit 3 Letter to Comdisco, Inc. Shareholders

tion. This is still true even if the equipment is sold under a tax advantaged transaction. Since most tax advantaged transactions are structured so that the equipment will have a zero net book value by the time any tax advantaged investor shares in the fair market value proceeds, this sharing will not have a significant effect on the margin of fair market value available to the Company over the net book value at lease termination.

Another method of evaluating our depreciation policy is to review the operating lease portfolio (which comprises 82% of the total lease portfolio) by comparing, by year of termination, net book value at lease termination to estimated fair market value at lease termination. The following table illustrates this comparison:

Operating Lease Portfolio at June 30, 1983 (000's omitted)

Fiscal Year of Termination	Net Book Value at Lease Termination	Estimated Fair Market Value at Lease Termination	Estimated Excess Fair Market Value
1983	$ 16,000	$ 22,000	$ 6,000
1984	30,000	53,000	23,000
1985	19,000	50,000	31,000
1986	14,000	46,000	32,000
1987	13,000	37,000	24,000
	$ 92,000	$208,000	$116,000

Our auditors, Peat, Marwick, Mitchell & Co., review and agree with the Company's depreciation policies.

Referring to the foregoing table, it should be noted that 71% of the Company's operating lease book value is represented by leases which terminate by September 30, 1985. This short time period increases the reliability of residual value estimates. Equally as important, the Company has historically realized more from the remarketing of leased computer equipment than the value carried on its books, resulting in additional profit at the point of remarketing.

(2) Revenue Recognition
The sale of leased equipment in a tax advantaged transaction is separate from the underlying user lease transaction and results in payments to the Company from the investor. Revenue is recognized from these transactions in accordance with one of two basic methods:

(a) For all equipment where the underlying user lease term is five years or longer, and generally for all 308X mainframe transactions, these investor payments are first applied to reduce the Company's investment in the equipment. Any excess over the investment is recorded in the period in which the tax advantaged transaction occurs. During fiscal 1982 and the nine months ended June 30, 1983, the Company generated $83,160,000 of such payments. The Company's investment in the equipment was reduced by $43,890,000 and the difference, $39,270,000, was recorded as financial services during this period.

(b) For equipment where the underlying user lease term is less than five years (except for 308X mainframe transactions) these investor payments are recognized in the period in which the tax advantaged lease transaction occurs. This accounting treatment is appropriate since the Company's depreciation policy results in net book values at the

C

86

Exhibit 3   Letter to Comdisco, Inc. Shareholders

end of the initial user lease term (typically 2–3 years) that already is less than fair market value estimates. To further reduce the Company's net book value for such equipment would materially understate current income and overstate future income by reducing or eliminating depreciation charges against future rental income.

Competition from IBM Credit Corporation

IBM has been Comdisco's single largest competitor for the entire 14 years Comdisco has been in business. Through its direct lease and rental programs, IBM has always been the dominant force in the computer leasing industry. IBM's increasing emphasis on generating equipment sales, however, is reflected in its withdrawal from the direct leasing business, which has resulted in a greatly expanding third party leasing market.

IBM Credit Corporation's (ICC) entry into the third party leasing business merely replaces part of the parent company's participation in leasing. ICC is participating in the third party market as a broker in much the same way as Comdisco. Comdisco has access to the same debt and equity markets as ICC, and on terms that will at most be only marginally less attractive to Comdisco than to ICC.

Tax Advantaged Investment Program

Our tax advantaged transactions have been carefully structured and documented. These transactions are bona fide investments with real economic substance and profit potential to the investor. They provide a valuable and effective way for individuals to provide capital for and participate in the equipment leasing industry. We take great pride in our reputation for providing a high quality computer leasing investment.

Like any tax advantaged investment, these transactions have certain tax risks, such as the possibility of IRS challenge and the risk of an adverse change in federal tax laws. We have made every effort to minimize these risks. Our nationally recognized tax counsel have provided their opinion that these transactions qualify as true leases for federal tax purposes under current law. We constantly monitor proposed federal tax changes, and we know of no imminent changes in federal tax laws or regulations affecting tax advantaged "wraparound" leases of computer equipment.

While these transactions have contributed substantially to Comdisco's profitability in recent years, our continued success in the computer equipment marketplace is not dependent on our ability to offer this specific form of transaction to investors. Nor does Comdisco's success depend on continuation of the status quo with respect to federal tax policy. We have employed and continue to employ a variety of transaction structures and have a history of adapting quickly to changes in the federal tax law and the marketplace. In fact, previous changes in federal tax laws and in the marketplace have often created significant opportunities for Comdisco.

Management Stockholdings

Management currently holds approximately 8,950,000 shares or 31% of the outstanding shares of the Company. These shares represent an ownership interest of approximately $240,000,000, based on the closing price on the New York Stock Exchange as of October 11, 1983. Over the years, sales of common stock have been made periodically by management. Tax liabilities created as a result of the exercise of stock options and sales by a retired senior executive who still owns approximately 650,000 shares account for a significant portion of these sales. The remaining sales are not significant when compared to current insider holdings.

87

Exhibit 3   Letter to Comdisco, Inc. Shareholders

Conclusion

In 1969, when we started Comdisco, we committed ourselves to building our business based on the principle of serving our customers with the highest degree of integrity and professionalism. Fortunately, over the years we have attracted talented individuals who share that commitment and who continue to value the principles of service, integrity and professionalism just as we did in 1969. We feel that our reputation and the trust that we have developed with our customers, our equity and debt investors, and our stockholders are our most valuable assets. We have not, and will not, compromise these principles in the conduct of our business.

Finally, it is important for you, our stockholders, to understand completely that Comdisco is stronger financially than it has ever been; that we have greater opportunities before us than at any time in our history; and that management is dedicated to retaining stockholder confidence and enhancing stockholder wealth.

Sincerely,

Kenneth N. Pontikes
(President)

Exhibit 4   Comdisco, Inc. Annual Report for Fiscal Year 1983 (abridged)

EXHIBIT 4

Comdisco, Inc. Annual Report for Fiscal Year 1983 (abridged)

To Our Stockholders

I am pleased to report that in fiscal 1983 your Company continued its outstanding growth and performance. Net earnings for fiscal 1983 of $51.8 million, or $1.78 per share, represented increases of 76% and 56%, respectively, over fiscal 1982 results. Total revenue increased 15% to $543.2 million. Your Company's continued success in the lease placement of IBM computer equipment, particularly 308X mainframes and 3380 disc storage devices, and in financial services activities were the primary reasons for the record results achieved. Dividends were increased 36% in fiscal 1983 from $.11 to $.15 per share, as adjusted for the 2-for-1 stock split distributed in March, 1983.

Leasing Activity. Leasing activity increased dramatically in fiscal 1983 as Comdisco entered into 3,470 new leases with total rentals in excess of $1 billion during the initial lease terms. This compares to 2,259 leases and over $700 million in total rentals for leases entered into during fiscal 1982. Comdisco leased to its customers 3380 disk storage devices and 3380 disk controllers with an initial cost in excess of $200 million in fiscal 1983. In addition the Company leased 308X mainframes having an aggregate purchase price of $289 million.

The large volume of 308X mainframe lease transactions did not correspondingly increase the Company's total revenue since these leases are required to be accounted for as direct financing leases. Under direct financing lease accounting only the net margins are recorded as revenue, not the gross rentals as under operating lease accounting (see Understanding Comdisco's Accounting for detailed explanation).

Pursuant to the Economic Recovery Tax Act of 1981, Comdisco elected in fiscal 1982 to sell tax benefits, including investment tax credits, to other corporations, and recorded the proceeds as financial services revenue. These "tax benefit transfers" increased both total revenue and earnings before taxes, but the corresponding reduction in investment

tax credits increased the effective income tax rate to 45.4%. In fiscal 1983 the large volume of 308X mainframe and 3380 disk storage equipment purchased for its leasing activity increased the amount of investment tax credit available to Comdisco. Because of changes in tax laws in late 1982 effectively eliminating tax benefit transfers, it was no longer attractive for Comdisco to enter into these transactions, so these investment tax credits were utilized for its own account. Investment tax credits of $22 million were earned in fiscal 1983, including $12 million in the fourth quarter, reducing the effective income tax rate to 12%.

Financial Services Activity. In fiscal 1982, proceeds from tax benefit transfers were recorded as financial services revenue. As I mentioned earlier, these tax benefit transfers had the effect of increasing revenue and income tax expense. In fiscal 1983, most of the financial services revenue was generated by the sale of leased equipment in the Company's tax advantaged transactions (see Understanding Comdisco's Accounting). In tax advantaged transactions, Comdisco retains any available investment tax credit. Equipment with a fair market value of $430.2 million was sold under tax advantaged transactions in fiscal 1983 compared to $253.0 million of equipment for the prior year.

Marketplace Perspective. In fiscal 1984, the data processing industry is expected to continue its annual growth rate of 15–25%. IBM Corporation continues to be the dominant factor in the computer leasing industry through its direct lease and rental programs.

However, in recent years IBM has been emphasizing the sale of its equipment, with less emphasis on direct leasing. This is reflected in IBM's pricing strategy which favors the purchase of equipment. For example, during fiscal 1983, IBM reduced lessee purchase option credits to make its leasing program even less attractive. In addition, IBM will eliminate, as of January 1, 1984 its practice of passing through investment tax credits to its lessees. IBM's reduced emphasis on direct leasing has led to

C

89

Exhibit 4   Comdisco, Inc. Annual Report for Fiscal Year 1983 (abridged)

increased user demand for third party lease financing, resulting in higher growth in the third party computer leasing marketplace. Your Company is successfully participating in this expanding market.

IBM Credit Corporation has entered the third party leasing market, replacing part of IBM's participation in this market. However, we do not expect this development to adversely affect our competitive position. We believe IBM Credit Corporation to be a reasonable competitor which will not take unacceptable risks nor assume unrealistic residual values. Also, Comdisco has access to the same debt and equity markets as IBM Credit Corporation. Finally, and of critical importance, users of computer equipment need to remarket existing equipment when new equipment is acquired. Because IBM Credit Corporation does not remarket displaced equipment, Comdisco still retains an advantage by virtue of its ability to remarket used equipment. No company is better situated to handle all of its customers' needs than Comdisco.

Activity in 308X mainframe and 3380 disk drives remains very strong, with your Company continuing to increase its market share. Comdisco's success in an expanding, competitive marketplace is directly attributable to its superior remarketing and lease financing capabilities.

Financial Condition and Liquidity. In fiscal 1983 Comdisco converted its $50 million of 13% convertible debentures into common stock and subsequently issued $250 million of 8% convertible debentures. As a result of these and other factors, Comdisco is in a stronger financial position than it has ever been. Stockholders' equity increased 110% to $91.5 million during fiscal 1983. At September 30, 1983 total assets were nearly $1 billion and cash and marketable securities exceeded $230 million. The continued improvement in your Company's financial condition was recognized by Moody's Investors Service, which raised Comdisco's bond rating for its convertible debentures to BA2 in fiscal 1983.

Personnel Changes. In fiscal 1983, the number of employees increased to 504, enhancing your Company's commitment to full customer service and helping to support continued growth. In November 1983, Raymond F. Sebastian was promoted to Executive Vice President from Senior Vice President-Corporate Development. Mr. Sebastian, an officer of Comdisco for eight years, will continue to oversee corporate development and take on additional administrative duties. In October 1983 Nicholas M. DiBari resigned his positions as Senior Vice President-Marketing and as a Director, for personal reasons. Mr. DiBari made valuable contributions to Comdisco's marketing structure and philosophy. Robert A. Bardagy has replaced Mr. DiBari as Senior Vice President-Marketing and as a Director. For the past six years, Mr. Bardagy has been responsible for the Company's market making and trading programs.

Other Activities. In fiscal 1983, the Company announced its Corporate Lease Line Program. The Corporate Lease Line Program allows the Company's customers to lease almost all types of capital equipment at attractive lease rates with very little administrative burden. The Company has the ability to administer the program based on the customer's requirements. This program is expected to make a substantial contribution to fiscal 1984 results. Comdisco Disaster Recovery Services has increased its capabilities to meet the growing demands for its services. The contributions of Comdisco Technical Services and Comdisco Maintenance Services assist the Company in providing the whole array of services required by a data processing operation. The Company's international operations continue to contribute significantly to our profitability. Finally, our ability to capitalize on opportunities both inside and outside of our basic industry has never been greater.

A recent misunderstanding of Comdisco has led to lower market prices for our common stock. Accordingly, we expanded this Annual Report to describe our key operations and our accounting policies in greater detail. By any measurement, there are few publicly-held companies that can match Comdisco's performance since its inception in 1969. For the last five years the Company's compound growth rate for net earnings was an outstanding 60%, while net earnings per share and total revenue had growth rates of 46% and 29%, respectively. In fiscal 1983 return on average equity was 37%, with a 5-year average return of 33%. Comdisco's record speaks for itself.

Exhibit 4   Comdisco, Inc. Annual Report for Fiscal Year 1983 (abridged)

I am proud of Comdisco's performance in fiscal 1983 and even prouder of the efforts and devotion of our employees. Without their outstanding efforts, we would not have achieved the success we have enjoyed. The support of our lenders, customers and you, our shareholders, is particularly gratifying. The first quarter of fiscal 1984 started out as our most active quarter ever, and I am confident that fiscal 1984 will prove to be Comdisco's most successful year to date.

Kenneth N. Pontikes
Chairman of the Board and President
November 28, 1983

Leasing's Four Fundamental Values

Initially, Comdisco was a computer equipment dealer, buying and selling equipment for its own account. Exceptional marketing capability helped make Comdisco the largest dealer in the industry by 1976.

By the late 1970's, market conditions had shifted and demand for computer leasing increased dramatically. Based on its exceptional marketing capability, Comdisco's emerging leasing operation quickly grew to become the Company's most significant business activity. Both dealer activity and the leasing operation—supported by unmatched remarketing capabilities—now contribute to Comdisco's overall success.

Today, Comdisco's fundamental business, the foundation on which its exceptional pattern of financial performance is based, is leasing—primarily the leasing of new and used IBM computer equipment. And, as business and institutions world-wide become more and more information driven, the demand for data processing systems will continue to grow.

Leasing is widely recognized as the most attractive alternative to purchasing multi-million dollar computer systems. Over the years, Comdisco has achieved leadership in the field, having built a lease portfolio of IBM equipment currently valued at approximately $1 billion.

The leasing business also creates values that enable Comdisco to capitalize on other related sources of revenue and earnings. At the core of Comdisco's business, there are four such fundamental values.

Initial User Lease—Value One

When Comdisco leases its new or used computer equipment to a customer, the customer's rental payments during the original lease term are the primary source of revenue. In fiscal 1983, for example, the Company entered into 3,470 leases having total lease payments of over $1 billion during the initial lease terms.

Lease contracts cannot be canceled, and the customer has full responsibility for maintenance and other expenses. Most leases have terms of two to five years.

These leases also allow Comdisco to finance its leasing growth through "nonrecourse debt." Typically, Comdisco takes an existing lease to a bank and assigns the stream of lease payments to the bank. In return, the bank gives Comdisco cash that is equal to the present value of the lease payment stream at market interest rates. The debt is nonrecourse because the bank looks to the lease payments to repay the loan. This nonrecourse debt for operating leases is recorded as "Discounted Lease Rentals" on Comdisco's Balance Sheet. Interest rates are fixed in this transaction, eliminating Comdisco's exposure to rate fluctuations. Comdisco retains ownership of the computer equipment.

Comdisco's continued success in computer leasing is supported by a variety of factors discussed in greater detail on the following pages of this Annual Report. Among them are a customer relationship with 70% of the *Fortune 500* companies, a proprietary data base containing information on all major data processing installations, a seasoned sales team with offices in key markets throughout the U.S., Canada and Europe, and a complete line of customer support services.

Remarketing Capacity—Value Two

Data processing technology is among the most dynamic in the history of world commerce. The marketplace has a virtually insatiable appetite for increased capacity and a constant stream of new technological advancements.

Exhibit 4   Comdisco, Inc. Annual Report for Fiscal Year 1983 (abridged)

With change as one of the few constants in the industry, Comdisco's unmatched capacity to remarket equipment is a fundamental component in the Company's formula for success. Indeed, leasing customers place a significant value on Comdisco's market making ability. As new products enter the marketplace, customers know that Comdisco has a unique capacity to remarket existing equipment, making it financially feasible to upgrade systems to a competitive, state-of-the-art level.

Comdisco's ability to capitalize on re-lease values and residual values is directly related to exceptional market penetration, its proprietary data base of marketing information, its professional sales force, and the Company's expertise in computer equipment and that equipment's life cycle.

Tax Benefits—Value Three

Tax benefits are an integral part of any leasing operation. Substantial tax benefits—particularly in the form of investment tax credits and accelerated depreciation deductions—are generated through Comdisco's acquisition of computer equipment.

Comdisco has a number of valuable alternatives concerning these tax benefits. Comdisco can claim the investment tax credits, thus reducing its own income tax. The Company can also choose to pass the investment tax credit through to the lessee in exchange for higher rentals. Or, as a third option, leveraged lease transactions with third party investors can also be arranged. This option has the effect of passing on all benefits of ownership, including tax and residual values. The compensation leasing companies typically receive is a lump sum payment and a share in the residual value of the leased equipment.

The capacity of the Company's basic leasing business, which generates significant tax benefits, allows Comdisco to capitalize on certain favorable tax laws. Such laws can be traced to the Congress' longstanding desire to provide industry with incentives for capital spending. Both investment tax credits and accelerated depreciation deductions are the product of laws that reflect this Congressional intent. Comdisco generates value by structuring transactions which permit the full utilization of the tax benefits associated with its equipment portfolio. Comdisco has demonstrated its ability to profitably

structure transactions in response to changes in tax laws. As long as Congress continues to encourage capital spending, the Company's control of equipment will enable it to continue structuring attractive tax-oriented transactions.

For example, in 1981 Congress devised "Safe Harbor Leasing" of equipment as a method for transferring tax benefits from one corporation to another. Called "tax benefit transfers," compensation for tax benefits was paid in a single lump sum at the beginning of the lease. Tax benefit transfers were, in effect, simply the sale of investment tax credits and depreciation benefits. In 1982, as part of the Tax Equity and Fiscal Responsibility Act of 1982 (TEFRA), Congress effectively eliminated Safe Harbor Leasing. In doing so, Congress did not change its desire to stimulate capital investment through tax incentives, as evidenced by the fact that in 1984 a new type of tax-oriented lease, the finance lease, will be permitted.

Despite the effective elimination of Safe Harbor Leasing, Comdisco continues to be in a position to generate value from significant investment tax credits and ownership rights to substantial amounts of equipment. While the laws have changed, the Congressional philosophy underlying tax-oriented leasing has not.

Tax Advantaged Transactions—Value Four

The fourth fundamental value of Comdisco's leasing activity is the tax advantaged transaction. In this alternative, Comdisco may sell equipment that is under an initial user lease to an independent third party. This is a completely separate transaction having no effect on the equipment user. The buyer is typically an individual or corporate investor who wants to share in the financial rewards of leasing—re-lease values, residual values and tax benefits.

When Comdisco sells computer equipment in a tax advantaged transaction, it receives an equity payment from the buyer in an amount equal to between 10% and 22% of the equipment's fair market value. In return for this equity payment, the new owner receives: (a) the accelerated depreciation benefits on the equipment, (b) a portion of the lease rentals in the sixth and seventh years after the sale is made, and (c) 100% of the equipment's value after the seventh year.

Exhibit 4   Comdisco, Inc. Annual Report for Fiscal Year 1983 (abridged)

The utilization of tax benefits, either by the Company for its own account or by an investor as a result of a tax advantaged transaction, results in a lower effective cost to the equipment user, which is in accordance with Congress' objective to stimulate capital expenditures.

These four values form the core of Comdisco's business—leasing activity, computer remarketing, tax benefits and tax advantaged transactions. Understanding these values is key to understanding Comdisco's growth potential and how the Company effectively minimizes the business risk in its operations.

Understanding Comdisco's Accounting

Lease Accounting

Comdisco accounts for its lease transactions in accordance with the rules set forth in Accounting for Leases (FASB 13) prescribed by the Financial Accounting Standards Board. FASB 13 contains guidelines for classifying lease transactions as one of the following three types:

- sales-type lease
- direct financing lease
- operating lease

A lease is classified and accounted for as sales-type or direct financing by Comdisco if it meets any one of the following criteria:

a. The lease transfers ownership of the property to the lessee (Comdisco's customer) by the end of the lease term;
b. The lease contains an option allowing the lessee to purchase the property at a bargain price;
c. The lease term is equal to 75% or more of the estimated economic life of the property; or
d. The present value of the rentals is equal to 90% or more of the fair market value of the leased property, less any related investment tax credit retained by Comdisco.

The majority of Comdisco's sales-type and direct financing leases are classified as such because they meet criterion d above.

If the leased equipment is new or purchased from the lessee (purchase/leaseback) and meets one or more of the preceding criteria, the lease is recorded as a direct financing lease; otherwise, the lease is

recorded as a sales-type lease. All other leases which do not meet one or more of the preceding criteria are classified and accounted for as operating leases. Operating leases are generally shorter term leases (2–4 years).

Sales-Type Lease. A sales-type lease is recorded in the income statement as "Sale of computer equipment," along with other sales. The amount recorded as a sale is the present value of the lease payments. The cost of the equipment less the present value of estimated residual value at lease termination, if any, is recorded in the income statement as "Cost of computer equipment."

Direct Financing Lease. It is Comdisco's policy to finance all of its direct financing leases on a nonrecourse basis. Therefore, the net margin for a direct financing lease is recorded as "other revenue." The net margin represents the sum of the proceeds from the financing of the lease plus the present value of estimated residual value at lease termination, if any, less the equipment cost.

The present value of the residual values of sales-type and direct financing leases and the present value of the noncancellable lease rentals, prior to their financing, are included in the balance sheets as "Net investment in sales-type and direct financing leases."

Operating Lease. Revenue under an operating lease is recorded as payments accrue, that is, on a monthly basis over the term of the lease. The depreciation expense is also recorded on a monthly basis and the equipment cost is recorded on the Company's balance sheet as "Leased computer equipment."

To summarize, the revenue recognition effects of the three different types of leases is as follows:

- For a sales-type lease, the present value of the lease rentals is recorded as "Sale of computer equipment" at the closing of the transaction.
- For a direct financing lease, the net margin is recorded as "Other revenue."
- For an operating lease, the monthly rentals are recorded as "Rental revenue" over the term of the lease.

Effect of Direct Financing Leases. In fiscal 1983 a substantial portion of leases written by Comdisco were recorded as direct financing leases. Because

C

93

Exhibit 4 Comdisco, Inc. Annual Report for Fiscal Year 1983 (abridged)

only the net margins on these leases are recorded, the total leasing volume that Comdisco transacted in fiscal 1983 is understated when compared to prior years when many fewer direct financing leases were recorded. The following table sets forth the cumulative increase in rental revenue that would have been recorded in recent fiscal years if Comdisco had recorded all direct financing leases as operating leases:

Fiscal Year	Rental Revenue (in thousands)		
	As Reported (A)	Increase (B)	Pro Forma
1979	$ 60,947	$ 9,634	$ 70,581
1980	80,979	14,612	95,591
1981	131,571	24,220	155,791
1982	206,592	65,284	271,876
1983	266,628	179,528	446,156

a. Column A represents rentals reported in the Company's income statement for the respective years.

b. Column B represents rentals due under direct financing leases that are not recorded as rental revenue because of the accounting treatment afforded direct financing leases.

As a result, the actual increase in the volume of leasing is not apparent from a review of the Company's income statement.

Residual Values. Residual value is an estimate of the value of the equipment that is expected to be realized at the end of the lease term for sales-type and direct financing leases. Comdisco records the present value of a conservative estimate of residual value.

Depreciation. All of Comdisco's leased equipment under operating leases is depreciated to zero within five years, with a higher rate applicable to the period covered by the initial user lease. Operating leases are depreciated to Comdisco's estimate of fair market value at lease termination. These conservative estimates are supported by forecasts prepared by International Data Corporation (IDC), a recognized expert in residual value projections for computer equipment. In fact, at September 30, 1983 IDC's fair market value projections are 242% of the equipment's net book value at lease termina-

tion. As a result of this conservative depreciation policy, the Company has constantly realized substantially more proceeds on the sale or re-lease of its equipment than its recorded book value.

The following table projects the runoff of the Company's September 30, 1983 operating lease portfolio. The table compares the net book value of the equipment to its estimated fair market value in the fiscal year in which the existing leases terminate. Fair market value represents IDC estimates of the equipment value at lease termination.

Comdisco, Inc.—Operating Lease Portfolio Runoff as of September 30, 1983

Fiscal Year of Termination	Fair Market Value Comparison to Net Book Value (in thousands)		
	Net Book Value at Termination	Estimated Fair Market Value at Termination	Estimated Excess Fair Market Value over Net Book Value
1984	$34,725	$70,234	$35,509
1985	15,665	43,682	28,017
1986	18,869	48,868	29,999
1987	13,820	36,525	22,705
1988	1,170	4,191	3,021
Total	**$84,249**	**$203,500**	**$119,251**

Tax Advantaged Transaction

While the specific terms and conditions of tax advantaged transactions vary, the following is a general description of a typical tax advantaged transaction:

1. At a date after the inception of the initial user lease and independent thereof, the Company may sell all or some of the leased equipment to a third party investor ("investor"). If the equipment is sold to an investor, the sale generally occurs three to nine months after the commencement of the initial user lease. The sales price equals the then current fair market value of the equipment and is paid in the form of:

   (a) cash and a negotiable, interest-bearing promissory note (due within two years) for 10–22% of the sales price (the "equity payment"), and

Exhibit 4 Comdisco, Inc. Annual Report for Fiscal Year 1983 (abridged)

(b) an installment note for the balance (90–78% of the sales price) payable over an 84-month period.

2. Simultaneously with the sale, the Company leases such equipment back from the investor for 84 months. The lease payments payable under the leaseback obligation generally are equal to the installment payments receivable under the installment note described in 1(b) above.

3. As part of the leaseback arrangement, during the 61st through 84th month of the leaseback period, the investor also shares in the re-lease proceeds that the company receives from subleasing the equipment. Upon the expiration of the leaseback period, the investor has the exclusive right to the equipment.

In summary, the Company has given up the accelerated depreciation benefits on the equipment for tax purposes, a portion of the rentals for months 61–84 and 100% of the equipment value after the 84th month in exchange for the non-refundable equity payment. This equity payment is the only portion of the tax advantaged transaction that is recorded by the Company.

Revenue Recognition. Revenue is recognized, according to the lease classification, in the following manner:

1. For equipment subject to operating leases, the equity payment is recognized as financial services revenue in the period in which the tax advantaged transaction occurs. The Company allocates as a cost a percentage of the net book value at the expiration of the initial user lease to the revenue from the tax advantaged transaction because of its decreased right to re-lease rentals. In all cases, the equipment sold under tax advantaged transactions is fully depreciated prior to the time the investor is entitled to share in re-lease rentals.

2. For sales-type and direct financing leases, the Company may record on its balance sheet an estimated residual value at the inception of the initial user lease. The equity payment is first applied to remove a portion of that residual value. The residual value is decreased because the Company's ability to recover such residual value is reduced by the rental sharing under the tax advantaged transaction. Any excess of the equity payment over the reduction of residual value is recorded as financial services revenue in the period in which the tax advantaged transaction occurs.

Lease accounting and tax advantaged transactions represent two of the more complex areas of Comdisco's accounting. See the footnotes to the Consolidated Financial Statements for additional information.

C

95

MANAGEMENT'S DISCUSSION AND ANALYSIS OF FINANCIAL CONDITION AND RESULTS OF OPERATIONS

Summary

Fiscal 1983 was the third consecutive year of record revenue and earnings for the Company. Total revenue for fiscal 1983 and 1982 was $543.2 million and $471.6 million, respectively. Net earnings increased from $29.4 million, or $1.14 per share, in fiscal 1982 to $51.8 million, or $1.78 per share, in fiscal 1983. The Company's continued success in the lease placement of IBM computer equipment, particularly 308X mainframes and 3380 disk storage devices, and in financial services activities were the primary reasons for the record results achieved.

Revenue

Total revenue increased 15% over the prior fiscal year. The increase in total revenue in fiscal 1983 was not as dramatic as the increase in fiscal 1982 despite the substantial increase in the number of lease transactions in fiscal 1983, primarily because of the different mix in lease transactions entered into in fiscal 1983. The lease classification, as determined by FASB Statement No. 13, "Accounting for Leases," has a significant effect on the manner in which revenue is recorded. During fiscal 1983, there was an active market for 308X mainframes, which

Exhibit 4   Comdisco, Inc. Annual Report for Fiscal Year 1983 (abridged)

were recorded as direct financing leases. In fiscal 1982, a larger percentage of leases were accounted for as operating leases. Under operating lease accounting, the gross rental is recognized in equal monthly amounts over the lease term as rental revenue. Since the Company finances most of its direct financing leases on a nonrecourse basis, the net margins are recorded as other revenue. The net margin represents the sum of the present value of the lease rentals, plus the present value of estimated residual value at lease termination, if any, less the equipment.

The growth of the Company's leasing activity continued on a strong upward trend in fiscal 1983. During fiscal 1983, the Company entered into 3,467 new leases with rental payments of $1.1 billion during the initial lease terms. This compared to 2,259 new leases and $702 million of rental payments during the initial lease term for the prior fiscal year. Rental revenue from equipment subject to operating leases increased 29% in comparison to the year earlier. The increase in operating leases in fiscal 1983 was primarily due to the high volume of lease placements of IBM's newest disk storage device, the 3380.

Revenue from the sale of computer equipment increased during fiscal 1983, primarily as a result of an active international market for 308X mainframes.

Financial services revenue for fiscal 1983 totaled $65.6 million, in comparison to $73.9 million in fiscal 1982 and $30.8 million in fiscal 1981. While the total financial services activity increased in volume during 1983, such increase is not reflected in financial services revenue in comparison to 1982. Pursuant to the Economic Recovery Tax Act of 1981, the Company elected in fiscal 1982 to sell tax benefits, including investment tax credits, to other corporations and recorded the proceeds as financial services revenue. In fiscal 1983, most of the financial services revenue was generated by the sales of leased equipment through the Company's tax advantaged transactions with the Company retaining any available investment tax credits on the equipment. In essence, in fiscal 1983, the investment tax credits associated with leasing were reflected in the reduced income tax rate, while in fiscal 1982, the sale of such benefits was reflected in

higher financial services revenue. Financial services revenue for fiscal 1983 and 1982 includes $6.0 million and $13.8 million, respectively, of net revenue generated by arranging leases between third parties.

Other revenue for fiscal 1983 totaled $39.8 million in comparison to $24.5 million in fiscal 1982 and $13.7 million in fiscal 1981. The increase in fiscal 1983 is primarily due to higher revenue from direct financing leases, interest income earned on short term investments and higher revenues from the Company's disaster recovery services.

Cost and Expenses

Total costs and expenses of $484.3 million for fiscal 1983 increased 16% over total costs and expenses of $417.8 million in fiscal 1982. Fiscal 1982 total costs and expenses were 49% higher than fiscal 1981. The increases were the result of the growth in the Company's leasing activities and the continuing expansion in the marketing of its services.

Interest expense for fiscal 1983 totaled $53.7 million in comparison to $47.2 million in fiscal 1982 and $33.7 million in fiscal 1981. The primary component is the interest expense associated with the discounting of operating leases. This represented 67%, 69% and 46% of total interest expense in fiscal 1983, 1982 and 1981, respectively. The Company finances leases by assigning the noncancellable rentals to financial institutions on a nonrecourse basis at fixed interest rates and receives from the lender the present value of the rental payments (the discounted amount). For operating leases, the Company recognizes interest expense over the term of the lease. The redemption of the Company's 13% Convertible Debentures Due 2001 reduced the Company's interest expense by approximately $5.3 million in fiscal 1983. Interest expense on the 8% convertible debentures issued May 1, 1983 totaled $8.2 million. The increases in interest expense in fiscal 1982 and fiscal 1981 were due to increased discounted lease rentals as a result of the growth in the Company's leased equipment portfolio.

Income Taxes

Income taxes as a percentage of earnings before income taxes were 11.9% in fiscal 1983 compared to 45.4% in fiscal 1982 and 26.8% in fiscal 1981. The higher effective tax rate in fiscal 1982 was

Exhibit 4   Comdisco, Inc. Annual Report for Fiscal Year 1983 (abridged)

attributable to lower investment tax credits due to the sale of such benefits by the Company as permitted under the Economic Recovery Tax Act of 1981. No significant tax benefit transfer leases were originated by the Company in fiscal 1983 and the Company retained the investment tax credits for its account, thereby reducing the effective tax rate to 11.9% in fiscal 1983. Note 10 of Notes to Consolidated Financial Statements provides details about the Company's income tax provisions and effective tax rates.

International Operations

The Company operates principally in three geographic areas: the United States, Europe and Canada. The Company has subsidiaries in Belgium, West Germany, Switzerland, the Netherlands, France, Sweden, Denmark, the United Kingdom and Canada. These subsidiaries offer services similar to those offered in the United States. A strong demand for IBM 308X processors, principally in Europe, resulted in an increase in revenue from international operations of 25% from $79.4 million in fiscal 1982 to $98.9 million in fiscal 1983. International revenues represented 18% of the Company's total revenue in fiscal 1983 and 17% in fiscal 1982.

Market and Dividend Information

The Company's common stock is traded on the New York Stock Exchange under the symbol CDO. The quarterly price range and dividends paid for fiscal year 1983 and 1982, adjusted to reflect the two-for-one and three-for-two common stock splits effected in March 1983 and March 1982, respectively, are shown below:

Qtr.	1983			1982		
	High	Low	Dvds.	High	Low	Dvds.
First	$18.38	$10.56	$.03	$ 9.00	$5.88	$.02
Second	27.13	16.56	.04	9.00	6.75	.03
Third	37.88	22.75	.04	9.63	7.75	.03
Fourth	42.00	34.25	.04	11.50	7.50	.03

At September 30, 1983, there were approximately 5,000 record holders of common stock.

Financial Condition

The Company's stockholders' equity increased substantially during fiscal 1983 as a result of the Company's record earnings and the conversion of

$50,000,000 of 13% convertible subordinated debentures. Cash and marketable securities totaled $232.6 million at September 30, 1983. In May 1983 the Company sold $250,000,000 of 8% convertible subordinated debentures, the primary reason for the increase in cash and marketable securities. The proceeds of the offering were used to finance the increase in the Company's leasing activities and to invest in short-term marketable securities.

At September 30, 1983, the Company had $40 million of available borrowing capacity under various lines of credit from commercial banks and no short term debt.

The Company's current financial resources and estimated cash flow from operations will be adequate to fund anticipated requirements for fiscal 1984. The major portion of funds required by the Company to finance its leasing operations is provided by assigning the noncancellable rentals to various financial institutions at fixed interest rates on a non-recourse basis. The Company's liquidity is aided by the maturation of its lease portfolio, since the remarketing of its leased equipment generates substantial funds. For example, the successful remarketing of equipment under leases which expire in fiscal 1984 is estimated to generate funds in excess of $50 million.

Total notes and debentures as a percentage of total capital (the sum of notes and debentures payable, discounted lease rentals and stockholders' equity) was 32%, 16% and 20% at September 30, 1983, 1982 and 1981, respectively.

Ratios

The following table presents ratios which illustrate the changes and trends in earnings for the last three fiscal years:

	1983	1982	1981
Return on average stockholders' equity	36.7%	39.2%	30.6%
Return on average assets	6.9%	6.2%	4.9%
Earnings before income taxes (as a percentage of revenue)	10.8%	11.4%	7.1%
Net earnings (as a percentage of revenue)	9.5%	6.2%	5.2%

97

Exhibit 4   Comdisco, Inc. Annual Report for Fiscal Year 1983 (abridged)

FIVE YEAR SELECTED FINANCIAL DATA

Years ended September 30,	1983	1982	1981	1980	1979
Consolidated Summary of Earnings (in thousands):					
Revenue:					
Rental	$ 266,628	$206,592	$131,571	$ 80,979	$ 60,947
Sale of computer equipment	171,138	166,705	125,384	149,708	149,983
Financial services	65,635	73,879	30,837	14,079	9,991
Other	39,779	24,454	13,746	8,348	4,355
Total revenue	543,180	471,630	301,538	253,114	225,276
Cost and expenses:					
Equipment depreciation, amortization and rental	214,439	160,523	99,413	68,328	47,698
Cost of computer equipment	151,573	149,654	111,784	134,595	128,470
Selling, general and administrative	64,655	60,402	35,313	24,219	21,284
Interest	53,673	47,242	33,657	16,988	13,319
Total costs and expenses	484,340	417,821	280,167	244,130	210,771
Earnings before income taxes	58,840	53,809	21,371	8,984	14,505
Income taxes	7,000	24,432	5,730	1,870	3,900
Net earnings	$ 51,840	$ 29,377	$ 15,641	$ 7,114	$ 10,605
Common and Common Equivalent Share Data					
Net earnings	$1.78	$1.14	$.68	$.33	$.54
Stockholders' equity	6.65	3.87	2.59	1.98	1.75
Average of common and common equivalent shares (in thousands)	29,502	28,973	24,539	22,102	19,858
Cash dividends paid	.15	.11	.09	.07	.06
Stock splits	2 for 1	3 for 2	5 for 4	—	3 for 2
Financial Position (in thousands)					
Total assets	$ 975,004	$536,679	$404,507	$229,170	$173,950
Total long-term debt	276,437	83,271	84,945	29,055	25,573
Discounted lease rentals	356,547	261,780	197,672	85,612	74,569
Stockholders' equity	191,487	91,056	58,746	43,565	35,508
Leasing Data					
Number of new leases	3,467	2,259	1,620	1,083	616
Total firm rents, initial lease term (in thousands)	$1,055,000	$702,000	$339,000	$183,000	$126,000

C

98

Exhibit 4   Comdisco, Inc. Annual Report for Fiscal Year 1983 (abridged)

CONSOLIDATED BALANCE SHEETS
(in thousands except number of shares)

Years Ended September 30,	1983	1982
Assets		
Cash and marketable securities (at cost of $205,053 in 1983 and $3,909 in 1982, which approximates market)	$232,560	$39,762
Receivables:		
Accounts and notes (net of allowance for doubtful accounts of $1,215 in 1983 and $628 in 1982)	74,830	41,368
Other	9,014	3,687
Inventory of computer equipment	59,681	35,382
Net investment in sales-type and direct financing leases	96,097	23,682
Leased computer equipment:		
Owned	671,697	502,494
Capitalized leases	24,353	24,158
Total leased equipment	696,050	526,652
Less accumulated depreciation and amortization	280,917	190,817
Net	415,133	335,835
Buildings, furniture and other (at cost less accumulated depreciation of $2,764 in 1983 and $1,897 in 1982)	9,068	6,062
Other assets and deferred charges	78,621	50,901
	$975,004	$536,679
Liabilities and Stockholders' Equity		
Note payable to bank	—	$2,385
Convertible subordinated debentures	250,000	50,000
Subordinated debentures	12,250	12,250
Accounts payable	58,963	19,110
Obligations under capital leases	14,187	18,636
Obligations under capital leases income taxes:		
Current	7,242	6,076
Deferred	18,121	30,121
Other liabilities	66,207	45,265
Discounted lease rentals	356,547	261,780
	783,517	445,623
Stockholders' equity:		
Common stock $.10 par value. Authorized 50,000,000 shares: issues outstanding 28,808,571 shares in 1983 (11,769,043 in 1982)	2,881	1,177
Additional paid-in capital	69,927	18,965
Deferred translation adjustment	(439)	(354)
Retained earnings	119,118	71,268
Total Stockholders' equity	191,487	91,056
	$975,004	$536,679

C

99

Exhibit 4   Comdisco, Inc. Annual Report for Fiscal Year 1983 (abridged)

CONSOLIDATED STATEMENTS OF EARNINGS

Years Ended September 30,	1983	1982	1981
Revenue			
Rental	**$266,628**	$206,592	$131,571
Sale of computer equipment	**171,138**	166,705	125,384
Financial services	**65,635**	73,879	30,837
Other	**39,779**	24,454	13,746
Total revenue	**543,180**	471,630	301,538
Cost and expenses			
Equipment depreciation, amortization and rental	**214,439**	160,523	99,413
Cost of computer equipment	**151,573**	149,654	111,784
Selling, general and administrative	**64,655**	60,402	35,313
Interest	**53,673**	47,242	33,657
Total costs and expenses	**484,340**	417,821	280,167
Earnings before income taxes	**58,840**	53,809	21,371
Income taxes	**7,000**	24,432	5,730
Net Earnings	**$ 51,840**	$ 29,377	$ 15,641
Net Earnings per Common and Common Equivalent Share	**$1.78**	$ 1.14	$.68

Exhibit 4 Comdisco, Inc. Annual Report for Fiscal Year 1983 (abridged)

CONSOLIDATED STATEMENT OF STOCKHOLDERS' EQUITY
(in thousands)

Years Ended September 30, 1983, 1982 and 1981	Common stock $.10 par value	Additional paid-in capital	Retained earnings	Deferred translation adjustment
Balance at September 30, 1980	$ 587	$ 14,167	$ 28,811	$ —
Net earnings	—	—	15,641	—
Dividends paid	—	—	(1,093)	—
Stock split	148	(148)	—	—
Stock options exercised	22	611	—	—
Balance at September 30, 1981	757	14,630	43,359	—
Cumulative amount as of September 30, 1981	—	—	—	(232)
Net earnings	—	—	29,377	—
Dividends paid	—	—	(1,468)	—
Stock split	391	(400)	—	—
Stock options exercised	14	835	—	—
Common stock issued	15	2,648	—	—
Translation adjustment	—	—	—	(122)
Income tax benefits resulting from exercise of non-qualified stock options	—	1,252	—	—
Balance at September 30, 1982	1,177	18,965	71,268	(354)
Net earnings	—	—	51,840	—
Dividends paid	—	—	(3,990)	—
Issuance of common stock upon conversion of 13% convertible debentures	256	51,782	—	—
Stock split	1,435	(1,435)	—	—
Stock options exercised	13	582	—	—
Employee Stock Purchase Plan	—	33	—	—
Translation adjustment	—	—	—	(85)
Balance at September 30, 1983	**$2,881**	**$ 69,927**	**$119,118**	**$ (439)**

Exhibit 4 Comdisco, Inc. Annual Report for Fiscal Year 1983 (abridged)

CONSOLIDATED STATEMENTS OF CHANGES IN FINANCIAL POSITION
(in thousands)

Years Ended September 30,	1983	1982	1981
Source of Funds			
From operations:			
Net earnings	$ 51,840	$ 29,377	$ 15,641
Noncash changes (credits) to operations:			
Depreciation and amortization	180,676	133,902	77,528
Increase in receivables	(38,789)	(12,849)	(5,531)
Investment in sales-type and direct financing leases	(72,415)	(5,792)	(11,732)
Income taxes	(10,834)	23,180	5,730
Increase in accounts payable and accrued liabilities	60,795	14,248	18,611
Other, net	5,636	474	(1,233)
Total provided from operations	176,909	182,540	99,014
Proceeds from issuance of subordinated debentures	245,250	—	48,560
Issuance of common stock upon conversion of 13% convertible debentures, net	53,365	—	—
Obligations under capital leases	1,984	5,663	14,249
Discounted lease rentals	257,096	145,626	183,557
Other	543	4,201	924
	735,147	338,030	346,304
Application of Funds			
Increase in leased equipment and inventory	282,341	190,180	202,002
Decrease in notes payable	2,385	1,060	33,460
Redemption of convertible debentures	50,000	—	—
Reduction of discounted lease rentals and obligations under capital leases	168,762	87,795	75,781
Purchase of subordinated debentures	—	—	2,162
Capitalized leases—computer equipment	1,984	5,663	14,249
Other assets and deferred charges	32,887	21,950	12,343
Cash dividends	3,990	1,468	1,093
	542,349	308,116	341,090
Increase in cash and marketable securities	192,798	29,914	5,214
Cash and marketable securities at beginning of year	39,762	9,848	4,634
Cash and marketable securities at end of year	$232,560	$ 39,762	$ 9,848

Exhibit 4 Comdisco, Inc. Annual Report for Fiscal Year 1983 (abridged)

NOTES TO CONSOLIDATED FINANCIAL STATEMENTS

1. Summary of Significant Accounting Policies

Principles of Consolidation: The accompanying consolidated financial statements include the accounts of the Company and its wholly-owned subsidiaries after elimination of inter-company accounts and transactions.

Inventory of Computer Equipment: Inventory of computer equipment is stated at the lower of cost or market.

Initial Direct Costs: Salesmen's commissions and other initial direct costs related to operating leases are deferred and amortized over the lease term.

Investment in Sales-Type and Direct Finance Leases: At lease commencement, the Company records the total lease rentals, estimated residual value of the leased equipment and unearned lease income as investment in sales-type and direct financing leases.

A. Sales-Type Leases
Revenue from sales-type leases is recorded as sale of computer equipment upon acceptance of the equipment by the customer. The amount of the sale is the present value of the lease payment. The carrying value of the equipment less the present value of the estimated residual value at lease termination, if any, is charged to cost of computer equipment. Unearned lease income represents the lease rentals plus the estimated residual value of the equipment less the present value of these amounts.

B. *Direct Financing Leases*
The total lease rentals plus the estimated residual value of lease termination, if any, less the equipment cost is recorded as unearned lease income.

The Company finances most sales-type and direct financing leases by assigning the noncancellable rentals on a nonrecourse basis. The proceeds from the assignment eliminate the total lease rentals receivable and related unearned income on sales-type and direct financing leases. Any gain or loss on the financing is recognized at the time of such financing. For leases which are not financed, unearned lease income is recognized as other revenue using the interest method over the lease term.

Leased Computer Equipment: Leased computer equipment under operating leases is recorded at cost. During the initial lease term, computer equipment is depreciated to the Company's estimate of fair market value at expiration of the initial lease term. Equipment sold under tax advantaged transactions is fully depreciated within five years. Equipment not sold under tax advantaged transactions is fully depreciated over the next lease term or five years from the date of acquisition, whichever is longer.

Financial Service Transactions: At a date after the inception of an initial user lease and independent thereof, the Company may sell some or all of the equipment to a third party investor. The sales price equals the then current fair market value of the equipment and is paid in the form of cash and a negotiable, interest-bearing promissory note (due within two years) for 10–22% of the sales price (the "equity payment"), and an installment note for the balance (90–78% of the sales price) payable over an 84- to 96-month period. Simultaneously with the sale, the Company leases such equipment back from the investor for 84 to 96 months. The lease payments payable under the leaseback obligation generally are equal to the installment payments receivable under the installment note. As part of the leaseback arrangement, from the 61st month of the leaseback period until the expiration of the leaseback, the investor shares in the release proceeds that the Company receives from subleasing the equipment. Upon the expiration of the leaseback period, the investor has the exclusive right to the equipment.

For equipment subject to sales-type and direct financing leases, the equity payment is first applied to remove a portion of the residual value of the equipment at the expiration of the initial user lease. The residual value is decreased because the Company's right to the full residual has been reduced by the tax advantaged transaction. Any excess of the equity payment over the reduction of residual value is recorded as financial services revenue in the period in which the tax advantaged transaction occurs.

For equipment subject to operating leases, the equity payment is recognized as financial services

C

103

Exhibit 4   Comdisco, Inc. Annual Report for Fiscal Year 1983 (abridged)

revenue in the period in which the tax advantaged transaction occurs. Against this revenue, the Company allocates as a cost a percentage of the net book value remaining at termination of the initial user lease. The balance of the net book value remaining at initial lease termination will be fully depreciated within five years from the date of equipment purchase.

In fiscal 1982 and the first quarter of fiscal 1983, the Company sold the tax benefits (investment tax credit and cost recovery allowances) on certain new equipment purchased for the Company's lease portfolio, under the provisions of the Economic Recovery Tax Act of 1981. The proceeds from the sale of tax benefits are recorded as financial services revenue. Also included in financial services revenue are fees for arranging lease transactions between third parties.

Income Taxes and Investment Tax Credit: Deferred income taxes are provided for income and expenses which are recognized in different periods for income tax purposes than for financial reporting purposes. Investment tax credits are accounted for on a flow-through basis.

Earnings Per Share: Earnings per common and common equivalent share are computed based on the weighted average number of common and common equivalent shares outstanding during each period including the effect of conversion of the 13% convertible subordinated debentures, after elimination of the related interest expense (net of tax), and after giving retroactive effect to the two-for-one stock split effected in March 1983. (See Note 11). Dilutive stock options included in the number of common and common equivalent shares are based on the treasury stock method. The number of common and common equivalent shares used in the computation of earnings per share for the years ended September 30, 1983, 1982 and 1981 were 29,501,678, 28,973,476 and 24,539,406, respectively.

2.   Investment in Sales-Type and Direct Financing Leases

The following table lists the components of the net investment in sales-type and direct financing leases as of September 30:

	1983	1982
Minimum lease payments	**$88,718**	$24,142
Estimated residual values of leased equipment	**29,863**	12,324
Net investment in equipment pending sale to third parties	**7,305**	—
Less unearned income	**29,789**	12,784
Net investment in sales-type and direct financing leases	**$96,097**	$23,682

Future minimum lease payments to be received as of September 30, 1983 are as follows:

Years ending September 30	Minimum lease payments receivable
	(in thousands)
1984	$24,844
1985	22,910
1986	20,696
1987	14,706
1988	5,562
	$88,718

3.   Leased Computer Equipment

Leased computer equipment at September 30, 1983 is comprised of the following:

Year lease commenced	Equipment cost	Accumulated depreciation	Net book value
1979	$20,357	$16,598	$3,759
1980	41,718	29,167	12,551
1981	146,118	96,179	49,939
1982	182,301	85,348	96,953
1983	281,203	35,518	245,685
	$671,697	$262,810	$408,887

An analysis of the operating lease portfolio by year the equipment was first available from the manufacturer follows below. This does not represent the year of purchase by the Company. The Company's depreciation policy generally depreciates computer equipment to zero within five years of the date of purchase.

Exhibit 4 Comdisco, Inc. Annual Report for Fiscal Year 1983 (abridged)

Year of delivery	Net book value
1970	$1,816
1973	8,244
1974	21,319
1975	58,656
1976	9,290
1978	58,556
1979	88,338
1980	42,543
1981	31,637
1982	88,488
	$408,887

4. Operating Leases

Rental revenue from operating leases is recognized in equal monthly amounts over the term of the lease. The following table summarizes the Company's future rentals receivable and payable under noncancellable operating leases existing at September 30, 1983 for computer equipment and rents payable for non-computer equipment and office space:

Year ending September 30	Computer equipment			Other rents payable
	Rents receivable on equipment		Rents payable on subleased equipment	
	Owned	Subleased		
	(in thousands)			
1984	$213,012	$28,334	$28,023	$2,430
1985	135,624	17,723	14,118	1,787
1986	63,488	7,309	4,340	831
1987	20,378	2,399	883	435
1988	1,345	275	60	250
	$433,847	$56,040	$47,424	$5,733

Total rental income and related expense for the years ended September 30, 1983, 1982 and 1981 applicable to computer sublease activities were as follows:

Years ended September 30	Rental income	Rental expense
	(in thousands)	
1983	$29,316	$33,694
1982	23,633	27,455
1981	24,152	22,415

5. Discounted Lease Rentals

Leased equipment owned by the Company is financed by assigning the noncancellable rentals to various lenders at fixed interest rates on a nonrecourse basis. The proceeds from the assignment of the lease rentals represent payments due under the lease discounted to their present value at the interest rate charged by the lender. The proceeds from the financing of equipment subject to sales-type and direct financing leases reduce the investment in sales-type and direct financing leases (see Note 1). The proceeds from the financing of equipment subject to operating leases is recorded on the balance sheet as Discounted Lease Rentals. Interest expense under these financings is computed under the interest method and amounted to $36,173,000, $32,527,000 and $15,468,000 in 1983, 1982 and 1981, respectively. In the event of default by the lessee, the lender has a first lien against the underlying leased equipment, with no further recourse against the Company.

The annual maturities of discounted lease rentals for the next five years are as follows:

Year ending September 30	Aggregate maturities
	(in thousands)
1984	$164,193
1985	113,318
1986	56,099
1987	20,528
1988	2,409
	$356,547

6. Capitalized Leases—Computer Equipment

The Company, as lessee, leases computer equipment from other parties which may be recorded as capitalized leases pursuant to FASB Statement No. 13. If the lease qualifies as a capital lease, the Company records as an asset the lesser of the fair market value of the equipment or the present value of the minimum lease payments. The Company amortizes the asset in a manner consistent with its normal depreciation policy for leased equipment.

Capitalized leases-computer equipment at September 30, is comprised of the following:

Exhibit 4   Comdisco, Inc. Annual Report for Fiscal Year 1983 (abridged)

	1983	1982
	(in thousands)	
Capitalized leases- computer equipment	$24,353	$24,158
Less accumulated computer amortization	18,107	15,354
Net capitalized leases- computer equipment	$ 6,246	$ 8,804

At September 30, 1983, the Company, as lessee, was obligated to pay rentals under those capitalized leases. The following table summarizes minimum rentals payable by the Company as lessee under capitalized leases:

Years ending September 30	Minimum rentals payable
	(in thousands)
1984	$7,527
1985	5,244
1986	2,807
1987	1,810
1988	521
Total minimum lease payments	17,909
Less imputed interest (9% to 17%)	3,722
Obligations under capital leases (present value of net minimum lease payments)	$14,187

The Company has subleased equipment under capitalized leases to others resulting in noncancellable sublease rental income of $10,532,000 due to the Company in the future.

7. Other Assets and Deferred Charges

During the third quarter of fiscal 1983, the Company began operations of a newly established, wholly owned subsidiary, Comdisco Resources, Inc. ("CRI"). CRI is primarily engaged, through joint ventures with established partners, in the acquisition of mineral and royalty rights in producing domestic oil and gas properties and in the acquisition of onshore leasehold interests primarily for resale to others for oil and gas exploration and development. At September 30, 1983, included in other assets and deferred charges are $22,959,000 of investments representing primarily onshore leasehold interests in unproved properties held for resale to others. For fiscal 1984, approximately $17,800,000 and

$9,000,000, respectively, has been budgeted for investment in proved producing domestic oil and gas properties and unproved onshore leasehold interests for resale to others for oil and gas exploration and development.

The Company, through its CFS subsidiary, has entered into certain computer equipment transactions in which it has leased equipment and in turn has subleased such equipment. In substantially all of these transactions, the lease term exceeds the sublease term. At September 30, 1983 and 1982, $19,336,000 and $21,258,000, respectively, of costs (representing the present value of the excess of lease payments over the initial sublease payments) were deferred in connection with such transactions and are included in other assets and deferred charges. These deferred costs will be recovered from remarketing the equipment after the expiration of the initial sublease. At September 30, 1983, the Company has firm noncancellable rentals under binding contracts totaling $9,102,000 as a result of remarketing a portion of this portfolio. All of these noncancellable rentals will be used to reduce the investment in the period such rentals are received.

8. Bank Borrowings and Compensating Balances

The Company has a revolving credit agreement which entitles it to borrow up to $15,000,000 on an unsecured basis. The agreement, which expires March 31, 1984, carries an interest cost of prime rate (11.0% at September 30, 1983) and includes a fee of 3/8% per annum of the average daily unused amount. If either the Company or the bank elects not to renew the agreement, the loan becomes a two-year term loan payable in equal quarterly installments with an interest cost of prime rate plus 1%. Under the agreement, the Company is required to maintain a defined debt to net worth ratio and dividend payments cannot exceed 20% of consolidated net earnings subsequent to September 30, 1980. At September 30, 1983, approximately $10,658,000 of retained earnings were available for payments of dividends.

In accordance with the terms of the agreement, the Company is required to maintain average cash balances with the bank equal to 5% of the $15,000,000 loan commitment. The amount of

106

Exhibit 4 Comdisco, Inc. Annual Report for Fiscal Year 1983 (abridged)

unused available borrowings under the agreement was $15,000,000 at September 30, 1983.

At September 30, 1983, the Company had an additional unused line of credit totaling $25,000,000 which bears interest at the prime rate. Under the agreement, the Company is required to maintain compensating balances equal to 5% of the outstanding borrowings.

9. Subordinated Debentures

8% Convertible Subordinated Debentures: In May 1983, the Company issued $250,000,000 of 8% convertible subordinated debentures ("Convertible Debentures") due in 2003. Issue costs of approximately $5,000,000 were deferred and are being amortized over 20 years. Each $1,000 principal amount may be converted into shares of common stock of the Company, prior to maturity, at the option of the Convertible Debenture holder at a conversion price of $36.50 per share.

The Convertible Debentures are not redeemable prior to November 1, 1984 unless the average closing price of the common stock is $51.10 for the twenty consecutive trading days ending on the fifth day preceding the date of notice of redemption. Thereafter, they are redeemable in full or in part at the option of the Company at an amount equal to 108.0% of the principal amount, with the premium on redemption declining 8% per annum commencing in 1984 through 1993, and redeemable thereafter at par.

13% Convertible Subordinated Debentures: On November 4, 1982, the Board of Directors announced the redemption of all of the Company's 13% Convertible Subordinated Debentures Due 2001 at a redemption price of $1,117 for each $1,000 principal amount, plus accrued and unpaid interest to December 6, 1982. Common stock issued upon conversion of $49,839,000 principal amount totaled 5,111,360 shares.

11½% Subordinated Debentures: At September 30, 1983, $12,250,000 of 11½% subordinated debentures due December 1, 1992 were outstanding. Annual sinking fund payments of $1,350,000 (9% of the aggregate original principal amount) commenced December 1, 1982 and are calculated to retire 90% of the issue prior to maturity. During fiscal

1981, the Company, in connection with future sinking fund requirements, acquired $2,750,000 principal amount of the outstanding debentures which resulted in a gain of $318,000 (net of income taxes of $270,000).

The annual maturities and sinking fund requirements of all the subordinated debentures for the next five years are as follows:

Years ending September 30	Aggregate maturities
	(in thousands)
1984	$ —
1985	1,300
1986	1,350
1987	1,350
1988	1,350

10. Income Taxes

The following data related to the provision for income taxes for the years ended September 30:

	1983	1982	1981
Current:			
Federal	$13,000	$ 6,252	$ —
State	6,000	1,076	—
	19,000	7,328	—
Deferred:			
Federal	(12,200)	16,281	4,216
State	(2,200)	273	553
Foreign	2,400	550	961
	(12,000)	17,104	5,730
Total tax provision	$7,000	$24,432	$ 5,730
Earnings before income taxes:			
Domestic	$51,869	$51,166	$18,992
Foreign	6,971	2,643	2,379
Total	$58,840	$53,809	$21,371

Income tax benefits of $900,000 resulting from the redemption of the 13% convertible debentures in fiscal 1983 and $1,252,000 resulting from the exercise of non-qualified stock options in fiscal 1982 were utilized to reduce the current Federal tax liability.

The reasons for the difference between the U.S. Federal income tax rate of 46% and the effective income tax rate were as follows:

Exhibit 4   Comdisco, Inc. Annual Report for Fiscal Year 1983 (abridged)

	Percentage of Pretax Earnings		
	1983	1982	1981
U.S. Federal income tax	**46.0%**	46.0%	46.0%
Increase (reduction) resulting from:			
Domestic International Sales Corporation tax benefit	—	(.1)	(1.2)
Reduction of deferred income taxes applicable to investment tax credit carrryforward	—	—	(20.4)
Investment tax credit	**(37.9)**	(2.0)	—
State income taxes, net of U.S. tax benefit	**3.5**	1.4	1.2
Other – net	**.3**	(.1)	1.2
	11.9%	45.4%	26.8%

The Company has not provided for income taxes on the unremitted earnings of the Domestic International Sales Corporation (DISC) subsidiary aggregating $4,253,000 through September 30, 1983, since the Company intends to postpone indefinitely the remittance of such earnings.

Deferred income taxes provided for timing differences were as follows:

	1983	1982	1981
Sale of tax benefits	**$(6,172)**	$38,661	$ —
Difference between depreciation for tax purposes and financial statement purposes	**(6,305)**	(18,125)	6,311
Deferred compensation expense	**1,264**	754	(754)
Deferred leasing income	**7,445**	2,934	(2,093)
Deferred leasing costs	**19**	1,518	1,164
Interest income on escrow account bonds not included in book income	**(7,972)**	—	—
Portion of undistributed earnings in DISC	—	(178)	(454)

	1983	1982	1981
Difference between leases accounted for as sales-type leases for financial statement purposes and operating leases for tax purposes	**211**	(23,601)	194
Reinstatement (reduction) of deferred income taxes applicable to:			
Investment tax credit carryforward	—	12,021	(4,356)
Tax net operating loss realization	—	—	2,323
Income tax benefit resulting from exercise of non-qualified stock options	—	—	1,903
Other – net	**(490)**	3,120	1,492
	$(12,000)	$17,104	$5,730

The Internal Revenue Service is examining the tax returns for the years 1980, 1981 and 1982. However, no final adjustments have been proposed and no provision for additional taxes is deemed necessary. The Company has settled all tax years through fiscal 1979.

11. Common Stock and Additional Paid-In Capital

On January 20, 1983, the Board of Directors declared a two-for-one split of the Company's common stock effective March 1983. On January 27, 1982 the Board of Directors declared a three-for-two split of the Company's common stock. On January 20, 1981 the Board of Directors of the Company declared a five-for-four split of the Company's common stock. All references in the financial statements and notes to the number of shares of common stock and per share amounts have been adjusted for the aforementioned stock splits.

On November 18, 1981, the Board of Directors approved the Settlement Agreement (the "Agree-

Exhibit 4   Comdisco, Inc. Annual Report for Fiscal Year 1983 (abridged)

ment") between the Company and participants in the Residual Incentive Compensation Plan (the "Plan") related to vested residual computer interests. The Plan provided in part for the allocation of a percentage interest in the residual value of computer equipment to the participants. The Agreement was approved by the stockholders on March 15, 1982 and, pursuant to the terms of the Agreement, the Company distributed to participants in accordance with the terms of the Plan the aggregate sum of $3,000,000 plus 300,000 shares of the Company's common stock.

Dividends on Common Stock: Common stock dividends paid were $.15 per share in 1983 compared with $.11 in 1982 and $.09 in 1981. Agreements with officers and directors who own approximately 29% (8,358,759 shares) of the outstanding common stock regarding waiver of their rights to certain cash dividends payable prior to February 1, 1983, have expired and have not been renewed.

At September 30, 1983, the Company has reserved the following number of common shares for future issuance:

1979 Stock Option Plan	542,851
1981 Stock Option Plan	1,474,200
Employees Stock Purchase Plan	196,430
Conversion of 8% Convertible Debentures	6,849,315
	9,062,796

12. Employee Benefit Plans

1979 Stock Option Plan: On November 18, 1981, the Board of Directors amended the Company's 1979 Stock Option Plan (the "1979 Plan") to qualify the plan as an incentive stock option plan in accordance with the provisions of the Economic Recovery Tax Act of 1981. All outstanding stock options, which retained their original option price, are eligible for treatment as incentive stock options subject to certain limitations as defined in the amended 1979 Plan.

1981 Stock Option Plan: On January 27, 1982, the stockholders approved the 1981 Stock Option Plan (the "1981 Plan") and 1,500,000 shares were reserved for issuance pursuant to the exercise of options under the 1981 Plan.

Employee Stock Purchase Plan: The Comdisco, Inc. Employee Stock Purchase Plan (the "Plan") was adopted by the Board of Directors on November 17, 1981 and 200,000 shares were reserved for issuance under the Plan.

The changes in the number of shares under the option plans during 1983, 1982 and 1981 were as follows:

	1983	1982	1981
	(in thousands except option price range)		
Number of shares:			
Shares under option beginning of year	986	1,024	1,722
Options granted	308	338	—
Options exercised	(133)	(376)	(698)
Shares under option end of year	1,161	986	1,024
Aggregate option price:			
Shares under option beginning of year	$4,967	$2,533	$3,257
Options granted	6,739	3,284	—
Option exercised	(596)	(850)	(724)
Shares under option end of year	$11,110	$4,967	$2,533
Options exercisable at end of year	238	116	328
Aggregate option price of exercisable options outstanding at end of year	$1,247	$295	$722
Options available for future grant at end of year	874	1,182	22
Option price range	$2.45–$21.88	$2.45–$9.69	$.68–$3.50

Profit Sharing Plan: The Company has a profit sharing plan covering all employees. Company contributions to the plan are based on a percentage of employees' compensation, as defined. Profit sharing payments are based on amounts accumulated on an individual employee basis. Profit sharing expense for the years ended September 30, 1983, 1982 and 1981 amounted to $834,000, $590,000 and $489,000, respectively.

C

109

Exhibit 4   Comdisco, Inc. Annual Report for Fiscal Year 1983 (abridged)

13. Commitments and Contingent Liabilities

At September 30, 1983, the Company was obligated under the following commitments: (1) to purchase computer equipment in the approximate aggregate amount of $58,782,000, (2) to sell computer equipment in the approximate aggregate amount of $9,370,000, and (3) to lease computer equipment to others with an aggregate initial term rental of approximately $86,133,000.

The Company has arranged for approximately $68,683,000 of letters of credit, primarily as guarantees for certain of the Company's sublease obligations and for future purchases of IBM equipment. The cost of such letters of credit range between ½% and ¾% per annum on the amount outstanding.

Accountant Report

The Stockholders and Board of Directors, Comdisco, Inc.:

We have examined the consolidated balance sheet of Comdisco, Inc. and subsidiaries as of September 30, 1983 and 1982 and the related consolidated statements of earnings, stockholders' equity and changes in financial position for each of the years in the three-year period ended September 30, 1983. Our examinations were made in accordance with generally accepted auditing standards and, accordingly, included such tests of the accounting records and such other auditing procedures as we considered necessary in the circumstances.

In our opinion, the aforementioned consolidated financial statements present fairly the financial position of Comdisco Inc. and subsidiaries at September 30, 1983 and 1982 and the results of their operations and the changes in their financial position for each of the years in the three-year period ended September 30, 1983, in conformity with generally accepted accounting principles applied on a consistent basis.

Peat, Marwick, Mitchell & Co.
Chicago, Illinois
November 9, 1983

Quarterly Financial Data

Summarized quarterly financial data for fiscal years ended September 30, 1983 and 1982 is as follows:

(in thousands of dollars except for per share amounts)

Quarter Ended:	December 31		March 31		June 30		September 30	
	1982	1981	1983	1982	1983	1982	1983	1982
Total revenue	$141,011	$121,189	$132,901	$118,309	$127,455	$94,691	$141,813	$137,441
Net earnings	12,531	9,604	10,334	5,934	13,199	5,824	15,776	8,015
Net earnings per common and common equivalent share	$.45	$.37	$.35	$.24	$.45	$.23	$.53	$.31

In the fourth quarter of fiscal 1983, the Company generated substantial investment tax credits, which resulted in an annual effective tax rate of 11.9%. This reduction in the income tax rate resulted in an increase of approximately $7,430,000 in net earnings ($.25 per share) for the fourth quarter of fiscal 1983.

The Computer Industry in 1992

It is mid-1992. The collection of industries under the heading "computer systems" (SIC 3571) grew dramatically during the 1970s and 1980s, but it is now in a state of turmoil. Most firms have suffered declines in earnings, and several—including industry giants IBM and Digital Equipment Corporation—have experienced large losses. Overall, profitability (as measured by return on equity) in the industry has fallen steadily from 23 percent in 1988 to 11 percent in 1991, and sales have been flat for the last two years. In the face of this turmoil, however, some firms with well-positioned product lines have managed to grow at a quick pace. For example, Sun Microsystems, a major player in the expanding market for workstations, experienced a 30 percent compounded annual growth rate from 1986 through 1991.

Standard and Poor's Corporation describes the situation as follows:

Computer manufacturers have become used to citing the reasons for the present malaise in the information technology business. These include the following:

1. *The spread of open system computer networks based on standard industry components that cannot command the gross profit margins inherent in proprietary designs. The gross margin associated with a mainframe computer sale can be as high as 70 percent; for personal computers (PCs) and workstations, it can be less than 30 percent.*
2. *A seemingly never-ending decline in the cost, and growth in the power of data processing equipment, which has further squeezed manufacturers' margins. A high performance workstation can cost less than $1000 for every million instructions per second (mips) of computer power. Mainframes typically cost more than $100,000 per mip. For many tasks, but not all, it is possible to substitute low-cost workstation power for mainframe power.*
3. *A slackening of demand for computer systems . . . [due to] saturation in some areas of the market, dissatisfaction with the results of continued computerization, and (in some countries) high interest rates.*[1]

To deal with the changes in the industry, some firms have abandoned product differentiation, cut prices, and focused on cost reduction. Some have undergone major restructurings. Several firms, including Apple and IBM, have formed new alliances.

This case was prepared by Professor Victor L. Bernard, and is based upon publicly available information. It was prepared as a basis for class discussion and is not intended to illustrate either an effective or ineffective management of a business situation.

1. *Standard and Poor's Industry Report Service (July 3, 1992), Vol. 3., No. 2, Sec. 2.*

The following brief sketches of four computing systems manufacturers help describe the variety of experience within the industry.

ATARI CORPORATION

Atari manufactures personal computers and video game systems. The firm's principle products are its Atari ST series of PCs, based on Motorola 68000 and 68030 series microprocessors and employing Atari's own TOS operating system with state-of-the-art graphical interface; its PC-compatible, MS-DOS based personal computers, including the one-pound Atari Portfolio and full-scale PCs driven by an 80386 microprocessor; Atari 8-bit microcomputers, which retail for less than $100; and video game systems. There are over 8000 software titles available for the ST computers, as well as a variety of peripherals. The fractions of net sales accounted for by the various product lines have been as follows:

	1991	1990	1989
Atari ST personal computers	.53	.59	.59
Atari PC compatible palm-top & personal computers	.10	.18	.17
Atari microcomputers	.03	.02	.06
Atari video game systems	.34	.21	.18

More than 80 percent of Atari's sales are in Europe, where it holds about 5 percent of the PC market, ranking behind IBM, Commodore, Olivetti, and Amstrad, and barely ahead of Apple Macintosh and Compaq. Until the second quarter of 1991, the company's principle products were manufactured in Taiwan, but that facility was sold. Since that time, various independent subcontractors have assembled the products, and some start-up problems were encountered. Atari intends to acquire another location for its manufacturing operations and resume in-house production.

Net sales declined 37 percent for Atari in 1991. In his letter to shareholders, Atari CEO Sam Tramiel (son of 46-percent owner Jack Tramiel) was straightforward: "I am quite displeased with the company's 1991 results, and hope that this message accurately conveys my dissatisfaction." Net income in 1991 reached its highest level since 1987, but only after inclusion of a $40.9 million pretax gain on the sale of its Taiwan manufacturing facility. Atari's ST sales continued the slide that began in 1990, as software producers—miffed by Atari's giveaway of prepackaged programs with ST computers—shifted their efforts to Apple and DOS systems.

Tramiel points to several corrections in Atari's strategy, all of which were in place or being put into place by the end of fiscal 1991. The changes include (1) cost reductions and careful monitoring of inventory levels, (2) refocusing of advertising to target specific audiences and reduce costs, and (3) redefining R&D, with a shift in emphasis to high volume production. Looking forward to late 1992, Atari is also ready to bring two

C
112

new products to market. One is the Falcon 030, a more powerful version of the ST computer; the other is Jaguar, the next-generation video game console.

A summary of Atari's recent financial performance appears in Exhibit 1. The company experienced a loss in the first quarter of 1992 equal to 11 percent of beginning equity. Analysts' forecasts for future performance are not available.

CRAY RESEARCH

Cray is the leading manufacturer of supercomputers, used in weather forecasting, aircraft and automotive design, scientific research, and seismic analysis. At the end of 1991, 324 Cray supercomputer systems were in use, including 68 installed in 1991. Approximately half of Cray sales for 1991 were in the U.S.; remaining sales were primarily in Western Europe and Pacific Asia. Cray is clearly the world leader in supercomputers, holding a market share in excess of 50 percent. However, it faces competition not only from other supercomputer manufacturers but also from the increasing power of "mini-supercomputers."

Cray supercomputers have generally relied on a single microprocessor. However, there has been a shift in high-speed computing toward massively parallel processing (MPP), which allows the simultaneous employment of many microprocessors. Cray has recently developed a partnership with Digital Equipment Corporation (DEC), to produce MPP implementations for sale by 1993. Cray also announced that, beginning in 1992, their EL systems will be sold not only through existing channels, but also through DEC's distribution network. The EL systems are "low-end" supercomputers, selling for approximately $350,000; some of its purchasers may ultimately upgrade to larger systems. Cray's high-end C90 systems sell for $30 million.

Cray also formed an alliance with Sun Microsystems that would facilitate seamless linkage of Cray computers and Sun workstations, as well as allow the use of Sun's SPARC chip in new Cray hardware. In the meantime, Cray introduced five new supercomputer systems in 1991. In their letter to shareholders, the CEO and COO labeled the market's response as "enthusiastic," and reported 58 new customers in 1991, more than in any previous year.

During 1991, Cray's revenues increased by seven percent, while profits increased only slightly. While such performance might normally be viewed as disappointing, Cray's letter to shareholders placed it in context: "These results came during what many observers are describing as the worst year overall in the computer industry's history." Based on Cray's performance relative to the industry, management indicated that "these results mean that we will not have to divert our attention in 1992 to 'rebuilding' or 'restructuring' efforts that have become almost commonplace in the industry."

During the first quarter of 1992, Cray installed 11 new and 2 used systems, generating sales of $165 million, up 15 percent over the first quarter of 1991. Nevertheless, net income fell 26 percent, to $3.9 million, reflecting lower volume in high-end systems. In mid-1992, Cray is just beginning to ship its top-of-the-line C90 systems at the rate of

C

113

about one per month. Analysts expect that Cray, which tends to make a big push to install systems before years' end, will see a pickup in earnings in the latter half of the year. Analysts forecast sales increases of 10 percent and 11 percent for 1992 and 1993, respectively, and return on equity of 13 to 14 percent in each year.

A summary of Cray's financial statements for recent years appears in Exhibit 2.

TANDEM COMPUTERS

Tandem operates within the niche of fault-tolerant mainframe and mid-range computer systems. Its products (labeled NonStop systems) are used in on-line transaction processing (OLTP) in banking, manufacturing, communications, distribution, brokerage and securities, and other industries. NonStop systems feature multiple independent processors, and are designed to continue operating through any single processor failure. (This is referred to as "continuous availability.") Beginning in 1990, Tandem produced a new fault-tolerant, high performance UNIX-based system, based on the high-speed Reduced Instruction Set Computing (RISC) technology. Through its subsidiary, Ungermann-Bass, Tandem also produces general-purpose local area networks. Almost half of Tandem's sales are within the U.S.; the remainder are primarily in Europe, with some in the Pacific Rim and elsewhere.

Tandem pioneered the fault-tolerant market and remains the acknowledged worldwide leader in fault-tolerant systems, with a 70 percent market share. However, it faces competition from Digital Equipment, Hewlett-Packard, Fujitsu, and Hitachi—all of which have entered the market in recent years—and from Stratus, a much smaller manufacturer. Moreover, some standard mid-range systems (produced by IBM and others) now have fault-tolerant capabilities, and so lines are blurring between the fault-tolerant market and mainstream systems market.

Tandem's revenues increased only slightly in 1991, and earnings declined. In the Tandem Annual Report for 1991, President and CEO James Treybig stated that "we are not satisfied with our financial results," and attributed the firm's difficulties to "the length and severity of a widespread recession." He indicated that the firm would "change the basic cost structure of [its] business" by reducing the size of its workforce, eliminating redundancies, increasing the leverage of sales and marketing efforts, and realigning the organization. Treybig indicated that Tandem would capitalize on opportunities in an OLTP marketplace that would continue to grow by "extending leadership in price/performance, open networking, and continuous availability." However, with the product cycle just beginning for some new RISC-based systems, substantial growth in Tandem sales could be a few quarters away.

In the first quarter of 1992, Tandem recorded an after-tax restructuring charge of $80 million, while sales rose only slightly. Thanks to that change, analysts expect the ROE to be only 4.3 percent in 1992, but to rise to 8.1 percent in 1993. Sales growth is projected at 4 to 5 percent for the next two years.

A summary of Tandem's recent financial statement data appears in Exhibit 3.

STRATUS COMPUTER

Like Tandem, Stratus produces fault-tolerant computer systems for use in OLTP, and is introducing a new generation of RISC-based fault-tolerant computers. Stratus systems consists of up to 32 processing modules connected via a high-speed communications link. The systems are used in the securities industry, banking, distribution, plant management, hotel reservation systems, and communications. Stratus is the only computer company in the world totally focused on continuous availability for OLTP; its 1991 annual report claims that, of their 150 largest bids of the year, "not one situation was reported where a competitor could show higher availability than Stratus."

Stratus was but a minor player in the fault-tolerant market until the mid- to late 1980s, but it now holds a 21 percent market share, second only to Tandem. More than half of Stratus sales are within the U.S., with Europe accounting for most other sales. Sales to IBM—which sells Stratus equipment on an OEM basis—accounted for 23 percent of Stratus sales in 1991, down from 26 percent in 1990 and 35 percent in 1989. Stratus is attempting to diversify its customer base, and expects increases in its sales to NEC (1.5 percent of 1991 sales) and others.

Stratus revenues for 1991 were up 11 percent, while earnings rose 34 percent. In its upbeat annual report to shareholders, Stratus emphasized what it considers its systems' unparalleled record of online applications availability, and indicated that "the growth of critical online applications is outpacing the abilities of most vendors to provide the levels of availability that customers actually need. This presents Stratus with the opportunity to capitalize on the trend that more businesses are becoming increasingly reliant on their online computer systems."

In the first quarter of 1992, sales growth slowed to "only" 9 percent, largely because of a dropoff of sales to IBM. However, earnings rose 40 percent. Analysts are projecting ROE of about 17 percent for 1992 and 1993, on sales growth of 13 percent in 1992 and 17 percent in 1993.

A summary of Stratus's recent financial statement data appears in Exhibit 4.

QUESTIONS

1. Profitability (as measured by return on equity) for the overall computer industry fell steadily from 23 percent in 1988 to 11 percent in 1991, and sales had been flat for the last two of those years. In early 1992, typical price-earnings ratios in the computer industry were within the range of 9 to 12, while typical price-to-book ratios stood at 1.0 to 1.4.

    Consider the factors that would determine the price-earnings ratios and price-to-book ratios for the four firms in the case. Based solely on the information in the case, would you expect price-earnings ratios and price-to-book ratios for each of the four firms to be higher than, lower than, or within the ranges considered typical for the industry at this time?

C

115

EXHIBIT 1

Atari Corporation – Common-Size Financial Statements and Selected Ratios

	1991	1990	1989	1988	1987
Cash	0.275	0.135	0.166	0.272	0.200
Receivables	0.318	0.352	0.324	0.297	0.196
Inventory	0.321	0.419	0.393	0.348	0.380
Other current assets	0.030	0.026	0.046	0.041	0.007
Total current assets	0.944	0.933	0.928	0.958	0.783
Plant, property, equip	0.038	0.050	0.042	0.025	0.128
Other long-term assets	0.018	0.017	0.030	0.017	0.089
Total assets	1.000	1.000	1.000	1.000	1.000
Notes payable	0.001	0.000	0.000	0.000	0.003
Other current liabilities	0.312	0.449	0.506	0.532	0.416
Total current liabilities	0.313	0.449	0.506	0.532	0.419
Long term debt	0.191	0.180	0.234	0.222	0.258
Other liabilities	0.000	0.000	0.000	0.000	0.000
Total liabilities	0.505	0.629	0.740	0.754	0.677
Shareholders' equity	0.495	0.371	0.260	0.246	0.323
Total liabilities and equity	1.000	1.000	1.000	1.000	1.000
Total assets (millions)	$253	$273	$331	$338	$518
Sales	1.000	1.000	1.000	1.000	1.000
Cost of sales	0.725	0.766	0.725	0.616	0.608
SGA expense	0.338	0.284	0.261	0.248	0.250
Operating income before depreciation	−0.063	−0.050	0.015	0.136	0.142
Depreciation	0.010	0.012	0.006	0.005	0.009
Interest expense	0.017	0.016	0.015	0.011	0.011
Nonoperating gain/loss	0.024	0.030	0.012	0.008	0.029
Special gain/loss	0.156	0.000	0.000	0.000	0.000
Income before tax	0.091	−0.047	0.006	0.129	0.152
Income tax provision	0.000	0.004	−0.004	0.042	0.062
Income before extraordinary items	0.092	−0.051	0.009	0.087	0.090
Net income	0.099	0.036	0.009	−0.188	0.116
Sales (millions)	$258	$411	$424	$452	$493
EBI/Sales	0.098	−0.044	0.015	0.091	0.094
Earnings/EBI	0.933	1.144	0.615	0.954	0.955
Sales turnover = sales/average assets	0.981	1.364	1.266	1.056	
Leverage = assets/equity (average)	2.320	3.222	3.953	3.415	
ROE = product of above	0.209	−0.223	0.047	0.314	

EBI = earnings before interest, net of tax. Tax effect of interest is assumed to be 40 percent.

EXHIBIT 2
Cray Research – Common-Size Financial Statements and Selected Ratios

	1991	1990	1989	1988	1987
Cash	0.034	0.071	0.072	0.182	0.194
Receivables	0.226	0.124	0.188	0.118	0.107
Inventory	0.227	0.191	0.212	0.238	0.214
Other current assets	0.030	0.024	0.007	0.005	0.006
Total current assets	0.517	0.409	0.479	0.543	0.520
Plant, property, equip	0.333	0.367	0.325	0.291	0.242
Other long-term assets	0.150	0.224	0.196	0.166	0.238
Total assets	1.000	1.000	1.000	1.000	1.000
Notes payable	0.006	0.039	0.053	0.009	0.010
Other current liabilities	0.186	0.177	0.175	0.192	0.176
Total current liabilities	0.192	0.216	0.227	0.201	0.186
Long term debt	0.100	0.112	0.151	0.111	0.120
Other liabilities	0.006	0.006	0.000	0.005	0.017
Total liabilities	0.297	0.334	0.378	0.317	0.323
Shareholders' equity	0.703	0.666	0.622	0.683	0.677
Total liabilities and equity	1.000	1.000	1.000	1.000	1.000
Total assets (millions)	$1,079	$944	$956	$991	$902
Sales	1.000	1.000	1.000	1.000	1.000
Cost of sales	0.333	0.306	0.289	0.272	0.252
SGA expense	0.348	0.356	0.370	0.330	0.321
Operating income before depreciation	0.320	0.338	0.341	0.398	0.426
Depreciation	0.131	0.137	0.130	0.110	0.105
Interest expense	0.009	0.010	0.011	0.010	0.013
Nonoperating gain/loss	0.009	0.022	0.023	0.031	0.029
Special gain/loss	0.005	−0.004	−0.061	0.000	0.000
Income before tax	0.193	0.209	0.162	0.309	0.338
Income tax provision	0.062	0.068	0.049	0.102	0.124
Income before extraordinary items	0.131	0.140	0.113	0.207	0.214
Net income	0.131	0.140	0.113	0.207	0.214
Sales (millions)	$862	$804	$785	$756	$687
EBI/Sales	0.135	0.144	0.118	0.211	0.219
Earnings/EBI	0.973	0.972	0.964	0.980	0.976
Sales turnover = sales/average assets	0.852	0.847	0.806	0.799	
Leverage = assets/equity (average)	1.458	1.553	1.532	1.471	
ROE = product of above	0.163	0.185	0.140	0.243	

EBI = earnings before interest, net of tax. Tax effect of interest is assumed to be 40 percent.

C

117

EXHIBIT 3

Tandem Computers – Common-Size Financial Statements and Selected Ratios

	1991	1990	1989	1988	1987
Cash	0.059	0.049	0.122	0.095	0.328
Receivables	0.258	0.264	0.259	0.270	0.263
Inventory	0.080	0.100	0.089	0.098	0.095
Other current assets	0.054	0.047	0.063	0.026	0.024
Total current assets	0.452	0.460	0.533	0.488	0.711
Plant, property, equip	0.331	0.341	0.276	0.317	0.261
Other long-term assets	0.218	0.199	0.190	0.194	0.028
Total assets	1.000	1.000	1.000	1.000	1.000
Notes payable	0.022	0.016	0.024	0.007	0.002
Other current liabilities	0.243	0.248	0.249	0.270	0.197
Total current liabilities	0.265	0.263	0.273	0.277	0.198
Long term debt	0.048	0.051	0.066	0.044	0.009
Other liabilities	0.041	0.045	0.050	0.029	0.047
Total liabilities	0.354	0.359	0.389	0.350	0.255
Shareholders' equity	0.646	0.641	0.611	0.650	0.745
Total liabilities and equity	1.000	1.000	1.000	1.000	1.000
Total assets (millions)	$1,932	$1,877	$1,619	$1,318	$967
Sales	1.000	1.000	1.000	1.000	1.000
Cost of sales	0.328	0.294	0.306	0.309	0.298
SGA expense	0.575	0.541	0.516	0.517	0.489
Operating income before depreciation	0.097	0.165	0.178	0.174	0.213
Depreciation	0.066	0.064	0.065	0.062	0.048
Interest expense	0.011	0.010	0.007	0.007	0.002
Nonoperating gain/loss	0.010	0.010	0.008	0.013	0.015
Special gain/loss	0.000	0.000	0.000	−0.007	0.000
Income before tax	0.030	0.100	0.114	0.111	0.179
Income tax provision	0.011	0.035	0.042	0.039	0.077
Income before extraordinary items	0.018	0.065	0.072	0.072	0.102
Net income	0.018	0.065	0.072	0.072	0.102
Sales (millions)	$1,922	$1,866	$1,633	$1,315	$1,035
EBI/Sales	0.023	0.069	0.075	0.075	0.102
Earnings/EBI	0.812	0.940	0.964	0.961	0.993
Sales turnover = sales/average assets	1.009	1.067	1.112	1.150	
Leverage = assets/equity (average)	1.554	1.595	1.591	1.449	
ROE = product of above	0.029	0.111	0.128	0.120	

EBI = earnings before interest, net of tax. Tax effect of interest is assumed to be 40 percent.

118

EXHIBIT 4
Stratus Computer – Common-Size Financial Statements and Selected Ratios

	1991	1990	1989	1988	1987
Cash	0.256	0.133	0.117	0.142	0.223
Receivables	0.348	0.379	0.417	0.375	0.356
Inventory	0.169	0.217	0.166	0.228	0.190
Other current assets	0.023	0.026	0.019	0.016	0.016
Total current assets	0.796	0.755	0.719	0.760	0.786
Plant, property, equip	0.171	0.199	0.245	0.209	0.196
Other long-term assets	0.033	0.046	0.036	0.030	0.018
Total assets	1.000	1.000	1.000	1.000	1.000
Notes payable	0.010	0.014	0.015	0.014	0.013
Other current liabilities	0.157	0.210	0.207	0.240	0.240
Total current liabilities	0.167	0.224	0.222	0.253	0.254
Long term debt	0.007	0.044	0.107	0.051	0.042
Other liabilities	0.010	0.014	0.000	0.000	0.000
Total liabilities	0.184	0.283	0.329	0.304	0.296
Shareholders' equity	0.816	0.717	0.671	0.696	0.704
Total liabilities and equity	1.000	1.000	1.000	1.000	1.000
Total assets (millions)	$385	$321	$274	$200	$145
Sales	1.000	1.000	1.000	1.000	1.000
Cost of sales	0.340	0.361	0.342	0.354	0.319
SGA expense	0.457	0.463	0.451	0.436	0.470
Operating income before depreciation	0.203	0.176	0.207	0.210	0.211
Depreciation	0.064	0.049	0.049	0.040	0.044
Interest expense	0.004	0.007	0.005	0.000	0.000
Nonoperating gain/loss	0.010	0.008	0.009	0.003	0.005
Special gain/loss	0.002	0.000	0.000	0.000	0.000
Income before tax	0.146	0.127	0.162	0.173	0.172
Income tax provision	0.035	0.036	0.058	0.062	0.066
Income before extraordinary items	0.111	0.092	0.104	0.111	0.105
Net income	0.111	0.092	0.104	0.111	0.105
Sales (millions)	$449	$404	$341	$265	$184
EBI/Sales	0.112	0.094	0.106	0.111	0.105
Earnings/EBI	0.985	0.970	0.982	1.000	1.000
Sales turnover = sales/average assets	1.271	1.357	1.441	1.537	
Leverage = assets/equity (average)	1.297	1.437	1.467	1.430	
ROE= product of above	0.183	0.179	0.219	0.243	

EBI = earnings before interest, net of tax. Tax effect of interest is assumed to be 40 percent.

C

119

In March 1989 Stuart Bell, Executive Vice President and CFO of CUC International, Inc., was concerned that the company's stock was seriously undervalued. He attributed the undervaluation to the investment community's concern about the quality of CUC's earnings:

> I am afraid our accounting is misunderstood by many investors. Recently, we have been forced to spend a lot of top management time and energy defending our policy in analysts' meetings. As a result we have been unable to focus investors' attention on our innovative business strategy and the tremendous cash-flow generating potential of our business. Concerns about our earnings quality are scaring new institutional investors from investing in our business. Many money managers tell me that they love our business concept but are afraid to buy our stock because they are worried about our accounting. The accounting is also giving short sellers an excuse to scare our current investors and drive down the stock price.

While Bell was convinced that CUC's accounting was appropriate, he wondered whether it was actually hurting, rather than helping, the company. What, if anything, should CUC do to shore up investors' confidence in the company?

BUSINESS HISTORY AND OPERATIONS

CUC International, located in Stamford, Connecticut, was a membership-based consumer services company. CUC marketed its membership programs to credit cardholders of major financial, retailing, and oil companies, including Chase Manhattan, Citibank, Sears, JC Penney, and Amoco. The company was formed in 1973 as Comp-U-Card of America, went public in 1983, and was renamed CUC International in 1987. As a result of its strong performance, the company was included in *Inc.* magazine's list of the fastest growing public companies in 1984 and 1986.

CUC's most popular product was Shoppers Advantage, introduced in 1981. Consumers paid an annual membership fee for this service, which entitled them to call the company's operators on a toll-free line, or to use on-line computer access seven days a week

This case was prepared by Professor Paul Healy of M.I.T. Sloan School and Professor Krishna Palepu of Harvard Business School as the basis for class discussion rather than to illustrate either effective or ineffective handling of an administrative situation. Copyright © 1992 by the President and Fellows of Harvard College. Harvard Business School case 9-192-099.

to inquire about, price, and/or buy brand-name products. Shoppers Advantage offered more than 250,000 brand-name and specialty items. Many members used the service principally as a reference for comparison pricing, not necessarily to purchase items directly. The company's large membership base allowed it to negotiate attractive discounts on the products offered in its catalog. As a result, the company guaranteed its subscribers the lowest prices available on goods it sold. If a member, after purchasing merchandise through CUC, sent an advertisement from an authorized dealer with a lower price within 30 days of placing an order, the company agreed to refund the difference. Members' purchase orders were executed through independent vendors who shipped the merchandise directly to customers, enabling the company to carry no inventory.

The firm acquired a large share of its new members through agreements with major credit card issuers, who provided CUC access to its list of cardholders. These individuals were solicited by three direct marketing approaches: billing statement inserts, solo mailings, and telemarketing. In billing statement insert programs, membership applications were enclosed in the monthly billing statements of credit card issuers. Solo mailings were membership offers mailed directly. Telemarketing involved following up mailings with telephone calls to explain membership offers further. CUC paid 10 percent to 20 percent of initial and renewal membership fees as a commission to the credit card company.

CUC incurred a large one-time cost for new member solicitations. Because only a small fraction of people reached through direct mail solicitations purchased the service, membership acquisition costs typically exceeded membership fees in the first year. For example, in 1989 the annual membership fee for Shoppers Advantage was $39, the average solicitation cost per new member was $29.37, commissions to the credit card companies were $6.63, and the average operating service cost per member was $5.00. Thus on average for each new member acquired, CUC incurred a cash outflow of $2 in the first year.

Members subscribed to Shoppers Advantage for a single year at a time. Renewals were automatically billed each year through the credit card company, and members could elect to cancel the service. There were thus no direct solicitation costs for renewing members. In 1989 CUC had a net cash inflow of $27.37 for each renewing member—membership fees were $39, and the commissions to the credit card companies and operating service costs totaled $11.63.[1] Membership renewal rates were therefore a key determinant of the profitability of the Shoppers Advantage program. The average annual renewal rate for Shoppers Advantage in recent years was 71 percent, making the program very profitable. This average was based on eight years' experience with the product since 1981. *Historical Data*

CUC capitalized on its Shoppers Advantage experience by introducing a variety of other membership-based products. These included: (1) Travellers Advantage—a travel membership created in 1988 to provide subscribers access to database information and reservations on discount airline travel, hotels and auto rental, tours, and cruises; (2) AutoVantage—provided subscribers with new car price and performance summaries,

---

1. The figures in this and the previous paragraph are from an analyst report by Brian E. Stack of Advest, Inc. dated October 30, 1989.

used car valuations, and parts and service discounts; and (3) Premier Dining—a service introduced in 1989 that offered subscribers two-for-one dining at mid- to upscale restaurants in major U.S. cities. The company made large marketing investments to build memberships in these new programs.

CUC's management explained the key elements of its business strategy as follows:

> *The company's expansion has been built on a foundation of creating, developing, and marketing a broad array of valuable services to consumers. . . . Aggressive marketing is an important strength. We sell our goods and services directly to millions of customers of major credit card issuers. Because our consumer services are a natural enhancement to personal financial services, more than 40 of the top 50 money center banks and a growing number of retailers and oil companies find it advantageous to work with CUC. . . . As competition heats up in the financial services industry, demand for CUC's services is likely to increase. Credit card issuers rely upon our services to draw new customers, increase card use, and raise average balances. They also use our services to differentiate their cards from others, and to tailor what they offer to appeal to different life-style and geographic preferences. Finally, card issuers benefit from the stream of membership commissions they receive from CUC.[2]*

By December 1988, CUC had approximately 12 million members enrolled in its programs. Revenues had grown from $45 million in the year ending January 31, 1984 (fiscal year 1984) to $198 million in the year ending January 31,1988 (fiscal 1988), and earnings had grown from $3 million to $17 million during this period. Exhibits 3 and 4 present the financial statements for the year ended January 31, 1988, and for the nine months ended October 31, 1988. Management expected the company to continue its rapid growth in the future, with revenues for the fiscal year ending January 31, 1989 projected to be approximately $270 million.

THE FINANCIAL REPORTING CONTROVERSY

CUC's management decided that because current marketing outlays provided significant future benefits, the company should capitalize membership solicitation costs in its financial statements, and amortize them over three years at rates of 40 percent, 30 percent, and 30 percent. This choice was endorsed by Ernst & Whinney, the company's auditors, and by the Securities and Exchange Commission when the company went public.

While it was unusual to capitalize marketing costs, CUC's managers believed that this decision was justified given the nature of the company's business and their confidence in future renewal rates. Bell explained the rationale behind CUC's accounting choice:

> *Many companies spend money on acquiring plant and equipment, and they capitalize these costs. Our business does not require major investments in plant and equipment. Instead, it requires investments in membership acquisitions. Because*

---

2. *Source: CUC's 1988 Annual Report.*

our membership renewal rates are so high and steady, I believe that it is important for accounting to reflect future benefits from spending money on membership acquisition in the current period. While expensing these costs is conservative, it fails to reflect their true nature.

In its accounting choice, CUC's management could not obtain much guidance from other companies' practices. Magazine publishers typically expensed costs of acquiring new subscribers, whereas insurance companies capitalized policy acquisition costs. Safecard Services, Inc., a credit-card registration company which also incurred large outlays for membership acquisition, capitalized its membership acquisition costs and amortized them over a ten-year period.

When CUC made the initial public stock offering, it had only a limited following among analysts and institutional investors. As the company grew larger, it sought to broaden its investor base. Some analysts, however, were concerned that capitalized marketing costs would subsequently have to be written off as losses because of high uncertainty about future renewal rates. They argued that deferring current marketing costs lowered the firm's earnings quality.

Analysts' concerns about the firm's accounting for marketing costs may have arisen from their experience with Safecard Services Inc. Safecard's capitalization of membership acquisition costs had been the subject of considerable controversy in the financial press. Safecard's decision to write off deferred marketing costs in 1987 may have heightened analysts' concerns about the value of CUC's capitalized marketing costs.

By early 1989 the company's stock had become a target of short sellers and its price began to suffer. As shown in Exhibit 1, short positions in the company rose from approximately 157,000 in November 1988 to more than 2,000,000 in March 1989.[3] While the stock market was generally on the upswing, CUC's stock price declined from $19.3 at the beginning of January 1988 to $16.3 at the beginning of March 1989. Exhibit 2 shows the stock price performance for CUC relative to the performance of the value-weighted OTC market index between January 1, 1988, and March 1, 1989. During this period CUC's stock price declined by 50 percent relative to the market. *Value Line Investment Survey* commented in its report on CUC dated March 17, 1989:

CUC International shares have taken a beating. The stock has fallen more than 35% since our last report three months ago. Wall Street's concern over the company's accounting methods . . . contributed to the stock price decline.

Management believed that the decline in CUC's stock performance could not be explained by either disappointing current operating performance or by forecasts of slower growth. Quarterly revenues and earnings grew steadily throughout 1988, and were consistent with *Value Line* analyst forecasts. In its March 18, 1988, report, *Value Line* forecasted that the company would have earnings of $5.5 million, $6 million, and $6.6 million in the quarters ending in April 1988, July 1988, and October 1988. Actual earnings in these quarters were $6 million, $6.6 million, and $6.9 million, respectively. The company projected that its growth would continue in the future—sales were projected

---

3. *Source:* Barron's Financial Weekly *(Down Jones News Service).*

to grow by 30 percent per year and operating cash flows would grow by 60 percent per year during the next five years. Finally, the firm was able to fund its substantial marketing outlays solely from operating cash flows during this period.

POSSIBLE MANAGEMENT RESPONSES

At least three options were available to CUC's management in responding to investors' concerns. One approach would be to adopt a more conservative policy to account for membership acquisition costs. By writing off previously capitalized expenses and adopting a policy of expensing future outlays as incurred, the firm would eliminate the major source of analysts' criticisms. However, such a move would seriously affect the company's balance sheet and income statement. More importantly, the accounting change would be unlikely to help management convince investors that current marketing outlays have future benefits.

An alternative strategy would be to provide expanded disclosure to justify the firm's capitalization of membership acquisition costs. This approach would involve identifying what type of information is likely to be most relevant and credible to investors. Further, it would require assessing whether the additional disclosures would provide proprietary information to competitors.

Finally, CUC could use corporate finance policies to enhance its stock price. Investors typically interpret cash payouts in the form of dividends and share repurchases as an indication of management's optimism about the firm's future cash flows. Such payouts, however, need to be planned in the context of the firm's investment needs for membership acquisitions.

One of the items on the agenda of CUC's upcoming board meeting was to consider proposals for dealing with the firm's communication challenge. Stu Bell was wondering which of the above options he should recommend.

QUESTIONS

1. What are the key success factors for CUC? How well does the company's management address them?
2. Is CUC's policy of capitalizing membership acquisition costs appropriate? Does this policy make the income statement more or less likely to reflect the company's operating performance?
3. Evaluate CUC's cash flow. Is the company financially healthy?
4. Why do you think CUC's investors are so concerned? Is CUC's stock undervalued?
5. What should Stu Bell do?

EXHIBIT 1

CUC International Shares Sold Short from January 1988 to March 1989

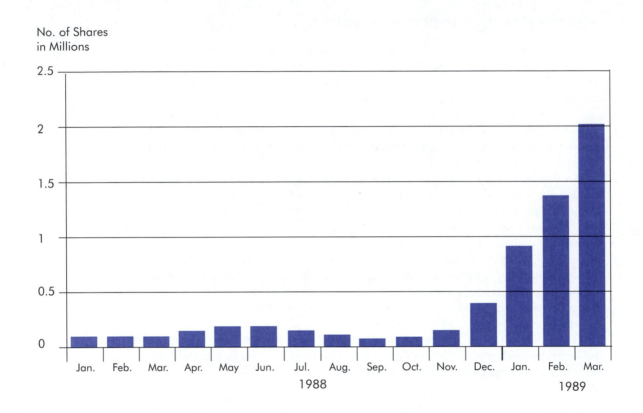

EXHIBIT 2

Cumulative Difference in Stock Returns for CUC International and the OTC Market Index in the Period January 4, 1988, to March 9, 1989

EXHIBIT 3

CUC International, Abridged Annual Report for the Year Ended January 31, 1988

CONSOLIDATED BALANCE SHEET

	January 31	
(Dollar amounts in thousands)	1988	1987
ASSETS		
Current Assets		
Cash and cash equivalents	$ 25,953	$ 14,810
Receivables, less allowance of $613 and $405	33,201	24,209
Prepaid expenses and other	3,468	3,288
Total Current Assets	62,622	42,307
Deferred membership charges, net	22,078	13,112
Prepaid solicitation costs	17,089	4,915
Prepaid commissions	6,267	8,127
Contract renewal rights, net	27,944	30,443
Excess of cost over net assets acquired, net	33,301	19,066
Properties, net	16,048	10,074
Other	1,519	4,416
Total Assets	$186,868	$132,460
LIABILITIES AND SHAREHOLDERS' EQUITY		
Current Liabilities		
Members' deposits	$ 4,997	$ 4,340
Accounts payable and accrued expenses	36,063	16,446
Federal and state income taxes	423	
Current portion of long-term obligations	1,404	5,011
Total Current Liabilities	42,887	25,797
Convertible subordinated debentures	12,000	22,000
Long-term obligations	3,767	5,120
Deferred income taxes	14,624	6,073
Other	1,229	1,268
Total Liabilities	74,507	60,258
Shareholders' Equity		
Common stock-par value $.01 per share; authorized 50 million shares; issued 19,683,567 and 17,820,338	197	178
Additional paid-in capital	82,271	59,550
Retained earnings	32,420	14,997
Treasury stock—398,230 and 398,091 shares, at cost	(2,527)	(2,523)
Total Shareholders' Equity	112,361	72,202
Total Liabilities and Shareholders' Equity	$186,868	$132,460

128

CONSOLIDATED STATEMENT OF INCOME

(Dollar amounts in thousands, except per share amounts)	Year Ended January 31		
	1988	1987	1986
Revenues			
Membership and service fees	$195,277	$138,149	$84,123
Other	3,180	3,610	3,342
Total Revenues	198,457	141,759	87,465
Expenses			
Operating	64,092	43,248	26,729
Marketing	68,937	56,496	35,042
General and administrative	31,729	23,342	14,572
Interest	2,259	2,663	1,507
Total Expenses	167,017	125,749	77,850
Operating Income	31,440	16,010	9,615
Acquisition costs			2,348
Income Before Income Taxes and Extraordinary Credit	31,440	16,010	7,267
Provision for income taxes	14,017	7,350	4,435
Income Before Extraordinary Credit	17,423	8,660	2,832
Extraordinary credit-utilization of tax loss carryforwards		1,041	3,589
Net Income	$ 17,423	$ 9,701	$ 6,421
Income Per Common Share			
Income before extraordinary credit	$.90	$.49	$.18
Extraordinary credit		.06	.23
Net Income Per Common Share	$.90	$.55	$.41

C

129

CONSOLIDATED STATEMENT OF CASH FLOWS

	Year Ended January 31		
(Dollar amounts in thousands)	1988	1987	1986
Operating Activities			
Net income	$17,423	$ 9,701	$ 6,421
Adjustments to reconcile net income to net cash provided by operating activities:			
Amortization of membership acquisition costs	44,641	35,501	20,237
Amortization of prepaid commissions	1,860	2,029	2,081
Amortization of contract rights and excess cost	3,423	2,199	
Deferred income taxes	11,712	5,553	442
Depreciation	2,506	2,582	1,969
Extraordinary credit and loss from discontinued operations			(1,475)
Change in operating assets and liabilities, net of acquisitions:			
Net (increase) decrease in receivables	(8,049)	(6,747)	3,795
Net increase (decrease) in members' deposits, accounts payable and accrued expenses and federal and state income taxes	12,755	(3,649)	(586)
Deferred membership income	9,629	14,366	9,052
Membership acquisition costs	(63,236)	(43,720)	(42,564)
Prepaid solicitation costs	(12,174)	(4,915)	
Prepaid commissions			(409)
Other, net	2,576	(1,748)	39
Net cash from (used in) operating activities	23,066	11,152	(998)
Investing Activities			
Acquisitions, net of cash acquired	(4,625)	(18,341)	
Acquisitions of properties	(7,586)	(5,078)	(4,345)
Proceeds from disposal of properties net of $3.2 million note receivable		783	
Disposals of marketable securities		1,933	2,724
Other, net			240
Net cash from (used in) investing activities	(12,211)	(20,703)	(1,381)

CONSOLIDATED STATEMENT OF CASH FLOWS (continued)

	Year Ended January 31		
(Dollar amounts in thousands)	1988	1987	1986
Financing Activities			
Issuance of Common Stock	5,326	6,220	613
Issuance of convertible subordinated debentures			15,000
Purchase of treasury stock		(2,377)	
Repayments of long-term obligations	(4,960)	(2,955)	(795)
Other, net	(78)		
Net cash from financing activities	288	888	14,818
Net Increase (Decrease) in Cash and Cash Equivalents	11,143	(8,663)	12,439
Cash and cash equivalents at beginning of year	14,810	23,473	11,034
Cash and cash equivalents at end of year	$25,953	$14,810	$23,473

NOTES TO CONSOLIDATED FINANCIAL STATEMENTS

Note 1. Summary of Significant Accounting Policies

Principles of Consolidation: The consolidated financial statements include the accounts of CUC International Inc. (formerly Comp-U-Card International Incorporated) and its wholly-owned subsidiaries. The Company operates in one business segment, providing a variety of services through individual, financial institution, credit union and group memberships. All significant intercompany transactions have been eliminated in consolidation.

Deferred Membership Charges, Net: Deferred membership charges is comprised of (in thousands):

January 31,	1988	1987
Deferred membership income	$(52,834)	$(43,205)
Unamortized membership acquisition costs	74,912	56,317
Deferred membership charges, net	$ 22,078	$ 13,112

The related membership fees and membership acquisition costs have been between $30 and $39 per individual member during the years ended January 31, 1988 and 1987. In addition, the annual renewal costs have remained between ten and twenty percent of annual membership fees for the same period.

Renewal costs consist principally of charges from sponsoring institutions and are amortized over the renewal period. Individual memberships are principally for a one-year period. These membership fees are recorded, as deferred membership income, upon acceptance of membership, net of estimated cancellations, and pro-rated over the membership period. The related initial membership acquisition costs are recorded as incurred and charged to operations as membership fees are recognized, allowing for renewals, over a three-year period. Such costs are amortized commencing with the beginning of the membership period, at the annual rate of 40%, 30% and 30%, respectively. Membership renewal rates are dependent upon the nature of the benefits and services provided by the Company in its various membership programs. Through January 31, 1988, membership renewal rates have been sufficient to generate future revenue in excess of deferred membership acquisition costs over the remaining amortization period.

Amortization of membership acquisition costs, including deferred renewal costs, amounted to $44.6 million, $35.5 million and $20.2 million for the years ended January 31, 1988, 1987, and 1986, respectively.

Prepaid Solicitation Costs: Prepaid solicitation costs consist of initial membership acquisition costs pertaining to membership solicitation programs that were in process at year end. Accordingly, no membership fees had been received or recognized at year end.

Prepaid Commissions: Prepaid commissions consist of the amount to be paid in connection with the termination of contracts with the Company's field sales force ($4.9 million and $5.8 million at January 31, 1988 and 1987, respectively) and the termination of special compensation agreements with an officer and former officer ($1.3 million and $1.6 million at January 31, 1988 and 1987, respectively). The amount relating to the termination of the field sales force is being amortized, using the straight-line method, over eight years and the amount relating to the termination of the special compensation agreement is being amortized ratably over ten years.

Contract Renewal Rights: Contract renewal rights represent the value assigned to contracts acquired in acquisitions and are being amortized over 9 to 16 years using the straight-line method.

Excess of Cost Over Net Assets Acquired: The excess of cost over net assets acquired is being amortized over 15 to 25 years using the straight-line method.

Earnings Per Share: Amounts per share have been computed using the weighted average number of common and common equivalent shares outstanding. The weighted average number of common and common equivalent shares outstanding was 19.4 million, 17.8 million and 15.8 million for the years ended January 31, 1988, 1987, and 1986, respectively. Fully diluted earnings per share did not differ significantly from primary earnings per share in any year.

Statement of Cash Flows: The Company adopted Financial Accounting Standards Board (FASB) "Statement of Cash Flows" in its fiscal 1988 financial statements and restated previously reported statements of changes in financial position for fiscal years 1987 and 1986. For purposes of the consolidated statement of cash flows, the Company considers all investments with a maturity of three months or less to be cash equivalents.

FINANCIAL HIGHLIGHTS

(In thousands, except per share amounts)

Year Ended January 31	1988	1987	1986	1985	1984
Total Revenues	$198,457	$141,759	$87,465	$65,947	$45,468
Net Income	17,423	9,701	6,421	4,214	3,184
Per Common Share:					
Net Income	$ .90	$ .55	$ .41	$ .28	$ .23
Book Value	5.83	4.14	2.33	1.94	1.70
Shareholders' Equity	$112,361	$ 72,202	$34,859	$28,673	$24,806
Number of Active Members	10,000	8,400	4,700	1,200	450

REPORT OF INDEPENDENT AUDITORS

Ernst & Whinney

Six Landmark Square, Suite 500
Stamford, Connecticut 06901

Board of Directors and Shareholders
CUC International Inc.
Stamford, Connecticut

We have examined the consolidated balance sheet of CUC International Inc. as of January 31, 1988 and 1987, and the related consolidated statements of income, shareholders' equity and cash flows for each of the three years in the period ended January 31, 1988. Our examinations were made in accordance with generally accepted auditing standards and, accordingly, included such tests of the accounting records and such other auditing procedures as we considered necessary in the circumstances.

In our opinion, the consolidated financial statements referred to above present fairly the consolidated financial position of CUC International Inc. at January 31, 1988 and 1987, and the consolidated results of operations and cash flows for each of the three years in the period ended January 31, 1988, in conformity with generally accepted principles applied on a consistent basis.

Ernst & Whinney

Stamford, Connecticut
March 30, 1988

C

133

Exhibit 4   CUC International, Abridged Interim Financial Statements

EXHIBIT 4

CUC International, Abridged Interim Financial Statements for Nine
Months Ended October 31, 1988

CONSOLIDATED BALANCE SHEET

(Dollar amounts in thousands)	October 31, 1988 (unaudited)	January 31, 1988
ASSETS		
Current Assets		
Cash and cash equivalents	$ 32,003	$ 25,953
Receivables	38,118	33,201
Other	4,164	3,468
Total Current Assets	74,285	62,622
Deferred membership charges, net	37,223	22,078
Prepaid solicitation costs	25,538	17,089
Prepaid commissions	5,397	6,267
Contract renewal rights and intangible assets, net	64,419	61,245
Properties, net	19,805	16,048
Other	2,040	1,519
Total Assets	$228,707	$186,868

Exhibit 4   CUC International, Abridged Interim Financial Statements

CONSOLIDATED BALANCE SHEET (continued)

(Dollar amounts in thousands)	October 31, 1988 (unaudited)	January 31, 1988
LIABILITIES AND SHAREHOLDERS' EQUITY		
Current Liabilities		
Members' deposits	$ 4,485	$ 4,997
Accounts payable and accrued expenses	50,017	36,063
Federal and state income taxes	1,264	423
Current portion of long-term obligations	1,494	1,404
Total Current Liabilities	57,260	42,887
Convertible subordinated debentures	12,000	12,000
Long-term obligations	2,673	3,767
Deferred income taxes	16,844	14,624
Other	1,402	1,229
Total Liabilities	90,179	74,507
Shareholders' Equity		
Common Stock	203	197
Other shareholders' equity	138,325	112,164
Total Shareholders' Equity	138,528	112,361
Total Liabilities and Shareholders' Equity	$228,707	$186,868

C

135

Exhibit 4 CUC International, Abridged Interim Financial Statements

CONSOLIDATED INCOME STATEMENT
(unaudited)

(In thousands, except per share amounts)	Three Months Ended October 31		Nine Months Ended October 31	
	1988	1987	1988	1987
Revenues				
Membership and service fees	$70,131	$50,696	$192,016	$143,409
Other	938	386	2,297	1,693
Total Revenues	71,069	51,082	194,313	145,102
Expenses				
Operating	24,320	16,258	64,123	47,608
Marketing	23,524	17,761	65,647	50,625
General and administrative	11,787	8,721	32,363	25,097
Total Expenses	59,631	42,740	162,133	123,330
Operating Income	11,438	8,342	32,180	21,772
Provision for income taxes	4,577	3,672	12,854	9,591
Net Income	$ 6,861	$ 4,670	$ 19,326	$ 12,181
Net Income Per Common Share	$.33	$.24	$.93	$.63
Weighted Average Number of Common and Common Equivalent Shares Outstanding	20,752	19,665	20,870	19,231

C

136

In early February 1993, Sir Geoffrey Mulcahy, Chairman of Kingfisher plc, was advised that Darty, the large French electrical retailer was searching for a buyer. Darty was an attractive partner for any retailer looking to expand in France because it was well positioned in the major urban areas of the country and because it had excellent growth possibilities in Europe. Mulcahy had been looking for a business combination with a French company for the last seven years and considered this the most promising opportunity that had arisen. He asked Brent Wilkinson, the Managing Director of Comet, Kingfisher's electrical retail chain, to form a task force to analyze the strategic fit between Kingfisher and Darty and to recommend a course of action.

THE RETAIL INDUSTRY IN FRANCE

The retail industry in France changed dramatically between 1960 and 1990. The early 1960s saw the development of large shopping centers that threatened the livelihood of small retailers. Political pressure from these small retailers led to the enactment of the Royer regulations, which imposed tight planning restrictions on large developments and effectively curtailed the creation of additional large complexes. However, it did not prevent the concentration of large retail chains. During the 1970s and 1980s the number of independent chains declined dramatically, until by the late 1980s the French market was dominated by only a few large firms (Leclerc, Carrefour, Intermarche, Auchan, and Casino). As a result of this increased concentration, power in the industry shifted from suppliers to the large chains. Intense competition between these chains led to lower prices in France, and some argue it was a major factor in keeping inflation rates low during the seven-year period 1986 through 1992.

Further changes to retailing in France, and in the remainder of Europe, were expected with the removal of trade barriers within the European Community (EC) in 1993. Foreign competitors would clearly benefit from the elimination of costly tariffs. They would also benefit from the simplification or elimination of customs documentation and reductions in border checks. These changes were expected to speed up crossborder transportation and further lower costs for foreign competitors, permitting retailers to source more widely, expanding customer choice, and increasing competition.

This case was prepared by Edouard De Vitry D'Avaucourt and Professor Paul Healy of the MIT Sloan School of Management for purposes of class discussion.

The effects of crossborder integration had already been seen in some areas in France. For example, French hypermarkets had spread to Spain, and English specialty products had been marketed heavily in France. While there was general agreement that this pattern would continue between European retailers, some analysts contended that U.K. retailers were unlikely to be successful in Europe, largely because of cultural and language differences. To support their view, they noted that very few British companies had expanded to Europe, and those that had ventured there, such as Marks and Spencer, had been unsuccessful.

DARTY

The Darty family opened its first electrical store in Paris in 1957. Ten years later the company decided to offer after-sales servicing to its customers. By 1973 Darty owned nine stores in the Paris area and was preparing to expand throughout France. To help finance this growth, the company went public in 1976. As a result, by 1987 the firm owned and operated 90 stores and was projecting still further growth, with plans to open six to ten new stores per year.

Darty was acquired by management and employees in 1988 for FF 7 billion. It was the largest management buyout ever completed in Europe, with financing arranged through Credit Lyonnais, one of the largest French banks. Following the buyout the company continued to grow impressively—by early 1993 it owned 130 stores and had a 12 percent share of the French electrical retailing market (see Exhibit 1 for market share data).

The firm's strategy, which has remained largely unchanged since 1973, is to have large well-located stores, offer low prices on an extensive product range, and provide customers with a strong level of service. The firm's stores are typically located in out-of-town retail parks with easy highway access. The average selling space per store is 11,000 square feet, larger than store sizes of most of Darty's French competitors, and also larger than typical store sizes of large electrical retailers in the U.K. Darty offers most major brands of VCRs and televisions, as well as laundry and other major appliances. It benchmarks its prices on those of its competitors, and pledges to match any competitor's price which is lower than that displayed in Darty stores. The firm's strong customer service unit provides home repair seven days a week on VCRs, televisions, and large kitchen appliances, as well as free delivery and loans of televisions and freezers if repairs cannot be completed on the spot.

Throughout the last twenty years Darty has maintained a consistent set of internal and external policies to support its price-choice-service strategy. Internally, it uses a standardized trading format for its stores, to maintain high quality service for customers. However, in other aspects of internal operations the firm gives store management considerable autonomy—the only centralized functions are for financing and human resource management. Externally, the firm has consistently advertised its price-choice-service strategy to customers using a variety of media. As a result, it has built a very strong image.

Darty's business strategy has been rewarded handsomely. Sales increased from FF 6,858 million in 1988 to FF 8,564 million in 1992, and pre-tax profits increased from FF 130 million to FF 443 million (see Exhibit 2 for a copy of the firm's financial statements).[1] This impressive performance occurred in spite of a recession in France in 1991, which caused Darty's sales to decline marginally in late 1991 and early 1992. However, the firm managed to maintain profits before taxes during this period, and actually increased its market share. In 1992 Darty's operating margin was 10.8 percent, significantly higher than margins for the leading electrical retailers in the U.S., U.K., and Japan.

Despite its success following the management buyout, Darty's management believed that the company was at a turning point. The continuing economic downturn in France was a source of concern given the firm's high debt levels. Further, the company had opportunities to expand further in France and in Europe but needed a partner with the financial resources to support this expansion.

KINGFISHER

Kingfisher was incorporated in September 1982 under the name Paternoster Stores plc. Two months later it changed its name to Woolworth Holdings when it acquired F. W. Woolworth. At this time the company's shares were listed on the London market at 50 pence (£ .5) per share. During the 1980s the group grew rapidly as a retailer, in part through an aggressive acquisition strategy. In 1984 it acquired Comet, in 1986 Record Merchandiser, and in 1987 Charley Brown's, Autocentre, and Superdrug. The group adopted its present name in 1989. As a result of its internal performance and its acquisitions, Kingfisher became one of the leading European retailers with around 2,000 outlets, more than 22 million square feet of selling space, and some 60,000 employees.

Kingfisher's major retail chains include:

- B&Q, a leading do-it-yourself chain in the U.K. Each of B&Q's stores carries more than 20,000 items for the house, garden, and car.
- Comet, the second largest electrical retailing group in the U.K., with 226 stores and 5,000 employees.
- Superdrug, a leading distributor of self-service health and personal care products. It operates 676 stores located in town centers and sells brand as well as private labels.
- F. W. Woolworth, a traditional British retail chain that sells low-cost entertainment products (video and audio), sweets, housewares, children's clothes, toys, and basic office supplies.

In addition, Kingfisher owns a number of smaller specialty chains, such as Charley Brown's, Autocentre, and Entertainment UK. Finally, Kingfisher has important interests in real estate through its subsidiary Chartwell Land.

d

139

---

1. *In February 1993 the exchange rate between French francs and pounds sterling was £1 = FF 7.96.*

Between 1982 and 1988 Kingfisher strategy has focused on building profits through increased volumes and improved productivity. High volumes are created through a policy of everyday low prices, which management believes leads to increased customer loyalty and market share. Higher volumes in turn translate into higher margins through increased productivity, enabling the firm to lower prices further to customers, creating a self-perpetuating cycle. To support its emphasis on everyday low prices, Kingfisher is committed to expanding square footage in all divisions to allow increased volume, and to developing information systems and logistics to help improve productivity. As part of this process it restructured Comet, moving many of the firm's stores from downtown areas to out-of-town retail parks in urban areas. The new stores are larger and offer better customer service than the older style stores.

Acquisition of Darty

In the course of its deliberations on the potential value of a merger with Darty, Kingfisher's task force identified several areas where Kingfisher could provide value to Darty:

- Kingfisher could provide the needed financing to support Darty's expansion in regions in France where it is currently under-represented. At present one-third of Darty's selling space is concentrated in the Île de France region, around Paris, where its market share is over 20 percent. Over the next six years, Darty would like to open 40 new stores in other regions. This should add at least 20 percent to Darty's selling space.
- Darty is likely to grow significantly in its existing markets over the coming few years, requiring additional financing. Darty's market share in new electrical products such as laser disc systems and large-screen televisions has been higher than its share in mature product categories. Further innovations, such as digital music systems and enhanced-definition video recorders and televisions, are likely to create even more demand for expansion.
- The French electrical market appears to be poised for strong growth following the anticipated economic recovery. Over the last ten years the industry has grown at a compound annual rate of 5.3 percent. However, during the current economic downturn the market has declined. Any economy-wide growth is likely to require further financial support from Kingfisher.

In addition to the financial strength that Kingfisher would add to Darty, the following areas of potential business synergy between the two firms were identified:

- Opportunities to source electrical products more effectively. Over the last decade there has been increased concentration among manufacturers of electrical products, many of which operate on a global basis. The formation of a global, or at least a European, electrical retailing business will enable retailers to source electrical products more effectively.

- Cost savings for Comet and Darty. These two firms are likely to be able to jointly develop management and in-store information systems, provide extended warranty services, and reduce capital costs for computers, potentially lowering administrative costs for Darty and Comet.
- Opportunities for Comet and Darty to expand jointly throughout Europe. Darty is clearly well positioned to expand its business in Europe, but will require financing. Comet is also considering its opportunities to expand in Europe.

Based on these estimated synergies, Kingfisher's treasury department proposed that the firm make an offer of up to FF 4.45 billion for Darty.

Takeover Task Force Deliberations

The task force created to evaluate the acquisition of Darty spent much of its time focused on the strategic value of Darty to Comet. However, there was considerable disagreement about the attractiveness of Darty as a takeover target. Some members argued that Darty's negative equity, low net profit margins, and high leverage made it a poor target. They pointed out that Kingfisher's treasury had valued Darty at only FF 4.45 billion, significantly lower than the FF 7 billion value of the firm at the time of the management buyout in 1988. Other task force members noted that Darty was the market leader in its industry and was therefore an attractive candidate.

Another issue raised by the task force arose from rumors that a French firm was also interested in acquiring Darty. Several members of the task force argued that this could create a takeover battle, which would lead the ultimate acquirer to overpay for Darty; therefore, Kingfisher should not enter a takeover battle. Other members pointed out that Darty is likely to be more valuable to a U.K. firm than to a comparable French acquirer, since British firms are permitted to deduct any goodwill recognized from owners' equity in a merger, leaving profits unaffected. In contrast, French firms are required to amortize any goodwill over a period of up to 40 years, regardless of whether the merger is financed with cash or with stock, thus lowering their income during this period. Consequently, some members argued that Kingfisher could actually afford to pay more for Darty than another French firm—they should be able to win any takeover battle without overpaying Darty's shareholders.

Finally, the task force was concerned about the impact of an acquisition on Kingfisher's financial position. Some members noted that Kingfisher would probably have to borrow to acquire Darty, and might need to raise additional debt in subsequent years to repay Darty's heavy debt burden and to finance its expansion plans. As a result, Kingfisher's leverage seemed certain to increase. Given the problems in the late 1980s and early 1990s faced by other companies that had financed acquisitions with debt, this was a source of concern. The task force was also not sure that it was an appropriate time for the company to finance an acquisition with equity, since Kingfisher's stock price had declined from £6 in early January to a current value of £5.10.

d

141

After a week of discussion many of the above issues were unresolved. Brent Wilkinson sat down to prepare his report for Sir Geoffrey Mulcahy. He knew that his report needed to clarify Darty's underlying financial performance, and to explain why the firm showed negative equity on its books. He also needed to address the question of what Kingfisher's strategy should be if a French competitor should bid for Darty. Finally, he had to make a recommendation on the form of financing that Kingfisher should use for any offer, and the financial impact of the alternatives on Kingfisher's balance sheet.

QUESTIONS

1. Assess and discuss the strategic fit between Darty and Kingfisher. What are the economic pros and cons of a combination?
2. How would you rate the underlying financial performance of Darty since the management buyout? Why does Darty have negative equity, and should this be a source of concern to the task force? Why is Kingfisher's valuation of Darty lower than its acquisition value in 1988?
3. If Kingfisher were a French company, what effect would goodwill amortization arising from a merger with Darty have on future earnings? Since Kingfisher does not have to amortize goodwill, how should this affect its valuation of Darty?
4. What impact would the acquisition have on the financial position of Kingfisher, assuming that it acquired Darty for (a) cash and for (b) stock?

d

EXHIBIT 1
1991 Market Shares in the Electrical Retailing Industry in France

Company	Format	Market Share	Number of Outlets	Sales (FF billion)
Darty	Electrical specialist	12	130	8.7
Carrefour	Department store	9	111	7.0[a]
Conforama	Furniture & electrical	7	153	5.0
BUT	Discount retailer	5	231	3.6
Fnac	Electrical specialist	3	37	2.6
Connexion	Electrical specialist	–	200	3.2[a]

Source of data: Kingfisher.

a.   Not all of these sales are for electrical products.

EXHIBIT 2
Darty Financial Statements

d

143

CONSOLIDATED INCOME STATEMENTS
for the years ended August 31, 1989 to 1992 (in FF million)

	1992	1991	1990	1989
Turnover	8,564	8,755	8,562	7,712
Cost of sales	(5,441)	(5,582)	(5,578)	(5,060)
Gross Margin	3,123	3,173	2,984	2,652
Net operating expenses	(2,210)	(2,242)	(2,180)	(1,962)
Other operating income	46	33	59	35
Income in associated COS	(21)	(27)	(22)	(6)
Earnings Before Interest	938	937	841	719
Interest expense (net)	(495)	(513)	(535)	(544)
Earnings Before Tax	443	424	306	175
Tax expense	(143)	(149)	(103)	(54)
Net income before minority int.	300	275	203	121
Minority interest	(27)	(27)	(25)	(20)
Net Income	273	248	178	101
Earnings per Share	124	113	82	46
Number of Shares	2,201,182	2,186,381	2,177,500	2,177,500

Exhibit 2   Darty Financial Statements

CONSOLIDATED BALANCE SHEETS
for the years ended August 31, 1989 to 1992 (FF million)

	1992	1991	1990	1989
Assets				
Fixed assets	2,163	2,091	2,059	1,918
Investments	46	66	27	85
	2,209	2,157	2,086	2,003
Current Assets				
Stocks	1,043	1,138	1,117	1,090
Debtors	514	525	580	644
Investments	871	1,033	523	139
Cash	154	184	173	102
	2,582	2,880	2,393	1,975
Total Assets	4,791	5,037	4,479	3,978
Liabilities and Equity:				
Current Liabilities				
Bank loans	406	637	303	82
Trade creditors	604	641	584	616
Taxes payable	414	413	408	296
Other creditors	116	103	108	98
Accruals	498	482	430	375
	2,038	2,276	1,833	1,467
Long-term liabilities	5,190	5,465	5,613	5,628
Deferred tax	(8)	3	4	12
Shareholders' Equity				
Common stock capital	882	882	871	871
Retained earnings	959	686	438	260
	1,841	1,568	1,309	1,131
Goodwill reserve	(4,312)	(4,312)	(4,312)	(4,289)
	(2,471)	(2,744)	(3,003)	(3,158)
Minority interest	42	37	32	29
Total Liabilities and Equity	4,791	5,037	4,479	3,978

Exhibit 2   Darty Financial Statements

CONSOLIDATED CASH FLOW STATEMENTS
for the years ended August 31, 1989 to 1992 (in FF million)

	1992	1991	1990	1989
Net Cash from Operations	1,494	965	1,138	981
Servicing Finance:				
Interest received	102	91	83	130
Interest paid	(883)	(315)	(613)	(614)
Dividends paid	(22)	(22)	(22)	(69)
Cash for Servicing Finance	(803)	(246)	(552)	(553)
Corporate taxation paid	(178)	(150)	(44)	(117)
Investing Activities:				
Acquisition of fixed assets	(188)	(157)	(250)	(220)
Acquisition of investments	(4)	(51)	(8)	(39)
Sale of fixed assets	23	21	31	30
Cash Outflow from Investing Activities	(169)	(187)	(227)	(229)
Cash Flow Before Financing	344	382	315	82
Issue of common stock	—	11	—	—
Increase (repay) loans	(305)	(206)	(81)	54
Net Cash Flow from Financing	(305)	(195)	(81)	54
Increase in Cash	39	187	234	136

NOTES TO FINANCIAL STATEMENTS
for the years ended August 31, 1989 to 1992 (in FF million)

1. Accounting Policies

Accounting conventions
The financial information of the group is prepared under the historical cost convention, except for short-term investments, which are carried at market value. The financial information has been restated using accounting policies generally accepted in the United Kingdom.

Basis of consolidation
The consolidated financial information incorporates the financial statements of the Company and its subsidiary undertakings. Associated companies are accounted for using the equity method. Goodwill arising is charged to reserves in the year of acquisition.

Exhibit 2   Darty Financial Statements

Depreciation

Depreciation of fixed assets is provided where necessary to reflect a reduction from book value to estimated residual value over the useful life of the asset to the Group. It is the Group's policy to maintain its properties in a state of good repair to prolong their useful lives. The estimated residual values of its freehold and leasehold buildings are not materially different from their carrying values. Accordingly, no provision for depreciation on these classes of assets is considered necessary.

Depreciation of other fixed assets is calculated on a straight-line basis with no residual values assumed. The annual rates applicable are:

Fixtures and fittings	5 to 10 years
Motor cars and other vehicles	3 to 4 years
Plant and equipment	5 years
Office furniture	3 to 10 years
Computer equipment	5 years

Leased assets

Assets under finance leases are capitalized and a corresponding liability is set up which is amortized over the life of the lease. The imputed interest cost is shown as part of interest expense.

Stocks

Stocks are stated at the lower of average cost or net realizable value. Cost includes appropriate overheads.

Short-term investments

Short-term investments are stated at market value.

Pensions

The Group contributes to State pension schemes by payment of social security costs in accordance with French legislation.

Deferred taxation

Provision is made for deferred taxation except where it is unlikely to become payable in the foreseeable future.

Turnover

Turnover represents retail sales and services supplied, and excludes transactions made between Group companies and value added tax.

Deferred income

Deferred income represents income received on service contracts which has not yet been recognized in the income statement.

Warranty provision

Provision is made for claims under warranty based on historical experience.

Exhibit 2   Darty Financial Statements

2. Profit on Ordinary Activities Before Taxation

Profit on ordinary activities before taxation is stated after charging the following:

	1992	1991	1990	1989
Staff costs:				
Wages and salaries	903	884	837	743
Social security costs	384	375	357	317
Employee profit sharing	81	78	72	62
	1,368	1,337	1,266	1,122
Operating leases:				
Land and buildings	94	93	87	79
Plant and equipment	22	26	27	28
Depreciation	88	92	84	68

3. Taxation

Annual tax on profit on the ordinary activities of the Group:

	1992	1991	1990	1989
Corporate taxes	154	150	111	71
Deferred taxation	(11)	(1)	(8)	(17)
	143	149	103	54

4. Long-Term Liabilities

	1992	1991	1990	1989
Amounts falling due after more than one year:				
Bank loans and overdrafts	4,623	4,926	5,128	5,232
Payable under finance leases	91	93	97	74
Deferred income	476	446	388	322
	5,190	5,465	5,613	5,628

The bank loans, overdrafts and obligations under finance leases fall due for repayment as follows:

	1992	1991	1990	1989
Between one and five years	2,588	1,985	1,483	1,022
After five years	2,126	3,034	3,742	4,284
	4,714	5,019	5,225	5,306

d

147

Exhibit 2   Darty Financial Statements

5. Cash Flow

	1992	1991	1990	1989
Reconciliation of operating profit to cash from operations:				
Profit before interest	938	937	841	719
Depreciation	88	92	84	68
Decrease in stock	95	(21)	(27)	(81)
Decrease in debtors	11	55	64	32
Increase in creditors	338	(123)	143	287
Associated undertakings	24	12	43	9
Unrealized profits on short-term investments	(5)	1	(4)	(58)
(Profit)/Loss on assets sales	5	12	(6)	5
Operating cash flow	1,494	965	1,138	981
Reconciliation of cash inflow to amounts shown in balance sheet:				
Closing cash	154	184	173	102
Closing investments	871	1,033	523	139
Closing short-term loans and overdrafts	(406)	(637)	(303)	(82)
	619	580	393	159
Opening cash	184	173	102	96
Opening investments	1,033	523	139	855
Opening short-term loans and overdrafts	(637)	(303)	(82)	(928)
	580	393	159	23
Net change in cash	39	187	234	136

Exhibit 3   Kingfisher Financial Statements

EXHIBIT 3
Kingfisher Financial Statements

CONSOLIDATED PROFIT AND LOSS ACCOUNTS
for the years 1989 to 1992 (in £ million)

	Jan. 30, 1993	Feb. 1, 1992	Feb. 2, 1991	Feb. 3, 1990
Turnover	3,547.9	3,388.8	3,235.4	2,910.0
Cost of sales	(2,401.5)	(2,264.3)	(2,170.8)	(1,967.7)
Gross profit	1,146.4	1,124.5	1,064.6	942.3
Selling expenses	(815.1)	(781.5)	(710.5)	(632.1)
Administrative expenses	(147.9)	(143.4)	(135.8)	(114.2)
Other operating income	46.3	32.2	26.7	47.4
Associated COS profits	2.2	1.8	0.4	–
Operating profit	231.9	233.6	245.4	243.4
Net interest	(0.7)	(11.8)	(30.1)	(36.0)
Exceptional items	(26.4)	5.9	37.2	87.3
Profit before tax	204.8	227.7	252.5	294.7
Provision for taxes	(56.9)	(61.5)	(63.7)	(63.3)
Profit after tax	147.9	166.2	188.8	231.4
Ordinary dividends	(75.1)	(63.4)	(55.3)	(50.6)
Extraordinary items	–	–	(4.4)	(5.8)
Retained profit	72.8	102.8	129.1	175.0
Earnings per share	30.1	35.2	42.1	52.6
Number of shares (in m)	492.0	471.6	448.1	439.9

d

149

Exhibit 3   Kingfisher Financial Statements

CONSOLIDATED BALANCE SHEETS
for the years 1989 to 1992 (in £ million)

	Jan. 30, 1993	Feb. 1, 1992	Feb. 2, 1991	Feb. 3, 1990
Fixed Assets:				
Tangibles	992.4	913.2	978.2	1,132.1
Investments	37.2	43.2	40.9	
	1,029.6	956.4	1,019.1	1,132.1
Current Assets:				
Development WIP	59.3	134.3	142.2	81.7
Stocks	571.7	505.0	509.0	463.9
Debtors	196.4	179.1	117.8	125.3
Prepayments	58.3	52.8	47.2	46.7
Investments	153.9	128.7	84.1	49.4
Cash and securities	161.7	210.0	75.1	52.8
	1,201.3	1,209.9	975.4	819.8
Total Assets	2,230.9	2,166.3	1,994.5	1,951.9
Current Liabilities:				
Bank loans	84.5	117.4	21.7	54.8
Notes & commercial paper	116.7	85.6	94.3	–
Trade creditors	292.4	228.6	233.9	247.4
Taxes payable	166.3	162.8	149.7	156.1
Accruals	226.1	212.9	207.5	198.5
Dividends	54.2	43.7	38.1	34.8
	940.2	851	745.2	691.6
Long-term liabilities	132.3	233	274.7	298.5
Provisions and deferred charges	0.6	–	–	–
Shareholders' Funds:				
Capital	124.7	120.8	113.5	110.0
Share premium account	150.3	117.2	55.7	27.6
Revaluation reserve	85.3	126.3	187.8	330.8
Other reserve	19.8	19.8	19.8	19.8
Profit & loss account	777.7	698.2	597.8	473.6
	1,157.8	1,082.3	974.6	961.8
Liabilities and Equity	2,230.9	2,166.3	1,994.5	1,951.9

Exhibit 3   Kingfisher Financial Statements

CONSOLIDATED CASH FLOW STATEMENTS
for the years 1990 to 1993 (in £ million)

	Jan. 30, 1993	Feb. 1, 1992	Feb. 2, 1991	Feb. 3, 1990
Net cash from operations	237.1	239.8	234.2	236.7
Servicing of Finance:				
Interest received	32.8	26.5	14.4	10.6
Interest paid	(36.0)	(46.2)	(52.5)	(50.1)
Dividends paid	(64.6)	(57.8)	(52.0)	(47.3)
Cash from servicing finance	(67.8)	(77.5)	(90.1)	(86.8)
Corporate taxation paid	(47.3)	(64.9)	(70.3)	(39.9)
Investing Activities:				
Purchase of subsidiary			(35.3)	(10.7)
Acquisition of fixed assets	(165.1)	(80.3)	(197.6)	(150.9)
Acquisition of investments	(4.0)	(6.0)	(40.5)	
Purchase of short-term investments	(36.9)	(3.1)	(20.8)	(17.4)
Sales of fixed assets	25.5	34.7	194.9	143.2
Cash from extraordinary items			(4.9)	(5.8)
Cash from investing activities	(180.5)	(54.7)	(104.2)	(41.6)
Cash flow before financing	(58.5)	42.7	(30.4)	68.4
Financing:				
Issue of common stock	9.8	17.7	3.9	1.1
Purchase of ST investments	14.1	(36.8)	(11.9)	(2.7)
Increase (repay) loans	(48.2)	(6.3)	94.0	(19.7)
Issue expenses	–	–	(0.2)	–
Net cash flow from financing	(24.3)	(25.4)	85.8	(21.3)
Increase in cash	(82.8)	17.3	55.4	47.1

NOTES TO FINANCIAL STATEMENTS
for the years 1989 to 1993 (in £ million)

1. Accounting Policies

Accounting conventions

The financial statements of the Company and its subsidiaries are made up to the Saturday nearest to 31st January each year. The financial statements of the Company and its subsidiaries are prepared under the historical cost convention, except for certain land and buildings which are included in the financial statements at valuation, and are prepared in accordance with applicable accounting standards.

d

151

Exhibit 3   Kingfisher Financial Statements

Basis of consolidation

The consolidated financial statements incorporate the financial statements of the Company, its subsidiary undertakings and associated undertakings. Subsidiaries acquired during the year are recorded under the acquisition method and their results are included from the date of acquisition. Associated undertakings are accounted for using the equity method. Goodwill arising is charged to reserves in the year of acquisition.

Depreciation

Depreciation of fixed assets is provided where necessary to reflect a reduction from book value to estimated residual value over the useful life of the asset to the Group. It is the Group's policy to maintain its properties in a state of good repair to prolong their useful lives. The Directors consider that, in the case of freehold and long leasehold properties, the estimated residual values at the end of their useful economic lives, based on prices prevailing at the time of acquisition or subsequent valuation, are not materially different from their current carrying values. Accordingly, no provision for depreciation on these classes of assets is considered necessary.

Depreciation of other fixed assets is calculated on a straight-line basis and the annual rates applicable to principal categories are:

Short leaseholds	over remaining period of lease
Tenant's improvements	over estimated useful life
Tenant's fixtures	between 10% and 15%
Computer equipment and electronic equipment	between 20% and 25%
Motor cars	25%
Commercial vehicles	33.33%

Disposal of land and buildings

Profits on disposal of land and buildings represent the difference between the net proceeds and the original cost of the land and buildings less any depreciation charged to the date of disposal based on the cost, and are shown after charging expenses attributable to the disposal.

Leased assets

All operating lease payments are charged to the income statement in the financial year to which the payments relate.

Capitalization of interest

Interest on borrowings to finance major property developments is included in the cost of the development where the Directors consider that it will be recoverable from the proceeds of the sale.

Foreign currencies

Income statement items are translated at average monthly exchange rates and assets and liabilities at rates of exchange ruling at the year end. Gains and losses on these translations are dealt with in the income statement. All other translation differences are reflected in reserves.

Property developments

Short-term property developments are stated at the lower of cost and net realizable value. Development profits on short-term contracts are taken when developments are sold. Long-term property developments are valued at cost plus attributable profit less provisions for foreseeable losses.

Stocks

Stocks are stated at the lower of cost and net realizable value. Cost includes appropriate overheads.

Investments

Investments are stated at the lower of cost and net realizable value. However, the difference between cost and net realizable value is not material.

Pensions

The Group operates defined benefit and defined contribution schemes for its employees. In each case a separate fund is being accumulated to meet the accruing liabilities. The assets of these funds are all held under trusts which are entirely separate from the Group's assets.

The cost of pensions in respect of the Group's defined benefit schemes is charged to the income statement so that it is spread over the working lives of the employees. Variations to pension costs caused by differences between the assumptions used and actual experience are spread over the working lives of the current employees at each actuarial valuation date.

Deferred taxation

Provision is made for deferred taxation except where the Directors consider it is unlikely to become payable in the foreseeable future.

Turnover

Turnover represents retail sales and services supplied together with rental income and turnover from property development activities. Turnover excludes transactions made between Group companies and value added tax.

2. Effect of Accounting Change for FRS3

The results for February 1, 1992, have been restated in accordance with FRS3. Under this statement, gains and losses on fixed assets are required to be reflected in the income statement as the difference between proceeds and net carrying cost (either depreciated historical cost or valuation). Kingfisher previously reported gains and losses as the difference between proceeds and depreciated historical cost. Reported figures from the prior year were (in £ m): Gross profit £1,124.5; Profit before tax £227.7; Profit after tax £166.2; and Retained profit £102.8.

d

153

Exhibit 3 Kingfisher Financial Statements

3. Profit on Ordinary Activities Before Taxation

Profit on ordinary activities before taxation is stated after charging the following:

	1993	1992	1991
Staff costs:			
Wages and salaries	421.2	403.5	372.5
Social security costs	27.9	27.4	25.2
Other pension costs	2.3	2.1	1.2
	451.4	433.0	398.9
Operating leases:			
Land and buildings	171.5	161.6	124.0
Plant and equipment	7.4	9.1	8.1
Depreciation	70.9	65.5	62.0

4. Exceptional Items

	1993	1992	1991
Write-down of Chartwell development property	26.4		
Profit on disposal of properties used by Kingfisher retail business		20.6	37.2
Cost of restructuring at Comet		(9.8)	
Cost of restructuring at Titles		(4.9)	
	26.4	5.9	37.2

5. Extraordinary Items

	1993	1992	1991
Abortive bid costs			2.1
Loss on disposal of interests in business			2.8
Less: tax credit			(0.5)
			4.4

Exhibit 3   Kingfisher Financial Statements

6. Taxation

Tax on profit on the ordinary activities of the Group for the year:

	1993	1992	1991
U.K. corporate tax	57.7	64.9	63.7
Relief for double taxation	(0.7)	(0.8)	(0.7)
Overseas taxation	3.0	2.1	1.9
Deferred taxation	1.6		3.0
Prior year adjustments	(5.3)	(5.4)	(4.2)
Associated undertakings	0.6	0.7	
	56.9	61.5	63.7

7. Long-Term Liabilities

	1993	1992	1991
Amounts falling due after more than one year:			
8.5% Convertible unsecured loan stock 2000	46.0	73.2	124.3
Zero coupon loan stock 2003	80.7	73.0	66.0
13.95% NZ dollar notes 1994		77.8	77.8
Less: amortized exchange gain		(6.6)	(4.7)
Loan notes 1994–1997	3.6	13.2	11.3
Medium term notes	2.0	2.4	
	132.3	233.0	274.7
These amounts fall due for repayment as follows:			
Between one and two years	4.6	71.7	
Between two and five years	1.0	12.3	83.4
After five years	126.7	149.0	191.3
	132.3	233.0	274.7

The Convertible unsecured loan stock 2000 is convertible in any of the years 1992 to 2000 into fully paid ordinary shares of the Company. The stock, unless previously converted, redeemed or purchased by the company, will be repaid at par on 31st October 2000.

The Zero coupon loan stock 2003 has an implicit interest rate of 10.3%, and unless redeemed earlier is repayable at par of £225.7 million on 28th April 2003.

The NZ dollar notes 1994 are repayable on 25th January 1994. Foreign exchange hedging arrangements are in place, as a result of which it is anticipated that an exchange gain of approximately £10 million will arise, and this gain is being amortized over the expected life of the notes.

Loan notes 1994–1997 bear interest rates between LIBOR and 1.5% below LIBOR.

d

155

Exhibit 3   Kingfisher Financial Statements

8. Cash Flow

	1993	1992	1991
Reconciliation of operating profit to cash from operations:			
Profit before interest	231.9	233.6	245.4
Exceptional items	(26.4)	5.9	37.2
Depreciation	70.9	65.5	62.0
Decrease in development WIP	32.3	13.0	(14.1)
Decrease in stock	(66.7)	4.0	(45.1)
Decrease in debtors	(26.2)	(58.7)	(0.1)
Increase in creditors	15.1	(2.5)	(7.3)
Net current assets of subsidiaries acquired			(6.2)
Associated undertakings	(2.2)	(1.8)	(0.4)
Profit on sales of fixed assets	8.4	(19.2)	(37.2)
Operating cash flow	237.1	239.8	234.2
Reconciliation of cash inflow to amounts shown in balance sheet:			
Closing cash	161.7	210.0	75.1
Closing short-term borrowings	(173.8)	(139.3)	(21.7)
	(12.1)	70.7	53.4
Opening cash	210.0	75.1	52.8
Opening short-term borrowings	(139.3)	(21.7)	(54.8)
	70.7	53.4	(2.0)
Net change in cash	(82.8)	17.3	(54.8)

Cash flow relating to exceptional profit on disposal of properties used by Kingfisher retail businesses is included in proceeds from sale of fixed assets. £2.7 million of the exceptional costs is included in operating cash flow.

Exhibit 3   Kingfisher Financial Statements

9. Business Analysis

	1993	1992	1991
Turnover:			
Retail sales	3,454.7	3,301.6	3,117.1
Property development sales	76.0	64.7	100.2
Rental income	53.2	58	56.5
Inter-segment rental income	(36.0)	(35.5)	(38.4)
	3,547.9	3,388.8	3,235.4
Profit Before Tax:			
B&Q	81.1	90.3	95.7
Comet	17.7	9.1	7.6
Woolworth	77.8	71.4	63
Superdrug	34.8	34.6	34.5
Other retail	3.0		
Restructuring provisions		(14.7)	
Chartwell Land:			
Development profits	(26.4)	1.9	11.6
Investment profits	34.5	37.2	42.8
Realization profits			
Other	(13.8)	(10.9)	(9.8)
Net interest	(0.7)	(11.8)	(30.1)
Property disposals	(3.2)	(11.4)	
Exceptional items			37.2
	204.8	195.7	252.5

Interest Coverage
Return on L-T cap.

Working Cap

LTD / Tot Cap

Richard Mandrell is a newly hired credit analyst, employed by a small but quickly growing insurance company that is becoming increasingly active in the market for private placements. In reviewing possible investments, the company considers what rating would have been assigned to similar bonds in the public markets. Such ratings play a significant role in determining the issues' yields and marketability. At this date, early 1991, AAA-rated corporate bonds are yielding, on average, about 9.4 percent, whereas BBB-rated corporates are yielding an average 10.2 percent. Some junk bonds are, of course, yielding much higher rates.

Analysis of prospective investments inevitably involves a degree of subjective business judgment. However, Mandrell is aware that, in the view of some, determination of an appropriate debt rating category for a particular issue is sometimes based largely on a few key financial ratios. In fact, several of Mandrell's competitors in the private placement market use purely quantitative debt scoring models as an important input to their credit analysis. Such an approach suggests that one could explain much of the variation in bond ratings based on a handful of financial ratios. Intrigued by that observation, Mandrell has decided to review a few recent public debt issues to see how well he can "predict" their current ratings based solely on a cursory review of the financial statements of the issuers.

The firms selected by Mandrell for analysis are all in the chemical industry: Fargo Chemical Company, Texas Gulf Corporation, MST Company, Boland Corporation, and Quotron Chemical Corporation. Despite their common industry membership, the five firms have widely varying capital structures and profitability.

The wide variation across the five firms' performance reflects the differences within the chemical industry. The prices of both inputs and outputs are volatile, and often they do not move in tandem. Thus, profitability critically depends on which prices are most important to a given firm. Some firms focus on basic chemicals—essentially, commodities that are similar across producers—and have little control over prices on either the input or output side of their market. Other firms focus on specialty chemicals. These firms tend to have highly differentiated products, specialized knowledge and processes, and close customer relations. In some cases, they are the sole supplier of a particular chemical. These firms are better insulated from changes in the prices of their inputs,

Prepared by Professor Victor L. Bernard, with the assistance of Mike Finn, Elise Kartchmar, and Hans Littooy. The firms on which the base is based are real, but the names have been disguised. The case was prepared as a basis for class discussion and is not intended to illustrate either an effective or ineffective management of a business situation.

because they have some ability to pass on such changes to their customers. Many chemical companies diversify across basic and speciality chemicals, sometimes achieving some manufacturing synergies in the process.

Profits in the chemical industry reached an all-time high in 1988 and 1989, due to favorable trends in prices. Sales grew by 10 percent, while net profit margins reached a healthy 8 percent and ROE moved to 17 percent. In 1990, however, the industry was not as fortunate. The prices in many input markets, including those for petroleum products, rose during the Gulf War. Simultaneously, a worldwide recession dampened demand for the outputs of chemical firms, including demand from the key sectors of construction and transportation. Sales growth in chemicals slowed significantly, and net profit margins fell below 7 percent. Several specialty chemical manufacturers maintained strong profits, but producers of basic chemicals struggled. With the world still in a recession in 1991, and the industry now facing some excess capacity due to the plant expansions that commenced during the highly profitable late 1980s, the near-term profitability picture for many chemical companies is only mediocre.

FARGO CHEMICAL COMPANY

Fargo Chemical is a leading international manufacturer and marketer of intermediate chemicals and specialty products. The company produces three principal chemicals: propylene oxide and derivatives, used in urethane foams and in solvents for furniture, auto, and construction industries; tertiary butyl alcohol and derivatives, used as an octane enhancer; and styrene, used in plastic and rubber components.

Fargo resulted from a spinoff of a major petroleum company in 1987; the majority of its shares remain in the control of that company. Earnings grew steadily in 1987 and 1988, but then fell in both 1989 and 1990, reflecting the generally difficult conditions in the chemical industry and the heightened price competition.

Fargo's long-term debt includes a half-dozen public and privately placed issues. The one for which Mandrell will attempt to "predict" a rating is a $100 million debenture, issued in 1990 and due in 2005. Like nearly all other long-term debt issued by Fargo, the debentures are unsecured, subordinated, and issued "for general corporate purposes." They are not callable.

Fargo's financial statements are presented in Exhibit 1.

TEXAS GULF CORPORATION

Texas Gulf Corporation is the smallest of the five chemical companies reviewed by Mandrell. It produces several highly integrated lines of commodity and specialty chemicals, and is a leading producer of chlorine, caustic soda, sodium chlorate, vinyl chloride monomer, and other chlorine-based and alcohol products. End uses for the products are diverse: housing and construction markets, solvents, plastics and fibers, consumer products, pulp and paper, and other uses.

Texas Gulf enjoyed extraordinary margins in 1988 and 1989. The profitability reflected not only the favorable relation of output to input prices, but also the efficiencies of Texas Gulf's highly integrated manufacturing process. Texas Gulf considers itself a low-cost producer of commodity and specialty chemicals, and claims that its productivity rates are among the highest in the industry. Nevertheless, Texas Gulf was not invulnerable to the downturn of 1990, with operating profits falling by nearly 25 percent.

In an effort to insulate itself from potential takeover, Texas Gulf undertook a recapitalization in April 1990, and followed that action with the adoption of a poison pill agreement. The recapitalization involved the distribution of a $30 dividend to shareholders, financed with a combination of $191 million of subordinated notes (issued to the shareholders), a $507 million term loan, and a smaller ($44 million) revolving credit agreement. The term loan and revolver were arranged with a group of financial institutions. The term loan is payable in quarterly installments through 1998.

The debt considered by Mandrell is the subordinated note issue. The notes are callable at par beginning 1995, and are due in 2000. Prepayment of the subordinated notes is prohibited while the bank debt remains outstanding. The notes are unsecured, but require that certain financial ratios be maintained.

Texas Gulf's financial statements are presented in Exhibit 2.

d

MST COMPANY

MST Company is the largest of the five firms considered here, and one of the largest chemical producers in the U.S. Its lines of business include agriculture, personal care products, food products, construction materials, plastics, resin products, rubber and process chemicals, and pharmaceuticals. In several of its lines of business, it holds major brand names.

MST is more widely diversified than others in the chemical industry, and therefore may be better insulated from the current industry conditions. Nevertheless, it experienced a decline in margins and a resulting dropoff in profits in 1990.

Among MST's many debt issues are $100 million of callable sinking fund debentures, issued for general corporate purposes. The debentures rank on a parity with nearly all of MST's other debt, and are unsecured and unsubordinated.

MST's financial statements appear in Exhibit 3.

BOLAND CORPORATION

Boland Corporation is a diversified manufacturer of chemicals, metals and materials, and defense-related products. Within its chemical operations, Boland produces industrial chemicals (including caustic soda, urethanes, and chlorines), performance chemicals, water sanitizing chemicals, and image-forming chemicals. Its metals products include a variety of copper and steel materials. The most important defense-related product is ammunition.

Boland's earnings grew steadily from 1985 through 1989. However, they fell by more than 30 percent in 1990, as Boland found itself selling products into those sectors of the economy most affected by the recession.

Boland's long-term debt consists of $341 million of notes, revolvers, and other debt arranged with a variety of financial institutions, plus $125 million of publicly held subordinated notes. It is the subordinated notes that Mandrell is attempting to rate. The notes were issued in 1987, are due in 1997, are not callable, and are unsecured. The notes were issued to reduce short-term bank debt incurred in early 1987 to finance working capital and long-term investments.

Boland's financial statements appear in Exhibit 4.

QUOTRON CHEMICAL CORPORATION

Quotron Chemical is a long-standing company engaged in the manufacturing and retailing of petrochemicals, propanes, and polyethylene products. Quotron ranks as the nation's largest propane retailer (24 percent of sales) and polyethylene producer (54 percent of sales). The polyethylene business tends to experience particularly volatile earnings, as the prices of the inputs (e.g., ethylene) and output (polyethylene) sometimes fail to move in tandem. The propane business is also subject to some randomness; for example, propane sales vary depending on the severity of winter weather.

Quotron's earnings, after having stagnated during the early and mid-1980s, grew dramatically in 1987 and 1988, largely as a product of strong demand and higher prices for polyethylene, polypropylene, and other petrochemical products. However, polyethylene margins fell in 1989 and a fire caused the shutdown of a major plant for the last half of the year—leaving Quotron operating profits down almost 40 percent. The plant resumed operations in the spring of 1990, but prices continued to swing in unfavorable directions, leading to another decline in operating profits.

In early 1989, the company undertook a number of actions to prevent a takeover. First, a leveraged recapitalization was arranged, involving the issue of a $50 per share dividend and a large increase in the firm's long-term debt. Secondly, a "poison pill" shareholders' rights plan was adopted. Third, an ESOP plan was adopted, resulting in the placement of 14 percent of the firm's shares in the hands of the ESOP trustee.

Quotron has more than a dozen issues of debt outstanding. Seven issues totaling $1.25 billion are unsubordinated; the remaining issues are subordinated. Mandrell has decided to consider one debt issue in each of these categories. The first is Quotron's largest debt issue: $500 million of unsecured subordinated debentures, issued in conjunction with the recapitalization in 1989 and due in 2004, callable after 1994 at prices that begin at 106.50 and decline over time to par. The other debt issue considered by Mr. Mandrell is Quotron's second largest: $300 million of unsecured unsubordinated sinking fund notes, dated 1988 and due in 2018, callable after 1991 at prices that begin at 108 and decline over the life of the issue to par.

Quotron's financial statements appear in Exhibit 5.

d

162

QUESTION

1. Based on the available information, estimate what rating would be assigned to each debt security described in the case.

d

Exhibit 1   Fargo Chemical Company – Financial Statements

EXHIBIT 1

Fargo Chemical Company – Financial Statements

INCOME STATEMENT

	Year Ended December 31			
($ millions, except per share data)	1990	1989	1988	1987
Sales	2,830	2,663	2,700	1,952
Cost of Goods Sold	1,993	1,749	1,704	1,335
Gross Profit	837	914	996	617
SG & A Expense	281	238	191	152
Operating Income Before Depreciation	556	676	805	465
Depreciation, Depletion, & Amortization	117	93	83	67
Operating Profit	439	583	722	398
Interest Expense	75	37	51	41
Non-Operating Income/Expense	73	56	92	64
Special Items	30	−3	0	0
Pretax Income	467	599	763	421
Total Income Taxes	159	194	269	164
Income Before Extraordinary Items	308	405	494	257
Extraordinary Items	43	0	0	0
Net Income	351	405	494	257

d

Exhibit 1   Fargo Chemical Company – Financial Statements

BALANCE SHEET

	as of December 31			
($ millions)	1990	1989	1988	1987
Assets:				
Cash & Equivalents	486	144	410	709
Net Receivables	593	409	477	363
Inventories	289	286	271	207
Other Current Assets	38	13	12	12
Total Current Assets	1,406	852	1,170	1,291
Gross PP & E	2,467	1,851	1,565	1,427
Accumulated Depreciation	699	588	487	443
Net PP & E	1,768	1,263	1,078	984
Investments at Equity	132	118	99	76
Other Investments	270	11	8	0
Deferred Charges	163	182	193	183
Other Assets	0	229	0	0
Total Assets	3,739	2,655	2,548	2,534
Liabilities:				
LT Debt Due in One Year	39	29	4	0
Notes Payable	40	102	256	650
Accounts Payable	225	151	113	122
Taxes Payable	45	48	71	31
Accrued Expenses	192	84	141	134
Other Current Liabilities	0	0	52	39
Total Current Liabilities	541	414	637	976
Long-Term Debt	1,181	390	271	166
Deferred Taxes	208	221	217	239
Other Liabilities	51	39	48	37
Total Noncurrent Liabilities	1,440	650	536	442
Total Liabilities	1,981	1,064	1,173	1,418
Equity:				
Common Stock	100	100	100	100
Capital Surplus	864	864	864	869
Retained Earnings	907	740	520	147
Less: Treasury Stock	113	113	109	0
Common (Total) Equity	1,758	1,591	1,375	1,116
Total Liabilities & Equity	3,739	2,655	2,548	2,534

d

Exhibit 2   Texas Gulf Corporation – Financial Statements

EXHIBIT 2

Texas Gulf Corporation – Financial Statements

INCOME STATEMENT

($ millions, except per share data)	Year Ended December 31			
	1990	1989	1988	1987
Sales	932	1,104	1,061	707
Cost of Goods Sold	646	742	689	498
Gross Profit	286	362	371	209
SG & A Expense	41	48	46	28
Operating Income Before Depreciation	245	315	325	181
Depreciation, Depletion, & Amortization	16	16	12	9
Operating Profit	229	299	313	172
Interest Expense	63	1	3	11
Non-Operating Income/Expense	3	2	3	1
Special Items	–18	0	0	0
Pretax Income	150	300	312	163
Total Income Taxes	55	108	119	71
Including Before Extraordinary Items	95	192	194	92
Extraordinary Items	0	0	0	-10
Net Income	95	192	194	82

Exhibit 2   Texas Gulf Corporation – Financial Statements

BALANCE SHEET

($ millions)	as of December 31			
	1990	1989	1988	1987
Assets:				
Cash & Equivalents	6	46	40	24
Net Receivables	118	117	127	95
Inventories	86	75	85	55
Prepaid Expenses	8	7	8	8
Total Current Assets	218	244	260	182
Gross PP & E	316	300	245	184
Accumulated Depreciation	101	91	76	64
Net PP & E	215	209	169	120
Deferred Charges	21	0	0	0
Other Assets	3	20	28	6
Total Assets	457	473	457	309
Liabilities:				
LT Debt Due in One Year	43	0	0	0
Accounts Payable	75	63	81	56
Taxes Payable	8	9	19	24
Accrued Expenses	35	27	28	20
Other Current Liabilities	0	6	0	0
Total Current Liabilities	161	106	128	100
Long-Term Debt	683	1	42	42
Deferred Taxes	36	36	31	25
Total Noncurrent Liabilities	720	37	73	66
Total Liabilities	881	143	201	166
Equity:				
Common Stock	0	1	1	1
Capital Surplus	2	36	27	23
Retained Earnings	−427	427	302	125
Less: Treasury Stock	0	134	74	7
Common (Total) Equity	−424	330	256	143
Total Liabilities & Equity	457	473	457	309

d

167

Exhibit 3   MST Company – Financial Statements

EXHIBIT 3
MST Company – Financial Statements

INCOME STATEMENT

($ millions, except per share data)	Year Ended December 31			
	1990	1989	1988	1987
Sales	8,995	8,681	8,293	7,639
Cost of Goods Sold	4,901	4,597	4,537	4,334
Gross Profit	4,094	4,084	3,756	3,305
SG & A Expense	2,485	2,342	2,135	1,957
Operating Income Before Depreciation	1,609	1,742	1,621	1,348
Depreciation, Depletion, & Amortization	700	664	666	646
Operating Profit	909	1,078	955	702
Interest Expense	208	204	193	188
Non-Operating Income/Expense	120	151	138	136
Special Items	0	0	0	32
Pretax Income	821	1,025	900	682
Total Income Taxes	263	336	302	237
Minority Interest	12	10	7	9
Net Income	546	679	591	436

d

168

Exhibit 3   MST Company – Financial Statements

BALANCE SHEET

($ millions)	as of December 31			
	1990	1989	1988	1987
Assets:				
Cash & Equivalents	204	253	221	223
Net Receivables	1,498	1,309	1,234	1,209
Inventories	1,270	1,197	1,170	1,081
Other Current Assets	541	489	472	490
Total Current Assets	3,513	3,248	3,097	3,003
Gross PP & E	7,620	6,937	6,926	6,730
Accumulated Depreciation	4,128	3,764	3,780	3,654
Net PP & E	3,492	3,173	3,146	3,076
Investments at Equity	248	204	205	240
Intangibles	1,425	1,682	1,790	1,953
Other Assets	558	297	223	183
Total Assets	9,236	8,604	8,461	8,455
Liabilities:				
LT Debt Due in One Year	118	44	128	119
Notes Payable	464	461	428	420
Accounts Payable	584	514	545	527
Taxes Payable	95	126	124	101
Accrued Expenses	929	777	755	633
Total Current Liabilities	2,190	1,922	1,980	1,800
Long-Term Debt	1,652	1,471	1,408	1,564
Deferred Taxes	640	621	588	584
Other Liabilities	665	649	685	606
Total Noncurrent Liabilities	2,957	2,741	2,681	2,754
Total Liabilities	5,147	4,663	4,661	4,554
Equity:				
Common Stock	329	164	164	164
Capital Surplus	714	877	874	872
Retained Earnings	4,609	4,144	3,714	3,382
Less: Treasury Stock	1,563	1,244	952	517
Common (Total) Equity	4,089	3,941	3,800	3,901
Total Liabilities & Equity	9,236	8,604	8,461	8,455

d

169

Exhibit 4   Boland Corporation – Financial Statements

EXHIBIT 4

Boland Corporation – Financial Statements

INCOME STATEMENT

($ millions, except per share data)	1990	1989	1988	1987
Sales	2,592	2,509	2,308	1,930
Cost of Goods Sold	1,936	1,811	1,664	1,337
Gross Profit	656	698	644	593
SG & A Expense	382	353	347	326
Operating Income Before Depreciation	274	345	297	267
Depreciation, Depletion, & Amortization	123	122	117	118
Operating Profit	151	223	180	149
Interest Expense	56	57	44	34
Non-Operating Income/Expense	25	22	15	12
Special Items	−4	4	0	0
Pretax Income	116	192	151	127
Total Income Taxes	32	68	53	49
Net Income	84	124	98	78

Year Ended December 31

d

170

Exhibit 4   Boland Corporation – Financial Statements

BALANCE SHEET

($ millions)	as of December 31			
	1990	1989	1988	1987
Assets:				
Cash & Equivalents	6	12	25	34
Net Receivables	419	453	437	362
Inventories	293	296	311	273
Other Current Assets	16	29	28	11
Total Current Assets	734	790	801	680
Gross PP & E	2,297	2,169	2,164	2,007
Accumulated Depreciation	1,468	1,388	1,363	1,280
Net PP & E	829	781	801	727
Investments at Equity	145	144	149	137
Intangibles	106	110	141	102
Other Assets	52	79	48	39
Total Assets	1,866	1,904	1,940	1,685
Liabilities:				
LT Debt Due in One Year	34	15	39	24
Notes Payable	70	140	172	26
Accounts Payable	222	255	223	200
Taxes Payable	9	4	4	11
Accrued Expenses	187	171	179	143
Total Current Liabilities	522	585	617	404
Long-Term Debt	466	501	474	392
Deferred Taxes	48	60	60	49
Other Liabilities	115	93	106	140
Total Noncurrent Liabilities	629	654	640	581
Total Liabilities	1,151	1,239	1,257	985
Equity:				
Common Stock	19	19	20	22
Capital Surplus	180	177	188	200
Retained Earnings	505	469	475	478
Common Equity	704	665	683	700
Preferred Stock	11	0	0	0
Total Equity	715	665	683	700
Total Liabilities & Equity	1,866	1,904	1,940	1,685

d

171

Exhibit 5   Quotron Chemical Corporation – Financial Statements

EXHIBIT 5
Quotron Chemical Corporation – Financial Statements

INCOME STATEMENT

	Year Ended December 31			
($ millions, except per share data)	1990	1989	1988	1987
Sales	2,618	2,637	2,884	2,525
Cost of Goods Sold	1,991	1,790	1,770	1,772
Gross Profit	627	847	1,114	753
SG & A Expense	217	224	207	232
Operating Income Before Depreciation	410	623	907	522
Depreciation, Depletion, & Amortization	155	147	147	142
Operating Profit	255	476	760	380
Interest Expense	269	297	116	83
Non-Operating Income/Expense	47	0	-26	6
Special Items	28	0	0	0
Pretax Income	61	178	618	303
Total Income Taxes	39	64	258	159
Income Before Discontinued Operations	21	114	360	144
Discontinued Operations	0	133	23	108
Net Income	21	247	383	252

d

Exhibit 5　Quotron Chemical Corporation – Financial Statements

BALANCE SHEET

($ millions)	as of December 31			
	1990	1989	1988	1987
Assets:				
Cash & Equivalents	13	104	219	25
Net Receivables	467	361	428	434
Inventories	366	304	339	316
Other Current Assets	51	99	354	61
Total Current Assets	897	868	1,339	836
Gross PP & E	2,905	2,513	1,943	2,037
Accumulated Depreciation	885	754	634	657
Net PP & E	2,020	1,759	1,309	1,380
Investments at Equity	32	129	60	60
Other Investments	34	39	39	107
Intangibles	83	94	26	62
Other Assets	156	115	135	137
Total Assets	3,222	3,004	2,908	2,581
Liabilities:				
LT Debt Due in One Year	14	8	3	21
Notes Payable	0	0	5	93
Accounts Payable	137	133	157	134
Taxes Payable	0	38	88	87
Accrued Expenses	277	324	326	242
Other Current Liabilities	0	0	1,141	0
Total Current Liabilities	428	503	1,720	577
Long-Term Debt	2,530	2,363	1,332	727
Deferred Taxes	230	160	174	150
Other Liabilities	135	151	88	82
Total Noncurrent Liabilities	2,895	2,674	1,594	959
Total Liabilities	3,323	3,176	3,315	1,536
Equity:				
Common Stock	220	159	57	75
Capital Surplus	0	0	0	29
Retained Earnings	−321	−331	-464	942
Common (Total) Equity	−101	−172	-407	1,045
Total Liabilities & Equity	3,222	3,004	2,908	2,581

d

173

Brenda Curtis, a buy-side analyst focusing on retail stocks, has watched her favorite industry suffer through turmoil and retrenchment during 1991. But while the industry faltered and Macy's filed for bankruptcy, one retailer—The Gap—was busy generating an almost-unheard-of ROE of 40 percent for the year ended January 1992. This San Francisco based marketer of casual clothing was labeled as "the nation's hottest retailer" by *Business Week* (March 9, 1992, cover story). Curtis has decided to take a harder look at The Gap to see what all the fuss is about.

The Gap's lofty P/E ratio of 35 and price-to-book ratio of 12 (based on a price in the $55 range) suggest that investors expect even more good things from The Gap in the future. Duff and Phelps analyst Carol I. Palmer labels The Gap a "buy," noting that relative to 1993 earnings forecasts, the P/E multiple was not unusually high, and yet five-year earnings growth was forecast "conservatively" at 17 percent, well above the 13 percent forecasted growth rate for the market as a whole. In speaking about The Gap's valuation, Palmer notes the following:

> *Discounting only five years of Gap cash flows (using a weighted average discount rate) and adding the residual value (present value of cash flows from 1996 on) and subtracting debt, we obtain a fair market value of $30 per share. However, since we feel strongly that The Gap is a long-term growth company, it is, therefore, appropriate to discount years beyond the next five, using a weighted average discount rate, into the "fair price"; a ten-year time-frame yields a fair market value of $55 per share. Note also that our forecast of fundamentals is conservative by the standards of both consensus opinion and the Company itself.[1]*

Palmer's optimism about the long run is buttressed by her view of The Gap's position within the industry. Few if any retailers had been so successful in recent years in executing their strategy and establishing their "look":

> *The Gap has established itself as a trend-setter in casual wear, at good prices, for younger consumers. Excellent management, systems, and merchandising support a continued leadership position. . . . We think the Company has mastered the right*

175

Prepared by Professor Victor L. Bernard, with the assistance of Elise Kartchmar. This case is based upon publicly available information. It was prepared as a basis for class discussion and is not intended to illustrate either an effective or ineffective management of a business situation.

1. *Duff and Phelps Company Analysis (April 1992). Duff & Phelps does not disclose the cost of capital estimate used in their model. However, analysts estimate The Gap's beta at approximately 1.30. Intermediate-term government bonds are yielding approximately 6.3 percent.*

mix of value-added, fashion merchandise and quality staples. This mix, combined with highly focused image-management (advertising, store layout, and locations), has made The Gap the definition of correctness in casual wear for a broad demographic group.[2]

Ironically, The Gap's notable success may be its greatest source of concern. *Business Week* notes that:

... plenty of rivals are regrouping to compete. Department store executives preach to employees about the need to "Gap-ize" the colors, fibers, and display of their wares. ... Giorgio Armani is looking to skim The Gap's biggest-spending customers with its new A/X Armani Exchanges, which offer stripped-down fashions with a European look at prices much lower than those at the top of Armani's line. ... The Limited Inc. has Gap-like "relaxed fit" jeans, sold in some stores with a sales tag whose design is strikingly like The Gap's. ... Dayton Hudson is experimenting with a chain called Everyday Hero that will have a distinctly Gap-like approach.[3]

Despite concerns about competitive forces in the retail industry, analyst Curtis is intrigued enough by Palmer's optimism to press on with her investigation of The Gap. The following paragraphs summarize the information at her disposal.

BUSINESS AT THE GAP

The Gap, Inc. is a specialty retailer of casual and active apparel for men, women, and children. Incorporated in 1969 as a retailer of Levi's jeans, records, and tapes, The Gap was restructured in 1984 under the guidance of merchandiser Mickey Drexler. Under Drexler, The Gap sought to provide stylish yet affordable apparel, primarily for the 20- to 45-year-old customer. GapKids was introduced in 1986 to serve the market for boys and girls aged 2 through 12. Selected GapKids stores include "babyGap" sections offering clothing for infants and toddlers. The Gap also owns Banana Republic, Inc., another specialty retailer emphasizing rugged and casual men's and women's apparel.

Gap, GapKids, and Banana Republic stores are located primarily in shopping malls throughout the U.S. As of April 1992, there were 1226 such stores, 1176 of which were located in the U.S. The remainder were located in Canada and the U.K.

Drexler's motto for The Gap is "Good style, good quality, good value." Analyst Palmer characterized The Gap's formula this way:

... mostly staple/commodity apparel, with some differentiated fashion merchandise, at highly competitive prices (given the reliable quality), in convenient locations; while the s.k.u. count is limited, the inventory is deep. To summarize, using The Gap's self-description: "intensely focused."[4]

2. *Ibid.*
3. Business Week, March 9, 1992. p. 63–64.
4. *Duff and Phelps Company Analysis (April 1992)*

The Gap's formula begins with its own New York designers, Lisa Schultz and John Fumiatti, who attempt to anticipate consumer desires for clothing that is stylish but basic, and faithful to The Gap "look." The Gap relies more on the vision of its designers and quick market tests than on quantitative consumer research. Designs are created approximately one year in advance of sale, in sufficient numbers to assure that Gap stores will receive a new collection of styles every two months; older clothing still unsold at that point is moved out quickly by slashing prices.

All clothing is manufactured under The Gap's private label, by over 450 suppliers. To control manufacturing quality, The Gap establishes specifications for each order and maintains a staff of 200 inspectors at the factory sites. In 1991, 38 percent of the clothing was produced domestically, and the rest in Hong Kong and other foreign countries. No single manufacturer accounted for more than 5 percent of the supply.

The Gap maintains little replenishment merchandise at the retail outlets. Instead, large inventories are maintained in distribution centers in California, Kentucky, Canada, the U.K., and (beginning in 1992) Maryland. Point-of-sale scanners permit tracking of inventory needs at each retail outlet, so that distribution centers can replenish stock quickly.

Gap stores are usually leased in shopping malls and are company-controlled, not franchised. Most Gap stores tend to be small by industry standards—often no more than 4000 square feet—but many of the newer outlets are larger: about 7000 square feet. They are more sparse than some specialty clothing outlets, but are well-lit, clean, and "shopper friendly," with wide aisles and readily accessible merchandise. Store layout and operations are controlled tightly by the corporation; one observer states that "there's no more room for creative expression at a Gap store than there is at a McDonald's— maybe less."[5] Each week, store windows and displays are rearranged, according to a specified company design, to maintain a fresh, new look even to frequent customers.

The Gap "look" is reinforced through advertising in lifestyle and fashion magazines, and in various outdoor media: bus shelters, mass transit posters, telephone kiosks, and so forth. Advertising campaigns are designed by The Gap's own in-house staff. The ads feature such well-known faces as Spike Lee, Joan Didion, and James Dean. Some of the black-and-white prints used in this campaign have won advertising awards. In 1991, The Gap kicked off a black-and-white television ad campaign, and intended to expand this campaign in 1992. Advertising costs were 1.5 percent, 1.2 percent, and 1.4 percent of sales in fiscal 1989, 1990, and 1991. Comparable amounts for direct competitors, such as the Limited, are not available.

Growth at The Gap has been phenomenal. Sales, which stood at about $850 million in 1986, rose to $2.5 billion in 1991. Over that same period, annual earnings rose from $68 million to $230 million. In 1991, The Gap brand became the Number 2 private label in the clothing business, behind Levi Strauss.

Much of the sales growth at The Gap has resulted from new store openings; the number of stores rose from 960 in 1989 to 1092 in 1990, and to 1216 in 1991. In addition, however, much growth is attributable to enhanced utilization of existing floor space.

5. Business Week, March 9, 1992, p. 61

The Gap, Inc.

Sales per square foot increased from $250 in 1986 to $481 in 1991; comparable store growth (i.e., growth ignoring the effects of new store openings and expansions) has been much higher than that of competitors. Below is a comparison of growth at The Gap with each of two competitors, The Limited and Petrie Stores. The Limited Inc. (owner of The Limited Stores, Express, Lane Bryant, Victoria's Secret, Structure, and others) was the second-fastest growing specialty retailer in fiscal 1991, behind The Gap. Petrie Stores (owner of Petrie's, Marianne's, Stuarts, and others), was among the more slowly growing firms in the specialty retail category.

	Sales ($ billions)			Sales per Square Foot ($)			Comparable Store Growth		
	Gap	Limited	Petrie	Gap	Limited	Petrie	Gap	Limited	Petrie
1991	2.519	6.281	1.355	481	302	N/D	13%	3%	3.5%
1990	1.933	5.376	1.282	438	309	N/D	14%	3%	1.7%
1989	1.587	4.750	1.258	389	323	N/D	15%	9%	2.0%
1986	0.848	3.223	1.198	250	277	N/D	12%	18%	N/D

N/D = not publicly disclosed

INDUSTRY CONDITIONS AND COMPETITION

The Gap's performance in the early 1990s was highly unusual within the retail sector. Retail businesses were hit hard by weak consumer confidence and a slowly growing economy. In real terms, sales declined from 1989 to 1990, and again from 1990 to 1991. Particularly hard hit were department stores, which experienced "probably the most trying period in [their] history."[6] Performance by general merchandisers was stronger, but still not overly impressive; ROEs for a composite of general merchandisers (K-Mart, Penney's, Sears, and Wal-Mart) averaged about 12 to 15 percent over the 1987–1991 period, not much different from the average for U.S. corporations in a typical year. Profitability at speciality retailers was highly variable, but healthy on average. ROEs for a specialty retailer composite (Gap, Limited, Melville, Nordstrom, and Petrie) ranged from 20 to 23 percent in 1987–1991.

Those firms who managed to find paths to profitability were the so-called "power retailers" or "New Wave retailers."[7] Included in this category were some specialty retailers (e.g., The Gap, The Limited, and Toys-R-Us) and other general merchandisers, including discount retailer Wal-Mart. The innovations that made these firms successful were varied, and included higher-margin niche strategies as well as everyday low pricing

6. Standard and Poor's Industry Surveys, June 4, 1992, p. R77.
7. Ibid., p. R81. The term "New Wave" retailer is attributed to Dr. Carl Steidtmann, Chief Economist of Management Horizons, a division of Price Waterhouse.

("value pricing") strategies. Most success stories, however, involved high inventory turns and high sales volume per square foot.

The Gap's 1991 10-K characterizes the specialty retail industry as "highly competitive," and acknowledges that the success of the Company's operations has increased the likelihood of imitation. Indeed, *Fortune* magazine states that "If imitation is the sincerest form of you-know-what, then The Gap is in the middle of an outright lovefest."[8]

On the subject of competition within the industry, Gap Chairman and CEO Donald Fisher says, "We don't worry. We have a distinct advantage in our name, our merchandise, and the number and location of our stores."[9] Is President Drexler worried? "Sure, but hey look, there aren't too many secrets in this business. It's just going to make us run a little harder."[10]

OUTLOOK

In their 1991 Letter to Shareholders, President Drexler and CEO Fisher described The Gap's outlook as follows:

Our challenges for 1992 and beyond begin with increasing market share through continued sales growth. To start working toward this goal we will open approximately 135 new stores in 1992. We will also continue the program to expand our locations by enlarging approximately 100 existing stores.

Along with building new stores and larger stores, . . . we plan to continue to grow our business through a concerted effort to increase consumer awareness of our four brands—Gap, GapKids, babyGap, and Banana Republic.

The Gap has stated goals of at least 20 percent annual sales and EPS growth; 30 percent ROE; and pretax margins of 10.5 to 11 percent. The growth is to be supported through capital expenditures of over $200 million per year beyond 1992.[11] In the foreseeable future, most of this will be devoted to investment in the U.S. However, international sales may become increasingly important. By the end of 1993, The Gap expects to have approximately 100 stores outside the U.S., primarily in Canada, but with an increasing presence in the U.K. Longer term, there is some possibility of expansion to Europe and Asia.

Analyst Michael Schiffman rated The Gap a strong buy, based on his optimism about short-run earnings performance, but still expressed some reasons to constrain enthusiasm about the long run:

The Gap has been a big beneficiary of changes in spending habits in the 1990s. Recessionary times have altered consumers' attitudes over the last couple of years. Expensive, impressive "labels" are out; value is in. . . . In the current environment, consumers have decided that a logo is not worth the extra cost.

g

179

8. Fortune, *December 2, 1991, p. 106.*
9. Business Week, *March 9, 1992, p. 60.*
10. Fortune, *op. cit.*
11. *Duff and Phelps Company Analysis (April 1992).*

Will these changes be long-lasting? That remains to be seen. It's not clear to us that people's attitudes have been permanently altered; that when prosperity returns, they will still flock to this retailer's stores in search of good quality at a value price. That's not to say the market for good-quality apparel at prices most people can afford to pay will disappear. We just don't think it will continue to grow by leaps and bounds over the next 3 to 5 years.[12]

Analyst Carol Palmer was more optimistic:

. . . The big question is whether The Gap can continue its recent record of success; more precisely, is its formula one for this recession (in which white-collar boomers are tightening their belts) or one for the decade of the '90s?

The market's worst fear about The Gap appears to be that, in an economic recovery, shoppers will trade up from The Gap for casual wear. In our opinion, consumers will merely complement Gap-shopping with more traditionally upscale shopping as they sense themselves gaining purchasing power. We think a better economy should serve to bolster The Gap's formidable consumer franchise.[13]

QUESTIONS

1. The Gap's return on equity for fiscal 1991 was extraordinarily high. Analyze the company's profitability, relative to prior years and relative to the competition. Which components of profitability provided the Gap with its "edge" in 1991? What appear to be the sources of that edge, and what does that suggest about The Gap's business strategy? What is your assessment of the sustainability of the company's profitability?
2. Forecast earnings and cash flows for The Gap for fiscal 1992.
3. With its stock price standing at $55 per share in early 1992, what must the market have in mind for The Gap? Using a valuation model—based either on discounted cash flow or discounted abnormal earnings—infer what possible combinations of profitability, growth, and cost of capital would be necessary to justify such a price.
4. Compare your assessment of prospects for profitability at The Gap with those reflected in the market price.

----

12. *Value Line report (February 28, 1992).*
13. *Duff and Phelps Company Analysis (April 1992).*

Exhibit 1   Excerpts from The Gap's 1991 Annual Report

EXHIBIT 1

Excerpts from The Gap's 1991 Annual Report

MANAGEMENT'S DISCUSSION AND ANALYSIS OF RESULTS OF OPERATIONS AND FINANCIAL CONDITION

RESULTS OF OPERATIONS

Net Sales

	Fiscal Year Ended		
	Feb. 1, 1992 (Fiscal 1991) 52 Weeks	Feb. 2, 1991 (Fiscal 1990) 52 Weeks	Feb. 3, 1990 (Fiscal 1989) 53 Weeks
Net Sales ($000)	$2,518,893	$1,933,780	$1,586,596
Total sales growth	30%	22%	27%
Growth in comparable store sales (52-week basis)	13%	14%	15%
Number of			
New stores	139	152	98
Expanded stores	79	56	7
Closed stores	15	20	38

The opening of new stores (less the effect of stores closed), and the expansion of existing stores, as well as the increase in comparable store sales contributed to total sales growth for the fiscal years 1991, 1990 and 1989.

Net sales per average square foot increased to $481 in 1991 from $438 in 1990 and $389 in 1989. Over the past two years, the Company has increased the average size of its new stores and expanded the size of some of its existing stores. This has resulted in a net increase in total square footage of 18% in 1991 and 17% in 1990.

Cost of Goods Sold and Occupancy Expenses

Cost of goods sold and occupancy expenses decreased as a percentage of net sales to 62.3% in 1991 from 64.2% in 1990 and 65.9% in 1989. The 1.9% decrease in 1991 was primarily a result of an increase in merchandise margins as a percentage of net sales. The 1.7% decrease in 1990 was the result of higher merchandise margins, somewhat offset by an increase in occupancy expenses as a percentage of net sales.

Operating Expenses

Operating expenses as a percentage of net sales were 22.9%, 23.4% and 22.9% for fiscal years 1991, 1990 and 1989. The .5% decrease in 1991 from 1990 was primarily due to lower payroll costs as a percentage of net sales, which reflected the positive leverage achieved on expenses through sales growth. The .5% increase in 1990 from 1989 was largely attributable to costs associated with the write off of fixed assets for store expansions and relocations.

Net Interest Expense

Net interest expense was $3,523,000 and $1,435,000 and $2,760,000 for fiscal years 1991, 1990 and 1989. The increase in 1991 over 1990 of $2,088,000 was due to increases in average net borrowings and average net interest rates. The decrease in 1990 from 1989 of $1,325,000 reflected lower average net borrowings and lower average net interest rates.

Hemisphere Closure

During the fourth quarter of 1989, the Company closed its Hemisphere stores resulting in a pretax charge to earnings of $10,785,000 ($.05 per share after tax). This charge represented the write down of related property and equipment, inventory, fourth quarter operating loss and a provision for occupancy expenses.

Income Taxes

The effective tax rate was 38.0% in 1991 compared with 39.0% in 1990 and 40.0% in 1989. The 1.0% decrease in the effective tax rate for 1991 was primarily due to a reduction in state taxes and net foreign taxes as a percentage of earnings before income taxes. The 1.0% decrease in 1990 was primarily due to a reduction in state taxes as a percentage of earnings before income taxes.

g

181

Exhibit 1 Excerpts from The Gap's 1991 Annual Report

LIQUIDITY AND CAPITAL RESOURCES

The following sets forth certain measures of the Company's liquidity:

	Fiscal Year		
	1991	1990	1989
Cash provided by operating activities ($000)	$333,696	$256,892	$118,093
Working capital ($000)	$235,537	$101,518	$129,139
Current ratio	1.71:1	1.39:1	1.69:1
Debt to equity ratio	.12:1	.04:1	.06:1

In 1991, capital expenditures totaled $227 million, net of construction allowances and dispositions (representing the addition of 139 new stores, the expansion of 79 stores and the remodeling of certain existing stores) which resulted in a net increase in store space of 876,100 square feet. The expenditures also included the construction of the Maryland distribution facility and an offsite data center. Capital expenditures were $200 million in 1990 and $94 million in 1989, a net increase in store space of 705,700 square feet in 1990 and 177,300 square feet in 1989.

In fiscal year 1992, the Company expects capital expenditures to total approximately $230 million, net of construction allowances, representing the addition of approximately 135 stores, the expansion of approximately 100 stores, and the remodeling of certain existing stores. Planned expenditures also include costs for administrative facilities and equipment. The Company expects to fund such capital expenditures by a combination of anticipated cash flow from operations, normal trade credit arrangements, and bank and other borrowings. New stores are generally expected to be leased.

In February 1991, the Company issued $75 million of 8.87% Senior Notes which are due in February 1995. Interest is payable quarterly. The Senior Notes are redeemable, in whole or in part, at any time after February 22, 1993, at the option of the Company.

The Company has a credit agreement which provides for a $250 million revolving credit facility until March 1995, at which time any outstanding borrowings can be converted to a four-year term loan. In addition, the credit agreement provides for the issuance of letters of credit during the three-year revolving period for up to $300 million at any one time.

Under the Company's 1988 program to repurchase up to 12,000,000 shares of its common stock, 40,460 shares were repurchased in 1991 for $1,004,000. To date, 10,484,528 shares have been repurchased for $92,454,000. Share amounts have been restated to reflect the two-for-one splits of common stock to stockholders of record on June 17, 1991 and September 17, 1990.

PER SHARE DATA

	Market Prices[a]				Cash Dividends[a]	
Fiscal	1991		1990		1991	1990
	High	Low	High	Low		
1st Quarter	$31½	$20	$17⅜	$12⁵⁄₃₂	$.062	$.048
2nd Quarter	36⅛	20³⁄₁₆	17⅜	13²¹⁄₃₂	.080	.048
3rd Quarter	47½	34¾	14¹⁄₃₂	10⁹⁄₃₂	.080	.062
4th Quarter	59	44¾	21¼	13¼	.080	.062
Year					$.302	$.22

The principal markets on which the Company's stock is traded are the New York and Pacific Stock Exchanges. The number of holders of record of the Company's common stock as of April 3, 1992 was 4,311.

(a) Restated to reflect the 2-for-1 splits of common stock to stockholders of record on June 17, 1991 and September 17, 1990.

Exhibit 1   Excerpts from The Gap's 1991 Annual Report

CONSOLIDATED STATEMENTS OF EARNINGS

($000 except per share amounts)	Fiscal 1991 52 Weeks		Fiscal 1990 52 Weeks		Fiscal 1989 53 Weeks	
Net sales	$2,518,893	100.0%	$1,933,780	100.0%	$1,586,596	100.0%
Costs and expenses						
Cost of goods sold and occupancy expenses	1,568,921	62.3%	1,241,243	64.2%	1,046,236	65.9%
Operating expenses	575,686	22.9%	454,180	23.4%	364,101	22.9%
Interest expense (net)	3,523	.1%	1,435	.1%	2,760	.2%
Hemisphere closure	—	—	—	—	10,785	.7%
Earnings before income taxes	370,763	14.7%	236,922	12.3%	162,714	10.3%
Income taxes	140,890	5.6%	92,400	4.8%	65,086	4.1%
Net earnings	$ 229,873	9.1%	$ 144,522	7.5%	$ 97,628	6.2%
Weighted average number of shares	142,139,577		141,500,888		141,080,200	
Earnings per share	$ 1.62	$ 1.02	$ .69			

See notes to consolidated financial statements.

g
183

Exhibit 1   Excerpts from The Gap's 1991 Annual Report

CONSOLIDATED BALANCE SHEETS

($000)	February 1, 1992	February 2, 1991
ASSETS		
Current Assets		
Cash and equivalents	$192,585	$66,716
Accounts receivable	7,962	9,609
Merchandise inventory	313,899	247,462
Prepaid expenses and other	51,402	41,268
Total Current Assets	565,848	365,055
Property and Equipment		
Leasehold improvements	394,835	289,266
Furniture and equipment	255,665	178,109
Construction-in-progress	86,967	60,992
	737,467	528,367
Accumulated depreciation and amortization	(189,727)	(144,819)
	547,740	385,548
Lease rights and other assets	33,826	28,297
Total Assets	$1,147,414	$776,900
LIABILITIES AND STOCKHOLDERS' EQUITY		
Current Liabilities		
Accounts payable	$ 158,317	$115,282
Accrued expenses	135,333	102,341
Income taxes payable	32,104	32,725
Current installments on long-term debt	2,500	12,500
Other current liabilities	2,057	689
Total Current Liabilities	330,311	263,537
Long-Term Liabilities		
Long-term debt	77,500	5,000
Other liabilities	16,773	18,945
Deferred lease credits	45,042	23,685
	139,315	47,630
Stockholders' Equity		
Common stock $.05 par value		
Authorized 240,000,000 shares; issued 153,007,862 and 151,708,098		
shares; outstanding 142,523,334 and 141,264,030 shares	7,650	7,585
Additional paid-in capital	124,683	91,185
Retained earnings	654,858	466,111
Foreign currency translation adjustment	575	5,667
Restricted stock plan deferred compensation	(17,524)	(13,365)
Treasury stock, at cost	(92,454)	(91,450)
	677,788	465,733
Total Liabilities and Stockholders' Equity	$1,147,414	$776,900

See notes to consolidated financial statements.

Exhibit 1   Excerpts from The Gap's 1991 Annual Report

CONSOLIDATED STATEMENTS OF CASH FLOWS

($000)	Fiscal 1991 52 Weeks	Fiscal 1990 52 Weeks	Fiscal 1989 53 Weeks
Cash Flows from Operating Activities			
Net earnings	$229,873	$144,522	$ 97,628
Adjustments to reconcile net earnings to net cash provided by operating activities			
Depreciation and amortization	82,133	61,473	43,769
Hemisphere closure	—	—	6,522
Deferred income taxes	(7,045)	(5,637)	(4,134)
Change in operating assets and liabilities			
Accounts receivable	1,643	(3,807)	108
Merchandise inventory	(66,559)	(3,980)	(50,214)
Prepaid expenses and other	(5,557)	(2,969)	(15,953)
Accounts payable	43,220	20,481	12,897
Accrued expenses	33,417	26,910	19,393
Income taxes payable	(574)	18,022	(27)
Other current liabilities	1,368	(26)	13
Other long-term liabilities	420	(2,802)	3,910
Deferred lease credits	21,357	4,705	4,181
Net cash provided by operating activities	333,696	256,892	118,093
Cash Flows from Investing Activities			
Net purchases of property and equipment	(236,521)	(193,734)	(88,398)
Net lease rights	(7,802)	(5,883)	(5,868)
Other assets	(1,382)	1,423	10,628
Net cash used for investing activities	(245,705)	(198,194)	(83,638)
Cash Flows from Financing Activities			
Issuance of long-term debt	75,000	—	—
Payments on long-term debt	(12,500)	(2,500)	(2,000)
Issuance of common stock	20,036	10,189	4,262
Repurchase of common stock	—	—	(213)
Purchase of treasury stock	(1,004)	(10,076)	(21,446)
Cash dividends paid	(41,126)	(29,625)	(22,857)
Net cash provided by (used for) financing activities	40,406	(32,012)	(42,254)
Effect of exchange rate changes on cash	(2,528)	1,245	219
Net increase (decrease) in cash and equivalents	125,869	27,931	(7,580)
Cash and equivalents at beginning of year	66,716	38,785	46,365
Cash and equivalents at end of year	$192,585	$ 66,716	$ 38,785

See notes to consolidated financial statements.

g

185

Exhibit 1   Excerpts from The Gap's 1991 Annual Report

NOTES TO CONSOLIDATED FINANCIAL STATEMENTS

For the Fifty-Two Weeks ended February 1, 1992 (Fiscal 1991), the Fifty-Two Weeks ended February 2, 1991 (Fiscal 1990) and the Fifty-Three Weeks ended February 3, 1990 (Fiscal 1989).

NOTE A: SUMMARY OF SIGNIFICANT ACCOUNTING POLICIES

The Company is an international specialty retailer selling casual and contemporary apparel. The consolidated financial statements include the accounts of the Company and its subsidiaries. Intercompany accounts and transactions have been eliminated.

Cash and equivalents represent cash and short-term, highly liquid investments with maturities of three months or less.

Merchandise inventory is stated at the lower of FIFO (first-in, first-out) cost or market.

Property and equipment are stated at cost. Depreciation and amortization are computed using the straight-line method over the estimated useful lives of the related assets or lease terms, whichever is less.

Lease rights are recorded at cost and are amortized over 12 years or the lives of the respective leases, whichever is less.

Costs associated with the opening of new stores are charged against earnings as incurred.

Deferred taxes are provided for those items reported in different periods for income tax and financial statement purposes. Tax credits reduce the current provision for income taxes in the year they are realized. The Company is required to adopt Statement of Financial Accounting Standards No. 109, Accounting for Income Taxes, during fiscal 1993. The impact on the current financial statements would have been immaterial if early adoption had been elected.

Foreign currency translation adjustments result from translating foreign subsidiaries' assets and liabilities to U.S. dollars using the exchange rates in effect at the balance sheet date. Resulting translation adjustments are included in stockholders' equity. Results of foreign operations are translated using the average exchange rates during the period.

Restricted stock awards represent deferred compensation and are shown as a reduction of stockholders' equity.

Earnings per share are based upon the weighted average number of shares of common stock outstanding during the period.

Certain reclassifications have been made to the 1990 and 1989 financial statements to conform with the classifications used in the 1991 financial statements.

NOTE B: LONG-TERM DEBT AND OTHER CREDIT ARRANGEMENTS

Long-Term Debt

($000)	Feb. 1, 1992	Feb. 2, 1991
8.87% Senior Notes, due February 1995	$75,000	$ —
Term Loan Agreement, unsecured, due in equal annual installments through July 1993	5,000	7,500
9.46% unsecured Term Loan due August 1991	—	10,000
	80,000	17,500
Less current installments	(2,500)	(12,500)
	$77,500	$ 5,000

Interest on the Senior Notes is payable quarterly. The Senior Notes are redeemable, in whole or in part, at anytime after February 22, 1993, at the option of the Company.

Interest on the Term Loan Agreement is at prime plus one-quarter of 1% or at LIBOR plus three-quarters of 1%, at the Company's option.

Other Credit Arrangements

The Company has a credit agreement with a syndicated bank group which provides for a $250 million revolving credit facility until March 2, 1995 at which time any outstanding borrowings can be converted to a four-year term loan. The revolving credit facility contains both auction and fixed spread borrowing options and serves as a back-up for the issuance of commercial paper. In addition, the credit agreement provides for the issuance of letters of credit during the three-year revolving period of up to $300 million at any one time.

At February 1, 1992, the Company had outstanding letters of credit totaling $148,634,000.

Borrowings under the Company's loan and credit agreements are subject to the Company maintain-

g

186

Exhibit 1   Excerpts from The Gap's 1991 Annual Report

ing certain levels of tangible net worth and financial ratios. Under the most restrictive covenant of these agreements, $376,918,000 of retained earnings were available for the payment of cash dividends at February 1, 1992.

Gross interest payments were $7,593,000, $4,477,000 and $4,501,000 in fiscal 1991, 1990 and 1989.

NOTE C: INCOME TAXES

Income taxes consisted of the following:

($000)	Fiscal 1991 52 Weeks	Fiscal 1990 52 Weeks	Fiscal 1989 53 Weeks
Currently Payable			
Federal income taxes	$125,181	$79,951	$55,236
Less tax credits	(6,879)	(1,392)	(1,282)
	118,302	78,559	53,954
State income taxes	24,354	18,011	15,604
Foreign income taxes	6,733	2,142	1,731
	149,389	98,712	71,289
Deferred			
Federal	(9,920)	(5,879)	(4,471)
State	1,421	(433)	(1,732)
	(8,499)	(6,312)	(6,203)
Total provision	$140,890	$92,400	$65,086

The foreign component of earnings before income taxes in fiscal 1991, 1990 and 1989 was $31,174,000, $23,377,000 and $11,974,000. Deferred federal and applicable state income taxes, net of applicable foreign tax credits, have not been provided for the undistributed earnings of foreign subsidiaries (approximately $38,791,000 at February 1, 1992) because the Company intends to permanently reinvest such undistributed earnings abroad.

The difference between the effective income tax rate and the United States federal income tax rate is summarized as follows:

	Fiscal 1991 52 Weeks	Fiscal 1990 52 Weeks	Fiscal 1989 53 Weeks
Federal tax rate	34.0%	34.0%	34.0%
State income taxes, less federal benefit	4.8	5.1	5.6
Other	(.8)	(.1)	.4
Effective tax rate	38.0%	39.0%	40.0%

In fiscal 1990 and 1989, accelerated depreciation decreased deferred tax assets by $4,719,000 and $2,797,000. In fiscal 1989, deferred compensation increased deferred tax assets by $4,547,000.

Income tax payments were $135,370,000, $74,790,000 and $73,682,000 in fiscal 1991, 1990 and 1989.

NOTE D: LEASES

The Company leases substantially all of its store premises, distribution and office facilities.

Leases relating to store premises, distribution and office facilities expire at various dates through 2025. The aggregate minimum annual lease payments under leases in effect on February 1, 1992 are as follows:

Fiscal Year	($000)
1992	$ 143,780
1993	139,434
1994	134,414
1995	129,422
1996	125,761
Thereafter	624,070
Total minimum lease commitment	$1,296,881

For leases which contain predetermined fixed escalations of the minimum rentals, the Company recognizes the related rental expense on a straight-line basis and includes the difference between the expense charged to income and amounts payable under the leases in deferred lease credits. At February 1, 1992 and February 2, 1991, this liability amounted to $27,400,000 and $19,700,000.

Cash or rent abatements received upon entering into certain store leases are recognized on a straight-line basis as a reduction to rent expense over the lease term. The unamortized portion is included in deferred lease credits.

Some of the leases relating to stores in operation at February 1, 1992 contain renewal options for periods ranging up to 20 years. Most leases also provide for payment of operating expenses, real estate taxes, and for additional rent based on a percentage of sales. No lease directly imposes any restrictions relating to leasing in other locations (other than radius clauses).

g
187

Exhibit 1   Excerpts from The Gap's 1991 Annual Report

Net rental expense for all operating leases was as follows:

	Fiscal 1991 52 Weeks	Fiscal 1990 52 Weeks	Fiscal 1989 53 Weeks
Minimum rentals	$137,721	$106,754	$ 88,386
Contingent rentals	30,473	24,666	20,463
	$168,194	$131,420	$108,849

NOTE I: QUARTERLY FINANCIAL INFORMATION (UNAUDITED)

Fiscal 1991 Quarter Ended

($000 except per share amounts)	May 4, 1991	Aug. 3, 1991	Nov. 2, 1991	Feb.1, 1992	Fiscal 1991
Net sales	$490,300	$523,056	$702,052	$803,485	$2,518,893
Gross profit	183,254	179,413	277,731	309,574	949,972
Net earnings	40,913	34,222	70,796	83,942	229,873
Net earnings per share	.29	.24	.50	.59	1.62

Fiscal 1990 Quarter Ended

($000 except per share amounts)	May 5, 1990	Aug. 4, 1990	Nov. 3, 1990	Feb. 2, 1991	Fiscal 1990
Net sales	$402,368	$404,996	$501,690	$624,726	$1,933,780
Gross profit	132,575	131,127	196,283	232,552	692,537
Net earnings	21,154	19,162	47,726	56,480	144,522
Net earnings per share	.15	.14	.33	.40	1.02

EXHIBIT 2

Comparative Five-Year Financial Summaries for The Gap, The Limited, and Specialty Retailers

THE GAP, INC.

INCOME STATEMENT

($ millions)	Jan. 1992	Jan. 1991	Jan. 1990	Jan. 1989	Jan. 1988
Sales	$2,519	$1,934	$1,587	$1,252	$1,062
Cost of Goods Sold	1,499	1,190	1,008	814	654
Gross Profit	1,020	744	578	438	408
Selling, General, and Administrative Expense	576	454	364	271	254
Operating Income Before Depreciation	444	290	214	167	154
Depreciation & Amortization	70	51	38	31	25
Operating Profit	374	238	176	136	129
Interest Expense	4	1	3	3	4
Shut-down and Restructuring Costs	0	0	–11	–7	0
Pretax Income	371	237	163	126	125
Total Income Taxes	141	92	65	52	55
Net Income	$ 230	$ 145	$ 98	$ 74	$ 70
Earnings per Share	$1.62	$1.02	$0.69	$0.51	$0.49
Dividends per Share	$0.30	$0.22	$0.17	$0.13	$0.13

Note: Depreciation and amortization above is less than that disclosed in The Gap's cash flow statement because it excludes amortization of deferred compensation.

Exhibit 2   Comparative Five-Year Financial Summaries for The Gap, The Limited, and Specialty Retailers

BALANCE SHEET

($ millions)	Jan. 1992	Jan. 1991	Jan. 1990	Jan. 1989	Jan. 1988
ASSETS					
Cash & Equivalents	$ 193	$ 67	$ 38	$ 46	$ 32
Net Receivables	8	10	6	6	9
Inventories	314	248	244	193	195
Other Current Assets	51	41	29	13	23
Total Current Assets	566	365	317	258	259
Gross Plant, Property & Equipment	738	528	352	286	234
Accumulated Depreciation	190	145	114	95	77
Net Plant, Property & Equipment	548	384	238	191	157
Other Assets	34	29	25	32	19
TOTAL ASSETS	1,147	777	580	481	434
LIABILITIES					
Long-Term Debt Due in One Year	3	13	3	2	2
Notes Payable	0	0	0	0	5
Accounts Payable	158	115	94	81	68
Taxes Payable	32	33	15	15	6
Accrued Expenses	135	102	75	53	47
Other Current Liabilities	2	1	1	1	1
Total Current Liabilities	330	264	187	152	129
Long-Term Debt	78	5	18	20	12
Other Liabilities	62	43	37	33	21
TOTAL LIABILITIES	470	311	242	205	161
EQUITY					
Common Stock	8	4	2	2	2
Capital Surplus	125	95	73	57	51
Retained Earnings	638	458	345	277	221
Less: Treasury Stock	93	92	81	60	0
TOTAL EQUITY	678	466	338	276	273
TOTAL LIABILITIES & EQUITY	$1,147	$777	$580	$481	$434

THE LIMITED, INC.

COMMON SIZE INCOME STATEMENT

	Jan. 1992	Jan. 1991	Jan. 1990	Jan. 1989	Jan. 1988
Sales	1.000	1.000	1.000	1.000	1.000
CGS	0.658	0.640	0.640	0.654	0.671
Gross Profit	0.342	0.360	0.360	0.346	0.329
SGA	0.193	0.196	0.194	0.200	0.186
Operating Income Before Depreciation	0.149	0.164	0.165	0.146	0.143
Depreciation and Amortization	0.035	0.034	0.034	0.033	0.030
Operating Profit	0.113	0.130	0.132	0.112	0.113
Interest Expense	0.010	0.011	0.012	0.015	0.011
Non-op. and Special Items	0.002	0.002	0.001	−0.002	0.003
Pretax Income	0.105	0.122	0.121	0.095	0.105
Income Taxes	0.041	0.047	0.048	0.036	0.040
Minority Interest	0.000	0.000	0.000	0.000	0.000
Income Before Extra Items	0.064	0.074	0.073	0.059	0.065
Extra Items and Discontinued Operations	0.000	0.000	0.000	0.000	0.000
Net Income	0.064	0.074	0.073	0.059	0.065
EBI/Sales	0.070	0.080	0.080	0.068	
Asset Turnover	1.997	2.032	2.081	2.226	
Leverage = assets/equity (average)	1.830	1.889	2.087	2.228	
Net Income/EBI	0.913	0.921	0.909	0.866	
ROE = product of above	0.235	0.285	0.317	0.293	
ROA = EBI/Assets	0.140	0.163	0.167	0.152	
Sustainable Growth	0.175	0.222	0.264	0.241	

EBI = earnings before interest, net of assumed 40% tax effect.
Sustainable growth rate is equal to ROE, multiplied by earnings retention rate.

SELECTED FINANCIAL STATEMENT DATA

(millions of $)	Jan. 1992	Jan. 1991	Jan. 1990	Jan. 1989	Jan. 1988
Net Receivables	736	670	596	532	95
Inventory	730	585	482	407	354
Net Property and Equipment	1,657	1,395	1,173	1,067	889
Total Assets	3,419	2,872	2,419	2,146	1,588
Total Equity	1,877	1,560	1,241	946	729
Sales	6,281	5,376	4,750	4,155	3,616
Cost of Goods Sold	4,133	3,440	3,041	2,717	2,426
Selling, General, & Admin. Expense	1,212	1,056	923	832	672
Operating Income Before Depreciation	935	880	785	606	518
Net Income	403	398	347	245	235

SPECIALTY RETAILERS INDUSTRY COMPOSITE

(including Gap, Limited, Melville, Petrie, and Nordstrom)

COMMON SIZE INCOME STATEMENT

	Jan. 1992	Jan. 1991	Jan. 1990	Jan. 1989	Jan. 1988
Sales	1.000	1.000	1.000	1.000	1.000
CGS	0.638	0.635	0.630	0.632	0.637
Gross Profit	0.362	0.365	0.370	0.368	0.363
SGA	0.252	0.253	0.251	0.253	0.250
Operating Income Before Depreciation	0.110	0.112	0.119	0.115	0.113
Depreciation and Amortization	0.026	0.025	0.024	0.024	0.023
Operating Profit	0.084	0.087	0.094	0.091	0.090
Interest Expense	0.007	0.008	0.008	0.008	0.009
Non-op and Special Items	0.005	0.005	0.004	0.004	0.009
Pretax Income	0.082	0.085	0.091	0.087	0.091
Income Taxes	0.032	0.030	0.033	0.031	0.035
Minority Interest	0.002	0.002	0.002	0.003	0.003
Income Before Extra Items	0.049	0.052	0.056	0.053	0.053
Extra Items and Discontinued Operations	0.000	0.000	0.000	0.004	0.000
Net Income	0.049	0.052	0.056	0.057	0.053
EBI/Sales	0.053	0.057	0.060	0.061	
Asset Turnover	2.141	2.153	2.175	2.190	
Leverage = Assets/equity (average)	1.874	1.889	1.869	1.860	
Net income/EBI	0.919	0.919	0.923	0.921	
ROE = Product of above	0.196	0.211	0.226	0.230	
ROA = EBI/Assets	0.114	0.122	0.131	0.134	
Sustainable Growth	0.058	0.062	0.058	0.054	

EBI = earnings before interest, net of assumed 40% tax effect.

Sustainable growth = ROE × earnings retention rate.

SELECTED FINANCIAL STATEMENT DATA

(millions of $)	Jan. 1992	Jan. 1991	Jan. 1990	Jan. 1989	Jan. 1988
Net Receivables	1,604	1,430	1,290	1,156	631
Inventory	3,578	3,067	2,558	2,316	1,986
Net Property and Equipment	4,456	3,874	3,200	2,878	2,476
Total Assets	11,588	10,104	8,635	7,749	6,622
Total Equity	6,230	5,344	4,576	4,192	3,534
Sales	23,220	20,172	17,819	15,734	13,771
Cost of Goods Sold	14,804	12,817	11,226	9,946	8,769
Selling, General, & Administrative Expense	5,855	5,096	4,480	3,984	3,442
Operating Income Before Depreciation	2,561	2,259	2,113	1,805	1,560
Net Income	1,132	1,047	990	889	730

I n February 1985, Peter Roberts, the research director of Exeter Group, a small Boston-based investment advisory service specializing in turnaround stocks, was reviewing the 1984 annual report of Harnischfeger Corporation (Exhibit 4). His attention was drawn by the $1.28 per share net profit Harnischfeger reported for 1984. He knew that barely three years earlier the company had faced a severe financial crisis. Harnischfeger had defaulted on its debt and stopped dividend payments after reporting a hefty $7.64 per share net loss in fiscal 1982. The company's poor performance continued in 1983, leading to a net loss of $3.49 per share. Roberts was intrigued by Harnischfeger's rapid turnaround and wondered whether he should recommend purchase of the company's stock (see Exhibit 3 for selected data on Harnischfeger's stock).

COMPANY BUSINESS AND PRODUCTS

Harnischfeger Corporation was a machinery company based in Milwaukee, Wisconsin. The company had originally been started as a partnership in 1884 and was incorporated in Wisconsin in 1910 under the name Pawling and Harnischfeger. Its name was changed to the present one in 1924. The company went public in 1929 and was listed on the New York Stock Exchange.

The company's two major segments were the P&H Heavy Equipment Group, consisting of the Construction Equipment and the Mining and Electrical Equipment divisions, and the Industrial Technologies Group, consisting of the Material Handling Equipment and the Harnischfeger Engineers divisions. The sales mix of the company in 1983 consisted of: Construction Equipment 32 percent; Mining and Electrical Equipment 33 percent, Material Handling Equipment 29 percent, and Harnischfeger Engineers 6 percent.

Harnischfeger was a leading producer of construction equipment. Its products, bearing the widely recognized brand name P&H, included hydraulic cranes and lattice boom cranes. These were used in bridge and highway construction and for cargo and other material handling applications. Harnischfeger had market shares of about 20 percent in hydraulic cranes and about 30 percent in lattice boom cranes. In the 1980s the construction equipment industry in general was experiencing declining margins.

Professor Krishna Palepu prepared this case as the basis for class discussion rather than to illustrate either effective or ineffective handling of an administrative situation. Copyright © 1985 by the President and Fellows of Harvard College. Harvard Business School case 9-186-160.

Electric mining shovels and excavators constituted the principal products of the Mining and Electrical Equipment Division of Harnischfeger. The company had a dominant share of the mining machinery market. The company's products were used in coal, copper, and iron mining. A significant part of the division's sales were from the sale of spare parts. Because of its large market share and the lucrative spare parts sales, the division was traditionally very profitable. Most of the company's future mining product sales were expected to occur outside the United States, principally in developing countries.

The Material Handling Equipment Division of Harnischfeger was the fourth largest supplier of automated material handling equipment, with a 9 percent market share. The division's products included overhead cranes, portal cranes, hoists, monorails, and components and parts. The demand for this equipment was expected to grow in the coming years as an increasing number of manufacturing firms emphasized cost reduction programs. Harnischfeger believed that the material handling equipment business would be a major source of its future growth.

Harnischfeger Engineers was an engineering services division engaged in design, custom software development, and project management for factory and distribution automation projects. The division engineered and installed complete automated material handling systems for a wide variety of applications on a fee basis. The company expected such automated storage and retrieval systems to play an increasingly important role in the "factory of the future."

Harnischfeger had a number of subsidiaries, affiliated companies, and licensees in a number of countries. Export and foreign sales constituted more than 50 percent of the total revenues of the company.

FINANCIAL DIFFICULTIES OF 1982

The machinery industry experienced a period of explosive growth during the 1970s. Harnischfeger expanded rapidly during this period, growing from $205 million in revenues in 1973 to $644 million in 1980. To fund this growth, the company relied increasingly on debt financing, and the firm's debt/equity ratio rose from 0.88 in 1973 to 1.26 in 1980. The worldwide recession in the early 1980s caused a significant drop in demand for the company's products starting in 1981 and culminated in a series of events that shook the financial stability of Harnischfeger.

Reduced sales and the high interest payments resulted in poor profit performance leading to a reported loss in 1982 of $77 million. The management of Harnischfeger commented on its financial difficulties:

There is a persistent weakness in the basic industries, both in the United States and overseas, which have been large, traditional markets for P&H products. Energy-related projects, which had been a major source of business of our Construction Equipment Division, have slowed significantly in the last year as a result of lower oil demand and subsequent price decline, not only in the U.S. but throughout the world. Lack of demand for such basic minerals as iron ore, copper and

h

194

bauxite have decreased worldwide mining activity, causing reduced sales for mining equipment, although coal mining remains relatively strong worldwide. Difficult economic conditions have caused many of our normal customers to cut capital expenditures dramatically, especially in such depressed sectors as the steel industry, which has always been a major source of sales for all P&H products.

The significant operating losses recorded in 1982 and the credit losses experienced by its finance subsidiary caused Harnischfeger to default on certain covenants of its loan agreements. The most restrictive provisions of the company's loan agreements required it to maintain a minimum working capital of $175 million, consolidated net worth of $180 million, and a ratio of current assets to current liabilities of 1.75. On October 31, 1982, the company's working capital (after reclassification of about $115 million long-term debt as a current liability) was $29.3 million, the consolidated net worth was $142.2 million, and the ratio of current assets to current liabilities was 1.12. Harnischfeger Credit Corporation, an unconsolidated finance subsidiary, also defaulted on certain covenants of its loan agreements, largely due to significant credit losses relating to the financing of construction equipment sold to a large distributor. As a result of these covenant violations, the company's long-term debt of $124.3 million became due on demand, the unused portion of the bank revolving credit line of $25.0 million became unavailable, and the unused short-term bank credit lines of $12.0 million were canceled. In addition, the $25.1 million debt of Harnischfeger Credit Corporation also became immediately due. The company was forced to stop paying dividends and began negotiations with its lenders to restructure its debt to permit operations to continue. Price Waterhouse, the company's audit firm, qualified its audit opinion on Harnischfeger's 1982 annual report with respect to the outcome of the company's negotiations with its lenders.

h

195

CORPORATE RECOVERY PLAN

Harnischfeger responded to the financial crisis facing the firm by developing a corporate recovery plan. The plan consisted of four elements: (1) changes in the top management, (2) cost reductions to lower the break-even point, (3) reorientation of the company's business, and (4) debt restructuring and recapitalization. The actions taken in each of these four areas are described below.

To deal effectively with the financial crisis, Henry Harnischfeger, then Chairman and Chief Executive Officer of the company, created the position of Chief Operating Officer. After an extensive search, the position was offered in August 1982 to William Goessel, who had considerable experience in the machinery industry. Another addition to the management team was Jeffrey Grade, who joined the company in 1983 as Senior Vice President of Finance and Administration and Chief Financial Officer. Grade's appointment was necessitated by the early retirement of the previous Vice President of Finance in 1982. The engineering, manufacturing, and marketing functions were also restructured to streamline the company's operations (see Exhibits 1 and 2 for additional information on Harnischfeger's current management).

To deal with the short-term liquidity squeeze, the company initiated a number of cost reduction measures. These included (1) reducing the workforce from 6,900 to 3,800; (2) eliminating management bonuses and reducing benefits and freezing wages of salaried and hourly employees; (3) liquidating excess inventories and stretching payments to creditors; and (4) permanent closure of the construction equipment plant at Escanaba, Michigan. These and other related measures improved the company's cash position and helped to reduce the rate of loss during fiscal 1983.

Concurrent with the above cost reduction measures, the new management made some strategic decisions to reorient Harnischfeger's business. First, the company entered into a long-term agreement with Kobe Steel, Ltd., of Japan. Under this agreement, Kobe agreed to supply Harnischfeger's requirements for construction cranes for sale in the United States as Harnischfeger phased out its own manufacture of cranes. This step was expected to significantly reduce the manufacturing costs of Harnischfeger's construction equipment, enabling it to compete effectively in the domestic market. Second, the company decided to emphasize the high technology part of its business by targeting for future growth the material handling equipment and systems business. To facilitate this strategy, the Industrial Technologies Group was created. As part of the reorientation, the company stated that it would develop and acquire new products, technology, and equipment and would expand its abilities to provide computer-integrated solutions to handling, storing, and retrieval in areas hitherto not pursued—industries such as distribution warehousing, food, pharmaceuticals, and aerospace.

While Harnischfeger was implementing its turnaround strategy, it was engaged at the same time in complex and difficult negotiations with its bankers. On January 6, 1984, the company entered into agreements with its lenders to restructure its debt obligations into three-year term loans secured by fixed as well as other assets, with a one-year extension option. This agreement required, among other things, specified minimum levels of cash and unpledged receivables, working capital, and net worth.

The company reported a net loss of $35 million in 1983, down from the $77 million loss the year before. Based on the above developments during the year, in the 1983 annual report the management expressed confidence that the company would return to profitability soon:

> We approach our second century with optimism, knowing that the negative events of the last three years are behind us, and with a firm belief that positive achievements will be recorded in 1984. By the time the corporation celebrates its 100th birthday on December 1, we are confident it will be operating profitably and attaining new levels of market strength and leadership.

During 1984 the company reported profits during each of the four quarters, ending the year with a pre-tax operating profit of $5.7 million, and a net income after tax and extraordinary credits of $15 million (see Exhibit 4). It also raised substantial new capital through a public offering of debentures and common stock. Net proceeds from the offering, which totaled $150 million, were used to pay off all of the company's restructured debt. In the 1984 annual report the management commented on the company's performance as follows:

> 1984 was the Corporation's Centennial year and we marked the occasion by rededicating ourselves to excellence through market leadership, customer service and improved operating performance and profitability.
>
> ⋮
>
> We look back with pride. We move ahead with confidence and optimism. Our major markets have never been more competitive; however, we will strive to take advantage of any and all opportunities for growth and to attain satisfactory profitability. Collectively, we will do what has to be done to ensure that the future will be rewarding to all who have a part in our success.

QUESTIONS

1. Identify all the accounting policy changes and accounting estimates that Harnischfeger made during 1984. Estimate, as accurately as possible, the effect of these on the company's 1984 reported profits.
2. What do you think are the motives of Harnischfeger's management in making the changes in its financial reporting policies? Do you think investors will see through these changes?
3. Assess the company's future prospects, given your insights from questions 1 and 2 and the information in the case about the company's turnaround strategy.

h

197

Exhibit 1 Harnischfeger Corporation Board of Directions in 1984

h
198

EXHIBIT 1
Harnischfeger Corporation Board of Directions in 1984

		Director Since	Current Term	Shares Owned
Edward W. Duffy	Chairman of the Board and Chief Executive Officer of United States Gypsum Company, manufacturer of building materials and products used in industrial processes, since 1983; Vice Chairman from 1981 to 1983; President and Chief Operating Officer from 1971 to 1981. Director, American National Bank and Trust Company of Chicago, Walter E. Heller International Corporation, W. W. Grainger, Inc., and UNR Industries, Inc. Age 64.	1981	1985	100
Herbert V. Kohler, Jr.	Chairman, Chief Executive Officer, and Director of Kohler Company, manufacturer of plumbing and specialty products, engines, and generators, since 1972; President since 1974. Age 44.	1973	1985	700
Taisuke Mori	Executive Vice Chairman and Director of Kobe Steel, Ltd., a Japanese manufacturer of steel and steel products, industrial machinery, construction equipment, aluminum, copper and alloy products, and welding equipment and consumables. Age 63.	1981	1985	None
William W. Goessel	President and Chief Operating Officer of the Corporation since 1982. Executive Vice President of Beloit Corporation from 1978 to 1982. Director, Goulds Pumps, Inc. Age 56.	1982	1986	15,000
Henry Harnischfeger	Chairman of the Board and Chief Executive Officer of the Corporation since 1970; President from 1959 to 1982. Director, First Wisconsin Corporation and First Wisconsin National Bank of Milwaukee. Age 60.	1945	1986	611,362
Karl F. Nygren	Partner in Kirkland & Ellis, attorneys, since 1959. Age 56.	1964	1986	2,000

	Director Since	Current Term	Shares Owned
John P. Gallagher	1979	1987	500
Jeffrey T. Grade	1983	1987	3,750
Donald Taylor	1979	1987	100
Frank A. Lee	1983	1987	None

John P. Gallagher — Senior lecturer, Graduate School of Business, University of Chicago. Director, IC Industries, Inc., Stone Container Corporation, UNR Industries, Inc., American National Bank and Trust Company of Chicago, and Walter E. Heller International Corporation. Age 67.

Jeffrey T. Grade — Senior Vice President/Finance and Administration and Chief Financial Officer of the Corporation since August 1, 1983. Vice President Corporate Finance of IC Industries from 1981 to 1983; Assistant Vice President from 1976 to 1981. Age 40.

Donald Taylor — President, Chief Operating Officer, and Director of Rexnord, Inc., a major manufacturer of industrial components and machinery, since 1978. Director, Johnson Controls, Inc., Marine Corporation, and Marine Bank, N.A. Age 56.

Frank A. Lee — Director of Foster Wheeler Corporation since 1971; Chairman of the Board from 1981 to 1982; President and Chief Executive Officer from 1978 to 1981. Director, Belco Pollution Control Corporation, International General Industries, Inc., and Banker's Life Insurance Co. Age 59.

Exhibit 2   Executive Compensation, Harnischfeger Corporation

EXHIBIT 2
Executive Compensation, Harnischfeger Corporation

The following table sets forth all cash compensation paid to each of the Corporation's five most highly compensated executive officers and to all executive officers as a group for services rendered to the Corporation and its subsidiaries during fiscal 1984.

		Cash Compensation
Henry Harnischfeger	Chairman of the Board and Chief Executive Officer	$ 364,004
William W. Goessel	President and Chief Operating Officer	280,000
C. P. Cousland	Senior Vice President and group executive, P&H Heavy Equipment	210,000
Jeffrey T. Grade	Senior Vice President-Finance and Administration and Chief Financial Officer	205,336
Douglas E. Holt	President, Harnischfeger Engineers, Inc.	152,839
All persons who were executive officers during the fiscal year as a group (14 persons)		2,159,066

1985 EXECUTIVE INCENTIVE PLAN

In December 1984, the board of directors established an Executive Incentive Plan for fiscal 1985 which provides an incentive compensation opportunity of 40% of annual salary for 11 senior executive officers only if the Corporation reaches a specific net after-tax profit objective; it provides an additional incentive compensation of up to 40% of annual salary for seven of those officers if the corporation exceeds the objective. The Plan covers the chairman, president, senior vice presidents; president, Harnischfeger Engineers, Inc.; vice president, P&H World Services; vice president; Material Handling Equipment; and secretary. Awards made in fiscal year 1984 are included in the compensation table above.

EXHIBIT 3
Harnischfeger Corporation, Selected Stock Price and Market Data

A. STOCK PRICES

	Harnischfeger's Stock Price			S&P 400 Industrials Index		
	High	Low	Close	High	Low	Close
January 4, 1985	9 1/8	8 6/8	9	186.4	181.8	182.2
January 11, 1985	10 6/8	8 7/8	10 5/8	188.2	182.2	182.8
January 18, 1985	11	10	10 4/8	191.9	186.9	191.3
January 25, 1985	11 2/8	10 1/8	11	199.7	191.3	198.6
February 1, 1985	11 5/8	10 7/8	11 2/8	201.8	198.6	200.0

Harnischfeger's stock beta = 0.95 (Value Line estimate)

B. MARKET DATA

	February 1985
Median P/E ratio of Dow Jones Industrials	10.9
Median P/E ratio of Value Line stocks	11.3
Median P/E ratio of machinery industry (construction and mining equipment)	10.0
Prime rate	10.5%
91-day Treasury bill rate	8.4%
30-year Treasury bond yield	11.4%
Moody's Aaa corporate bond yield	12.0%

h

Exhibit 4   Harnischfeger Corporation 1984 Annual Report (abridged)

EXHIBIT 4
Harnischfeger Corporation 1984 Annual Report (abridged)

TO OUR SHAREHOLDERS

The Corporation recorded gains in each quarter during fiscal 1984, returning to profitability despite the continued depressed demand and intense price competition in the world markets it serves.

For the year ended October 31, net income was $15,176,000 or $1.28 per common share, which included $11,005,000 or 93¢ per share from the cumulative effect of a change in depreciation accounting. In 1983, the Corporation reported a loss of $34,630,000 or $3.49 per share.

Sales for 1984 improved 24% over the preceding year, rising to $398.7 million from $321 million a year ago. New orders totaled $451 million, a $101 million increase over 1983. We entered fiscal 1985 with a backlog of $193 million, which compared to $141 million a year earlier.

ALL DIVISIONS IMPROVED

All product divisions recorded sales and operating improvements during 1984.

Mining equipment was the strongest performer with sales up over 60%, including major orders from Turkey and the People's Republic of China. During the year we began the implementation of the training, engineering and manufacturing license agreement concluded in November, 1983 with the People's Republic of China, which offers the Corporation long-term potential in modernizing and mechanizing this vast and rapidly developing mining market.

Sales of material handling equipment and systems were up 10% for the year and the increasingly stronger bookings recorded during the latter part of the year are continuing into the first quarter of 1985.

Sales on construction equipment products showed some signs of selective improvement. In the fourth quarter, bookings more than doubled from the very depressed levels in the same period a year ago, although the current level is still far below what is needed to achieve acceptable operating results for this product line.

FINANCIAL STABILITY RESTORED

In April, the financial stability of the Corporation was improved through a public offering of 2.15 million shares of common stock, $50 million of 15% notes due April 15, 1994, and $100 million of 12% subordinated debentures due April 15, 2004, with two million common stock purchase warrants.

Net proceeds from the offering totaled $149 million, to which we added an additional $23 million in cash, enabling us to pay off all of our long-term debt. As a result of the refinancing, the Corporation gained permanent long-term capital with minimal annual cash flow requirements to service it. We now have the financial resources and flexibility to pursue new opportunities to grow and diversify.

Furthermore, should we require additional funds, they will be available through a $52 million unsecured three-year revolving credit agreement concluded in June with ten U.S. and Canadian banks. An $80 million product financing capability was also arranged through a major U.S. bank to provide financing to customers purchasing P&H products.

OUTLOOK

Throughout 1985 we believe we will see gradual improvements in most of our U.S. and world markets.

For our mining excavator product line, coal and certain metals mining are expected to show a more favorable long-term outlook in selected foreign requirements and our capability to source equipment from the U.S., Japan or Europe places us in a strong marketing position. In the U.S., we see only a moderate strengthening in machinery requirements for coal, while metals mining will remain weak.

Continuing shipments of the Turkish order throughout 1985 will help to stabilize our plant utilization levels and improve our operating results for this product line.

In our material handling and systems markets, particularly in the U.S., we are experiencing a moderately strong continuation of the improved bookings which we began to see in the third and fourth quarters of last year.

Exhibit 4 Harnischfeger Corporation 1984 Annual Report (abridged)

In construction lifting equipment markets, we expect modest overall economic improvement in the U.S., which should help to absorb the large numbers of idle lifting equipment that have been manufacturer, distributor and customer inventories for the last three years. As this overhang on the market is reduced we will see gradual improvement in new sales. Harnischfeger traditionally exports half of its U.S.-produced lifting products. However, as with mining equipment, the continued strength of the U.S. dollar severely restricts our ability to sell U.S.-built products in world markets.

In addition to the strong dollar and economic instability in many foreign nations, overcapacity in worldwide heavy equipment manufacturing remains a serious problem in spite of some exits from the market as well as consolidations within the industry.

The Corporation continues to respond to severe price competition through systematic cost reduction programs and through expanded sourcing of P&H equipment from our European operation and, most importantly, through our 30-year association with our Japanese partner, Kobe Steel, Ltd. P&H engineering and technology have established world standards for quality and performance for construction cranes and mining equipment, which customers can expect from every P&H machine regardless of its source. More than a dozen new models of foreign-sourced P&H construction cranes will be made available for the first time in the U.S. during 1985, broadening our existing product lines and giving competitive pricing to our U.S. distributors and customers.

To improve our future operating results, we restructured our three operating divisions into two groups. All construction and mining related activities are in the new "P&H Heavy Equipment Group." All material handling equipment and systems activities are now merged into the "Industrial Technologies Group." More information on these Groups is reported in their respective sections.

We are pleased to announce that John P. Moran was elected Senior Vice President and Group Executive, Industrial Technologies Group, and John R. Teitgen was elected Secretary and General Counsel.

In September Robert F. Schnoes became a member of our Board of Directors. He is President and Chief Executive Officer of Burgess, Inc. and of Ultrasonic Power Corporation, and a member of the Board of Signode Industries, Inc.

BEGINNING OUR SECOND CENTURY

1984 was the Corporation's Centennial year and we marked the occasion by rededicating ourselves to excellence through market leadership, customer service and improved operating performance and profitability.

Our first century of achievement resulted from the dedicated effort, support and cooperation of our employees, distributors, suppliers, lenders, and shareholders, and we thank all of them.

We look back with pride. We move ahead with confidence and optimism. Our major markets have never been more competitive; however, we will strive to take advantage of any and all opportunities for growth and to attain satisfactory profitability. Collectively, we will do what has to be done to ensure that the future will be rewarding to all who have a part in our success.

Henry Harnischfeger
Chairman of the Board

William W. Goessel
President

January 31, 1985

h

203

Exhibit 4   Harnischfeger Corporation 1984 Annual Report (abridged)

MANAGEMENT'S DISCUSSION & ANALYSIS

RESULTS OF OPERATIONS

1984 Compared to 1983

Consolidated net sales of $399 million in fiscal 1984 increased $78 million or 24% over 1983. Sales increases were 62% in the Mining and Electrical Equipment Segment, and 10% in the Industrial Technologies Segment. Sales in the Construction Equipment Segment were virtually unchanged reflecting the continued low demand for construction equipment world-wide.

Effective at the beginning of fiscal 1984, net sales include the full sales price of construction and mining equipment purchased from Kobe Steel, Ltd. and sold by the Corporation, in order to reflect more effectively the nature of the Corporation's transactions with Kobe. Such sales aggregated $28.0 million in 1984.

The $4.0 million increase in Other Income reflected a recovery of certain claims and higher license and technical service fees.

Cost of Sales was equal to 79.1% of net sales in 1984 and 81.4% in 1983; which together with the increase in net sales resulted in a $23.9 million increase in gross profit (net sales less cost of sales). Contributing to this increase were improved sales of higher-margin replacement parts in the Mining Equipment and Industrial Technologies Segments and a reduction in excess manufacturing costs through greater utilization of domestic manufacturing capacity and economies in total manufacturing costs including a reduction in pension expense. Reductions of certain LIFO inventories increased gross profit by $2.4 million in 1984 and $15.6 million in 1983.

Product development selling and administrative expenses were reduced, due to the funding of R&D expenses in the Construction Equipment Segment pursuant to the October 1983 Agreement with Kobe Steel, Ltd., to reductions in pension expenses and provision for credit losses, and to the absence of the corporate financial restructuring expenses incurred in 1983.

Net interest expense in 1984 increased $2.9 million due to higher interest rates on the outstanding funded debt and a reduction in interest income.

Equity in Earnings (Loss) of Unconsolidated Companies included 1984 income of $1.2 million of Harnischfeger Credit Corporation, an unconsolidated finance subsidiary, reflecting an income tax benefit of $1.4 million not previously recorded.

The preceding items, together with the cumulative effect of the change in depreciation method described in Financial Note 2, were included in net income of $15.2 million or $1.28 per common share, compared with net loss of $34.6 million or $3.49 per share in 1983.

The sales orders booked and unshipped backlogs of orders of the Corporation's three segments are summarized as follows (in million of dollars):

Orders Booked	1984	1983
Industrial Technologies	$132	$106
Mining and Electrical Equipment	210	135
Construction Equipment	109	109
	$451	$350
Backlogs at October 31		
Industrial Technologies	$ 79	$ 71
Mining and Electrical Equipment	91	50
Construction Equipment	23	20
	$193	$141

1983 Compared to 1982

Consolidated net sales of $321 million in fiscal 1983 were $126 million or 28% below 1982. This decline reflected, for the second consecutive year, the continued low demand in all markets served by the Corporation's products, with exports even more severely depressed due to the strength of the dollar. The largest decline was reported in the Construction Equipment Segment, down 34%; Mining and Electrical Equipment Segment shipments were down 27%, and the Industrial Technologies Segment, 23%.

Cost of Sales was equal to 81.4% of net sales in 1983 and 81.9% in 1982. The resulting gross profit

Exhibit 4   Harnischfeger Corporation 1984 Annual Report (abridged)

was $60 million in 1983 and $81 million in 1982, a reduction equal to the rate of sales decrease.

The benefits of reduced manufacturing capacity and economies in total manufacturing costs were offset by reduced selling prices in the highly competitive markets. Reductions of certain LIFO inventories increased gross profits by $15.6 million in 1983 and $7.2 million in 1982.

Product development, selling and administrative expenses were reduced as a result of expense reduction measures in response to the lower volume of business and undertaken in connection with the Corporation's corporate recovery program, and reduced provisions for credit losses, which in 1982 included $4.0 million in income support for Harnischfeger Credit Corporation.

Net interest expense was reduced $9.1 million from 1982 to 1983, due primarily to increased interest income from short-term cash investments and an accrual of $4.7 million in interest income on refundable income taxes not previously recorded.

The Credit for Income Taxes included a federal income tax benefit of $5 million, based upon the recent examination of the Corporation's income tax returns and refund claims. No income tax benefits were available for the losses of the U.S. operations in 1983.

The losses from unconsolidated companies recorded in 1983 included $0.5 million in Harnischfeger Credit Corporation; $2.1 million in Cranetex, Inc., a Corporation-owned distributorship in Texas; and $0.8 million in ASEA Industrial Systems Inc., then a 49%-owned joint venture between the Corporation and ASEA AB and now 19%-owned with the investment accounted for on the cost method.

The preceding items were reflected in a net loss of $34.6 million or $3.49 per share.

LIQUIDITY AND FINANCIAL RESOURCES

In April 1984, the Corporation issued in public offerings 2,150,000 shares of Common Stock, $50 million principal amount of 15% Senior Notes due in 1994, and 100,000 Units consisting of $100 million principal amount of 12% Subordinated Debentures due in 2004 and 2,000,000 Common Stock Purchase Warrants.

The net proceeds from the sales of the securities of $149 million were used to prepay substantially all of the outstanding debt of the Corporation and certain of its subsidiaries.

During the year ended October 31, 1984, the consolidated cash balances increased $32 million to a balance of $96 million, with the cash activity summarized as follows (in million of dollars):

Funds provided by operations	$10
Funds returned to the Corporation upon restructuring of the Salaried Employees' Pension Plan	39
Debt repayment less the proceeds of sales of securities	(9)
Plant and equipment additions	(6)
All other changes—net	(2)
	$32

In the third quarter of fiscal 1984 the Corporation entered into a $52 million three-year revolving credit agreement with ten U.S. and Canadian banks. While the Corporation has adequate liquidity to meet its current working capital requirements, the revolver represents another step in the Corporation's program to strengthen its financial position and provide the required financial resources to respond to opportunities as they arise.

h

205

Exhibit 4   Harnischfeger Corporation 1984 Annual Report (abridged)

CONSOLIDATED STATEMENT OF OPERATIONS

(Dollar amounts in thousands except per share figures)	Year Ended October 31		
	1984	1983	1982
Revenues:			
Net sales	**$398,708**	$321,010	$447,461
Other income, including license and technical service fees	**7,067**	3,111	5,209
	405,775	324,121	452,670
Cost of Sales	**315,216**	261,384	366,297
Operating Income	**90,559**	62,737	86,373
Less:			
Product development, selling and administrative expenses	**72,196**	85,795	113,457
Interest expense—net	**12,625**	9,745	18,873
Provision for plant closing	**—**	—	23,700
Income (Loss) Before Provision (Credit) for Income Taxes, Equity Items and Cumulative Effect of Accounting Change	**5,738**	(32,803)	(69,657)
Provision (Credit) for Income Taxes	**2,425**	(1,400)	(1,600)
Income (Loss) Before Equity Items and Cumulative Effect of Accounting Change	**3,313**	(31,403)	(68,057)
Equity items:			
Equity in earnings (loss) of unconsolidated companies	**993**	(3,397)	(7,891)
Minority interest in (earnings) loss of consolidated subsidiaries	**(135)**	170	(583)
Income (Loss) Before Cumulative Effect of Accounting Change	**4,171**	(34,630)	(76,531)
Cumulative Effect of Change in Depreciation Method	**11,005**	—	—
Net Income (Loss)	**$ 15,176**	$(34,630)	$ (76,531)
Earnings (Loss) per Common and Common Equivalent Share:			
Income (Loss) before cumulative effect of accounting change	**$ .35**	$(3.49)	$(7.64)
Cumulative effect of change in depreciation method	**.93**	—	—
Net income (loss)	**$1.28**	$(3.49)	$(7.64)
Pro forma Amounts Assuming the Changed Depreciation Method Had Been Applied Retroactively:			
Net (loss)		$ (33,918)	$ (76,695)
(Loss) per common share		$(3.42)	$(7.65)

(The accompanying notes are an integral part of the financial statements.)

Exhibit 4   Harnischfeger Corporation 1984 Annual Report (abridged)

CONSOLIDATED BALANCE SHEET

	October 31	
(Dollar amounts in thousands except per share figures)	**1984**	1983
Assets		
Current Assets:		
Cash and temporary investments	**$ 96,007**	$ 64,275
Accounts receivable	**87,648**	63,740
Inventories	**144,312**	153,594
Refundable income taxes and related interest	**1,296**	12,585
Other current assets	**5,502**	6,023
Prepaid income taxes	**14,494**	14,232
	349,259	314,449
Investments and Other Assets:		
Investments in and advances to:		
Finance subsidiary, at equity in net assets	**8,849**	6,704
Other companies	**4,445**	2,514
Other assets	**13,959**	6,411
	27,253	15,629
Operating Plants:		
Land and improvements	**9,419**	10,370
Buildings	**59,083**	60,377
Machinery and equipment	**120,949**	122,154
	189,451	192,901
Accumulated depreciation	**(93,259)**	(107,577)
	96,192	85,324
	$472,704	$415,402

(continued)

h

207

Exhibit 4   Harnischfeger Corporation 1984 Annual Report (abridged)

CONSOLIDATED BALANCE SHEET (continued)

(Dollar amounts in thousands except per share figures)	October 31 1984	1983
Liabilities and Shareholders' Equity		
Current Liabilities:		
Short-term notes payable to banks by subsidiaries	$ 9,090	$ 8,155
Long-term debt and capitalized lease obligations payable within one year	973	18,265
Trade accounts payable	37,716	21,228
Employee compensation and benefits	15,041	14,343
Accrued plant closing costs	2,460	6,348
Advance payments and progress billings	20,619	15,886
Income taxes payable	1,645	3,463
Account payable to finance subsidiary	—	3,436
Other current liabilities and accruals	29,673	32,333
	117,217	123,457
Long-Term Obligations:		
Long-term debt payable to:		
Unaffiliated lenders	128,550	139,092
Finance subsidiary	—	5,400
Capitalized lease obligations	7,870	8,120
	136,420	152,612
Deferred Liabilities and Income Taxes:		
Accrued pension costs	57,611	19,098
Other deferred liabilities	5,299	7,777
Deferred income taxes	6,385	134
	69,295	27,009
Minority Interest	2,400	2,405
Shareholders' Equity:		
Preferred stock $100 par value—authorized 250,000 shares:		
Series A $7.00 cumulative convertible preferred shares: authorized, issued and outstanding 117,500 shares in 1984 and 100,000 shares in 1983	11,750	10,000
Common stock, $1 par value—authorized 25,000,000 shares: issued and outstanding 12,283,563 shares in 1984 and 10,133,563 shares in 1983	12,284	10,134
Capital in excess of par value of shares	114,333	88,332
Retained earnings	19,901	6,475
Cumulative translation adjustments	(10,896)	(5,022)
	147,372	109,919
	$472,704	$415,402

(The accompanying notes are an integral part of the financial statements.)

Exhibit 4 Harnischfeger Corporation 1984 Annual Report (abridged)

CONSOLIDATED STATEMENT OF CHANGES IN FINANCIAL POSITION

(Dollar amounts in thousands)	Year Ended October 31,		
	1984	1983	1982
Funds Were Provided by (Applied to):			
Operations:			
Income (loss) before cumulative effect of accounting change	$ **4,171**	$ (34,630)	$(76,531)
Cumulative effect of change in depreciation method	**11,005**	—	—
Net income (loss)	**15,176**	(34,630)	(76,531)
Add (deduct) items included not affecting funds:			
Depreciation	**8,077**	13,552	15,241
Unremitted (earnings) loss of unconsolidated companies	**(993)**	3,397	7,891
Deferred pension contributions	**(500)**	4,834	—
Deferred income taxes	**6,583**	(3,178)	1,406
Reduction in accumulated depreciation resulting from change in depreciation method	**(17,205)**	—	—
Other—net	**(2,168)**	(67)	2,034
Decrease in operating working capital (see below)	**7,039**	11,605	72,172
Add (deduct) effects on operating working capital of:			
Conversion of export and factored receivable sales to debt	**—**	23,919	—
Reclassification to deferred liabilities:			
Accrued pension costs	**—**	14,264	—
Other liabilities	**—**	5,510	—
Foreign currency translation adjustments	**(6,009)**	(1,919)	(5,943)
Funds provided by operations	**10,000**	37,287	16,270
Financing, Investment and Other Activities:			
Transactions in debt and capitalized lease obligations —Long-Term debt and capitalized lease obligations:			
Proceeds from sale of 15% Senior Notes and 12% Subordinated Debentures, net of issue costs	**120,530**	—	—
Other increases	**1,474**	—	25,698
Repayments	**(161,500)**	(760)	(9,409)
Restructured debt	**—**	158,058	—
Debt replaced, including conversion of receivable sales of $23,919, and short-term bank notes payable of $9,028	**—**	(158,058)	—
	(39,496)	(760)	16,289
Net increase (repayment) in short-term bank notes payable	**2,107**	(3,982)	(2,016)
Net increase (repayment) in debt and capitalized lease obligations	**(37,389)**	(4,742)	14,273

(continued)

h

209

Exhibit 4   Harnischfeger Corporation 1984 Annual Report (abridged)

CONSOLIDATED STATEMENT OF CHANGES IN FINANCIAL POSITION (continued)

	Year Ended October 31,		
(Dollar amounts in thousands)	1984	1983	1982
Issuance of:			
Common stock	21,310	—	449
Common stock purchase warrants	6,663	—	—
Salaried pension assets reversion	39,307	—	—
Plant and equipment additions	(5,546)	(1,871)	(10,819)
Advances to unconsolidated companies	(2,882)	—	—
Other—net	269	1,531	848
Funds provided by (applied to) financing, investment and other activities	21,732	(5,082)	4,751
Increase in Cash and Temporary Investments Before Cash Dividends	$ 31,732	$ 32,205	$21,021
Cash Dividends	—	—	(2,369)
Increase in Cash and Temporary Investments	$ 31,732	$ 32,205	$ 18,652
Decrease (Increase) in Operating Working Capital (Excluding Cash Items, Debt and Capitalized Lease Obligations):			
Accounts receivable	$ (23,908)	$ (5,327)	$ 42,293
Inventories	9,282	56,904	26,124
Refundable income taxes and related interest	11,289	(2,584)	(6,268)
Other current assets	259	10,008	(439)
Trade accounts payable	16,488	(1,757)	(3,302)
Employee compensation and benefits	698	(15,564)	(3,702)
Accrued plant closing costs	(3,888)	(14,148)	20,496
Other current liabilities	(3,181)	(15,927)	(3,030)
Decrease in operating working capital	$ 7,039	$ 11,605	$ 72,172

(The accompanying notes are an integral part of the financial statements.)

h

Exhibit 4   Harnischfeger Corporation 1984 Annual Report (abridged)

CONSOLIDATED STATEMENT OF SHAREHOLDERS' EQUITY

(Dollar amounts in thousands except per share figures)	Preferred Stock	Common Stock	Capital in Excess of Par Value of Shares	Retained Earnings	Cumulative Translation Adjustments	Total
Balance at October 31, 1981	$10,000	$10,085	$ 87,932	$120,005	$ —	$228,022
Cumulative translation adjustments through October 31, 1981					(1,195)	(1,195)
Issuance of Common Stock:						
10,000 shares to Kobe Steel, Ltd.		10	91			101
38,161 shares under stock purchase and dividend reinvestment plans		39	309			348
Net (loss)				(76,531)		(76,531)
Cash dividends paid on:						
Preferred stock				(350)		(350)
Common stock $.20 per share				(2,019)		(2,019)
Translation adjustments, net of deferred income taxes of $128					(2,928)	(2,928)
Balance at October 31, 1982	10,000	10,134	88,332	41,105	(4,123)	145,448
Net (loss)				(34,630)		(34,630)
Translation adjustments, including deferred income taxes of $33					(899)	(899)
Balance at October 31, 1983	10,000	10,134	88,332	6,475	(5,022)	109,919
Issuance of:						
2,150,000 shares of common stock		2,150	19,160			21,310
2,000,000 common stock purchase warrants			6,663			6,663
17,500 shares of Series A $7.00 cumulative convertible preferred stock in discharge of dividends payable on preferred stock	1,750			(1,750)		—
Net income				15,176		15,176
Translation adjustments, net of deferred income taxes of $300					(5,874)	(5,874)
Other			178			178
Balance at October 31, 1984	$11,750	$12,284	$114,333	$ 19,901	$(10,896)	$147,372

(The accompanying notes are an integral part of the financial statements.)

h

211

Exhibit 4   Harnischfeger Corporation 1984 Annual Report (abridged)

FINANCIAL NOTES

Note 1

Summary of Significant Accounting Policies:

Consolidation—The consolidated financial statements include the accounts of all majority-owned subsidiaries except a wholly-owned domestic finance subsidiary, a subsidiary organized in 1982 as a temporary successor to a distributor, both of which are accounted for under the equity method, and a wholly-owned Brazilian subsidiary, which is carried at estimated net realizable value due to economic uncertainty. All related significant intercompany balances and transactions have been eliminated in consolidation.

Financial statements of certain consolidated subsidiaries, principally foreign, are included, effective in fiscal year 1984, on the basis of their fiscal years ending September 30; previously, certain of such subsidiaries had fiscal years ending July (See Note 2). Such fiscal periods have been adopted by the subsidiaries in order to provide for a more timely consolidation with the Corporation.

Inventories—The Corporation values its inventories at the lower of cost or market. Cost is determined by the last-in, first-out (LIFO) method for inventories located principally in the United States, and by the first-in, first-out (FIFO) method for inventories of foreign subsidiaries.

Operating Plants, Equipment and Depreciation—Properties are stated at cost. Maintenance and repairs are charged to expense as incurred and expenditures for betterments and renewals are capitalized. Effective in 1981, interest is capitalized for qualifying assets during their acquisition period. Capitalized interest is amortized on the same basis as the related asset. When properties are sold or otherwise disposed of, the cost and accumulated depreciation are removed from the accounts and any gain or loss is included in income.

Depreciation of plants and equipment is provided over the estimated useful lives of the related assets, or over the lease terms of capital leases, using, effective in fiscal year 1984, the straight-line method for financial reporting, and principally accelerated methods for tax reporting purposes. Previously, accelerated methods, where applicable, were also

used for financial reporting purposes (See Note 2). For U.S. income tax purposes, depreciation lives are based principally on the Class Life Asset Depreciation Range for additions, other than buildings, in the years 1973 through 1980, and on the Accelerated Cost Recovery System for all additions after 1980.

Discontinued facilities held for sale are carried at the lower of cost less accumulated depreciation or estimated realizable value, which aggregated $4.9 million and $3.6 million at October 31, 1984 and 1983, respectively, and were included in Other Assets in the accompanying Balance Sheet.

Pension Plans—The Corporation has pension plans covering substantially all of its employees. Pension expenses of the principal defined benefit plans consist of current service costs of such plans and amortization of the prior service costs and actuarial gains and losses over periods ranging from 10 to 30 years. The Corporation's policy is to fund at a minimum the amount required under the Employee Retirement Income Security Act of 1974.

Income Taxes—The consolidated tax provision is computed based on income and expenses recorded in the Statement of Operations. Prepaid or deferred taxes are recorded for the difference between such taxes and taxes computed for tax returns. The Corporation and its domestic subsidiaries file a consolidated federal income tax return. The operating results of Harnischfeger GmbH are included in the Corporation's U.S. income tax returns.

Additional taxes are provided on the earnings of foreign subsidiaries which are intended to be remitted to the Corporation. Such taxes are not provided on subsidiaries' unremitted earnings which are intended to be permanently reinvested.

Investment tax credits are accounted for under the flow-through method as a reduction of the income tax provision, if applicable, in the year the related asset is placed in service.

Reporting Format—Certain previously reported items have been conformed to the current year's presentation.

Note 2

Accounting Changes:

Effective November 1, 1983, the Corporation includes in its net sales products purchased from

Exhibit 4   Harnischfeger Corporation 1984 Annual Report (abridged)

Kobe Steel, Ltd. and sold by the Corporation, to reflect more effectively the nature of the Corporation's transactions with Kobe. Previously only the gross margin on Kobe-originated equipment was included. During fiscal year 1984 such sales aggregated $28.0 million. Also, effective November 1, 1983, the financial statements of certain foreign subsidiaries are included on the basis of their fiscal years ending September 30 instead of the previous years ending July 31. This change had the effect of increasing net sales by $5.4 million for the year ended October 31, 1984. The impact of these changes on net income was insignificant.

In 1984, the Corporation has computed depreciation expense on plants, machinery and equipment using the straight-line method for financial reporting purposes. Prior to 1984, the Corporation used principally accelerated methods for its U.S. operating plants. The cumulative effect of this change, which was applied retroactively to all assets previously subjected to accelerated depreciation, increased net income for 1984 by $11.0 million or $.93 per common and common equivalent share. The impact of the new method on income for the year 1984 before the cumulative effect was insignificant.

As a result of the review of its depreciation policy, the Corporation, effective November 1, 1983, has changed its estimated depreciation lives on certain U.S. plants, machinery and equipment and residual values on certain machinery and equipment, which increased net income for 1984 by $3.2 million or $.27 per share. No income tax effect was applied to this change.

The changes in accounting for depreciation were made to conform the Corporation's depreciation policy to those used by manufacturers in the Corporation's and similar industries and to provide a more equitable allocation of the cost of plants, machinery and equipment over their useful lives.

Note 3

Cash and Temporary Investments:

Cash and temporary investments consisted of the following (in thousands of dollars):

	October 31, 1984	1983
Cash—in demand deposits	$ 2,155	$11,910
—in special accounts principally to support letters of credit	4,516	—
Temporary investments	89,336	52,365
	$96,007	$64,275

Temporary investments consisted of short-term U.S. and Canadian treasury bills, money market funds, time and certificates of deposit, commercial paper and bank repurchase agreements and bankers' acceptances. Temporary investments are stated at cost plus accrued interest, which approximates market value.

Note 4

Long-Term Debt, Bank Credit Lines and Interest Expense:

Outstanding long-term debt payable to unaffiliated lenders was as follows (in thousands of dollars):

	October 31, 1984	1983
Parent Company:		
15% Senior Notes due April 15, 1994	$ 47,700	$ —
12% Subordinated Debentures, with an effective interest rate of 16.3%; sinking fund redemption payments of $7,500 due annually on April 15 in 1994–2003, and final payment of $25,000 in 2004	100,000	—
Term Obligations— Insurance company debt:		
9% Notes	—	20,000
9 7/8 Notes	—	38,750
8 7/8 Notes	—	40,500
Bank debt, at 105% of prime	—	25,000
Paper purchase debt, at prime or LIBOR, plus 1¼%	—	18,519
9.23% Mortgage Note due monthly to April, 1998	4,327	4,481
	152,027	147,250

h

213

Exhibit 4   Harnischfeger Corporation 1984 Annual Report (abridged)

	October 31,	
	1984	1983
Consolidated Subsidiaries:		
Notes payable to banks in German marks	—	9,889
Contract payable in 1985–1989, in South African rands, with imputed interest rate of 12%	**1,024**	—
Other	—	36
	153,051	157,175
Less: Amounts payable within one year	**644**	17,799
Unamortized discounts	**23,857**	284
Long-Term Debt—excluding amounts payable within one year	**$128,550**	$139,092

Note 5

Harnischfeger Credit Corporation and Cranetex, Inc.

Condensed financial information of Harnischfeger Credit Corporation ("Credit"), an unconsolidated wholly-owned finance subsidiary, accounted for under the equity method, was as follows (in thousands of dollars):

Balance Sheet	October 31,	
	1984	1983
Assets:		
Cash and temporary investments	**$ 404**	$19,824
Finance receivables—net	**4,335**	11,412
Factored account note and current account receivable from parent company	—	8,836
Other assets	**4,181**	661
	$8,920	$40,733
Liabilities and Shareholder's Equity:		
Debt payable	**$ —**	$32,600
Advances from parent company	**950**	—
Other liabilities	**71**	1,429
	1,021	34,029
Shareholder's equity	**7,899**	6,704
	$8,920	$40,733

Statement of Operations	Year Ended October 31,		
	1984	1983	1982
Revenues	**$1,165**	$2,662	$9,978
Less:			
Operating Expenses	**1,530**	3,386	14,613
Provision (credit) for income taxes	**(1,560)**	(222)	180
Net income (loss)	**$1,195**	$(502)	$(4,815)

Credit's purchases of finance receivables from the Corporation aggregated $1.1 million in 1984, $46.7 million in 1983 and $50.4 million in 1982. In 1982, Credit received income support of $4.0 million from the Corporation.

In 1982, the Corporation organized Cranetex, Inc. to assume certain assets and liabilities transferred by a former distributor of construction equipment, in settlement of the Corporation's and Credit's claims against the distributor and to continue the business on an interim basis until the franchise can be transferred to a new distributor. The Corporation recorded provisions of $2.5 million in 1983 and $2.3 million in 1982 and Credit recorded a provision of $6.7 million in 1982, for credit losses incurred in the financing of equipment sold to the former distributor.

The condensed balance sheet of Cranetex, Inc. was as follows (in thousand of dollars):

	October 31,	
	1984	1983
Assets:		
Cash	**$ 143**	$ 49
Accounts receivables	**566**	428
Inventory	**2,314**	3,464
Property and equipment	**1,547**	1,674
	$4,570	$5,615
Liabilities and Deficit:		
Loans payable	**$4,325**	$6,682
Other liabilities	**338**	620
	4,663	7,302
Shareholder's (deficit), net of accounts and advances payable to parent company	**(93)**	(1,687)
	$4,570	$5,615

Exhibit 4 Harnischfeger Corporation 1984 Annual Report (abridged)

The net losses of Cranetex, Inc. of $.2 million in 1984, $2.1 million in 1983 and $1.0 million in 1982 were included in Equity in Earnings (Loss) of Unconsolidated Companies in the Corporation's Statement of Operations.

Note 6

Transactions with Kobe Steel, Ltd. and ASEA Industrial Systems Inc.

Kobe Steel, Ltd. of Japan ("Kobe"), has been a licensee for certain of the Corporation's products since 1955, and has owned certain Harnischfeger Japanese construction equipment patents and technology since 1981. As of October 31, 1984, Kobe held 1,030,000 shares or 8.4% of the Corporation's outstanding Common Stock (See Note 13). Kobe also owns 25% of the capital stock of Harnischfeger of Australia Pty. Ltd., a subsidiary of the Corporation. This ownership appears as the minority interest on the Corporation's balance sheet.

Under agreements expiring in December 1990, Kobe pays technical service fees on P&H mining equipment produced and sold under license from the Corporation, and trademark and marketing fees on sales of construction equipment outside of Japan. Net fee income received from Kobe was $4.3 million in 1984, $3.1 million in 1983, and $3.9 million in 1982; this income is included in Other Income in the accompanying Statement of Operations.

In October 1983, the Corporation entered into a ten-year agreement with Kobe under which Kobe agreed to supply the Corporation's requirements for construction cranes for sale in the United States as it phases out its own manufacture of cranes over the next several years, and to make the Corporation the exclusive distributor of Kobe-built cranes in the United States. The Agreement also involves a joint research and development program for construction equipment under which the Corporation agreed to spend at least $17 million over a three-year period and provided it does so, Kobe agreed to pay this amount to the Corporation. Sales of cranes outside the United States continue under the contract terms described in the preceding paragraph.

The Corporation's sales to Kobe, principally components for mining and construction equipment, excluding the R&D expenses discussed in the preceding paragraph, approximated $5.2 million, $10.5 million and $7.0 million during the three years ended October 31, 1984, 1983 and 1982, respectively. The purchases from Kobe of mining and construction equipment and components amounted to approximately $33.7 million, $15.5 million and $29.9 million during the three years ended October 31, 1984, 1983 and 1982, respectively, most of which were resold to customers (See Note 2).

The Corporation owns 19% of ASEA Industrial Systems Inc. ("AIS"), an electrical equipment company controlled by ASEA AB of Sweden. The Corporation's purchases of electrical components from AIS aggregated $11.2 million in 1984 and $6.1 million in 1983 and its sales to AIS approximated $2.6 million in 1984 and $3.8 million in 1983.

The Corporation believes that its transactions with Kobe and AIS were competitive with alternative sources of supply for each party involved.

Note 7

Inventories

Consolidated inventories consisted of the following (in thousand of dollars):

| | October 31, | |
	1984	1983
At lower of cost or market (FIFO method):		
Raw materials	$ 11,003	$ 11,904
Work in process and purchased parts	88,279	72,956
Finished goods	79,111	105,923
	178,393	190,783
Allowance to reduce inventories to cost on the LIFO method	(34,081)	(37,189)
	$144,312	$153,594

Inventories valued on the LIFO method represented approximately 82% of total inventories at both October 31, 1984 and 1983.

Inventory reductions in 1984, 1983 and 1982 resulted in a liquidation of LIFO inventory quantities carried at lower costs compared with the current cost of their acquisitions. The effect of these liquidations was to increase net income by 2.4 million or $.20

h

215

Exhibit 4   Harnischfeger Corporation 1984 Annual Report (abridged)

per common share in fiscal 1984, and to reduce the net loss by approximately $15.6 million or $1.54 per share in 1983, and by $6.7 million or $.66 per share in 1982; no income tax effect applied to the adjustment in 1984 and 1983.

Note 8

Accounts Receivable

Accounts receivable were net of allowances for doubtful accounts of $5.9 million and $6.4 million at October 31, 1984 and 1983, respectively.

Note 9

Research and Development Expense

Research and development expense incurred in the development of new products or significant improvements to existing products was $5.1 million in 1984 (net of amounts funded by Kobe Steel, Ltd.) $12.1 million in 1983 and $14.1 million in 1982.

Note 10

Foreign Operations

The net sales, net income (loss) and net assets of subsidiaries located in countries outside the United States and Canada and included in the consolidated financial statements were as follows (in thousands of dollars):

| | Year Ended October 31, | | |
	1984	1983	1982
Net sales	$78,074	$45,912	$69,216
Net income (loss) after minority interests	828	(1,191)	3,080
Corporation's equity in total net assets	17,734	7,716	7,287

Foreign currency transaction losses included in Cost of Sales were $2.7 million in 1984, $1.2 million in 1983 and $1.3 million in 1982.

Note 11

Pension Plans and Other Postretirement Benefits

Pension expense for all plans of the Corporation and its consolidated subsidiaries was $1.9 million in

1984, $6.5million in 1983 and $12.2 million in 1982.

Accumulated plan benefits and plan net assets for the Corporation's U.S. defined benefit plans, at the beginning of the fiscal years 1984 and 1983, with the data for the Salaried Employees' Retirement Plan as in effect on August 1, 1984, were as follows (in thousands of dollars):

	1984	1983
Actuarial present value of accumulated plan benefits:		
Vested	$52,639	$108,123
Nonvested	2,363	5,227
	$55,002	$113,350
Net assets available for benefits:		
Asset s of the Pension Trusts	$45,331	$112,075
Accrued contributions not paid to the Trusts	16,717	12,167
	$62,048	$124,242

The Salaried Employees' Retirement Plan, which covers substantially all salaried employees in the U.S., was restructured during 1984 due to overfunding of the Plan. Effective August 1, 1984, the Corporation terminated the existing plan and established a new plan which is substantially identical to the prior plan except for an improvement in the minimum pension benefit. All participants in the prior plan became fully vested upon its termination. All vested benefits earned through August 1, 1984 were covered through the purchase of individual annuities at a cost aggregating $36.7 million. The remaining plan assets, which totaled $39.3 million, reverted to the Corporation in cash upon receipt of regulatory approval of the prior plan termination from the Pension Benefit Guaranty Corporation. For financial reporting purposes, the new plan is considered to be a continuation of the terminated plan. Accordingly, the $39.3 million actuarial gain which resulted from the restructuring is included in Accrued Pension Costs in the accompanying Balance Sheet and is being amortized to income over a ten-year period commencing in 1984. For tax reporting purposes, the asset reversion will be

Exhibit 4   Harnischfeger Corporation 1984 Annual Report (abridged)

treated as a fiscal 1985 transaction. The initial unfunded actuarial liability of the new plan, computed as of November 1, 1983, of $10.3 million is also included in Accrued Pension Costs.

In 1982 and 1983, the Pension Trusts purchased certain securities with effective yields of 13% and 12%, respectively, and dedicated these assets to the plan benefits of a substantial portion of the retired employees and certain terminated employees with deferred vested rights. These rates, together with 9% for active employees in 1984, 8% in 1983 and 7¼% in 1982, were the assumed rates of return used in determining the annual pension expense and the actuarial present value of accumulated plan benefits for the U.S. plans.

The effect of the changes in the investment return assumption rates for all U.S. plans, together with the 1984 restructuring of the U.S. Salaried Employees' Plan, was to reduce pension expense by approximately $4.0 million in 1984 and $2.0 million in 1983, and the actuarial present value of accumulated plan benefits by approximately $60.0 million in 1984. Pension expense in 1983 was also reduced $2.1 million from the lower level of active employees. Other actuarial gains, including higher than anticipated investment results, more than offset the additional pension costs resulting from plan changes and interest charges on balance sheet accruals in 1984 and 1983.

The Corporation's foreign pension plans do not determine the actuarial value of accumulated benefits or net assets available for retirement benefits as calculated and disclosed above. For those plans, the total of the plans' pension funds and balance sheet accruals approximated the actuarially computed value of vested benefits at both October 31, 1984 and 1983.

The Corporation generally provides certain health care and life insurance benefits for U.S. retired employees. Substantially all of the Corporation's current U.S. employees may become eligible for such benefits upon retirement. Life insurance benefits are provided either through the pension plans or separate group insurance arrangements. The cost of retiree health care and life insurance benefits, other than the benefits provided by the pension plans, is expensed as incurred; such costs approximated $2.6 million in 1984 and $1.7 million in 1983.

Note 12

Income Taxes

Domestic and foreign income (loss) before income tax effects was as follows (in thousands of dollars):

| | Year Ended October 31, | | |
	1984	1983	1982
Domestic	$1,578	$(35,412)	$(77,600)
Foreign:			
Harnischfeger GmbH	432	(2,159)	(475)
All other	3,728	4,768	8,418
	4,160	2,609	7,943
Total income (loss) before income tax effects, equity items and cumulative effect of accounting change	$5,738	$(32,803)	$(69,657)

Provision (credit) for income taxes, on income (loss) before income tax effects, equity items and cumulative effect of accounting change, consisted of (in thousands of dollars):

	1984	1983	1982
Currently payable (refundable):			
Federal	$ —	$(7,957)	$(9,736)
State	136	297	70
Foreign	2,518	3,379	5,376
	2,654	(4,281)	(4,290)
Deferred (prepaid):			
Federal	—	2,955	2,713
State and foreign	(229)	(74)	(23)
	(229)	2,881	2,690
Provision (credit) for income taxes	$2,425	$(1,400)	$(1,600)

During 1983 an examination of the Corporation's 1977–1981 federal income tax returns and certain refund claims was completed by the Internal Revenue Service, and as a result, a current credit for federal income taxes of $8.0 million was recorded in 1983, $3.0 million of which was applied to the reduction of prepaid income taxes.

h

217

Exhibit 4   Harnischfeger Corporation 1984 Annual Report (abridged)

In 1984, tax credits fully offset any federal income tax otherwise applicable to the year's income, and in 1983 and 1982, the relationship of the tax benefit to the pre-tax loss differed substantially from the U.S. statutory tax rate due principally to losses from the domestic operations for which only a partial federal tax benefit was available in 1982. Consequently, an analysis of deferred income taxes and variance from the U.S. statutory rate is not presented.

Unremitted earnings of foreign subsidiaries which have been or are intended to be permanently reinvested were $19.1 million at October 31, 1984. Such earnings, if distributed, would incur income tax expense of substantially less than the U.S. income tax rate as a result of previously paid foreign income taxes, provided that such foreign taxes would become deductible as foreign tax credits. No income tax provision was made in respect of the tax-deferred income of a consolidated subsidiary that has elected to be taxed as a domestic international sales corporation. The Deficit Reduction Act of 1984 provides for such income to become nontaxable effective December 31, 1984.

At October 31, 1984, the Corporation had federal tax operating loss carry-forwards of approximately $70.0 million, expiring in 1998 and 1999, for tax return purposes, and $88.0 million for book purposes. In addition, the Corporation had for tax purposes, foreign tax credit carry-forwards of $3.0 million (expiring in 1985 through 1989), and investment tax credit carry-forwards of $1.0 million (expiring in 1997 through 1999). For book purposes, tax credit carry-forwards approximately $8.0 million. The carry-forward will be available for the reduction of future income tax provisions, the extent and timing of which are not determinable.

Differences in income (loss) before income taxes for financial and tax purposes arise from timing differences between financial and tax reporting and relate to depreciation, consolidating eliminations for inter-company profits in inventories, and provisions, principally, for warranty, pension, compensated absences, product liability and plant closing costs.

REPORT OF INDEPENDENT ACCOUNTANTS

Milwaukee, Wisconsin
November 29, 1984

To the Directors and Shareholders of Harnischfeger Corporation:

In our opinion, the financial statements, which appear on pages 18 to 34 of this report, present fairly the consolidated financial position of Harnischfeger Corporation and its subsidiaries at October 31, 1984 and 1983, and the results of their operations and the changes in their financial position for each of the three years in the period ended October 31, 1984, in conformity with generally accepted accounting principles consistently applied during the period except for the change, with which we concur, in the method of accounting for depreciation expense as described in Note 2 on page 23 of this report. Our examinations of these statements were made in accordance with generally accepted auditing standards and accordingly included such tests of the accounting records and such other auditing procedures as we considered necessary in the circumstances.

Price Waterhouse

The President's Message in Hawkeye Bancorporation's 1984 Annual Report was exceptionally blunt:

Dear Shareholder:

Hawkeye Bancorporation has long had a philosophy of planning for the future. Everyone in the Company puts in writing what he or she intends to do in the coming year. From those individual commitments we build our subsidiary operating plans. We like to say what was accomplished occurred because we planned it that way. What has occurred is history and to constantly be looking backwards for guidance in the future is similar to trying to drive an automobile by watching only the rear-view mirror.

Nineteen eighty-four is a year that caused us all to question our basic philosophies and beliefs. On January 2, 1984, our operating plan, based on individual commitments, showed we would earn $2.15 a share for the year. We ended 1984 with earnings of $.12 a share. Our cash dividend was cut 73%. We did not pay a stock dividend. The contribution to our employee stock ownership trust was cut 50%. On January 2, 1984, our stock was selling at $17 a share—on December 31st, $8.25. In July, we thought we were strong enough to acquire United Central Bancshares. By December, it was decided each company should go its own way.

What happened? What caused a company with 16 straight years of outstanding performance to stumble as we did in 1984?

On a loan portfolio of about $1 billion, from 1967 until 1981, our losses averaged under $1.5 million, or about one-half of what the average bank in the United States experienced. One year in our annual report, we stated we had never suffered a direct loan loss to an Iowa farmer over a ten-year period. In 1982, our loan losses went to 44/100ths of 1%, or about $4.1 million, and for the first time in our Company's history we did not have a per share earnings increase. We were concerned, but thought 1983 would be better. In 1983, our losses increased to $6.1 million, and by year-end 1984, we had provided nearly $21 million for anticipated loan losses.

Hawkeye Bancorporation, by its ownership of county-seat trade center banks, has probably the largest concentration of agricultural loans of any major banking organization. In sheer size, we are in the top 15 of the largest agricultural lenders in the

This case was prepared by Associate in Research Jane Palley Katz, under the supervision of Professor Krishna G. Palepu and Professor G. Peter Wilson as the basis for class discussion rather than to illustrate either effective or ineffective handling of an administrative situation. Copyright © 1991 by the President and Fellows of Harvard College. Harvard Business School case 9-192-064.

United States. Approximately 30% of all our loans are direct loans to Iowa farmers, compared with 11% for Banks of Iowa and 7% for Norwest Corporation. We have another 30% in agri-business loans and to merchants in our county-seat markets.

We are being bombarded by the press, the radio, and television news as to the poor state of agriculture here in the Midwest. Our Iowa legislature has Iowa's economy as its number one debating issue. President Reagan's attitude seems to be one of "hands off"; let the natural forces boil down the industry to a point where only the toughest can survive.

With this scenario, what can we do? There is no better answer than the old saying, "When the going gets tough, the tough get going."

For 1985, I have ten goals for this Company to accomplish:

1. *We are going to remain the leader in banking in Iowa. We can't do this if we champion pessimism and talk only of gloom and despair and how miserable we all are. This Company, with one voice, is going to talk about accomplishments and the opportunities available if we are willing to take what is being offered. Bad times present as many or more opportunities than good times.*

2. *Our strong and active Political Action Committee is going to work with the Iowa Legislature in pursuing legislative changes that will aid the distressed Iowa farmer by voluntary mortgage extensions, interest buy-downs, and a better tax environment for economic expansion. We will support the proposed World Trade Center.*

3. *We will bring all the resources necessary to control loan losses. In 1984, we added 26 new senior loan officers to our bank subsidiaries, plus a specialist in loan workout problems. In 1985, we will add another loan review officer and greatly expand our in-house loan training program. Every bank is under pressure to know its loans—to know its exposures and communicate with its borrowers.*

4. *We will remain as Iowa's number one agricultural lender. Agriculture may be having a tough time, but this is our business—our life. We aren't going to walk away from our farm customers. The State of Iowa is built on agriculture. Our Company is built on agricultural lending.*

5. *In each community where we have a bank, we will promote industrial development. Nineteen eighty-five will be a year in which we will place special emphasis on this area.*

6. *We will continue our emphasis on being a sales organization with broadened products. If we are in a state with no population growth, then we had better sell more product and expand our markets to wider areas.*

7. *We have shown that our Investor Centers can sell. We have over $120 million in sweep accounts, including a new tax-exempt fund. In 1985, we are introducing mutual funds and universal life insurance as part of our Investor Center product line.*

8. *In 1984, the operations of our 28 property and casualty agencies were consolidated into one large centralized agency, and now, instead of representing 109*

companies, we represent "CIGNA." Nineteen eighty-five is the year of increased profitability and service from these agencies.

9. *Our banks will remain strongly capitalized, and the Parent Company financially sound. Hawkeye anticipates entering the capital markets in 1985 to further strengthen its equity base.*

10. *Each individual in this Company is to give a year of special effort: a special effort in our own individual work—doing it right, doing it on time, a special effort in co-operating with one another. A company with 43 separate subsidiaries causes people and efforts to cross one another's territory many times in a year. We will make a special effort to find ways to cut costs. Not quick fixes, which may save money this year but impair long-term goals, but little and big savings, which can be accomplished by awareness on everyone's part. We will make a special effort to sell with everyone aware of our product line and willing to ask for the business.*

There isn't much doubt about our most valuable asset. When the going gets tough, we aren't looking at brick and mortar—we aren't looking at new computers and systems—we aren't looking for government help and bailouts. When the going gets tough, we look at ourselves. We are the ones who can cause it to happen. Nineteen eighty-five is the year we are going to cause it to happen.

Sincerely,
Paul D. Dunlap, President

h

221

COMPANY BACKGROUND

Hawkeye Bancorporation (Hawkeye) was founded by Paul D. Dunlap, a born-and-bred farm banker, in 1966, when he acquired 80 percent of the voting stock of Lyon County State Bank in Rock Rapids, Iowa. By 1984, Hawkeye had become the largest Iowa-based bank-holding company, with $1.9 billion in total assets and operating 36 banks in 89 locations across the state. Hawkeye also owned seven subsidiaries offering computer services, farm management, investment management, mortgage banking, insurance products, real estate brokerage, and credit card services.

Unlike most other bank holding companies, Hawkeye had no lead bank. Instead, it owned a collection of banks whose assets ranged from $30 million to $75 million, each of which had a large share in its individual market. With each of these affiliated banks, Hawkeye had five-year management contracts that automatically continued from year to year, unless terminated. They required Hawkeye to perform for each bank various services such as managing bond investment accounts; recruiting personnel; supervising loan activities; planning and arranging for publication or production of advertising and promotional projects; recommending and implementing adequate auditing, bookkeeping, and clerical systems; supervising placement of insurance coverages; advising department heads concerning operating economics, efficiency methods, and business developments; submitting periodic criticisms and evaluations concerning all aspects of operations; and assisting in the standardization of commercial forms and compliance with government regulations.

Most of Hawkeye's subsidiary banks were located in Iowa's rural areas and in county seat cities, which were typically the hub of each county's agricultural and financial activities. This focus meant that Hawkeye depended directly on the local agricultural economy. In some rural areas, its banks had issued loans to a large percentage of all the local farms and businesses. In addition, Hawkeye was the state's largest originator of student loans. Approximately 30 percent of its loan portfolio consisted of student loans, which were backed by state insurance and federal reinsurance guarantees.

In 1984, Iowa law did not permit branch banking, although a limited number of offices could be established within a specified geographic area, with prior approval of the banking regulatory authorities. Several proposals were afloat to allow interstate banking, but local bankers and banking regulators were divided on their merits. As of 1984, interstate banking was still prohibited in Iowa. Like all banks, Hawkeye was affected by the monetary and fiscal policies of the United States, and particularly those of the Federal Reserve System, of which eight Hawkeye banks were members.

From 1974 to 1984, Hawkeye's strategy had embraced growth through acquisition. During that time Hawkeye acquired 23 subsidiary banks, which had provided well over half of its asset growth. An analyst for Dain Bosworth, Inc. commented on this strategy:

Premiums to book value are typically paid for these banks; as a result, goodwill amounts to about $34 million, or 25% of the $133 million shareholders' equity at [1983] year-end. While this figure is high, it has allowed Hawkeye to develop the strongest banking franchise in the state. The banks are allowed to operate with considerable autonomy, and profitability incentives are used to encourage high performance. Volume-sensitive operations, such as data processing and credit cards, are centralized for efficiency, and corporate-level management has developed products and market plans with a unified Hawkeye theme, while still allowing individual bank autonomy to continue.[1]

However, one observer was less optimistic, remarking that Hawkeye "has taken over a number of banks that were on the brink of financial disaster."[2] Moreover, Hawkeye's Parent Company statements in its 1984 Annual Report showed that dividends from subsidiary banks had declined more than 50 percent since 1982. The Annual Report also revealed that six Hawkeye banks showed a negative return on assets in 1984. In fact, these six banks required cash transfusions from parent to subsidiary.[3]

THE IOWA ECONOMY

The Iowa economy was deeply rooted in agriculture. Most years, the state ranked first or second in the United States in the production of corn, soybeans, and hogs. In 1984,

h

222

1. Steven R. Schroll, "Hawkeye Bancorporation: Report," Dain Bosworth, Inc., March 9, 1984.
2. Lisabeth Weiner, "With Fewer Farm Loans, Banks of Iowa Recovers Sooner than Its Competitors," American Banker, August 27, 1984, p. 12.
3. Jay McCormick, "When Backbone Meets Belly Button," Forbes, May 6, 1985, p. 40.

Iowa farmers earned more than $9 billion from crops and livestock, including $1.7 billion from corn and $2 billion from soybeans. They produced 27 percent of America's pork and 9 percent of its grain-fed beef. The commodity markets of Iowa's four major products—corn, soybeans, hogs, and cattle—were very cyclical and interdependent, although it was considered unusual for these markets to be at the same point in the cycle at the same time. Furthermore, a significant portion of agricultural production was destined for export to foreign markets. In 1984, Iowa recorded agricultural exports of $3.4 billion, 10 percent of the United States total agricultural exports and top among all midwestern states.

The Iowa economy consisted of more than farms. In 1984, manufacturing accounted for 27 percent of total state income, wholesale and retail trade for 19 percent, services for 17 percent, and government services for 14 percent. The general condition of the national and global economy also affected the state, particularly through interest rates and the demand for agricultural products.

The early 1980s were an especially difficult period for the Iowa economy. The national recession, high interest rates, low commodity prices, weak exports, and the vicissitudes of Mother Nature combined to batter businesses in the state's rural communities. Holmes Foster, chief executive officer of Banks of Iowa, one of Hawkeye's principal competitors, noted:

> *The first signs of trouble came in 1981, when farmers began to feel the effects of the recession and stopped buying big-ticket items such as farm equipment. As the big-ticket business dwindled, job shops, which manufactured farm machinery parts, saw their business fade. Real estate, construction, and even service industries also began to slow down, reflecting the nationwide recession.*[4]

Net farm income, personal income, and Iowa's gross state product all declined during this period. The number of large tractors sold in the state declined by more than 50 percent, and the number of combines sold fell by more than 60 percent. By 1984, the average value of Iowa farm real estate had fallen to $1,499 an acre, down from $1,811 in 1980. The state unemployment rate stood at 7 percent, well above the 1979 rate of 4.1 percent, though below the high of 8.5 percent reached in 1982.[5] Gross state product stagnated at $16.3 billion, below the high of $17.3 billion achieved in 1979, though greater than the $15.6 billion recorded in 1982.[5] The Federal Reserve Bank's tight money policies, which had contributed to the national recession and high interest rates, also began to have their intended effect on inflation, as price increases slowed substantially.

Hawkeye's 1984 Annual Report noted that Iowa's four principal commodities experienced mixed results for that year. Although the corn crop was relatively good, the year-end price per bushel was at its lowest level since 1977, and, at $2.44, it was below the $2.99 estimated cost of production.[6] Iowa was, again, the number one soybean-producing state, and price levels were profitable during the first half of the year, but they de-

h

223

....

4. *Weiner, op. cit., p. 12.*
5. *All gross state product figures as in 1974 constant dollars.*
6. *Data from Hawkeye Annual Report, 1984, p. 3. Cost estimates are based on production of 115 bushels per acre, slightly above the 1984 rate of 112 bushels per acre.*

clined to $5.50 per bushel by year-end, also less than the estimated production cost. Whereas pork producers experienced losses in 7 out of 12 months, Hawkeye managers expected a recovery and greater profitability in 1985, based on lower feed costs and a 5 percent reduction in nationwide hog numbers. Beef producers also weathered a marginal year, but profitability was expected to increase in 1985.

MARKET VALUE OR BOOK VALUE?

While total shareholder equity fell 5.6 percent between year-end 1983 and 1984, Hawkeye's stock price took an even more dramatic tumble. During 1983, and even through the first quarter of 1984, the stock traded in a range between $14.25 and $20.00. In the third quarter of 1984, the price slipped to between $12.00 and $14.00. By year-end 1984, it had plunged to $8.25 per share. With this drop, the ratio of Hawkeye's market value to book value fell precipitously to .41, down from .85 in 1980.

Analyst Assessment of Hawkeye

Stock market analysts had been very enthusiastic in their assessment of Hawkeye. In a 1983 report, one analyst wrote:

> We recommend purchase of Hawkeye Bancorporation by investors seeking undervalued growth stocks. . . . [It] offers investors prospects of good long-term capital appreciation, above-average dividend yield and, in our opinion, minimal downside risk. In view of the extremely high P/E multiples currently accorded many unseasoned technology and "emerging" types of stocks, we regard Hawkeye as an exceptional value. The company has an impressive earnings record, a leadership position within Iowa in the rapidly changing financial services marketplace, and prospects of strong and consistent earnings during the remainder of the 1980s.[7]

In March 1984, Hawkeye was endorsed by another analyst:

> We are encouraged by the Company's continual expansion program and the growth in new services provided at these banks. This growth has slowed earnings per share gains, but is preparing the Company to be an even stronger competitor in the future. The year 1984 will be another challenging year, but we expect improving loan quality and 7%–8% loan growth before any acquisitions to generate earnings per share in the $2.15 area, a 15% gain. Trading at 7.6 times our estimate and a 4% discount to the $16.92 book value, we would buy the stock for a high-quality, long-term holding.[8]

Management Assessment of Hawkeye

In December 1984, Hawkeye's board decided to reduce its quarterly dividend by 73 percent, to 7¢ a common share from 26¢. After the meeting, Paul Dunlap said to the press,

7. Gary L. Wirt, "Broker Reports—Hawkeye Bancorporation," The Wall Street Transcript, June 13, 1983, p. 1.

8. Schroll, op. cit.

"Hawkeye Bancorp. remains financially sound, and the actions we are taking will ensure that we stay that way."[9] In the 1984 Annual Report, company officials were cautiously optimistic about the future:

The outlook for 1985, though rigorous, appears more hopeful than 1984. Land prices may be approaching their lows in "real terms." Net returns to land are reaching the historically high 10% level, which could mark the end of net worth deterioration due to falling land values. Efforts are being made to stem the rise in the U.S. dollar, and future erosion of buying power for U.S. grain should be contained. Substantial improvements in profit margins for livestock producers are anticipated in 1985. And, finally, there are 90 million new mouths to feed every year.

PROSPECTS FOR 1985

On April 28, 1985, Thomas Huston, Iowa Banking Superintendent, announced that a new buyer for the failed Peoples State Bank in Odebolt, Iowa, had been secured, but that the state's bank troubles were not over:

I think we're done [closing banks] for April, but you should expect to be back for another announcement by mid-May. It won't be very long before we close another one. I don't care what other people say, we are not near the bottom and things aren't getting better. We have nothing in place to straighten this situation out. I don't see much that we can do about it, but be assured we are going to close more banks in this state.[10]

At the end of 1984, Huston had estimated that 14 Iowa banks would close during 1985. By April, 1985, he was predicting five additional closings, remarking, "I hope its's not worse than that."[11]

h

225

QUESTIONS

1. Evaluate Hawkeye's business. What are the key success factors in managing the company?
2. By year-end 1984, Hawkeye's market value to book value ratio had fallen to 0.41. There appeared to be at least two reasons for this low ratio. First, the stock market had assessed the values of some of Hawkeye's balance sheet items to be lower than their book values. Second, and more generally,the stock market was pessimistic about Hawkeye's future prospects.

   (a) Identify balance sheet items that might account for differences between the market and book values.

   (b) How optimistic are you about Hawkeye's turnaround strategy (as outlined in the President's Message)?

   (c) Is Hawkeye's stock a good buy?

---

9. *"Hawkeye Bancorp. Reduces Its Quarterly 73%, to 7 Cents a Share,"* Wall Street Journal, *December 28, 1984, p. 23.*
10. *"Hair-Raising Search Locates Firm to Buy, Reopen Bank in Iowa,"* Omaha World Herald, *April 28, 1985.*
11. *Ibid.*

Exhibit 1   Excerpts from Hawkeye Bancorporation Annual Report, 1984

EXHIBIT 1

Excerpts from Hawkeye Bancorporation Annual Report, 1984

FINANCIAL REVIEW

The following discussion and analysis is presented to provide pertinent information about Hawkeye Bancorporation's financial performance, including principal factors affecting the results of operations and any significant changes in financial position. The discussion is intended to be read in conjunction with the Consolidated Financial Statements and with other comparative statistical information presented in this annual report.

Results of Operations

Nineteen eighty-four marked the first year Hawkeye Bancorporation experienced a decline in net income. Net income for 1984 was $917 thousand—a 94% decrease from the 1983 net income of $14.5 million and a 93% decrease from the 1982 net income of $13.9 million.

The decline in earnings was the result of an abnormal increase in the loan loss provision as well as other credit-related losses and expenses. The 1984 loan loss provision was $20.7 million versus $5.3 million for 1983 and $4.7 million for 1982. Problem loans impacted net income in a variety of other areas in 1984. Interest income not recognized due to nonaccrual and restructured loans was $3.7 million, and writedowns and expenses on other real estate that are included in other noninterest expenses totaled approximately $2 million.

For the prior five years, operating expenses and loan loss provisions combined averaged 78% of gross income (net interest income plus noninterest income). In 1984 operating expenses and loan loss provision rose to 102% of gross income. The other major areas impacting net income in 1984 compared to 1983 were:

- $3.4 million increase in net interest income;
- $3.7 million increase in noninterest income;
- $5.5 million increase in noninterest expense;
- $5.1 million of income tax benefit not recorded due to the consolidated net operating loss carryforward position of the Company.

Primary earnings per share of $.12, compared to $1.88 for 1983 and $2.00 for 1982, reflected the decline in earnings as well as the 133 thousand—and an 892 thousand share increase in weighted average shares outstanding.

Total average assets continued to increase, which, along with the earnings decline, had a negative impact on return on average assets (ROA). In 1984 ROA was .05%, a decline from .80% and .92% in 1983 and 1982, respectively. Return on equity (ROE) for 1984 was .69% compared to 11.43% in 1983 and 12.64% in 1982. Both ratios reflect the low level of earnings due to abnormal loan losses in 1984. The makeup of 1984, 1983, and 1982 primary earnings per share is presented in the following table:

Exhibit 1   Excerpts from Hawkeye Bancorporation Annual Report, 1984

	1984	1983	1982
Net interest income	$7.65	$7.34	$6.99
Provision for loan losses	(2.64)	(.69)	(.68)
Noninterest income	3.41	2.99	2.85
Noninterest expenses	(8.66)	(8.10)	(7.66)
Income tax credit	.36	.34	.50
Primary earnings per share	$ .12	$1.88	$2.00

Shareholders' Equity and Capital Planning

Total average equity to average assets remained a strong 7.0% for the year, compared to 7.0% for 1983 and 7.3% for 1982. Year-end equity to assets was 6.5%, well above the regulators' requirement of 6.0% for bank holding companies and the Keefe Bank Index of 6.1%. In 1982 and 1983, 965 thousand shares of common stock were issued for bank acquisitions.

In 1984, Hawkeye offered $5 million in long-term debt by marketing five-year 12½% notes through the Investor Centers in each bank. This ability to raise capital is a major strength in capital management and one that is available for Hawkeye through its large network of banks. In 1983, capital was increased $15 million through a private placement of long-term debt with six insurance companies.

Hawkeye will continue to maintain a strong capital base. Management anticipates it will enter the capital markets in 1985, given favorable market conditions.

Net Interest Income

The total of interest income minus the total of interest expense equals net interest income. There are three factors that affect the dollar amount of net interest income: a change in the dollar amount (or volume) of interest-earning assets or interest-bearing liabilities; a change in the rate paid or earned on these interest-bearing items; and a change in the mixture of volume and rates.

An analysis of the components of net interest income is more meaningful if the income from tax-exempt securities is adjusted to a taxable equivalent basis. This adjustment increases net interest income to an amount that would be realized if that income were taxable. From 1983 to 1984, taxable equivalent net interest income increased $1.2 million to $74.0 million.

Total average earning assets increased $62.6 million, and average interest-bearing liabilities increased $77.4 million. Because interest-bearing liabilities increased more than interest-earning assets, a $751 thousand negative volume change resulted. Rates earned on interest-earning assets increased 16 basis points, compared to a 17-basis-point increase in interest-bearing liabilities. Since average earning assets were approximately $135 million greater than total average interest-bearing liabilities, this resulted in a positive change due to rates. The $751 thousand negative change due to volume and the $1.954 million positive change due to rates resulted in a $1.203 million positive change to net interest income on a taxable equivalent basis.

Net interest margin (net interest income on a taxable equivalent basis divided by average earning assets) was 4.42% for 1984, a 10-basis-point decline from 1983 and a

h

227

Exhibit 1   Excerpts from Hawkeye Bancorporation Annual Report, 1984

42-basis-point decline from 1982. This decline was caused by an increase in interest charged off and interest not recognized due to nonaccrual and restructured loans of $3.7 million for the year ended December 31, 1984. This compares to $2.4 million in 1983.

Liquidity and Interest Rate Sensitivity Analysis

Two key measures of the soundness of a bank are liquidity to meet the needs of borrowers and depositors and interest rate sensitivity, a measure of the bank's exposure to changes in market interest rate levels. By both of these measures, the Company maintained its high level of safety and soundness in 1984.

Liquidity management practices include formal, quarterly cash flow projections prepared by each of the Company's 36 affiliate banks. These forecasts are then monitored daily by both the bank and by Hawkeye Investment Management, Inc., the Company's investment management subsidiary. Liquidity goals are established based on these projections, and actual liquidity sources are secured based on the goals and ongoing cash flow trends.

Hawkeye's primary liquidity reserve consists of overnight and very short-term investment assets. In this category are federal funds sold and deposits in other banks, which totaled $52 million at year-end 1984, and marketable investment securities due within one year, which totaled $219 million. Secondary liquidity is provided by the $507 million of commercial and agricultural loans and $108 million of other loans due within one year. The sum of these primary and secondary liquidity sources at December 31, 1984, was $886 million, equal to 55% of total deposits. At year-end 1983, this total was $828 million, or 52% of total deposits.

A third source of liquidity to Hawkeye is temporary borrowing by the Company or by the affiliate banks. Hawkeye Bancorporation maintains access to operating and term loans from several domestic and foreign financial institutions. These borrowings remained virtually unchanged during 1984. At the bank level, liquidity needs can be met by temporarily purchasing federal funds, borrowing from the Federal Reserve System's discount window, or by purchasing large deposits of commercial customers or public bodies. The Company's long-standing policy has been to reserve this bank-level borrowing capability, keeping it available for periods of heavy loan demand or large withdrawals. Very little use was made of these liquidity sources in 1984.

Hawkeye's primary tool for managing interest margins is interest sensitivity and analysis—an ongoing comparison of present and prospective interest income with present and prospective interest expense. Analysis of the amounts and yields of the various asset and liability categories, maturing or repricing in various future periods, serves as the basis for establishing loan rates and terms as well as deposit pricing to protect and enhance interest margins.

The key goal of interest-sensitivity management is to protect against unfavorable changes in margins arising from changes in the general level of interest rates. This is achieved by balancing the amount of assets maturing or repricing in any future period with the amount of liabilities maturing or repricing in the same period. Any imbalance in any future period is referred to as a "gap."

A detailed, monthly analysis of one-day, one-month, three-month, six-month, and one-year prospective gaps is provided to each Hawkeye affiliate bank. Consolidated companywide data are provided to Hawkeye Investment Management. Together, the affil-

h

228

Exhibit 1   Excerpts from Hawkeye Bancorporation Annual Report, 1984

iate banks, Hawkeye Investment Management, and the Company's financial staff establish asset and liability management policies and investment portfolio programs to minimize companywide exposure to adverse changes in interest rates.

The consolidated total of rate-sensitive assets on December 31, 1984, was $886 million, or 98% of the $908 million of rate-sensitive liabilities. One year ago, rate-sensitive assets were 96% of rate-sensitive liabilities. This nearly perfectly balanced position was maintained throughout the year to further ensure that the Company's ability to meet its customers' needs would not be impaired by unforeseen swings in market interest rates.

Noninterest Income

The Company continues to emphasize a strong sales orientation, offering a broad range of financial services. Investor Centers located in the banks serve as the marketing center, providing customers access to the wide range of financial services. As Hawkeye continues to develop new products and deregulation continues, more and more opportunity is available to invest funds at high rates of interest for a broad range of investors, from the small saver to the investor who needs tax-exempt income. The Company's product line has developed from the days of passbook savings as the only short-term savings alternative to include interest-bearing checking accounts, high-yielding certificates of deposit with virtually any maturity date, money market savings, interest-bearing checking accounts for businesses through SWEEP accounts, tax-exempt interest for checking accounts through a SWEEP fund, discount brokerage and mutual fund services, a broad range of insurance products, Hawkeye real estate centers, and farm management.

Noninterest income rose to an all-time high of $26.8 million in 1984, an increase of 16% over the prior year's figure of $23.1 million. Most categories realized significant increases. Fee income had the largest increase, 28% over the total from 1983, and 41% higher than 1982. Service charge income was 17% higher than the 1983 total and 31% higher than the 1982 total. Both of these increases reflect the continuing efforts by the banks to establish equitable charges for services used and the widening product array, which provides a broader base for generation of fee income.

Trust fees continued to increase. The 1984 total of $2.0 million was 17% higher than 1983 and 45% higher than 1982. This was due to the continued development of new trust business and a rise in the market value of trust assets on which certain fee income was based. An increase of 12% was realized in insurance, real estate, and advisory services income from 1984 to 1983, and 28% over 1982. Life insurance commissions and investment advisory fees were the biggest contributors to this increase.

Noninterest income has grown at a compound growth rate of 28% over the past five years. As a percent of average earning assets, noninterest income has grown from 1.05% in 1979 to 1.60% in 1984. In addition, noninterest-income coverage of noninterest expenses had increased steadily to 39% in 1984, from 31% in 1979.

Noninterest Expenses

Noninterest expenses totaled $68.0 million for 1984, 9% over $62.4 million in 1983 and 27% over $53.4 million in 1982.

The largest expense category was salaries and employee benefits. The small 3% increase in this category from 1984 to 1983 is the result of concentrated efforts to reduce costs. The ratio of employee benefit expense to salary expense fell to 19%, compared to 25% in 1983 and 23% in 1982. This reflects the change in the amount contributed to the

h

229

Exhibit 1   Excerpts from Hawkeye Bancorporation Annual Report, 1984

Employee Stock Ownership Plan. Prior to 1984, 10% of qualified compensation was contributed to the Plan. During 1984, that amount was reduced to 5%. There were 1,620 full-time-equivalent employees at year-end, compared to 1,602 in 1983 and 1,482 in 1982. Other noninterest expense increased 18% over 1983 and 30% over 1982. Expenses and writedowns related to other real estate owned were the largest contributor to this increase, totaling over $2 million in 1984.

Data processing expenses, the second-largest contributor to the other noninterest expense increases, grew $1.0 million, or 44%, from 1983 to 1984, and $1.4 million, or 76%, from 1982 to 1984. This reflects the expanded use of data processing services to support new fee-based products and more credit card and student loan activity.

All other expense categories rose modestly or declined from 1983 to 1984. A cost-savings program has been instituted in 1985 which should continue to minimize noninterest-expense growth. Noninterest expense was held to a 22% compound growth rate for the past five years, compared to noninterest income, which has compounded at a 28% growth rate for the same period.

Investment Portfolio

The investment portfolio plus federal funds sold and other short-term investments totaled $587 million at year-end 1984, down $66 million from year-end 1983. The average balance of these categories during 1984 was $610 million, down slightly from the 1983 average of $628 million. The decline in average investments was used to fund the 1984 increase in loans.

Measured in terms of average daily balances, investments in U.S. Treasury and Government Agency issues were $348 million in 1984, $53 million, or 18%, higher than in 1983. This increase in high-quality investments and the funding of loan growth was accomplished primarily by reducing the average investments in municipals to $215 million, $41 million less than in 1983, or a decrease of 16%. Federal funds and other short-term investments declined to an average of $47 million in 1984, $30 million lower than the average in 1983.

The average tax equivalent yield on the investment portfolio was 12.35% in 1984, up slightly from the 1983 average of 12.25%. At year-end 1984, the average maturity of the portfolio was 3.5 years, compared to 3.7 years at year-end 1983. Approximately 41% of the portfolio matures in 1985 and carries an average tax equivalent yield of 11.41%.

The credit quality of the investment portfolio remains high with 65% in U.S. Treasury and Government Agency securities and 48% of the municipal portfolio rated "A" or better. Nonrated issues constitute 50% of tax-exempt investments, but the majority of these bonds are either Iowa municipals or industrial revenue bonds negotiated directly with customers of Hawkeye banks. Only .2% of the tax exempts were rated lower than "Baa."

Loans

Hawkeye's loan portfolio increased 5% during 1984 to $1.073 billion at year-end, compared to $1.021 billion at year-end 1983 and $931 million at year-end 1982. The loan-to-deposit ratio, which averaged 65% in 1983, expanded to 67% in 1984.

The loan portfolio continues to be well diversified among four major categories. At year-end 1984, commercial loans accounted for 31% of the portfolio, agricultural 27%, real estate 25%, and installments 17%. This is a normal mix of loans for the Company, reflecting the trade center, county seat markets on which the Company has built its base

Exhibit 1   Excerpts from Hawkeye Bancorporation Annual Report, 1984

of banks. The average rate of return on the portfolio was 13.2% in 1984, compared to 13.1% in 1983 and 14.6% in 1982. Due to nonaccrual and restructured loans, a total of $3.7 million of interest was not recorded in 1984, compared to $2.4 million in 1983. The Company's policy dictates that any loan that is past due 90 days or more will not accrue interest unless the loan is both well secured and in the process of collection.

Management of Hawkeye continues to stress asset quality. The Company's loan quality-control procedures are under the supervision of the Senior Vice President of Credit Administration, who also heads the Company's loan committee. All loans too large for the lending capacity of the originating affiliate bank are reviewed and acted on by the loan committee, and approved loans are then participated throughout the Company. In addition, all lines of credit above $1 million are reviewed annually by the loan committee. Loan reviews are conducted in each bank by the Credit Administration staff, and there is a constant review of the problem and watch loan lists of each affiliate bank. Management's long-standing policy has been to lend only to customers in the local market of its 36 banks. Hawkeye has no loans to foreign countries or loans to "national" credits. This policy has been and continues to be adhered to.

Loan Loss Provision and Nonperforming Assets

The loan loss provision for 1984 was the highest in the Company's history. Net loan charge-offs totaled $16.9 million in 1984, compared to $6.1 million in 1983 and $4.1 million in 1982. Net charge-offs as a percent of average loans were 1.58%, .62%, and .49% for 1984, 1983, and 1982, respectively. The 1984 ratio of 1.58% compares to the 1984 Keefe Bank Index of .46%. The allowance for loan losses totaled $15.1 million, $11.0 million, and $9.4 million on December 31, 1984, 1983, and 1982, respectively. The allowance as a percent of total loans increased to a strong 1.4%, compared to 1.3% for the Keefe Bank Index. Provision for loan losses totaled $20.7 million in 1984, $5.3 million in 1983, and $4.7 million in 1982. This large provision reflects the abnormal level of charge-offs as well as the increased allowance, all of which mirror the depressed Iowa agricultural economy. Nonperforming assets, including nonaccrual and restructured loans and other real estate, increased to 4.5% of total loans and other real estate at year-end 1984, compared to 2.4% in 1983 and 1.5% in 1982. Seven of the Company's thirty-six affiliate banks accounted for 70% of consolidated net loan losses in 1984. Of these banks, three are new to the Hawkeye system in the past two years and represent 35% of consolidated net loan losses.

The allowance for loan losses is established through charges to earnings. The provision for loan losses is determined by Management through a continuous evaluation of each affiliate bank's loan portfolio relative to a number of factors, including historical experience, results of internal loan reviews, reports received from regulatory agencies, and the existing level of the allowance for loan losses. Management's conservative philosophy is reflected in the nonaccrual loan policy, the dramatic increase in loan charge-offs, and the increased balance in the allowance for loan losses.

Deposits

Prior to 1980, noninterest-bearing checking accounts, savings accounts earning interest at 5¼%, and certificates of deposit at regulated lower rates were the only investment opportunities available to savers. Nineteen eighty-two and nineteen eighty-three saw the introduction of Super NOW accounts, savings accounts that earn money market rates of interest, and unregulated interest rates on certificates of deposit. The attractive-

h

231

Exhibit 1 Excerpts from Hawkeye Bancorporation Annual Report, 1984

ness of these higher-yielding instruments caused a shift in deposit categories from 1982 to 1983. However, little change was seen in the deposit categories from 1983 to 1984, although an increase in certificates of deposit was caused by a decline in interest rates during the last half of 1984, which prompted customers to shift funds to certificates of deposit and thus lock in higher rates of interest.

The average cost of deposits remained relatively unchanged from 1984 to 1983. The cost of funds for 1984 was 8.96%, compared to 8.90% for 1983 and 10.30% for 1982, reflecting rates which were at an all-time high in 1982. These current lower rates reflect the larger volume of deposits that are interest sensitive and, therefore, more closely match current money market rates.

Average demand deposits, an interest-free source of funds, dropped to 12% of total deposits, down from 13% in 1983 and 15% in 1982. Total deposits were up $19 million, or 1% above 1983. The Company continued to maintain a very stable base of core deposits of 95% in 1984 and 1983.

h

Exhibit 1   Excerpts from Hawkeye Bancorporation Annual Report, 1984

CONSOLIDATED BALANCE SHEETS
(in Thousands)

December 31,	1984	1983
ASSETS		
Cash and due from banks	$ 96,056	$ 82,614
Interest-bearing deposits in other banks	13,100	22,596
Investment securities (market value 1984—$519,392; 1983—$573,151) (Note 3)	533,453	589,997
Federal funds sold and securities purchased under agreements to resell	40,679	40,876
Loans (Note 4):		
Commercial	331,099	315,615
Agricultural	289,382	278,045
Real estate	270,902	259,422
Installment	181,958	167,531
Total loans	1,073,341	1,020,613
Less allowance for loan losses	15,085	10,953
Net loans	1,058,256	1,009,660
Premises and equipment, at cost:		
Land	6,204	5,624
Buildings	33,103	31,175
Equipment	17,956	17,110
	57,263	53,909
Less accumulated depreciation	15,194	12,503
	42,069	41,406
Accrued interest receivable	47,991	45,702
Excess of cost over net assets of consolidated subsidiaries	34,616	34,191
Other assets	47,635	33,999
Total assets	$1,913,855	$1,901,041

(continued)

h

233

Exhibit 1 Excerpts from Hawkeye Bancorporation Annual Report, 1984

CONSOLIDATED BALANCE SHEETS (continued)

December 31,	1984	1983
LIABILITIES		
Deposits:		
Noninterest bearing	$ 208,808	$ 213,499
Interest bearing	1,411,433	1,387,603
Total deposits	1,620,241	1,601,102
Short-term borrowings:		
Federal funds purchased and securities sold under agreements to repurchase	6,011	13,596
Other (Note 5)	42,956	41,297
Long-term debt (Note 5)	86,361	80,594
Other liabilities (Note 6)	33,024	31,745
Total liabilities	1,788,593	1,768,334
Commitments and contingencies (Note 9)		
SHAREHOLDERS' EQUITY (Notes 5, 11, 12 and 15)		
Preferred stock (liquidation preference 1984—$28,207)	233	249
Common stock (shares outstanding 1984—6,214; 1983—6,097)	18,643	18,292
Capital surplus	75,431	75,746
Retained earnings	30,955	38,420
Total shareholders' equity	125,262	132,707
Total liabilities and shareholders' equity	$1,913,855	$1,901,041

CONSOLIDATED STATEMENTS OF INCOME
(In Thousands Except Per Share)

Years Ended December 31,	1984	1983	1982
INTEREST INCOME			
Loans	$140,032	$128,745	$121,919
Investment securities:			
Taxable	39,127	32,198	19,348
Non-taxable	16,422	19,036	19,252
Federal funds sold and other	4,816	7,486	12,391
Total interest income	200,397	187,465	172,910
INTEREST EXPENSE			
Deposits	125,338	117,109	107,789
Federal funds purchased and other	1,312	1,579	4,591
Other short-term borrowings	4,421	4,656	4,463
Long-term debt	9,304	7,530	7,432
Total interest expense	140,375	130,874	124,275

(continued)

Exhibit 1   Excerpts from Hawkeye Bancorporation Annual Report, 1984

CONSOLIDATED STATEMENTS OF INCOME (continued)

Years Ended December 31,	1984	1983	1982
Net interest income	60,022	56,591	48,635
Provision for loan losses (Note 4)	20,712	5,340	4,694
Net interest income after provision for loan losses	39,310	51,251	43,941
OTHER INCOME			
Insurance, real estate and advisory services	7,009	6,251	5,461
Trust and agency services	1,973	1,689	1,365
Service charges	3,523	3,009	2,696
Fees	10,987	8,577	7,797
Investment security gains (losses)	51	(104)	50
Other	3,210	3,642	2,450
Total other income	26,753	23,064	19,819
OTHER EXPENSES			
Salaries and employee benefits (Note 7)	32,686	31,841	26,466
Occupancy	5,153	4,594	4,000
Furniture and equipment	5,444	5,009	3,860
Other (Note 14)	24,673	20,980	19,028
Total other expenses	67,956	62,424	53,354
Income (loss) before income taxes	(1,893)	11,891	10,406
Income tax credit (Note 6)	2,810	2,585	3,488
Net income	$ 917	$ 14,476	$ 13,894
Average number of shares and equivalents (Note 13):			
Primary	7,846	7,713	6,954
Fully diluted	8,974	8,543	7,726
Earnings per share (Note 13):			
Primary	$.12	$1.88	$2.00
Fully diluted	$.10	$1.69	$1.80

Exhibit 1   Excerpts from Hawkeye Bancorporation Annual Report, 1984

CONSOLIDATED STATEMENTS OF CHANGES IN FINANCIAL POSITION
(In Thousands)

Years Ended December 31,	1984		1983		1982	
	Funds Provided From	Funds Used For	Funds Provided From	Funds Used For	Funds Provided From	Funds Used For
Operations:						
Net Income	$ 917		$ 14,476		$ 13,894	
Depreciation	3,888		3,283		2,355	
Amortization	3,336		4,357		2,013	
Accretion of discount	(792)		(1,158)		(1,224)	
Provision for loan losses	20,712		5,340		4,694	
Deferred income taxes	(3,310)		(1,528)		1,685	
Total from operations	24,751		24,770		23,417	
Cash dividends		$ 8,382		$ 7,837		$ 6,712
Issuance of common stock	1,631		7,250		9,862	
Preferred stock conversions		1,611		3,749		
Treasury stock					2,413	2,250
	26,382	9,993	32,020	11,586	35,692	8,962
Cash and due from banks	9,303		33,066		4,239	
Investment securities	66,052			76,166		40,678
Federal funds sold and securities purchased under agreements to resell	197		28,945		44,360	
Gross loans		41,944		43,258		58,272
Loans charged off		17,691		6,806		4,747
Premises and equipment		4,475		6,313		7,936
Accrued interest receivable		1,416		2,826		4,488
Excess of cost over net assets of consolidated subsidiaries		1,280		4,987		3,416
Net assets of subsidiaries acquired		1,824		9,940		27,396
Other assets		14,189		5,202		6,433
Deposits		12,573	93,856		64,353	
Federal funds purchased and securities sold under agreements to repurchase		8,790		26,586		1,952
Other short-term borrowings	1,659			12,903	20,592	
Long-term debt	6,838	1,097	15,279	1,280	5,842	2,600
Accrued interest payable	1,015		1,309			1,037
Accrued taxes		834	1,849			2,984
Other liabilities	3,848		1,347			2,967
Other, net	812		182			1,210
Total	$116,106	$116,106	$207,853	$207,853	$175,078	$175,078

h

236

Exhibit 1   Excerpts from Hawkeye Bancorporation Annual Report, 1984

NOTES TO FINANCIAL STATEMENTS

(Dollars in Thousands Except Per Share)

1. Significant Accounting Policies

The accounting and reporting policies of Hawkeye Bancorporation ("Company") and its subsidiaries conform with generally accepted accounting principles. The following is a summary of the significant policies.

(a) Principles of Consolidation

The consolidated financial statements include the accounts of the Company and all subsidiaries. All material intercompany transactions have been eliminated in consolidation. In the Parent Company financial statements, investments in subsidiaries are accounted for using the equity method of accounting.

The excess of cost over the net assets acquired in purchase transactions is being amortized on the straight-line method over twenty-five to forty years. Accumulated amortization is $4,067 and $3,212 at December 31, 1984 and 1983, respectively.

The intangible value of the core deposit base acquired in purchase transactions is included in other assets and totals, net of amortization, $10,666 and $10,888 at December 31, 1984 and 1983, respectively. The core deposit intangibles are amortized over their estimated lives, which average approximately fifteen years. Accumulated amortization at December 31, 1984 and 1983 totaled $1,520 and $877, respectively.

(b) Investment Securities

Investment securities are stated at cost, adjusted for amortization of premiums and accretion of discount, both computed on the straight-line method. Gains or losses on the sales of securities are recognized upon disposition based on the adjusted cost of the specific securities sold.

(c) Allowance for Loan Losses

The allowance for loan losses is based on management's review of individual bank loan portfolios, including known problem loans, analysis of regulatory examinations and the possible impact of economic conditions in the market area served. The allowance is maintained at a level believed adequate by management to absorb any potential losses in the portfolio.

(d) Recognition of Interest on Loans

Interest on loans is accrued and credited to operating income based upon the principal amount of the loan.

The Company and its subsidiaries do not accrue interest on loans whose ultimate collectibility is considered doubtful. A loan is placed on nonaccrual when the loan is past due 90 days or more, unless the loan is well secured and in the process of collection. When previously accrued interest is deemed to be uncollectible, interest credited to income in the current year is reversed and interest accrued in prior years is charged to the allowance for loan losses.

h

237

Exhibit 1   Excerpts from Hawkeye Bancorporation Annual Report, 1984

(e) Premises and Equipment

Depreciation of premises and equipment is computed, primarily on the straight-line method, over the estimated useful lives of the assets as follows:

Buildings . . . . 10–50 years
Equipment . . . . 3–25 years

The cost of improvements is capitalized, and expenditures for maintenance and repairs are charged to expense as incurred. Gains or losses on dispositions are included in income.

(f) Other Real Estate Owned

Other real estate owned or acquired through customers' loan defaults is included in other assets at the lower of the fair market value or the recorded investment in the related loan. Expenses, gains or losses incurred due to the holding or selling of other real estate owned are reflected in current period earnings when incurred.

(g) Income Taxes

When income and expenses are recognized in different periods for financial reporting purposes other than for purposes of computing income taxes currently payable, deferred income taxes are provided as a result of such timing differences.

The subsidiaries have computed their provisions for income taxes at statutory rates. The Parent Company has accrued in its income statement the difference between the aggregate amount of the subsidiaries' provisions and the consolidated income tax provision.

Investment tax credits are accounted for under the flow-through method.

3. Investment Securities

At December 31, 1984 and 1983, the investment securities at adjusted cost and market value are shown below:

	1984		1983	
	Adjusted Cost	Market	Adjusted Cost	Market
U.S. Government Obligations, including U.S. Government Agencies	$344,163	$349,624	$344,004	$345,965
Obligations of state and political subdivisions	$189,290	$169,768	$245,993	$227,186
TOTAL	$533,453	$519,392	$589,997	$573,151

A total of $80,895 and $84,807 of Industrial Development Revenue bonds are included in obligations of state and political subdivisions at December 31, 1984 and 1983, respectively.

The adjusted cost of securities pledged to collateralize public and trust deposits, securities sold under agreements to repurchase, funds borrowed and for other purposes required by law were $84,902 and $70,296 at December 31, 1984 and 1983, respectively.

h

238

Exhibit 1   Excerpts from Hawkeye Bancorporation Annual Report, 1984

SUPPLEMENTAL FINANCIAL DATA
(Dollars in Thousands Except Per Share)

RISK ELEMENTS

Balances December 31,	1984	1983	1982	1981	1980
Nonaccrual loans	$29,214	$13,080	$8,503	$2,575	$1,588
Accruing loans past due 90 days or more as to interest or principal payments	$10,590	$13,500	$9,416	$4,278	$2,677
Restructured loans*	$ 7,495	$ 4,738	$1,872	$992	
Loans which are current but where there are serious doubts as to the ability of the borrower to meet the repayment terms	$ 5,501				
Repossessed other real estate*	$11,724	$ 6,851	$3,814	$1,277	

*Not available for 1980.

SUMMARY OF LOAN LOSS EXPERIENCE

For Years Ended December 31,	1984	1983	1982	1981	1980
Daily average loans	$1,062,842	$982,887	$833,558	$704,897	$582,398
Allowance for loan losses at beginning of year	$ 10,953	$ 9,388	$7,274	$ 6,980	$ 5,561
Loans charged off:					
Commercial	7,559	2,228	2,203	954	554
Agricultural	8,296	3,268	1,342	241	14
Real estate	947	558	409	121	41
Installment	889	752	793	663	526
Total loans charged off	$ 17,691	6,806	4,747	1,979	1,135
Recoveries:					
Commercial	473	388	468	73	72
Agricultural	121	122	10	2	56
Real estate	52	13	2	14	25
Installment	165	168	144	113	96
Total recoveries	811	691	624	202	249
Net loans charged off	16,880	6,115	4,123	1,777	886
Additions to allowance charged to expense	20,712	5,340	4,694	1,062	1,110
Allowances of acquired subsidiaries at dates of acquisition	300	2,340	1,543	1,009	1,195
Allowance for loan losses at end of year	$ 15,085	$ 10,953	$ 9,388	$ 7,274	$ 6,980
Ratio of net loan losses to daily average loans	1.58%	.62%	.49%	.25%	.15%

Note: The amount of the addition to the allowance charged to operating expense was based on management's review of the individual bank loan portfolios, including known problem loans, analysis of regulatory examinations and evaluation of current and anticipated economic conditions in the market area served.

The Home Depot, Inc.

The difference between a company with a concept and one without is the difference between a stock that sells for 20 times earnings and one that sells for 10 times earnings. The Home Depot is definitely a concept stock, and it has the multiple to prove it – 27-28 times likely earnings in the current fiscal year ending this month. On the face of it, The Home Depot might seem like a tough one for the concept-mongers to work with. It's a chain of hardware stores. But, as we noted in our last visit to the company in the spring of '83, these hardware stores are huge warehouse outlets – 60,000 to 80,000 feet in space. You can fit an awful lot of saws in these and still have plenty of room left over to knock together a very decent concept.

And in truth, the warehouse notion is the hottest thing in retailing these days. The Home Depot buys in quantum quantities, which means that its suppliers are eager to keep within its good graces and hence provide it with a lot of extra service. The company, as it happens, is masterful in promotion and pricing. The last time we counted, it had 22 stores, all of them located where the sun shines all the time.

Growth has been sizzling. Revenues, a mere $22 million in fiscal '80, shot past the quarter billion mark three years later. As to earnings, they have climbed from two cents in fiscal '80 to an estimated 60 cents in the fiscal year coming to an end [in January 1985].

Its many boosters in the Street, moreover, anticipate more of the same as far as the bullish eye can see. They're confidently estimating 30% growth in the new fiscal year as well. Could be. But while we share their esteem for the company's merchandising skills and imagination, we're as bemused now as we were the first time we looked at The Home Depot by its rich multiple. Maybe a little more now than then.[1]

The above report appeared on January 21, 1985, in "Up & Down Wall Street," a regular column in *Barron's* financial weekly.

COMPANY BACKGROUND

Bernard Marcus and Arthur Blank founded The Home Depot in 1978 to bring the warehouse retailing concept to the home center industry. The company operated retail "do-

This case was prepared by Professor Krishna Palepu as the basis for class discussion rather than to illustrate either effective or ineffective handling of an administrative situation. Copyright © 1988 by the President and Fellows of Harvard College. Harvard Business School case 9-188-148.1.

1. *Reprinted with permission from Barron's, January 21, 1985.*

it-yourself" (DIY) warehouse stores which sold a wide assortment of building materials and home improvement products. Sales, which were on a cash-and-carry basis, were concentrated in the home remodeling market. The company targeted as its customers individual homeowners and small contractors.

The Home Depot's strategy had several important elements. The company offered low and competitive prices, a feature central to the warehouse retailing concept. The Home Depot's stores, usually in suburbs, were also the warehouses, with inventory stacked over merchandise displayed on industrial racks. The warehouse format of the stores kept the overhead low and allowed the company to pass the savings to customers. Costs were further reduced by emphasizing higher volume and lower margins with a high inventory turnover. While offering low prices, The Home Depot was careful not to sacrifice the depth of merchandise and the quality of products offered for sale.

To ensure that the right products were stocked at all times, each Home Depot store carried approximately $4,500,000 of inventory, at retail, consisting of approximately 25,000 separate stock-keeping units. All these items were kept on the sales floor of the store, thus increasing convenience to the customer and minimizing out-of-stock occurrences. The company also assured its customers that the products sold by it were of the best quality. The Home Depot offered nationally advertised brands as well as lesser known brands carefully chosen by the company's merchandise managers. Every product sold by The Home Depot was guaranteed by either the manufacturer or by the company itself.

The Home Depot complemented the above merchandising strategy with excellent sales assistance. Since the great majority of the company's customers were individual homeowners with no prior experience in their home improvement projects, The Home Depot considered its employees' technical knowledge and service orientation to be very important to its marketing success. The company pursued a number of policies to address this need. Approximately 90% of the company's employees were on a full-time basis. To attract and retain a strong sales force, the company maintained salary and wage levels above those of its competitors. All the floor sales personnel attended special training sessions to gain thorough knowledge of the company's home improvement products and their basic applications. This training enabled them to answer shoppers' questions and help customers in choosing equipment and material appropriate for their projects. Often, the expert advice the sales personnel provided created a bond that resulted in continuous contact with the customer throughout the duration of the customer's project.

Finally, to attract customers, The Home Depot pursued an aggressive advertising program utilizing newspapers, television, radio, and direct mail catalogues. The company's advertising stressed promotional pricing, the broad assortment and depth of its merchandise, and the assistance provided by its sales personnel. The company also sponsored in-store demonstrations of do-it-yourself techniques and product uses. To increase customers' shopping convenience, The Home Depot's stores were open seven days a week, including weekday evenings.

Fortune magazine commented on The Home Depot's strategy as follows:

Warehouse stores typically offer shoppers deep discounts with minimal service and back-to-basics ambiance. The Home Depot's outlets have all the charm of a freight yard and predictably low prices. But they also offer unusually helpful customer service. Although warehouse retailing looks simple, it is not: As discounting cuts into gross profit margins, the merchant must carefully control buying, merchandising, and inventory costs. Throwing in service, which is expensive and hard to systematize, makes the job even tougher. In the do-it-yourself (DIY) segment of the industry – which includes old-style hardware stores, building supply warehouses, and the everything-under-one-roof home centers – The Home Depot is the only company that has successfully brought off the union of low prices and high service.[2]

The Home Depot's strategy was successful in fueling an impressive growth in the company's operations. The first three Home Depot stores, opened in Atlanta in 1979, were a quick success. From this modest beginning, the company grew rapidly and went public in 1981. The company's stock initially traded over-the-counter and was listed on the New York Stock Exchange in April 1984. Several new stores were opened in markets throughout the Sunbelt, and the number of stores operated by The Home Depot grew from 3 in 1979 to 50 by the end of fiscal 1985. As a result, sales grew from $7 million in 1979 to $700 million in 1985. Exhibit 1 provides a summary of the growth in the company's operations. The company's stock price performance during 1985 is summarized in Exhibit 2.

h

243

INDUSTRY AND COMPETITION

The home improvement industry was large and growing during the 1980s. The industry sales totaled approximately $80 billion in 1985 and strong industry growth was expected to continue, especially in the do-it-yourself (DIY) segment, which had grown at a compounded annual rate of 14 percent over the last 15 years. With the number of two-wage-earner households growing, there was an increase in families' average disposable income, making it possible to increase the frequency and magnitude of home improvement projects. Further, many homeowners were undertaking these projects by themselves rather than hiring a contractor. Research conducted by the Do-It-Yourself Institute, an industry trade group, showed that DIY activities had become America's second most popular leisure-time activity after watching television.

The success of warehouse retailing pioneered by The Home Depot attracted a number of other companies into the industry. Among the store chains currently operating in the industry were Builders Square (a division of K Mart), Mr. HOW (a division of Service Merchandise), The Home Club (a division of Zayre Corp.), Payless Cashways (a division of W.R. Grace), and Hechinger Co. Most of these store chains were relatively new and not yet achieving significant profitability.

....
2. *Reprinted with permission from Fortune, February 1988, p. 73.*

Among The Home Depot's competitors, the most successful was Hechinger, which had operated hardware stores for a long time and recently entered the do-it-yourself segment of the industry. Using a strategy quite different from The Home Depot's, Hechinger ran gleaming upscale stores and aimed at high profit margins. As of the end of fiscal 1985, the company operated 55 stores, located primarily in southeastern states. Hechinger announced that it planned to expand its sales by 20 to 25 percent a year by adding 10 to 14 stores a year. A summary of Hechinger's recent financial performance is presented in Exhibit 3.

THE HOME DEPOT'S FUTURE

While The Home Depot had achieved rapid growth every year since its inception, fiscal 1985 was probably the most important in the company's seven-year history. During 1985 the company implemented its most ambitious expansion plan to date by adding 20 new stores in eight new markets. Nine of these stores were acquired from Bowater, a competing store chain which was in financial difficulty. As The Home Depot engaged in major expansion, its revenues rose 62 percent from $432 million in fiscal 1984 to $700 million in 1985. However, the company's earnings declined in 1985 from the record levels achieved during the previous fiscal year. In fiscal 1985, The Home Depot earned $8.2 million, or $0.33 per share, as compared with $14.1 million or $0.56 per share in fiscal 1984.

Bernard Marcus, The Home Depot's chairman and chief executive officer, commented on the company's performance as follows:

> *Fiscal 1985 was a year of rapid expansion and continued growth for The Home Depot. Feeling the time was ripe for us to enhance our share of the do-it-yourself market, we seized the opportunity to make a significant investment in our long-term future. At the same time, we recognized that our short-term profit growth would be affected.*

The Home Depot's 1985 annual report (Exhibit 4) provided more details on the firm's financial performance during the year.

As fiscal 1985 came to a close, The Home Depot faced some critical issues. The competition in the do-it-yourself industry was heating up. The fight for market dominance was expected to result in pressure on margins, and industry analysts expected only the strongest and most capable firms in the industry to survive. Also, The Home Depot had announced plans for further expansion that included the opening of nine new stores in 1986. The company estimated that site acquisition and construction would cost about $6.6 million for each new store, and investment in inventory (net of vendor financing) would require an additional $1.8 million per store. The company needed significant additional financing to implement these plans.

Home Depot relied on external financing—both debt and equity—to fund its growth in 1984 and 1985. However, the significant drop in its stock price in 1985 made further equity financing less attractive. While the company could borrow from its line of credit, it had to make sure that it could satisfy the interest coverage requirements (see Note 3 in Exhibit 4 for a discussion of debt covenant restrictions). Clearly, generating more cash from its own operations would be the best way for Home Depot to invest in its growth on a sustainable basis.

QUESTIONS

1. Evaluate Home Depot's business strategy. Do you think it is a viable strategy in the long run?
2. Analyze Home Depot's financial performance during the fiscal years 1983–1985. Compare Home Depot's performance in this period with Hechinger's performance. (You may use the ratios and the cash flow analysis in Exhibit 3 in this summary.)
3. How productive were Home Depot's stores in the fiscal years 1983–1985? (You may use the statistics in Exhibit 1 in this analysis.)
4. Home Depot's stock price dropped by 23 percent between January 1985 and February 1986, making it difficult for the company to rely on equity capital to finance its growth. Covenants on existing debt (discussed in Note 3 of Exhibit 4) restrict the magnitude of the company's future borrowing. Given these constraints, what specific actions should Home Depot take with respect to its current operations and growth strategy? How can the company improve its operating performance? Should the company change its strategy? If so, how?

h

245

EXHIBIT 1
The Home Depot, Inc. – Summary of Performance During Fiscal Years 1981–1985

h

246

EXHIBIT 2

The Home Depot's Common Stock Price and Standard & Poor's 500 Composite Index from January 1985 to February 1986

Date	Home Depot Stock Price	S&P 500 Composite Index
1/2/85	$17.125	165.4
2/1/85	16.375	178.6
3/1/85	19.000	183.2
4/1/85	17.000	181.3
5/1/85	18.000	178.4
6/3/85	16.125	189.3
7/1/85	13.000	192.4
8/1/85	12.625	192.1
9/2/85	11.875	197.9
10/1/85	11.375	185.1
11/1/85	10.750	191.5
12/2/85	11.000	200.5
1/2/86	12.625	209.6
2/3/86	13.125	214.0
Cumulative Return:	−23.4%	29.4%

The Home Depot's β = 1.3 (Value Line *estimate*).

EXHIBIT 3
The Home Depot, Inc. – Summary of Financial Performance of Hechinger Company

I. HECHINGER'S FINANCIAL RATIOS

	Year Ending		
	February 1, 1986	February 2, 1985	January 28, 1984
Profit Before Taxes/Sales (%)	7.80	9.40	9.80
× Sales/Average Assets	1.48	1.72	2.02
× Average Assets/Average Equity	2.21	2.12	1.79
× (1 – Average Tax Rate)	0.62	0.55	0.54
= Return on Equity (%)	15.80	18.90	19.10
× (1 – Dividend Payout Ratio)	0.93	0.95	0.95
= Sustainable Growth Rate (%)	14.70	18.00	18.10
Gross Profit/Sales (%)	29.30	30.10	32.10
Selling, General and Administrative Expenses/Sales (%)	21.60	21.10	22.90
Interest Expenses/Sales (%)	2.10	1.30	0.70
Interest Income/Sales (%)	2.20	1.70	1.30
Inventory Turnover	4.50	4.50	4.40
Average Collection Period[a] (Days)	32.00	33.00	35.00
Average Accounts Payable Period[b] (Days)	58.00	61.00	63.00

a. Assumed 365 days in the fiscal year.
b. Payables also include accrued wages and expenses. Purchases are computed as cost of sales plus increase in inventory during the year. Assumed 365 days in the fiscal year.

II. HECHINGER'S CASH FLOW

(Dollars in Thousands)	Year Ending		
	February 1, 1986	February 2, 1985	January 28, 1984
Cash Provided from Operations			
Net earnings	$23,111	$20,923	$16,243
Items not requiring the use of cash or marketable securities:			
Depreciation and amortization	6,594	4,622	3,429
Deferred income taxes	1,375	2,040	1,515
Deferred rent expense	2,321	2,064	1,463
	33,401	29,649	22,650
Cash Invested in Operations			
Accounts receivable	4,657	7,905	7,954
Merchandise inventories	17,998	8,045	20,596
Other current assets	4,891	3,760	1,304
Accounts payable and accrued expenses	(6,620)	(12,099)	(9,767)
Taxes on income – current	285	3,031	(575)
	21,211	10,642	19,512
Net Cash Provided from Operations	12,190	19,007	3,138
Cash Used for Investment Activities			
Expenditures for property, furniture and equipment, net of disposals, and other assets	(36,037)	(25,531)	(16,346)
Cash Used to Pay Dividends to Shareholders	(1,550)	(1,091)	(868)
Cash Provided from Financing Activities			
Proceeds from public offering of 8½% converted subordinated debentures, net of expenses	—	85,010	—
Proceeds from public offering of common stock net of expenses	28,969	—	13,439
Proceeds from sale and leaseback transactions under operating leases	—	8,338	6,874
Increase (decrease) in long-term debt	—	(4,750)	6,366
Decrease in short-term debt	—	—	(318)
Exercise of stock options including income tax benefit	180	674	611
Decrease in capital lease obligations	(311)	(280)	(254)
	28,838	88,992	26,718
Increase in Cash and Marketable Securities	$ 3,441	$81,377	$12,642

EXHIBIT 4

The Home Depot, Inc.—Abridged Annual Report for Fiscal Year 1985

A *Letter to Our Shareholders:*

Fiscal 1985 was a year of rapid expansion and continued growth for The Home Depot. Feeling the time was ripe for us to enhance our share of the do-it-yourself market, we seized the opportunity to make a significant investment in our long-term future. At the same time, we recognized that our short-term profit growth would be affected.

The Home Depot intends to be the dominant factor in every market we serve. The key to our success has been that upon entering a new market, we make a substantial commitment—opening multiple stores, providing excellent customer service, creating highly visible promotions, and growing the entire market. We turn the novice into a do-it-yourselfer and enable the expert to do more for less money.

From shortly before the end of fiscal 1984 to the close of fiscal 1985, The Home Depot entered eight new markets—Dallas, Houston, Jacksonville, San Diego, Los Angeles, Shreveport, Baton Rouge and Mobile—in a period of approximately 13 months. In that time, the number of Home Depot stores rose dramatically, from 22 to 50, including 9 stores acquired in the Bowater acquisition which had not been in our original plan. Twenty of these stores were opened during the past fiscal year alone. During this time span, we have become the only national warehouse retailing chain serving markets across the Sunbelt.

This expansion program required a tremendous investment of capital expenditures and inventory, as well as in personnel. As a result, our net earnings declined from record levels achieved during the previous fiscal year. In fiscal 1985, The Home Depot earned $8,219,000, or $.33 per share, as compared with $14,122,000, or $.56 per share, in fiscal 1984. However, as The Home Depot engaged in this major thrust forward, it also increased its market share and market presence as revenues rose 62% from $432,779,000 in fiscal 1984 to $700,729,000 in fiscal 1985.

Despite our significant investments, we still continue to be in a very strong financial condition. In Decem-

ber, The Home Depot replaced a prior $100 million bank credit line with an eight-year decreasing revolving credit agreement of $200 million. In addition, we are pursuing sale-and-leaseback negotiations for an aggregate of approximately $50 million for ten of our stores. These sources of additional funds, along with internally generated cash flow, will provide us with an ample financial foundation to continue to underwrite our growth over the next several years.

We are also quite proud that The Home Depot achieved its substantial gain in sales and market share in what turned out to be a very difficult year for our industry and retailing in general. The do-it-yourself "warehouse" industry, which we pioneered only a few short years ago, has recently attracted many competitors, some of whom have already fallen by the wayside, having mistaken our dramatic success as a path towards easy profits. Now the industry is faced with a situation when only the strongest and most capable will survive. As this process continues, we expect to encounter additional cost competition in the fight for market dominance. However, with our strengths—both financial and our successful ability to develop a loyal customer base—we are confident that The Home Depot will emerge an even stronger company.

We have never doubted The Home Depot's ability to be a leader in our business. We have the market dominance, the superior retailing concepts and the necessary foundation of experienced management. Further, we have the determination to maintain our position.

Looking at some of our markets individually, clearly our most difficult environment has been in Houston, where the oil-related economy is undergoing painful contractions combined with particularly fierce industry competition. This has caused our newly-opened stores to operate at a sub par level. In Dallas/Fort Worth, the stores we acquired at the end of fiscal 1984 have not yet generated the profits we expect. Such difficult market conditions demand a flexible

h

250

reaction both in merchandising and operations. Recognizing the future potential of both of these markets, our management team is addressing the issues and feels confident that the final outcome will be positive.

In the other markets entered this year, the situation has been considerably more positive. There, our stores are experiencing growth much closer to our historical patterns.

In support of our California and Arizona operations, a West Coast division was inaugurated to facilitate a timely response to the demands of that marketplace. With management personnel in place, this division is now responsible for the merchandising and operations of all stores in the western states.

Other highlights of the past year's activities include the progress we have made in expanding our management team, and the computer systems we installed into our operations to enhance our efficiency.

During the year, we completed the store price look-up phase of our management information system. This facilitates tracking individual items' sales through our registers, resulting in a more concise method of inventory reorder and margin management with the information now available.

During the coming year we will be testing a perpetual inventory tie-in with our price look-up system, eliminating pricing of our merchandise at the store level. The latter is being tested in several stores presently and hopefully will be expanded to include all of our stores by year end. This will have a significant effect on labor productivity at the store level.

The Home Depot is always looking for ways in which to do things better, priding ourselves on our flexibility and ability to innovate and to react to changing conditions. Whether it is a matter of developing state-of-the-art computer systems, reevaluating our store layouts or adapting to fast-changing markets and new types of merchandising, flexibility has always been a Home Depot characteristic.

In fiscal 1986, The Home Depot will continue to expand, but at a much more moderate pace. We plan to open nine new stores. These stores will be in existing markets except for two locations in the new market of San Jose, California.

When we open stores in existing markets, sharing advertising costs and operational expenses, we achieve a faster return than stores in new markets. With this in mind, in January 1986, we withdrew from the Detroit market and delayed the opening of stores in San Francisco. These stores were targeted for a substantial initial loss in earnings that would have been necessary to achieve market dominance. From our standpoint, these new markets would have had the combined effect of diluting our personnel and negatively affecting our earnings.

It has always been Home Depot's philosophy to maintain orderly growth and achieve market dominance as we expand to new markets. Indeed, growth for growth's sake has never been and never will be our objective. We intend to invest prudently and expand aggressively in our business and our markets only when such expenditures meet our criteria for long-term profitability.

We are quite optimistic about our company's future—both for fiscal 1986 and for the years to follow. Essential to this optimism is the fact that The Home Depot has consistently proven that we can grow the market in every geographical area we enter. Simply, this means that we do not have to take business away from hardware stores and other existing home-improvement outlets, but rather, to create new do-it-yourselfers out of those who have never done their own home improvements.

Our philosophy is to educate our customers on how to be do-it-yourselfers. Our customers have come to expect The Home Depot's knowledgeable sales staff to guide them through any project they care to undertake, whether it be installing kitchen cabinets, constructing a deck, or building an entire house. Our sales staff knows how to complete each project, what tools and material to include, and how to sell our customers everything they need.

The Home Depot traditionally holds clinics for its customers in such skills as electrical wiring, carpentry, and plumbing, to name a few. Upon the successful completion of such clinics, our customers are confident in themselves and in The Home Depot. This confidence allows them to attempt increasingly advanced and complex home improvements.

Concerning our facilities, Home Depot's warehouse retailing concept allows us to carry a truly fantastic

h

251

selection of merchandise and offer it at the lowest possible prices. Each of our stores ranges from about 65,000 to over 100,000 square feet of selling space, with an additional 4,000 to 10,000 square feet of outdoor selling area. In these large stores, we are able to stock all the materials and tools needed to build a house from scratch, and to landscape its grounds. With each store functioning as its own warehouse, with a capacity of over 25,000 different items, we are able to keep our prices at a minimum while providing the greatest selection of building materials and name brand merchandise.

For the majority of Americans, their home is their most valuable asset. It is an asset that consistently appreciates. It is also an asset in need of ongoing care and maintenance. By becoming do-it-yourselfers, homeowners can significantly enhance the value of their homes. We at The Home Depot have found that by successfully delivering this message, we have created loyal and satisfied customers. And by maintaining leadership in our markets, we have established a sound basis on which to build a future of growth with profitability.

The Home Depot management and staff are dedicated to the proposition that we are—and will remain—America's leading do-it-yourself retailer.

Bernard Marcus
Chairman and
Chief Executive Officer

Arthur M. Blank
President and
Chief Operating Officer

h

CONSOLIDATED STATEMENTS OF EARNINGS

	Fiscal Year Ended		
	February 2, 1986 (52 weeks)	February 3, 1985 (53 weeks)	January 29, 1984 (52 weeks)
Net Sales (note 2)	$700,729,000	$432,779,000	$256,184,000
Cost of Merchandise Sold	519,272,000	318,460,000	186,170,000
Gross Profit	181,457,000	114,319,000	70,014,000
Operating Expenses:			
Selling and store operating expenses	134,354,000	74,447,000	43,514,000
Preopening expenses	7,521,000	1,917,000	2,456,000
General and administrative expenses	20,555,000	12,817,000	7,376,000
Total Operating Expenses	162,430,000	89,181,000	53,346,000
Operating Income *EBIT*	19,027,000	25,138,000	16,668,000
Other Income (Expense):			
Net gain on disposition of property and equipment (note 7)	1,317,000	—	—
Interest income	1,481,000	5,236,000	2,422,000
Interest expense (note 3)	(10,206,000)	(4,122,000)	(104,000)
	(7,408,000)	1,114,000	2,318,000
Earnings Before Income Taxes	11,619,000	26,252,000	18,986,000
Income Taxes (note 4)	3,400,000	12,130,000	8,725,000
Net Earnings	$ 8,219,000	$ 14,122,000	$ 10,261,000
Earnings per Common and Common Equivalent Share (note 5)	$ .33	$ .56	$ .41
Weighted Average Number of Common and Common Equivalent Shares	25,247,000	25,302,000	24,834,000

h

253

CONSOLIDATED BALANCE SHEETS

	February 2, 1986	February 3, 1985
ASSETS		
Current Assets:		
Cash, including time deposits of $43,374,000 in 1985	$ 9,671,000	$ 52,062,000
Accounts receivable, net (note 7)	21,505,000	9,365,000
Refundable income taxes	3,659,000	—
Merchandise inventories	152,700,000	84,046,000
Prepaid expenses	2,526,000	1,939,000
Total current assets	190,061,000	147,412,000
Property and Equipment, at Cost (note 3):		
Land	44,396,000	30,044,000
Buildings	38,005,000	3,728,000
Furniture, fixtures, and equipment	34,786,000	18,162,000
Leasehold improvements	23,748,000	11,743,000
Construction in progress	27,694,000	14,039,000
	168,629,000	77,716,000
Less accumulated depreciation and amortization	7,813,000	4,139,000
Net property and equipment	160,816,000	73,577,000
Cost in Excess of the Fair Value of Net Assets Acquired, net of accumulated amortization of $730,000 in 1985 and $93,000 in 1984 (note 2)	24,561,000	25,198,000
Other	4,755,000	3,177,000
	$380,193,000	$249,364,000
LIABILITIES AND STOCKHOLDERS' EQUITY		
Current Liabilities:		
Accounts payable	$ 53,881,000	$ 32,356,000
Accrued salaries and related expenses	5,397,000	3,819,000
Other accrued expenses	13,950,000	10,214,000
Income taxes payable (note 4)	—	626,000
Current portion of long-term debt (note 3)	10,382,000	287,000
Total current liabilities	83,610,000	47,302,000
Long-Term Debt, Excluding Current Installments (note 3):		
Convertible subordinated debentures	100,250,000	100,250,000
Other long-term debt	99,693,000	17,692,000
	$199,943,000	$117,942,000

(continued)

	February 2, 1986	February 3, 1985
Other Liabilities	**861,000**	1,320,000
Deferred Income Taxes (note 4)	**6,687,000**	2,586,000
Stockholders' Equity (note 5):		
Common stock, par value $.05. Authorized: 50,000,000 shares; issued and outstanding – 25,150,063 shares at February 2, 1986 and 25,055,188 shares at February 3, 1985	**1,258,000**	1,253,000
Paid-in capital	**48,900,000**	48,246,000
Retained earnings	**38,934,000**	30,715,000
Total stockholders' equity	**89,092,000**	80,214,000
Commitments and Contingencies (notes 5, 6 and 8)	**$380,193,000**	$249,364,000

CONSOLIDATED STATEMENTS OF CHANGES IN FINANCIAL POSITION

	Fiscal Year Ended		
	February 2, 1986	February 3, 1985	January 29, 1984
Sources of Working Capital:			
Net earnings	**$8,219,000**	$14,122,000	$ 10,261,000
Items which do not use working capital:			
Depreciation and amortization of property and equipment	**4,376,000**	2,275,000	903,000
Deferred income taxes	**3,612,000**	1,508,000	713,000
Amortization of cost in excess of the fair value of net assets required	**637,000**	93,000	—
Net gain on disposition of property and equipment	**(1,317,000)**	—	—
Other	**180,000**	77,000	59,000
Working capital provided by operations	**15,707,000**	18,075,000	11,936,000
Proceeds from disposition of property and equipment	**9,469,000**	861,000	3,000
Proceeds from long-term borrowings	**92,400,000**	120,350,000	4,200,000
Proceeds from sale of common stock, net	**659,000**	814,000	36,663,000
	$118,235,000	$140,100,000	$ 52,802,000

(continued)

CONSOLIDATED STATEMENTS OF CHANGES IN FINANCIAL POSITION (continued)

	Fiscal Year Ended		
	February 2, 1986	February 3, 1985	January 29, 1984
Uses of Working Capital:			
Additions to property and equipment	$ **99,767,000**	$50,769,000	$ 16,081,000
Current installments and repayments of long-term debt	**10,399,000**	6,792,000	52,000
Acquisition of Bowater Home Center, Inc., net of working capital of $9,227,000 (note 2):			
Property and equipment	**—**	4,815,000	—
Cost in excess of the fair value of net assets acquired	**—**	25,291,000	—
Other assets, net of liabilities	**—**	(913,000)	—
Other, net	**1,728,000**	2,554,000	252,000
Increase in working capital	**6,341,000**	50,792,000	36,417,000
	$118,235,000	$140,100,000	$ 52,802,000
Changes in Components of Working Capital:			
Increase (decrease) in current assets:			
Cash	**(42,391,000)**	$29,894,000	$ 13,917,000
Receivables, net	**15,799,000**	7,170,000	1,567,000
Merchandise inventories	**68,654,000**	25,334,000	41,137,000
Prepaid expenses	**587,000**	1,206,000	227,000
	42,649,000	63,604,000	56,848,000
Increase (decrease) in current liabilities:			
Accounts payable	**21,525,000**	10,505,000	17,150,000
Accrued salaries and related expenses	**1,578,000**	(93,000)	2,524,000
Other accrued expenses	**3,736,000**	2,824,000	341,000
Income taxes payable	**(626,000)**	(657,000)	406,000
Current portion of long-term debt	**10,095,000**	233,000	10,000
	36,308,000	12,812,000	20,431,000
Increase in Working Capital	$ **6,341,000**	$ 50,792,000	$ 36,417,000

h

SELECTED FINANCIAL DATA

	Fiscal Year Ended				
	February 2, 1986	February 3, 1985[a]	January 29, 1984	January 30, 1983	January 31, 1982
Selected Consolidated Statement of Earnings Data:					
Net sales	$700,729,000	$432,779,000	$256,184,000	$117,645,000	$51,542,000
Gross profit	181,457,000	114,319,000	70,014,000	33,358,000	14,735,000
Earnings before income taxes and extraordinary item	11,619,000	26,252,000	18,986,000	9,870,000	1,963,000
Earnings before extraordinary item	8,219,000	14,122,000	10,261,000	5,315,000	1,211,000
Extraordinary item-reduction of income taxes arising from carryforward of prior years' operating losses	—	—	—	—	234,000
Net earnings	$ 8,219,000	$ 14,122,000	$10,261,000	$5,315,000	$1,445,000
Per Common and Common Equivalent Share:					
Earnings before extraordinary item	$ .33	$ .56	$ .41	$ .24	$.06
Extraordinary item	—	—	—	—	.01
Net earnings	$ .33	$ .56	$ .41	$ .24	$ .07
Weighted average number of common and common equivalent shares	25,247,000	25,302,000	24,834,000	22,233,000	21,050,000
Selected Consolidated Balance Sheet Data:					
Working capital	$106,451,000	$100,110,000	$ 49,318,000	$ 12,901,000	$ 5,502,000
Total assets	380,193,000	249,364,000	105,230,000	33,014,000	16,906,000
Long-term debt	199,943,000	117,942,000	4,384,000	236,000	3,738,000
Stockholders' equity	89,092,000	80,214,000	65,278,000	18,354,000	5,024,000

a.   53-week fiscal year; all others were 52-week fiscal years.

h

MANAGEMENT'S DISCUSSION AND ANALYSIS OF RESULTS OF OPERATIONS AND FINANCIAL CONDITION

The data below reflect the percentage relationship between sales and major categories in the Consolidated Statements of Earnings and selected sales data of the percentage change in the dollar amounts of each of the items.

h

258

	Fiscal Year[a]			Percentage Increase (Decrease) of Dollar Amounts	
	1985	1984	1983	**1985 v. 1984**	1984 v. 1983
Selected Consolidated Statements of Earnings Data:					
Net sales	**100.0%**	100.0%	100.0%	**61.9%**	68.9%
Gross profit	**25.9**	26.4	27.3	**58.7**	63.3
Cost and expenses:					
Selling and store operating	**19.2**	17.2	17.0	**80.5**	71.1
Preopening	**1.1**	.4	.9	**292.3**	(21.9)
General and administrative	**2.9**	3.0	2.9	**60.4**	73.8
Net gain on disposition of property and equipment	**(.2)**	—	—	**—**	—
Interest income	**(.2)**	(1.2)	(.9)	**(71.7)**	116.2
Interest expense	**1.4**	.9	—	**147.6**	3,863.5
	24.2	20.3	19.9	**92.9**	72.6
Earnings before income taxes	**1.7**	6.1	7.4	**(55.7)**	38.3
Income taxes	**.5**	2.8	3.4	**(72.0)**	39.0
Net earnings	**1.2%**	3.3%	4.0%	**(41.8%)**	37.6%
Selected Consolidated Sales Data:					
Number of customer transactions	**23,324,000**	14,256,000	8,479.000	**63.6%**	68.1%
Average amount of sale per transaction	**$30.04**	$30.36	$30.21	**(1.1)**	.5
Weighted average weekly sales per operating store	**$ 342,500**	$ 365,500	$ 360,300	**(6.3)**	1.4

a. Fiscal years 1985, 1984 and 1983 refer to the fiscal years ended February 2, 1986, February 3, 1985 and January 29, 1984, respectively. Fiscal 1984 consisted of 53 weeks while 1985 and 1983 each consisted of 52 weeks.

Results of Operations

For an understanding of the significant factors that influenced the Company's performance during the past three fiscal years, the following discussion should be read in conjunction with the consolidated financial statements appearing elsewhere in this annual report.

Fiscal Year Ended February 2, 1986 Compared to February 3, 1985

Net sales in fiscal year 1985 increased 62% from $432,779,000 to $700,729,000. The growth is attributable to several factors. First, the Company opened 20 new stores during 1985 and closed one store. Second, second-year sales increases were realized from the three new stores opened in 1984 and from the nine former Bowater Home Center stores acquired during 1984. Third, comparable store sales increases of 2.3% were achieved despite comparing the 52-week 1985 fiscal year to the sales of the 53-week 1984 fiscal year, due in part to the number of customer transactions increasing by 64%. Finally, the weighted average weekly sales per operating store declined 6% in 1985 due to the significant increase in the ratio of the number of new stores to total stores in operation—new stores have a lower sales rate than mature stores until they establish market share.

Gross profit in 1985 increased 59% from $114,319,000 to $181,457,000. This increase was due to the increased sales and was partially offset by a reduction in the gross profit margin from 26.4% to 25.9%. The reduction is primarily due to lower margins achieved while establishing market presence in new markets.

Cost and expenses increased 93% during 1985 and, as a percent of sales, increased from 20.3% to 24.2%. The increase in selling and store operating, preopening expenses and net interest expense is due to the opening of 20 new stores, the costs associated with the former Bowater Home Center stores, and the related cost of building market share. The large percentage of new stores which have lower sales but fixed occupancy and certain minimum operating expenses tends to cause the percentage of selling and store operating costs to increase as a percentage of sales. The net gain on disposition of property and equipment is discussed fully in note 7 to the financial statements.

Earnings before income taxes decreased 56% from $26,252,000 to $11,619,000 resulting from the increase in operating expenses to support the Company's expansion program. The Company's effective income tax rate declined from 46.2% to 29.3% resulting from an increase in investment and other tax credits as a percentage of the total tax provision. As a percentage of sales, earnings decreased from 3.3% in 1984 to 1.2% in 1985 due to the increase in operating expenses as discussed above.

Fiscal Year Ended February 3, 1985 Compared to January 29, 1984

Net sales in fiscal 1984 increased 69% from $256,184,000 to $432,779,000. The growth was attributable to several factors. First, the company opened three new stores during fiscal 1984. Second, the Company had sales of $9,755,000 from the nine former Bowater Home Center stores acquired on December 3, 1984. Third, second-year sales increases were realized from the nine stores opened during fiscal 1983. Fourth, comparable store sales increases of 14% were due in part to 53 weeks in fiscal 1984 compared to 52 weeks in fiscal 1983 and in part to the number of customer transactions increasing by 63%. Finally, excluding the sales of the former Bowater Home Center stores, the weighted average weekly sales per operating store increased 6% to $383,500 in fiscal 1984.

Gross profit in fiscal 1984 increased 63% from $70,014,000 to $114,319,000. This net increase was due to the increased sales and was partially offset by a reduction in the gross profit margin from 27.3% to 26.4%. The reduction in the gross profit percentage is largely the result of the purchase of a high proportion of promoted merchandise by customers in the second quarter.

Costs and expenses increased 73% during fiscal 1984. As a percent of sales, costs and expenses increased from 19.9% to 20.3% due to increased selling, store operating, general and administrative expenses. This planned increase was in preparation of the Company's future expansion. Interest expense increased significantly as a result of the

h

259

issuance of substantial debt during fiscal 1984 to fund the Company's expansion. These increases were partially offset by reduced preopening expenses and increased interest income resulting from temporary investment of the proceeds of the debt financing.

Earnings before income taxes increased 38% from $18,986,000 to $26,252,000 resulting from the factors discussed above. Such pretax earnings, however, were reduced by a loss from the Bowater stores of approximately $1,900,000 from date of acquisition (December 1984) to year end. The Company's effective income tax rate increased slightly from 46.0% to 46.2% resulting principally from less investment and other tax credits as a percentage of the total tax provision. As a percentage of sales, earnings decreased from 4.0% in fiscal 1983 to 3.3% in fiscal 1984. The decline is a result of the company's reduced gross profit percentage and increases in the operating expenses discussed above.

Impact of Inflation and Changing Prices

Although the Company cannot accurately determine the precise effect of inflation on its operations, it does not believe inflation has had a material effect on sales or results of operations. The Company has complied with the reporting requirements of the Financial Accounting Standards Board Statement No. 33 in note 10 to the financial statements. Due to the experimental techniques, subjective estimates and assumptions, and the incomplete presentation required by this accounting pronouncement, the Company questions the value of the required reporting.

Liquidity and Capital Resources

Cash flow generated from existing store operations provided the Company with a significant source of liquidity since sales are on a cash-and-carry basis. In addition, a significant portion of the Company's inventory is financed under vendor credit terms. The Company has supplemented its operating cash flow from time to time with bank credit and equity and debt financing. During fiscal 1985, $88,000,000 of working capital was provided by the revolving bank credit line, $4,400,000 from industrial revenue bonds, and approximately $15,707,000 from operations. In addition, during fiscal 1985, the Company entered into a new credit agreement for a $200,000,000 revolving credit facility with a group of banks.

The Company has announced plans to open nine new stores during fiscal 1986, two in the new market of northern California and the balance in existing markets. The cost of this store expansion program will depend upon, among other factors, the extent to which the Company is able to lease second-use store space as opposed to acquiring leases or sites and having stores constructed to its own specifications. The Company estimates that approximately $6,600,000 per store will be required to acquire sites and construct facilities to the Company's specifications and that approximately $1,700,000 will be required to open a store in leased space plus any additional costs of acquiring the lease. These estimates include costs for site acquisition, construction expenditures, fixtures and equipment, and in-store minicomputers and point-of-sale terminals. In addition, each new store will require approximately $1,800,000 to finance inventories, net of vendor financing. The Company believes it has the ability to finance these expenditures through existing cash resources, current bank lines of credit which include a $200,000,000 eight-year revolving credit agreement, funds generated from operations, and other forms of financing, including but not limited to various forms of real estate financing and unsecured borrowings.

NOTES TO CONSOLIDATED FINANCIAL STATEMENTS

1. Summary of Significant Accounting Policies

Fiscal Year

The Company's fiscal year ends on the Sunday closest to the last day of January and usually consists of 52 weeks. Every five or six years, however, there is a 53-week year. The fiscal year ended February 2, 1986 (1985) consisted of 52 weeks, the year ended February 3, 1985 (1984) consisted of 53 weeks and the year ended January 29, 1984 (1983) consisted of 52 weeks.

Principles of Consolidation

The consolidated financial statements include the accounts of the Company and its wholly owned subsidiary. All significant intercompany transactions have been eliminated in consolidation. Certain reclassifications were made to the 1984 balance sheet to conform to current year presentation.

Merchandise Inventories

Inventories are stated at the lower of cost (first-in, first-out) or market, as determined by the retail inventory method.

Depreciation and Amortization

The Company's buildings, furniture, fixtures, and equipment are depreciated using the straight-line method over the estimated useful lives of the assets. Improvements to leased premises are amortized on the straight-line method over the life of the lease or the useful life of the improvement, whichever is shorter.

Investment Tax Credit

Investment tax credits are recorded as a reduction of Federal income taxes in the year the credits are realized.

Store Preopening Costs

Non-capital expenditures associated with opening new stores are charged to expense as incurred.

Earnings Per Common and Common Equivalent Share

Earnings per common and common equivalent share are based on the weighted average number of shares and equivalents outstanding. Common equivalent shares used in the calculation of earnings per share represent shares granted under the Company's employee stock option plan and employee stock purchase plan.

Shares issuable upon conversion of the 8½% convertible subordinated debentures are also common stock equivalents. Shares issuable upon conversion of the 9% convertible subordinated debentures would only be included in the computation of fully diluted earnings per share. However, neither shares issuable upon conversion of the 8½% nor the 9% convertible debentures were dilutive in any year presented, and thus neither were considered in the earnings per share computations.

h

261

2. Acquisition

On December 3, 1984 the Company acquired the outstanding capital stock of Bowater Home Center, Inc. (Bowater) for approximately $38,420,000 including costs incurred in connection with the acquisition. Bowater operated nine retail home center stores primarily in the Dallas, Texas metropolitan area. The acquisition was accounted for by the purchase method and, accordingly, results of operations have been included with those of the Company from the date of acquisition. Cost in excess of the fair value of net assets acquired amounted to approximately $25,291,000, which is being amortized over forty years from date of acquisition using the straight-line method.

The following table summarizes, on a pro forma, unaudited basis, the estimated combined results of operations of the Company and Bowater for the years ended February 3, 1985 and January 29, 1984, as though the acquisition were made at the beginning of fiscal year 1983. This pro forma information does not purport to be indicative of the results of operations which would have actually been obtained if the acquisition had been effective on the dates indicated.

	Fiscal Year Ended	
	February 3, 1985	January 29, 1984*
	(Unaudited)	
Net sales	$482,752,000	$274,660,000
Net earnings	9,009,000	6,913,000
Earnings per common and common equivalent share	.36	.28

*Includes the operations and pro forma adjustments from the date of inception of Bowater's operations in August, 1983.

3. Long-Term Debt and Lines of Credit

Long-term debt consists of the following:

	February 2, 1986	February 3, 1985
8½% convertible subordinated debentures, due July 1, 2009, convertible into shares of common stock of the Company at a conversion price of $26.50 per share. The debentures are redeemable by the Company at a premium from July 1, 1986 to July 1, 1995, will retire 70% of the issue prior to maturity. Interest is payable semi-annually.	$86,250,000	$86,250,000
9% convertible subordinated debentures, due December 15, 1999, convertible into shares of common stock of the Company at a conversion price of $16.90 per share. The debentures are redeemable by the Company at a premium from December 15, 1986 to December 15, 1994. An annual mandatory sinking fund of $2,000,000 per year is required from 1994 to 1998. Interest is payable semi-annually.	14,000,000	14,000,000
Total convertible subordinated debentures	**100,250,000**	100,250,000

	February 2, 1986	February 3, 1985
Revolving credit agreement. Interest may be fixed for any portion outstanding for up to 180 days, at the Company's option, based on a CD rate plus ¾%, the LIBOR rate plus ½% or at the prime rate.	88,000,000	—
*Variable Rate Industrial Revenue Bond (see note 7)	10,100,000	10,100,000
*Variable Rate Industrial Revenue Bond, secured by a letter of credit, payable in sinking fund installments from December 1, 1991 through December 1, 2010	4,400,000	—
9⅝% Industrial Revenue Bond, secured by a letter of credit, payable on December 1, 1993, with interest payable semi-annually	4,200,000	4,200,000
*Variable Rate Industrial Revenue Bond, secured by land, payable in annual installments of $233,000 with interest payable semi-annually	3,267,000	3,500,000
Other	108,000	179,000
Total long-term debt	210,325,000	118,229,000
Less current portion	10,382,000	287,000
Long-term debt, excluding current portion	$199,943,000	$117,942,000

*The interest rates on the variable rate industrial revenue bonds are related to various short-term municipal money market composite rates.

h

263

Maturities of long-term debt are approximately $10,382,000 for fiscal 1986 and $234,000 for each of the next four subsequent years.

During the fiscal year ended February 2, 1986, the Company entered into a new unsecured revolving line of credit for a maximum of $200,000,000, subject to certain limitations, of which $88,000,000 is outstanding at year-end. Commitment amounts under the agreement decrease by $15,000,000 on July 31, 1990, by $20,000,000 each six months from that date through January 31, 1993, by $35,000,000 on July 31, 1993, and with the remaining $50,000,000 commitment expiring on January 31, 1994. Maximum borrowings outstanding within the commitment limits may not exceed specified percentages of inventories, land and buildings, and fixtures and equipment, all as defined in the Agreement. Under certain conditions, the commitments may be extended and/or increased. An annual commitment fee of ¼% to ⅜% is required to be paid on the unused portion of the revolving line of credit. Interest rates specified may be increased by a maximum of ⅜ of 1% based on specified ratios of interest rate coverage and debt to equity.

Under the revolving credit agreement, the Company is required, among other things, to maintain during fiscal year 1985 a minimum tangible net worth (defined to include the convertible subordinated debentures) of $150,000,000 (increasing annually to $213,165,000 by January 3, 1989), a debt to tangible net worth ratio of no more than 2 to 1, a current ratio of not less than 1.5 to 1, and a ratio of earnings before interest expense and income taxes to interest expense, net, of not less than 2 to 1. The Company was in compliance with all restrictive covenants as of February 2, 1986. The restrictive covenants related to the letter of credit agreements securing the industrial revenue bonds and the convertible subordinated debentures are no more restrictive than those under the revolving line of credit agreement.

Interest expense in the accompanying consolidated statements of earnings is net of interest capitalized of $3,429,000 in fiscal 1985 and $1,462,000 in fiscal 1984.

4. Income Taxes

The provision for income taxes consists of the following:

	Fiscal Year Ended		
	February 1, 1986	February 3, 1985	January 29, 1984
Current:			
Federal	**$(578,000)**	$9,083,000	$6,916,000
State	**366,000**	1,539,000	1,096,000
	(212,000)	10,622,000	8,012,000
Deferred:			
Federal	**3,306,000**	1,464,000	713,000
State	**306,000**	44,000	—
	3,612,000	1,508,000	713,000
Total	**$3,400,000**	$12,130,000	$8,725,000

The effective tax rates for fiscal 1985, 1984, and 1983 were 29.3%, 46.2%, and 46.0%, respectively. A reconciliation of income tax expense at Federal statutory rates to actual tax expense for the applicable fiscal years follows:

	Fiscal Year Ended		
	February 2, 1986	February 3, 1985	January 29, 1984
Income taxes at Federal statutory rate, net of surtax exemption	**$5,345,000**	$12,076,000	$8,734,000
State income taxes, net of Federal income tax benefit	**363,000**	855,000	592,000
Investment and targeted jobs tax credits	**(2,308,000)**	(800,000)	(747,000)
Other, net	**—**	(1,000)	146,000
	$3,400,000	$12,130,000	$8,725,000

Deferred income taxes arise from differences in the timing of reporting income for financial statement and income tax purposes. The sources of these differences and the tax effect of each are as follows:

	Fiscal Year Ended		
	February 2, 1986	February 3, 1985	January 29, 1984
Accelerated depreciation	**$2,526,000**	$1,159,000	$713,000
Interest capitalization	**855,000**	349,000	—
Other, net	**231,000**	—	—
	$3,612,000	$1,508,000	$713,000

5. Leases

The Company leases certain retail locations, office, and warehouse and distribution space, equipment, and vehicles under operating leases. All leases will expire within the next 25 years; however, it can be expected that in the normal course of business, leases will be renewed or replaced. Total rent expense, net of minor sublease income for the fiscal years ended February 2, 1986, February 3, 1985 and January 29, 1984 amounted to approximately $12,737,000, $6,718,000 and $4,233,000, respectively. Under the building leases, real estate taxes, insurance, maintenance, and operating expenses applicable to the leased property are obligations of the Company. Certain of the store leases provide for contingent rentals based on percentages of sales in excess of specified minimums. Contingent rentals for fiscal years ended February 2, 1986, February 3, 1985 and January 29, 1984 were approximately $650,000, $545,000 and $111,000.

The approximate future minimum lease payments under operating leases at February 2, 1986 are as follows:

Fiscal Year	
1986	**$ 16,093,000**
1987	16,668,000
1988	16,345,000
1989	16,086,000
1990	16,129,000
Thereafter	171,455,000
	$252,776,000

h

265

7. Disposition of Property and Equipment

During the fourth quarter of fiscal year 1985, the Company disposed of certain properties and equipment at a net gain of $1,317,000. The properties represented real estate located in Detroit, Houston and Tucson, and the equipment represented the trade-in of cash registers of current generation point of sale equipment. Under the terms of the Detroit real estate sale, the purchaser will either assume the bond obligations of the Company of $10,100,000 after February 2, 1986 or pay the Company the funds disbursed under the bonds in order for the Company to prepay the total amount outstanding. Included in accounts receivable at February 2, 1986 is $13,800,000 related to these transactions.

8. Commitments and Contingencies

At February 2, 1986, the Company was contingently liable for approximately $5,300,000 under outstanding letters of credit issued in connection with purchase commitments.

The Company has litigation arising from the normal course of business. In management's opinion, this litigation will not materially affect the Company's financial condition.

h

266

9. Quarterly Financial Data (Unaudited)

The following is a summary of the unaudited quarterly results of operations for fiscal years ended February 2, 1986 and February 3, 1985:

	Net Sales	Gross Profit	Net Earnings	Net Earnings per Common and Common Equivalent Share
Fiscal year ended February 2, 1986:				
First Quarter	$145,048,000	$ 36,380,000	$ 1,945,000	$ .08
Second Quarter	174,239,000	45,572,000	2,499,000	.10
Third Quarter	177,718,000	46,764,000	1,188,000	.05
Fourth Quarter	203,724,000	52,741,000	2,587,000	.10
	$700,729,000	$181,457,000	$ 8,219,000	$ .33
Fiscal year ended February 3, 1985:				
First Quarter	$ 95,872,000	$ 25,026,000	$ 3,437,000	$ .14
Second Quarter	119,068,000	29,185,000	3,808,000	.15
Third Quarter	100,459,000	27,658,000	3,280,000	.13
Fourth Quarter	117,380,000	32,450,000	3,597,000	.14
	$432,779,000	$114,319,000	$14,122,000	$ .56

AUDITORS' REPORT

The Board of Directors and Stockholders,
The Home Depot, Inc.:

We have examined the consolidated balance sheets of The Home Depot, Inc. and subsidiary as of February 2, 1986 and February 3, 1985 and the related consolidated statements of earnings, stockholders' equity, and changes in financial position for each of the years in the three-year period ended February 2, 1986. Our examinations were made in accordance with generally accepted auditing standards, and, accordingly, included such tests of the accounting records and such other auditing procedures as we considered necessary in the circumstances.

In our opinion, the aforementioned consolidated financial statements present fairly the financial position of The Home Depot, Inc. and subsidiary at February 2, 1986 and February 3, 1985, and the results of their operations and the changes in their financial position for each of the years in the three-year period ended February 2, 1986, in conformity with generally accepted accounting principles applied on a consistent basis.

PEAT, MARWICK, MITCHELL & CO.
Atlanta, Georgia
March 24, 1986

Research analyst Doug Chase has been reviewing the pricing and financial performance of Japanese and U.S. firms. He recognizes that financial ratios differ significantly between firms from the two countries. For example, rates of return on assets tend to be much lower for Japanese firms. Price multiples also tend to differ dramatically. As of December 1990, the average P/E ratio in Japan was 36.6, or about two and one-half times higher than the U.S. average of 15.9. During the three years that preceded the decline of Japanese stock prices in 1990, the difference was even more dramatic: Japanese P/E ratios averaged nearly four times those in the U.S.

The question in Chase's mind is to what extent the differences between the Japanese and U.S. numbers are "real," as opposed to artifacts of differences in accounting. For example, higher P/E ratios in Japan could indicate that (1) Japanese stocks are still relatively overpriced, even after the "crash" of 1990; (2) real growth in earnings is justifiably expected to be higher in Japan than the U.S.; and/or (3) Japanese earnings are calculated more conservatively than in the U.S.[1]

Chase is aware of research indicating that, in the aggregate, accounting differences can explain part, but not all, of the differences in Japanese and U.S. PE ratios as of the end of 1990.[2] However, such estimates are based on crude assumptions, and Chase is interested in investigating the issue more carefully at a firm-specific level. He has decided to examine the financial statements of Fujitsu and IBM, to discern to what extent the price multiples of the two firms differ only as a result of accounting choices.

Even though they both operate in the computer industry, Fujitsu and IBM have dramatically different PE ratios. On March 31, 1991, Fujitsu's stock traded at a multiple of approximately 26 times earnings for the fiscal year ended on that date. (The stock price was 1180 yen per share, while earnings per primary share stood at 45.60 yen.) IBM's PE ratio at December 31, 1990 (based on a price of $115 and 1990 EPS of $10.51) was approximately 11. The stock prices of both firms have been falling during 1991; as the end of the year approaches, Fujitsu is trading at approximately 22 times 1990 earnings, while IBM is trading at 8 times earnings.

....

Prepared by Professor Victor L. Bernard with the Assistance of Christine Botosan and Marlene Plumlee. The case is based on publicly available information.

1. *Another possibility is that the cost of equity capital is justifiably lower in Japan. However, unless any differential could be attributed to lower risk in Japan, such a possibility rests on the assumption that constraints on capital movements prevent equilibration of required returns across the U.S. and Japanese capital markets. At least in the 1990s, one could question the plausibility of that assumption.*

2. *For more detail, see K. French and J. Poterba, "Were Japanese Stock Prices Too High?" Journal of Financial Economics (October 1991): 337–364.*

Chase wondered not only about what might explain Fujitsu's relatively higher PE ratio, but also about how the two firms' price-to-book ratios could be reconciled with their relative degrees of profitability. Chase is aware that price-to-book ratios should vary across firms according to variation in their expected future ROEs and growth opportunities. He also knows that since current ROEs are related to future ROEs, there is—at least in the U.S.—a positive relation between price-to-book ratios and current ROEs.[3] However, a comparison of U.S. and Japanese corporations seems to contradict this relation. Specifically, Japanese corporations have, at least during the 1980s and early 1990s, maintained higher price-to-book ratios than their U.S. counterparts while generating lower ROEs. IBM and Fujitsu present a case in point. Fujitsu's price-to-book ratio at the end of its fiscal 1990 was about 1.85, while IBM stood at 1.6. However, Fujitsu's ROE for the year was much lower: 7 percent versus IBM's 14 percent. Chase wondered what might explain the apparent anomaly and also why the market was paying 1.85 times book value for a firm that generated an ROE of only 7 percent. In 1990, an investor could have acquired long-term Japanese government bonds at face value, and expected a yield of approximately 7 percent with little or no risk involved.

FINANCIAL ACCOUNTING IN JAPAN

There are several accounting-related factors that could affect comparison of Japanese and U.S. financial ratios. A brief summary of some of the factors is as follows:

- *Conservative earnings calculations in Japan.* Japanese corporations tend to be more conservative in accounting than their U.S. counterparts. One important reason for this is that, in Japan, income reported to shareholders is the same as that reported to income tax authorities. Another possibility is that Japanese firms, with close ties to some of their key suppliers of capital, may not (at least historically) have been as concerned as U.S. firms about using public financial statements as a vehicle for communicating their prospects. Thus, Japanese firms may be able to report conservative measures of income, perhaps for tax purposes, without serious concerns that doing so will harm their ability to raise capital.

  Conservatism in accounting can arise in many ways. One important source of conservatism in Japan involves depreciation methods: depreciation is more accelerated there than in the U.S. There is also a greater tendency to immediately expense costs that would be not be written off in the U.S., in part through the use of a variety of "special reserves" (e.g., special reserves for bad debts and provisions for anticipated costs).

- *Cross-firm holdings.* Japanese firms are organized in related groups called *keiretsu*. A firm typically owns shares in many of the other members of the network. When one firm owns less than 20 percent of another's shares, as is often the case, then

---

3. *For some evidence on this issue, see Penman, "An Evaluation of Accounting Rate-of-Return,"* Journal of Accounting, Auditing, and Finance *(Spring 1991): 233–255.*

income from the affiliate is recorded under the cost method—that is, only dividend income is recorded. As a result, any appreciation in the value of the investment is not recorded in earnings.

Even if a Japanese firm owns more than 20 percent but less than 50 percent of another firm, the equity in the earnings of the other firm is typically not recorded by the parent in the "parent-only" financials. (In the consolidated financials, this is not the case; the equity method is used there.) Since many of the published PE ratios are based on parent-only financials, the failure to use the equity method tends to inflate such ratios.

- *Unrecorded appreciation in land values.* Accounting for land in Japan is no different from that in the U.S.: land is carried at cost. However, the impact of that accounting differs because real estate prices in Japan have risen more than those in the U.S. over the past few decades. Professor Tak Wakasugi of the University of Tokyo has estimated that land held by Japanese corporations exceeded recorded book values by factors ranging from 16 to 25 over the 1974–1986 period. Taking the appreciation in land values as a given, it could partially explain high price-to-book ratios and high price-to-earnings ratios for Japanese corporations. However, the unrecorded appreciation justifies such high multiples only if it translates into high expected future earnings growth.

i

271

IBM IN 1991

IBM is the world's largest manufacturer of data processing equipment and systems; sales for 1990 were nearly $70 billion. Sales of computers, workstations, and peripherals constituted 63 percent of that amount; software, maintenance, and other services accounted for an additional 34 percent of sales. Approximately 39 percent of sales were in the U.S.

IBM is a major player in nearly all markets for information processing equipment. IBM dominates in the market for mainframes and brought a new entrant to that market in September 1990—the ES/9000. In the minicomputer market, IBM offers the AS/400, the most widely sold computer in its class. In the personal computer market, IBM faces heavy competition but now offers its PS/2 as the encore to the PS/1, the most popular desktop computer in history. In the young but quickly growing market for high-performance workstations, IBM (after developing the prevailing technology) lags behind Sun and other competitors, but introduced RISC System/6000, managing to capture a 7 percent market share. IBM's operations are supported with a large commitment to research and development—R&D expenditures were $6.6 billion in 1990 and $6.8 billion in 1989.

The combination of the Gulf War, higher interest rates, and weakening worldwide economies presented IBM with a challenging environment for sales in 1990. Nevertheless, sales increased again, by 10 percent, and EPS increased by 62 percent over the poor performance of 1989. The earnings increase brought EPS to a level similar to that maintained from 1983 through 1988. However, IBM's 14 percent ROE for 1990 was a far cry from the 25 percent registered six years earlier.

The year 1991 proved difficult for IBM. As the year opened, analysts expected earnings to be in the range of $8 to $11 per share, but those forecasts fell as the mainframe market weakened and IBM faced stiff competition in other markets, including those for workstations and PCs. IBM's stock price, which rose to $140 in January, fell throughout the year and stood at $86 by early December. Sales for the year were expected to decline for the first time since 1946. By December 1991, analysts forecast that the small profits of the first three quarters would be more than offset by a fourth-quarter accounting charge (pertaining to retirement benefits), bringing 1991 earnings to a loss of about $3.30 per share. Earnings before the fourth-quarter charge were forecast at $0.70 a share.

In November 1991, IBM announced a dramatic restructuring that would free its major business units to operate more autonomously. The restructuring also involves cutting the workforce by 20,000 positions, or about 5 percent of all employees. IBM's restructuring was greeted as good news on Wall Street, but some observers felt that IBM's changes were only indicative of a decade-long transition from high-margin mainframe products to low-margin, standards-based products. "The profit implications of that are pretty clear," stated Frank Gens of Technology Investment Strategies Corp.[4]

The changes at IBM, in conjunction with the impact of new products and upgrades in the mainframe, personal computer, and workstation markets are expected by analysts to contribute to a substantial rebound in 1992. As the end of 1991 approaches, analysts expect 1992 EPS to come in at over $7 a share—lower than EPS during much of the 1980s, but a dramatic increase over 1991. Over the long run, earnings are expected to increase as IBM operates more efficiently, employs its mainframes within network systems, and links with other firms (e.g., Apple) on software development. Value Line forecasts EPS to hit $15 a share at some point during the 1994–96 time frame.

FUJITSU IN 1991

Fujitsu is the world's second largest computer manufacturer. Sales of data processing equipment accounted for 72 percent of total sales in fiscal 1990; other products included communications equipment (17 percent of sales) and semiconductors and related electronic devices (11 percent of sales). Fujitsu is the majority owner of Amdahl, a U.S.-based manufacturer of IBM-compatible mainframes, and ICL PLC, the U.K.'s largest computer company and a manufacturer of UNIX-based open computer systems. Total sales for fiscal 1991 were 3 trillion yen, or approximately $21 billion (based on the rate of exchange at March 29, 1991). Thus, Fujitsu is about one-third the size of IBM. Approximately 73 percent of Fujitsu's 1990 sales were in Japan.

Fujitsu competes in many markets, but its mainstays are mainframes, minicomputers, and supercomputers. In Japan, Fujitsu holds the number one share in each of those markets. Fujitsu was slow to recognize the potential of the PC market, but now has products in that arena. Fujitsu spends heavily on R&D: 340 billion yen in fiscal 1990, up from 292 billion yen in the previous year. It is developing HDTV technologies that it believes

---

4. R. Hamilton, "IBM stung by market shifts," Computer World (June 24, 1991): 125.

hold great promise for the long run. Fujitsu's chairman and former pilot Takuma Yama-moto is said to "want nothing less than to take on number 1 IBM . . . in dogfights every-where in the world."[5]

After several years of dramatic earnings growth, profits fell at Fujitsu in fiscal 1990, from 48.6 to 45.7 yen per share. Fujitsu management attributed the decline to the slow-down in worldwide economic growth. Mainframe sales grew at a 20 percent rate despite the recession, but semiconductor sales were slower, with lower profit margins.

Fujitsu's stock price languished during much of 1991, falling from a high of 1290 yen in March to 901 yen in August. As the turn of the year approached, Fujitsu's managers were forecasting sales for the fiscal year ending March 1992 would rise to 3.6 trillion yen, but that net profit would decline again slightly, to 44.7 yen per share. Forecasts be-yond March 1992 are not yet available.

QUESTIONS

1. Consider the issues confronted by analyst Doug Chase. Identify and discuss some of the major reasons why the PE ratio for Fujitsu is so much higher than that for IBM, with a focus on the extent to which accounting issues play a role. Also consider why Fujitsu's price-to-book ratio is higher than IBM's, even though its current ROE is lower.
2. What evidence is there that Fujitsu's accounting is more conservative than IBM's? To what extent are differences between IBM accounting and Fujitsu accounting apparent upon reading their descriptions of accounting policies? What does a comparison of the cash flows of the two firms reveal about this issue? Do differences in depreciation accounting methods really have a large impact on price multiples, as is claimed in the financial press? To what extent does the numerator of price multiples reflect appre-ciation in assets that does not impact the denominator?

i

273

5. B. Schlender, "How Fujitsu will tackle the giants," Fortune (June 1, 1991): 82.

EXHIBIT 1
Excerpts from IBM Financial Statements for Year Ended
December 31, 1990

REPORT OF INDEPENDENT ACCOUNTANTS

To the Stockholders and Board of Directors   January 29, 1991
of International Business Machines Corporation

In our opinion, the accompanying consolidated financial statements present fairly in all
material respects the financial position of International Business Machines Corporation
and its subsidiaries at December 31, 1990 and 1989, and the results of their operations
and their cash flows for each of the three years in the period ended December 31,1990,
in conformity with generally accepted accounting principles. These financial statements
are the responsibility of the company's management; our responsibility is to express an
opinion thereon based on our audits. We conducted our audits in accordance with generally accepted auditing standards which require that we plan and perform the audit to
obtain reasonable assurance about whether such statements are free of material misstatement. An audit includes examining, on a test basis, evidence supporting the amounts
and disclosures in the financial statements, assessing the accounting principles used and
significant estimates made by management, and evaluating the overall financial statement presentation. We believe that our audits provide a reasonable basis for the opinion
expressed above.

As discussed in the note regarding Taxes, the company changed its method of
accounting for income taxes in 1988. We concur with this change.

Price Waterhouse
153 East 53rd Street
New York, N.Y. 10022

CONSOLIDATED FINANCIAL STATEMENTS

CONSOLIDATED STATEMENT OF EARNINGS

For the year ended December 31:	1990	1989	1988
(Dollars in millions except per share amounts)			
Revenue:			
Sales	$43,959	$41,586	$39,959
Support services	11,322	9,858	9,285
Software	9,952	8,424	7,927
Rentals and financing	3,785	2,842	2,510
	69,018	62,710	59,681
Cost:			
Sales	19,401	18,001	17,499
Support services	6,617	5,701	4,971
Software	3,126	2,694	2,110
Rentals and financing	1,579	1,305	1,068
	30,723	27,701	25,648
Gross Profit	38,295	35,009	34,033
Operating Expenses:			
Selling, general and administrative	20,709	21,289	19,362
Research, development and engineering	6,554	6,827	5,925
	27,263	28,116	25,287
Operating Income	11,032	6,893	8,746
Other Income, principally interest	495	728	996
Interest Expense	1,324	976	709
Earnings before Income Taxes	10,203	6,645	9,033
Provision for Income Taxes	4,183	2,887	3,542
Net Earnings before Cumulative Effect of Accounting Change	6,020	3,758	5,491
Cumulative Effect of Change in Accounting for Income Taxes	—	—	315
Net Earnings	$6,020	$3,758	$5,806
Per share amounts:			
Before cumulative effect of accounting change	$10.51	$6.47	$9.27
Cumulative effect of change in accounting for income taxes	—	—	.53
Net earnings	$10.51	$6.47	$9.80

Average number of shares outstanding:
1990—572,647,906
1989—581,102,404
1988—592,444,409

i

275

Exhibit 1   Excerpts from IBM Financial Statements for Year Ended December 31, 1990

CONSOLIDATED STATEMENT OF FINANCIAL POSITION

At December 31	1990	1989
(Dollars in millions)		
Assets		
Current Assets:		
Cash	$ 1,189	$ 741
Cash equivalents	2,664	2,959
Marketable securities, at cost, which approximates market	698	1,261
Notes and accounts receivable—trade, net of allowances	20,988	18,866
Other accounts receivable	1,656	1,298
Inventories	10,108	9,463
Prepaid expenses and other current assets	1,617	1,287
	38,920	35,875
Plant, Rental Machines and Other Property	53,659	48,410
Less: Accumulated depreciation	26,418	23,467
	27,241	24,943
Investments and Other Assets:		
Software, less accumulated amortization (1990, $5,873; 1989, $4,824)	4,099	3,293
Investments and sundry assets	17,308	13,623
	21,407	16,916
	$87,568	$77,734
Liabilities and Stockholders' Equity		
Current Liabilities:		
Taxes	$ 3,159	$ 2,699
Short-term debt	7,602	5,892
Accounts payable	3,367	3,167
Compensation and benefits	3,014	2,797
Deferred income	2,506	1,365
Other accrued expenses and liabilities	5,628	5,780
	25,276	21,700
Long-Term Debt	11,943	10,825
Other Liabilities	3,656	3,420
Deferred Income Taxes	3,861	3,280
Stockholders' Equity:		
Capital stock, par value $1.25 per share	6,357	6,341
Shares authorized: 750,000.000		
Issued: 1990—571,618,795;1989—574,775,560		
Retained earnings	33,234	30,477
Translation adjustments	3,266	1,698
	42,857	38,516
Less: Treasury stock, at cost (Shares: 1990—227,604; 1989—75,723)	25	7
	42,832	38,509
	$87,568	$77,734

CONSOLIDATED STATEMENT OF CASH FLOWS

For the year ended December 31:	1990	1989	1988
(Dollars in millions)			
Cash Flow from Operating Activities:			
Net earnings	$6,020	$3,758	$5,806
Adjustments to reconcile net earnings to cash provided from operating activities:			
Depreciation	4,217	4,240	3,871
Amortization of software	1,086	1,185	893
Loss (gain) on disposition of investment assets	32	(74)	(133)
(Increase) in accounts receivable	(2,077)	(2,647)	(2,322)
Decrease (increase) in inventory	17	(29)	(1,232)
(Increase) in other assets	(3,136)	(1,674)	(1,587)
Increase in accounts payable	293	870	265
Increase in other liabilities	1,020	1,743	519
Net cash provided from operating activities	7,472	7,372	6,080
Cash Flow from Investing Activities:			
Payments for plant rental machines and other property	(6,509)	(6,414)	(5,390)
Proceeds from disposition of plant, rental machines and other property	804	544	409
Investment in software	(1,892)	(1,679)	(1,318)
Purchases of marketable securities and other investments	(1,234)	(1,391)	(2,555)
Proceeds from marketable securities and other investments	1,687	1,860	4,734
Net cash used in investing activities	(7,144)	(7,080)	(4,120)
Cash Flow from Financing Activities:			
Proceeds from new debt	4,676	6,471	4,540
Payments to settle debt	(3,683)	(2,768)	(3,007)
Short-term borrowings less than 90 days—net	1,966	228	1,028
Payments to employee stock plans—net	(76)	(29)	(11)
Payments to purchase and retire capital stock	(415)	(1,759)	(992)
Cash dividends paid	(2,774)	(2,752)	(2,609)
Net cash used in financing activities	(306)	(609)	(1,051)
Effect of Exchange Rate Changes on Cash and Cash Equivalents	131	(158)	(201)
Net Change in Cash and Cash Equivalents	153	(475)	708
Cash and Cash Equivalents at January 1	3,700	4,175	3,467
Cash and Cash Equivalents at December 31	$3,853	$3,700	$4,175
Supplemental Data:			
Cash paid during the year for:			
Income taxes	$3,315	$3,071	$3,405
Interest	$2,165	$1,605	$1,440

NOTES TO CONSOLIDATED FINANCIAL STATEMENTS

Significant Accounting Policies

Principles of Consolidation The consolidated financial statements include the accounts of International Business Machines Corporation and its U.S. and non-U.S. subsidiary companies. Investments in joint ventures and other companies in which IBM does not have control, but has the ability to exercise significant influence over operating and financial policies (generally greater than 20% ownership) are accounted for by the equity method. Other investments are accounted for by the cost method.

Translation of Non-U.S. Currency Amounts For non-U.S. subsidiaries which operate in a local currency environment, assets and liabilities are translated to U.S. dollars at year-end exchange rates. Income and expense items are translated at average rates of exchange prevailing during the year. Translation adjustments are accumulated in a separate component of stockholders' equity. For non-U.S. subsidiaries and branches which operate in U.S. dollars or whose economic environment is highly inflationary, inventories and plant, rental machines and other property are translated at approximate rates prevailing when acquired. All other assets and liabilities are translated at year-end exchange rates. Inventories charged to cost of sales and depreciation are remeasured at historical rates. All other income and expense items are translated at average rates of exchange prevailing during the year. Gains and losses which result from remeasurement are included in earnings.

Revenue Revenue is recognized from sales or sales-type leases when the product is shipped, from software when the program is shipped or as monthly license fees accrue, from support services (primarily maintenance services) over the contractual period or as the services are performed from rentals under operating leases in the month in which they accrue, and from financing at level rates of return over the term of the lease or receivable.

Software Costs related to the conceptual formulation and design of licensed programs are expensed as research and development. Costs incurred subsequent to establishment of technological feasibility to produce the finished product are generally capitalized. The annual amortization of the capitalized amounts is the greater of the amount computed based on the estimated revenue distribution over the products' revenue-producing lives or the straight-line method, but not in excess of six years. Costs to support or service licensed programs are charged against income as incurred or when related revenue is recognized, whichever occurs first.

Depreciation Plant, rental machines and other property are carried at cost and depreciated over their estimated useful lives using the straight-line method.

Goodwill Goodwill is amortized on a straight-line basis over the periods estimated to be benefited, currently not exceeding five years.

Retirement Plans and Other Postretirement Benefits Current service costs of retirement plans are accrued currently. Prior service costs resulting from improvements in the plans are amortized over the average remaining service period of employees expected to receive benefits. Postretirement health care and life insurance benefits are fully accrued, principally at retirement.

Selling Expenses Selling expenses are charged against income as incurred.

Income Taxes Income tax expense is based on reported earnings before income taxes. Deferred income taxes reflect the impact of temporary differences between the amount of assets and liabilities recognized for financial reporting purposes and such amounts recognized for tax purposes.

In accordance with Statement of Financial Accounting Standards (SFAS) 96, which the company adopted in 1988, these deferred taxes are measured by applying currently enacted tax laws. Deferred investment tax credits are being amortized as a reduction of income tax expense over the average useful life of the applicable classes of property.

Inventories Raw materials, finished goods and work in process are stated at the lower of average cost or market.

Cash Equivalents All highly liquid investments with a maturity of three months or less at date of purchase are considered to be cash equivalents.

Restructuring and Other Actions In December 1989, the company announced a series of actions to reduce costs, expenses and structure.

As a result, the 1989 earnings include a charge, recorded in the fourth quarter, of $2,420 million ($1,500 million after tax or $2.58 per share). $1,335 million of this relates to the costs of facility consolidations and capacity reductions and changes in the valuation and recovery periods of special investments. This amount is included in selling, general and administrative expense. Costs of $500 million associated with employee separations and relocations are also included in selling, general and administrative expense.

Costs of $585 million represent a charge related to the adoption of new guidelines to provide for the earlier recognition of costs in both hardware and software due to the pace of technological change and the company's success in shortening its product cycles. These charges are included in research, development and engineering expenses and in cost of software.

In 1988, $870 million was included in selling, general and administrative expense for manufacturing and headquarters consolidations.

Marketable Securities At December 31:	1990	1989
(Dollars in millions)		
U.S. government securities	$ 92	$ 201
Time deposits and other bank obligations	373	419
Non-U.S. government securities and other fixed-term obligations	233	641
Total	$698	$1,261
Market value	$698	$1,263

Inventories At December 31:	1990	1989
(Dollars in millions)		
Current inventories:		
Finished goods	$ 2,851	$ 2,915
Work in process	7,051	6,394
Raw materials	206	154
Total current inventories	10,108	9,463
Work in process included in plant, rental machines and other property	1,498	1,364
Total inventories	$11,606	$10,827

Plant, Rental Machines and Other Property

At December 31:	1990	1989
(Dollars in millions)		
Land and land improvements	$ 1,645	$ 1,507
Buildings	13,792	12,333
Plant, laboratory and office equipment	35,155	31,064
	50,592	44,904
Less: Accumulated depreciation	24,916	22,017
	25,676	22,887
Rental machines and parts	3,067	3,506
Less: Accumulated depreciation	1,502	1,450
	1,565	2,056
Total	$27,241	$24,943

Investments and Sundry Assets At December 31:	1990	1989
(Dollars in millions)		
Net investment in sales-type leases[†]	$16,914	$12,728
Less: Current portion (net) classified as notes and accounts receivable—trade	5,682	4,332
	11,232	8,396
Prepaid pension cost	1,045	655
Installment payment receivable	896	912
Investments in business alliances	703	660
Mortgage investments	529	509
Goodwill, less accumulated amortization (1990, $406; 1989, $283)	383	392
Other investments and sundry assets*	2,520	2,099
Total	$17,308	$13,623

[†]These leases relate to IBM equipment and are for terms generally ranging from three to five years. Net investment in sales-type leases includes unguaranteed residual values of approximately $1,350 million and $1,100 million at December 31,1990 and 1989, and is reflected net of unearned income at these dates of approximately $3,600 million and $2,600 million, respectively.

*Includes, at cost, an investment of $400 million in 7.35% preferred stock of MCI Communications Corporation, which is not convertible, nor is it planned to be publicly traded. MCI has the option to redeem all or part of this issue at any time.

Finance Subsidiaries

The company's wholly owned finance subsidiaries consist of IBM Credit Corporation and several non-U.S. finance subsidiaries. IBM Credit Corporation offers a wide range of financing services for IBM customers and business partners. Financing products, which are directly related to the sale of IBM products, include leases, installment payment loans and remarketer financing. The non-US. finance subsidiaries offer lease financing of selected IBM Products and in some cases finance installment receivables.

Exhibit 1   Excerpts from IBM Financial Statements for Year Ended December 31, 1990

The following schedule depicts the combined financial information for these finance subsidiaries, of which IBM Credit Corporation accounts for more than 70% of the net earnings These wholly owned subsidiaries are consolidated in the accompanying financial statements. Financing activity in countries in which the company does not have a finance subsidiary is not included.

Financial position at December 31:	1990	1989
(Dollars in millions)		
Assets:		
Cash and cash equivalents	$ 307	$ 315
Receivables—net	3,421	2,796
Net investment in capital leases	9,702	7,350
Equipment under operating leases—net	2,082	2,030
Other	499	246
Total Assets	$16,011	$12,737

	1990	1989*
(Dollars in millions)		
Liabilities and Stockholders' Equity:		
Short- term debt	$ 4,743	$ 3,482
Deferred taxes and accruals	1,355	1,214
Due to IBM and affiliates	2,641	1,648
Long-term debt	6,006	5,291
Stockholder's equity	1,266	1,102
Total Liabilities and Stockholder's Equity	$16,011	$12,737

Earnings for the years ended December 31:	1990	1989	1988
(Dollars in millions)			
Financing and other income	$1,992	$1,332	$914
Interest and other expenses	1,649	1,098	791
Provision for income taxes	112	75	26
Net earnings	$ 231	$ 159	$ 97†

*Reclassified to conform with 1990 presentation
†1988 net earnings before cumulative effect of accounting change for income taxes.

Taxes

	1990	1989	1988
(Dollars in millions)			
Earnings before income taxes:			
U.S. operations	$ 2,359	$ (851)	$1,945
Non-U.S. operations	7,844	7,496	7088
	$10,203	$6,645	$9,033
Provision for income taxes:			
U.S. operations	$ 913	$ (501)	$ 533
Non-U.S. operations	3,270	3,388	3,009
	4,183	2,887	3,542
Social security, real estate, personal property and other taxes	3,017	2,562	2,528
Total	$ 7,200	$5,449	$6,070

Exhibit 1 Excerpts from IBM Financial Statements for Year Ended December 31, 1990

The components of the provision for income taxes are as follows:

	1990	1989	1988
(Dollars in millions)			
U.S. Federal:			
Current	$ 379	$ 476	$ 79
Deferred	(44)	(1,247)	(86)
Net deferred investment tax credits	(95)	(101)	(125)
	240	(872)	(132)
Non-U.S.:			
Current	3,375	3,025	3,562
Deferred	446	824	87
	3,821	3,849	3,649
U.S. State and local:			
Current	16	107	12
Deferred	106	(197)	13
	122	(90)	25
Total provision	$4,183	$2,887	$3,542

In 1988, the company implemented Statement of Financial Accounting Standards (SFAS) 96. This standard calls for adjustment of deferred tax assets and liabilities whenever there is a change in enacted tax rates, with a corresponding adjustment being reflected in income tax expense for that period. Previous rules called for recording these assets and liabilities at the current rate, with no subsequent adjustment for tax rate changes.

The cumulative effect of adopting SFAS 96 for the periods ended prior to January 1, 1988, which amounted to a benefit of $315 million, has been included in 1988 net earnings.

Deferred income taxes reflect the impact of temporary differences between the amount of assets and liabilities recognized for financial reporting purposes and such amounts recognized for tax purposes. The principal items making up the deferred tax provision in 1990 included $573 million related to the partial turnaround of deferred tax assets arising from the 1989 U.S. restructuring charge, $343 million for sales-type leases and installment sales, $276 million for deferred software costs, and $173 million for retirement benefits. These amounts were offset by $205 million of deferred tax benefits associated with the alternative minimum tax and $197 million for depreciation. In 1989, the principal items included

$904 million related to the restructuring charge and $159 million for deferred inventory overhead, offset by $339 million for sales-type leases and installment sales and $230 million for deferred software costs. In 1988, the principal items included $283 million for sales-type leases and installment sales and $175 million for deferred software costs, offset by $182 million of deferred tax benefits associated with the alternative minimum tax.

The consolidated effective income tax rate was 41.0% in 1990, 43.4% in 1989, and 39.2% in 1988. In 1990, 1989, and 1988, the higher effective tax rate on earnings of non-U.S. operations accounted for 5.9, 12.6, and 6.6 percentage points, respectively, of the difference between the effective rate and the U.S. federal statutory rate of 34.0%.

Rental Expense and Lease Commitments Rental expense, including amounts charged to inventories and fixed assets, amounted to $1,903 million in 1990, $1,765 million in 1989 and $1,566 million in 1988.

Minimum rental commitments, in millions of dollars, under noncancellable leases for 1991 and thereafter are as follows: 1991, $1,558; 1992, $1,342; 1993, $1,161; 1994, $967; 1995, $850; and after 1995, $3,938. These leases are principally for the rental of office premises.

Other Liabilities Other liabilities consist principally of indemnity and retirement plan reserves for non-U.S. employees.

Retirement Plans The company and its subsidiaries have retirement plans covering substantially all employees. The total cost of all plans for 1990, 1989 and 1988 was $94 million, $328 million and $460 million, respectively.

Pension cost in 1990 was lower than in 1989 principally due to the growth in the expected return on plan assets exceeding the growth in annual interest and service cost. Pension cost in 1989 was lower than in 1988 principally due to changes in actuarial assumptions in the U.S. and several non-U.S. plans, partially offset by amendments to the U.S. plan.

Annual cost is determined using the Projected Unit Credit actuarial method. Prior service cost is amortized on a straight-line basis over the average remaining service period of employees expected to receive benefits. An assumption is made for modified career average plans that the average earnings base period will be updated to the years prior to retirement.

It is the company's practice to fund amounts for pensions sufficient to meet the minimum requirements set forth in applicable employee benefit and tax laws, and such additional amounts the company may determine to be appropriate from time to time. The assets of the various plans include corporate equities, government securities, corporate debt securities and income-producing real estate.

The tables below provide information on the status of the U.S. retirement plan, and selected non-U.S. plans which represent approximately 98% of the total non-U.S. accumulated benefit obligations.

The ranges of assumptions used for the non-U.S. plans reflect the different economic environments within the various countries.The expected long-term rates of return on plan assets used in the calculation of net periodic pension cost ranged from 5% to 12% in both 1990 and 1989 and from 5% to 11% in 1988. Measurement of the 1990 and 1989 projected benefit obligation was based on discount rates, ranging from 4½% to 10% and long-term rates of compensation increase ranging from 3% to 8½%.

i

283

The funded status at December 31 was as follows:

	U.S. Plan		Non-U.S. Plans	
	1990	1989	1990	1989
(Dollars in millions)				
Actuarial present value of benefit obligations:				
Vested benefit obligation	$(13,112)	$(11,642)	$ (9,022)	$ (6,892)
Accumulated benefit obligation	$(13,146)	$(11,708)	$(10,347)	$ (8,056)
Projected benefit obligation	$(17,091)	$(15,451)	$(14,338)	$(11,582)
Plan assets at fair value	22,225	22,867	12,382	11,231
Projected benefit obligation less than (in excess of) plan assets	5,134	7,416	(1,956)	(351)
Unrecognized net (gain) loss	(2,665)	(4,902)	459	(1,108)
Unrecognized prior service cost	1,323	1,092	332	241
Unrecognized net asset established at January 1, 1986	(2,747)	(2,951)	(152)	(163)
Prepaid (accrued) pension cost recognized in the statement of financial position	$1,045	$ 655	$ (1,317)	$ (1,381)

Exhibit 1   Excerpts from IBM Financial Statements for Year Ended December 31, 1990

Net periodic pension cost for the years ended December 31 included the following components:

	U.S. Plan			Non-U.S. Plans		
	1990	1989	1988	1990	1989	1988
(Dollars in millions)						
Service cost—benefits earned during the period	$ 573	$ 562	$ 579	$ 575	$ 501	$ 482
Interest cost on the projected benefit obligation	1,309	1,194	1,120	837	679	648
Return on plan assets:						
Actual	(160)	(3,950)	(2,058)	665	(1,315)	(1,003)
Deferred	(1,859)	2,214	456	(1,644)	564	340
Net amortizations	(253)	(174)	(152)	(5)	2	5
Net periodic pension cost	$ (390)	$ (154)	$ (55)	$ 428	$ 431	$ 472
Total net periodic pension cost for all non-U.S. plans				$ 484	$ 482	$ 515

EXHIBIT 2

Excerpts from Fujitsu Financial Statements for Year Ended March 31, 1991

INDEPENDENT AUDITORS' REPORT

Showa Ota & Co.
Certified Public Accountants

To the Board of Directors
FUJITSU LIMITED

We have examined the consolidated balance sheets of Fujitsu Limited and its consolidated subsidiaries (the "Group") as of March 31, 1990 and 1991, and the related consolidated statements of income, of shareholders' equity and of changes in financial position for each of the years in the five-year period ended March 31, 1991, all expressed in Japanese yen. Our examinations were made in accordance with auditing standards generally accepted in Japan and, accordingly, included such tests of the accounting records and such other auditing procedures as we considered necessary under the circumstances.

In our opinion, the aforementioned consolidated financial statements present fairly the financial position of the Group as of March 31, 1990 and 1991, and the results of its operations and changes in its financial position for each of the years in the five-year period ended March 31, 1991, in conformity with accounting principles generally accepted in Japan applied on a consistent basis.

The accompanying consolidated financial statements expressed in United States dollars have been translated into dollars solely for the convenience of the reader. We have reviewed the translation and, in our opinion, the consolidated financial statements expressed in yen have been translated into dollars on the basis set forth in Note 2 of the Notes to the Consolidated Financial Statements.

Tokyo, Japan
June 27, 1991

CONSOLIDATED FINANCIAL STATEMENTS

CONSOLIDATED BALANCE SHEETS

	Yen (millions)		U.S. dollars (thousands)
March 31	1990	1991	1991
Assets			
Current assets:			
Cash	133,899	188,235	1,335,000
Time deposits (Note 7)	128,029	222,130	1,575,390
Marketable securities (Note 4)	32,154	22,413	158,958
Receivables, trade	736,905	866,272	6,143,773
Allowance for doubtful accounts	(7,434)	(15,511)	(110,007)
Inventories (Note 5)	585,546	711,392	5,045,333
Other current assets	37,876	84,579	599,851
Total current assets	1,646,975	2,079,510	14,748,298
Investments and long-term loans:			
Unconsolidated subsidiaries and affiliates (Note 6)	298,734	327,548	2,323,036
Other (Note 4, 6, 7)	195,950	226,415	1,605,780
	494,684	553,963	3,928,816
Property, plant and equipment, at cost (Note 7):			
Land	83,490	96,351	683,340
Buildings	407,909	473,697	3,359,553
Machinery and equipment	1,309,716	1,518,021	10,766,106
Construction in progress	45,392	72,317	512,887
	1,846,507	2,160,386	15,321,886
Accumulated depreciation	(1,020,750)	(1,179,425)	(8,364,716)
	825,757	980,961	6,957,170
Intangible assets (Note 8)	3,949	122,736	870,468
	2,971,365	3,737,170	26,504,752
Liabilities and Shareholders' Equity			
Current liabilities:			
Short-term bank loans (Note 7)	368,162	674,780	4,785,674
Current portion of long-term debt (Note 7)	90,608	34,343	243,567
Payables, trade	378,093	469,307	3,328,418
Accrued expenses	184,311	228,052	1,617,390
Customers' advances	15,720	26,896	190,752
Accrued income taxes	68,407	66,915	474,575
Employees' savings deposits	66,855	68,194	483,645
Other current liabilities	111,254	117,463	833,071
Total current liabilities	1,283,409	1,685,950	11,957,092

Exhibit 2   Excerpts from Fujitsu Financial Statements for Year Ended March 31, 1991

	Yen (millions)		U.S. dollars (thousands)
March 31	1990	1991	1991
Long-term liabilities:			
Long-term debt (Note 7)	333,481	577,794	4,097,830
Accrued severance indemnities	51,963	68,491	485,752
Provision for loss on repurchase of computers	126,857	127,597	904,943
Other long-term liabilities	328	3,818	27,078
	512,629	777,700	5,515,603
Minority interests in consolidated subsidiaries	90,199	114,221	810,078
Shareholders' equity:			
Common stock:			
Authorized—5,000,000,000 shares			
Issued (¥50 par value)			
1990—1,802,358,518 shares	216,193		
1991—1,812,101,715 shares		221,415	1,570,319
Capital surplus	386,787	392,790	2,785,745
Legal reserve	15,658	17,381	123,270
Retained earnings	466,490	527,713	3,742,645
Total shareholders' equity	1,085,128	1,159,299	8,221,979
	2,971,365	3,737,170	26,504,752

The accompanying Notes to the Consolidated Financial Statements are an integral part of these statements.

Exhibit 2   Excerpts from Fujitsu Financial Statements for Year Ended March 31, 1991

CONSOLIDATED STATEMENTS OF INCOME

Years ended March 31	Yen (millions)					U.S. dollars (thousands)
	1987	1988	1989	1990	1991	1991
Net sales	1,789,417	2,046,802	2,387,442	2,549,773	2,971,462	21,074,199
Operating costs and expenses:						
Cost of goods sold	1,232,722	1,339,183	1,527,908	1,578,343	1,820,554	12,911,731
Selling, general and administrative expenses	494,526	588,098	673,685	776,086	936,713	6,643,355
	1,727,248	1,927,281	2,201,593	2,354,429	2,757,267	19,555,086
Operating Income	62,169	119,521	185,849	195,344	214,195	1,519,113
Other (income)/ expenses:						
Interest charges	31,502	28,680	32,176	39,044	66,159	469,213
Interest received	(7,771)	(8,923)	(14,185)	(15,752)	(25,541)	(181,142)
Dividends received	(1,929)	(1,557)	(1,665)	(2,023)	(2,029)	(14,390)
Other, net (Note 11)	(7,645)	(4,727)	14,371	3,859	22,033	156,262
	14,157	13,473	30,697	25,128	60,622	429,943
Income before income taxes	48,012	106,048	155,152	170,216	153,573	1,089,170
Income taxes (Note 12)	30,522	73,407	97,462	99,102	91,204	646,837
	17,490	32,641	57,690	71,114	62,369	442,333
Equity in income of unconsolidated subsidiaries and affiliates	5,841	12,860	18,709	21,216	23,722	168,241
	23,331	45,501	76,399	92,330	86,091	610,574
Minority interests in income of consolidated subsidiaries	1,722	3,386	6,451	5,572	3,418	24,241
Net income	21,609	42,115	69,948	86,758	82,673	586,333
	Yen					U.S. dollars
Net income per share:						
Primary	13.8	25.4	40.1	48.6	45.7	0.324
Fully diluted	13.4	23.5	36.8	45.4	42.2	0.299
Cash dividends per share	8.0	8.0	9.0	9.0	10.0	0.071

The accompanying Notes to the Consolidated Financial Statements are an integral part of these statements.

i

288

CONSOLIDATED STATEMENTS OF CHANGES IN FINANCIAL POSITION

Years ended March 31	Yen (millions)					U.S. dollars (thousands)
	1987	1988	1989	1990	1991	1991
Source of working capital:						
Net income for the year	21,609	42,115	69,948	86,758	82,673	586,333
Charges/(credits) to income not affecting working capital:						
Depreciation	140,559	136,762	160,635	194,722	225,073	1,596,262
Provision for severance indemnities	6,990	8,694	9,125	11,201	22,092	156,681
Provision for loss on repurchase of computers	75,506	70,095	74,156	54,929	60,651	430,149
Minority interests in net income of consolidated subsidiaries	1,722	3,386	6,451	5,572	3,418	24,241
Equity in income of unconsolidated subsidiaries and affiliates	(5,841)	(12,860)	(18,709)	(21,216)	(23,722)	(168,241)
Other	4,018	11,673	7,054	13,382	29,638	210,199
Total provided by operations	244,563	259,865	308,660	345,348	399,823	2,835,624
Proceeds from long-term debt	45,094	82,149	91,375	124,368	288,757	2,047,922
Increase in common stock and capital surplus	39,120	127,057	81,004	57,611	11,225	79,610
Equity in income of unconsolidated subsidiaries and affiliates	5,841	12,860	18,709	21,216	23,722	168,241
Increase/(decrease) in retained earnings resulting from changes of interest in consolidated subsidiaries and from adopting the equity accounting method	(971)	(4,977)	(4,489)	(3,462)	(115)	(816)
Decrease in investments in and long-term loans to unconsolidated subsidiaries and affiliates	749	6,883	3,629	6,820	2,155	15,284
Decrease of property, plant and equipment	7,627	6,473	7,996	9,388	13,006	92,241
Increase/(decrease) resulting from consolidation of additional subsidiaries	(23)	868	4,187	—	(1,953)	(13,851)
Total source of working capital	342,000	491,178	511,071	561,289	736,620	5,224,255

(continued)

CONSOLIDATED STATEMENTS OF CHANGES IN FINANCIAL POSITION (continued)

Years ended March 31	Yen (millions)					U.S. dollars (thousands)
	1987	1988	1989	1990	1991	1991
Application of working capital:						
Acquisition of property, plant and equipment	141,879	190,843	283,944	331,057	397,521	2,819,298
Reduction of long-term debt	29,508	42,508	53,060	63,942	36,577	259,411
Conversion of convertible bonds into common stock	33,977	75,683	23,538	43,012	7,867	55,794
Increase in investments in and long-term loans to unconsolidated subsidiaries and affiliates	9,036	21,201	54,063	32,030	30,969	219,638
Payment of severance indemnities	3,503	3,557	4,503	4,700	5,564	39,461
Reversal of provision for loss on repurchase of computers	75,866	71,667	53,326	51,706	59,911	424,901
Cash dividends	12,022	12,973	13,852	15,975	17,147	121,610
Other, net	7,539	17,922	48,161	12,781	151,070	1,071,419
Total application of working capital	313,330	436,354	534,447	555,203	706,626	5,011,532
Increase/(decrease) in working capital	28,670	54,824	(23,376)	6,086	29,994	212,723
Increase/(decrease) in working capital elements:						
Cash and time deposits	33,409	64,083	61,674	(43,238)	148,437	1,052,745
Marketable securities	7,464	67,539	(65,183)	7,935	(9,741)	(69,085)
Receivables, trade	45,344	39,885	88,780	137,656	121,290	860,213
Inventories	18,615	54,151	15,971	106,706	125,846	892,525
Other current assets	9,502	7,291	1,691	(20,141)	46,703	331,227
Short-term bank loans and current portion of long-term debt	(46,006)	(26,583)	(40,933)	(72,159)	(250,353)	(1,775,553)
Payables, trade	(23,889)	(59,995)	(31,136)	(39,972)	(91,214)	(646,908)
Accrued expenses	(2,585)	(24,528)	(26,667)	(29,532)	(43,741)	(310,220)
Customers' advances	958	(213)	3,757	(5,785)	(11,176)	(79,262)
Accrued income taxes	(11,394)	(38,272)	(1,234)	(4,871)	(1,491)	(10,574)
Employees' savings deposits	(8,063)	(7,561)	(7,690)	(8,700)	(1,339)	(9,497)
Other current liabilities	5,315	(20,973)	(22,406)	(21,813)	(6,209)	(44,036)
Increase/(decrease) in working capital	28,670	54,824	(23,376)	6,086	29,994	212,723

The accompanying Notes to the Consolidated Financial Statements are an integral part of these statements.

NOTES TO THE CONSOLIDATED FINANCIAL STATEMENTS

1. Significant accounting policies

(a) Basis of presenting consolidated financial statements

The accompanying consolidated financial statements of Fujitsu Limited and its consolidated subsidiaries (the "Group") have been prepared in accordance with accounting principles and practices generally accepted in Japan, and rules of the Japanese Securities Exchange Act. Accounting principles and practices adopted by the foreign subsidiaries in the respective countries basically conform to those adopted by the Company in Japan. Further, certain items have been reclassified for the convenience of the reader outside Japan.

Accounting principles and practices adopted by the Group are being accommodated to International Accounting Standards ("IAS"). Where certain differences exist between IAS and accounting practices which the Group has adopted are set out in the relevant notes on accounting policies below.

The statements of changes in financial position for the five years ended March 31, 1991 have been prepared for the purpose of inclusion in this annual report in accordance with the method recommended by the Japanese Institute of Certified Public Accountants.

(b) Principles of consolidation

The consolidated financial statements include the accounts of the Company and those of its consolidated subsidiaries, whether directly or indirectly controlled. All inter-company accounts and transactions have been eliminated on consolidation.

Investments in major affiliates have been stated at cost plus equity in undistributed earnings and reserves. Net consolidated income includes the Company's equity in the current net earnings (losses) of such companies, after elimination of unrealized inter-company profits. Investments in the remaining unconsolidated subsidiaries and affiliates, which are not material, are carried at cost.

(c) Marketable securities

Marketable securities (current and non-current) are stated at the lower of cost or market value, cost being determined by the moving average method.

(d) Allowance for doubtful accounts

The allowance for doubtful accounts is provided at an estimated amount of probable debt accounts that is sufficient to cover the possible losses.

(e) Inventories

Finished goods are stated at cost not in excess of the market. Cost is determined by the actual cost method, the moving average method and the first-in, first-out method ("FIFO").

Work in progress is stated at actual cost and cost determined by FIFO.

Raw materials are stated at cost not in excess of the market. Cost is determined by the moving average method, the most recent purchase price method and FIFO.

(f) Property, plant and equipment, and depreciation

Property, plant and equipment, including renewals and additions, are carried at cost. When retired or otherwise disposed of, the cost and related depreciation are cleared from the respective accounts and the net difference, less any amounts realized on disposal, is reflected in earnings.

Depreciation is computed by the declining balance method at rates based on estimated useful lives of the assets, according to general class, type of construction and use.

Maintenance and repairs, including minor renewals and improvements, are charged to income as incurred.

(g) Pension plan and accrued severance indemnities

Employees who terminated their service with the Group are generally entitled to pension payments or lump-sum severance indemnities based on current basic rate of pay and length of service.

The Group in Japan has a contributory pension plan with insurance companies and trust banks to supplement the public welfare pension plan and entitles employees upon retirement to receive either a lump-sum payment or regular payments for life or a combination of both.

Most foreign subsidiaries have defined benefit pension plans covering substantially all of their employees.

i

291

The cost of benefit for pension payment and lump-sum severance indemnities is currently funded or accrued.

The recorded liability for employee's severance indemnities plus the pension funds were sufficient to state the Group's maximum liability for employee service to the balance sheet date.

(h)   Provision for loss on repurchase of computers

A certain proportion of the computers manufactured by the Group is sold to Japan Electronic Computer Company Limited ("JECC") and other leasing companies and financial institutions for leasing to ultimate users under contracts which provide for the Group to repurchase the computers if they are returned by the users after being used for a certain period. Based on past experience, an estimated amount for loss which arises on repurchase is provided at the point of sales and is charged to income.

(i)   Revenue recognition

Sales of telecommunication and computer systems are mainly recognized at the time of acceptance by the customers, while sales of personal equipment and electronic devices are taken when the products are shipped.

(j)   Income taxes

Whereas IAS No. 12 requires the tax effect accounting method, income taxes have been accrued on the basis of actual income tax liabilities and no provision is made for deferred taxes arising from timing differences between financial and tax reporting, with the exception of certain foreign subsidiaries.

In consolidating such foreign subsidiaries as recognize deferred taxes, no adjustment is made in the accompanying consolidated financial statements.

(k)   Translation of foreign currency accounts

Current receivables and payables denominated in foreign currencies are translated into Japanese yen at exchange rates in effect at the respective balance sheet dates. Non-current receivables and payables denominated in foreign currencies are translated into Japanese yen at historical exchange rates.

The accounts of foreign subsidiaries are translated into Japanese yen at applicable fiscal year-end rates. Income and expenses are translated at the average rate during the year.

(l)   Appropriation of retained earnings

Cash dividends, transfers to legal reserve and bonuses to directors and statutory auditors are recorded in the financial year during which a proposed appropriation of retained earnings is approved by the Board of Directors and/or shareholders.

(m) Legal reserve

The Japanese Commercial Code provides that an amount not less than 10 per cent of cash dividends paid be appropriated as a legal reserve until such reserve equals 25 per cent of stated capital. The legal reserve may be used to reduce a deficit or may be transferred to stated capital, but is not available for distribution as dividends.

(n)   Income per share

Net income per share is based on the weighted average number of shares of common stock outstanding during the respective years. Fully diluted net income per share is computed assuming that all convertible bonds converted during the year or outstanding at the end of the year were converted, and warrants exercised during the year or outstanding at the end of the year were exercised at the beginning of the year or from the time they were issued.

2. U.S. dollar amounts

The Company and its domestic consolidated subsidiaries maintain the account records in yen. The U.S. dollar amounts included in the accompanying financial statements and notes thereto represent the arithmetic results of translating yen into dollars at a rate of ¥141 to $1, the approximate rate of exchange on March 29, 1991. The inclusion of such dollar amounts is solely for the convenience of the reader and is not intended to imply that the assets and liabilities which originated in yen have been or could readily be converted, realized or settled in dollars at ¥141 to $1 or at any other rate.

3. Acquisition

In November 1990, the Company acquired an 80% share of STC International Computers Limited, the top of U.K. information systems suppliers, for Stg £700 million in cash. At the same time, STC International Computers Limited was renamed ICL PLC ("ICL"). The acquisition was accounted for as a purchase. Accordingly, ICL's results of the operations were included in the accompanying consolidated financial statements from the date of acquisition. The excess of the purchase price over the fair value of net assets acquired, as recognized as goodwill, is being amortized on a straight-line basis over 20 years.

4. Marketable securities

The current and noncurrent portfolios of marketable securities at March 31, 1990 and 1991 which were included in marketable securities and in investments and long-term loans—other, were as follows:

	Yen (millions)		U.S. dollars (thousands)
	1990	1991	1991
Current:			
Book value	9,183	9,723	68,957
Market value	9,276	9,688	68,709
Gross unrealized gains	93	(35)	(248)
Noncurrent:			
Book value	56,069	66,446	471,248
Market value	289,649	282,502	2,003,560
Gross unrealized gains	233,580	216,056	1,532,312

5. Inventories

Inventories at March 31, 1990 and 1991 consisted of the following:

	Yen (millions)		U.S. dollars (thousands)
	1990	1991	1991
Finished goods	256,618	309,720	2,196,596
Work in progress	262,501	309,563	2,195,482
Raw materials	66,427	92,109	653,255
	585,546	711,392	5,045,333

6. Investments in unconsolidated subsidiaries and affiliates

Summarized financial information in respect of unconsolidated subsidiaries and affiliates which are accounted for on an equity basis is shown below for the two years ended March 31, 1991:

	Yen (millions)		U.S. dollars (thousands)
	1990	1991	1991
Current assets	772,756	772,267	5,477,071
Other assets, including property, plant and equipment	527,051	551,170	3,909,007
	1,299,807	1,323,437	9,386,078
Current liabilities	459,354	429,730	3,047,731
Long-term liabilities	183,837	173,975	1,233,865
Net assets	656,616	719,732	5,404,482
Net sales	878,371	986,747	6,998,206
Net income	64,097	72,248	512,397

Of unconsolidated subsidiaries and affiliates which are accounted for on an equity basis, the stocks of six companies have quoted on the market values at March 31, 1990 and 1991, respectively, as follows:

	Yen (millions)		U.S. dollars (thousands)
	1990	1991	1991
Book value	273,159	301,920	2,141,277
Market value	932,413	713,697	5,061,681

Included in investments and long-term loans—other at March 31, 1990 and 199,1 respectively, was an amount of ¥19,373 million ($137 million) representing the Company's 29.49 per cent investment in JECC. The Company does not regard JECC as an affiliate as it is unable to exercise significant influence over JECC's affairs. JECC's principal business is the leasing of computers and peripheral computer equipment which it purchases from its seven shareholders. At March 31, 1991 JECC's issued share capital was ¥65,700 million ($466 million) and its net sales for the year then ended amounted to ¥265,089 million ($1,880 million).

7. Short-term bank loans and long-term debt

Short-term bank loans at March 31, 1990 and 1991 consisted of:

	Yen (millions)		U.S. dollars (thousands)
	1990	1991	1991
Loans, principally from banks, with interest rates ranging from 5.75 per cent, to 18.25 per cent:			
Secured	5,941	2,620	18,582
Unsecured	362,221	672,160	4,767,092
	368,162	674,780	4,785,674

8. Intangible assets

As of March 31, 1991 intangible assets principally consisted of goodwill. The balance amount of goodwill at March 31, 1991 was ¥118,633 million ($841 million) and ¥6,531 million ($46 million) was charged in income. Goodwill is being amortized on a straight-line basis over periods not exceeding 20 years.

Other intangible assets at March 31, 1990 and 1991 were payments to utility companies, public corporations and municipal authorities to secure services. These tangible assets are mainly amortized over five years on a straight-line basis.

9. Contingent liabilities

Contingent liabilities at March 31, 1991 in respect of notes discounted in the ordinary course of business and loans guaranteed amounted to ¥179 million ($1 million) and ¥67,401 million ($478 million), respectively. Loans guaranteed included the guarantee for bank loans of JECC, the principal leasing company to which the Group sells its computers (see Note 1), of ¥2,569 million ($18 million).

10. Supplementary balance sheets information

The balances with unconsolidated subsidiaries and affiliates were as follows:

	Yen (millions)		U.S. dollars (thousands)
	1990	1991	1991
Receivables, trade	73,615	69,801	495,043
Payables, trade	24,032	28,375	201,241

11. Supplementary income statement information

	Yen (millions)					U.S. dollars (thousands)
	1987	1988	1989	1990	1991	1991
Depreciation	140,559	136,762	160,635	194,722	225,073	1,596,262
Provisions for employees' severance indemnities and pension costs	15,084	17,330	19,246	23,841	36,344	257,759
Other (income)/expenses—other, net for the five years ended March 31, 1991 consisted of the following:						
Net foreign exchange losses/(gains)	2,250	3,982	4,710	(10,350)	5,521	39,156
Net loss on disposal of fixed assets	1,542	1,920	4,246	4,178	4,238	30,057
Profit on sale of shares in connection with the listing of subsidiaries	(5,548)	(8,469)	—	—	(1,971)	(13,979)
Expenses for issue and offering of securities	401	2,047	1,592	2,615	3,601	25,539
Other, net	(6,290)	(4,207)	3,823	7,416	10,644	75,489
	(7,645)	(4,727)	14,371	3,859	22,033	156,262

Other, net in the year ended March 31, 1991 comprised the amortization of goodwill and the loss arising from the revision of the Group's regulations of retirement allowance, whose amounts were ¥6,531 million and ¥8,271 million, respectively.

12. Income taxes

The effective income tax rates on income before income taxes in the accompanying consolidated financial statements differ from the normal statutory rate in Japan. The principal reasons for such differences are (a) the accounting policy of not providing for deferred income taxes arising from timing differences between financial and tax reporting; and (b) certain expenses which are not deductible for income tax purposes.

i

295

On April 17, 1985, Bill Ahern sat in his office and contemplated a difficult judgment he had to make in the next two days. Two weeks before, Bill had been asked to be an arbitrator in a dispute between the Owner-Player Committee (OPC, the representatives of the owners of the 26 major league baseball teams in collective bargaining negotiations) and the Professional Baseball Players Association (PBPA, the players' union).

The issue Ahern had to resolve was the profitability of the major league baseball teams. The players felt they should share in the teams' profits; the owners maintained, however, that most of the teams were actually losing money each year, and they produced financial statements to support that position. The players, who had examined the owners' statements, countered that the owners were hiding profits through a number of accounting tricks and that the statements did not accurately reflect the economic reality. Ahern's decision on the profitability issue was important because it would affect the on-going contract negotiations, particularly in the areas of minimum salaries and team contributions to the players' pension fund.

On April 9, Ahern met with the OPC and the representatives of the PBPA. They explained they wanted him to focus on the finances of the Kansas City Zephyrs Baseball Club, Inc. This club was selected for review because both sides agreed its operations were representative, yet it was a relatively clean and simple example to study: the baseball club entity was not owned by another corporation, and it did not own the stadium the team played in. Furthermore, no private financial data would have to be revealed because the corporation was publicly owned. Ahern's task was to review the Zephyrs' financial statements, hear the owners' and players' arguments, and then reach a decision as to the profitability of the team by Friday, April 19.

MAJOR LEAGUE BASEBALL

Major league baseball in the United States was comprised of a number of components bound together by sets of agreements and contractual relationships. At the heart of major

Research Assistant Joseph P. Mulloy prepared this case under the supervision of Professors Kenneth A. Merchant and Krishna G. Palepu as the basis for class discussion rather than to illustrate either effective or ineffective handling of an administrative situation. The case is based on publicly available information. Copyright © 1987 by the President and Fellows of Harvard College. Harvard Business School case 9-187-088.

league baseball were the 26 major league teams. Each team operated as an independent economic unit in such matters as contracting for players, promoting games and selling tickets, arranging for the use of a stadium and other needed facilities and services, and negotiating local broadcasting of games. The teams joined together to establish common rules and playing schedules, and to stage championship games.

The business of most teams was limited exclusively to their major league activities. Very few integrated vertically by owning their own stadium or minor league teams. Most teams were organized as partnerships or privately held corporations, although a few were subunits of larger corporations. While baseball was often thought of as a big business, the individual teams were relatively small. For most of them, annual revenues were between $20 million and $30 million.

Each team maintained an active roster of 24 players during the playing season, plus 16 minor league players "on option," who might see major league action during the season. This made a total of 40 players on major league contracts for each team at any one time. Each team played a schedule of 162 games during the season, 81 at home and 81 away.

Collectively, the team owners established most of the regulations that governed the industry. The covenant that bound them was the Major League Agreement (MLA), to which was attached the Major League Rules. The rules detailed all the procedures the clubs agreed on, including the rules for signing, trading, and dealing with players.

Under the MLA, the owners elected a commissioner of baseball for a seven-year term. The commissioner acted as a spokesperson for the industry, resolved disputes among the clubs and the other baseball entities, policed the industry, and enforced the rules. The commissioner had broad powers to protect the best interests of the game. The commissioner also administered the Major Leagues Central Fund, under which he negotiated and received the revenues from national broadcast contracts for major league games. About one-half of the fund's revenues were passed on directly to the teams in approximately equal shares.

Within the overall structure of major league baseball, the 26 teams were organized into two leagues each with its own president and administration. The American League had 14 teams and the National League had 12 teams, of which one was the Kansas City Zephyrs. Each league controlled the allocation and movement of its respective franchises. In addition to authorizing franchises, the leagues developed the schedule of games, contracted for umpires, and performed other administrative tasks. The leagues were financed through a small percentage share of club ticket revenues and receipts from the World Series and pennant championship games.

In addition to the major league teams, U.S. baseball included about 150 minor league teams located throughout the United States, Canada, and Mexico. Minor league teams served a dual function: they were entertainment entities in their own right, and they were training grounds for major league players. Through Player Development Contracts, the major league teams agreed to pay a certain portion of their affiliated minor league teams' operating expenses and player salaries.

MEETING WITH THE ZEPHYRS' OWNERS

Bill Ahern spent Tuesday reviewing the history of major league baseball and the relationships among the various entities that make up the major leagues. Then he met with the Zephyrs owners' representatives on Wednesday.

The owners' representatives gave Ahern a short history of the team and presented him with the team's financial statements for the years 1983 and 1984 (shown in Exhibits 1 and 2). The current owner was a corporation with five major shareholders, which bought the team on November 1, 1982, for $24 million. The Zephyrs did not own any of their minor league teams or their stadium, but two of the Zephyrs' owners were part owners of the private corporation that owned the baseball stadium.

Ahern studied the financial statements for a short time, and then he met with Keith Strong, the owners' lawyer. The conversation can be summarized by the following exchange:

Bill: I would like to know more about the controversial items in your financial statements. First, could you please explain your players' salaries expense entries?

Keith: Sure. Here is a list of our roster players and what we paid them last year [see Exhibit 3]. The number we show on our 1984 income statement is the total expense of $10,097,000. Most of the expense represents cash outflows in 1984. The only exception is shown in the last column of this exhibit. For our highest paid players, we have agreed to defer a portion of their salary for 10 years. That helps save them taxes and provides them with some income after their playing days are over.

Bill: What is the nonroster guaranteed contract expense?

Keith: That is also player salary expense, but we break it out separately because the salaries are paid to players who are no longer on our active roster. The salaries are amounts we owe to players whom we released who had long-term guaranteed contracts. The amount of $750,000 represents the amount we still owe at the end of 1984 to two players [shown in Figure A on the next page]. Joe Portocararo, one of our veteran pitchers, signed a four-year guaranteed contract last year, but before the season started he suffered a serious injury, and Joe and the team jointly decided it was best he retire. We released U. R. Wilson in spring training, hoping that another team would pick him up and pay his salary, but none did.

We still owe these players the amounts in their contracts. We decided to expense the whole amount in 1984 because they are not active players; they are not serving to bring in our current revenues. We felt it was more meaningful and conservative to recognize these losses now, as they result from the effects of past decisions that did not turn out well.

Bill: Okay. Let's move on to roster depreciation expense.

Keith: When the team was bought in 1982, $12 million—50 percent of the purchase price—was designated as the value of the player roster at that time. This amount was capitalized and is being amortized over six years.

Figure A Calculation of Nonroster Guaranteed Contract Expense ($000)

	Amounts Owed			
Player	1984	1985	1986	Total
Joe Portocararo	$300.0	$350.0	$400.0	$1,050.0
U. R. Wilson	200.0			200.0
				$1,250.0

Bill: Why 50 percent?

Keith: That is the maximum percentage that the Internal Revenue Code will allow when purchasing a sports team.

Bill: I see. Is there anything else in the statements that the players dispute?

Keith: No, I don't think so. The rest of our accounting is very straightforward. Most of our revenues and expenses result directly from a cash inflow or outflow.

Bill: Well, that answers all my questions. Thank you.

Keith: I have just one more thing to say concerning baseball finances in general. People seem to think that we generate huge profits since we have a relative monopoly, but it should be obvious that the professional baseball leagues do not exist in order to carry out traditional cartel functions. The rules and regulations governing the clubs comprising the league are essential to the creation of the league as an entity and have virtually nothing to do with pricing policies of the individual clubs. The objective of the cooperative agreements is not to constrain the economic competition among them, but rather to create the league as a joint venture that produces baseball during a season of play. Without such rules of conduct, leagues would not exist.

When this meeting was completed, Bill Ahern felt he understood the owners' accounting methods well enough.

MEETING WITH THE PLAYERS

The following Monday, Ahern met with the PBPA representatives and their lawyer, Paul Hanrahan. They presented Ahern with income statements for the years 1983 and 1984 as they thought they should be drawn up (Exhibit 4). As Ahern studied them, he found the players' version of the financial statements showed profits before tax of $2.9 million for 1983 and $3.0 million for 1984 as compared to the losses of $2.4 million and $2.6 million on the owners' statements.

Ahern's conversation with Paul Hanrahan went approximately as follows:

Bill: The income statements you have given me are very similar to those of the owners except for a few items.

Paul: That's true—most of the expenses are straightforward. There are only a few areas we dispute, but these areas can have a significant impact on the overall profitability of the team. We feel that the owners have used three techniques to "hide" profits: (1) roster depreciation, (2) overstated player salary expense, and (3) related-party transactions.

Bill: Let's start with roster depreciation. Why have you deleted it?

Paul: We feel it gives numbers that aren't meaningful. The depreciation expense arises only when a team is sold, so you can have two identical teams that will show dramatically different results if one had been sold and the other had not. We also don't think the depreciation is real because most of the players actually improve their skills with experience, so if anything, there should be an increase in roster value over time, not a reduction as the depreciation would lead you to believe.

Bill: Okay. I understand your reasoning. I'll have to think about that. Let's move on to the next issue.

Paul: That's player salary expense. We think the owners overstate player expense in several ways. One is that they expense the signing bonuses in the year they're paid. We feel the bonuses are just a part of the compensation package, and that for accounting purposes, the bonuses should be spread over the term of the player's contract.

We gathered information on the bonuses paid in the last four years and the contract terms [Exhibit 5]. Then we adjusted the owners' income statements by removing the bonuses from the current roster salary expense and by adding an "amortization of bonuses" line. The net effect of this one adjustment on 1984, for example, was an increase in income of $373,000.[1]

Bill: But the owners have really paid out all the bonuses in cash, and there is no guarantee that the players will complete their contracts.

Paul: That's partly true. Some players get hurt and are unable to compete effectively. But the number of players who do not complete their contracts is very small, and we think it is more meaningful to assume that they will continue to play over the term of their contract.

Bill: Okay. What's next?

Paul: A second adjustment we made to the players' salary line was to back out the deferred portion of the total compensation. Many of the players, particularly those who are higher paid, receive only about 80 percent of their salaries in any given year. They receive the rest ten years later [see Exhibit 3]. We feel that since the team is paying this money over a long period of time, it is misleading to include the whole amount as a current expense. This adjustment increased 1984 income for the Zephyrs by $1,521,000. No salary expense deferred from prior years was added back in because that form of contract is a relatively recent phenomenon.

K

301

---

1. *$1,320,000 less $947,000.*

Bill: I've looked at some of the contracts, and it says very clearly that the player is to receive, say, $500,000, of which $100,000 is deferred to the year 1984. Doesn't that indicate that the salary expense is $500,000?

Paul: No. The team has paid only $400,000 in cash.

Bill: Doesn't the team actually set money aside to cover the future obligation?

Paul: Some teams do, and in such cases, I think we would agree that it is appropriate to recognize that amount as a current expense. But the Zephyrs don't set any money aside.

Bill: Okay. You made a third adjustment to the players' salaries.

Paul: Yes, we think the salaries due to players who are no longer on the roster should be recognized when the cash is paid out, not when the players leave the roster. Unless that is done, the income numbers will vary wildly depending on when these players are released and how large their contracts are. Furthermore, it is quite possible that these players' contracts will be picked up by another team, and the Zephyrs would then have to turn around and recognize a large gain because the liability it has set up would no longer be payable.

Bill: Okay. Let's go to the last area: related-party transactions. You have listed Stadium Operations at about 80 percent of what the owners charged. Why is that?

Paul: You probably know that two of the Zephyrs' owners are also involved with the stadium corporation. But what you probably don't know is that they are the sole owners of that stadium company. We think that the stadium rent is set to overcharge the team and help show a loss for the baseball operations.

Bill: How did you get your numbers?

Paul: This wasn't easy, but we looked at what other teams pay for their stadiums. Every contract is slightly different, but we are sure that two of the five shareholders in the team are earning a nice gain on the stadium-pricing agreement.

Just for your own edification, this is not the only type of related-party transaction where the owners can move profits around. A few of the teams are owned by broadcasting organizations, and as a result, they report no local broadcasting revenues. Their individual losses are consolidated into the overall major league position, thus the overall loss is overstated. I know it's hard to do, but an objective look must be taken at all these related-party transactions if baseball's true position is to be fairly stated.

The overall effect of all these adjustments we have made to the Zephyrs' income statements changes losses to profits. In 1984, the change is from a loss of $1.7 million to a profit of $1.4 million. In the labor negotiations, the owners keep claiming that they're losing money and can't afford the contract terms we feel are fair. We just don't think that's true. They are "losing money" only because they have selected accounting methods to hide their profits.

Bill: Well, you've given me a lot to think about. There are a lot of good arguments on both sides. Thank you for your time. I'll have my answer for you soon.

BILL'S DECISION

By Wednesday, April 17, Bill was quite confused. To clarify the areas of disagreement, he prepared the summaries shown in Exhibit 6; but whereas the sets of numbers were clear, the answers to the conflicts were not. Bill had expected this arbitration to be rather straightforward, but instead he was mired in difficult issues involving the accounting unit, depreciation, amortization of intangibles, and related-party transactions. Now he was faced with a tight deadline, and it was not at all obvious to him how to define "good accounting methods" for the Zephyrs Baseball Club.

QUESTIONS

1. How should Bill Ahern resolve the accounting conflict between the owners and players?
2. How much did the Kansas City Zephyrs Baseball Club earn in 1983 and 1984?

EXHIBIT 1
Kansas City Zephyrs Baseball Club, Inc.—Income Statements, Owners' Figures (000s omitted)

	Year Ending October 31	
	1983	1984
Operating Revenues:		
Game Receipts	$16,526.0	$18,620.0
National Television	2,360.8	2,730.8
Local Broadcasting	3,147.9	3,575.1
Concessions	2,886.3	3,294.3
Parking	525.1	562.0
Other	786.9	843.9
Total Revenues	$26,233.0	$29,626.1
Operating Expenses:		
Spring Training	$ 545.0	$ 594.0
Team Operating Expenses:		
Players' Salaries:		
Current Roster	9,111.0	10,097.0
Nonroster Guaranteed Contract Expense	0.0	1,250.0
Coaches' Salaries	756.9	825.7
Other Salaries	239.0	260.8
Miscellaneous	2,655.9	2,897.3
Player Development	2,996.0	3,269.0
Team Replacement:		
Roster Depreciation	2,000.0	2,000.0
Scouting	672.8	734.0
Stadium Operations	4,086.0	4,457.0
Ticketing and Marketing	1,907.0	2,080.0
General and Administrative	3,541.0	3,663.0
Total Operating Expense	$28,510.6	$32,127.8
Income from Operations	(2,277.6)	(2,501.7)
Other Income (Expense)	(96.0)	(101.0)
Income Before Taxes	(2,373.6)	(2,602.7)
Federal Income Tax Benefit	855.9	944.2
Net Income (Loss)	$(1,517.7)	$(1,658.5)

EXHIBIT 2
Kansas City Zephyrs Baseball Club, Inc.—Balance Sheets, Owners' Figures (000s omitted)

	Year Ending October 31	
	1983	1984
ASSETS		
Current Assets:		
Cash	$ 488.0	$ 561.0
Marketable Securities	6,738.0	7,786.1
Accounts Receivable	598.0	681.2
Notes Receivable	256.0	234.0
Total Current Assets	8,080.0	9,262.3
Property, Plant & Equipment	1,601.0	1,892.0
Less Accumulated Depreciation	(359.0)	(511.0)
Net PP&E	1,242.0	1,381.0
Initial Roster	12,000.0	12,000.0
Less Accumulated Depreciation	(4,000.0)	(6,000.0)
Net Initial Roster	8,000.0	6,000.0
Other Assets	2,143.0	4,123.2
Franchise	6,500.0	6,500.0
Total Assets	$25,965.0	$27,266.5
LIABILITIES AND SHAREHOLDERS' EQUITY		
Current Liabilities:		
Accounts Payable	$ 909.2	$1,020.2
Accrued Expenses	1,207.5	1,461.8
Total Current Liabilities	2,116.7	2,482.0
Long-Term Debt	7,000.0	8,073.7
Other Long-Term Liabilities	2,443.3	3,964.3
Shareholders' Equity:		
Common Stock, par value $1 per share, 500,000 shares issued	500.0	500.0
Additional Paid-In Capital	10,000.0	10,000.0
Retained Earnings	3,905.0	2,246.5
Total Liabilities and Shareholders' Equity	$25,965.0	$27,266.5

Exhibit 3 Detailed Players' Salary Summary—1984

EXHIBIT 3

Detailed Players' Salary Summary—1984 (000s omitted)

Roster Player	Signing Bonus	Base Salary	Performance and Attendance Bonuses	Total Compensation	Portion of 1984 Salary Deferred Until 1994
Bill Hogan	$ 500.0	$ 850.0	$ 250.0	$ 1,600.0	$ 250.0
Corby Megorden	300.0	600.0	225.0	1,125.0	200.0
Manuel Vasquez	200.0	500.0	100.0	800.0	150.0
Jim Showalter		600.0	100.0	700.0	200.0
Scott Van Buskirk	150.0	400.0	100.0	650.0	150.0
Jerry Hyde	150.0	400.0	50.0	600.0	150.0
Dave Schafer		355.0	50.0	405.0	130.0
Leslie Yamshita		300.0	37.5	337.5	100.0
Earl McLain		220.0	37.5	257.5	50.0
Shannon Saunders		210.0	37.5	247.5	50.0
Gary Blazin		190.0	37.5	227.5	40.0
Rich Hayes		160.0	25.0	185.0	30.0
Sam Willett		140.0	17.5	157.5	21.0
Chuck Wright	20.0	115.0	12.5	147.5	
Jim Urquart		115.0	12.5	127.5	
Bill Schutt		115.0	12.5	127.5	
Mike Hegarty		115.0	12.5	127.5	
Bruce Selby		110.0	12.5	122.5	
Dave Kolk		110.0	12.5	122.5	
Bill Kelly		110.0	12.5	122.5	
Dave Carr		110.0	12.0	122.0	
Tom O'Conner		110.0	5.0	115.0	
Jake Luhan		110.0		110.0	
Ray Woolrich		100.0		100.0	
John Porter		100.0		100.0	
Dusty Rhodes		100.0		100.0	
Lynn Novinger		100.0		100.0	
Bill Williams		95.0		95.0	
Jim Sedor		95.0		95.0	
Ralph Young		95.0		95.0	
Ed Marino		95.0		95.0	
Ray Spicer		90.0		90.0	
Eric Womble		90.0		90.0	
Ron Gorena		90.0		90.0	
Gene Johnston		90.0		90.0	
Jack Zollinger		90.0		90.0	
Ken Karr		90.0		90.0	
Tom Crowley		80.0		80.0	
Joe Matt		80.0		80.0	
Bill Brunelle		80.0		80.0	
Roster Player Salary	$1,320.0	$7,605.0	$1,172.0	$10,097.0	$1,521.0

k

306

EXHIBIT 4

Kansas City Zephyrs Baseball Club, Inc.—Income Statements, Players' Figures (000s omitted)

	Year Ending October 31	
	1983	1984
Operating Revenues:		
Game Receipts	$16,526.0	$18,620.0
National Television	2,360.8	2,830.8
Local Broadcasting	3,147.9	3,475.1
Concessions	2,886.3	3,294.3
Parking	525.1	562.0
Other	786.9	843.9
Total Revenues	$26,233.0	$29,626.1
Operating Expenses:		
Spring Training	$545.0	$594.0
Team Operating Expenses:		
Players' Salaries:		
Current Roster	5,897.4	7,256.5
Nonroster Guaranteed Contract Expense	0.0	500.0
Amortization of Bonuses	716.0	947.0
Coaches' Salaries	756.9	825.7
Other Salaries	239.0	260.8
Miscellaneous	2,655.9	2,897.3
Player Development	2,996.0	3,269.0
Team Replacement: Scouting	672.8	734.0
Stadium Operations	3,300.0	3,500.0
Ticketing and Marketing	1,907.0	2,080.0
General and Administrative	3,541.0	3,663.0
Total Operating Expenses	$23,227.0	$26,527.3
Income from Operations	3,006.0	3,098.8
Other Income (Expense)	(96.0)	(101.0)
Income Before Taxes	2,910.0	2,997.8
Provision for Federal Income Taxes[a]	1,338.6	1,379.0
City and State Taxes	236.0	253.0
Net Income	$ 1,335.4	$ 1,365.8

a. Tax rate assumed to be 46%.

k

307

Exhibit 5   Summary of Signing Bonuses

EXHIBIT 5

Summary of Signing Bonuses ($000)

	Bonuses for Contracts Starting in			
Contract Length (Years)	1981	1982	1983	1984
4	$240	$550	$350	$800
3	210	200	250	200
2	360	250	170	320

EXHIBIT 6
Summary of Items of Disagreement Between Owners and Players ($000)

Items of Dispute	1983			1984		
	Owners	Players	Difference	Owners	Players	Difference
Roster depreciation	2,000.0	0.0	2,000.0	2,000.0	0.0	2,000.0
Current roster salary	$9,111.0	$5,897.4	$3,213.6	$10,097.0	$7,256.5	$2,840.5
Amortization of signing bonuses	0.0	716.0	(716.0)	0.0	947.0	(947.0)
Nonroster guaranteed contract expense	0.0	0.0	—	1,250.0	500.0	750.0
Stadium operations	4,086.0	3,300.0	786.0	4,457.0	3,500.0	957.0
Total effect on net income			$5,283.6			$5,600.5

Effect on Net Income (before tax)	1983	1984
Income before tax per Owners' Financial Statements (Exhibit 1)	($2,373.6)	($2,602.7)
Total items of disagreement	5,283.6	5,600.5
Income before tax per Players' Financial Statements (Exhibit 4)	$2,910.0	$2,997.8

k

309

In late 1993, most analysts agreed that Eastman Kodak, the world's largest manufacturer of film and photo products, was struggling. Kodak had watched its market share for film in the U.S. decline from 95 percent in the late 1970s to less than 85 percent in the 1980s and early 1990s. Further, its profits were stagnant, and its balance sheet was heavily loaded with debt. Many of its difficulties could be linked to the successful entry into the U.S. market of Fuji, Japan's photographic giant. Despite repeated efforts by Kodak's management to restructure its business to respond to the Fuji challenge, many analysts felt that the company's problems were unlikely to be solved without some fundamental rethinking of its business strategy.

To prepare for a reassessment of its business plan, in October 1993, Kay Whitmore, Kodak's CEO, requested a review of any available information on Fuji. He wanted to understand more clearly why Fuji had been so successful during the past ten years, what was known about their future plans, and whether there were important lessons that Kodak could learn.

In late October, Dr. Chuck Schallhorn, the firm's Business Research Director and expert on Fuji and Japanese business practices, was asked to prepare a briefing to respond to CEO Whitmore's request. Chuck formed a task force to look into these issues and to do a competitive analysis of Kodak and Fuji. He requested the team to focus on comparing the imaging and information groups for the two firms, since these areas account for approximately 60 percent of Kodak's sales and 50 percent of its profits and are where competition with Fuji is most intense.

THE PHOTOGRAPHIC INDUSTRY

The photographic industry is composed of several closely related segments, including cameras, photographic film, photographic paper, photo finishing services, and photo finishing equipment (see Exhibit 1 for U.S. sales). In 1989 the U.S. accounted for an estimated 31 percent of the total consumption of photographic products and services, Western Europe for 23 percent, Japan for 16 percent, and the rest of the world for about 30 percent.

The largest and most profitable segments of the photo industry are the photo film and paper segments. These segments are highly concentrated due to significant technological and know-how barriers to entry. The major players are Kodak, Fuji, Agfa, Polaroid,

This case was prepared by Raguvir Gurumurthy and Paul M. Healy, with help from Renu Nallicheri and Eleanor Westney. Special thanks are due to Dr. Charles Schalhorn, Director of Business Research Group in Kodak, for his insightful comments and help in arranging meetings with relevant Kodak executives.

and Konica (see Exhibit 2 for the U.S. market share of color film and photographic paper for these firms). Jacques Kaufman, an industry consultant, estimates that gross margins on film exceed 50 percent.[1] Photographic paper has slightly lower, but nonetheless impressive, margins. In contrast, the photo finishing services segment is fragmented, with intense competition and low margins, and the hardware and equipment segments are not highly profitable.

Demand for film and photo paper in the U.S. during the 1980s grew by approximately 4 percent per year, reaching a record level of 17 billion exposures in 1991. However, in 1992 conventional picture-taking in the U.S. declined for the first time in at least three decades. The recession, competition from video camcorders, and changing demographics were all to blame.

New Developments in the Photo Industry

A number of new developments had an impact on the film and photo paper segments of the industry in the early 1990s. These include the increase in market share of private-label generic film which competes with the traditional brand products, the emergence of single-use disposable 35mm cameras, and technological changes in imaging. Private label generic 35mm film, lower in price than major brands, was first introduced in the mid-1980s. Although generic film is lower in quality, it is often difficult for an average consumer to readily distinguish the difference. It therefore appeals to consumers who are not highly quality conscious. The branded companies have responded to this challenge in three ways—by dramatically improving the quality of their images so that consumers can detect quality differences more easily; by tightening their cost structures in readiness for a price war; and, in Kodak's case, by issuing discount coupons to promote sales of its film.

The second important development in the industry was the emergence of single-use disposable 35mm cameras. These cameras are ideal for taking pictures on vacation or special occasions. More importantly, their quality is high, with pictures being comparable to those from 35mm point-and-shoot models. Consequently, they have been highly successful, with 1991 U.S. sales increasing by 50 percent, from 10 million to 15 million units. In 1992, global sales of these cameras were approximately 90 million units, of which Fuji's sales were 55 million. As the quality of their pictures improves, these cameras are expected to become even more popular.

Finally, changes in imaging technology are likely to have significant consequences for film and photo paper demand. Imaging includes all functions relating to the capture, storage, manipulation, transmission, and display of images. Silver halide-based photographic systems have traditionally been the dominant imaging technology. However, recent advances in electronic imaging are beginning to challenge photographic technology. Hybrid systems which combine electronic and silver-based imaging are also becoming popular. Research into these new imaging technologies has been undertaken by photo

1. Forbes, *August 30, 1993*

companies such as Kodak and Fuji, by specialists in electronic imaging such as Sony, Canon, Ricoh, and Toshiba, and by specialists in commercial imaging and private label products such as DuPont and 3M. In the late 1980s, several photographic companies concluded that the photographic business was doomed due to developments in electronic imaging. However, by the early 1990s electronic imaging had not yet had a strong impact on photography because of the lower quality of the images as well as the prohibitive cost of electronic imaging equipment in comparison to silver-based systems. Electronic imaging has been used primarily for industrial applications. Analysts predict that it will ultimately complement, but probably not replace, conventional consumer photography.

EASTMAN KODAK COMPANY

In 1880, forty years after photography was invented by Louis Daguerre, George Eastman commercialized its use for consumers. Eastman developed the first snapshot camera, the Kodak, in 1888 and for the next five decades his company pioneered the creation of markets for black-and-white film and paper. In the 1930s, Kodachrome film was introduced, making color images available for a wide range of applications. Fifty years later, Kodak announced the development of film-based digital imaging with its Photo CD system.

Currently, Kodak is a diversified manufacturer and marketer of imaging, chemical, and pharmaceutical products with 1992 net sales of $20.2 billion. The company's three divisions are based on its core strengths in imaging and chemistry.

- The Imaging and Information Division is divided into imaging (amateur, motion picture, and professional films, photographic papers, chemicals and equipment for photographic imaging) and information (graphic arts films, microfilms, copiers, printers, and other equipment for information management). These segments account for 57 percent of corporate sales and 50 percent of operating profit.
- The Chemicals Division is subdivided into four groups: olefin, acetyl, polyester, and specialty and fine chemicals, which together account for 18 percent of total sales and 23 percent of profits.
- The Health Division includes pharmaceuticals, consumer health products, products for radiography markets and households, do-it-yourself products, and personal care products. It accounts for 25 percent of sales and 27 percent of profits. In the late 1980s Sterling Drugs was acquired, in part because of the noncyclical nature of its business and because it provided opportunities to apply Kodak's expertise in "wet chemistry."

Imaging and Information Businesses

Kodak's imaging and information businesses span all parts of the imaging chain, from image capture and manipulation to storage and output, and include products that are chemistry-based, electronic, and "hybrids" that combine both. As the CEO of Kodak

k

313

states: "Our principal business is in images. Recording images, storing images, transmitting images and delivering image outputs is our competitive advantage."[2]

In 1985 the Imaging and Information Division was restructured into 17 autonomous business units. This effectively transformed the division from a function-based organization into one based on product lines. Unit managers were encouraged to compete aggressively for both incremental business and internal resources. While these strategic business units helped Kodak to improve revenues, they led to replication of administrative functions as product managers built their own SG&A base, duplicating resources at corporate headquarters. Between 1980 and 1990 Kodak's SG&A expenses increased from 20 percent to 29 percent of sales. Most of this increase is attributable to the Imaging and Information Division, particularly following its reorganization in 1985.

As can be seen from the company's financial statements (presented in Exhibit 3), Kodak's financial performance was disappointing throughout much of the 1980s and 1990s. Much of this can be attributed to poor performance in the Imaging and Information Division, where the company continued to gear its expense structure (particularly selling, administrative, and R&D) to an industry growth rate of 5–7 percent, a rate not realized during this period.

Responses to Poor Performance in Imaging and Information

Kodak responded to the poor performance in its Imaging and Information Division by downsizing these businesses, selling nonessential assets, reorganizing its business units, and changing top management. To reduce its cost base in the core imaging and information businesses, in 1991 the firm formed a consolidated Imaging and Information Organization, designed to contain costs and to align resources within a single strategic framework. In the same year it also initiated the first phase of an early retirement program. The following year, the second phase of the retirement program was completed.

While the above measures helped reduce Kodak's costs, competitive pressures and expenses associated with a more aggressive advertising program for photographic products masked the savings. Consequently, on January 19, 1993, CEO Kay Whitmore announced additional steps to deal with the company's expense structure, primarily in the Imaging and Information Division. The plan requires the reallocation of R&D resources in the division on the basis of highest priority, with cancellation of a number of projects; a substantial reduction of infrastructure costs, particularly administrative expense; continued scrutiny of capital spending; and the consolidation of equipment manufacturing operations. As a result of these steps, employment is to be reduced by approximately 20,000, largely involuntarily, saving at least $200 million in 1993 pretax profits. At a mid-January meeting for analysts and investors, management scaled down its long term unit growth expectations for the core imaging and information businesses from 5–7 percent to 2–4 percent, and announced that the above changes would adjust overhead, R&D, and capital expenditures to levels appropriate for such sales growth.

....

2. *Eastman Kodak Annual Report, 1992*

Other changes in response to poor performance included the sale of several peripheral businesses, such as Atex, Estek, Videk, Interactive Systems, and the Eastman Kodak Credit Corporation. Proceeds from these sales and internal cash flows were used in 1992 to repay $1 billion of the debt raised to finance the Sterling Drug acquisition. Kay Whitmore announced in 1993 that there would be additional divestitures of businesses that had no clear strategic fit with the company.

As part of the overall restructuring, Kodak reorganized its operations globally around five regionally-focused business divisions, representing Asia/Pacific, Europe, Africa and the Middle East, Latin America, and the U.S. and Canada. Each division was to be responsible for strategy, the development of new technology and new markets, and financial results. Finally, the firm made a number of management and management compensation changes. In January 1993 senior management compensation was changed so that remuneration would be tied more directly to cash generation and asset utilization. Around the same time, Christopher Steffen, an aggressive cost cutter and turnaround expert with experience at Chrysler and Honeywell, was appointed CFO. Steffen, however, stayed with Kodak for less than a month.

FUJI PHOTO FILM CO., LTD.

Since its founding in 1934 as Japan's first manufacturer of motion picture film, Fuji has advanced into virtually every field of communications to become an integrated imaging enterprise. Fuji is the world's second largest and Japan's largest film and photo paper maker. It has an estimated 70 percent domestic market share, and a 15 percent to 20 percent worldwide share. Besides film and photo paper, Fuji is a major manufacturer of video and audio tapes, floppy disks, compact cameras, and camcorders. Commercial products such as film processing machines, printing and publishing equipment, medical equipment, and data storage equipment are now the fastest growing areas for the company and account for over 40 percent of total sales. Fuji Xerox, a joint venture with Rank Xerox and an affiliate of Fuji, is a major maker of copy machines and other types of office equipment.

Fuji is organized around three main business segments, each of which has grown impressively in the past five years:

- The Commercial Products Division manufactures products in graphic arts, medical imaging, office automation, and motion picture film.
- The Magnetic Products Division develops audio and video tapes, and floppy disks.
- The Consumer Photographic Products Division, the largest in terms of sales and profits, is responsible for film, still, video, and disposable camera products. It has a 70 percent share of the Japanese film market and an 80 percent share of the disposable camera market.

In 1991 Fuji's sales were $7.4 billion, an increase of more than 16 percent over 1990 (see Exhibit 4 for a summary of Fuji's financial statements presented under U.S. GAAP). The firm also had significant cash reserves which gave it financial flexibility and enabled it to raise any needed additional funds at low cost. This financial success has been achieved through sustained efforts to improve the quality of its manufacturing operations, international expansion, and development of a strong research capability.

Manufacturing Quality

Fuji's manufacturing priority is to maintain high product quality. In 1990 investment in manufacturing facilities increased by more than 16 percent. Much of this investment was used to develop new state-of-the-art facilities, both in domestic and offshore plants. These efforts are coordinated and driven by small groups within manufacturing called "Result Management" committees. Their collective goal has been to promote plant automation while keeping the number of workers constant; Fuji's manufacturing staff has not noticeably increased in size in the past decade.

International Expansion

Fuji has also made significant progress in globalizing its business over the last few years, expanding its marketing and manufacturing operations overseas. It has constructed new manufacturing facilities in the Netherlands. Fuji Photo Film B.V., Fuji's Dutch subsidiary, began producing presensitized plates and color film and paper at a new facility in Tilsburg in 1990. In the U.S., in Greenwood, South Carolina, the subsidiary Fuji Photo Film, Inc. began production of presensitized plates and processing videotape in 1991.

On a consolidated basis, including factories overseas, Fuji's exports account for 40 percent of total sales. The two large markets, North America and Europe, account for 75 percent of total exports. Fuji does not provide geographical segment data in its financial reports. However, it appears that it prices its products in the international markets quite differently than in its domestic market. Exhibit 5 shows the pricing of color paper shipments of Japanese manufacturers for domestic use and for export. Photographic paper exported from Japan is sold for less than one-third of the price in the domestic market. Thus, although the volume of Fuji's exports has grown impressively since the mid-1980s, in terms of value this growth is not as impressive.

Investment in R&D

The firm's investments in R&D have always been about 7 percent of sales.[3] Some have argued that one reason Fuji is able to maintain this high commitment to R&D, particularly for long-term projects, is because of its ownership structure. As shown in Exhibit 6, much of the firm's stock is owned by a small number of large institutions, which are usually viewed as being less concerned about short-term performance than many U.S. institutional or retail investors.

Fuji's R&D funds are used to support six laboratories which conduct research into general-use film, magnetic products, medical information, printing, industrial materials, and office automation. For the past decade, Fuji has invested particularly heavily in

---

3. *This figure represents Fuji's reported R&D spending. However, this may be an underestimate of actual outlays because many Japanese companies use suppliers to perform some of their research and development. These outlays may then be treated as cost of sales rather than R&D in the financial report.*

R&D to develop core competence in electronic imaging. It recently established Fuji Film Micro Devices Co., Ltd. to design, develop, and manufacture devices used in image processing. Fuji's multi-faceted electronic imaging strategy also includes aggressively pursuing joint ventures with companies that are already active in the field. For example, Fuji and DuPont entered into a joint venture agreement for the development and manufacture of color electronic publishing systems for printing and graphic applications. This joint venture acquired De La Rue Company PLC, a member of the Crossfield Electronics Group, to further expand into graphic arts and the medical diagnostic business. Fuji has partnered with Toshiba for the design of a memory card to be used in Fuji's digital still product line. Most recently, Fuji Film Micro Devices entered into a joint venture with Zoron Corp., a California venture film company that produced a device which can compress still video images by a factor of 16:1.

To further leverage its investments in electronic imaging, Fuji created the I&I (Imaging and Information) Concept in 1990 to develop information technology products for imaging applications and to focus on the potential uses of digital technology in the imaging industry. Since then Fuji has introduced an array of innovative new products in fields ranging from audio-visual communications to medicine and education. These new products have not only added a new dimension to the imaging industry but have also enabled Fuji to strengthen its corporate image as one of the foremost innovators of imaging technology.

Despite its heavy investments in electronic imaging technology, Fuji's has not neglected its research in photographic products. For example, it has continued investing heavily to make continuous improvements in traditional films.

COMPETITION BETWEEN KODAK AND FUJI

Eastman Kodak has dominated the market for photographic film in the U.S. for nearly 100 years. This dominance has been challenged recently, however, by Japanese suppliers such as Fuji, Konica, and others. As a result, Kodak's market share declined from over 95 percent of the consumer film market in the 1970s to roughly 83 percent in 1988. Competition between Fuji and Kodak has become intense.

Fuji's early strategy in competing in the U.S. market was to offer film of satisfactory quality at prices considerably lower than those of Kodak. However, in the early 1980s Fuji improved the quality of its film to a level comparable to and sometimes superior to that of Kodak.

Kodak responded to Fuji's aggressive moves in three ways. First, it retaliated by attacking Fuji in Japan, where it has proceeded to build a presence. Kodak decided to build market share in consumer film products, establish a technology base to tap into Japan's strengths, and to strengthen its alliances with Japanese companies. Kodak even established an R&D facility in Japan in the mid-1980s to hire local engineers and become a Japanese company. Kodak's second response was to significantly improve the quality of its amateur film and introduce 400 and 1000 speed films. Finally, it became more competitive in its pricing in the U.S.

As Kodak stepped up its marketing efforts, Fuji responded by also increasing its U.S. marketing. For example, it became the official photographer of the 1984 Olympics in Los Angeles and has used the Fuji film blimp extensively at major sports events. It also increased the color saturation of its films, a move widely applauded by U.S. photographers. Currently, Fuji film continues to be less expensive than the corresponding Kodak film at most retail outlets in Europe and the U.S., despite the fluctuating dollar-yen exchange rate (see Exhibit 7). In Japan, however, this pattern is reversed: Fuji film is comparably—or higher—priced than that of Kodak.

Fuji has been active in both the private label and branded markets in the U.S. By supplying films to the private label market, Fuji has been able to increase its sales volume and thus reduce costs through economies of scale. In the branded market, Fuji has been gaining market share in the U.S. by pricing aggressively and building distribution channels through the acquisition of photo finishers and minilabs. For example, Fuji recently acquired a photo finishing laboratory in North Carolina. In addition, as mentioned above, Fuji has set up a plant in Greenwood, South Carolina, to manufacture videotape and presensitized printing plates. It is believed that the current purpose of the Greenwood plant is to learn how to do business in the U.S.

Both Kodak and Fuji have been losing money in electronic photography. However, the two companies appear to be following somewhat different strategies in the new technology. Kodak believes that electronic photography will not take business away from conventional photography within the foreseeable future, since there are innumerable conventional cameras on the market, electronic systems are not yet able to produce an acceptable hard print, and there are many relatively undeveloped markets. Therefore, Kodak has decided to concentrate on its traditional photography business while still continuing to invest in electronic imaging. Fuji has decided to adopt a more aggressive two-pronged investment strategy, emphasizing both electronic imaging and photography.

QUESTIONS

1. Compare the financial performance of Kodak and Fuji for the period 1982 to 1992.
2. What factors explain any observed differences in operating performance for the two firms?
3. How do differences in financing strategies affect the performance of the two firms? To what extent are any differences in financing strategies explained by institutional or structural differences between the U.S. and Japan (such as differences in tax rates, financial markets, and corporate governance)?
4. Does your analysis of Fuji and Kodak provide any insights as to how Kodak could restructure to compete more effectively with Fuji?

EXHIBIT 1

U.S. Consumption of Cameras, Photographic Products, and Services[a]

(millions of dollars, manufacturers' sales level)	1989	1993	Avg. Annual Growth Rate, 1989–1993 (%)
Photographic and Photofinishing Materials and Services	9,200	12,312	7
Silver Halide-Sensitized Film, Paper, and Plates	6,920	9,261	7
Micrographic Equipment and Services	1,918	2,223	3
Still Cameras and Other Photo Equipment	1,462	1,779	4
X-ray Film	1,100	1,214	2
Microfilm	410	475	3
Photofinishing Equipment	242	294	4
TOTAL	21,252	27,558	5.9

a.   Source: SRI International; Wolfman Report, 1989 and Imaging Technology/Markets, Inc.

k

EXHIBIT 2
U.S. Market Shares for Color Film Manufacturers and Photographic Paper Suppliers

	Percent of Total Market	
Company	1984	1988
Color Film Manufacturers[a]		
Eastman Kodak Company	88.0	83.0
Fuji Photo Film Co., Ltd.	7.0	12.0
Konica Corporation	3.0	3.0
3M Company	1.0	1.0
Other	1.0	1.0
TOTAL	100.0	100.0
Photographic Paper Suppliers[b]		
Eastman Kodak Company	64.0	61.0
Fuji Photo Film Co., Ltd.	10.3	16.0
Konica Corporation	9.8	9.0
Agfa-Gevaert AG	9.0	7.5
Mitsubishi Paper Mills, Ltd.	5.7	5.5
Other	1.2	1.0
TOTAL	100.0	100.0

a. Source: SRI International: Wolfman Report, 1989, and Imaging Technology/Markets, Inc.

b. Source: Imaging Technology/Markets

k

320

EXHIBIT 3

Eastman Kodak Company – Consolidated Financial Statements

CONSOLIDATED STATEMENT OF INCOME
for the years ended December 31, 1982 to 1992

(in $ millions)	1982	1983	1984	1985	1986	1987	1988	1989	1990	1991	1992
Sales	10,815	10,170	10,600	10,631	11,550	13,305	17,034	18,398	18,908	19,419	20,183
Cost of Goods Sold	6,120	6,305	6,049	6,153	6,554	7,012	8,580	9,822	9,637	9,985	10,392
Gross Profit	4,695	3,865	4,551	4,478	4,996	6,293	8,454	8,576	9,271	9,434	9,791
Research and Development	710	746	838	976	1,059	992	1,147	1,253	1,329	1,494	1,587
SG and A	2,125	2,024	2,119	2,378	2,693	3,190	4,495	4,857	5,098	5,565	5,869
Restructuring Costs	0	0	0	563	520	0	0	875	0	1,605	220
Earnings from Operations	1,860	1,095	1,594	561	724	2,111	2,812	1,591	2,844	770	2,115
Litigation Costs	0	0	0	0	0	0	0	0	888	0	0
Investment Income	(117)	(122)	(140)	(129)	(129)	(83)	(132)	(148)	(167)	(109)	(174)
Interest Expense	89	117	114	183	200	181	697	895	812	819	813
Other Expense (Income)	16	12	(51)	(23)	55	29	11	(81)	54	49	(125)
Pretax Profit	1,872	1,088	1,671	530	598	1,984	2,236	925	1,257	11	1,601
Income Taxes	710	455	701	198	224	806	839	396	554	(6)	607
Effect of Accounting Change											152
Net Earnings	1,162	633	970	332	374	1,178	1,397	529	703	17	1,146
Per share data:											
Net Income	3.17	1.52	2.54	0.97	1.11	3.52	4.31	1.63	2.17	0.05	3.53
Dividends	1.58	1.58	1.60	1.62	1.63	1.71	1.90	2.00	2.00	2.00	2.00
Stock Price (year end)	38.25	33.88	31.88	33.75	45.75	45.13	45.13	41.13	41.63	48.25	40.50
Year end number shares (000)	372.4	372.5	350.3	338.5	338.7	324.4	324.2	324.4	324.6	324.9	325.9
Other items:											
Advertising Expense	401	390	430	411	470	545	1,027	1,067	1,073	1,209	1,352
Labor Expense	4,446	4,340	4,148	4,482	4,912	4,645	5,469	5,877	5,783	6,105	6,293
Depreciation & Amortization	575	652	758	838	956	962	1,057	1,181	1,168	1,329	1,393
No. of Employees (000)	137	126	124	129	121	124	145	138	134	133	133

Exhibit 3   Eastman Kodak Company – Consolidated Financial Statements

CONSOLIDATED STATEMENT OF FINANCIAL POSITION
for the years ended December 31, 1982 to 1992

Exhibit 3 Eastman Kodak Company – Consolidated Financial Statements

(in $ millions)	1982	1983	1984	1985	1986	1987	1988	1989	1990	1991	1992
Cash and Equivalents	1,018	1,562	1,011	813	613	954	1,075	1,279	916	924	560
Receivables	1,829	1,779	2,050	2,346	2,563	3,086	4,071	4,245	4,333	4,348	3,984
Inventories	2,101	1,710	1,758	1,940	2,072	2,178	3,025	2,507	2,425	2,311	2,379
Other Current Assets	341	369	312	578	563	477	513	560	934	675	482
Current Assets	5,289	5,420	5,131	5,677	5,811	6,695	8,684	8,591	8,608	8,258	7,405
Gross Plant	9,344	10,049	10,775	12,047	12,919	13,789	15,667	16,774	17,648	19,034	19,840
Accumulated Depreciation	4,286	4,801	5,386	6,070	6,643	7,126	7,654	8,146	8,670	9,432	10,005
Net Plant	5,058	5,248	5,389	5,977	6,276	6,663	8,013	8,628	8,978	9,602	9,835
Other Assets	275	260	258	488	815	1,093	6,267	6,433	6,550	6,310	5,898
Total Assets	10,622	10,928	10,778	12,142	12,902	14,451	22,964	23,652	24,136	24,170	23,138
Accounts Payable	342	380	375	526	520	717	921	784	942	935	902
Income Taxes Payable	261	204	268	156	209	380	411	338	588	292	505
Debt in Current Liabilities	256	181	324	725	1,162	1,019	1,834	2,862	2,956	2,610	1,736
Other Current Liabilities	1,287	1,407	1,339	1,918	1,900	1,959	2,684	2,589	2,677	3,062	2,855
Current Liabilities	2,146	2,172	2,306	3,325	3,791	4,075	5,850	6,573	7,163	6,899	5,998
Long-Term Debt	350	416	409	988	911	2,212	7,779	7,376	6,989	7,597	7,202
Deferred Income Tax Credits	446	606	723	1,048	1,209	1,408	1,565	1,690	1,830	1,490	1,069
Other Liabilities	139	214	203	219	603	743	990	1,371	1,406	2,080	2,312
Long-Term Liabilities	935	1,236	1,335	2,255	2,723	4,363	10,334	10,437	10,225	11,167	10,583
Total Liabilities	3,081	3,408	3,641	5,580	6,514	8,438	16,184	17,010	17,388	18,066	16,581
Stockholders' Equity	7,541	7,520	7,137	6,562	6,388	6,013	6,780	6,642	6,748	6,104	6,557
Total Debt and Equity	10,622	10,928	10,778	12,142	12,902	14,451	22,964	23,652	24,136	24,170	23,138

Exhibit 3   Eastman Kodak Company – Consolidated Financial Statements

CASH FLOW STATEMENT
for the years ended December 31, 1987 to 1992

	1987	1988	1989	1990	1991	1992
Net earnings	1,178	1,397	529	703	17	1,146
Adjustments:						
Depreciation and amortization	995	1,183	1,326	1,309	1,477	1,539
Deferred taxes	193	160		(192)	(153)	1
Loss on sale of properties				154	131	148
Increase in receivables	(535)	(503)	(174)	(88)	(15)	216
Decrease in inventories	(106)	(507)	518	82	114	(150)
Increase in other liabilities	606	10	334	414	755	271
Effect of accounting change						(152)
Other items, net	(350)	(694)	(236)	35	145	347
Total adjustments	803	(351)	1,768	1,714	2,454	2,220
Operating cash flows	1,981	1,046	2,297	2,417	2,471	3,366
Cash from investing activities:						
Sale of properties	303	265	322	83	53	85
Additions to properties	(1,652)	(1,914)	(2,118)	(2,037)	(2,135)	(2,092)
Sterling Drug acquisition		(4,781)				
Sale of investments				10	33	189
Purchase marketable securities	(394)	(329)	(356)	(128)	(60)	(159)
Sale of marketable securities	288	684	406	126	102	114
Other items	22	16	10	90	16	3
Investment cash flow	(1,433)	(6,059)	(1,736)	(1,856)	(1,991)	(1,860)
Cash from financing activities:						
Increase in short-term debt	(178)	413	652	114	(111)	(629)
Issue long-term debt	1,537	5,432	1,085	1,691	1,535	549
Repay long-term debt	(132)	(71)	(1,371)	(2,102)	(1,207)	(1,184)
Dividends to shareowners	(568)	(600)	(649)	(649)	(649)	(650)
Treasury stock purchases	(978)					
Other items	(3)	2	5	1	2	16
Financing cash flow	(322)	5,176	(278)	(945)	(430)	(1,898)
Exchange rate effect on cash	40	(17)	(36)	24	(2)	(17)
Net change in cash	266	146	247	(360)	48	(409)

k

323

Exhibit 3   Eastman Kodak Company – Consolidated Financial Statements

k

324

BUSINESS SEGMENT INFORMATION
for the years ended December 31, 1982 to 1992

(in $ millions)	1982	1983	1984	1985	1986	1987[a]	1988	1989	1990	1991	1992
Sales – Imaging											
Inside the U.S.						2,875	2,906	3,096	2,936	2,847	2,971
Outside the U.S.						3,331	3,736	3,902	4,192	4,228	4,444
Total Imaging	8,935	8,097	8,380	8,531	9,408	6,206	6,642	6,998	7,128	7,075	7,415
Sales – Information											
Inside the U.S.						2,324	2,517	2,651	2,506	2,380	2,375
Outside the U.S.						1,170	1,420	1,549	1,634	1,588	1,688
Total Information						3,494	3,937	4,200	4,140	3,968	4,063
Sales – Chemicals											
Inside the U.S.						1,961	2,260	2,473	2,399	2,449	2,602
Outside the U.S.						674	863	1,049	1,189	1,291	1,325
Total Chemicals	2,151	2,285	2,464	2,348	2,378	2,635	3,123	3,522	3,588	3,740	3,927
Sales – Health											
Inside the U.S.						658	2,104	2,375	2,541	2,760	3,027
Outside the U.S.						548	1,493	1,634	1,808	2,157	2,054
Total Health						1,206	3,597	4,009	4,349	4,917	5,081
Earnings											
Imaging	1,655	813	1,266	378	497	1,231	1,280	821	1,611	489	1,216
Information	205	214	281	183	227	225	311	(360)	5	(688)	(151)
Chemicals						378	630	643	602	538	494
Health						244	591	487	626	433	588
Assets											
Imaging	7,887	7,555	7,926	9,387	10,309	6,836	7,937	7979	6,611	6,586	6,391
Information						3,814	4,319	4331	3,939	3,844	3,808
Chemicals	2,001	2,124	2,054	2,136	2,266	2,548	2,967	3238	3,952	4,035	4,255
Health						1,100	7,278	7793	8,142	8,353	8,227
Capital Expenditures											
Imaging	1,035	710	818	1,244	1,124	821	854	902	679	606	631
Information						390	393	453	468	537	552
Chemicals	465	179	152	251	314	395	515	514	610	602	467
Health						46	152	249	280	390	442

a. In 1987 Kodak changed its method of business segment reporting by separating the information and imaging segments of its business. Previously, both imaging and photographic operations had been reported as a single segment. In 1987 it also introduced health as a new segment with the acquisition of Sterling Drugs.

Exhibit 3 Eastman Kodak Company – Consolidated Financial Statements

GEOGRAPHIC SEGMENT INFORMATION
for the years ended December 31, 1982 to 1992

(in $ millions)	1982	1983	1984	1985	1986	1987	1988	1989	1990	1991	1992
Sales											
U.S.	8,039	8,201	8,836	8,717	8,959	9,866	12,325	13,176	13,075	13,459	14,197
Canada and Latin America	1,043	799	791	794	876	1,033	1,562	1,657	1,642	1,833	1,998
Europe	2,589	2,093	2,067	2,164	2,800	3,475	4,383	4,811	5,377	5,302	5,417
Asia, Africa, Australia	669	534	533	520	796	1,192	1,898	1,692	1,724	1,972	2,158
Earnings											
U.S.	1,554	939	1,467	364	350	1,302	1,851	785	1,698	108	1,480
Canada and Latin America	166	66	94	53	65	185	264	239	290	270	265
Europe	76	(30)	(14)	113	302	553	591	470	675	222	283
Asia, Africa, Australia	60	23	34	1	22	59	121	98	184	178	128
Assets											
U.S.	8,274	8,600	8,482	9,560	9,543	10,498	17,486	17,749	17,705	17,548	16,925
Canada and Latin America	670	635	689	688	759	894	1,242	1,324	1,336	1,254	1,417
Europe	1,935	1,878	1,850	2,121	2,339	2,930	3,539	3,855	4,321	4,308	3,890
Asia, Africa, Australia	373	358	388	453	918	1,190	1,420	1,449	1,450	1,428	1,555

Exhibit 3   Eastman Kodak Company – Consolidated Financial Statements

NOTES TO 1992 CONSOLIDATED FINANCIAL STATEMENTS

Basis of Consolidation. The consolidated financial statements include the accounts of Eastman Kodak Company and its majority owned subsidiary companies. Intercompany transactions are eliminated and net earnings are reduced by the portion of earnings of subsidiaries applicable to minority interests.

Translation of Non-US Currencies. Effective January 1, 1992, the local currency is the "functional currency" for translating the accounts of most subsidiary companies outside the US. The US dollar will continue to be used for reporting operations in highly inflationary economies. This change did not have a material effect on the Company's statement of financial position as of January 1, 1992.

Inventories. Inventories are valued at cost, which is not in excess of market. The cost of most US inventories is determined by the last-in-first-out (LIFO) method. The cost of other inventories is determined by the first-in-first-out (FIFO), or average cost method. The LIFO reserve was $1,008 million in 1992, $949 million in 1991, $1,011 million in 1990, $1,063 million in 1989, and $976 million in 1988.

Goodwill. The excess of the Company's costs of its consolidated investments over the value ascribed to the equity of such companies at the time of acquisition is amortized over the future periods benefitted but not exceeding 40 years. Goodwill amortization was $146 million in 1992, $148 million in 1991, $141 million in 1990, $145 million in 1989, and $126 million in 1988.

Investments. Included in noncurrent assets are investments in joint ventures which are managed as integral parts of the Company's segment operations and are accounted for on an equity basis. The Company's share of the earnings of these joint ventures is included in the earnings from operations for the related segments.

Sales. Sales represent revenue from sales of products and services, equipment rentals, and other operating fees.

Depreciation. Depreciation expense is provided based on historical cost and the estimated useful lives of the assets. The Company generally uses the straight-line method for calculating the provision for depreciation. For assets in the United States acquired prior to January 1, 1992, the provision for depreciation is generally calculated using accelerated methods.

Property Retirements. When assets are retired or otherwise disposed of, the cost of such assets and the related accumulated depreciation are removed from the accounts. Any profit or loss on retirement, or other disposition, is reflected in earnings.

Income Taxes. Effective January 1, 1992, deferred income taxes reflect the impact of temporary differences between the assets and liabilities recognized for financial reporting purposes and amounts recognized for tax purposes. Deferred taxes are based on tax laws as currently enacted. Between 1988 and 1992, the US corporate tax rate was 34%. Prior to 1992 the Company used the deferred method of recording deferred taxes. The income statement item which has consistently given rise to deferred tax provisions during the last five years is depreciation. The depreciation effect on deferred taxes was $70 million in 1992, $64 million in 1991, $58 million in 1990, $59 million in 1989, and $58 million in 1988.

k

326

EXHIBIT 4
Fuji Photo Film Company, Ltd. – Consolidated Financial Statements

CONSOLIDATED STATEMENT OF INCOME
for the years 1982 to 1992

(in ¥ trillion)	1982	1983	1984	1985	1986	1987	1988	1989	1990	1991	1992
Domestic Sales		405.1	433.4	465.6	489.1	525.4	571.5	609.4	656.6	683.8	693.3
Overseas Sales		228.4	235.8	282.8	269.8	289.5	305.0	319.1	408.3	433.6	449.0
Total Sales	587.5	633.6	669.2	748.4	758.8	814.9	876.5	928.5	1064.9	1117.4	1142.3
Cost of Goods Sold	324.4	355.9	379.2	410.2	426.0	443.6	479.4	493.7	560.1	592.8	610.1
Gross Profit	263.0	277.7	290.0	338.2	332.8	371.3	397.1	434.8	504.8	524.7	532.2
SG and A	111.5	122.9	132.8	155.5	157.9	178.1	196.3	222.9	267.6	278.9	290.7
Research and Development	31.6	37.4	39.8	42.2	44.3	50.2	55.0	56.8	59.5	68.2	75.0
Operating Income	120.0	117.4	117.5	140.5	130.6	143.0	145.8	155.2	177.7	177.6	166.5
Interest and Dividend Income	(6.8)	(11.3)	(13.0)	(18.0)	(20.4)	(20.9)	(22.6)	(27.4)	(38.9)	(43.2)	(33.3)
Interest Expense	13.0	11.6	10.8	10.1	9.8	9.2	9.7	12.3	19.9	23.0	22.1
Other Income/Expense		2.9	5.0	5.4	6.0	5.6	2.3	2.9	0.8	7.2	10.7
Income Before Taxes	113.8	114.2	114.6	143.0	135.2	149.1	156.4	167.4	195.9	190.6	167.0
Income Taxes	63.3	63.5	66.4	85.1	80.1	86.2	87.7	97.0	109.5	99.6	93.0
Net Earnings—Consolidated	50.4	50.7	48.3	57.9	55.1	62.9	68.6	70.4	86.4	91.0	73.9
Earnings—Non-Consolidated	6.7	7.5	8.1	8.2	7.1	9.1	13.4	12.9	3.8	3.8	1.8
Net Earnings—Total	57.1	58.2	56.3	66.1	62.2	72.0	82.0	83.3	90.3	94.8	75.7
Per share data[a]:											
Net Income	117.24	119.00	114.55	134.46	126.29	145.29	164.23	164.65	176.20	184.95	147.46
Dividends	7.14	7.14	8.64	10.14	10.14	10.14	10.52	10.89	12.40	14.09	17.50
Stock price (year end)	1,216	1,525	1,262	1,607	2,359	2,907	2,419	4,157	3,391	3,090	2,570
Average number shares (000)	487,420	491,720	491,720	491,720	492,335	495,410	499,492	505,938	512,355	512,458	513,328
Other data											
Number of employees (000)	15.9	16.3	16.7	16.9	17.2	17.7	18.2	19.7	21.9	23.7	24.9
Depreciation & Amortization	25.9	32.5	36.6	39.2	44.1	47.9	50.8	57.4	61.5	76.5	85.7

a. Per share values are adjusted for the effect of stock distributions

k
328

CONSOLIDATED STATEMENT OF FINANCIAL POSITION
(for the years 1982 to 1992)

(in ¥ trillion)	1982	1983	1984	1985	1986	1987	1988	1989	1990	1991	1992
Cash	111.2	153.0	168.1	258.0	302.9	353.1	417.8	401.4	446.0	441.4	509.4
Receivables	117.9	126.9	132.9	143.4	134.3	148.9	154.5	175.4	206.0	214.3	217.4
Inventories	121.5	132.4	139.2	142.9	136.7	140.2	138.3	162.3	180.0	192.9	192.5
Other Current Assets	16.9	14.4	18.3	25.4	23.1	24.8	27.0	32.6	37.4	51.5	39.5
Current Assets	367.5	426.7	458.5	569.8	597.0	666.9	737.6	771.8	869.3	900.0	958.8
Gross Plant	313.1	357.6	400.0	444.7	480.8	527.9	590.3	677.9	814.2	933.6	1,055.3
Accumulated Depreciation	171.1	195.0	220.6	250.4	280.6	315.7	351.0	394.1	451.8	501.3	575.4
Net Plant	142.0	162.5	179.4	194.3	200.2	212.2	239.3	283.8	362.5	432.3	479.9
Investments	95.7	101.5	120.2	126.0	129.3	144.7	174.0	237.6	269.9	266.8	226.7
Other Assets	19.9	21.4	20.6	20.6	21.7	22.3	20.5	27.3	27.9	33.4	32.7
Total Assets	625.1	712.2	778.8	910.7	948.2	1,046.2	1,171.4	1,320.6	1,529.6	1,632.5	1,698.1
Trade Payables	57.0	57.3	60.9	77.0	73.8	78.2	90.8	97.9	113.6	118.0	109.6
Other Payables	17.0	15.9	13.5	18.8	17.8	27.2	20.6	33.7	51.1	50.8	42.7
Taxes Payable	38.3	28.4	36.1	57.5	39.2	47.2	42.2	51.0	57.0	46.2	40.8
LT Debt Repayable	49.7	49.7	50.2	71.9	73.3	74.3	85.1	92.0	103.8	184.9	181.9
Other	51.1	53.1	56.8	58.6	63.2	67.7	71.0	74.2	82.8	80.5	86.0
Current Liabilities	213.1	204.3	217.5	283.8	267.3	294.6	309.7	348.7	408.4	480.4	461.0
Long-Term Debt	16.4	58.4	39.3	38.3	34.6	27.9	45.8	69.4	100.2	44.9	54.7
Pension Costs	60.4	60.6	61.1	60.9	60.1	58.8	57.4	57.1	58.6	59.0	60.6
Other LT Debt	0.0	0.0	21.3	27.2	28.1	32.1	37.3	23.9	44.9	49.3	50.2
LT Liabilities	76.8	119.1	121.8	126.4	122.8	118.8	140.5	150.4	203.7	153.1	165.4
Total Liabilities	289.9	323.4	339.3	410.2	390.1	413.4	450.2	499.1	612.1	633.5	626.5
Owners' Equity	1.5	1.7	1.8	1.9	1.9	2.1	2.1	2.6	3.4	3.5	4.6
Minority Interest	333.7	387.1	437.7	498.6	556.1	630.7	719.2	818.9	914.1	995.5	1,067.1
Debt and Equity	625.1	712.2	778.8	910.7	948.2	1,046.2	1,171.4	1,320.6	1,529.6	1,632.5	1,698.1

CONSOLIDATED STATEMENT OF CASH FLOWS
for the years 1989 to 1992

(in ¥ trillion)	1989	1990	1991	1992
Cash Flows from Operating Activities				
Net income	83.3	90.3	94.8	75.7
Adjustments for non-cash items:				
Depreciation and amortization	59.7	68.2	84.4	91.6
Deferred income taxes	(2.7)	2.1	0.0	0.0
Equity earnings	(10.7)	(0.7)	(0.7)	1.4
Increase in receivables	(15.6)	(21.4)	(12.5)	(2.5)
Increase in inventories	(19.4)	(10.1)	(18.6)	1.0
Increase in payables	3.8	8.3	5.9	(8.2)
Increase in taxes payable	8.2	5.7	(10.6)	(5.4)
Other	1.5	(6.8)	0.0	(2.7)
Cash flows from operating activities	108.0	135.7	142.8	150.9
Cash from Investing Activities				
Purchase of property	(85.7)	(109.9)	(166.3)	(139.0)
Purchase of investments	(43.0)	(4.6)	(6.6)	0.9
Acquisition	(21.4)			
Other	(10.1)	(4.4)	(2.9)	(2.9)
Cash from investing activities	(160.4)	(118.9)	(175.8)	(141.0)
Cash from Financing Activities				
Issue long-term debt	16.7	32.9	24.4	21.2
Repay long-term debt	(0.2)	(0.2)	(0.2)	(0.2)
Increase short-term debt	24.1	(0.9)	12.1	(11.1)
Dividends paid	(5.5)	(5.9)	(6.9)	(8.1)
Exercise of warrants	0.0		0.4	5.1
Cash from financing activities	35.2	25.8	29.8	6.8
Exchange rate effects	0.8	1.9	(1.8)	(0.1)
Increase (decrease) in cash	(16.3)	44.5	(5.1)	16.6

k

329

NOTES TO 1992 CONSOLIDATED FINANCIAL STATEMENTS

Fuji Photo Film Co., Ltd. (the parent company) and its domestic subsidiaries maintain their records and prepare their financial statements in accordance with accounting principles generally accepted in Japan, and its foreign subsidiaries in conformity with those conventions of the countries of their domicile. Certain reclassifications and adjustments, including those relating to the tax effects of timing differences and the accrual of certain expenses, have been incorporated in the accompanying consolidated financial statements to conform with accounting principles generally accepted in the United States of America. These adjustments were not recorded in the statutory books of account.

Significant accounting policies, after reflecting adjustments for the above, are as follows:

Principles of consolidation and accounting for investments in affiliated companies

The consolidated financial statements include the accounts of the parent company and, with minor exceptions, those of its majority-owned subsidiaries (together, the Company). All significant intercompany transactions and accounts are eliminated.

The Company's investments in affiliated companies (20 percent to 50 percent owned companies and unconsolidated subsidiaries), in which the ability to exercise significant influence exists, are stated at cost plus equity in undistributed earnings; consolidated net income includes the Company's equity in the current net earnings (losses) of such companies, after elimination of unrealized intercompany profits.

The excess of the cost over the underlying net equity of investments in consolidated subsidiaries and affiliated companies accounted for on an equity basis, which is recognized as goodwill, is amortized on a straight-line basis principally over the period estimated to be benefited, for a maximum of twenty years.

Foreign currency translations

Asset and liability accounts of foreign subsidiaries and affiliates are translated at appropriate year-end current rates. Revenue and expense amounts are translated at rates prevailing at the time of the transaction and the resulting translation adjustments are accumulated and reported as a separate component of shareholders' equity.

Foreign currency receivables and payables are translated at appropriate year-end current rates and the resulting translation gains and losses are credited or charged to income currently.

Financial Instruments

The Company enters into foreign exchange contracts with banks as hedges against foreign currency receivables and payables. The discount or premium on a forward contract is included in determining net income over the life of the forward contract. Currency swap agreements are accounted for in a manner similar to the accounting for forward contracts. Interest rate swap agreements involve the exchange of fixed and floating rate interest payment obligations without the exchange of the underlying principal amounts. Net amounts paid or received are reflected as adjustments to the interest expense.

Cash equivalents

For purposes of the statement of cash flows, the Company considers all highly liquid investments which are readily convertible into cash and/or mature within three months or less to be cash equivalents.

k

330

Marketable securities

Marketable securities (current and non-current), including equity securities, are valued at the lower of aggregate cost or market; other investments are stated at cost or less.

Realized gains or losses on the sale of marketable securities are based on the average cost of all the shares of each security held at the time of sale.

Certificates of deposit and marketable securities purchased under agreements to resell

The Company enters into agreements with financial institutions to resell certificates of deposit and marketable securities at predetermined selling prices and dates. Such certificates and securities are stated at cost, which approximates market. The difference between purchase cost and predetermined selling price is accounted for as interest and is accrued on a straight-line basis.

Inventories

Inventories are valued at the lower of cost or market, cost being determined generally by the moving-average method, except that the cost of principal raw materials is determined by the last-in, first-out method.

In connection with the purchasing of silver for anticipated manufacturing requirements, the Company enters into forward silver purchase contracts in order to reduce the risk associated with price fluctuations. These forward contracts are accounted for as hedges, and gains or losses are deferred and shown as a reduction or addition to the cost of the silver acquired.

Property, plant and equipment and depreciation

Property, plant and equipment is stated at cost. Depreciation of property, plant and equipment is computed principally by the declining-balance method at rates based on estimated useful lives of the assets according to general class, type of construction and use.

Pension and severance plans

Employees of the parent company and subsidiaries in Japan who terminate employment are entitled, under most circumstances, to lump-sum payments and/or pension payments as described below, determined by reference to current basic rate of pay, length of service and conditions under which the termination occurs. The minimum payment is an amount based on voluntary retirement. In addition to the minimum payment based on voluntary retirement, employees receive additional benefits for retirement due to age limit, death or other defined reasons. With respect to directors' resignations, lump-sum severance indemnities, calculated by using a stipulated formula, are normally paid subject to approval of the shareholders.

The parent company and certain subsidiaries in Japan have non-contributory defined benefit pension plans funded with a trust bank and insurance companies. The funding policy is to make contributions that are actuarially determined to provide the plans with sufficient assets to meet future benefit payment requirements.

The parent company and certain subsidiaries in Japan also have a defined benefit pension plan covering substantially all of their employees. The plan consists of two parts: a governmental welfare contributory pension plan which would be otherwise provided by the Japanese government, and an additional non-contributory defined benefit pension plan. The pension benefits are determined based on years of service and the compensation amounts as stipulated in the regulations. The contributions are funded in conformity

k

331

with the requirements regulated by Japanese Welfare Pension Insurance Law. The contributions to the plan are funded with trustee pension funds.

Most subsidiaries outside Japan have various retirement plans covering substantially all of their employees, which are primarily defined contribution plans. The funding policy for the defined contribution plans is to annually contribute an amount equal to a certain percent of the participants' annual salaries.

Income taxes

Deferred income taxes are provided with respect to timing differences between financial and tax reporting in accordance with Accounting Principles Board Opinion No. 11.

In February 1992, the Financial Accounting Standards Board issued Statement of Financial Accounting Standards No. 109 (SFAS 109), "Accounting for Income Taxes," which requires an asset and liability approach for financial accounting and reporting for income taxes. SFAS 109 supersedes SFAS 96, "Accounting for Income Taxes," and amends or supersedes other relevant accounting pronouncements. In the case of the Company, SFAS 109 must be adopted no later than its fiscal year beginning October 21, 1993. The Company has not decided when it will adopt SFAS 109 or the method of adoption. However, the Company does not expect that adoption of SFAS 109 will have a material effect on its consolidated financial statements.

Net income per share

The computation of net income per share is based on the average number of shares outstanding each year, appropriately adjusted for any free distribution of common stock. Net income per share of common stock assuming full dilution is determined on the assumption that convertible bonds outstanding were converted into common stock at the beginning of the year or at the time of debt issuance, if later.

Common stock distributions

On occasion, the Company may make, by resolution of the Board of Directors, a free distribution of common stock. Such distribution is accounted for either by a transfer of the applicable par value from additional paid-in capital to the common stock account or with no entry if free shares are distributed from the portion of previously issued shares accounted for as excess of par value in the common stock account.

Under the Commercial Code of Japan, as amended with effect from April 1, 1991, a stock dividend is effected by an appropriation of retained earnings to the common stock account by resolution of the general stockholders' meeting and the free share distribution with respect to the amount as appropriated by resolution of the Board of Directors.

Exhibit 5   Color Paper Shipments of Japanese Manufacturers for 1991

EXHIBIT 5
Color Paper Shipments of Japanese Manufacturers for 1991

	Export	Domestic Shipments
Square Meters	203,020,417	112,697,979
Monetary Value (000 yen)	63,911,764	113,445,143
Yen/Square Meter	315	1,007

Source: MITI, MOF statistics, Photo Market (Japan) 1991, casewriter's analysis

EXHIBIT 6
The Ten Largest Shareholders of Fuji Photo Film as of October 1992[a]

Shareholders	Percentage of Shares Owned
Nippon Life Insurance	6.7
Mitsui Trust & Banking	6.6
Sakura Bank	4.5
Sumitomo Trust & Banking	3.5
Yasuda Trust & Banking	2.8
Toyo Trust & Banking	2.5
Yokohama Bank	2.2
Daisel Chemical[b]	2.0
Mitsui Marine & Fire Insurance	1.8
Mitsubishi Trust & Banking	1.8
Total	34.4

a.   Source: Nikkei Corporation Information, Spring 1993, Nikkei Economic Daily
b.   Daisel was the third largest supplier for Fuji.

EXHIBIT 7
Financial Market Data

Yen to Dollar Comparison from 1982 to 1991

1991	1990	1989	1988	1987	1986	1985	1984	1983	1982
179.09	191.21	188.52	169.36	175.20	194.61	220.23	246.13	243.10	259.23

Source: International Financial Statistics Yearbook, 1993

T his *Winston-Salem company sells affordable Southern comfort: fully furnished and carpeted mobile homes for as little as $10,000. Robert Sauls, the 59-year-old founder and chairman, was an orphaned boy who never finished high school. Through acquisitions, Sauls has built the retailer into the industry's largest, with annual sales ballooning to about $180 million in four years. The company sells the homes, built primarily by Fleetwood Enterprises and Redman Industries, to rural blue-collar workers in the Southeast. "Our people buy in good times and bad," says Sauls. If he can raise the capital, he foresees a doubling of sales in four to five years. The stock recently sold at 6.5 times estimated 1988 earnings.*

Jane Edwards, Director of Research at a small Boston-based investment management firm specializing in growth stocks, noted the above review of Manufactured Homes in the February 15, 1988 issue of *Fortune* magazine's Companies To Watch column. She knew that attractive growth stocks are hard to find and wondered whether Manufactured Homes would be a good addition to her firm's growth stock portfolio. She checked the recent performance of Manufactured Homes' common stock and noted that the stock performed favorably relative to the stock market (see Exhibit 1). Jane Edwards asked her assistant Peter Herman to gather additional information on the company and to write a report analyzing the company's recent financial statements.

COMPANY BACKGROUND AND MARKETING FOCUS

Herman's preliminary research on Manufactured Homes indicated that the company was founded in 1975 with two retail outlets for mobile homes. The company grew rapidly and by March 31, 1987, had a network of 120 retail outlets located in seven southeastern states. Eighty-five percent of the company's retail centers were located in North Carolina, South Carolina, Alabama, Georgia, and Florida, with the remaining sales centers in Virginia and West Virginia. The company went public in 1983 and was listed on the American Stock Exchange in January 1987.

Professor Krishna G. Palepu prepared this case as the basis for class discussion rather than to illustrate either effective or ineffective handling of an administrative situation. Copyright © 1989 by the President and Fellows of Harvard College. Harvard Business School case 9-190-090.

The southeastern U.S. was the country's fastest-growing market for mobile homes due to suitable climate, the easy availability of vacant land for mobile-home parks, and the region's demographics. Potential customers for manufactured homes included individuals seeking a single-family primary residence but lacking the ability to purchase conventional housing, retirees, and those wanting a second home for vacation purposes.

The company targeted individuals in the low income category, which was a segment of the manufactured homes market in the company's seven-state operating area. The company's customers were typically between the ages of 18 and 40, blue-collar workers in manufacturing, service, and agricultural industries, and earned approximately $20,000 per year. Many of them were seeking single-family accommodations for their families and turned to manufactured homes because conventional low-cost housing was becoming increasingly less affordable.

Manufactured homes came in a wide variety of styles, including both single and multi-sectional units. They typically had a living room, a kitchen and dining area, and bedrooms and baths, with a wide variety in the size, number and layout of rooms among the various models. The single-sectional homes ranged in size from 588 to 1008 square feet and retailed at prices between $10,000 and $25,000, with the majority selling below $17,000. The multi-sectional homes were 960–2016 square feet and sold at prices ranging from $17,000 to $40,000. Single-sectional homes represented most of the company's sales. While approximately 30 percent of all unit sales in the industry in 1986 were multi-sectional homes, they represented only about 20 percent of Manufactured Homes' unit volume.

The company believed that its focus on the lower end of the market had two advantages. First, since its customers were seeking to fulfill an essential housing need, sales were less affected by changes in general economic conditions. Second, the company's repossession rates were significantly lower than those of the industry since its customers were likely to work very hard to keep their primary residences even when times were bad.

REVENUES

Most of Manufactured Homes' sales were credit sales where the customer paid a down payment of 5 to 10 percent of the sales price and entered into an installment sales contract with the company to pay the remaining amount over periods ranging from 84 to 180 months. The company generally sold the majority of its retail installment contracts to unrelated financial institutions on a recourse basis. Under this agreement, Manufactured Homes was responsible for payments to the financial institution if the customer failed to make the payments specified in the installment contract.

While the installment sale interest rate that Manufactured Homes charged its customers was limited by competitive conditions, it was typically higher than market interest rates. Therefore, the financial institutions to whom these contracts were sold on a recourse basis usually paid the company the stated principal amount of the contract and a portion of the differential between the stated interest rate and the market rate. (The remainder of the interest rate differential was retained by the financial institutions as a security against credit losses and was paid to the company in proportion to customer payments received. The reserve required varied up to seven percent of the aggregate amount financed, including principal and interest.) The company therefore had two sources of revenue: the sale of homes (sales revenue), and the interest rate "spread" (finance participation income).

Peter Herman noted that Financial Accounting Board's Statement 77 (FASB-77) governs the accounting treatment for installment sales receivables that are transferred by a company to a third party on a recourse basis. Transfers of receivables that are subject to recourse must be reported as sales if the following three conditions are satisfied:

1. The seller unequivocally surrenders the receivable to the buyer.
2. The seller's remaining obligations to the buyer under the recourse provision must be subject to reasonable estimation on the date of the transfer of the receivable. For this purpose, the seller should be able to estimate:
   (a) The amount of bad debts and related costs of collection and repossession, and
   (b) The amount of prepayments. If the seller cannot make these estimates reasonably well, a transfer of the receivable cannot be reported as a sale.
3. The seller cannot be required to repurchase the receivable from the buyer except in accordance with the recourse provision.

If any of the above conditions is not satisfied, the seller of the receivable must report the proceeds from the transfer as a loan against the receivable.

337

FINANCIAL PERFORMANCE

Manufactured Homes' revenues increased rapidly in recent years, from $11 million in 1983 to $120 million in 1986. In the company's 1986 annual report, Robert Sauls, the CEO, forecasted the company's growth to continue and expected the 1987 revenues to be $140–$145 million. Herman noted that the company's sales for the first nine months of 1987 exceeded this forecast. The company's latest 10-Q statement reported $148 million revenues for the nine months ended September 30, 1987.

Based on the performance in the first nine months of 1987, the *Value Line Investment Survey* forecasted that Manufactured Homes would achieve $180 million revenues and $6 million net income (or $1.65 per share) in 1987, and $210 million revenues and $7.5 million net income (or $2.00 per share) in 1988. *Value Line* commented on the company's near term prospects as follows:[1]

> *We look forward for [per] share net [income] to advance 20% in 1988, despite a difficult selling environment. Industrywide shipments for the company's core Carolina markets were down in the December quarter and are likely to remain soft*

---

1. *Reprinted with permission from* Value Line Investment Survey, *February 26, 1988.*

in the year ahead. We think, however, that Manufactured Homes will nevertheless find growth opportunities. True, the number of retail centers probably won't increase much this year. On the other hand, the rapid expansion of retail centers over the past five years has put in place a large number of dealerships that have plenty of opportunity for increasing volume.

Management is seeking to average 100 units per store as these sales locations mature. At the end of 1986, stores were selling 47 units per year on average, and that figure rose 20% for the first nine months of 1987. Although the market will be very competitive this year, we think the company's special attention to the low-end of the market, to which many large competitors pay less attention, will give Manufactured Homes a solid niche position. Adding in the reduced tax rate, we think full year [per] share net [income] may well reach the $2.00 mark.

Volume buying gives this retailer an edge. Because Manufactured Homes buys in bulk, it can negotiate lower prices from the manufacturers it deals with. And by passing the savings on to customers, the company is able to underprice smaller, "mom and pop" outlets. Furthermore, because of its size, the company is able to more efficiently handle inventory financing and mortgage assistance for its customers.

Before making a final recommendation to Edwards, Herman wanted to take a detailed look at Manufactured Homes' financial statements for the fiscal year 1986 (Exhibit 2) and the interim statements for the first nine months of 1987 (Exhibit 3).

QUESTIONS

1. Identify the accounting policies of Manufactured Homes which have the most significant impact on the company's financial statements. What are the key assumptions behind these policies? Do you think that these assumptions are justified?
2. Evaluate the company's financial and operating performance during 1986 and the first nine months of 1987.
3. Given the company's business strategy, accounting policies, and recent performance, what is your assessment of its current condition and future potential?

EXHIBIT 1
Performance of Manufactured Homes' Common Stock and S&P 500 Stock Index
Relative to Their Levels on January 2, 1987

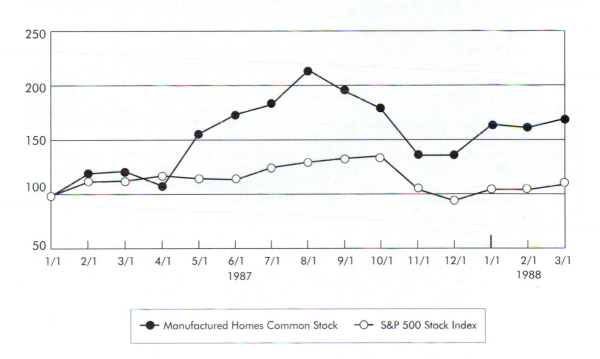

	Manufactured Homes' Stock Price	S&P 500
January 2, 1987	$ 9.000	246.45
March 1, 1988	14.875	267.82
Value Line estimated β	1.05	1.0

EXHIBIT 2

Manufactured Homes, Annual Report for the Year Ended December 31, 1986

Chairman's Letter to Stockholders

The year 1986 was a period of significant accomplishment for your company which served to strengthen our leadership position in the manufactured homes industry. The results achieved were the culmination of a corporate development plan set in motion years ago. For the fourth consecutive year revenues reached record levels, $120 million compared with $80 million in 1985. We are now one of the largest retailers of manufactured, single-family homes in the nation.

As part of our long-term efforts to increase market share, we added 39 retail outlets, bringing the total to 114 at year end. We now have retail outlets in seven states that combined represent approximately 40 percent of the total U.S. market for manufactured homes.

We continue to be primarily a sales and marketing company with manufacturing and retail financing on a limited basis to support the company's growth plan.

We completed a major financing in April 1986 and a second financing in February 1987, both managed by Wertheim Schroder and Company, that totaled $43 million. A portion of the proceeds was used to pay down variable rate debt associated with inventory financing with fixed rate debt and save money in the process. The remainder of the proceeds is to be used for general corporate purposes.

We were pleased at the recognition we received for the growth we have achieved over the last four years as both *Business Week* and *INC. Magazine* included our company in their lists of the fastest growing companies in America. Some describe our growth as explosive. We, however, consider these accomplishments a direct result of a well-structured and carefully executed corporate development plan. Our plans for growth are founded on the basic premise that expansion not exceed our ability to manage our affairs.

From $11 million in revenues in 1983 and a position of near obscurity in the industry, our progress has led us to a position of leadership in the industry.

While we are extremely pleased with our revenue performance, we are also mindful that we must operate profitably. Net earnings per share for 1986 were only 53 cents. The sharp decline in 1986 earnings is directly related to a fourth quarter net loss of $1,347,642. Charges against earnings in the fourth quarter for losses on credit sales and other charges totaling more than three million dollars, coupled with the cost of strengthening your company's position in the marketplace, created a temporary setback in earnings while establishing a basis for a strong 1987.

A strategic plan can only be confirmed as correct when tested by adversity; and last year was something of an acid test for our industry. During 1986, many retailers, in hopes of gaining greater market share, or in some cases hoping for survival, engaged in excessive price cutting. In addition, financial institutions in response to concern over the economy in some geographic areas tightened their policies. We not only dealt with the problems that confronted us but turned some into opportunities.

Over the years management has made it a practice to monitor the various retailers of the manufactured homes in our operating area. First, we wanted to understand our competition; and second, we were looking for acquisition candidates. From a large list of companies, we singled out those that best met our standards of performance. We wanted only those firms with superior management and sales teams. We were able to acquire two of these firms on favorable terms and left management in place.

As a result we succeeded in not only enlarging our market penetration in our traditional states of North Carolina, South Carolina, Georgia, Florida and Alabama, but were able to enter new markets with nine retail outlets in Virginia and West Virginia and six additional outlets in Alabama.

Our independent dealer network continues to grow, and now numbers 26 in five states. The independent dealer program offers important advantages and opportunities. Because of the advantages we bring

m

340

to these small dealers, we continue to receive more requests to join our team.

During the last half of 1986 we sacrificed short-term results to increase market share. We attained that share and as expected it cost us dearly. Selling, general and administrative expense increased from an average of $4.5 million in the first and second quarters to $6 million in the third quarter and to $8 million in the fourth quarter.

As we look to 1987, it is with the knowledge that we are working from a solid foundation. Our financial position is strong. Our debt service requirements are manageable without impairing future earnings performance. Our retail network continues to mature, and sales by location will increase.

Our goal in 1987 is to maintain our market share and show a substantial increase in profit margins. Your Board of Directors has shown confidence in our ability to perform by authorizing me to give you a conservative estimate of our 1987 revenues. Our first quarter revenues are expected to be $32 million with earnings per share of 24 cents. If current economic conditions continue, we expect 1987 revenues to be $140-145 million. The expected significant increase in margins should make this a great year.

I am grateful for the confidence and support of our employees, financial institutions, suppliers and customers; and to you, our shareholders, I would like to say a special "Thanks!"

Robert M. Sauls
Chairman of the Board, President
and Chief Executive Officer

Operating Philosophy

We are convinced that a company is no better than the people selected to manage its affairs. Quality of product and service are vital to any successful enterprise; but again without quality managers and line employees, the business will not succeed. Manufactured Homes has consistently sought and employed only the highest quality individuals at every level within the organization.

It is our practice to provide our employees, at all levels with suitable working conditions and remunera-

tion. We ask only that they perform to the highest level of ability and be innovative in terms of how we can best operate our business.

We believe that the results of the past four years speak for themselves in terms of the invaluable contributions made by our management team and employees.

Industry Profile

The manufactured homes industry is fragmented. At this time there are approximately 10,000 manufactured home retailers throughout the nation, most of which fall into the category of "mom and pop" operations. The industry is presently undergoing a period of transition and consolidation. More and more of the smaller firms, lacking volume buying power and adequate capitalization, are disappearing or becoming a part of a larger company like Manufactured Homes.

The industry has always been competitive but has become more so in recent years. The continuing increases in the average price of conventional housing have forced low income families to seek other alternatives. And more and more are turning to manufactured homes, which have much more to offer than an apartment with the added advantage of equal to lower monthly payments.

In the past, the manufactured home industry suffered from consumer misconceptions created in large part by the use of the term "mobile home." While manufactured homes can be transported from place to place, only five percent are ever relocated once in place. In addition, 60 percent of all homes sold are placed on private property.

Furthermore, the features offered in today's homes are equal to that found in conventional housing but at far less cost.

Industry estimates indicate there are 12 million people living in 6 million manufactured homes. Because of the quality and price advantage, this number is expected to increase on a year-to-year basis for the foreseeable future.

As competition for market share increases, companies like Manufactured Homes will benefit if for no other reason than the financial advantages volume buying affords. This is the primary reason so many

m

341

independent dealers are actively seeking a working relationship with our company. The same can be said of those companies willing to be acquired.

Retail Operations

During 1986 we sold 6,239 new and used homes, a 61 percent increase over the previous year. These sales generated $113 million in revenues or 46 percent above the previous year. With our enlarged retail network in place, we anticipate that sales will again reach record levels in 1987.

The potential market for manufactured homes includes individuals seeking a single-family residence, but lacking the ability to purchase conventional housing. In addition, these homes are sold to retirees and those wanting a second home for vacation purposes. The latter two groups are increasing in great numbers as our population grows older. However, for our company we have concentrated on a single portion of the marketplace, those individuals in the low income category. This market segment is in great numbers in our seven-state operating area as well as other parts of the nation.

Manufactured Homes had its beginning 11 years ago in Winston-Salem, North Carolina. We began with one retail outlet. Our initial growth took place in North Carolina and eventually South Carolina. These two states accounted for 90 percent of sales in 1985. To continue to market only in these two states eventually could have resulted in corporate stagnation. In 1983, the year we became a publicly-held company, we began to formulate what might be best termed as a geographic expansion plan. The real question was, in which states could we operate most effectively and profitably.

Our initial planning went beyond the southeastern states, which remain the largest single regional source of manufactured home sales. We looked at a number of states including Texas which, at the time, was the number one state in manufactured home sales. After careful evaluation, we concluded that our interests and those of our stockholders would best be served in the southeastern portion of the United States. Texas was the most tempting, but it was obvious to management that the reward was not worth the risk; and as time has proven, Texas

has become a graveyard for many manufactured home retail companies.

Like many other retail businesses, presence in the marketplace is critical. After determining to concentrate in the seven states management selected, North Carolina, South Carolina, Georgia, Alabama, Florida, Virginia and West Virginia, we moved aggressively to open new retail outlets and acquire others. In 1983, we had 13 retail outlets; in 1984, the number was 32 and as of March 31, 1987 it's 120.

One of the major keys to success for our company is the insistence that our retail people listen to the customers in terms of interior design and features. When we sense a major trend developing, we go to our suppliers seeking what eventually becomes an entire new line of homes.

We also provide important incentives for our retail managers and sales force. Our base salaries are among the finest in the industry, and we add to that a bonus incentive plan tied directly to margin performance. When times require, we can deal with competitive pricing, but our goal is to maximize sales without sacrificing margins.

Manufacturing

We acquired a manufacturing facility but not as a means of competing with the major manufacturers. In fact, last year we were the largest single retailer of Fleetwood and Redman homes, two of the nation's largest builders of manufactured homes. We acquired the facility to safeguard the company during periods when demand for homes outpaced supply. It also provides the opportunity to manufacture especially designed homes in smaller numbers, thereby eliminating the major commitment that would be required by unaffiliated suppliers.

The firm we acquired was Craftsman Homes, and we continue to manufacture under this brand name. When we acquired the company in 1985, it was producing one home per day. That operation is now producing ten floors per day. Large numbers of our customers have been asking for more entertainment features in the home. With our manufacturing capabilities, we have responded with a home we call the Entertainment Center, and sales have been most rewarding.

We have no immediate need nor intention to enlarge this facility. As it stands, manufacturing can make important contributions, but we can also put this operation on hold without damage to either revenues or earnings.

Financial Considerations

Believing that interest rates will eventually return to the double digit range, we have been successful in replacing our variable rate debt with fixed rate debt. In April 1986, we completed an $18 million private placement of 9% convertible subordinated notes, due 2001. The notes are convertible into common stock at $17.50 per share. The notes were purchased by Prudential Insurance Company of America and Equity-Linked Investors.

In February 1987, we completed a private placement of $25 million of unsecured senior notes in two series. Series A notes, due 1990, were issued in the amount of $15 million at an interest rate of 8.64%. Series B notes, due 1992, were issued in the amount of $10 million at an interest rate of 9.42%. The entire placement was managed by Wertheim Schroder and Co. and purchased by Prudential Insurance Company of America, and we are gratified with the trust they have placed in the future of Manufactured Homes.

There are four key elements that bear on our financial performance related to the sale of homes. These elements are repossessions, recourse financing, loan losses and finance participation.

In almost all cases mortgages executed by the Company are sold to financial institutions. At this moment all of the elements mentioned come into play. The recourse financing provision requires that the Company reassume ownership of the home when the buyer becomes in default of mortgage payments. We knew this when the company was started 11 years ago, and the actions required to deal with this situation are a part of each year's operating plan.

The possibility of repossessions is another reason for selecting the low income segment of the marketplace. Families in this category will make extreme sacrifices to save their homes. We experience one of the lowest repossession rates in the industry. Of the homes returned, we move quickly to renovate and refurbish them and have them resold, normally within 60 to 90 days, at a price equal to or greater than the loan payoff.

We also make provisions for those instances when loan losses do occur. Based on our historical experience, we now maintain a financial reserve equal to 1.7 percent of total net contingent liability for credit sales. Our annual loan loss provisions have consistently exceeded actual losses by more than 20 percent, even though homes which have been sold for four or more years are seldom repossessed. Finance participation is an important source of income for the Company. Simply, funds derived from finance participation is the "spread" between the finance charges included in the mortgage agreement initiated by the Company and those required by the financial institution. A portion of the "spread" is paid in cash to the Company and the remainder over the life of the mortgage contract. The portion retained by the financial institution is accounted for by discounting to present value based on the time period, normally 120 to 180 months, required to actually collect the funds.

Financial Services Subsidiary

Plans for our finance operations, MANH Financial Services Corp., are similar in nature to that for our manufacturing division. The company did not enter this business segment to compete with the financial institutions that have historically provided our mortgage banking requirements. This new entity will be employed primarily to facilitate financing agreements with our banks.

Financial Services does have mortgage lending capabilities that will only be employed at those times when our conventional banking arrangements are unable to act on a timely basis. Again, like our manufacturing operations, management has no intention of expanding Financial Services. As it exists now, it provides the Company with the flexibility required to deal quickly with mortgage finance transactions.

m

343

Selected Financial Data

Years Ended December 31,	1986	1985	1984	1983	1982
Operating Results:					
Revenues	$120,264,954	$79,525,988	$36,195,802	$10,986,036	$7,477,966
Earnings (loss) before cumulative effect of change in accounting principle[1]	2,033,425	3,718,325	2,694,529	536,881	(59,570)
Earning (loss) per share	.53	.98	.77	.21	(.03)
Net earnings (loss)	2,033,425	3,213,754	2,694,529	536,881	(59,570)
Net earnings (loss) per share	.53	.85	.77	.21	(.03)
Financial Position at Year-End:					
Total assets	$81,377,803	$50,944,924	$17,660,984	$6,836,087	$5,025,130
Long-term debt	18,609,987	1,082,543	400,000	—	491,280
Stockholders' equity	14,167,119	11,052,759	7,633,005	4,938,654	733,195
Working capital	15,111,883	4,820,912	4,819,203	3,699,184	(147,124)

Quarterly Financial Data (unaudited)

Quarter	First	Second	Third	Fourth	Total
1986[2]:					
Revenues	$23,324,633	$29,724,418	$33,295,241	$33,920,662	$120,264,954
Net earnings (loss)	641,702	1,562,205	1,177,160	(1,347,642)	2,033,425
Net earnings (loss) per share	.17	.40	.30	(.36)	.53
Average shares and equivalents	3,850,277	3,944,518	3,922,406	3,733,968	3,864,161
1985:					
Revenues	$10,965,457	$22,103,134	$24,083,556	$22,373,841	$ 79,525,988
Earnings before cumulative effect of change in accounting principle[1]	741,395	1,312,511	1,112,714	551,705	3,718,325
Earnings per share	.21	.34	.29	.14	.98
Net earnings	236,824	1,312,511	1,112,714	551,705	3,213,754
Net earnings per share	.08	.34	.29	.14	.85
Proforma amounts:					
Net earnings	741,395	1,312,511	1,112,714	551,705	3,718,325
Net earnings per share	.21	.34	.29	.14	.98
Average shares and equivalents	3,488,968	3,820,016	3,870,857	3,838,486	3,802,693

[1]See Note 2 of notes to consolidated financial statements for information regarding a change in accounting principle for finance participation income in 1985.

[2]During the fourth quarter of 1986, the Company provided approximately $3,000,000 for losses on credit sales, primarily due to industry conditions, which are causing unusually high costs relating to the repossession of homes. In addition, the Company incurred abnormal costs in the fourth quarter of approximately $300,000 relating primarily to the write-off of previously recognized finance participation income. The aggregate provision for these items amounted to approximately $3,300,000 in the fourth quarter. The Company cannot determine the extent to which these fourth quarter provisions may be applicable to the first, second and third quarter of 1986.

Common Stock Prices and Dividend Information

The Company's common stock is traded on the American Stock Exchange under the symbol MNH.

	1986		1985	
	High	Low	High	Low
First	15 3/4	10	8 3/4	4 3/8
Second	16 1/2	12 1/4	13 1/4	8 1/4
Third	15	9 3/4	15 3/8	10 1/2
Fourth	12	8 7/8	14	8 3/4

The Company has never paid a cash dividend and does not intend to for the foreseeable future. The weighted average number of shares outstanding for 1986 was 3,660,048 shares, for 1985 and 1984, 3,488,968 shares, for 1983, 2,588,518 shares and for 1982, 2,100,000 shares. The approximate number of stockholders at March 1987 was 2,000.

m

MANAGEMENT DISCUSSION AND ANALYSIS

Results of Operations

1986 Versus 1985

The Company's net sales in 1986 were $106,095,667 compared with $68,674,779 in 1985, an increase of $37,420,888 or 54%.

The Company's program of managed sales growth resulted in greater penetration due to:

	1986	1985	Increase
An increase of 44% in the number of company-owned and operated sales centers	92	64	28
A 100% expansion of the MANH Independent Retailer network	22	11	11
A total increase of 52% in sales centers for the year	114	75	39

The total number of new and used homes sold in 1986 was 6,239, a 61% increase over the 3,866 homes sold in 1985. New home sales for both years were 87% of total home sales.

A manufactured home sales center usually experiences a five-year growth and development period. The Manufactured Homes (AMEX Symbol: MNH) sales center should develop a sales production level of at least 100 new homes per year at maturity, although this average annual sales volume can vary widely by geographic location. The Company in 1986 averaged 47 new sales per sales center versus 45 in 1985. The average reflects the rapid expansion of new sales centers. Approximately 47% of the average potential capacity per sales center had been achieved, leaving significant growth potential within the Company's current sales center network without the need for significantly increasing the number of sales centers.

New home sales were 80% single-wides in 1986, as compared with 84% in 1985. This reflects a shift to more double-wides resulting from the acquisition of

two subsidiaries. In addition, a number of our customers are able to purchase double-wide homes since interest rates are lower. However, the primary emphasis of MNH's marketing plan continues to be towards the less expensive, single-wide home which fits the economic capability of a significant percentage of potential customers within the MNH market area of the five southeastern states, plus Virginia and West Virginia.

The average MNH selling price of new homes by Company sales centers for 1986 was $17,300 versus $17,400 in 1985. The gross profit margins were unchanged for 1985.

Craftsman Manufactured Homes, Inc., a wholly owned subsidiary of MNH, expanded its production capability from one production line to two. Revenues in 1986 were in excess of $15,746,000 of which $7,489,000 were direct sales to non-affiliated dealers with $8,257,000 being sold to Company sales centers for resale. The Company purchased the manufacturing facility in September 1985. The Craftsman manufacturing subsidiary sold 481 homes directly to dealers not associated with MNH in 1986 as compared with 130 homes in 1985.

Repossessions and Early Pay-offs

Manufactured housing, as an industry, has been significantly impacted by the slow economic growth of the economy coupled with an extended period of low interest rates. These factors are reflected by a year-to-year decrease in 1986 of 15% in manufactured homes sold throughout the Company's market area.

Lower interest rates have resulted in two noticeable shifts within the housing industry: (1) certain owners may select conventional homes over manufactured homes; and (2) an intensive marketing effort by financial institutions for mortgage refinancing has resulted in many home owners refinancing their mortgages at lower interest rates, which for MNH usually means a mortgage prepayment.

The Company's experience relative to prepayments of home mortgages, until 1986, had been minor. However, late in 1986, prepayments became a recognized concern. Prepayment of mortgages caused management to reevaluate certain assumptions resulting in a significant increase in the reserve for

m

346

credit losses related to mortgage prepayments in order to address the prospects of mortgage interest rates continuing to remain at present levels of 8½ to 9½ percent.

Repossessions of homes result primarily from customers' inability to meet their mortgage payment commitment. Approximately 70% of all MNH credit sales are with recourse, which means the Company will buy back from the financial institution holding a customer's mortgage those homes repossessed by the mortgage holder which were originally sold by MNH subsidiaries.

The Company's experience related to repossessions has shown very little change during the past ten years. However, during the fourth quarter of 1986, approximately $2,000,000 of repossession expense and interest chargebacks were experienced and charged off. Therefore, a charge to earnings, for both prepayments and repossessions, was made and the reserve for credit losses was increased to $3,000,000 at December 31, 1986.

One of the causes of the $2,000,000 charge was the refusal of some unrelated financial institutions to refinance the repossession that occurred in their portfolio, and a second cause was that the Company had to finance them through MANH Financial Services thereby having an immediate charge in finance participation on the pay-off and not recognizing the finance participation income of the resale.

During the first three quarters of 1986, the provision for credit losses was approximately 1% of net sales. Due to the recent fourth quarter charges, management will increase the provision for losses for 1987 to 1½% of net sales as a precautionary measure against future repossession and early pay-off.

Finance Participation

Finance participation was $12,084,108 in 1986 versus $9,715,558 in 1985, a 24.4% increase. As a percentage of net sales, it was 11.4% in 1986 compared with 14.1% in 1985. Several factors caused the percentage of decrease in realized finance participation: (1) increased cash sales; (2) increased non-recourse sales where no finance participation is received; (3) contributions of manufacturing to the sales volume where no finance participation is received; and (4) a decrease in the interest rate

spread earned by the Company when the sales contracts are sold to financial institutions. The decreased "spread" was the most important factor in 1986 as two major financial institutions changed their "retail rate" and reduced the "spread" received by the Company by 33%.

Finance participation is an important part of the Company's revenue. This source of revenue is monitored closely and alternative sources of financing are considered for customer mortgage funding on an ongoing basis.

Insurance

The Company earns commissions for writing homeowner insurance policies at the time of sale of the home and from renewal premiums. Income from insurance sales was $721,758 in 1986 compared with $413,282 in 1985, a 75% increase.

Selling, General and Administrative

The Company's selling, general and administrative expense (SG&A) has historically ranged around 17% of revenue. This range varies according to the Company's growth pattern and marketing emphasis.

In 1986, the significant factors affecting the Company's SG&A expense, which was 19% of revenue, were that: (1) the Company initiated a second production line at its manufacturing plant; (2) acquired two additional subsidiaries — Piggy Bank Homes of Alabama and Jeff Brown Homes in Virginia and West Virginia, in mid-September 1986; (3) initiated two additional operating subsidiaries — AAA Mobile Homes (formerly part of MNH), and MANH Independent Retailers Corp. (formerly spread among several subsidiaries for operational purposes); (4) opened 13 new company sales centers; added 11 independent dealers to the retail network; and (5) formed MANH Financial Services Corp. as of October 1986. This expansion and realignment of subsidiaries, which occurred mostly during the fourth quarter, were part of an overall marketing strategy to more effectively penetrate the Company's market. The significant increase in sales over 1985 of 54% resulted from staffing an additional 13 company-owned sales centers, with special emphasis on bonus programs to sell aged inventory and homes received in trade for new sales, as well as improving the percentage of homes which were sold with recourse. This aggressive marketing program was designed to achieve momentum for a strong 1987, but increased SG&A expense significantly at the same time.

Several other cost factors effecting SG&A expense were: (1) An increase in liability insurance rates on policy renewals during 1986 at an annual rate 40% higher than in 1985, or approximately an additional $350,000; and (2) the cost incurred during the year related to the completion of a 15-month standardization of accounting procedures and data processing enhancement program which centralized the Company's management information with on-line capability to each subsidiary. This is a significant step forward in better data management and timely preparation of financial information.

Interest Expense

Interest expense increased $1,543,352 to $3,367,940 in 1986 from $1,824,588 in 1985, or 85%. The increase resulted from a $12,536,000 increase in total inventory and approximately an $8,000,000 increase in total receivables directly related to the expansion of 39 sales centers in 1986.

Income Taxes

The Company's effective income tax rate was 49.8% in 1986 compared to 47.2% in 1985. This increase resulted primarily from the elimination of investment tax credits under the Tax Reform Act of 1986.

Organization

Each of the Company's nine subsidiaries are profit centers. Each subsidiary has its own chief executive officer with total profit and loss responsibility. The Company's long-range plan for growth is by strategic acquisitions, expanding market share, and developing management talent through a newly organized salesperson training program, all to meet the need of providing low-cost housing to the American consumer.

Manufacturing

Craftsman Manufactured Homes, Inc., the MNH manufacturing subsidiary, commenced operations in

September 1985. It has grown from virtually a start-up operation to a sales volume in excess of $15,000,000 in 1986. Approximately 57% of the 1,119 homes manufactured were sold to and through Company related sales centers. The balance of the homes were sold to non-related independent retailers. The Craftsman plant operates two production lines with a plant capacity of approximately 3,500 floors (multi-section homes require more than one floor) per year.

Financial Services

MANH Financial Services Corp. was organized on October 14, 1986 to facilitate the marketing of new, repossessed and pre-owned homes. Two major retail financial sources curtailed the purchase of conditional sales contracts which resulted in slow response to contract applications and therefore lost sales. The Company responded with the formation of MANH Financial Services Corp. to operate on a limited basis. The growth of this subsidiary will depend largely on whether or not the unrelated financial institutions continue to service the Company's growth.

1985 Versus 1984

The Company's net sales for 1985 were $68,674,779 compared to $30,480,571 for 1984, an increase of 125%. The majority of this increase was due to the addition of eight retail sales centers during the first quarter and the acquisition of Country Squire Mobile Homes, Inc. on March 22, 1985, with 20 retail sales centers. The Company also opened seven retail sales centers in the second quarter, six in the third quarter, and two in the fourth quarter. Volume increases in sales centers which were in operation at the end of 1984 also occurred while the average sales price per unit remained fairly constant from 1984 to 1985. The Company's purchase of a manufacturing facility on September 4, 1985, contributed approximately 7% of the 1985 sales increase.

Finance participation income for 1985 was $9,715,558 compared to $5,221,279, an increase of 86%. This was less than the percentage increase in sales due to three factors: (1) The election to discount the unreceived portion of finance participation

m
348

income to its present value; (2) Country Squire earned significantly less finance participation income than the other retail groups, primarily because of non-recourse sales; and, (3) the inclusion of manufacturing sales which do not earn finance participation income. Insurance commissions, interest and other revenues increased proportionally in relation to the increase in sales.

Cost of sales as a percentage increased approximately 2% in 1985. This increase was due to the substantial increase in sales to independent retailers which traditionally have lower margins, and a slight decrease in margins at Company-owned sales centers. Selling, general and administrative expenses increased in 1985 as a result of increased sales volume and reflect the increase in number of sales centers and additional personnel to support our continued growth. Provision for losses on credit sales remained relatively constant as a percentage of net sales from 1984 to 1985. Interest rates were generally lower in 1985; however, total interest cost increased significantly due to increased inventories to support the added sales centers.

Liquidity and Capital Resources

The Company, in April 1986, sold $18,000,000 of 9% convertible subordinated notes due May 15, 2001. The proceeds were used primarily to reduce floor plan notes payable and to significantly improve the Company's liquidity. During 1986, the Company purchased Jeff Brown Homes, Inc. with nine sales centers and Piggy Bank Homes of Alabama, Inc. with six sales centers, added 13 Company-owned sales centers, formed a finance

company subsidiary with an initial capitalization of $500,000, expanded the principal offices of its wholly-owned subsidiary, Tri-County Homes, Inc., and opened a second production line at its manufacturing facility, using funds generated from the sale of the subordinated notes and from operations.

At December 31, 1986, the Company had available $1,000,000 in a bank line of credit and $8,000,000 in unused floor plan lines of credit. On February 13, 1987, the Company sold $25,000,000 of unsecured senior notes due in 1990 and 1992 bearing interest at a blended rate of 8.95%. The proceeds have been partially used to reduce floor plan notes payable.

Although working capital increased significantly in 1986, operations used working capital of $2,956,041 compared to providing working capital of $2,847,026 in 1985 and $2,599,953 in 1984. The use of working capital by operations in 1986 was principally due to the interest rate spread applicable to finance participation and significant reductions in deferred income taxes applicable to the provision for credit losses and finance participation income.

The Tax Reform Act of 1986 will benefit the Company through a reduction of the corporate income tax rate. However, beginning January 1, 1987, the Act will require the Company to accelerate the payment of Federal income taxes. However, the Company believes that funds to be generated by operations, combined with credit lines currently available, will be sufficient to satisfy capital needs for current operations.

m

349

CONSOLIDATED BALANCE SHEET

December 31,	1986	1985
ASSETS		
Current Assets		
Cash and cash equivalents:		
Cash and temporary investments	$2,486,024	$2,968,837
Contract proceeds receivable from financial institutions (Note 9)	11,496,078	5,189,535
Total cash and cash equivalents	13,982,102	8,158,372
Finance participation receivable – current portion (Note 2)	2,691,497	2,486,001
Deferred finance participation income	(801,511)	(523,038)
Net finance participation receivable	1,889,986	1,962,963
Other receivables (Note 4)	3,746,863	2,057,674
Refundable income taxes (Note 11)	778,971	—
Inventories (Notes 5 and 9)	38,163,712	25, 628,156
Prepaid expenses	538,419	408,124
Deferred income taxes (Note 11)	761,262	436,496
Total current assets	59,861,315	38,651,785
Finance participation receivable – noncurrent portion (Note 2)	16,128,799	10, 269,713
Deferred finance participation income	(3,923,178)	(2,968,629)
Net finance participation receivable	12,205,621	7,301,084
Property, plant and equipment at cost (Notes 6 and 10)	7,504,272	5,467,164
Accumulated depreciation and amortization	(2,410,812)	(1,555,427)
Net property, plant and equipment	5,093,460	3,911,737
Excess of costs over net assets of acquired companies less amortization (Note 3)	2,107,874	973, 860
Other assets	2,109,533	106,458
	$81,377,803	$50,944,924

December 31,	1986	1985
LIABILITIES AND STOCKHOLDERS' EQUITY		
Current Liabilities		
Notes payable	$1,099,971	$ —
Long-term debt – current installments (Note 10)	810,901	1,100,624
Floor plan notes payable (Note 9)	35,207,386	27,468,153
Accounts payable	4,899,250	2,210,560
Income taxes (Note 11)	—	1,828,234
Accrued expenses and other liabilities (Note 8)	2,731,924	1,223,302
Total current liabilities	44,749,432	33,830,873
Long-term debt – noncurrent installments (Note 10)	18,609,987	1,082,543
Reserve for losses on credit sales (Note 7)	3,000,000	1,863,992
Deferred income taxes (Note 11)	851,265	3,114,757
Total liabilities	67,210,684	39,892,165
Stockholders' Equity (Notes 10 and 12)		
Common stock — $.50 par value per share; authorize 10,000,000 shares; issued and outstanding 3,733,968 shares in 1986 and 3,488,968 shares in 1985	1,866,984	1,744,484
Additional paid-in capital	3,508,351	2,549,916
Retained earnings	8,791,784	6,758,359
Total stockholders' equity	14,167,119	11,052,759
Commitments and contingent liabilities (Notes 3 and 13)		
	$81,377,803	$50,944,924

m

351

CONSOLIDATED STATEMENTS OF EARNINGS

Years Ended December 31,	1986	1985	1984
Revenues:			
Net sales	$106,095,667	$68,674,779	$30,480,571
Finance participation income	12,084,108	9,715,558	5,221,279
Insurance commissions	721,758	413,282	231,618
Interest	338,447	163,663	123,564
Other	1,024,974	558,706	138,770
Total revenues	120,264,954	79,525,988	36,195,802
Costs and expenses:			
Cost of sales	86,212,901	56,222,412	24,324,851
Selling, general and administrative	22,852,093	13,639,942	5,895,891
Provision for losses on credit sales (Note 7)	3,777,900	793,497	253,004
Interest	3,367,940	1,824,588	570,527
Total costs and expenses	116,210,834	72,480,439	31,044,273
Earnings before income taxes	4,054,120	7,045,549	5,151,529
Income taxes (Note 11)	2,020,695	3,327,224	2,457,000
Earnings before cumulative effect of change in accounting principle (Note 2)	2,033,425	3,718,325	2,694,529
Cumulative effect on prior years of change in accounting principle for finance participation (Notes 2 and 11)	—	(504,571)	—
Net earnings	$2,033,425	$3,213,754	$2,694,529
Earnings per share:			
Before cumulative effect of change in accounting principle	$.53	$.98	$.77
Cumulative effect on prior years of change in accounting principle for finance participation	—	(.13)	—
Net earnings per share — primary	$.53	$.85	$.77
Net earnings per share — fully diluted	$.53	$.84	$.77
Proforma amounts assuming retroactive application of the change in accounting principle (Note 2):			
Net earnings	$2,033,425	$3,718,325	$2,365,334
Net earnings per share — primary	$.53	$.98	$.68

CONSOLIDATED STATEMENTS OF CHANGES IN FINANCIAL POSITION

Year Ended December 31,	1986	1985	1984
Working capital was provided by			
Operations:			
Net earnings	$2,033,425	$3,213,754	$2,694,529
Adjustments for items not requiring (providing) working capital:			
Depreciation and amortization	946,858	556,23 6	210,699
Noncurrent deferred income taxes	(2,197,061)	78,637	1,412,812
Provision for losses on credit sales, net of actual charges	699,343	(217,402)	134,614
Issuance of nonqualified stock options	142,000	206,000	—
Finance participation income	(12,084,108)	(9,715,558)	(5,221,279)
Collections, current and deferred finance participation income portion of finance participation receivable	7,503,502	8,725,359	3,316,397
Other	—	—	52,181
Working capital provided (used) by operations	(2,956,041)	2,847,026	2, 599,953
Proceeds from long-term debt	18,396,000	1,651,822	400,000
Exercise of stock options	938,935	—	—
Decrease in other assets	—	4,024	—
	16,378,894	4,502,872	2,999,953
Working capital was used for			
Net assets, exclusive of working capital of $806,363 in 1985 and deficits in working capital of $1,109,080 in 1986 and $140,604 in 1984, of acquired companies (Note 3)	1,285,935	422,179	1,220,198
Additions to property, plant and equipment	1,917,489	2,756,178	580,259
Current installments and repayment of long-term debt	1,071,308	1,322,806	70,423
Additions to other assets and excess costs	1,813,191	—	9,054
	6,087,923	4,501,163	1,879,934
Increase in working capital	$10,290,971	$ 1,709	$1,120,019
Changes in working capital, by component			
Cash and cash equivalents	$ 5,823,730	$6,136,129	$ 579,418
Finance participation receivable – current portion	(72,977)	1,193,013	569,838
Other receivables	1,689,189	1,715,543	233,696
Refundable income taxes	778,971	—	—
Inventories	12,535,556	17,448,795	5,616,654
Prepaid expenses	130,295	371,403	25,918
Deferred income taxes	324,766	102,710	203,000
Notes payable	(1,099,971)	—	—
Long-term debt -current installments	289,723	(900,624)	(200,000)
Floor plan notes payable	(7,739,233)	(22,962,163)	(3,986,435)
Accounts payable	(2,688,690)	(1,896,668)	(219,293)
Income taxes	1,828,234	(620,489)	(1,207,745)
Accrued expenses and other liabilities	(1,508,6 22)	(585,940)	(495,032)
Increase in working capital	$10,290,971	$ 1,709	$ 1,120,019

m

353

NOTES TO CONSOLIDATED FINANCIAL STATEMENTS

December 31, 1986, 1985 and 1984

Note 1
Summary of Significant Accounting Policies

Principles of Consolidation and Nature of Business

The consolidated financial statements include the accounts of Manufactured Homes, Inc. and all sub-sidiaries, each wholly-owned, and hereafter referred to collectively as the "Company." All significant intercompany items are eliminated.

The Company is engaged principally in the retail sale of new and used manufactured single-family homes.

Inventories

Inventories are stated at the lower of cost or market, with cost being determined using the specific unit method for new and used manufactured homes and average cost for materials and supplies.

Property, Plant and Equipment

Depreciation of property, plant and equipment is provided principally by the straight-line method over the estimated useful lives of the respective assets. Amortization of leasehold improvements is provided by the straight-line method over the shorter of the lease terms or the estimated useful lives of the improvements.

Income Taxes

Deferred income taxes are recognized for income and expense items that are reported in different periods for financial reporting and income tax pur-poses.

Income Recognition

A sale is recognized when payment is received or, in the case of credit sales, when a down payment (gen-erally 10% of the sales price) is received and the Company and the customer enter into an install-ment contract. Installment contracts are normally payable over periods ranging from 120 to 180 months. Credit sales represent the majority of the Company's sales.

Under existing financing arrangements, the majority of installment contracts are sold, with recourse to unrelated financial institutions at an agreed upon rate which is below the contractual interest rate of the installment contract. At the time of sale, the Company receives immediate payment for the stated principal amount of the installment contract and a portion of the finance participation resulting from the interest rate differential. The remainder of the interest rate differential is retained by the finan-cial institution as security against credit losses and is paid to the Company in proportion to customer pay-ments received by the financial institution. The Com-pany accounts for these transactions as sales in accordance with Statement of Financial Accounting Standards No. 77, "Reporting by Transferors for Transfers of Receivables with Recourse," and recog-nizes finance participation income equal to the dif-ference between the contractual interest rates of the installment contracts and the agreed upon rates to the financial institutions; the portion retained by the financial institutions is discounted for estimated time of collection and carried at its present value (see Note 2).

Reserve for Losses on Credit Sales

Estimated losses arising from the recourse provi-sions of the Company's financing arrangements with unrelated financial institutions are provided for currently based on historical loss experience and current economic conditions and consist of esti-mated future rebates of finance participation income due to prepayment or repossession, esti-mated future losses on installment contracts repur-chased from financial institutions and estimated future losses on installment contracts transferred to new purchasers in lieu of repossession. Actual losses are charged to the reserve when incurred.

Excess of Costs over Net Assets of Acquired Companies

The excess of costs over net assets of acquired com-panies is being amortized over 30 years on the straight-line method.

Earnings per Share

Primary earnings per share are based on the weighted average number of common and common equivalent shares outstanding. Such average shares are as follows:

Years Ended December 31,	1986	1985	1984
Outstanding shares	3,660,048	3,488,968	3,488,968
Equivalent shares	204,113	313,725	—
	3,864,161	3,802,693	3,488,968

The equivalent shares in 1986 and 1985 represent the shares issuable upon exercise of stock options and warrants after the assumed repurchase of common shares with the related proceeds at the average price during the period. Common equivalent shares were not considered in 1984 as the resulting dilution was insignificant.

Fully diluted earnings per share are based on the weighted average number of common and common equivalent shares outstanding plus the common shares issuable upon the assumed conversion of the convertible subordinated notes and elimination of the applicable interest expense less related income tax benefit. In determining equivalent shares, the assumed repurchase of common shares is at the higher of the average or period-end price.

Note 2
Accounting Change

Prior to 1985, the Company recognized finance participation income without discounting for the estimated time of collection of the portion retained by the unrelated financial institutions as security against credit losses. However, in 1985 the Company adopted the practice whereby the portion of finance participation income retained by the financial institutions is recorded at its present value based upon estimated time of collection. The Company believes the new method is preferable since it more accurately reflects the value of the finance participation receivable at the date the installment contracts are sold to the financial institutions.

As a result of this change, earnings in 1985, before the cumulative effect of the change on prior years, were decreased by $538,466 ($.14 per share). Net earnings were further decreased by $504,571 ($.13 per share), which represents the cumulative effect of the change on prior years. Proforma net earnings and earnings per share amounts reflecting retroactive application of the change are shown in the consolidated statements of earnings.

Note 3
Acquisitions

On January 6, 1984, Manufactured Homes, Inc. acquired the outstanding common stock of Tri-County Homes, Inc., a retailer of manufactured housing located in eastern North Carolina. The purchase agreement required cash payments of $400,000 and potential earn-out payments of $600,000, all earned at December 31, 1984. The acquisition has been accounted for as a purchase and, accordingly, the operations of Tri-County are included in the consolidated financial statements of Manufactured Homes, Inc. beginning in 1984. Effective March 22, 1985, Manufactured Homes, Inc. acquired the outstanding common stock of Country Squire Mobile Homes, Inc., a retailer of manufactured housing located principally in South Carolina. The purchase agreement required cash payments of $873,000 and includes potential earn-out payments of $1,960,000 over the period 1985 to 1990. The potential earn-out is based on a percentage of Country Squire's pre-tax earnings as defined. At December 31, 1986, $642,947 ($396,000 in 1986 and $246,947 in 1985) of the potential earn-out had been earned and recorded as an adjustment of the purchase price. The acquisition has been accounted for as a purchase and, accordingly, the operations of Country Squire are included in the consolidated financial statements of Manufactured Homes, Inc. since March 22, 1985. The following unaudited proforma data presents the results of operations of the Company and Country Squire as if the acquisition had occurred at January 1, 1984.

Years Ended December 31,	1985	1984
Total revenues	$87,729,677	$59,696,534
Net earnings	3,090,464	2,812,632
Net Earnings per share:		
Primary	$ .81	$ .81
Fully diluted	$ .80	$ .81

m

355

In September 1986, Manufactured Homes, Inc. acquired the outstanding common stock of two companies engaged in the retail sale of manufactured homes. The purchase agreements required aggregate cash payments of $151,000 and potential earn-out payments of $874,000 over the period 1987 to 1992. The potential earn-outs are based on a percentage of the respective companies' pre-tax earnings as defined. The acquisitions have been accounted for as purchases and, accordingly, their operations, which are not material, are included in the consolidated financial statements of Manufactured Homes, Inc., since September 1986. At date of acquisition, one company had operating loss carryforwards of $612,049 and to the extent utilized, the income tax reductions will be accounted for as adjustments of the purchase price. At December 31, 1986, $324,510 (tax benefit of $159,226) of the carryforwards had been utilized.

The net assets, exclusive of working capital of $806,363 in 1985 and deficits in working capital of $1,109,080 in 1986 and $140,604 in 1984, of the acquired companies were as follows:

Years Ended December 31,	1986	1985	1984
Finance participation receivable	$ 323,931	$1,337,147	$1,172,853
Property, plant and equipment	169,092	747,092	131,367
Other assets	493,089	23,403	61,016
Long-term debt	(202,752)	(353,527)	(70,423)
Reserve for losses on credit sales	(436,665)	(1,675,000)	(74,615)
Other liabilities	—	(679,524)	—
Excess of costs over net assets of acquired companies	939,240	1,022,588	—
	$1,285,935	$ 422,179	$1,220,198

Note 4
Other Receivables

Other receivables consist of the following:

December 31,	1986	1985
Manufacturers' volume bonuses	$1,979,021	$1,557,029
Sundry	1,767,842	500,645
	$3,746,863	$2,057,674

Note 5
Inventories

Inventories consist of the following:

December 31,	1986	1985
New manufactured homes	$31,920,134	$22,766,030
Used manufactured homes	4,971,040	2,068,099
Materials and supplies	1,272,538	794,027
	$38,163,712	$25,628,156

Note 6
Property, Plant and Equipment

The cost and estimated useful lives of the major classifications of property, plant and equipment are as follows:

	Estimated Useful Life	December 31, 1986	December 31, 1985
Land	—	$ 735,329	$ 620,083
Buildings	15–20 yrs.	1,660,321	849,427
Manufactured homes— office units	5–7 yrs.	1,048,571	1,013,543
Leasehold improvements	3–5 yrs.	615,319	
Furniture & equipment	3–10 yrs.	1,921,101	1,108,123
Vehicles	3–5 yrs.	1,485,222	1,124,154
Signs	3–7 yrs.	38,409	185,196
		$7,504,272	$5,467,164

Note 7
Reserve for Losses on Credit Sales

An analysis of the reserve for losses on credit sales follows:

Years Ended December 31,	1986	1985	1984
Balance at beginning of year	$1,863,992	$ 406,394	$197,165
Amount at date of acquisition applicable to acquired companies, less actual charges of $69,236 in 1986 and $604,403 in 1985	367,429	1,070,597	74,615
Provision for losses	3,777,900	793,497	253,004
Actual charges	(3,009,321)	(406,496)	(118,390)
Balance at end of year	$3,000,000	$1,863,992	$406,394

Note 8
Accrued Expenses and Other Liabilities

A summary of accrued expenses and other liabilities follows:

December 31,	1986	1985
Payroll and related costs	$1,580,235	$ 697,287
Other	1,151,689	526,015
	$2,731,924	$1,223,302

Note 9
Floor Plan Notes Payable

A substantial portion of the Company's new manufactured home inventories are financed through floor plan arrangements with certain unrelated financial institutions. A summary of floor plan notes payable follows:

December 31,	Rate	Floor Plan Lines	1986	1985
General Electric Credit Corporation	Prime + 1.75 (9.25%)	$27,052,000	$22,601,520	$17,183,988
ITT Diversified Credit Corporation	Prime + 2.00 (9.50%)	7,200,000	5,869,438	5,224,373
CIT Financial Services	Prime + 2.00 (9.50%)	4,000,000	3,958,932	1,761,854
Whirlpool Acceptance Corporation	Prime + 1.50 (9.00%)	1,500,000	1,210,586	—
U.S. Home Acceptance	Prime (7.50%)	1,000,000	36,680	815,066
Citicorp Acceptance Company, Inc.	Prime + 2.00 (9.50%)	975,000	—	1,706,728
Others	Various	1,850,000	1,530,230	776,144
		$43,577,000	$35,207,386	$27,468,153

The floor plan liability at December 31, 1986 is collateralized by inventories and contract proceeds receivable from financial institutions. The floor plan arrangements generally require periodic partial repayments with the unpaid balance due upon sale of the related collateral.

The weighted average interest rate paid on the outstanding floor plan liability was 10.9%, 11.0%, and 14.7% for 1986, 1985, and 1984, respectively. The maximum amount outstanding at any month end during each year was $35,207,386 for 1986, $27,468,153 for 1985, and $4,508,319 for 1984, with a weighted average balance outstanding for each year of approximately $25,500,000, $16,000,000 and $3,750,000, respectively.

Note 10
Long-Term Debt

A summary of long-term debt follows:

December 31,	1986	1985
9% convertible subordinated notes payable, due in annual installments of $1,800,000 beginning May 15, 1992 through May 15, 2001	$18,000,000	—
Note payable, due in monthly installments of $66,667 through October 1, 1987, interest at prime rate (7½% at December 31, 1986) and collateralized by property, plant and equipment with a depreciated cost of $1,160,640	666,670	1,466,667
Obligation payable in January 1988, interest at the prime rate (7½% at December 31, 1986) and collateralized by the common stock of Country Squire Mobile Homes, Inc. (Note 3)	396,000	—
Obligation payable in annual installments of $200,000 through April 15, 1987, repaid in 1986	—	400,000
Various notes payable, due in monthly installments, including interest at rates ranging from 8% to 18%	358,218	316,500
	19,420,888	2,183,167
Less current installments	810,901	1,100,624
	$18,609,987	$1,082,543

The aggregate annual maturities of the long-term debt for the five years following December 31, 1986 are: 1987, $810,901; 1988, $508,497; 1989, $53,498; 1990, $33,255; 1991, $14,737.

Pursuant to an agreement dated April 25, 1986 (the "1986 Agreement"), the Company sold its Convertible Subordinated Notes due May 15, 2001, in the amount of $18,000,000 to two lenders. The proceeds from these notes have been used principally to reduce floor plan notes payable. The notes are convertible into shares of the Company's common stock at the conversion price of $17.50 per share. The conversion price is subject to adjustment in the event of stock dividends, stock splits, payment of extraordinary distributions, granting of options or sale of additional shares of common stock. The notes are subject to prepayment at the option of the Company between October 28, 1986 and May 15, 1996 at 100% of par if for a specified period preceding the written notice of prepayment the closing market price per share of the Company's common stock is equal to or greater than a percentage of the conversion price. Such percentage decreases from 200% through May 15, 1989 to 110% at May 15, 2001. The 1986 Agreement contains various restrictive covenants which include, among other things, maintenance of a minimum level of working capital as defined, maintenance of a minimum level of net earnings available for fixed charges as defined, consolidated current assets as defined, equal or greater than senior debt, payment of cash dividends and the creation of additional indebtedness.

Subsequent to December 31, 1986 and pursuant to an agreement dated February 13, 1987 (the "1987 Agreement"), the Company sold the Prudential Insurance Company of America Series A and Series B Senior notes in the aggregate of $25,000,000. The Series A notes in the amount of $15,000,000 bear interest at the rate of 8.64% and are due February 15, 1990. The Series B notes in the amount of $10,000,000 bear interest at the rate of 9.42% and are due February 15, 1992. The proceeds from these notes have been used partially to reduce floor plan notes payable and the remainder added to corporate funds. The 1987 Agreement also contains restrictive financial covenants. The 1987 Agreement financial covenants were changed to reflect more accurately the Company's current financial structure.

Concurrent with the execution of the 1987 Agreement, the financial covenants contained in the 1986 Agreement were amended to conform to the covenants in the 1987 Agreement. At December 31, 1986, the Company was in compliance with the various restrictive covenants in the 1986 Agreement with the exception of the net earnings available for fixed charges covenant. The Company was in compliance with all of the restrictive covenants in the 1986 Agreement, as amended. Retained earnings available for the payment of cash dividends amounted to $1,516,712 at December 31, 1986.

Note 11
Income Taxes

Income taxes are reflected in the consolidated statements of earnings as follows:

Years Ended December 31,	1986	1985	1984
Before cumulative effect of change in accounting principle	$2,020,695	$3,327,224	$2,457,000
Cumulative effect on prior years of change in accounting principle	—	(449,989)	—
	$2,020,695	$2,877,235	$2,457,000

Components of income tax expense (benefit) are as follows:

Years Ended December 31,	1986	1985	1984
Current:			
State	$ 550,653	$ 342,085	$ 166,000
Federal	3,942,668	2,366,685	1,075,000
	4,493,321	2,708,770	1,241,000
Deferred:			
State	(305,198)	20,529	143,000
Federal	(2,167,428)	147,936	1,073,000
	(2,472,626)	168,465	1,216,000
	$2,020,695	$2,877,235	$2,457,000

m

359

A reconciliation of the statutory Federal income tax rate with the Company's actual income tax rate follows:

Years Ended December 31,	1986	1985	1984
Statutory Federal income tax rate	46.0%	46.0%	46.0%
State income tax rate less applicable Federal income tax benefit	3.2	3.2	3.2
Investment and jobs tax credit	—	(1.2)	(.4)
Nontaxable items – net	1.1	(.2)	.2
Other – net	(.5)	(.6)	(1.3)
Actual income tax rate	49.8%	47.2%	47.7%

The sources of deferred income tax expenses (benefits) and their tax effects are as follows:

Years Ended December 31,	1986	1985	1984
Provision for losses on credit sales	$(1,622,079)	$743,032	$705,000
Finance participation income	(778,939)	(521,030)	453,000
Operating loss and tax credit carryforwards	—	—	244,000
Manufacturers' volume bonuses	(105,058)	(32,062)	(203,000)
Depreciation	103,519	50,415	17,000
Accrued compensation	63,027	(101,434)	—
Allowance for doubtful account	—	29,544	—
Other – net	(133,096)	—	—
	$(2,472,626)	$168,465	$1,216,000

The operating loss and tax credit carryforwards in 1984 represent the reinstatement of deferred tax credit recognized in previous years for financial reporting purposes.

The Tax Reform act of 1986 will benefit the Company through a reduction of the statutory Federal income tax rate.

Note 12
Common Stock

In connection with a public offering of common stock in 1983, the Company sold to the primary underwriter warrants to purchase 142,500 shares of common stock at a price equal to 120% of the public offering price. The warrants are exercisable for a four-year period beginning in 1984 at $3.84 per share. On June 14, 1983, the Board of Directors approved an Incentive Stock Option Plan and reserved 608,900 shares of the Company's authorized common stock for award to officers, directors and key employees. Under the Plan, options are granted at the discretion of a committee appointed by the Board of Directors and may be either incentive stock options or nonqualified stock options. Incentive options must be at a price equal to or greater than fair market value at date of grant. Nonqualified options may be at a price lower than fair market value at date of grant. The Plan expires June 13, 1993.

Activity and price information regarding the plan follows:

	Shares	Option Price Range
Balance December 31, 1983	104,750	$2.40– $3.20
Granted	119,250	$2.40– $3.75
Canceled	(20,500)	$3.20
Balance December 31, 1984	203,500	$2.40– $3.75
Granted	297,600	$4.06–$11.25
Canceled	(5,250)	$2.40– $3.75
Balance December 31, 1985	495,850	$2.40–$11.25
Granted	32,300	$11.00–$17.50
Exercised	(245,000)	$2.40– $4.06
Canceled	(18,250)	$2.70–$10.38
Balance December 31, 1986	264,900	$2.40–$17.50

At December 31, 1986, options for 17,000 shares were currently exercisable. The remaining options become exercisable through the expiration date of the Plan. The excess, if any, of the fair market value at date of grant over the exercise price of nonqualified options is considered compensation and is charged to operations as earned. For 1986 and 1985, the charge to operations was $142,000 and $206,000, respectively. No options were granted at prices lower than fair market value prior to 1985.

At December 31, 1986, 1,534,971 shares of the Company's authorized common stock were reserved for issuance as follows: 142,500 shares for the outstanding warrants, 363,900 shares for the Incentive Stock Option Plan, and 1,028,571 shares for the convertible subordinated notes.

Note 13
Commitments and Contingent Liabilities

The Company leases office space, the majority of its retail sales centers and certain equipment under noncancellable operating leases that expire over the next five years. Total rental expense under such leases amounted to $1,335,809 in 1986, $888,719 in 1985, and $433,759 in 1984. Approximately 10%, 18%, and 22%, respectively, of such amounts were paid to the Company's majority stockholder and the officers of certain subsidiaries.

Future minimum payments under noncancellable operating leases as of December 31, 1986 follow:

Year Ending December 31,	Minimum Payments
1987	$1,298,346
1988	787,572
1989	498,572
1990	312,510
1991	192,912
	$3,089,912

At December 31, 1986 the Company was contingently liable as guarantor on approximately $180 million (net) of installment sales contracts sold to financial institutions on a recourse basis. [Case writer's note: This contingent liability was $150 million at December 31, 1985, $116 million at December 31, 1984, and $45 million at December 31, 1983.]

Note 14
Supplementary Income Statement Information

Advertising costs amounted to $1,569,658, $1,021,978 and $311,285 in 1986, 1985 and 1984, respectively. Maintenance and repairs, depreciation and amortization of intangible assets, preoperating costs and similar deferrals, taxes, other than payroll and income taxes, and royalties did not exceed 1% of revenues in 1986, 1985 or 1984.

REPORT OF INDEPENDENT CERTIFIED PUBLIC ACCOUNTANTS

THE BOARD OF DIRECTORS AND STOCKHOLDERS
MANUFACTURED HOMES, INC.:

We have examined the consolidated balance sheets of Manufactured Homes, Inc. and subsidiaries as of December 31, 1986 and 1985 and the related consolidated statements of earnings, stockholders' equity and changes in financial position for each of the years in the three-year period ended December 31, 1986. Our examinations were made in accordance with generally accepted auditing standards and, accordingly, included such tests of the accounting records and such other auditing procedures as we considered necessary in the circumstances.

In our opinion, the aforementioned consolidated financial statements present fairly the financial position of Manufactured Homes, Inc. and subsidiaries at December 31, 1986 and 1985 and the results of their operations and the changes in their financial position for each of the years in the three-year period ended December 31, 1986, in conformity with generally accepted accounting principles consistently applied during the period except for the change, with which we concur, in the method of recording the uncollected portion of finance participation income as explained in Note 2 to the consolidated financial statements.

PEAT, MARWICK, MITCHELL & CO.
Charlotte, North Carolina
March 10, 1987

EXHIBIT 3

Manufactured Homes, Consolidated Financial Statements for the First Nine Months of 1987

CONSOLIDATED BALANCE SHEETS (unaudited)

	September 30, 1987	December 31, 1986
ASSETS		
Current Assets:		
Cash and cash equivalents:		
Cash and temporary investments (includes) $5,212,849 of restricted cash in 1987	$9,311,240	$2,486,024
Contract proceeds receivable from financial institutions	17,435,191	11,496,098
Total cash and cash equivalents	26,746,431	13,982,102
Finance participation receivable - current portion	4,572,042	2,691,497
Deferred finance participation income	(1,208,275)	(801,511)
Net finance participation receivable	3,363,767	1,889,986
Installment sales contracts held for resale (less unearned interest of $3,648,675)	2,382,573	—
Other receivables	6,343,052	3,746,863
Refundable income taxes	—	778,971
Inventories	41,638,452	38,163,712
Prepaid expenses	587,749	538,419
Deferred income taxes	1,000,262	761,262
Total current assets	82,062,286	59,861,315
Finance participation receivable - noncurrent portion	25,020,194	16,128,799
Deferred finance participation income	(5,984,910)	(3,923,178)
Net finance participation receivable	19,035,284	12,205,621
Property, plant and equipment, at cost	9,248,065	7,504,272
Accumulated depreciation and amortization	(3,166,445)	(2,410,812)
Net property, plant and equipment	6,081,620	5,093,460
Deferred income taxes	1,847,735	—
Excess of costs over net assets of acquired companies, less amortization	2,130,099	2,107,874
Other assets	1,446,657	2,109,533
	$112,603,681	$81,377,803

m

Exhibit 3   Manufactured Homes, Consolidated Financial Statements for the First Nine Months of 1987

	September 30, 1987	December 31, 1986
LIABILITIES AND STOCKHOLDERS' EQUITY		
Current liabilities:		
Notes payable	$ —	$ 1,099,971
Long-term debt—current installments	90,038	810,901
Floor plan notes payable.	28,306,796	35,207,386
Accounts payable	8,181,736	4,899,250
Income taxes	2,469,015	—
Accrued expenses and other liabilities	5,351,963	2,731,924
Total current liabilities	44,399,548	44,749,432
Long-term debt - noncurrent installments	43,000,000	18,609,987
Reserve for losses on credit sales	4,850,000	3,000,000
Deferred income taxes	—	851,265
Total liabilities	92,249,548	67,210,684
Stockholder's equity:		
Common stock—$.50 par value per share; authorized 10,000 shares; issued and outstanding 3,777,168 shares in 1987 and 3,733,968 in 1986	1,888,584	1,866,984
Additional paid-in capital	3,830,314	3,508,351
Retained earnings	14,635,235	8,791,784
Total stockholders' equity	20,354,133	14,167,119
	$112,603,681	$81,377,803

m

363

CONSOLIDATED STATEMENT OF EARNINGS (unaudited)

	Three Months Ended September 30,		Nine Months Ended September 30,	
	1987	1986	1987	1986
Revenues:				
Net sales	$44,590,244	$29,464,161	$126,599,392	$76,396,868
Finance participation income	8,439,473	3,277,085	18,895,975	8,629,223
Insurance commissions	291,868	180,870	976,128	465,577
Interest	373,415	98,327	925,116	230,602
Other	534,916	121,378	786,971	221,448
Total revenues	54,229,916	33,141,821	148,183,582	85,943,718
Costs and expenses:				
Cost of sales	36,325,647	23,741,484	101,997,757	61,554,367
Selling, general and administrative	10,806,534	5,905,930	27,973,865	14,823,385
Provision for losses on credit sales	1,096,027	294,716	3,203,913	772,417
Interest	1,568,906	877,531	4,416,596	2,303,482
Total costs and expenses	49,797,114	30,819,661	137,592,131	79,453,651
Earnings before income taxes	4,432,802	2,322,160	10,591,451	6,490,067
Income taxes	2,038,000	1,145,000	4,748,000	3,109,000
Net earnings	$2,394,302	$1,177,160	$5,843,451	$3,381,067
Net earnings per share:				
Primary	$ .60	$ .30	$ 1.48	$ .87
Fully diluted	$ .53	$ .28	$ 1.31	$ .83

m

364

CONSOLIDATED STATEMENTS OF CHANGES IN FINANCIAL POSITION (unaudited)

	Nine Months Ended September 30	
	1987	**1986**
Working capital was provided by:		
Operations:		
Net earnings	$ 5,843,451	$ 3,381,067
Adjustments for items not requiring (providing) working capital:		
Depreciation and amortization	921,388	664,769
Noncurrent deferred income taxes	(2,699,000)	(345,000)
Provision for losses on credit sales, net of actual changes	1,850,000	(318,539)
Issuance of nonqualified stock options	39,000	106,500
Finance participation income	(18,895,975)	(8,629,223)
Collections and net change in noncurrent portion of finance participation receivable	12,066,312	5,019,381
Working capital used by operations	(874,824)	(121,045)
Proceeds from long-term debt	25,000,000	18,000,000
Exercise of stock options	304,563	1,060,805
Decrease in other assets	662,876	—
	25,092,615	18,939,760
Working capital was used for:		
Net assets, exclusive of working capital, of acquired companies:		
Finance participation receivable	—	349,749
Property and equipment	—	212,716
Other assets	—	509,514
Long-term debt	—	(257,571)
Reserve for losses on credit sales	—	(436,664)
Deferred income taxes	—	78,486
Excess of costs over net assets of acquired companies	—	867,849
	—	1,324,079
Additions to property, plant and equipment	1,851,773	1,365,703
Current installments and repayment of long-term debt	609,987	1,015,876
Additions to other assets and excess costs	80,000	879,665
	2,541,760	4,585,323
Increase in working capital	$22,550,855	$14,354,437
Changes in working capital, by component:		
Cash and cash equivalents	$12,764,329	$ 6,425,144
Finance participation receivable - current portion	1,473,781	239,967
Installment sales contracts held for resale	2,382,573	—
Other receivables	2,596,189	2,818,093
Refundable income taxes	(778,971)	—
Inventories	3,474,740	6,923,301
Prepaid expenses	49,330	59,791
Deferred income taxes	239,000	52,001
Notes payable	1,099,971	(1,391,500)
Long-term debt - current installments	720,863	167,046
Floor plan notes payable	6,900,590	1,424,866
Accounts payable	3,282,486)	(2,811,331)
Income taxes	(2,469,015)	1,820,226
Accrued expenses and other liabilities	(2,620,039)	(1,373,167)
Increase in working capital	$22,550,855	$14,354,437

Notes to Consolidated Financial Statements

1. Pursuant to an agreement dated February 13, 1987, the Company sold to Prudential Insurance Company of America Series A and Series B Senior notes in the aggregate of $25,000,000. The Series A notes in the amount of $15,000,000 bear interest at the rate of 8.64% and are due February 15, 1990. The Series B notes in the amount of $10,000,000 bear interest at the rate of 9.42% and are due February 15, 1992. The proceeds from these notes have been used partially to reduce floor plan notes payable and to fund the Company's finance subsidiary with the remainder added to working capital.

2. On August 18, 1987, the Company's finance subsidiary sold, with recourse, a portfolio of retail installment sales contracts with a principal balance of approximately $8,300,000 to an unrelated financial institution. As a result, the Company recognized, in the third quarter, finance participation income, net of discounts and estimated future servicing costs, of $1,688,690. The terms of the sale required the Company to provide to the unrelated financial institution as security against credit losses, an irrevocable reducing letter of credit in the amount of $3,000,000 secured by a six-month renewable certificate of deposit equal in amount to the letter of credit. At September 30, 1987, approximately $2,200,000 of the proceeds from the sale was held in an escrow account pending receipt, from the appropriate state agencies, of the titles to certain of the new and pre-owned homes securing the retail installment sales contracts in accordance with the terms of the sale.

3. Primary earnings per share are based on the weighted average number of common and common equivalent shares outstanding. Such average shares are as follows:

	Three Months Ended September 30,		Nine Months Ended September 30,	
	1987	1986	1987	1986
Outstanding shares	3,773,894	3,726,427	3,758,245	3,635,137
Equivalent shares	205,159	195,979	187,848	272,150
	3,979,053	3,922,406	3,946,093	3,907,287

The equivalent shares represent shares issuable upon exercise of stock options and warrants after the assumed repurchase of common shares with the related proceeds at the average price during the period.

Fully diluted earnings per share are based on the weighted average number of common and common equivalent shares outstanding plus the common shares issuable upon the assumed conversion of the convertible subordinated notes and elimination of the applicable interest expense less related income tax benefit. In determining equivalent shares, the assumed repurchase of common shares is at the higher of the average or period-end price.

4. Certain amounts in the 1986 financial statements have been reclassified to conform to the presentation adopted in 1987.

5. In the opinion of management, all adjustments which are necessary for a fair presentation of operating results are reflected in the accompanying interim financial statements. All such adjustments are considered to be of a normal recurring nature.

Management's Discussion and Analysis of Financial Condition and Results of Operations

Results of Operations

The Company's net sales for the three-month period ended September 30, 1987 were $44,590,244 compared to $29,464,161 for the comparable period of 1986, an increase of 51%. Net sales for the nine-month period ended September 30, 1987 were $126,599,392 compared to $76,396,868 for the comparable period of 1986, an increase of 66%. These increases are due primarily to the acquisitions in September 1986 of Jeff Brown Homes, Inc., with nine retail sales centers, and Piggy Bank Homes of Alabama, Inc., with six retail sales centers, and the opening of 24 additional retail centers between September 30, 1986 and September 30, 1987. In addition, the average number of homes sold per retail sales center for the three-month and the nine-month periods ended September 30, 1987 increased by 28% and 20% respectively, over the corresponding periods of 1986.

Finance participation income for both the three-month and the nine-month periods ended September 30, 1987 was greater as a percentage of net sales than in the comparable periods of 1986 due primarily to improved financing terms from third-party finance sources and the sale in August 1987 of a portfolio of retail installment sales contracts with a principal balance of approximately $8,300,000, which resulted in finance participation income of $1,688,690 net of discounts and estimated future servicing costs. This portfolio consisted of retail installment sales contracts originated during 1987 and the fourth quarter of 1986. Insurance commissions increased as a percentage of net sales due to added emphasis being placed on this revenue source. Interest income increased significantly due to an improved cash position in 1987 and the interest earned on retail installment sales contracts while held in the Company's finance subsidiary. Other income increased primarily due to a gain of $400,000 recognized in September 1987 on the cancellation of a lease on one of the Company's sales centers.

Cost of sales increased as a percentage of net sales for the three-month period ended September 30, 1987 as compared to the corresponding period of 1986 primarily as a result of extremely competitive market conditions. For the nine-month period ended September 30, 1987, cost of sales as a percentage of net sales was unchanged from the comparable period of 1986. Selling, general and administrative expenses were higher, as a percentage of total revenues, for both the three-month and nine-month periods ended September 30, 1987 as a result of expenses incurred for the following activities: the acquisitions in September 1986 of Piggy Bank Homes of Alabama, Inc. and Jeff Brown Homes, Inc.; the segregation and expanded operations of MANH Independent Retailers Corp. and AAA Mobile Homes, Inc. as separate subsidiaries of the Company; the increased number of retail sales centers; and the establishment in October 1986 of the Company's finance subsidiary.

The provision for losses on credit sales, as a percentage of total revenues, increased significantly for both the three-month and nine-month periods ended September 30,1987 as compared to the corresponding periods of 1986, primarily as a result of industry-wide problems which became evident in the second half of 1986 and which caused the Company to incur increased costs relating to the prepayment of retail installment sales contracts, the repossession of homes and the resale of repossessed homes.

Interest rates were generally lower in 1987; however, total interest expense increased significantly in 1987 due to increased borrowings to support additional retail sales centers and to fund the activities of the Company's finance subsidiary.

Liquidity and Capital Resources

Liquidity and capital resources were greater at September 30, 1987 than at September 30, 1986 due to the sale in February 1987 of $25,000,000 of unsecured senior notes due in 1990 and 1992 bearing interest at a blended rate of 8.95% and to increased floor plan lines of credit. At September 30, 1987, the Company had available $3,000,000 in a bank line of credit and approximately $18,500,000 in unused floor plan lines of credit. In addition, the Company filed a registration statement with the Securities and Exchange Commission on September 22, 1987 for the proposed sale by the Company of 1,200,000 shares of its previously unissued common stock. Due to recent events in the financial market place, the status of this proposed sale is now uncertain.

The Tax Reform Act of 1986 is benefiting the Company through a reduction of the corporate income tax rate. However, beginning January 1, 1987, the Act required the Company to change from the reserve method to the direct write-off method for providing for losses on credit sales, which is requiring the Company to accelerate the payment of federal income taxes. However, the Company believes that funds to be generated by operations, combined with financial resources and credit lines currently available, will be sufficient to satisfy capital needs for current operations.

m

Morlan International, Inc.

*W*e *are not subject to changes in customer needs, technological change, or foreign competition. We are recession-resistant. We are unique.*

Morlan International's 1985 Annual Report

This month we've found an intriguing little company at a low price which has been showing lively growth from, of all things, cemetery management. It's hard to think of death on these beautiful first days of summer, but this company takes care of needs that don't go away. It is well-run, sports an excellent growth record, and a reasonable P/E multiple. . . . This pick surfaced when we were researching our July cover story for OTC Review, *"The 100 Fastest-Growing Companies on NAS-DAQ.". . . Looking in areas others haven't noticed can turn up the best values, and we think this month's pick is the most special among the fast-growers.*

Special Situations, *OTC Review*, June 24, 1985

BUSINESS

In 1986 Morlan International and Service Corporation International (SCI) were the only publicly-traded cemetery and funeral service firms. By September 30, 1986, Morlan owned 28 cemeteries and 10 funeral homes in geographically concentrated areas. Morlan also manufactured concrete burial vaults, primarily to serve the needs of its cemetery operations. SCI was considerably larger, owning 309 funeral homes, 75 cemeteries, and 50 flower shops.

Cemeteries

Cemetery operations were similar to real estate development. Morlan bought land, secured zoning permits, subdivided the property into burial plots, constructed mausoleums and roads, planted grass, and maintained the site in perpetuity. Plots were sold on both an "at need" and "pre-need" basis. Traditionally, pre-need sales of burial plots were aggressively marketed by most cemetery companies. Customers usually paid for these

This case was prepared by Professors Krishna G. Palepu and G. Peter Wilson as the basis for class discussion rather than to illustrate either effective or ineffective handling of an administrative situation. Copyright © 1991 by the President and Fellows of Harvard College. Harvard Business School case 9-192-075.

plots within one to five years via regular monthly installment payments. Because the average purchase was made by people in their thirties and forties, customers typically waited many years before they (were) moved in. To ensure that cemetery grounds were maintained, state laws required that a portion of the proceeds from cemetery sales be assigned to perpetual endowment trusts. These trusts were managed by unrelated parties and the earnings from the trust funds were used to maintain the cemeteries.

Starting in 1983 Morlan began to also market merchandise and burial services on a pre-need basis. Merchandise includes mausoleums, lawn crypts, grave markers, burial vaults, and caskets. Funeral services or "openings and closings" included digging graves, lowering a casket, filling in holes, setting the grave marker or tombstones, replacing the sod and other related services. A large portion of Morlan's pre-need merchandise and burial service sales were made to customers who previously purchased a cemetery plot. These sales were referred to as "reloadings" by industry analysts.

In 1986 over 90 percent of Morlan's revenues were derived from cemetery operations. A large portion of these revenues were attributable to sales made on a pre-need basis.

Funeral Operations

In 1986 less than 10 percent of Morlan's revenues were derived from funeral operations—embalming, coordinating services, cremating, and delivery. Traditionally these services were sold on a need basis, but recently pre-need services have become popular. Morlan's 1986 annual report indicates that they are considering offering consumers a burial insurance program that will pay for funeral services purchased under a pre-need contract.

Growth Through Acquisitions

Morlan's major growth in recent years was achieved by acquiring family-owned funeral homes and cemeteries. As the company's 1986 annual report stated, "the aggressive, but carefully supervised acquisition program undertaken by Morlan since 1984 has played a major role in rapidly expanding revenues, operating earnings, trust funds and land available for resale." Among the factors considered by the company in making an acquisition were the property's ability to complement regionally located Morlan facilities so as to produce economies of scale in marketing and delivering services, the area's demographic characteristics, and the number of annual internments.

Larry Miller, Morlan's president, explained the company's acquisitions strategy: "We look for growth areas, for more established cemeteries that have a significant number of internments every year and a substantial trust fund. . . . If you have a significant number of internments and trust funds, you have the heritage to begin working the funeral systems off of." As the *OTC Review* added, "Heritage is a jargon in death-related businesses for the fact that if someone has buried a family member in one cemetery, other family members may want to be buried there too. Morlan sends sales people to visit those family members."[1] A major objective of the sales people was to market merchandise and services to these potential customers on a pre-need basis. To motivate sales people, Morlan paid them a generous cash commission when a customer agreed to sign a pre-need sales agreement.

Morlan's rapid growth attracted considerable attention. For example, the *New York Post* commented in its Market Beat section:

> *Traditionally, the funeral and cemetery business has been characterized by mom-and-pop operations. These small family-owned businesses serve a local clientele. Nearly 70 percent of the 15,000 funeral homes in the country are sole proprietorships; 80 percent of the 10,000 active cemeteries have staffs less than nine people. Despite this fragmentation, annual revenues for this industry exceeded $5 billion. In an industry in which no single company controls more than 5 percent of the market, Morlan has become a major force thanks to its innovative marketing and strategic acquisitions. Evidence of Morlan's marketing and managerial skills is exemplified by the success of its "pre-need program." People like the idea of making a decision in a non-apprehensive guilt-free environment. This apparently relieves the survivors of making emotion-laden decisions under stressful conditions. It also makes economic sense, since it locks in the cost of burial regardless of subsequent inflationary developments.*[2]

ACCOUNTING POLICIES

One of Morlan's key accounting policies concerns the recognition of revenues from the pre-need sales. The company's annual report explained the policy: "Revenues from the sale of cemetery lots and related merchandise and services are recorded when customer contracts are signed with concurrent recognition of related cost of sales determined by allocation of cost of land, firm contracts for purchase of merchandise and cost studies of rendering services, including an allowance for estimated inflation."

While the above policy was endorsed by Morlan's auditors, some analysts were critical. For example, *Barron's* financial weekly commented:

> *. . . It appears that Morlan's earnings growth depends heavily on a liberal method of accounting. It's a method that industry heavyweight SCI (Service Corporation International) says, point blank, it would never use, . . . And what does Service Corp do about booking pre-need services? It doesn't book a dime of sales until the service is actually performed. Others in the industry agree this is the way to do it. "You can't book a service because you don't know what it's going to cost you 20 years from now," explains a funeral industry veteran, who asked his name be withheld. "You should only book services that you can deliver now."*

m

371

---

1. *Special Situations*, OTC Review, June 24, 1985.
2. *"Grave Prospects Cheer Morlan,"* New York Post, March 26, 1986.

Morlan's president, Larry Miller, disagrees. He claims that SCI's refusal to book such sales reflects a lack of understanding of the pre-need marketplace. Indeed, Miller says he hopes that states will change laws on refunds on pre-sold funerals so that Morlan can book those sales as well. He conceded that it's difficult to match costs with pre-need burial revenue. "No one knows," he agrees. "If costs were to change, we could just allocate some of the year's trust earnings to that particular account."[3]

FUTURE POTENTIAL

In 1986, Morlan's management was very upbeat in its assessment of the company's future growth potential. The company's chairman and chief executive officer stated: "When we tell people we manage cemeteries, they snicker. But like the candy bar Snickers, you take a bite and it tastes oh-so-sweet. I believe this industry is where life insurance industry was in the thirties. My wife hasn't seen me this excited in twenty years."[4]

Management's optimism was echoed by some industry analysts. One analyst summed it up as follows: "Bad jokes aside, it's an excellent business to be in—the cemetery industry. Seriously, while those high-tech wonders teeter on the edge of bankruptcy, Morlan is racking up an extraordinary record. . . . Morlan may be unknown, but they indeed have an able management team, a shrewd strategy, and good old-fashioned cash flow. And yes, everyone is a possible customer—235 million people!"[5]

QUESTIONS

1. Describe the various economic transactions that Morlan undertakes to implement its pre-need sales programs. How are these transactions reflected in the company's income statement and balance sheet? How well does the company's accounting reflect the economics of the pre-need sales programs? Where does management judgment play a critical role in this accounting?
2. Analyze Morlan's profitability and financial position. What are the strengths and weaknesses?
3. Evaluate the company's growth strategy. What are the current and future cash flow implications of this strategy? What are the potential risks, if any, for investors in Morlan's stock?

3. "Anticipating the Worst: Morlan Cashes in on the Funeral Business," William M. Alpert, Barron's, August 25, 1986.
4. Special Situations, OTC Review, June 24, 1985.
5. "Morlan International: Cash Flow, Expansion, and 235 Million Potential Customers," Penny Stock Journal, July 1985.

Exhibit 1   Morlan International, Inc., Abridged 1986 Annual Report

EXHIBIT 1
Morlan International, Inc., Abridged 1986 Annual Report

LETTER TO SHAREHOLDERS AND INVESTORS

Fiscal 1986 results were both stimulating and satisfying for the Morlan International management team.

We were stimulated by the fact that our ambitious program to acquire successful cemeteries and funeral homes in strategically situated geographic clusters—launched only two years ago—is starting to provide rewarding returns.

We were satisfied in that 1986 operating revenues increased by more than 50% and net earnings rose approximately 80%, exclusive of land sale gains which distort year-to-year results.

Before we accelerated our acquisition activities in 1984, Morlan operated 15 cemeteries and one funeral home in five states. Operations were supervised by a modest management team located at corporate headquarters in Philadelphia. Our trust funds totalled $17 million.

Management could have been content to manage existing operations and remain a respected and profitable regional company. But in reviewing the highly fragmented state of this $5 billion industry—where most funeral homes and cemeteries are family-owned enterprises and no company controls more than five percent of the market—we saw opportunities to grow and to eventually achieve national stature. This growth could benefit our customers and our shareholders.

To implement a comprehensive long-range plan in an orderly manner, we had to insure that:

1. Acquired companies could readily become profitable under Morlan's management and lend themselves to cluster development in geographically defined regions;
2. Sufficient capital would be available to finance this strategy;
3. Management depth would be strengthened;
4. Our organization would be further developed to professionally accommodate our planned growth.

What have been the results of this plan?

- In the past two years we have added 13 cemeteries and five funeral homes in five states, culminating this year in our $7.6 million purchase of a large Denver funeral home/cemetery operation plus acquisitions in Atlanta and Palm Beach, Florida.
- Because of a significantly broadened customer base, increased pre-need sales—in addition to our acquisitions—have swelled trust funds to the current $50 million total.
- Emphasis on evaluating trust funds on a net after-tax total return basis has lowered Morlan's effective income tax rate from last year's 46% to 27% for this year. The portfolio currently includes more tax-free investments and high quality, dividend-oriented common stocks.

m

373

Exhibit 1   Morlan International, Inc., Abridged 1986 Annual Report

- The Company successfully completed a $16.5 million 20-year subordinated debenture offering, bearing interest at 8% and convertible at $9. Proceeds were used to repay existing debt which carried higher rates. Thereafter, Morlan was able to restructure its debt and increase its lines of credit to $50 million on more favorable terms.

Improved Financial Resources

Morlan generates sufficient cash from operations to fund current operating requirements, including all debt service. Lines of credit will be used to finance acquisitions, construct funeral homes on or near existing cemeteries and pay for major capital improvement projects.

Our financial resources are periodically strengthened through the sale of land not needed for operations during the succeeding 50 years. Land sale gains vary from year to year and may distort financial comparisons. For example, because Morlan gained almost $1.2 million from land sales in fiscal 1985 but only $226,000 in fiscal 1986, net earnings for the two years appear essentially level, with an increase of only 10% in 1986. A more meaningful comparison would be to compare earnings on a year-to-year basis—exclusive of land sale gains. That comparison reveals net earnings, without the inclusion of land sales, increased approximately 80%.

This significant surge of growth during the past two years has challenged management's ability to oversee and control geographically varied operations from a single corporate location. We recognize that such challenges create opportunities. During 1986 we strengthened our eastern, midwestern and western regional offices, adding key management personnel. We welcomed the opportunity to promote deserving executives from within our management group and to hire top industry talent from outside our company. Regional management is well equipped to exercise the necessary control over cemetery and funeral home operations in these areas. We are now increasingly able to coordinate the Company's expanding activities and devise and adopt strategies for future growth.

Growth of Pre-Need Sales

Morlan greatly enhanced its sales force during the year, adding salespeople and concentrating on a new telemarketing approach and more intensified direct mail and multi-media advertising programs. These educated, energetic and well trained salespeople understand the sensitivity associated with selling cemetery and funeral products and related services. Our small company attitude continues to emphasize approaching potential customers with concern and compassion.

More than 80% of our cemetery sales involve selling in advance of actual need. We regard pre-need selling as a "win-win" program, in which both Morlan and its customers equally benefit from each transaction. The Company receives payments which are profitably invested in trust funds for long periods of time. Consumers rationally and economically arrange for appropriate services and related equipment well in advance of actual need, thereby relieving survivors of making difficult, sometimes costly decisions in times of extreme duress.

Respected organizations, institutions and the general public are becoming increasingly aware of the financial and emotional benefits to be derived from pre-need planning and purchasing. Advance purchase of funeral services is also becoming popular. Morlan is considering offering a life insurance program as a means of providing funeral and other services and products more economically to consumers.

Exhibit 1   Morlan International, Inc., Abridged 1986 Annual Report

We are purchasing and constructing funeral homes on or near Morlan-owned cemeteries as a convenience to bereaved families and their friends and to accommodate all customer needs at one location.

To summarize, fiscal 1986 was an additional year of growth and solid accomplishment. By remaining alert to industry trends and capitalizing on the many opportunities available to us, we have broadened our financial base, strengthened our management structure and become a major presence in a stable and promising industry.

Needless to say, we could not have taken these important strides without the dedication and diverse talents of our employees, the support of our customers and the loyalty of our valued shareholders. We hope to continue rewarding you for your confidence in Morlan by successfully executing our growth strategies in fiscal 1987 and beyond.

Marvin N. Demchick   Lawrence Miller
Chairman   President

MANAGEMENT'S DISCUSSION AND ANALYSIS OF FINANCIAL CONDITION AND RESULTS OF OPERATIONS

The cash generated from current year operations is one of the major indicators of the Company's financial stability. Operating profits, trust income earned, distributions from trust funds and collection of accounts receivable are the major items generating operating cash. Cash generated from operations before extraordinary items increased from $2,137,400 in 1984 to $3,589,500 in 1985 and $3,531,100 in 1986. The 68% increase in 1985 is attributable primarily to the sale of land in Colorado. The 2% decrease in 1986 is attributable to reduced land sale proceeds. Excluding the effect of the land sales, 1986 had a 36% increase in cash generated from operations which was primarily due to the new acquisitions. Operating profitability is demonstrated by analyzing certain financial relationships, including operating earnings before gains on sale of assets.

	Year Ended September 30,		
	1986	1985	1984
Operating earnings before gain on sale of assets	**$4,068**	$2,775	$2,734
Gains on sale of assets	**226**	1,175	56

The increase in operating earnings before the gain on sale of assets in 1986 was primarily due to acquisitions consummated during April, May and December 1985. In addition, the Company had transition costs for 1986 which relate to the acquisitions made during that period.

Cemetery lots and merchandise are generally sold with payment terms ranging from one to five years. Increasing sales result in increasing accounts receivable and require the use of operating funds. Selling and administrative costs are paid in the year of sale. The Company has estimated that it will be required to deposit approximately $2,500,000 into trust funds mandated by the laws of various states in which the Company conducts its

Exhibit 1   Morlan International, Inc., Abridged 1986 Annual Report

cemetery and funeral home operations. In addition, in fiscal 1987, the Company is required to pay approximately $1,000,000 in principal payments on debt primarily incurred to finance the acquisition of additional cemeteries and funeral homes. The Company anticipates that approximately $4,900,000 of accounts receivable generated by the Company's operations to be paid in fiscal 1987 will be sufficient to satisfy these obligations.

The Company's business generally does not require major expenditures for the purchase of capital equipment. During 1984 and 1985, the majority of capital purchases resulted from a decision to modernize cemetery equipment. A significant portion of the Company's capital purchases is financed through bank borrowings. A large portion of 1985 and 1986 capital expenditures was financed from operationally generated cash. The debt to equity ratio at September 30, 1984, 1985, and 1986 was as follows:

	September 30,		
	1986	1985	1984
Debt to Equity Ratio	**3.5 to 1**	3.3 to 1	3.3 to 1

Traditionally, the Company has been able to finance acquisitions with bank debt, purchase money mortgages and relatively small down payments. In fiscal 1985 and 1986, the Company financed several acquisitions by borrowings under its credit lines. These borrowings are the primary reason for the increase in the Company's debt to equity ratio. During August 1986, the Company completed a $16,500,000 offering of subordinated debentures. These funds were used to repay bank debt.

The trust funds have in the past helped to act as an inflation hedge against increasing interest rates. The Company closely monitors payments to its trust funds and reductions in the related merchandise liability. Upon acquisition of many cemeteries, the Company assumes a liability to make payments into a trust fund and a liability to purchase cemetery merchandise. The Company's policy is to systematically reduce its merchandise liability by purchasing merchandise or increasing the amount paid into trust funds. The cemetery merchandise liability decreased more than $831,000 from 1981 to 1984. From 1984 to 1985 the merchandise liability increased as a result of acquisitions which more than offset the reduction by the Company of its merchandise liability for its existing properties. During 1986 the merchandise liability was again reduced by $1,141,000.

The Company's operating revenues have increased during each of the past five years. The percent of increase ranged from a low of 4% from 1980 to 1981 to a high of approximately 19% from 1984 to 1985; 1983 and 1984 increases were 16% and 13%, respectively. The increase in operating revenues was generated primarily from cemetery acquisitions. Price increases represented a minor amount of the increase in operating revenues during the past three years.

The Company's policy of growth through acquisition was the most significant contributor to a five-year trend of increased earnings before extraordinary items. Increased operating and selling expenses as a percentage of revenues in 1984 and 1985 resulted from the purchase of management contracts for the operation of four Ohio cemeteries. Net earnings have fluctuated as a percentage of operating revenues primarily because of gains on sale of assets consisting primarily of land sales, high interest rates during prior

Exhibit 1   Morlan International, Inc., Abridged 1986 Annual Report

years, and the added interest costs of debt incurred to finance acquisitions and the extraordinary items during 1983 and 1984. During 1986, the Company changed its trust funds investment goals to tax free investments from taxable investments. This reduced the effective tax rate to 26%.

The Tax Reform Act of 1986 affects the Company in that investment tax credits will no longer be available to offset income tax expense. Included in current year income tax expense is $85,000 of investment tax credits. Of this amount $25,000 will be reversed and included in income tax expense in the first quarter of fiscal 1987.

FIVE-YEAR COMPARATIVE SUMMARY OF SELECTED FINANCIAL DATA
(Dollars in thousands, except per share amounts)

	Year Ended September 30,				
	1986	1985	1984	1983	1982
Statement of Earnings Data:					
Operating revenues	$24,810	$16,071	$13,475	$11,905	$10,256
Gain on sale of land	226	1,175	56	—	185
	25,036	17,246	13,531	11,905	10,441
Earnings from operations	1,713	1,468	842	631	546
Earnings before extraordinary item	1,713	1,468	842	631	546
Extraordinary item	—	—	(178)	235	—
Net earnings	$ 1,713	$ 1,468	$ 664	$ 866	$ 546
Earnings per share:					
Before extraordinary items	$.32	$.28	$.18	$.12	$.11
Extraordinary item	—	—	(.04)	.05	—
Net earnings	$.32	$.28	$.14	$.17	$.11

	September 30,				
	1986	1985	1984	1983	1982
Balance Sheet Data:					
Total assets	$39,109	$24,648	$18,540	$16,660	$14,809
Notes payable and subordinated debentures	23,159	12,407	9,955	8,175	8,014
Stockholders' equity	8,766	5,709	4,288	3,755	3,313
Trust Funds (1)	45,355	24,646	19,875	16,233	13,900

1. The majority of the trust funds of the Company are not included in the Consolidated Financial Statements. The Company receives substantially all of the income earned from these trust funds.

377

Exhibit 1   Morlan International, Inc., Abridged 1986 Annual Report

CONSOLIDATED BALANCE SHEETS

	September 30,	
	1986	1985
Assets		
Land and Improvements Held for Sale, including cemetery management agreements of $2,135,000—1986 and $2,249,000—1985	**$15,296,000**	$11,542,400
Accounts Receivable, less allowances of $2,338,000—1986 and $1,685,000—1985	**12,771,700**	7,857,600
Building and Equipment	**8,053,300**	3,648,500
Cash	**608,400**	603,000
Water Rights	**619,400**	619,400
Other Assets, Prepaid Expenses and Inventories	**1,759,700**	376,700
	$39,108,500	$24,647,600
Liabilities and Stockholders' Equity		
Notes Payable	**$ 6,659,300**	$12,407,200
Accounts Payable	**1,567,000**	831,500
Accrued Expenses	**1,767,500**	1,280,900
Cemetery Merchandise and Care Liability	**472,900**	1,614,000
Deferred Taxes	**3,376,200**	2,804,500
Convertible Subordinated Debentures	**16,500,000**	—
Stockholders' Equity:		
Preferred Stock, par value $.01 a share:		
Series C:		
Authorized 1,000,000 shares		
Issued and outstanding 40,000 shares	**400**	400
Series D:		
Authorized 200,000 shares		
Issued and outstanding 53,333 shares	**500**	—
Common Stock, par value $.01 a share:		
Authorized 9,000,000 shares		
Issued 4,292,194 shares—1986; 3,547,638 shares—1985	**42,900**	35,500
Additional Capital	**3,620,000**	2,146,700
Retained Earnings	**5,488,800**	3,878,600
	9,152,600	6,061,200
Less:		
Employee Subscription Receivable	**—**	(148,500)
Common Shares in Treasury, at cost: 213,016—1986; 180,000—1985	**(387,000)**	(203,200)
	8,765,600	5,709,500
	$39,108,500	$24,647,600

Exhibit 1   Morlan International, Inc., Abridged 1986 Annual Report

CONSOLIDATED STATEMENTS OF EARNINGS

	Year Ended September 30,		
	1986	1985	1984
Revenues:			
Operating	**$24,810,100**	$16,070,600	$13,474,800
Gain on sale of land	**226,100**	1,175,000	56,000
	25,036,200	17,245,600	13,530,800
Costs and Expenses:			
Operating and selling	**14,572,800**	8,989,200	7,518,000
General and administrative	**6,169,300**	4,306,900	3,223,100
	20,742,100	13,296,100	10,741,100
Operating Earnings	**4,294,100**	3,949,500	2,789,700
Interest Expense	**1,980,400**	1,331,500	1,199,000
Earnings Before Income Taxes and Extraordinary Items	**2,313,700**	2,618,000	1,590,700
Income Taxes	**601,000**	1,149,800	749,000
Earnings Before Extraordinary Items	**1,712,700**	1,468,200	841,700
Extraordinary Items, less income tax (benefit) of ($158,000)—1984	**—**	—	(177,800)
Net Earnings	**$ 1,712,700**	$ 1,468,200	$ 663,900
Net Earnings Per Share:			
Before extraordinary items	**$.32**	$.28	$.18
Extraordinary items	**—**	—	(.04)
	$.32	$.28	$.14

See notes to consolidated financial statements.

m

Exhibit 1   Morlan International, Inc., Abridged 1986 Annual Report

CONSOLIDATED STATEMENTS OF CHANGES IN FINANCIAL POSITION

	Year Ended September 30,		
	1986	1985	1984
Funds Provided By:			
Operations:			
Earnings before extraordinary items	$ **1,712,700**	$ 1,468,200	$ 841,700
Add items not requiring financial resources:			
Depreciation and amortization	**768,300**	549,200	378,300
Cost of land sold	**478,400**	483,200	326,400
Deferred income taxes	**571,700**	1,088,900	591,000
Total funds provided by operations before			
extraordinary items	**3,531,100**	3,589,500	2,137,400
Extraordinary items			(177,800)
Total funds provided by operations	**3,531,100**	3,589,500	1,959,600
Decrease (increase) in inventories	**77,400**	58,700	(82,900)
Increase (decrease) in accounts payable and			
accrued expenses	**483,100**	(73,700)	(383,400)
Issuance of preferred stock	**236,600**	—	—
Issuance of common stock	**1,244,600**	1,500	24,400
Decrease in subscriptions receivable	**148,500**	—	—
Decrease (increase) in cash	**(5,400)**	(73,100)	23,300
Other	**243,100**	29,900	(2,400)
	5,959,000	3,532,800	1,538,600
Funds Used For:			
Increase in accounts receivable	**1,965,000**	274,200	797,100
Decrease in cemetery merchandise and care liability	**1,115,400**	665,200	473,500
Purchase of buildings and equipment	**2,066,800**	773,700	395,500
Purchase of land and improvements	**109,600**	211,600	—
Acquisition of subsidiaries-net	**10,109,200**	2,932,800	—
Cost of issuance of convertible subordinated			
debentures	**1,058,800**	—	—
Purchase of cemetery management agreements	**—**	1,079,000	1,497,800
Purchase of treasury stock	**183,800**	48,200	155,000
Payment of dividends on preferred stock	**102,500**	—	—
	16,711,100	5,984,700	3,318,900
Increase in Notes Payable and Convertible			
Subordinated Debentures	**$10,752,100**	$ 2,451,900	$1,780,300

m
380

Exhibit 1   Morlan International, Inc., Abridged 1986 Annual Report

	Year Ended September 30,		
	1986	1985	1984
Summary of Changes in Notes Payable and Convertible Subordinated Debentures:			
Additional borrowings	**4,117,200**	575,200	1,317,900
Repayments	**5,028,700**	1,922,000	918,800
	(911,500)	(1,346,800)	399,100
Acquisition debt	**9,490,000**	4,552,400	1,414,400
Repayment of acquisition debt	**14,326,400**	753,700	33,200
	(4,836,400)	3,798,700	1,381,200
Increase in convertible subordinated debentures	**16,500,000**	—	—
Increase in notes payable and convertible subordinated debentures	**10,752,100**	2,451,900	1,780,300
Balance at beginning of year	**12,407,200**	9,955,300	8,175,000
Balance at end of year	**$23,159,300**	$12,407,200	$9,955,300

NOTES TO CONSOLIDATED FINANCIAL STATEMENTS

Years ended September 30, 1986, 1985, and 1984

A. Summary of Significant Accounting Policies

(1) *Description of Business*—Morlan International, Inc. and its subsidiaries own and operate cemeteries and funeral homes and market cemetery and funeral products and services directly to retail customers.

(2) *Principles of Consolidation*—The consolidated financial statements include the accounts of the Company and its subsidiaries, all of which are wholly-owned. All material intercompany accounts and transactions have been eliminated.

(3) *Revenue Recognition*—Morlan markets its products and services primarily on a pre-need basis to customers who wish to make appropriate provisions prior to death and on an at-need basis to customers who have not made such provisions.

Revenues from the sale of cemetery lots and related merchandise and services are recorded when customer contracts are signed with concurrent recognition of related cost of sales determined by allocation of cost of land, firm contracts for purchase of merchandise and cost studies of rendering services, including an allowance for estimated inflation.

Revenue from the sale of funeral plans is recognized in the year of sale to the extent that such sales price is not refundable (generally -0- to 15%) and the remainder is recognized in the year the funeral is performed. Selling costs including sales commissions are expensed in the year of sale.

Pre-tax earnings from the sale of funeral plans and pre-need grave opening contracts which are deferred until the service is performed amounted to $2,640,000—1986, $555,000—1985, and $755,000—1984.

Exhibit 1   Morlan International, Inc., Abridged 1986 Annual Report

(4) *Trust Funds*—The Company is required to establish trust funds to meet certain statutory requirements providing for the delivery of merchandise, services and perpetual care of cemetery property. These trust funds are established because State laws require percentages of amounts collected from sales of funeral services, cemetery merchandise and services and burial lots to be deposited until such time as the related merchandise is used or the service is performed. Perpetual care trust funds are required to provide for the recurring maintenance of cemetery land. The Company is not permitted to distribute any principal deposits of the perpetual care funds.

The majority of trust fund assets of the Company are not included in the Consolidated Balance Sheet. These assets, at cost, totaled $45,355,000 at September 30, 1986. Gross trust fund revenues which are recorded by the Company when earned and included in operating revenues, amounted to $3,270,000—1986, $2,050,000—1985 and $1,750,000—1984. At September 30, 1986 and 1985, the market value exceeded the recorded amounts of trust fund assets by $1,160,000 and $430,000 respectively.

(5) *Depreciation*—Depreciation is computed by the straight-line method over the estimated useful lives of the related assets.

(6) *Income taxes*—The Company and its subsidiaries file a consolidated tax return. Investment tax credits are accounted for by the flow-through method. Deferred taxes result from the use of different methods for financial and tax reporting purposes, primarily the use of the installment method of accounting for accounts receivable and the use of accelerated methods of recording depreciation expense for income tax purposes.

(7) *Inventories*—Inventories are valued at the lower of cost (first-in, first-out method) or market.

(8) *Water Rights*—Water rights represent interests in water and irrigating companies which entitle the Company to draw water from reservoirs for use in irrigating cemeteries. No amortization of these rights is being made as management believes they have a continuing value.

(9) *Cemetery Management Agreements*—Cemetery management agreements represent the cost of acquiring the right to manage certain cemeteries in the State of Ohio. These costs are being amortized over 20 years. The land is owned by a separate not-for-profit cemetery association.

(10) *Quasi-Reorganization*—A deficit of $1,895,700 was transferred to additional capital on October 1, 1980.

B. Acquisitions

During fiscal 1986 the Company acquired substantially all the cemetery and funeral operations of the Olinger Group in Denver, Colorado, Crest Lawn Memorial Park in Atlanta, Georgia, and Palm Beach Memorial Park and Town & Country Funeral Home in Palm Beach, Florida for aggregate consideration of $9,490,000 and 53,333 shares of the Company's Series D Preferred Stock.

During fiscal 1985 the Company acquired Hillcrest Cemetery in West Palm Beach, Florida, Forest Hills and Calvary Cemeteries in Kansas City, Missouri, and sales and management contracts for Miami Valley and Valley View Cemeteries in Dayton, Ohio for an aggregate cost of approximately $2,700,000. During fiscal 1984 sales and management

Exhibit 1   Morlan International, Inc., Abridged 1986 Annual Report

contracts for Sunset Hills Cemeteries in Canton, Ohio were acquired for approximately $1,300,000.

Each of the preceding acquisitions was accounted for by the purchase method of accounting and the total purchase price was assigned to the net tangible assets acquired.

Unaudited proforma financial information is presented below as if each of these acquisitions had occurred at the beginning of the year preceding the date of acquisition. Adjustments have been made, primarily for interest charges attributable to the financing of the purchases:

	1986	1985	1984
Revenues	$26,428,200	$24,174,700	$16,486,000
Earnings Before Extraordinary Items	1,735,900	1,489,600	595,000
Net Earnings	1,735,900	1,489,600	417,200
Net Earnings per Share	.32	.29	.09

Management of the Company might have made different decisions with respect to operations, and the results of operations might have differed substantially had these companies actually been acquired at the beginning of the fiscal year.

C. Accounts Receivable

	1986	1985
Installment contracts receivable	$10,957,500	$8,331,200
Deferred interest income	(1,110,900)	(1,134,100)
Allowance for contract cancellations	(2,338,000)	(1,685,400)
	7,508,600	5,511,700
Excess of funeral home trust funds over statutory requirements	2,434,700	
Notes and advances-related parties	2,189,200	1,688,500
Other	639,200	657,400
	$12,771,700	$7,857,600

Accounts receivable mature as follows: $4,927,800—1987; $2,625,300—1988; $1,689,200—1989; $1,022,100—1990; and $693,100—1991.

Exhibit 1   Morlan International, Inc., Abridged 1986 Annual Report

F. Notes Payable

	1986	1985
Revolving credit loan due 1989	$ 746,600	$ 6,064,000
Acquisition notes payable, collateralized by real estate, interest at 5% to prime plus 1% due in installments to May 2002	4,139,700	4,770,400
Notes Payable, interest at 6% to prime plus 2% due in installments to 1992	1,362,700	1,082,900
Notes Payable, interest at 6% to 13% due in installments to 1994	388,700	448,800
Other	21,600	41,100
	$6,659,300	$12,407,200

Under the terms of the revolving credit loan, the Company may borrow amounts subject to a borrowing base formula (as defined) at the rate of 1½% in excess of the prime commercial rate charged by the bank. The maximum commitment is $10,300,000. Substantially all of the Company's assets are pledged as collateral for the notes payable.

Maturities of notes payable during the next five years are as follows:

Year	Amount
1987	$1,058,200
1988	823,300
1989	1,484,000
1990	685,200
1991	579,700
Thereafter	2,028,900

G. Convertible Subordinated Debentures

The 8% Convertible Subordinated Debentures are due August 1, 2006; interest is paid semi-annually on February 1 and August 1. The Debentures are convertible at any time prior to maturity, unless previously redeemed, into shares of the Company's Common Stock at a conversion price of $9.00 a share, subject to adjustment under certain conditions. The Debentures are callable at the option of the Company under certain conditions beginning August 1, 1988 at 108% of face value and decreasing ratably to 100% of face value after July 31, 1993.

Sinking fund payments as follows are required to provide for retirement of the debentures:

1996–2000	$ 750,000 each year
2001–2005	$1,250,000 each year

Exhibit 1   Morlan International, Inc., Abridged 1986 Annual Report

J. Major Segments of Business

The Company conducts cemetery and funeral service operations throughout the United States. The following table shows certain segment information of the Company's 1986 consolidated operations.

	Cemetery	Funeral	Corporate	Consolidated
Net revenues	$20,942,700	$3,873,700	$ 219,800	$25,036,200
Operating income	$ 6,056,300	$ 609,400	($2,371,600)	$ 4,294,100
Capital expenditures	$ 1,432,100	$ 633,000	$ 1,700	$ 2,066,800
Depreciation and amortization	$ 633,300	$ 81,800	$ 53,200	$ 768,300
Identifiable assets	$30,074,000	$6,753,100	$2,281,400	$39,108,500

The Company did not have material segments during 1985 and 1984.

L. Income Taxes

	1986	1985	1984
Current:			
Federal	—	$ 10,900	
State	$ 29,300	50,000	—
	29,300	60,900	—
Deferred:			
Federal	$530,400	1,009,300	$669,600
State	41,300	79,600	79,400
	571,700	1,088,900	749,000
Extraordinary items	—	—	(158,000)
	$601,000	$1,149,800	$591,000

Exhibit 1   Morlan International, Inc., Abridged 1986 Annual Report

O. Quarterly Financial Data (Unaudited)

1986	1st Quarter	2nd Quarter	3rd Quarter	4th Quarter
Revenues	$4,336,400	$6,418,700	$7,080,600	$7,200,500
Operating earnings	640,500	1,004,400	1,443,900	1,205,300
Earnings before extraordinary items	216,600	290,000	654,600	551,500
Net earnings	216,600	290,000	654,600	551,500
Earnings per share:				
Before extraordinary items	.04	.06	.12	.10
Net	.04	.06	.12	.10

1985	1st Quarter	2nd Quarter	3rd Quarter	4th Quarter
Revenues	$4,691,800	$3,620,900	$4,145,000	$4,787,800
Operating earnings	1,718,200	625,900	790,100	815,300
Earnings before extraordinary items	727,300	157,900	235,200	347,800
Net earnings	727,300	157,900	235,200	347,800
Earnings per share:				
Before extraordinary items	.15	.03	.04	.06
Net	.15	.03	.04	.06

The gain on sale of land of $1,175,000 occurred in the first quarter of 1985, and the gain of $226,100 occurred in the third quarter of 1986.

m

Exhibit 1   Morlan International, Inc., Abridged 1986 Annual Report

Report of Independent Certified Public Accountants

Board of Directors and Stockholders
Morlan International, Inc.
Philadelphia, Pennsylvania

We have examined the consolidated balance sheets of Morlan International, Inc. and subsidiaries as of September 30, 1986 and 1985, and the related statements of earnings, stockholders' equity and changes in financial position for each of the three years in the period ended September 30, 1986. Our examinations were made in accordance with generally accepted auditing standards and, accordingly, included such tests of the accounting records and such other auditing procedures as we considered necessary in the circumstances.

In our opinion, the consolidated financial statements referred to above present fairly the financial position of Morlan International, Inc. and subsidiaries as of September 30, 1986 and 1985, and the results of their operations and the changes in their financial position for each of the three years in the period ended September 30, 1986, in conformity with generally accepted accounting principles applied on a consistent basis.

Touche Ross & Co.
Certified Public Accountants
Philadelphia, Pennsylvania
December 8, 1986

m

387

Exhibit 2   Morlan Stock Price Index and OTC Composite Stock Price Index

EXHIBIT 2
Morlan Stock Price Index and OTC Composite Stock Price Index

Indices from the end of December 1985 to the end of December 1986
with value of both at beginning of period set at 100.

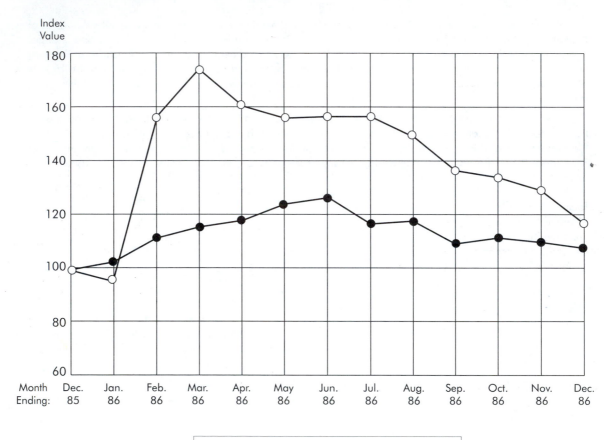

	12/31/85	12/31/86	Change
Morlan's Stock Price	$4.875	$5.625	15.4%
OTC Composite Index	325	349	7.4%

The Murray Ohio Manufacturing Company

In March 1985, Dianne Simmons, director of research for the Commonwealth Investment Group, called David McIntosh, a newly joined analyst, into her office and presented a request:

> *David, I just received the 1984 annual report and proxy statement of The Murray Ohio Manufacturing Company. A few years ago we bought Murray's stock for our equity income fund. As you know, that fund is marketed to dividend-oriented investors. It's been a good investment so far, thanks to Murray's excellent dividend payment record. I think, though, that it's time for us to take a fresh look at Murray's recent performance and future prospects.*
>
> *I want you to analyze the company's 1984 annual report [Exhibit 3] and make a recommendation. You may find the information on the company's board reported in the proxy statement useful [Exhibit 1]. I've also collected some information for you on Murray's stock price in recent months [Exhibit 2]. And here's some background information on the company's business.*

BUSINESS

Murray Ohio Company was based in Brentwood, a suburb of Nashville, Tennessee. The company's stock was listed on the New York Stock Exchange.

Murray Ohio manufactured and sold power mowers and bicycles. During the 1982–1984 period the shares of these two product lines in the company's sales and operating profits were as follows:

	Sales			Profits		
	1982	1983	1984	1982	1983	1984
Power Mowers	54%	53%	62%	73%	68%	88%
Bicycles	46%	47%	38%	27%	32%	12%

Source: Murray Ohio's 1984 annual report

Murray produced all its products in a 57-acre manufacturing facility located in Lawrenceburg, Tennessee.

Professor Krishna Palepu prepared this case as the basis for class discussion rather than to illustrate either effective or ineffective handling of an administrative situation. Copyright © 1987 by the President and Fellows of Harvard College. Harvard Business School case 9-187-178.

Bicycles

Murray began as a bicycle manufacturer in 1936. The company produced a complete line of bicycles ranging from sidewalk bicycles for small children to lightweight racing bicycles. The bicycles were sold under both the Murray brand name and the private labels of major retailers. Substantially all of the company's bicycles were distributed through department stores, discount stores, toy stores, and other mass merchandise outlets.

In 1984 Murray manufactured approximately one-third of the bicycles made in the United States. The company competed with several domestic bicycle manufacturers including Huffy, Roadmaster, Columbia, and Ross.

INDUSTRY TRENDS.   The demand for bicycles was largely dependent on discretionary income. Thus, higher income consumers comprised a major portion of the market. The maturation of the baby boom generation into their peak earning years and the growing incidence of two-income households as a result of more women in the work force had increased this pool of "upscale" consumers in recent years. Another factor that positively affected the demand was migration of the population to the West and the South, where the weather and access to recreational areas are favorable for outdoor activities.

The bicycle industry grew at a compound annual growth rate of 7.8 percent during the ten-year period 1972–1982 and 0.6 percent during the five years 1977–1982. Domestic shipments of bicycles and parts rebounded strongly in 1983 from one of the industry's worst years in more than a decade. Constant dollar shipments increased an estimated 15 percent in 1983, then slowed to a 4 percent increase in 1984. Much of the slowdown in 1984 domestic shipments was attributable to competition from low-priced imports from the Far East. Even though demand remained strong in 1984, a 50 percent rise of imports in 1984 adversely affected the domestic producers of bicycles.

The following table summarizes the total shipment data for the bicycle industry:

	Bicycle and Parts Shipments				
(in millions of dollars)	1980	1981	1982	1983	1984
Domestic	649	733	565	644	683
Imports	281	327	208	329	494

Source: U.S. Department of Commerce, Bureau of the Census

The long-term demand for bicycles was expected to remain strong. Domestic producers' share of the market would depend on their ability to be cost competitive with foreign producers, particularly those in Taiwan. Import growth would also be influenced by the value of the dollar. In addition, pressure on Taiwanese exporters in the form of proposed tariff legislation and other trade remedies could result in voluntary cutbacks by the exporters. Based on these factors, domestic bicycle shipments were expected to grow at a rate of 3 percent in 1985 and 3.5 percent annually for the five years thereafter.

Power Mowers

Murray entered the power mower market in 1968 and by 1984 had become one of the largest U.S. manufacturers of power mowers. The company had a full line of walk-behind and riding mowers. Some of these models also accepted attachments such as snow blowers, plows, and tillers. Murray also offered a line of tillers to complement its power mower products.

Through 1984 Murray's power mowers were marketed through major national and regional chains, primarily under the Murray label. In early 1985 the company formed a new marketing subsidiary, Sabre Corporation, to sell mowers to outdoor power equipment dealers. These dealers participated in a large share of the higher priced mower market in which Murray was not previously represented.

INDUSTRY TRENDS.   According to the 1982 Census of Manufacturers, 152 firms produced lawn and garden equipment in the United States. However, many of these producers were small and had fewer than 20 employees. In addition to Murray, the major domestic manufacturers included Western International, Roper, MTD, and Aircap. Lawn mower producers tended to specialize in one of two distribution markets: the high-volume, low-to-medium price mass merchandisers, which accounted for about two-thirds of industry sales, or the higher priced independent retailers, who serviced equipment in addition to selling it. Sales through national department stores had been declining since 1978 as specialty retailers and hardware stores were handling a greater share of the market.

Demand for lawn and garden equipment, like demand for other household durables, was closely related to the level of real disposable income and to the health of the housing market. Between 1972 and 1979, constant dollar shipments of lawn and garden equipment increased at a compound annual rate of 5.5 percent. Record high interest rates from 1979 through 1982 severely depressed the housing market, and constant dollar shipments of lawn and garden equipment declined 31 percent to their lowest level since 1972. The recovery began in 1983 as real disposable income and housing starts rebounded. The expansion continued in 1984 with an estimated 12 percent increase in lawn and garden equipment shipments.

The balance of trade in lawn and garden equipment was historically very favorable for U.S. producers. In recent years, however, imports began to make inroads into the U.S. market. In 1984, estimated U.S. imports of lawn and garden equipment increased 178 percent, continuing a trend begun in 1979 when a Japanese producer, Honda, entered the market for lawn mowers.

The following table summarizes recent trends in the lawn and garden equipment industry:

	Lawn and Garden Equipment Shipments				
(in millions of dollars)	1980	1981	1982	1983	1984
Domestic	2419	2270	2387	2536	2956
Imports	26	30	40	66	184

Source: U.S. Department of Commerce, Bureau of the Census

Constant dollar shipments of lawn and garden equipment were expected to increase at a compound annual growth rate of 4 percent between 1984 and 1989. Growth in housing starts, an increase in real disposable income, and an increase in replacement demand were expected to contribute to this growth. Due to its leading position in the world markets, the U.S. industry was expected to expand exports as world economies recovered and as the value of the dollar dropped. U.S. imports of lawn and garden equipment were also expected to continue to increase, especially in the lower priced models.

FINANCIAL PERFORMANCE

Between 1975 and 1979 Murray's sales grew 158 percent, from $126.6 million to $327.1 million; the company's reported profits grew by 125 percent, from $4.7 million to $10.6 million. During this period, the company had relatively stable profitability, with an average return on sales (ROS) of 3.5 percent, and an average return on equity (ROE) of 13.5 percent.

In contrast to the steady growth during the last half of the 1970s, Murray's performance became erratic beginning in 1980 as foreign competition in its product markets increased significantly. Between 1979 and 1983, the company's sales and profits grew by only 31 percent and 16 percent, respectively. Further, the company's average profitability showed a significant decline. The average ROS and ROE from 1980 to 1983 were 2.6 percent and 10.8 percent, respectively. (See Exhibit 3 for more data on the performance from 1975 to 1983.)

1984 was a challenging year for Murray Ohio. The company's management explained:

> The past year, 1984, was a difficult one for our company. While total sales were basically flat with 1983, earnings were down considerably. Two factors primarily accounted for this earnings decline.
>
> First, bicycle imports were up over 55 percent in 1984. This increase, which has been sold almost totally to the mass market merchants, adversely affected our bicycle pricing, production levels, and sales.

Secondly, stronger domestic competition in both our product lines, bicycles and power mowers, increased pressures on our pricing and resulted in a tightening of our profit margins.

The mower segment of Murray's business performed significantly better than the bicycle segment. Following a record sales performance in 1983, Murray's mower sales increased to a new high in 1984, up 15 percent. In contrast, bicycle sales decreased 19 percent in 1984, and operating profits for the year declined by 72 percent.

Murray Ohio's management announced that it would take several steps to improve its future performance: (1) adopting an aggressive bicycle pricing structure to regain market share; (2) improving manufacturing productivity through process modernization, manufacturing resources planning, and better manpower utilization; (3) introducing new and innovative products, including the new Sabre mower line aimed at the power equipment dealers; and (4) working with other domestic producers to lobby the U.S. Congress to increase import tariffs on bicycles.

While these steps were viewed as necessary to prevent further erosion in the company's market share, management realized that profit margin pressure was likely to continue, at least in the short term. Further, the productivity improvement program was expected to require significant capital expenditure outlays. The company increased its capital expenditures in 1984 by 86 percent to $10.9 million, and expected to invest comparable amounts in 1985 as well. Management summed up their view of the future:

We recognize the difficult journey before us. Our past record, however, shows one of success and profitability. With a solid balance sheet and the full commitment of our resources and people, we look forward to the challenges that lie ahead. Our people continue to be our greatest strength. Their innovativeness, team-work, and support provide the company with the impetus it needs. In these times of change, their support and assistance are immeasurable.

DIVIDEND POLICY

David McIntosh knew that the Commonwealth Investment Group had found Murray Ohio's stock attractive for Commonwealth's equity income fund because of its reliable dividend policy. Murray's dividend per share grew steadily from $0.67 in 1975 to $1.20 in 1980. Despite the company's mixed performance between 1980 and 1984, dividends remained constant. As the company's annual report stated, Murray's management was proud of the company's dividend history—it had paid them quarterly without a reduction for the past 49 consecutive years. McIntosh wondered whether Murray Ohio would be able to maintain this record given the company's changed business circumstances. Has the nature of Murray's business changed enough to warrant a reevaluation of its dividend policy? If the company decided to change its longstanding policy, how would investors react?

QUESTIONS

1. Analyze Murray Ohio's recent financial performance and cash flows. Can the company afford to maintain its current dividend if operating conditions remain about the same?

2. Evaluate management's business strategy for the future. What does this strategy imply for the company's future cash requirements? Given this new strategy, is the company more or less likely to maintain its current dividend policy?

3. Is there an alternative strategy that is better than management's proposed strategy for increasing shareholders' value? Is the company's current management likely to pursue this alternative strategy? If not, is the company an attractive takeover target?

4. What are the implications for current stockholders of Murray Ohio? What should the Commonwealth Investment Group do?

m

EXHIBIT 1
The Murray Ohio Manufacturing Company—Board of Directors, 1984

Name	Principal Occupation, Business Experience, and Other Directorships in Public Companies (1)	Age on April 2, 1985	Beginning Year, Period of Service
John N. Anderson (2)	President and Chief Executive Officer of the Company. Director of Third National Bank, Nashville, Tennessee.	60	1979
Lovic A. Brooks, Jr.	Senior Partner in the firm of Constangy, Brooks & Smith, Atlanta, Georgia (attorneys). Constangy, Brooks & Smith has performed legal services for the Company for many years and is expected to continue to do so.	57	1972
Sam M. Fleming (2)	Retired. Former Chairman of the Board, Third National Bank, Nashville, Tennessee. Director of Hillsboro Enterprises, Inc., Nashville, Tennessee.	76	1965
Robert A. Flesher	Retired. Former Vice Chairman of the Board of the Company.	66	1966
Charles W. Geny (2)	Vice President, Alexander & Alexander, Incorporated, Nashville, Tennessee (insurance and bonds).	71	1972
William M. Hannon (2)	Chairman of the Board and retired Chief Executive Officer of the Company. Director of Third National Bank, Nashville, Tennessee.	65	1955
Thomas M. Hudson	Investments. Retired Senior Vice President of the The Robinson-Humphrey Company, Inc. (an investment banking firm). The Robinson-Humphrey Company, Inc. has performed investment banking services for the Company for many years and is expected to continue to do so. Director of the United Cities Gas Company, Nashville, Tennessee.	63	1980
William C. Keyes	Retired. Former Senior Executive Vice President of the Company. Director of Commerce Union Bank, Nashville, Tennessee.	65	1966
H. Theodore Meyer (3)	Partner in the firm of Jones, Day, Reavis & Pogue, which has performed legal services for the Company for many years and is expected to continue to do so.	49	1985
Gerald E. Sheridan	President, Sheridan Construction Co., Nashville, Tennessee.	60	1983
G. Cromer Smotherman (2)	Executive Vice President and Chief Operating Officer of the Company. Director of First National Bank of Lawrenceburg, Lawrenceburg, Tennessee.	59	1971
David K. Wilson	President, Cherokee Equity Corporation, Nashville, Tennessee (holding company). Director of First American National Bank, Winners Corporation, and Genesco, Inc., all located in Nashville, Tennessee, and Torchmark Corporation, Birmingham, Alabama.	65	1983

All directors and officers of the company as a group (26 persons, including those named above) own 10.4 percent of the company's common stock.

EXHIBIT 2
The Murray Ohio Manufacturing Company—Stock Prices, January 1984–March 1985

Month	Murray Ohio's Stock Price at Month End	Standard and Poor's 400 Industrial Index at Month End
1984		
January	21 6/8 .75	184
February	21 4/8 .50	177
March	22 4/8	180
April	22 5/8 .625	182
May	21 5/8	171
June	23 2/8 .25	175
July	20 2/8	171
August	20 7/8 .875	189
September	21 2/8	187
October	20 2/8	187
November	19 2/8	183
December	19 4/8	186
1985		
January	20 5/8	201
February	20 5/8	203
March	20 3/8 .375	202

Murray Ohio's Common Stock ß = 0.8 (Value Line estimate).

Interest rates at the beginning of 1985:
3-month Treasury bills: 8.8%
20-year Treasury bonds: 11.7%

m

396

EXHIBIT 3

The Murray Ohio Manufacturing Company—1984 Annual Report (Abridged)

LETTER TO SHAREHOLDERS

March 4, 1985

The past year, 1984, was a difficult one for our Company. While total sales were basically flat with 1983, earnings were down considerably. Two factors primarily accounted for this earnings decline.

First, bicycle imports were up over 55% in 1984. This increase, which has been sold almost totally to the mass market merchants, adversely affected our bicycle pricing, production levels, and sales.

Secondly, stronger domestic competition in both our product lines, bicycles and power mowers, increased pressures on our pricing and resulted in a tightening of our profit margins.

Net sales for the year were $383,589,000, a 1% decrease from 1983. Power mower sales, however, were up 15%, with bicycle sales down 19%.

Earnings, after nonrecurring adjustments for 1984, were $7,826,000, a 37% decrease from 1983. The majority of this decrease, as stated above, was due to the bicycle segment of our business. Earnings per share, after nonrecurring adjustments, decreased 43% to $2.01 from $3.53 in 1983. The difference between the percent change in earnings and earnings per share is a result of the June, 1983 equity offering of 770,000 shares of common stock.

The 1984 nonrecurring adjustments are benefits arising from the elimination of a provision for deferred taxes of our international sales operations (DISC) and an accounting change in the method for recognizing investment tax credits. These benefits resulted in earnings of $920,000 and $1,404,000, respectively, or $.24 and $.36 per share.

The declining profitability experienced in 1984 presented Murray with a difficult challenge that we are determined to face. In the third quarter report, we announced the first step in our program to improve profitability. This step involves an aggressive bicycle pricing structure aimed at maintaining our necessary production levels and at regaining market share lost to imports. Our pricing stance has shown success and will help Murray regain lost market share in 1985.

Productivity and Marketing—Steps for the Future

While putting a pricing structure in place to regain bicycle market share, we began major programs in two areas—productivity and marketing—to improve our profitability in both of our product lines. Neither program will create overnight success, but both will help keep Murray on solid ground and a strong course for the future.

Murray's productivity program involves several facets—process modernization, Manufacturing Resources Planning (MRP), and improved manpower productivity.

Our 1984 capital expenditures amounted to $10,878,000, an 86% increase over 1983. This increase strengthened our continuing program of process modernization. Major investments included the installation of modern tube cutting equipment, robot welders, a computer aided design system, and the initial phase of a state of the art press room. The commitment to the modernization of our facilities is one that will continue, and we are projecting comparable expenditures in 1985.

In 1984, we also began installation of a Manufacturing Resources Planning (MRP) System. The MRP System will lead to reduced inventory levels and better control and utilization of our manufacturing facility and processes. Such efficiency will improve our cost of operations.

With regards to marketing, Murray has always been innovative in product introductions. We have been successful in introducing BMX, mountain bikes, and freestyle bicycles into the mass market. Murray revolutionized the riding mower market when we entered this industry in 1968 in both performance

m

397

and design, and we have continued as an innovator in this industry. In 1984, we reaffirmed our commitment to this type of innovation.

Bicycles and power mowers continue to be viable products for the consumer. We recognize the need to intensify our efforts to compete in these markets. At the same time, we are analyzing our present and related markets for expansion opportunities. This effort is continuing, and its benefits are beginning to show in our marketing plans.

One result of this market analysis was the introduction of our Sabre mower line for the spring of 1985. The Sabre line will target the outdoor power equipment dealer who participates in a large share of the mower market in which Murray is not currently represented. This new line, which will be sold directly to the dealer, offers him high quality merchandise with the ability to improve profit margins. Murray will continue such expansion or diversification moves as prove correct for our business future.

Our power mower products continue to meet with great success. The 1985 Murray line has been well received by our customers, and we expect the momentum created by our steady mower sales rise over the past 15 years to be maintained.

This year again, we were pleased to be selected to receive the Sears "Partners in Progress Award." We were one of only 23 suppliers to receive this award for the third consecutive year. The award is presented for overall excellence as a manufacturer of products for Sears. Sears has a total of over 12,000 suppliers.

We and our industry continue to make every effort in Washington to draw attention to the unfair competition we face from imported bicycles. The industry was successful in May with having H.R. 5754 introduced in the House of Representatives. This Bill provides for a 24% duty on imported bicycles and bicycle parts, a duty comparable to that in foreign markets. No action was taken on this Bill, and it will be reintroduced in the new session of Congress. It is the aim of the domestic industry to have our Government recognize and control the flood of unfairly traded import bicycles coming into this country.

If the economy continues on its present course, our sales for 1985 should improve. While our plans for 1985 and the future will help offset our 1985 pricing structure, we expect continued profit margin pressure.

Board of Director Changes

At the February 1985 Board Meeting, we regretfully accepted the resignation of Eugene T. Kinder, a recently retired partner in the law firm of Jones, Day, Reavis & Pogue. Though leaving our Board, Mr. Kinder will continue to be available as requested to render the excellent counsel that he has given Murray in his 12 years on the Board.

H. Theodore Meyer, also a partner of Jones, Day, Reavis & Pogue and currently Secretary of Murray Ohio, was elected to fill the vacant position. His election continues the tradition since 1925 of having a member of this firm on our Board.

Solid Record for the Future

We recognize the difficulty of the journey before us. Our past record, however, shows one of success and profitability. With a solid balance sheet and the full commitment of our resources and people we look forward to the challenges that lie ahead.

Our people continue to be our greatest source of strength. Their innovativeness, team-work, and support provide the Company with the impetus that it needs. In these times of change, their support and assistance are unmeasurable.

Very truly yours,

W. M. Hannon
Chairman of the Board

John N. Anderson
President and Chief Executive Officer

G. Cromer Smotherman
Executive Vice President and
Chief Operating Officer

FINANCIAL REVIEW

Sales in 1984 were $384 million, which was within 1% of the company's all-time record sales year of 1983. This included an increase of over 15% from the company's previous record for its power mower line, while bicycle sales were adversely impacted by import competition to record a 19% decrease from 1983.

Net income and earnings per common share were $7.8 million and $2.01, respectively, each after non-recurring adjustments. This resulted in profit margins of 2.04% and return on average shareholders' equity of 7.05%.

Murray Ohio has spent approximately $59 million during the past ten years to modernize and automate its facilities, to increase the productive efficiency and to expand the plant capacity. This included a significant increase in 1984 to further pursue the goals stated above.

During this ten-year period, the company has significantly expanded both its power mower and bicycle production capacities at Lawrenceburg, including additions of 600,000 square feet. Other expenditures were for research and development facilities, and an expansion to the corporate office. Another $9.7 million is budgeted for capital expenditures in 1985.

Total long-term debt at the end of 1984 was $23.0 million or 16.9% of total capitalization. This compares to $26.0 million and 19.2% for 1983. Working capital stands at $86.5 million at December 31, 1984, resulting in a current ratio of 2.2 to 1.

Shareholders' equity per share has increased every year for the last ten years to $28.93 at December 31, 1984, an increase of 91% for the ten-year period.

Murray Ohio paid cash dividends of $1.20 per common share in 1984. Murray is proud of its history of paying regular quarterly dividends without a reduction for the past 49 consecutive years. During this period Murray's stock became listed on the New York Stock Exchange and the Midwest Stock Exchange in 1969 and 1971, respectively, and continues to be so listed. Prior to 1969 Murray was listed on the American Stock Exchange.

Murray Ohio's cash payout over the past ten-year period has averaged 43% of net income. At year end, 3,896,670 shares of the company's common stock were outstanding. Of this total, 1,113,041 shares (29%), were owned by directors, officers, and current employees.

TEN YEARS OF GROWTH

Summary of Operations	1984	1983	1982	1981
Net Sales	$383,589,105	$386,493,993	$288,642,358	$332,278,451
Power Mowers and Accessories	236,421,047	205,036,387	155,415,363	161,076,211
Bicycles and Accessories	147,079,185	181,377,604	133,138,347	170,619,908
Other Products	88,873	80,002	88,648	582,332
Cost of Products Sold	335,374,269	327,134,491	245,394,295	283,353,873
Depreciation and Amortization	3,635,096	3,361,666	3,253,897	2,876,664
Interest Expense	4,689,476	4,336,223	6,847,499	7,217,509
Income Before Income Taxes	9,129,558	22,527,621	9,429,651	17,180,728
Federal and State Income Taxes	2,708,000(b)	10,153,000	4,337,000	8,090,000
Income Before Cumulative Effect of Change in Accounting Principle	6,421,558	12,374,621	5,092,651	9,090,728(d)
Cumulative Effect of Change in Accounting Principle for Investment Tax Credit	1,404,000	—	—	—
Net Income (a)	7,825,558(b)	12,374,621	5,092,651	9,090,728(d)
Percent of Net Income to Net Sales	2.04%	3.20%	1.76%	2.74%
Return on Average Shareholder's Equity	7.05%	13.02%	6.39%	11.96%
Earnings per Common Share Before Cumulative Effect of Change in Accounting Principle	1.65	3.53	1.63	2.93(d)
Cumulative Effect of Change in Accounting Principle for Investment Tax Credit	.36	—	—	—
Earnings per Common Share (a, c, e)	2.01(b)	3.53	1.63	2.93(d)
Cash Dividends Paid	4,649,740	4,118,992	3,701,465	3,674,103
Cash Dividends Declared and Paid per Common Share (e)	1.20	1.20	1.20	1.20
Common Shares Outstanding at Year End (net of Treasury Shares) (c, e)	3,896,670	3,873,748	3,134,565	3,099,527
Number of Shareholders (h)	4,813	4,802	5,203	4,711
Average Number of Employees	3,500	3,403	2,868	3,534

Financial Condition at Year End				
Total Assets	$209,777,365	$188,845,331	$171,732,458	$173,521,388
Current Assets	157,938,259	142,782,974	127,822,330	132,297,984
Current Liabilities	71,395,177	48,140,763	58,037,639	62,352,490
Current Ratio	2.2 to 1	3.0 to 1	2.2 to 1	2.1 to 1
Working Capital	86,543,082	94,642,211	69,784,691	69,945,494
Shareholders' Equity	112,721,223	109,368,410	80,741,336	78,713,813
Shareholders' Equity per Common Share (e)	28.93	28.23	25.76	25.40
Property, Plant and Equipment (net)	50,794,929	44,778,715	42,628,946	39,721,024
Capital Expenditures	10,878,234	5,862,985	6,277,156	6,104,077
Total Amount of Long-Term Debt	22,978,225	26,014,300	29,075,375	30,131,450
Long-Term Debt as a Percentage of Total Capitalization	16.9%	19.2%	26.5%	27.7%

(a) Pro forma based on revised method of accounting for investment tax credit, applied retroactively:

	1984	1983	1982	1981	1980	1979	1978	1977	1976	1975
Net Income (000's)	6,422	12,521	5,184	9,242	8,566	10,704	7,936	8,435	5,768	4,850
Earning per Common Share	1.65	3.57	1.66	2.98	2.76	3.46	2.56	2.73	1.86	1.57

b)   Income taxes, net income, and earnings per common share for 1984 include the nonrecurring effect of the reversal of certain deferred taxes. Refer to the financial statements and management's discussion and analysis for further explanation.

(c) Earnings per common share are computed based on the average common shares outstanding each year. The average common shares for 1983 (3,505,567) were significantly different from the common shares outstanding at year end due to the issuance in June 1983 of 770,000 common shares.

1980	1979	1978	1977	1976	1975
$294,745,956	$327,137,268	$254,113,710	$212,773,180	$150,815,365	$126,655,353
153,706,766	165,313,297	136,748,819	100,660,828	63,342,453	46,862,481
139,178,541	161,823,971	117,364,891	112,112,352	87,472,912	79,792,872
1,860,649	—	—	—	—	—
251,746,135	283,699,952	220,067,742	181,971,227	127,930,166	106,560,985
2,742,559	2,668,797	2,453,631	1,643,479	1,577,229	1,440,611
7,534,174	4,979,286	3,875,387	1,787,587	1,549,272	1,878,782
15,878,660	20,108,133	15,264,403	16,155,618	11,164,297	9,272,287
7,405,000	9,480,000	7,464,000	7,916,000	5,425,000	4,544,000
8,473,660	10,628,133	7,800,403	8,239,618	5,739,297	4,728,287
—	—	—	—	—	—
8,473,660	10,628,133	7,800,403	8,239,618	5,739,297	4,728,287
2.87%	3.25%	3.07%	3.87%	3.81%	3.73%
11.95%	16.42%	13.33%	15.46%	11.79%	10.41%
2.73	3.43	2.52	2.66	1.85	1.53
—	—	—	—	—	—
2.73	3.43	2.52	2.66	1.85	1.53
3,643,351	3,185,688	3,071,258	2,777,681	2,252,703	2,041,374
1.20	1.05	1.00	.90	.73	.67
3,099,527	3,099,527	3,094,563	3,094,563	3,093,154	3,093,079
5,002	4,874	4,872	4,728	4,663	4,713
3,106	3,676	3,350	3,050	2,423	2,212
$162,593,699	$165,676,630	$137,954,695(f)	$118,184,974	$96,521,505	$77,703,626(g)
123,774,401	128,536,269	104,553,999(f)	92,158,408	74,098,444	56,496,582(g)
56,045,182	62,951,762	41,929,128	47,978,918	31,202,317	15,060,145
2.2 to 1	2.0 to 1	2.5 to 1	1.9 to 1	2.4 to 1	3.8 to 1
67,729,219	65,584,507	62,624,871(f)	44,179,490	42,896,127	41,436,437(g)
73,271,961	68,498,679	60,922,713	56,087,652	50,497,987	46,894,095
23.64	22.10	19.69	18.12	16.32	15.16
36,563,771	34,071,357	30,560,878	24,692,169	20,408,767	19,747,300
5,322,612	6,891,287	7,648,408	5,962,610	2,335,131	1,600,299
31,177,525	32,213,600	33,249,675(f)	12,470,000	13,480,000	14,485,000(g)
29.9%	32.0%	35.3%	18.2%	21.1%	23.6%

d) Net income in 1981 was reduced by $3,047,000 ($.98 per common share) due to the change to the LIFO, from the FIFO, method of accounting for inventories.

(e) Adjusted for the 3-for-2 stock split distributed August 31, 1977.

(f) Includes a long-term loan of $20,000,000 at 9¼% annual interest.

(g) Includes a long-term loan of $5,000,000 at 10¼% annual interest.

(h) Represents the number of shareholders of record as of the approximate December 15, dividend record date of each respective year.

QUARTERLY RESULTS OF OPERATIONS

In Thousands of Dollars (except for per share data)

Comparison of Quarterly Results for Years Ended December 31, 1984, and December 31, 1983

| | Net Sales | | | | | | | |
| | Power Mowers and Accessories | | Bicycles and Accessories | | Other Products | | Total | |
Quarter	1984	1983	1984	1983	1984	1983	1984	1983
1st	$114,820	$104,446	$ 40,664	$33,918	$22	$ 6	$155,506	$138,370
2nd	94,213	70,445	39,775	48,387	50	16	134,038	118,848
3rd	12,641	11,561	32,908	48,759	11	46	45,560	60,366
4th	14,747	18,584	33,732	50,314	6	12	48,485	68,910
Total	$236,421	$205,036	$147,079	$181,378	$89	$80	$383,589	$386,494

| | Income | | | | | | | | | |
| | Gross Profit[1] | | Income (Loss) Before Cumulative Effect of Accounting Change | | Net Income (Loss) | | Earnings (Loss) per Common Share Before Cumulative Effect of Accounting Change | | Earnings (Loss) per Common Share | |
Quarter	1984	1983	1984[3]	1983	1984[3]	1983	1984[3]	1983[2,3]	1984[3]	1983[2,3]
1st	$18,688	$17,625	$4,340	$4,953	$5,744	$4,953	$1.12	$1.58	$1.48	$1.58
2nd	15,147	16,943	2,460	4,296	2,460	4,296	.63	1.37	.63	1.37
3rd	4,782	10,146	285	1,693	285	1,693	.07	.44	.07	.44
4th	6,300	11,570	(663)	1,433	(663)	1,433	(.17)	.37	(.17)	.37
Total	$44,917	$56,284	$6,422	$12,375	$7,826	$12,375	$1.65	$3.53	$2.01	$3.53

(1) Gross Profit represents net sales less those costs directly related to the manufacturing process (i.e. labor, and overhead costs consumed within the factory).

(2) Due to the sale of the Common Shares (See Note J), average common shares outstanding for the year differed from the average common shares outstanding for each quarterly period. Earnings per common share for each period is computed by dividing total net income by the period's average common shares outstanding. As a result, the sum of earnings per common share for the individual quarters will not equal the per share amount for the year. The additional shares caused earnings per share to increase by a smaller percentage than total net income.

(3) Net income for the third quarter ended September 30, 1984 and for the year ended December 31, 1984 reflects the reversal of $920,000, or $.24 per common share, (after deductions of expenses relating to employee fringe benefits) of deferred taxes provided in prior years for the company's export sales through its Domestic International Sales Corporation (DISC).

The company changed its method of accounting for investment tax credit effective January 1, 1984. The cumulative effect of the accounting change increased 1984 first quarter earnings per common share by $.36. Other than the cumulative effect, there was no material impact on net income and earnings per common share in any quarter of 1984.

Refer to the Financial Statements and Management's Discussion and Analysis for further explanation.

Common Stock: Market and Dividend Information

	1984 Price Range			1983 Price Range		
Quarter	High	Low	1984 Dividends Paid	High	Low	1983 Dividends Paid
1st	24 5/8	20 3/8	$ .30	$23 3/4	$20	$ .30
2nd	23 3/8	21 1/8	.30	30 1/2	23 1/4	.30
3rd	23 3/4	20	.30	31 1/4	26 1/8	.30
4th	21 5/8	18 3/8	.30	29 3/8	22	.30
Total	24 5/8	18 3/8	$1.20	$31 1/4	$20	$1.20

The most restrictive provisions of the company's long-term debt agreements place certain restrictions (which do not currently limit any existing or presently contemplated company policies) on the payment of dividends and the purchase or redemption of the company's Common Shares.

STATEMENT OF FINANCIAL POSITION

	December 31	
	1984	1983
ASSETS		
Current Assets		
Cash	$ 1,424,761	$ 1,318,101
Trade accounts receivable, less allowance of $300,000	28,339,695	41,974,966
Other accounts receivable	501,387	764,285
Inventories	123,360,661	95,673,256
Company Common Shares acquired for employees' stock plans, at cost	767,737	777,518
Prepaid expenses	796,138	1,142,561
Deferred federal income tax benefits	1,163,467	1,132,287
Refundable federal income taxes	1,584,413	—
Total Current Assets	157,938,259	142,782,974
Property, Plant and Equipment		
Land	758,122	708,121
Buildings	31,054,300	27,619,109
Machinery and equipment	53,154,907	47,477,011
Allowances for depreciation and amortization (deduction)	(34,172,400)	(31,025,526)
	50,794,929	44,778,715
Deferred Charges, Investments and Other Assets	1,044,177	1,283,642
	$209,777,365	$188,845,331

(continued)

m

403

STATEMENT OF FINANCIAL POSITION (continued)

	December 31	
	1984	1983
LIABILITIES AND SHAREHOLDERS' EQUITY		
Current Liabilities		
Notes payable to banks	$ 32,348,675	$1,190,454
Accounts payable and other liabilities	24,015,784	25,459,837
Reserves for product warranty and product liability	1,400,000	1,300,000
Accrued payroll, commissions, and other compensation	8,722,810	12,803,699
Accrued interest, payroll taxes and other taxes	1,387,602	1,494,495
Federal and state income taxes	444,231	2,831,203
Portion of long-term debt due within one year	3,076,075	3,061,075
Total Current Liabilities	71,395,177	48,140,763
Long-Term Debt—less portion shown as current liability		
Notes payable to insurance companies:		
10 1/4% notes	2,075,000	2,400,000
9 1/4% notes	16,000,000	18,000,000
8% notes	1,750,000	2,000,000
6 1/4% notes	750,000	1,125,000
Other notes payable	93,225	84,300
Lease obligations	2,310,000	2,405,000
	22,978,225	26,014,300
Deferred Credits		
Investment tax credit	—	2,121,877
Obligations under deferred compensation plans and other deferred credits	705,685	747,427
Deferred federal income taxes	1,977,055	2,452,554
	2,682,740	5,321,858
Shareholders' Equity		
Serial Preferred Shares, no par value: Authorized 500,000 shares; issued—none		
Common Shares, par value $2.50 a share: Authorized 8,000,000 shares; Issued—3,904,565 shares in 1984 and 1983	9,761,413	9,761,413
Additional paid-in capital	42,292,504	42,804,155
Retained earnings	60,848,757	57,672,939
	112,902,674	110,238,507
Less cost of Common Shares held in treasury (7,895 shares in 1984 and 30,817 shares in 1983)	(181,451)	(870,097)
	112,721,223	109,368,410
	$209,777,365	$188,845,331

See notes to financial statements.

STATEMENT OF INCOME

	Year Ended December 31		
	1984	1983	1982
Net sales	$383,589,105	$386,493,993	$288,642,358
Deductions from (additions to) income			
Cost of product sold (exclusive of depreciation and amortization)	335,374,269	327,134,491	245,394,295
Provision for depreciation and amortization	3,635,096	3,361,666	3,253,897
Selling, general and administrative expenses	30,941,548	30,070,404	23,729,181
Interest on long-term debt	2,438,759	2,627,100	2,711,077
Interest on short-term borrowings	2,250,717	1,709,123	4,136,422
Interest income	(180,842)	(936,412)	(12,165)
	374,459,547	363,966,372	279,212,707
Income before income taxes	9,129,558	22,527,621	9,429,651
Federal and state income taxes	3,628,000	10,153,000	4,337,000
Reversal of deferred taxes	(920,000)	—	—
Net income taxes	2,708,000	10,153,000	4,337,000
Income before cumulative effect of change in accounting principle	6,421,558	12,374,621	5,092,651
Cumulative effect of change in accounting principle for investment tax credit	1,404,000	—	—
Net income	7,825,558	12,374,621	5,092,651
Earnings per common share:			
Before cumulative effect of change in accounting principle	$1.65	$3.53	$1.63
Cumulative effect of change in accounting principle for investment tax credit	.36	—	—
Earnings per common share	$2.01	$3.53	$1.63
Pro forma based on revised method of accounting for investment tax credit, applied respectively:			
Net income	$ 6,421,558	$12,520,798	$5,184,024
Earnings per common share	$1.65	$3.57	$1.66
Average common shares outstanding	3,889,345	3,505,567	3,115,750
Retained earnings at beginning of year	$ 57,672,939	$ 49,417,310	$ 48,026,124
Add:			
Net income	7,825,558	12,374,621	5,092,651
Deduct:			
Cash dividends paid, $1.20 per common share each year	4,649,740	4,118,992	3,701,465
Retained earnings at end of year	$60,848,757	$57,672,939	$49,417,310

See notes to financial statements.

m

405

STATEMENT OF CHANGES IN WORKING CAPITAL

	Year Ended December 31		
	1984	1983	1982
Source of working capital			
From operations:			
Net income	**$ 7,825,558**	$ 12,374,621	$ 5,092,651
Non-cash charges (credits):			
Cumulative effect of change in accounting principle for investment tax credit	**(1,404,000)**	—	—
Provision for depreciation and amortization	**3,635,096**	3,361,666	3,253,897
Deferred income taxes, non-current	**(118,474)**	1,364,331	1,782,871
Other	**88,084**	243,269	97,787
Total from operations	**10,026,264**	17,343,887	10,227,206
Net book value of property, plant and equipment disposals	**1,226,924**	351,550	115,337
Decrease (increase) in investments	**239,735**	(15,711)	51,496
Increase in long-term debt	**40,000**	—	—
Issuance of common stock	**—**	21,270,179	603,205
Tax benefits for non-qualified stock options exercised	**308,105**	—	—
Treasury shares reissued under stock option plans	**688,646**	—	—
Other	**37,675**	15,907	—
	12,567,349	38,965,812	10,997,244
Application of working capital			
Additions to property, plant and equipment	**10,878,234**	5,862,985	6,277,156
Decrease in long-term debt	**3,076,075**	3,061,075	1,056,075
Cash dividends	**4,649,740**	4,118,992	3,701,465
Stock options exercised from repurchased stock	**181,202**	71,445	—
Stock options exercised from treasury shares	**668,407**	—	—
Treasury shares acquired	**—**	870,097	—
Reclassification of deferred investment tax credit	**717,877**	—	—
Reclassification of deferred taxes	**357,025**	—	—
Other	**137,918**	123,698	123,351
	20,666,478	14,108,292	11,158,047
Increase (decrease) in working capital	**(8,099,129)**	24,857,520	(160,803)
Working capital at beginning of year	**94,642,211**	69,784,691	69,945,494
Working capital at end of year	**$86,543,082**	$94,642,211	$69,784,691

m

406

STATEMENT OF CHANGES IN WORKING CAPITAL (continued)

| | Year Ended December 31 | | |
	1984	1983	1982
Changes in components of working capital			
Increase (decrease) in working capital assets:			
Cash	$106,660	$(134,612)	$(148,491)
Accounts receivable	(13,898,169)	16,175,577	3,312,330
Inventories	27,687,405	(723,170)	(8,896,653)
Refundable federal income taxes	1,584,413	—	—
Other	(325,024)	(357,151)	1,257,160
	15,155,285	14,960,644	(4,475,654)
Increase (decrease) in working capital liabilities:			
Notes payable to banks	31,158,221	(27,104,946)	1,748,236
Accounts payable and other liabilities	(1,444,053)	6,708,503	(1,366,321)
Reserves for product warranty and product liability	100,000	200,000	—
Accrued payroll, commissions, and other compensation	(4,080,889)	6,239,607	(3,481,353)
Accrued interest, payroll taxes, and other taxes	(106,893)	126,068	(500,166)
Federal and state income taxes	(2,386,972)	1,928,892	(725,247)
Portion of long-term debt due within one year	15,000	2,005,000	10,000
	23,254,414	(9,896,876)	(4,314,851)
Increase (decrease) in working capital	$(8,099,129)	$24,857,520	$(160,803)

See notes to financial statements.

m

407

NOTES TO FINANCIAL STATEMENTS

Note A—Accounting Policies

The accounting policies that affect the more significant elements of the company's financial statements are summarized below. Certain reclassifications have been made in the financial statements to conform to the 1984 presentation.

Inventories—Inventories are stated at the lower of cost (last-in, first-out method) or market. The company adjusts the carrying value on a current basis for potential losses from obsolete or slow-moving inventories.

Property, Plant and Equipment—Property, plant and equipment are carried at cost. The company provides for depreciation of property, plant and equipment on annual rates, applied generally by the straight-line method, designed to amortize the cost of the respective assets over the period of their esti-

mated useful lives (buildings—20 to 40 years; machinery and equipment—15 years). Structural die costs are capitalized and amortized up to 3 years. When properties are disposed of, the related costs and accumulated depreciation are removed from the accounts at the time of disposal, and the resulting gain or loss is reflected in income.

Product Warranty and Product Liability—These costs are expensed in the year in which they are incurred. The related reserves are reviewed at each year end for reasonableness of possible future costs applicable to the current year's products.

Federal Income Taxes—Deferred taxes are provided with respect to timing differences resulting from those items for which the period of reporting for income tax purposes is different from the period of reporting for financial statement purposes. Effective for 1984, the company adopted the flow-through method of accounting for investment tax credits. In prior years investment credit had been amortized over a ten-year period for financial reporting, but taken for the full amount of the credit in the year in which the credits were available for tax purposes.

Earnings per Common Share—Earnings per Common Share is calculated by dividing net income by the weighted average number of Common Shares outstanding during the year. The only Common Share equivalents are stock options which have no material dilutive effect on earnings per common share.

Note B—Federal and State Income Taxes

Federal income tax returns filed by the company have been examined and approved by the Internal Revenue Service through the year ended December 31, 1979.

The provision for federal and state income taxes is composed of the following:

	1984	1983	1982
Federal income tax currently payable:			
Gross	$3,405,740	$ 8,866,388	$2,409,611
Investment and other credits	(976,220)	(847,365)	(451,788)
Net	2,429,520	8,019,023	1,957,823
Reversal of DISC deferred taxes	(920,000)	—	—
State income tax currently payable	502,150	1,002,000	325,000
Deferred federal income tax	696,330*	1,131,977*	2,054,177*
	$2,708,000	$10,153,000	$4,337,000

*Accelerated depreciation methods resulted in $1,027,943, $976,510 and $820,609 of deferred tax for the years 1984, 1983 and 1982, respectively. Tool and die amortization methods resulted in deferred tax of $365,811 for 1984. The DISC resulted in $406,275 of deferred tax in 1982.

Reconciliation of U.S. statutory tax rate to effective rate:

	1984
Statutory tax rate	46.0%
Investment tax credits (net of recapture)	(6.0)
PAYSOP tax credit	(4.1)
State income taxes (net of federal tax benefit)	3.0
Other (net)	.8
Subtotal	39.7
Reversal of DISC deferred taxes	(10.0)
Effective tax rate	29.7)

The effective tax rate for 1983 and 1982 was not significantly different from the statutory rate.

Net income for the third quarter ended September 30, 1984 and for the year ended December 31, 1984 reflects the reversal of $920,000, or $.24 per common share, (after deductions of expenses relating to employee fringe benefits and related tax effects) of deferred taxes provided in prior years for the company's export sales through its Domestic International Sales Corporation (DISC). As a result of tax legislation enacted in 1984, the potential payment of these taxes has been eliminated. In accordance with a pronouncement of the Financial Accounting Standards Board, the entire reversal is reflected in the third quarter results.

Note C—Accounting Change (Investment Tax Credit)

Effective January 1, 1984, the company changed to the flow-through method of accounting for investment tax credits. The deferred method had been used in prior years. The change was made to conform to predominant U.S. industry practice. The flow-through method includes these credits in income in the year earned, while the deferred method amortized the credits over a ten-year period. This change in accounting method (after deductions of expenses relating to fringe benefits and related tax effects) increased 1984 net income by approximately $103,000 for credits earned during the year, and by $1,404,000 for the cumulative effect of the change; earnings per common share was increased by $.03 and $.36, respectively. Pro forma net income and earnings per common share amounts reflecting retroactive application of this change are shown on the Statement of Income.

Note D—Long-Term Debt

The company negotiated long-term loans of $6,000,000 at 6¼% annual interest during 1967, $5,000,000 at 8% during 1972, $5,000,000 at 10¼% during 1975, and $20,000,000 at 9¼% during 1978, with groups of insurance companies. Under the provisions of the loan agreements, the company is required to maintain current assets of not less than 150% of current liabilities.

The 6¼% notes mature in equal annual installments from September 1972 to September 1987. The 8% notes mature in equal annual installments from December 1973 to December 1992. The 10¼% notes mature in equal annual installments from April 1977 to April 1991. The 9¼% notes mature in equal annual installments from June 1984 to June 1993.

Capitalized Lease Agreements—During 1971 and 1978, the company entered into lease obligations with the Industrial Development Board of the Town of Franklin, Tennessee, for the lease of its office building and an addition thereto. The lease obligation, in an original amount of $1,600,000, will be repaid over a twenty-year term ending in 1991. The second lease obligation, also in the amount of $1,600,000, will be repaid in total in 1998. The company will own the buildings at the expiration of the lease, and has the option to purchase the underlying land at its market value after July 31, 1992.

Future maturities of long-term debt are as follows:

	Notes	Lease Obligations	Total
1985	$2,981,075	$95,000	$3,076,075
1986	2,981,075	100,000	3,081,075
1987	2,981,075	105,000	3,086,075
1988	2,606,075	115,000	2,721,075
1989	2,575,000	120,000	2,695,000
1990 and later	9,525,000	1,870,000	11,395,000

Rental expense and other future lease commitments are not considered to be material.

In early 1985, the company entered into a lease obligation with the Industrial Development Board of the City of Lawrenceburg, Tennessee, for the lease of environmental control facilities at its factory.

This lease obligation, in an original amount of $2,500,000, will be repaid over a fifteen-year term ending in 2000. The bondholder has the option to redeem the bonds after the tenth year. The company will own the facility upon the redemption of the bonds. This lease obligation is not included in the above maturity schedule.

Note E—Company Stock Plans

Eligible employees may contribute up to 5% of their base compensation to the company's stock purchase plan. The company may contribute an additional 50% of the employees' contributions. The company made such contributions for portions of 1982 and 1983, and for all of 1984. At December 31, 1984, 1,092 of the 2,220 employees eligible to participate in this plan were participants. There were 35,669 and 37,357 Common Shares held for this purpose at December 31, 1984 and 1983, respectively.

Unissued Common Shares of the company are reserved for issuance under stock option plans authorized by the shareholders during 1969, 1973, 1979 and 1984. The terms of the plans provide that qualified or non-qualified options may be issued to key employees, including officers, of the company at a price not less than the market value of the shares at the date of grant. The options generally become exercisable one year from the date of grant ratably over the succeeding four years and expire not later than ten years from the date of grant. The qualified options must be exercised in order of grant dates. The company makes no charges to income in connection with these options.

A summary of option activity follows.

Options	Shares	Option Prices
Outstanding January 1, 1984	283,982	$9.33 – 28.00
Exercised during 1984	(65,237)	$9.33 – 12.25
Expired during 1984	(9,422)	$11.50 – 28.00
Outstanding December 31, 1984	209,323	$9.33– 28.00

m

409

Options	Shares	Option Prices
Exercisable:		
December 31, 1984	167,193	
December 31, 1983	204,107	
December 31, 1982	190,731	
Exercised during 1983	8,374	$9.33 – 20.88
Exercised during 1982	-0-	

There were 513,369 and 203,947 unoptioned shares at December 31, 1984 and 1983, respectively.

Stock appreciation rights may be granted in tandem with options granted under the company's stock option plans. The amounts recorded each year by the company as income or expense attributable to these stock appreciation rights are insignificant.

The company has maintained since 1970 a Contingent Supplemental Retirement Benefit Plan pursuant to which additional retirement benefits may be awarded on an annual basis in amounts and to key employees of the company as designated by the Compensation Committee of the Board of Directors. Payment of such benefits is contingent upon certain employment conditions.

Note F—Pension Plans

The company has noncontributory pension plans which cover substantially all of its employees. The company makes annual contributions to the plans equal to the amounts accrued for pension expense in the prior year.

The total pension expense was $1,654,100, $2,417,400 and $2,552,900 for 1984, 1983 and 1982, respectively. The decreases in pension expense have resulted principally from the increased assumed rate of return and changes in the employment levels. The company's consulting actuary has estimated certain information for the 1984 and 1983 plan years as follows:

	1984	1983
Date of actuarial valuation:		
Hourly Plan	January 1, 1984	January 1, 1983
Salary Plan	December 1, 1983	December 1, 1982
Net assets available for plan benefits	$47,151,444	$41,586,931
Actuarial present value of plan benefits:		
Vested	27,463,800	27,411,600
Non-Vested	4,496,200	4,362,600
Assumed rate of return*:		
Hourly Plan	8.0%	7.0%
Salary Plan	8.5%	7.0%

Used in determining the actuarial present value of plan benefits, which would have been approximately $5,900,000 higher had the rate remained at 7%. Actual plan benefits were not affected.

In addition to providing pension benefits, the company provided certain health care and life insurance benefits for retired employees and their dependents. Substantially all of the company's employees who retire under the company's retirement plans may become eligible for these benefits. The cost of retiree health care and life insurance benefits is recognized as an expense as incurred. For 1984, these costs totaled approximately $261,000.

Note G—Short-Term Credit Arrangements

Under lines of credit arrangements for short-term debt with eleven financial institutions, the company may borrow up to $111,100,000 on such terms as may be mutually agreeable. These arrangements do not have termination dates but are reviewed annually for renewal. At December 31, 1984, the unused portion of the credit lines was $78,751,325.

Under various informal and unrestricted arrangements with the financial institutions, compensating balances are maintained at varying terms against credit lines and related borrowings. During 1984, such compensating balances averaged approximately $2,830,000 and were satisfied substantially by float.

Note I—Business Segment Information

The components of revenue, operating profit and other data by business segments are set forth within the following table for the years ended:

December 31, 1984	Power Mowers and Accessories	Bicycles and Accessories	Other Products	Total
Net Sales	$236,421,047	$147,079,185	$88,873	$383,589,105
Operating Profit (loss)	24,533,300	3,352,581	(27,349)	27,858,532
General and Administrative Expense (1)	8,721,454	5,316,076	1,968	14,039,498
Interest (2)	3,222,125	1,467,173	178	4,689,476
Income (Loss) Before Taxes	$12,589,721	$(3,430,668)	$(29,495)	$9,129,558
Identifiable Assets (3)	$119,534,386	$49,353,639	$54,766	$168,942,791
General Corporate Assets				40,834,574
				$209,777,365
Depreciation and Amortization Expense	$1,797,348	$1,613,597	$-0-	$3,410,945
General Depreciation Expense				224,151
				$3,635,096
Identifiable Capital Expenditures	$5,792,543	$4,246,449	$-0-	$10,038,992
General Capital Expenditures				839,242
				$10,878,234

December 31, 1983	Power Mowers and Accessories	Bicycles and Accessories	Other Products	Total
Net Sales	$205,036,387	$181,377,604	$80,002	$386,493,993
Operating Profit (Loss)	25,057,921	12,000,318	(4,639)	37,053,600
General and Administrative Expense (1)	6,505,761	3,682,691	1,304	10,189,756
Interest (2)	2,595,403	1,740,577	243	4,336,223
Income (Loss) Before Taxes	$15,956,757	$6,577,050	$(6,186)	$22,527,621
Identifiable Assets (3)	$84,424,799	$51,061,136	$305,592	$135,791,527
General Corporate Assets				53,053,804
				$188,845,331
Depreciation and Amortization Expense	$1,632,805	$1,537,759	$4,027	$3,174,591
General Depreciation Expense				187,075
				$3,361,666
Identifiable Capital Expenditures	$2,682,958	$2,954,450	$-0-	$5,637,408
General Capital Expenditures				225,577
				$5,862,985

December 31, 1982	Power Mowers and Accessories	Bicycles and Accessories	Other Products	Total
Net Sales	$155,415,363	$133,138,347	$88,648	$288,642,358
Operating Profit (Loss)	18,603,595	7,086,836	(230,795)	25,459,636
General and Administrative Expense (1)	5,815,558	3,365,070	1,858	9,182,486
Interest (2)	4,577,197	2,269,850	452	6,847,499
Income (Loss) Before Taxes	$8,210,840	$1,451,916	$(233,105)	$9,429,651
Identifiable Assets (3)	$94,912,121	$39,142,707	$348,421	$134,403,249
General Corporate Assets				37,329,209
				$171,732,458

(continued)

411

December 31, 1984	Power Mowers and Accessories	Bicycles and Accessories	Other Products	Total
Depreciation and Amortization Expense	$1,643,064	$1,426,993	$3,811	$3,073,868
General Depreciation Expense				180,029
				$3,253,897
Identifiable Capital Expenditures	$2,099,488	$4,115,209	$-0-	$6,214,697
General Capital Expenditures				62,459
				$6,277,156

(1) General and administrative expenses were directly allocated by segment where reasonable bases existed with the remainder of these expenses allocated based upon the ration of the segment's net sales to total net sales. Interest income, receipts from an antitrust settlement and losses on capital disposals are included in general and administrative expenses. The combination of these items increased general and administrative expenses by $806,000 in 1984, while the same items decreased this category by $1,466,000 in 1983, resulting in $2,272,000 of the total change in general and administrative expenses between the two years. The balance of the increase was composed of a number of different items. The above mentioned items were insignificant in 1982.

(2) Interest expense was partially allocated using the ratio of the segment's identifiable assets to total assets with the portion of interest related to general assets allocated based upon the ratio of the segment's net sales to total net sales.

(3) Identifiable assets by segment includes both assets directly identified with those operations including finished and in-process inventories and an allocable share of jointly used assets. General assets consist of cash, receivables and other unallocable assets.

Of the company's total revenue, its three largest customers provided $69 million, $43 million and $43 million, respectively in 1984, while one customer provided $79 million and $68 million in 1983 and 1982, respectively, from purchases of both power mowers and bicycles.

Note J—Change in Capital Accounts

A summary of changes in capital accounts for 1984, 1983 and 1982 follows.

	Common Shares Outstanding		Additional Paid-In Capital	Treasury Shares
	Number	Amount		
Balance at January 1, 1982	3,099,527	$7,748,818	$22,938,871	—
Stock issued to Stock Purchase Plan	35,038	87,595	515,610	
Credit attributable to deferred compensation			33,132	
Balance at December 31, 1982	3,134,565	7,836,413	23,487,613	—
Stock options exercised from repurchased stock			(71,445)	
Additional common stock issued less cost of issue	770,000	1,925,000	19,345,179	
Treasury shares acquired	(30,817)			(870,097)
Credit attributable to deferred compensation			42,808	
Balance at December 31, 1983	3,873,748	9,761,413	42,804,155	(870,097)
Stock options exercised from repurchased stock			(181,202)	
Treasury shares reissued under stock options plans	22,922		(668,407)	688,646
Tax benefits of non-qualified stock options exercised			308,105	
Credit attributable to deferred compensation			29,853	
Balance at December 31, 1984	3,896,670	$9,761,413	$42,292,504	(181,451)

The company sold 770,000 Common Shares in a public offering during June 1983. The company's net proceeds from this sale totaled $21,270,179. Had these shares been issued at the beginning of 1983 and the proceeds applied to short-term debt at that time, earnings per common share for 1983 would have been $3.31 as compared to the reported amount of $3.53.

Note K—Inventories and Cost of Sales

The inventory components are as follows:

	1984	1983
Finished and in-process products	$121,931,069	$90,822,673
Raw materials	6,695,859	8,859,494
Manufacturing supplies	1,582,733	1,392,089
	130,209,661	101,074,256
Less allowance to reduce carrying value to LIFO basis	(6,849,000)	(5,401,000)
Inventory at LIFO	$123,360,661	$95,673,256

During 1982, certain inventory quantities were reduced, resulting in a liquidation of LIFO quantities carried at the cost prevailing in the prior year. The effect was to increase 1982 net profit by approximately $130,000.

Note L—Non-Monetary Transactions

During 1983 and 1982 the company exchanged certain inventory for advertising services to be received. These transactions resulted in no significant gain or loss. At December 31, 1984, 1983 and 1982, the unused amounts of $577,000, $935,000 and $1,321,000, respectively, were classified as prepaid expenses.

Note M—Miscellaneous Receipts and Charges

Selling, general and administrative expenses include miscellaneous receipts and charges which normally are insignificant. However, in the second quarter of 1984 and the first quarter of 1983 the company received approximately $85,000 and $628,000, respectively, for distributions from a class action antitrust settlement involving certain members of the corrugated container industry. In the fourth quarter of 1984, the company recorded an expense of $998,000 due to the write-off of an inoperative machine.

m

413

REPORTS OF INDEPENDENT ACCOUNTANTS AND MANAGEMENT

Report of Independent Accountants

Board of Directors and Shareholders
The Murray Ohio Manufacturing Company
Brentwood, Tennessee

We have examined the statement of financial position of The Murray Ohio Manufacturing Company as of December 31, 1984 and 1983, and the related statement of income, retained earnings and changes in working capital for each of the three years in the period ended December 31, 1984. Our examinations were made in accordance with generally accepted auditing standards and, accordingly, included such tests of the accounting records and such other auditing procedures as we considered necessary in the circumstances.

In our opinion, the financial statements referred to above present fairly the financial position of The Murray Ohio Manufacturing Company at December 31, 1984 and 1983, and the results of its operations and changes in working capital for each of the three years in the period ended December 31, 1984, in conformity with generally accepted accounting principles applied on a consistent basis, except for the change, with which we concur, in the method of accounting for investment tax credits as described in Note C of Notes to Financial Statements.

Ernst and Whinney
Nashville, Tennessee
January 28, 1985

Report of Management

The management of The Murray Ohio Manufacturing Company is responsible for the integrity of all information and representation contained in the financial statements and other sections of this Annual Report. The Company's financial statements are based on generally accepted accounting principles and as such include amounts based on management's judgment and estimates.

The company has a system of internal accounting controls which is designed to provide reasonable assurance that assets are safeguarded, transactions are executed in accordance with management's authorization and financial records are reliable as a basis for preparation of financial statements. The system includes the selection and training of qualified personnel, an organizational structure which permits the delegation of authority and responsibility, the establishing and disseminating of accounting and business policies and procedures and an extensive internal audit program. There are limits inherent in all systems of internal control and a recognition that the cost of such systems should not exceed the benefits to be derived. We believe the company's systems provide this appropriate balance.

The company's independent accountants, Ernst & Whinney, have examined the financial statements. As independent accountants, they also provide an objective review of management's discharge of its responsibility to report operating results and financial condition. They obtain and maintain an understanding of the company's systems and procedures and perform such tests and other procedures, including tests of the internal accounting controls, as they deem necessary to enable them to express an opinion on the fairness of the financial statements.

The Board of Directors pursues its oversight role for the financial statements through its Audit Committee composed of three outside directors. The Audit Committee meets as necessary with management, the internal auditors and the independent accountants. The independent accountants and internal auditors have free access to the Audit Committee without the presence of management representatives to discuss internal accounting controls, auditing and financial reporting matters.

MANAGEMENT'S DISCUSSION AND ANALYSIS OF THE SUMMARY OF OPERATIONS

Sales for 1984 remained basically constant with 1983 as a result of a 15% increase in power mower sales which represented 62% of total sales and a 19% decrease in bicycle sales which represented the remaining 38% of total sales. In 1983 power mower sales represented 53% and bicycle sales represented 47% of total sales. The increase in 1984 power mower sales was attributable to increased volume. The company's bicycle pricing, production levels and sales have been adversely affected by increased bicycle imports and heightened domestic bicycle competition. Net income as a percentage of sales decreased to 2.0% in 1984 from 3.2% in 1983.

Net income for 1984 was down 37% reflecting narrower operating margins than were experienced in 1983 and 1982 for power mowers and especially bicycles. Operating profit as a percentage of sales for power mowers was 10.4%, 12.2% and 12.0% for 1984, 1983 and 1982, respectively. Bicycle operating profit as a percentage of sales was 2.3%, 6.6% and 5.3% for 1984, 1983 and 1982, respectively. Increased domestic competition in both product lines contributed to the narrower operating margins. However, the increasing volume of imports, principally from Taiwan, had an added impact upon the bicycle operating profit for 1984. The decrease in earnings per common share was greater than the corresponding decrease in net income for 1983 to 1984 due to the increase in the average number of common shares outstanding resulting from the sale of additional common shares in June 1983.

Net income for 1984 reflects the reversal of $920,000, or $.24 per common share (after deductions of expenses relating to employee fringe benefits and related tax effects), of deferred taxes provided in prior years for the company's export sales through its Domestic International Sales Corporation (DISC). As a result of tax legislation enacted in 1984, the liability for potential payment of these taxes has been eliminated. For further explanation refer to Note B of Notes to Financial Statements.

m

414

Effective January 1, 1984, the company changed to the flow-through method of accounting for investment tax credits. The deferred method had been used in prior years. This change in accounting method (after deductions of expenses relating to employee fringe benefits and related tax effects) increased 1984 net income by approximately $103,000 ($.03 per common share) for credits earned during the year, and by approximately $1,404,000 ($.36 per common share) for the cumulative effect of the change. For further information refer to the Statement of Income and Note C of Notes to Financial Statements.

The company experienced an exceptional year in both sales and net income for 1983. The sales and net income increases in 1983 from 1982 were attributable primarily to increased sales volume resulting from the general improvement in the economy. Both the bicycle and power mower product lines contributed to the increased sales and net income in 1983. Net income as a percentage of sales increased to 3.2% in 1983 from 1.8% in 1982.

Selling, general and administrative expenses for 1984 remained relatively constant compared to 1983. Selling, general and administrative expenses for 1984 and 1983 were reduced by approximately $85,000 and $628,000, respectively, for distributions received from a class action antitrust settlement involving certain members of the corrugated container industry. In 1984 an expense of $998,000 was recorded due to the write-off of an inoperative machine. Increased advertising expenditures along with increased costs associated with increased sales caused the company's 1983 selling, general and administrative expenses to increase $6.3 million (26.7%) from 1982.

Interest expense on short-term borrowings reflects an increase for 1984 as compared to 1983 as a result of higher levels of average borrowing at higher interest rates. Short-term borrowings increased in 1984 from 1983 due to higher average inventory levels experienced during 1984 and the use of the proceeds from the common stock offering to repay short-term borrowings in 1983 as later discussed.

Inventories at December 31, 1984 are considerably higher than at December 31, 1983, primarily due to power mower inventory levels reflecting an expectation of increased orders for the 1985 riding mower lines. Notes payable have correspondingly increased due to the increased inventory levels.

Accounts receivable outstanding at year-end decreased in 1984 compared to 1983 primarily due to decreased sales experienced in the fourth quarter in 1984. Traditionally, sales in the last 45 days of the year cause receivables to be correspondingly higher.

Accrued payroll, commissions and other compensation decreased from $12.8 million in 1983 to $8.7 million in 1984. This decrease principally resulted from decreased net income, year-end employment levels and related employee fringe benefits.

The effective income tax rate of 29.7% was significantly lower that the effective rates of 45.1% for 1983 and 46% for 1982. The effective tax rate for 1984 differs from the statutory rate principally because of tax credits and the impact of the reversal of DISC taxes. The company continues to review, and adopt where appropriate, methods of tax accounting, all within tax regulations, which allow the company to defer payment of tax and thus increase its cash flow.

The company's business cycle imposes fluctuating demands on its cash flow, due to the temporary buildup of inventory in anticipation of, and receivables subsequent to, shipping during the peak seasonal periods. The company has in the past used lines of credit arrangements for short-term debt to meet its cash flow demands. These arrangements, the details of which are further discussed in Note G of Notes to Financial Statements, provide the company with immediate and continued sources of liquidity.

During June 1983, the company sold an additional 770,000 shares of Common Stock in a public offering at $29.25 per share. The net proceeds to the company, totaling approximately $21 million were used to repay outstanding short-term instruments pending application to the company's working capital requirements. Decreased interest expense on short-term borrowings and increased interest income for 1983 reflect the use of the proceeds from the sale of Common Stock.

In addition to cash flow and existing lines of credit, management believes that alternatives are available

m

415

to the company to meet future cash needs. These may include additional short-term debt, commercial paper, or equity securities. The company's strong debt to equity ratio should place it in a favorable position to issue new debt or equity securities. The company reviews these alternatives relative to current market and economic conditions on a continuing basis.

Capital expenditures for 1984 amounted to $10.9 million as compared to $5.9 million in 1983. Major expenditures included modern tube cutting equipment, robot welders, a computer aided design system and the initial phase of a state of the art press room. The company has budgeted $9.7 million for its 1985 capital expenditures. This budget is based on current economic conditions, and is subject to change in the event of significant changes in the general economy and/or the company's performance. This budget includes projects for further modernization and automation of production processes, and for continued vertical integration. These projects are anticipated to be financed principally from working capital sources. In early 1985, the company entered into a 2.5 million Industrial Development Revenue Bond financing for environmental control facilities at its factory. Refer to Note D of Notes to Financial Statements for further information.

Virtually all costs and expenses are subject to normal inflationary pressures and the company is continually seeking ways to cope with its impact. The effects of inflation on the company's operations are summarized and discussed in Note H of Notes to Financial Statements.

m

In August 1990 Lawrence J. Ellison, CEO of Oracle Systems Corporation, was facing increasing pressure from analysts about the method the company used to recognize revenue in its financial reports. Analysts' major concerns were clearly articulated by a senior technology analyst at Hambrecht & Quist, Inc. in San Francisco:

> *Under Oracle's current set of accounting rules, Oracle can recognize any revenue they believe will be shipped within the next twelve months. . . . Many other software firms have moved to booking only the revenue that has been shipped.*

Given its aggressive revenue-recognition policy and relatively high amount of accounts receivable, many analysts argued that Oracle's stock was a risky buy. As a result, the company's stock price had plummeted from a high of $56 in March to around $27 in mid-August. This poor stock performance concerned Larry Ellison for two reasons. First, he worried that the firm might become a takeover candidate, and second that the low price made it expensive for the firm to raise new equity capital to finance its future growth.

ORACLE'S BUSINESS AND PERFORMANCE

Since its formation in California in June 1977, Oracle Systems Corporation has grown rapidly to become the world's largest supplier of database management software. Its principal product is the ORACLE relational database management system, which runs on a broad range of computers, including mainframes, minicomputers, microcomputers, and personal computers. The company also develops and distributes a wide array of products to interface with its database system, including applications in financial reporting, manufacturing management, computer aided systems engineering, computer network communications, and office automation. Finally, Oracle offers extensive maintenance, consulting, training, and systems integration services to support its products.

Oracle's leadership in developing software for database management has enabled it to achieve impressive financial growth. As reported in Exhibit 1, the company's sales grew from $282 million in 1988 to $971 million two years later. Larry Ellison was proud of this rapid growth and committed to its continuance. He often referred to Genghis Khan as his inspiration in crushing competitors and achieving growth.

....

This case was prepared for class discussion by Cholthicha Srivisal and Paul M. Healy of the MIT Sloan School of Management.

The primary factors underlying Oracle's strong performance have been its successes in R&D and its committed sales force. The firm's R&D triumphs are proudly noted in the 1990 annual report:

In 1979, we delivered ORACLE, the world's first relational database management system and the first product based on SQL. In 1983, ORACLE was the first database management system to run on mainframes, minicomputers, and PCs. In 1986, ORACLE was the first database management system with distributed capability, making access to data on a network of computers as easy as access on a single computer.

We continued our tradition of technology leadership in 1990, with three key achievements in the area of client-server computing. First, we delivered software that allows client programs to automatically adapt to the different graphical user interfaces on PCs, Macintoshes, and workstations. Second, we delivered our complete family of accounting applications running as client programs networked to an ORACLE database server. Third, the ORACLE database server set performance records of over 400 transactions per second on mainframes, 200 transactions per second on minicomputers, and 20 transactions per second on PCs.

Oracle's sales force has also been responsible for its success. The sales force is compensated on the basis of sales, giving it a strong incentive to aggressively court large corporate customers. In some cases salespeople even have been known to offer extended payment terms to a potentially valuable customer to close a sale.

Oracle's growth slowed in early 1990. In March the firm announced a 54 percent jump in quarterly revenues (relative to 1989's results)—but only a 1 percent rise in earnings (see Exhibit 2 for quarterly results for 1989 and 1990). Management explained that several factors contributed to this poor performance. First, the company had recently redrawn its sales territories and, as a result, for several months salespeople had become unsure of their new responsibilities, leaving some customers dissatisfied. Second, there were problems with a number of new products, such as Oracle Financials, which were released before all major bugs could be fixed. However, the stock market was unimpressed by these explanations, and the firm's stock price dropped by 31 percent with the earnings announcement.

REVENUE RECOGNITION

The deterioration in its financial performance prompted analysts to question Oracle's method of recognizing revenues. For example, one analyst commented:

Oracle's accounting practices might have played a role in the low net income results. The top line went up over 50%, though the net bottom line did not do so well, because Oracle's running more cash than it should be as a result of financial mismanagement. The company's aggressive revenue-recognition policy and relatively high amount of accounts receivables make the stock risky.

Oracle's major revenues come from licensing software products to end users, and from sublicensing agreements with original equipment manufacturers (OEMs) and software value-added relicensors (VARs). Initial license fees for the ORACLE database management system range from $199 to over $5,500 on micro- and personal computers, and from $5,100 to approximately $342,000 on mini- and mainframe computers. License fees for Oracle Financial and Oracle Government Financial products range from $20,000 to $513,000, depending on the platform and number of users. A customer may obtain additional licenses at the same site at a discount. Oracle recognizes revenues from these licenses when a contract has been signed with a financially sound customer, even though shipment of products has not occurred.

OEM agreements are negotiated on a case-by-case basis. However, under a typical contract Oracle receives an initial nonrefundable fee (payable either upon signing the contract or within 30 days of signing) and sublicense fees based on the number of copies distributed. Under VAR agreements the company charges a development license fee on top of the initial nonrefundable fee, and it receives sublicense fees based on the number of copies distributed. Sublicense fees are usually a percentage of Oracle's list price. The initial nonrefundable payments and development license fees under these arrangements are recorded as revenue when the contracts are signed. Sublicense fees are recorded when they are received from the OEM or VAR.

Oracle also receives revenues from maintenance agreements under which it provides technical support and telephone consultation on the use of the products and problem resolution, system updates for software products, and user documentation. Maintenance fees generally run for one year and are payable at the end of the maintenance period. They range from 7.5 percent to 22 percent of the current list price of the appropriate license. These fees are recorded as unearned revenue when the maintenance contract is signed and are reflected as revenue ratably over the contract period.

The major questions about Oracle's revenue recognition concern the way the firm recognizes revenues on license fees. There is no currently accepted standard for accounting for these types of revenues.[1] However, Oracle tends to be one of the more aggressive reporters. The firm's days receivable exceed 160 days, substantially higher than the average of 62 days receivable for other software developers (see Exhibit 3 for a summary of days receivable for other major software developers in 1989 and 1990). As a result, some analysts argue that the firm should recognize revenue when software is delivered rather than when a contract is signed, consistent with the accounting treatment for the sale of products. In addition, the collectibility of license fees is considered questionable by some analysts, who have urged the firm to recognize revenue only when there is a reasonable basis for estimating the degree of collectibility of a receivable. Estimates by Oracle's controller indicate that if Oracle were to change to a more conservative revenue recognition policy, the firm's days receivable would fall to about 120 days.

---

1. *The Financial Accounting Standards Board was considering the issue of revenue recognition for software developers at this time. It was widely expected that the Board would make a pronouncement on the topic early in 1991.*

MANAGEMENT'S CONCERNS

Oracle's management was concerned about analysts' opinions and the downturn in the firm's stock. The company had lost credibility with investors and customers due to its recent poor performance and its controversial accounting policies.

One of the items on the agenda at the upcoming board meeting was to consider proposals for changing the firm's revenue recognition method and for dealing with its communication challenge. Ellison knew that his opinion on this question would be influential. As he saw it, the company had three alternatives. One was to modify the recognition of license fees so that revenue would be recognized only when substantially all the company's contractual obligations had been performed. However, he worried that such a change would have a negative impact on the firm's bottom line and further depress the stock price. A second possibility was to wait until the FASB announced its position on software revenue recognition before making any changes. Finally, the company could make no change and vigorously defend its current accounting method. Ellison carefully considered which alternative made the most sense for the firm.

QUESTIONS

1. What factors might have led analysts to question Oracle Systems' method of revenue recognition in mid-1990? Are these legitimate concerns?
2. Estimate the earnings impact for Oracle from recognizing revenue at delivery, rather than when a contract is signed.
3. What accounting or communication changes would you recommend to Oracle's Board of Directors?

Exhibit 1 Oracle Systems Corporation – Consolidated Financial Statements

EXHIBIT 1
Oracle Systems Corporation – Consolidated Financial Statements

CONSOLIDATED BALANCE SHEETS
As of May 31, 1990 and 1989 (in $000, except per share data)

	1990	1989
ASSETS		
CURRENT ASSETS:		
Cash and cash equivalents	$ 44,848	$ 44,893
Short-term investments	4,980	4,500
Receivables		
Trade, net of allowance for doubtful accounts of $28,445 in 1990 and $16,829 in 1989	468,071	261,989
Other	28,899	16,175
Prepaid expenses and supplies	22,459	9,376
Total current assets	569,257	336,933
PROPERTY, net	171,945	94,455
COMPUTER SOFTWARE DEVELOPMENT COSTS, net of accumulated amortization of $14,365 in 1990 and $6,180 in 1989	33,396	13,942
OTHER ASSETS	12,649	14,879
TOTAL ASSETS	$787,247	$460,209
LIABILITIES AND STOCKHOLDERS' EQUITY		
CURRENT LIABILITIES:		
Notes payable to banks	$ 31,236	$ 9,747
Current maturities of long-term debt	11,265	13,587
Accounts payable	64,922	51,582
Income taxes payable	18,254	14,836
Accrued compensation and related benefits	61,164	39,063
Customer advances and unearned revenues	42,121	15,403
Other accrued liabilities	32,417	23,400
Sales tax payable	22,193	8,608
Deferred Income taxes	—	2,107
Total current liabilities	283,572	178,333
LONG-TERM DEBT	89,129	33,506
OTHER LONG-TERM LIABILITIES	4,936	5,702
DEFERRED INCOME TAXES	22,025	12,114
STOCKHOLDERS' EQUITY:		
Common stock, $.01 par value-authorized, 200,000,000 shares; outstanding: 131,138,302 shares in 1990 and 126,933,288 shares in 1989	388	346
Additional paid-in capital	118,715	84,931
Retained earnings	267,475	150,065
Accumulated foreign currency translation adjustments	1,007	(4,788)
Total stockholders' equity	387,585	230,554
TOTAL LIABILITIES AND STOCKHOLDERS' EQUITY	$787,247	$460,209

O

421

Exhibit 1   Oracle Systems Corporation – Consolidated Financial Statements

CONSOLIDATED STATEMENTS OF INCOME
For the Years Ended May 31, 1990 to 1988 (in $000, except per share data)

	1990	1989	1988
REVENUES			
Licenses	$689,898	$417,825	$205,435
Services	280,946	165,848	76,678
Total revenues	970,844	583,673	282,113
OPERATING EXPENSES			
Sales and marketing	465,074	272,812	124,148
Cost of services	160,426	100,987	51,241
Research and development	88,291	52,570	25,708
General and administrative	67,258	34,344	17,121
Total operating expenses	781,049	460,713	218,218
OPERATING INCOME	189,795	122,960	63,895
OTHER INCOME (EXPENSE):			
Interest income	3,772	2,724	2,472
Interest expense	(12,096)	(4,318)	(1,540)
Other income (expense)	(8,811)	(1,121)	152
Total other income (expense)	(17,135)	(2,715)	1,084
INCOME BEFORE PROVISION FOR INCOME TAXES	172,660	120,245	64,979
PROVISION FOR INCOME TAXES	55,250	38,479	22,093
NET INCOME	$117,410	$81,766	$42,886
EARNINGS PER SHARE	$ .86	$ .61	$ .32
NUMBER OF COMMON AND COMMON EQUIVALENT SHARES OUTSTANDING	136,826	135,066	132,950

Exhibit 1   Oracle Systems Corporation – Consolidated Financial Statements

CONSOLIDATED STATEMENTS OF CASH FLOWS
For the Years Ended May 31, 1990 to 1988 (in $000)

	1990	1989	1988
CASH FLOWS FROM OPERATING ACTIVITIES			
Net income	$117,410	$ 81,766	$ 42,886
Adjustments to reconcile net income to net cash provided by operating activities:			
Depreciation and amortization	44,078	23,156	12,973
Provision for doubtful accounts	16,625	9,211	4,839
Increase in receivables	(227,046)	(149,900)	(74,777)
Increase in prepaid expenses & supplies	(12,834)	(5,684)	(1,458)
Increase in accounts payable	12,491	25,236	12,854
Increase income taxes payable	3,002	6,821	7,940
Increase in other accrued liabilities	42,166	38,057	21,420
Increase in customer advances and unearned revenues	25,786	6,496	5,682
Increase (decrease) in deferred taxes	7,728	(10,857)	8,170
Increase (decrease) in other non-current liabilities	(766)	1,938	—
Net cash provided by operating activities	28,640	26,240	40,529
CASH FLOWS FROM INVESTING ACTIVITIES			
Increase in short-term investments	(480)	2,998	(7,498)
Capital expenditures	(89,275)	(68,428)	(30,959)
Capitalization of computer software development costs	(27,639)	(10,526)	(4,447)
Increase in other assets	(1,116)	(2,084)	(481)
Purchase of a business	—	(6,650)	—
Net cash used for investing activities	(118,510)	(84,690)	(43,385)
CASH FLOWS FROM FINANCING ACTIVITIES			
Notes payable to banks	21,156	10,305	(169)
Proceeds from issuance of long-term debt	68,530	37,539	1,445
Payments of long-term debt	(34,239)	(6,205)	(3,638)
Proceeds from common stock issued	18,460	11,060	4,712
Tax benefits from stock options	15,366	10,593	3,992
Net cash provided by financing activities	89,273	63,292	6,342
EFFECT OF EXCHANGE RATE CHANGES ON CASH	552	(1,061)	69
NET INCREASE (DECREASE) IN CASH	**(45)**	**3,781**	**3,555**
CASH: BEGINNING OF YEAR	44,893	41,112	37,557
CASH: END OF YEAR	**$44,848**	**$44,893**	**$41,112**

O

423

Exhibit 1   Oracle Systems Corporation – Consolidated Financial Statements

EXCERPTS FROM NOTES TO CONSOLIDATED FINANCIAL STATEMENTS

1. Organization and Significant Accounting Policies

Organization

Oracle Systems Corporation (the Company) develops and markets computer software products used for database management, applications development, decision support, programmer tools, computer network communication, end user applications, and office automation. The Company offers maintenance, consulting, and training services in support of its clients' use of its software products.

Basis of Financial Statements

The consolidated financial statements include the Company and its subsidiaries. All transactions and balances between the companies are eliminated.

Business Combination

In November 1988, the Company's subsidiary, Oracle Complex Systems Corporation, acquired all of the outstanding shares of Falcon Systems, Inc., a systems integrator, for $13,714,000 in cash and $4,600,000 in notes which become due November 1, 1991. The acquisition was accounted for as a purchase and the excess of the cost over the fair value of assets acquired was $5,648,000, which is being amortized over 5 years on a straight-line method. Pro forma results of operations, assuming the acquisition had taken place June 1, 1987, would not differ materially from the Company's actual results of operations.

Software Development Costs

Effective June 1, 1986, the Company began capitalizing internally generated software development costs in compliance with Statement of Financial Accounting Standards No. 86, "Accounting for the Costs of Computer Software to be Sold, Leased or Otherwise Marketed." Capitalization of computer software development costs begins upon the establishment of technological feasibility for the product. Capitalized software development costs amounted to $27,639,000, $10,526,000, and $4,447,000 in fiscal 1990, 1989, and 1988, respectively.

Amortization of capitalized computer software development costs begins when the products are available for general release to customers, and is computed product by product as the greater of: (a) the ratio of current gross revenues for a product to the total of current and anticipated future gross revenues for the product, or (b) the straight-line method over the remaining estimated economic life of the product. Currently, estimated economic lives of 24 months are used in the calculation of amortization of these capitalized costs. Amortization amounted to $8,185,000, $3,504,000, and $2,345,000 for fiscal years ended May 31, 1990, 1989, and 1988, respectively, and is included in sales and marketing expenses.

Statements of Cash Flows

The Company paid income taxes in the amount of $33,731,000, $29,006,000, and $711,000 and interest expense of $8,026,000, $4,274,000 and $1,540,000 during the fiscal years ended 1990, 1989, and 1988, respectively. The Company purchased equipment under capital lease obligations in the amount of $17,616,000, $4,692,000, and $4,108,000 in fiscal 1990, 1989 and 1988, respectively.

Exhibit 1   Oracle Systems Corporation – Consolidated Financial Statements

Revenue Recognition

The Company generates several types of revenue including the following:

License and Sublicense fees. The Company licenses ORACLE products to end users under license agreements. The Company also has entered into agreements whereby the Company licenses Oracle products and receives license and sublicense fees from original equipment manufacturers (OEMs) and software value-added relicensors (VARs). The minimum amount of license and sublicense fees specified in the agreements is recognized either upon shipment of the product or at the time such agreements are effective (which in most instances is the date of the agreement) if the customer is creditworthy and the terms of the agreement are such that the amounts are due within one year and are nonrefundable, and the agreements are noncancellable. The Company recognizes revenue at such time as it has substantially performed all of its contractual obligations. Additional sublicense fees are subsequently recognized as revenue at the time such fees are reported to the Company by the OEMs and VARs.

Maintenance Agreements. Maintenance agreements generally call for the Company to provide technical support and certain systems updates to customers. Revenue related to providing technical support is recognized proportionately over the maintenance period, which in most instances is one year, while the revenue related to systems updates is recognized at the beginning of each maintenance period.

Consulting, Training, and Other Services. The Company provides consulting services to its customers; revenue from such services is generally recognized under the percentage of completion method.

O

2. Short-Term Debt

	Year Ended May 31	
Short term debt (in $000) consists of:	1990	1989
Unsecured revolving lines of credit	$18,198	$5,955
Other	13,038	3,792
Total	$31,236	$9,747

At May 31, 1990, the Company had short-term unsecured revolving lines of credit with two banks providing for borrowings aggregating $42,000,000, of which $18,198,000 was outstanding. These lines expire in September 1990 ($2,000,000), November 1990 ($10,000,000), and January 1991 ($30,000,000). Interest on these borrowings is based on varying rates pegged to the banks' prime rate, cost of funds, or LIBOR. The Company also had other unsecured short-term indebtedness to banks of $13,038,000 at May 31, 1990, payable upon demand. The average interest rate on short-term borrowings was 9.4% at May 31, 1990.

The Company is required to maintain certain financial ratios under the line of credit agreements. The Company was in compliance with these financial covenants at May 31, 1990.

Exhibit 1   Oracle Systems Corporation – Consolidated Financial Statements

3. Long-Term Debt

At May 31, 1990, the Company had long-term unsecured revolving lines of credit with four banks providing for borrowings aggregating $135,000,000, of which $61,460,000 was outstanding. Of the $61,460,000 outstanding, $58,210,000 was classified as long-term debt and $3,250,000 was classified as current maturities of long-term debt. These lines of credit expire in December 1991 ($60,000,000), March 1992 ($15,000,000), July 1992 ($20,000,000), January 1991 ($20,000,000), and March 1991 ($20,000,000). The Company has the option to convert $20,000,000 of its line expiring in January of 1991 and $8,000,000 of that expiring in March of 1991 into two term loans which would mature in 1993. Interest on these borrowings vary based on the banks' cost of funds rates. At May 31, 1990 the interest rate on outstanding domestic and foreign currency borrowings ranged from 8.6% to 15.6%. The aggregate amount available under these lines of credit at May 31, 1990 was $73,540,000.

Under the line-of-credit agreements, the Company is required to maintain certain financial ratios. At May 31, 1990 the Company was in compliance with these financial covenants.

Subsequent to May 31, 1990, the Company obtained two additional unsecured revolving lines of credit, one which expires May 1992 ($20,000,000) and one which expires January 1991 ($20,000,000).

4. Stockholders' Equity

Stock Option Plan

The Company's stock option plan provides for the issuance of incentives stock options to employees of the Company and nonqualified options to employees, directors, consultants, and independent contractors of the Company. Under the terms of this plan, options to purchase up to 23,335,624 shares of Common Stock may be granted at not less than fair market value, are immediately exercisable, become vested as established by the Board (generally ratably over four to five years), and generally expire ten years from the date of grant. The Company has the right to repurchase shares issued upon the exercise of unvested options at the exercise price paid by the stockholder should the stockholder leave the Company prior to the scheduled vesting date. At May 31, 1990, 271,300 shares of Common Stock outstanding were subject to such repurchase rights. Options to purchase 5,005,720 common shares were vested at May 31, 1990.

Non-Plan Options

In addition to the above option plan, nonqualified stock options to purchase a total of 5,712,000 common shares have been granted to employees and directors of the Company. These options were granted at the fair market value as determined by the Board of Directors, became exercisable immediately, vest either immediately (for directors) or ratably over a period of up to five years (for individuals other than directors) and generally expire ten years from the date of grant. The Company has the right to repurchase shares issued upon the exercise of unvested options at the exercise price paid by the stockholder should the stockholder leave the Company prior to the scheduled vesting date. Options to purchase 160,000 common shares were vested as of May 31, 1990.

As of May 31, 1990, the Company had reserved 11,135,194 shares of Common Stock for exercise of options.

Exhibit 1   Oracle Systems Corporation – Consolidated Financial Statements

Stock Purchase Plan

In October 1987, the Company adopted an Employee Stock Purchase Plan and reserved 8,000,000 shares of Common Stock for issuance thereunder. Under this plan, the Company's employees may purchase shares of Common Stock at a price per share that is 85% of the lesser of the fair market value as of the beginning or the end of the semi-annual option period. Through May 31, 1990, 2,326,772 shares have been issued and 5,673,228 shares are reserved for future issuances under this plan.

REPORT OF INDEPENDENT PUBLIC ACCOUNTANTS

To Oracle Systems Corporation:

We have audited the accompanying consolidated balance sheets of Oracle Systems Corporation (a Delaware corporation) and subsidiaries as of May 31, 1990 and 1989 and the related consolidated statements of income, stockholders' equity, and cash flows for each of the three years in the period ended May 31, 1990. These financial statements are the responsibility of the company's management. Our responsibility is to express an opinion on these financial statements based on our audits. We conducted our audits in accordance with generally accepted auditing standards. Those standards require that we plan and perform the audit to obtain reasonable assurance about whether the financial statements are free of material misstatement. An audit includes examining, on a test basis, evidence supporting the amounts and disclosures in the financial statements. An audit also includes assessing the accounting principles used and significant estimates made by management, as well as evaluating the overall financial statement presentation. We believe that our audits provide a reasonable basis for our opinion.

In our opinion, the financial statements referred to above present fairly, in all material respects, the financial position of Oracle Systems Corporation and subsidiaries as of May 31, 1990 and 1989 and the results of their operations and their cash flows for each of the three years in the period ended May 31, 1990, in conformity with generally accepted accounting principles.

Our audits were made for the purpose of forming an opinion on the basic financial statements taken as a whole. The schedules listed under Item 14(a)2. are presented for purposes of complying with the Securities and Exchange Commission's rules and are not part of the basic financial statements. These schedules have been subjected to the auditing procedures applied in the audit of the basic financial statements and, in our opinion, fairly state in all material respects the financial data required to be set forth therein in relation to the basic financial statements taken as a whole

ARTHUR ANDERSEN & CO.
SAN JOSE, CALIFORNIA
JULY 9, 1990

EXHIBIT 2

Oracle Systems Corporation – Review of Quarterly Results in Fiscal 1989 and 1990 (in $000 except per share data)

	Fiscal 1990 Quarter Ended			
	Aug. 31 1989	Nov. 30 1989	Feb. 28 1990	May 31 1990
Revenues	$175,490	$209,023	$236,165	$350,166
Net income	11,679	28,491	24,282	52,958
Earnings per share[a]	$ .09	$ .21	$ .18	$ .39

	Fiscal 1989 Quarter Ended			
	Aug. 31 1988	Nov. 30 1988	Feb. 28 1989	May 31 1989
Revenues	$90,639	$123,745	$153,354	$215,935
Net income	7,067	17,189	23,964	33,546
Earnings per share[a]	$ .05	$ .13	$ .18	$ .25

a.   Adjusted to reflect the two-for-one stock splits in the third quarter of fiscal 1988 and the first quarter of fiscal 1990.

EXHIBIT 3

Days Receivable for Selected Companies in the Software Industry for 1989–90

Company	1989	1990
Borland International Corp.	49	45
Lotus Development Corp.	64	64
Microsoft Corp.	51	56
Novell Corp.	85	81
Average	62	62

Marsha Henderson is a loan officer at a large regional bank. She is approached in November 1988 by Lewis Poole, the Vice President of Finance for Pageturner Bookstores, Inc., a franchiser of retail bookstores. Poole is interested in obtaining a $300,000 loan, preferably unsecured. Henderson's bank has had no prior dealings with this company. However, she is favorably impressed by Poole. Moreover, based on his description, Pageturner Bookstores appears to be a quickly growing business.

Given the small size of the possible loan involved, Henderson cannot afford to devote much time to the lending decision. Nevertheless, given that Pageturner appears to hold the potential for substantial growth, it appears that serious consideration of the case is merited.

Poole has furnished to Henderson a document entitled "Pageturner Bookstores Business and Financing Plan." From that document and Henderson's conversation with Poole, she garners the information on the following pages. As she does so, she wonders how difficult the decisions will be. Will Pageturner easily qualify or not qualify for a loan? Or will it be a tough call? If a loan were offered, what kind of loan might be appropriate and how should it be structured? Would collateral be required? What covenants would be required?

CORPORATE STRUCTURE

Pageturner Bookstores is a bookstore franchiser formed in the late 1960s by entrepreneurs in Collegetown, a small city in New England. Pageturner's purpose is to help retail booksellers, through franchising, operate profitable community bookstores. Its franchise network now includes more than 120 stores, with average annual per-store sales in the range of $250,000 to $300,000.

Since 1981, the majority of the outstanding shares of Pageturner Bookstores have been held by PBI, a holding company owned by founders and managers of Pageturner. The remaining shares (14 percent in 1988) are held by franchisees. Beyond Pageturner Bookstores, PBI's only asset is 100 percent ownership of Pageturner-Collegetown, the

This case was prepared by Professor Victor L. Bernard as a basis for class discussion and is not intended to illustrate either an effective or ineffective management of a business situation. The name of the company on which the case is based has been disguised. Assistance of company personnel is gratefully acknowledged.

only company-owned retail bookstore in the network. In addition to acting as the parent organization for Pageturner Bookstores and Pageturner-Collegetown, PBI seeks to develop experience and expertise in the area of retail franchise management in order to apply these assets in the future to ventures other than bookstores.

Pageturner-Collegetown, formed in the early 1970s, is located in Collegetown. It has generated very strong sales volume—around $1 million annually—even though its asset base is not much larger than that of the typical store. However, it has not been profitable. In terms of operations, it is viewed as a "model" store, and serves as a training center for both new and existing owners of franchises.

CORPORATE OPERATIONS AND GOALS

Pageturner Bookstores, Inc. sells business format franchises to establish new retail bookstores and provides management, operational, technical, and promotional support to existing franchised stores. Pageturner's network ranks among the largest retail bookstore chains in the United States, and is the largest franchise chain.

Pageturner Bookstores are general, community-oriented retail bookstores featuring complete selection and a full range of services. They are located primarily in neighborhood shopping centers and outdoor malls in 33 states throughout the United States.

Pageturner franchises are sold for an initial fee of $21,000. After opening, franchisees remit royalties (based on a percentage of franchisee sales) to Pageturner Bookstores, Inc. Franchisees choose to operate within the Pageturner network rather than "go it alone" for at least four reasons. First, Pageturner offers the use of its name. Second, it offers expertise and service in a variety of areas: site evaluation and selection; lease negotiations; store set-up and design; store operating systems (including software); initial training and continuing education programs for both franchise owners and staff; financial planning and management; and ongoing operational assistance. Third, it offers economies of scale in purchasing. Fourth, it offers the benefits of some regional and national advertising programs and marketing materials. To support the franchisees, Pageturner Bookstores' regional managers are in frequent phone and face-to-face contact with the franchisees.

The company's broad goal is to be *the* "independent" bookseller of the 1990s. The company expects that competitive pressures will increasingly encourage a market for conversion franchising whereby existing bookstores will seek the advantages of a national organization. Although this is as yet an unproved opportunity for Pageturner Bookstores, the company believes that its programs and services will secure its position as the organization most poised to capitalize on the conversion market.

The company's specific goal is to accomplish at least $100 million in retail sales during 1992. To achieve this, a total of 200 franchised locations need to be in place by 1992, requiring approximately 20 new stores to be opened each year.

NATURE OF FRANCHISE AGREEMENTS

A Pageturner franchise can be established with a franchisee investment of approximately $100,000—including the initial franchise fee of $21,000, fixtures of $20,000 to $25,000, and inventory of $40,000 to $60,000. The inventory is purchased through Pageturner at cost; fixtures are purchased through Pageturner at a modest markup. Of the $21,000 (nonrefundable) franchise fee, $7,500 is received prior to site development, and $13,500 is due within six weeks of opening. Amounts billed for inventory and fixtures are due eight weeks prior to opening (typically prior to the time Pageturner actually pays for those costs). In 1987, Pageturner recorded revenues from initial franchise fees of $264,000, revenues from sales of inventory to new stores of $582,000, and revenues from sales of fixtures (primarily to new stores) of $325,000. The initial franchise fees are separately identified in Pageturner's income statement; the remaining sales to new stores are included in "Franchise revenue and sales to franchisees." The combined revenues related to new store openings ($264,000 of initial franchise fees and $907,000 of sales to new franchisees) accounted for more than half of total 1987 revenues of $2,155,000. (See Exhibit 1)

After opening, Pageturner receives royalties (typically as a percentage of sales), which are determined in accordance with a 15-year renewable franchise contract. The royalty percentage varies across franchisees, largely as a result of rate increases that have occurred over time. However, typical percentages range from 1.5 to 2.5 percent. Royalty income in 1987 was $457,000. In that year, "Franchise revenue and sales to franchisees" also included revenues from advertising fees of $155,000, and revenues from various other goods and services totaling $245,000.

Pageturner Bookstores' final source of income is generated by retaining a portion of amounts paid by magazine publishers for display space. Publishers typically pay approximately $.05 per magazine (labeled a "Retail Display Allowance," or RDA) for such space. As franchiser, Pageturner Bookstores tracks activity and bills the magazine publishers on a quarterly basis. Pageturner Bookstores retains approximately one-third of the amounts received from publishers, and transfers the remainder to the franchisees (typically after receipt from the publishers). The amount retained is labeled "Retail service income" in Pageturner's financial statements; such income totaled $127,000 in 1987.

COMPETITION

Pageturner's major competitors are Waldenbooks (owned by K-Mart) and B. Dalton Bookseller (owned by Barnes and Noble Bookstores). They operate company-owned stores in large regional malls.

Pageturner's competitive strategy could be viewed as combining the economies of a large bookstore chain with the benefits of local ownership. Pageturner franchisees, which tend to be located in neighborhood shopping centers, attempt to maintain an advantage by offering a well-trained, professional, knowledgeable staff and wider selection than the chains. Turnover among Pageturner franchisee employees is much lower than that experienced by competitors.

Useful data on the performance of competitors is difficult to obtain. Waldenbooks' financial data are consolidated within K-Mart's much larger organization, and B. Dalton Bookseller is owned by a privately-held firm. Similar circumstances describe others in the industry: Crown Books is consolidated within Dart Group; Doubleday Book Shops are consolidated within Bertelsmann, AG; Encore Books is consolidated within Rite Aid. Some bookstore chains, such as Anderson Brothers, are privately held rather than consolidated within larger organizations. Data on some privately-held bookstores are available in aggregated form from Dun and Bradstreet. However, neither these nor any of the above-mentioned groups are directly comparable to a pure franchiser.

FINANCIAL PERFORMANCE AND GOALS

Pageturner Bookstores, Inc. has experienced dramatic increases in revenues for several years. However, after producing profits of $35,000 and $45,000 in 1985 and 1986, respectively, the company experienced a loss of $71,000 in 1987. In its Business and Financing Plan, Pageturner explains the loss as follows:

> *The operating loss experienced by the company in 1987 primarily resulted from two factors. These were a temporary hesitation by prospective new franchise owners because of the unsettled economic circumstances of last fall and increased expenses associated with the addition of franchiser staff during the summer of 1987. During 1987 sixteen new franchises were sold when at least twenty-two were budgeted, and new positions were created for a Vice President of Franchise Operations, three regional managers, a Franchise Development Manager and a secretary.*

Pageturner's (unaudited) interim reports for 1988 indicate a pretax profit through September of $27,000. CFO Poole is projecting a pretax profit for the year as a whole of $132,000. Pretax earnings are forecast at $227,000 for 1989, and $336,000 in 1990. (Detailed projections appear in Exhibit 2.)

The projected increases in future earnings are based on expectations that the franchisee network will soon reach the point where ongoing franchise operating revenues can cover the company's expenses without requiring a contribution from the sales of new franchises. In its Business and Financing Plan, Pageturner depicts the path of "operating margin" and "operating expense" as follows:

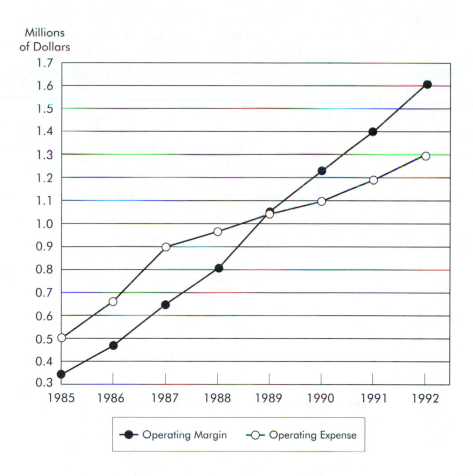

Millions of Dollars

Operating Margin   Operating Expense

The Business and Financing Plan noted progress towards Pageturner's financial goals in 1988, as indicated below. Note that sales and income figures are based on projections for the calendar year, given information available as of October 1988.

- *Retail sales is expected to surpass $40 million.*
- *Income from operating stores is projected to reach a level sufficient to cover the costs attributable to providing supporting services to franchised stores.*
- *The organizational infrastructure of the company was completed with the hiring of Lewis Poole as Vice President of Finance. In the future, new staff will be required only as franchised locations and retail sales increase.*
- *Minimum inventory investment for new stores was increased by 50 percent to $60,000 to encourage higher sales from new, larger stores.*
- *A computerized retail operating system was installed in ten franchised stores serving as test locations for the entire organization.*

> • *A pilot program for collecting co-operative advertising monies from publishers on behalf of individual stores began in September.*

The Business and Financing Plan also stated that the company had adopted five short-term goals for 1988-1989:

> • *Earn a 100 percent pre-tax return on equity.*
> • *Accentuate responsive service to franchise owners.*
> • *Emphasize training and support programs for mature stores.*
> • *Make the trademark more visible in the industry as well as in the retail marketplace.*
> • *Institute a computerized retail management system for franchised stores.*

REQUEST FOR FINANCING

Pageturner's Business and Financing Plan includes the following request for financing:

> *During the past five years the company has increased its revenues fivefold while following a course of investing profits in its own growth and development. Currently the infrastructure of franchising staff and store support programs has been established, and beginning in 1989 the revenue stream from opening stores will pay for the company's expenses without requiring a contribution from the sale of new franchises.*
>
> *Although the company has had some borrowing experience, the growth of the company has primarily been funded internally. The purchase and expansion of the company owned store and the increase of accounts receivable that naturally occurs with growth have all been funded in this manner. The distinct seasonality of the business, with the bulk of earnings being generated in the fourth quarter, exacerbates the difficulties created by short-term financing.*
>
> *Now that the company's revenue stream and earnings can justify and support the repayment of long-term debt, financing in the amount of $300,000 is sought. Procurement of this financing on a long-term basis will benefit the company in a number of ways. It will be used to:*
>
> > • *Capture cash discounts from suppliers of over $20,000 annually*
> > • *Reduce accounts payable and strengthen the company's working capital position*
> > • *Enhance supplier relationships and increase operating efficiencies in purchasing and payables management*
>
> *The company intends to satisfy its capital needs of $300,000 by structuring this financing in either of two ways:*
>
> > • *Debentures of a ten to fifteen year period, the exact terms of which would be negotiated with the lender. Our preference is for the security to be callable*

after a five year period with the usual call premium. A sinking fund for the security could be established if deemed necessary.

- *Installment note for a five to ten year period. The next five years are expected to be ones of rapid earnings growth for the company and will require a continuing strong working capital position. During that period the company will establish a strong financial position through its earnings stream.*

The request for financing indicates that Pageturner anticipates a borrowing rate of approximately 12 percent. As of October 1988, the yield on 3-month T-bills is 7.8 percent; the yield on 10-year T-bonds is 9.0 percent. The prime rate is 10.1 percent.

The Business and Financing Plan also furnishes a detailed history of prior borrowings. It indicates that in 1984, 1985, and 1986, Pageturner Bookstores or the affiliated Collegetown bookstore had borrowed from another large regional bank four times, in amounts ranging from $25,000 to $100,000, for periods ranging from two months to four years. Each loan had been repaid on or before its due date. The most recent financing occurred in December 1987; at that time Pageturner Bookstores issued a $150,000 note to its primary supplier, to be repaid within 12 months. Pageturner prefers to avoid dependence on its supplier for financing because it could potentially affect flexibility in purchasing. The loan from the supplier had largely been repaid as of September 1988.

GENERAL PROJECTIONS

Current expectations about earnings growth for the economy as a whole, the retail sector, and retail bookstores are reflected in the following P/E ratios and earnings forecasts:

	P/E ratio	Forecast change in earnings for 1989
S&P 500 composite	12.0	+12.0%
Retail stores composite	14.7	+22.2%
Retail stores: specialty	17.1	+20.7%
Publishing	24.9	+25.6%

HISTORICAL AND PRO FORMA FINANCIAL STATEMENTS

Included in the Business and Financing Plan are Pageturner's financial statements for 1987 (audited by a Big Eight public accounting firm and given a "clean opinion") and projected partial financial statements for 1988 and 1989. Excerpts appear in Exhibits 1 and 2. In discussions with CFO Poole, loan officer Henderson has acquired the following additional knowledge about the financial statements:

Accounting change. Starting in 1988, Poole excludes from the income statement the revenues and costs of inventory delivered to new stores, since those amounts are always offsetting, and to maintain consistency with the handling of inventory for existing franchisees. Note that after franchises are established, they acquire inventory directly from the supplier. Thus, there are and never have been any purchases of inventory and sales to ongoing franchisees recorded by Pageturner.

Cost allocations. In its internal records, Pageturner tracks some costs according to whether they are more closely related to new store development or support of existing stores. In 1987, cost of goods sold includes the cost of inventory sold to new stores ($582,000), the cost of fixtures sold primarily to new stores ($280,000), advertising costs ($164,000), and other costs for existing stores ($190,000) and new stores ($5,000). Selling and administrative expenses of approximately $57,000 were deemed allocable to new store openings; the remainder of the costs were incurred in the process of servicing existing stores ($216,000) and general administration ($312,000). Management fees are billed to Pageturner Bookstores, Inc. by its parent, PBI, primarily for salaries of PBI owner/managers and employees. In 1987, $67,000 of these costs were deemed allocable to new store development, $247,000 to ongoing store operations, and $106,000 to general administration.

Accounts receivable consist primarily of two components. The first (and largest) component includes amounts due from Pageturner stores primarily for royalties. The second component includes gross amounts due from magazine publishers for Retail Display Allowances ("RDA receivables").

Receivables from affiliates include amounts due primarily from Pageturner-Collegetown, but also from PBI. The receivables from Pageturner-Collegetown represent advances used to help cover operating expenses.

Notes receivable are amounts due from franchisees.

Accounts payable consist of amounts due to various suppliers for items purchased by Pageturner on behalf of the franchisees. Also included are "Payables-RDA," representing amounts due to franchisees under the Retail Display Allowance program.

Franchise deposits includes amounts received from franchisees prior to store opening but not yet recognized as Franchise Fee Income.

QUESTIONS

1. Describe Pageturner's business strategy and evaluate its key risks and opportunities.
2. Why does Pageturner have a cash flow problem? That is, why is it in need of external financing and incapable (currently) of funding its own operations?
3. Assume that you are willing to loan to Pageturner only on a secured basis. Evaluate Pageturner's collateral and indicate whether it would be sufficient to support a loan of the size requested.
4. Would you grant a loan to Pageturner? If a loan were offered, what type of loan would be appropriate and how should it be structured?

Exhibit 1   Pageturner Bookstores, Inc.—Financial Statements

EXHIBIT 1

Pageturner Bookstores, Inc.—Financial Statements

BALANCE SHEETS

	December 31	
	1987	1986

ASSETS

Current assets

Cash	$ 23,308	$ 44,006
Accounts receivable, less allowance for doubtful accounts of $6,000 in 1987 and 1988	648,463	453,133
Accounts receivable from affiliate	152,319	122,344
Common stock subscriptions receivable	—	9,510
Notes receivable	17,970	21,484
Inventories	29,083	9,928
Prepaid expense	13,329	18,498
Total current assets	884,472	678,903
Notes receivable, interest at 10% to 16%, due in varying amounts through 1997	29,241	20,914

Property and equipment

Furniture and fixtures	88,578	82,277
Leasehold improvements	1,275	1,275
	89,853	83,552
Accumulated depreciation and amortization	−23,761	−23,276
Net property and equipment	66,092	60,276
	$979,805	$760,093

LIABILITIES AND EQUITY

Current liabilities

Accounts payable	$688,788	$538,536
Notes payable (Note 2)	12,350	2,500
Deferred revenue—franchise deposits	95,418	80,903
Long term debt due within one year (Note 3)	62,500	0
	859,056	621,939
Long-term debt (Note 3)	18,254	16,506
Total liabilities	877,310	638,445

Commitments and contingencies (Note 4)

(continued)

p

437

Exhibit 1 Pageturner Bookstores, Inc.—Financial Statements

	December 31	
	1987	1986
Stockholders' equity		
Common stock, no par value125,000 shares authorized; 114,149 and 108,017 shares issued in 1987 and 1986, respectively	142,990	81,170
Common stock subscribed:		
4,669 and 951 shares in 1987 and 1986, respectively	46,690	9,510
Less subscriptions receivable	(46,690)	0
Retained Earnings	(40,495)	30,968
Total shareholders' equity	102,495	121,648
	$979,805	$760,093

STATEMENT OF OPERATIONS

	Year ended December 31		
	1987	1986	1985
Revenues			
Franchise revenue and sales to franchisees	$1,764,662	$1,541,146	$1,370,977
Initial franchise fees	264,000	257,000	185,000
Retail service income	126,291	72,951	75,415
	2,154,953	1,871,097	1,631,392
Expenses[a]			
Cost of goods sold	1,221,150	1,083,314	1,010,695
Selling and administrative	584,710	425,761	357,589
Management fee charged by affiliate (Note 5)	420,556	317,509	227,657
	2,226,416	1,826,584	1,595,941
Income (loss) before charge in lieu of income taxes and extraordinary item	(71,463)	44,513	35,451
Charge in lieu of income taxes (Note 6)	0	2,000	6,000
Income (loss) before extraordinary item	(71,463)	42,513	29,451
Extraordinary item: Tax effect of utilization of net operating loss carryforward	0	2,000	6,000
Net income (loss)	$ (71,463)	$ 44,513	$ 35,451

a. Expenses include depreciation of $6300, $6000, and $6988 in 1987, 1986, and 1985, respectively.

Exhibit 1 Pageturner Bookstores, Inc.—Financial Statements

NOTES TO FINANCIAL STATEMENTS

1. Basis of presentation and summary of significant accounting policies

Basis of presentation—PBI owns 90% of Pageturner Bookstores, Inc. (Company). The operations of the Company are comprised of bookstore franchising.

Significant accounting policies

Inventories—Inventories are stated at the lower of cost (first-in, first-out method) or market.

Property and equipment—Property and equipment are stated at cost and are depreciated over the estimated useful lives of the assets on the straight-line method.

Investment tax credits—Investment tax credits are accounted for using the flow-through method.

Sale of franchises—The Company records initial franchise fees after the franchise agreement has been signed and all services or conditions relating to the sale have been substantially performed. Until these services have been substantially performed, receipts from franchisees are recorded as deferred revenue-franchise deposits.

2. Notes payable

Notes payable at December 31, 1987 and 1986 consist of the following:

	1987	1986
Note payable to a stockholder of PBI, due in monthly installments of $2,067 through March, 1988, including interest at 10.5%	$12,350	$ —
Demand note payable, due in monthly installments of $2,500 through January, 1987, plus interest at a bank's prime rate (7.5% at December 31, 1986) plus 2%, secured by substantially all assets of the Company	—	2,500
	$12,350	$2,500

3. Long-term debt

Long-term debt at December 31, 1987 and 1986 consists of the following:

	1987	1986
Note payable to a stockholder of PBI, with interest at the prime rate (7.5% at December 31, 1986)	$ —	$16,506
Note payable due in monthly installments of $6,250 through January, 1989, plus interest at the prime rate (8.75% at December 31, 1987) plus 2.5%, secured by substantially all assets of the Company	68,750	—
Other long term debt	12,004	—
Less: Long-term debt within one year	(62,500)	—
	$18,254	$16,506

Exhibit 1   Pageturner Bookstores, Inc.—Financial Statements

4. Lease commitments and contingent liabilities

Rent expense was $59,000, $33,000 and $38,000 in 1987, 1986, and 1985, respectively.

The Company leases its administrative facilities under a lease that expires in May, 1991. Minimum annual rentals are as follows:

Years ending December 31

1988	$ 62,000
1989	66,000
1990	71,000
1991	24,000
	$223,000

At December 31, 1987, the Company was contingently liable as primary lessee (in event of default by the assignee) for rentals of franchisee locations in the amounts of $39,000 and $5,000 for 1988 and 1989, respectively.

5. Affiliated company transactions

Included in the expenses of the Company are management fees of $420,556 by PBI. These fees are an allocation of salaries and wages to the Company.

During 1987, the Company issued 6,182 shares of common stock, of which 2,500 shares were issued to PBI.

Franchise revenue of $7,000 in 1987, $6,000 in 1986, and $5,000 in 1985 has been charged to Pageturner–Collegetown, which is a subsidiary of PBI and a franchisee of the Company.

A stockholder of PBI provided professional services to the Company of $29,321 in 1987 and $39,096 in 1986.

6. Income taxes

The Company's taxable income (loss) is included in the consolidated income tax returns of its parent company, PBI. Income taxes are provided or allocated to the Company by the parent company based on the ratio of the Company's income before income taxes to the consolidated income before income taxes.

At December 31, 1987, the Company has net operating loss carryforwards for financial statement purposes of approximately $40,000. These net operating loss carryforwards are available to offset future income for financial statement purposes. During the years ended December 31, 1986 and 1985, net operating loss carryforwards of $13,545 and $35,451, respectively, were utilized to offset financial statement income. In 1986, the effective tax rate for financial statement purposes varied from statutory rates due to utilization of investment tax credit carryforwards.

Net operating loss carryforwards for income tax purposes at December 31, 1987, amounted to approximately $74,000 and expire in the amounts of $24,000 and $50,000 through December 31, 1997 and 2002, respectively. The difference between the financial reporting and income tax loss carryforwards results from the use of accelerated depreciation for income tax purposes, which resulted in cumulative tax depreciation exceeding cumulative financial statement depreciation by $34,000 at December 31, 1987.

EXHIBIT 2

Pageturner Bookstores, Inc.—1988 Interim Financial Statements and Pro Forma Projections

PRE-AUDIT BALANCE SHEET
September 27, 1988

		September 27, 1988
ASSETS		
Current Assets		
Cash	$ 73,000	
Notes Receivable	91,000	
Accounts Receivable Trade	281,000	
Accounts Receivable Affiliates	249,000	
Inventory and Prepaid Expenses	147,000	
Total Current Assets		841,000
Fixed Assets		
Office Furniture & Equipment		82,000
Total Assets		$923,000
LIABILITIES & OWNERS EQUITY		
Current Liabilities		
Accounts Payable Trade	252,000	
Accounts Payable RDA	98,000	
Franchise Deposits	379,000	
Notes Payable	18,000	
Total Current Liabilities		747,000
Total Liabilities		747,000
Owners Equity		
Common Stock	190,000	
Retained Earnings	(40,000)	
YTD Income	26,000	
Total Owners Equity		176,000
Total Liabilities & Owners Equity		$923,000

PRO FORMA INCOME STATEMENTS
Three Years Ended December 1988

	1986 Total	Year to Date September 1987	1987 4th Qtr	Year End Total	Year to Date September 1988	1988 4th Qtr Projected	Year End Projected
Revenues (1)	944,000	798,000	494,000	1,292,000	1,169,000	467,000	1,633,000
Cost of Goods (1)	155,000	187,000	160,000	347,000	303,000	82,000	385,000
Expenses	744,000	756,000	260,000	1,016,000	839,000	280,000	1,119,000
Pre-tax Income	45,000	(145,000)	74,000	(71,000)	27,000	105,000	132,000

PRO FORMA BALANCE SHEET

	December 31, 1988
Current Assets	
Cash	$ 35,680
Notes Receivable	88,000
Accounts Receivable Trade	380,000
Accounts Receivable Affiliates	260,000
Inventory & Prepaid Expenses	40,000
Total Current Assets	803,680
Fixed Assets	
Office Furniture & Equipment	95,000
Total Assets	$898,680
Current Liabilities	
Accounts Payable Trade	120,000
Accounts Payable RDA	90,000
Franchise Deposits	95,000
Notes Payable	12,000
Total Current Liabilities	317,000
Long Term Liabilities	300,000
Total Liabilities	$617,000
Owners Equity	
Common Stock	189,680
Retained Earnings	92,000
Total Owners Equity	$281,680
Total Liabilities & Owners Equity	$898,680

p

443

PRO FORMA INCOME STATEMENT
Year Ended 1989

	1st Qtr	2nd Qtr	3rd Qtr	4th Qtr	Total
Revenues					
Franchise Operations	300,000	318,000	334,000	343,000	1,295,000
Franchise Development	84,000	126,000	126,000	84,000	420,000
Office and Administrative	6,000	6,000	5,000	5,000	22,000
Total Revenues	390,000	450,000	465,000	432,000	1,737,000
Cost of Goods Sold					
Franchise Operations	68,000	56,000	68,000	56,000	248,000
Franchise Development	10,000	11,000	11,000	10,000	42,000
Total Cost of Goods	78,000	67,000	79,000	66,000	290,000
Operating Expenses					
Franchise Operations	105,000	124,000	115,000	122,000	466,000
Franchise Development	39,000	49,000	42,000	41,000	171,000
Office and Administrative	141,000	146,000	147,000	149,000	583,000
Total Expenses	285,000	319,000	304,000	312,000	1,220,000
Contribution					
Franchise Operations	127,000	138,000	151,000	165,000	581,000
Franchise Development	35,000	66,000	73,000	33,000	207,000
Office and Administrative	(135,000)	(140,000)	(142,000)	(144,000)	(561,000)
Pre-Tax Profit	27,000	64,000	82,000	54,000	227,000

F orget Florida. Today's underdeveloped land hype centers on good old New England. The affluent young and upwardly mobile lust not for perpetual sunshine but for "unspoiled" woodland and farmland plots close to Boston, Providence or New York. An urban yearning for the bucolic.

Who's there to sell wide-open spaces to cramped but credit worthy city dwellers? Patten Corp., a $35 million installment land sales company based in Stamford, VT. A nice business? So it seems. In 1986 Patten's reported net per share was $1.40, vs. 47 cents in 1985. In the first six months of fiscal 1987, Patten's property sales rose 110%, while reported earnings increased 53%. Patten's stock–recently listed on the Big Board–jumped from a split-adjusted $4 a share in early 1986 to around $19 in late December. . . .

Trouble is, Patten's earnings suffer serious shrinkage when scrutinized. And the asset side of the company's balance sheet looks a bit bloated. Patten records 100% of its land sales as revenues, even though it typically receives just 10% to 50% of the amount in cash. Therefore, the quality of its earnings is suspect.[1]

During the last week of December 1986, when the above comments were published in *Forbes* magazine, Patten's share price dropped from $18.250 to $15.875 in frenzied trading on the New York Stock Exchange, representing a loss of approximately $19.5 million dollars in the market value of the company's stock.

BUSINESS METHODS AND PERFORMANCE

Patten Corporation acquired large undeveloped rural properties, subdivided these properties into parcels averaging approximately 15 acres, and sold them. The company's primary customers were residents of metropolitan areas who sought to own rural land for vacation or retirement home sites and investment. Most of the land that the company purchased and resold was two to five hours' driving time from major metropolitan areas such as Boston, Hartford, New York City, and Philadelphia.

....

This case was prepared by Professor Krishna Palepu as the basis for class discussion rather than to illustrate either effective or ineffective handling of an administrative situation. Copyright © 1987 by the President and Fellows of Harvard College. Harvard Business School case 9-188-027.

1. *Excerpts from "Old Game, New Twist," Forbes, January 12, 1987. Reprinted with permission. The issue became available on the newsstands in the last week of December 1986.*

Acquisition of Land

The Company employed a staff of approximately 46 acquisition specialists in its 13 regional offices. The acquisition staff in each office systematically contacted all major property owners and real estate brokers in its territory. Patten's objective was to develop strong relationships with these property owners and brokers so that it would be the first party to see a property when it became available for purchase.

Once an appropriate property was located, Patten entered into a purchase agreement with the seller. Generally, the company agreed to make a small down payment and to pay the balance on closing after all necessary governmental approvals were obtained. The time between execution of a purchase agreement and closing was usually two to six months. By requiring that all regulatory approvals be obtained prior to closing and by making only a small down payment upon signing purchase agreements, the company held a large number of properties under contract without expending significant amounts of cash.

After contracting for, but prior to acquiring a property, the company completed a survey, designed a subdivision plan, conducted soil tests if feasible, reviewed applicable environmental and zoning laws and regulations, and received all necessary regulatory approvals to permit subdivision and sale of the property. After acquisition, Patten made only minor improvements and rarely built on or otherwise developed the land it sold. Because of the extended escrow period, the company could turn over its properties rapidly, with the period from acquisition to resale generally being one to twelve weeks. This strategy to reduce the time it actually owned any given property minimized the market risk associated with holding real estate.

Marketing of Land

Patten's marketing activities were targeted by geography and customer demographics. To sell parcels of land from a property, the company usually advertised in major newspapers in metropolitan areas located within a two to five hour drive of the property. When a property contained a large number of parcels, the company also conducted a direct mail campaign using brochures describing available parcels.

The company's advertisements and direct mail campaigns were designed to cause prospective customers to call for more information. A sales representative answered each call, discussed the property with the prospective purchaser, attempted to ascertain the customer's needs and whether an available parcel would be suitable for that person, and arranged an appointment for the customer to visit the property. Patten offered no premiums or other inducements for such visits.

Patten's typical customer was 38 years old with an annual income of $30,000–$50,000, married, and owned a home. The company attempted to match the profile of its sales representatives to its customer profile because it felt that sales success depended on a high degree of trust and personal identification that developed between the customer and the company representative during the customer's visit. The typical Patten sales representative was 36 years old, earned an annual income of $40,000, was married, and owned a home.

The company's marketing strategy was very successful. In 1986, the sales staff converted 25 percent of initial customer calls to appointments to visit properties, and 45 percent of customers who made a visit purchased a property. Patten attributed its marketing success to its careful targeting of customers and its strategy of ensuring that, before visiting the properties offered by the company, the customers had:

- taken the time to look for land offers in a newspaper;
- made a long distance call to receive additional information on an advertisement of interest;
- made an appointment to visit a property without the offer of any premiums, gifts, or other inducements;
- driven anywhere from two to five hours to view the property.

After deciding to purchase a parcel of land, the customer entered into a contract and paid Patten a deposit equal in most cases to 10 percent of the purchase price. The closing usually occurred within two to four weeks after payment of the deposit. Upon closing, the company delivered to the buyer a warranty deed and a recent survey of the property.

During fiscal 1986, 90 percent of the parcels were sold at prices ranging from $5,000 to $40,000, and the average sales price of all parcels sold was $19,327. This price represented an average price per acre of $1,282, as compared with an average acquisition cost to Patten of $579 per acre.

p
447

Customer Financing

Patten offered up to 90 percent financing of the purchase price of a parcel to all qualified customers. The company viewed its customer financing offer as a marketing tool because it removed the difficulty most customers would have in obtaining financing to purchase undeveloped land in an area often outside their home state. In 1986, 21 percent of Patten's customers paid cash for their property, while 79 percent used the company's financing.

In general, customers who utilized Patten's financing paid 10–50 percent of the purchase price in cash, and the balance was represented by promissory notes. Notes were secured by first mortgages on the parcels sold. Rates of interest charged by the company on notes from customers were approximately 4–5 percent over the prime rate. The company's own borrowing cost usually was 0.5–2 percent above prime. As a result, the company's portfolio of notes receivable, which amounted to $18.6 million at the end of 1986, was an important source of income to the company. Since customer financing was an important marketing tool and a source of stable interest income, the company had plans to increase the proportion of sales which it financed.

Before granting financing, Patten performed substantially the same type of credit review of the customer as a lending institution would undertake. The company considered the delinquency and default rate on its notes receivable to be low by industry standards. In approximately 90 percent of default cases, the company forgave the note in exchange for title to the parcel.

Recent Performance

Patten's well-focused land acquisition and marketing strategy led to the company's rapid growth in recent years. The company's sales grew from $11.2 million in fiscal 1984 to $33.3 million in 1986. During the same period, the reported profits grew from $0.47 million (40 cents per share) to $3.95 million ($1.40 per share). In November 1985 the company went public and was listed on the New York Stock Exchange.

The success of Patten's land retailing strategy has attracted considerable attention and favorable comments from financial analysts. For example, Kurt Fenerman and Terence York, analysts with Drexel Burnham Lambert Inc., stated in their November 1986 report on Patten:

> *Patten is in the midst of a dramatic earnings expansion driven by an exciting retailing concept. The management team is young and aggressive. Growth is fueled by both existing and new (regional) offices. Inventory turnover remains very high by design, reducing risk. Profit margins are the highest of any stock we follow, and are rising. If there is risk to our earnings estimates, which have already been raised five times this year, it is that they are too low.*[2]

As a result of investors' favorable assessment of the company's performance and future prospects, Patten's stock price rose rapidly in 1986. In 1986 the company split the stock two-for-one in response to the rapid stock price increase.

THE ACCOUNTING CONTROVERSY

Since only a small portion of Patten's revenues were from cash sales, how to record the noncash sales was an important financial reporting policy decision. The company recorded a sale of real estate and recognized revenue when a minimum of 10 percent of sales proceeds was received and collectability of the balance was reasonably assured. The excess of sales price over legally binding deposits received was recorded as contract receivables or notes receivable. All related costs were recorded when a sale was recorded. Patten's 1986 Annual Report (Exhibit 1) provides more details on the company's revenue recognition and other accounting policies.

Accounting Rules

Under Generally Accepted Accounting Principles (GAAP) for retail land sales (as stated in Statement No. 66 of the Financial Accounting Standards Board), Patten's revenue recognition method was considered appropriate if *all* of the following conditions were met:

1. The buyer signs a legally bound contract for the land purchase, and pays a nonrefundable down-payment of 10 percent or more of the sales price.
2. The seller's collection experience on similar sales indicates that at least 90 percent

---

2. *Excerpts from "Research Abstracts: Patten Corporation" by Kurt A. Fenerman and Terence M. York, Drexel Burnham Lambert Inc., November 4, 1986.*

of the receivables will be collected in full. A down-payment of 20 percent or more is an acceptable substitute for the experience test.

3. The seller's receivable for the property sold is not subject to subordination of new loans.

4. The seller is not obliged to construct amenities or other facilities, or complete any improvements for lots which have been sold.

Patten's revenue recognition policy was not valid if one or more of the above tests were not met. When that occurred, several accounting alternatives were available, all of which recognized revenues less rapidly. For example, if all criteria except the last one were met, sales and profits could be recognized by the percentage-of-completion method, in proportion to the work performed over time by the seller. If only the first criterion was met, revenues and profits could be recognized under the installment sales method, in proportion to the cash payments received from the buyer.

Patten's management was responsible for judging which of the above accounting alternatives was appropriate given the company's business circumstances. Management was also responsible for estimating an allowance to cover potential defaults on any receivables recognized. The company's management was expected to use its knowledge of the industry, the firm's business strategy, and the characteristics of its customers in making these judgments. The firm's auditors were responsible for verifying the appropriateness of the managers' accounting choices and bad debt estimates.

Forbes' Criticism

In the article "Old Game, New Twist," cited at the beginning of the case, *Forbes* magazine criticized Patten's accounting as aggressive. The article explained:

> *Of Patten's customers, 80% buy their land on time, signing notes that obligate them to pay off loans at an adjustable interest rate, currently 12.5%. Patten includes these notes receivable among its assets and records them at face value. In 1986 this amounted to more than $17 million. Patten allows for possible losses on the notes, but for a laughably small amount: $10,000. Delinquency rates have been low so far, but that's often true in the early stages of these installment land deals.*
>
> *Patten's accounting techniques are, to put it mildly, aggressive. The company says it actually received 35% of reported revenues as cash down payments in 1986. That's $12.2 million. But subtract the company's costs and expenses from this figure – just the costs of real estate sold, for example, amounted to $15 million – and it becomes clear that Patten is operating on a negative cash flow. This explains why Patten has such a heavy debt load: 70% of total capitalization.*
>
> *Negative cash flow and go-go accounting have burned some nasty holes in investors' pockets over the years. Remember Punta Gorda Isles, a Florida land sales and development company? Its stock traded as high as 16 in 1981, before its similarly obscured negative cash flow came to light. Now the shares languish at 2. Then there is Thousand Trails, a company that sold lifetime campground memberships. It was hot in 1984, following three years of 40% annual revenue growth.*

Trails' stock climbed to 29 a share. Soon, however, membership sales evaporated. The stock recently traded around 2½.[3]

Patten's Response

In response to the criticism by *Forbes,* Patten issued a press release defending the company's revenue recognition policy. In this press release, Donald Dion Jr., Executive Vice President and Treasurer of Patten Corporation, stated, "Our financial statements and accounting policies have been audited by Arthur Young & Company, a 'Big Eight' public accounting firm. Arthur Young & Company has issued an unqualified opinion on our financial statements for each of the past four years."

Dion also stated that the delinquency rate has always been low in the company's 20-year history with mortgage note customers. "The delinquency rate on our mortgage note portfolio has been low throughout inflationary periods and recessions," he said. "Over the past five years, losses on our mortgage note portfolio have not been material."

The company also attempted to allay investors' concerns raised by the *Forbes* article through a series of meetings with security analysts. The "Heard on the Street" column of the *Wall Street Journal* commented on investor reaction to Patten's efforts:

Patten Corp, a land sales company whose rapid growth made it the third best performing stock on the New York Stock Exchange last year, has held analysts' meetings in Boston, New York and San Francisco this week to counter negative news report about its finances. The good news is that the stock went up 1⅝ during the course of the meetings, closing yesterday at 18¾. The bad news is that there are still plenty of questions about Stamford, VT-based Patten's growth prospects.[4]

QUESTIONS

1. Explain how Patten's revenue recognition policy affects its income statement and balance sheet. Given Patten's business, its strategy, and the accounting rules, is this policy justified?
2. If Patten recognized revenues from land sales when it received cash from its customers, what would have been the company's approximate revenues and net income for the year ended March 31, 1986? Do you think these numbers represent the company's economic performance better or worse than the numbers reported by the company?
3. What is your evaluation of Patten's financial condition as of March 31, 1986? Can Patten withstand the adverse investor reaction resulting from Forbes' criticism of the company's accounting?
4. What actions can Patten's management take to respond to Forbes' criticism and increase investors' confidence in the company's accounting policies? What are the pros and cons of each of these actions? What actions, if any, would you recommend?

---

3. *Reprinted with permission.*
4. *Excerpts from "Patten Summons Analysts to Dispel Doubts, But Its Growth Prospects Remain," Heard on the Street, Randall Smith, Wall Street Journal, January 29, 1987. Reprinted with permission.*

Exhibit 1　Patten Corporation Abridged Annual Report for 1986

EXHIBIT 1
Patten Corporation Abridged Annual Report for 1986

FINANCIAL HIGHLIGHTS

(000's omitted except per share data)	1986	1985	% Change
Operating Results			
Revenues:			
Sales of Real Estate	$33,263	$18,549	79
Interest Income	1,694	645	163
Total Revenues	34,957	19,194	82
Pre-Tax Income (a)	8,810	2,272	288
Net Income	3,951	852	364
Net Income Per Common Share	1.40	.47	198
Weighted Average Number of Common and			
Common Equivalent Shares Outstanding	2,829	1,820	55
Financial Position			
Current Assets	$15,353	$ 6,777	127
Current Liabilities	8,467	5,440	56
Working Capital	6,886	1,337	415
Total Assets	35,304	13,985	152
Shareholders' Equity	14,848	2,289	549
Operating Ratios			
Gross Profit Margin	54.8%	48.2%	14
Pre-Tax Margin	25.2%	11.8%	114
Net Margin	11.3%	4.4%	157
Long-Term Debt/Total Capital (b)	28.5%	53.0%	46
Return on Beginning Equity	172.6%	59.3%	191
Return on Average Total Assets	16.0%	7.5%	113

a.　income before income taxes and minority interests
b.　includes long-term debt, equity interests of minority shareholders in subsidiaries and shareholders' equity

Exhibit 1   Patten Corporation Abridged Annual Report for 1986

LETTER TO SHAREHOLDERS

Fellow Shareholders:

It is my pleasure to report that the year ended March 31, 1986 was one of exceptional achievement and profitability for Patten Corporation.

The Company's revenues reached $35 million, up 82.3% over 1985 revenues of $19.2 million. Net income rose to $3,951,000 or $1.40 per share, from $852,000 or $.47 per share.

Fourth quarter revenues of $9.7 million were 146% ahead of $4 million for the same period last year. Net income rose 33X to $1,053,000 or $.27 per share, from $32,000 or $.02 per share.

Your Company has never been in a better financial position. As a result of the initial public offering of Patten Corporation Common Stock in November 1985 and fiscal 1986 net income, shareholders' equity grew to $14.8 million from $2.3 million. Working capital reached a record $6.9 million and total assets were up 152% to an all-time high of $35.3 million.

Revenues increased 99% in the five offices that were opened throughout 1985 and 1986.

Vertical & Horizontal Expansion

Among the factors contributing to the Company's strong financial performance were faster-than-expected growth in our existing offices, unusually dry weather, and the addition of 15 qualified acquisition professionals, bringing the acquisition staff to 46.

During 1986, a total of five new offices opened in Concord, New Hampshire; Bangor, Maine; York, Pennsylvania; Montpelier, Vermont; and Brooklyn, Connecticut. Continuing geographic diversification allows a more varied product mix and lessens the effect of seasonal fluctuations.

In addition to our ongoing program of gradual geographic and new market expansion, each regional office continues to develop its own specialized market area and products. After successful testing in 1986, each office will increase its residential and bulk acreage sales efforts in 1987, in addition to maintaining its significant rate of growth in the sale of large country parcels and specialized products.

The Bangor, Maine office is currently successful in marketing 40-acre parcels, while Sleepy Hollow Lake, New York continues to specialize in small lakefront parcels within a 2½-hour drive of New York City. Our York, Pennsylvania office is in a strategic location for providing the 3-million-person Philadelphia-Baltimore-District of Columbia market with properties in Maryland, Virginia, West Virginia, and Pennsylvania.

The Patten People

Each Patten office is headed by a regional president with bottom-line responsibility for acquisition and sales teams throughout his area. We have continued to strengthen our management team at all levels through advancement, training, and a rigorous recruiting program.

Michael Sanders joined the Company as Executive Vice President of Acquisitions and comes to us with 12 years experience in the acquisition of rural properties. He will oversee our continuing geographic expansion and work with the regional presidents on the development of acquisition managers.

On May 1, 1986, Jeffrey B. Lavin, C.P.A., joined Patten Corporation to serve as the Company's Chief Financial Officer, and will be working closely with the Executive Vice President of Finance and the regional presidents to coordinate financial planning and control. He has ten years of public accounting experience.

Joseph R. O'Brien, Gary P. Sumner and Raymond A. Lamoureaux were promoted to regional presidents of the Bangor, Maine; York and Stroudsburg, Pennsylvania; and Brooklyn, Connecticut offices, respectively. Each of these men has worked for the Company for several years.

In Memphis, William J. Britton III brought 25 years of real estate experience, including extensive knowledge of the Tennessee market, when he joined the Patten team to spark our expansion into the mid-south. His appointment and the promotions to regional president illustrate Patten's balanced approach to strengthening its management team.

A Commitment to Conservation

Since year-end, we established the Patten Environmental Trust, a non-profit corporation designed to protect the environment through the creation of forever-wild areas. We believe that the free enterprise

Exhibit 1   Patten Corporation Abridged Annual Report for 1986

approach to land conservation will be the most effective in the long run. The formation of this Trust is a reflection of the unique spirit, attitudes, and commitments that have made Patten Corporation the leader in its market.

Looking Ahead

There is every reason to believe that the exceptional achievement and performance of Patten Corporation will continue.

- At least 16 offices should be open by the end of 1987. Since the end of 1986, we expanded operations to the mid-south market by opening an office in Memphis, Tennessee.
- While new offices will contribute to our success in 1987, most of our growth in the next fiscal year will continue to come from our established offices where we expect to further increase the quality of our acquisition of sales staffs.
- On March 31, 1986, the Company held options on 33,366 acres of land at an aggregate purchase price of $17.7 million, as compared with $11.2 million four months earlier, placing the Company in the strongest inventory position in its history.
- The average selling price of a parcel in 1986 rose 68% to $19,300 from $11,500 a year earlier. We believe this is a reflection of our improving pricing policies and product mix.

- Several sales managers are now ready to assume responsibility for new offices. It is our goal to prepare a minimum of six managers for this role within the next twelve months.

In May of 1986, Patten Corporation successfully completed an offering of $30 million of 7¼% convertible subordinated debentures to the public through Drexel Burnham Lambert, Incorporated, First Albany Corporation and Morgan Keegan and Company, Inc.

This offering provides us with funds to increase working capital to support expansion of the Company's business, to increase the amount of customer mortgages retained by the Company, and to open new offices.

We appreciate your support and confidence since our initial public offering on November 21, 1985. The results of the past year, and those we expect in the future, would not be possible without the continued, dedicated efforts of our employees and the support of our customers and Shareholders.

Sincerely,

Harry S. Patten, President
Chairman, Board of Directors
May 21, 1986

p

453

FINANCIAL STATISTICS

(000's omitted except in per share and operating data)

Operating Results for the Years Ended March 31,	1986	1985	1984	1983	1982
Revenues:					
Sales of Real Estate	$33,263	$18,549	$11,186	$ 4,315	$2,822
Interest Income	1,694	645	293	111	84
Total Revenues	34,957	19,194	11,479	4,426	2,906
Income from Operations	8,658	2,006	1,459	732	105
Income Before Income Taxes and Minority Interests	8,810	2,272	1,557	842	282
Provision for Income Taxes	4,184	971	729	338	94
Net Income	$ 3,951	$ 852	$ 475	$ 386	$ 188
Net Income per Common Share	1.40	.47	.26	.21	.10

(continued)

Exhibit 1   Patten Corporation Abridged Annual Report for 1986

Operating Results for the Years Ended March 31,	1986	1985	1984	1983	1982
Weighted Average Number of Common and Common Equivalent Shares Outstanding	2,829	1,820	1,820	1,820	1,820
Financial Position on March 31					
Current Assets	$15,353	$ 6,777	$ 4,604	$ 2,055	$1,464
Current Liabilities	8,467	5,440	3,532	1,072	1,151
Working Capital	6,886	1,337	1,072	983	313
Total Assets	35,304	13,985	8,635	3,490	2,246
Long Term Debt	5,908	3,414	2,070	700	236
Shareholders' Equity	14,848	2,289	1,437	962	576
Operating Ratios					
Gross Profit Margin	54.8%	48.2%	46.4%	51.9%	47.2%
Net Margin	11.3%	4.4%	4.1%	8.7%	6.5%
Long-Term Debt/Total Capital (a)	28.5%	53.0%	53.7%	38.8%	29.1%
Return on Beginning Equity	172.6%	59.3%	49.3%	67.0%	48.4%
Return on Average Total Assets	16.0%	7.5%	7.8%	13.5%	9.5%
Operating Data					
Average Sale Price per Parcel	$19,327	$11,521	$10,310	$10,396	$6,006
Number of Parcels Sold	1,721	1,610	1,085	415	470
Total Acres Sold	25,935	14,084	10,537	5,706	6,928
Number of Offices at End of Period	13	8	6	3	1

Price Range of Common Stock

The Company's Common Stock is traded in the Over-The-Counter market under the symbol "PATN." The following table sets forth the range of high and low bit quotations per share of Common Stock from the initial public offering of Common Stock on November 21, 1985 through February 3, 1986, as reported by the National Association of Securities Dealers Automated Quotation ("NASDAQ") System, and the range of high and low sale prices since February 4, 1986, as reported on the NASDAQ National Market System. Quotations represent prices between dealers, and do not reflect retail mark-ups, mark-downs or commissions and, for periods prior to February 4, 1986, may not represent actual transactions.

Fiscal 1986:	High	Low
Third Quarter (from November 21)	10 5/8	9 7/8
Fourth Quarter (through February 3)	15 1/8	10 1/4
Fourth Quarter (from February 4)	20	14 1/2

The Company has not paid any cash dividend on its Common Stock to date and does not intend to pay dividends in the foreseeable future. As of April 16, 1986, there were 358 holders of record of Common Stock.

a. Includes long-term debt, equity interests of minority shareholders in subsidiaries and shareholders' equity

Exhibit 1   Patten Corporation Abridged Annual Report for 1986

MANAGEMENT'S DISCUSSION AND ANALYSIS

Fiscal 1986 vs. Fiscal 1985

Sales of real estate increased by $14.7 million, or 79.3%, from $18.5 million to $33.3 million. This increase was primarily attributable to an increase in the total acres sold from 14,084 to 25,935, and an increase in the average sale price per parcel from $11,521 to $19,327. The number of parcels sold increased from 1,610 to 1,721. Sales by existing offices (offices open during all of fiscal 1985 and 1986) increased 99% from $12.8 million to $25.5 million. Sales also increased due to the opening of regional offices in Bangor, Maine and Concord, New Hampshire. In addition, the Company opened a new office in Stroudsburg, Pennsylvania to replace an office in Milford, Pennsylvania. The Company sold 4,441 acres in bulk parcels (100 acres or more) resulting in $2.7 million of bulk acreage sales in fiscal 1986 as compared with no such sales in the prior year. The number of regional offices was 13 and 8 at March 31, 1986 and 1985, respectively.

Interest income increased from $645,000 to $1.7 million. This was due primarily to an increase in the amount of notes receivable retained by the Company, as well as an increase in the total amount of notes receivable originated by the Company.

Gross margin on sales of real estate improved from 48.2% to 54.8% as a result of the Company's ability to increase the sale prices of parcels without reducing sales volume, and to allocate certain fixed acquisition expenses over a greater volume of properties sold. In addition, the financial resources provided by the Company's initial public offering in November 1985 increased the Company's ability to make acquisitions.

Selling, general and administrative expenses increased by $3.6 million, or 52.3%, from $6.7 million to $10.3 million primarily due to the expansion of the Company's operations, resulting in an increase in advertising, marketing and selling expenses of $784,000, or 26.1%. In addition, as a result of increased sales volume, personnel costs and other variable expenses increased. Selling, general and administrative expenses decreased as a percentage of total revenues from 35.1% to 29.3%, primarily reflecting increased sales volume.

Interest expense rose from $846,000 to $1.0 million. This reflects an increase in the amount of borrowings outstanding, partially offset by a decrease in the weighted average interest rates on borrowings.

The effective income tax rate increased from 42.7% to 47.5%, reflecting a lower proportion of investment tax credits and surtax exemptions relative to income before income taxes.

Net income increased $3.1 million, or 364%, from $852,000 to 3.9 million. The increase in earnings is primarily due to increased revenues, improved gross margins, and lower selling, general and administrative expenses as a percentage of total revenues.

Fiscal 1985 vs. Fiscal 1984

Sales of real estate increased by $7.3 million, or 66%, from $11.2 million to $18.5 million. This increase was primarily attributable to the opening of an additional regional office at Sleepy Hollow Lake, New York. Sales in existing offices (offices open during all of both fiscal 1984 and 1985) increased from $9.3 million to $11.0 million, or 19%. The number of parcels sold increased from 1,085 to 1,610, and the average sale price per parcel increased from $10,310 to $11,521. The number of regional offices was eight and six at March 31, 1985 and 1984, respectively.

The Company also broadened the types of real estate parcels available for sale to include water-view property, such as ocean-front, lake-front and fishing rivers, and primary home sites. In fiscal 1985, the Company was involved in selling a large volume of lake-front parcels at Sleepy Hollow Lake in New York, the majority of which were less than one acre.

Interest income increased from $293,000 to $645,000. This was due primarily to an increase in the amount of notes receivable originated by the Company.

Gross margin on sales of real estate improved from 46.4% to 48.2%, primarily as a result of an increased proportion of sales of higher-margin and higher-priced lake-front and ocean-view properties.

Exhibit 1   Patten Corporation Abridged Annual Report for 1986

Selling, general and administrative expenses increased by $3.0 million, or 82%, from $3.7 million to $6.7 million and increased as a percentage of total revenues from 32.3% to 35.1%, primarily reflecting increased advertising, marketing and sales costs incurred in part in connection with the development of a new direct mail program. Selling, general and administrative expenses also increased as a result of the addition of acquisition and marketing personnel and increased salaries.

Interest expense increased from $321,000 to $846,000, reflecting an increase in the amount of borrowing outstanding. The weighted average interest rates on borrowing outstanding during the periods did not vary materially.

The effective income tax rate declined from 46.8% to 42.7%, primarily reflecting a higher proportion of investment tax credits and surtax exemptions relative to income before income taxes.

Net income increased to $852,000 from $475,000, reflecting the opening of additional regional offices, increased revenues, and improved gross margins.

Liquidity and Capital Resources

The Company's capital resources are provided from both internal and external sources. These funds support the Company's operations, including the acquisition and holding of land, and allow it to offer financing to its customers.

The Company typically advances only a small down payment when signing a contract to acquire property. At March 31, 1986, the Company had contracted to purchase approximately $17.7 million of property against which it had made down payments of $499,000. In most cases, the Company is not required to advance the full purchase price until all regulatory approvals for the subdivision and sale of land have been obtained and certain other conditions have been satisfied. The Company further reduces its capital requirements by marketing and selling properties promptly, with the period from acquisition to sale generally being one to 12 weeks.

The Company finances a substantial portion of its sales (approximately 64% of its sales in fiscal 1986) and pledges or holds the related notes it receives. As of March 31, 1986, approximately $18.6 million of notes receivable were held by the Company. Approximately 47% of these notes were pledged as collateral for the Company's bank loans, with the Company being entitled to borrow amounts totaling 70–80% of the outstanding principal of pledged notes. Until the end of calendar 1985, the Company sold the notes it did not hold to banks at face amount, and receives as interest income the difference between the coupon rate on the notes sold (usually 4–5% over the banks' prime lending rate) and the banks' prime lending rate plus 3%. The Company was required to guarantee the repayment of each note sold to banks, although in some cases the Company was only required to guarantee the repayment of a note until one-half of the term of the note expired or one-half of the amount due on the note was paid, whichever occurred later. As of March 31, 1986, the Company was subject to contingent liabilities under such guarantees of approximately $10.9 million. The determination to pledge rather than to sell notes receivable is made by the Company in part, as discussed below, to defer income taxes. The Company has increased, and intends to continue increasing, the proportion of its sales which it finances and intends to retain or pledge rather than sell the receivables generated. The Company continues to have the ability to sell a substantial portion of its notes if required for liquidity purposes.

Cash flow provided by the Company's operations (which includes net income plus non-cash deductions from net income) was $1.7 million, $2.5 million and $8.8 million for the years ended March 31, 1984, 1985 and 1986, respectively. However, as a result of increasing sales and the Company's mortgage financing activities over the three-year period, net funds used for the Company's operations were $2.4 million, $856,000 and $9.3 million, respectively. The increase in funds used for operations during fiscal 1986 was due primarily to the Company's decision to finance a greater percentage of customer purchases and to hold all of the notes receivable it originated. Notes receivable retained by the Company totaled $2.6 million, $4.0 million and $13.6 million for the years ended March 31, 1984, 1985 and 1986, respectively. The Company's growth in its real estate operations and its mortgage financing activities have been funded through cash flow generated from operations, borrowings under secured and unsecured lines of credit, sales of notes receivable to banks and the approximately $7.2 mil-

Exhibit 1   Patten Corporation Abridged Annual Report for 1986

lion of net proceeds from the public offering of 850,000 shares of its Common Stock in November 1985. The Company increased the aggregate amounts available under its lines of credit from $6.5 million at March 31, 1984 to $16.4 million at March 31, 1986, approximately 65% of which required the security of existing real estate mortgage notes and inventory. At March 31, 1986, approximately $6.1 million remained available for additional borrowings under such lines of credit.

A portion of the Company's liquidity is provided through the use of the installment sale method of reporting income from property sales for income tax purposes, the effect of which is to defer income taxes, thereby increasing available cash. Under current tax law, the Company is able to pledge its installment notes receivable to secure loans from banks without accelerating the tax liability attribut-

able to such notes. Legislative proposals have been made which, if they were to become effective, would require the Company to accelerate the tax liability attributable to its installment notes upon their pledge to banks and prevent the Company from continuing to increase its liquidity in this manner.

Based upon its current financial condition and credit relationships, the Company believes that it has, or can obtain, adequate financial resources to satisfy its liquidity and capital requirements for the foreseeable future at anticipated rates of growth.

Effects of Inflation

Management believes that inflationary increases in costs of sales and operations can normally be absorbed by increases in the price of properties sold. To date, inflationary effects have had little impact on the Company.

p

Exhibit 1   Patten Corporation Abridged Annual Report for 1986

CONSOLIDATED BALANCE SHEET

	March 31	
	1986	1985
ASSETS		
Current assets:		
Cash	$ 1,578,361	$ 658,016
Contracts receivable	2,939,417	1,078,813
Notes receivable, current portion (Notes 2 and 5)	1,328,374	693,161
Inventory (Notes 4 and 5)	7,172,050	2,921,772
Due from officers and other related parties (Note 8)	1,016,998	1,125,770
Other current assets	1,318,126	299,498
Total current assets	15,353,326	6,777,030
Property and equipment, net (Notes 3 and 5)	2,716,147	1,087,820
Notes receivable (Notes 2 and 5)	17,234,488	5,746,639
Due from officers and other related parties (Note 8)	—	373,296
Total assets	$35,303,961	$13,984,785
LIABILITIES AND SHAREHOLDERS' EQUITY		
Current liabilities:		
Accounts payable	$ 1,277,173	$ 588,297
Accrued liabilities	383,631	176,430
Income taxes payable (Note 7)	253,632	10,848
Notes payable (Note 4)	5,487,592	3,719,982
Current portion of long-term debt (Note 5)	1,065,223	944,611
Total current liabilities	8,467,251	5,440,168
Long-term debt (Note 5)	5,908,498	3,413,837
Deferred income taxes (Note 7)	6,080,531	2,103,107
Commitments and contingencies (Notes 6 and 10)		
Equity interests of minority shareholders in subsidiaries (Note 11)	—	738,564
Shareholders' equity (Notes 4 and 11):		
Preferred Stock, $.01 par value, 1,000,000 shares authorized: none issued and outstanding at March 31, 1986 and 1985	—	—
Common Stock, $.01 par value, 10,000,000 shares authorized: 3,900,000 shares issued and outstanding at March 31, 1986 and 1,820,000 at March 31, 1985	39,000	18,200
Capital in excess of par value	8,586,958	—
Retained earnings	6,221,723	2,270,909
Total shareholders' equity	14,847,681	2,289,109
Total liabilities and shareholders' equity	$35,303,961	$13,984,785

Exhibit 1   Patten Corporation Abridged Annual Report for 1986

CONSOLIDATED STATEMENT OF INCOME

	Years Ended March 31		
	1986	1985	1984
Revenues			
Sales of real estate (Notes 6 and 8)	$33,262,613	$18,548,630	$11,185,870
Interest income	1,693,923	645,335	293,238
	34,956,536	19,193,965	11,479,108
Cost and expenses			
Cost of real estate sold (Notes 6 and 8)	15,028,396	9,606,072	5,993,651
Selling, general and administrative expense	10,258,788	6,736,083	3,705,471
Interest expense	1,011,513	846,074	320,953
	26,298,697	17,188,229	10,020,075
Income from operations	8,657,839	2,005,736	1,459,033
Other income (Note 8)	151,847	266,560	98,298
Income before income taxes and minority interests	8,809,686	2,272,296	1,557,331
Provision for income taxes (Note 7)	4,184,086	970,583	729,424
Income before minority interests	4,625,600	1,301,713	827,907
Minority interests in earnings of subsidiaries	674,786	449,341	353,259
Net income	$ 3,950,814	$ 852,372	$ 474,648
Net income per common share	$1.40	$.47	$.26
Weighted average number of common and common equivalent shares used to calculate net income per common share	2,829,303	1,820,000	1,820,000

CONSOLIDATED STATEMENT OF SHAREHOLDERS' EQUITY

(Note 11)	Years Ended March 31		
	1986	1985	1984
Class A Preferred Stock, no par value			
Balance beginning of period	—	—	—
Issuance of stock dividend on April 9, 1985	$2,289,000	—	—
Exchange for Common Stock, $.01 par value, on November 21, 1985	(2,289,000)	—	—
Balance end of period	—	—	—
Preferred Stock, $.01 par value			
Balance beginning of period	—	—	—
Balance end of period	—	—	—

(continued)

p

459

Exhibit 1   Patten Corporation Abridged Annual Report for 1986

CONSOLIDATED STATEMENT OF SHAREHOLDERS' EQUITY (continued)

	Years Ended March 31		
	1986	1985	1984
Common Stock, no par value			
Balance beginning of period	—	—	$3,627
Transfer to Common Stock, $.01 par value, for retroactive effect of reincorporation in Massachusetts on October 8, 1985	—	—	(3,627)
Balance end of period	—	—	—
Common Stock, $.01 par value			
Balance beginning of period	$18,200	$18,200	—
Transfer from Common Stock, no par value, and retained earnings for retroactive effect of reincorporation in Massachusetts on October 8, 1985 and for exchange of Class A Preferred Stock on November 21, 1985	—	—	$18,200
Shares issued for acquisition of minority interests	12,300	—	—
Shares issued in public offering	8,500	—	—
Balance end of period	$39,000	$18,200	$18,200
Capital in Excess of par Value			
Balance beginning of period	—	—	—
Excess of book value of minority interests acquired over par value of Common Stock, $.01 par value, issued for acquisition of minority interests	$1,410,645	—	—
Shares issued in public offering	7,176,313	—	—
Balance end of period	$8,586,958	—	—
Retained Earnings			
Balance beginning of period	$2,270,909	$1,418,537	$ 958,462
Issuance of stock dividend on April 9, 1985	(2,289,000)	—	—
Transfer to Common Stock, $.01 par value, for retroactive effect of reincorporation in Massachusetts on October 8, 1985	—	—	(12,284)
Exchange of Class A Preferred Stock for Common Stock, $.01 par value, on November 21, 1985	2,289,000	—	(2,289)
Net income for the period	3,950,814	852,372	474,648
Balance end of period	$6,221,723	$2,270,909	$1,418,537

Exhibit 1   Patten Corporation Abridged Annual Report for 1986

CONSOLIDATED STATEMENT OF CHANGES IN FINANCIAL POSITION

	Years Ended March 31		
	1986	1985	1984
Operations			
Net income	$ 3,950,814	$ 852,372	$ 474,648
Add (deduct) items not affecting cash:			
Depreciation	246,923	230,122	135,989
Deferred income taxes	3,977,424	933,686	693,155
Minority interests in earnings of subsidiaries	674,786	449,341	353,259
Cash payments on notes receivable	1,493,406	948,591	656,773
Proceeds from sale of notes receivable to banks	5,751,952	4,932,513	3,280,280
Notes receivable originated during the period	(19,368,420)	(8,909,141)	(5,840,366)
Increase (decrease) in:			
Accounts payable and accrued liabilities	896,077	100,324	509,183
Income taxes payable	242,784	(21,355)	23,896
Decrease (increase) in:			
Contracts receivable	(1,860,604)	113,749	(441,689)
Inventory	(4,250,278)	(330,029)	(2,173,230)
Other current assets	(1,018,628)	(156,419)	(113,168)
Net funds used for operations	(9,263,764)	(856,246)	(2,441,270)
Investments			
Purchase of property and equipment, net	(1,875,250)	(284,042)	(823,873)
Decrease (increase) in amount due from officers and other related parties, net	482,068	(1,606,608)	—
Decrease in investment in affiliates	—	—	39,087
Acquisition of equity interests of minority shareholders in subsidiaries	(1,422,945)	—	—
Other, net	9,595	(30,667)	(101,666)
Net funds used for investments	(2,806,532)	(1,921,317)	(886,452)
Financing			
Addition to short-term borrowings	1,767,610	1,291,817	1,869,396
Addition to long-term debt	4,209,243	2,030,384	1,714,781
Reduction in long-term debt	(1,593,970)	(148,453)	(126,330)
Issuance of common stock	8,607,758	—	—
Net funds provided by financing	12,990,641	3,173,748	3,457,847
Increase in cash	$ 920,345	$ 396,185	$ 130,125

p
461

Exhibit 1   Patten Corporation Abridged Annual Report for 1986

NOTES TO CONSOLIDATED FINANCIAL STATEMENTS

1. Significant Accounting Policies

Principles of Consolidation

The financial statements include the accounts of Patten Corporation (the Company) and all majority owned subsidiaries. All intercompany transactions are eliminated.

Business

The Company acquires large underdeveloped rural properties, subdivides these properties into parcels, and markets and sells the parcels to persons living in metropolitan areas. Generally, the Company makes only minor improvements and rarely builds on or otherwise develops the land it sells. In fiscal 1986 the Company began a program of acquiring large properties for bulk acreage sales.

Inventory

Inventory is stated at the lower of cost or market, with cost being determined on a specific cost basis considering relative fair values. Cost includes cost of real estate, improvements and capitalizable purchase costs.

Property and Equipment

Property and equipment are recorded at cost. Depreciation is computed on both the straight-line and accelerated methods based on the estimated useful lives of the related assets.

Contracts Receivable and Revenue Recognition

The Company records a sale of real estate and recognizes revenue when a minimum of 10% of the sales proceeds has been received and collectability of the balance can be reasonably assured. The excess of sales price over legally binding deposits received is recorded as contracts receivable. All related costs are recorded when the sale is recorded. The amount of delinquent contracts receivable at March 31, 1986 is not material.

Income Taxes

Deferred income taxes are provided for those items of revenue and expense which are recognized for financial reporting in different periods than for income tax purposes. Investment tax credits are accounted for as a reduction of the provision for income taxes in the year in which they arise.

Net Income per Common Share

Net income per common share was determined by dividing net income by the weighted average number of common shares and, in fiscal 1986, common equivalent shares outstanding during each period after giving retroactive effect to the common stock dividends as of April 9, 1985 and August 21, 1985, the exchange of common shares pursuant to the reincorporation of the Company in Massachusetts on October 8, 1985, and the issuance of 228,900 shares of Common Stock, $.01 par value, in exchange for 1,000 shares of Class A Preferred Stock on November 21, 1985. The common equivalent shares reflect the dilutive impact of shares reserved for outstanding stock options and common stock purchase warrants. (See Note 11).

Exhibit 1   Patten Corporation Abridged Annual Report for 1986

Presentation

The format of the statement of changes in financial position for the years ended March 31, 1985 and 1984 has been changed to conform to the 1986 presentation.

2. Notes Receivable

The weighted average interest rate on notes receivable is approximately 13.8% and 14.2% at March 31, 1986 and 1985, respectively. The interest rates on these notes at March 31, 1986 range from 9.5% to 19%. As of March 31, 1986, the amount of outstanding notes receivable held by the Company which were delinquent, with delinquency defined as notes receivable with payments more than 30 days past due, was approximately 0.6% or $104,000. Notes receivable are shown net of an allowance for possible losses on notes receivable of $10,000, in the accompanying consolidated balance sheet as of March 31, 1986. The amount of notes receivable written off in the years ended March 31, 1986, 1985 and 1984 was not material.

Installments due on notes receivable during each of the five fiscal years subsequent to March 31, 1986 are as follows:

March 31, 1987	$ 1,328,374
March 31, 1988	1,412,710
March 31, 1989	1,504,613
March 31, 1990	1,491,521
March 31, 1991	1,462,209
Thereafter	11,363,435

3. Property and Equipment

Property and equipment consist of the following:

	March 31	
	1986	1985
Land and buildings	$383,500	$196,000
Building improvements	543,948	377,930
Office equipment, furniture and fixtures	577,752	252,491
Aircraft	1,362,034	454,174
Vehicles	432,642	226,313
	3,299,876	1,506,908
Accumulated depreciation	583,729	419,088
	$2,716,147	$1,087,820

Exhibit 1   Patten Corporation Abridged Annual Report for 1986

4. Notes Payable

The Company has borrowings with various banks which are used to finance inventory purchases and the carrying of notes receivable and to fund operations.

Significant financial data related to the Company's notes payable to banks are as follows:

	Years Ended March 31		
	1986	1985	1984
Total lines of credit available	$8,400,000	$9,500,000	$6,000,000
Borrowings outstanding at end of period	$4,891,586	$3,481,521	$2,211,739
Weighted average interest rate on borrowings outstanding at end of period	10.5%	12%	12%
Average amounts outstanding during the period	$4,090,262	$2,930,345	$1,514,156
Maximum amount borrowed during the period	$5,078,045	$3,481,521	$2,211,739
Weighted average interest rate during the period (determined by dividing interest expense on notes payable to banks by average borrowings of notes payable to banks)	11%	12%	11.8%

All line of credit arrangements may be withdrawn at the option of the banks. There are no significant compensating balance requirements or legal restrictions as to the withdrawal of funds. Under the terms of certain of these line of credit arrangements, the Company is prohibited from the payment of dividends on its outstanding Common Stock and is required to maintain working capital of $1,300,000 or more, a current ratio of at least 1 to 1 and a debt to equity ratio not greater than 5.5 to 1.

In addition, at March 31, 1986 and 1985, $596,006, and $238,461, respectively, is owed to unaffiliated individuals from whom the Company purchased property. The notes evidencing the borrowings are secured primarily by the property purchased, with the balance being paid off as such property is sold by the Company. The interest rates on these notes at March 31, 1986 range from 10% to 12%.

In May of 1985, the Company arranged for a $500,000 term loan to refinance a portion of the current notes payable. Accordingly, $500,000 of notes payable at March 31, 1985 have been classified as long-term debt in the accompanying consolidated balance sheet.

5. Long-Term Debt

Long-term debt consists of the following:

	March 31	
	1986	1985
Mortgage notes secured by certain inventory, property and equipment with interest rates ranging from 8% to 14% fixed and prime plus 1½% variable. Maturities range from 1987 to 1999.	$ 491,983	$ 631,711
Notes payable under long-term available lines of credit of $8,000,000 secured by mortgages held by the Company with total outstanding principal balances aggregating $7,386,000 and $3,251,223 at March 31, 1986 and 1985, respectively. Interest rates are variable ranging from prime (9%) plus 1% to prime plus 2% with the total principal scheduled for repayment through March 1996 (see debt covenants in Note 4).	5,363,467	2,641,125
Notes secured by various equipment with interest payable at rates ranging from 8.5% to 14% fixed and prime plus 1% variable. Maturities range from 1986 through 1989	951,033	415,728
Notes secured by irrevocable letters of credit issued by a commercial bank with interest rates ranging from 9% to 10%. Maturities range from 1988 to 1992. Total letters of credit outstanding to secure such obligations amount to $302,310 at March 31, 1986.	167,238	169,884
Notes payable refinanced to long-term, bearing interest at prime plus 1½%, due May 1986	—	500,000
	6,973,721	4,358,448
Less current maturities	1,065,223	944,611
Long-term debt	$ 5,908,498	$ 3,413,837

p

465

Installments due on long-term debt during each of the five fiscal years subsequent to March 31, 1986 are as follows:

March 31, 1987	$1,065,223
March 31, 1988	886,153
March 31, 1989	702,512
March 31, 1990	479,123
March 31, 1991	462,472
Thereafter	3,378,238

Exhibit 1   Patten Corporation Abridged Annual Report for 1986

6. Agent Agreement

During the year ended March 31, 1985, the Company entered into an agreement under which the Company acted as sole agent for the sale of subdivided land owned by another party. Under the terms of the agreement, the Company received 50% of the sales proceeds for each lot as compensation. The Company also had an option to acquire any remaining unsold lots at specified prices provided that less than 80% of the total lots were sold. The Company was obligated to acquire all remaining unsold lots when 80% of the total lots were sold.

Sales of real estate and cost of real estate sold for the year ended March 31, 1985 include $3,339,990 and $1,652,200, respectively, in order to recognize the substance of the above agreement. On April 17, 1985, the Company acquired the remaining unsold lots at a cost of $584,450. All lots were sold during the year ended March 31, 1986.

7. Income Taxes

The provisions for income taxes consist of the following:

| | Years Ended March 31 | | |
	1986	1985	1984
Federal:			
Current	$ 47,758	$ 21,303	$ 13,189
Deferred	3,366,762	757,427	555,675
State:			
Current	158,496	15,594	23,080
Deferred	611,070	176,259	137,480
	769,566	191,853	160,560
Total	$4,184,086	$970,583	$729,424

The reason for the differences between the provision for income taxes and the amount which results from applying the federal statutory tax rate of 46% to income before income taxes and minority interests are as follows:

| | Years Ended March 31 | | |
	1986	1985	1984
Income tax expense at statutory rate	$4,052,456	$1,045,256	$716,372
Increase in income tax expense due to inclusion of state taxes	415,566	103,601	86,702
Investment tax credits	(258,593)	(100,781)	(40,455)
Impact of graduated federal tax rates	(116,831)	(77,493)	(33,195)
Other	91,488	—	—
	$4,184,086	$ 970,583	$729,424

Exhibit 1 Patten Corporation Abridged Annual Report for 1986

The sources of deferred income taxes were as follows:

	Years Ended March 31		
	1986	1985	1984
Recording of sales for financial reporting purposes when at least 10% of the proceeds are received while the sales are not recorded for tax purposes until actual closing and title passage	$ 525,982	$ 20,541	$ 64,463
Installment sales treatment of notes receivable for tax purposes	3,344,304	898,206	606,511
Excess of depreciation for tax purposes over that for financial reporting purposes	107,546	14,939	22,181
	$3,977,832	$933,686	$693,155

8. Related Party Transactions

The Company performed various management services for related entities which are owned in part by an officer and shareholder of Patten Corporation and one of which is owned in part by a director. Such fees amounted to $60,200, $89,700 and $130,000 for the years ended March 31, 1986, 1985 and 1984, respectively, and are reflected as other income in the consolidated statement of income.

The Company pays maintenance costs for certain facilities to a corporation owned by an officer and shareholder of Patten Corporation. Total maintenance expense of $55,000, $78,000 and $41,000 for the years ended March 31, 1986, 1985 and 1984, respectively, was incurred under this agreement.

Since June 1984, the Company has acted as general partner in a partnership which manages two rental properties. As a result of various consulting activities with this partnership, net fees of $3,500 and $172,294 were earned and are reflected as other income in the consolidated statement of income for the years ended March 31, 1986 and 1985, respectively.

During the years ended March 31, 1986 and 1985, the Company sold certain parcels of land to entities controlled by related parties. The consolidated statement of income for the years ended March 31, 1986 and 1985 includes sales of real estate of $153,903 and $872,243, respectively, and cost of real estate sold of $130,782 and $546,513, respectively, associated with these sales. At March 31, 1986 and 1985, the Company held 10% demand notes receivable totaling $575,770 and $681,221, respectively, from these related parties.

In October 1985, the Company sold its regional office building in Bangor, Maine to a general partnership of which the regional managers of the Bangor office and Harry S. Patten are the sole general partners. The sales price amounted to $132,500 which equaled book value of the property. Subsequent to the sale, the Company has rented the office building from the partnership. The total rent expense paid by the Company for the Bangor office through March 31, 1986 was $5,200.

Exhibit 1   Patten Corporation Abridged Annual Report for 1986

Effective on April 1, 1984, the Company sold its 51% interest in Patten Southeast Corporation to Harry S. Patten for $25,296, representing the book value of such interest. Prior to April 1, 1984, the Company conducted real estate acquisition and sales activities in South Carolina through Patten Southeast Corporation. The Company determined to sell its interest in Patten Southeast Corporation, which no longer engages in the purchase of real estate but continues to hold mortgages on properties it sold. At March 31, 1986 and 1985, Patten Southeast Corporation owed $331,189 and $258,989, respectively to the Company.

During the fiscal years 1986, 1985 and 1984, the Company made interest free demand loans to Harry S. Patten in the amounts of $642,628, $1,255,120 and $736,926, respectively. All of such loans have been repaid in full to the Company.

As a result of the above transactions and certain other advances to and from officers and other related parties, the consolidated balance sheets include the following:

	March 31, 1986	March 31, 1985	
	Current	Current	Noncurrent
Accounts receivable from officers and other related parties	$1,049,652	$1,178,815	$439,548
Accounts payable to officers and other related parties	(32,654)	(53,045)	(66,252)
	$1,016,998	$1,125,770	$373,296

9. Supplementary Income Statement

Supplementary income statement information is as follows:

	Years Ended March 31		
	1986	1985	1984
Advertising costs	$1,562,423	$1,511,921	$691,751
Taxes, other than payroll and income taxes	$547,747	$195,407	$210,306

10. Commitments and Contingent Liabilities

At March 31, 1986, the Company had contracted to purchase approximately $17.7 million of property against which it had made down payments of $499,000. In most cases, the Company is not required to advance the full purchase price until all regulatory approvals for the subdivision and sale of land have been obtained and certain other conditions have been satisfied.

Exhibit 1   Patten Corporation Abridged Annual Report for 1986

The Company and its subsidiaries have discounted notes receivable in conjunction with property sales. In the event of default of future payment by a property owner, the Company and its subsidiary that discounted the note would have direct responsibility for satisfying any outstanding balance. In each case, a security interest in the property securing the note is maintained; accordingly, the Company may repossess the property to satisfy the note. No material losses have occurred in the past as subsequent disposition of repossessed properties has created a gain due to inflationary effects on price and the equity that returns to the guarantor in the event of default. Of the total of all loans acquired by the bank and outstanding at March 31, 1986, approximately 5% were over 30 days' delinquent as of March 31, 1986. As of March 31, 1986, the Company's contingent liability was approximately $10,950,000.

11. Shareholders' Equity, Minority Interests, Stock Option Plan and Warrants

As of April 9, 1985, the Company's Board of Directors authorized a stock dividend on its outstanding 795,550 shares of Common Stock of 1,000 shares of Class A 8% Redeemable Preferred Stock (liquidation preference $2,289,000) and 795,550 shares of Common Stock to Harry S. Patten, its sole shareholder at that time (such share amounts and all other share amounts discussed in these financial statements reflect the stock dividend, reincorporation and exchange transactions discussed below in this Note 11). Transfer restrictions were imposed on all stock of the Company requiring that shareholders who desire to transfer any stock of the Company must first offer such stock to the Company at a formula price. The formula price for the Common Stock is its net book value as of the close of the month ended next prior to the date of the offer. The formula price for the Class A 8% Redeemable Preferred Stock is its liquidation value.

As of August 21, 1985, the Company's Board of Directors declared a 59.11% Common Stock dividend on each share of its issued and outstanding Common Stock on that date.

As of September 1, 1985, the Company acquired the minority interests in seven of its subsidiaries in exchange for an aggregate of 1,230,000 shares of the Company's Common Stock. In each case, the owner of the minority interest in the subsidiary was the regional manager in charge of operations of such subsidiary. One owner of a minority interest was issued 50,000 shares of Common Stock which are held in escrow contingent upon future earnings of the subsidiary. The number of shares of the Company's Common Stock issued to each regional manager in exchange for the minority interest was determined by negotiations among such regional managers and the Company. The value of the shares of the Company's Common Stock exchanged for such minority interests was based on the book value of the minority interests ($1,422,945 as of September 1, 1985).

This transaction has resulted in the Company owning 100% of these subsidiaries. Consolidated financial statements of the Company subsequent to September 1, 1985 include all of the net income of these subsidiaries. Previously issued financial statements of the Company included all of the assets, liabilities, revenues and expenses of these subsidiaries, but only the Company's proportionate share of equity and net income of the subsidiaries. Assuming the acquisition had been made as of April 1, 1984, pro forma consolidated net income and net income per common share would have been as follows:

p

469

Exhibit 1   Patten Corporation Abridged Annual Report for 1986

| | Years Ended March 31 | |
	1986	1985
Net income	$4,625,600	$1,301,713
Net income per common share	$1.37	$.43
Weighted average number of common and common equivalent shares used to calculate net income per common share	3,368,394	3,050,000

On October 8, 1985, the Company reincorporated in Massachusetts by merging into a wholly-owned subsidiary which was organized on September 18, 1985. In connection with this reincorporation and merger, each share of the Company's Common Stock was exchanged for 10,000 shares of Common Stock, $.01 par value, and each share of its Class A 8% Redeemable Preferred Stock was exchanged for one share of Class A Preferred Stock.

On November 21, 1985, the Company exchanged the 1,000 shares of its Class A Preferred Stock held by Harry S. Patten for 228,900 shares of its Common Stock, $.01 par value. Such exchange was based on a liquidation preference of $2,289 per share of preferred stock, as provided in the Company's Articles of Organization, and the public offering price of the Company's Common Stock. At the same time, the Company's Articles of Organization were amended to eliminate the restrictions on the transfer of the Company's capital stock.

As a result of the above transactions, $14,573 has been transferred to Common Stock, $.01 par value, from retained earnings in the accompanying statement of shareholders' equity as of March 31, 1984.

All references to numbers of shares of Common Stock and per share amounts have been adjusted to reflect the stock dividend of 795,550 shares as of April 9, 1985 and the 59.11% stock dividend authorized by the Company's Board of Directors on each share of the Company's Common Stock outstanding as of August 21, 1985, pursuant to which each share of Common Stock outstanding was exchanged for 10,000 shares of Common Stock.

By consent of the sole Shareholder and Directors of the Company on September 30, 1985, the Company adopted an employee incentive stock option plan. Under the plan, options may be granted at prices not less than the fair market value on the date of grant. On November 20, 1985, the Board of Directors granted options to purchase an aggregate of 145,500 shares of the Common Stock of the Company to 53 employees, at an exercise price of $10.00 per share. The options expire in 1995. As of March 31, 1986, no options have been exercised under the plan, and no options were exercisable. As of March 31, 1986, 225,000 shares of Common Stock were reserved for issuance under the plan. As of March 31, 1986, 176 employees of the Company were eligible to participate in the plan and 53 employees were actually participating in the plan.

On November 21, 1985, the Company issued five-year warrants to purchase up to an aggregate of 50,000 shares of Common Stock at $12.00 per share. The warrants may be exercised as to all or any less number of shares of Common Stock commencing on November 21, 1986.

On November 21, 1985, the Company sold 850,000 shares of Common Stock in an initial public offering. Net proceeds to the Company amounted to $7,184,813.

Exhibit 1   Patten Corporation Abridged Annual Report for 1986

12. Quarterly Financial Information (Unaudited)

Summarized quarterly financial information (in 000's except for per share information) for the years ended March 31, 1986 and 1985 is as follows:

	Three Months Ended			
	June 30, 1985	Sept. 30, 1985	Dec. 31, 1985	March 31, 1986
1986				
Sales of real estate	$6,223	$10,728	$7,262	$9,050
Interest income	278	322	423	671
Gross profit	3,451	6,099	3,809	4,876
Net income	479	1,537	882	1,053
Net income per common share	.26	.69	.27	.27

	Three Months Ended			
	June 30, 1984	Sept. 30, 1984	Dec. 31, 1984	March 31, 1985
Sales of real estate	$2,048	$ 6,480	$6,304	$3,717
Interest income	118	138	153	236
Gross profit	766	3,387	3,040	1,750
Net income	(150)	565	406	32
Net income per common share	(.08)	.31	.22	.02

REPORT OF INDEPENDENT CERTIFIED PUBLIC ACCOUNTANTS

Board of Directors and Shareholders
Patten Corporation

We have examined the accompanying consolidated balance sheet of Patten Corporation at March 31, 1986 and 1985 and the related consolidated statements of income, changes in financial position and shareholders' equity for each of the three years in the period ended March 31, 1986. Our examinations were made in accordance with generally accepted auditing standards and, accordingly, included such tests of the accounting records and such other auditing procedures as we considered necessary in the circumstances.

In our opinion, the statements mentioned above present fairly the consolidated financial position of Patten Corporation at March 31, 1986 and 1985 and the consolidated results of operations and changes in financial position for each of the three years in the period ended March 31, 1986, in conformity with generally accepted accounting principles applied on a consistent basis during the period.

ARTHUR YOUNG & COMPANY
Worcester, Massachusetts
April 22, 1986

It is May 1989. Power Line, Inc., the large Cleveland-based manufacturing concern, has been attempting to gain control of troubled Raymond Barry Corporation for 18 months. After acquiring an initial stake in Barry for $5 per share and setting off a price runup, Power Line expanded its holdings to nearly 15 percent during April 1989, at prices in excess of $8 a share. Further purchases would trigger Barry's "poison pill" unless a friendly acquisition can be arranged. Early this month, a hostile offer of $10 a share for the remaining shares was rebuked, but Barry indicated that an offer of $13 might be of interest. With Power Line now poised to offer $12.40, management believes a successful, and friendly, tender offer is in the making.

Power Line is in contact with you and others at PNC Bancorp, in an effort to arrange a financing commitment for the proposed acquisition. In addition to requesting funds to back the acquisition, Power Line has a need to finance ongoing working capital requirements and pre-existing bank debt.

As a commercial lending officer with PNC Bancorp, you are to analyze the merger and the financing proposal suggested by management and decide on whether the financing should be provided and, if so, how it should be structured.

OVERVIEW OF POWER LINE AND RAYMOND BARRY

Power Line is a diversified manufacturer with 1988 earnings of $15 million on sales of $177 million. The largest of its four divisions, Hydroforce, manufactures power tools and other equipment; Power Line also manufactures a variety of hydraulic products and systems. Most of the company's sales are in the U.S. and Europe.

Barry is a California-based manufacturer of vibration control equipment. Through its Stor-Rite Inc. subsidiary, Barry also manufactures and sells office filing systems, filing cabinets, and other office equipment. Barry had been a consistently profitable firm for many years, but problems at Stor-Rite have recently caused profits to plummet. Those difficulties have combined with the burden of debt assumed in a 1988 restructuring to leave Barry at barely above breakeven. (The restructuring included a variety of takeover

Adapted by Johannes L. Homan and Professor Victor L. Bernard from a case prepared by PNC Bancorp using information taken from PNC files and public sources. Although the case is based upon a real situation, the names of firms and persons involved have been altered for pedagogical purposes. The case was prepared as a basis for class discussion and is not intended to illustrate either an effective or ineffective management of a business situation.

defenses: a leveraged recapitalization and associated special dividend, establishment of an ESOP, termination of the pension plan, and adoption of a "poison pill" stock rights plan.) Barry peddled the Stor-Rite division during the spring of 1988 and entered into an agreement to sell it to a group of private investors for $34 million. However, further losses at Stor-Rite and the investors' difficulty in arranging financing scuttled the deal. In the meantime, the directors of Raymond Barry are being sued by four of the company's shareholders, who feel the directors breached their fiduciary trust by implementing the company's restructuring plan. Barry's stock price, as high as $25 a share in recent years, fell to $5 in early 1989.

ANTICIPATED MERGER TRANSACTION

Power Line has created a wholly-owned holding company, PLI Acquisition Inc., to acquire the shares of Raymond Barry. With a 14.8 percent stake already in place, Power Line expects an offer of $12.40 a share will result in the tendering of substantially all remaining shares. The support of Barry management is expected, in part because Power Line has no intention to sell any of Raymond Barry's operations, including its troubled Stor-Rite Inc. division. Richard Kimle, chairman and chief executive officer of Power Line, commented:

We don't expect to close any plants or move any work. The Raymond Barry businesses will stay exactly where they are under current management. Our approach is to work with existing management teams and to take things from there. That's what I've done all my life: walk into existing management teams, find out who the good people are, and go to work. It's true Raymond Barry has been trying to sell [Stor-Rite], and, in some aspects, it does seem to be a different product and technology from what Power Line is used to. But if I acquire this company, I have to address the question of how I get a return on the investment for my shareholders, and selling off Stor-Rite would not help me much. The new manager of the division, hired last October, is already taking a number of aggressive steps to turn that business around, and I like what I hear.

Barry Chairman Ralph Smith had explicitly spurned Power Line's overtures as recently as late March, when he wrote that ". . . we believe that the sale of the company at this time would be particularly inopportune. Having gone through the rigors and disruption of a partial restructuring in 1988, we are now in a period of consolidation and rebuilding." However, a friendly deal now appears in the making. Natale Carlson, Raymond Barry's chief financial officer, said the company's board will review Power Line's offer "plus appropriate alternatives" in the next two weeks. Carlson added that although Raymond Barry has had problems recently, the company has a "proud and profitable history. . . . We're also number 1 or number 2 in most of our markets."

At first glance, synergies from the merger are not apparent, since there are few overlaps in the two firm's product lines. A few of Barry's products from its Allied Engineering division, including hydraulic clamps for punch presses and other devices, overlap those of Power Line's Hydroforce workholding device unit, but even those units are basically complementary. However, Power Line management sees some benefit of joining their marketing network, especially their thousands of industrial distributorships, with Barry's OEM-focused business. Potential synergies include:

- The ability to introduce Barry's workholding and vibration equipment to foreign markets through Power Line's worldwide distribution network, made up of over 6,000 distributors and original equipment manufacturer (OEM) marketers.
- The potential for Power Line's Hydroforce division to move from the position of number 3 producer to number 1 producer in its industry.
- The potential for Power Line to leverage its knowledge of hydraulics through further development of Barry's products.
- The opportunity to exploit the growth potential available to vibration control equipment in Europe, where there are no resident competitors.

At $12.40 per share, completion of the tender offer, including fees, would require $112 million. Power Line would also expect to refinance $20 million of existing debt. Once the tender offer and resulting merger are consummated, Power Line would require another $30 million to refinance Raymond Barry debt. Thus, the total financing involved is expected to be $162 million. Due to uncertainties about the amount of refinancing ultimately required and the desire to maintain financial flexibility, Power Line has requested a total commitment of $200 million. In initial discussions with PNC, one possibility raised was a five-year amortizing revolving credit facility, under which the maximum outstanding debt permitted would decline from the initial $200 million to, say, $110 million over four years.

If the loan commitment is approved, all pre-existing bank debt of Power Line and Raymond Barry would be repaid and canceled. PNC Bancorp and other members of the financing syndicate would become, initially, the sole bankers for the merged company.

POWER LINE'S BUSINESS

Power Line's largest customers consist mainly of OEMs. Smaller OEMs and end users are serviced by a worldwide network of more than 6,000 distributors. In addition, through direct contact with 200 central purchasing operations working with its Hydroforce and Value Electrical units, Power Line serves more than 20,000 hardware and do-it-yourself consumer outlets.

Power Line operates internationally, with 35 percent of fiscal year 1988 sales occurring in Europe, 11 percent in Japan, 45 percent in the U.S., and 9 percent in the rest of the world. To support its international presence, the company owns manufacturing and engineering operations in three foreign countries in addition to its facilities in the U.S. Marketing, sales, purchasing, and technical assistance for its customers is provided through 21 legal entities worldwide.

Power Line, Inc.

In April 1989, Power Line liquidated its equity investment in Kraft-Werke GmbH by selling to a majority shareholder. At a price of $19.8 million, or approximately a 20 percent premium over market price, Power Line realized a significant gain on its investment.

Power Line has four primary divisions: Hydroforce, Transpower, Value Electrical, and Energy Absorption Systems. In general, products are based on hydraulics, electric power, electronic control, and sensor technologies. Sales and profits in millions of the four divisions over the last two years are as follows:

	1988		1987	
	Sales	Operating Income	Sales	Operating Income
Hydroforce	$124.8	$22.0	$101.2	$14.5
Transpower	36.5	6.7	26.8	4.1
Value Electrical	12.6	1.9	—	—
Energy Absorption Systems	3.2	−2.4	1.4	−1.2
General corporate expense		−3.0		−4.5
Other income (expense)		−3.5		−2.6
Total	$177.1	$21.7	$129.4	$10.1

Hydroforce

The Hydroforce division of Power Line includes three subdivisions: High Force Tools, Engineered Products, and Production Automation. Through Power Line's extensive international network, the High Force Tools line sells approximately 4,000 products worldwide to a broad range of industrial and construction markets. The Engineered Products line manufactures customized products designed to meet the individual requests of a variety of OEMs. The Production Automation line designs components and systems to meet specific needs for automating the setup of injection molding, metal forming, and metal cutting machines.

Most of Hydroforce's products are sold in North America through a network of industrial distributors. Hydroforce benefited from a market share in the U.S. in excess of 50 percent in fiscal 1988, but is looking to expand its current domestic customer base through product innovation and niche marketing.

In the 1988 Power Line annual report, management was "bullish" about Hydroforce's future prospects. When combined with other units in the company, and assuming "reasonable worldwide economic growth," they stated that sales should expand by 20 percent while maintaining a return on operating capital of 20 percent. (As measured by Power Line, the comparable return in 1988 was 19 percent.) Vehicles for improvement were said to be "new marketing thrusts, new products, continued attention to improve customer service and prudent management of operating expenses." If a major recession occurs, goals of steady sales and a 15 percent return were considered reasonable.

Transpower Hydraulics

The Transpower division of Power Line provides customized hydraulic products and systems for OEMs in the transportation, agricultural, and medical equipment industries.

Transpower manufactures three major products. First, 80 percent of Transpower sales come from its cab-tilt systems for cab-over-engine trucks, where it holds a 90 percent market share in the U.S. and Europe, and is looking for increased presence in Japan. Second, Transpower manufactures cab suspensions (sold to UPS and others), which improve driver comfort and reduce fatigue. Third, the division produces hydraulic actuator systems for automobile convertible tops in the U.S. and Europe.

Value Electrical

The Value Electrical division was integrated into Power Line as a result of an acquisition in February 1988. VE manufactures electrical consumable items, commodity tools, sophisticated benders, and other specialty tools. Customers include the electrical contractor, OEM, and do-it-yourself consumer markets.

When Value Electrical was integrated into Power Line, it brought an extensive manufacturers' representatives organization with it, which complemented Hydroforce's electrical tool line. This resulted in substantial volume growth. VE plans to use its representatives organization as a springboard for its products as well as selected other Power Line products by tapping the worldwide electrical construction and do-it-yourself markets.

Energy Absorption Systems

Energy Absorption Systems was created in 1986, and manufactures a variety of systems and components which control the hydraulic motion on mobile off-highway, municipal, and industrial equipment. Major products include joy-stick controls for rough terrain forklift equipment and automated flow controls for road spreaders.

RAYMOND BARRY'S BUSINESS

Raymond Barry's two major operating divisions are the Engineered Products Group and Stor-Rite. Engineered Products Group earned a pretax operating profit of $9.6 million on sales of $113 million and assets of $78 million in 1988. Operating profits stood at

$7.2 million in 1987, and $10.2 million in 1986. Stor-Rite lost $4.8 million in pretax operating profits on sales of $88 million and assets of $47 million during 1988. Operating profits were $7.9 million in 1987 and $3.1 million in 1986. (Operating profits are before interest, include non-interest other income, and exclude Barry's gain on restructuring.)

Engineered Products Group

The Engineered Products Group is a manufacturer of engineered components and systems to control vibration and other dynamic forces; it also makes specialized products which improve the efficiency, productivity, and safety of industrial equipment. Subdivisions of this group include Boston Controls, Palmer-Johnson, Line Automation, Allied Engineering, and Maximum Products.

Boston Controls designs, manufactures, and markets engineered components and systems for the control of dynamic forces and motions, which include vibration, shock, and structure-born noise. Its primary and customers include OEMs of machinery and equipment, manufacturers of aircraft, defense and aerospace contractors, and other consumers of industrial equipment who require noise or vibration control and reduction. Products are marketed internationally through a network of Barry's own sales engineers, independent sales engineering representatives, specialized distributors, foreign licensees, and joint ventures.

Palmer-Johnson designs, manufactures, and sells fiberoptic systems and related products. Major customers include OEMs and end users of robotics, factory automation, instrumentation, microscopy, and machine safety. Marketing is conducted internationally through distributors, representatives, and a joint venture.

The Line Automation division designs, manufactures, and sells robotic end-of-arm devices and intelligent sensor systems. In the U.S., products are directly marketed; independent distributors and representatives are used for foreign markets. A Line Automation unit being "incubated" inside Boston Controls' Smalltown, Massachusetts plant should eventually benefit from growing demand for robot end-effectors and similar products.

Allied Engineering engages in the design and manufacture of clamping, holding, positioning, and locating parts for manufacturing operations, and proprietary products for vibration and noise control in manufacturing facilities. The Maximum Products division produces mechanical variable-speed drives and accessories, couplings and linear actuators. Both Allied Engineering and Maximum Products sell to OEMs and end users in a variety of industries.

Stor-Rite Inc.

Stor-Rite Inc. manufactures and sells integrated filing systems for all types of records, documents, and data. The products include specialized filing systems, filing cabinets, filing devices, color-coded file folders, workstations, work surfaces, and accessories to improve all areas of office efficiency, including data processing, systems and programming, word processing, telecommunications, micrographic and individual workstation environments, and conventional paper applications. Primary customers include commercial and governmental end users; products are sold through Stor-Rite's field sales organization, which includes a small network of independent representatives in the secondary market throughout the U.S. as well as office product wholesalers and computer accessory catalog resellers. Stor-Rite also markets through wholly-owned subsidiaries in Canada, West Germany, Australia, and the United Kingdom; these subsidiaries are aided by sales representatives and dealers.

Stor-Rite's disappointing performance during 1988 was attributed in part to a three-month delay in the commencement of one U.S. government contract, and a four-month freeze on procurements at the Department of Defense. (U.S. government sales account for 25 percent of Stor-Rite's total sales.) By the fourth quarter of 1988, government sales recovered, but not to historical levels; commercial sales also declined during the year. Overall, sales were down 15 percent from the levels generated in 1987 and 1986.

Stor-Rite operations have now been placed under the control of the previous manager of its successful Canadian operations. The business is being refocused and will be more like the Canadian division, with a focus on integrated filing systems for the office and computer media and less emphasis on computer furniture. Barry's new President and CEO, John Walvoord, states that "even though we recognize that the full implementation of this new strategy will require additional time and resource allocation, we are convinced that the potential returns are well worth the effort, and we are optimistic about Stor-Rite's medium and long-term prospects."

QUESTIONS

1. Consider the advisability from the bank's perspective of financing Power Line's acquisition of Raymond Barry. How risky would this loan be? If a loan were granted, how might it be structured to contain the risks?

EXHIBIT 1

Summary Consolidated Financial Results for Power Line, Inc. and Raymond Barry Corporation

POWER LINE, INC.

($000,000)	Six Months Ended		Fiscal Year Ended		
	2/88	2/89	8/86	8/87	8/88
Income Statement Information (Continuing Operations Only)					
Net Sales	$ 78.8	$105.0	$113.0	$129.4	$177.1
Costs/Expenses	69.3	91.2	103.6	119.3	155.4
Net Profit	6.0	8.5	.8	6.5	14.5
Balance Sheet Information					
Current Assets	$ 77.2	$ 94.2	$ 79.4	$ 64.5	$ 81.0
Total Assets	148.1	164.0	100.6	102.1	149.7
Current Liabilities	45.8	61.5	39.7	32.4	48.8
Long Term Debt	31.1	23.9	12.1	5.4	26.0
Stockholders' Equity	64.5	73.4	43.2	57.0	70.0

RAYMOND BARRY CORPORATION

	Six Months Ended		Fiscal Year Ended		
	3/88	3/89	12/86	12/87	12/88
Income Statement Information					
Revenues	$ 55.7	$ 52.2	$198.3	$210.7	$203.7
Costs/Expenses	53.8	50.5	184.5	195.2	199.8
Net Profit	1.1	0.9	7.0	.4	1.3
Balance Sheet Information					
Current Assets	$ 83.0	$ 76.8	$ 74.2	$ 79.1	$ 76.3
Total Assets	140.0	129.2	133.1	137.9	130.9
Current Liabilities	28.4	36.0	0.8	26.9	42.3
Long Term Debt	4.4	33.9	1.4	.5	30.2
Stockholders' Equity	97.4	49.2	90.2	97.0	48.5

Exhibit 2   Power Line, Inc. – Excerpts from 1988 Annual Report

EXHIBIT 2

Power Line, Inc. – Excerpts from 1988 Annual Report

CONSOLIDATED INCOME STATEMENT
(In thousands of dollars)

	Fiscal Year Ended August 31,		
	1988	1987	1986
Net Sales	$177,054	$129,449	$113,039
Cost of Products Sold	–101,488	–72,892	–64,311
Gross Profit	75,566	56,557	48,728
Operating Expenses:			
Engineering	6,713	5,769	5,037
Selling and Administrative	43,709	38,039	34,433
Operating Profit	25,144	12,749	9,258
Other Expense:			
Interest Expense	3,701	3,700	2,982
Foreign Currency Exchange (Gains)	–249	–1,098	–3,121
Earnings before Taxes	21,692	10,147	9,397
Income Taxes	8,375	3,775	3,615
Equity Earnings	1,230	100	0
Earnings from Continuing Operations	14,547	6,472	5,782
Discontinued Operations:			
Net Income from Discontinued Operations	0	209	–1,777
Net Loss on Disposition	0	–8,300	0
Earnings from Discontinued Operations	0	–8,091	–1,777
Earnings (Loss) Before Extraordinary Items	14,547	–1,619	4,005
Extraordinary Items	650	0	0
Net Earnings (Loss)	15,197	–1,619	4,005
Primary EPS:			
Continuing Operations	$2.25	$1.27	$1.18
Discontinued Operations	0.00	–1.59	–0.39
Earnings Before Extraordinary Items	2.25	–0.32	0.79
Extraordinary Items	0.10	0.00	0.00
	2.35	–0.32	0.79

Exhibit 2 Power Line, Inc. – Excerpts from 1988 Annual Report

CONSOLIDATED BALANCE SHEETS
(In thousands of dollars)

	Fiscal Year Ended	
	8/31/88	8/31/87
ASSETS		
Current Assets:		
Cash & equivalents	$ 2,265	$ 7,335
Accounts receivable, net	37,530	30,125
Inventories	34,810	23,928
Prepaid expenses & income tax	6,380	3,134
Total Current Assets	80,985	64,522
Other Assets:		
Equity investments	11,788	10,733
Prepaid income taxes	0	1,596
Miscellaneous	4,293	6,034
Total Other Assets	16,081	18,363
Property, Plant & Equipment (cost):		
Land	1,596	1,648
Buildings	13,049	9,783
Machinery & Equipment	24,650	17,224
Less: Accumulated Depreciation	−12,769	−11,309
Net Property, Plant & Equipment	26,526	17,346
Intangible Assets:		
Excess cost over acquired assets	17,213	541
Other intangibles	8,889	1,352
Total Intangible Assets	26,102	1,893
Total Assets	$149,694	$102,124

p
482

Exhibit 2   Power Line, Inc. – Excerpts from 1988 Annual Report

	Fiscal Year Ended	
	8/31/88	8/31/87

LIABILITIES & OWNERS' EQUITY

Liabilities

Current Liabilities:

	8/31/88	8/31/87
Short term borrowing (unsecured):		
Bank loans	$ 8,918	$ 6,194
Commercial paper	10,076	3,561
Trade accounts payable	13,454	10,723
Payrolls, commissions & withholdings	6,269	4,979
Other accrued liabilities	5,700	5,832
Income taxes	4,208	1,005
Current maturities of long term debt	187	69
Total Current Liabilities	48,812	32,363
Long Term Debt	25,976	5,363
Deferred Liabilities & Credits	4,943	7,386
Total Liabilities	79,731	45,112

Owners' Equity

	8/31/88	8/31/87
Capital Stock:		
Class A (par $.20)	1,009	812
Class B (par $.20)	258	448
Additional Capital	22,305	22,115
Retained Earnings	45,986	32,040
Cumulative Translation Adjustment	942	1,888
Treasury Stock	–215	–291
Notes Receivable from Officer	–322	0
Total Owners' Equity	69,963	57,012
Total Liabilities & Owners' Equity	$149,694	$102,124

Exhibit 2   Power Line, Inc. – Excerpts from 1988 Annual Report

CONSOLIDATED STATEMENT OF CASH FLOWS
(In thousands of dollars)

	Fiscal Year		
	1988	1987	1986
Cash Flows from Operating Activities			
Cash received from customers	$173,329	$132,663	$117,646
Cash paid to suppliers and employees	−154,823	−116,792	−103,611
Net cash paid on forward exchange contracts	−510	−1,232	−178
Net cash flows from discontinued operations	0	2,149	−2,839
Interest paid	−3,344	−3,694	−3,039
Income taxes paid	−3,006	−2,986	−2,164
Net Cash Provided by Operating Activities	11,646	10,108	5,815
Cash Flows from Investing Activities			
Proceeds from the sale of fixed assets	1,210	1,102	433
Additions to fixed assets	−8,577	−6,697	−4,553
Cash used to purchase subsidiaries	−31,439	−1,883	−68
Dividends received from Kraft-Werke	275	0	0
Net Cash Used by Investing Activities	−38,531	−7,478	−4,188
Cash Flows from Financing Activities			
Net short-term borrowings (payment)	9,330	−3,853	840
Proceeds on issuance of long-term debt	30,750	0	10,400
Proceeds from IPO of stock	0	18,378	0
Other stock transactions	119	168	72
Principal payments on long-term debt	−16,800	−7,472	−11,492
Dividends paid	−1,232	−1,089	−967
Capital stock repurchased	−168	−8	−109
Preferred stock redemption	0	−3,924	0
Net Cash Provided by Financing Activities	21,999	2,200	−1,256
Effect of Exchange Rate Changes on Cash	−184	333	486
Net Increase (Decrease) in Cash & Equivalents	−5,070	5,163	857

p
484

Exhibit 2   Power Line, Inc. – Excerpts from 1988 Annual Report

SELECTED FOOTNOTES

Note 1. Summary of Accounting Policies

The consolidated financial statements include the accounts of the parent company and its subsidiaries. All intercompany balances, transactions and profits are eliminated in consolidation.

Inventories are stated at the lower of cost or market. Cost is determined using the last-in, first-out (LIFO) method for substantially all inventories in the United States (approximately 44% and 35% of total inventories in 1988 and 1987, respectively) and the first-in, first-out (FIFO) method for all other inventories. Inventories are comprised of material, direct labor and manufacturing overhead.

Depreciation is provided over the useful lives of plant and equipment using the straight line method for financial reporting purposes. Accelerated methods are used for deferred income taxes applicable to the difference in depreciation charges.

Excess of cost over net assets acquired (Goodwill) primarily arising from an acquisition (True Tools, Inc. – Note 2) is being amortized on a straight line basis over forty years.

Other intangibles (also primarily arising from the acquisition) are being amortized on a straight line basis over periods from three to twelve years.

The Company does not provide for income taxes which would become payable upon remission of earnings from outside the United States because it is management's intention to reinvest substantially all of these undistributed earnings.

Note 2. Acquisition

Effective February 1988, the Company acquired all of the outstanding common stock of True Tools, Inc. and related assets for cash of $31.44 million, including acquisition expenses. The acquisition was recorded using the purchase method of accounting. Of the total purchase price, approximately $15.25 million was assigned to the assets acquired, $9.36 million to liabilities assumed, $8.36 million to identified intangible assets and $16.92 million to the excess of cost over net assets acquired. Power incorporated True Tools into its Value Electrical division.

Note 3. Foreign Currency Translation

Prior to September 1, 1986, the Company had identified the U.S. dollar as the functional currency for all operations worldwide. Effective September 1, 1986 the Company changed the functional currency used as the basis for financial reporting of its operations outside the United States from the U.S. dollar to the applicable local currency.

Had the Company adopted local currency as its functional currency for FY 1986, earnings from continuing operations before income taxes would have been $5.1 million compared to $9.4 million, and earnings from continuing operations after income taxes would have been $2.3 million compared to $5.8 million.

Note 4. Inventories

Current replacement costs of inventories stated on the LIFO method were greater than the carry amounts by approximately $7.9 million and $7.5 million at August 31, 1988 and 1987, respectively.

Reductions of inventory quantities during the year ended 8/31/86 resulted in liquidations of LIFO inventory quantities carried at lower costs prevailing in prior years as compared

Exhibit 2   Power Line, Inc. – Excerpts from 1988 Annual Report

with the costs of FY 1986 purchases. The effect of this reduction was to increase earnings from continuing operations by $93,000 in FY 1986.

The disposition of the Hawk Automotive Division during 1987 resulted in the reduction of domestic inventory quantities causing the liquidation of LIFO inventories. This resulted in $1.53 million being credited to discontinued operations.

Note 5. Short Term Borrowing and Lines of Credit

The Company has various lines of credit with banks aggregating approximately $41 million. The amount of unused available borrowing under the various lines of credit was approximately $24 million at August 31, 1988.

Note 6. Long Term Debt

Aggregate maturities of term debt are:

1989	$ 187,000
1990	738,000
1991	15,119,000
1992	10,119,000

In 1988, the Company refinanced a majority of its outstanding long term debt by entering into a new revolving credit agreement with nine participating banks. The agreement provides for borrowing up to $55 million through December 22, 1990 and $30 million through December 22, 1991, of which $25 million was outstanding at August 31, 1988. Under the terms of the agreement, the loans may, at the Company's option, be either domestic dollar loans or Eurodollar loans or a combination thereof.

The credit agreement contains usual requirements and restrictions concerning liens on assets, sales of assets, borrowing and shareholders' equity. In addition, the credit agreement requires the Company to maintain certain ratios of total liabilities to shareholders' equity, cash flow from operations to current maturities on long term debt and earnings to interest charges.

Note 7. Shareholders' Equity

In August 1987, the Company completed a public offering including over 1.27 million shares of its Class A common stock. The net proceeds to the Company, aggregating $18.38 million, were used to reduce borrowing under the Company's revolving credit agreement, to retire 10% subordinated notes then outstanding and added to the general funds.

Note 8. Leases

The Company and its subsidiaries lease certain facilities, equipment and vehicles under various operating lease agreements over periods of one to eleven years.

Aggregate minimum rental obligations under operating leases with an initial term greater than one year during the next five fiscal years and after are: 1989—$2.471 million; 1990—$1.414 million; 1991—$898,000; 1992— $685,000; 1993 and after—$529,000.

Total rent expense under operating leases charged to continuing operations was $3.27 million, $2.98 million and $2.58 million in 1988, 1987, and 1986, respectively.

Exhibit 2   Power Line, Inc. – Excerpts from 1988 Annual Report

Note 9. Income Taxes

Following are the components of income taxes ($000):

	1988	1987	1986
Current			
Federal	$ 402	$ 946	$ 659
Foreign	5,125	2,562	1,569
State	203	60	27
Deferred			
Federal	$1,423	—	$1,310
Foreign	26	107	50
State	206	—	—
	$7,375	$3,675	$3,615
Tax expense attributable to equity investments	(100)	—	—
Extraordinary credit from tax loss carryforwards	650	—	—
Income tax benefits credited directly to equity	450	100	—
Income tax on earnings from continuing operations, exclusive of equity investments	$8,375	$3,775	$3,615

The Company has available tax credit carryforwards of approximately $2.2 million expiring in various years from 1991 to 2001.

Note 10. Discontinued Operations/Subsequent Events

In March 1987, the Company sold certain assets of its Hawk Automotive Division for an equity interest in Kraft-Werke, which it subsequently sold back to Kraft-Werke GmbH in April 1989.

Net sales and related income taxes of the discontinued operations amounted to $50,942,000 and ($2,175,000) in FY 1986 and $16,349,000 and $247,000 in FY 1987, respectively.

Note 11. Contingencies

In April 1988, the Ohio Department of Natural Resources found volatile organic compounds in residential wells near the Company's plant in Cleveland, Ohio. Since that time, the Company has underwritten the cost of drilling wells in a variety of locations in order to better understand the nature of the contamination and characterize the hydrology in the area. The resolution of this matter is ongoing and is expected to take some time. Based on tests completed to date, management does not believe that the resolution of this matter will have a material impact on the Company's financial position.

Exhibit 3   Raymond Barry Corporation – Excerpts from 1988 Annual Report

EXHIBIT 3
Raymond Barry Corporation – Excerpts from 1988 Annual Report

CONSOLIDATED BALANCE SHEETS
(In thousands of dollars)

	December 31,		
	1988	1987	1986
ASSETS			
Current Assets:			
Cash & short-term investments	$ 3,746	$ 12,961	$ 15,222
Accounts receivable, net	32,740	37,246	28,729
Inventories	25,928	23,487	25,485
Tax benefit of dividend to ESOP	4,316	0	0
Current deferred taxes	7,680	3,697	3,047
Other current assets	1,877	1,742	1,734
Total Current Assets	76,287	79,133	74,217
Property, Plant and Equipment, Net	40,396	43,955	45,411
Intangibles	10,019	11,066	10,135
Other Assets	4,163	3,742	3,352
Total Assets	$130,865	$137,896	$133,115
LIABILITIES & OWNERS' EQUITY			
Liabilities			
Current Liabilities:			
Notes payable	$ 0	$ 397	$ 4,215
Accounts payable	13,829	10,628	8,383
Accrued compensation & benefits	8,685	7,008	9,649
Other accrued liabilities	12,905	8,071	7,182
Income taxes payable	6,669	513	1,089
Current portion of long-term debt	205	235	235
Total Current Liabilities	42,293	26,852	30,753
Long-Term Debt	30,159	4,528	1,391
Deferred Income Taxes	8,605	8,513	7,839
Deferred Compensation	1,346	980	564
Minority Interest	0	0	2,330
Commitments and Contingencies	0	0	0
Total Liabilities	82,403	40,873	42,877

Exhibit 3   Raymond Barry Corporation – Excerpts from 1988 Annual Report

CONSOLIDATED BALANCE SHEETS (continued)

	December 31,		
	1988	1987	1986
Owners' Equity			
Preferred Stock	0	0	0
Common Stock (par value $1)	10,713	9,188	9,188
Additional Capital	46,461	20,961	21,223
Earnings Retained	4,216	82,649	79,227
Foreign Currency Translation Adjustments	3,961	3,259	1,377
Common Treasury Stock (at cost)	−16,889	−19,034	−20,777
Total Owners' Equity	48,462	97,023	90,238
Total Liabilities & Owners' Equity	$130,865	$137,896	$133,115

CONSOLIDATED INCOME STATEMENTS
(In thousands of dollars)

	1988	1987	1986
Revenues:			
Net sales	$201,682	$205,694	$195,142
Other income	2,062	5,045	3,157
	203,744	210,739	198,299
Costs and Expenses:			
Cost of sales	127,453	125,171	112,461
Selling, general and administrative expenses	70,884	69,538	70,924
Gain from restructuring	−2,405	0	0
Interest expense	3,824	538	1,083
	199,756	195,247	184,468
Earnings Before Income Taxes	3,988	15,492	13,831
Provision for income taxes	2,687	7,130	6,795
Net Earnings	$1,301	$8,362	$7,036

Exhibit 3   Raymond Barry Corporation – Excerpts from 1988 Annual Report

CONSOLIDATED STATEMENTS OF CASH FLOWS
(In thousands of dollars)

	1988	1987	1986
Operating Activities			
Net Earnings	$1,301	$8,362	$7,036
Adjustments to reconcile net income to net cash provided by operating activities:			
Depreciation of fixed assets	7,235	7,094	6,840
Employee benefit expense paid in stock	1,003	1,314	1,326
(Gain) loss on sale of fixed assets	699	−570	106
Decrease (increase) in accounts receivable	4,722	−7,565	3,124
Decrease (increase) in inventories	−2,291	2,671	482
Increase (decrease) in accounts payable and accrued expenses	17,015	−728	−259
Other – net	−2,833	355	−259
Net Cash Provided by Operating Activities	26,851	10,933	18,396
Investing Activities			
Additions to property, plant and equipment	−5,235	−7,008	−6,121
Proceeds from disposal of fixed assets	899	2,330	57
Other - net	173	−22	369
Net Cash Provided by Investing Activities	−4,163	−4,700	−5,695
Financing Activities			
Sale of common stock to ESOP	24,019	0	0
Borrowing on revolving facility and term loan	76,019	0	0
Other borrowings	0	3,160	1,563
Repayments on revolving facility and term loan	−50,019	0	0
Other debt repayments	−365	−3,642	−1,797
Net increase in foreign overdraft facility	−397	−902	−288
Cash dividends paid:			
Special	−78,486	0	0
Quarterly	−2,519	−4,893	−5,240
Purchase of treasury stock	−176	0	−22,323
Purchase of minority interest	0	−2,303	0
Exercise of stock options	8	22	123
Net Cash Provided by Financing Activities	−31,916	−8,558	−27,962
Net change in cash	−9,228	−2,325	−15,261

Exhibit 3   Raymond Barry Corporation – Excerpts from 1988 Annual Report

SELECTED NOTES TO 1988 FINANCIAL STATEMENTS

1. Selected accounting policies

Inventory is accounted for using the LIFO method at Stor-Rite and for certain inventories at Engineered Products; in total, these account for approximately two-thirds of the Company's inventory. Remaining inventories are accounted for using the FIFO method. If all inventories were accounted for at FIFO cost, they would have been $6.5 million and $5.7 million higher than reported for 1988 and 1987, respectively. A liquidation of inventory carried at LIFO cost at Stor-Rite caused cost of sales to be lower than it would have been, based on currently prevailing prices; the effect was to increase net income by $0.5 million.

Property, plant, and equipment is depreciated using the straight-line method.

Income taxes are based upon earnings reported for financial reporting purposes. Deferred income taxes result from timing differences in the recognition of revenues and expenses for tax and financial reporting purposes. Excluding a 1988 tax benefit from the tax-deductible payment of dividends to the Company's ESOP, taxes currently due were $6.6 million and $7.8 million in 1988 and 1987, respectively. Deferred taxes, related principally to methods of accounting for depreciation, inventory, and accruals, caused tax expense to be lower than these amounts by $3.9 million and $0.6 million in 1988 and 1987. Thus, income tax expense was $2.7 million and $7.1 million in 1988 and 1987. The Company's effective tax rate in 1988 (67 percent) exceeded the U.S. statutory rate (34 percent) as the result of nondeductible expenses including excise tax on pension plan reversion (16 percent), state income taxes (8 percent), foreign taxes (7 percent), and other effects (2 percent).

2. Restructuring of operations

During 1988, the Company (1) entered into a new Credit Agreement; (2) terminated its domestic pension plan; (3) created, funded, and sold 1.5 million shares to a new Employee Stock Option Plan (ESOP); and (4) paid a special dividend of $8/share.

The ESOP was established with a loan from the Company in the amount of $24 million. With these funds, the ESOP purchased from the Company 1.5 million newly issued shares at $15.75 per share. The loan to the ESOP was subsequently repaid from the proceeds of the ESOP's share of the special dividend and a portion of the proceeds from the termination of the pension plan.

The pension plan terminated in 1988 included $27 million of funds in excess of amounts necessary to settle accrued benefits. Of this amount, $11.4 million reverted to the ESOP plan, and $15.4 million remained as a gain before income taxes. When reduced by excise taxes and other restructuring costs, including legal fees and severance pay, the termination generated a gain before income taxes of 2.4 million, and an after-tax gain of $0.8 million. Benefits accrued under the terminated pension plan were satisfied in full through the purchase of annuity contracts and lump sum cash payments.

The special dividend required cash of $78.5 million, which was financed with borrowings of $46 million under the Credit Agreement, cash on hand, and proceeds from the sale of shares to the ESOP.

The Credit Agreement is a $68 million revolving credit facility, reduced quarterly to $29 million by January 1, 1993. The interest rate is the bank's prime rate plus 1.5 percent. Since the Credit Agreement assumed completion of the entire plan of restructuring, including the sale of Stor-Rite that was never consummated, the agreement must be modified, and the credit line reduced. Discussions with lenders have begun.

Exhibit 4   Power Line, Inc. – Company-Prepared Financial Projections

EXHIBIT 4
Power Line, Inc. – Company-Prepared Financial Projections

ASSUMPTIONS

Projections for Power Line are based on the following assumptions provided by management:

- 1989 fiscal year-end financials combine Power Line's projected August 31, 1989 results with Raymond Barry's December 31, 1988 year-end results.

- Raymond Barry's Stor-Rite performs at breakeven during 1990 and 1991 and then is sold at year-end 1991 for $40 million. The gain on the sale is $24.71 million.

- Sales growth for the merged companies ranges from 11.5 percent to 13.3 percent during the years 1990–1994. The exception is 1992, when the effects of the 1991 sale of Stor-Rite Inc. cause sales to decrease 8.1 percent.

- Individually, sales growth attributable to Power Line's pre-merger businesses is projected to be 17 percent in 1990, 14 percent in both 1991 and 1992, 15 percent in 1993, and 14 percent in 1994. This compares with 24 percent expected in 1989 and 36 percent in 1988. For Raymond Barry, sales growth is projected to be 0 percent in 1990, 8 percent in 1991, 36 percent in 1992, and 10 percent in both 1993 and 1994. This compares with projected flat sales in 1989 after a 3 percent decline in 1988, which resulted from the loss of certain government sales.

- Cost of Goods Sold as a percentage of sales ranges from 60 percent to 60.9 percent during the years 1990–1994.

- SG&A Expense grows 3.4 percent in 1990 and 1991, declines 22.6 percent in 1992 due to the Stor-Rite Inc. divestiture, and increases 6.1 percent and 6.2 percent in 1993 and 1994, respectively.

- Other Operating Income derived from lease revenue Raymond Barry is receiving from unrelated parties is $1.5 million in 1990, $1.7 million in 1991, $1.9 million in 1992, $2.1 million 1993, and $2.0 million in 1994.

- The tax rate is 40 percent.

- Common Dividends of $0.12 per share, or $1.6 million, will be paid each year from 1990 to 1994.

- Capital Expenditures will be $13 million in 1990, $11.5 million in 1991, $14 million in 1992, and $15 million in both 1993 and 1994.

- Working capital accounts as a percentage of sales are not expected to fluctuate and will remain at historical levels.

- $31 million of long-term debt is incurred in 1990 in order to finance increases in working capital and to refinance $20.3 million in notes payable.

Exhibit 4   Power Line, Inc. – Company-Prepared Financial Projections

PRO FORMA BALANCE SHEET FOR POWER LINE/RAYMOND BARRY CORP.
(In thousands of dollars)

	Fiscal Year Ending August 31,					
	1989	1990	1991	1992	1993	1994
Cash & Marketable Securities	$ 6,000	$ 6,000	$ 6,000	$ 6,000	$ 15,805	$ 89,448
Accounts Receivable	79,517	87,535	86,884	96,550	112,712	125,287
Inventories	63,876	70,874	68,405	74,672	85,094	97,569
Other Current Assets	14,542	14,542	13,001	13,001	13,001	13,001
Total Current Assets	163,935	178,951	174,290	190,223	226,612	325,305
Net Plant & Equipment	66,977	69,053	54,048	56,582	58,992	60,124
Land	2,346	2,346	1,781	1,781	1,781	1,781
Goodwill	83,391	81,311	79,231	77,152	75,072	72,992
Other Intangibles	17,317	15,932	12,058	10,706	9,354	8,002
Other Assets	13,816	13,816	13,016	13,016	13,016	13,016
Total Assets	$347,782	$361,409	$334,424	$349,460	$384,827	$481,220
Accounts Payable & Accruals	$59,489	$67,950	$60,792	$69,401	$78,606	$87,666
Other	12,599	0	0	0	0	0
Income Taxes Payable	12,823	9,243	16,935	18,147	23,772	29,542
Total Current Liabilities	84,911	77,193	77,727	87,548	102,378	117,208
L-T Debt	164,149	164,448	87,491	44,205	0	0
Deferred Income Taxes	2,463	3,309	385	1,708	3,334	5,284
Other Deferrals	4,808	4,808	4,808	4,808	4,808	4,808
Total Liabilities	256,331	249,758	170,411	138,269	110,520	127,300
Total Equity	91,451	111,651	164,013	211,191	274,307	353,920
Total Liabilities and Equity	$347,782	$361,409	$334,424	$349,460	$384,827	$481,220

Exhibit 4   Power Line, Inc. – Company-Prepared Financial Projections

PRO FORMA INCOME STATEMENT FOR POWER LINE/RAYMOND BARRY CORP.
(In thousands of dollars)

Fiscal Year Ending August 31,

	1989	1990	1991	1992	1993	1994
Sales	$424,100	$478,792	$533,729	$490,400	$555,442	$626,589
Cost of Goods Sold	255,050	291,584	323,973	295,711	333,265	375,953
Gross Profit	169,050	187,208	209,756	194,689	222,177	250,636
SG&A Expense	124,000	128,316	132,898	102,494	108,867	115,919
Other Operating Income	1,300	1,500	1,700	1,900	2,100	2,000
Amortization of Goodwill/Intangibles	1,692	3,357	3,357	3,357	3,357	3,357
Operating Profit	44,658	57,035	75,201	90,738	112,053	133,360
Interest Expense (Income)	6,886	18,500	15,116	7,243	1,990	-4,196
Other Expense	127	0	0	0	0	0
Gain on Sale – Kraft-Werke & Stor-Rite	6,218	0	24,710	0	0	0
Earnings Before Taxes	43,863	38,535	84,795	83,495	110,063	137,556
Provision for Income Taxes	19,200	16,756	30,853	34,741	45,368	56,365
Equity in Kraft-Werke	1,425	0	0	0	0	0
Net Income	$26,088	$21,779	$53,942	$48,754	$64,695	$81,191
Common Dividends	$1,578	$1,578	$1,578	$1,578	$1,578	$1,578

PRO FORMA FUNDS FLOW STATEMENT FOR POWER LINE/RAYMOND BARRY CORP.

Exhibit 4 Power Line, Inc. – Company-Prepared Financial Projections

Fiscal Year Ending August 31,

	1989	1990	1991	1992	1993	1994
Net Income	$26,088	$21,779	$53,942	$48,754	$64,695	$81,191
Depreciation Expense	13,037	10,924	11,216	11,467	12,589	13,868
Amortization of Intangibles	1,692	3,357	3,357	3,357	3,357	3,357
Other Noncash Items	−8,232	−847	−27,634	1,323	1,626	1,950
	32,585	35,213	40,881	64,901	82,267	100,366
Increase in Debt	105,213	−12,300	−76,957	−43,286	−44,205	0
Increase in Accounts Receivable	9,247	8,018	−652	9,666	16,162	12,574
Increase in Inventories	3,138	6,998	−2,469	6,267	10,422	12,475
Increase in Other Current Assets	8,372	0	−1,541	0	9,805	73,643
Increase in Accounts Payable	−1,353	8,461	−7,158	8,609	9,205	9,060
Increase in Other Current Liabilities	1,946	−3,580	7,692	1,212	5,625	5,770
Total Sources of Funds	117,634	12,778	−30,880	15,503	16,503	16,504
Fixed Capital Investment	15,192	13,000	11,500	14,000	15,000	15,000
Other	−1,204	−1,800	−3,958	−75	−75	−74
Proceeds of Kraft-Werke & Star-Rite	−13,213	0	−40,000	0	0	0
Acquisition of Raymond Barry	115,281	0	0	0	0	0
Common Dividends	1,578	1,578	1,578	1,578	1,578	1,578
Total Uses of Funds	$117,634	$12,778	$(30,880)	$15,503	$16,503	$16,504

Ⅰt is late 1986, and within the month Revco will undergo a leveraged buyout. As an analyst for a large high-yield bond fund, Jacqueline Walker is engaged in an analysis of Revco's situation. On the surface, Revco appears to offer the type of debt security Walker's fund is currently looking for: yields in the 12 to 14 percent range on intermediate maturities, with risks that are significant but manageable. However, she hopes to offer a more complete assessment after further investigation. She intends to produce some forecasts of cash flows and earnings, along with sensitivity analyses, that can be used to help assess the probability that Revco could face difficulty meeting obligations to debtors after the buyout. If the fund takes a position in the debt, it would also be useful to have earnings forecasts to benchmark the subsequent performance of Revco, as reports are released.

At this time, financial reports are available from Revco through the quarter ended August 23, 1986, and a variety of information is also available from the prospectus for the LBO securities and the firm's proxy statement issued prior to the vote on the buyout. Earnings for the quarter ended November 16, 1986 have not yet been announced, but Walker, like others following the firm, is aware that EPS is likely to be in the range of $.25 to $.35 per share. (Details underlying that estimate are not yet available.) Walker plans to contact a representative from the CFO's office, but only after she uses her initial analysis to frame the questions of highest priority.

COMPANY BACKGROUND

Revco is the nation's largest discount drugstore chain, operating 2,049 stores in 30 states at August 23, 1986. The stores sell not only prescription and over-the-counter drugs, but also health and beauty aids, toiletries, vitamins, tobacco products, sundries, and a broad line of other products. Since 1984, Revco has also operated a chain of "deep-discount" retail stores (Odd Lot Stores), that specialize in low-priced promotional goods, manufacturers' overruns, and close-out merchandise.

Earnings and sales for Revco grew steadily through 1984. However, earnings for the years ended in May 1985 and May 1986 failed to reach the earlier levels. At least part

This case, which is based upon publicly available information, was prepared by Professor Victor L. Bernard as a basis for class discussion and is not intended to illustrate either an effective or ineffective management of a business situation. Selected information is based on published materials that are not disclosed in the case for pedagogical reasons.

of the difficulty concerns the operations of Odd Lot, which suffered operating losses in 1985 and 1986. The difficulties of the last two years, in conjunction with the accompanying management turmoil, have led to the leveraged buyout. Revco Chairman and CEO Sidney Dworkin believes an LBO offers the best prospect for him to guide the company successfully through the currently trying times.

DRUGSTORE INDUSTRY CONDITIONS

The drugstore industry includes both small, independently owned pharmacies and chain stores. The former compete largely on the basis of personalized service, while the latter focus on price competition and an offering of a wide variety of general merchandise. Increasingly, the cost efficiencies of the major chains—Revco, Eckerd, Walgreen, Fays, Genovese, Perry, Rite Aid, and others—have permitted them to dominate. As a group, these chains have been steadily profitable for a number of years. Between 1974 and 1984, Revco's peers (the six chains mentioned above other than Revco) produced a combined margin—EBIT/sales—that was between 4.2 percent and 6.0 percent, with an average of about 5.2 percent. Of course, individual company margins have been more variable than the overall industry margin, with a standard deviation of about 1.3 percent. When margins in the 5 percent range are combined with the high asset turnover for these firms—typically between 2.5 and 3—the average pretax return on assets has been a respectable 14 to 15 percent. Moreover, although earnings did fall during the recession of the mid-1970s and early 1980s, the decline was quite moderate relative to most industries.

As the industry moved through the mid-1980s, pressures on earnings mounted and the industry experienced a substantial amount of consolidation and restructuring. The six-chain Revco peer group experienced a decline in margin from 6 percent in 1984 to less than 5 percent in 1986. Pharmacies found themselves in direct competition with health maintenance organizations, and they faced constraints on third-party reimbursement of drug costs. In the major population centers, drugstore chains opened a number of "deep discount stores," and other retailers—including food stores and mass merchandisers—opened pharmacies on their premises. A number of "combo" stores were created that paired grocery stores and drugstores and offered customers both low prices and convenient, one-stop shopping. By 1986, the intense competition had driven some to exit the deep discount end of the market, but overall, growth continued.

Restructuring in the industry arose in the form of a number of leveraged buyouts. In some cases (e.g., Jack Eckerd Corp.), managers and other private investors combined to take the firms private. Other buyouts involved takeovers. For example, K-Mart bought Payless Drugstores, while Kroger Co. acquired Hook Drugs. Information about the major takeover buyouts of the mid-1980s, including prior profitability of the chains involved, is as follows:

Firm and Fiscal Year Preceding Buyout	Sales in Year Prior to Buyout (millions)	EBIT/Sales		Sales Turnover		Buyout Value, as Multiple of:	
		Prior Year	Two Prior Years	Prior Year	Two Prior Years	Sales	EBIT
Jack Eckerd Corp.–1985	$2,508	.052	.076	2.3	2.3	.55	10.6
Thrifty Corp.–1985	1,405	.052	.051	3.0	3.0	.75	14.3
Hook Drugs, Inc.–1984	351	.048	.054	3.6	3.6	.50	10.4
Payless Drug Stores – 1984	855	.068	.061	2.5	2.5	.70	10.1

BUSINESS AT REVCO

Revco's major focus—75 percent of sales—is on "necessity items" such as drugs, health and beauty aids, and toiletries; management believes this focus helps protect them from downturns in the economy. Prescription drugs, which generate margins much higher than other products at Revco, accounted for 31 percent of total Drugstore division sales in 1986, up slightly from 1984 and 1985. Revco believes its prescription drugs constitute a higher fraction of sales than all other chains in the industry.

Revco was a pioneer in discount merchandising, advertising its "everyday low prices" strategy—that is, prices always below manufacturers' suggested retail prices and very few "special sales"—as early as the 1950s. Revco was also among the first to offer seven-day shopping, with stores open 12 hours Monday through Saturday and 8 hours on Sunday. Aside from competition on price and convenience, Revco's stated competitive strategy involves careful attention to location. Revco drugstores are small to medium sized by current industry standards, and are typically located in strip shopping centers in cities with populations of 25,000 or less. Most of these are in the Midwest, Southwest, and Southeast. Revco believes its prime locations in smaller markets tend to protect it from the competition of the deep discount stores, which require a large population center to support profitable operations.

Although Revco is a relatively old drugstore chain, having begun operations in 1956, 75 percent of its stores are either new or have been expanded and/or remodeled within the last five years. As the result of new store openings, acquisitions, and closures, the Revco chain has grown from 1,514 stores at the end of fiscal 1981 to its current size of 2,049 stores.

During fiscal 1986, more than 130 new stores were opened. The cost of opening a new store (including inventory and fixtures) averages about $300,000. Plans for further expansion are in place, with approximately 100 stores to be opened in each of the next five years. Details of Revco's growth follow.

r

499

Revco D.S., Inc.

Fiscal Year Ended May 31	Number of Stores	Gross Retail Square Footage (in 000s)	Increase in Gross Square Footage
1981	1,514	11,448	—
1982	1,593	12,227	7%
1983	1,661	12,849	5%
1984	1,778	13,909	8%
1985	1,898	15,148	9%
1986	2,031	16,694	10%
8/23/86	2,049	16,900	1%

While adding new stores, Revco also reviews existing operations and divests itself of underperforming stores. Prior to 1985 such divestitures were rare, but during 1985 and 1986 a total of 69 stores were closed; approximately 100 stores are scheduled to be closed in the near future.

In late fiscal 1985, Revco began to experiment with a price-reduction program on non-prescription goods, which reduced gross margins. The anticipated increases in sales volume were not forthcoming, and Revco abandoned the program in mid-fiscal 1986.

Acquisition of Odd Lot Stores

Revco entered the field of merchandising close-out goods at the end of fiscal 1984 with its acquisition of Odd Lot for $113 million. Odd Lot acquires merchandise through manufacturers who have discontinued a product line or for other reasons wish to dispose of a large supply of inventory, wholesalers or manufacturers who have terminated business, and other channels. The merchandise consists of housewares, toys, stationery, snacks, gifts, health and beauty aids, and various other items. Odd Lot then sells these items in its 153 stores in the Midwest and Northeast at prices substantially below normal retail. Odd Lot faces competition from about 500 stores operated by 25 chains throughout the nation.

Since its acquisition, Odd Lot has provided about 5 percent of Revco sales. However, it has been a major drag on profits. In 1985, Odd Lot suffered a $53 million pre-tax loss, including a $35 million inventory writedown. In 1986, Odd Lot posted a pre-tax loss of $15.5 million. During the first quarter of fiscal 1987, Odd Lot again generated a loss, this time in the amount of $2.2 million.

Revco's 1986 Status and Projections for Future

Revco's recent performance has been mixed. Operating margins (EBIT/sales) fell to 3.4 percent and 4.7 percent for 1985 and 1986, respectively, with EPS coming in at $1.06 and $1.54. However, there were some signs that Revco would improve in fiscal 1987.

The last half of fiscal 1986 was relatively strong, with an EPS of $1.24 per share, as compared to $.32 in the last half of fiscal 1985 and $.44 in the first half of 1986. The improvement reflected improved margins after the abandonment of the experimental price reduction program, and gains in pharmacy sales. However, the first quarter of fiscal 1987 was weak (EPS of $.20), as sales softened throughout the industry and problems at Odd Lot continued. Revco's recent history of sales, earnings, and EPS is shown below.

Revco Quarterly Sales, Earnings, and Related Data: 1980–1986 and First Quarter of 1987

Sales (millions)

Quarter Ended	1980	1981	1982	1983	1984	1985	1986	1987
August	$228	$269	$332	$379	$453	$511	$586	$628
November	240	279	341	392	481	527	602	
February	272	321	383	439	571	605	708	
May	353	441	499	583	723	753	848	
Annual sales	$1,093	$1,310	$1,555	$1,793	$2,228	$2,396	$2,744	

Earnings (millions) and Related Data

Quarter Ended	1980	1981	1982	1983	1984	1985	1986	1987
August	$7.63	$9.14	$9.82	$11.97	$16.42	$15.30	$9.29	$6.39
November	8.06	9.54	10.20	12.68	18.32	10.36	5.53	
February	10.32	12.09	12.47	16.07	28.29	16.35	19.66	
May	12.90	14.35	17.16	25.75	30.38	–3.10	22.46	
Annual earnings	$38.91	$45.12	$49.65	$66.47	$93.41	$38.91	$56.94	
Annual EBIT	73.05	85.32	97.52	129.50	177.58	81.13	$128.16	
EBIT/Sales	.067	.065	.063	.072	.080	.034	.047	
Pretax ROA	.215	.209	.203	.228	.254	.098	.138	
ROE	.196	.194	.186	.201	.228	.086	.134	

Earnings per Share

Quarter Ended	1980	1981	1982	1983	1984	1985	1986	1987
August	.25	.30	.32	$.39	$.44	$.42	$.27	$.20
November	.26	.31	.33	.41	.50	.28	.17	
February	.34	.39	.41	.52	.77	.44	.60	
May	.42	.47	.56	.81	.83	–.08	.68	
Annual EPS	$1.28	$1.47	$1.61	$2.13	$2.54	$1.06	$1.72	

Looking ahead, *Value Line*'s Jerome Kaplan is forecasting EPS for fiscal 1987 of $1.90, on sales of $3 billion. Kaplan's quarterly forecasts of EPS are $.25, $.75, and $.70 for the second, third, and fourth quarters, respectively. He is more optimistic long-term, projecting that sales will rise to $4,150 million by 1990, with earnings of $115 million,

Revco D.S., Inc.

or $3.55 per share. These forecasts ignore the effects of higher interest from LBO debt, changes in the number of shares outstanding, and presumably some other LBO impacts; it is unclear to what extent Kaplan is already factoring in some efficiency improvements discussed in the LBO proposal. He also has not considered the impact of the Tax Reform Act of 1986, which would reduce federal corporate income tax rates for Revco from 46 percent in 1986 to about 40 percent in fiscal 1987, and 34 percent thereafter.

Revco management does not typically make public projections of sales or earnings, but they did so in the 1986 proxy statement used to inform shareholders prior to the vote on the LBO. The projections given below are the same shown to prospective investors and lenders; they were prepared by Revco management and were not subject to review or approval by any other parties. Managers assumed an annual increase in net sales of 12 percent and a profit before interest, taxes, and depreciation of 7.7 percent for 1988 through 1991. The projected sales growth assumes that sales will increase at existing stores, and that new stores will be added at a rate that would add 10 percent to retail space each year.

Projected Consolidated Financial Data of Revco

(dollars in thousands, except per share data)	Fiscal Year Ending in				
	1987	1988	1989	1990	1991
Net sales	$3,017,181	$3,379,243	$3,784,752	$4,238,922	$4,747,593
Operating profit before depreciation	207,579	260,202	291,426	326,397	365,565
Depreciation	36,505	38,505	40,505	42,505	44,505
Net interest expense	31,691	30,700	27,900	27,500	26,200
Earnings before income taxes	139,383	190,997	223,021	256,392	294,860
Income taxes	66,555	87,858	102,590	117,940	135,636
Net earnings	$ 72,828	$ 103,139	$ 120,431	$ 138,452	$ 159,224
Average shares outstanding	32,500,000	32,626,000	32,706,000	32,796,000	32,906,000
Per common share:					
Net earnings	$2.24	$3.16	$3.68	$4.22	$4.84
Cash dividends	$ .80	$ .80	$ .80	$ .80	$ .80

The projections are not intended to reflect certain factors. Most important, they do not include the impact of LBO financing, LBO-related divestitures, or any adjustments to accounts that would be required at the time of the LBO. They also ignore the impact of the Tax Reform Act of 1986.

THE LEVERAGED BUYOUT PROPOSAL

Revco's difficulties of the last two years have been accompanied by some turmoil among internal management, and between managers and dissident shareholders. By March of 1986, a group of insiders led by Chairman Sidney Dworkin and President William Edwards began discussions about the possibility of a leveraged buyout. An initial offer of $33 per share was rejected by a committee representing outside shareholders, but an offer of $38.50 a share was subsequently approved. The buyout is scheduled to become effective on December 29, 1986.

Events Leading Up to the LBO

Although Revco is a publicly traded company, with only 3 percent of the stock in the hands of CEO Sidney Dworkin, the firm is widely recognized as one that operates as a family business. Dworkin, a Wayne State University graduate with a degree in accounting, had started with the company's predecessor, Regal D.S., Inc., in 1956. By the mid 1960s, the fast-growing company had gone public as Revco, and Dworkin had become its CEO.

Dworkin's sons were both employed by Revco. Marc Dworkin joined the firm in 1968, at age 22, and eventually become executive vice-president for marketing. Elliot Dworkin joined the firm in 1972, at age 23, and later became vice-president of purchasing.

Although Revco grew quickly and became the nation's largest drugstore chain, Sidney Dworkin was criticized for nepotism. There was further criticism in 1983, when Revco was sued for the deaths of 38 infants, allegedly caused by vitamins produced and sold by one of Revco's subsidiaries.

During 1984, in an effort to defend the firm against potential acquirers, Dworkin merged Revco with Odd Lot Stores, Inc. Odd Lot was owned by close friends of Dworkin, Bernard Marden and Isaac Perlmutter. The merger placed 12 percent of Revco's shares in those friendly hands. However, within weeks of the consummation of the merger, Marden and Perlmutter began to complain that Sidney and Elliot Dworkin were mismanaging Odd Lot. Ultimately, Revco bought out Marden and Perlmutter in an effort to settle the conflict.

In the meantime, as losses at Odd Lot continued to mount, so did criticism of Dworkin. The Revco board forced Dworkin to hire Edwards, a man who had rejuvenated a small Detroit drugstore chain, as its new president and COO. Local investment banker Glenn Golenberg convinced Dworkin that the best strategy for re-establishing control was to take the firm private. A plan to do so was arranged, with a large portion of equity financing for the LBO contributed by Salomon Brothers and an outside investment group, Transcontinental Corporation.

Revco D.S., Inc.

Planned Improvements in Operations

In the buyout proposal, Revco management listed a number of reasons to expect that profitability in the future would be stronger than in 1985 and 1986. Expected sources of improvement are as follows:

1. *Divestiture program.* Revco states that it is determined to divest itself of substantially all operations other than drugstores and Odd Lot. These include several distribution centers and other real property that could be sold (or sold and leased back). In addition, approximately 100 drugstores will be sold. The operations subject to divestiture generated sales of $250 million during fiscal 1986, and EBITDA of $24 million. Book value of the operations was $176 million.

    Sales under the plan are projected to generate after-tax proceeds of $255 million, all of which would be used to pay down LBO debt. The bank LBO covenants require that Revco "use its best efforts" to dispose of assets other than inventory that will yield net proceeds of at least $255 million by the second quarter of fiscal 1989.

2. *Expansion plan.* Approximately 100 new stores will be opened each year for the next five years, primarily in smaller cities.

3. *Reduced capital expenditures.* In light of the recent remodeling of many of Revco's stores, management expects to operate effectively with capital expenditures of not more than $37.5 million in fiscal 1987—a constraint imposed as a covenant in the LBO bank debt. Beyond 1987, and until the debt is retired in 1992, the covenant states that capital expenditures will not exceed $30 million, or a smaller amount (depending on the level of earnings before interest and depreciation). Capital expenditures in 1986 were $95 million.

4. *Inventory and selling expense reduction programs.* Revco already has begun efforts to reduce inventory and selling expenses. It expects a return to inventory-to-sales ratios consistent with historical experience, and projects a resulting $75 million reduction in inventory by the end of fiscal 1987, relative to what would otherwise exist. Selling, general, and administrative expenses are expected to be $24 million lower in fiscal 1987 than otherwise would have existed.

    The covenants of the LBO bank debt require that the ratio of inventory to sales be held below 20 percent at interim quarters, and below 17 percent at the end of each fiscal year.

5. *Resolution of Odd Lot controversy.* In an effort to end controversy over the management of Odd Lot, Revco repurchased the shares of Odd Lot's previous owners (Marden and Perlmutter) in July 1985 for $22.50.[1] Revco management expects that resolution of the Odd Lot controversy will improve operations, as it will no longer be necessary to divert senior management time and energy to the dispute with Marden and Perlmutter.

---

1. Marden and Perlmutter subsequently sued, claiming that Revco and Dworkin had intentionally depressed the earnings of Revco to lower the price. The plaintiffs sought to enjoin Revco from consummating the buyout and also requested compensation for damages. A request for a preliminary injunction was denied in early December 1986, and Revco believes the complaints are without merit.

504

The covenants of the LBO bank debt require that if in any year Odd Lot does not generate EBIT in excess of 5 percent of its total assets, it must be sold within six months.

Financial Structure of the Buyout Proposal

The LBO will involve $1.449 billion of financing, as described below. Most of this ($1.253 billion) will be used to buy the outstanding shares of Revco, excluding treasury stock, at a price of $38.50 per share. An additional $117 million will be used to retire existing debt with average interest rates of 10 percent, and $78 million will cover fees and expenses in connection with underwriting newly issued securities, structuring the deal, and so forth.

The proceeds to finance the $1.449 billion LBO derive from the following sources:

1. *$11 million cash from Revco.*
2. *$455 million bank term loan.* Interest rate of 2.75% over LIBOR, which now stands at 6.5%. The bank debt is to be retired periodically, with annual payments scheduled as follows:

Fiscal Year	Scheduled Payments (millions)	Remaining Principal (millions)
1987	$45.0	$410.0
1988	142.5	267.5
1989	117.5	150.0
1990	50.0	100.0
1991	60.0	40.0
1992	40.0	0.0

After taking into account the scheduled payments of principal on the bank term loan, interest expense on the loan is expected to be $18 million during the remaining five months of fiscal 1987, and $34 million during fiscal 1988.

3. *$834 million issue of securities to public*, consisting of:
   - $400 million senior subordinated notes. Interest rate 13.125%, due 1994.
   - $210 million subordinated notes. Interest rate 13.30%, due 1996.
   - $94 million junior subordinated notes. Interest rate 13.30%, due in annual payments of $19 million commencing 1997. Each $1,000 note issued in conjunction with 4 shares of common stock and 4 common stock puts.
   - $130 million cumulative preferred stock. Dividend rate 15.25%.
4. *$85 million convertible preferred stock.* To be acquired by New York Life, Morgan Guaranty, and others; dividend 12%. Each $39 of preferred stock can be converted into one share of common.
5. *$30 million junior preferred stock.* To be acquired by Transcontinental (a consortium of outside investors) and Salomon Brothers. Dividend rate 17.6%.

6. *$34.3 million common stock.* The holders of the new common stock, after the LBO, will be:

Management (primarily Sidney Dworkin and William Edwards)	$10.2 million
Transcontinental	18.9
Salomon Brothers	4.8
Golenberg and Co	0.5
Total	$34.3

Management's ownership share will increase significantly from its current 3 percent. Even including common stock issued in conjunction with junior subordinated notes and assuming conversion of preferred stock into common stock, management would still have a 19.5 percent stake in the post-LBO company. However, in terms of wealth invested, managers' ownership will be reduced. Management's current 3 percent interest in the stock is worth roughly $41 million, based on the buyout price of $38.50. Of this amount, $10.2 million will be invested in the buyout of Revco ($1.6 million from Sidney Dworkin).

Accounting and Tax Implications of the Buyout Proposal

When the buyout occurs, the book values of all assets will be adjusted to reflect current value, using the same purchase accounting used when acquisitions take place. As a result, several assets will be written up: inventory, plant and other long-lived tangible assets, and (primarily) goodwill. Revco's prospectus for the LBO financing indicates that if the associated writeups had been made retroactively, depreciation and amortization would have been higher by $35.4 million in 1986, and by $8.2 million in the first quarter of fiscal 1987. However, for tax purposes, the transaction is considered nontaxable to the corporation: there is to be no writeup of corporate assets, and therefore no adjustment to deductible expenses.

Other relevant Revco financial information is given in Exhibits 1 and 2.

QUESTIONS

1. Analyze Revco's profitability for 1986. How strong does profitability in the Drugstore division appear to be, relative to competitors? Does Revco appear to have a competitive advantage in that line of business? What is your assessment of Revco's prospects for future profitability?
2. Jacqueline Walker has at her disposal a pre-LBO management projection and a pre-LBO analyst forecast. Discuss how much emphasis she should place on this information as she proceeds with her analysis.
3. Forecast sales and earnings for fiscal 1987 and fiscal 1988.
4. Forecast cash from operations for fiscal 1987 and fiscal 1988.
5. How much "margin for error" is in the Revco LBO? That is, how much could cash flows fall from your forecasted level before Revco would default on its debt payments?

EXHIBIT 1
Excerpts from Revco D.S. Audited Financial Statements for Year Ended May 31, 1986

CONSOLIDATED BALANCE SHEETS

(Dollars in Thousands)	May 31, 1986	June 1, 1985
ASSETS		
Current assets:		
Cash, including temporary cash investments	$ 45,074	$ 8,152
Accounts receivable—less allowance for doubtful accounts of $3,074 and $1,543, respectively	68,534	75,429
Inventories	501,956	491,583
Prepaid expenses	24,022	26,271
Total current assets	639,586	601,435
Property and plant	428,031	344,590
Less accumulated depreciation and amortization	126,684	101,738
Property and plant, net	301,347	242,852
Other assets	46,021	30,605
	$986,954	$874,892
LIABILITIES AND STOCKHOLDERS' EQUITY		
Current liabilities:		
Short-term borrowings	$ —	$120,939
Current portion of long-term debt	4,490	4,117
Accounts payable, trade	155,179	144,769
Accounts payable, other	21,904	21,452
Accrued salaries and wages	22,705	18,998
Other accrued liabilities	42,861	27,216
Federal, state and local income taxes	6,442	7,706
Total current liabilities	253,581	345,197
Long-term debt, less current portion	304,885	44,781
Deferred income taxes	35,958	27,640
Stockholders' equity:		
Common stock, par value one dollar per share. Authorized 100,000,000; issued 36,742,762 and 36,640,741 shares, respectively)	36,743	36,641
Additional paid-in capital	41,764	39,194
Retained earnings	411,729	381,519
	490,236	457,354
Treasury stock, at cost	(97,706)	(80)
Total stockholders' equity	392,530	457,274
	$986,954	$874,892

See accompanying notes to consolidated financial statements.

507

CONSOLIDATED STATEMENTS OF EARNINGS

(Dollars in Thousands Except Per Share Amounts)

	Fiscal Years Ended		
	May 31, 1986	June 1, 1985	June 2, 1984
Net sales	$2,743,178	$2,395,640	$2,227,510
Cost of sales, including occupancy costs	2,022,275	1,794,734	1,602,150
Warehouse, selling, administrative and general expenses	595,560	519,781	447,777
	2,617,835	2,314,515	2,049,927
Operating profit	125,343	81,125	177,583
Interest expense	(28,989)	(14,796)	(6,402)
Interest income	2,465	1,777	3,363
Unusual items	2,815	—	—
	(23,709)	(13,019)	(3,039)
Earnings before income taxes	101,634	68,106	174,544
Income taxes:			
Federal			
Current	21,501	17,441	64,351
Deferred	14,399	5,659	8,759
	35,900	23,100	73,110
State and local	8,800	6,100	8,023
	44,700	29,200	81,133
Net earnings	$ 56,934	$ 38,906	$ 93,411
Net earnings per common share	$1.72	$1.06	$2.54

See accompanying notes to consolidated financial statements.

CONSOLIDATED STATEMENTS OF CHANGES IN FINANCIAL POSITION

(Dollars in Thousands)	Fiscal Years Ended		
	May 31, 1986	June 1, 1985	June 2, 1984
Sources of working capital:			
Net earnings	$ 56,934	$ 38,906	$ 93,411
Items which do not use (provide) working capital:			
Depreciation and amortization	33,701	28,250	22,534
Loss (gain) on disposals of property and equipment	299	273	(21)
Gains on sales of divisions, net of tax	(6,166)	—	—
Deferred income taxes	8,546	5,375	9,665
Compensation on restricted stock plans	195	367	499
Working capital provided by operations	93,509	73,171	126,088
Proceeds from long-term debt	261,399	10,453	—
Proceeds from sales of property and equipment	1,795	6,345	1,005
Proceeds from stock plans	1,397	327	617
Federal income tax benefits derived from stock option plans	771	133	555
Other	8,739	—	100
	$367,610	$ 90,429	$128,365
Uses of working capital:			
Purchase of Carls Drug Co., Inc., excluding working capital:	23,164	—	—
Purchases of common stock for treasury	98,778	—	—
Additions to property and equipment	82,415	90,173	57,880
Cash dividends	26,724	29,282	21,859
Reductions in long-term debt	5,043	5,080	7,040
Other changes, net	1,719	3,998	2,676
Increase (decrease) in working capital	129,767	(38,104)	38,910
	$367,610	$90,429	$128,365
Changes in components of working capital:			
Increase (decrease) in current assets:			
Cash, including temporary cash investments	$36,922	$(10,439)	$(32,747)
Receivables, net	(6,895)	21,749	6,975
Inventories	10,373	19,712	142,358
Prepaid expenses	(2,249)	7,654	2,232
	38,151	38,676	118,818
Increase (decrease) in current liabilities:			
Short-term borrowings	(120,939)	70,031	49,108
Current portion of long-term debt	373	541	(115)
Accounts payable	10,862	7,256	33,155
Accrued liabilities	19,352	5,411	1,723
Federal, state and local income taxes	(1,264)	(6,459)	(3,963)
	(91,616)	76,780	79,908
Increase (decrease) in working capital	$129,767	$(38,104)	$38,910

509

NOTES TO CONSOLIDATED FINANCIAL STATEMENTS

May 31, 1986, June 1, 1985 and June 2, 1984

1. Summary of Significant Accounting Policies

(a) Basis of Consolidation

The consolidated financial statements include the accounts of the Company and its subsidiaries, substantially all of which are wholly-owned. All significant intercompany profits, transactions and balances are eliminated in consolidation.

(b) Fiscal Year

The Company's fiscal year ends on the Saturday closest to May 31. The fiscal years ended May 31, 1986 and June 1, 1985 consisted of fifty-two weeks, while the fiscal year ended June 2, 1984 consisted of fifty-three weeks.

(c) Inventories

Inventories consist principally of merchandise purchased for resale and are based on physical inventories taken on or about the end of each fiscal year.

Inventories are stated at the lower of cost or replacement market. The cost of approximately 90% of all inventories is determined on a last-in, first-out (LIFO) basis.

(d) Property, Equipment and Leasehold Improvements

Depreciation is provided in full for the cost of depreciable properties at rates based on the estimated useful lives of the individual items in the various classes of assets. The rates so determined are applied principally on a straight-line basis. Leasehold improvements are amortized over the life of the related asset or the term of the lease, whichever is shorter. Depreciation and amortization expense includes amortization associated with capitalized leases.

(e) Goodwill

The difference between the purchase price and the value of the net assets of acquired subsidiaries is included in other assets and amortized on a straight-line basis over a 40-year period.

(f) Store Pre-opening Expenses

Expenses for preparation of new stores are charged to administrative and general expense when incurred.

(g) Income Taxes

Deferred income taxes are provided to reflect differences in the timing of transactions for financial reporting and tax purposes.

2. Proposed Buyout

On August 15, 1986, the Company's Board of Directors approved a merger agreement between the Company and Anac Holding Corporation. Anac Holding Corporation was formed by an investor group led by certain executive officers of the Company. In the merger, Company common stockholders will receive $38.50 per share in cash. The agreement is subject to financing and other conditions, including the approval of holders of a majority of outstanding common stock. The proposal will be submitted to stockholders later in calendar year 1986.

3. Inventories

In the fourth quarter of 1985, inventories of video game cartridges, computer peripherals and other merchandise purchased by a subsidiary of the Company were written down by $35 million. The write-down reduced 1985 net earnings by $18 million, or $.49 per share.

If the FIFO method of inventory accounting had been used, inventories would have been approximately $128,100,000 and $118,000,000 higher than reported at the end of fiscal 1986 and 1985, respectively.

r

EXHIBIT 2

Revco D.S. Unaudited Financial Statements for Quarter Ended August 23, 1986

CONDENSED CONSOLIDATED BALANCE SHEETS

(Dollars in Thousands)	August 23, 1986	May 31, 1986
	(Unaudited)	
ASSETS		
Current assets:		
Cash, including temporary cash investments	$ 39,233	$ 45,074
Accounts receivable—trade and other	71,081	71,608
Less allowance for doubtful accounts	3,149	3,074
	67,932	68,534
Inventories	512,575	501,956
Prepaid expenses	31,826	24,022
Total current assets	651,566	639,586
Property, equipment and leasehold improvements, at cost	434,184	428,031
Less accumulated depreciation and amortization	134,655	126,684
	299,529	301,347
Other assets	46,773	46,021
	$997,868	$986,954
LIABILITIES AND STOCKHOLDERS' EQUITY		
Current liabilities:		
Current portion of long-term debt	$ 4,365	$ 4,490
Accounts payable	188,924	177,083
Other current liabilities	75,654	72,008
Total current liabilities	268,943	253,581
Long-term debt less current portion	304,432	304,885
Deferred income taxes	37,897	35,958
Stockholders' equity:		
Common stock, par value one dollar per share. Authorized 100,000,000 shares; issued 36,744,903 and 36,742,762 at August 23, 1986 and May 31, 1986, respectively	36,745	36,743
Additional paid-in capital	42,031	41,764
Retained earnings	405,144	411,729
	483,920	490,236
Treasury stock (at cost)	(97,324)	(97,706)
Total stockholders' equity	386,596	392,530
	$997,868	$986,954

See accompanying notes to condensed consolidated financial statements.

CONDENSED CONSOLIDATED STATEMENTS OF EARNINGS
(Unaudited)

(Dollars in Thousands, Except Per share Amounts)

	For the Twelve-Week Periods Ended	
	August 23, 1986	August 24, 1985
Net sales	$ 627,910	$ 585,500
Costs and expenses:		
Cost of sales, including occupancy costs	465,342	435,569
Warehouse, selling, administrative and general expenses	143,419	128,545
Interest expense	7,448	4,825
Interest income	(518)	(305)
Total costs and expenses	615,691	568,634
Earnings before income taxes	12,219	16,866
Income taxes	5,834	7,581
Net earnings	$ 6,385	$ 9,285
Earnings per common share	$.20	$.27
Dividends paid per common share	$.20	$.20
Average number of shares outstanding	32,501,596	34,581,013

See accompanying notes to condensed consolidated financial statements.

CONDENSED CONSOLIDATED STATEMENTS OF CHANGES IN FINANCIAL POSITION
(Unaudited)

(Dollars in Thousands)

	For The Twelve-Week Periods Ended	
	August 23, 1986	August 24, 1985
Sources of working capital:		
Net earnings	$ 6,385	$ 9,285
Items which do not use working capital:		
Depreciation and amortization	8,593	7,354
Other items	2,103	2,379
Working capital provided by operations	17,081	19,018
Proceeds from stock plans	51	46
Proceeds from sale of property and equipment	565	66
Proceeds from long-term debt	—	35,000
Treasury stock transferred to profit sharing and savings plan	600	—
	$18,297	$54,130

(continued)

CONDENSED CONSOLIDATED STATEMENTS OF CHANGES IN FINANCIAL POSITION
(Continued)

(Dollars in Thousands)

	For The Twelve-Week Periods Ended	
	August 23, 1986	August 24, 1985
Uses of working capital:		
Purchase of common stock for treasury	$ —	$ 98,458
Net non-current assets of acquired company	—	22,493
Additions to property and equipment	7,492	19,721
Cash dividends	12,970	13,784
Reductions in long-term debt	453	609
Other changes, net	764	2,168
Decrease in working capital	(3,382)	(103,103)
	$18,297	$ 54,130
Changes in components of working capital:		
Increase (decrease) in current assets:		
Cash, including temporary cash investments	$ (5,841)	$ 2,646
Receivables, net	(602)	(15,941)
Inventories	10,619	21,544
Prepaid expenses	7,804	12,219
	11,980	20,468
Increase (decrease) in current liabilities:		
Short-term borrowings	—	101,794
Current portion of long-term debt	(125)	449
Accounts payable	11,841	5,172
Other current liabilities	3,646	16,156
	15,362	123,571
Decrease in working capital	$ (3,382)	$(103,103)

See accompanying notes to condensed consolidated financial statements.

In April 1992, Stanley Bradshaw, president and chief executive officer of Roosevelt Financial Group, was puzzled that the stock market's valuation of the company was far below the net market value of Roosevelt's equity estimated by the company. The company calculated net market value by adjusting stockholders' equity for differences between actual market values and the historical cost basis for all of its assets, liabilities, and off-balance-sheet items, and disclosed it in the company's financial statements. Although the difference between the stock market valuation and net market value was smaller than it had been a year ago, it was still substantial. Clearly, investors did not fully appreciate the value of Roosevelt's business or its operating strategy. Bradshaw was considering what actions, if any, he should initiate to increase investors' confidence in the company's market value estimates.

THE COMPANY BACKGROUND

Roosevelt Financial Group was a publicly traded thrift holding company whose sole asset was Roosevelt Bank, a $2.1 billion thrift headquartered in St. Louis, Missouri. The bank operated 21 full-service branches in Missouri and Illinois. Incorporated as a mutual savings and loan in 1924, the bank converted to stock ownership in 1987. The company's stock traded on the over-the-counter market and was quoted in the NASDAQ National Market System. The principal elements of Roosevelt's operating strategy were to (1) concentrate lending efforts on single-family residential loans while holding those loans and most other assets in a securitized form, (2) focus on retail deposits as a primary funding source while marketing fee-based consumer financial products to the bank's growing customer base, and (3) control exposure to interest rate risk.

The company was subject to broad federal regulation because, as a federally chartered savings bank, the company's savings deposits were insured and backed by the full faith and credit of the U.S. Government. The passage of the Financial Institutions Reform, Recovery, and Enforcement Act of 1989 (FIRREA) significantly changed and increased the regulatory structure and oversight of savings institutions. In particular,

Professor Mary E. Barth and Professor Krishna G. Palepu prepared this case as the basis for class discussion rather than to illustrate either effective or ineffective handling of an administrative situation. Copyright © 1992 by the President and Fellows of Harvard College. Harvard Business School case 9-192-138.

FIRREA transferred the previous regulatory authority of the Federal Home Loan Bank Board and Federal Savings and Loan Insurance Corporation to the Office of Thrift Supervision (OTS) and the Federal Deposit Insurance Corporation. The company was required, among other things, to file periodic reports with these regulatory bodies, to engage only in activities that were prescribed by federal laws and regulations, and to maintain certain required levels of regulatory capital (as defined by the regulations) and other financial ratios. Exhibit 1 shows the typical structure of financial statements for U.S. commercial banks and thrifts.

During the 1980s, a large number of thrifts failed. Many problems that plagued the thrift industry related to mismanaging (or lack of managing) interest-rate and credit risk. Bradshaw believed that Roosevelt had implemented strategies that substantially mitigated each of these risks and therefore was worthy of investor confidence.

Credit risk for thrifts arose because typically a thrift's lending activities were geographically concentrated. By increasing investments in securitized assets and holding only a small portion of its originated loans, Roosevelt diversified its geographic credit risk.

Interest-rate risk arose principally because a thrift's basic business was to obtain funds from short-term savings deposits and invest in long-term residential mortgage loans, which often had fixed interest rates. Because of the difference in duration between a thrift's assets and liabilities, and its high leverage, interest-rate changes could have a large impact on a thrift's financial position if interest-rate risk was not properly managed. For example, in a period of rising interest rates, thrifts' liabilities (deposits) turned over frequently at increasing interest rates while their assets (loans) earned a fixed return that was established in periods of lower interest rates. In a period of declining rates, prepayment options on mortgages permitted homeowners to prepay high-interest-rate mortgages and to refinance at lower rates. Each reduced the interest-rate spread, resulting in a deteriorated financial condition.

Because of the interest-rate risk inherent in thrifts' basic business, Roosevelt developed an operating and investing strategy to manage interest-rate risk. Bradshaw believed interest-rate risk management to be one of the most important top management responsibilities of thrift institutions and thus focused much of his management's attention on achieving interest-rate matching. His primary strategy for managing interest-rate risk was to match the weighted average maturities of assets, liabilities, and off-balance sheet items. In implementing this strategy, Roosevelt utilized internal and external methods, including acquisition of savings deposits, issuance of fixed-rate collateralized debt, investment in adjustable-rate home loans and securities, interest-rate exchange agreements, U.S. Treasury bond and Eurodollar time deposit financial futures contracts, and options contracts on financial futures.

Excerpts from Roosevelt's 1991 Form 10K and Annual Report, including the company's consolidated balance sheets, statements of operations and cash flows, and letter to stockholders, are given in Exhibit 2. Exhibit 3 summarizes the basis for recognizing Roosevelt's major assets and liabilities in the financial statements.

ROOSEVELT'S VOLUNTARY REPORTING OF NET MARKET VALUE

In 1992, most Generally Accepted Accounting Principles (GAAP) for thrifts were based on historical cost accounting. Bradshaw was troubled by his belief that historical cost accounting did not reflect the underlying economic results of Roosevelt's operating strategy because it did not capture the effects of changing interest rates or the interactions among various financial instruments on a timely basis. Thus, Roosevelt management found it difficult to communicate its achievements to investors. Roosevelt management based the bank's transactions on economics and then tried to work within the accounting rules to tell the bank's story the "right" way. As Lloyd Garrison, executive vice president and chief financial officer stated, "Roosevelt is a live example of a situation where GAAP doesn't tell the whole story."

To Roosevelt management, the right way was to measure the net market value of the bank's assets and liabilities and disclose that amount to the public. Roosevelt's management explained it in the 1990 Annual Report:

> We at Roosevelt have always taken great pride in managing the company in a manner designed to enhance its true economic value. While tangible book value is an important relative measure, the economic value of the company would be better measured by an assessment of the market values of all its assets, liabilities, and off-balance sheet items and the resulting computation of Roosevelt's net market value. While net market value has been an illusive concept for many financial institutions, it is both meaningful and useful for Roosevelt, given that market values can be quickly ascertained for 80 percent of its assets and many of its liabilities.

Beginning in 1989, Roosevelt calculated an estimate of the net market value of its assets and liabilities and disclosed it, together with sensitivity to increases or decreases of 100 and 200 interest basis points,[1] in the Management's Discussion and Analysis section of the company's annual Forms 10K and quarterly Forms 10Q filed with the Securities and Exchange Commission (SEC). Exhibit 4 presents the disclosures made in 1990, the four quarters of 1991, and the first quarter of 1992. The calculation took account of interest-rate risk management by netting together all assets and liabilities. If an asset decreased in market value because of interest rate changes and interest-rate risk was properly matched, there would be an offsetting increase in the value of a liability. The effect on net market value would then be zero.

Exhibit 5 presents an excerpt from the company's 1991 Form 10K that explains the net market value calculation.

Financial Accounting Debate

Whereas Roosevelt's management voluntarily disclosed its estimate of net market value, other thrifts continued to use historical cost accounting. However, the thrift industry

r

517

---

1. *A basis point is 1/100 of 1%.*

problems in the early 1980s prompted some observers to question the usefulness of historical cost accounting. As a result, the merits of requiring all thrifts to report market value information were hotly debated by the accounting profession.

Several newly issued Financial Accounting Standards Board (FASB) standards required disclosures of market value information, suggesting that the FASB believed the information was useful to financial statement users, yet few standards required recognition based on market values. For example, in 1990, the FASB issued Statement of Financial Accounting Standards (SFAS) No. 105, requiring disclosure of information about financial instruments with off-balance-sheet risk, and in late 1991, it issued SFAS 107, requiring disclosure of market values of all financial instruments beginning in 1993. Investment securities of financial institutions were specifically a subject of the market value accounting debate. In 1990, the American Institute of Certified Public Accountants issued a Statement of Position recommending guidance on reporting for debt securities held as assets, including investment securities. In June 1991, the FASB added to its agenda this special issue as a limited scope project. During its deliberations, the FASB changed its position on accounting for investment securities several times and, by April 1992, had not reached a consensus on the appropriate accounting treatment.

Much of the debate focused on using market value accounting for financial institutions, although broader application was also under consideration. In testimony before the Senate Committee on Banking, Housing, and Urban Affairs (September 10, 1990), SEC Chairman Richard Breeden suggested that a move to market value accounting for financial institutions, as well as all publicly held companies, was appropriate. In that testimony, he stated that "the presumption that market-based information is the most relevant financial data attribute should be recognized." Critics of market value accounting asserted that the resulting financial statement volatility and the questionable reliability of market value data would reduce the reliability of financial statements. Unwarranted volatility was of particular concern for financial institutions required to maintain specified levels of regulatory capital. Kelly Holthus, president of the American Bankers Association, argued,

> *Recent suggestions that banks convert to a market value accounting concept will, if adopted, cause banks' financial results to be volatile and unreliable. If management, in turn, makes decisions based on such volatile and unreliable financial information, then the very safety and soundness of the banking industry could be in jeopardy.*

Bradshaw disagreed with the critics of market value accounting. In a speech to the SEC, he stated,

> *We believe that market value information is not only relevant—it is invaluable for most decision makers. We strongly urge both FASB and the Commission to provide guidance as well as impetus for the increased use of market value information. . . . We believe that the proper and full use of market value information is not a source of volatility. At most, market value information simply acknowledges the existing volatility within the financial condition of reporting entities. We believe that this information is in itself extremely valuable to decision makers.*

Investor Reaction to Roosevelt's Voluntary Disclosure

In choosing voluntarily to disclose net market value, Roosevelt's management was hoping that investors would better appreciate the true economics of the company. Management was particularly concerned about the negative impression that investors had about the thrift industry as a whole and wanted to use the net market value disclosure to underscore Roosevelt's financial strengths.

Thus far, Roosevelt's efforts had met with mixed success. For some reason, investors did not totally accept the disclosed estimates of net market value. The company's stock price was consistently much lower than the bank's estimate of net market value. Exhibit 6 shows the relation between the estimated net market value per share and the company's stock price from 1989 to 1991. The discrepancy after the December 31, 1991 disclosures was still 14 percent of net market value; net market value per share was $14.77, yet the company's stock price was only $12.63. Although Mr. Bradshaw did not expect the two amounts to be exactly the same (because, for example, there were several assets not included in the company's calculation), he could not understand why there was such a large negative discrepancy.

Roosevelt's management had already taken some action to increase the credibility of its net market value estimates. First, the company stepped up its efforts to educate, on a one-on-one basis, analysts who followed the company about the importance of the net market value disclosure. Second, the company emphasized that its procedures for net market value estimation were very similar to those required by the OTS for all thrifts' regulatory reporting under Thrift Bulletin 13. Third, to underscore its belief the company's stock was undervalued, Roosevelt's management initiated a stock repurchase plan.

Bradshaw wondered whether further action was necessary to convince stock market participants of his company's operating strategy effectiveness and the credibility of the net market value estimate. He strongly believed that the company's stock was undervalued because of inadequate communication and wanted to identify courses of action to improve communication with investors.

QUESTIONS

1. Evaluate Roosevelt's business and strategy. What are the key success factors for Roosevelt? Is the company's management addressing them properly?
2. Evaluate the procedure used by Roosevelt to estimate net market value.
3. Do you think voluntary disclosure of market value estimates is helpful to Roosevelt? What do you think of the way they have selected to do it?
4. Why do you think Roosevelt's stock price differs from net market value? What should Mr. Bradshaw do?

EXHIBIT 1
Typical Structure of Financial Statements for Commercial Banks and Thrifts

Assets and Liabilities Percentages:	Commercial Banks	Thrifts
Assets		
Cash	9.0%	1.5%
Loans:		
Mortgages	—	53.9
Mortgage-backed securities	—	16.0
Commercial and industrial	23.5	2.4
Real estate	20.0	—
Consumer	13.4	4.8
Other	10.1	—
Securities:		
U.S. government and federal agency	14.8	4.3
State and local	3.8	.1
Other	.4	8.0
Other assets	5.0	9.0
Total	100.0%	100.0%
Liabilities		
Transaction deposits	24.0%	4.7%
Savings deposits	21.0	18.6
Time deposits	31.0	51.8
Borrowings	13.0	18.8
Other liabilities	4.0	1.7
Capital	7.0	4.4
Total	100.0%	100.0%

Income and Expenses Percentages:	Commercial Banks	Thrifts
Income		
Net on interest on loans	62.0%	59.1%
Net interest on mortgage-backed securities	—	13.9
Interest on securities	16.0	11.6
Other interest	7.0	8.3
Other operating income	15.0	7.1
Total operating income	100.0%	100.0%
Expenses		
Operating expenses	44.0%	23.5%
Interest paid depositors	46.0	60.1
Other interest costs	10.0	16.4
Total operating expenses	100.0%	100.0%

Sources: 1988 Fact Book of Savings Institutions *and* Money and Banking

r

520

Exhibit 2   Excerpts from Roosevelt Financial Group's 1991 Annual Report

EXHIBIT 2

Excerpts from Roosevelt Financial Group's 1991 Annual Report

1991 LETTER TO STOCKHOLDERS

We are pleased by Roosevelt's performance during 1991, and we are gratified that we continued to buck the trend. The past three years have been a period dominated by record bank and thrift failures and large reversals of fortune for many of those financial institutions that have survived. In 1991 nonperforming assets continued to plunder the earnings of financial institutions throughout the country. The year was also marked by the elimination of payments to shareholders by many companies, as they adjusted to the fulfillment of promises of toughness made by Congress when it enacted FIRREA. The adjustment to rational banking practices has taken quite a toll on many institutions.

For Roosevelt, however, 1991 represented another year of uninterrupted progress in its continuing story of outstanding asset quality, improving performance and increasing shareholder value. In an environment marked by regulatory pressure and hampered by weakened real estate markets, Roosevelt's financial results for 1991 are further evidence that our disciplined approach, our penchant for safety and our innovation continue to serve shareholders well.

While the Company reported a net loss for the year due to the write-off of its remaining goodwill, during 1991 Roosevelt demonstrated improved earnings capabilities by concentrating on increasing the efficiency of its core operations and continually seeking out new sources of revenue. General and Administrative expenses were held in check during 1991 at $26.9 million, versus $27.0 million for 1990. In addition, total deposits, an increasingly attractive funding source throughout 1991, increased both in dollars and as a percentage of total liabilities. Further, retail revenues (retail banking fees plus gross profit from the insurance agency) were up 45% to $3.7 million. As a result, tangible net income[a] increased to $1.55 per share in 1991 with further growth expected during 1992 as efforts to increase efficiency continue to show results.

Anticipating the recently proposed 4% minimum leverage capital requirement, Roosevelt was able to use its increased earnings capabilities to build and maintain capital at levels comfortably in excess of all fully phased-in capital requirements while still paying an attractive dividend of 60 cents a share during 1991. At December 31, 1991, Roosevelt reported, on a fully phased-in basis, tangible and core capital ratios of 4.11% and a risk-based capital ratio of 10.58%. We have always felt that the burden of any increased regulatory capital requirements should not be borne on the backs of our shareholders. Our performance in 1991 indicates our ability to live up to that ideal.

The earnings momentum achieved during 1991 has not been at the expense of safety or asset quality considerations. At December 31, 1991, Roosevelt had 73.5% of its assets in cash, interest-bearing deposits, mortgage-backed securities, and commercial paper as well as other highly rated financial instruments. These assets, virtually devoid of credit risk and extremely liquid, provide stable and predictable returns while permitting management to be nimble in responding to changing market conditions when managing

r

521

---

a. Tangible net income is calculated by adding back the $16.321 million ($3.03 per share) goodwill write-off to net income.

Exhibit 2 Excerpts from Roosevelt Financial Group's 1991 Annual Report

Roosevelt's balance sheet. During 1991 Roosevelt continued to improve on its already outstanding nonperforming assets numbers as its ratio of nonperforming assets to total assets improved to .18% at December 31, 1991, from .35% at December 31, 1990. Total nonperforming assets, already minimal at $8.4 million, were reduced 54% to $3.8 million over the same period. Reducing these impediments to future performance lends further stability and predictability to Roosevelt's future earnings capabilities.

The year 1991 was another period of uninterrupted progress in building shareholder value as well. From December 31, 1990, through December 31, 1991, Roosevelt's tangible book value per share increased 9% from $15.65 to $17.04. In last year's annual report, Roosevelt introduced a measure designed to reflect the true economic value of the company more accurately: its "netmarket value."[b] Over the past three years, Roosevelt's net market value per share has increased from $13.14 at December 31, 1989, to $13.46 and then to $14.77 at December 31, 1990 and 1991, respectively. Taking advantage of the relative disparity between the market price of Roosevelt's common stock and these two measures of value, we continued to repurchase stock under our ongoing stock repurchase program throughout 1991. During the year, we repurchased 309,900 shares, leaving Roosevelt with 5,299,123 shares issued and outstanding at December 31, 1991. Roosevelt has now repurchased 415,950 of the 575,000 shares authorized at the inception of its stock repurchase program in August 1990. The stock repurchase program continues to be one of the best methods available to make meaningful enhancements to shareholder value. Roosevelt will continue to repurchase its stock in 1992, subject to market conditions, reflecting the confidence of the Board of Directors and Management in both its financial prospects and its current value.

More than at any other time in recent memory, we look to the future with great expectations. Our operating environment has improved significantly since the return to our markets of sound banking principles and rational pricing brought on by FIRREA and sensible, consistently applied regulatory guidance. Our 1991 financial results demonstrate that our performance will not be governed by prevailing economic conditions, freeing us from excessive concern over the duration or intensity of the current recession. The continued progress of our cost control and efficiency efforts gives us additional confidence that we will demonstrate yet improved operating performance in 1992 and the capacity to sustain that trend in future years.

Clarence M. Turley, Jr.
Chairman of The Board

Stanley J. Bradshaw
President and Chief Executive Officer

March 2, 1992

....

b. *Roosevelt's net market value is calculated by adjusting stockholders' equity for differences between actual market values and the historical cost basis for all of its assets, liabilities, and off-balance sheet items. For a more detailed discussion, see Roosevelt's Form 10-K for the year ended December 31, 1991.*

Exhibit 2 Excerpts from Roosevelt Financial Group's 1991 Annual Report

CONSOLIDATED BALANCE SHEETS

	At December 31,	
	1991	1990
ASSETS		
Cash	$ 12,386,970	$ 17,694,857
Interest-bearing deposits	9,093,733	4,330,213
Securities purchased under agreements to resell	128,729,924	—
Mortgage-backed and investment grade securities, carried at market value (cost of $310,602,226 and $134,752,481 at December 31, 1991, and 1990, respectively)	315,008,234	135,276,537
Investment securities, net (approximate market value of $106,654,423 and $74,117,477 at December 31, 1991 and 1990, respectively)	105,004,702	73,577,894
Mortgage-backed securities, net (approximate market value of $1,044,277,077 and $1,614,460,845 at December 31, 1991 and 1990, respectively)	986,924,659	1,586,591,626
Loans receivable, net	476,949,079	446,464,315
Investment in real estate, net	8,418,822	13,078,853
Stock in Federal Home Loan Bank	17,775,700	21,168,500
Office properties and equipment, net	12,041,293	10,760,664
Accrued income and other assets	47,538,729	51,389,554
Cost in excess of fair value of net assets acquired, net	—	16,320,978
	$2,119,871,845	$2,376,653,991
LIABILITIES AND STOCKHOLDERS' EQUITY		
Savings deposits	$1,356,039,264	$1,334,623,551
Mortgage-backed bonds	341,800,526	455,639,868
Securities sold under agreements to repurchase	300,923,899	426,633,213
Advances from Federal Home Loan Bank	—	19,000,058
Note payable to bank	—	1,140,000
Accrued expenses and other liabilities	30,823,057	35,498,007
Total liabilities	$2,029,586,746	$2,272,534,697
Commitments and contingencies		
Stockholders' equity:		
Serial preferred stock: Authorized 1,000,000 shares at December 31, 1991 and 1990, outstanding—none	—	—
Common stock ($.01 par value): Authorized 10,000,000 shares at December 31, 1991 and 1990, issued and outstanding 5,299,123 shares at December 31, 1991 and 5,609,023 at December 31, 1990	52,991	56,090
Paid-in capital	42,859,831	45,678,765
Retained earnings—substantially restricted	47,510,807	58,722,265
	90,423,629	104,457,120
Unamortized restricted stock awards	(138,530)	(337,826)
Total stockholders' equity	90,285,099	104,119,294
	$2,119,871,845	$2,376,653,991

r

523

Exhibit 2 Excerpts from Roosevelt Financial Group's 1991 Annual Report

CONSOLIDATED INCOME STATEMENTS

	Year Ended December 31,		
	1991	1990	1989
Interest Income:			
Mortgage-backed securities	$110,968,456	$179,807,535	$187,318,424
Loans receivable	46,449,785	47,525,612	51,157,371
Securities carried at market value	19,490,524	861,749	—
Investment securities	9,696,588	8,802,740	26,235,237
Securities purchased under agreement to resell	2,660,442	1,296,024	—
Other	3,485,579	5,601,431	6,005,495
Total interest income	$192,751,374	$243,895,091	$270,716,527
Interest expense:			
Savings deposits, net	94,279,348	101,292,691	96,611,619
Mortgage-backed bonds	36,742,575	48,153,495	74,642,956
Securities sold under agreements to repurchase	15,943,903	45,153,873	35,401,902
Interest rate exchange agreements, net	7,168,470	9,356,680	5,611,955
Advances from Federal Home Loan Bank	94,457	1,971,957	5,665,376
Total interest expense	154,228,753	205,928,696	217,933,808
Net interest income	38,522,621	38,066,395	52,792,719
Provision for losses on loans	593,339	1,246,750	1,070,778
Net interest income after provision for losses on loans	37,929,282	36,819,645	51,711,941
Noninterest income (loss):			
Provision for losses on real estate acquired for development and sale	—	(1,000,000)	(4,224,420)
Loss on securities held for sale, net	—	(12,441,459)	(12,154,253)
Net gain (loss) from financial instruments	(2,106,907)	4,882,579	736,369
Options expense	(1,043,363)	(1,222,008)	(423,235)
Gross profit - insurance agency	1,638,995	1,132,217	1,035,038
Retail banking fees	2,015,002	1,445,465	1,353,125
State tax settlement	—	—	2,384,475
Other	719,044	897,690	1,652,259
Total noninterest income (loss)	1,222,771	(6,305,516)	(9,640,642)
Noninterest expense:			
General and administrative:			
Compensation and employee benefits	11,390,869	12,200,180	11,956,358
Occupancy	5,740,750	4,723,367	5,500,012
Advertising	780,734	1,095,884	1,128,584
Federal insurance premiums	3,004,402	2,523,176	2,449,849
Other	5,977,612	6,409,792	7,991,881
Total general and administrative	26,894,367	26,952,399	29,026,684
Amortization of cost in excess of fair value of net assets acquired	—	2,428,656	1,785,372
Provision for losses on foreclosed real estate	—	1,093,681	1,762,380
Total noninterest expense	26,894,367	26,952,399	29,026,684

r

524

Exhibit 2   Excerpts from Roosevelt Financial Group's 1991 Annual Report

CONSOLIDATED INCOME STATEMENTS (continued)

	Year Ended December 31,		
	1991	1990	1989
Income before income taxes and cumulative effect of change in accounting principle	12,347,686	39,393	9,496,863
Income tax expense (benefit)	3,996,214	(923,825)	3,894,916
Income before cumulative effect of change in accounting principle	8,351,472	963,218	5,601,947
Cumulative effect of change in accounting principle	(16,320,978)	—	—
Net income (loss)	$ (7,969,506)	$ 923,218	$ 5,601,947
Earnings (loss) per share:			
Income before cumulative effect of change in accounting principles	$1.55	$ 0.17	$0.97
Cumulative effect of change in accounting principle	(3.03)	—	—
Net income (loss) per share	$ (1.48)	$ 0.17	$0.97
Pro forma amounts assuming the change in accounting principle is applied retroactively:			
Net income	$ 8,351,472	$ 1,493,725	$ 5,249,269
Earnings per share	$1.55	$0.26	$0.91

r

525

CONSOLIDATED STATEMENTS OF CASH FLOWS

	Year Ended December 31,		
	1991	1990	1989
Cash flows from operating activities:			
Net income (loss)	$ (7,969,506)	$ 963,218	$ 5,601,947
Adjustments to reconcile net income (loss) to net cash provided by (used in) operating activities:			
Cumulative effect of change in accounting principle	16,320,978	—	—
Depreciation and amortization	1,407,382	1,109,681	1,296,345
Amortization of premiums (discounts), net	(918,910)	1,256,725	(10,437,673)
(Increase) decrease in accrued interest receivable	1,634,381	8,237,258	(5,681,833)
Increase (decrease) in accrued interest payable	(6,643,274)	(10,610,110)	1,597,434
Provision for losses on loans and real estate	593,339	3,340,431	7,057,578
Loss on securities held for sale, net	-	12,441,459	12,154,253
Net increase in mortgage-backed and investment grade securities carried at market value	(59,796,846)	(16,543,295)	-
Increase (decrease) in income taxes	(5,453,028)	2,910,904	(5,102,931)
Change in other assets and other liabilities, net	1,577,982	(1,765,148)	586,526
Other, net	3,457,908	(2,380,437)	(1,639,388)
Net cash provided by (used in) operating activities	$ (55,789,594)	$ (1,039,314)	$ 5,432,258

(continued)

Exhibit 2   Excerpts from Roosevelt Financial Group's 1991 Annual Report

CONSOLIDATED STATEMENTS OF CASH FLOWS (continued)

	Year Ended December 31,		
	1991	1990	1989
Cash flows from investing activities:			
Principal payments on mortgage-backed securities	$140,155,416	$154,195,815	$132,846,123
Principal payments on loans receivable	87,674,117	70,074,895	83,113,342
Proceeds from sales of mortgage-backed securities	799,142,478	518,430,246	458,121,188
Proceeds from sales of investment securities	42,127,234	103,976,390	312,219,073
Proceeds from sales of securities held for sale	—	23,639,559	51,262,895
Proceeds from maturities of investment securities	284,715,228	710,638,380	696,734,724
Net proceeds from sales of real estate acquired through foreclosure	2,390,215	2,710,489	5,885,991
Investment in mortgage-backed securities	(457,152,194)	(253,068,765)	(898,114,415)
Originations and purchases of loans receivable	(109,194,076)	(131,220,793)	(26,380,361)
Purchase of investment securities	(407,646,650)	(828,685,838)	(909,767,841)
Sales of (investment in) real estate acquired for development and sale	3,058,522	328,027	3,963,072
Purchase of office properties and equipment	(1,510,896)	(1,973,800)	(1,270,327)
Sale (purchase) of stock in FHLB	3,392,800	(2,076,400)	2,744,400
Acquisition of cash–Hannibal Mutual	9,349,034	—	—
Net cash provided by (used in) interest activities	$396,501,228	$366,968,205	$(88,642,136)
Cash flows from financing activities:			
Maturity on mortgage-backed bonds		$(390,000,000)	
Repurchase on mortgage-backed bonds	$(63,218,000)	(21,205,000)	$(16,700,000)
Proceeds from FHLB advances	—	—	45,000,000
Principal payments on advances from FHLB	(20,000,000)	—	(46,799,631)
Proceeds from (repayment of) note payable to bank	(1,140,000)	1,140,000	—
Fees paid for interest rate floor/cap agreements	—	—	(8,779,140)
Excess of savings deposits receipts over withdrawals	3,605,222	50,480,402	15,368,058
Increase (decrease) in securities sold under agreements to repurchase, net	(125,709,314)	(27,941,254)	125,917,821
Proceeds from issuance of stock, net	—	1,058,329	—
Repurchase of common stock	(2,822,033)	(914,028)	—
Cash dividends paid	(3,241,952)	(4,536,766)	(4,457,933)
Net cash provided by (used in) financing activities	$(212,526,077)	$(391,918,317)	$109,549,175
Net increase (decrease) in cash and cash equivalents	128,185,557	(25,989,426)	26,339,297
Cash and cash equivalents at beginning of year	$ 22,025,070	$ 48,014,496	$ 21,675,199
Cash and cash equivalents at end of year	$150,210,627	$ 22,025,070	$ 48,014,496
Supplemental disclosures of cash flow information:			
Interest credited to savings deposits	$67,791,121	$69,221,610	$63,269,542
Payments (receipts) during the period for:			
Interest	160,872,027	214,914,786	218,213,604
Income taxes (refunds)	(1,380,605)	(4,449,376)	5,575,000
Noncash investing & financing activities:			
Noncash transfers to trading portfolio	119,934,851	117.968,409	—
Defeasance of mortgage-backed bonds	(52,181,627)	—	—
Acquisition of loans–Hannibal Mutual	(7,806,763)	—	—
Acquisition of deposits–Hannibal Mutual	17,810,491	—	—
Acquisition of other assets–Hannibal Mutual	(654,784)	—	—

EXHIBIT 3

Roosevelt Financial Group's Basis for Financial Statement Recognition of
Major Assets and Liabilities, December 31, 1991 and 1990

Assets	Basis
Cash	bank balances
Interest bearing deposits	amount paid
Securities:	
Under agreements to resell	market quotes
Mortgage-backed and investment grade	market quotes
Investment	amortized cost
Mortgage-backed	amortized cost
Loans receivable	amounts lent less allowance for loan losses
Investment in real estate	lower of cost or market
FHLB stock	cost
Office properties and equipment	depreciated cost

Liabilities	
Savings deposits	face amount of accounts
Mortgage-backed bonds	amount received
Securities sold under repurchase agreements	amount received
Advances from FHLB	amount received

Source: 1991 Form 10K

527

Exhibit 4   Roosevelt Financial Group's Net Market Value

EXHIBIT 4
Roosevelt Financial Group's Net Market Value, Including Sensitivity to 100 and 200 Basis Point Increases and Decreases in Interest Rates

Basis Point Changes in Interest Rates:	−200	−100	BASE	+100	+200
December 31, 1990					
Net market value	$76,229	$76,400	**$75,507**	$76,307	$73,349
Increase (decrease) in net market value from base	722	893		800	(2,158)
Shares outstanding			5,609,023		
March 31, 1991					
Net market value	87,224	82,040	**80,141**	79,471	78,743
Increase (decrease) in net market value from base	7,083	1,899		(670)	(1,398)
Shares outstanding			5,512,023		
June 30, 1991					
Net market value	79,355	81,020	**81,100**	81,113	78,388
Increase (decrease) in net market value from base	(1,745)	(80)		13	(2,712)
Shares outstanding			5,302,323		
September 30, 1991					
Net market value	84,277	83,768	**82,100**	78,820	75,661
Increase (decrease) in net market value from base	2,177	1,668		(3,280)	(6,439)
Shares outstanding			5,302,232		
December 31, 1991					
Net market value	74,621	81,061	**78,281**	76,291	74,041
Increase (decrease) in net market value from base	(3,660)	2,780		(1,990)	(4,240)
Shares outstanding			5,299,123		
March 31, 1992					
Net market value	87,130	85,205	**83,524**	80,495	74,916
Increase (decrease) in net market value from base	3,606	1,681		(3,029)	(8,608)
Shares outstanding			5,257,423		

Sources: Forms 10K and 10Q

528

r

Exhibit 5   Description of Roosevelt's Net Market Value Estimation

EXHIBIT 5
Description of Roosevelt's Net Market Value Estimation

The Company's primary objective regarding Asset/Liability Management is to position the Company such that changes in interest rates do not have a material adverse impact upon the net market value of the Company. Net market value is calculated by adjusting stockholders' equity for differences between actual market values and the historical cost basis for all of the Company's assets, liabilities and off-balance sheet items. Net market value, as calculated by the Company and presented herein, should not be confused with the value of the Company's stock or of the amounts distributable to stockholders in connection with a sale of the Company or in the unlikely event of its liquidation. The Company's primary strategy for accomplishing its Asset/Liability Management objective is achieved by matching the weighted average maturities of assets, liabilities and off-balance sheet items (duration matching). In assessing success in this regard, the Company will determine the net market value by assigning market values to assets, liabilities and off-balance sheet items, including the estimated income tax effects of differences between market values and historical cost based values. The Company's methodology in determining market values is discussed in subsequent paragraphs.

The net market value for the Company at December 31, 1991 was $78.3 million as compared to $75.5 million at December 31, 1990. The net increase of $2.8 million in the net market value for the Company from December 31, 1990 to December 31, 1991 is comprised of various components. The gross increase in the market value was $8.8 million. Such gross increase resulted primarily from earnings before the cumulative effect of change in accounting principle of $8.4 million. This gross increase was offset by transactions which decrease the net market value of the Company, such as the repurchase of common stock totaling $2.8 million and the payment of $3.2 million in cash dividends on common stock.

To measure the impact of interest rate changes, the Company recalculates the net market value assuming instantaneous, permanent parallel shifts in the yield curve of both up and down 100, 200, 300, and 400 basis points, or eight separate calculations. Larger increases or decreases in the net market value of the company as a result of these interest rate changes represent greater interest rate risk than do smaller increases or decreases in net market value. In connection with those recalculations, the Company acknowledges the probable changes in cash flows of its assets, liabilities and off-balance sheet positions that would be expected in those various interest-rate environments. Accordingly, the Company adjusts the pro forma net market values as it believes appropriate on the basis of historical experience and its business judgment. The Company endeavors to maintain a position where it experiences no material change in net market value as a result of assumed 100 and 200 basis point increases and decreases in interest rates. Utilizing this measurement concept, the interest rate risk of the Company at December 31, 1991 is as follows:

	(Dollars in thousands) (unaudited)				
Basis point changes in interest rates	−200	−100	Base	+100	+200
Net market value	$74,621	$81,061	$78,281	$72,291	$74,041
Increase (decrease) in net market value from base	$ (3,660)	$ 2,780		$ (1,990)	$ (4,240)

r

529

Exhibit 5   Description of Roosevelt's Net Market Value Estimation

Management believes that the above method of measuring and managing interest rate risk is consistent with the Office of Thrift Supervision (OTS) December 1990 proposed regulation regarding an interest rate risk component of required regulatory capital. According to the proposed regulation, thrift institutions would calculate a market value of portfolio equity (MVPE) which is analogous to the Company's net market value. Pursuant to the proposed regulation, institutions would be required to maintain additional capital equal to 50% of the maximum decline in MVPE caused by either a 200 basis point increase or decrease in interest rates. The Company believes that the adoption of this proposed additional capital requirement for interest rate risk would not have a material effect on the Company.

The calculation of net market value adjusts stockholders' equity, as determined by generally accepted accounting principles, for differences between market values (determined as discussed below) and the historical cost basis of all assets, liabilities and off-balance sheet items.

For all securitized assets and securitized liabilities, market value is derived from quotations received from exchange markets or dealer markets. Similarly, for all off-balance sheet items such as financial futures contracts, options on financial futures contracts, interest rate exchange agreements and cap and floor agreements, market values are derived from quotations received from exchange markets or dealer markets.

For loans, deposit liabilities and other borrowings, market value is determined by calculating the present value of the Company's estimate of future cash flows using a market interest rate deemed by the Company to be commensurate with the type of instrument involved. Purchase accounting discounts and deferred fee income are considered to be reductions in the historical cost basis of the related assets.

The market value of deposit liabilities does not assign any value to a possible core deposit intangible. The Company services mortgage loans for other investors; however, no value has been assigned for this activity. In the unlikely event of liquidation, the net market value could be effected by the liquidation account established by the Bank in its conversion to capital stock form in 1987 and the restoration to taxable income of the Bank's bad debt reserves for income tax purposes.

Office properties and equipment are valued at historical cost reduced by accumulated depreciation. Investment in real estate is valued at the lower of net realizable value or historical cost. Material prepaid expenses and deferred gain on sale/leaseback of office buildings are subtracted from or added to stockholders' equity for purposes of this calculation.

Source: 1991 Form 10K

Exhibit 6   Roosevelt's Per Share Amounts

EXHIBIT 6
Roosevelt's Per Share Amounts: Book Value of Equity, Disclosed Net Market Value, and Stock Price, 1989–1992

Date	Book Value of Equity	Net Market Value	Stock Price[a]	Stock Price Based on OTC Bank Index [b]
December 31, 1989	$19.24	$13.14	$10.50	$10.50
December 31, 1990	18.56	13.46	8.50	8.76
March 31, 1991	18.87	14.54	9.25	9.43
June 30, 1991	19.38	15.30	9.50	9.87
September 30, 1991	19.51	15.48	9.88	9.62
December 31, 1991	17.04	14.77	12.63	11.27
March 31, 1992	17.53	15.89	13.38	11.38

a. Stock price is at date contemporaneous with date company filed 10K or 10Q with the SEC.

b. Represents what Roosevelt's stock price would have been had it moved exactly with the OTC Bank Index.

r

In late January 1991, Didier Pineau-Valencienne, CEO and Chairman of the French firm Groupe Schneider, was frustrated at his lack of success in building a closer working relationship between his company and Square D, Schneider's American counterpart in the electrical equipment industry. Convinced that a global market was developing for electrical equipment, Pineau-Valencienne believed that Schneider needed to become a major player in the U.S. market to maintain its future competitive position. Given the lack of success in partnering with Square D, he was considering the option of acquiring the company.

THE ELECTRICAL EQUIPMENT INDUSTRY

The electrical equipment industry generates revenue from new construction as well as from the maintenance of existing equipment. Demand for both closely follows general economic conditions. The 1990 economic slump hit the electrical manufacturing segment in the United States severely. However, by early 1991 analysts expected prospects for the industry to brighten with the predicted upturn in the economy and the construction market.

Two related trends dominated the industry in 1990: globalization and industry concentration. The first of these has led many U.S. firms to expand internationally to take advantage of market growth in Western Europe and Pacific Rim countries. These international opportunities have been enhanced by the globalization of product standards in the industry. The most widely accepted standards in the U.S. were developed by the National Electrical Manufacturers Association (NEMA). European products conformed to a different set of standards, developed by the International Electrical Commission (IEC) in Geneva. However, many in the industry expected that the move toward a unified Europe, set for 1992, would ultimately lead IEC standards to become dominant in the world.

The second major trend in the industry, concentration of manufacturing and research capabilities, resulted from increasing costs of development and production as well as from globalization. The development of a new product line costs between $46 million

This case was prepared by Edouard De Vitry D'Avaucourt, under the supervision of Professor Paul Healy. Additional comments and information were provided by Professors Paul Asquith from the MIT Sloan School of Management and Anant Sundaram from the Amos Tuck School.

and $74 million (FF 250 million to FF 400 million). Globalization of markets and product standards enabled firms to take advantage of economies of scale, using their expertise and technologies to create common products for domestic and international markets.

SQUARE D COMPANY

Square D is a major supplier of electrical equipment, services, and systems in the U.S. (see Exhibit 1 for Square D's U.S. market shares). The company was incorporated in 1903 and has grown steadily since then. It currently owns and operates 18 manufacturing plants in 11 foreign countries. Operations are concentrated in two segments: electrical distribution and industrial control. The electrical distribution segment manufactures products and systems used to transmit electricity from power lines to outlets for residential, commercial, industrial, or other types of buildings. The industrial control segment manufactures products and provides services to control power used by electrical devices or processes.

One of Square D's strengths is its network of independent electrical distributors, or wholesalers, which market its products. Individual distributors, selected by Square D, provide products and services to all types of clients (contractors, utilities, industrial users, and original equipment manufacturers). This extensive network is the result of many years of relationship building, and is the envy of most of Square D's competitors.

Square D's major competitors include ABB, Westinghouse, Siemens, Allen Bradley, General Electric, and Schneider (through its subsidiaries Télémécanique and Merlin Gerin). These companies compete across a number of segments. In late 1990, *US Industrial Outlook* ranked Square D second in the U.S. industrial control business after Allen Bradley. In electrical distribution, the company ranks third in the U.S. market behind Westinghouse and General Electric.

Square D has had an impressive financial track record—it has been profitable for each of the last 59 years. In the mid-1980s, however, company performance indicators began to deteriorate, prompting the Board to make a change in top management. Jerre Stead joined Square D as president and COO in 1987, was elected CEO in 1988, and was appointed Chairman of the Board in 1989. Stead led a revitalization plan to restore the company's performance and help it face the new industry challenges. Under the plan the following restructuring changes were made:

- Some facilities in the U.S. and Canada were closed, and others were consolidated.
- The firm's businesses were reorganized into three externally focused sectors serving industrial control, electrical distribution, and international markets.
- The resources generated by redeployments and disposal of operations not closely related to the core were used to strengthen core businesses.

Thanks to these efforts, Square D weathered the 1990 recession better than many of its competitors. In 1990, Square D's sales were $1.7 billion (see Exhibit 2 for financial statements), 71 percent in the electrical distribution segment (85 percent of operating earnings) and 29 percent in the industrial control segment (15 percent of operating earnings). By early 1991 analysts were expressing optimism about the industry's prospects for late 1991 and 1992, especially those for Square D. *Value Line* noted that "a stronger economy, a rebound in housing, and positive operating leverage . . . could enable earnings per share to surge to $5.50 or so in 1992 (from $4.73 in 1990)."

GROUPE SCHNEIDER

Schneider was founded in October 1886 as a partnership and was transformed into a corporation (société anonyme) in 1966. It is one of the largest industrial groups in France and is ranked 184 in Fortune's 500 (worldwide ranking).

In 1981, with the arrival of Pineau-Valencienne as chairman and CEO of the group, Schneider embarked on an ambitious restructuring program. The first stage of the program was to divest all loss-making businesses (shipbuilding, railways, and telephone equipment), which had historically generated much of the firm's sales. The sale of these businesses allowed the group to simplify its operational structure and to strengthen its finances. In the second stage of the restructuring Schneider focused on two core businesses:

- Electrical equipment manufacturing for power distribution and automation of industrial complexes (56 percent of sales, 85 percent of operating profits in 1990)
- Electrical building contracting (44 percent of sales, 15 percent of operating profits in 1990)

As a result of the restructuring efforts, Schneider transformed itself from a diversified holding company into an industrial group focused on electrical equipment, engineering, and contracting. The company was organized around four major industrial subsidiaries:

- *Merlin Gerin*—Manufacturer of high-, medium-, and low-voltage equipment, as well as process control systems
- *Télémécanique*—Manufacturer of automation systems and equipment
- *Jeumont Schneider*—Manufacturer of electrical and electronic engineering equipment
- *Spie Batignolles*—Provider of electrical contracting and civil engineering services

With sales of 51 billion francs (financial statements are presented in Exhibit 3) and 85,000 employees throughout the world in 1990, Schneider ranked second or third in most segments of the global electrical equipment industry.

In the late 1980s, Pineau-Valencienne became convinced that the industry was moving more toward a global industry. In his communications with analysts, he emphasized that IEC standards would gain influence in the U.S. and would become the worldwide standard. In addition, he believed that increasing R&D and manufacturing costs would encourage international concentration. Consequently, Schneider began a third restructuring stage—geographical diversification. This move was initiated with two major acquisitions in 1989:

- Spie Batignolles acquired 15 percent of DAVY, the leading British engineering company.
- Schneider acquired a controlling interest in Federal Pioneer, the leading Canadian electrical equipment manufacturer.

The Relationship Between Schneider and Square D

Schneider became interested in Square D in 1988. In September 1988, Pineau-Valencienne arranged a meeting between the top executives of the two companies, during which Schneider presented its vision of a possible joint venture. After this presentation, operational meetings were scheduled from fall 1988 to spring 1989 to determine the product lines most suitable for such a joint venture. To protect the information exchanged, the companies entered into a confidentiality agreement in late October 1988. This restricted the use and public disclosure of confidential information received during the discussions, but it did not contain any "standstill" provisions limiting purchase of securities or business combination proposals.

Very early in the negotiations it became clear that the two CEOs diverged in their understanding of the nature of the relationship. Pineau-Valencienne had hoped that Schneider would acquire an equity position in Square D to cement the relationship. Stead, however, made it very clear that he did not welcome this, and requested that Square D's independence be respected. In correspondence on September 25, 1989, Pineau-Valencienne made his views very clear, connecting the future of the joint venture discussions to Square D's agreeing to Schneider acquiring a 20 percent interest in Square D. As a result, joint venture discussions between the two firms terminated. Frustrated over this standstill, in September 1990 Pineau-Valencienne indicated to Stead that Schneider's interests in Square D had changed from a joint venture to a "friendly cash merger transaction." Square D's Board subsequently became increasingly hostile to Schneider's proposals.

At the same time that Schneider was making overtures to Square D, Square D was organizing legal defenses against hostile takeovers. In 1989 it moved to Delaware, where state laws require hostile bidders to have a minimum of 85 percent of the shares tendered to effect a takeover. In addition, it created poison pill amendments to fight potential unsolicited bids, including a Common Stock Purchase Plan (see Exhibit 4 for details).

During November 1990, unusual activity was noticeable in Square D's stock. Rumors of a takeover led to a jump in volume and increased the share price from $36.50 on October 22 to $49.75 on November 7 (see Exhibit 5). On November 6, 1990, Stead discussed the unusual activity in a phone conversation with Pineau-Valencienne, who expressed an interest in having the opportunity to propose a transaction to Square D if any other parties were given such an opportunity.

On February 1, 1991, *Value Line Investments Survey* made the following comments:

Square D stock is trading on takeover speculation, as it has for the past three months. Square D has several attractions (including positions in selected electrical equipment markets), and could well be a tempting takeover target, especially to a foreign company trying to establish or to enlarge a market presence in the U.S. An acquirer might be willing to pay $70 a share or more for the company. But after three months of unusually heavy trading in the stock, during which time all of its outstanding shares theoretically have changed hands, no evidence of a pending buyout attempt has appeared. If none is eventually forthcoming, we'd expect the stock to gradually drift lower, perhaps to the range of $40–$45 a share. At this juncture, only speculative investors should be holding these shares.

Potential Acquisition of Square D

One option that Pineau-Valencienne was considering was to make a bid for Square D. After two years of contacts with Square D, he had a number of ideas for synergies and sources of value that could result from a full combination of the two companies. These included:

- Rationalizing R&D efforts between the two companies and sharing the benefits of existing technologies;
- Providing access to larger distribution channels for both companies;
- Rationalizing manufacturing capabilities; and
- Expanding Square D's product lines by selling products developed by Télémécanique or Merlin Gerin.

Lazard Frères, the financial advisor of Schneider, was asked to analyze the stand-alone value of Square D as well as its value to Schneider. To determine Square D's stand-alone value, Lazard Frères prepared a set of base assumptions for the firm's future performance as an independent entity. They projected that (a) sales would grow 3.5 percent in 1991 and 7 percent per year thereafter; (b) EBIT would be 15–16 percent of sales; (c) net working capital would continue to be 11–13 percent of sales; (d) projected capital expenditures would be 5 percent of sales; and (e) depreciation expenses would remain at 4 percent of sales between 1991 and 1997, and 4.3 percent thereafter. Based on the synergies between Schneider and Square D, Lazard Frères estimated that Square D could save approximately $60 million per year in expenses (after tax) if it were combined with Schneider. In addition, the disposal of some of Square D's unrelated assets could generate $150 million in cash. Other data relevant to the valuation of Square D is presented in Exhibit 6.

One other issue that Pineau-Valencienne was concerned about in a possible acquisition of Square D was its effect on Schneider's income. Under French accounting, Schneider would have to amortize goodwill, regardless of whether the offer was cash or stock-financed. Lazard Frères estimated that asset and liability revaluations under an acquisition would be minimal, implying that there would be significant goodwill amorti-

S

537

zation charges, even if the maximum period of 40 years was chosen. Pineau-Valencienne expected that many analysts would react negatively to the resulting dilution of earnings.

Didier Pineau-Valencienne felt he had to make a quick decision. There were rumors that Square D already had been approached by a number of other companies about a business combination. Pineau-Valencienne was very concerned that other competitors could gain control of Square D, leaving Schneider with few opportunities to gain access to the U.S. market.

QUESTIONS

1. Assess and discuss the strategic fit between Square D and Schneider. What are the economic pros and cons of a combination?
2. Evaluate the base assumptions Lazard Frères made for valuing Square D.
3. Estimate the value of Square D as an independent company. What is the company worth to Schneider?
4. What would be the effect of the acquisition on Schneider's future earnings, assuming that it was forced to pay the full value of Square D? Should Schneider be concerned about this effect?
5. If you were Mr. Pineau-Valencienne in late January 1991, what would you do? Would you offer a bid for Square D? If so, how much would you bid, and would you make your offer friendly or hostile?

Exhibit 1   Schneider and Square D Market Shares, U.S. and Europe

EXHIBIT 1
Schneider and Square D Market Shares, U.S. and Europe

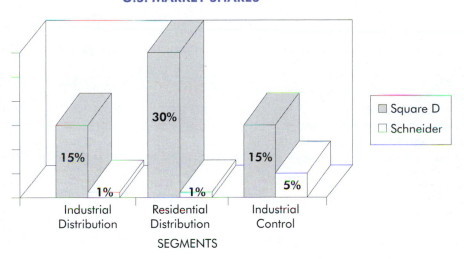

U.S. MARKET SHARES

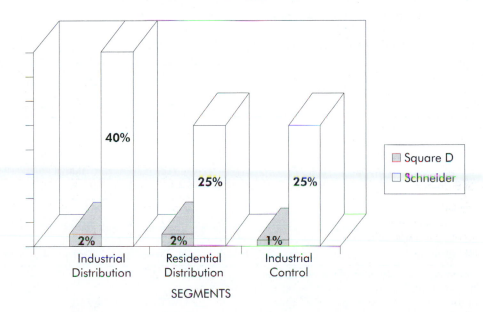

EUROPEAN MARKET SHARES

Exhibit 2   Selected Pages from Square D's 1990 Annual Report

EXHIBIT 2
Selected Pages from Square D's 1990 Annual Report

CONSOLIDATED FINANCIAL STATEMENTS

CONSOLIDATED STATEMENTS OF NET EARNINGS

(Amounts in thousands, except per share)	Year Ended December 31		
	1990	1989	1988
Net Sales	$1,653,319	$1,598,688	$1,497,772
Costs and Expenses:			
Cost of products sold	1,088,977	1,027,348	979,591
Selling, administrative and general	385,903	369,726	338,962
Restructuring charge	—	26,320	—
Operating Earnings	178,439	175,294	179,219
Non-Operating Income	34,740	17,106	17,255
Interest Expense	(28,760)	(31,438)	(22,082)
Earnings from Continuing Operations before Income Taxes	184,419	160,962	174,392
Provision for Income Taxes	67,773	59,856	63,310
Earnings from Continuing Operations	116,646	101,106	111,082
Discontinued Operations:			
(Loss) earnings from operations, net of income tax (benefit) expense: 1990—$(1,188); 1989—$(1,086); 1988—$3,831	(312)	798	7,852
Gain on disposal, net of other provisions; net of income taxes of $1,865	4,391	—	—
Earnings from Discontinued Operations	4,079	798	7,852
Net Earnings	120,725	101,904	118,934
Preferred Dividend, Net of Income Taxes	6,176	3,300	—
Net Earnings Available for Common Shareholders	$ 114,549	$ 98,604	$ 118,934
Earnings per Common Share:			
Primary:			
Continuing operations	$ 4.76	$ 3.95	$ 4.15
Discontinued operations	.18	.03	.29
Net Earnings	$ 4.94	$ 3.98	$ 4.44
Fully Diluted:			
Continuing operations	$ 4.57	$ 3.88	$ 4.13
Discontinued operations	.16	.03	.29
Net Earnings	$ 4.73	$ 3.91	$ 4.42
Weighted Average Number of Common Shares Outstanding:			
Primary	23,181	24,763	26,776
Fully diluted	25,088	25,809	27,016

Exhibit 2   Selected Pages from Square D's 1990 Annual Report

CONSOLIDATED BALANCE SHEETS

	December 31,	
(Dollars in thousands, except per share)	1990	1989

ASSETS

Current Assets:		
Cash and short-term investments	$ 244,933	$ 66,348
Receivables, less allowances (1990—$23,759; 1989—$18,556)	305,241	314,123
Inventories	159,109	151,316
Prepaid expenses	12,664	15,206
Prepaid income taxes	4,714	—
Deferred income tax benefit	34,988	26,459
Net assets of discontinued operation	—	117,116
Total Current Assets	761,649	690,568
Investment in Leveraged Leases	137,182	133,344
Property, Plant and Equipment:		
Land	24,477	22,216
Buildings and improvements	222,105	212,992
Equipment	552,785	501,531
Property, Plant and Equipment—at cost	799,367	736,739
Less accumulated depreciation	349,265	318,261
Property, Plant and Equipment—net	450,102	418,478
Net Assets of Discontinued Operations	36,681	52,949
Excess of Purchase Price Over Net Assets of Businesses Acquired, Less		
Amortization (1990—$13,769; 1989— $12,978)	51,391	50,528
Other Assets	22,744	26,718
Total Assets	$1,459,749	$1,372,585

LIABILITIES AND COMMON SHAREHOLDERS' EQUITY

Current Liabilities:		
Short-term debt	$ 123,871	$ 263,730
Current maturities of long-term debt	15,067	10,174
Accounts payable and accrued expenses	220,575	200,686
Income taxes	—	10,327
Dividends payable	12,633	11,893
Total Current Liabilities	372,146	496,810
Long-Term Debt	244,820	123,420
Deferred Income Taxes	82,381	74,464
Deferred Income Taxes—Leveraged Leases	127,699	112,473
Other Liabilities	14,000	—
Minority Interest	10,941	9,295
Preferred Stock, No Par Value, Authorized 6,000,000 Shares; Issued		
1,709,402 Shares, Outstanding 1,701,822 Shares, Cumulative		
Series A ESOP Convertible Preferred Stock	$ 124,568	$ 125,000

(continued)

S

541

Exhibit 2   Selected Pages from Square D's 1990 Annual Report

(Dollars in thousands, except per share)	December 31, 1990	1989
Note Receivable from ESOP Trust	(25,000)	(125,000)
Unearned ESOP Compensation	(95,400)	—
Common Shareholders' Equity:		
Common stock, par value $1.66⅔, authorized 100,000,000 shares	49,601	49,409
Additional paid-in capital	130,401	120,211
Retained earnings	773,126	713,225
Cumulative translation adjustments	3,262	(8,788)
Treasury stock—at cost	(352,796)	(317,934)
Total Common Shareholders' Equity	603,594	556,123
Total Liabilities and Common Shareholders' Equity	$1,459,749	$1,372,585

CONSOLIDATED STATEMENTS OF CASH FLOWS

(Dollars in thousands)	Year Ended December 31, 1990	1989	1988
Cash and Short-Term Investments at January 1	$ 66,348	$ 65,855	$ 94,488
Cash and Short-Term Investments Were Provided from (Used for):			
Operating Activities:			
Earnings from Continuing Operations	116,646	101,106	111,082
Add (deduct) non-cash items included in earnings from continuing operations:			
Depreciation and amortization	59,300	49,443	45,174
Deferred income taxes	1,707	(25,147)	(8,506)
Deferred income taxes—leveraged leases	15,226	23,445	25,683
(Gain) loss on sale of property, plant and equipment	(1,011)	1,936	657
(Gain) loss on foreign exchange	(2,222)	964	(52)
Minority interest	1,646	985	1,047
Other credits to earnings—net	—	(15)	(63)
Current Items (net of effects of purchase of businesses):			
Receivables	13,501	(58,515)	(20,789)
Inventories	(1,285)	26,568	(52,795)
Prepaid expenses	2,769	12,027	1,635
Accounts payable and accrued expenses	(7,312)	16,736	20,316
Income taxes	(15,253)	(3,319)	8,243
Net cash provided from continuing operations	183,712	146,214	131,632
Net cash (used for) provided from discontinued operations	(484)	2,971	721
Net cash provided from operating activities	183,228	149,185	132,353

Exhibit 2   Selected Pages from Square D's 1990 Annual Report

(Dollars in thousands)	Year Ended December 31,		
	1990	1989	1988
Investing Activities:			
Increase in investment in leveraged leases	$ (3,838)	$ (2,876)	$ (4,829)
Purchase of businesses, net of $103 of cash acquired	—	(9,271)	—
Property additions	(83,117)	(80,024)	(70,419)
Proceeds from sale of business	175,476	—	—
Proceeds from sale of property, plant and equipment	21,774	6,186	14,222
Decrease (increase) in other investments	1,281	(12,794)	24,692
Net cash provided from (used for) investing activities	111,576	(98,779)	(36,334)
Financing Activities:			
Net (decrease) increase in short-term debt	(143,983)	142,262	44,430
Increase in long-term debt	27,883	614	11,066
Reductions in long-term debt	(14,412)	(21,580)	(17,910)
Proceeds of note receivable from ESOP trust	125,000	—	—
Loan to ESOP trust	(25,000)	—	—
Cash dividends paid on common stock	(50,128)	(50,590)	(54,601)
Cash dividends paid on preferred stock	(9,956)	(5,000)	—
Common stock issued	6,602	8,929	6,349
Purchase of treasury stock	(34,916)	(126,778)	(111,394)
Redemption of preferred stock	(432)	—	—
Treasury stock issued	54	114	256
Net cash used for financing activities	(119,288)	(52,029)	(121,804)
Effect of Exchange Rate Changes on Cash	3,069	2,116	(2,848)
Net Increase (Decrease) in Cash and Short-Term Investments	178,585	493	(28,633)
Cash and Short-Term Investments at December 31	$244,933	$ 66,348	$ 65,855

See accompanying notes to consolidated financial statements.

S

543

Exhibit 2   Selected Pages from Square D's 1990 Annual Report

NOTES TO CONSOLIDATED FINANCIAL STATEMENTS

(Dollars in thousands, except per share)

A. Summary of Significant Accounting Policies

Principles of Consolidation
The financial statements include the accounts of the company and all majority-owned subsidiaries. Investments in unconsolidated affiliates are accounted for by the equity method. All significant intercompany accounts and transactions have been eliminated. The statements are based on years ended December 31, except for substantially all international subsidiaries whose fiscal years end November 30.

Cash and Short-Term Investments
Cash consists of cash in banks and time deposits. Short-term investments consist of a variety of highly liquid short-term instruments with purchased maturities of generally three months or less. Short-term investments are carried at cost, which approximates market.

Inventories
Inventories are stated at the lower of cost or market. Cost of inventories is determined using the last-in, first-out (LIFO) method for substantially all domestic inventories and certain international inventories. The first-in, first-out (FIFO) method is used for substantially all international inventories.

Property, Plant and Equipment
Depreciation of property, plant and equipment is provided on a straight-line basis over the estimated useful lives of the assets. Accelerated methods are used for income tax purposes.

Businesses Acquired
The excess of purchase price over net assets of businesses acquired is amortized on a straight-line basis over not more than forty years.

Income Taxes
Income taxes are accounted for in accordance with APB No. 11. The Financial Accounting Standards Board has issued Statement No. 96, which will change the accounting for income taxes; the company will adopt this statement no later than January 1, 1992.

Off-Balance Sheet Financial Instruments
The company enters into a variety of financial instruments in the management of its exposure to changes in interest rates and foreign currency rates. These instruments include interest rate swap agreements and foreign exchange contracts. These financial instruments do not represent a material off-balance sheet risk in relation to the financial statements.

Earnings per Common Share
Primary earnings per common share are determined by dividing the weighted average number of common shares outstanding during the year into net earnings after deducting

S

544

Exhibit 2   Selected Pages from Square D's 1990 Annual Report

after-tax dividends attributable to preferred shares. Common share equivalents in the form of stock options and convertible debt are excluded from the calculation since they do not have a material dilutive effect on per share figures. Fully diluted earnings per share reflect the conversion of all convertible preferred stock and common stock equivalents into common stock.

Reclassifications

Certain amounts in the 1989 and 1988 financial statements have been reclassified to conform to the current year's financial statement presentation.

B. Discontinued Operations

As of June 30, 1990, the company reported its General Semiconductor Industries (GSI) business as a discontinued operation, and as of September 30, 1989, the company reported its Yates Industries (Yates) copper foil business as a discontinued operation. Accordingly, the consolidated financial statements of the company have been reclassified to report separately the net assets and operating results of these discontinued operations. Financial results for periods prior to the dates of discontinuance have been restated to reflect continuing operations.

In January 1990, the company concluded the sale of its Yates operations in Europe and its 50 percent joint venture interest in Japan. In April 1990, the company completed the sale of its Yates operation in Bordentown, N.J. Total gross proceeds from the sale of all Yates operations were $175,476. The proceeds from the sale of Yates operations and the associated costs approximated management's original estimates. Management is actively pursuing the sale of the GSI business.

A gain from the sale of Yates, offset by provisions for a loss on the prospective sale of GSI and costs associated with other previously discontinued businesses, resulted in a gain of $4,391, net of income taxes, in the second quarter of 1990 from discontinued operations. The gain on the sale of Yates is net of a $14,000 provision for long-term environmental costs. The gain from the sale of Yates' foreign locations included a gain of $6,895 from the recognition of cumulative translation adjustments.

Net assets of discontinued operations were $36,681 and $170,065 at December 31, 1990 and 1989, respectively. These amounts consist of current assets; property, plant and equipment; other noncurrent assets; and current and concurrent liabilities.

Sales applicable to the discontinued operations prior to the dates of discontinuance were $16,158, $124,121 and $159,000 in 1990, 1989 and 1988, respectively. Interest expense of $249, $2,730 and $2,246, net of income taxes, was allocated to the discontinued operations prior to dates of discontinuance based on net assets for 1990, 1989 and 1988, respectively. The operating results of GSI from the date of discontinuance to December 31, 1990 were immaterial.

C. Restructuring Charge

In 1989, a restructuring charge of $17,511 net of taxes, or $.71 per share, was incurred by the company as a part of a plan to rationalize and improve profitability of several

S

Exhibit 2   Selected Pages from Square D's 1990 Annual Report

businesses and product lines both in the United States and abroad. The charge is principally comprised of costs associated with product, facility and organizational rationalization of the electrical distribution segment; product rationalization of the industrial control segment; plant consolidation and organizational restructuring in Canada; reorganization in Europe; and marketing restructuring.

D. Acquisitions

In 1989, the company acquired Crisp Automation, Inc. of Dublin, Ohio. Crisp Automation is a designer of process controls and factory automation systems and operates as part of the Square D Automation Products business. Also in 1989, the company acquired Electrical Specialty Products (ESP) of Montevallo, Alabama. ESP is a manufacturer of electrical connectors and operates as part of the Square D Connectors business. These acquisitions were accounted for as purchases; their sales and net earnings for the periods prior to the dates of acquisition were not material.

G. Inventories

Inventories valued by the last-in, first-out (LIFO) method aggregated $83,941 and $65,017 at December 31, 1990 and 1989, respectively. If the first-in, first-out (FIFO) method had been used, inventories would have been $138,120 and $140,076 higher than reported in the accompanying consolidated balance sheets at December 31, 1990 and 1989, respectively.

Inventories are maintained by element of cost; therefore, it is not practical to determine major classes such as finished goods, work in process and raw materials.

H. Lease Commitments

The company rents various warehouse and office facilities and certain equipment, principally computers and vehicles, under lease arrangements classified as operating leases.

Future minimum rental payments under noncancelable operating leases with initial terms of one year or more as of December 31, 1990 are:

1991	$10,160
1992	7,266
1993	5,520
1994	4,473
1995	975
Remainder	1,224
Total	$29,618

Exhibit 2 Selected Pages from Square D's 1990 Annual Report

J. Debt

Long-term debt consists of:

	1990	1989
ESOP Notes, 7.7%, due on various dates to 2004	$120,400	$ —
Senior Notes, 10.0%, due 1995	75,000	75,000
Industrial Revenue Bonds, 5.6% to 8.8%, due on various dates to 2004	25,715	26,610
First Mortgage Notes, 9.0% to 9.2%, due on various dates to 2009	10,825	11,119
Subordinated Convertible Notes, 9.0%, due 1992 (net of unamortized discount at 13.0%: 1990—$220, 1989—$376)	2,787	4,096
Payable to banks; average rate 1990—13.8%, 1989—10.3%; due on various dates to 1996	1,114	2,423
Other debt: average rate 1990—14.4%, 1989—12.7%; due on various dates to 2000	24,046	14,346
Subtotal	259,887	133,594
Less current maturities	15,067	10,174
Total	$244,820	$123,420

The aggregate annual maturities of long-term debt for the years 1991 through 1995 are $15,067, $14,642, $14,968, $13,877 and $82,187, respectively.

The Employee Stock Ownership Plan (ESOP) Notes include $25,000 of direct borrowings by the company, the proceeds from which have been advanced in the form of a loan to the company's ESOP. Direct borrowings of the ESOP, aggregating $95,400 as of December 31, 1990, have been guaranteed by the company and accordingly, are reported as long-term debt of the company. See Note Q for further discussion.

Industrial Revenue Bonds of $9,115 and the First Mortgage Notes are secured by the property and equipment acquired with the proceeds of the financings.

The Subordinated Convertible Notes are convertible at a rate of 28.57 shares for each one thousand dollars of principal. The company has reserved 85,934 shares of common stock for the conversion.

The company has entered into revolving credit agreements in which twelve of its principal banks participate. The agreements provide for up to $180,000 of revolving credit through 1994. The credit is available in both the domestic and euro markets.

Short-term debt includes bank borrowings of $33,611 and $19,438 and commercial paper of $70,260 and $214,292 at December 31, 1990 and 1989, respectively. Additionally, short-term debt includes a master note agreement of $20,000 and $30,000 at December 31, 1990 and 1989, respectively.

The company has additional unused short-term lines of credit which aggregated $69,501 at December 31, 1990.

S

547

Exhibit 2   Selected Pages from Square D's 1990 Annual Report

K. Income Taxes

Pre-tax income from continuing operations is as follows:

	1990	1989	1988
United States	$163,674	$142,855	$155,453
International	20,745	18,107	18,939
Total	$184,419	$160,962	$174.392

Income tax provisions for continuing operations are as follows:

	1990	1989	1988
Current:			
U.S. Federal	$ 33,452	$ 46,784	$ 35,261
International	7,999	4,752	3,989
State	9,037	9,902	6,625
	50,488	61,438	45,875
Deferred:			
U.S. Federal	17,189	(1,375)	17,475
International	(869)	1,479	228
State	965	(1,686)	(268)
	17,285	(1,582)	17,435
Total	$ 67,773	$ 59,856	$ 63,310

The components of the deferred income tax provision are as follows:

	1990	1989	1988
Leasing subsidiary income	$ 17,077	$ 22,502	$ 25,256
401(k) contributions	4,383	—	—
State tax	965	(1,686)	(268)
Tax over book depreciation	2,535	1,301	751
Deferred taxable income on installment sales	—	(13,006)	(5,615)
Alternative minimum tax	—	8,484	1,634
Funding of group health insurance trust	—	(6,863)	(11,634)
Restructuring charge	—	(4,510)	—
Other	(7,675)	(7,804)	7,311
Deferred Income Tax Expense (Benefit)	$ 17,285	$ (1,582)	$ 17,435

Exhibit 2   Selected Pages from Square D's 1990 Annual Report

A reconciliation between the statutory and effective tax rates for continuing operations is as follows:

	1990	1989	1988
U.S. Federal statutory rate	34.0%	34.0%	34.0%
State income taxes, net of Federal benefit	3.6	3.4	2.4
Rate reduction	—	—	(2.5)
U.S. tax on international dividend	0.4	0.3	4.2
International rate differential	0.1	(0.9)	(2.6)
Leasing subsidiary	(0.1)	(0.2)	(0.8)
Restructuring charge	—	0.6	—
Other	(1.3)	—	1.6
Effective tax rate	36.7%	37.2%	36.3%

No provisions have been made for possible international withholding and U.S. income taxes payable on the distribution of approximately $120,009 of undistributed earnings which have been or will be reinvested abroad or are expected to be returned to the United States in tax-free distributions. Provisions for taxes have been made for all earnings which the company presently plans to repatriate.

S

549

L. Supplementary Earnings Statement Information

	1990	1989	1988
Non-Operating Income:			
Interest income	$25,501	$14,497	$9,666
Settlement of lawsuit	5,695	—	—
Income from leveraged leases	5,273	6,694	8,219
Gain (loss) on sale of property, plant and equipment	1,005	(1,933)	(673)
Other non-operating (expense) income	(2,734)	(2,152)	43
Total	$34,740	$17,106	$17,255
Research and Development	$55,384	$44,720	$46,533
Maintenance and Repairs	47,328	49,572	47,131
Advertising	26,584	25,933	19,586
Rents	22,857	23,238	19,958
Foreign Currency Transaction (Loss) Gain	(1,423)	292	2,343

O. Pension Plans

The company's domestic operations maintain several pension plans, primarily defined benefit pension plans covering substantially all employees for normal retirement benefits at age 65. Defined benefits for salaried employees are based on a final average com-

Exhibit 2 Selected Pages from Square D's 1990 Annual Report

pensation formula and hourly plans are based on an amount per year of service formula. The company makes annual contributions to the plans in accordance with ERISA and IRS regulations, including amortization of past service cost over the average remaining service life of active employees.

In 1989 the company adopted SFAS No. 87 for its significant international pension plans. For the company's international pension plans that have not adopted SFAS No. 87, the excess of vested benefits over fund assets is insignificant. The company makes annual contributions to the plans in accordance with the laws and regulations of the respective international taxing jurisdictions in which the company operates.

Components of net periodic pension cost for the company's domestic and international pension plans consist of the following:

	1990	1989	1988
Service cost—benefits earned during period	$12,409	$11,039	$9,515
Net deferral and amortization	(42,253)	24,976	(11,621)
Interest on projected benefit obligation	28,547	25,796	25,414
Actual return on plan assets	10,809	(55,795)	(14,388)
Net periodic pension cost	$ 9,512	$ 6,016	$ 8,920

The net periodic pension cost attributable to the company's significant international pension plans was $843 and $1,000 in 1990 and 1989, respectively.

The following tables set forth the company's domestic and international pension plans' funded status and amounts recognized in the company's balance sheet at December 31:

	Overfunded Plans		Underfunded Plans	
	1990	1989	1990	1989
Actuarial present value of benefit obligations:				
Vested employees	$(193,615)	$(194,793)	$(96,325)	$(90,466)
Non-vested employees	(12,169)	(6,073)	(15,407)	(3,251)
Total accumulated benefit obligation	(205,784)	(200,866)	(111,732)	(93,717)
Additional amounts related to projected salary increases	(35,705)	(45,637)	(3,949)	(3,095)
Projected benefit obligation	(241,489)	(246,503)	(115,681)	(96,812)
Fair value of plan assets (primarily common equities and fixed income instruments)	245,953	267,184	75,493	68,884
Projected benefit obligation less than (in excess of) plan assets	4,464	20,681	(40,188)	(27,928)
Unrecognized net (gain) loss	(7,583)	(15,018)	9,451	8,442
Unrecognized prior service cost	(6,374)	(6,934)	17,281	4,673
Unrecognized net liability existing at the date of initial adoption of SFAS No. 87	6,604	1,682	1,378	4,569
(Accrued) Prepaid Pension Cost	$ (2,889)	$ 411	$(12,078)	$(10,244)

Exhibit 2   Selected Pages from Square D's 1990 Annual Report

The economic assumptions used in determining the actuarial present value of the projected benefit obligation of the domestic plans were:

	1990	1989
Weighted average discount rate	9.0%	8.3%
Rate of increase in future compensation levels	5.3	5.3
Rate of return on plan assets	10.0	10.0

The assumed rates for the company's international plans, which reflect the economic conditions of each plan, generally varied from U.S. rates by 1.0 percent to 2.0 percent.

Total pension expense for all plans was $10,914, $8,073 and $12,962 for 1990, 1989 and 1988, respectively. Actuarial assumptions were revised in 1990, 1989 and 1988 principally to update the investment return and rates of pay increase to levels more reflective of current economic conditions. These and other changes increased pension expense in 1990 by approximately $920 and reduced pension expense in 1989 and 1988 by approximately $5,838 and $1,218, respectively.

P. Post-Retirement Benefits

The company provides health plan coverage and life insurance benefits for retired employees of substantially all of its domestic operations. Substantially all of the company's employees may become eligible for these benefits when they retire from active employment with the company. The cost of retiree health coverage is recognized as an expense when claims are paid. The cost of life insurance benefits is recognized as an expense as premiums are paid. These costs totaled $6,165 in 1990, $5,075 in 1989 and $3,982 in 1988.

The Financial Accounting Standards Board has issued Statement of Financial Accounting Standards No. 106, "Employers' Accounting for Post-Retirement Benefits Other Than Pensions." This Statement will require accrual of post-retirement benefits during the years an employee provides services. While the impact of this new standard has not been fully determined, the change will result in significantly greater expense being recognized for these benefits. The company plans to adopt this Statement in 1993.

T. Segment and Geographic Information

The company is engaged in the manufacture and sale of electrical distribution products, systems and services and industrial control products, systems and services, and operates in virtually every major marketing area in the world. Major manufacturing plants are located throughout the United States and in Europe, Latin America, Canada, Australia and Thailand.

The electrical distribution segment primarily consists of the manufacture and sale of products, systems and services used in the distribution of electricity. Distribution equipment is used principally in distributing electricity from the end of transmission lines to points of utilization within residential, commercial, industrial or other types of buildings. Distribution products include industrial molded case circuit breakers, miniature circuit breakers, load centers, safety switches, metering devices, switchboards, panelboards, motor control centers, low and medium voltage switchgear, busways and raceways, dry type transformers and power and cast resin transformers.

S

551

Exhibit 2   Selected Pages from Square D's 1990 Annual Report

The industrial control segment mainly consists of the manufacture and sale of control products, systems and services that control the electricity used in the operation of power utilization devices or processes. Control equipment includes motor starters, contactors, push buttons, adjustable frequency motor controllers and sensors. Other products in this segment include programmable controllers, cell controllers, electronic computerized control and data-gathering systems, uninterruptible power systems, power protection equipment, infrared radiation thermometers and pyrometers and snap dome switches and keyboards.

Substantially all products of the electrical distribution and industrial control segments are marketed through the company's own marketing organization and distributed through a system of strategically located warehouses. The majority of all sales are made directly to authorized electrical distributors who, in turn, market the products to electrical contractors, electrical utilities, large industrial plants and other classes of trade.

Sales between geographic areas and industry segments are based on prices approximating current market values. Net sales to a group of customers under common control, for both industry segments, were $161,015 in 1990, $161,156 in 1989 and $176,700 in 1988.

Financial information by industry segment for the three years ended December 31, 1990 is summarized as follows:

Industry Segments	1990	1989	1988
Sales			
Electrical Distribution:			
Unaffiliated customers	$1,170,420	$1,117,619	$1,057,359
Intercompany	18,203	13,083	10,484
	1,188,623	1,130,702	1,067,843
Industrial Control:			
Unaffiliated customers	482,899	481,069	440,413
Intercompany	63,919	51,923	49,244
	546,818	532,992	489,657
Eliminations	(82,122)	(65,006)	(59,728)
Consolidated	$1,653,319	$1,598,688	$1,497,772
Operating Earnings			
Electrical Distribution	$ 152,280	$ 143,541	$ 138,229
Industrial Control	26,302	31,614	40,046
Eliminations	(143)	139	944
Consolidated	$ 178,439	$ 175,294	$ 179,219
Identifiable Assets			
Electrical Distribution	$ 920,781	$ 755,253	$ 701,973
Industrial Control	503,079	447,913	418,247
Eliminations	(792)	(646)	(835)
Identifiable Assets of Continuing Operations	$1,423,068	$1,202,520	$1,119,385
Net Assets of Discontinued Operations	36,681	170,065	181,338
Consolidated	$1,459,749	$1,372,585	$1,300,723

Exhibit 2   Selected Pages from Square D's 1990 Annual Report

Industry Segments	1990	1989	1988
Depreciation and Amortization Expense			
Electrical Distribution	$ 36,688	$ 29,815	$ 26,345
Industrial Control	22,612	19,628	18,829
Capital Additions			
Electrical Distribution	$ 54,763	$ 50,323	$ 43,980
Industrial Control	39,125	30,125	27,975

Effective September 30, 1989, the company changed its reportable segments from Electrical Equipment and Electronic Products to Electrical Distribution Products, Systems and Services and Industrial Control Products, Systems and Services.

   Financial information by geographic area for the three years ended December 31, 1990 is summarized as follows:

Geographic Areas	1990	1989	1988
Sales			
United States:			
Unaffiliated customers	$1,332,390	$1,321,769	$1,256,009
Intercompany	73,646	62,253	47,479
	1,406,036	1,384,022	1,303,488
Europe:			
Unaffiliated customers	138,836	115,678	105,471
Intercompany	22,617	23,691	25,207
	161,453	139,369	130,678
Latin America:			
Unaffiliated customers	78,867	68,178	53,242
Intercompany	1,300	1,217	1,761
	80,167	69,395	55,003
Other International			
Unaffiliated customers	103,226	93,063	83,050
Intercompany	447	256	620
	103,673	93,319	83,670
Eliminations	(98,010)	(87,417)	(75,067)
Consolidated	$1,653,319	$1,598,688	$1,497,772
Operating Earnings			
United States	$ 164,155	$ 163,202	$ 156,791
Europe	3,555	212	4,098
Latin America	10,445	12,547	11,212
Other International	650	(463)	3,942
Eliminations	(366)	(204)	3,176
Consolidated	$ 178,439	$ 175,294	$ 179,219

(continued)

S

Exhibit 2   Selected Pages from Square D's 1990 Annual Report

Geographic Areas	1990	1989	1988
Identifiable Assets			
United States	$1,131,085	$ 952,865	$ 883,334
Europe	158,637	120,483	109,297
Latin America	65,847	62,171	62,924
Other International	70,203	69,357	64,886
Eliminations	(2,704)	(2,356)	(1,056)
Identifiable Assets of Continuing			
Operations	1,423,068	1,202,520	1,119,385
Net Assets of Discontinued			
Operations	36,681	170,065	181,338
Consolidated	$1,459,749	$1,372,585	$1,300,723

Exhibit 2   Selected Pages from Square D's 1990 Annual Report

SELECTED FINANCIAL DATA

	1990	1989	1988	1987	1986	1985
Summary of Operations						
Net sales	$1,653,319	$1,598,688	$1,497,772	$1,330,784	$1,274,932	$1,223,193
Cost of products sold	1,088,977	1,027,348	979,591	838,749	820,457	787,310
Selling, administrative and general expenses	385,903	369,726	338,962	287,386	267,066	237,790
Restructuring charge	—	26,320	—	11,192	—	—
Non-operating income	34,740	17,106	17,255	17,590	26,670	14,486
Interest expense	28,760	31,438	22,082	19,699	24,977	21,191
Earnings from continuing operations before income taxes	184,419	160,962	174,392	191,348	189,102	191,388
Provision for income taxes	67,773	59,856	63,310	75,736	85,191	89,465
Earnings from continuing operations	116,646	101,106	111,082	115,612	103,911	101,923
Earnings (loss) from discontinued operations, net of income taxes	4,079	798	7,852	(5,611)	(4,983)	(14,735)
Net earnings	120,725	101,904	118,934	110,001	98,928	87,188
Financial Information						
Working capital	$ 389,503	$ 193,758	$ 178,399	$ 192,693	$ 204,083	$ 202,076
Property, plant and equipment—at cost	799,367	736,739	673,946	630,754	606,757	570,538
Total assets	1,459,749	1,372,585	1,300,723	1,252,819	1,178,826	1,118,473
Long-term debt	244,820	123,420	135,467	141,085	166,389	201,028
Common shareholders' equity	603,594	556,123	636,029	679,711	670,789	606,139
Capital additions	93,888	80,448	71,955	35,356	71,617	61,880
Depreciation and amortization	59,300	49,443	45,174	42,277	38,548	32,430
Share Data						
Earnings per common share:						
Primary:						
Continuing operations	$4.76	$3.95	$4.15	$4.01	$3.59	$3.53
Discontinued operations	.18	.03	.29	(.19)	(.17)	(.51)
Net earnings	4.94	3,98	4.44	3.82	3.42	3.02
Fully diluted:						
Continuing operations	4.57	3.88	4.13	3.98	3.56	3.50
Discontinued operations	.16	.03	.29	(.19)	(.17)	(.50)
Net earnings	4.73	3.91	4.42	3.79	3.39	3.00
Cash dividends declared per common share	2.20	2.00	1.94	1.86	1.84	1.84
Common shares outstanding at December 31	22,886	23,489	25,691	27,660	28,966	28,864
Common shareholders' equity per share	$26.37	$23.68	$24.76	$24.57	$23.16	$21.00

S

555

(continued)

Exhibit 2   Selected Pages from Square D's 1990 Annual Report

SELECTED FINANCIAL DATA (continued)

	1990	1989	1988	1987	1986	1985
Key Financial Relationships						
Gross profit	34.1%	35.7%	34.6%	37.0%	35.6%	35.6%
Current ratio	2.0:1	1.4:1	1.5:1	1.7:1	1.9:1	1.8:1
Average total debt to average total equity	66.2%	55.7%	38.2%	29.0%	39.2%	40.5%
Average long-term debt to average capital	23.3%	13.6%	15.6%	16.7%	22.0%	19.8%

All financial data for the periods prior to 1990 have been restated for discontinued operations.

All financial data for the periods prior to 1988 have been restated for the consolidation of a majority-owned subsidiary.

S

Exhibit 3   Schneider Financial Statements and Accounting Policies

EXHIBIT 3
Schneider Financial Statements and Accounting Policies

STATEMENT OF INCOME

(in FF million for the year ended December 31)	1990	1989	1988
Net sales	**49,884**	**45,127**	**40,493**
Cost of goods sold, personnel and administrative expenses	(44,978)	(41,008)	(36,766)
Depreciation and amortization	(1,565)	(1,166)	(1,272)
Operating expenses	**(46,543)**	**(42,174)**	**(38,038)**
Operating income	**3,341**	**2,953**	**2,455**
Interest expense – net	(832)	(757)	(182)
Income before non-recurring items, amortization of goodwill, taxes and minority interest	**2,509**	**2,196**	**2,273**
Non-recurring items:			
Gains on disposition of assets – net	419	550	484
Other non-recurring income and expense – net	(367)	(343)	(642)
Income before taxes, employee profit-sharing, amortization of goodwill and minority interests	**2,561**	**2,403**	**2,115**
Employee profit-sharing	(158)	(130)	(126)
Income taxes	(802)	(912)	(701)
Net income of fully consolidated companies before amortization of goodwill	**1,601**	**1,361**	**1,288**
Amortization of goodwill	(236)	(235)	(345)
Net income of fully consolidated companies	**1,365**	**1,126**	**943**
Group's share of income of companies accounted for by the equity method	**4**	**17**	**(53)**
Minority interests	(445)	(266)	(330)
Net income (Schneider SA share)	**924**	**877**	**560**
Net income (Schneider SA share) per share – in FF	62.96	63.06	48.85
Net income (Schneider SA share) per share after dilution – in FF	61.65	60.53	N/A

S

557

Exhibit 3   Schneider Financial Statements and Accounting Policies

BALANCE SHEET

(in FF million for the year ended December 31)	1990	1989	1988
ASSETS			
Current Assets			
Cash and equivalents	1,841.3	3,400.3	1,579.6
Marketable securities	3,020.9	1,924.3	1,243.7
Accounts receivable – trade	14,597.4	14,987.3	13,998.5
Other receivables and prepaid expenses	4,738.1	3,876.5	4,054.9
Deferred taxes	407.5	290.2	236.9
Inventories and work in process	7,712.6	7,159.0	29,715.3
Total current assets	**32,317.8**	**31,637.6**	**50,828.9**
Non-Current Assets			
Property, plant and equipment	14,293.9	13,107.5	12,019.7
Accumulated depreciation	(6,691.5)	(6,365.6)	(6,409.5)
Property, plant and equipment – net	7,602.4	6,741.9	5,610.2
Investments accounted for by the equity method	175.9	135.7	244.9
Other equity investments	1,727.9	571.3	684.6
Other investments	573.0	618.3	909.8
Total investments	2,476.8	1,325.3	1,839.3
Intangible assets – net	147.5	153.5	115.0
Goodwill – net	7,032.8	6,087.8	5,596.8
Total non-current assets	**17,259.5**	**14,308.5**	**13,161.3**
Total assets	**49,577.3**	**45,946.1**	**63,990.2**
LIABILITIES AND SHAREHOLDERS' EQUITY			
Current Liabilities			
Accounts payable – trade	9,867.9	9,614.6	8,440.8
Taxes and benefits payable	4,822.5	4,795.8	3,748.4
Other payables and accrued liabilities	5,230.4	4,332.2	3,405.5
Short-term debt	3,120.5	3,165.8	3,081.3
Customer prepayments	2,509.5	3,848.3	27,606.1
Total current liabilities	**25,547.2**	**25,756.7**	**46,282.1**
Long-term debt	9,958.4	7,345.9	7,712.1
of which: convertible bonds	3,950.2	1,108.8	500.5
Provisions for contingencies	3,942.6	3,890.0	3,758.8
Invested Capital	**24,030.1**	**20,189.4**	**17,708.1**
Capital stock	1,414.4	1,397.2	1,146.3
Retained earnings	6,091.1	5,344.6	3,046.6
Shareholders' Equity	**7,505.5**	**6,741.8**	**4,192.9**
Minority interests	2,623.6	2,211.7	2,044.3
Total shareholders' equity and minority interests	**10,129.1**	**8,953.5**	**6,237.2**
Total liabilities and shareholders' equity	**49,577.3**	**45,946.1**	**63,990.2**

STATEMENT OF CASH FLOWS

(in FF million for the year ended December 31)	1990	1989
I. Operating activities		
Net income of fully consolidated companies	1,368.5	1,143.7
Depreciation, amortization and provisions, net of recoveries	2,164.0	2,283.0
(Gains) on disposals of assets	(418.7)	(550.1)
Others	(0.8)	(28.7)
Net cash provided by operating activities before changes in operating assets and liabilities	**3,113.0**	**2,847.9**
Decrease (increase) in accounts receivable	(944.4)	1,170.4
Inventories and work in process	675.4	(1,708.6)
Increase (decrease) in accounts payable	578.7	(16.3)
Other current assets and liabilities	(1,681.4)	736.0
Net change in operating assets and liabilities	**(1,371.7)**	**181.5**
Net cash provided by operating activities	**1,741.3**	**3,029.4**
II. Investing activities		
Disposals of fixed assets	712.9	1,394.8
Purchases of property, plant and equipment and intangible assets	(2,589.5)	(2,154.3)
Financial investments	(2,788.2)	(1,068.8)
Other long-term investments	125.5	13.4
Net cash used in investing activities	**(4,539.3)**	**(1,814.9)**
III. Financing activities		
Reduction in long-term debt	(1,626.4)	(3,045.2)
New borrowings	1,508.7	2,435.1
Convertible bonds issued	2,655.6	634.7
Common stock issued	71.9	1,877.0
Dividends paid:		
Schneider SA shareholders	(174.6)	(126.1)
Minority interests	(116.5)	(69.7)
Net cash provided by financing activities	**2,318.7**	**1,705.8**
IV. Net effect of exchange rate and other changes	**13.8**	**178.5**
Net increase (decrease) in cash and cash equivalents (I + II + III + IV)	**(465.5)**	**3,098.8**
Cash and cash equivalents at beginning of year	**3,424.9**	**326.1**
at end of year	**2,959.4**	**3,424.9**

The following notes are an integral part of these financial statements.

Exhibit 3 Schneider Financial Statements and Accounting Policies

SELECTED NOTES TO FINANCIAL STATEMENTS

1. ACCOUNTING PRINCIPLES

The consolidated financial statements of Schneider SA have been prepared in accordance with French generally accepted accounting principles and with the international accounting principles recommended by the International Accounting Standards Committee (I.A.S.C.). The differences between these principles and U.S. GAAP are explained in Note l.m), below.

The financial statements of consolidated subsidiaries, which are prepared in accordance with accounting principles generally accepted in the countries in which they operate, have been restated in accordance with the principles applied by the Group.

a) Consolidation principles

All significant companies that are controlled directly or indirectly by Schneider SA have been fully consolidated.

Companies over which Schneider SA exercises significant influence have been accounted for by the equity method.

As an exception to the above principles, Banque Morhange, in which the Group holds a majority interest but whose operations are not material in relation to the Group as a whole, has also been consolidated by the equity method.

In accordance with French generally accepted accounting principles, joint ventures in which the Group is the managing partner are fully consolidated by Schneider SA, after deducting the other partners' share in the income or loss of the joint venture. In cases where the Group is not the managing shareholder, only Schneider SA's share of the income or loss is accounted for, except for two contracts which are consolidated by the proportional method.

Goodwill is amortized out of income over a maximum of forty years based on estimated useful life.

b) Translation of the financial statements of foreign subsidiaries

The financial statements of foreign subsidiaries are translated into French francs as follows:
- Assets and liabilities are translated at year-end exchange rates;
- Income statement and cash flow items are translated at average exchange rates.

Differences arising on translation are recorded under shareholders' equity.

c) Translation of foreign currency transactions

With the exception of the transactions described below, foreign currency debts and receivables are translated into French francs at year-end exchange rates. As allowed under French law, translation differences are recorded in the income statement under interest income and expense.

Exchange gains as well as carrybacks and carryforwards related to forward purchases and sales of foreign currency used to hedge the Group's trading commitments are deferred and recognized at the same time as the gain or loss on the underlying transaction.

Gains and losses on unhedged forward currency transactions are credited or charged to income. The gain or loss corresponds to the difference between the forward exchange rate provided for in the contract and the exchange rate prevailing at year end for purchases and sales made in the same currency and according to the same term.

In cases where a speculative currency position is considered to exist due to the future interest on fixed to variable currency swaps, the interest is discounted on the basis of the fixed rate and stated at the exchange rate prevailing at year end for cash transactions. The translation difference is credited or charged to income.

d) Financial instruments based on exchange and interest rates

The Group uses financial instruments based on exchange and interest rates. The methods used to account for these instruments are described above.

Exhibit 3   Schneider Financial Statements and Accounting Policies

e) Long-term contracts

Income from long-term contracts is recognized by the percentage-of-completion method, based on the financial status of the contract. Probable losses upon completion of a given contract are provided for in full as soon as they become known. The cost of work in process includes costs relating directly to the contracts and a percentage of overheads.

The estimated cost of the remaining work on contracts expected to generate a loss does not take account of any income from claims, except where such claims have been accepted by the customer and the latter has no major financing problems. Contracts in progress are therefore stated at the lower of cost or realizable value.

In accordance with the logic underlying the percentage-of-completion method, work in process is matched with customer prepayments received upon presentation of a schedule of work performed to date. However, prepayments in connection with the work in process include:
- Prepayments to finance production;
- Prepayments for work in process on contracts which are still in the early stages and for which it is not possible to make any estimate of probable income or losses; and
- Contracts scheduled to last less than twelve months.

f) Research and development expenditures

Internally-financed research and development expenditures are charged to income for the period.

g) Deferred taxes

Deferred taxes corresponding to timing differences between the recognition of income and expenses in the consolidated financial statements and for tax purposes are accounted for by the liability method.

h) Provisions for retirement bonuses

The Group's liability for retirement bonuses is calculated taking into account projected future compensation levels. The method used is in accordance with the Financial Accounting Standards Board (FASB) Statement of Financial Accounting Standards No. 87.

Part of the Group's liability for retirement bonuses is provided for and part is funded by an insured plan. The provisions are calculated for all eligible employees and the same discount and indexation rates are used for all Group companies that have adopted this method. For the insured plan, the current value of the plan assets has been calculated and provision has been made for any unfunded liability.

i) Marketable securities

Almost all marketable securities represent conventional short-term instruments (commercial paper, mutual funds and related securities). They are stated at cost. In the case of bonds and other debt instruments, cost includes accrued interest.

j) Inventories and work in process

Inventories and work in process are stated at weighted average cost. Any difference between cost and realizable value is provided for.

The cost of work in process, semi-finished and finished products includes direct materials and labor costs, sub-contracting costs incurred up to the balance sheet date and a percentage of production overheads

k) Property, plant and equipment

Land, buildings and equipment are stated at cost. Assets held at the time of a legal revaluation are stated at revalued cost. An equivalent amount is recorded in shareholders' equity, under retained earnings or revaluation reserve, and is written back to income in an amount matching the corresponding depreciation and disposals, so that the revaluation has no impact on income.

In the case of subsidiaries operating in high-inflation countries, the impact of legal revaluations is eliminated on consolidation and the resulting translation differences are recorded in retained earnings.

S

561

Exhibit 3   Schneider Financial Statements and Accounting Policies

Property, plant and equipment is depreciated on a straight-line basis over the estimated useful lives of the assets.

Property, plant and equipment acquired under a capital lease is capitalized on the basis of the cost of the asset concerned and depreciated in accordance with the above principles. An obligation in the same amount is recorded on the liabilities side of the balance sheet.

l) Non-consolidated equity investments and other investments

Non-consolidated equity investments and other investments are stated at cost, except for investments held at the time of the 1977 legal revaluation. Each year, the carrying value is compared to fair value and any difference is provided for. Fair value is determined by reference to the Group's share in the underlying net assets, the expected future profitability and business prospects of the investee company, and – in the case of listed securities – the market value of the stock.

m) Differences between Schneider SA accounting principles and U.S. GAAP

The main differences between the accounting principles described above and U.S. GAAP are as follows:

Write-ups

As mentioned in Note l.k. above, the Company has performed certain write-ups which are contrary to U.S. GAAP. The write-ups have no impact on income but do affect shareholders' equity.

Consolidation

As indicated in Note a, Banque Morhange, whose operations are not material in relation to the Group as a whole, has been accounted for by the equity method.

Provisions for contingencies

In U.S. GAAP, the part of these provisions related to operating cycles would be considered as accrued liabilities.

Customer prepayments

In the consolidated financial statements, customer prepayments are recorded as a separate component of current liabilities. Under U.S. GAAP, work in process in an amount equal to the cost of the work performed for which no income or loss has been recognized.

Deferred taxes

In December 1987, the FASB issued a new standard concerning the accounting treatment of deferred taxes. The application of this standard is not compulsory in 1990. The Company has not yet decided the date at which it will start applying this standard and, in view of the complexity of the new rules, has not determined the impact that its application would have had on the 1990 financial statements as presented.

Non-recurring income and expense

Non-recurring income and expense includes items that the Company considers to be non-recurring but that would be treated as operating income and expense under U.S. GAAP. In addition, under U.S. GAAP, the amortization of goodwill would have been accounted for under income from continuing operations.

These reclassifications would have the following impact on income from continuing operations:

(in FF million)	1990	1989
Income from continuing operations, before tax	2,509	2,196
Non-recurring income other than extraordinary items	(237)	85
Amortization of goodwill	(236)	(235)
Income from continuing operations, before tax, according to U.S. GAAP	2,036	2,046

S

562

EXHIBIT 4   Square D Common Stock Purchase Plan

EXHIBIT 4
Square D Common Stock Purchase Plan

The firm's Articles of Incorporation were modified in August 1988 as follows:

The Company adopted a new Share Purchase Rights Plan and declared a dividend distribution of one new common purchase right on each outstanding share of Square D common stock. The rights are exercisable only if someone acquires 20 percent or more of the company's common stock or announces a tender offer. At any time a person or group acquires 20 percent or more of the company's outstanding common stock and prior to that person acquiring 50 percent or more of the company's common stock, the company may exchange the rights (other than rights owned by such 20 percent or greater shareholder) in whole or in part for one share of common stock per right. If a person or group acquires 20 percent or more of the common stock, or certain events occur, each right not owned by the 20 percent or greater shareholder becomes exercisable for the number of shares of the company having a market value of twice the exercise price of the right. If the company is acquired in a merger or other business combination transaction or 50 percent or more of its assets or earning power are sold at any time after the rights become exercisable, the rights entitle a holder to buy a number of shares of common stock of the acquiring company having a market value of twice the exercise price of each right.

Exhibit 5   Selected Square D Stock Data for the Fourth Quarter 1990a

EXHIBIT 5

Selected Square D Stock Data for the Fourth Quarter 1990[a]

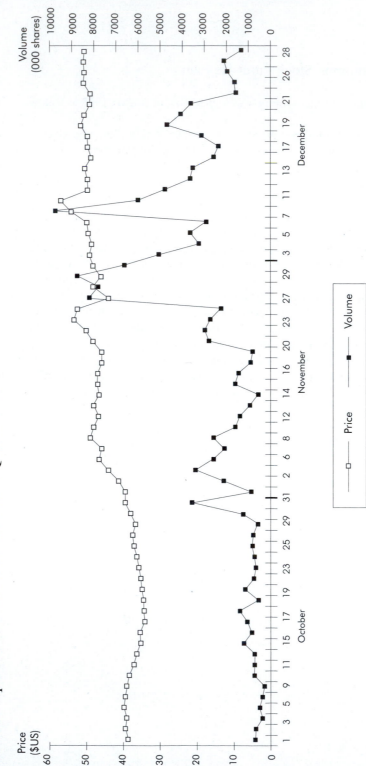

a. In late 1990, approximately 23 million shares were outstanding.

Exhibit 6   Valuation Data for Square D

EXHIBIT 6
Valuation Data for Square D

....

Square D equity beta	0.95
Moody's corporate bond average yield in February 1991 for major ratings:	
Aaa	8.83%
Aa	9.16%
A	9.38%
Ba	10.07%
Prime rate in February 1991	8.8%
Treasury bills rates in February 1991 (3 months)	6.0%
Government 30-year treasuries rates in February 1991	8.25%
Square D commercial paper rating in February 1991 (on a scale from P3 to P1, P1 being the best rating)	P1
Square D corporate bonds rating in February 1991	Aa3
US federal statutory tax rate in 1990	34.0%
State income tax rate, net of federal benefit in 1990	3.6%

....

S

Siemens

Siemens, Munich's conglomerate in electrical and electronic equipment, is one of the 30 largest public corporations in the world, and the largest electrical/electronics company in Europe. Siemens entered the 1990s having shown steadily increasing sales in recent years, maintaining 19 major business segments, and producing a variety of products that span the consumer and industrial sectors. Siemens' output ranges from nuclear power plants to computers; from factory automation equipment to washing machines; from electronic automotive components to locomotives; from fiber-optic telecommunications networks to lasers. In short, if it involves electricity or electronics, Siemens probably produces it.

While the magnitude and growth of Siemens' revenue is impressive, Siemens' profitability is not, at least by U.S. standards. Siemens' profit margin has been only about 2.5 percent and return on equity was only 8 to 10 percent for each of the five years ended in 1992. In contrast, the U.S.'s General Electric has (ignoring the effect of an accounting change in 1991) posted profit margins of 7 to 8 percent, with returns on equity of 16 to 21 percent.

Siemens' mediocre profit performance has been attributed to everything from "lethargy" to a "cavalier attitude towards profitability" to a greater concern for social responsibility than earnings.[1] On this last score, one senior Siemens executive was quoted as saying, "Unlike GE, we are not committed first to making money. We are committed to our workers, our markets, and to technical leadership."[2]

Weak profitability and concern for social responsibility may make good press. However, security analyst Connie Bishop is questioning whether, in real economic terms, Siemens is any less profitable than its international competitors. Bishop knows that there are a variety of ways in which German accounting provides substantial flexibility to management, especially if managers' incentives are to keep reported profits low. Moreover, the multiples at which Siemens stock trades suggest there may be more to Siemens' profit than meets the eye. Its price-to-book multiple has hovered around 2 for years—much higher than Bishop would normally expect of a U.S. common stock with a return on equity as low as Siemens' 8 to 10 percent.

Prepared by Professor Victor L. Bernard with the assistance of Todd Hassen and Marlene Plumlee. This case is based on publicly available information. It was prepared as a basis for class discussion and is not intended to illustrate either an effective or ineffective management of a business situation.

1. See "Papa Siemens," Forbes (May 28, 1990), pp. 98, 100–102; "Half Way There," The Economist (July 4, 1992), pp. 60–61.
2. "Papa Siemens," Forbes (May 28, 1990), pp. 98, 100–102.

SIEMENS: THE COMPANY

Siemens is a DM 78 billion firm operating in many lines of business. The two largest segments are computers (Siemens Nixdorf Informationssysteme, or SNI) and Public Communications Networks, specializing in telephone network systems. Each of these two segments generated sales in 1992 of about DM 13 billion. Other large segments, ranging from DM 5 billion to DM 8 billion in sales, are producers of a variety of electrical and electronic products and systems—involved in power generation, power distribution, systems automation and control, engineering, and many other products and services for the government, corporate, and consumer sectors.

Siemens' common stock is widely held and traded on several European exchanges; its preferred stock is held by the Siemens family. The company is governed by a 21-person Supervisory Board, chaired in 1992 by Heribald Naerger. Approximately half of the Board consists of high-level corporate executives; laborers (mechanics, technicians, etc.) fill the remaining seats, as is typical in Germany.

Siemens' record of mediocre profitability is longstanding. It has been referred to as "dangerously unwieldy,"[3] too beholden to its key customer, the German government, and maintaining a "civil service mentality."[4] It has at times amassed so much cash as to be labeled jokingly as "a bank with sidelines in electricals."[5]

Siemens' apparently weak profit performance has, of course, not gone unnoticed. In 1990, one writer put it this way:

> In many respects the incentive to maximize profits hasn't been overpowering at Siemens. The company is takeover-proof by virtue of a two-tiered share structure that protects the voting rights of the Siemens family heirs. The result is an ingrained outlook that is heavily institutional, overcautious and, if not scornful of the bottom line, at least somewhat cavalier about profitability. "More than other German companies," [CEO] Kaske explains, "we have a great sense of social responsibility and want to be a long-staying partner of the German economy."
>
> The partnership has yielded mutual benefits. Siemens has been the preferred and protected provider on many fat-margin German infrastructure projects. . . . But what happens now? The West German government is having to pry open its markets. . . . Siemens' best customer, the West German state-owned telephone monopoly Deutsche Bundepost, will at long last throw open the equipment market to all comers. . . . Siemens has found the competition somewhat unnerving. . . . Certainly, too, it has been having a very tough time in the U.S.[6]

Siemens CEO Karlheinz Kaske launched a reorganization in 1990; when he reached mandatory retirement in 1992, the restructuring was accelerated by new CEO Heinrich

3. "Half Way There," The Economist (July 4, 1992), pp. 60–61.
4. "The New Generation at Siemens," Business Week (March 9, 1992), pp. 46–48.
5. "Half Way There," The Economist (July 4, 1992), pp. 60–61.
6. "Papa Siemens," Forbes, May 28, 1990, pp. 98, 100–102.

von Pierer. Von Pierer brought a different attitude to Siemens. "Technology can't be a goal in itself; we have to earn money," he stated.[7] In his first year at the helm, however, the profitability picture did not change much. The computer group SNI continued to show losses in 1992, as did the semiconductor group (exact amounts are not disclosed). Overall, 1992 earnings as a fraction of sales stood at 2.5 percent and ROE stood at 10 percent, representing only slight improvement over prior years.

FINANCIAL ACCOUNTING IN GERMANY

Unlike the approach in the U.S., financial accounting rules in Germany are largely dictated by law.[8] The legal prescriptions are contained within the *Handelsgesetzbuch* (HGB), revised in 1985 in large part to codify existing practices. In Germany, financial accounting and tax accounting are directly linked; in fact, tax deductions are allowable only if they are also reflected as expenses in the published financial statements.

The guiding principle underlying German financial accounting is *"Vorsicht,"* which can be translated as prudence. The principle requires the recognition of losses even when they are not yet realized, but precludes the recognition of unrealized gains. Historically, the objective of the principle was to protect creditors by avoiding overstatement of a firm's equity "cushion." In the past, banks provided most of the capital to the German corporate sector.

Consistent with the *Vorsicht* principle, German accounting adheres closely to historical cost. Moreover, German companies can establish accruals for "foreseeable risks" that would not be allowed under U.S. GAAP. Such accruals are sometimes labeled "hidden reserves" because they can be aggregated with other accruals and are not visible in financial statements.

Profit measures in Germany are directly linked to not only taxes but also dividends. Management is permitted unilaterally to retain not more than half of net income within the firm; any retention beyond that point must be approved by shareholders. Moreover, any earnings retained are taxed at a higher rate than earnings distributed as dividends.

In 1985, Germany adopted the Fourth and Seventh Directives of the European Community, which in principle shifted German accounting closer to the British "true and fair" model. However, how large a shift actually occurred is an empirical question, and research shows no support for the existence of a shift.[9]

The tables below compare the recent reported profitability of German and U.S. corporations as a whole; German and U.S. corporations in the electrical industry; and Sie-

7. *"The New Generation at Siemens,"* Business Week (March 9, 1992), pp. 46–48.

8. For a more detailed description of financial accounting in Germany, see F. Choi and G. Mueller, International Accounting, *second edition* (Englewood Cliffs: Prentice-Hall, 1992) or Harris, T., M. Lang, and H. P. Moeller, *"The Value Relevance of German Accounting Measures,"* Journal of Accounting Research (Autumn 1994), pp. 187–209.

9. Harris, T., M. Lang, and H. P. Moeller, *"The Value Relevance of German Accounting Measures,"* Journal of Accounting Research (Autumn 1994), pp. 187–209.

mens and GE. Note that profitability appears lower for the German firms at every level of aggregation: the firm level, the industry level, and the national level. In fact, at the national level over the 1988–1992 period as a whole, net profit margins were only approximately half as great in Germany as in the U.S.

Profitability: German Corporations vs. U.S. Corporations

	1992	1991	1990	1989	1988
Germany					
Pretax margin	0.024	0.035	0.043	0.051	0.044
Net margin	0.011	0.018	0.021	0.026	0.020
Pre-interest ROA	0.024	0.031	0.035	0.042	0.034
ROE	0.061	0.092	0.104	0.126	0.096
U.S.					
Pretax margin	0.050	0.049	0.065	0.076	0.086
Net margin	0.029	0.028	0.039	0.047	0.057
Pre-interest ROA	0.044	0.044	0.057	0.063	0.072
ROE	0.100	0.086	0.121	0.143	0.168

Profitability: German Electrical Industry vs. U.S. Electrical Industry

	1992	1991	1990	1989	1988
German Firms					
Pretax margin	0.050	0.055	0.052	0.047	0.045
Net margin	0.032	0.034	0.034	0.028	0.028
Pre-interest ROA	0.034	0.038	0.048	0.033	0.030
ROE[a]	0.136	0.149	0.131	0.103	0.104
U.S. Firms					
Pretax margin	0.095	0.075	0.106	0.102	0.096
Net margin	0.053	0.046	0.070	0.068	0.066
Pre-interest ROA	0.037	0.042	0.052	0.061	0.059
ROE[b]	0.142	0.129	0.139	0.183	0.179

a. German industry profitability is heavily influenced by Siemens, which accounts for 90 percent of industry assets, and Vorwerk and Co. Vorwerk accounts for only 3 percent of the industry shareholder equity, but (in 1992) 30 percent of the industry profits. Excluding Vorwerk, industry ROE would be .10, .11, and .10 in 1992, 1991, and 1990, respectively.
b. GE accounts for 73 percent of industry shareholders' equity and 86 percent of industry assets in 1992.

Profitability: Germany's Siemens vs. U.S.'s General Electric

	1992	1991	1990	1989	1988
Siemens					
Pretax margin	.041	.047	.045	.046	.042
Net margin	.025	.025	.026	.026	.018
ROA	.033	.033	.037	.035	.027
ROE	.096	.096	.095	.085	.061
GE					
Pretax margin	.110	.105	.104	.107	.097
Net margin	.083	.081	.082	.073	.069
ROA	.042	.049	.053	.057	.054
ROE	.201	.205	.198	.189	.183

Source: Worldscope Disclosure

ANALYSTS' VIEWS OF SIEMENS PROFITABILITY

In the 1960s, the German Institute of Financial Analysts (assigned the acronym DVFA, based on the German title) developed a method to adjust reported earnings that was intended to mitigate the influence of transitory impacts on earnings. The DVFA states that the adjusted earnings number should provide "a more relevant appraisal of the real income of the firm." The calculation eliminates gains/losses designated as unusual or nonrecurring, including (but not limited to) accounting changes, translation gains/losses, writeups and some writedowns of assets, special depreciation, and gains/losses on large assets sales. It also eliminates pension expenses other than service costs, amortization of goodwill, and some transfers to/from "hidden reserves."

The so-called "DVFA earnings" are often calculated with the help of German corporate managers, using information not available in the published financial statements; some managers even publish a DVFA earnings figure directly. However, Siemens managers do not publish a DVFA earnings number, and provide no input to the analysts' DVFA calculation. The DVFA earnings for Siemens is compared below with the reported earnings. (No further details are available.)

	Reported Earnings (in DM millions)	DVFA Earnings (in DM millions)
1992	1,955	2,510
1991	1,792	2,210
1990	1,668	2,426
1989	1,577	2,361
1988	1,391	2,027

Whether Siemens' accounting practices are considered conservative might to some extent be revealed through the pricing of the firm's securities. As shown below, in recent years Siemens has tended to trade at a higher PE multiple than GE. However, GE's price/book multiple has tended to be higher, and was nearly twice as high at the end of 1992:

	PE Ratio				Price/Book Ratio			
	1989	1990	1991	1992	1989	1990	1991	1992
Siemens	20.1	17.3	18.2	17.8	1.7	1.6	1.9	1.7
GE	14.8	11.9	15.2	15.7	2.8	2.4	3.1	3.1

Siemens: lethargic performer, or more profitable than it appears?

The press appears to take for granted that Siemens' profitability is only mediocre. However, if German managers face incentives to constrain profitability, the German financial accounting system may permit the flexibility to allow that. Thus, there looms the possibility that Siemens' profitability is stronger than it looks.

Analyst Connie Bishop wonders whether a detailed analysis of Siemens' financial statements would reveal whether Siemens' profitability is as weak as it appears on the surface. She recognizes that if Siemens' reporting strategy reflects a response to incentives to "hide" profitability, it may be difficult to gauge their performance accurately. A summary of GE's 1992 financial performance and excerpts from Siemens' 1992 financial statements follow.

QUESTIONS

1. Summarize the forces that might influence Siemens' financial reporting policies.
2. Identify areas of potential flexibility in Siemens' measurement of profitability. What indications are there that Siemens has or has not used its flexibility to enhance or reduce its reported profitability?
3. In 1992, Siemens' PE ratio is slightly higher than GE's, but Siemens' price-to-book ratio is much lower. What does this suggest about the firms' relative prospects for future growth and future rates of profitability? What features of accounting could possibly lead to this set of relations?

Exhibit 1   Financial Summary: General Electric Company

EXHIBIT 1
Financial Summary: General Electric Company

($ in millions)	GE consolidated		GE only	
	12/31/92	12/31/91	12/31/92	12/31/91
Sales revenue	$57,073	$54,629	$38,755	$38,319
Cost of sales, excluding depreciation	25,562	25,217	26,934	26,467
Gross margin	31,511	29,412	11,821	11,852
Depreciation and amortization	2,818	2,654	1,483	1,429
Cost of insurance claims	1,957	1,623	0	0
Provision for loan losses	1,056	1,102	0	0
Other costs and expenses	12,494	10,834	5,319	5,422
Earnings before interest and tax	13,186	13,199	5,019	5,001
Interest expense	6,860	7,401	768	893
Earnings of GECS			1,499	1,275
Minority interest	53	72	13	39
Pretax income	6,273	5,726	5,737	5,344
Provision for taxes	1,968	1,742	1,432	1360
Income from operations	4,305	3,984	4,305	3,984
Income from discontinued operations	420	451	420	451
Income before accounting change	4,725	4,435	4,725	4,435
Accounting change	0	−1,799	0	−1,799
Net income	4,725	2,636	4,725	2,636
Working capital from operations	9,589	9,291	5,464	4,759
Cash from operations	9,508	7,105	4,573	3,626

(continued)

S

Exhibit 1　Financial Summary: General Electric Company

($ in millions)	GE consolidated		GE only	
	12/31/92	12/31/91	12/31/92	12/31/91
Cash	$ 3,129	$ 1,971	$ 1,189	$ 1,046
Marketable securities	62,198	45,223	32	41
Current receivables	7,150	7,324	7,462	7,569
Inventory	4,574	5,321	4,574	5,321
Financing receivables	67,413	62,975	0	0
Equipment leased to others	9,395	7,552	0	0
Plant, property & equipment	23,711	22,381	21,978	21,045
Accumulated depreciation	12,719	11,601	12,046	11,070
PPE-net	10,992	10,780	9,932	9,975
Investment in GECS	0	0	8,884	7,758
Other assets	28,025	25,362	16,002	15,440
Total assets	192,876	166,508	48,075	47,150
Short term debt	56,389	51,350	3,448	3,482
Other current liabilities	64,086	49,507	10,631	10,726
Total current liabilities	120,475	100,857	14,079	14,208
Long-term liabilities	47,598	42,750	10,187	10,906
Total liabilities	168,073	143,607	24,266	25,114
Minority interest	1,344	1,218	350	353
Total shareholders' equity	23,459	21,683	23,459	21,683
Total liabilities and equity	192,876	166,508	48,075	47,150
Stock price (close of year)	85.50	76.50		
EPS before accounting change	5.02	4.58		

NOTES:

1. GE's consolidated financial statements include GE Capital Services (GECS); in the GE financial statements, GE Capital Services is accounted for using the equity method.

2. Most of GE's plant and equipment is depreciated using the sum-of-years' digits method.

3. Virtually all of GE's U.S. inventory is accounted for by the LIFO method; FIFO is used for non-U.S. inventories. If valued on a FIFO basis, inventories would be higher in 1992 (1991) by $1,808 ($2,012).

4. Goodwill is amortized on a straight-line basis over its estimated useful life, not to exceed 40 years. Goodwill at the end of 1992 (1991) was approximately $7,700 ($7,600) for GE on a consolidated basis, and $5,900 ($5,800) for GE only.

5. An accounting change took place in 1991, to account for a previously unrecognized liability for employee post-retirement health and life insurance benefits of $2,710 ($1,999 net of deferred tax effect).

6. GE's pension fund was overfunded (relative to projected benefits) by approximately $6,200 ($5,800) at the end of 1992 (1991). As a result, pension income exceeded pension expense by $586 ($696) in 1992 (1991); ongoing service cost for pensions was $494 ($446) in 1992 (1991).

Exhibit 2   Excerpts from Siemens 1992 Annual Report

EXHIBIT 2
Excerpts from Siemens 1992 Annual Report

WORLDWIDE CONSOLIDATED FINANCIAL STATEMENTS

CONSOLIDATED BALANCE SHEET

| | | as of September 30 | |
(in millions of DM)	Note	1992	1991
ASSETS			
Intangibles, fixed assets and investments			
Intangible assets	(5)	435	275
Property, plant and equipment	(5)		
At cost		46,762	43,660
Less accumulated depreciation		(28,960)	(27,206)
		17,802	16,454
Investments	(6)	2,657	2,660
		20,894	19,389
Current assets			
Inventories	(7)	26,275	24,774
Less advances received from customers		(19,993)	(16,535)
		6,282	8,239
Receivables and miscellaneous assets	(8)		
Accounts receivable – trade		14,459	14,387
Other receivables and miscellaneous assets		10,445	8,818
		24,904	23,205
Marketable securities and notes	(9)	16,600	15,088
Other liquid assets		3,077	3,478
		50,863	50,010
Prepaid expenses		43	69
Total assets		71,800	69,468
SHAREHOLDERS' EQUITY AND LIABILITIES			
Shareholders' equity			
Capital stock of Siemens AG	(10)		
Common stock (total number of votes 55,025,662)	.	2,752	2,593
Preferred stock (total number of votes 923,634)		46	46
		2,798	2,639
Additional paid-in capital	(10)	8,590	6,244
Retained earnings		6,991	7,735
Unappropriated consolidated net income		727	686
Minority interests		1,235	1,345
		20,341	18,649

(continued)

S

575

Exhibit 2 Excerpts from Siemens 1992 Annual Report

CONSOLIDATED BALANCE SHEET (continued)

		as of September 30	
(in millions of DM)	Note	1992	1991
Accrued liabilities	(11)		
Pension plans and similar commitments		14,761	13,957
Other accrued liabilities		20,220	20,137
		34,981	34,094
Debt	(12)	4,531	4,575
Other liabilities	(12)		
Accounts payable – trade		4,854	4,912
Additional liabilities		6,675	6,851
		11,529	11,763
Deferred income		418	387
Total shareholders' equity and liabilities		71,800	69,468

CONSOLIDATED STATEMENT OF INCOME

		for fiscal years ended September 30	
(in millions of DM)	Note	1992	1991
Net sales		78,509	73,008
Change in inventories and additions to self-produced plant and equipment	(13)	3,204	3,300
Total operating performance		81,713	76,308
Other operating income	(14)	5,326	5,089
Cost of materials	(15)	(35,450)	(32,360)
Personnel costs	(16)	(33,873)	(31,817)
Depreciation and amortization		(4,613)	(4,400)
Other operating expenses	(17)	(11,826)	(11,107)
Net income from investment in other companies		56	(153)
Net interest income	(18)	1,864	1,859
Income before income taxes		3,197	3,419
Income taxes	(19)	(1,242)	(1,627)
Net income		1,955	1,792
Appropriation of net income		1,955	1,792
Minority interests in net income of consolidated subsidiaries		(203)	(155)
Minority interests in net loss of consolidated subsidiaries		43	211
Balance brought forward from prior year		6	–
Transfers to retained earnings		(1,074)	(1,162)
Unappropriated consolidated net income (dividend of Siemens AG)		727	686

Exhibit 2   Excerpts from Siemens 1992 Annual Report

STATEMENT OF CHANGES IN FINANCIAL POSITION

(in millions of DM)	for fiscal years ended September 30	
	1992	1991
Cash flow		
Net income	1,955	1,792
Depreciation, amortization and write-downs	4,735	4,440
Increase in medium- and long-term accrued liabilities	189	565
	6,879	6,797
Funds invested in operating assets		
Capital expenditures for property, plant and equipment	(5,560)	(5,003)
Expenditures for acquisition of investments	(3,014)	(592)
Increase in inventories	(910)	(2,042)
Increase in receivables	(2,121)	(2,648)
Change in miscellaneous balance sheet items	134	816
	(11,471)	(9,469)
Financing from operations		
Increase in advances received from customers	3,247	1,808
Increase in other liabilities	109	325
	3,356	2,133
Other financing activities		
Increase in paid-in capital	2,505	351
Reduction of debt	(158)	(593)
	2,347	(242)
Change in liquid assets	1,111	(781)
Included therein: Marketable securities and notes	1,512	(598)
Other liquid assets	(401)	(183)
Liquid assets at September 30	19,677	18,566

S

577

Exhibit 2   Excerpts from Siemens 1992 Annual Report

CONSOLIDATED FINANCIAL STATEMENTS – NOTES

(1) Principles of consolidation

The worldwide consolidated financial statements include virtually all the domestic (German) and foreign subsidiaries. In addition to Siemens AG, 67 (1991: 57) subsidiaries in Germany and 224 (1991: 231) subsidiaries in foreign countries have been consolidated. 320 (1991: 306) companies that are either inactive or have a low business volume are not included in the consolidated financial statements, because they have little or no significance for the presentation of Siemens' overall position. Their sales account for less than three percent of consolidated sales. In addition, we have omitted retirement benefit corporations, whose assets are assigned for a specific purpose, as well as those companies whose shares were acquired exclusively for investment purposes.

Investments in 36 (1991: 50) associated companies and in two subsidiaries which we had already recorded at our proportionate interest in their net worth in fiscal 1991, have been accounted for using the equity method. An additional 137 (1991: 131) other associated companies were not accounted for in this manner because of their relative immateriality.

The principal subsidiaries and associated companies are listed on pages 46 and 47, including their sales, shareholders' equity and earnings. A complete list of our holdings is being filed with the Commercial Registries of the Berlin-Charlottenburg and Munich District Courts.

In consolidating our investment in subsidiaries, we offset the purchase price against the value of Siemens' interests in the shareholders' equity of the consolidated subsidiaries at the time of their acquisition or initial consolidation. Any resulting goodwill is offset against retained earnings. The same principles are applied in consolidating companies under the equity method. Our share in the net income of the companies accounted for under this method is shown in the statement of income under net income from investment in other companies.

In the consolidated financial statements, we eliminate intercompany profits as well as sales, expenses and income within the Siemens organization and all receivables and liabilities between consolidated companies. Since the intercompany profits of the companies accounted for under the equity method are insignificant, they are not eliminated. Interim statements are used for consolidated subsidiaries whose fiscal year differs from that of Siemens AG.

(2) Foreign currency translation

In the individual financial statements, we translate receivables and liabilities in foreign currency at the rate existing at the transaction date or the rate at the balance sheet date, whichever is lower. When foreign currency receivables and liabilities of our subsidiaries outside Germany have been hedged by forward exchange transactions, they are valued at the corresponding hedging rate.

Accruals are established to cover impending losses from hedging operations.

In the consolidated financial statements, intangible assets, property, plant and equipment, and investment in subsidiaries and other companies of our foreign subsidiaries are translated at historical exchange rates. Their other assets and liabilities are translated at the year-end current rate (the average of the buying and selling rates).

Revenues and expenses included in the statement of income are translated at average rates for the year, except for depreciation, amortization and write-downs on intangibles, fixed assets and investments, which are translated at historical rates.

When our subsidiaries' financial statements are translated into German marks, the resulting balance is recorded in one of two ways in accordance with the convention of conservatism. A net translation loss is charged against earnings, while a net translation gain is offset by an accrual for exchange risks, which is used to cover translation losses in subsequent years.

(3) Principles of accounting and valuation

The financial statements of Siemens AG and its domestic and foreign subsidiaries are prepared according to uniform principles of accounting and valuation. To ensure uniformity of valuation within the worldwide Siemens consolidated financial state-

Exhibit 2   Excerpts from Siemens 1992 Annual Report

ments, the tax-deductible valuation adjustments and special reserves included in the individual financial statements of the domestic companies have been reversed in the consolidated financial statements. In accordance with §17 of the German DM Opening Balance Sheet Act (DMBilG), the special reserves in the individual financial statements of the companies in the new German federal states have been offset against the special loss accounts and allocated to the retained earnings of the worldwide consolidated financial statements. Valuations in the statements of companies accounted for under the equity method that deviate from these uniform principles have not been adjusted on the basis of immateriality.

Insofar as intangible assets have been acquired for consideration, they are carried at acquisition cost and are amortized up to a maximum of five years. Any goodwill resulting from consolidation is offset against retained earnings.

Property, plant and equipment is recorded at acquisition or production cost, less scheduled depreciation. Depreciation is taken on residential, office and factory buildings for a maximum of 50 years, on technical equipment and machinery for a maximum of 10 years, and on other equipment and plant and office equipment, in general, over five years. Equipment leased to customers is depreciated according to the useful lives of the product groups. In the Federal Republic of Germany, we use the declining balance method for the depreciation of property, plant and equipment to the extent possible under the tax laws, at the maximum allowable rates, switching to the straight-line method as soon as the latter results in higher depreciation. Additional depreciation is taken where a write-down in book value is deemed necessary. Minor fixed assets are fully expensed in the year of acquisition.

Significant investments in associated companies are accounted for using the equity method, thereby reflecting our proportionate interest in their net worth. Interests in nonconsolidated subsidiaries and other associated and related companies are valued at the lower of cost or market. Loans made as investments and bearing nominal or no interest are stated at their discounted cash value.

Materials, supplies, merchandise for resale, and advances to suppliers are carried in inventories at the lower of cost or market. Work in process and finished products are stated at production cost. Production cost includes materials, direct labor and production overhead which must be capitalized in accordance with the provisions of the German tax laws. The cost of unbilled contracts is valued according to the same principles. We use the LIFO method for certain metals. Purchases from consolidated companies are stated in inventory according to the uniform capitalization policy required by the German Commercial Code. A reasonable and sufficient allowance is made for declines in value due to slow-moving items, technical obsolescence and reductions in fair value.

Receivables and miscellaneous assets are carried at the lower of cost or market. Accounts receivable due after one year which bear nominal or no interest have been discounted.

Marketable securities and notes are stated at the lower of cost or market. In Germany, lower valuations are retained to the extent permissible under the tax laws.

Accrued liabilities include reasonable and sufficient allowance for all perceivable risks. In Germany, the accruals for pension plans are set up according to actuarial principles, using the method of computation provided for in the German Income Tax Act. Foreign subsidiaries establish accruals for pension plans, as required, according to comparable principles.

Deferred taxes are recorded following the liability method. These taxes are provided for the temporary differences between the financial reporting basis and the tax basis of the consolidated assets and liabilities. Deferred assets and liabilities are netted, with any resulting credit balance being recorded as an accrual for deferred taxes. A net deferred tax receivable balance will be recorded only if it is derived from consolidation entries.

Intangibles, fixed assets and investments of our subsidiaries in the highly inflationary economies of Argentina and Brazil are recorded at acquisition or production cost and translated at historical exchange rates. Other assets and liabilities are stated at their current value or replacement cost and translated at the year-end current rate (the average of the buying and selling rates). The difference

Exhibit 2   Excerpts from Siemens 1992 Annual Report

between this amount and the lower acquisition or production cost is, as a rule, largely neutralized by translation at the prevailing year-end current rate.

For improved clarity of the consolidated financial statements, the inflationary components contained within interest income (expense) and within foreign exchange gains (losses) have been eliminated from the financial statements of our subsidiaries in countries with highly inflationary economies and reclassified to other operating expenses.

Certain items on the consolidated balance sheet and in the consolidated statement of income have been combined to provide greater clarity. These items are shown separately in the Notes to consolidated financial statements.

The consolidated financial statements are denominated in millions of German marks (DM).

(4) Acquisition of subsidiaries and associated companies

Goodwill in the amount of DM1,934 million, which resulted from the initial consolidation of equity interests in subsidiaries and associated companies, was offset against retained earnings.

(5) Intangible assets and property, plant and equipment

(in millions of DM)	9/30/91	Additions	Reclassifications	Retirements	9/30/92	Accumulated depreciation/amortization	Net value as of 9/30/92	Net value as of 9/30/91	Depreciation/amortization during the fiscal year
Intangible assets	971	411	—	450	932	497	435	275	248
Property, plant and equipment									
Land, equivalent rights to real property, and buildings, including buildings on land not owned	12,442	955	380	174	13,603	5,083	8,520	7,837	521
Technical equipment and machinery	11,985	1,081	421	802	12,685	9,436	3,249	2,961	1,083
Other equipment, plant and office equipment	14,836	2,357	259	1,570	15,882	12,382	3,500	3,325	2,248
Equipment leased to customers	2,961	649	(6)	647	2,957	2,047	910	896	501
Advances to suppliers and construction in progress	1,436	1,276	(1,054)	23	1,635	12	1,623	1,435	12
	43,660	6,318	—	3,216	46,762	28,960	17,802	16,454	4,365
	44,631	6,729	—	3,666	47,694	29,457	18,237	16,729	4,613

Additions to intangible assets and property, plant and equipment during the fiscal year amounted to DM6,729 (1991: DM8,651) million, which include the opening balance amounts of DM1,072 million attributable to companies included in the consolidated financial statements for the first time.

Exhibit 2   Excerpts from Siemens 1992 Annual Report

(6) Investments

(in millions of DM)	9/30/91	Additions	Reclassifi-cations	Retire-ments	9/30/92	Accumulated write-downs	Accumulated equity-adjustment	Net value as of 9/30/92	Net value as of 9/30/91
Interests in subsidiaries	718	337	29	250	834	158	(95)	581	640
Interests in associated companies	2,876	81	(18)	201	2,738	—	(1,349)	1,389	1,494
Miscellaneous invest-ments	805	315	(11)	78	1,031	344	—	687	526
	4,399	733	—	529	4,603	502	(1,444)	2,657	2,660

The additions to interests in subsidiaries and associated companies relate predominantly to the acquisition of equity interests.

Retirements in interests in subsidiaries resulted primarily from their initial consolidation. Retirements in interests in associated companies mainly include the sale of the equity interest in Fides Industrie-Beteiligungsgesellschaft GmbH, Munich.

Our share in the net income of subsidiaries and associated companies accounted for under the equity method amounted to DM36 (1991: DM92) million during the fiscal year.

Miscellaneous investments include interests in other companies, as well as loans, primarily residential construction loans.

Write-downs of DM89 million on interests in subsidiaries and of DM33 million on miscellaneous investments were made during the fiscal year.

(7) Inventories

(in millions of DM)	9/30/92	9/30/91
Materials and supplies	2,448	2,512
Work in process	4,489	4,798
Finished products and merchandise	5,140	5,478
Cost of unbilled contracts	12,598	11,055
Advances to suppliers	1,600	931
	26,275	24,774

(8) Receivables and miscellaneous assets

(in millions of DM)	9/30/92	Due after one year	9/30/91	Due after one year
Accounts receivable – trade	14,459	981	14,387	1,657
Other receivables and miscellaneous assets				
Receivables from nonconsolidated subsidiaries	2,249	32	1,259	46
Receivables from associated and related companies	2,753	1,499	2,202	992
Miscellaneous assets	5,443	713	5,357	947
	10,445	2,244	8,818	1,985
	24,904	3,225	23,205	3,642

Miscellaneous assets include our interests in subsidiaries in the amount of DM1,308 (1991: DM1,473) million, which were acquired exclusively as financial investments. This item also includes a large amount of accrued interest income.

(9) Marketable securities and notes

(in millions of DM)	9/30/92	9/30/91
Treasury stock	57	13
Stock certificates	1,850	1,733
Fixed-income securities	13,264	11,580
Notes	1,429	1,762
	16,600	15,088

In fiscal 1992, Siemens AG purchased 608,369 shares of common stock, with a total par value of DM30 million, or 1.2% of the capital stock, at an average price of DM639.80 per share, in order to offer them to employees for purchase. Including the 32,505 shares of treasury stock held at the begin-

S

581

Exhibit 2   Excerpts from Siemens 1992 Annual Report

ning of the fiscal year, 476,364 shares, with a total par value of DM24 million, or 0.9% of the capital stock, were sold to employees at a preferential price of DM391 per share. At the close of the fiscal year, 164,510 shares of common stock, having a total par value of DM8 million, or 0.3% of the capital stock, remained in treasury. They are valued at DM347 per share.

The fixed-income securities include shares of investment funds in the amount of DM3,965 (1991: DM3,604) million.

Our security holdings include debentures and bonds issued by Siemens companies.

For tax reasons, write-downs of DM108 million made in prior years were not reversed in fiscal 1992, although the market price of such securities increased during the year. This reduced net income in fiscal 1992 by DM45 million.

(10) Capital stock and additional paid-in capital

The capital stock of Siemens AG amounts to DM2,798 million and is divided into 55,025,662 common shares and 923,634 preferred shares, each with a par value of DM50. Each share is entitled to one vote. Under conditions set forth in the Articles of Association, preferred stock is entitled to six votes per share in a second vote that may be demanded by the holders of preferred stock.

(11) Accrued liabilities

The accruals for pension plans at Siemens AG and its domestic subsidiaries provide for the contractual retirement benefits of employees and retirees not subject to collective bargaining agreements. In addition, the accruals provide for 80% of the retirement benefits of employees covered by such collective bargaining agreements as well as their claims for transitional payments. Retirement benefit corporations in Germany provide for the remainder of Siemens AG's pension obligations to employees subject to collective bargaining agreements and to their surviving dependents. In addition, accruals are established for the retirement benefits of the employees and retirees of our foreign subsidiaries, unless the obligations are covered by pension funds. Moreover, the obligations of our U.S. subsidiaries to provide

postretirement benefits other than pensions for active and retired employees are shown here.

The pension commitments of Siemens AG and its subsidiaries are fully covered by accruals for pension plans and the funds of the retirement benefit corporations.

Other accrued liabilities include DM2,131 (1991: DM2,106) million in provisions for taxes. In addition, this item consists primarily of accruals for personnel costs, warranty obligations, anticipated losses on contracts, penalties for contract performance delays, and expenses for contracts already billed.

(12) Debt and other liabilities

(in millions of DM)	9/30/92	Due within one year	9/30/91	Due within one year
Debt				
Bonds and debentures	2,225	3	1,213	3
Loans from banks	1,920	1,498	2,344	1,775
Notes and other loans	386	99	1,018	761
	4,531	1,600	4,575	2,539
Other liabilities				
Accounts payable – trade	4,854	4,640	4,912	4,652
Additional liabilities				
Liabilities to non-consolidated subsidiaries	239	165	524	479
Liabilities to associated and related companies	310	272	444	302
Miscellaneous liabilities	6,126	5,494	5,883	5,205
	6,675	5,931	6,851	5,986
	11,529	10,571	11,763	10,638

Debt increased as a result of the 8% U.S. dollar bonds with warrants issued by Siemens Capital Corporation.

Tax liabilities totaling DM961 (1991: DM989) million are included in miscellaneous liabilities. This item also contains liabilities amounting to DM995 (1991: DM988) million mandated by the social security program, which consist of outstanding statutory social welfare contributions and statutory retirement benefit obligations in foreign countries.

Exhibit 2   Excerpts from Siemens 1992 Annual Report

(13) Change in inventories and additions to self-produced plant and equipment

Change in inventories and additions to self-produced plant and equipment totaled DM3,204 (1991: DM3,300) million, of which DM1,124 (1991: DM1,700) million relates to the increase in inventories of finished products and work in process and in the cost of unbilled contracts. DM2,080 (1991: DM1,600) million in additions to self-produced plant and equipment was capitalized.

(14) Other operating income

Other operating income includes, in particular, foreign exchange and securities gains, income from various services, subsidies for research and development, Berlin sales tax benefits and capital investment grants, income from the reversal of accruals, and gains on the sale of investments.

(15) Cost of materials

The cost of materials amounted to DM35,450 (1991: DM32,360) million. This included DM26,775 (1991: DM24,110) million for materials, supplies, and merchandise purchased for resale, and DM8,675 (1991: DM8,250) million for purchased services from third parties.

(16) Personnel costs

Personnel costs consist of wages and salaries totaling DM27,043 (1991: DM25,373) million, statutory social welfare contributions and expenses related to employee benefits of DM4,396 (1991: DM4,103) million, and expense for pension plans of DM2,434 (1991: DM2,341) million.

(17) Other operating expenses

Other operating expenses include the expenses for write-downs on investments, marketable securities and notes totaling DM465 (1991: DM110) million and miscellaneous taxes in the amount of DM477 (1991: DM553) million.

The translation of financial statements into German marks resulted in a loss of DM138 (1991: DM255) million in fiscal 1992.

Furthermore, other operating expenses consist mainly of administrative, marketing and selling expenses such as rentals, travel expenses, sales commissions, insurance and other overhead; addi-

tions to accruals; securities and foreign exchange losses; and bad debt expenses.

(18) Net interest income

Interest and similar income of DM2,706 (1991: DM2,885) million exceeded interest and similar expenses of DM842 (1991: DM1,026) million by DM1,864 (1991: DM1,859) million. Interest and similar income includes DM216 (1991: DM135) million attributable to subsidiaries. The interest expense attributable to subsidiaries is not significant.

(19) Income taxes

Income taxes include German corporate income and local income taxes, as well as the comparable foreign taxes relating to income. Such taxes are determined in accordance with the tax laws applicable to the individual companies. In addition, income taxes include the deferred taxes resulting from temporary differences. Income tax expense was reduced by DM40 (1991: DM98) million in tax credits that relate to income from investments in domestic companies. Taxes not based on income, at DM477 (1991: DM553) million, are included in other operating expenses.

(20) Segment information

Siemens is a supplier of electronic and electrical products, systems and equipment. Activities in other lines of business are not significant.

Sales and capital expenditures of the domestic and foreign subsidiaries are assigned to the Group that has the worldwide responsibility for that business activity. Net sales in the table below include intersegment shipments.

By business segment

(in millions of DM)	Net sales		Capital expenditures	
	1992	1991	1992	1991
Power Generation (KWU)	6,570	4,955	523	394
Power Transmission and Distribution	5,568	5,307	219	221
Industrial and Building Systems	8,717	8,774	272	214
Drives and Standard Products	6,686	6,522	316	420
Automation	5,811	5,680	216	237
Private Communication Systems	5,383	5,105	516	431

S

583

Exhibit 2   Excerpts from Siemens 1992 Annual Report

By business segment (continued)

(in millions of DM)	Net sales 1992	Net sales 1991	Capital expenditures 1992	Capital expenditures 1991
Public Communication Networks	13,165	11,260	472	434
Defense Electronics	1,460	1,679	52	76
Automotive Systems	2,540	2,127	241	219
Transportation Systems	2,718	2,141	132	79
Medical Engineering	7,887	7,429	347	375
Semiconductors	1,881	2,029	470	345
Passive Components and Electron Tubes	1,488	1,591	116	139
Electromechanical Components	855	832	87	68
Audio and Video Systems	261	249	16	14
SN I	13,010	12,125	712	708
Osram	3,119	2,971	310	328
Other	1,251	1,446	543	301
Less intersegment shipments	(9,861)	(9,214)	—	—
	78,509	73,008	5,560	5,003

Our 202 operating companies outside Germany earned net income of DM562 million in fiscal 1992, compared with DM652 million in 1991. A regional breakdown of the net sales and capital expenditures of Siemens AG and its domestic and foreign subsidiaries is shown in the table below.

By region

(in millions of DM)	Net sales 1992	Net sales 1991	Capital expenditures 1992	Capital expenditures 1991
Germany	56,339	51,245	3,568	3,105
Attributable to exports	(19,864)	(17,982)		
Europe excluding Germany	23,485	23,338	1,160	1,061
Included therein: European Community	(15,183)	(14,761)	(782)	(680)
North America	8,716	8,517	515	502
Latin America	1,417	1,563	92	115
Asia	2,582	2,715	184	183
Other regions	1,178	1,100	41	37
Less intersegment shipments	(15,208)	(15,470)	—	—
	78,509	73,008	5,560	5,003

Berlin and Munich, December 14, 1992

Siemens Aktiengesellschaft

The Managing Board

The consolidated financial statements, which we have audited in accordance with professional standards, comply with the German legal provisions. With due regard to the generally accepted accounting principles, the consolidated financial statements present a true and fair view of the Siemens group's assets, liabilities, financial position and earnings. The general review of the Managing Board is consistent with the consolidated financial statements.

KPMG Deutsche Treuhand-Gesellschaft
Aktiengesellschaft
Wirtschaftsprüfungsgesellschaft

Berlin and Frankfurt on Main
Munich, January 5, 1993

Schnicke	Dr. Schulz
Wirtschaftsprüfer	Wirtschaftsprüfer

(independent auditors)

Southwestern Fuel Systems, Inc.

Andrea Williamson is employed in the corporate finance department of a large brokerage house. On September 9, 1983, Williamson meets with Donald Trotter, President of Southwestern Fuel Systems, Inc. Southwestern's primary business is the production of plants that convert corn, milo, and other feedstocks into "power alcohol," which can be blended with or used as an alternative to gasoline. Southwestern's power alcohol business has existed only since the summer of 1982, but Southwestern has already reported sales of $23 million for 1982, and $25 million for the first half of 1983. The business has been profitable, with net margins of 24 percent in 1982 and 31 percent in the first half of 1983. The firm's stock, sold over-the-counter, has soared from $3 per share in July 1982 to over $22 in September 1983.

Trotter explains to Williamson that Southwestern is seeking cash to fund its rapid expansion. He is optimistic about the long-run profitability of the power alcohol industry, and is proud of being among the early entrants in the business. Trotter is interested in discussing the possibility of engaging Williamson's firm to underwrite an equity offering, or otherwise assist in obtaining financing.

Williamson speaks with Trotter long enough to obtain a brief overview of the business and a package of financial data that he brought to the meeting. Williamson indicates that she and her colleagues will review the situation and decide soon whether they might be able to assist Southwestern. She also lets Trotter know that she may be contacting him with some more detailed questions about Southwestern's strategy and operations.

COMPANY BACKGROUND AND OPERATIONS

Southwestern has operated under various names since 1919. Initially a mining company, it later engaged in gambling in Nevada and then entered a period of inactivity. In 1981, the corporate shell was reactivated to acquire a coal mining operation in Missouri. On June 30, 1982, the corporation acquired Ethanol Energy Engineering (EEE), a New Mexico corporation. It was through EEE that Southwestern entered the power alcohol industry.

At the time it was acquired by Southwestern, the principal assets of EEE were processes, designs, techniques, and formulae for the manufacture and production of ethanol from feedstock. EEE owners had already designed ethanol plants in Idaho and Utah, as well as the first plant to become operative in New Mexico. EEE's President and CEO,

Prepared by Professor Victor L. Bernard. The case is based upon a real situation, but the names of firms and persons involved have been changed. The case was prepared as a basis for class discussion and is not intended to illustrate either an effective or ineffective management of a business situation.

Jack Green, is a nationally prominent engineer who has served as president of the Utah Society of Professional Engineers and as majority leader of his state legislature. Green is now an outside director of Southwestern, and his engineering firm continues to serve as a subcontractor to EEE.

For the year 1982, 74 percent of Southwestern's sales and nearly all of its earnings were accounted for by EEE's ethanol plant construction activity. Most of the remaining sales and earnings were derived from the mining operations.

Ethanol Operations

Power alcohol of the ethanol variety can be made from a variety of readily available sources of sugar and starch, including corn, milo, and potatoes. Power alcohol is typically blended with gasoline (in a ratio of 90 percent gasoline and 10 percent alcohol); the blended mixture can be used to fuel standard internal combustion engines.

The power alcohol and blended gasoline industry is in its infancy. Southwestern management reports that production of alcohol fuel became economically viable as the result of tax incentives and the rise in oil prices in the late 1970s and early 1980s. Since the production cost of power alcohol exceeds that for gasoline in the early 1980s, the tax incentives are important. They include energy tax credits and investment tax credits for the owners of alcohol production facilities, and exemptions from gasoline tax for consumers of blended gasoline. One exemption, included in the Crude Oil Windfall Profits Tax Act of 1980, allows consumers to escape the 5 cent per gallon federal gasoline tax through 1992. There is another exemption for the 10 cent per gallon New Mexico gasoline tax, under a state provision to be phased out from 1987 through 1991. Given that one gallon of power alcohol yields 10 gallons of blended gasoline, it permits the ultimate consumer of that amount to escape tax of $1.50 in New Mexico (exemptions of 5 cents and 10 cents on each of ten gallons of blended fuel).

As ethanol production plants are designed and built by EEE, it contracts to sell the output of the plants. The contracts require the purchaser to acquire all the ethanol that the plant can produce, at per-gallon prices equal to the lowest available wholesale price of gasoline in the purchaser's area, plus 10 times the available federal and state tax exemptions, less 20 cents.

Thus, given the 15-cent-per-gallon exemption available in New Mexico, purchasers would be required to pay $1.30 above the wholesale price. They should be able to sell the product for more, once it is blended with gasoline. Contracts arranged in 1982 continue in force through 1988, and are renewable thereafter. During that period, the operations of the plants will be managed by a company that is owned by Southwestern officers. For its part, EEE must guarantee that the plants will be built by a prespecified date and meet a prespecified production capacity.

Once the contracts to sell ethanol are arranged, EEE assigns the contracts and sells the associated ethanol production facility to limited partnerships. In addition to proceeds from sales of plants, EEE receives a periodic royalty commission equal to 7 percent of the gross revenue of the plant. The partnerships are attracted to the acquisition of ethanol production facilities, at least in part, because they intend to qualify for tax incentives. Specifically, the Internal Revenue Service allows acquirers of certain energy production facilities to qualify for a 10 percent investment tax credit and a 10 percent energy credit on the full purchase price of the plant, so long as certain conditions are met. The contracts between EEE and the limited partnerships require a 20 percent down payment, with the remainder financed with notes carrying an interest rate of 13 percent and payable in equal monthly installments over eight years. Notes representing 5 percent of the purchase price are issued on a recourse basis, with the remainder being non-recourse. If the ethanol plants are sufficiently profitable, all of the notes could be retired with cash generated through operations.

A portion of Southwestern's ethanol plant construction activity has been financed by industrial revenue bonds issued by the local municipalities, and the Company expects to be able to rely on this type of financing in the future. Debt service on the bonds is to be provided by proceeds from the sale of plants.

Southwestern began construction of ethanol plants in New Mexico in 1982, and expanded to Louisiana during 1983. Southwestern reports that as of the end of 1982, it had sold five ethanol production facilities for $17.5 million. During the first six months of 1983, sales of ethanol plants were reported at $22.5 million.

Mining Operations

Southwestern, through its wholly-owned mining subsidiary, is involved in strip-mining operations in Missouri. Additional equipment and land have enabled Southwestern to reach an annual production level capacity of 480,000 tons of coal. At that production level, Southwestern's reserves would last for approximately 26 years. Actual production in 1982 was 230,000 tons, dampened to some extent by mild winter weather and reduced demand for heat. Over 90 percent of that production was devoted to fulfilling the obligations of one contract with the city of Independence, Missouri. Southwestern believes that, because of its quality advantage and the costs of shipping coal from other locations, it will be able to continue selling to this city for the indefinite future.

Mined-over land is reclaimed by Southwestern on a scheduled basis. No charge of improper or inadequate reclamation activities has ever been asserted against Southwestern.

Other Operations

Southwestern owns a 100 percent interest in Supersweep, Inc., which holds the rights to an additive used in oil drilling. The natural fiber-based product is added to drilling fluid to help "sweep" debris from the oil well. Supersweep is an alternative to asbestos materials, which are known to be carcinogenic, and gels, which are more expensive. Moreover, unlike other additives, Supersweep tends to help "plug" holes that develop in the walls of oil wells and thus cause a loss of drilling fluid. Based on 18 months of testing in the field, Southwestern management believes Supersweep to be an improvement over existing additives. Production and sale of Supersweep is expected to impact the overall performance of the company by late 1984. The current market for "sweeps" is about $250 million annually in the U.S., and about $900 million worldwide.

Ownership and Corporate Governance

Although some of Southwestern's shares are traded in the over-the-counter market, most of the shares are held by officers, directors, and other key investors, and are restricted from sale. The restricted shares were issued in return for a contribution of previously outstanding shares, in the form of a one-for-five reverse split during 1982. As a result of the split, the public shareholders' proportional share of the firm increased. At the end of 1982, approximately 2 million of the total 10.6 million total outstanding shares were in the hands of the public.

Directors, officers, and key investors include the following:

Gerald Bard, age 68; Chairman of the Board of Southwestern since 1981 and President; founder and Chairman of the mining subsidiary; holds 11 percent of Southwestern stock.

Donald Trotter, age 35; Director of Southwestern since 1981 and Executive Vice President; Vice President of the mining subsidiary and its predecessor corporation since 1980; formerly involved in real estate development, retail merchandising, and energy marketing; graduate electrical engineer; holds 12 percent of Southwestern stock.

Orville Wright, age 57; Director of Southwestern since 1981 and Secretary/Treasurer; CPA and senior partner of local firm; owns 2 percent of Southwestern stock.

Arnold Kilmer, age 39; Director of Southwestern since 1983 and President of mining subsidiary and its predecessor corporation since 1977; owns 13 percent of stock.

Dr. Steven Mellow, age 53; economist and outside director of Southwestern; owns less than 1 percent of Southwestern stock.

John Cearney, age 44; attorney and outside director of Southwestern; owns 4 percent of Southwestern stock.

Jack Green, age 51; engineer and outside director of Southwestern; President of EEE; owns less than 1 percent of Southwestern stock.

William Kilmer (relative of Director Arnold Kilmer); Vice President of the mining subsidiary and its predecessor corporation since 1976; owns 13 percent of Southwestern stock.

Thomas Capton; local investor with no position as director or officer of Southwestern; owns 12 percent of Southwestern stock.

As a group, officers and directors of Southwestern received $218,000 in compensation and remuneration during 1982. None received more than $50,000.

The holders of the restricted stock of the corporation (including all of the above persons) hold options to acquire up to 1.4 million shares in 1984 and 1 million shares annually from 1985 through 1992 at their par value of $.08 each if certain earnings goals are met. Specifically, these holders can purchase a fraction of these maximum allowable shares equal to the percentage by which earnings per share exceed the prior year level. Thus, for example, when the maximum allowable shares are 1 million in 1985, and the earnings per share increases by 50 percent, the holders of restricted stock would be allowed to buy up to 500,000 shares at 8 cents each.

COMPETITION

Price is the overriding concern in the marketability of power alcohol, and a primary contributing factor in determining price is state tax incentives. At the current time, power alcohol is readily marketable in states with favorable tax treatment. To date, there are only a small number of power alcohol producers, none of which has produced in large quantities. By continuing to build its plants in states offering the greatest tax benefits, Southwestern expects to be able to actively compete in the market for power alcohol.

STOCK PRICE ACTIVITY

The following chart summarizes stock price behavior for Southwestern, for High Plateau Inc. (a small, very thinly traded stock and the only other publicly traded firm devoted to power alcohol production), and the OTC index.

End of Month:	Southwestern	High Plateau	OTC Composite Index
July 1982	$3.19	$1.69	167.35
Aug 1982	3.63	3.13	177.71
Sept 1982	4.06	3.25	187.65
Oct 1982	6.31	3.19	212.63
Nov 1982	9.38	3.63	232.31
Dec 1982	13.43	4.31	232.41
Jan 1983	14.88	4.94	248.35
Feb 1983	16.50	4.63	260.67
Mar 1983	15.00	3.88	270.80
April 1983	16.50	3.38	293.06
May 1983	22.63	4.88	308.73
June 1983	21.00	4.88	318.70
July 1983	22.63	5.88	303.96
Aug 1983	23.00	6.63	292.42

OUTLOOK

In his 1982 letter to shareholders, Chairman and President Gerald Bard had this to say about Southwestern's outlook:

It is our belief that our company has tremendous potential for the 1980s and be-yond, and that actions implemented with regard to diversification in 1981 and 1982 have yielded, and will continue to yield, beneficial results. We will continue to be pleasingly aggressive in our attempt to make their investment in our com-pany one in which our shareholders may take pride.

QUESTIONS

1. What are the key areas of flexibility in the accounting for Southwestern? What finan-cial reporting choices have the managers adopted in those areas? How well does Southwestern's financial reporting reflect the underlying economics of the firm? What is your assessment of Southwestern's quality of earnings? *are geal fir analy.*
2. Based on Southwestern's current stock price, what must the market expect in terms of future earnings and growth prospects?
3. What should Andrea Williamson recommend to her director about the possibility of assisting Southwestern in an equity issue? What risks might such a venture involve? Does Southwestern appear to offer good potential for appreciation to clients of Ms. Williamson's investment house?

S

590

Risk

Exhibit 1   Southwestern Fuel Systems, Excerpts from 6/30/83 10-Q

EXHIBIT 1
Southwestern Fuel Systems, Excerpts from 6/30/83 10-Q

1. FINANCIAL STATEMENTS (UNAUDITED)

CONSOLIDATED BALANCE SHEET

	June 30, 1983	December 31, 1982
ASSETS		
Current Assets		
Cash	$ 1,567,633	$ 2,889,495
Accounts receivable:		
Trade	5,118,050	403,270
Other	1,863,880	41,233
Notes receivable:		
Current installments of long-term notes receivable	1,496,708	664,814
Officers and stockholders	1,474	45,000
Escrowed industrial revenue bond proceeds	5,855,497	3,556,536
Costs and estimated earnings in excess of billings on uncompleted contracts	1,292,500	424,875
Inventories	3,014,018	353,324
Bond escrow fund	475,673	492,200
Prepaid expenses	173,708	106,333
Deferred income taxes, current	143,513	141,215
Total current assets	$21,002,655	$ 9,118,295
Property, Plant and Equipment		
Land	240,093	197,605
Buildings and improvements	742,423	525,926
Machinery and equipment	11,095,244	10,748,234
Trucks, autos, furniture, and fixtures	565,630	440,798
Construction in process	171,410	—
	12,814,800	11,912,563
Less accumulated depreciation	3,334,702	2,679,610
Total property, plant and equipment	$ 9,480,098	$ 9,232,953
Other Assets		
Notes receivable	26,389,791	13,460,186
Mining permit costs and deposits	427,464	526,147
Bond issue costs, net of amortization	2,180,071	1,034,818
Bond escrow fund—principal	2,405,000	1,180,000
Intangible assets	714,464	673,950
Other	147,922	79,986
Total other assets	$32,264,712	$16,955,087
Total assets	$62,747,465	$35,306,335

S

591

Exhibit 1   Southwestern Fuel Systems, Excerpts from 6/30/83 10-Q

CONSOLIDATED BALANCE SHEET (continued)

	June 30, 1983	December 31, 1982

LIABILITIES AND STOCKHOLDERS' EQUITY

Current Liabilities

Current maturities of long-term debt:	$ 818,132	$ 972,208
Notes payable:		
Banks	1,523,138	902,151
Stockholders	108,772	108,772
Other	806,250	103,125
Accounts payable:		
Trade	5,357,135	2,540,665
Other	—	990,000
Deposit on contract	—	664,870
Accrued liabilities	1,181,096	1,115,457
Deferred interest income, net of amortization of $642,937 and $10,722	904,860	420,673
Income taxes	100,924	59,442
Total current liabilities	10,800,307	7,877,363
Long-term debt, net of current maturities	25,667,467	13,675,586
Deferred income tax, noncurrent	8,401,807	4,029,741
Accrued land reclamation costs	137,982	151,768
Deferred income on joint venture	345,203	345,203
Deferred sales tax payable	988,005	451,895
Total liabilities	46,340,771	26,531,556

Stockholders' Equity

Common stock, $.08 par value, authorized 50,000,000 shares, issued 10,577,575 shares	846,206	846,206
Additional paid-in capital	1,850,676	1,850,676
Excess of par value over stated capital of subsidiary acquired	(334,072)	(334,072)
	2,362,810	2,362,810
Retained earnings	14,043,884	6,411,969
Total stockholders' equity	16,406,694	8,774,779
Total liabilities and stockholders' equity	62,747,465	35,306,335

Exhibit 1   Southwestern Fuel Systems, Excerpts from 6/30/83 10-Q

CONSOLIDATED STATEMENT OF INCOME
Six Months Ended June 30, 1983 and 1982

	Three Months Ended June 30		Six Months Ended June 30	
	1983	1982	1983	1982
Sales	$12,739,555	$2,250,243	$24,899,467	$4,515,261
Cost of Sales	6,344,175	1,822,012	11,963,917	3,558,476
Gross Profit	6,395,380	428,231	12,935,550	956,785
Operating Expenses	350,585	338,551	1,783,856	640,020
Income from Operations	6,044,795	89,680	11,151,694	316,765
Other Income				
Interest Income	415,521	61,071	860,415	88,194
Miscellaneous	16,914	1,882	19,806	5,387
Total Other Income	432,435	62,953	880,221	93,581
Net Income Before Taxes	6,477,230	152,633	12,031,915	410,346
Provision for Income Taxes				
Current	122,340	12,830	30,232	31,472
Deferred	1,810,154	5,560	4,369,768	10,857
Total Provision for Taxes	1,932,494	18,390	4,400,000	42,329
Net Income	$ 4,544,736	134,243	$ 7,631,915	368,017
Net Earnings per Share	$ .41	$ .01	$ .68	$ .03

CONSOLIDATED STATEMENT OF CHANGES IN FINANCIAL POSITION
Six Months Ended June 30, 1983 and 1982

	1983	1982
Sources of Working Capital		
Funds provided from operations:		
Net income	$ 7,631,915	$ 368,017
Items not requiring working capital:		
Depreciation and amortization	667,422	422,992
Deferred income taxes, noncurrent	4,372,166	9,084
Provision for land reclamation costs	(13,786)	13,485
Total funds provided from operations	12,657,717	813,578
Increase in deferred sales tax payable	536,110	—
Current installments of long-term notes receivable	831,895	—
Proceeds from long-term debt	13,650,000	118,658
Capital contributed	—	675,000
Disposition of property, plant and equipment	—	1,282
Total Sources of Working Capital	27,675,722	1,608,518

(continued)

S

593

Exhibit 1   Southwestern Fuel Systems, Excerpts from 6/30/83 10-Q

CONSOLIDATED STATEMENT OF CHANGES IN FINANCIAL POSITION (continued)

	1983	1982
Uses of Working Capital		
Increase in long-term note receivable	13,761,500	—
Reduction of mining permit costs and deposits	(97,444)	—
Industrial revenue bond issue costs	1,156,345	—
Increase in bond escrow fund - principal	1,225,000	—
Additions to property, plant and equipment	902,237	898,214
Reduction of long-term debt	1,658,119	222,461
Acquisition of other assets	33,550	724,613
Investment in joint venture	75,000	—
Total Application of Working Capital	18,714,307	1,845,288
Increase (Decrease) in Working Capital	$ 8,961,415	$ (236,770)
Increase (Decrease) in Working Capital Components		
Current Assets:		
Cash	$(1,321,862)	$1,226,563
Accounts receivable	6,493,901	183,345
Notes receivable	831,895	(180,000)
Escrowed industrial revenue bond proceeds	2,298,960	—
Costs and estimated earnings in excess of billings on uncompleted contracts	867,625	—
Inventories	2,660,694	(314,758)
Bond escrow fund-interest	(16,527)	(48,469)
Prepaid expenses	67,375	47,690
Deferred income taxes, current	2,298	43,227
Increase (Decrease) in Current Assets	11,884,359	957,598
Current Liabilities:		
Current maturities of long-term debt	(154,076)	(222,169)
Notes payable	1,324,112	961,500
Accounts payable	1,826,470	123,353
Deposit on contract	(664,870)	—
Accrued liabilities	65,639	296,138
Deferred interest income	484,187	—
Income taxes	41,482	35,546
Increase (Decrease) in Current Liabilities	2,922,944	1,194,368
Increase (Decrease) in Working Capital	$ 8,961,415	$(236,770)

Exhibit 1　Southwestern Fuel Systems, Excerpts from 6/30/83 10-Q

2. EXCERPTS FROM MANAGEMENT'S DISCUSSION AND ANALYSIS OF FINANCIAL CONDITION AND RESULTS OF OPERATIONS FOR SIX MONTHS ENDED 6/30/83

LIQUIDITY AND CAPITAL RESOURCES

During the six months ended June 30, 1983, the Company has utilized its internally generated funds, short-term borrowings from banks and finance companies, and proceeds from industrial revenue bond issues to finance property, plant and equipment additions and its acquisition of mining permits. A comparison of internally generated funds to capital expenditures for the six months ended June 30, 1983 and 1982 is as follows:

	Six Months Ended June 30	
(000 Omitted)	1983	1982
Total funds provided from operations	$14,676	$ 813
(Decrease) increase in cash	(1,322)	(1,227)
(Decrease) increase in receivables	6,494	(3)
(Decrease) increase in inventories	2,661	315
(Increase) decrease in payable and accruals	(1,892)	1,194
(Increase) decrease in contract deposits	665	—
Other	51	(42)
Net funds provided from operations before capital expenditures	21,333	1,050
Additions to property, plant and equipment and mining permit costs	(805)	(898)
Long-term receivables	(13,762)	—
Net funds provided for operating transactions	$ 6,766	$ 152

RESULTS OF OPERATIONS

Net sales for the six months ended June 30, 1983 include sales of ethanol plants, coal sales and other sales in the amounts of $22,518,320, $2,300,268 and $80,879, respectively. Net sales for the comparative period ended June 30, 1982, do not include sales of ethanol plants since such operations were commenced during the quarter ended December 31, 1982. Gross margins on coal sales decreased from 12% for the months ended June 30, 1982 to 2% for the comparable period ended in 1983.

Increased net earnings for the six months ended June 30, 1983 when compared to the comparable period ended June 30, 1982 are attributed principally to the net earnings before taxes generated from plant sales effected by Ethanol Energy Engineering, Inc., in the amount of $14,067,616 since net earnings before taxes on income for the Company as a whole increased to $12,031,915 during the six months ended June 30, 1983, as compared to net earnings before taxes on income for the six months ended June 30, 1982, in the amount of $410,346.

Exhibit 2   Southwestern Fuel Systems, Excerpts from 12/31/82 10-K

EXHIBIT 2
Southwestern Fuel Systems, Excerpts from 12/31/82 10-K

1. SELECTED FINANCIAL DATA

FIVE-YEAR SUMMARY OF SELECTED FINANCIAL DATA

	1982	1981	1980	1979	1978
Net sales	$23,200,661	$4,677,501	$3,624,201	$2,601,829	$ 848,695
Net earnings	5,585,124	475,913	315,064	182,522	3,775
Net earnings per common share	.55	.05	.03	.02	—
Cash dividends per common share	—	—	—	—	—
Total assets	$35,306,335	$6,986,941	$2,910,951	$2,112,414	$1,241,526
Long-term debt	$13,675,586	$3,577,990	$ 570,249	$ 914,975	$ 692,279

2. FINANCIAL STATEMENTS AND SUPPLEMENTARY DATA

ACCOUNTANT'S REPORT

The Board of Directors
Southwestern Fuel Systems, Inc.

We have examined the consolidated financial statements of Southwestern Fuel Systems, Inc. and subsidiaries as listed in the accompanying index. Our examinations were made in accordance with generally accepted auditing standards and, accordingly, included such tests of the accounting records and such other auditing procedures as we considered necessary in the circumstances. In connection with our examinations of the consolidated financial statements, we also examined the supporting schedules as listed in the accompanying index.

In our opinion, the aforementioned consolidated financial statements present fairly the financial position of Southwestern Fuel Systems, Inc. and subsidiaries at December 31, 1982 and 1981 and the results of their operations and the changes in their financial position for each of the years in the three year period ended December 31, 1982, in conformity with generally accepted accounting principles applied on a consistent basis. Also in our opinion, the related supporting schedules, when considered in relation to the basic consolidated financial statements taken as a whole, present fairly in all material respects the information set forth therein.

BIG EIGHT & CO.

Kansas City, Missouri
March 11, 1983

Exhibit 2   Southwestern Fuel Systems, Excerpts from 12/31/82 10-K

CONSOLIDATED BALANCE SHEET
December 31, 1982 and 1981

	December 31	
	1982	1981
ASSETS		
Current Assets		
Cash	2,889,495	14,211
Accounts receivable:		
Trade	403,270	231,532
Officers and stockholders	—	30,625
Other	41,233	9,786
Notes receivable:		
Current installments of long-term notes receivable	664,814	—
Officers and stockholders	45,000	170,000
Other	—	10,000
Escrowed industrial revenue bond issue proceeds (note F)	3,556,536	—
Costs and estimated earnings in excess of billings on uncompleted contracts (note C)	424,875	—
Inventories (note B)	353,324	732,935
Bond escrow fund-interest (note F)	492,200	50,795
Prepaid expenses	106,333	15,545
Deferred income taxes, current	141,215	10,192
Total current assets	9,118,295	1,275,621
Property, Plant and Equipment (note F)		
Land	197,605	127,861
Buildings and improvements	525,926	245,433
Machinery and equipment	10,748,234	5,602,256
Trucks, autos, furniture, and fixtures	440,798	360,527
	11,912,563	6,336,077
Less accumulated depreciation	2,679,610	1,807,898
Net property, plant and equipment	9,232,953	4,528,179
Other Assets		
Notes receivable (note C)	13,460,186	—
Mining permit costs and deposits	526,147	403,277
Bond issue costs, net of amortization	1,034,818	264,326
Bond escrow fund-principal (note F)	1,180,000	430,000
Intangible assets, net of amortization	673,950	—
Reorganization costs and other	79,986	85,538
Total other assets	16,955,087	1,183,141
	35,306,335	6,986,941

S

597

(continued)

Exhibit 2   Southwestern Fuel Systems, Excerpts from 12/31/82 10-K

CONSOLIDATED BALANCE SHEET (continued)

	December 31	
	1982	1981
LIABILITIES AND STOCKHOLDERS' EQUITY		
Current Liabilities		
Current maturities of long-term debt (note F)	972,208	626,424
Notes payable:		
Banks (note E)	902,151	392,600
Stockholders	108,772	16,272
Other	103,125	106,875
Accounts payable:		
Trade	2,540,665	521,606
Other	990,000	—
Deposit on contract	664,870	—
Accrued liabilities	1,115,457	245,756
Deferred interest income, net of amortization of $10,722 (note C)	420,673	—
Income taxes	59,442	63,296
Total current liabilities	7,877,363	1,972,829
Long-term debt, net of current maturities (note F)	13,675,586	3,577,990
Deferred income taxes, non-current	4,029,741	6,964
Accrued land reclamation costs	151,768	104,238
Deferred income on joint venture	345,203	—
Sales tax payable (note C)	451,895	—
Total liabilities	26,531,556	5,662,021
Stockholders' Equity		
Common stock, $.08 per value, authorized 50,000,000 shares, issued 10,577,575 shares in 1982 and 44,001,836 shares in 1981	846,206	3,520,147
Additional paid-in capital	1,850,676	—
Excess of par value over stated capital of subsidiary acquired	(334,072)	(3,022,072)
	2,362,810	498,075
Retained earnings	6,411,969	826,845
Total stockholders' equity	8,774,779	1,324,920
Commitments and contingencies (note G)		
Total liabilities and shareholders' equity	35,306,335	6,986,941

Exhibit 2   Southwestern Fuel Systems, Excerpts from 12/31/82 10-K

CONSOLIDATED STATEMENTS OF EARNINGS

	Year Ended December 31		
	1982	1981	1980
Revenues			
Ethanol plant sales, net of discount of $431,395 (note C)	$17,068,605	—	—
Coal sales	6,084,751	$4,677,501	$3,624,201
Other	47,305	—	—
	23,200,661	4,677,501	3,624,201
Cost of Revenue			
Ethanol plant sales	6,946,452	—	—
Coal sales	5,286,271	3,531,861	2,966,163
Other	114,605	—	—
	12,347,328	3,531,861	2,966,163
Gross profit	10,853,333	1,145,640	658,038
General and administrative expenses	855,424	214,508	80,149
Operating income	9,997,909	931,132	577,889
Other income (expense):			
Interest income	86,086	136,957	13,852
Interest expense, net of interest capitalized of $114,796 in 1982	(688,927)	(547,388)	(230,414)
Miscellaneous, net	132,489	343	(9,625)
Earnings before income taxes	9,527,557	521,044	351,702
Income tax expense (benefit) (note D):			
Current	50,679	33,271	40,136
Deferred	3,891,754	11,860	(3,498)
Total income tax expense	3,942,433	45,131	36,638
Net earnings	$ 5,585,124	$ 475,913	$ 315,064
Net earnings per share	$ .55	$ .05	$ .03

See accompanying notes to consolidated financial statements

S

599

Exhibit 2   Southwestern Fuel Systems, Excerpts from 12/31/82 10-K

CONSOLIDATED STATEMENTS OF CHANGES IN FINANCIAL POSITION

	Year Ended December 31		
	1982	1981	1980
Sources of Working Capital			
Working capital provided by operations:			
Net earnings	$ 5,585,124	$ 475,913	$ 315,064
Items which do not use (provide) working capital:			
Depreciation and amortization	941,794	721,842	488,163
Deferred income tax expense (benefit), non-current	4,022,777	14,923	(1,111)
Provision of land reclamation costs	47,530	33,338	50,528
Working capital provided by operations	10,597,225	1,246,016	852,644
Contributions to capital	675,000	—	—
Increase in deferred income	345,203	—	—
Increase in deferred sales tax payable	451,895	—	—
Current installments and payment of notes receivable	664,814	—	—
Additions to long-term debt	10,843,415	3,673,000	538,635
Proceeds from retirements of property, plant and equipment	14,792	7,648	2,890
Proceeds from sale of treasury stock	—	20,000	—
Issuance of common stock	1,189,735	223,728	74,200
Other	—	996	—
	$24,782,079	$5,171,388	$1,468,369
Uses of Working Capital			
Increase in long-term notes receivable	$14,125,000	—	—
Additions to mining permit costs and deposits	126,403	$ 207,975	$ 133,267
Industrial revenue bond issue costs	803,159	280,509	—
Increase in bond escrow fund—principal	750,000	430,000	—
Reorganization costs incurred	10,446	83,507	—
Additions to property, plant and equipment	5,606,276	2,641,525	1,251,973
Current installments and repayment of long-term debt	745,819	665,260	862,989
Acquisition of treasury stock	—	—	20,000
Acquisition of intangible assets of subsidiary	673,950	—	—
Other	2,886	—	3,355
Increase (decrease) in working capital	1,938,140	862,612	(803,215)
	$24,782,079	$5,171,388	$1,468,369

Exhibit 2   Southwestern Fuel Systems, Excerpts from 12/31/82 10-K

	Year Ended December 31		
	1982	1981	1980
Changes in Components of Working Capital			
Increase (decrease) in current assets:			
Cash	$ 2,875,284	$ (12,017)	$ (25)
Accounts receivable	172,560	246,290	(64,278)
Notes receivable	529,814	180,000	—
Escrow industrial revenue bond issue proceeds	3,556,536	—	—
Costs and estimated earnings in excess of billings on uncompleted contracts	424,875	—	—
Inventories	(379,611)	693,557	(27,086)
Bond escrow fund—interest	441,405	50,795	—
Prepaid expenses	90,788	9,590	(11,474)
Deferred income taxes	131,023	3,063	2,387
	$ 7,842,674	$1,171,278	$ (100,476)
Increase (decrease) in current liabilities:			
Current maturities of long-term debt	345,784	17,336	33,530
Notes payable	598,301	49,344	349,403
Accounts payable	3,009,059	135,926	239,373
Deposit on contract	664,870	—	—
Accrued liabilities	869,701	91,303	49,386
Deferred interest income	420,673	—	—
Income taxes	(3,854)	14,757	31,047
	5,904,534	308,666	702,739
	$ 1,938,140	$ 862,612	$ 803,215

See accompanying notes to consolidated financial statements.

S

601

NOTES TO CONSOLIDATED FINANCIAL STATEMENTS

(A) Accounting Policies and Principles

Accounting for Construction Contracts of Ethanol Plants
Revenues earned and costs related to the construction of ethanol plants are recognized based on the Company's estimates of the completion of each contract, subject to the receipt of an adequate down payment, the execution of a completed contract or purchase order and when collection of the sales price is reasonably assured. When such plants are completed, as certified by an independent engineer, the Company makes an accrual for estimated future warranty costs covering possible costs to be incurred under the warranty periods of the sales contracts. Such warranty costs are included in accounts payable in the accompanying balance sheet at December 31, 1982. No revenue is recorded until contracts are substantially in progress.

Exhibit 2   Southwestern Fuel Systems, Excerpts from 12/31/82 10-K

Property, Plant and Equipment

Property, plant and equipment are recorded at cost. Expenditures for repairs and maintenance are charged to operations as incurred.

Depreciation is calculated using the straight-line and accelerated methods for financial reporting purposes, based upon the estimated useful lives of depreciable assets. For income tax purposes, additions to property, plant and equipment prior to December 31, 1980 are depreciated in the same manner as for financial reporting purposes. Additions after that date are being depreciated under the accelerated cost recovery system for income tax purposes.

Bond Issue Costs

Bond issue costs, consisting primarily of underwriter's fees and legal fees incurred by the Company in conjunction with the issuance of industrial revenue bonds, have been capitalized and are being amortized on a level-yield method over the life of the bonds.

Income Taxes

Southwestern Fuel Systems, Inc. and its subsidiaries file a consolidated income tax return. Certain items are accounted for differently for financial reporting purposes than for income tax purposes. Deferred income taxes have been provided in recognition of these timing differences.

Investment tax credits arising from the acquisition of assets used in the business are accounted for using the "flow-through" method, which recognizes the benefit as a reduction in the income tax provision in the year in which the related assets are placed in service.

Earnings per Share

Earnings per share data is based upon the weighted average number of shares of common stock outstanding during the year adjusted retroactively for the contribution of 34,100,000 shares held by officers and directors in July and November, 1982 and the shares issued as a result of the acquisition of Southwestern Mining and Reclamation by Southwestern Fuel Systems, Inc. in May, 1981. Weighted average shares outstanding have been adjusted for warrants outstanding, which constitute common stock equivalents, when the effect of such is dilutive.

(B) Inventories

Inventories, accounted for at the lower of cost or market on a FIFO basis, consisted of the following at December 31, 1982 and 1981:

	1982	1981
Coal	45,985	408,832
Spare parts	155,669	259,033
Supplies	41,017	24,640
Other	110,653	40,430
	$353,324	$732,935

Exhibit 2   Southwestern Fuel Systems, Excerpts from 12/31/82 10-K

(C) Contract Costs and Notes Receivable

Contract costs on uncompleted contracts at December 31, 1982 amounted to $424,875. There were no billings outstanding under these contracts.

During the year ended December 31, 1982, the Company's subsidiary, EEE, sold five eth-anol plants for a total purchase price of $17,500,000, of which $3,375,000 was paid in cash and the balance of $14,125,000 was represented by notes receivable from the pur-chasers. The notes receivable of $14,125,000 ($664,814 shown as a current asset) are due in equal monthly installments over 96 months, commencing in May and June of 1983, and bear interest at the rate of 13%. As neither principal or interest payments on these notes commence for six months from the date the notes were issued, the notes and related sales price were discounted for such period. Aggregate discounts netted against the sales price of the plants during the year ended December 31, 1982, amounted to $431,395. Such discount is being recognized on a level-yield basis over the payment abatement period.

Sales tax charged on the sale of ethanol plants is payable as the sales proceeds are received. Unpaid sales tax on the sale of ethanol plants at December 31, 1982 aggre-gated $588,405, of which $136,510 is included in current liabilities under the caption "accrued liabilities" and the balance of $451,895, which is payable after one year, is included as a noncurrent liability.

(D) Income Taxes

The components of consolidated income tax expense (benefit) for the years ended December 31, 1982, 1981 and 1980 are as follows:

	1982	1981	1980
Taxes currently payable:			
Federal	11,988	26,271	29,694
State	38,691	7,000	10,442
Total currently payable	50,679	33,271	40,136
Deferred taxes:			
Federal	3,629,254	1,765	(727)
State	262,500	10,095	(2,771)
Total deferred taxes	3,891,754	11,860	(3,498)
Total income tax expense	3,942,433	45,131	36,638

The sources of timing differences relating to the deferred income tax provision (benefit) during the years ended December 31, 1982, 1981 and 1980 and the tax effect of each are as follows:

	1982	1981	1980
Gain from sale of ethanol plants for finan-cial reporting purposes in excess of gain recognized for tax purposes under the installment method	3,938,383	—	—

Exhibit 2   Southwestern Fuel Systems, Excerpts from 12/31/82 10-K

	1982	1981	1980
Gain from sale of coal fines for tax purposes not recognized for financial reporting purposes	(131,590)	—	—
Depreciation for tax purposes in excess of depreciation for financial reporting purposes	465,215	117,624	—
Provision for land reclamation costs charged to expense for financial reporting purposes not deductible for tax purposes	(23,147)	(16,236)	(24,607)
Balance carried forward	4,248,861	101,388	(24,607)
Investment tax credit recognized for tax purposes in excess of (less than) amount recognized for financial reporting purposes	(307,670)	(70,584)	16,956
Other	(49,437)	(18,944)	4,153
Total tax effect of timing differences	3,891,754	11,860	(3,498)

The consolidated provision for income tax expense has been provided at effective rates of 41.4%, 8.7% and 10.4% for the years ended December 31, 1982, 1981 and 1980, respectively. The reasons for the difference between the effective income tax rates and the statutory Federal income tax rate of 46% are as follows:

	1982	1981	1980
Expected "normal" income tax rate	46.0%	46.0%	46.0%
Statutory depletion	—	(16.2	(26.0
Surtax exemption	(0.2)	(3.7)	(5.5)
Investment tax credit	(6.3)	(20.9)	(11.6)
New jobs credit	(0.1)	(3.6)	(1.7)
Minimum tax	—	5.0	8.0
Other, net	2.0	2.1	1.2
Total tax effect of timing differences	41.4%	8.7%	10.4%

The Company has available investment tax credit carryovers for income tax purposes amounting to $340,804 at December 31, 1982. Such credits expire in 1997. No investment tax credit carryovers exist for financial reporting purposes.

(E) Short-Term Debt

Short-term borrowings with banks at December 31, 1982 and 1981 amounted to $902,151 and $392,600, respectively. Such short-term notes are written for periods ranging from 30 to 180 days and bear interest at rates ranging from 13.0% to 17.5%.

Exhibit 2   Southwestern Fuel Systems, Excerpts from 12/31/82 10-K

(F) Long-Term Debt

The components of long-term debt at December 31, 1982 and 1981 are as follows:

	1982	1981
Installment notes payable, due in monthly payments in 1983 through 1986, bearing interest at 10% to 16.5%, secured by property, plant and equipment with a depreciated cost of $7,654,341.	3,782,794	704,414
Industrial revenue bonds, due in annual installments through 1991, bearing interest at 10.5% to 13.25%, secured by a security interest in ethanol plants sold in 1982, as well as a contingent security interest in the related notes receivable in the event of and during the continuance of any default on the bonds	7,500,000	—
Industrial revenue bonds due in quarterly installments in 1983 through 1994, bearing interest at 10% to 14%, secured by a security interest in all real estate, improvements, fixtures, machinery and equipment financed with Bond proceeds and a partially improved tract of real estate being contributed by the Company to the project	3,365,000	3,500,000
Total	14,647,794	4,204,414
Less current maturities	972,208	626,424
Total long-term debt	13,675,586	3,577,990

At December 31, 1982, an additional $3,556,536 of industrial revenue bond proceeds remained in escrow pending release to the Company upon the submission and approval of documentation related to the construction of the ethanol plants completed during 1982.

Maturities of long-term debt for the next five years are as follows:

1983	972,208
1984	948,260
1985	843,975
1986	658,187
1987 and thereafter	11,225,164
	14,647,794

(G) Commitments and Contingencies

Coal lease agreements as executed by the Company's subsidiary, Southwestern Mining, provide for minimum annual advance royalty payments which are charged to operations as incurred.

S

605

Exhibit 2   Southwestern Fuel Systems, Excerpts from 12/31/82 10-K

Southwestern Mining is a party to a contract with the City of Independence, Missouri to supply 5,137,000 tons of coal for a fifteen-year period from January 1, 1980 through December 31, 1994, at prices subject to price negotiations on an annual basis. Total sales to the City of Independence during the years ended December 31, 1982, 1981 and 1980 amounted to $5,078,389, $4,045,604 and $3,480,498, respectively. No other individual customer accounted for more than 10% of Southwestern Mining's total coal sales revenue.

(H) Segment Data

The following table shows business segment information for the year ended December 31, 1982.

	Ethanol Plant Ethanol	Mining Operations	Other	Total
Net sales	17,068,605	6,084,751	47,305	23,200,661
Earnings (loss) before income taxes	10,049,484	71,712	(593,639)	9,527,557
Taxes on income				3,942,433
				5,585,124
Depreciation and amortization	24,083	861,971	55,740	941,794
Capital expenditures	1,063,614	1,382,663	3,159,999	5,606,276
Identifiable assets	22,362,787	7,095,437	5,848,111	35,306,335

Amounts included above under the caption "other" reflect the operations and assets of Supersweep, Inc. and corporate assets and expenses of the Company and its other subsidiaries. There were no inter-segment sales for the year ended December 31, 1982. Prior to the year ended December 31, 1982, the Company had only one reportable segment (mining operations).

Thousand Trails, Inc.

It is late 1984. Thousand Trails, Inc., the national leader in the private membership campground resort industry, has generated an exceptional record of growth in sales and earnings since its creation in 1969. The OTC market has responded with enthusiasm: the Company's stock, which traded at less than $4 per share (adjusted for splits) at the end of 1981, rose to more than $10 by the end of 1982, $16 a share by the end of 1983, and $26 by October 31, 1984. At that price, the stock was selling at approximately 15 times anticipated 1984 earnings.

POTENTIAL ACQUISITION

Thousand Trails now announces that it is "involved in preliminary merger discussions with an unnamed party concerning a transaction whereby Thousand Trails might be acquired." The Company emphasizes that no agreement in principle or letter of intent has been negotiated, and that in any case a definitive agreement would be subject to shareholder approval. Immediately after the announcement, Thousand Trails' stock price hits an all-time high of $29.50.

In discussing the development, a vice-president of a local (Seattle) brokerage firm states that "this is very positive for the campground industry" and that several members of the industry, including Thousand Trails, American Adventures, All Season, and U.S. Vacations, all deserve to be trading at higher prices. On the other hand, a research analyst with a national brokerage house noted that investors remain nervous about difficulties faced by some firms in this industry in prior years—for example, some firms were accused by various state attorneys of using high-pressure sales techniques. She noted that "while earnings growth has been above average the past two or three years . . . I don't think investors forget right away."

Although it has not been announced publicly, some outsiders are already aware that the potential suitor is Weyerhaeuser Co., which has been seeking income outside the timber products industry. J. P. Weyerhaeuser, the retired Weyerhaeuser executive, is on the Thousand Trails board. The most talked-about arrangement is a deal in which Weyerhaeuser would trade 1.3 of its shares for one share of Trails stock. That would put the buyout in the range of $35 to $38 per share, with a total value of about $370 million.

At Weyerhaeuser, it is evident just how preliminary are the discussions of a possible acquisition. Diversification is of interest to some board members, and it is possible that some Weyerhaeuser land might be available for development as campgrounds. How-

---

Prepared by Professor Victor L. Bernard. The case was prepared as a basis for class discussion and is not intended to illustrate either an effective or ineffective management of a business situation.

ever, the extent to which such development could create opportunities for sales beyond that which Thousand Trails could generate independently has not yet been closely examined. A variety of other important issues also remain to be considered carefully. One question is how much anticipated sales growth and associated profitability was already impounded in the price of Thousand Trails as a stand-alone enterprise, before the preliminary discussions were announced. Further progress on an acquisition would require some assurance that the market expectations are reasonable. Another question is how much sales prospects would need to be enhanced (or costs of generating sales reduced) to justify extending an offer of, say, $35 a share.

As the discussion of the potential acquisition proceeds, one industry observer suggests that Thousand Trails' earnings calculations deserve a hard look. An acquisition in the range of 17 times earnings, for a company whose earnings are growing so quickly, may not appear unreasonably expensive at first blush. However, the observer suggests that Thousand Trails' accounting appears aggressive on at least a couple of key dimensions. First, Thousand Trails records all revenue from sales activity as soon as sales contracts are signed. Second, profit from such sales is calculated on the assumption that the camping "preserves" will ultimately fill to capacity. However, not all agree that such policies are a cause for concern. One industry insider indicates that Thousand Trails' financial reporting is consistent with industry standards.

t

THE COMPANY

Thousand Trails, Inc. is the pioneer and largest member of the private membership campground resort industry. It calls itself "America's Private National Park System." The Company acquires land, develops and operates camping preserves, and sells family memberships that grant the right to use the preserves. Each preserve includes not only individual campsites but also various other amenities. A fully-developed reserve would include swimming pools, shuffleboard courts, horseshoe pits, fishing facilities, tennis courts, indoor recreation centers, trading posts, chapels, hiking trails, and perhaps a lodge. One-half of each preserve is maintained in its natural wilderness state.

The Company is based in Bellevue, Washington, and commenced operations during the late 1960s and early 1970s with a handful of preserves in Washington state. In the late 1970s and early 1980s, Thousand Trails expanded to Oregon and California. Subsequent expansions encompassed Texas, the Midwest, and the East Coast. Now, in 1984, the Company is operating a 42-resort network located in 16 states and British Columbia. The total number of memberships stands at 68,000. More than half of these have been sold within the last three years.

Thousand Trails Memberships

Standard Thousand Trails memberships sell for an initial fee of $6500; annual dues now stand at $238 and are adjusted annually for inflation. In return for these payments, three generations of the member's family receive exclusive use of existing and future campground facilities for an unlimited number of visits up to two weeks' duration per visit.

The annual dues are intended to cover operating costs for the preserves, and a share of general corporate overhead. The Company estimates that the annual dues are sufficient to cover such costs when memberships reach 40 percent of total campground capacity. Projections of total capacity are based on the assumption that a preserve can accommodate ten families per campsite without overcrowding. Given the 22,400 campsites in the current system, Thousand Trails estimates its current capacity at 224,000 memberships, and thus considers itself at about 30 percent of capacity, on average.

Membership in the Thousand Trails network conveys no interest in real estate, nor does it guarantee that existing preserves will be developed fully. Thus, the Company has the ability to alter the planned amenities for a campground. Chairman Jim Jensen puts it this way: "Let's say we had a campground where the master plan was used to develop 800 to 900 campsites and the accompanying amenities. If circumstances later suggested the master plan has been overly optimistic, we simply wouldn't fully develop that property, or incur the expenses of the original plan."[1]

Marketing

Marketing has been the key to success for the company. In the words of an American Marketing Association newsletter, "Thousand Trails virtually created an industry, basically through application of pure marketing."[2] CEO Jensen is a direct sales expert, having once worked for an encyclopedia company.

Thousand Trails' target market includes older couples and families. The typical Thousand Trails member is over 50 years old, with annual family income of about $30,000. The campgrounds are marketed as scenically-located, safe, secure, clean, and peaceful alternatives to crowded public campgrounds. The image that Thousand Trails intends to convey is evident in its choice of official spokespersons, Roy Rogers and Dale Evans. Those within the Company sometimes jokingly refer to the preserves as a "poor man's country club."

Memberships are sold through direct mail (41 percent and 54 percent of sales in 1980 and 1984, respectively), member referral (37 percent and 26 percent of sales in 1980 and 1984), advertising, and telemarketing. Those contacted via direct mail and telemarketing are guaranteed a prize if they will attend a 90-minute sales presentation. Typical prizes are telephone/clock radios (retail value $100); two sleeping bags ($60); and clocks ($150). Since only about 9 percent of those attending the presentation ultimately purchase a membership, marketing is a major expense for Thousand Trails.

Thousand Trails memberships have traditionally been marketed to families that own recreational vehicles (RVs), and those families live in their RVs while they visit the campgrounds. In the state of Washington, where Thousand Trails has operated for more

t

609

1. "Heard on the Street," Wall Street Journal (November 14, 1984)
2. AMA Newsletter, Puget Sound Chapter (1984)

than 10 years, memberships have now been sold to 5 percent of all RV owners. Given that there are approximately 7 million RV owners in the United States, there may be opportunities for substantial further growth within that market. Nevertheless, in an effort to expand its membership network more quickly, Thousand Trails began extending memberships in 1982 to non-RV owners, who would then rent Company-owned RVs during their campground stays. CEO Jensen states that "these new memberships have proven to be very popular with the public. More and more people want to experience the great outdoors at a campground. But not all have made the investment in a recreational vehicle. By making travel trailers available to families, we have vastly increased our target market." Indeed, about half of 1984 sales were to non-RV owners.

Within the last three years, Thousand Trails has also expanded geographically. Specifically, Thousand Trails expanded to Texas in 1982, and within the last two years established campgrounds in the Midwest (Illinois, Indiana, Ohio, Missouri, Wisconsin, and Michigan) and the East Coast (Pennsylvania, Virginia, North Carolina, and Florida). In an effort to control costs and increase marketing efficiencies, Thousand Trails expects to open only 15 to 20 new preserves over the next three years.

Financing the Memberships

Most memberships are sold on an installment basis. (The fraction of new membership sales on an installment basis was 74 percent, 82 percent, and 88 percent in 1982, 1983, and 1984, respectively.) The installment contracts are written with initial terms of 24 to 84 months (average 71 months in 1984), require an average down payment of $1045, and carry an average interest rate of 14.8 percent in 1984. Thousand Trail salespersons are given considerable latitude in deciding to whom the company will grant financing; the Company imposes only a few blanket requirements. Family income must be at least $15,000. The minimum down payment is $800, but in some cases even that can be financed. A major credit card or checking account is not required. The Company concedes that it has little recourse against those who fail to make payments, other than to cut off their membership privileges. Nevertheless, the Company reports that in 1984, 93 percent of all payments were received on or before their due date, and, on average, only 1.6 percent of accounts were more than 32 days overdue.

Financial Performance Through 1984

Although 1984 has yet to close, earnings for the year are not difficult to anticipate; the second and third quarters of the year are the key to annual performance, and Thousand Trails Chairman and CEO Jim Jensen has been forthcoming with statements about the likely path of fourth quarter sales and earnings. In fact, those close to the firm have access to essentially the same information reflected in the attached excerpts from the 1984 annual report, as well as other background information like that presented above. It is on the basis of such information that the process of considering the questions surrounding the potential Thousand Trails acquisition commences.

QUESTIONS

a gen'l fin analysis

1. Evaluate Thousand Trails' financial reporting policies. How well do they reflect the underlying economics of the firm? What is your assessment of Thousand Trails' quality of earnings?
2. Assume that Thousand Trails continues to exist as a stand-alone entity, and that it will sell enough memberships within the next ten years to fill the capacity of the existing campground network. Under this scenario, what might the firm's common stock be worth in late 1984? Would it be sufficient to justify the acquisition price now under consideration? Or would substantial other growth or synergies from acquisition be needed to render the price a reasonable one?
3. On the basis of the available information, does an acquisition at a price of $35 to $38 per share appear fair to the buyer? to the seller? What key issues would need to be addressed to answer the question more confidently?

t

611

Exhibit 1   Thousand Trails, Inc. – Excerpts from 1984 Annual Report

EXHIBIT 1
Thousand Trails, Inc. – Excerpts from 1984 Annual Report

Management's Letter to Shareholders

The 1984 Thousand Trails Annual Report is dedicated to our members because it is our members who have made possible the growth and development of the Company. Without their enthusiastic support and desire to share the Thousand Trails experience with their friends, the Company would not be where it is today.

Thousand Trails' more than 68,000 member families are the lifeblood of the Company. Our faith in our existing and future members allows us to envision a future with one million member families from coast to coast.

Our confidence in our members is not based on theory, but on information gathered over Thousand Trails' 15-year history. For instance, we know that 49 percent of our members have fully paid for their memberships. Financial institutions marvel that 93 percent of our installment receivable payments are received on or before the scheduled due date. Those familiar with installment receivable financing are equally impressed by the fact that in 1984, delinquencies of 32 days or more averaged only 1.6 percent of the entire receivable portfolio. These record results are a testimony to both the members' *ability* to pay as well as their *willingness* to pay. We know

that willingness to pay is a direct result of member satisfaction with the high quality of products and services they receive.

Financial Highlights

1984 was another year of record sales and earnings for your Company. Sales of memberships increased 46 percent, from $80.0 million in 1983 to $117.0 million this past year. Total revenues from all sources increased 49 percent, from $100.3 million in 1983 to $149.6 million in 1984. Net earnings grew from $12.0 million in 1983 to $19.1 million in 1984, an increase of 59 percent. Earnings per share increased 45 percent, from $1.21 in 1983 to $1.76 in 1984.

Thousand Trails 5-Year Compounded Growth Table

Sales	40.5%
Earnings	46.9%
Return on average equity	28.1%

Record operating results were not the only financial achievements of the Company during the year. The Company restructured and expanded its bank

Thousand Trails Membership Receivables Table

(Dollars in Thousands)	1980	1981	1982	1983	1984
Average membership contracts receivable	$19,656	$30,488	$46,292	$71,619	$115,138
Average 32-day delinquency as a percent of membership contracts receivable	2.73%	1.87%	1.79%	1.72%	1.62%
Accounts written off as a percentage of average membership contracts receivable	3.3%	3.7%	2.9%	2.7%	1.6%
Membership contracts receivable written off (net)	$655	$1,118	$1,343	$1,899	$1,827

Exhibit 1   Thousand Trails, Inc. – Excerpts from 1984 Annual Report

credit arrangement in 1984 to provide for a $125.0 million bank line of credit. Subsequent to year-end, the Company sold $75 million of seven-year subordinated notes which will provide increased flexibility for growth. Proceeds of the issue were used to reduce bank indebtedness.

Market Size

Prior to 1983, most Thousand Trails memberships were sold to families who owned their own recreational vehicles (RVs). The RV market is growing rapidly, representing today more than 7 million owners. Even throughout the recent recession, the RV industry enjoyed successive annual increases in sales, with 1984 shipments of new RV units topping the 400,000 mark.

In 1983, the Company introduced a concept throughout its system which enables families who do not own their own RV to participate in the Thousand Trails experience through the use of fully furnished and equipped, Company-owned travel trailers. This strategy to expand the Company's market universe has been so successful that of the 18,625 new memberships sold in 1984, more than 56 percent were sold to customers choosing this type of membership. As a result, the market for Thousand Trails memberships has increased from the 7 million RV owners to more than 27 million American families whose socio/economic profile matches closely that of the Thousand Trails member.

1984 Strategies

Last year we asked you to share with us the vision of creating "America's Private National Park System." In 1984, Thousand Trails made great strides towards realizing its goal of a coast-to-coast network of resorts. In a period of only 12 months, we acquired fourteen new properties, entered eight new states, and established a strong presence in two major new markets, the Midwest and East Coast of the United States. This was a very aggressive endeavor for the Company. The 1984 expansion of the resort network into these regions was in planning for three years and recognizes the need to establish a "network" of resorts rather than one or two properties. By clustering property acquisitions within new geographic regions, Thousand Trails is able to offer its members easy access to multiple resort camping. Our reception in these new areas was greater than expected, with sales in 1984 in the Midwest and East Coast of

approximately $20.0 million and 1985 sales expected to exceed $50.0 million.

Marketing Costs

One of the results of our rapid expansion was the anticipated increase in our marketing costs as a percent of sales revenues. These higher marketing costs are due to several factors:

1. In new markets we do not have the membership base to generate referral business, which is the Company's most cost efficient source of sales.

2. It takes a number of months of training by experienced Thousand Trails sales personnel to develop an effective sales team at new locations.

3. When sales are begun at a new location, some parts of the resort are still under development, which creates a natural and expected "wait and see" attitude in the minds of many potential members.

Our experience has proven that marketing costs generally decline in the second and third years after the initial opening of a property for sales. Therefore, although marketing costs will tend to be higher in 1985 than they were in 1984, we anticipate a decrease in these costs in 1986.

Future Expansion Strategy

Having secured a foothold in the Midwest and East Coast markets, the Company intends to open only five to seven new resorts per year in each of the next three years. This slower rate of growth is expected to result in reduced costs and greater marketing efficiencies beginning in 1986.

Conclusion

1984 was a year of great growth for your Company. It was a year that marked the creation of several new business units, which will be discussed in detail in this report. It was also a year of major reorganization resulting in a streamlined and more efficient organizational structure.

Because of our successful 1984 expansion and excellent financial results, we are well postured to continue the development of "America's Private National Park System."

As always, we appreciate your support.

Sincerely,

C. James Jensen
Chairman of the Board and Chief Executive Officer

Exhibit 1   Thousand Trails, Inc. – Excerpts from 1984 Annual Report

MANAGEMENT'S DISCUSSION AND ANALYSIS OF FINANCIAL CONDITION AND RESULTS OF OPERATIONS

The following table provides historical information on membership sales and resorts owned by the Company:

Year Ended December 31,	1980	1981	1982	1983	1984
Units of membership sales:					
Camping	7,704	7,585	9,743	9,989	**8,037**
Vacation	—	—	377	3,852	**10,588**
Total	7,704	7,585	10,120	13,841	**18,625**
Operating Resorts:					
Selling	12	15	16	21	**30**
Non-Selling	1	—	3	4	**6**
Resorts under initial development	1	—	2	3	**6**
Total resorts owned	14	15	21	28	**42**

Membership Sales

Revenues from membership sales during the three years ended December 31, 1982, 1983 and 1984 were $56,454,000, $79,971,000 and $116,983,000, respectively. Increases in revenues from membership sales were a result of increases in the number of memberships sold and increases in the average membership price from $5,600 in 1982 to $5,800 in 1983, and to $6,300 in 1984. Increases in the number of total memberships sold in 1983 and 1984 from the prior periods were due primarily to the addition of five selling resorts in 1983 and nine selling resorts in 1984, accounting for 16% and 25% of the total memberships sold in such years, respectively, and to the availability of vacation memberships.

Marketing expenses as a percentage of sales were 44.1% in 1982 and 44.0% in 1983 and increased to 46.3% in 1984. Compensation paid to sales personnel represented approximately 35% of marketing expenses in each of these years. The increase in marketing costs as a percentage of sales in 1984 was due primarily to the commencement of sales activities at 10 of the 11 new operating resorts. New selling resorts tend to have higher marketing costs than the more established selling resorts. Marketing expenses for new selling resorts in new geographic market areas also tend to be higher than for new resorts in established market areas. Nine of the new selling resorts opened in 1984 were in geographical areas in which the Company had not previously marketed memberships.

Resort land and improvement costs attributable to membership sales were $8,389,000 (14.9% of sales) in 1982, $13,047,000 (16.3% of sales) in 1983 and $17,842,000 (15.3% of sales) in 1984. The average land and improvement costs expensed per membership sold in 1982, 1983 and 1984 were approximately $830, $940 and $940, respectively. The percentage increase in 1983 compared with 1982 was due primarily to the sale of more memberships in California, where land and improvement costs are typically higher than the Company's overall average. The percentage decrease in 1984 compared with 1983 resulted from a $500 increase in the average membership sales price.

Exhibit 1   Thousand Trails, Inc. – Excerpts from 1984 Annual Report

The Company expenses resort land and improvement costs based on the ratio of memberships sold to total memberships planned by the Company to be available for sale in each region. The number of memberships planned for sale is derived from the Company's estimate that its resorts can support 10 memberships per campsite without overcrowding. As a result, since inception, the Company has used a 10 to 1 ratio in expensing land and improvement costs attributable to membership sales. For the Company to amortize fully in accordance with its accounting practices the total of incurred and all estimated future land and improvement costs with respect to the planned 22,452 campsites for its current 36 operating resorts, it would be necessary for it to sell approximately 224,520 memberships, of which 68,660 memberships (31%) were outstanding as of December 31, 1984. If in the future it appears that this number of memberships cannot be sold because of market or usage constraints, the Company will reassess planned future development at its resorts and, if necessary, increase the rate at which it expenses land and improvement costs against subsequent sales, which would adversely affect profit margins and earnings, unless offset in whole or in part by increases in the membership sales prices.

General and administrative expenses as a percentage of membership sales have decreased from 15.2% in 1982 to 14.8% in 1983, and to 12.6% in 1984. These decreases are primarily the result of economies obtained from increases in sales.

The Company provides for estimated losses on installment sales based on its historical collection experience. The provision for doubtful accounts as a percentage of membership sales increased from 4.0% in 1982 to 5.0% in 1983 and 1984 as a result of the increase in the number of sales made on the installment basis, but remained constant as a percentage of the financed portion of installment sales. Installment sales were 74% of sales in 1982, 82% of sales in 1983 and 88% of sales in 1984. Delinquent receivables (defined as receivables more than 32 days past due), as a percentage of the total contracts receivable portfolio of the Company, have averaged approximately 1.8% during each of these three years.

The Company has been able to offset the impact of inflation on its operations through increases in the membership sales prices and increases in annual dues for new members.

Resort Operations

Revenues from resort operations continued to increase as the base of members grew from 27,620 on January 1, 1982 to 68,660 at December 31, 1984. After allocating to marketing expenses certain costs related to membership sales, resort operations generated a profit during 1982 and 1983, increasing from $325,000 in 1982 to $489,000 in 1983. As a result of the addition of 11 new operating resorts in 1984, resort operations incurred a loss of $588,000 in that year because new resorts initially have a relatively small base of members paying dues. To support its sales activities and maintain member satisfaction, it is the philosophy of the Company to provide facilities and a complete staff at all resorts regardless of the number of memberships sold at any particular resort. The Company does not anticipate any significant earnings contribution from resort operations during the next few years as it continues to expand its resort network.

Interest Income and Expense

The Company charges interest on the unpaid portion of its membership contracts receivable portfolio at fixed rates which averaged approximately 14.8% in 1982, 1983 and

Exhibit 1   Thousand Trails, Inc. – Excerpts from 1984 Annual Report

1984. Interest income increased from $6,622,000 in 1982 to $10,147,000 in 1983, and to $16,067,000 in 1984, due to the substantial increases in the Company's membership contracts receivable portfolio. The total contracts receivable portfolio increased from $56,114,000 at December 31, 1982 to $143,153,000 at December 31, 1984.

The Company finances its acquisition and development of resorts through borrowings under its bank line of credit and seller-financed real estate contracts. Seller financing of resort acquisitions accrues interest at fixed rates, generally ranging from 9% to 11%. Financing under the Company's bank line of credit bears interest at variable rates which averaged 12.8% in 1984.

The average cost to the Company of all borrowed funds over the past three years has varied but decreased from 15.2% in 1982 to 11.7% in 1983, and increased to 11.9% in 1984. An increase in interest rates would adversely affect the Company's earnings because interest costs on borrowings under the bank line of credit fluctuate.

Liquidity and Capital Resources

The Company believes that the number of memberships that may be sold within a region is limited by campsite capacity at, and the size of the market area for, each resort within the region. Accordingly, to continue to generate additional growth in membership sales, it is necessary for the Company to add new resorts as well as to continue development of existing resorts. Substantial costs are incurred to acquire and develop resorts prior to membership sales and usage by members. Revenues from membership sales are recorded in full at the time of sale, although cash flow from memberships sold on installment contracts (constituting 88% of total membership sales in 1984) is received over a number of years.

The following table presents the historical cash flow of the Company:

(in thousands) Year Ended December 31,	1982	1983	1984
Cash received from operations:			
Membership sales	$22,582	$27,738	$30,549
Collections on contracts receivable, including interest	19,278	28,619	44,060
Dues and resort revenues	7,336	10,507	15,586
Other	133	211	1,288
	49,329	67,075	91,483
Principal operating expenditures	(37,077)	(52,782)	(74,906)
Cash provided by operations before debt service and resort acquisition and development	12,252	14,293	16,577
Cash expended for resort acquisition and development	(12,631)	(20,609)	(59,316)
Interest expense	(4,203)	(3,957)	(4,984)
Principal payments on debt related to resort properties	(2,388)	(4,337)	(4,688)
Cash used in operations	($6,970)	($14,610)	($52,411)

Exhibit 1   Thousand Trails, Inc. – Excerpts from 1984 Annual Report

Although cash provided by operations before debt service and resort acquisition and development has increased over the past three years, internally generated cash flow has not been sufficient to fund the Company's operations because of expenditures to expand the Company's resort network. The Company's decision to offer a number of resorts in the new market areas of the Midwestern and Eastern United States in 1984 required acquisition and development of a substantial number of properties.

The Company also spent $2,562,000, $4,331,000 and $13,480,000 in 1982, 1983 and 1984, respectively, for purchase of construction and operating equipment, a portion of which was financed through borrowings secured by such equipment. These expenditures include approximately $1,384,000 in 1983 and $6,744,000 in 1984 for purchase of rental trailers.

The principal sources of cash to fund expansion over the past three years have been bank borrowings of $8,646,000 and proceeds from the sale of common stock of $4,161,000 in 1982, bank borrowings of $851,000 and proceeds from the sale of common stock of $17,756,000 in 1983, and bank borrowings of $63,284,000 in 1984.

During 1985, the Company anticipates spending approximately $37,000,000 for additional development of its 36 operating resorts and six resorts under initial development, approximately $15,000,000 for acquisition and development of new resorts, and approximately $8,000,000 for additional rental trailers.

t

Exhibit 1   Thousand Trails, Inc. – Excerpts from 1984 Annual Report

CONSOLIDATED FINANCIAL STATEMENTS

CONSOLIDATED BALANCE SHEETS

Year Ended December 31,	1983	1984
ASSETS		
Current Assets:		
Cash	$ 770,000	$ 1,644,000
Membership contracts receivable, net of allowance of $1,111,000 and $1,797,000	19,271,000	27,426,000
Inventory and other assets	3,625,000	6,409,000
Total Current Assets	23,666,000	35,479,000
Membership contracts receivable, net of allowance of $3,638,000 and $7,005,000	63,102,000	106,925,000
Operating Resorts:		
Land	17,702,000	28,981,000
Improvements	64,580,000	119,417,000
	82,282,000	148,398,000
Costs attributable to membership sales	(38,466,000)	(55,661,000)
	43,816,000	92,737,000
Resorts Under Initial Development, at Cost	6,592,000	9,830,000
Resort Operating Equipment, Net of Accumulated Depreciation of $1,060,000 and $2,217,000	2,688,000	9,356,000
Investment in Real Estate, at Cost	2,773,000	3,203,000
Construction and Other Equipment, Net of Accumulated Depreciation of $2,114,000 and $2,902,000	2,605,000	5,596,000
Other Assets, at Cost	6,525,000	6,644,000
	$151,767,000	$269,770,000

Exhibit 1   Thousand Trails, Inc. – Excerpts from 1984 Annual Report

CONSOLIDATED BALANCE SHEETS (continued)

Year Ended December 31,	1983	1984
LIABILITIES AND SHAREHOLDERS' EQUITY		
Current Liabilities:		
Accounts payable	$ 2,415,000	$ 5,980,000
Accrued salaries	3,714,000	6,110,000
Prepaid membership dues	1,887,000	2,706,000
Other liabilities	1,180,000	3,322,000
Current portion of long-term debt	5,896,000	9,359,000
Deferred income taxes	7,026,000	9,197,000
Total Current Liabilities	22,118,000	36,674,000
Long-Term Debt	47,343,000	112,895,000
Deferred Income Taxes	22,007,000	35,856,000
Deferred Rental Revenue		3,428,000
Commitments and Contingencies (Note G)		
Shareholders' Equity:		
Common Stock, no par value—Authorized, 15,000,000 shares; Issued and outstanding, 10,197,145 and 10,658,476	29,358,000	30,934,000
Retained Earnings	30,941,000	49,983,000
	60,299,000	$ 80,917,000
	$151,767,000	$269,770,000

See notes to consolidated financial statements.

t

619

Exhibit 1   Thousand Trails, Inc. – Excerpts from 1984 Annual Report

CONSOLIDATED STATEMENTS OF EARNINGS

Year Ended December 31,	1982	1983	1984
Membership Sales	$56,454,000	$79,971,000	$116,983,000
Costs Attributable to Membership Sales:			
Marketing expenses	24,892,000	35,209,000	54,181,000
Resort land and improvement costs	8,389,000	13,047,000	17,842,000
General and administrative expenses	8,612,000	11,827,000	14,730,000
Provision for doubtful accounts	2,241,000	3,977,000	5,880,000
	44,134,000	64,060,000	92,633,000
Income from Membership Sales	12,320,000	15,911,000	24,350,000
Resort Operations:			
Membership dues	4,982,000	7,355,000	10,551,000
Resort revenue and rental income	2,015,000	2,749,000	5,264,000
	6,997,000	10,104,000	15,815,000
Less—			
Maintenance and operations expense	3,860,000	5,709,000	10,107,000
Cost of resort revenue	1,839,000	2,400,000	3,743,000
General and administrative expenses	973,000	1,506,000	2,553,000
	6,672,000	9,615,000	16,403,000
Income (Loss) from Resort Operations	325,000	489,000	(558,000)
Other Income (Expense):			
Interest income	6,622,000	10,147,000	16,067,000
Interest expense	(4,203,000)	(3,957,000)	(5,124,000)
Other	35,000	42,000	691,000
	2,454,000	6,232,000	11,634,000
Earnings Before Deferred Income Taxes	15,099,000	22,632,000	35,396,000
Deferred Income Taxes	7,338,000	10,628,000	16,286,000
Net Earnings	$7,761,000	$12,004,000	$ 19,110,000
Net Earnings Per Share:			
Primary	$.97	$1.23	$1.78
Fully diluted	$.89	$1.21	$1.76

See notes to consolidated financial statements.

t
620

Exhibit 1   Thousand Trails, Inc. – Excerpts from 1984 Annual Report

CONSOLIDATED STATEMENTS OF SHAREHOLDERS' EQUITY

	Common Stock		Retained Earnings
	Shares	Amount	
Balance, January 1, 1982	$ 6,873,565	$6,588,000	$11,277,000
Debenture conversions	114,239	286,000	
Issuance of common stock	1,221,435	4,378,000	
Foreign currency translation			(96,000)
Net earnings			7,761,000
Balance, December 31, 1982	8,209,239	11,252,000	18,942,000
Debenture conversions	116,704	296,000	
Issuance of common stock	1,871,202	17,810,000	
Foreign currency translation			(5,000)
Net earnings			12,004,000
Balance, December 31, 1983	10,197,145	29,358,000	30,941,000
Debenture conversions	**230,135**	**587,000**	
Issuance of common stock	**231,196**	**989,000**	
Foreign currency translation			**(68,000)**
Net earnings			**19,110,000**
Balance, December 31, 1984	**$10,658,476**	**$30,934,000**	**$49,983,000**

t

621

Exhibit 1   Thousand Trails, Inc. – Excerpts from 1984 Annual Report

CONSOLIDATED STATEMENTS OF CHANGES IN FINANCIAL POSITION

Year Ended December 31,	1982	1983	1984
Operations:			
Cash Received—			
Membership sales	$ 22,582,000	$ 27,738,000	$ 30,549,000
Collections on contracts receivable, including interest	19,278,000	28,619,000	44,060,000
Dues and resort revenues	7,336,000	10,507,000	15,586,000
Other	133,000	211,000	1,288,000
	49,329,000	67,075,000	91,483,000
Cash Expended—			
Marketing expenses	23,211,000	32,832,000	48,653,000
General and administrative expenses	7,739,000	11,325,000	12,510,000
Resort maintenance and operations	6,127,000	8,625,000	13,743,000
	37,077,000	52,782,000	74,906,000
Cash provided by operations before debt service and resort acquisition and development	12,252,000	14,293,000	16,577,000
Cash expended for resort acquisition and development	(12,631,000)	(20,609,000)	(59,316,000)
Interest expense	(4,203,000)	(3,957,000)	(4,984,000)
Principal payments on debt related to resort properties	(2,388,000)	(4,337,000)	(4,688,000)
Cash used in operations	(6,970,000)	(14,610,000)	(52,411,000)
Other Sources (Uses) of Cash:			
Issuance of common stock	4,161,000	17,756,000	989,000
Proceeds of borrowings collateralized by contracts receivable	8,646,000	851,000	63,284,000
Purchase of resort operating equipment, net of related borrowings of $1,008,000, $1,302,000 and $3,165,000	(313,000)	(1,711,000)	(5,953,000)
Purchase of construction and other equipment, net of related borrowings of $64,000, $86,000 and $96,000	(1,177,000)	(1,232,000)	(4,266,000)
Principal payments on notes payable and credit line arrangements	(735,000)	(1,109,000)	(306,000)
Investment in preferred stock	(3,000,000)		
Other, net	(81,000))	122,000	(463,000)
	7,501,000	14,677,000	53,285,000
Increase in Cash	531,000	67,000	874,000
Cash:			
Beginning of year	172,000	703,000	770,000
End of year	$ 703,000	$ 770,000	$ 1,644,000

See notes to consolidated financial statements.

Exhibit 1   Thousand Trails, Inc. – Excerpts from 1984 Annual Report

NOTES TO CONSOLIDATED FINANCIAL STATEMENTS

General

The Company and its subsidiaries operate membership-based destination resort campgrounds in the United States and Canada. All significant intercompany transactions and balances have been eliminated in the accompanying financial statements.

NOTE A. Significant Accounting Policies

Revenue Recognition

The Company sells memberships for cash or on an installment basis. Membership sales are recorded in full upon execution of membership contracts. Installment sales require a down payment of at least ten percent of the sales price. All marketing costs and an allowance for estimated contract collection losses (based on historical loss occurrence rates) are recorded currently.

Certain membership contracts provide for prepaid use by members of Company-owned rental trailers. Revenue attributable to prepaid use is recorded as deferred rental revenue and recognized over the period of expected use.

Members are assessed annual dues which are used for resort maintenance and operations, member services and related general and administrative expenses. The Company establishes dues at rates intended to fully provide for such expenses when active memberships sold reach approximately 40 percent of total memberships available for sale. Membership contracts provide for annual adjustment of dues to reflect increases in the Consumer Price Index.

Operating Resorts

Operating resort land and improvement costs, including the estimated costs to fully develop the resorts, are aggregated by geographical region and recorded as a cost of membership sales based upon the ratio of actual memberships sold within each region to the total memberships planned for sale within the region. The maximum number of memberships which will be sold in a geographical region is determined based on members' historical use of the Company's resorts in that region. The Company currently plans to sell ten memberships for each campsite. Resort utilization statistics are reviewed on a regular basis, and the number of total planned memberships available for sale will be revised if future experience indicates the ten-to-one ratio is no longer appropriate. As of December 31, 1984, the Company had 68,660 members, which represented approximately one-third of the total memberships planned for sale in its 36 operating resorts.

Resorts under Initial Development

Resorts under initial development are classified as operating resorts when development has been completed to the extent that the resorts are reflected in the Company's marketing program as available for use by members.

Investment in Real Estate

Land acquired in excess of that necessary for operating resorts is classified as investment in real estate. Real estate contiguous to operating resorts is infrequently used but is generally available for use by members until disposition or further development. Certain parcels of the real estate contiguous to operating resorts are subject to land use permits obtained in connection with development of the resorts. Prior to disposition or develop-

Exhibit 1   Thousand Trails, Inc. – Excerpts from 1984 Annual Report

ment of such parcels, the Company will be required to obtain waivers or modifications of such permits from local governmental authorities.

Depreciation

Depreciation of equipment is provided on the straight-line method over the assets' respective useful lives.

Foreign Currency Translation

The Company translates the financial statements of its Canadian subsidiary into U.S. dollars at exchange rates in effect as of the balance sheet dates. Unrealized translation gains and losses are included in retained earnings.

Earnings per Share

Earnings per share of common stock are computed based on weighted average common and equivalent shares outstanding during the year retroactively restated for the three-for-two stock split payable to shareholders of record on May 22, 1984. Stock options, warrants and rights to purchase stock are included in the computation of earnings per share when dilutive. The effect of an assumed conversion of the Company's convertible subordinated debentures is also included in the computation of fully diluted earnings per share.

Reclassifications

Certain reclassifications have been made in the 1982 and 1983 financial statements to conform with 1984 classifications.

NOTE B. Membership Contracts Receivable

Membership contracts receivable bear interest at an average rate of 14.8% and currently are written with initial terms of 24 to 84 months (average 71 months in 1984). The Company has no obligation to refund monies received or to provide further services to members in the event a membership is cancelled for nonpayment of contractual obligations.

Scheduled aggregate annual principal payments on membership contracts are as follows:

Year ended December 31	
1985	$29,223,000
1986	28,828,000
1987	26,683,000
1988	22,516,000
1989	16,605,000
1990	11,678,000
1991	7,620,000

The Company received principal payments in excess of scheduled payments in 1982, 1983 and 1984 of $1,139,000, $2,249,000 and $9,800,000, respectively, by utilizing early payment incentive programs.

Substantially all membership contracts receivable are pledged as collateral for debt.

Exhibit 1   Thousand Trails, Inc. – Excerpts from 1984 Annual Report

NOTE C. Long-Term Debt and Line of Credit

Long-term debt and line of credit consist of the following:

Year ended December 31,	1983	1984
Real estate contracts and capitalized leases, 6.5% to 13.25% (average 9.7%), payable in aggregate monthly installments of $491,000 and $587,000 including interest	$23,096,000	$ 28,604,000
Notes, 6% to 14.5% (average 12.4%), payable in monthly installments of approximately $60,000 and $46,000 including interest	1,967,000	1,378,000
Equipment and other contracts, 8.8% to 18.6% (average 13.1%), payable in aggregate monthly installments of $116,000 and $182,000 including interest	2,492,000	3,955,000
13% convertible subordinated debentures	651,000	—
	28,206,000	33,937,000
Line of credit	25,033,000	88,317,000
	53,239,000	122,254,000
Current portion	(5,896,000)	(9,359,000)
	$47,343,000	$112,895,000

Substantially all of the Company's assets are pledged as collateral for the above debt. Aggregate annual principal payments are as follows:

Year ended December 31	
1985	$9,359,000
1986	9,692,000
1987	8,841,000
1988	10,449,000
1989	17,867,000

NOTE D. Deferred Income Taxes

The provision for deferred income taxes consists of the following:

Year ended December 31,	1982	1983	1984
Federal	$6,563,000	$ 9,539,000	$14,434,000
Foreign and state	775,000	1,089,000	1,852,000
	$7,338,000	$10,628,000	$16,286,000

Exhibit 1   Thousand Trails, Inc. – Excerpts from 1984 Annual Report

The income tax provision was reduced by investment tax credits of $66,000 in 1982, $226,000 in 1983 and $934,000 in 1984. Investment tax credits are recorded as a reduction of the income tax provision in the year available.

The tax effect of items reported in different periods for financial statement and income tax purposes is as follows:

Year ended December 31,	1982	1983	1984
Installment sales	$9,200,000	$13,309,000	**$18,514,000**
Capitalized interest	805,000	211,000	**1,379,000**
Resort land and improvement costs	(1,642,000)	(4,033,000)	**(1,877,000)**
Decrease (increase) in tax basis net operating loss carryforward	(1,138,000)	977,000	**(2,079,000)**
Other, net	113,000	164,000	**349,000**
	$7,338,000	$10,628,000	**$16,286,000**

NOTE G. Commitments and Contingencies

Certain of the Company's resorts have been developed and must be operated in compliance with the provisions of applicable land use permits. Management believes the Company is in compliance with such permits and, in the future, will make applications for new permits or for modifications of existing permits as considered necessary for resort operations or for further development.

The Company has operating lease obligations of approximately $975,000 annually until 1994.

NOTE H. Costs and Expenses

The Company capitalizes interest as a component of the cost of significant improvements to resorts. Total interest costs were $6,756,000 in 1982, $6,411,000 in 1983 and $11,007,000 in 1984, of which $2,553,000, $2,454,000 and $5,883,000, respectively, were capitalized.

Certain resort operating costs are incurred to provide support for the Company's marketing program and classified as marketing expenses as follows:

Year ended December 31	
1982	$963,000
1983	1,234,000
1984	3,040,000

Exhibit 1   Thousand Trails, Inc. – Excerpts from 1984 Annual Report

Report of Independent Certified Public Accountants

Board of Directors and Shareholders
Thousand Trails, Inc., Seattle, Washington

We have examined the consolidated balance sheets of Thousand Trails, Inc. and subsidiaries as of December 31, 1983 and 1984, and the related statements of earnings, shareholders' equity and changes in financial position for each of the three years in the period ended December 31, 1984. Our examinations were made in accordance with generally accepted auditing standards and, accordingly, included such tests of the accounting records and such other auditing procedures as we considered necessary in the circumstances.

In our opinion, the consolidated financial statements referred to above present fairly the financial position of Thousand Trails, Inc. and subsidiaries as of December 31, 1983 and 1984, and the results of their operations and the changes in their financial position for each of the three years in the period ended December 31, 1984, in conformity with generally accepted accounting principles applied on a consistent basis.

TOUCHE ROSS & CO.
Certified Public Accountants

Seattle, Washington
February 7, 1985

t

She needs to
wipe that
brown stuff
off her nose!

The Timberland Company

I t is December 1993. The year thus far has been disappointing for several leading companies in the footwear industry, with flat earnings and falling stock prices at Nike, Reebok, and Stride Rite. Against this background, however, a few firms that cater to the market for a rugged outdoor look have turned in an exceptional performance. Wolverine Worldwide, producer of Hush Puppies and the Wilderness sport boot, is enjoying its strongest earnings in a decade, and has watched its stock price more than triple since mid-1992. Analysts are projecting even more earnings improvement in 1994 and beyond, and Wolverine's price is standing at 17 times earnings of the last four quarters.

Even more impressive has been the performance of The Timberland Company. After the family-run business was joined by several new managers, it turned in its strongest earnings ever in 1992, and is topping itself again in 1993. EPS for the first three quarters stands at $1.38, up 86 percent over 1992's record performance. Analysts project EPS for the year at $2.05 to $2.10, and they expect 1994 EPS to be in the range of $3.10 to $3.35. Timberland's stock price, which opened the year at $19, rose to above $83, and stands now at $62—an overall increase good enough to rank Timberland as the NYSE's best performer of the year. Company morale could not be higher; at the Timberland plant in North Carolina, employees declare their aspiration for the company's stock price by sporting "95 in 95" buttons.

COMPANY BACKGROUND

The Timberland Company designs, develops, manufactures, and markets premium quality footwear, accessories, and apparel under the Timberland® label. These products are sold through specialty stores and upscale department and shoe stores in 28 countries worldwide. In addition, the company sells its products in six specialty stores (operated or licensed by the company) and ten company-operated factory outlets devoted exclusively to Timberland merchandise.

The company was incorporated in Delaware in 1978, and is the successor to Abington Shoe Company, a Massachusetts firm dating back to 1933. Nathan Swartz and his family acquired the Abington company in the fifties and manufactured private-label shoes for national manufacturers for nearly 10 years. In the sixties they introduced injection-molding technology to fuse soles to leather uppers without stitching. In 1973, the family set up a factory in Newmarket, New Hampshire, and manufactured the first guaranteed waterproof boots under the Timberland brand. In 1978, with more than 80 per-

Prepared by Professor Charles M. C. Lee and revised by Professor Victor L. Bernard. This case is based on publicly available information. It is prepared as a basis for class discussion and is not intended to illustrate either an effective or ineffective management of a business situation.

cent of the company's footwear carrying the Timberland name, the company dropped its unbranded lines and incorporated as The Timberland Company.

Today, the Swartz family continues to run the business and controls 64 percent of the stock. Sidney Swartz is chairman, president, and CEO. His son, Jeffrey B. Swartz, joined the firm as director of operations in 1986 and became chief operating officer in 1991. In the early 1990s the family brought in managers from outside to staff sales, marketing, and financial positions. The company began coordinating design, production, and marketing functions under firm cost controls.

The company now offers a variety of shoes and boots for men and women, including heavy duty and lightweight trail boots. Over the past few years, approximately 83 percent of its sales came from footwear (boots, shoes, and sandals); the rest came from the sale of apparel and accessories (waterproof and rugged outerwear, sweaters, shirts, pants, shorts, and skirts). The company has built its product lines with classic rugged styles which provide durability and quality. In marketing its products, the company has consistently stressed the workmanship and detailing incorporated into its products, which are designed to provide lasting protection from the elements.

The firm's philosophy is reflected in the company's 1992 10K filing, which reads in part: "The company believes that by providing the highest quality products to consumers at competitive prices, it will continue to increase sales." As *Investor Daily*'s John A. Jones puts it, "From the world's first guaranteed waterproof leather boots to high-tech boat shoes worn by some of the 1992 America's Cup crews, Timberland has held the high ground as a maker of top-quality outdoor shoes and apparel."[1]

OPERATIONS

Timberland has increased its sales steadily for years by capitalizing on its core business and expanding its domestic and international presence through increased consumer awareness of the Timberland brand. Once the producer of a single product—the waterproof leather boot—Timberland now markets a full line through an integrated brand presentation. For example, within department stores Timberland products are presented as a group in "concept shops" or "concept corners." The product line remains consistent, whether it be in such concept shops, Timberland specialty shops, or outlet stores.

The Timberland brand is reinforced through heavy regional print and television advertising—with a significant stepup in the latter category in late 1992—emphasizing the workmanship, detailing, and ruggedness of its merchandise. Advertising costs for 1992 totaled $11.0 million, as compared to $9.2 million for 1991 and $9.3 million for 1990. This advertising is reinforced with a variety of in-store promotions, point-of-purchase displays, and a cooperative advertising program with retailers, as well as retail sales clerk training and other incentive programs. Other marketing efforts include sponsorship of sporting events such as the annual Iditarod dog sled race (from Anchorage to Nome, Alaska) and not-for-profit organizations such as The Wilderness Society.

Timberland sells its products both domestically and internationally, with 63 percent of sales in the U.S. in 1992. It provides four showrooms for wholesalers (New York, Chi-

t

630

---

1. John A. Jones, "Timberland's Classic Outdoor Gear Has Worldwide Sales," Investor Daily *(October 8, 1992): p. 32*

cago, Dallas, and Atlanta) and employs its own sales force to service domestic retailers. The company-owned specialty stores, which sell only Timberland products, are located in six cities across the U.S. Timberland's ten outlet stores, selling factory seconds and close-out merchandise, are located in the Northeast. Internationally, Timberland sells through distributors, commission agents, and six subsidiaries in Europe, Australia, and New Zealand. The company also owns four specialty shops in Europe and one in New Zealand.

Timberland manufactures the majority of its footwear products in leased facilities located in Tennessee, North Carolina, Puerto Rico, and the Dominican Republic. By concentrating within the U.S., Timberland has less exposure to U.S. import restrictions and duties than many of its competitors. However, certain products are sourced from South America, Europe, and the Far East, and Timberland has recently increased the fraction of goods produced outside the U.S. to 30 percent. Raw materials are procured from both domestic and foreign sources. Nearly all leather comes from the U.S., with the largest supplier servicing 34 percent of Timberland's needs.

COMPETITION IN THE FOOTWEAR INDUSTRY

In its 1992 10-K, Timberland characterizes the footwear industry as "highly competitive" and "subject to rapid changes in consumer preference." The Company also notes that "although the industry is fragmented to a great degree, many of the company's competitors are larger and have substantially greater resources than Timberland."

The U.S. footwear industry includes a large number of firms, with 1992 sales of publicly traded firms in excess of $10 billion. Major players include Nike (1992 sales of $3.4 billion); Reebok International ($3.0 billion); Brown ($1.8 billion); Stride Rite ($585 million); Genesco ($539 million); J. Baker ($532 million); and L.A. Gear ($430 million). For the group as a whole, sales are projected to increase by 16 percent in 1993 and 13 percent for 1994 and the foreseeable future.

Timberland's boot products competitors are located principally in the U.S. There are three major competitors in the category of classic boots, two in sports boots, and six in hiking boots. In its 1992 10-K, Timberland states that these competing companies "have been in the business longer than Timberland and have strong market identities." One such company is Wolverine World Wide, the owner of the Hush Puppy casual footwear line, the Wolverine workboot, and the Wilderness sport boot. Competing boot manufacturers also include Justin Industries, Genesco, Nocona, Tony Lama, and others.

Product performance and quality (including continuing technological improvements), product identity, and product design, styling, and pricing are all important elements of competition in the markets for footwear, apparel, and accessories. Although changing fashion trends generally affect demand for particular footwear products, the company believes that demand for its products is less sensitive to fashion trends because the products are designed primarily to reflect their functionality and performance characteristics.

Selected financial statistics for the last two fiscal years for Timberland and four other industry members appear in the following table. The four other companies reported per-

	Timberland	Nike Inc.	Reebok International	Stride Rite	Wolverine World Wide
Fiscal Year Ended:	12/31/92	5/31/93	12/31/92	11/27/92	1/2/93
Sales	$291,368	$3,930,984	$3,022,627	$585,926	$293,136
Gross profit	107,858	1,543,991	1,213,323	254,872	86,950
EBIT	24,527	620,255	278,044	100,707	10,115
Earnings*	12,919	365,016	114,818	61,506	4,620
Assets	194,117	2,187,463	1,345,346	383,524	204,011
Equity	104,600	1,646,326	838,656	271,535	100,128
Gross margin	0.370	0.393	0.401	0.435	0.297
EBIT/sales	0.084	0.158	0.092	0.172	0.035
Asset turnover	1.586	1.936	2.184	1.638	1.433
Receivables/assets	.278	.305	.311	.218	.253
Inventory/assets	.363	.271	.322	.341	.315
Plant/assets	.168	.178	.095	.047	.150
Pretax ROA	0.134	0.306	0.201	0.281	0.049
ROE (average equity)	0.130	0.245	0.138	0.240	0.044
EPS	$1.20	$4.74	$1.28	$1.20	$0.69
Recent stock price	$62	$50	$31	$18	$29
Shares for EPS	10,788	77,008	89,702	51,255	6,686
Market capitalization	$668,856	$3,850,380	$2,780,748	$922,590	$193,894
Trailing PE**	34	12	28	15	19
Price/book**	5.57	2.12	3.30	3.13	2.09
Estimated beta	0.90	1.45	1.60	1.35	1.00
Fiscal Year Ended:	12/31/91	5/31/92	12/31/91	11/29/91	12/31/91
Sales	$226,082	$3,405,211	$2,734,474	$574,379	$282,749
Gross profit	79,792	1,316,122	1,089,839	245,594	88,143
EBIT	17,539	552,483	419,181	108,266	9,453
Earnings	8,085	329,218	234,711	65,960	4,422
Assets	173,274	1,872,861	1,422,283	332,090	205,078
Equity	93,412	1,331,995	823,537	240,427	110,385
Gross margin	0.353	0.387	0.399	0.428	0.312
EBIT/sales	0.078	0.162	0.153	0.188	0.033
Asset turnover	1.317	2.880	1.936	1.921	1.432
Pretax ROA	0.102	0.467	0.297	0.362	0.048
ROE (average equity)	0.090	0.278	0.258	0.313	0.041

*Earnings exclude extraordinary items and discontinued operations.
**PE and price/book based on most recent price, most recent four quarters' earnings, and most recent book value.

formance in the most recent fiscal year that ranged from highly profitable (e.g., Nike's operating margin [EBIT/sales] of 16 percent and ROE of 25 percent) to quite weak (Wolverine World Wide's operating margin of 3.5 percent and ROE of 4.4 percent). In 1992 the industry as a whole generated an operating margin of 9.2 percent with an ROE of 16.4 percent. Since 1978, the industry operating margin has ranged from 5.9 to 9.2 percent, with an average of 7.8 percent. ROEs have ranged from 9 percent in 1985 to 39 percent in 1988, with an average of 15 percent.

TIMBERLAND'S RECENT PERFORMANCE

The first half of 1992 was difficult for cyclical consumer goods in general and the footwear industry in particular, primarily because an expected recovery from the recession of 1991 never materialized. Nevertheless, Timberland managed to stay in the black in the first quarter (in contrast to the experience of the prior year) and turned in a strong enough second half to make 1992 the most profitable year ever. Timberland's sales, earnings, and EPS for the last seven years are shown below.

	1993	1992	1991	1990	1989	1988	1987
Net Sales (millions):							
March	$ 70.61	$ 52.79	$ 45.78	$ 37.85	$ 30.14	$ 26.13	$ 21.22
June	84.85	57.67	44.96	38.04	30.52	30.21	23.49
September	140.26	92.28	72.03	68.44	51.06	41.53	31.08
December		88.62	63.30	51.98	44.42	34.72	31.19
Total		291.36	226.07	196.31	156.14	132.59	106.98
Net Income (millions):							
March	$ 2.332	$ 0.851	$ 0.094	$ 0.761	$ 0.323	$1.647	$1.116
June	1.912	0.364	−0.542	0.505	−0.476	2.066	1.224
September	11.241	6.887	5.212	5.172	4.065	3.980	2.861
December		4.817	3.321	1.416	2.468	0.384	2.517
Total		12.919	8.085	7.854	6.380	8.077	7.718
Common Share Earnings:							
March	$0.22	$0.08	$0.01	$0.07	$0.03	$0.16	$0.15
June	0.18	0.03	−0.05	0.05	−0.04	0.20	0.17
September	1.00	0.63	0.48	0.48	0.38	0.38	0.27
December		0.44	0.31	0.13	0.23	0.04	0.24
Annual EPS		1.18	0.75	0.73	0.60	0.76	0.85

Some analysts began to note the good news at Timberland early in 1992. Lloyd Kanev of Smith Barney attributed the gains over the prior year to the company's broader management expertise in the 1990s. "Management is a bit tighter and controls are improved," Kanev said. "And they've got a niche out there."[2] After earnings were reported for the third quarter of 1992, analyst Jeff Feinberg of Fidelity explained that new COO Jeffrey Swartz was "transforming the company."[3]

The latter half of 1992 was also good to other major players in the boots market. Wolverine World Wide, after losing money in the first two quarters, turned in a respectable fourth quarter. Genesco, after operating at near break-even in the first two quarters, did well enough in the second half to make 1992 its best year since 1989.

If 1992 was a good year for Timberland, 1993 has been nothing short of sensational. Buoyed by strong sales and record profits in the first three quarters, Timberland's stock soared to a high of $85.37 on November 10, 1993, before falling back to the low $60s in mid-December.

The strong sales at Timberland reflect a continuing shift in consumer preferences from athletic footwear to a rugged outdoor look. Analyst Alice Ruth of Montgomery Securities notes that the market "has really been moving toward Timberland."[4] Wolverine Worldwide is feeling the benefits as well, as earnings appear headed for the strongest showing since 1983.

Meanwhile, producers of name-brand athletic footwear are feeling the effects of a shift in tastes. Nike's sales for the quarter ended May 31, 1993 were up 16 percent relative to the prior year, but earnings were up only 9 percent. Reebok's sales and earnings for the second quarter of 1993 were both down 6 percent. By the autumn of 1993, as Timberland recorded its most profitable quarter in history, Nike's sales fell 8 percent and Reebok's declined 6 percent relative to the comparable quarter of the prior year. The table opposite presents detailed financial data for Timberland's last five quarters, accumulated from 10-Qs.

STOCK PRICES AND FUTURE PROSPECTS

Timberland's meteoric stock price increase during 1993 came after years of languishing in the $8 to $20 range. As the year opened, the moves were gradual, going from $19 in early January to the $30s during July—shortly after second-quarter earnings were announced on July 29, the price hit $39. Over the next three weeks, the stock reached $55, and when shoe dealers and buyers met at the Expo West show in Reno on August 22, rumors circulated that Nike was considering acquiring Timberland. Timberland and Nike executives were quick to deny that any takeover talks had transpired, but nevertheless the stock price remained at its elevated level.

2. *Ibid.*

3. Mark Tedeschi, *"Timberland Logs Record Results in Third Quarter,"* Footwear News *(November 2, 1992): p. 21.*

4. Jeff Siegel, *"Value-Oriented Footwear Seen Bumping Athletics as '93's King of the Hill,"* Footwear News *(July 19, 1993): p. 28.*

Fiscal Quarter Ending	10/1/93	7/2/93	3/31/93	12/31/92	9/30/92
Cash	$ 556	$ 1,500	$ 2,028	$ 1,220	$ 573
Receivables	115,289	70,221	50,982	54,141	74,159
Inventories	96,813	101,334	80,375	70,542	76,909
Other current assets	15,648	12,576	12,608	11,967	7,912
Total current assets	228,306	185,631	145,993	137,870	159,553
Net property & equipment	43,502	39,241	34,496	32,669	33,735
Goodwill	18,350	18,544	18,738	18,931	19,100
Other assets	4,491	4,499	4,687	4,647	5,090
Total assets	$294,649	$247,915	$203,914	$194,117	$217,478
Notes payable	$ 50,578	$ 22,789	$ 7,808	$ 6,851	$ 29,115
Accounts payable	26,957	29,150	21,798	14,121	17,694
Other current liabilities	31,091	21,367	21,621	22,471	20,391
Total current liabilities	108,626	73,306	51,227	43,443	67,200
Deferred income taxes	4,650	4,551	4,126	4,541	7,086
Long term debt	60,986	61,159	41,369	41,533	41,741
Total liabilities	174,262	139,016	96,722	89,517	116,027
Shareholder equity	120,387	108,899	107,192	104,600	101,451
Total liabilities & equity	$294,649	$247,915	$203,914	$194,117	$217,478
Net sales	$140,261	$84,849	$70,606	$88,625	$92,281
Cost of goods sold	90,415	54,263	43,139	54,847	57,382
Gross profit	49,846	30,586	27,467	33,778	34,899
Selling, general & administrative expenses	30,450	25,540	22,084	24,360	22,578
Other expense	–61	–670	–529	–595	–832
Interest expense	1,771	1,388	1,210	1,434	1,651
Income before tax	17,564	2,988	3,644	7,389	9,838
Provision for income taxes	6,323	1,076	1,312	2,572	2,951
Net income	11,241	1,912	2,332	4,817	6,887
Earnings per share	1.00	0.18	0.22	0.45	0.64
Gross margin	0.36	0.36	0.39	0.38	0.38
EBIT/sales	0.14	0.05	0.07	0.10	0.12
Net margin	0.08	0.02	0.03	0.05	0.07

t

635

By mid-November, with the record third-quarter earnings now known, the price soared above 80, and Barron's began to question whether "this maker of outdoor shoes and boots [is] really worth over twice sales, 7.8 times book value and 40 times earnings."[5] Indeed, the industry average price-to-book ratio stood at only 2.5, and the average PE ratio was only 12.1—close to its long-run average.

5. As quoted in Reuter's news release (November 14, 1993)

Others, however, remained undaunted by Timberland's ratios. For example, Lydia Miller, Director of SBC Portfolio Management International, argued in late November that "Timberland sales are on the rise, and management has taken more control of inventories to cut costs and fatten profit margins."[6] Timberland's earnings, she noted, have started to break out. For 1993, she expects $2.20 a share, up from $1.18 per share last year. For 1994, she sees $3 to $3.50 per share. With Timberland positioned right where it wants to be, and the economy continuing to bubble along,[7] who's to say such optimism is unwarranted?

QUESTIONS

use genl fin analysis

1. Analyze Timberland's recent profitability. Discuss the sources of improvement in earnings and the sustainability of the improvement.
2. Forecast Timberland sales and earnings for 1993 and 1994 to gain some sense of the assumptions underlying Lydia Miller's forecasts of earnings per share. Is a continuation of present trends sufficient to produce the forecast? What does Ms. Miller appear to assume about the sustainability of Timberland's competitive advantage?
3. With its stock price standing at $80 per share in late 1993, what must the market have in mind for Timberland? Using a valuation model—based either on discounted cash flow or discounted abnormal earnings—infer what possible combinations of profitability, growth, and cost of capital would be necessary to justify such a price. Compare your assessment of prospects for profitability at Timberland with those reflected in the market price.
4. Compare Timberland's trailing PE and price-to-book ratio with the others in the industry. How could the differences be explained?

3-5 pg w/ graphs & charts

---

6. Business Week (November 22, 1993): p. 124.
7. Real GNP is growing at a rate of about 3 percent; interest rates remain relatively low (with intermediate government bond rates at about 6 percent); and inflation appears under control at 3.1 percent.

Exhibit 1   The Timberland Company, Excerpts from 1992 Annual Report

EXHIBIT 1
The Timberland Company, Excerpts from 1992 Annual Report

To Our Shareholders

1992 was a good year for The Timberland Company. Our Company realized record revenues and record income during a time of lingering worldwide recession. Even more important to me than just the financial results was the coming together of our team. We're still a young company and our management team is evolving and maturing. I see very positive results from the leadership of our Chief Operating Officer and Executive Vice President, Jeffrey B. Swartz. A little parental pride I believe is in order, though I hold him more accountable than any other member of the team.

The revenue increase is a clear reflection of the growing worldwide strength of the Timberland brand. In response to two fundamental strategies, our unique retail approach and the integration of the entire product line, our brand is taking a more powerful form everywhere in the world.

Our specialty stores and the Concept Shop Program are increasingly effective marketing and brand-building tools. We will continue to push hard to expand distribution with the right partners and to work even more closely with our strategic retail allies. Through great suppliers and committed retailers, we will continue to satisfy Timberland customers.

In 1992 we clearly met our customers' expectations. Our sales increased 29%, to $291.4 million. More important, profits were up 60%, to $12.9 million, or $1.18 per share. Our thanks to the shareholders for their confidence and patience while we implemented the programs that helped us achieve those results. We accomplished them, in part, through better management of working capital. Our 1992 debt-to-capital ratio improved to 33%, while inventories and receivables both dropped as a percentage of sales.

We have five major responsibilities—to our stockholders, our employees, our business partners, our community and, especially, our consumers who deserve great quality and value with service beyond expectation. We have an aggressive business plan for 1993. Our employees and business partners are solidly behind the Timberland product. Our standards are high because our customers count on us for protection in a sometimes harsh world. I am confident that, with the support of a unified team, we will deliver. Thanks for your past support.

Sincerely,

Sidney W. Swartz
Chairman and Chief Executive Officer

637

Exhibit 1   The Timberland Company, Excerpts from 1992 Annual Report

MANAGEMENT'S DISCUSSION AND ANALYSIS OF FINANCIAL CONDITION AND RESULTS OF OPERATIONS

Results of Operations

(Amounts in Thousands Except Per Share Data)	Year Ended December 31,					
	1992	%	1991	%	1990	%
Net sales	$291,368	100.0%	$226,082	100.0%	$196,319	100.0%
Gross profit	107,858	37.0	79,792	35.3	71,388	36.4
Total operating expenses	82,016	28.1	62,390	27.6	54,801	27.9
Operating income	25,842	8.9	17,402	7.7	16,587	8.5
Interest expense	5,528	1.9	5,822	2.6	6,484	3.3
Net income	12,919	4.4%	8,085	3.6%	7,854	4.0%
Earnings per share	$ 1.18		$ .75		$ .73	
Weighted average shares outstanding	10,922		10,791		10,692	

1992 Compared to 1991

Net sales in 1992 were $291.4 million, a 29% increase over the $226.1 million reported in fiscal 1991. This increase was primarily attributable to an overall increase in the volume of footwear, apparel and accessory units sold.

Historically, the Company's revenues and earnings have been more heavily weighted to the second half of the year, primarily the third quarter.

Gross profit as a percentage of net sales was 37.0% in 1992 as compared to 35.3% in 1991. This increase resulted from a combination of significant reductions in the level of markdowns in 1992 compared to 1991, which was affected by an aggressive inventory reduction program, increased production levels, increased efficiencies in manufacturing and sourcing, and a favorable sales mix.

Total operating expenses increased by 31% to $82.0 million in 1992 from $62.4 million in 1991. The increased spending was attributable to a higher level of selling and general and administrative expenses, as the Company invested further in infrastructure and increased marketing in support of current and future sales growth.

Interest expense in 1992 decreased by $.3 million from 1991 due primarily to lower interest rates.

1991 Compared to 1990

Net sales in 1991 were $226.1 million, an increase of 15% over the $196.3 million reported in 1990. This increase was attributable to an overall increase in footwear and apparel units sold.

Gross profit as a percentage of net sales was 35.3% in 1991 as compared to 36.4% in 1990. This decrease was primarily a result of increased manufacturing and sourcing costs. In the first half of 1991, the Company experienced reduced margins as a result of significant markdowns associated with its inventory reduction program which commenced in the second half of 1990. Although the gross profit margin declined for the year, the fourth quarter margin increased to 38.6% of net sales compared to 36.1% in the same period of 1990. Fourth quarter margin improvement resulted from increased manufacturing efficiencies and significantly fewer markdown sales, as less of the Company's revenues were generated in connection with its inventory reduction program.

Total operating expenses increased by 14% to $62.4 million in 1991 from $54.8 million in 1990. This comparative dollar increase in spending was attributable to a higher level of selling and general and administrative expenses to support the sales growth and the continued development of information systems. Despite the increased spending in 1991, operating expenses as a percentage of sales decreased to 27.6% from 27.9%.

Interest expense in 1991 decreased by $.7 million from 1990 due to a combination of lower average borrowings and lower interest rates.

For an analysis of the change in the effective tax rates from 1990 to 1992, see notes to the consolidated financial statements.

t

Exhibit 1   The Timberland Company, Excerpts from 1992 Annual Report

CONSOLIDATED BALANCE SHEETS
As of December 31, 1992 and 1991

(Dollars in Thousands)

Assets	1992	1991
Current assets		
Cash and equivalents	$1,220	$7,509
Accounts receivable, net of allowance for doubtful accounts of $1,821 in 1992 and $1,675 in 1991	54,141	48,043
Inventories	70,542	58,311
Prepaid expenses	4,501	4,988
Deferred and refundable income taxes *do we break this down*	7,466	4,196
Total current assets	137,870	123,047
Property, plant and equipment, at cost	57,820	46,583
Less accumulated depreciation and amortization	(25,151)	(16,834)
Net property, plant and equipment	32,669	29,749
Excess of cost over fair value of net assets acquired, net	18,931	19,608
Other assets, net	4,647	5,066
	$194,117	$177,470

Liabilities and Stockholders' Equity	1992	1991
Current liabilities		
Notes payable	$6,851	$759
Current maturities of long-term obligations	2,643	2,715
Accounts payable	14,121	12,372
Accrued expenses		
Payroll and related	5,933	4,444
Interest and other	8,096	5,976
Income taxes payable	5,799	9,171
Total current liabilities	43 443	35,437
Long-term obligations, less current maturities	41,533	44,199
Deferred income taxes	4,541	4,422
Stockholders' equity		
Preferred stock, $.01 par value; 2,000,000 shares authorized; none issued	—	—
Class A Common Stock, $.01 par value; 30,000,000 shares authorized; 7,549,015 shares issued and outstanding in 1992 and 7,483,958 shares in 1991	75	75
Class B Common Stock, $.01 par value; 15,000,000 shares authorized; 3,238,686 shares issued and outstanding in 1992 and 3,240,955 shares in 1991	32	32
Additional paid-in capital	53,758	53,293
Retained earnings	51,585	38,666
Cumulative translation adjustment	(850)	1,346
	104,600	93,412
	$194,117	$177,470

Exhibit 1 The Timberland Company, Excerpts from 1992 Annual Report

CONSOLIDATED STATEMENTS OF INCOME
For the Years Ended December 31, 1992, 1991 and 1990

(Amounts in Thousands Except Per Share Data)

	1992	1991	1990
Net sales	$291,368	$226,082	$196,319
Cost of goods sold	183,510	146,290	124,931
Gross profit	107,858	79,792	71,388
Operating expenses			
Selling	51,846	40,815	37,193
General and administrative	29,493	20,898	16,931
Amortization of goodwill	677	677	677
Total operating expenses	82,016	62,390	54,801
Operating income	25,842	17,402	16,587
Other expense (income)			
Interest expense	5,528	5,822	6,484
Other, net	1,315	(137)	(912)
Total other expense	6,843	5,685	5,572
Income before income taxes	18,999	11,717	11,015
Provision for income taxes	6,080	3,632	3,161
Net income	$12,919	$8,085	$7,854
Earnings per share	$1.18	$.75	$.73
Weighted average shares and share equivalents outstanding	10,922	10,791	10,692

The accompanying notes are an integral part of these consolidated financial statements.

Exhibit 1   The Timberland Company, Excerpts from 1992 Annual Report

CONSOLIDATED STATEMENTS OF CASH FLOWS
For the Years Ended December 31, 1992, 1991 and 1990

(Dollars in Thousands)

	1992	1991	1990
Cash flows from operating activities:			
Net income	**$12,919**	$ 8,085	$ 7,854
Adjustments to reconcile net income to net cash provided (used) by operating activities:			
Deferred income taxes	**119**	(3,748)	(1,010)
Depreciation and amortization	**7,959**	6,304	5,247
Increase (decrease) in cash from changes in working capital items:			
Accounts receivable	**(6,210)**	(6,499)	(5,248)
Inventories	**(13,892)**	10,607	(7,438)
Prepaid expenses	**202**	(149)	(1,742)
Accounts payable	**1,841**	5,724	(7,484)
Accrued expenses	**3,712**	2,326	1,250
Income taxes	**(6,642)**	4,975	—
Net cash provided (used) by operating activities	**8**	27,625	(8,571)
Cash flows from investing activities:			
Additions to property, plant and equipment, net	**(11,774)**	(7,540)	(7,530)
Other, net	**1,616**	(747)	(623)
Net cash used in investing activities	**(10,158)**	(8,287)	(8,153)
Cash flows from financing activities:			
Net borrowings (payments) under short-term credit facilities	**6,352**	(11,188)	11,900
Issuance of term notes and capital lease obligations	**—**	—	3,008
Payments on long-term debt and capital lease obligations	**(2,711)**	(2,646)	(2,316)
Issuance of common stock	**465**	231	140
Net cash provided (used) by financing activities	**4,106**	(13,603)	12,732
Effect of exchange rate changes on cash	**(245)**	219	526
Net increase (decrease) in cash and equivalents	**(6,289)**	5,954	(3,466)
Cash and equivalents at beginning of year	**7,509**	1,555	5,021
Cash and equivalents at end of year	**$ 1,220**	$ 7,509	$ 1,555
Supplemental disclosures of cash flow information:			
Interest paid	**$5,699**	$5,877	$6,621
Income taxes paid	**12,356**	2,899	3,903

The accompanying notes are an integral part of these consolidated financial statements.

Exhibit 1   The Timberland Company, Excerpts from 1992 Annual Report

NOTES TO CONSOLIDATED FINANCIAL STATEMENTS

(Dollars in Thousands)

1. SUMMARY OF SIGNIFICANT ACCOUNTING POLICIES

Basis of Consolidation

The consolidated financial statements include the accounts of the Company and its subsidiaries. All intercompany transactions have been eliminated in consolidation.

Reclassifications

Certain prior year amounts have been reclassified to conform with the current year presentation.

Recognition of Revenue

Revenue is recognized upon shipment of product to customers.

Translation of Foreign Currencies

The Company translates financial statements denominated in foreign currency by translating balance sheet accounts at the end of period exchange rate and income statement accounts at the average exchange rate for the period. Translation gains and losses are recorded in stockholders' equity, and transaction gains and losses are reflected in income.

Foreign Currency Options

The Company has entered into foreign currency option and forward contracts (5.3 million pounds sterling, 27.0 million French francs and 1.2 million Deutsche marks) to hedge foreign currency commitments through 1993. Gains and losses on these contracts will be recognized when the offsetting gains and losses on the hedged transactions occur. The unrealized net gain (loss) deferred on such contracts as of December 31, 1992 and 1991 was approximately $495 and $(1,179), respectively. Unrealized gains or losses are determined based on the difference between the settlement and year end spot rates.

Cash and Equivalents

Cash equivalents consist of short-term, highly liquid investments which have original maturities of three months or less.

Inventories

Inventories are stated at the lower of cost (first-in, first-out) or market.

Property, Plant and Equipment

Property, plant and equipment are depreciated using the straight-line method over the estimated useful lives of the assets or over the terms of the related leases, if such periods are shorter. The principal estimated useful lives are: building and improvements, 4 to 30 years; machinery and equipment, 3 to 10 years; lasts, patterns and dies, 5 years.

Excess of Cost Over Fair Value of Net Assets Acquired

The excess of cost over the fair value of net assets acquired is being amortized on a straight-line basis over periods of 40 and 20 years. Accumulated amortization amounted to $3,865 and $3,188 at December 31, 1992 and 1991, respectively.

Income Taxes

Income taxes are provided on income as reported in the financial statements, regardless of the period in which the income is recognized for tax purposes.

Earnings Per Share

Earnings per share are calculated by dividing net income for each period by the weighted average number of common shares and equivalents outstanding during each period.

Exhibit 1   The Timberland Company, Excerpts from 1992 Annual Report

2. FAIR VALUE OF FINANCIAL INSTRUMENTS

The estimated fair values of the Company's financial instruments are as follows:

| | December 31, | | | |
| | 1992 | | 1991 | |
	Carrying or Contract Amount	Fair Value	Carrying or Contract Amount	Fair Value
Cash and equivalents	$ 1,220	$ 1,220	$ 7,509	$ 7,509
Notes payable	6,851	6,851	759	759
Long-term obligations	44,176	49,075	46,914	52,157
Foreign currency contracts	17,590	16,780	31,840	33,680

3. INVENTORIES

Inventories consist of the following:

| | December 31, | |
	1992	1991
Raw materials	$10,802	$11,295
Work-in-process	6,761	5,172
Finished goods	52,979	41,844
	$70,542	$58,311

4. PROPERTY, PLANT AND EQUIPMENT

Property, plant and equipment consist of the following:

| | December 31, | |
	1992	1991
Land and improvements	$ 633	$ 575
Building and improvements	14,640	13,757
Machinery and equipment	33,490	25,351
Lasts, patterns and dies	9,057	6,900
	$57,820	$46,583

5. INCOME TAXES

The components of the provision for income taxes are as follows:

| | Year Ended December 31, | | | | | |
| | 1992 | | 1991 | | 1990 | |
	Current	Deferred	Current	Deferred	Current	Deferred
Federal	$6,356	$(2,887)	$2,606	$(1,000)	$1,745	$(1,394)
State	2,514	(193)	843	184	573	155
Puerto Rico	454	281	276	577	180	1,077
Foreign	(445)	—	146	—	575	250
	$8,879	$(2,799)	$3,871	$ (239)	$3,073	$ 88

The deferred tax provision consists of the following:

| | Year Ended December 31, | | |
	1992	1991	1990
Increase in reserves not currently deductible	$(2,709)	($1,015)	$(1,325)
Tax depreciation over (under) book depreciation	(239)	357	374
Puerto Rico tollgate taxes	281	625	604
Undistributed foreign earnings	(47)	(51)	122
Other, net	(85)	(155)	313
	$(2,799)	$ (239)	$ 88

The provision for income taxes differs from the amount computed using the statutory federal income tax rate of 34% due to the following:

| | Year Ended December 31, | | |
	1992	1991	1990
Federal income tax at statutory rate	$6,460	$3,984	$3,745
Net reduction in federal tax due to tax exempt earnings in Puerto Rico	(3,341)	(2,138)	(3,759)
Puerto Rico and state taxes, net of applicable federal benefit	908	1,050	2,170
Purchase accounting adjustments	230	230	279
Losses of foreign subsidiaries	2,395	576	426
Foreign sales corporation	(508)	—	—
Other, net	(64)	(70)	300
Total provision for income taxes	$6,080	$3,632	$3,161

The Company's consolidated income before taxes included earnings from its subsidiary in Puerto Rico, which are substantially exempt from Puerto Rico and federal income taxes under an exemption which expires in 2002. However, if the earnings were remitted to Timberland, they would be subject to a Puerto Rico tollgate tax not to exceed 10%. Deferred tollgate taxes have been provided on all of the accumulated earnings of the subsidiary in Puerto Rico. Deferred income taxes are also provided on the undistributed earnings of Timberland's foreign subsidiaries.

Income (loss) before income taxes from foreign operations was $(5,563), $(1,267) and $20 for the years ended December 31, 1992, 1991 and 1990, respectively. At December 31, 1992, the Company had $5,713 of foreign operating loss carryforwards available to offset future foreign taxable income. Of these operating loss carryforwards, $800 will expire in 1996 and $2,345 will expire in 1997.

t

643

Exhibit 1   The Timberland Company, Excerpts from 1992 Annual Report

6. NOTES PAYABLE

The Company has an unsecured committed revolving credit agreement (the "Agreement") expiring October 4, 1994 with a group of banks that provides for revolving credit loans of up to $50,000 subject to a borrowing base formula. At December 31, 1992, the amount available under this formula was $50,000; however, the Company had no outstanding borrowings under the Agreement at year end.

Additionally, the Company had uncommitted lines of credit available from certain banks totalling $27,000 at December 31, 1992, of which $3,100 was outstanding at year end. Borrowings under these lines are at prevailing money market rates (3.93% at December 31, 1992).

At December 31, 1992, the balance outstanding under all short-term borrowing arrangements was $6,851. At December 31, 1991, the balance outstanding under the Company's credit facility was $759. Average borrowings under all short-term credit arrangements were $16,997 in 1992, $11,391 in 1991 and $17,689 in 1990. The weighted average interest rates were 5.88%, 8.66% and 9.62% in 1992, 1991 and 1990, respectively.

7. LONG-TERM OBLIGATIONS

Long-term obligations consist of the following:

	December 31, 1992	1991
Senior notes	$35,000	$35,000
Industrial revenue bonds	5,345	5,345
Note payable	1,500	3,000
Capitalized lease obligations (Note 8)	2,331	3,569
	44,176	46,914
Less – current maturities	(2,643)	(2,715)
	$41,533	$44,199

The senior notes bear interest at a rate of 9.7% and mature on December 1, 1999. Commencing December 1, 1995, annual redemption payments of $7,000 are required until maturity. The note agreement places limitations on the payment of cash dividends and contains other financial and operational covenants.

The Company's long-term obligations at December 31, 1992, excluding capitalized lease obligations, are scheduled to become due as follows:

1993	$ 1,500
1994	5,345
1995	7,000
1996	7,000
1997	7,000
Thereafter	14,000
	$41,845

8. LEASE COMMITMENTS

The Company leases manufacturing facilities, retail stores, showrooms and equipment under noncancellable operating and capital leases expiring at various dates through 2015. The approximate minimum rental commitments under all noncancellable leases as of December 31, 1992, are as follows:

	Capital	Operating
1993	$1,322	$5,063
1994	791	4,401
1995	504	4,203
1996	—	3,862
1997	—	3,044
Thereafter	—	14,445
Total minimum lease payments	2,617	$35,018
Less – amount representing interest	(286)	
Present value of net minimum lease payments	2,331	
Less – current maturities	(1,143)	
	$1,188	

Property and accumulated depreciation on equipment held under capital leases were $6,419 and $3,368, respectively, at December 31, 1992 and $6,731 and $2,512, respectively, at December 31, 1991.

Rental expense for all operating leases was $6,635, $5,444 and $4,572 for the years ended December 31, 1992, 1991 and 1990, respectively.

Exhibit 1   The Timberland Company, Excerpts from 1992 Annual Report

INDEPENDENT AUDITORS' REPORT

**To the Board of Directors and Stockholders of
The Timberland Company:**

We have audited the accompanying consolidated balance sheet of The Timberland Company and subsidiaries as of December 31, 1992 and the related statements of income, changes in stockholders' equity, and cash flows for the year then ended. These financial statements are the responsibility of the Company's management. Our responsibility is to express an opinion on these financial statements based on our audit. The Company's consolidated balance sheet as of December 31, 1991 and the related statements of income, changes in stockholders' equity, and cash flows for the two-year period then ended, were audited by other auditors whose report dated February 12, 1992, expressed an unqualified opinion on those statements.

We conducted our audit in accordance with generally accepted auditing standards. Those standards require that we plan and perform the audit to obtain reasonable assurance about whether the financial statements are free of material misstatement. An audit includes examining, on a test basis, evidence supporting the amounts and disclosures in the financial statements. An audit also includes assessing the accounting principles used and significant estimates made by management, as well as evaluating the overall financial statement presentation. We believe that our audit provides a reasonable basis for our opinion.

In our opinion, such 1992 consolidated financial statements present fairly, in all material respects, the financial position of the Company at December 31, 1992, and the results of its operations and its cash flows for the year then ended in conformity with generally accepted accounting principles.

DELOITTE & TOUCHE
Boston, Massachusetts
February 11, 1993

t

645

A profit of $12 thousand on sales of $3.6 million might appear meager, but it is cause for celebration at Vitronics Corporation in the first quarter of 1994. Vitronics has not seen a first quarter profit or an annual profit since 1990. The early performance of 1994 supports management's belief that, at last, the firm has turned the corner. Analysts at Barclay Investments, which had underwritten Vitronics' 1992 public offering, are labeling the Corporation as "an attractive business recovery candidate." Moreover, the Corporation has arranged to finance receivables with Riviera Finance, after having previously relied on such funding from the New England Growth Fund, the purchaser of the firm's convertible debentures in 1993. Vitronics is now seeking a line of credit from a bank to replace and extend the funding from Riviera.

THE COMPANY

Vitronics Corporation describes itself as "an innovative company specializing in the design, engineering, and assembly of state-of-the-art thermal processing equipment and environmentally-safe cleaning equipment." Its primary product line, including UNITHERM, UNITHERM II, and ISOTHERM, consists of force convection ovens called "solder reflow systems" that are used in the soldering of electronic components to printed circuit boards (PCBs). The Company also produces an equipment line, ENVIRO-CLEAN, used to clean PCBs; in contrast to the chlorofluorocarbon-based solvents used by many, the Vitronics cleaning system does not deplete the earth's ozone layer.

Vitronics, headquartered in Newmarket, New Hampshire, was incorporated in 1981. Its invention at that time of infrared solder technology helped it develop a reputation as an industry pioneer. Later in the decade, it introduced the first semi-aqueous cleaning system (requiring no environmentally harmful chlorofluorocarbons) for PCBs. Vitronics currently enjoys a 25 percent worldwide market share for solder reflow systems, and a 65 percent market share for non-ozone-depleting cleaning systems. About 42 percent of Vitronic's 1993 sales were domestic; 46 percent were in Japan and Southeast Asia; 12 percent were in Europe, mainly the U.K.

The Company's primary manufacturing facility is located in Newmarket, but some manufacturing takes place in the firm's U.K. affiliate. Vitronics markets its products in

Prepared by Professor Victor L. Bernard. This case is based on publicly available information, and discussions with company personnel. It was prepared as a basis for class discussion and is not intended to illustrate either an effective or ineffective management of a business situation.

the U.S. through two direct sales people and a network of 20 manufacturers' representatives. The U.K. facility handles sales in the U.K. and Europe. Sales in Japan are handled directly by a wholly-owned subsidiary, the Juki Corporation, and Southeast Asia is serviced through 26 distributors.

The market for SMT solder reflow systems and cleaning systems includes computer manufacturers and a variety of other manufacturers that use electronic components. Vitronics customers include IBM, Intel, Motorola, AT&T, Hughes Aircraft, General Electric, Chrysler, General Motors, DuPont, and several other U.S.-based manufacturers. Vitronics' foreign customers include such major names as Fujitsu, Hitachi, Mitsubishi, NEC, Siemens, Phillips, and Olivetti.

THE INDUSTRY AND ITS TECHNOLOGY

Prior to the 1980s, electronics manufacturers attached components to PCBs with pins that were passed through pre-drilled holes and then fixed in place by passing the bottom of the PCB through a bath of molten solder. Under this approach, only one side of the board was usable. In 1981, an alternative approach emerged: surface mount technology (SMT). With SMT, no pins are used. Instead, solder paste is placed on electronic components at that point where they are to be attached to the PCB. The components are positioned on the board, placed on a conveyor belt, and then passed through an oven that melts the solder. This "solder reflow" process must be tightly controlled, to assure an even distribution of the proper amount of heat. The solder then cools and solidifies, bonding the components to the PCB. SMT permits the production of smaller, more complex, and double-sided PCBs; it is also less expensive and more reliable than the preceding "through-hole" technology.

In the market for SMT cleaning systems, there are several options to replace the existing chlorofluorocarbon-based approaches. Vitronics' entrants in the cleaning system replacement market are based on semi-aqueous systems, which the company believes will appeal to high-volume producers that require reliability and performance. In light of the international ban on ozone-depleting chlorofluorocarbons, scheduled to be imposed by 1995 in 87 nations (including the U.S.), Vitronics expects the replacement market to offer high potential.

Competition in the SMT capital equipment industry is heated. Barclay Investments analyst John C. Ball, in his July 14, 1994 review of Vitronics, put it this way: "[The industry] is cyclical and highly competitive, with too many suppliers vying for too few dollars. Furthermore, while technological superiority used to be the predominant requirement for sale, now price, reliability, ability to meet delivery schedules, and technological performance have become the prerequisites." Vitronics' competition from within the U.S. comes from BTU International, a $37 million dollar producer of various thermal processing equipment, including solder reflow systems; Conceptronics, a $13 million producer of various SMT capital equipment, including solder reflow systems and cleaners; and Electrovert/USA, a privately held firm. Other competition comes from companies in England, France, and Germany. Finally, three Japanese companies compete with Vitronics within Japan, but they have not extended their distribution channels beyond that country.

VITRONICS' RECENT DIFFICULTIES AND RESTRUCTURING

The Company's reputation as a state-of-the-art manufacturer helped it grow quickly during the 1980s, with sales reaching the $20 million level by 1989. In that year, net income was $0.830 million. However, as the 1990s opened, Vitronics was caught unprepared by the industry shift to "forced convection" solder reflow technology. The forced convection technology used motor-driven fans to transfer pressurized, heated gas to PCBs passing through the solder reflow ovens. This approach permitted tighter control of the heating process. The industry shift, in combination with a worldwide recession, turmoil in the electronics industry, and reduced capital spending by electronics manufacturers led to reduced earnings at Vitronics in 1990, and large losses in 1991 and 1992. By the end of 1992, Vitronics' difficulties were sufficiently severe that it stood in default on its bank term agreement, and was permitted to operate only under a standstill agreement with the bank. As a result, Deloitte & Touche rendered a "going concern opinion" on the 1992 financials, stating that there was "substantial doubt about the Company's ability to continue as a going concern."

Vitronics took several steps to overcome the difficulties they confronted. First, they introduced a line of force-convection solder reflow systems. The first of these systems, UNITHERM, was delivered in late 1991 and incorporated a new heater and cell design that Vitronics labels "revolutionary," and for which patents are pending. This system was followed by UNITHERM II and ISOTHERM, both introduced during the first quarter of 1994. Sales of these two products exceeded $600,000 in that quarter. The ISOTHERM system earned Vitronics the 1994 Vision Award from *SMT Magazine*. Management believes that its new product lines have permitted Vitronics to regain the technological lead in the industry.

Second, during 1993, Vitronics' U.S. manufacturing operations were consolidated in one building, saving about $300,000 in annual facility charges. Manufacturing operations were also revamped to reduce production time from 6 to 8 weeks to 10 days. Such streamlining, in conjunction with the development of new product lines and reductions in material and labor costs, leads management to believe that they can now sell solder reflow systems at the lowest prices in the industry while still generating a profit.

Third, Vitronics introduced new selling tools, techniques, and sales literature.

Vitronics continued to operate at a loss during 1992 and 1993. Nevertheless, after Deloitte & Touche was dismissed as auditor on Christmas Eve of 1992, Vitronics received an unqualified opinion from Coopers and Lybrand for 1992 and 1993. Operations were financed with the help of an equity offering in 1992 and placement of a subordinated convertible loan with the New England Growth Fund in 1993. By the end of 1993, management concluded in their Letter to Shareholders that "while we may not be out of the woods yet, we can point to substantial progress in reducing losses and improving the sales picture."

Vitronics was not alone in its difficulties. BTU International, its chief U.S. competitor, suffered a huge loss in 1991 ($14 million on sales of $22 million) and a smaller loss in 1992. By 1993, BTU returned to profitability, enjoying a 41 percent gross margin and a net income of $1.0 million on sales of $37 million. Conceptronics, on the other hand, continued to struggle even in 1993, reporting a loss of $1.0 million on sales of $13 million. Condensed operating statements for Vitronics, BTU, and Conceptronics in 1993 are as follows:

	Vitronics	BTU International	Conceptronics
Net sales (in millions)	$12.8	$37.0	$13.0
Cost of sales	(9.2)	(21.8)	(9.5)
Gross profit	3.5	15.2	3.6
Selling, general, administrative, and other operating expense	(3.7)	(10.9)	(4.2)
Research and development	(0.9)	(2.6)	(0.3)
Income (loss) from operations	(1.1)	1.7	(0.9)
Net interest expense and other non-operating income/expense	(0.2)	(0.5)	(0.1)
Income (loss) before taxes	(1.3)	1.1	(1.0)
Net income (loss)	($ 1.4)	$ 1.0	($ 1.0)
Total assets	$ 4.7	$25.8	$ 6.6
Shareholders' equity	$ 1.0	$ 9.3	$ 3.9
Market capitalization at 12/31/93	$ 6.9	$18.0	$ 2.7

As Vitronics and its competitors confronted the turmoil in their industry, a direct struggle arose between Vitronics and Conceptronics. Conceptronics was founded by a former Vitronics employee, Edward Furtek, who invented a patented method and apparatus used in Vitronics' solder reflow systems. Vitronics sued Conceptronics in November 1991, alleging that Conceptronics was using the method and apparatus even though the patents had been assigned by Furtek to Vitronics. The courts found in favor of Vitronics on one of two patents involved and scheduled a trial in July 1994 to settle factual claims surrounding the second. Conceptronics, in turn, sued Vitronics for "abuse and tortious interference with business relations," a claim dismissed in 1993. Subsequently, Conceptronics sued again, alleging that Vitronics' patents were obtained by fraud. In referring to the litigation as a whole, Vitronics indicates in the 1993 annual report that it is "very optimistic that we will prevail in this action."

VITRONICS' OBJECTIVES AND OUTLOOK

Vitronics management believes it can improve profitability through pursuit of four objectives. First, it expects to realize increased penetration of the U.S. market for SMT capital equipment as new customers recognize the value of Vitronics' leading-edge technology in controlling costs in the electronics industry. Second, it will pursue niche markets where price sensitivity is less severe. Third, it plans to expand marketing channels in Europe and the Pacific Rim. Fourth, it intends to continue its strategy of low-cost leadership, with a focus on procurement of materials at lower cost through high-volume buying.

Barclay Investments forecasts 1994 net income at $0.6 million on sales of $15 to $17 million. Management considers sales forecasts in the $17 to $18 million range reasonable for 1995, with net income approaching $1.5 million. Management's objective for pretax margin is 9 percent to 10 percent by 1996.

Although improved profitability would help ease Vitronic's needs for cash, it continues to consider several possibilities for financing. In January 1994, the New England Growth Fund loaned Vitronics $350,000, secured with a pledge of accounts receivable. That loan was repaid in March, and a new $750,000 receivables factoring facility was established with Riviera Finance. The facility can be used on an as-needed basis, subject to the finance company's approval of particular accounts receivable. Management views reliance on Riviera Finance as temporary, since the cost of funds from that source is extremely high (20 percent), and is seeking a regular line of credit with a bank.

V

651

QUESTIONS

1. Assess Vitronics' vulnerability to distress, and its opportunity for turnaround. Evaluate how much deterioration Vitronics could withstand in 1994 without confronting severe cash flow problems.
2. From the perspective of a banker, evaluate the risks and opportunities associated with granting a line of credit to Vitronics. Has Vitronics' financial health improved sufficiently to warrant such credit? As a banker, how would you respond to a request for such credit from Vitronics?

Exhibit 1   Vitronics Corporation First Quarter Report, April 2, 1994

EXHIBIT 1

Vitronics Corporation First Quarter Report, April 2, 1994

Dear Stockholder:

Enclosed please find selective financial information for the three months ended April 2,1994 and April 3, 1993.

Sales for the quarter ended April 2,1994 were $3,584,000 versus $4,380,000 for the same period in 1993. Bookings for the three months ended April 2, 1994 were $3,628,000 versus $2,535,000 for the same period in 1993. Backlog as of April 2, 1994 was $2,177,000 versus $1,173,000 as of April 3,1993 and $2,133,000 as of December 31,1993.

Revenue in the first quarter of 1994 decreased from the same period in 1993 due to a continuation of the economic slowdown in Europe and increased competition. Bookings during the first quarter were strong in the U.S. and Southeast Asia. We are beginning to see some activity in Europe that, if it continues, will be beneficial during the balance of 1994.

Gross margin for the three months ended April 2, 1994 was 34.2% versus 27.9% for the same period in 1993. The higher margin is due to decreased operating costs, reduced material costs of the Unitherm™ product line and improved manufacturing efficiencies. The margin increase was partially offset by the product mix in the first quarter of 1994 and also by a larger percentage of foreign sales, where discounting reduced the gross margin.

Operating expenses for the three months ended April 2, 1994 were $1,117,000 versus $1,284,000 for the same period in 1993. The decrease in spending is primarily due to a number of cost containment programs in place to keep spending at a minimum and in line with the sales level. Any increase in expenditures is attributed to sales and marketing activities. We also have maintained level spending in our research and development activities and introduced our new Unitherm™ II and Isotherm™ products in the first quarter of 1994 at the NEPCON West show. Bookings have already exceeded $600,000 for the two new products, with shipments expected in the second quarter of 1994.

The Company had non-operating expenses of $97,000 for the first quarter of 1994 compared to $37,000 for the same period in 1993. The nonoperating expenses for 1994 are composed of interest expense, sales cash discounts and patent defense costs relating to the Conceptronic patent suit.

Net income for the quarter was $12,000 compared to a net loss of $(97,000) for the same period in 1993. Net income per share was $.00 compared to a net loss per share of $(.01) for the same period in 1993.

During January 1994, the Company pledged receivables and received a $350,000 loan from New England Growth Fund, which was fully repaid at the end of March 1994. We continue to search for a working capital line of credit with a bank but as we continue this search, we have obtained a factoring facility of $750,000 for accounts receivable financing on an as-needed basis subject to the factor's approval of particular accounts receivable submitted by the Company.

We are pleased with the increased domestic and international business during the last two quarters. We continue to hold the line on operating expenses as we progress into 1994, and with increased business activity, we believe we are well positioned to capitalize on this opportunity during 1994.

We thank you for your continued support.

James J. Manfield, Jr.
Chairman of the Board and
Chief Executive Officer

Ronald W. Lawler
President and
Chief Operating
Officer

May 12,1994

Vitronics Corporation is an innovative company specializing in the design, engineering and assembly of state-of-the-art thermal processing equipment and environmentally safe cleaning equipment.

Vitronics' Common Stock trading symbol on the American Stock Exchange Is VTC.

Exhibit 1   Vitronics Corporation First Quarter Report, April 2, 1994

CONDENSED CONSOLIDATED STATEMENT OF OPERATIONS
(Unaudited)
(000's omitted except per share amounts)

	Three Months Ended	
	April 2, 1994	April 3, 1993
Net sales	$3,584	$4,380
Cost of goods sold	2,358	3,156
Gross profit	1,226	1,224
Selling, general and administrative expenses	857	995
Research and development costs	260	289
	1,117	1,284
Income (Loss) from operations	109	(60)
Other expenses	(97)	(37)
Income (Loss) before income tax	12	(97)
Income tax benefit	—	—
Net Income (Loss)	$ 12	$ (97)
Net Income (Loss) per common share	$.00	$(.01)
Weighted average number of common and common equivalent shares used in calculation of income (loss) per common share	7,388	7,379

BALANCE SHEET DATA
(000's omitted)

	April 2, 1994	April 3, 1993
ASSETS		
Current assets	$4,099	$5,689
Property and equipment (net)	297	417
Other assets	179	214
	$4,575	$6,320
LIABILITIES AND STOCKHOLDERS' EQUITY		
Current liabilities	$2,041	$3,979
Long-term liabilities	1,456	54
Stockholders' equity	1,078	2,287
	$4,575	$6,320

V

653

Exhibit 2   Vitronics Corporation, Excerpts from 1993 Annual Report

EXHIBIT 2
Vitronics Corporation, Excerpts from 1993 Annual Report

LETTER TO SHAREHOLDERS

Vitronics Corporation has completed a difficult year of rebuilding in 1993. While we may not be out of the woods yet, we can point to substantial progress in reducing losses and improving the sales picture.

We were able to stabilize our sales level and actually saw 1993 sales increase by 3% over 1992. We were also able to increase our gross profit percentage from 16% to 28% by aggressively attacking our material and direct labor cost components. We significantly improved manufacturing efficiency and reduced our manufacturing production time from 6–8 weeks to ten days. This improvement allowed us to consolidate our U.S. manufacturing operation into one building. We also continue to be very aggressive in our sales and marketing efforts. In spite of lower Research & Development expenditures, we have continued an aggressive and responsive development program, culminating in the introduction of two new reflow machines in February 1994.

We have also completely paid off Fleet Bank and continue to have discussions with several banks to obtain a line of credit for Vitronics. We are currently managing our cash very tightly and continue to work with our customers for deposits and early payment of shipments. We also continue to work with our vendors to schedule material and cash flow in a very efficient manner. To date, both are working favorably.

Sales for the year ended December 31, 1993 were $12,778,000 versus $12,373,000 for 1992. Net loss was $1,357,000 versus a net loss of $2,965,000 for 1992. Included in the 1993 loss was $290,000 of restructuring costs relating to consolidation of our U.S. manufacturing into one building and severance costs. The Company wrote off $130,000 of goodwill relating to the Gram Corporation acquisition in 1988. Bookings for the year were $11,893,000 versus $14,109,000 for 1992. Backlog at December 31, 1993 was $2,133,000 versus $3,018,000 at December 31, 1992. Bookings for the fourth quarter were $3,654,000, which were higher than any of our previous quarters in 1993.

Our UNITHERM product line that was introduced in August 1991 has made tremendous strides in helping Vitronics regain lost market share in the reflow business. We continue to perform very well with our key customers and to regain other key customers such as IBM and AT&T. We have also been able to enhance and improve the operating performance of the UNITHERM line with the introduction of our enhanced cooling and lower nitrogen consumption. We were also able to make a major design and development effort to introduce two new reflow machines at Nepcon West in late February 1994. These were all development efforts that were part of the 1993 research and development costs.

Our semi-aqueous product line remained flat in 1993, but we have seen increased business with our aqueous cleaner line in the second half of 1993. We continue to feel optimistic that with the total elimination of CFC production and usage by the end of 1995, that demand for alternative cleaning methods will increase. Our product line has been fully developed and awaiting the orders.

The patent lawsuit against Conceptronic is in the discovery stage. No trial date has been set, but the judge has given Conceptronic some additional time. We continue to push for as early a trial date as possible. After finding in favor of Vitronics by way of a

Exhibit 2 Vitronics Corporation, Excerpts from 1993 Annual Report

summary judgment and determining that the Conceptronic system performed substantially the same function as the apparatus disclosed in the patent, the only issue was whether the structure was substantially equivalent. The courts have also confirmed that Conceptronic was precluded from challenging the validity of our patents in litigation. We also received, in early December 1993, a favorable summary judgment from the U.S. District Court of the State of New Hampshire with respect to the counterclaim filed by Conceptronic relating to abusive process allegedly based on Vitronics' filing of its claim for patent infringement—the court dismissed such claims in their entirety. We continue to feel very confident and optimistic that we will prevail in this action and we continue to pursue this case very aggressively.

In closing, we have come through a tough 1991 and 1992 and a rebuilding year in 1993. Although 1993 was not a profitable year, our losses have been reduced substantially. We look forward to 1994 and feel optimistic that we have regained our momentum. This turnaround could not have taken place without all the support and help of our employees, customers, vendors and shareholders.

James J. Manfield, Jr.
Chairman of the Board and
Chief Executive Officer

Ronald W. Lawler
President and
Chief Operating Officer

CONSOLIDATED FINANCIAL STATEMENTS

CONSOLIDATED STATEMENTS OF OPERATIONS
(Dollars in thousands except share amounts)

| | Year Ended December 31 | | |
	1993	1992	1991
Net sales	$ 12,778	$ 12,373	$ 14,312
Costs of goods sold	9,248	10,385	10,107
Gross profit	3,530	1,988	4,205
Selling, general and administrative expenses	3,338	3,778	4,679
Research and development costs	860	1,130	1,928
Non-recurring charges	420	—	711
	4,618	4,908	7,318
Loss from operations	(1,088)	(2,920)	(3,113)
Non-operating expense, net	232	94	35
Loss before taxes	(1,320)	(3,014)	(3,148)
Income taxes (credit)	37	(49)	(896)
Net loss	$ (1,357)	$ (2,965)	$ (2,252)
Loss per common share	$(.18)	$(.70)	$(.57)
Weighted average number of common and common equivalent shares used in calculation of earnings per common share	7,379,000	4,216,000	3,929,000

655

Exhibit 2   Vitronics Corporation, Excerpts from 1993 Annual Report

CONSOLIDATED BALANCE SHEETS
(Dollars in thousands except share amounts)

	December 31	
	1993	1992
ASSETS		
CURRENT ASSETS:		
Cash and cash equivalents	$ 172	$1,256
Accounts receivable – less allowance for doubtful accounts of $120 and $124	1,696	1,990
Inventories	2,159	2,256
Refundable taxes	20	209
Other current assets	241	337
TOTAL CURRENT ASSETS	4,288	6,048
PROPERTY AND EQUIPMENT	318	477
OTHER ASSETS	190	230
	$4,796	$6,755
LIABILITIES AND STOCKHOLDERS' EQUITY		
CURRENT LIABILITIES:		
Accounts payable	$1,026	$1,481
Other current liabilities	696	1,310
Current maturities of long-term liabilities	470	1,528
TOTAL CURRENT LIABILITIES	2,192	4,319
LONG-TERM LIABILITIES – net of current maturities	1,605	54
COMMITMENTS:		
STOCKHOLDERS' EQUITY: Common stock, $.01 par value: Authorized 20,000,000 shares; issued and outstanding 7,378,538	74	74
Additional paid-in capital	5,311	5,329
Foreign currency translation adjustment	(219)	(211)
Accumulated deficit	(4,167)	(2,810)
	999	2,382
	$4,796	$6,755

See notes to consolidated financial statements.

Exhibit 2   Vitronics Corporation, Excerpts from 1993 Annual Report

CONSOLIDATED STATEMENTS OF CASH FLOWS
(Dollars in thousands)

	Year Ended December 31		
	1993	1992	1991
CASH FLOWS FROM OPERATING ACTIVITIES:			
Net loss	$(1,357)	$(2,965)	$(2,252)
Adjustments to reconcile net loss to net cash provided by (used for) operating activities:			
Depreciation and amortization	279	404	1,021
Gain on sale of assets	(42)	(179)	(129)
Deferred income taxes	—	360	(13)
Equity in (earnings) loss of affiliate	—	—	(86)
Writedown of non-current marketable equity securities	130	—	100
Changes in current assets and liabilities:			
Accounts receivable	294	417	1,036
Inventories	97	270	922
Other current assets	96	(24)	12
Accounts payable	(90)	53	225
Income taxes	189	649	(1,186)
Other current liabilities	(614)	77	(202)
Total adjustments	339	2,027	1,700
Net cash provided by (used for) operating activities	(1,018)	(938)	(552)
CASH FLOWS FROM INVESTING ACTIVITIES:			
Additions to property and equipment	(65)	(92)	(534)
Disposals of property and equipment	74	332	230
Decrease (increase) in other assets	(177)	(21)	(64)
Loan to affiliated company	—	—	100
Proceeds on sale of investment	—	100	—
Net cash provided by (used for) investing activities	(168)	319	(268)
CASH FLOWS FROM FINANCING ACTIVITIES:			
Long-term borrowing	1,200	—	—
Government grant for property and equipment	—	—	133
Payments of long-term debt	(1,072)	(1,112)	(288)
Rights offering	(18)	1,321	—
Net cash provided by (used for) financing activities	110	209	(155)
Foreign currency translation adjustment	(8)	264	(39)
CASH AND CASH EQUIVALENTS:			
Net decrease	(1,084)	(146)	(1,014)
Balance, beginning of year	1,256	1,402	2,416
Balance, end of year	$ 172	$ 1,256	$ 1,402

See notes to consolidated financial statements.

V

657

Exhibit 2   Vitronics Corporation, Excerpts from 1993 Annual Report

NOTES TO CONSOLIDATED FINANCIAL STATEMENTS

Three Years Ended December 31, 1993

A. Summary of Significant Accounting Policies

The Company is engaged in the business of designing, manufacturing and marketing equipment used primarily in the manufacture and assembly of electronic components. The significant accounting policies employed are as follows:

1992 & 1993 Operations

During 1992, the Company experienced significant, unanticipated losses due to a number of factors including a decrease in sales and an increase in product costs and was not in compliance with its term loan agreement. As a result, the Company operated under a series of standstill agreements in 1992. These matters raised substantial doubt about the Company's ability to continue as a going concern at the time the financial statements for the year ended December 31, 1991 were released. Subsequently, the Company raised $1,321,000 in a rights offering and $1,200,000 through the issuance of a subordinated debenture and repaid its outstanding bank debt. The Company has experienced additional losses during 1993. On April 8, 1994, the Company obtained a commitment for a factoring facility of $750,000 under which the Company may obtain accounts receivable financing on a pre-approved basis. In addition, the holder of the Company's Subordinate Debentures has indicated, without commitment, it is willing to continue to provide accounts receivable collateralized financing to the Company similar to and under similar terms and conditions to the loan it extended to the Company in January, 1994 as described in Note F. Management believes these possible financing sources combined with its existing cash balances and anticipated cash flow from operations will be adequate to meet its working capital requirements during 1994. However, there can be no assurances that the Company will be able to access funds under these financing arrangements or that the Company operations will generate adequate cash flows.

Principles of consolidation

The consolidated financial statements include the accounts of the Company and its wholly-owned subsidiaries. All significant intercompany balances, transactions and profits have been eliminated.

Cash equivalents

The Company considers all highly liquid debt instruments with a maturity of three months or less to be cash equivalents.

Inventories

Inventories are stated at the lower of cost (first-in, first-out method) or market.

Property and equipment

Property and equipment are recorded at cost. Depreciation is provided using the straight-line method over the estimated useful lives of the applicable assets. Expenditures

Exhibit 2   Vitronics Corporation, Excerpts from 1993 Annual Report

for maintenance and repairs are charged to expense as incurred, whereas expenditures for renewals and betterments are capitalized. Upon sale or other disposition of assets, the cost and related accumulated depreciation are removed from the accounts and any resulting gain or loss is reflected in income.

The estimated useful lives used to compute depreciation are as follows:

Description	Years
Machinery and equipment	3–8
Furniture and fixtures	5–8

Leasehold improvements are amortized over the life of the lease, including extensions, but not in excess of the maximum useful lives of the improvements.

Other assets

Included in other assets are patents and debenture costs associated with the issuance of long-term debt. Patents and debenture costs are being amortized on the straight-line method over their estimated useful lives ranging from three to seven years.

Foreign currency translation

All assets and liabilities of the Company's United Kingdom subsidiary, Vitronics Europe Limited (VEL), are translated at exchange rates in effect at December 31, 1993. Income and expenses are translated at average rates for the year. The resulting differences, due to changing exchange rates, are charged or credited to "Foreign Currency Translation Adjustments" included as part of Stockholders' Equity. Gains and losses from foreign currency transactions are included in earnings.

Revenue recognition

Sales are recognized when products are shipped, except for customers where bill and hold arrangements are requested, in which case revenue is recognized when the product is ready for shipment. Revenues from 1993 bill and hold arrangements were approximately $210,000.

Research and development costs

All research and development costs are charged to operations as incurred.

Warranties

The Company's products are generally under warranty against defects in material and workmanship for a one-year period. Estimated warranty costs are accrued in the same period as products are shipped.

Income taxes

The Company has adopted the liability method of accounting for income taxes, as set forth in Statement of Financial Accounting Standards No. 109, *Accounting for Income Taxes* (SFAS 109), effective January 1, 1993. The cumulative effect of adopting this statement as of January 1, 1993 was immaterial to the results of operations for the year ended December 31, 1993. Previous to January 1, 1993, the Company had appropriately accounted for taxes under APB #11. SFAS 109 is an asset and liability approach

V

659

that requires the recognition of deferred tax assets and liabilities for the expected future tax consequences of events that have been recognized in the Company's financial statements or tax returns. In estimating future tax consequences, SFAS 109 generally considers all expected future events other than future enactments of changes in the tax law or rates. Deferred tax assets are recognized, net of any valuation allowance, for deductible temporary differences and operating loss and credit carryforwards. Deferred tax expense represents the change in the deferred tax assets and liabilities.

Loss per share

The loss per share is based on the weighted average number of common and common equivalent shares (where dilutive) outstanding during the year.

B. Inventories

Inventories consisted of (in thousands):

	December 31	
	1993	1992
Finished goods	$ 308	$ 58
Work in process	473	523
Raw materials	1,378	1,675
	$2,159	$2,256

C. Property and Equipment

Property and equipment consisted of (in thousands):

	December 31	
	1993	1992
Machinery and equipment	$1,063	$1,313
Furniture and fixtures	389	409
Leasehold improvements	418	367
	1,870	2,089
Less accumulated depreciation and amortization	1,552	1,612
	$ 318	$ 477

Exhibit 2 Vitronics Corporation, Excerpts from 1993 Annual Report

D. Other Assets

Other assets consisted of (in thousands):

	December 31	
	1993	1992
Patents	$ 201	$ 178
Goodwill	—	183
Other assets	155	20
	356	381
Less accumulated amortization	166	151
	$ 190	$ 230

E. Other Current Liabilities

Other current liabilities consisted of (in thousands):

	December 31	
	1993	1992
Accrued sales commissions	$ 194	$ 303
Accrued payroll and related taxes	80	121
Accrued warranty costs	130	152
Other	292	734
	$ 696	$1,310

F. Indebtedness

Long-term liabilities consisted of (in thousands):

	December 31	
	1993	1992
Bank term loan	$ —	$ 684
U.K. term loan, interest at bank base rate plus 3%	261	317
Notes payable, primarily to vendors, interest ranging from 0%–12%	565	493
Subordinated Convertible Debenture interest at 10%	1,200	—
Unamortized government grants	49	88
	2,075	1,582
Less current maturities	470	1,528
Total long-term liabilities – net of current maturities	$1,605	$ 54

Exhibit 2   Vitronics Corporation, Excerpts from 1993 Annual Report

The bank term loan was classified as short-term in 1992 because of failure to maintain certain financial covenants. This loan was paid off on October 4, 1993.

On October 1, 1993, the Company received $1,200,000 from an investment fund. This was a convertible subordinated debenture with interest rate of 10% convertible into 2,400,000 shares of Vitronics common stock. Quarterly principal payments of $33,333 are to be made beginning on June 30, 1995 and continuing through December 31, 1997, at which time any unpaid principal will be due. The agreement calls for mandatory prepayment on the occurrence of certain events and contains certain financial covenants, the most restrictive of which is that the Company must maintain a ratio of consolidated net earnings to cover interest charges of not less than 1:1 and that the Company must maintain a debt to equity ratio not greater than 3:1. The Company was in violation of a covenant under the agreement for which a waiver was received.

In January 1994, the Company pledged receivables and received a $350,000 loan at 12% interest from New England Growth Fund I, L.P. This loan was repaid subsequent to December 31, 1993.

Borrowings under the U.K. term loan are collateralized by a first position in all of the assets of VEL, the Company's United Kingdom subsidiary, and guaranteed by the parent company. The interest rate was 8.5% at December 31, 1993. As a result of a cross-default covenant, these borrowings have been classified in current maturities at December 31, 1992. At December 31, 1993, this has been classified as long-term debt.

VEL received government grants in order to subsidize the acquisition of equipment and leasehold improvements and to stimulate employment. To the extent that the grant is capital in nature, it is amortized over 5 years, the equipment's useful life. Repayment of the grant may be forgiven if specified levels of capital investment and employment are maintained. Because the Company has not met its personnel requirements under the grant, the Company may be obligated to repay the unamortized portion of the grant ($49,000) to the government.

In 1993 and 1992, approximately $365,000 and $317,000, respectively, of accounts payable were converted to long-term Notes Payable, $71,000 of which can be converted into 142,000 shares of common stock.

As of December 31, 1993, aggregate maturities of long-term liabilities were as follows (in thousands):

1994	$ 470
1995	289
1996	244
1997	185
1998	887
	$2,075

Exhibit 2   Vitronics Corporation, Excerpts from 1993 Annual Report

G. Income Taxes

The provision for income taxes consisted of (in thousands):

	Year Ended December 31		
	1993	1992	1991
Currently payable (refundable):			
Federal	$ (53)	$(360)	$(717)
Foreign	—	(49)	(166)
State	—	—	—
	(53)	(409)	(883)
Deferred (prepaid):			
Federal	—	360	(13)
Foreign	90	—	—
State	—	—	—
	90	360	(13)
	$ 37	$ (49)	$(896)

Reconciliations of income taxes at the statutory rate to the effective rate reflected in the financial statements were as follows:

	Year Ended December 31		
	1993	1992	1991
Statutory income tax rate	(34.0%)	(34.0%)	(34.0%)
Net losses without tax benefit	20.9	28.8	—
Research and development costs	—	—	(2.8)
Goodwill amortization	3.6	3.6	3.9
Foreign taxes	6.8	—	2.3
Other	5.5	—	2.1
	2.8	(1.6)	(28.5%)

V

663

Exhibit 2   Vitronics Corporation, Excerpts from 1993 Annual Report

The 1993 foreign deferred tax provision represents an adjustment of prior year amounts. The components of the net deferred tax assets and liabilities were as follows (in thousands):

	December 31, 1993	January 1, 1993
Deferred tax assets:		
Inventory reserves	$116	$126
Accounts receivable reserves	40	40
Workman's compensation and benefits reserves	25	15
Depreciation	66	56
Capital loss carryforwards	193	202
Net operating loss carryforwards	1,176	1,306
Research and development credits	199	199
Total deferred tax asset	1,815	1,944
Valuation allowance	(1,815)	(1,944)
Net deferred tax assets	$ —	$ —

The Company has placed a full valuation allowance against the deferred tax asset due to the uncertainty regarding the utilization of these benefits in future returns.

The Company currently has net operating loss and capital loss carryforwards for federal income tax purposes of approximately $2,942,249 and $483,000, respectively, and R&E credits of approximately $199,000, all expiring in the years 2007 and 2008.

The Company is currently under audit by the Internal Revenue Service for the year ended December 31, 1990. The Company feels any adjustments resulting from the audit would be immaterial to the financial statements.

H. Operating Lease Commitments

The Company leases its facilities and certain equipment under operating leases ranging up to 5 years with renewal and purchase options. The leases provide for monthly rental payments plus, in certain situations, payments for real estate taxes, insurance and maintenance. Rental expense for property, machinery and equipment charged to operations was $463,000, $434,000 and $503,000 for the years ended December 31, 1993, 1992 and 1991, respectively.

At December 31, 1993, future minimum payments applicable to non-cancelable operating leases with initial terms of one year or more were as follows (in thousands):

1994	$ 264
1995	249
1996	239
1997	197
1998	137
Thereafter	23
	$1,109

*A*merican investors should take a close look at the Polish stock market. No other market in the world can offer more attractive rates of return! Look at Wedel, for instance. This company is the market leader in the Polish candy industry. It is very profitable and has the backing and marketing expertise of Pepsico. At the current price of 145,000 zlotys per share, Wedel is trading at a PE of less than 3. This is a real bargain for foreign investors!

So says Krzysztof Piotrkowska, director of a brokerage firm in Warsaw. At first blush, Piotrkowska appears to have a point. In 1991, Wedel generated a return on equity in excess of 40 percent, while the average ROE for the U.S. candy industry was "only" 15.9 percent. Yet, despite Wedel's high level of profitability, it trades at only 1.16 times book value, while the typical American food manufacturer trades at 2 to 3 times book value and 20 times earnings.

COMPANY BACKGROUND

E. Wedel is the leading Polish manufacturer of confectionery and one of the leading producers of biscuits. It produces several different types of products, including sweets, plain chocolate, chocolate-covered sweets and wafers, biscuits, and jellies. The company sells its products primarily in the Polish market, and holds nearly 30 percent of the market for chocolate products and a significant share of markets for chocolate-covered products, chocolate-like products, and biscuits. Expressed in terms of U.S. dollars, 1991 sales were approximately $115 million.

The company was founded in 1851 and named for Emil Wedel, the son of the founder; it remained with the Wedel family until the end of World War II, when it was nationalized. Originally a regional chocolate manufacturer, Wedel significantly ex-

Prepared by Heitor Martins and Professor Victor L. Bernard. The assistance of Mr. Jarek Szewczyk of E. Wedel is gratefully acknowledged. This case is based upon publicly available information. It was prepared as a basis for class discussion and is not intended to illustrate either an effective or ineffective management of a business situation.

panded its operations during the communist period. Through a series of acquisitions, the company became the largest national producer of chocolates and also diversified into sweets and biscuit manufacturing. After the collapse of the communist government in 1989, and in light of Wedel's strong past performance and high profitability, the Polish government chose Wedel as one of the first companies to be privatized. In October and November of 1991, the government, while retaining a 20 percent interest in the company, sold the remaining interest to Pepsico, Inc., Wedel employees, and private investors. In November 1991, Wedel was listed for the first time at the Warsaw Stock Exchange.

POLISH POLITICAL AND ECONOMIC ENVIRONMENT

From the period after World War II until 1989, Poland was under single-party communist rule, and the government controlled almost all aspects of Polish economic life. Dissatisfaction with the Polish economy helped spur the rise of the independent trade union Solidarity during the 1970s; strikes and public protests ensued, leaving Poland on the verge of chaos by 1981. At that time, Solidarity was outlawed and its leaders arrested, as the communist regime turned to a series of ultimately failed economic reforms. Solidarity eventually re-emerged, forced partially free elections in 1989, and emerged from those elections as the dominant political force in Poland.

Fully free elections were held in 1990 and 1991, but have not produced political stability. The new parliament is composed of numerous political parties, none of which controls more than a small fraction of the seats. However, the Solidarity government (headed by the end of 1990 by newly-elected President Lech Walesa) has taken steps toward a recovery program aimed at controlling the accelerating inflation and transforming the economy to a Western style system within two or three years. The plan includes tight monetary policy, elimination of price controls, a phase-out of government subsidies, liberalization of foreign trade, maintenance of more realistic exchange rates, reform of the legal system, and privatization of state-owned companies. Throughout 1990, government efforts were focused primarily on economic stabilization. Raging inflation and devaluation of the Polish zloty was slowed fairly quickly, but at the cost of a deep recession and increasing social unrest.

The Economy in 1991–1992

The recession continued during 1991, with real gross domestic product falling 9 percent, but structural reforms and privatization were finally viewed as more pressing issues. Looking ahead, economists expected a decline in real GDP of −2.0 percent in 1992, but a return to modestly positive growth in 1993. Behavior of key economic indicators in Poland from 1987 through 1991 and forecasts for the next two years are as follows:

Macroeconomic Indicators in Poland	Recent Years					Forecasted	
	1987	1988	1989	1990	1991	1992	1993
Population (million)	37.8	37.9	38.0	38.2	38.3	38.5	38.6
Real GDP (% change)	−1.2%	2.5%	−1.3%	−12.0%	−9.0%	−2.0%	1.3%
Industrial production (% change)	3.4%	5.3%	−0.5%	−23.0%	−11.9%	−3.0%	2.1%
Balance of trade ($ billion)	1	1.1	0.6	2.1	0.0	0.45	0.8
Unemployment (million)				1.1	2.2	3.5	n.a.
Exchange Rate (Zl/$)	265.1	430.6	1439.2	9500	10576	n.a.	n.a.

Source: The Economist Intelligence Unit

Data on recent inflation in Poland is shown below. After having witnessed rampant inflation in 1989 and 1990, the Poles saw the rate slow considerably in 1991. Over the last three months of 1991, the consumer price index rose by "only" 3.1 to 3.2 percent per month. Inflation is expected to be "only" about 40 to 50 percent per year over the next two years.

Poland's Consumer Price Index, 1989–1991
(1985 = 100)

	1989	1990	1991
First quarter	327	4246	7337
Second quarter	420	4943	8424
Third quarter	703	5810	9743
Fourth quarter	1765	6891	11198
Average for year	746	5385	9680

Source: International Monetary Fund

As one would expect based on Poland's high inflation rate, the Polish zloty has weakened substantially relative to most other currencies. By January 1990, the attempt to maintain the zloty at a fixed exchange rate had obviously failed, and the Solidarity government devalued the currency to a rate of Zl 9500 per U.S. dollar. In late 1991, Poland moved to a free floating exchange rate; in June 1992 the zloty traded at a rate of 14,000 per dollar.

The Privatization Program

The privatization process in Poland started in 1989, soon after Solidarity assumed control of the government. Various modes of privatization were adopted: (1) liquidation of companies followed by the sale or lease of assets, (2) employee and management buyouts, (3) formation of joint-ventures with private companies, generally of foreign origin, (4) sale of companies to private investors, and (5) initial public offerings.

The majority of the smaller companies in the Polish economy, especially in the service sector, were privatized during the early 1990s. However, the government has not been as successful in transferring medium and large size manufacturing companies to the private initiative. In 1992 the public sector still accounts for over 75 percent of Poland's industrial production. The failure to privatize can be attributed to the lack of profitability of many government-owned enterprises, the strong opposition of labor unions, the lack of well developed capital markets, the low level of private savings in Poland, and/or the relative lack of interest among foreign investors.

PEPSICO'S INVESTMENT IN E. WEDEL

When E. Wedel was privatized in the latter half of 1991, it was largely through the sale of shares to Pepsico, Inc. of the United States. The shares issued in Wedel's privatization were classified as both preferred (35 percent) and common (65 percent). Preferred shares carry the same dividend rights as common shares, but entitle shareholders to five votes instead of one. Preferred shares were sold to Pepsico at a price of Zl224,000, while common shares were sold at Zl130,000. Employees were allowed to buy common shares at a 50 percent discount. Wedel shares were distributed as follows:

Recipient of Shares	Preferred Shares Acquired	Common Shares Acquired	Fraction of Shares Held	Total Votes Controlled	Fraction of Voting Rights
Pepsico, Inc.	1,120,000	832,000	61.0%	6,432,000	83.75%
Polish government		416,000	13.0	416,000	5.17
Wedel employees		416,000	13.0	416,000	5.17
Private investors		416,000	13.0	416,000	5.17
	1,120,000	2,080,000	100.0%	7,680,000	100.00%

The Polish government retained ownership of much of Wedel's real estate and buildings. These properties are currently leased by the company, and there is a high probability that the basic rates or rules of payment for these leases will be changed in the future. There is also uncertainty concerning the government's ownership of these properties due to potential claims from previous owners. However, the government assumed entire responsibility for any losses that these claims may cause. It also accepted responsibility for any potential environmental liabilities, and promised to provide up to U.S.$950,000, if needed, in order to upgrade the conditions at Wedel's facilities, mostly by pollution control and asbestos removal at factory sites.

While the Polish government retained a 20 percent interest in Wedel, it agreed to transfer 5 percent of Wedel's shares to Pepsico at no additional cost in 1994. The government also agreed not to sell any of its remaining 15 percent interest during the next five years without previous approval from Pepsico. At the same time, Pepsico agreed not to sell any portion of its interest in Wedel during the next five years without prior approval from the Polish government. Pepsico agreed further to acquire any shares that may be issued in the future, until it increases its current ownership, 61 percent of all outstanding shares, to 67 percent. Finally, it was established that preferred shares would automatically be converted into common shares, with only one vote, whenever Pepsico became the owner of 75 percent of total outstanding shares.

WEDEL'S PUBLIC FLOAT AND POLAND'S STOCK MARKET

As noted above, 20 percent of Wedel's shares were sold to the public in the IPO in late October and early November 1991. Sold initially at Zl130,000, Wedel's stock opened on November 26 on the Warsaw Exchange at Zl180,000, joining a dozen other formerly state-owned enterprises. The Exchange had been in existence only since April 1991, but the government expected to add at least one new company to it each month. Shares are made available to not only Poles but also foreign investors. Trading sessions were held initially once a week, and, since January 1992, have been held twice a week. Price movements are limited to 10 percent per session.

Despite Poles' enthusiasm for capitalism, the performance of the stock market has been quite poor. The volume of transactions has been erratic and prices have been dropping steadily. At the end of June 1992, almost all stocks were trading below their initial listing prices and the Warsaw Stock Exchange (WIG) index had dropped 38 percent since the first session. The following table provides an overview of the performance of the Warsaw Stock Exchange and of Wedel stock. Note that after opening in late November at 180,000 zlotys, Wedel's price fell in May 1992 to 130,000—the same as its IPO price.

THE BUSINESS OF E. WEDEL, S.A.

Wedel produces a variety of products, but the primary ones—accounting for nearly 80 percent of revenue—are chocolate and chocolate-covered products. Other main products include biscuits and sweets. Exports accounted for less than 5 percent of sales.

E. Wedel has been a household name in chocolate in Poland since the 1920s; few if any brand names are better known in the country. Between the two world wars Wedel won international awards for its chocolate and flew chocolate to company-owned stores in London, Paris, and throughout Poland. Today, the name E. Wedel still plays an essential role in its marketing of high-quality, premium-priced speciality chocolates in boxes,

E. Wedel, S.A.

Month	Warsaw Stock Exchange			Wedel Stock		
	Number of Trading Sessions	WIG Index (end of month)	Total Volume (Zl 000's)	Per Share Price (end of month)	Volume (Zl 000's)	Volume as Percent of Total
April 1991	3		1,210,290			
May 1991	3	95.6	4,793,770			
June 1991	4	86.1	8,512,140			
July 1991	5	84.4	16,230,918			
Aug. 1991	4	74.7	11,000,605			
Sept. 1991	4	66.9	21,370,763			
Oct. 1991	5	89.3	65,208,983			
Nov. 1991	4	79.9	57,287,945	180,000	3,000,000	5.24%
Dec. 1991	4	86.4	106,225,112	180,000	35,501,664	33.42%
Jan. 1992	8	86.9	68,329,830	187,000	16,161,260	23.65%
Feb. 1992	8	87.6	113,104,677	160,000	12,752,942	11.28%
March 1992	9	83.0	172,888,999	135,000	22,349,100	12.93%
April 1992	8	71.9	127,386,361	134,000	13,107,040	10.29%
May 1992	8	68.0	107,699,062	130,000	17,255,740	16.02%
June 1992	8	62.0	91,134,080	145,000	23,264,449	25.53%

wafers, luxury chocolate bars, and other candy bars. The company produces chocolates using old, proven recipes and believes that, in the confectionary goods market, quality is more important to customers than price. Seventy percent of its products are sold to wholesalers and various retail shops in Poland, but Wedel maintains a small number of its own retail outlets, including an exquisite shop at the site of one of the original company factories, on Szpitalna Street in Warsaw.

About 95 percent of E. Wedel's sales are domestic, and its immediate plans are to continue focusing on that market. Within Poland, it competes with several companies, primarily Wawel and Goplana. Wawel is preparing to be privatized as an independent Polish company, and the government also hopes to privatize Goplana, perhaps with the aid of a foreign partner. Financial data on these companies' performance is not available. However, their products sell at somewhat lower prices than E. Wedel's, and their brand names do not enjoy the same reputation. E. Wedel expects strong competition in the future from foreign firms, including Suchard, Nestlé, Mars, and Alpina. As a group, these foreign firms already hold a 37 percent market share in confectionary goods in Poland, and some are successful in marketing their goods at premium prices.

Material costs, which comprise a large majority of cost of sales, are important to Wedel. The materials include sugar, milk powder, condensed milk, cocoa beans, potato syrup, confectionary fat, and other ingredients, many of which must be imported. As the result of the reforms in the Polish economy, E. Wedel has for the last two years been able to procure supplies through any channels it desires, and there are many suppliers of the required materials. The company employs approximately 3,000 workers, but labor costs comprise only a small fraction of total product costs. (The typical worker in the Polish food processing industry earned the equivalent of only about $150/month in 1991.[2])

Pepsico, Inc. plans on introducing a number of important changes at E. Wedel. The changes include:

- *Increased marketing activity*. Pepsico will step up advertising, including creative television advertising. Some of it will focus on reinforcing product quality and heritage of the E. Wedel name, while advertising of some new products will be designed specifically to appeal to young, active consumers.
- *Expansion of distribution channels*. Pepsico is committed to investing $7 million in strengthening distribution networks over the next five years.
- *Plant modernization*. Pepsico will spend $27 million over five years on modernization of manufacturing facilities for the traditional confectionary and biscuit product lines. The modernization is intended to help E. Wedel reduce costs—an important step in an increasingly competitive environment.
- *Manufacture of salty snacks*. Pepsico will spend $22 million over five years (most within the first two years) on the construction of what will be the most modern plant in Europe for the manufacture of Frito-Lay "salty snacks." These products, which will be marketed under the name Frito-Lay Poland, include Ruffles potato chips, Fritos corn chips, Chee-tos corn curls, and other snacks. Pepsico will team with farmers in Poland to enhance the productivity of potato production in the local area.

The Pepsico investments in E. Wedel will be treated as purchases of additional issues of new stock.

COMPARISON OF WEDEL AND AMERICAN FOOD PROCESSORS

It is difficult to compare Wedel's performance to those of American companies for several reasons. Poland has not operated as a market economy, and Wedel was under government management until late 1991. Wedel focuses on the confectionary business, while such businesses in the U.S. tend to be located within more diversified food companies. Finally, as explained below, the financial reporting approaches are different.

Based on 1991 results, Wedel appears on the surface to be performing substantially better than the average American company in the food industry. Despite being significantly less leveraged, Wedel was able to provide a return on equity almost 4 times higher

W

671

2. *Source:* The Industrial Statistic Yearbook, 1991, United Nations.

E. Wedel, S.A.

than publicly traded small American food processors, and its operating margin was 5.3 times as high. Even so, American firms were trading at high multiples while Wedel was selling at only slightly above book value. Some key financial ratios for Wedel and for the American food processors follow.

Financial Ratios	Wedel[a]	American Food Processors[b]	
		Large[c]	Small[d]
Operating Profit Margin	29.3%	12.4%	5.6%
Net Profit Margin	15.7%	5.0%	1.7%
Return on Equity	41.0%	21.1%	10.8%
Debt to Equity Ratio	.06	.57	.58
Price/Sales Ratio	.38	.91	.36
Price Earnings Ratio	2.8	18.3	21.3
Price to Book Value	1.2	3.9	2.3

a. Wedel ratios based on 1991 financial statements and stock price of Zl145,000.
b. American data extracted from the Value Line Industry Review for 1991.
c. Large firms include publicly traded companies with market values of more than $1 billion.
d. Small firms include publicly traded companies with market value of less than $1 billion.

WEDEL'S FINANCIAL REPORTING

E. Wedel's "Principles of the Financial Account," given in Exhibit 1, are different from those used in the U.S. but share some of the features of systems used in the U.K. and Australia. The basic rule applied is a historical cost convention, except for fixed assets, which are revalued periodically. Upon revaluation, fixed asset balances and associated accumulated depreciation accounts are increased to an approximation of their current cost, with an equivalent increase recorded in shareholders' equity. Depreciation expense is then computed based on the revalued balances. Inventory, which consists primarily of raw materials, is accounted for at cost.

In addition to using accounting conventions that differ from those in most other countries, Wedel's terminology, as translated into English, differs from that in the U.S. For example, "cost of sales" refers to selling commissions, and "financial costs" is the term for interest expense.

The "Principles of the Financial Account" in Exhibit 1 are derived from Wedel's prospectus for the 1991 IPO. The same principles were also applied in financial statements issued after the IPO. Exhibit 2 presents excerpts from the prospectus, including financial statements for 1988, 1989, 1990, and the first half of 1991. The entire 1991 Annual Review (except for the Polish version of the text) appears in Exhibit 3, and additional 1991 data appear in Exhibit 4.

CASE QUESTIONS

1. Evaluate E. Wedel's profitability. Is it as strong as it appears at first blush? Is it possible to determine (at least approximately) how reported profitability has been distorted by the high levels of inflation in Poland? What is your assessment of the quality of E. Wedel's financial reporting?

2. On the basis of the information in the case, do you agree with Mr. Piotrkowska that the current price of 145,000 zlotys per share is an exceptional bargain?

Exhibit 1 Accounting Conventions Used by E. Wedel

EXHIBIT 1

Accounting Conventions Used by E. Wedel

Principles of the Financial Account

General Principles

The principles of the financial account applied at E. WEDEL S.A. are congruent with legal regulations.

The basic rule applied to the financial information is a historical cost convention, except for fixed assets, the value of which has been increased for required periods according to the rules, and by the coefficients set by the State Central Statistical Office.

Sales

The value of sales is calculated on a basis of amounts invoiced to the customers, and includes turnover taxes.

An exception from this principle is applied for the year 1988, where the sales were calculated on the basis of payments collected before January the 25th of the next year.

For the sake of congruence of the data, the value of sales for each period was calculated on the basis of the same principle, that is, on the accrual basis.

Plant and Equipment

Fixed assets are valued on the basis of the purchase or manufacturing cost and are gradually depreciated according to the average life of the asset involved. The coefficients for depreciation are set by the President of the State Central Statistical Office and published in Dziennik Urzędowy.

In the audited period the assets were revalued three times.

The financial statements include the revalued assets.

The detailed revaluation of fixed assets on the day before the day of transformation of the Company into joint stock company required by law—as set in §11 sec. 1 of the instruction of the Council of Ministers dated December 19, 1989 concerning classification of assets as tangibles or intangibles, principles and coefficients of depreciation and rules for valuation of fixed assets—had not been done in due time. The instruction was followed in the first six months of 1991.

Equipment is valued on the basis of acquisition or manufacturing cost.

A consistent method of depreciation was applied within the examined period, which was 100% of value at the moment of giving from the stock. The stock taking of fixed assets and equipment has been conducted in each of the years between 1988 and 1990.

The investments are valued at purchase cost at the day of purchase and they are periodically revalued after completion, in the same way as fixed assets. Financial assets are valued at the purchase cost.

Current Assets

The inventories of raw materials are valued at the actual purchase price.

Production in process is valued on the basis of cost of direct materials consumed, according to the production norms standards.

Finished goods are valued at the technical cost of manufacturing, i.e. direct cost and factory overheads.

Goods for sale are valued on the basis of sale price diminished by a margin of profit.

The inventory of the elements of current assets has been done in the first six months of 1991, except for stocks for which there are books kept in quantities as well.

Until the end of 1989 cash and cash equivalents were classified separately for Polish and foreign currencies.

Transactions in foreign currencies were recalculated into zlotys at the exchange rate on the day of the transaction.

Liquid assets disclosed in the Balance Sheet of June 30, 1991 are exactly the same as in accounting books and bank statements.

Accounts receivable and accounts payable were taken from WEDEL's accounting books, and noncollected accounts receivable are unconfirmed.

Exhibit 1   Accounting Conventions Used by E. Wedel

The Scope of the Examination

E. WEDEL's financial statements for the years 1988, 1989, and 1990 were reviewed by the auditors registered at the Ministry of Finance and employed by the Treasury Chambers in Warsaw and Ciechanów. Therefore our examination for those years was only selective because we based our opinion on verified statements, whereas full examination has been carried out for the period of the first six months of 1991.

For the reason of changes in many disclosure structures, accounting standards, and definitions throughout the period of 1988–1990, the classification structure of presentation of financial and accounting data has been unified.

Despite the above, the customary examination has been carried out with an aim at confronting accounting data in the books with the reality of and congruence with legal regulations.

Neither one of the financial statements presented herein includes the value of land which belongs to the State Treasury and has been only used by state-owned enterprise transformed into E.WEDEL S.A. A formal solution of this problem, i.e. property rights of the Company for the land and buildings, may result in increased cost to be paid for the land and buildings, rents for a lease of land and buildings, and taxes for the land and buildings.

E. WEDEL's Management Board assured us with a statement that the accounting books contain all the assets and financial obligations, and that they take into consideration any reasonable risk.

Auditor's Report

The Balance Sheet, Profit & Loss Account, and Sources and Applications of Funds Analysis for E. Wedel, S.A. were examined for a period of 1988–1990 and a period of the first six months of 1991.

The scope of the examination and the summary of principles of financial account applied at E. Wedel S.A. are presented above.

We express here our conviction that our examination gives a rational basis for our opinion.

The financial statements presented here give, in our opinion, a true and fair view of the financial position of E. Wedel S.A.

PROVIDUM S.A.

W

675

EXHIBIT 2

Excerpts from E. Wedel Prospectus for Initial Public Offering, November 1991

FINANCIAL STATEMENTS, 1988 THROUGH FIRST HALF OF 1991

BALANCE SHEET   (in millions of zlotys)

	12/31/88	12/31/89	12/31/90	6/30/91
A. ASSETS				
1. FIXED ASSETS				
a. Machinery and Equipment (Note I)	5,549	79,751	215,857	211,626
b. Investments and Investments Grants	418	3,170	9,900	36,599
c. Intangibles	2	1	2,042	3,231
d. Financial Fixed Assets	87	102	202	202
2. CURRENT ASSETS				
a. Inventories (Note II)	4,606	22,781	79,192	102,928
b. Accounts Receivable	4,321	42,733	54,704	90,029
c. Short-Term Securities	–	—	461	1,518
d. Cash	1,047	4,412	9,067	20,349
3. PREPAID EXPENSES	—	—	—	—
4. LOSS	—	—	—	—
TOTAL ASSETS	**16,030**	**152,950**	**371,425**	**466,482**
B. LIABILITIES				
1. SHAREHOLDERS EQUITY (Note III)				
a. Creation Fund and Enterprise's Fund	5,633	6,911	18,727	—
b. Shareholders' Equity	—	—	—	160,000
c. Reserve Fund	—	—	—	75,403
d. Revaluation of Fixed Assets	2,746	76,880	192,587	—
e. Retained Profit or Retained Loss	5	215	—	—
2. LONG-TERM LIABILITIES				
a. Long-Term Bank Loans (Note IV)	—	—	14,782	33,669
3. SHORT-TERM LIABILITIES				
a. Accounts Payable	1,787	29,525	19,993	16,819
b. Short-Term Creditors	1,330	7,711	42,790	12,988
c. Other Liabilities	2,935	19,894	47,988	65,907
d. Long-Term Liabilities to Be Paid (Note IV)	—	—	8,008	8,008
4. DEFERRED INCOME AND ACCRUALS	2	2	69	7,965
5. RETAINED PROFIT	1,592	11,812	26,481	85,723
TOTAL LIABILITIES	**16,030**	**152,950**	**371,425**	**466,482**

W
676

PROFIT AND LOSS ACCOUNT

(in millions of zlotys)

	12/31/88	12/31/89	12/31/90	6/30/91
Sales (Note I)	38,024	141,470	653,200	584,619
Turnover Tax	−6,847	−23,062	−100,674	−89,283
Grants and Other Subventions (Note II)	519	318	63	1,875
Net Sales	31,696	118,726	553,156	497,211
Cost	−22,160	−74,491	−331,309	−300,650
Administrative Expenses	−2,090	−9,293	−55,085	−26,884
Cost of Sales	−309	−929	−6,158	−5,921
Operating Profit	7,137	34,013	160,604	163,756
Additional Sales	78	783	1,379	−129
Net Financial Income	75	3,515	1,044	1,331
Financial Cost	−132	−3,024	−18,090	−14,495
Profit	7,158	35,287	144,937	150,463
Extraordinary Losses	−33	−136	−1,154	−1,857
Extraordinary Profit	15	41	2,377	875
Profit Before Tax	7,140	35,192	146,160	149,481
Income Tax	−4,284	−13,853	−53,097	−54,561
Other Taxes from Profit	−273	−804	−35,724	−9,087
Profit After Tax	2,583	20,535	57,339	85,833
Dividend to the State Treasury	−	−1,399	−4,576	—
Employees' Fund (Note III)	−991	−7,324	−26,282	—
Welfare Contribution	—	—	—	—
Supervisory Boards' Contribution	—	—	—	−110
Net Profit	1,592	11,812	26,282	85,723

Exhibit 2   Excerpts from E. Wedel Prospectus for Initial Public Offering, November 1991

SOURCES AND APPLICATIONS OF FUNDS (in millions of zlotys)

	12/31/88	12/31/89	12/31/90	6/30/91
A. SOURCES OF FUNDS				
Internal Sources				
Profit After Tax	2,583	20,535	57,339	85,833
Depreciation	252	427	6,701	8,126
Reserves and Accrued Income	—	—	67	7,896
Other Internal Sources	96	1	205	18
Subtotal	**2,931**	**20,963**	**64,312**	**101,873**
External Sources				
Credits and Long-Term Loans	—	—	22,790	18,887
Securities Sold	30	15	—	—
Other External Sources	—	4	22	—
Subtotal	30	19	22812	18887
TOTAL SOURCES OF FUNDS	**2,961**	**20,982**	**87,124**	**120,760**
B. APPLICATION OF FUNDS				
Employees' Fund and Welfare Contributions	991	7,324	26,282	—
Dividend to Treasury of State	—	1,399	4,576	—
Investments	737	3,344	36,309	34,193
Conversion into Share Capital and Bonds	115	30	100	—
Other Applications	139	11	—	110
TOTAL APPLICATION OF FUNDS	**1,982**	**12,108**	**67,267**	**34,303**
Surplus on Sources	979	8,874	19,857	86,457
Change in Inventories	1,568	18,175	56,411	23,736
Change in Account Receivable	1,945	38,412	11,971	35,325
Change in Liabilities	–2,226	–51,078	–53,641	15,057
Change in Cash and Cash Equivalents	-308	3,365	5,116	12,339
TOTAL CHANGES	**979**	**8,874**	**19,857**	**86,457**

The company has not issued any bonds.

NOTES TO BALANCE SHEET

NOTE I: PLANT AND EQUIPMENT

	12/31/88	12/31/89	12/31/90	6/30/91
Beginning value	11,388	169,390	480,639	474,448
Depreciation	−5,839	−89,639	−264,782	−262,822
Net Value	5,549	79,751	215,857	211,626
Buildings:				
Beginning value	5,171	81,806	198,222	198,253
Depreciation	−1,102	−18,670	−48,750	−50,953
Net Value	4,069	63,136	149,472	147,300
Machinery and equipment:				
Beginning value	6,217	87,584	282,417	276,195
Depreciation	−4,737	−70,969	−216,032	−211,869
Net Value	1,480	16,615	66,385	64,326

CHANGES IN PLANT AND EQUIPMENT, 1/1/91–6/30/91   (in millions of zlotys)

	Beginning Value	Depreciation	Net Value
Beginning balance	480,639	264,782	215,857
Increases			
Investments	6,216	0	6,216
Decreases		0	
Cancellation or sale	−854	−835	−19
Corrections	−11,553	−9,417	−2,136
Depreciation computations	0	8,292	−8,292
Ending Balance	474,448	262,822	211,626

NOTE II: INVENTORY. Inventory consists of raw materials (approximately 80 percent); work-in-process (approximately 8 percent); and finished goods (approximately 12 percent).

NOTE III: SHAREHOLDERS' EQUITY. At the moment of transformation of the state-owned enterprise into a joint stock company, all accounts have been transformed into Shareholders' Equity and Reserve Fund.

NOTE IV: DEBT. Long-term debt (including current maturities) is denoted primarily in Deutschmarks.

NOTES TO PROFIT AND LOSS ACCOUNT

NOTE I: EARNINGS FROM SALES   (in millions of zlotys)

	12/31/88	12/31/89	12/31/90	6/30/91
Domestic Sales	35,664	133,816	607,985	559,978
including profit margin	470	1,874	12,563	13,875
Export Sales	2,360	7,654	45,215	24,641
including transferrable currencies	2,353	7,648	45,063	24,641
TOTAL	38,024	141,470	653,200	584,619

Expressed in terms of 1990 prices for confectionary items, sales (in millions) were Zl 1,096,275, Zl 744,840l, Zl 653,200, and Zl 384,871 for the periods ended 12/31/88, 12/31/89, 12/31/90, and 6/30/91, respectively.

NOTE II: GRANTS AND OTHER SUBVENTIONS. This account contains refund of turnover tax exempts on export in 1988 and 1989, refund of custom duty and agriculture subvention in 1990, agriculture subvention in 1991.

NOTE III: EMPLOYEES' FUND. This account contains 175 million zlotys compensation for Management Board and Workers' Council.

W

Exhibit 3   E. Wedel 1991 Annual Review

EXHIBIT 3

E. Wedel 1991 Annual Review

LETTER TO SHAREHOLDERS

I am both pleased and honored to be able to write to you, Wedel's new shareholders, in your new company's first Annual Review for its first year as a newly privatized company with its partner, PepsiCo Foods International. This Annual Review is indeed an historic document, the first such Review that your company will prepare for you each year.

I would like to take this opportunity to welcome you as shareholders and to say how much your company is looking forward to a long, rewarding relationship with one of its most important constituencies—you. This sense of partnership leads me to the subject of my letter, which is the equally important partnership between E. Wedel S.A. and PepsiCo Foods International (PFI).

In the 140 years since it was founded, Wedel has become one of the leading institutions in Poland and has earned an enviable reputation through the widely acclaimed quality of its sweet products. Those products, including chocolate, biscuits and candies, have been enjoyed by generations of Poles and are a fitting testament to the principles upon which Wedel has prospered over the years. We were proud to recognize the 140th anniversary at the early September 1991 celebrations.

When PFI, the international snack food division of PepsiCo, Inc., purchased 40% of the shares of Wedel on August 22, 1991, as part of the Polish government's privatization program, we fully understood the obligation to strengthen and grow this great company and its products. We take seriously our commitment of continued support and future investment in Wedel, and we intend to make Wedel the first and greatest Polish full-snack company.

We were also enthusiastic and optimistic about the partnership we were forming—a Partnership in a Proud Tradition. And we still are. We believed then—and believe even more strongly today—that the partnership with Wedel would become recognized as the model for the development of private enterprises in Poland.

I am pleased to report to you that we are encouraged by the early results of this unprecedented venture. Already, our strategic partnership is successfully applying PFI's financial and technical expertise to help maintain Wedel's tradition of national leadership.

Although we must not be too influenced by one set of results, we can be encouraged by Wedel's 1991 performance: We achieved a net profit of Pzl.163.0 billion, on net sales of Pzl.1,035 billion. These results are particularly impressive in view of the challenging economic conditions in Poland during the country's transition to a market economy.

But this is only the start. We plan to strengthen Wedel's national leadership position by investing capital, technology, and management expertise and by reinvesting profits into Wedel to build for you a stronger, more valuable company.

When we formed our partnership, PFI committed to invest US$56 million in Wedel during the first five years to expand and upgrade existing sweet production facilities, develop a nationwide distribution system for Wedel products and to build a new plant for the production of salty snacks. This strategy is designed, first, to strengthen areas in which Wedel is already established; second, to develop an efficient distribution system to handle the anticipated additional volume; and third, to introduce new salty snack products.

Already, the pace of our investment in Wedel has accelerated. In keeping with our commitment to strengthen Wedel's operations, we are now spending a total of US$17 million in the first year of the partnership, more than the US$15.2 million originally planned, on a number of projects. We are in the process of upgrading and modernizing the production facilities at the Wedel plant and Plonsk biscuit plant to increase capacity for the production of Wedel's most popular chocolate, biscuit and candy products. We are also transforming existing space at Plonsk into a modern distribution centre for Wedel products.

W

681

Exhibit 3   E. Wedel 1991 Annual Review

But this is not all. We also are beginning construction of a new manufacturing plant for salty snacks, which is scheduled for completion in April 1993. This modern plant will employ 125 workers initially, increasing to 400–500 in four years, and will be at the core of a new sister company, Frito-Lay Poland, which we have formed for the salty snack business. Frito-Lay Poland will benefit directly from PFI's global technical and marketing strengths. We begin operations next month, when a full line of five different salty snacks is launched. In time, Wedel shareholders will profit from the value Frito-Lay Poland will add to your shares.

We already have begun an environmental program to improve working conditions at all of our facilities in Poland. This program is based on the results of an independent study performed according to standards followed by European Community countries.

PFI's investment in Wedel goes much beyond new factories and equipment, and includes research and development efforts. Wedel has begun an agricultural program working with farmers in Poland to improve crop yields and ensure the best quality potato crops. This will enable us to purchase more potatoes from more local farmers, which in turn will provide more jobs on the farms and reduce the company's costs. Both are important benefits to Poland.

As we help to improve the local sources for potatoes and other crops, we will be able to increase our volume of salty snack foods and reach our goal of US$100 million in sales by 1996. Simultaneously, we are developing marketing programs to increase consumer demand in Poland for Wedel's most popular sweet snacks. We know they are a treasure and intend to enhance them.

In recognition of the valuable contribution of our employees, we have retained all those employed as of August 22, 1991, and given each an 80% wage increase, and have maintained all existing welfare programs at your company. In addition, each Wedel employee received a 1,000,000 zloty bonus in recognition of the 140th anniversary.

By investing PFI's capital and by reinvesting Wedel's profits in new factories, research and technology, as well as in our people, we will continue to strengthen Wedel's already strong name. The road ahead is

not easy, but we are confident that, working together, we can overcome all challenges.

And that's what our partnership is really all about: working together to build a better future for Wedel and, more importantly, for Poland.

I look forward to reporting our progress to you for many years to come.

James H. O'Neal
Chairman,
Supervisory Board
E. Wedel S.A.

4 April 1992

REVIEW OF OPERATIONS

Our operations are divided into two complementary businesses: sweets and biscuits, in both of which Wedel already is well established; and salty snacks, which the company is introducing to Poland next month.

Sweets and Biscuits Business

While Wedel is acknowledged as Poland's leading manufacturer of chocolate and candy and one of the country's leading producers of sweet biscuits, there is considerable room for growth in these businesses. A comparison of Poland's per capita consumption of these products of 3.6 kilos per year shows that it lags behind consumption in Germany, Belgium, and Britain. This represents an opportunity to increase consumption of Wedel products, especially since the name enjoys unprecedented recognition in the marketplace—a 95 percent level of awareness among most age groups.

Even so, competition from other Polish and foreign manufacturers is growing and expected to increase, particularly in chocolate products, because these other companies also have recognized the latent demand in Poland.

We are addressing the changes in the sweet snack business and this increased competition with a series of initiatives and investments that include manufac-

Exhibit 3   E. Wedel 1991 Annual Review

turing improvements, distribution enhancement and marketing innovation. We are confident these actions will strengthen Wedel's leadership position.

We will provide increased resources to support such popular products as Ludsudowaz Zorzechani, Ptasie Mieczko, and Wedel Torte, among others, ensuring that the consumer will find these products on store shelves wherever and whenever they want them. As part of this plan, we will extend the popular products, or brands, with a variety of sizes and new packaging.

The introduction of new products will stimulate the sweet snacks market and increase Wedel's total sales in the expanded market. In 1991, the introduction of two new biscuit lines helped to maintain strong sales in that market. Other new products, planned for introduction in 1992, will help increase sales of chocolate and candy lines.

As PFI has demonstrated in virtually every country where it has operations, the youth market represents a major opportunity for increased sales. Our plans include increased marketing efforts directed at teenagers and young people, with products at prices they can afford.

Increasing Wedel's share of the Polish sweet snack market will remain a major priority for years, and we plan to increase our market share in domestic regions beyond our traditional strengths. We also intend to expand the export of Wedel sweet snacks to other parts of the world.

Salty Snacks Business

Wedel's total sales and profits are expected to increase considerably in 1992 with the launch this month of Frito-Lay Poland and its full line of salty snacks. We will take advantage of the natural synergies between the sweet and salty snacks businesses to help us efficiently expand Wedel into Poland's first full-snack enterprise.

Poland's per capita consumption of salty snacks also lags behind that of other countries, such as Greece, Spain, Italy and Portugal. Again, this offers great opportunity for growth as more Polish consumers are encouraged to eat more salty snacks. Young

people are the predominant salty snacks consumer group in Poland's $90 million a year market, and the competition is primarily from German companies along with only one Polish challenger.

We will take advantage of PFI's worldwide strengths in research, technology, and marketing to build a market leadership position for the Frito-Lay line of products. The first step already has been taken with the introduction of Fritos™, Ruffles™, Chee-tos™, Bocabits™ and Drakis™ snacks that are currently manufactured overseas with specially designed packaging for Poland. These imports will help to build a sufficient market base for the new salty snack plant we are building, scheduled to be operational in April 1993. This plant will have the capacity to produce up to 600 million bags of potato, corn, and other salty snack products annually.

Our emphasis on domestic manufacturing will have a significant, positive impact upon other sectors, including agriculture. We have begun an agricultural research program to ensure the highest yield from the finest quality potato crops. Together with the new potato storage facility opening this year, this program will ensure a sufficient domestic source of key ingredients for Frito-Lay Poland, for which we anticipate sales of $100 million by 1996.

Single-serve packages and attractive advertising will help increase the product appeal among young people, the key consumer group. Wedel's expanding distribution capabilities will also be used to ensure wide availability of the Frito-Lay snacks for consumers.

The steps already taken have laid the foundation for a self-fulfilling sequence of events: we're investing in Wedel's existing businesses while constructing new facilities for new products; we're building increased storage and distribution capacity to handle the increased volume that will result from our marketing, advertising, packaging and selling efforts to increase consumer demand; and, as demand grows, we'll increasingly draw on domestic sources of higher and higher quality potatoes and other raw materials.

We believe this will create a bright future for Wedel and its shareholders, and contribute significantly in building Poland's new national economy.

W

683

Exhibit 3   E. Wedel 1991 Annual Review

FINANCIAL STATEMENT, E. WEDEL, S.A.

(in entirety, as presented in Annual Review)

WYNIKI FINANSOWE ZA ROK 1991	FINANCIAL HIGHLIGHTS
(w miliardach złotych)	(in PZL Billion)

BILANS	1991	BALANCE SHEET	1991
Aktywa:		Assets:	
Środki pieniężne i należności	112.8	Cash and Receivables	112.8
Zapasy	112.2	Inventories	112.2
Środki trwałe (netto)	264.8	Fixed Assets (Net)	264.8
Inne aktywa	16.4	Other Assets	16.4
W sumie	506.2	Total	506.2
Pasywa i kapitał własny:		Liabilities and Owners' Equity:	
Zobowiązania bieżące	85.6	Payable to Suppliers and Others	85.6
Zobowiązania długoterminowe	22.9	Long Term Debt	22.9
Kapitał własny	397.7	Owners' Equity	397.7
W sumie	506.2	Total	506.2

RACHUNEK WYNIKÓW	1991	INCOME STATEMENT	1991
Przychody ze sprzedaży	1,220.2	Gross Sales	1,220.2
Podatek obrotowy	185.0	Turnover Tax	185.0
Przychody ze sprzedaży netto	1,035.2	Net Sales	1,035.2
Kost operacyjny	731.4	Operating Expenses	731.4
Zysk operacyjny	303.8	Operating Profit	303.8
Odsetki, koszty finansowe i inne	28.0	Interest and Financing Costs/Other	28.0
Zysk przed opodatkowaniem	275.8	Profit Before Tax	275.8
Podatki płacone z zysku	112.8	Tax	112.8
Zysk netto	163.0	Net Income After Tax	163.0

W

684

Exhibit 4   E. Wedel 1991 Statement of Sources and Applications of Funds

EXHIBIT 4
E. Wedel 1991 Statement of Sources and Applications of Funds
(available from E. Wedel, but excluded from 1991 Annual Review)

STATEMENT OF SOURCES AND APPLICATIONS OF FUNDS   (in millions of zlotys)

	1990	1991
A. SOURCES OF FUNDS		
Internal Sources		
Profit After Tax	57,339	162,693
Depreciation	6,701	19,479
Reserves and Accrued Income	67	401
Other Internal Sources	205	82
Subtotal	**64,312**	**182,655**
External Sources		
Credits and Long-Term Loans	22,790	8,123
Securities Sold	—	—
Other External Sources	22	139
Subtotal	22812	8,262
TOTAL SOURCES OF FUNDS	**87,124**	**190,917**
B. APPLICATION OF FUNDS		
Employees' Fund and Welfare Contributions	26,282	—
Dividend to Treasury of State	4,576	—
Investments, including Capital Expenditures	36,309	75,743
Repayment of Long-Term Credits	—	36,662
Other Applications	100	6,384
TOTAL APPLICATION OF FUNDS	**67,267**	**118,789**
Surplus on Sources	19,857	72,128
Change in Inventories	56,411	37,415
Change in Accounts Receivable	11,971	5,417
Change in Short-Term Liabilities	−53,641	−11,363
Change in Cash and Cash Equivalents	5,116	40,659
TOTAL CHANGES	**19,857**	**72,128**

W

685

p a r t 5

Compaq Computer Corporation

Compaq Computer Corporation is a world leader in the design, development, manufacturing and marketing of PC servers, desktop, portable and notebook personal computers, and network laser printers. 1992 Annual Report

1992 Annual Report and 10-K Excerpts Financial Highlights Letter to Stockholders Nature of Business Selected Consolidated Financial Data Management's Discussion and Analysis of Financial Condition and Results of Operations Report of Independent Accountants Consolidated Financial Statements Notes to Consolidated Financial Statements

Compaq Computer Corporation
Financial Highlights

	1992	1991	1990
	(in thousands, except per share amounts)		
Sales	$4,099,758	$3,271,367	$3,598,768
Gross margin	1,194,734	1,217,791	1,540,882
Net income	213,152	130,869	454,910
Earnings per common and common equivalent share:			
Primary	2.58	1.49	5.14
Assuming full dilution	2.52	1.49	5.12
Working capital	1,359,091	1,144,634	1,044,899
Total assets	3,142,393	2,826,386	2,717,529
Stockholders' equity	2,006,691	1,930,704	1,859,013

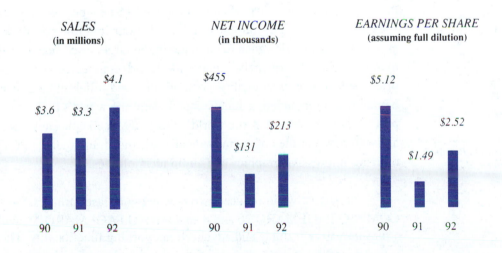

SALES (in millions) — $3.6 (90), $3.3 (91), $4.1 (92)

NET INCOME (in thousands) — $455 (90), $131 (91), $213 (92)

EARNINGS PER SHARE (assuming full dilution) — $5.12 (90), $1.49 (91), $2.52 (92)

To Our Stockholders:

In 1992 Compaq entered a new era as a leader in the personal computer industry. As the year began, we saw an exciting opportunity to gain market share and improve Compaq's financial results by adopting aggressive new strategies. We developed a bold plan to introduce a broad range of high quality products from entry-level to high-end, to price our products competitively, to implement the best customer support program in the industry, and to expand our distribution channels. Then we challenged our worldwide organization to make it happen.

Our people responded. They achieved new economies and efficiencies with fewer resources. They introduced a record number of new Compaq products – more than 80 models from entry-level to high-end performance PCs, servers, and network printers. They built and shipped products in record volumes to meet overwhelming global demand. Their creativity, enthusiasm and hard work helped us maintain our equilibrium and expand our vision of the future. Compaq regained momentum, captured market share, and achieved substantial gains in sales and earnings.

In June Compaq staged one of the most dramatic product rollouts in the history of the industry when it introduced 16 new personal computers – 45 models in all. The introduction included our first low-cost desktop and notebook PCs designed to compete in the large, price-sensitive PC market. These were entirely Compaq-designed, engineered and tested to offer the levels of functionality, compatibility and reliability that users demand. Also included in June's launch were the world's highest performance desktop PC, the world's most advanced color notebook PC and two new families of technologically advanced, upgradable PCs offering impressive graphics and audio technologies.

In August we introduced two new network laser printers, the COMPAQ PAGEMARQ 20 and the COMPAQ PAGEMARQ 15, which offer innovative features and advanced networking functionality. Their output capabilities make them the fastest desktop printers available today. These products incorporate state-of-the-art technology for which Compaq has been granted a number of patents. In the first 30 days following their announcement, Compaq printers received 11 top industry awards.

In October Compaq solidified its leadership in PC servers by introducing the world's fastest PC server, the COMPAQ SYSTEMPRO/XL, which features high speed at an attractive price to make it a leader in its class. It offers exceptional performance and simplified server management for demanding database applications. The COMPAQ ProSignia, also introduced in October, combines high performance and low price for the best value in the market. It is dramatically less expensive than comparable competitive products, yet outperforms them significantly.

Throughout the year we made impressive additions to our distribution channels. Compaq products are now sold in 85 countries through a vast network of marketing partners that includes a variety of dealers, retailers, value-added resellers, distributors and systems integrators. The total number of outlets for Compaq products has more than doubled to 10,600 worldwide.

Each of our employees contributed to the year's many achievements, which also include:
- Strengthening service and support with more than a dozen new programs through CompaqCare, the PC industry's most comprehensive U.S. customer service and support program
- Extending the industry's first three-year warranty on PC products
- Shipping 1.5 million PCs worldwide
- Dramatically reducing costs and cutting overhead per unit by 63 percent
- Winning numerous prestigious product awards worldwide
- Maintaining product quality during rapid growth.

Our winning strategy and employees' hard work paid off. Compaq's market share of PC unit sales worldwide doubled to 7.2 percent. Revenue grew to $4.1 billion, a 25 percent increase from 1991. Net income was $213.2 million, an increase of 63 percent from 1991. Earnings per share grew 69 percent to $2.52 on a fully diluted basis.

Compaq's gains in market share and profitability affirm our plans for the 1990s. The results tell us that the strategy we put in place a year ago – to make Compaq the acknowledged leader in the PC industry and the standard of quality, innovation, performance, value, reliability and support – is succeeding.

1992 SYSTEMS TECHNOLOGY FIRSTS:

-NetFlex Controller

-TriFlex System Architecture

-Automatic Server Recovery

-INSIGHT Manager

1992 DISTRIBUTION % of Outlets

16% Retail   15% Value-Added Resellers/ Systems Integrators

69% Dealers

COMPAQCARE 1992 ACCOMPLISHMENTS

-3-year warranty/on-site service

-Wide range of support providers

-Free hotline support seven days a week/24 hours a day

-Remote Diagnostic Utility with every PC product

-Wide range of self-help tools

-Self maintenance program

-Customer training

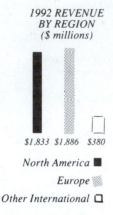

*1992 REVENUE
BY REGION
($ millions)*

$1,833 $1,886 $380

North America ■
Europe ▨
Other International ☐

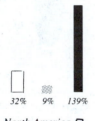

*1992 REVENUE
GROWTH BY REGION*

32%   9%   139%

North America ☐
Europe ▨
Other International ■

Still, we have hard work ahead. The PC market experienced dramatic price declines in 1992, which are likely to continue in 1993. Additional pricing actions will put further pressure on gross profit margins. In order to maintain or increase profitability, we must control our costs and increase our unit sales substantially.

We are ready for the challenge. Compaq expects the PC market to sustain the enthusiasm that greeted our wave of new products in 1992. Our engineering and design teams plan additional leadership products in 1993, continuing our tradition of technological innovation in exciting new areas like multimedia and personal digital assistant products, as well as PCs using Intel's Pentium microprocessor. We will pursue component sourcing and manufacturing strategies that allow us to remain price competitive and enhance our share of the market. We will bring manufacturing output into line with demand and solve the backlog problems that confronted us in 1992. We know that the growth of our business requires close management of manufacturing utilization, inventory, receivables, and distribution channels.

Our goal is simple: We want to be the leading supplier of PCs and PC servers in all customer segments worldwide. We intend to accomplish that goal by leading the industry in developing new products, pricing competitively, controlling costs, supporting customers and expanding distribution. Compaq understands the dynamics of the industry and is poised to move decisively to exploit new opportunities. In the process, we will continue to raise the standards by which quality, performance, and customer support are measured in the industry.

Eckhard Pfeiffer
President and Chief Executive Officer
March 5, 1993

General

Compaq Computer Corporation, founded in 1982, designs, develops, manufactures, and markets personal computers, PC systems, printers, and related products. The Company operates in one principal industry segment across geographically diverse markets. As used herein, the term "Company" means Compaq Computer Corporation and its consolidated subsidiaries, unless the context indicates otherwise.

Strategy

In 1992 the Company implemented aggressive changes in its business strategy. These changes focused on increasing the Company's market share by expanding sales to new endusers while maintaining its existing customer base. The Company introduced broad-based new programs in pricing, product development, distribution and marketing, and service and support, while continuing to emphasize its traditional areas of strength--product quality and innovation. The Company believes its key to success is leveraging the Company's engineering talent, purchasing power, manufacturing capabilities, and distribution strengths to bring to market high-quality cost-competitive products with different features in different price ranges. This strategy will enable the Company to offer appropriate products to many types of customers.

Compaq Products

The Company's personal computer products consist of desktop personal computers, battery-powered notebook computers, and AC-powered portable computers. The Company also produces tower PC systems that store and manage data in network environments and high performance laser printers designed for network environments. The Company's products are available with a broad variety of functions and features designed to accommodate a wide range of user needs.

In 1992 sales of desktop, notebook, and portable personal computers with accompanying options accounted for almost 90% of the Company's revenue with more than half of its revenue stemming from desktop personal computers and options for desktop computers. In June the Company introduced 16 new personal computers--45 models in all, including the Company's first low-cost desktop and notebook PCs, the world's highest performance desktop PC, and the Company's first color notebook PC as well as two new families of advanced and upgradable PCs offering graphic and audio technologies. The Company's leading unit seller in 1992 was the COMPAQ ProLinea 3/25s Personal Computer, introduced in June. The Company's most popular notebook product in 1992 was the COMPAQ LTE Lite 25 notebook computer, introduced in January 1992.

In its tower PC systems product line, in October 1992 the Company introduced the COMPAQ SYSTEMPRO/XL the world's fastest PC server, as well as the COMPAQ ProSignia, a cost effective tower machine for small business network environments. The Company's leading unit seller in 1992 in its tower PC systems product line was the COMPAQ SYSTEMPRO/LT 486/33 introduced in October 1991.

The Company entered the PC network printer market in August 1992 with the introduction of two new network laser printers--the COMPAQ PAGEMARQ 20 and PAGEMARQ 15 printers, which are the fastest desktop printers available today. These printers incorporate technology for which the Company has been granted a number of patents.

The Company offers a number of related options products for its PC, systems, and printer products, including the COMPAQ ProLiant external disk storage system, which holds up to 7.35 billion bytes of data and allows users to expand the storage capacity of their PC networks to almost 30 billion bytes through the use of multiple ProLiant systems.

Product Development

The Company is actively engaged in the design and development of additional products and enhancements to its existing products. Since personal computer technology develops rapidly, the Company's continued success is dependent on the timely introduction of new products with the right price and features. Its engineering effort focuses on new and emerging technologies as well as design features that will increase efficiency and lower production costs. In 1992 the Company focused on technological developments for PC products related to color and monochrome active matrix flat panels, power conservation, communication devices, and component densification, as well as new technologies applicable to future products in the area of personal computers with full-motion video and stereo sound, pen-based PCs, and other small form-factor devices. In that same period the Company focused on connectivity and compatibility issues, technological developments for systems products related to server systems management from remote locations, and other new technologies applicable to future products in its printer line. During 1992, 1991, and 1990, the Company expended approximately $173 million, $197 million, and $186 million, respectively, on research and development.

Manufacturing and Materials

The Company's manufacturing operations consist of manufacturing finished products and various circuit boards from components and subassemblies that the Company acquires from a wide range of vendors. The Company's principal manufacturing operations are located in Houston, Texas; Erskine, Scotland; and Singapore. Products sold in Europe are manufactured primarily in the Company's facilities in Erskine, Scotland and Singapore. Products sold in the U.S. are primarily manufactured in the Company's facilities in Houston, Texas and Singapore.

The Company believes that there is a sufficient number of competent vendors for most components, parts, and subassemblies. A significant number of components, however, are purchased from single sources due to technology, availability, price, quality, or other considerations. Key components and processes currently obtained from single sources include certain of the Company's displays, microprocessors, mouse devices, keyboards, disk drives, printers and printer components, application specific integrated circuits and other custom chips, and certain processes relating to construction of the plastic housing for the Company's computers. In addition, new products introduced by the Company often initially utilize custom components obtained from only one source until the Company has evaluated whether there is a need for an additional supplier. In the event that a supply of a key single-sourced material, process, or component were delayed or curtailed, the Company's ability to ship the related product in desired quantities and in a timely manner could be adversely affected. The Company believes that the suppliers whose failure to meet the Company's orders could have a material adverse effect on the Company include Intel Corporation and Conner Peripherals, Inc. The Company attempts to mitigate these potential risks by working closely with key suppliers on product plans, strategic inventories, and coordinated product introductions.

Materials and components are normally acquired through purchase orders, as is common in the industry, typically covering the Company's requirements for periods averaging 90 days. From time to time the Company has experienced significant price increases and limited availability of certain components that are available from multiple sources, such as dynamic random-access memory devices. At times the Company has been constrained by parts availability in meeting product orders. Any similar occurrences in the future could have an adverse effect on the Company's operating results.

Marketing and Distribution

The Company distributes its products principally through third-party computer resellers. The Company's products are sold to large and medium-sized business and government customers through dealers, value-added resellers, and systems integrators and to small business and home customers through dealers and consumer channels. In 1992 the Company continued its expansion into new distribution channels, such as consumer electronics outlets and office product superstores, to address the needs of small business and individual consumers. In the first half of 1993 the Company will begin to distribute products directly to customers in the U.S. through a mail order catalogue featuring a variety of personal computers, printers, and software products.

In 1992 European sales constituted 46% of the Company's total revenues with an almost equal amount from sales in North America. The Company's Europe Division, based in Munich, Germany, focuses on opportunities in Europe as well as in parts of Africa and the Middle East.

In March 1992 the Company introduced notebook, desktop, and systems products designed for the Japanese market. The Company continues to expand its international business through entry into new countries, and the Company's highest growth areas are in Asia and Latin America. For further geographic information for 1992, 1991, and 1990, see Note 14 of Notes to Consolidated Financial Statements.

Service and Support

The Company provides support and warranty repair to its customers through full-service computer dealers and independent third-party service companies. In 1992 Compaq announced CompaqCare, a number of customer service and support programs, most notably a three-year warranty on PC products (excluding monitors and batteries) and round-the-clock lifetime telephone technical support at no additional charge to the customer.

Patents, Trademarks and Licenses

The Company held 146 patents (including 18 design patents) and had 125 patent applications (including 10 design patent applications) pending with the United States Patent and Trademark Office at the close of 1992. In addition, the Company has registered certain trademarks in the United States and in a number of foreign countries. While the Company believes that patent and trademark protection plays an important part in its business, the Company relies primarily upon technological expertise, innovative talent, marketing abilities, and management skills of its employees.

The Company has from time to time entered into cross-licensing agreements with other companies holding patents to technology used in the Company's products. The Company holds a license from IBM for all patents issuing on applications filed prior to July 1, 1993. Texas Instruments, Inc. ("TI") has granted the Company an option to acquire a patent license, which would result in an increase in the Company's royalty payments. TI has notified the Company that the option period has begun to run and the Company is evaluating TI's offer. The Company's failure to enter into a license agreement could result in litigation with TI. Because of technological changes in the computer industry, extensive patent coverage, and the rapid rate of issuance of new patents, certain components of the Company's products may unknowingly infringe patents of others. The Company believes, based in part on industry practices, that if any infringements do exist, the Company will be able to modify its products to avoid infringement or obtain licenses or rights under such infringed patents on terms not having a material adverse effect on the Company.

Seasonal Business

Although the Company does not consider its business to be highly seasonal, the Company in general experiences seasonally higher revenues and earnings in the first and fourth quarters of the year. The Company anticipates that the seasonality of its sales may increase as it expands the consumer retail portion of its business.

Working Capital

Information regarding the Company's working capital position and practices is set forth on page 10 of this Form 10-K under the caption "Liquidity and Capital Resources."

Customers

No customer of the Company accounted for 10% or more of sales for 1992. Computerland, Inc. and Intelligent Electronics, Inc. accounted for 9% and 8% of 1992 sales, respectively.

Backlog

The Company's resellers typically purchase products on an as-needed basis. Resellers frequently change delivery schedules and order rates depending on market conditions. Unfilled orders ("backlog") can be, and often are, canceled at will and without penalties. The Company attempts to fill orders on the requested delivery schedules; however, in 1992 the Company experienced significant demand for certain products that it was unable to produce on a timely basis. In the Company's experience, the actual amount of product backlog at any particular time is not a meaningful indication of its future business prospects since backlog rapidly becomes balanced as soon as supply begins meeting demand.

Competition

The computer industry is intensely competitive with many U.S., Japanese, and other international companies vying for market share. The principal elements of competition are price, product performance, product quality and reliability, service and support, marketing and distribution capability, and corporate reputation. While the Company believes that its products compete favorably based on each of these elements, the Company could be adversely affected if its competitors introduce innovative or technologically superior products or offer their products at significantly lower prices than the Company or if the Company is unable to fill orders on a timely basis for an extended period. No assurance can be given that the Company will have the financial resources, marketing and service capability, or technological knowledge to continue to compete successfully.

Environmental Laws and Regulations

Compliance with laws enacted for protection of the environment to date has had no material effect upon the Company's capital expenditures, earnings, or competitive position. Although the Company does not anticipate any material adverse effects in the future based on the nature of its operations and the purpose of such laws and regulations, there can be no assurance that such laws or future laws will not have a material adverse effect on the Company.

Employees

At December 31, 1992, the Company had approximately 9,500 full-time regular employees and 1,800 temporary and contract workers.

Selected Consolidated Financial Data

The following data have been derived from consolidated financial statements that have been audited by Price Waterhouse, independent accountants. The information set forth below is not necessarily indicative of the results of future operations and should be read in conjunction with the consolidated financial statements and notes thereto appearing elsewhere in this Annual Report on Form 10-K.

	Year ended December 31,				
	1992	1991	1990	1989	1988
	(in thousands, except per share amounts)				
Consolidated Statement of Income Data:					
Sales	$4,099,758	$3,271,367	$3,598,768	$2,876,062	$2,065,562
Cost of Sales	2,905,024	2,053,576	2,057,886	1,715,243	1,233,283
	1,194,734	1,217,791	1,540,882	1,160,819	832,279
Research and development costs	172,948	197,277	185,726	132,474	74,859
Selling, general, and administrative expense	698,589	721,622	706,060	538,721	397,363
Unrealized gain on investment in affiliated company			(34,532)	(13,691)	(9,683)
Other income and expenses, net	27,795	144,856	42,195	18,776	2,893
	899,332	1,063,755	899,449	676,280	465,432
Income from consolidated companies before provision for income taxes	295,402	154,036	641,433	484,539	366,847
Provision for income taxes	97,483	42,932	216,205	165,010	119,296
Income from consolidated companies	197,919	111,104	425,228	319,529	247,551
Equity in net income of affiliated company	15,233	19,765	29,682	13,771	7,691
Net income	$ 213,152	$ 130,869	$ 454,910	$ 333,300	$ 255,242
Earnings per common and common equivalent share:-					
Primary	$ 2.58	$ 1.49	$ 5.14	$ 3.89	$ 3.15
Assuming full dilution	2.52	1.49	5.12	3.88	3.13

	1992	1991	December 31, 1990	1989	1988
			(in thousands)		
Consolidated Balance Sheet Data:					
Total assets	$3,142,393	$2,826,386	$2,717,529	$2,090,389	$1,589,997
Long-term debt		73,456	73,996	274,434	274,930
Stockholders' equity	2,006,691	1,930,704	1,859,013	1,171,635	814,554

Management's Discussion and Analysis of Financial Condition and Results of Operations

The following discussion should be read in conjunction with the consolidated financial statements.

Results of Operations

The following table presents, as a percentage of sales, certain selected consolidated financial data for each of the three years in the period ended December 31, 1992.

	Year ended December 31,		
	1992	1991	1990
Sales	100.0%	100.0%	100.0%
Cost of sales	70.9	62.8	57.2
Gross margin	29.1	37.2	42.8
Research and development costs	4.2	6.0	5.2
Selling, general, and administrative expense	17.0	22.1	19.6
Other income and expense, net	.7	4.4	.2
	21.9	32.5	25.0
Income from consolidated companies before provision for income taxes	7.2%	4.7%	17.8%

Sales

Revenue for 1992 increased approximately 25% over the prior year as compared with a decline of 9% in 1991 from 1990. North American revenue, which includes Canada, increased 32% during 1992, compared with a decline of 16% in 1991 from 1990. European revenue increased 9% during 1992 compared to a decline of 5% in 1991 from 1990. Other international revenue, excluding Canada, increased 139% during 1992, compared with an increase of 19% in 1991 from 1990. International revenue, excluding Canada, represented 55% of total revenue in 1992 as compared with 58% in 1991 and 54% in 1990.

The personal computer industry is highly competitive and marked by frequent product introductions, continual improvement in product price/performance characteristics, and a large number of competitors. The

Company significantly altered its product line in 1992 by introducing new notebook, desktop, and server products in June and September 1992 and entering the network printer market with two network printers in August 1992. Additional server products were introduced in October 1992. More than 53% of the Company's unit sales and approximately 50% of the Company's revenue from sales of units in 1992 were derived from products introduced after May 1992. These new products have been designed to allow the Company to lower its product costs while maintaining the quality and reliability for which the Company's products have been known, thereby increasing the Company's ability to compete on price and value.

The lower prices of the Company's new products, as well as price reductions in June and October 1992 on existing products have substantially lowered the Company's average unit sales prices. The Company's increase in revenue in 1992 reflects strong unit sales of the Company's personal computers. In 1992 the Company's worldwide unit sales increased 78% while they held stable in 1991. The Company believes that the personal computer industry as a whole experienced significant increases in unit sales in 1992, with unit growth worldwide increasing approximately 15% in contrast to a 4% increase in 1991. Unit growth did not translate directly into revenue growth because of significantly lower unit prices. Third-party estimates indicate that industry revenue increased by approximately 5% worldwide in 1992.

Gross Margin

Gross margin as a percentage of sales continued to decline in 1992. The gross margin percentage declined to 29.1% in 1992, from 37.2% in 1991, and from 42.8% in 1990, primarily as a result of industrywide competitive pressures and associated pricing and promotional actions outpacing the Company's ability to reduce cost. Although the Company continues to aggressively pursue the reduction of product costs both at the supplier and manufacturing levels, expected pricing actions in 1993 will result in further reductions of gross margin.

The Company's operating strategy and pricing take into account changes in exchange rates over time; however, the Company's results of operations may be significantly affected in the short-term by fluctuations in foreign currency exchange rates. When the value of the dollar strengthens against other currencies, revenues from sales in those currencies translate into fewer dollars. The opposite effect occurs when the dollar weakens.

The Company attempts to reduce the impact of currency movements on net income primarily through the use of forward exchange contracts that are used to hedge a portion of the net monetary assets of its international subsidiaries. The Company also utilizes forward exchange contracts and foreign currency options to hedge certain capital expenditures and inventory purchases. In the third quarter of 1992, the Company began to hedge a portion of the probable anticipated sales of its international marketing subsidiaries through the use of purchased currency options.

The translation gains and losses relating to the financial statements of the Company's international subsidiaries, net of offsetting gains and losses associated with hedging activities related to the net monetary assets of these subsidiaries, are included in other income and expense and were a net loss of $11.2 million in 1992, a net gain of $4.1 million in 1991, and a net loss of $21.4 million in 1990. The gains associated with the hedging of anticipated sales of the Company's international marketing subsidiaries, net of premium costs associated with the related purchased currency options, are included in revenue and were $2.8 million in 1992.

Operating Expenses

Research and development costs declined in absolute dollars (to $173 million from $197 million) in 1992 as compared to 1991 due to a more focused approach to the Company's research and development projects. The

Company's research and development costs had increased in 1991 from 1990 both absolutely and as a percentage of sales. Because the personal computer industry is characterized by rapid product cycles and price cuts on older products, the Company believes that its long-term success is directly related to its ability to bring new products to market on a timely basis and to reduce the costs of new and existing products. Accordingly, it is committed to continuing a significant research and development program and research and development costs are likely to be relatively stable in absolute dollars in 1993.

Selling, general, and administrative expense declined in 1992 due to lower general and administrative expense partially offset by higher selling expense. The decrease in general and administrative expense was primarily the result of cost reductions from the Company's 1991 restructuring. Selling expense increased in connection with the introduction of new products, the entry into new markets (both domestically and internationally), the expansion of distribution channels, a new emphasis on advertising and customer service, and technical support. The Company anticipates that selling expenses will continue to increase in 1993--at least in absolute dollars--as a result of the Company's marketing program and the continuing expansion of its geographic markets.

The Company formally introduced its Japanese marketing subsidiary in March 1992 and has introduced several products tailored to the Japanese market. Due to the size and potential significance of the Japanese market, the introductory costs were and will continue to be significant in comparison to revenue generated. Furthermore, ongoing costs necessary to penetrate successfully new international markets will cause additional selling, general, and administrative expense.

As a result of the changes in the personal computer industry resulting from intense price competition, the Company has taken steps to reduce costs and more efficiently focus its resources. The Company believes its ability to control operating expenses is an important factor in its ability to be price competitive and accordingly continues to pursue cost reduction alternatives throughout the Company. In an environment of increased efforts to penetrate new markets, greater diversity of distribution channels, and increased customer support, the Company may not be successful in identifying areas to cut additional costs.

Other Items

Interest expense, net of interest and dividend income from investment of excess funds, was $11.6 million, $5.4 million, and $19.1 million in 1992, 1991, and 1990, respectively. The fluctuation in net interest expense is due primarily to declines in interest rates earned on investable cash, reduced interest expense associated with lower average borrowings, and changes in interest expense associated with financing resellers' inventories.

In each of the third quarters of 1992 and 1991 the Company recorded restructuring charges associated principally with reducing the number of employees and consolidating and streamlining operations. The charges totaled $73 million in 1992 and $135 million in 1991. In addition, in 1992 and 1991 the Company had charges related to the disposition or write-downs of the carrying value of certain fixed assets.

In the third quarter of 1992 the Company sold its equity interest in Conner Peripherals, Inc. ("Conner") realizing a gain of $85.7 million. The Company's ownership in Conner created an after-tax contribution to the Company's net income of $10.1 million in 1992, $13 million in 1991, and $19.6 million in 1990. In 1990 the Company recorded a pretax gain of $27.1 million on the sale by Conner of new equity securities and an additional pretax gain of $7.5 million on the conversion by Conner of its outstanding debentures into common stock.

The Company's effective tax rate was 33.0% in 1992, 27.9% in 1991, and 33.7% in 1990. The Financial Accounting Standards Board has issued a Statement that will change the method of determining reported income tax expense. The Company will apply the provisions of this Statement in 1993. Application of the provisions of this Statement will have minimal impact on the Company's financial statements.

Liquidity and Capital Resources

At December 31, 1992, the Company had working capital of approximately $1.4 billion, including approximately $357 million of cash and short-term investments. Approximately $834 million consists of inventory, which is not as liquid as other current assets.

On May 16, 1991, the Company's Board of Directors authorized the Company to repurchase up to ten million shares of its common stock on the open market. During 1991 the Company purchased three million shares of its common stock at an aggregate cost of $95.5 million. During the first nine months of 1992 the Company completed the program by purchasing the remaining seven million shares of its common stock at an aggregate cost of $202.2 million.

During 1992 the Company repaid a $73.5 million mortgage loan.

In 1992 the Company discontinued joint technology development with Silicon Graphics, Inc. ("SGI") and entered into a cross-license for technology previously exchanged by the two companies. In addition, SGI paid the Company $150 million and the Company transferred to SGI the 5% convertible preferred stock of SGI that it had acquired in 1991 for $135 million.

The Company estimates that capital expenditures for land, buildings, and equipment during 1993 will be approximately $140 million. Such expenditures are currently expected to be funded from a combination of available cash balances, internally generated funds, and, if necessary, financing arrangements. Although the Company fully expects that such expenditures will be made, it has commitments for only a small portion of such amounts.

During 1992 the Company funded its capital expenditures and other investing activities with cash generated from operations and previously accumulated cash balances as well as the cash generated by the sale of its equity investment in Conner and its transaction with SGI. The Company's ability to fund its activities from operations is directly dependent on its rate of growth, inventory management, the terms and financing arrangements under which it extends credit to its customers, and the manner in which it finances any capital expansion. In December 1992 and January 1993 the Company entered into credit agreements with two banks in which the banks agreed to extend committed lines of credit aggregating $100 million to the Company. At February 24, 1993, the lines of credit were unused and fully available. The Company anticipates entering into additional financing arrangements in the first half of 1993 for utilization if additional operating funds are needed.

Factors that May Affect Future Results

The personal computer industry is characterized by intense price competition. In early 1993 a number of the Company's competitors lowered their prices dramatically, and additional pricing actions likely will occur in the future. In order to maintain or increase its market share, the Company must continue to price its products competitively, which will lower revenue per unit and cause declines in gross margin. To compensate for the impact on its revenue and profitability, the Company must substantially increase unit volumes as well as aggressively reduce its costs. While the Company believes its new pricing and product strategy has created demand for its products and the Company is actively engaged in cost reduction programs, if the Company does not achieve significant volume increases and cost reductions, there will be an adverse impact on revenue and profitability.

To respond to the increase in demand for the Company's products in 1992, the Company increased the utilization of its manufacturing capacity. The Company, however, experienced shortages of certain components that impeded its ability to meet all of its demand. In order to increase its production, the Company has significantly increased its level of inventory. If the Company is unable to manage its inventory position or anticipate demand accurately, maintaining this inventory level may result in increased obsolescence and affect its ability to meet cost reduction goals.

Because of the pace of technological advances in the personal computer industry, the Company must design and develop new and more sophisticated products in relatively short time spans. The Company designs many of its own components for its products. Across the Company's product range, however, certain elements of product strategy are dependent on technological developments by other manufacturers. There can be no assurance that the Company will obtain the delivery of the technology needed to introduce new products in a timely manner or will be able to obtain any competitive advantage in access to such technology. The Company's product strategy focuses in part on marketing products with distinctive features that appeal to a variety of purchasers. If the Company were unable to develop and launch new products in a timely fashion, this failure could have a material adverse effect on the Company's business.

In 1992 the Company broadened its distribution in order to identify and pursue new market opportunities, including the home, education, and small business markets as well as new geographic markets. Certain of the Company's sales in 1992 were to newly appointed distributors and new locations for sale of the Company's products. Offering its products through a variety of distribution channels, including distributors, electronics superstores, and mail order, requires the Company to increase the level of direct sales and support interface with customers. There can be no assurance, however, that this new direction will be effective, or that the requisite service and support to ensure the success of these new channels can be achieved without significantly increasing overall expenses. While the Company anticipates that the number of outlets for its products will continue to increase in 1993, a reduction in the growth of new outlets could affect demand.

The Company's primary means of distribution remains third-party resellers. The Company's business could be adversely affected in the event that the generally weak financial condition of third-party computer resellers worsens. In the event of the financial failure of a major reseller, the Company could experience disruptions in its distribution as well as the loss of the unsecured portion of any outstanding accounts receivable. The Company believes that the expansion of its distribution channels will help mitigate any potential impact on its sales.

General economic conditions have an impact on the Company's business and financial results. Many of the markets in which the Company sells its products are currently experiencing economic recession and the Company cannot predict when these conditions will improve or if conditions in these and other markets will decline. The personal computer market showed unusual robustness despite weak economic conditions in 1992, and there can be no assurance that growth will continue at the same pace in 1993. The value of the U.S. dollar also affects the Company's results. When the U.S. dollar strengthens against other currencies, sales made in those currencies translate into less revenue in U.S. dollars; and when the U.S. dollar weakens, sales made in those currencies translate into more revenue. Correspondingly, costs and expenses incurred in non-U.S. dollar currencies increase when the U.S. dollar weakens and decline when the U.S. dollar strengthens. The Company attempts to reduce the impact of changes in currency exchange rates through forward and option currency contracts. Should the U.S. dollar sustain a strengthening position against currencies in which the Company sells its products or a weakening exchange rate against currencies in which the Company incurs costs, particularly the Japanese yen, the Company's sales or its costs would be adversely affected.

While the effects of the 1992 restructuring will help the Company control its selling, general, and administrative expense in certain areas, several factors, including a new marketing focus directed towards end-user purchasers, are anticipated to cause an increase in such expenses in 1993 in absolute terms although the Company anticipates that these expenses may decline as a percentage of sales during 1993.

Because of the foregoing factors, as well as other factors affecting the Company's operating results, past financial performance should not be considered to be a reliable indicator of future performance, and investors should not use historical trends to anticipate results or trends in future periods.

REPORT OF INDEPENDENT ACCOUNTANTS

To the Stockholders and Board of Directors of
Compaq Computer Corporation

In our opinion, the consolidated financial statements listed in the accompanying index present fairly, in all material respects, the financial position of Compaq Computer Corporation and its subsidiaries at December 31, 1992 and 1991, and the results of their operations and their cash flows for each of the three years in the period ended December 31, 1992, in conformity with generally accepted accounting principles. These financial statements are the responsibility of the Company's management; our responsibility is to express an opinion on these financial statements based on our audits. We conducted our audits of these statements in accordance with generally accepted auditing standards which require that we plan and perform the audit to obtain reasonable assurance about whether the financial statements are free of material misstatement. An audit includes examining, on a test basis, evidence supporting the amounts and disclosures in the financial statements, assessing the accounting principles used and significant estimates made by management, and evaluating the overall financial statement presentation. We believe that our audits provide a reasonable basis for the opinion expressed above.

PRICE WATERHOUSE

Houston, Texas
January 25, 1993

COMPAQ COMPUTER CORPORATION
CONSOLIDATED BALANCE SHEET

ASSETS

	December 31, 1992	December 31, 1991
	(in thousands)	
Current assets:		
Cash and short-term investments	$ 356,747	$ 452,174
Accounts receivable, less allowance of $24,733,000 and $18,265,000	986,735	624,376
Inventories	834,406	436,824
Prepaid expenses and other current assets	141,083	269,203
Total current assets	2,318,971	1,782,577
Investment in affiliated company		142,057
Property, plant, and equipment, less accumulated depreciation	807,653	883,765
Other assets	15,769	17,987
	$3,142,393	$2,826,386

LIABILITIES AND STOCKHOLDERS' EQUITY

	December 31, 1992	December 31, 1991
Current liabilities:		
Accounts payable	$ 516,323	$ 195,582
Income taxes payable	36,073	33,103
Other current liabilities	407,484	409,258
Total current liabilities	959,880	637,943
Long-term debt		73,456
Deferred income taxes	175,822	184,283
Commitments and contingencies		
Stockholders' equity:-		
Preferred stock: $.01 par value; 10,000,000 shares authorized; none outstanding		
Common stock: $.01 par value; 400,000,000 shares authorized; 79,829,488 shares and 84,201,515 shares issued and outstanding	798	842
Capital in excess of par value	399,693	536,814
Retained earnings	1,606,200	1,393,048
Total stockholders' equity	2,006,691	1,930,704
	$3,142,393	$2,826,386

The accompanying notes are an integral part of these financial statements.

COMPAQ COMPUTER CORPORATION
CONSOLIDATED STATEMENT OF INCOME

	Year ended December 31,		
	1992	1991	1990
	(in thousands, except per share amounts)		
Sales	$4,099,758	$3.271,367	$3,598,768
Cost of sales	2,905,024	2,053,576	2,057,886
	1,194,734	1,217,791	1,540,882
Research and development costs	172,948	197,277	185,726
Selling, general, and administrative expense	698,589	721,622	706,060
Unrealized gains on investment in affiliated company			(34,532)
Other income and expense, net	27,795	144,856	42,195
	899,332	1,063,755	899,449
Income from consolidated companies before provision for income taxes	295,402	154,036	641,433
Provision for income taxes	97,483	42,932	216,205
Income from consolidated companies	197,919	111,104	425,228
Equity in net income of affiliated company	15,233	19,765	29,682
Net income	$ 213,152	$ 130,869	$ 454,910
Earnings per common and common equivalent share:			
Primary	$ 2.58	$ 1.49	$ 5.14
Assuming full dilution	$ 2.52	$ 1.49	$ 5.12

The accompanying notes are an integral part of these financial statements.

COMPAQ COMPUTER CORPORATION

CONSOLIDATED STATEMENT OF CASH FLOWS

	Year ended December 31,		
	1992	1991	1990
	(in thousands)		
Cash flows from operating activities:			
Cash received from customers	$3,594,786	$3,325,465	$3,536,984
Cash paid to suppliers and employees	(3,641,655)	(2,822,648)	(2,721,070)
Interest and dividends received	32,404	32,301	26,889
Interest paid	(42,137)	(36,907)	(46,728)
Income taxes paid	(2,816)	(104,001)	(140,294)
Net cash provided by (used in) operating activities	(59,418)	394,210	655,781
Cash flows from investing activities:			
Purchases of property, plant, and equipment, net	(159,215)	(188,746)	(324,859)
Proceeds from sale of investment in Conner Peripherals, Inc.	241,427		
Investment in Silicon Graphics, Inc.	135,000	(135,000)	
Other, net	13,004	(16,636)	(1,747)
Net cash provided by (used in) investing activities	230,216	(340,382)	(326,606)
Cash flows from financing activities:			
Purchases of treasury shares	(215,505)	(82,275)	
Proceeds from sale of equity securities	56,836	22,637	22,645
Repayment of borrowings	(73,456)	(540)	(30,561)
Net cash used in financing activities	(232,125)	(60,178)	(7,916)
Effect of exchange rate changes on cash	(34,100)	23,824	(47,872)
Net increase (decrease) in cash	(95,427)	17,474	273,387
Cash and short-term investments at beginning of year	452,174	434,700	161,313
Cash and short-term investments at end of year	$ 356,747	$ 452,174	$ 434,700
Reconciliation of net income to net cash provided by operating activities:			
Net income	$ 213,152	$ 130,869	$ 454,910
Depreciation and amortization	159,510	165,824	135,305
Provision for bad debts	13,654	8,542	3,878
Equity in net income of affiliated company	(15,233)	(19,765)	(29,682)
Unrealized gain on investment in affiliated company			(34,532)
Gain on sale of investment in affiliated company	(85,709)		
Deferred income taxes	34,128	(9,639)	40,443
Loss on disposal of assets	14,408	4,200	4,887
Exchange rate effect	11,236	(4,136)	21,422
Income tax refund	51,400		
Other changes in net current assets	(455,964)	118,315	59,150
Net cash provided by (used in) operating activities	($ 59,418)	$ 394,210	$ 655,781

COMPAQ COMPUTER CORPORATION

CONSOLIDATED STATEMENT OF STOCKHOLDERS' EQUITY

| | Common stock | | Capital in excess of | Retained | |
	Shares	Par value	par value	earnings	Total
			(in thousands, except for shares)		
Balance, December 31, 1989	78,545,808	$ 785	$363,581	$ 807,269	$1,171,635
Issuance pursuant to stock option plans	1,394,413	14	22,631		22,645
Issuance on conversion of convertible subordinated debentures	6,149,426	62	197,461		197,523
Compensation expense associated with grant of nonqualified stock options			200		200
Tax benefit associated with stock options			12,100		12,100
Net income				454,910	454,910
Balance, December 31, 1990	86,089,647	861	595,973	1,262,179	1,859,013
Issuance pursuant to stock option plans	1,111,868	11	22,626		22,637
Purchases of treasury shares	(3,000,000)	(30)	(95,474)		(95,504)
Tax benefit associated with stock options			13,689		13,689
Net income				130,869	130,869
Balance, December 31, 1991	84,201,515	842	536,814	1,393,048	1,930,704
Issuance pursuant to stock option plans	2,627,973	26	56,810		56,836
Purchases of treasury shares	(7,000,000)	(70)	(202,206)		(202,276)
Compensation expense associated with grant of nonqualified stock options			62		62
Tax benefit associated with stock options			8,213		8,213
Net income				213,152	213,152
Balance, December 31, 1992	79,829,488	$ 798	$399,693	$1,606,200	$2,006,691

COMPAQ COMPUTER CORPORATION

NOTES TO CONSOLIDATED FINANCIAL STATEMENTS

Note 1 - Significant Accounting Policies:

The Company has adopted accounting policies which are generally accepted in the industry in which it operates. Set forth below are the Company's more significant accounting policies.

Principles of consolidation -

The consolidated financial statements include the accounts of Compaq Computer Corporation and its wholly owned subsidiaries. The investment in Conner Peripherals, Inc., which represented a less than majority interest, was accounted for under the equity method. All significant intercompany transactions have been eliminated.

Inventories -

Inventories are stated at the lower of cost or market, cost being determined on a first-in, first-out basis.

Property, plant, and equipment -

Property, plant, and equipment are stated at cost. Major renewals and improvements are capitalized; minor replacements, maintenance, and repairs are charged to current operations. Depreciation is computed by applying the straight-line method over the estimated useful lives of the related assets, which are 30 years for buildings and range from three to ten years for equipment. Leasehold improvements are amortized over the shorter of the useful life of the improvement or the life of the related lease.

Intangible assets -

Licenses and trademarks are carried at cost less accumulated amortization, which is being provided on a straight-line basis over the economic lives of the respective assets.

Warranty expense -

The Company provides currently for estimated cost which may be incurred under product warranties.

Revenue recognition -

The Company recognizes revenue at the time products are shipped to its customers. Provision is made currently for estimated product returns which may occur under programs the Company has with its third-party resellers and floor planning arrangements with third-party finance companies.

Foreign currency -

The Company uses the U.S. dollar as its functional currency. Financial statements of the Company's foreign subsidiaries are translated to U.S. dollars for consolidation purposes using current rates of exchange for monetary assets and liabilities and historical rates of exchange for nonmonetary assets and related elements of expense. Revenue and other expense elements are translated at rates which approximate the rates in effect on the transaction dates. Gains and losses from this process are included in results of operations.

The Company hedges certain portions of its foreign currency exposure through the use of forward exchange contracts and option contracts. Generally, gains and losses associated with currency rate changes on forward exchange contracts are recorded currently, while the interest element is recognized over the life of each contract. However, to the extent such contracts hedge a commitment for capital expenditures or inventory purchases, no gains or losses are recognized, and the rate at the time the forward exchange contract is made is, effectively, the rate used to determine the U.S. dollar value of the asset when it is recorded. In addition, during 1992 the Company began to hedge a portion of its probable anticipated sales of its international marketing subsidiaries using purchased foreign currency options. Realized and unrealized gains and the net premiums on these options are deferred and recognized as a component of sales in the period that the related sales occur.

Income taxes -

The provision for income taxes is computed based on the pretax income included in the consolidated statement of income. Deferred taxes result from differences in the timing of recognition of revenue and expenses for tax and financial reporting purposes. Research and development tax credits are recorded to the extent allowable as a reduction of the provision for federal income taxes in the year the qualified research and development expenditures are incurred.

The Financial Accounting Standards Board has issued a Statement which will change the method of determining reported income tax expense. The Company will apply the provisions of this Statement in 1993. Application of the provisions of this Statement will have minimal impact on the Company's financial statements.

Note 2 - Short-term Investments:

The Company held the following short-term investments:

	December 31, 1992	December 31, 1991
	(in thousands)	
Money market instruments	$133,926	$321,527
Commercial paper and other investments	135,324	120,010
	$269,250	$441,537

All such investments are carried at cost plus accrued interest, which approximates market, have maturities of three months or less and are considered cash equivalents for purposes of reporting cash flows.

Note 3 - Inventories:

Inventories consisted of the following components:

	December 31, 1992	December 31, 1991
	(in thousands)	
Raw material	$351,373	$193,843
Work-in-process	124,042	36,450
Finished goods	358,991	206,531
	$834,406	$436,824

Note 4 - Prepaid Expenses and Other Current Assets:

During the early part of 1992, the Company sold its $135 million equity interest in Silicon Graphics, Inc. (SGI) and discontinued the joint technical development agreement with SGI. The transaction resulted in no material gain or loss to the Company. The Company's $135 million equity interest in SGI was included in prepaid expenses and other current assets at December 31, 1991.

Note 5- Investment in Conner Peripherals, Inc.:

In 1992 the Company sold its equity interest in Conner Peripherals, Inc. (Conner) realizing a gain of $85.7 million.

During 1990 Conner issued approximately six million shares of common stock. The per share price of the newly issued shares was higher than the then per share carrying value of the Company's investment in Conner. The increases in the carrying value of the Company's investment in Conner resulting from this stock issuance caused a pretax gain of $27.1 million in 1990. Additionally, in 1990 Conner converted its outstanding debentures into common stock giving rise to a similar pretax gain of $7.5 million.

The Company made disk drive purchases from Conner during 1992 through the date it sold its equity interest and during 1991 and 1990 of approximately $149 million, $197 million, and $255 million, respectively. At December 31, 1991, the Company had balances owing to Conner of $19 million. While the Company controlled approximately 20% of the equity securities of Conner, the Company believes that purchases from Conner were made at market prices.

Note 6 - Property, Plant, and Equipment:

Property, plant, and equipment are summarized below:

	December 31, 1992	December 31, 1991
Land	$ 75,455	$ 70,028
Buildings	531,849	510,049
Machinery and equipment	547,942	615,353
Furniture and fixtures	53,408	54,217
Leasehold improvements	19,768	27,183
Construction-in-progress	55,709	45,652
	1,284,131	1,322,482
Less-accumulated depreciation	476,478	438,717
	$ 807,653	$ 883,765

Depreciation expense totaled approximately $159 million, $164 million, and $134 million in 1992, 1991, and 1990, respectively.

Note 7 - Other Current Liabilities:

The estimated costs which may be incurred under product warranties of approximately $73 million and $39 million were included in other current liabilities at December 31, 1992 and 1991, respectively.

Note 8 - Credit Agreement:

In December 1992 and January 1993 the Company entered into credit agreements with two banks in which the banks agreed to extend short-term committed lines of credit aggregating $100 million to the Company.

Note 9 - Long-term Debt:

On May 4, 1988, the Company issued $200 million of 6 1/2% convertible subordinated debentures due 2013. Approximately $199 million remained outstanding at December 31, 1989. During 1990 substantially all of the outstanding debentures were converted to 6,149,426 shares of the Company's common stock. Deferred debt issuance costs of $3.6 million were charged to capital in excess of par value as a result of the conversion of debentures in 1990.

During 1992 the Company repaid its outstanding mortgage note which had a 9.77% interest rate.

Note 10 - Other Income and Expense:

Other income and expense consisted of the following components:

	Year ended December 31,		
	1992	1991	1990
		(in thousands)	
Restructuring charge	$73,000	$135,000	
Interest and dividend income	(32,404)	(32,301)	($ 26,889)
Interest expense	44,031	37,703	45,986
Realized gain on investment in affiliated company	(85,709)		
Currency exchange (gains) losses, net	11,236	(4,136)	21,422
Loss on disposition of assets, net	14,408	4,200	4,887
Other, net	3,233	4,390	(3,211)
	$27,795	$144,856	$42,195

On October 23, 1991, the Company announced a major restructuring of its operations and a reorganization into distinct product divisions. The restructuring plan included, among other things, a reduction of the Company's worldwide workforce of approximately 14% and provided for the consolidation and streamlining of certain operations. The estimated cost of the restructuring plan, $135 million, was recorded by the Company in the third quarter of 1991 and included approximately $39 million for expenses related to the worldwide reduction in workforce. The restructuring charge also included $63 million for expenses associated with facility rearrangements, consolidations, and writedowns; $20 million for manufacturing equipment disposals and product line consolidations; and $13 million for miscellaneous charges associated with the restructuring. In the third quarter of 1992 the Company recorded $73 million in additional restructuring charges in conjunction with additional plans for consolidating and streamlining operations. The 1992 restructuring charges consisted of approximately $31 million of charges associated with the worldwide reduction of workforce and $42 million related to facility rearrangements, consolidations, and writedowns. Other current liabilities at December 31, 1992 and 1991 included a reserve related to these restructurings of $54 million and $83 million, respectively.

Interest aggregating approximately $3.5 million, $6.2 million, and $8.9 million was capitalized and added to the cost of the Company's property, plant, and equipment in 1992, 1991, and 1990, respectively.

Note 11 - Provision for Income Taxes:

Domestic income (loss) from consolidated companies before provision for income taxes was $99 million, ($33) million, and $332 million in 1992, 1991, and 1990, respectively. The foreign component of income before provision for income taxes was $196 million, $187 million, and $309 million in 1992, 1991, and 1990, respectively. The components of related income taxes were as follows:

	Year ended December 31,		
	1992	1991	1990
		(in thousands)	
U.S. federal income tax:			
Current	$36,617	$17,478	$ 98,962
Deferred	29,896	(4,487)	38,838
Foreign income taxes:			
Current	26,745	32,798	73,711
Deferred	4,232	(5,152)	1,605
State income taxes	(7)	2,295	3,089
	$97,483	$42,932	$216,205

Total income tax expense for 1992, 1991, and 1990 resulted in effective tax rates of 33%, 27.9%, and 33.7%, respectively. The reasons for the differences between these effective tax rates and the U.S. statutory rate of 34% are as follows:

	Year ended December 31,		
	1992	1991	1990
Tax expense at U.S. statutory rate	$100,437	$52,372	$218,075
Research and development tax credits	(3,048)	(8,826)	(7,893)
Foreign tax effect, net	101	6,076	5,828
Tax exempt Foreign Sales Corporation income	(1,439)	(6,914)	(7,891)
Provision for tax on equity in net income of affiliated company	5,179	6,720	10,092
Other, net	(3,747)	(6,496)	(2,006)
	$ 97,483	$42,932	$216,205

Deferred and prepaid taxes result from differences in the timing of revenue and expenses for tax and financial reporting purposes. The sources and tax effects of these differences are as follows:

	Year ended December 31,		
	1992	1991	1990
Unremitted earnings of foreign subsidiaries	$35,585	$44,034	$36,057
Intercompany profits not included in net income for financial reporting purposes	(5,329)	31,494	(16,180)
Realized gain on sale of affiliated company	(49,631)		
Unrealized gains on investment in affiliated company			12,069
Equity in net income of affiliated company	5,752	6,720	10,092
Depreciation	2,157	4,895	20
Unrealized currency exchange (gains) losses	9,293	(5,297)	3,978
Restructuring charge	11,359	(35,642)	
Warranty reserve	(6,677)	98	(2,950)
Difference arising from different tax and financial reporting year ends	14,818	(36,915)	(2,185)
Other, net	16,801	(19,026)	(458)
	$34,128	($ 9,639)	$40,443

Deferred tax assets of approximately $77 million and $121 million were included in prepaid expenses and other current assets at December 31, 1992 and 1991, respectively. Accounts receivable at December 31, 1991 included $51 million of refundable U.S. federal income taxes.

Note 12 - Earnings Per Share:

Primary earnings per common and common equivalent share and earnings per common and common equivalent share assuming full dilution were computed using the weighted average number of shares outstanding adjusted for the incremental shares attributed to outstanding options to purchase common stock and assuming the conversion of the outstanding convertible subordinated debentures at the beginning of the period. All share and per-share information has been retroactively restated in the accompanying financial data to reflect the two-for-one stock split effected in the form of a 100% stock dividend declared by the Company in May 1990. Shares used in computing earnings per share were as follows:

	Year ended December 31,		
	1992	1991	1990
		(in thousands)	
Primary	82,641	88,098	89,225
Assuming full dilution	84,726	88,098	89,639

Note 13 - Stockholders' Equity and Employee Benefit Plans:

Equity incentive plans -

At December 31, 1992, there were 23,010,498 shares of common stock reserved by the Board of Directors for issuance under the Company's employee stock option plans. Options are generally granted at the fair market value of the common stock at the date of grant and generally vest over four to five years. In limited circumstances, options may be granted at prices less than fair market value and may vest immediately. Options granted under the plans must be exercised not later than ten years from the date of grant. Options on 6,884,730 shares were exercisable at December 31, 1992. The following table summarizes activity under the plans for each of the three years in the period ended December 31, 1992:

	Shares	Price per share
Options outstanding, December 31, 1989	11,763,844	
Options granted	2,884,626	$37.87- 62.25
Options lapsed or cancelled	(360,731)	
Options exercised	(1,394,413)	.25- 52.75
Options outstanding, December 31, 1990	12,893,326	
Options granted	4,415,600	23.88- 69.75
Options lapsed or cancelled	(1,662,937)	
Options exercised	(1,111,868)	22.25- 73.50
Options outstanding, December 31, 1991	14,534,121	
Options granted	2,745,525	23.63- 42.38
Options lapsed or cancelled	(703,456)	
Options exercised	(2,606,575)	.25- 47.19
Options outstanding, December 31, 1992	13,969,615	

There were 9,040,883; 11,082,952; and 3,847,035 shares available for grants under the plans at December 31, 1992, 1991, and 1990, respectively.

In 1987 the stockholders approved the Stock Option Plan for Non-Employee Directors (the Director Plan). At December 31, 1992, there were 458,602 shares of common stock reserved for issuance under the Director Plan. Pursuant to the terms of the plan, each non-employee director is entitled to receive options to purchase common stock of the Company upon initial appointment to the Board (initial grants) and upon subsequent re-election to the Board (annual grants). Initial grants are exercisable during the period beginning one year after initial appointment to the Board and ending ten years after the date of grant. Annual grants vest over two years and are exercisable thereafter until the tenth anniversary of the date of grant. Both initial grants and annual grants have an exercise price equal to the fair market value of the Company's stock on the date of grant. Additionally, pursuant to the terms of the Director Plan, non-employee directors may elect to receive stock options in lieu of all or a portion of the annual retainer to be earned. Such options are granted at 50% of the price of the Company's common stock at the date of grant and are exercisable during the period beginning one year after the grant date and ending ten years after the date of grant. Options totaling 121,084 were exercisable under the Director Plan at December 31, 1992. Activity under the plan for each of the three years in the period ended December 31, 1992 was as follows:

	Shares	Price per share
Options outstanding, December 31, 1989	40,000	
Options granted	75,690	$30.50-61.00
Options outstanding, December 31, 1990	115,690	
Options granted	37,292	17.88-35.76
Options outstanding, December 31, 1991	152,982	
Options granted	27,895	12.69-25.38
Options exercised	(21,398)	40.25-43.00
Options outstanding, December 31, 1992	159,479	

There were 299,123; 327,018; and 364,310 shares available for grants under the plan at December 31, 1992, 1991, and 1990, respectively.

Pursuant to a plan adopted by the Board of Directors in 1986, the Company granted to selected officers and key employees options on shares of Conner stock owned by the Company. Such options, which were granted at $.09 per share, vested ratably over four years and expire ten years from the date of grant. During 1992 options on 193,499 shares were exercised and no options lapsed or were cancelled. At December 31, 1992, options on 105,178 shares of Conner common stock were exercisable and outstanding.

Compaq Computer Corporation Investment Plan -

The Company has an Investment Plan available to all domestic employees and intended to qualify as a deferred compensation plan under Section 401(k) of the Internal Revenue Code of 1986. Employees may contribute to the plan up to 14% of their salary with a maximum of $8,728 in 1992 ($8,994 in 1993). The Company will match employee contributions for an amount up to 6% of each employee's base salary. Contributions are invested at the direction of the employee in one or more funds or can be directed to purchase common stock of the Company at fair market value. Company contributions generally vest over three years although Company contributions for those employees having five years of service vest immediately. Company contributions are charged to expense in accordance with their vesting. Amounts charged to expense were $13 million, $11.6 million, and $8.3 million in 1992, 1991, and 1990, respectively.

Incentive Compensation Plan -

The Company adopted an incentive compensation plan for the majority of its employees beginning in the second half of 1992. Provision for payments to be made under the plan is based on 6% of net income from operations, as defined, and is payable in August and February. The amount expensed under the plan was $8.3 million in 1992.

Stock Repurchases -

On May 16, 1991, the Company's Board of Directors authorized the Company to repurchase up to ten million shares of its common stock on the open market. During 1992 and 1991 the Company repurchased seven million and three million shares of its common stock, respectively, at an aggregate cost of $202.2 million and $95.5 million, respectively. The shares are held by the Company as treasury stock and accounted for using the par value method.

Post Retirement and Post Employment Benefits -

The Financial Accounting Standards Board has issued Statements requiring accrual basis accounting for post retirement and post employment benefits offered to employees. The Company currently offers very limited post retirement and post employment benefits and accordingly the provisions of the Statements will have minimal impact on the Company's financial statements when applied in 1993.

Stockholder Rights Plan -

The Board of Directors adopted a Stockholder Rights Plan in May 1989 which in certain limited circumstances would permit stockholders to purchase securities at prices which would be substantially below market value.

Note 14 - Certain Market and Geographic Data:

Compaq Computer Corporation designs, develops, manufactures, and markets personal computers. The Company has subsidiaries in various foreign countries which manufacture and sell the Company's products in their respective geographic areas. Summary information with respect to the Company's geographic operations in 1992, 1991, and 1990 follows:

1992	United States and Canada	Europe	Other countries (in thousands)	Eliminations	Consolidated
Sales to customers	$1,833,175	$1,886,109	$380,474		$4,099,758
Intercompany transfers	898,997	49,844	536,695	($1,485,536)	
	$2,732,172	$1,935,953	$917,169	($1,485,536)	$4,099,758
Income from operations	$ 37,415	$ 73,956	$142,531	($ 2,059)	$ 251,843
Corporate income, net					43,559
Pretax income					$ 295,402
Identifiable assets	$2,006,643	$ 961,316	$322,847	($ 505,160)	$2,785,646
General corporate assets					356,747
Total assets					$3,142,393
1991					
Sales to customers	$1,387,758	$1,724,621	$158,988		$3,271,367
Intercompany transfers	838,156	16,490	360,851	($1,215,497)	
	$2,225,914	$1,741,111	$519,839	($1,215,497)	$3,271,367
Income (loss) from operations	($ 29,049)	$ 100,993	$133,163	$ 12,343	$ 217,450
Corporate expenses, net					(63,414)
Pretax income					$ 154,036
Identifiable assets	$1,824,721	$ 695,808	$125,085	($ 271,402)	$2,374,212
General corporate assets					452,174
Total assets					$2,826,386

1990

Sales to customers	$1,657,640	$1,807,499	$133,629		$3,598,768
Intercompany transfers	1,018,981	26,540	329,653	($1,375,174)	
	$2,676,621	$1,834,039	$463,282	($1,375,174)	$3,598,768
Income from operations	$ 414,297	$ 169,280	$121,713	($ 29,327)	$ 675,963
Corporate expenses, net					(34,530)
Pretax income					$ 641,433
Identifiable assets	$1,565,876	$ 662,942	$129,403	($ 75,392)	$2,282,829
General corporate assets					434,700
Total assets					$2,717,529

In each year, the Company's hedging activities are designed to reduce the effects of changes in the value of the U.S. dollar relative to the currencies of those countries in which the Company's international subsidiaries operate.

Cumulative retained earnings of international subsidiaries were $406 million and $345 million at December 31, 1992 and 1991, respectively.

Products are transferred between countries at prices which are intended to approximate those that would be charged to unaffiliated customers in the respective countries. Transactions with one of the Company's resellers accounted for 10% of consolidated sales in 1990.

Note 15 - Commitments and Contingencies:

Litigation -

The Company and certain of its current and former officers and directors are named in a consolidated, alleged class action, lawsuit brought in federal court in Houston on behalf of persons who purchased Compaq stock or held certain types of options during the period December 4, 1990 through May 14, 1991. The complaint alleges, among other things, that the defendants, through certain public statements, misled investors respecting (i) deterioration in the Company's markets and the demand for its products, (ii) the inadequacy of the Company's foreign currency hedging mechanisms to protect it from the rising value of the dollar, (iii) marketing problems such as pricing pressure from competitors and reduced dealer loyalty, and (iv) other industry, competitive and Company conditions. Individual suits making similar allegations have been brought by certain stockholders in Texas state court. The ultimate liability, if any, which may result from these lawsuits cannot be determined at this time. However, management believes that the outcome of this litigation will not have a material adverse effect on the financial condition of the Company.

The Company is also subject to legal proceedings and claims which arise in the ordinary course of its business. Management does not believe that the outcome of any of those matters will have a material adverse effect on the Company's financial condition.

Off-balance sheet risk and concentration of credit risk -

At December 31, 1992 and 1991, respectively, the Company had entered into forward exchange contracts with financial institutions to sell net amounts of $381 million and $325 million of foreign currencies and also had entered into foreign currency option contracts relating to the hedges of certain portions of its foreign currency exposure of the net monetary assets of its international subsidiaries and to hedge purchase commitments. Forward exchange contracts, which are valued in U.S. dollars based on the respective year-end spot rate, had maturity dates ranging from one day to six months. In the event of a failure to honor one of these contracts by one of the banks with which the Company had contracted, management believes any loss would be limited to the exchange rate differential from the time the contract was made until the time it was compensated. At December 31, 1992, the Company had entered into option contracts to sell currency to hedge a portion of its probable anticipated sales over the next nine months of its international marketing subsidiaries. The net unrealized gain deferred on these contracts at December 31, 1992 totaled $25.5 million and if realized will be recognized in the periods that the related sales occur. To the extent the Company has such options outstanding, the amount of any loss resulting from a breach of contract would be limited to the amount of premiums paid for the options and the unrealized gain, if any, related to such contracts.

The Company's cash and short-term investments and accounts receivable are subject to potential credit risk. The Company's cash management and investment policies restrict investments to low risk, highly-liquid securities and the Company performs periodic evaluation of the relative credit standing of the financial institutions with which it deals.

The Company distributes products primarily through third-party resellers and as a result maintains individually significant accounts receivable balances from various major resellers. The Company evaluates the credit worthiness of its resellers on an ongoing basis and may, from time to time, tighten credit terms to particular resellers. Such tightening may take the form of shorter payment terms, requiring security, reduction of credit availability, or the deauthorization of a reseller. In addition the Company uses various risk transfer instruments such as credit insurance, factoring, and flooring planning with third-party finance companies; however, there can be no assurance that these arrangements will be sufficient to avoid significant accounts receivable losses or will continue to be available. While the Company believes that its distribution strategies will serve to minimize the risk associated with the loss of a reseller or the decline in sales to a reseller due to tightened credit terms, there can be no assurance that disruption to the Company's sales and profitability will not occur. If the financial condition and operations of these resellers deteriorate, the Company's operating results could be adversely affected. At December 31, 1992, the receivable balances from the Company's two largest resellers represented approximately 15% of accounts receivable.

The Company's resellers typically purchase products on an as-needed basis through purchase orders. Various of the Company's resellers finance a portion of their inventories through third-party finance companies. Under the terms of the financing arrangements, the Company may be required, in limited circumstances, to purchase certain products from the finance companies. At December 31, 1992 and 1991, amounts owed to third-party finance companies by the Company's resellers under such arrangements aggregated approximately $180 million and $175 million, respectively. Additionally, the Company has on occasion guaranteed a portion of certain resellers' outstanding balances with third-party finance companies. Guarantees aggregating $14.4 million and $18 million were outstanding at December 31, 1992 and 1991, respectively. During the ten years that the Company has supported these financing programs, claims under these arrangements have been negligible. The Company makes provisions for estimated product returns and bad debts which may occur under these programs.

Lease Commitments -

The Company leases certain manufacturing and office facilities and equipment under noncancelable operating leases with terms from one to 30 years. Rent expense for 1992, 1991, and 1990 was $34.8 million, $38.5 million, and $37.3 million, respectively.

The Company's minimum rental commitments under noncancelable operating leases at December 31, 1992 were as follows:

Year	Amount
1993	$ 26,062
1994	19,991
1995	15,379
1996	8,779
1997	7,732
Thereafter	42,493
	$120,436

Note 16 - Selected Quarterly Financial Data (not covered by report of independent accountants):

The table below sets forth selected financial information for each quarter of the last two years.

	1st quarter	2nd quarter	3rd quarter	4th quarter
1992				
Sales	$783,048	$826,976	$1,067,105	$1,422,629
Gross margin	262,343	249,933	299,737	382,721
Net income	45,326	28,996	49,365	89,465
Earnings per common and common equivalent share:				
Primary	.53	.35	.61	1.11
Assuming full dilution	.53	.35	.61	1.10
1991				
Sales	$970,751	$717,845	$ 709,370	$ 873,401
Gross margin	401,653	247,660	243,458	325,020
Net income	114,278	20,285	(70,256)	66,562
Earnings per common and common equivalent share:				
Primary	1.26	.23	(.82)	.77
Assuming full dilution	1.26	.23	(.82)	.77

During the first six months of 1991 the Company estimated that its effective tax rate would be 34%. During the third quarter of 1991, the Company incurred a $135 million restructuring charge which substantially reduced the forecast of 1991 pretax earnings. Consequently, the Company revised its estimated effective tax rate downward to 28%. The actual effective tax rate for 1991 was 27.9%. The full benefit of the lower rate was recorded in the third quarter of 1991 and had the effect of reducing the loss per share for the quarter by approximately $.13. The 1992 third quarter restructuring and other special charges were offset by the gain on the sale of the equity interest in Conner; accordingly, there was no similar effect in 1992.

There were no other unusual or infrequently occurring items or adjustments, other than normal recurring adjustments, in any of the quarters presented.